D0204347

The Oxford French Minidictionary

SECOND EDITION

FRENCH–ENGLISH

ENGLISH–FRENCH

FRANÇAIS–ANGLAIS

ANGLAIS–FRANÇAIS

Michael Janes
Dora Carpenter
Edwin Carpenter

Oxford   New York

OXFORD UNIVERSITY PRESS

Oxford University Press, Great Clarendon Street, Oxford OX2 6DP

Oxford New York
Athens Auckland Bangkok Bogota Bombay
Buenos Aires Calcutta Cape Town Dar es Salaam
Delhi Florence Hong Kong Istanbul Karachi
Kuala Lumpur Madras Madrid Melbourne
Mexico City Nairobi Paris Singapore
Taipei Tokyo Toronto Warsaw
and associated companies in
Berlin Ibadan

Oxford is a trade mark of Oxford University Press

1st Edition 1986
2nd Edition 1993
Reissued 1997

British Library Cataloguing in Publication Data

Data available

Library of Congress Cataloging in Publication Data

Data available

ISBN 0-19-860140-9

3 5 7 9 10 8 6 4 2

Printed in Great Britain by
Charles Letts (Scotland) Ltd., Dalkeith, Scotland

Preface

This is the second edition of *The Oxford French Minidictionary*. It remains largely the work of Michael Janes, the compiler of the first edition, but some entries have been substantially revised and we have been able to incorporate a large proportion of new material. We hope to have kept to the aim of the original: to provide users requiring a compact dictionary with the maximum amount of useful material.

Dora Latiri-Carpenter
Edwin Carpenter
January 1993

Contents

Introduction

When you look up a word, you will find a pronunciation, a grammatical part of speech, and the translation. Sometimes more than one translation is given, and material in brackets in *italics* is included to help you choose the right one. For example, under **cabin** you will see (*hut*) and (*in ship, aircraft*). When a word has more than one part of speech, this can affect the translation. For example **praise** is translated one way when it is a verb (*v.t.*) and another way when it is a noun (*n.*).

A swung dash (∼) represents the entry word, or the part of it that comes before a vertical bar (as in **libert|y**). You will see it in examples using the entry word and words based on it. For example, under **good** you will find **as ∼ as** and **∼-looking**.

Translations are given in their basic form. You will find tables at the end showing verb forms. Irregular verbs are marked on the French to English side with †. This side also shows the plurals of nouns and the feminine forms of adjectives when they do not follow the normal rules.

Proprietary terms

This dictionary includes some words which are, or are asserted to be, proprietary terms or trade marks. The presence or absence of such assertions should not be regarded as affecting the legal status of any proprietary name or trade mark.

Pronunciation of French

Phonetic symbols

Vowels

i	v*ie*	y	vêt*u*
e	pr*é*	ø	p*eu*
ɛ	l*ai*t	œ	p*eu*r
a	pl*a*t	ə	*d*e
ɑ	b*a*s	ɛ̃	mat*in*
ɔ	m*o*rt	ɑ̃	s*an*s
o	m*o*t	ɔ̃	b*on*
u	gen*ou*	œ̃	*lun*di

Consonants and semi-consonants

p	*p*ayer	ʒ	*j*e
b	*b*on	m	*m*ain
t	*t*erre	n	*n*ous
d	*d*ans	l	*l*ong
k	*c*ou	r	*r*ue
g	*g*ant	ɲ	a*gn*eau
f	*f*eu	ŋ	campi*ng*
v	*v*ous	j	*y*eux
s	*s*ale	w	*ou*i
z	*z*éro	ɥ	h*u*ile
ʃ	*ch*at		

Notes: ' before the pronunciation of a word beginning with *h* indicates no liaison or elision.

An asterisk immediately following an apostrophe in some words like **qu'*** shows that this form of the word is used before a vowel or mute 'h'.

Abbreviations · Abréviations

abbreviation	*abbr., abrév.*	abréviation
adjective(s)	*a. (adjs.)*	adjectif(s)
adverb(s)	*adv(s).*	adverbe(s)
American	*Amer.*	américain
anatomy	*anat.*	anatomie
approximately	*approx.*	approximativement
archaeology	*archaeol.,*	archéologie
	archéol.	
architecture	*archit.*	architecture
motoring	*auto.*	automobile
auxiliary	*aux.*	auxiliaire
aviation	*aviat.*	aviation
botany	*bot.*	botanique
computing	*comput.*	informatique
commerce	*comm.*	commerce
conjunction(s)	*conj(s).*	conjonction(s)
cookery	*culin.*	culinaire
electricity	*electr., électr.*	électricité
feminine	*f.*	féminin
familiar	*fam.*	familier
figurative	*fig.*	figuré
geography	*geog., géog.*	géographie
geology	*geol., géol.*	géologie
grammar	*gram.*	grammaire
humorous	*hum.*	humoristique
interjection(s)	*int(s).*	interjection(s)
invariable	*invar.*	invariable
legal, law	*jurid.*	juridique
language	*lang.*	langue
masculine	*m.*	masculin
medicine	*med., méd.*	médecine
military	*mil.*	militaire
music	*mus.*	musique
noun(s)	*n(s).*	nom(s)
nautical	*naut.*	nautique
oneself	*o.s.*	se, soi-même
proprietary term	*P.*	marque déposée
pejorative	*pej., péj.*	péjoratif

philosophy	*phil.*	philosophie
photography	*photo.*	photographie
plural	*pl.*	pluriel
politics	*pol.*	politique
possessive	*poss.*	possessif
past participle	*p.p.*	participe passé
prefix	*pref., préf.*	préfixe
preposition(s)	*prep(s)., prép(s).*	préposition(s)
present participle	*pres. p.*	participe présent
pronoun	*pron.*	pronom
relative pronoun	*pron. rel.*	pronom relatif
psychology	*psych.*	psychologie
past tense	*p.t.*	passé
something	*qch.*	quelque chose
someone	*qn.*	quelqu'un
railway	*rail.*	chemin de fer
religion	*relig.*	religion
relative pronoun	*rel. pron.*	pronom relatif
school, scholastic	*schol., scol.*	scolaire
singular	*sing.*	singulier
slang	*sl.*	argot
someone	*s.o.*	quelqu'un
something	*sth.*	quelque chose
technical	*techn.*	technique
television	*TV*	télévision
university	*univ.*	université
auxiliary verb	*v. aux.*	verb auxiliaire
intransitive verb	*v.i.*	verbe intransitif
pronominal verb	*v. pr.*	verbe pronominal
transitive verb	*v.t.*	verbe transitif

FRANÇAIS–ANGLAIS
FRENCH–ENGLISH

A

a /a/ *voir* **avoir.**

à /a/ *prép.* (*à + le* = **au,** *à + les* = **aux**) in, at; (*direction*) to; (*temps*) at; (*jusqu'à*) to, till; (*date*) on; (*époque*) in; (*moyen*) by, on; (*prix*) for; (*appartenance*) of; (*mesure*) by. **donner**/*etc.* **à qn.,** give/*etc.* to s.o. **apprendre**/*etc.* **à faire,** learn/*etc.* to do. **l'homme à la barbe,** the man with the beard. **à la radio,** on the radio. **c'est à moi**/*etc.*, it is mine/*etc.* **c'est à vous**/*etc.* **de,** it is up to you/*etc.* to; (*en jouant*) it is your/*etc.* turn to. **à six km d'ici,** six km. away. **dix km à l'heure,** ten km. an *ou* per hour. **il a un crayon à la main,** he's got a pencil in his hand.

abaissement /abɛsmã/ *n.m.* (*baisse*) drop, fall.

abaisser /abese/ *v.t.* lower; (*levier*) pull *ou* push down; (*fig.*) humiliate. **s'~** *v. pr.* go down, drop; (*fig.*) humiliate o.s. **s'~ à,** stoop to.

abandon /abãdɔ̃/ *n.m.* abandonment; desertion; (*sport*) withdrawal; (*naturel*) abandon. **à l'~,** in a state of neglect. **~ner** /-one/ *v.t.* abandon, desert; (*renoncer à*) give up, abandon; (*céder*) give (**à,** to). **s'~ner à,** give o.s. up to.

abasourdir /abazurdir/ *v.t.* stun.

abat-jour /abaʒur/ *n.m. invar.* lampshade.

abats /aba/ *n.m. pl.* offal.

abattement /abatmã/ *n.m.* dejection; (*faiblesse*) exhaustion; (*comm.*) allowance.

abattis /abati/ *n.m. pl.* giblets.

abattoir /abatwar/ *n.m.* slaughterhouse, abattoir.

abattre† /abatr/ *v.t.* knock down; (*arbre*) cut down; (*animal*) slaughter; (*avion*) shoot down; (*affaiblir*) weaken; (*démoraliser*) dishearten. **s'~** *v. pr.* come down, fall (down). **se laisser ~,** let things get one down.

abbaye /abei/ *n.f.* abbey.

abbé /abe/ *n.m.* priest; (*supérieur d'une abbaye*) abbot.

abcès /apsɛ/ *n.m.* abscess.

abdi|quer /abdike/ *v.t./i.* abdicate. **~cation** *n.f.* abdication.

abdom|en /abdomɛn/ *n.m.* abdomen. **~inal** (*m. pl.* **~inaux**) *a.* abdominal.

abeille /abɛj/ *n.f.* bee.

aberrant, **~e** /abɛrã, -t/ *a.* absurd.

aberration /abɛrasjɔ̃/ *n.f.* aberration; (*idée*) absurd idea.

abêtir /abetir/ *v.t.* make stupid.

abhorrer /abore/ *v.t.* loathe, abhor.

abîme /abim/ *n.m.* abyss.

abîmer /abime/ *v.t.* damage, spoil. **s'~** *v. pr.* get damaged *ou* spoilt.

abject /abʒɛkt/ *a.* abject.

abjurer /abʒyre/ *v.t.* abjure.

ablation /ablɑsjɔ̃/ *n.f.* removal.

ablutions /ablysjɔ̃/ *n.f. pl.* ablutions.

aboiement /abwamɑ̃/ *n.m.* bark(ing). **~s**, barking.

abois (aux) /(oz)abwa/ *adv.* at bay.

abolir /abɔlir/ *v.t.* abolish. **~ition** *n.f.* abolition.

abominable /abɔminabl/ *a.* abominable.

abond|ant, ~ante /abɔdɑ̃, -t/ *a.* abundant, plentiful. **~amment** *adv.* abundantly. **~ance** *n.f.* abundance; (*prospérité*) affluence.

abonder /abɔ̃de/ *v.i.* abound (en, in). **~ dans le sens de qn.**, completely agree with s.o.

abonn|er (s') /(s)abɔne/ *v. pr.* subscribe(à, to). **~é, ~ée** *n.m., f.* subscriber; season-ticket holder. **~ement** *n.m.* (à un journal) subscription; (de bus, théâtre, etc.) season-ticket.

abord /abɔr/ *n.m.* access. **~s**, surroundings. **d'~**, first.

abordable /abɔrdabl/ *a.* (prix) reasonable; (personne) approachable.

abordage /abɔrdaʒ/ *n.m.* (accident: naut.) collision. **prendre à l'~**, (navire) board, attack.

aborder /abɔrde/ *v.t.* approach; (lieu) reach; (problème etc.) tackle. —*v.i.* reach land.

aborigène /abɔriʒɛn/ *n.m.* aborigine, aboriginal.

aboutir /abutir/ *v.i.* succeed, achieve a result. **~ à**, end (up) in, lead to. **n'~ à rien**, come to nothing.

aboutissement /abutismɑ̃/ *n.m.* outcome.

aboyer /abwaje/ *v.i.* bark.

abrasi|f, ~ve /abrazif, -v/ *a. & n.m.* abrasive.

abrégé /abreʒe/ *n.m.* summary.

abréger /abreʒe/ *v.t.* (texte) shorten, abridge; (mot) abbreviate, shorten; (visite) cut short.

abreuv|er /abrœve/ *v.t.* water; (fig.) overwhelm (de, with). **s'~er** *v. pr.* drink. **~oir** *n.m.* watering-place.

abréviation /abrevjasjɔ̃/ *n.f.* abbreviation.

abri /abri/ *n.m.* shelter. **à l'~**, under cover. **à l'~ de** sheltered from.

abricot /abriko/ *n.m.* apricot.

abriter /abrite/ *v.t.* shelter; (recevoir) house. **s'~** *v. pr.* (take) shelter.

abroger /abrɔʒe/ *v.t.* repeal.

abrupt /abrypt/ *a.* steep, sheer; (fig.) abrupt.

abruti, ~e /abryti/ *n.m., f.* (fam.) idiot.

abrutir /abrytir/ *v.t.* make ou drive stupid, dull the mind of.

absence /apsɑ̃s/ *n.f.* absence.

absent, ~e /apsɑ̃, -t/ *a.* absent, away; (chose) missing. —*n.m., f.* absente. **il est toujours ~**, he's still away. **d'un air ~**, absently. **~éisme** /-teism/ *n.m.* absenteeism. **~éiste** /-teist/ *n.m./f.* absentee.

absenter (s') /(s)apsɑ̃te/ *v. pr.* go ou be away; (sortir) go out, leave.

absolu /apsɔly/ *a.* absolute. **~ment** *adv.* absolutely.

absolution /apsɔlysjɔ̃/ *n.f.* absolution.

absor|ber /apsɔrbe/ *v.t.* absorb; (temps etc.) take up. **~bant, ~bante** *a.* (travail etc.) absorbing; (matière) absorbent. **~ption** *n.f.* absorption.

absoudre /apsudr/ *v.t.* absolve.

absten|ir (s') /(s)apstənir/ *v. pr.* abstain. **s'~ir de**, refrain from. **~tion** /-ɑ̃sjɔ̃/ *n.f.* abstention.

abstinence /apstinɑ̃s/ *n.f.* abstinence.

abstr|aire /apstrɛr/ *v.t.* abstract. **~action** *n.f.* abstraction. **faire**

~**action de,** disregard. ~**ait,** ~**aite** *a.* & *n.m.* abstract.

absurd|e /apsyrd/ *a.* absurd. ~**ité** *n.f.* absurdity.

abus /aby/ *n.m.* abuse, misuse; (*injustice*) abuse. ~ **de confiance,** breach of trust. ~ **sexuel,** sexual abuse.

abuser /abyze/ *v.t.* deceive. —*v.i.* go too far. **s'**~ *v. pr.* be mistaken. ~ **de,** abuse, misuse; (*profiter de*) take advantage of; (*alcool etc.*) over-indulge in.

abusi|f, ~**ve** /abyzif, -v/ *a.* excessive; (*usage*) mistaken.

acabit /akabi/ *n.m.* **du même** ~, of that same.

académicien, ~**ne** /akademisjɛ̃, -jɛn/ *n.m., f.* academician.

académ|ie /akademi/ *n.f.* academy; (*circonscription*) educational district. **A**~**ie,** Academy. ~**ique** *a.* academic.

acajou /akaʒu/ *n.m.* mahogany.

acariâtre /akarjɑtr/ *a.* cantankerous.

accablement /akabləmɑ̃/ *n.m.* despondency.

accabl|er /akable/ *v.t.* overwhelm. ~**er d'impôts,** burden with taxes. ~**er d'injures,** heap insults upon. ~**ant,** ~**ante** *a.* (*chaleur*) oppressive.

accalmie /akalmi/ *n.f.* lull.

accaparer /akapare/ *v.t.* monopolize; (*fig.*) take up all the time of.

accéder /aksede/ *v.i.* ~ **à,** reach; (*pouvoir, requête, trône, etc.*) accede to.

accélér|er /akselere/ *v.i.* (*auto.*) accelerate. —*v.t.,* **s'**~**er** *v. pr.* speed up. ~**ateur** *n.m.* accelerator. ~**ation** *n.f.* acceleration; speeding up.

accent /aksɑ̃/ *n.m.* accent; (*sur une syllabe*) stress, accent; (*ton*) tone. **mettre l'**~ **sur,** stress.

accent|uer /aksɑ̃tɥe/ *v.t.* (*lettre,*

syllabe) accent; (*fig.*) emphasize, accentuate. **s'**~**uer** *v. pr.* become more pronounced, increase. ~**uation** *n.f.* accentuation.

accept|er /aksɛpte/ *v.t.* accept. ~**er de,** agree to. ~**able** *a.* acceptable. ~**ation** *n.f.* acceptance.

acception /aksɛpsjɔ̃/ *n.f.* meaning.

accès /aksɛ/ *n.m.* access; (*porte*) entrance; (*de fièvre*) attack; (*de colère*) fit; (*de joie*) (out)burst. **les** ~ **de,** (*voies*) the approaches to. **facile d'**~, easy to get to.

accessible /aksesibl/ *a.* accessible; (*personne*) approachable.

accession /aksɛsjɔ̃/ *n.f.* ~ **à,** accession to.

accessit /aksesit/ *n.m.* honourable mention.

accessoire /akseswar/ *a.* secondary. —*n.m.* accessory; (*théâtre*) prop.

accident /aksidɑ̃/ *n.m.* accident. ~ **de train/d'avion,** train/plane crash. **par** ~, by accident. ~**é** /-te/ *a.* damaged *ou* hurt (in an accident); (*terrain*) uneven, hilly.

accidentel, ~**le** /aksidɑ̃tɛl/ *a.* accidental.

acclam|er /aklame/ *v.t.* cheer, acclaim. ~**ations** *n.f. pl.* cheers.

acclimat|er /aklimate/ *v.t.,* **s'**~**er** *v. pr.* acclimatize; (*Amer.*) acclimate. ~**ation** *n.f.* acclimatization; (*Amer.*) acclimation.

accolade /akolad/ *n.f.* embrace; (*signe*) brace, bracket.

accommodant, ~**e** /akɔmɔdɑ̃, -t/ *a.* accommodating.

accommodement /akɔmɔdmɑ̃/ *n.m.* compromise.

accommoder /akɔmɔde/ *v.t.* adapt (**à,** to); (*cuisiner*) prepare; (*assaisonner*) flavour. **s'**~ **de,** put up with.

accompagn|er /akɔ̃paɲe/ v.t. accompany. **s'∼er de**, be accompanied by. **∼ateur, ∼atrice** *n.m., f.* (*mus.*) accompanist; (*guide*) guide. **∼ement** *n.m.* (*mus.*) accompaniment.

accompli /akɔ̃pli/ a. accomplished.

accompl|ir /akɔ̃plir/ v.t. carry out, fulfil. **s'∼ir** v. pr. be carried out, happen. **∼issement** *n.m.* fulfilment.

accord /akɔr/ *n.m.* agreement; (*harmonie*) harmony; (*mus.*) chord. **être d'∼**, agree (**pour,** to). **se mettre d'∼**, come to an agreement, agree. **d'∼!**, all right!, OK!

accordéon /akɔrdeɔ̃/ *n.m.* accordion.

accord|er /akɔrde/ v.t. grant; (*couleurs etc.*) match; (*mus.*) tune. **s'∼er** v. pr. agree. **s'∼er avec**, (*s'entendre avec*) get on with. **∼eur** *n.m.* tuner.

accoster /akɔste/ v.t. accost; (*navire*) come alongside.

accotement /akɔtmɑ̃/ *n.m.* roadside, verge; (*Amer.*) shoulder.

accoter (s') /(s)akɔte/ v. pr. lean (**à,** against).

accouch|er /akuʃe/ v.i. give birth (**de,** to); (*être en travail*) be in labour. —v.t. deliver. **∼ement** *n.m.* childbirth; (*travail*) labour. (*médecin*) **∼eur** *n.m.* obstetrician. **∼euse** *n.f.* midwife.

accoud|er (s') /(s)akude/ v. pr. lean (one's elbows) on. **∼oir** *n.m.* armrest.

accoupl|er /akuple/ v.t. couple; (*faire copuler*) mate. **s'∼er** v. pr. mate. **∼ement** *n.m.* mating, coupling.

accourir /akurir/ v.i. run up.

accoutrement /akutrəmɑ̃/ *n.m.* (*strange*) garb.

accoutumance /akutymɑ̃s/ *n.f.* habituation; (*méd.*) addiction.

accoutum|er /akutyme/ v.t. accustom. **s'∼er** v. pr. get accustomed. **∼é a.** customary.

accréditer /akredite/ v.t. give credence to; (*personne*) accredit.

accro /akro/ *n.m./f.* (*drogué*) addict; (*amateur*) fan.

accroc /akro/ *n.m.* tear, rip; (*fig.*) hitch.

accroch|er /akroʃe/ v.t. (*suspendre*) hang up; (*attacher*) hook, hitch; (*déchirer*) catch; (*heurter*) hit; (*attirer*) attract. **s'∼er** v. pr. cling, hang on; (*se disputer*) clash. **∼age** *n.m.* hanging; hooking; (*auto.*) collision; (*dispute*) clash; (*mil.*) encounter.

accroissement /akrwasmɑ̃/ *n.m.* increase (**de,** in).

accroître /akrwatr/ v.t., **s'∼** v. pr. increase.

accroup|ir (s') /(s)akrupir/ v. pr. squat. **∼i** a. squatting.

accru /akry/ a. increased, greater.

accueil /akœj/ *n.m.* reception, welcome.

accueill|ir† /akœjir/ v.t. receive, welcome; (*aller chercher*) meet. **∼ant, ∼ante** a. friendly.

acculer /akyle/ v.t. corner. **∼ à**, force ou drive into ou against ou close to.

accumul|er /akymyle/ v.t., **s'∼** v. pr. accumulate, pile up. **∼ateur** *n.m.* accumulator. **∼ation** *n.f.* accumulation.

accus /aky/ *n.m. pl.* (*fam.*) battery.

accusation /akyzasjɔ̃/ *n.f.* accusation; (*jurid.*) charge. **l'∼**, (*magistrat*) the prosecution.

accus|er /akyze/ v.t. accuse (**de,** of); (*blâmer*) blame (**de,** for); (*jurid.*) charge (**de,** with); (*fig.*) show, emphasize. **∼er reception de,** acknowledge receipt of. **∼ateur, ∼atrice** a. incriminating; *n.m., f.* accuser. **∼é, ∼ée** a. marked; *n.m., f.* accused.

acerbe /asɛrb/ a. bitter.

acéré /asere/ a. sharp.

achalandé /aʃalɑ̃de/ a. **bien ~**, well-stocked.

acharné /aʃarne/ a. relentless, ferocious. **~ement** n.m. relentlessness.

acharner (s') /(s)aʃarne/ v. pr. **s'~ sur**, set upon; (poursuivre) hound. **s'~ à faire**, keep on doing.

achat /aʃa/ n.m. purchase. **~s**, shopping. **faire l'~ de**, buy.

acheminer /aʃmine/ v.t. dispatch, convey. **s'~ vers**, head for.

achet|er /aʃte/ v.t. buy **~er à**, buy from; (pour) buy for. **~eur, ~euse** n.m., f. buyer; (client de magasin) shopper.

achèvement /aʃɛvmɑ̃/ n.m. completion.

achever /aʃve/ v.t. finish (off). **s'~** v. pr. end.

acid|e /asid/ a. acid, sharp. —n.m. acid. **~ité** n.f. acidity. **~ulé** a. slightly acid.

acier /asje/ n.m. steel. **aciérie** n.f. steelworks.

acné /akne/ n.f. acne.

acolyte /akɔlit/ n.m. (péj.) associate.

acompte /akɔ̃t/ n.m. deposit, part-payment.

à-côté /akote/ n.m. side-issue. **~s**, (argent) extras.

à-coup /aku/ n.m. jolt, jerk. **par ~s**, by fits and starts.

acoustique /akustik/ n.f. acoustics. —a. acoustic.

acqu|érir† /akerir/ v.t. acquire, gain; (biens) purchase, acquire. **~éreur** n.m. purchaser. **~isition** n.f. acquisition; purchase.

acquiescer /akjese/ v.i. acquiesce, agree.

acquis, ~e /aki, -z/ n.m. experience. —a. acquired; (fait) established; (faveurs) secured. **~ à**, (projet) in favour of.

acquit /aki/ n.m. receipt. **par ~ de conscience**, for peace of mind.

acquitt|er /akite/ v.t. acquit; (dette) settle. **s'~er de**, (promesse, devoir) carry out. **s'~er envers**, repay. **~ement** n.m. acquittal; settlement.

âcre /akr/ a. acrid.

acrobate /akrɔbat/ n.m./f. acrobat.

acrobatie /akrɔbasi/ n.f. acrobatics. **~ aérienne**, aerobatics.

acrobatique /-tik/a. acrobatic.

acte /akt/ n.m. act, action, deed; (théâtre) act; (de naissance, mariage) certificate. **~s**, (compte rendu) proceedings. **prendre ~ de**, note.

acteur /aktœr/ n.m. actor.

acti|f, ~ve /aktif, -v/ a. active. —n.m. (comm.) assets. **avoir à son ~f**, have to one's credit ou name. **~vement** adv. actively.

action /aksjɔ̃/ n.f. action; (comm.) share; (jurid.) action. **~naire** /-jɔner/ n.m./f. shareholder.

actionner /aksjone/ v.t. work, activate.

activer /aktive/ v.t. speed up; (feu) boost. **s'~** v. pr. hurry, rush.

activiste /aktivist/ n.m./f. activist.

activité /aktivite/ n.f. activity. **en ~**, active.

actrice /aktris/ n.f. actress.

actualiser /aktɥalize/ v.t. update.

actualité /aktɥalite/ n.f. topicality. **l'~**, current events. **les ~s**, news. **d'~**, topical.

actuel, ~le /aktɥɛl/ a. present; (d'actualité) topical. **~lement** adv. at the present time.

acuité /akɥite/ n.f. acuteness.

acupunc|ture /akypɔ̃ktyr/ n.f. acupuncture. **~eur** n.m. acupuncturist.

adage /adaʒ/ n.m. adage.

adapt|er /adapte/ v.t. adapt;

(*fixer*) fit. **s'∼er** *v. pr.* adapt (o.s.). (*techn.*) fit, **∼ateur,** **∼atrice** *n.m., f.* adapter; *n.m.* (*électr.*) adapter. **∼ation** *n.f.* adaptation.

additif /aditif/ *n.m.* (*note*) rider; (*substance*) additive.

addition /adisjɔ̃/ *n.f.* addition; (*au café etc.*) bill; (*Amer.*) check. **∼nel,** **∼nelle** /-jɔnɛl/ *a.* additional. **∼ner** /-jɔne/ *v.t.* add; (*totaliser*) add (up).

adepte /adɛpt/ *n.m./f.* follower.

adéquat, ∼e /adekwa, -t/ *a.* suitable.

adhérent, ∼e /aderɑ̃, -t/ *n.m., f.* member.

adhé|rer /adere/ *v.i.* adhere, stick (à, to). **∼rer à,** (*club etc.*) be a member of; (*s'inscrire à*) join. **∼rence** *n.f.* adhesion. **∼sif, ∼sive** *a. & n.m.* adhesive. **∼sion** *n.f.* membership; (*accord*) adherence.

adieu (*pl.* **∼x**) /adjø/ *int. & n.m.* goodbye, farewell.

adipeu|x, ∼se /adipø, -z/ *a.* fat; (*tissu*) fatty.

adjacent, ∼e /adʒasɑ̃, -t/ *a.* adjacent.

adjectif /adʒɛktif/ *n.m.* adjective.

adjoindre /adʒwɛ̃dr/ *v.t.* add, attach; (*personne*) appoint. **s'∼** *v. pr.* appoint.

adjoint, ∼e /adʒwɛ̃, -t/ *n.m., f. & a.* assistant. **∼ au maire,** deputy mayor.

adjudant /adʒydɑ̃/ *n.m.* warrant-officer.

adjuger /adʒyʒe/ *v.t.* award; (*aux enchères*) auction. **s'∼** *v. pr.* take.

adjurer /adʒyre/ *v.t.* beseech.

admettre† /admɛtr/ *v.t.* let in, admit; (*tolérer*) allow; (*reconnaître*) admit; (*candidat*) pass.

administrati|f, ∼ve /administratif, -v/ *a.* administrative.

administr|er /administre/ *v.t.* run, manage; (*justice, biens, antidote, etc.*) administer. **∼ateur, ∼atrice** *n.m., f.* administrator, director. **∼ation** *n.f.* administration. **A∼ation,** Civil Service.

admirable /admirabl/ *a.* admirable.

admirati|f, ∼ve /admiratif, -v/ *a.* admiring.

admir|er /admire/ *v.t.* admire. **∼ateur, ∼atrice** *n.m., f.* admirer. **∼ation** *n.f.* admiration.

admissible /admisibl/ *a.* admissible; (*candidat*) eligible.

admission /admisjɔ̃/ *n.f.* admission.

adolescen|t, ∼te /adolesɑ̃, -t/ *n.m., f.* adolescent. **∼ce** *n.f.* adolescence.

adonner (s') /(s)adɔne/ *v. pr.* **s'∼ à,** devote o.s. to; (*vice*) take to.

adopt|er /adɔpte/ *v.t.* adopt. **∼ion** /-psjɔ̃/ *n.f.* adoption.

adopti|f, ∼ve /adɔptif, -v/ *a.* (*enfant*) adopted; (*parents*) adoptive.

adorable /adɔrabl/ *a.* delightful, adorable.

ador|er /adɔre/ *v.t.* adore; (*relig.*) worship, adore. **∼ation** *n.f.* adoration; worship.

adosser /adɔse/ *v.t.* **s'∼** *v. pr.* lean back (à, **contre,** against).

adouc|ir /adusir/ *v.t.* soften; (*boisson*) sweeten; (*personne*) mellow; (*chagrin*) ease. **s'∼r** *v. pr.* soften; mellow; ease; (*temps*) become milder. **∼ssant** *n.m.* (*fabric*) softener.

adresse /adrɛs/ *n.f.* address; (*habileté*) skill.

adresser /adrɛse/ *v.t.* send; (*écrire l'adresse sur*) address; (*remarque etc.*) address. **∼ la parole à,** speak to. **s'∼ à,** address; (*aller voir*) go and ask ou see; (*bureau*) enquire at; (*viser, intéresser*) be directed at.

adroit, **~e** /adrwa, -t/ *a.* skilful, clever. **~ement** /-tmã/ *adv.* skilfully, cleverly.

aduler /adyle/ *v.t.* adulate.

adulte /adylt/ *n.m./f.* adult. —*a.* adult; (*plante, animal*) fully-grown.

adultère /adylter/ *a.* adulterous. —*n.m.* adultery.

advenir /advənir/ *v.i.* occur.

adverbe /adverb/ *n.m.* adverb.

adversaire /adverser/ *n.m.* opponent, adversary.

adverse /advers/ *a.* opposing.

adversité /adversite/ *n.f.* adversity.

aérateur /aeratœr/ *n.m.* ventilator.

aér|er /aere/ *v.t.* air; (*texte*) lighten. **s'~er** *v.pr.* get some air. **~ation** *n.f.* ventilation.

aérien, **~ne** /aerjɛ̃, -jɛn/ *a.* air; (*photo*) aerial; (*câble*) overhead; (*fig.*) airy.

aérobic /aerobik/ *m.* aerobics.

aérodrome /aerodrom/ *n.m.* aerodrome.

aérodynamique /aerodinamik/ *a.* streamlined, aerodynamic.

aérogare /aerogar/ *n.f.* air terminal.

aéroglisseur /aeroglisœr/ *n.m.* hovercraft.

aérogramme /aerogram/ *n.m.* airmail letter; (*Amer.*) aerogram.

aéronautique /aeronotik/ *a.* aeronautical. —*n.f.* aeronautics.

aéronavale /aeronaval/ *n.f.* Fleet Air Arm; (*Amer.*) Naval Air Force.

aéroport /aeropor/ *n.m.* airport.

aéroporté /aeroporte/ *a.* airborne.

aérosol /aerosol/ *n.m.* aerosol.

aérospat|ial (*m. pl.* **~iaux**) /aerospasjal, -jo/ *a.* aerospace.

affable /afabl/ *a.* affable.

affaibl|ir /afeblir/ *v.t.*, **s'~ir** *v.pr.* weaken. **~issement** *n.m.* weakening.

affaire /afer/ *n.f.* matter, affair; (*histoire*) affair; (*transaction*) deal; (*occasion*) bargain; (*firme*) business; (*jurid.*) case. **~s**, affairs; (*comm.*) business; (*effets*) belongings. **avoir ~ à**, (have to) deal with. **c'est mon ~**, **ce sont mes ~s**, that is my business. **faire l'~**, do the job. **tirer qn. d'~**, help s.o. out. **se tirer d'~**, manage.

affair|er (s') /(s)afere/ *v.pr.* bustle about. **~é** *a.* busy.

affaiss|er (s') /(s)afese/ *v.pr.* (*sol*) sink, subside; (*poutre*) sag; (*personne*) collapse. **~ement** /-ɛsmã/ *n.m.* subsidence.

affaler (s') /(s)afale/ *v.pr.* slump (down), collapse.

affam|er /afame/ *v.t.* starve. **~é** *a.* starving.

affect|é /afɛkte/ *a.* affected. **~ation**[1] *n.f.* affectation.

affect|er /afɛkte/ *v.t.* (*feindre, émouvoir*) affect; (*destiner*) assign; (*nommer*) appoint, post. **~ation**[2] *n.f.* assignment; appointment, posting.

affect|if, **~ve** /afɛktif, -v/ *a.* emotional.

affection /afɛksjɔ̃/ *n.f.* affection; (*maladie*) ailment. **~ner** /-jɔne/ *v.t.* be fond of.

affectueu|x, **~se** /afɛktɥø, -z/ *a.* affectionate.

affermir /afermir/ *v.t.* strengthen.

affiche /afiʃ/ *n.f.* (*public*) notice; (*publicité*) poster; (*théâtre*) bill.

affich|er /afiʃe/ *v.t.* (*annonce*) put up; (*événement*) announce; (*sentiment etc, comput.*) display. **~age** *n.m.* billposting; (*électronique*) display.

affilée (d') /(d)afile/ *adv.* in a row, at a stretch.

affiler /afile/ *v.t.* sharpen.

affil|ier (s') /(s)afilje/ *v. pr.* become affiliated. **~iation** *n.f.* affiliation.

affiner /afine/ *v.t.* refine.

affinité /afinite/ *n.f.* affinity.

affirmati∣f, **∼ve** /afirmatif, -v/ *a.* affirmative. —*n.f.* affirmative.

affirm∣er /afirme/ *v.t.* assert. **∼ation** *n.f.* assertion.

affleurer /aflœre/ *v.i.* appear on the surface.

affliction /afliksjɔ̃/ *n.f.* affliction.

afflig∣er /afliʒe/ *v.t.* grieve. **∼é à** distressed. **∼é de**, afflicted with.

affluence /aflyɑ̃s/ *n.f.* crowd(s).

affluent /aflyã/ *n.m.* tributary.

affluer /aflye/ *v.i.* flood in; (*sang*) rush.

afflux /afly/ *n.m.* influx, flood; (*du sang*) rush.

affol∣er /afɔle/ *v.t.* throw into a panic. **s'∼er** *v. pr.* panic. **∼ant**, **∼ante** *a.* alarming. **∼ement** *n.m.* panic.

affranch∣ir /afrɑ̃ʃir/ *v.t.* stamp; (à la machine) frank; (*esclave*) emancipate; (*fig.*) free. **∼issement** *n.m.* (*tarif*) postage.

affréter /afrete/ *v.t.* charter.

affreu∣x, **∼se** /afrø, -z/ *a.* (laid) hideous; (*mauvais*) awful. **∼sement** *adv.* awfully, hideously.

affriolant, **∼e** /afrijɔlã, -t/ *a.* enticing.

affront /afrɔ̃/ *n.m.* affront.

affront∣er /afrɔ̃te/ *v.t.* confront. **s'∼er** *v. pr.* confront each other. **∼ement** *n.m.* confrontation.

affubler /afyble/ *v.t.* rig out (**de**, in).

affût /afy/ *n.m.* à l'**∼**, on the watch (**de**, for).

affûter /afyte/ *v.t.* sharpen.

afin /afɛ̃/ *prép. & conj.* **∼ de/que**, in order to/that.

africain, **∼e** /afrikɛ̃, -ɛn/ *a. & n.m., f.* African.

Afrique /afrik/ *n.f.* Africa. **∼ du Sud**, South Africa.

agacer /agase/ *v.t.* irritate, annoy.

âge /ɑʒ/ *n.m.* age. **quel ∼ avez-vous?**, how old are you? **∼ adulte**, adulthood. **∼ mûr**, middle age. **d'un certain ∼**, past one's prime.

âgé /ɑʒe/ *a.* elderly. **∼ de cinq ans/***etc.*, five years/*etc.* old.

agence /aʒɑ̃s/ *n.f.* agency, bureau, office; (*succursale*) branch. **∼ d'interim**, employment agency. **∼ de voyages**, travel agency.

agenc∣er /aʒɑ̃se/ *v.t.* organize, arrange. **∼ement** *n.m.* organization.

agenda /aʒɛ̃da/ *n.m.* diary; (*Amer.*) datebook.

agenouiller (s') /(s)aʒnuje/ *v. pr.* kneel (down).

agent /aʒã/ *n.m.* agent; (*fonctionnaire*) official. **∼ (de police)**, policeman. **∼ de change**, stockbroker.

agglomération /aglɔmerasjɔ̃/ *n.f.* built-up area, town.

aggloméré /aglɔmere/ *n.m.* (*bois*) chipboard.

agglomérer /aglɔmere/ *v.t.*, **s'∼** *v. pr.* pile up.

agglutiner /aglytine/ *v.t.*, **s'∼** *v. pr.* stick together.

aggraver /agrave/ *v.t.*, **s'∼** *v. pr.* worsen.

agil∣e /aʒil/ *a.* agile, nimble. **∼ité** *n.f.* agility.

agir /aʒir/ *v.i.* act. **il s'agit de faire**, it is a matter of doing; (*il faut*) it is necessary to do. **dans ce livre il s'agit de**, this book is about. **dont il s'agit**, in question.

agissements /aʒismã/ *n.m. pl.* (*péj.*) dealings.

agité /aʒite/ *a.* restless, fidgety; (*trouble*) agitated; (*mer*) rough.

agit∣er /aʒite/ *v.t.* (*bras etc.*) wave; (*liquide*) shake; (*troubler*) agitate; (*discuter*) debate. **s'∼er** *v. pr.* bustle about; (*enfant*) fidget; (*foule, pensées*) stir. **∼ateur**,

~**atrice** *n.m.*, *f.* agitator.
~**ation** *n.f.* bustle; (*trouble*)
agitation.

agneau (*pl.* ~**x** /aɲo/ *n.m.* lamb.

agonie /agɔni/ *n.f.* death throes.

agoniser /agɔnize/ *v.i.* be dying.

agraf|e /agraf/ *n.f.* hook; (*pour
papiers*) staple. ~**er** *v.t.* hook
(up); staple. ~**euse** *n.f.* stapler.

agrand|ir /agrɑ̃dir/ *v.t.* enlarge.
s'~ir *v. pr.* expand, grow.
~**issement** *n.m.* extension; (*de
photo*) enlargement.

agréable /agreabl/ *a.* pleasant.
~**ment** /-əmɑ̃/ *adv.* pleasantly.

agré|er /agree/ *v.t.* accept. ~**er à**,
please. ~**é à** *a.* authorized.

agrég|ation /agregɑsjɔ̃/ *n.f.* agré-
gation (*highest examination for
recruitment of teachers*). ~**é**,
~**ée** /-ʒe/ *n.m.*, *f.* agrégé (*teacher
who has passed the agrégation*).

agrément /agremɑ̃/ *n.m.* charm;
(*plaisir*) pleasure; (*accord*) assent.

agrémenter /agremɑ̃te/ *v.t.* embellish (**de**, with).

agrès /agrɛ/ *n.m. pl.* (gymnastics)
apparatus.

agress|er /agrese/ *v.t.* attack.
~**eur** /-ɛsœr/ *n.m.* attacker;
(*mil.*) aggressor. ~**ion** /-ɛsjɔ̃/
n.f. attack; (*mil.*) aggression.

agressi|f, ~**ve** /agresif, -v/ *a.*
aggressive. ~**vité** *n.f.* aggres-
siveness.

agricole /agrikɔl/ *a.* agricultural;
(*ouvrier etc.*) farm.

agriculteur /agrikyltœr/ *n.m.*
farmer.

agriculture /agrikyltyr/ *n.f.* agriculture, farming.

agripper /agripe/ *v.t.*, **s'~ à**,
grab, clutch.

agroalimentaire /agrɔalimɑ̃tɛr/
n.m. food industry.

agrumes /agrym/ *n.m. pl.* citrus
fruit(s).

aguerrir /agerir/ *v.t.* harden.

aguets (aux) /(o)zagɛ/ *adv.* on the
look-out.

aguicher /agiʃe/ *v.t.* entice.

ah /a/ *int.* ah, oh.

ahurir /ayrir/ *v.t.* dumbfound.
~**issement** *n.m.* stupefaction.

ai /e/ *voir* avoir.

aide /ɛd/ *n.f.* help, assistance, aid.
—*n.m./f.* assistant. **à l'~ de**, with
the help of. ~ **familiale**, home
help. ~**-mémoire** *n.m. invar.*
handbook of facts. ~ **sociale**,
social security; (*Amer.*) welfare.
~ **soignant**, ~ **soignante** *n.m.*,
f. auxiliary nurse. **venir en ~ à**,
help.

aider /ede/ *v.t./i.* help, assist. ~ **à
faire**, help to do. **s'~ de**, use.

aïe /aj/ *int.* ouch, ow.

aïeul, ~**e** /ajœl/ *n.m.*, *f.* grand-
parent.

aïeux /ajø/ *n.m. pl.* forefathers.

aigle /ɛgl/ *n.m.* eagle.

aigr|e /ɛgr/ *a.* sour, sharp; (*fig.*)
sharp. ~**e-doux**, ~**e-douce** *a.*
bitter-sweet. ~**eur** *n.f.* sourness;
(*fig.*) sharpness. ~**eurs d'estomac**, heartburn.

aigrir /egrir/ *v.t.* embitter;
(*caractère*) sour. **s'~** *v. pr.* turn
sour; (*personne*) become embittered.

aigu, ~**ë** /egy/ *a.* acute; (*objet*)
sharp; (*voix*) shrill. (*mus.*) **les
~s**, the high notes.

aiguillage /eguijaʒ/ *n.m.* (*rail.*)
points; (*rail.*, *Amer.*) switches.

aiguille /eguij/ *n.f.* needle; (*de
montre*) hand; (*de balance*)
pointer.

aiguill|er /eguije/ *v.t.* shunt; (*fig.*)
steer. ~**eur** *n.m.* pointsman;
(*Amer.*) switchman. ~**eur du
ciel**, air traffic controller.

aiguillon /eguijɔ̃/ *n.m.* (*dard*)
sting; (*fig.*) spur. ~**ner** /-jɔne/ *v.t.*
spur on.

aiguiser /eg(ɥ)ize/ *v.t.* sharpen;
(*fig.*) stimulate.

ail /aj/ (pl. **~s**) n.m. garlic.

aile /ɛl/ n.f. wing.

ailé /ele/ a. winged.

aileron /ɛlrɔ̃/ n.m. (de requin) fin.

ailier /elje/ n.m. winger; (Amer.) end.

aille /aj/ voir aller¹.

ailleurs /ajœr/ adv. elsewhere. **d'~**, besides, moreover. **par ~**, moreover, furthermore. **partout ~**, everywhere else.

aïoli /ajɔli/ n.m. garlic mayonnaise.

aimable /ɛmabl/ a. kind. **~ment** /-əmã/ adv. kindly.

aimant¹ /ɛmã/ n.m. magnet. **~er** /-te/ v.t. magnetize.

aimant², **~e** /ɛmã, -t/ a. loving.

aimer /eme/ v.t. like; (d'amour) love. **j'aimerais faire**, I'd like to do. **~ bien**, quite like. **~ mieux ou autant**, prefer.

aine /ɛn/ n.f. groin.

aîné, **~e** /ene/ a. eldest; (entre deux) elder. —n.m., f. eldest (child); elder (child). **~s** n.m. pl. elders. **il est mon ~**, he is older than me ou my senior.

ainsi /ɛ̃si/ adv. thus; (donc) so. **~ que**, as well as; (comme) as. **et ~ de suite**, and so on. **pour ~ dire**, so to speak, as it were.

air /ɛr/ n.m. air; (mine) look, air; (mélodie) tune. **~ conditionné**, air-conditioning. **avoir l'~ de**, look like. **avoir l'~ de faire**, appear to be doing. **en l'~**, (up) in the air; (promesses etc.) empty.

aire /ɛr/ n.f. area. **~ d'atterrissage**, landing-strip.

aisance /ɛzɑ̃s/ n.f. ease; (richesse) affluence.

aise /ɛz/ n.f. joy. —a. **bien ~ de/que**, delighted about/that. **à l'~**, (sur un siège) comfortable; (pas gêné) at ease; (fortuné) comfortably off. **mal à l'~**, uncomfortable; ill at ease. **aimer ses ~s**, like one's comforts. **se**

mettre à l'~, make o.s. comfortable.

aisé /eze/ a. easy; (fortuné) well-off. **~ment** adv. easily.

aisselle /ɛsɛl/ n.f. armpit.

ait /ɛ/ voir avoir.

ajonc /aʒɔ̃/ n.m. gorse.

ajourn|er /aʒurne/ v.t. postpone; (assemblée) adjourn. **~ement** n.m. postponement; adjournment.

ajout /aʒu/ n.m. addition.

ajouter /aʒute/ v.t. & s'~ v. pr. add (à, to). **~ foi à**, lend credence to.

ajust|er /aʒyste/ v.t. adjust; (coup) aim; (cible) aim at; (adapter) fit. **s'~er** v. pr. fit. **~age** n.m. fitting. **~é** a. close-fitting. **~ement** n.m. adjustment. **~eur** n.m. fitter.

alambic /alãbik/ n.m. still.

alanguir (s') /(s)alɑ̃gir/ v. pr. grow languid.

alarme /alarm/ n.f. alarm. **donner l'~**, sound the alarm.

alarm|er /alarme/ v.t. alarm. **s'~** v. pr. become alarmed (de, at). **~iste** /alarmist/ a. & n.m. alarmist.

albâtre /albɑtr/ n.m. alabaster.

albatros /albatros/ n.m. albatross.

album /albɔm/ n.m. album.

albumine /albymin/ n.f. albumin.

alcali /alkali/ n.m. alkali.

alcool /alkɔl/ n.m. alcohol; (eau de vie) brandy. **~ à brûler**, methylated spirit. **~ique** a. & n.m./f. alcoholic. **~isé** a. (boisson) alcoholic. **~isme** n.m. alcoholism.

alcootest /alkɔtɛst/ n.m. (P.) breath test; (appareil) breathalyser.

alcôve /alkov/ n.f. alcove.

aléa /alea/ n.m. hazard.

aléatoire /aleatwar/ a. uncertain; (comput.) random.

alentour /alɑ̃tur/ adv. around. **~s** n.m. pl. surroundings. **aux ~s de**, round about.

alerte /alɛrt/ a. agile. —n.f. alert. **~ à la bombe**, bomb scare.

alerter /alɛʀte/ v.t. alert.

algarade /algaʀad/ n.f. altercation.

algèbre /alʒɛbʀ/ n.f. algebra. **~ébrique** a. algebraic.

Alger /alʒe/ n.m./f. Algiers.

Algérie /alʒeʀi/ n.f. Algeria.

algérien, ~ne /alʒeʀjɛ̃, -jɛn/ a. & n.m., f. Algerian.

algue /alg/ n.f. seaweed. **les ~s**, (bot.) algae.

alias /aljɑs/ adv. alias.

alibi /alibi/ n.m. alibi.

aliéné, ~e /aljene/ n.m., f. insane person.

alién|er /aljene/ v.t. alienate; (céder) give up. **s'~er** v. pr. alienate. **~ation** n.f. alienation.

aligner /aliɲe/ v.t. (objets) line up, make lines of; (chiffres) string together. **~ sur**, bring into line with. **s'~** v. pr. line up. **s'~ sur**, align o.s. on. **alignement** /-əmɑ̃/ n.m. alignment.

aliment /alimɑ̃/ n.m. food. **~aire** /-tɛʀ/ a. food; (fig.) bread-and-butter.

aliment|er /alimɑ̃te/ v.t. feed; (fournir) supply; (fig.) sustain. **~ation** n.f. feeding; supply(ing); (régime) diet; (aliments) groceries.

alinéa /alinea/ n.m. paragraph.

aliter (s') /(s)alite/ v. pr. take to one's bed.

allaiter /alete/ v.t. feed. **~ au biberon**, bottle-feed. **~ au sein**, breast-feed; (Amer.) nurse.

allant /alɑ̃/ n.m. verve, drive.

allécher /aleʃe/ v.t. tempt.

allée /ale/ n.f. path, lane; (menant à une maison) drive(way). **~s et venues**, comings and goings.

allégation /alegasjɔ̃/ n.f. allegation.

allég|er /aleʒe/ v.t. make lighter; (poids) lighten; (fig.) alleviate. **~é** a. (diététique) light.

allègre /alɛgʀ/ a. gay; (vif) lively, jaunty.

allégresse /alegʀɛs/ n.f. gaiety.

alléguer /alege/ v.t. put forward.

Allemagne /almaɲ/ n.f. Germany. **~ de l'Ouest**, West Germany.

allemand, ~e /almɑ̃, -d/ a. & n.m., f. German. —n.m. (lang.) German.

aller¹† /ale/ v.i. (aux. être) go. **s'en ~** v. pr. go away. **~ à**, (convenir à) suit; (s'adapter à) fit. **~ faire**, be going to do. **comment allez-vous?**, (comment) ça va?, how are you? ça va!, all right! il va bien, he is well. **il va mieux**, he's better. **allez-y!**, go on! **allez!**, come on! allons-y!, let's go!

aller² /ale/ n.m. outward journey; **~ (simple)**, single (ticket); (Amer.) one-way (ticket). **~ (et) retour**, return journey; (Amer.) round trip; (billet) return (ticket); (Amer.) round trip (ticket).

allerg|ie /alɛʀʒi/ n.f. allergy. **~ique** a. allergic.

alliage /aljaʒ/ n.m. alloy.

alliance /aljɑ̃s/ n.f. alliance; (bague) wedding-ring; (mariage) marriage.

allié, ~e /alje/ n.m., f. ally; (parent) relative (by marriage).

allier /alje/ v.t. combine; (pol.) ally. **s'~** v. pr. combine; (pol.) become allied; (famille) become related (à, to).

alligator /aligatɔʀ/ n.m. alligator.

allô /alo/ int. hallo, hello.

allocation /alɔkasjɔ̃/ n.f. allowance. **~ (de) chômage**, unemployment benefit. **~s familiales**, family allowance.

allocution /alɔkysjɔ̃/ n.f. speech.

allongé /alɔ̃ʒe/ a. elongated.

allongement /alɔ̃ʒmɑ̃/ n.m. lengthening.

allonger /alɔ̃ʒe/ v.t. lengthen; (bras, jambe) stretch (out). **s'~** v.

pr. get longer; (*s'étendre*) stretch (o.s.) out.

allouer /alwe/ *v.t.* allocate.

allum|er /alyme/ *v.t.* light; (*radio, lampe, etc.*) turn on; (*pièce*) switch the light(s) on in; (*fig.*) arouse. **s'∼er** *v. pr.* (*lumière*) come on. **∼age** *n.m.* lighting; (*auto.*) ignition. **∼e-gaz** *n.m. invar.* gas lighter.

allumette /alymɛt/ *n.f.* match.

allure /alyʁ/ *n.f.* speed, pace; (*démarche*) walk; (*prestance*) bearing; (*air*) look. **à toute ∼**, at full speed. **avoir de l'∼**, have style.

allusion /alyzjɔ̃/ *n.f.* allusion (à, to); (*implicite*) hint (à, at). **faire ∼ à**, allude to; hint at.

almanach /almana/ *n.m.* almanac.

aloi /alwa/ *n.m.* **de bon ∼**, sterling; (*gaieté*) wholesome.

alors /alɔʁ/ *adv.* then. —*conj.* so, then. **∼ que**, when, while; (*tandis que*) whereas. **ça ∼!**, well! **et ∼?**, so what?

alouette /alwɛt/ *n.f.* lark.

alourdir /aluʁdiʁ/ *v.t.* weigh down.

aloyau (*pl.* **∼x**) /alwajo/ *n.m.* sirloin.

alpage /alpaʒ/ *n.m.* mountain pasture.

Alpes /alp/ *n.f. pl.* **les ∼**, the Alps.

alpestre /alpɛstʁ/ *a.* alpine.

alphab|et /alfabɛ/ *n.m.* alphabet. **∼étique** *a.* alphabetical.

alphabétiser /alfabetize/ *v.t.* teach to read and write.

alphanumérique /alfanymeʁik/ *a.* alphanumeric.

alpin, ∼e /alpɛ̃, -in/ *a.* alpine.

alpinis|te /alpinist/ *n.m./f.* mountaineer. **∼me** *n.m.* mountaineering.

altér|er /alteʁe/ *v.t.* falsify; (*abîmer*) spoil; (*donner soif à*) make thirsty. **s'∼er** *v. pr.* deteriorate. **∼ation** *n.f.* deterioration.

alternati|f, ∼ve /altɛʁnatif, -v/ *a.* alternating. —*n.f.* alternative. **∼vement** *adv.* alternately.

altern|er /altɛʁne/ *v.t./i.* alternate. **∼ance** *n.f.* alternation. **en ∼ance**, alternately. **∼é a.** alternate.

Altesse /altɛs/ *n.f.* Highness.

alt|ier, ∼ière /altje, -jɛʁ/ *a.* haughty.

altitude /altityd/ *n.f.* altitude, height.

alto /alto/ *n.m.* viola.

aluminium /alyminjɔm/ *n.m.* aluminium; (*Amer.*) aluminum.

alvéole /alveɔl/ *n.f.* (*de ruche*) cell.

amabilité /amabilite/ *n.f.* kindness.

amadouer /amadwe/ *v.t.* win over.

amaigr|ir /amegʁiʁ/ *v.t.* make thin(ner). **∼issant, ∼issante** *a.* (*régime*) slimming.

amalgam|e /amalgam/ *n.m.* combination. **∼er** *v.t.* combine, amalgamate.

amande /amãd/ *n.f.* almond; (*d'un fruit à noyau*) kernel.

amant /amã/ *n.m.* lover.

amarr|e /amaʁ/ *n.f.* (*mooring*) rope. **∼es**, moorings. **∼er** *v.t.* moor.

amas /ama/ *n.m.* heap, pile.

amasser /amase/ *v.t.* amass, gather; (*empiler*) pile up. **s'∼** *v. pr.* pile up; (*gens*) gather.

amateur /amatœʁ/ *n.m.* amateur. **∼ de**, lover of. **d'∼**, (*péj.*) amateurish. **∼isme** *n.m.* amateurism.

amazone (en) /(ãn)amazon/ *adv.* side-saddle.

Amazonie /amazɔni/ *n.f.* Amazonia.

ambages (sans) /(sãz)ãbaʒ/ *adv.* in plain language.

ambassade /ãbasad/ *n.f.* embassy.

ambassa|deur, ∼drice /ãbasadœʁ, -dʁis/ *n.m., f.* ambassador.

ambiance /ãbjãs/ *n.f.* atmosphere.

ambiant, **~e** /ɑ̃bjɑ̃, -t/ *a.* surrounding.

ambigu, **~ë** /ɑ̃bigy/ *a.* ambiguous. **~ité** /-qite/ *n.f.* ambiguity.

ambitieu|x, **~se** /ɑ̃bisjø, -z/ *a.* ambitious.

ambition /ɑ̃bisjɔ̃/ *n.f.* ambition. **~ner** /-jɔne/ *v.t.* have as one's ambition (**de**, to).

ambivalent, **~e** /ɑ̃bivalɑ̃, -t/ *a.* ambivalent.

ambre /ɑ̃br/ *n.m.* amber.

ambulanc|e /ɑ̃bylɑ̃s/ *n.f.* ambulance. **~ier**, **~ière** *n.m., f.* ambulance driver.

ambulant, **~e** /ɑ̃bylɑ̃, -t/ *a.* itinerant.

âme /ɑm/ *n.f.* soul. **~ sœur**, soul mate.

amélior|er /ameljɔre/ *v.t., s'~er* *v. pr.* improve. **~ation** *n.f.* improvement.

aménag|er /amenaʒe/ *v.t.* (*arranger*) fit out; (*transformer*) convert; (*installer*) fit up; (*territoire*) develop. **~ement** *n.m.* fitting out; conversion; fitting up; development; (*modification*) adjustment.

amende /amɑ̃d/ *n.f.* fine. **faire ~ honorable**, make an apology.

amend|er /amɑ̃de/ *v.t.* improve; (*jurid.*) amend. **s'~er** *v. pr.* mend one's ways. **~ement** *n.m.* (*de texte*) amendment.

amener /amne/ *v.t.* bring; (*causer*) bring about. **~ qn. à faire**, cause sb. to do. **s'~** *v. pr.* (*fam.*) come along.

amenuiser (s') /(s)amənɥize/ *v. pr.* dwindle.

amer, **amère** /amer/ *a.* bitter.

américain, **~e** /amerikɛ̃, -ɛn/ *a. & n.m., f.* American.

Amérique /amerik/ *n.f.* America. **~ centrale/latine**, Central/Latin America. **~ du Nord/Sud**, North/South America.

amertume /amertym/ *n.f.* bitterness.

ameublement /amœbləmɑ̃/ *n.m.* furniture.

ameuter /amøte/ *v.t.* draw a crowd of; (*fig.*) stir up.

ami, **~e** /ami/ *n.m., f.* friend; (*de la nature, des livres, etc.*) lover. —*a.* friendly.

amiable /amjabl/ *a.* amicable. **à l'~** *adv.* amicably; *a.* amicable.

amiante /amjɑ̃t/ *n.m.* asbestos.

amic|al (*m. pl.* **~aux**) /amikal, -o/ *a.* friendly. **~alement** *adv.* in a friendly manner.

amicale /amikal/ *n.f.* association.

amidon /amidɔ̃/ *n.m.* starch. **~ner** /-ɔne/ *v.t.* starch.

amincir /amɛ̃sir/ *v.t.* make thinner. **s'~** *v. pr.* get thinner.

amir|al (*pl.* **~aux**) /amiral, -o/ *n.m.* admiral.

amitié /amitje/ *n.f.* friendship. **~s**, kind regards. **prendre en ~**, take a liking to.

ammoniac /amɔnjak/ *n.m.* (*gaz*) ammonia.

ammoniaque /amɔnjak/ *n.f.* (*eau*) ammonia.

amnésie /amnezi/ *n.f.* amnesia.

amnistie /amnisti/ *n.f.* amnesty.

amniocentèse /amnjosɛtɛz/ *n.f.* amniocentesis.

amocher /amɔʃe/ *v.t.* (*fam.*) mess up.

amoindrir /amwɛ̃drir/ *v.t.* diminish.

amollir /amɔlir/ *v.t.* soften.

amonceler /amɔ̃sle/ *v.t.*, **s'~** *v. pr.* pile up.

amont (en) /(ɑ̃n)amɔ̃/ *adv.* upstream.

amorc|e /amɔrs/ *n.f.* bait; (*début*) start; (*explosif*) fuse, cap; (*de pistolet d'enfant*) cap. **~er** *v.t.* start; (*hameçon*) bait; (*pompe*) prime.

amorphe /amɔrf/ *a.* (*mou*) listless.

amortir /amɔrtir/ *v.t.* (*choc*)

cushion; (*bruit*) deaden; (*dette*) pay off; (*objet acheté*) make pay for itself.

amortisseur /amɔrtisœr/ *n.m.* shock absorber.

amour /amur/ *n.m.* love. **pour l'~de,** for the sake of. **~-propre** *n.m.* self-respect.

amouracher (s') /(s)amuraʃe/ *v. pr.* become infatuated (**de,** with).

amoureu|x /~se /amurø, -z/ *a.* (*ardent*) amorous; (*vie*) love. —*n.m.*, *f.* lover. **~x de qn.,** in love with s.o.

amovible /amɔvibl/ *a.* removable.

ampère /ɑ̃pɛr/ *n.m.* amp(ere).

amphibie /ɑ̃fibi/ *a.* amphibious.

amphithéâtre /ɑ̃fiteɑtr/ *n.m.* amphitheatre; (*d'université*) lecture hall.

ample /ɑ̃pl/ *a.* ample; (*mouvement*) broad. **~ment** /-əmɑ̃/ *adv.* amply.

ampleur /ɑ̃plœr/ *n.f.* extent, size; (*de vêtement*) fullness.

ampli /ɑ̃pli/ *n.m.* amplifier.

amplifi|er /ɑ̃plifje/ *v.t.* amplify; (*fig.*) expand, develop. **s'~er** *v.pr.* expand, develop. **~icateur** *n.m.* amplifier.

ampoule /ɑ̃pul/ *n.f.* (*électrique*) bulb; (*sur la peau*) blister; (*de médicament*) phial.

ampoulé /ɑ̃pule/ *a.* turgid.

amput|er /ɑ̃pyte/ *v.t.* amputate; (*fig.*) reduce. **~ation** *n.f.* amputation; (*fig.*) reduction.

amuse-gueule /amyzgœl/ *n.m. invar.* appetizer.

amus|er /amyze/ *v.t.* amuse; (*détourner l'attention de*) distract. **s'~er** *v. pr.* enjoy o.s.; (*jouer*) play. **~ant, ~ante** *a.* (*blague*) funny; (*soirée*) enjoyable, entertaining. **~ement** *n.m.* amusement; (*passe-temps*) diversion. **~eur** *n.m.* (*péj.*) entertainer.

amygdale /amidal/ *n.f.* tonsil.

an /ɑ̃/ *n.m.* year. **avoir dix/etc. ans,** be ten/*etc.* years old.

anachronisme /anakrɔnism/ *n.m.* anachronism.

analgésique /analʒezik/ *a. & n.m.* analgesic.

analog|ie /analɔʒi/ *n.f.* analogy. **~ique** *a.* analogical; (*comput.*) analogue.

analogue /analɔg/ *a.* similar.

analphabète /analfabɛt/ *a. & n.m./f.* illiterate.

analy|se /analiz/ *n.f.* analysis; (*de sang*) test. **~ser** *v.t.* analyse. **~ste** *n.m./f.* analyst. **~tique** *a.* analytical.

ananas /anana(s)/ *n.m.* pineapple.

anarch|ie /anarʃi/ *n.f.* anarchy. **~ique** *a.* anarchic. **~iste** *n.m./f.* anarchist.

anatom|ie /anatɔmi/ *n.f.* anatomy. **~ique** *a.* anatomical.

ancestral (*m. pl.* **~aux**) /ɑ̃sɛstral, -o/ *a.* ancestral.

ancêtre /ɑ̃sɛtr/ *n.m.* ancestor.

anche /ɑ̃ʃ/ *n.f.* (*mus.*) reed.

anchois /ɑ̃ʃwa/ *n.m.* anchovy.

ancien, ~ne /ɑ̃sjɛ̃, -jɛn/ *a.* old; (*de jadis*) ancient; (*meuble*) antique; (*précédent*) former, ex-, old; (*dans une fonction*) senior. —*n.m., f.* senior; (*par l'âge*) elder. **~ combattant,** ex-serviceman. **~nement** /-jɛnmɑ̃/ *adv.* formerly. **~neté** /-jɛnte/ *n.f.* age; seniority.

ancr|e /ɑ̃kr/ *n.f.* anchor. **jeter/lever l'~e,** cast/weigh anchor. **~er** *v.t.* anchor; (*fig.*) fix. **s'~er** *v.pr.* anchor.

andouille /ɑ̃duj/ *n.f.* sausage filled with chitterlings; (*idiot. fam.*) nitwit.

âne /ɑn/ *n.m.* donkey, ass; (*imbécile*) ass.

anéantir /aneɑ̃tir/ *v.t.* destroy; (*exterminer*) annihilate; (*accabler*) overwhelm.

anecdot|e /anɛkdɔt/ *n.f.* anecdote. **~ique** *a.* anecdotal.

aném|ie /anemi/ n.f. anaemia. **∼ié**, **∼ique** adjs. anaemic.

ânerie /anri/ n.f. stupidity; (parole) stupid remark.

ânesse /anɛs/ n.f. she-ass.

anesthés|ie /anɛstezi/ n.f. (opération) anaesthetic. **∼ique** a. & n.m. (substance) anaesthetic.

angle /ɑ̃ʒ/ n.m. angel. **aux ∼es** in seventh heaven. **∼élique** a. angelic.

angélus /ɑ̃ʒelys/ n.m. angelus.

angine /ɑ̃ʒin/ n.f. throat infection.

anglais, **∼e** /ɑ̃glɛ, -z/ a. English. —n.m., f. Englishman, Englishwoman. —n.m. (lang.) English.

angle /ɑ̃gl/ n.m. angle; (coin) corner.

Angleterre /ɑ̃glətɛr/ n.f. England.

anglicisme /ɑ̃glisism/ n.m. anglicism.

angliciste /ɑ̃glisist/ n.m./f. English specialist.

anglo- /ɑ̃glo/ préf. Anglo-.

anglophone /ɑ̃glɔfɔn/ a. English-speaking. —n.m./f. English speaker.

anglo-saxon, **∼ne** /ɑ̃glɔsaksɔ̃, -ɔn/ a. & n.m., f. Anglo- Saxon.

angoiss|e /ɑ̃gwas/ n.f. anxiety. **∼ant**, **∼ante** a. harrowing. **∼é** a. anxious. **∼er** v.t. make anxious.

anguille /ɑ̃gij/ n.f. eel.

anguleux, **∼se** /ɑ̃gylø/ a. (traits) angular.

anicroche /anikrɔʃ/ n.f. snag.

anim|al (pl. **∼aux**) /animal, -o/ n.m. animal. —a. (m. pl. **∼aux**) animal.

anima|teur, **∼trice** /animatœr, -tris/ n.m., f. organizer, leader; (TV) host, hostess.

anim|é /anime/ a. lively; (affairé) busy, (être) animate. **∼ation** n.f. liveliness; (affairement) activity; (cinéma) animation.

animer /anime/ v.t. liven up;

(mener) lead; (mouvoir, pousser) drive; (encourager) spur on. **s'∼** v. pr. liven up.

animosité /animozite/ n.f. animosity.

anis /anis/ n.m. (parfum, boisson) aniseed.

ankylos|er (s') /(s)ɑ̃kiloze/ v. pr. go stiff. **∼é** a. stiff.

anneau (pl. **∼x**) /ano/ n.m. ring; (de chaîne) link.

année /ane/ n.f. year.

annexe /anɛks/ a. attached; (question) related. (bâtiment) adjoining. —n.f. annexe; (Amer.) annex.

annex|er /anɛkse/ v.t. annex; (document) attach. **∼ion** n.f. annexation.

annihiler /aniile/ v.t. annihilate.

anniversaire /anivɛrsɛr/ n.m. birthday; (d'un événement) anniversary. —a. anniversary.

annonc|e /anɔ̃s/ n.f. announcement; (publicitaire) advertisement; (indice) sign. **∼er** v.t. announce; (dénoter) indicate. **s'∼er bien/mal**, look good/bad. **∼eur** n.m. advertiser; (speaker) announcer.

Annonciation /anɔ̃sjasjɔ̃/ n.f. l'∼, the Annunciation.

annuaire /anɥɛr/ n.m. year-book. **∼ (téléphonique)**, (telephone) directory.

annuel, **∼le** /anɥɛl/ a. annual, yearly. **∼lement** adv. annually, yearly.

annuité /anɥite/ n.f. annual payment.

annulaire /anɥlɛr/ n.m. ring-finger.

annul|er /anɥle/ v.t. cancel; (contrat) nullify; (jugement) quash. **s'∼er** v. pr. cancel each other out. **∼ation** n.f. cancellation.

anodin, **∼e** /anɔdɛ̃, -in/ a. insignificant; (blessure) harmless.

anomalie /anɔmali/ n.f. anomaly.

ânonner /anɔne/ v.t./i. mumble, drone.

anonymat /anɔnima/ n.m. anonymity.

anonyme /anɔnim/ a. anonymous.

anorak /anɔrak/ n.m. anorak.

anorexie /anɔreksi/ n.f. anorexia.

anorm|al (m. pl. ~aux) /anɔrmal, -o/ a. abnormal.

anse /ɑ̃s/ n.f. handle; (baie) cove.

antagonis|me /ɑ̃tagɔnism/ n.m. antagonism. **~te** n.m./f. antagonist; a. antagonistic.

antan (d') /(d)ɑ̃tɑ̃/ a. of long ago.

antarctique /ɑ̃tarktik/ a. & n.m. Antarctic.

antenne /ɑ̃tɛn/ n.f. aerial; (Amer.) antenna; (d'insecte) antenna; (succursale) agency; (mil.) outpost; (auto., méd.) emergency unit. **à l'~,** on the air. **sur l'~ de,** on the wavelength of.

antérieur /ɑ̃terjœr/ a. previous, earlier; (placé devant) front. **~ à,** prior to. **~ement** adv. earlier. **~ement à,** prior to. **antériorité** /-jɔrite/ n.f. precedence.

anthologie /ɑ̃tɔlɔʒi/ n.f. anthology.

anthropolo|gie /ɑ̃trɔpɔlɔʒi/ n.f. anthropology. **~gue** n.m./f. anthropologist.

anthropophage /ɑ̃trɔpɔfaʒ/ a. cannibalistic. —n.m./f. cannibal.

anti- /ɑ̃ti/ préf. anti-.

antiadhési|f, **~ve** /ɑ̃tiadezif, -v/ a. non-stick.

antiaérien, **~ne** /ɑ̃tiaerjɛ̃, -jɛn/ a. anti-aircraft. **abri ~,** air-raid shelter.

antiatomique /ɑ̃tiatɔmik/ a. **abri ~,** fall-out shelter.

antibiotique /ɑ̃tibjɔtik/ n.m. antibiotic.

anticancéreu|x, **~se** /ɑ̃tikɑ̃sero, -z/ a. (anti-)cancer.

antichambre /ɑ̃tiʃɑ̃br/ n.f. waiting-room, antechamber.

anticipation /ɑ̃tisipasjɔ̃/ n.f. **d'~,** (livre, film) science fiction. **par ~,** in advance.

anticipé /ɑ̃tisipe/ a. early.

anticiper /ɑ̃tisipe/ v.t./i. **~ (sur),** anticipate.

anticonceptionnel, **~le** /ɑ̃tikɔ̃sɛpsjɔnɛl/ a. contraceptive.

anticorps /ɑ̃tikɔr/ n.m. antibody.

anticyclone /ɑ̃tisyklon/ n.m. anticyclone.

antidater /ɑ̃tidate/ v.t. backdate, antedate.

antidote /ɑ̃tidɔt/ n.m. antidote.

antigel /ɑ̃tiʒɛl/ n.m. antifreeze.

antihistaminique /ɑ̃tiistaminik/ a. & n.m. antihistamine.

antillais, **~e** /ɑ̃tijɛ, -z/ a. & n.m., f. West Indian.

Antilles /ɑ̃tij/ n.f. pl. **les ~,** the West Indies.

antilope /ɑ̃tilɔp/ n.f. antelope.

antimite /ɑ̃timit/ n.m. moth repellent.

antipath|ie /ɑ̃tipati/ n.f. antipathy. **~ique** a. unpleasant.

antipodes /ɑ̃tipɔd/ n.m. pl. antipodes. **aux ~ de,** (fig.) poles apart from.

antiquaire /ɑ̃tikɛr/ n.m./f. antique dealer.

antiqu|e /ɑ̃tik/ a. ancient. **~ité** n.f. antiquity; (objet) antique.

antirouille /ɑ̃tiruj/ a. & n.m. rustproofing.

antisémit|e /ɑ̃tisemit/ a. anti-Semitic. **~isme** n.m. anti-Semitism.

antiseptique /ɑ̃tisɛptik/ a. & n.m. antiseptic.

antithèse /ɑ̃titɛz/ n.f. antithesis.

antivol /ɑ̃tivɔl/ n.m. anti-theft lock ou device.

antre /ɑ̃tr/ n.m. den.

anus /anys/ n.m. anus.

anxiété /ɑ̃ksjete/ n.f. anxiety.

anxieu|x, **~se** /ɑ̃ksjø, -z/ a. anxious. —n.m., f. worrier.

août /u(t)/ *n.m.* August.

apais|er /apeze/ *v.t.* calm down, (*douleur*, *colère*) soothe (*faim*) appease. **s'~er** *v. pr.* (*tempête*) die down. **~ement** *n.m.* appeasement; soothing. **~ements** *n.m. pl.* reassurances.

apanage /apanaʒ/ *n.m.* l'~ de, the privilege of.

aparté /aparte/ *n.m.* private exchange; (*théâtre*) aside. en ~, in private.

apath|ie /apati/ *n.f.* apathy. **~ique** *a.* apathetic.

apatride /apatrid/ *n.m./f.* stateless person.

apercevoir† /apɛrsəvwar/ *v.t.* see. **s'~ de**, notice. **s'~ que**, notice *ou* realize that.

aperçu /apɛrsy/ *n.m.* general view *ou* idea; (*intuition*) insight.

apéritif /aperitif/ *n.m.* aperitif.

à-peu-près /apøprɛ/ *n.m. invar.* approximation.

apeuré /apœre/ *a.* scared.

aphone /afɔn/ *a.* voiceless.

aphte /aft/ *n.m.* mouth ulcer.

apit|oyer /apitwaje/ *v.t.* move (to pity). **s'~oyer sur**, feel pity for. **~oiement** *n.m.* pity.

aplanir /aplanir/ *v.t.* level; (*fig.*) smooth out.

aplatir /aplatir/ *v.t.* flatten (out). **s'~** *v. pr.* (*s'allonger*) lie flat; (*s'humilier*) grovel; (*tomber: fam.*) fall flat on one's face.

aplomb /aplɔ̃/ *n.m.* balance; (*fig.*) self-possession. **d'~**, (*en équilibre*) steady, balanced.

apogée /apɔʒe/ *n.m.* peak.

apologie /apɔlɔʒi/ *n.f.* vindication.

a posteriori /aposterjori/ *adv.* after the event.

apostolique /apɔstɔlik/ *a.* apostolic.

apostroph|e /apɔstrɔf/ *n.f.* apostrophe; (*appel*) sharp address. **~er** *v.t.* address sharply.

apothéose /apoteoz/ *n.f.* final triumph.

apôtre /apotr/ *n.m.* apostle.

apparaître† /aparɛtr/ *v.i.* appear. **il apparaît que**, it appears that.

apparat /apara/ *n.m.* pomp. **d'~**, ceremonial.

appareil /aparɛj/ *n.m.* apparatus; (*électrique*) appliance; (*anat.*) system; (*téléphonique*) phone; (*dentaire*) brace; (*auditif*) hearing-aid; (*avion*) plane; (*culin.*) mixture. **l'~ du parti**, the party machinery. **c'est Gabriel à l'~**, it's Gabriel on the phone. **~(-photo)**, camera. **~ électroménager**, household electrical appliance.

appareiller¹ /apareje/ *v.i.* (*navire*) cast off, put to sea.

appareiller² /apareje/ *v.t.* (*assortir*) match.

apparemment /aparamã/ *adv.* apparently.

apparence /aparãs/ *n.f.* appearance. **en ~**, outwardly; (*apparemment*) apparently.

apparent, ~e /aparã, -t/ *a.* apparent; (*visible*) conspicuous.

apparenté /aparãte/ *a.* related; (*semblable*) similar.

appariteur /aparitœr/ *n.m.* (*univ.*) attendant, porter.

apparition /aparisjɔ̃/ *n.f.* appearance; (*spectre*) apparition.

appartement /apartəmã/ *n.m.* flat; (*Amer.*) apartment.

appartenance /apartənãs/ *n.f.* membership (à, of), belonging (à, to).

appartenir† /apartənir/ *v.i.* belong (à, to) **il lui/vous/***etc.* **appartient de**, it is up to him/you/*etc.* to.

appât /apa/ *n.m.* bait; (*fig.*) lure. **~er** /-te/ *v.t.* lure.

appauvrir /apovrir/ *v.t.* impoverish. **s'~** *v. pr.* grow impoverished.

appel /apɛl/ *n.m.* call; (*jurid.*) appeal; (*mil.*) call-up. **faire ~**, appeal. **faire ~ à**, (*recourir à*) call on; (*invoquer*) appeal to; (*évoquer*) call up; (*exiger*) call for. **faire l'~**, (*scol.*) take the register; (*mil.*) take a roll-call. **~ d'offres**, (*comm.*) invitation to tender. **faire un ~ de phares**, flash one's headlights.

appelé /aple/ *n.m.* conscript.

appel|er /aple/ *v.t./i.* call; (*nécessiter*) call for. **s'~er** *v. pr.* be called. **~é à**, (*désigné à*) marked out for. **en ~er à**, appeal to. **il s'appelle**, his name is. **~lation** /apelasjɔ̃/ *n.f.* designation.

appendic|e /apẽdis/ *n.m.* appendix. **~ite** *n.f.* appendicitis.

appentis /apɑ̃tis/ *n.m.* lean-to.

appesantir /apəzɑ̃tir/ *v.t.* weigh down. **s'~** *v. pr.* grow heavier. **s'~ sur**, dwell upon.

appétissant, **~e** /apetisɑ̃, -t/ *a.* appetizing.

appétit /apeti/ *n.m.* appetite.

applaud|ir /aplodir/ *v.t./i.* applaud. **~ir à**, applaud. **~isse-ments** *n.m. pl.* applause.

applique /aplik/ *n.f.* wall lamp.

appliqué /aplike/ *a.* painstaking.

appliquer /aplike/ *v.t.* apply; (*loi*) enforce. **s'~** *v. pr.* apply o.s (à, to). **s'~ à**, (*concerner*) apply to.

applicable /-abl/ *a.* applicable.

application /-asjɔ̃/ *n.f.* application.

appoint /apwẽ/ *n.m.* contribution. **d'~**, extra. **faire l'~**, give the correct money.

appointements /apwɛ̃tmɑ̃/ *n.m. pl.* salary.

apport /apɔr/ *n.m.* contribution.

apporter /apɔrte/ *v.t.* bring.

apposer /apoze/ *v.t.* affix.

appréciable /apresjabl/ *a.* appreciable.

appréc|ier /apresje/ *v.t.* appreciate; (*évaluer*) appraise.

~iation *n.f.* appreciation; appraisal.

appréhen|der /apreɑ̃de/ *v.t.* dread, fear; (*arrêter*) apprehend. **~sion** *n.f.* apprehension.

apprendre† /aprɑ̃dr/ *v.t./i.* learn; (*être informé de*) hear of. **~ qch. à qn.**, teach s.o. sth. (*informer*) tell s.o. sth. **~ à faire**, learn to do. **~ à qn. à faire**, teach s.o. to do. **~ que**, learn that; (*être informé*) hear that.

apprenti, **~e** /aprɑ̃ti/ *n.m.*, *f.* apprentice.

apprentissage /aprɑ̃tisaʒ/ *n.m.* apprenticeship; (*d'un sujet*) learning.

apprêté /aprete/ *a.* affected.

apprêter /aprete/ *v.t.*, **s'~** *v. pr.* prepare.

apprivoiser /aprivwaze/ *v.t.* tame.

approba|teur, **~trice** /aprɔ-batœr, -tris/ *a.* approving.

approbation /aprɔbasjɔ̃/ *n.f.* approval.

approchant, **~e** /aprɔʃɑ̃, -t/ *a.* close, similar.

approche /aprɔʃ/ *n.f.* approach.

approché /aprɔʃe/ *a.* approximate.

approcher /aprɔʃe/ *v.t.* (*objet*) move near(er) (**de**, to); (*personne*) approach. **—v.i.** **~** (**de**), approach. **s'~ de**, approach, move near(er) to.

approfond|ir /aprɔfɔ̃dir/ *v.t.* deepen; (*fig.*) go into thoroughly. **~i** *a.* thorough.

approprié /aprɔprije/ *a.* appropriate.

approprier (s') /(s)aprɔprije/ *v. pr.* appropriate.

approuver /apruve/ *v.t.* approve; (*trouver louable*) approve of; (*soutenir*) agree with.

approvisionn|er /aprɔvizjɔne/ *v.t.* supply. **s'~er** *v. pr.* stock up. **~ement** *n.m.* supply.

approximati|f, **~ve** /aprɔksi-matif, -v/ *a.* approximate. **~vement** *adv.* approximately.

approximation /aprɔksimasjɔ̃/ n.f. approximation.

appui /apɥi/ n.m. support; (de fenêtre) sill; (pour objet) rest. à l'~ de, in support of. prendre ~, support o.s. on.

appuie-tête /apɥitɛt/ n.m. head-rest.

appuyer /apɥije/ v.t. lean, rest; (presser) press; (soutenir) support, back. —v.i. ~ sur, press (on); (fig.) stress. s'~ sur, lean on; (compter sur) rely on.

âpre /apr/ a. harsh, bitter. ~ au gain, grasping.

après /aprɛ/ prép. after; (au-delà de) beyond. —adv. after(wards); (plus tard) later. ~ avoir fait, after doing. ~ qu'il est parti, after he left. ~ coup, after the event. ~ tout, after all. d'~, (selon) according to. ~-demain adv. the day after tomorrow. ~-guerre n.m. postwar period. ~-midi n.m./f. invar. afternoon. ~-rasage n.m. aftershave. ~-ski n.m. moonboot. ~-vente a. after-sales.

a priori /aprijɔri/ adv. in principle, without going into the matter. —n.m. preconception.

à-propos /aprɔpo/ n.m. timeliness; (fig.) presence of mind.

apte /apt/ a. capable (à, of).

aptitude /aptityd/ n.f. aptitude, ability.

aquarelle /akwarɛl/ n.f. water-colour, aquarelle.

aquarium /akwarjɔm/ n.m. aquarium.

aquatique /akwatik/ a. aquatic.

aqueduc /akdyk/ n.m. aqueduct.

arabe /arab/ a. Arab; (lang.) Arabic; (désert) Arabian. —n.m./f. Arab. —n.m. (lang.) Arabic.

Arabie /arabi/ n.f. ~ Séoudite, Saudi Arabia.

arable /arabl/ a. arable.

arachide /araʃid/ n.f. peanut.

araignée /arɛɲe/ n.f. spider.

arbitr|e /arbitr/ n.m. referee; (cricket, tennis) umpire; (maître) arbiter; (jurid.) arbitrator. ~age n.m. arbitration; (sport) refereeing. ~er v.t. (match) referee; (jurid.) arbitrate.

arbor|er /arbɔre/ v.t. display; (vêtement) sport.

arbre /arbr/ n.m. tree; (techn.) shaft.

arbrisseau (pl. ~x) /arbriso/ n.m. shrub.

arbuste /arbyst/ n.m. bush.

arc /ark/ n.m. (arme) bow; (voûte) arch. ~ de cercle, arc of a circle.

arcade /arkad/ n.f. arch. ~s, arcade, arches.

arc-boutant (pl. arcs-boutants) /arkbutɑ̃/ n.m. flying buttress.

arc-bouter (s') /(s)arkbute/ v. pr. lean (for support), brace o.s.

arceau (pl. ~x) /arso/ n.m. hoop; (de voûte) arch.

arc-en-ciel (pl. arcs-en-ciel) /arkɑ̃sjɛl/ n.m. rainbow.

archaï|que /arkaik/ a. archaic.

arche /arʃ/ n.f. arch. ~ de Noé, Noah's ark.

archéolo|gie /arkeɔlɔʒi/ n.f. archaeology. ~gique a. archaeological. ~gue n.m./f. archaeologist.

archer /arʃe/ n.m. archer.

archet /arʃɛ/ n.m. (mus.) bow.

archétype /arketip/ n.m. archetype.

archevêque /arʃəvɛk/ n.m. archbishop.

archi- /arʃi/ préf. (fam.) tremendously.

archipel /arʃipɛl/ n.m. archipelago.

architecte /arʃitɛkt/ n.m. architect.

architecture /arʃitɛktyr/ n.f. architecture.

archiv|es /aʀʃiv/ *n.f. pl.* archives. **~iste** *n.m./f.* archivist.

arctique /aʀktik/ *a. & n.m.* Arctic.

ardemment /aʀdamɑ̃/ *adv.* ardently.

ard|ent, ~ente /aʀdɑ̃, -t/ *a.* burning; (*passionné*) ardent; (*foi*) fervent. **~eur** *n.f.* ardour; (*chaleur*) heat.

ardoise /aʀdwaz/ *n.f.* slate.

ardu /aʀdy/ *a.* arduous.

are /aʀ/ *n.m.* are (= 100 square metres).

arène /aʀɛn/ *n.f.* arena. **~(s),** (*pour courses de taureaux*) bullring.

arête /aʀɛt/ *n.f.* (*de poisson*) bone; (*bord*) ridge.

argent /aʀʒɑ̃/ *n.m.* money; (*métal*) silver. **~ comptant,** cash. **prendre pour ~ comptant,** take at face value. **~ de poche,** pocket money.

argent|é /aʀʒɑ̃te/ *a.* silver(y); (*métal*) (silver-)plated. **~erie** /aʀʒɑ̃tʀi/ *n.f.* silver-ware.

argentin, ~e /aʀʒɑ̃tɛ̃, -in/ *a. & n.m., f.* Argentinian, Argentine.

Argentine /aʀʒɑ̃tin/ *n.f.* Argentina.

argil|e /aʀʒil/ *n.f.* clay. **~eux, ~euse** *a.* clayey.

argot /aʀgo/ *n.m.* slang. **~ique** /-ɔtik/ *a.* (*terme*) slang; (*style*) slangy.

arguer /aʀgɥe/ *v.i.* **~ de,** put forward as a reason.

argument /aʀgymɑ̃/ *n.m.* argument. **~er** /-te/ *v.i.* argue.

aride /aʀid/ *a.* arid, barren.

aristocrate /aʀistɔkʀat/ *n.m./f.* aristocrat.

aristocrat|ie /aʀistɔkʀasi/ *n.f.* aristocracy. **~ique** /-atik/ *a.* aristocratic.

arithmétique /aʀitmetik/ *n.f.* arithmetic. —*a.* arithmetical.

armateur /aʀmatœʀ/ *n.m.* shipowner.

armature /aʀmatyʀ/ *n.f.* framework; (*de tente*) frame.

arme /aʀm/ *n.f.* arm, weapon. **~s,** (*blason*) arms. **~ à feu,** firearm.

armée /aʀme/ *n.f.* army. **~ de l'air,** Air Force. **~ de terre,** Army.

armement /aʀməmɑ̃/ *n.m.* arms.

armer /aʀme/ *v.t.* arm; (*fusil*) cock; (*navire*) equip; (*renforcer*) reinforce; (*photo.*) wind on. **~ de,** (*garnir de*) fit with. **s'~ de,** arm o.s. with.

armistice /aʀmistis/ *n.m.* armistice.

armoire /aʀmwaʀ/ *n.f.* cupboard; (*penderie*) wardrobe; (*Amer.*) closet.

armoiries /aʀmwaʀi/ *n.f. pl.* (coat of) arms.

armure /aʀmyʀ/ *n.f.* armour.

arnaque /aʀnak/ *n.f.* (*fam.*) swindling. **c'est de l'~,** it's a swindle *ou* con (*fam.*). **~r** *v.t.* swindle, con (*fam.*).

arnica /aʀnika/ *n.f.* (*méd.*) arnica.

aromate /aʀɔmat/ *n.m.* herb, spice.

aromatique /aʀɔmatik/ *a.* aromatic.

aromatisé /aʀɔmatize/ *a.* flavoured.

arôme /aʀom/ *n.m.* aroma.

arpent|er /aʀpɑ̃te/ *v.t.* pace up and down; (*terrain*) survey. **~eur** *n.m.* surveyor.

arqué /aʀke/ *a.* arched; (*jambes*) bandy.

arraché (à l') /(al)aʀaʃe/ *adv.* with a struggle, after a hard struggle.

arrache-pied (d') /(d)aʀaʃpje/ *adv.* relentlessly.

arrach|er /aʀaʃe/ *v.t.* pull out *ou* off; (*plante*) pull *ou* dig up; (*cheveux, page*) tear *ou* pull out; (*par une explosion*) blow off. **~er à,** (*enlever à*) snatch from; (*fig.*) force *ou* wrest from. **s'~er qch.,**

arraisonner /araɛzɔne/ v.t. inspect.

arrangeant, ~e /arɑ̃ʒɑ̃, -t/ a. obliging.

arrangement /arɑ̃ʒmɑ̃/ n.m. arrangement.

arranger /arɑ̃ʒe/ v.t. arrange, fix up; (*réparer*) put right; (*régler*) sort out; (*convenir à*) suit. **s'~** v. pr. (*se mettre d'accord*) come to an arrangement; (*se débrouiller*) manage (**pour,** to).

arrestation /arɛstazjɔ̃/ n.f. arrest.

arrêt /arɛ/ n.m. stopping (**de,** of); (*lieu*) stop; (*pause*) pause; (*jurid.*) decree. **~s,** (*mil.*) arrest. **à l'~,** stationary. **faire un ~,** (make a) stop. **sans ~,** without stopping. **~ maladie,** sick leave. **~ de travail,** (*grève*) stoppage; (*méd.*) sick leave. **rester** *ou* **tomber en ~,** stop short.

arrêté /arɛte/ n.m. order.

arrêter /arɛte/ v.t./i. stop; (*date, regard*) fix; (*appareil*) turn off; (*appréhender*) arrest. **~** v. pr. stop. **(s')~ de faire,** stop doing.

arrhes /ar/ n.f. pl. deposit.

arrière /arjɛr/ n.m. back, rear; (*football*) back. *—a. invar.* back, rear. **à l'~,** in *ou* at the back. **en ~,** behind; (*marcher*) backwards. **en ~ de,** behind. **~-boutique,** n.f. back room (of the shop). **~-garde** n.f. rearguard. **~-goût** n.m. after-taste. **~-grand-mère** n.f. great-grandmother. **~-grand-père** (pl. **~-grands-pères**) n.m. great-grandfather. **~-pays** n.m. backcountry. **~-pensée,** n.f. ulterior motive. **~-plan** n.m. background.

arriéré /arjere/ a. backward. *—n.m.* arrears.

arrimer /arime/ v.t. rope down; (*cargaison*) stow.

arrivage /arivaʒ/ n.m. consignment.

arrivant, ~e /arivɑ̃, -t/ n.m., f. new arrival.

arrivée /arive/ n.f. arrival; (*sport*) finish.

arriver /arive/ v.i. (aux. être) arrive, come; (*réussir*) succeed; (*se produire*) happen. **~ à,** (*atteindre*) reach. **~ à faire,** manage to do. **en ~ à faire,** get to the stage of doing. **il arrive que,** it happens that. **il lui arrive de faire,** he (sometimes) does.

arriviste /arivist/ n.m./f. self-seeker.

arrogan|t, ~te /arɔgɑ̃, -t/ a. arrogant. **~ce** n.f. arrogance.

arroger (s') /(s)arɔʒe/ v. pr. assume (without justification).

arrondir /arɔ̃dir/ v.t. (make) round; (*somme*) round off. **s'~** v. pr. become round(ed).

arrondissement /arɔ̃dismɑ̃/ n.m. district.

arros|er /aroze/ v.t. water; (*repas*) wash down; (*rôti*) baste; (*victoire*) celebrate with a drink. **~age** n.m. watering. **~oir** n.m. watering-can.

arsenal (pl. **~aux**) /arsənal, -o/ n.m. arsenal; (*naut.*) dock-yard.

arsenic /arsənik/ n.m. arsenic.

art /ar/ n.m. art. **~s et métiers,** arts and crafts. **~s ménagers,** domestic science.

artère /artɛr/ n.f. artery. **(grande) ~,** main road.

artériel, ~le /arterjɛl/ a. arterial.

arthrite /artrit/ n.f. arthritis.

arthrose /artroz/ n.f. osteo-arthritis.

artichaut /artiʃo/ n.m. artichoke.

article /artikl/ n.m. article; (*comm.*) item, article. **à l'~ de la mort,** at death's door. **~ de fond,** feature (article). **~s d'ameublement,** furnishings. **~s de voyage,** travel requisites *ou* goods.

articul|er /artikyle/ *v.t.* **s'~er** *v. pr.* articulate. **~ation** *n.f.* articulation; (*anat.*) joint.

artifice /artifis/ *n.m.* contrivance.

artificiel, ~le /artifisjɛl/ *a.* artificial. **~lement** *adv.* artificially.

artill|erie /artijri/ *n.f.* artillery. **~eur** *n.m.* gunner.

artisan /artizɑ̃/ *n.m.* artisan, craftsman. **l'~ de**, (*fig.*) the architect of. **~al** (*m. pl.* **~aux**) /-anal, -o/ *a.* of *ou* by craftsmen, craft; (*amateur*) homemade. **~at** /-ana/ *n.m.* craft; (*classe*) artisans.

artist|e /artist/ *n.m./f.* artist. **~ique** *a.* artistic.

as¹ /a/ *voir* avoir.

as² /as/ *n.m.* ace.

ascendant¹, ~e /asɑ̃dɑ̃, -t/ *a.* ascending, upward.

ascendant² /asɑ̃dɑ̃/ *n.m.* influence. **~s**, ancestors.

ascenseur /asɑ̃sœr/ *n.m.* lift; (*Amer.*) elevator.

ascension /asɑ̃sjɔ̃/ *n.f.* ascent. **l'A~**, Ascension.

ascète /asɛt/ *n.m./f.* ascetic.

ascétique /asetik/ *a.* ascetic.

aseptique /asɛptik/ *a.* aseptic.

aseptis|er /asɛptize/ *v.t.* disinfect; (*stériliser*) sterilize. **~é** (*péj.*) sanitized.

asiatique /azjatik/ *a. & n.m./f.*, **Asiate** /azjat/ *n.m./f.* Asian.

Asie /azi/ *n.f.* Asia.

asile /azil/ *n.m.* refuge; (*pol.*) asylum; (*pour malades, vieillards*) home.

aspect /aspɛ/ *n.m.* appearance; (*fig.*) aspect. **à l'~ de**, at the sight of.

asperge /aspɛrʒ/ *n.f.* asparagus.

asper|ger /aspɛrʒe/ *v.t.* spray. **~sion** *n.f.* spray(ing).

aspérité /asperite/ *n.f.* bump, rough edge.

asphalt|e /asfalt/ *n.m.* asphalt. **~er** *v.t.* asphalt.

asphyxie /asfiksi/ *n.f.* suffocation.

asphyxier /asfiksje/ *v.t.*, **s'~** *v. pr.* suffocate, asphyxiate; (*fig.*) stifle.

aspic /aspik/ *n.m.* (*serpent*) asp.

aspirateur /aspiratœr/ *n.m.* vacuum cleaner.

aspir|er /aspire/ *v.t.* inhale; (*liquide*) suck up. —*v.i.* **~er à**, aspire to. **~ation** *n.f.* inhaling; suction; (*ambition*) aspiration.

aspirine /aspirin/ *n.f.* aspirin.

assagir /asaʒir/ *v.t.*, **s'~** *v. pr.* sober down.

assaill|ir /asajir/ *v.t.* assail. **~ant** *n.m.* assailant.

assainir /asenir/ *v.t.* clean up.

assaisonn|er /asɛzɔne/ *v.t.* season. **~ement** *n.m.* seasoning.

assassin /asasɛ̃/ *n.m.* murderer; (*pol.*) assassin.

assassin|er /asasine/ *v.t.* murder; (*pol.*) assassinate. **~at** *n.m.* murder; (*pol.*) assassination.

assaut /aso/ *n.m.* assault, onslaught. **donner l'~ à**, **prendre d'~**, storm.

assécher /asefe/ *v.t.* drain.

assemblée /asɑ̃ble/ *n.f.* meeting; (*gens réunis*) gathering; (*pol.*) assembly.

assembl|er /asɑ̃ble/ *v.t.* assemble, put together; (*réunir*) gather. **s'~er** *v. pr.* gather, assemble. **~age** *n.m.* assembly; (*combinaison*) collection; (*techn.*) joint. **~eur** *n.m.* (*comput.*) assembler.

assener /asene/ *v.t.* (*coup*) deal.

assentiment /asɑ̃timɑ̃/ *n.m.* assent.

asseoir† /aswar/ *v.t.* sit (down), seat; (*affermir*) establish; (*baser*) base. **s'~** *v. pr.* sit (down).

assermenté /asɛrmɑ̃te/ *a.* sworn.

assertion /asɛrsjɔ̃/ *n.f.* assertion.

asservir /asɛrvir/ *v.t.* enslave.

assez /ase/ *adv.* enough; (*plutôt*) quite, fairly. **~ grand/rapide** *etc.*, big/fast/*etc.* enough (pour, to). **~ de**, enough. **j'en ai ~ (de)**, I've had enough (of).

assid|u /asidy/ *a.* (zèle) assiduous; (régulier) regular. **~u auprès de**, attentive to. **~uité** /-ɥite/ *n.f.* assiduousness; regularity. **~ûment** *adv.* assiduously.

assiéger /asjeʒe/ *v.t.* besiege.

assiette /asjɛt/ *n.f.* plate; (équilibre) seat. **~ anglaise**, assorted cold meats. **~ creuse/plate**, soup-/dinner-plate. **ne pas être dans son ~**, feel out of sorts.

assiettée /asjete/ *n.f.* plateful.

assigner /asiɲe/ *v.t.* assign; (limite) fix.

assimil|er /asimile/ *v.t.*, **s'~er** *v. pr.* assimilate. **~er à**, liken to; (classer) class as. **~ation** *n.f.* assimilation; likening; classification.

assis, ~e /asi, -z/ *voir* **asseoir**. **—a.** sitting (down), seated.

assise /asiz/ *n.f.* (base) foundation. **~s**, (tribunal) assizes; (congrès) conference, congress.

assistance /asistãs/ *n.f.* audience; (aide) assistance. **l'A~** (publique), government child care service.

assistant, ~e /asistã, -t/ *n.m., f.* assistant; (univ.) assistant lecturer. **~s**, (spectateurs) members of the audience. **~ social, ~e sociale**, social worker.

assist|er /asiste/ *v.t.* assist. **—v.i. ~er à**, attend, be (present) at; (scène) witness. **~é par ordinateur**, computer-assisted.

association /asɔsjasjɔ̃/ *n.f.* association.

associé, ~e /asɔsje/ *n.m., f.* partner, associate. **—a.** associate.

associer /asɔsje/ *v.t.* combine (à, with). **~ qn. à**, (projet) involve s.o. in; (bénéfices) give s.o. a share of. **s'~ v. pr.** (sociétés associées) become associated, join forces (à, with); (s'harmoniser) combine (à,

with). **s'~ à**, (joie de qn.) share in; (opinion de qn.) share; (projet) take part in.

assoiffé /aswafe/ *a.* thirsty.

assombrir /asɔ̃bri̇r/ *v.t.* darken; (fig.) make gloomy. **s'~ v. pr.** darken; become gloomy.

assommer /asɔme/ *v.t.* knock out; (tuer) kill; (animal) stun; (fig.) overwhelm; (ennuyer. fam.) bore.

Assomption /asɔ̃psjɔ̃/ *n.f.* Assumption.

assorti /asɔrti/ *a.* matching; (objets variés) assorted.

assort|ir /asɔrti̇r/ *v.t.* match (à, with, to). **~ir de**, accompany with. **s'~ir (à)**, match. **~iment** *n.m.* assortment.

assoup|ir (s') /(s)asupi̇r/ *v. pr.* doze off; (s'apaiser) subside. **~i** *a.* dozing.

assouplir /asupli̇r/ *v.t.* make supple; (fig.) make flexible.

assourdir /asurdi̇r/ *v.t.* (personne) deafen; (bruit) deaden.

assouvir /asuvi̇r/ *v.t.* satisfy.

assujettir /asyʒeti̇r/ *v.t.* subject, subdue. **~ à**, subject to.

assumer /asyme/ *v.t.* assume.

assurance /asyrãs/ *n.f.* (self-)assurance; (garantie) assurance; (contrat) insurance. **~-maladie** *n.f.* health insurance. **~s sociales**, National Insurance. **~-vie** *n.f.* life assurance ou insurance.

assuré, ~e /asyre/ *a.* certain, assured; (sûr de soi) (self-)confident, assured. **—n.m., f.** insured. **~ment** *adv.* certainly.

assurer /asyre/ *v.t.* ensure; (fournir) provide; (exécuter) carry out; (comm.) insure; (stabiliser) steady; (frontières) make secure. **~ à qn. que**, assure s.o. that. **~ qn. de**, assure s.o. of. **~ la gestion de**, manage. **s'~ de/que**, make sure of/that. **s'~ qch.**, (se procurer) secure ou

ensure sth. **assureur** /-œr/
n.m. insurer.

astérisque /asterisk/ *n.m.* asterisk.

asthm|e /asm/ *n.m.* asthma.
~atique *a.* & *n.m./f.* asthmatic.

asticot /astiko/ *n.m.* maggot.

astiquer /astike/ *v.t.* polish.

astre /astr/ *n.m.* star.

astreignant, **~e** /astreɲɑ̃, -t/
a. exacting.

astreindre /astrɛ̃dr/ *v.t.* **~ qn. à
qch.,** force sth. on s.o. **~ à faire,**
force to do.

astringent, **~e** /astrɛ̃ʒɑ̃, -t/ *a.*
astringent.

astrolo|gie /astrɔlɔʒi/ *n.f.* astro-
logy. **~gue** *n.m./f.* astrologer.

astronaute /astronot/ *n.m./f.*
astronaut.

astronom|ie /astronomi/ *n.f.*
astronomy. **~e** *n.m./f.* astro-
nomer. **~ique** *a.* astronomical.

astuce /astys/ *n.f.* smartness;
(*truc*) trick; (*plaisanterie*) wisecrack.

astucieu|x, **~se** /astysjø, -z/ *a.*
smart, clever.

atelier /atalje/ *n.m.* workshop; (*de
peintre*) studio.

athé|e /ate/ *n.m./f.* atheist. **—a.**
atheistic. **~isme** *n.m.* atheism.

athl|ète /atlɛt/ *n.m./f.* athlete.
~étique *a.* athletic. **~étisme**
n.m. athletics.

atlantique /atlɑ̃tik/ *a.* Atlantic.
—n.m. A~, Atlantic (Ocean).

atlas /atlɑs/ *n.m.* atlas.

atmosph|ère /atmɔsfɛr/ *n.f.* at-
mosphere. **~érique** *a.* atmo-
spheric.

atome /atom/ *n.m.* atom.

atomique /atɔmik/ *a.* atomic.

atomiseur /atɔmizœr/ *n.m.* spray.

atout /atu/ *n.m.* trump (card);
(*avantage*) great asset.

âtre /ɑtr/ *n.m.* hearth.

atroc|e /atrɔs/ *a.* atrocious. **~ité**
n.f. atrocity.

atroph|ie /atrɔfi/ *n.f.* atrophy.
~ié *a.* atrophied.

attabler (s') /(s)atable/ *v. pr.* sit
down at table.

attachant, **~e** /ataʃɑ̃, -t/ *a.*
likeable.

attache /ataʃ/ *n.f.* (*agrafe*) fastener; (*lien*) tie.

attach|é /ataʃe/ *a.* **être ~é à,**
(*aimer*) be attached to. **—n.m., f.**
(*pol.*) attaché. **~é-case** *n.m.* attaché case. **~ement** *n.m.* attach-
ment.

attacher /ataʃe/ *v.t.* tie (up);
(*ceinture, robe, etc.*) fasten;
(*étiquette*) attach. **~ à,** (*attribuer
à*) attach to. **—v.i.** (*culin.*) stick.
s'~ à, (*se lier à*) become attached
to; (*se consacrer à*) apply o.s.
to.

attaque /atak/ *n.f.* attack.
(*cérébrale*), stroke. **il va en
faire une ~,** he'll have a fit. **~ à
main armée,** armed attack.

attaqu|er /atake/ *v.t./i.,* **s'~er à,**
attack; (*problème, sujet*) tackle.
~ant, **~ante** *n.m., f.* attacker;
(*football*) striker; (*football,
Amer.*) forward.

attardé /atarde/ *a.* backward;
(*idées*) outdated; (*en retard*) late.

attarder (s') /(s)atarde/ *v. pr.*
linger.

atteindre† /atɛ̃dr/ *v.t.* reach;
(*blesser*) hit; (*affecter*) affect.

atteint, **~e** /atɛ̃, -t/ *a.* **~ de,**
suffering from.

atteinte /atɛ̃t/ *n.f.* attack (**à, on**).
porter ~ à, make an attack on.

attel|er /atle/ *v.t.* (*cheval*) harness;
(*remorque*) couple. **s'~er à,** get
down to. **~age** *n.m.* harnessing;
coupling; (*bêtes*) team.

attelle /atɛl/ *n.f.* splint.

attenant, **~e** /atnɑ̃, -t/ *a.* **~
(à),** adjoining.

attendant (en) /(ɑ̃n)atɑ̃dɑ̃/ *adv.*
meanwhile.

attendre /atɑ̃dr/ *v.t.* wait for;

(*bébé*) expect; (*être le sort de*) await; (*escompter*) expect. —*v.i.* wait. **~ que tu fasse**, wait for s.o. to do. **s'~ à**, expect.

attendr|ir /atɑ̃driːr/ *v.t.* move (to pity). **s'~ir** *v. pr.* be moved to pity. **~issant**, **~issante** *a.* moving.

attendu /atɑ̃dy/ *a.* (*escompté*) expected; (*espéré*) long-awaited. **~ que**, considering that.

attentat /atɑ̃ta/ *n.m.* murder attempt. **~ (à la bombe)**, (bomb) attack.

attente /atɑ̃t/ *n.f.* wait(ing); (*espoir*) expectation.

attenter /atɑ̃te/ *v.i.* **~ à**, make an attempt on; (*fig.*) violate.

attenti|f, **~ve** /atɑ̃tif, -v/ *a.* attentive; (*scrupuleux*) careful. **~f à**, mindful of; (*soucieux*) careful of. **~vement** *adv.* attentively.

attention /atɑ̃sjɔ̃/ *n.f.* attention; (*soin*) care. **~**, watch out (for)! **faire ~ à**, (*professeur*) pay attention to; (*marche*) mind. **faire ~ à faire**, be careful to do. **~né** /-jɔne/ *a.* considerate.

attentisme /atɑ̃tism/ *n.m.* wait-and-see policy.

atténuer /atenɥe/ *v.t.* (*violence*) tone down; (*douleur*) ease; (*faute*) mitigate. **s'~** *v. pr.* subside.

atterrer /atere/ *v.t.* dismay.

atterr|ir /aterir/ *v.i.* land. **~issage** *n.m.* landing.

attestation /atɛstasjɔ̃/ *n.f.* certificate.

attester /atɛste/ *v.t.* testify to. **~ que**, testify that.

attifé /atife/ *a.* (*fam.*) dressed up.

attirail /atiraj/ *n.m.* gear.

attirance /atirɑ̃s/ *n.f.* attraction.

attirant, **~e** /atirɑ̃, -t/ *a.* attractive.

attirer /atire/ *v.t.* draw, attract; (*causer*) bring. **s'~** *v. pr.* bring upon o.s.; (*amis*) win.

attiser /atize/ *v.t.* (*feu*) poke; (*sentiment*) stir up.

attitré /atitre/ *a.* accredited; (*habituel*) usual.

attitude /atityd/ *n.f.* attitude; (*maintien*) bearing.

attraction /atraksjɔ̃/ *n.f.* attraction.

attrait /atrɛ/ *n.m.* attraction.

attrape-nigaud /atrapnigo/ *n.m.* (*fam.*) con.

attraper /atrape/ *v.t.* catch; (*habitude, style*) pick up; (*duper*) take in; (*gronder: fam.*) tell off.

attrayant, **~e** /atrɛjɑ̃, -t/ *a.* attractive.

attrib|uer /atribɥe/ *v.t.* award; (*donner*) assign; (*imputer*) attribute. **s'~uer** *v. pr.* claim. **~ution** *n.f.* awarding; assignment. **~utions** *n.f. pl.* attributions.

attrister /atriste/ *v.t.* sadden.

attroup|er (s') /(s)atrupe/ *v. pr.* gather. **~ement** *n.m.* crowd.

au /o/ *voir* **à**.

aubaine /oben/ *n.f.* (stroke of) good fortune.

aube /ob/ *n.f.* dawn, daybreak.

aubépine /obepin/ *n.f.* hawthorn.

auberg|e /obɛrʒ/ *n.f.* inn. **~e de jeunesse**, youth hostel. **~iste** *n.m./f.* innkeeper.

aubergine /obɛrʒin/ *n.f.* aubergine; (*Amer.*) egg-plant.

aucun, **~e** /okœ̃, okyn/ *a.* no, not any; (*positif*) any. —*pron.* none, not any; (*positif*) any. **des deux**, neither of the two. **d'~s**, some. **~ement** /okynmɑ̃/ *adv.* not at all.

audace /odas/ *n.f.* daring; (*impudence*) audacity.

audacieu|x, **~se** /odasjø. -z/ *a.* daring.

au-delà /odla/ *adv.*, **~ de** *prép.* beyond.

au-dessous /odsu/ *adv.*, **~ de** *prép.* below; (*couvert par*) under.

au-dessus /ɔdsy/ *adv.*, **~ de** *prép.* above.

au-devant /odvã(də)/ *prép.* **aller ~ de** qn., go to meet s.o.

audience /odjãs/ *n.f.* audience; (*d'un tribunal*) hearing; (*intérêt*) attention.

Audimat /odimat/ *n.m.* (P.) **l'~,** the TV ratings.

audiotypiste /odjotipist/ *n.m./f.* audio typist.

audio-visuel, **~le** /odjovizɥɛl/ *a.* audio-visual.

audi|teur, **~trice** /oditœr, -tris/ *n.m., f.* listener.

audition /odisjõ/ *n.f.* hearing; (*théâtre, mus.*) audition. **~ner** /-jone/ *v.t./i.* audition.

auditoire /oditwar/ *n.m.* audience.

auditorium /oditɔrjɔm/ *n.m.* (*mus., radio*) recording studio.

auge /oʒ/ *n.f.* trough.

augment|er /ogmãte/ *v.t./i.* increase; (*employé*) increase the pay of. **~ation** *n.f.* increase. **~ation (de salaire),** (pay) rise; (*Amer.*) raise.

augure /ogyr/ *n.m.* (*devin*) oracle. **être de bon/mauvais ~,** be a good/bad sign.

auguste /ogyst/ *a.* august.

aujourd'hui /oʒurdɥi/ *adv.* today.

aumône /omon/ *n.f.* alms.

aumônier /omonje/ *n.m.* chaplain.

auparavant /oparavã/ *adv.* before(hand).

auprès (de) /oprɛ(də)/ *prép.* by, next to; (*comparé à*) compared with; (*s'adressant à*) to.

auquel, ~le /okɛl/ *voir* **lequel**.

aura, aurait /ora, orɛ/ *voir* **avoir**.

auréole /oreɔl/ *n.f.* halo.

auriculaire /orikyler/ *n.m.* little finger.

aurore /orɔr/ *n.f.* dawn.

ausculter /ɔskylte/ *v.t.* examine with a stethoscope.

auspices /ɔspis/ *n.m. pl.* auspices.

aussi /osi/ *adv.* too, also; (*comparaison*) as; (*tellement*) so. —*conj.* (*donc*) therefore. **~ bien que,** as well as.

aussitôt /osito/ *adv.* immediately. **~ que,** as soon as. **~ arrivé/levé/***etc.*, as soon as one has arrived/got up/*etc.*

aust|ère /ɔster/ *a.* austere. **~érité** *n.f.* austerity.

austral (*m. pl.* **~s**) /ɔstral/ *a.* southern.

Australie /ɔstrali/ *n.f.* Australia.

australien, **~ne** /ɔstraljɛ̃, -jɛn/ *a. & n.m., f.* Australian.

autant /otã/ *adv.* (*travailler, manger, etc.*) as much (**que, as**). **~ de,** (*quantité*) as much (**que, as**); (*nombre*) as many (**que, as**); (*tant*) so much; so many. **~ faire,** one had better do. **d'~ plus que,** all the more since. **en faire ~,** do the same. **pour ~,** for all that.

autel /otɛl/ *n.m.* altar.

auteur /otœr/ *n.m.* author. **l'~ du crime,** the person who committed the crime.

authentifier /otãtifje/ *v.t.* authenticate.

authenti|que /otãtik/ *a.* authentic. **~cité** *n.f.* authenticity.

auto /oto/ *n.f.* car. **~s tamponneuses,** dodgems, bumper cars.

auto- /oto/ *préf.* self-, auto-.

autobiographie /otobjɔgrafi/ *n.f.* autobiography.

autobus /otɔbys/ *n.m.* bus.

autocar /otɔkar/ *n.m.* coach.

autochtone /otɔktɔn/ *n.m./f.* native.

autocollant, **~e** /otɔkɔlã, -t/ *a.* self-adhesive. —*n.m.* sticker.

autocratique /otɔkratik/ *a.* autocratic.

autocuiseur /otɔkyizœr/ *n.* pressure cooker.

autodéfense /otɔdefɑ̃s/ *n.f.* self-defence.

autodidacte /otɔdidakt/ *a.* & *n.m./f.* self-taught (person).

auto-école /otɔekɔl/ *n.f.* driving school.

autographe /otɔgraf/ *n.m.* autograph.

automate /otɔmat/ *n.m.* automaton, robot.

automatique /otɔmatik/ *a.* automatic. **∼ment** *adv.* automatically.

automat|iser /otɔmatize/ *v.t.* automate. **∼ion** /-mɑsjɔ̃/ *n.f.* **∼isation** *n.f.* automation.

automne /otɔn/ *n.m.* autumn; *(Amer.)* fall.

automobil|e /otɔmobil/ *a.* motor, car. —*n.f.* (motor) car. l'**∼e**, *(sport)* motoring. **∼iste** *n.m./f.* motorist.

autonom|e /otɔnom/ *a.* autonomous. **∼ie** *n.f.* autonomy.

autopsie /otɔpsi/ *n.f.* post-mortem, autopsy.

autoradio /otɔradjo/ *n.m.* car radio.

autorail /otɔraj/ *n.m.* railcar.

autorisation /otɔrizɑsjɔ̃/ *n.f.* permission, authorization; *(permis)* permit.

autoris|er /otɔrize/ *v.t.* authorize, permit; *(rendre possible)* allow (of). **∼é** *a.* *(opinions)* authoritative.

autoritaire /otɔritɛr/ *a.* authoritarian.

autorité /otɔrite/ *n.f.* authority. **faire ∼**, be authoritative.

autoroute /otɔrut/ *n.f.* motorway; *(Amer.)* highway.

auto-stop /otɔstɔp/ *n.m.* hitch-hiking. **faire de l'∼**, hitch-hike. **prendre en ∼**, give a lift to. **∼peur**, **∼peuse** *n.m.,f.* hitch-hiker.

autour /otur/ *adv.*, **∼ de** *prép.* around. **tout ∼**, all around.

autre /otr/ *a.* other. **un ∼ jour**/*etc.*, another day/*etc.* —*pron.* **un ∼**, **une ∼**, another (one). l'**∼**, the other (one). **les autres**, the others; *(autrui)* others. **d'∼s**, (some) others. l'**un l'∼**, each other. l'**un et l'∼**, both of them. **∼ chose**/**part**, sth./somewhere else. **qn.**/**rien d'∼**, s.o./nothing else. **quoi d'∼?**, what else? **d'∼ part**, on the other hand. **vous ∼s Anglais**, you English. **d'un jour**/*etc.* **à l'∼**, *(bientôt)* any day/*etc.* now. **entre ∼s**, among other things.

autrefois /otrəfwa/ *adv.* in the past.

autrement /otrəmɑ̃/ *adv.* differently; *(sinon)* otherwise; *(plus)* far more. **∼ dit**, in other words.

Autriche /otriʃ/ *n.f.* Austria.

autrichien, ∼ne /otriʃjɛ̃, -jɛn/ *a.* & *n.m.,f.* Austrian.

autruche /otryʃ/ *n.f.* ostrich.

autrui /otrɥi/ *pron.* others.

auvent /ovɑ̃/ *n.m.* canopy.

aux /o/ *voir* **à**.

auxiliaire /oksiljɛr/ *a.* auxiliary. —*n.m./f.* *(assistant)* auxiliary. —*n.m.* *(gram.)* auxiliary.

auxquel|s, ∼les /okɛl/ *voir* **lequel**.

aval (en) /(ɑ̃n)aval/ *adv.* downstream.

avalanche /avalɑ̃ʃ/ *n.f.* avalanche.

avaler /avale/ *v.t.* swallow.

avance /avɑ̃s/ *n.f.* advance; *(sur un concurrent)* lead. **∼ (de fonds)**, advance. **à l'∼**, **d'∼**, in advance. **en ∼**, early; *(montre)* fast. **en ∼ (sur)**, *(menant)* ahead (of).

avancement /avɑ̃smɑ̃/ *n.m.* promotion.

avanc|er /avɑ̃se/ *v.i.* move forward, advance; *(travail)* make progress; *(montre)* be fast; *(faire saillie)* jut out. —*v.t.* *(argent)* advance; *(montre)* put forward. **s'∼er** *v. pr.* move forward, advance; (*se hasarder*) commit o.s. ~é, ~ée *a*. advanced; *n.f.* projection.

avanie /avani/ *n.f.* affront.

avant /avɑ̃/ *prép* & *adv.* before. —*a. invar.* front. —*n.m.* front; (*football*) forward. ~ **de faire**, before doing. ~ **qu'il (ne) fasse**, before he does. **en** ~, (*mouvement*) forward. **en** ~ **(de)**, (*position, temps*) in front (of). ~ **peu**, before long. ~ **tout**, above all. **bien** ~ **dans**, very deep(ly) *ou* far into. ~**bras** *n.m. invar.* forearm. ~**centre** *n.m.* centreforward. ~**coureur** *a. invar.* precursory, foreshadowing. ~**dernier**, ~**dernière** *a.* & *n.m., f.* last but one. ~**garde** *n.f.* (*mil.*) vanguard; (*fig.*) avant-garde. ~**goût** *n.m.* foretaste. ~**guerre** *n.m.* pre-war period. ~**hier** /-tjɛr/ *adv.* the day before yesterday. ~**poste** *n.m.* outpost. ~**première** *n.f.* preview. ~**propos** *n.m.* foreword. ~**veille** *n.f.* two days before.

avantag|**e** /avɑ̃taʒ/ *n.m.* advantage; (*comm.*) benefit. ~**er** *v.t.* favour; (*embellir*) show off to advantage. ~**eu**|**x**, ~**se** /avɑ̃taʒø, -z/ *a.* attractive.

avar|**e** /avar/ *a.* miserly. —*n.m./f.* miser. ~**e de**, sparing of. ~**ice** *n.f.* avarice.

avarié /avarje/ *a.* (*aliment*) spoiled.

avaries /avari/ *n.f. pl.* damage.

avatar /avatar/ *n.m.* (*fam.*) misfortune.

avec /avɛk/ *prép.* with; (*envers*) towards. —*adv.* (*fam.*) with it *ou* them.

avenant, ~e /avnɑ̃, -t/ *a.* pleasing.

avenant (à l') /(al)avnɑ̃/ *adv.* in a similar style.

avènement /avɛnmɑ̃/ *n.m.* advent. (*d'un roi*) accession.

avenir /avnir/ *n.m.* future. **à l'**~, in future. **d'**~, with (future) prospects.

aventur|**e** /avɑ̃tyr/ *n.f.* adventure; (*sentimentale*) affair. ~**eux**, ~**euse** *a.* adventurous; (*hasardeux*) risky. ~**ier**, ~**ière** *n.m., f.* adventurer.

aventurer (s') /(s)avɑ̃tyre/ *v. pr.* venture.

avenue /avny/ *n.f.* avenue.

avérer (s') /(s)avere/ *v. pr.* prove (to be).

averse /avɛrs/ *n.f.* shower.

aversion /avɛrsjɔ̃/ *n.f.* aversion.

avert|**ir** /avertir/ *v.t.* inform; (*mettre en garde, menacer*) warn. ~**i** *a.* informed. ~**issement** *n.m.* warning.

avertisseur /avertisœr/ *n.m.* (*auto.*) horn. ~ **d'incendie**, firealarm.

aveu (*pl.* ~**x**) /avø/ *n.m.* confession. **de l'**~ **de**, by the admission of.

aveugl|**e** /avœgl/ *a.* blind. —*n.m./f.* blind man, blind woman. ~**ement** *n.m.* blindness. ~**ément** *adv.* blindly. ~**er** *v.t.* blind.

aveuglette (à l') /(al)avœglɛt/ *adv.* (*à tâtons*) blindly.

avia|**teur, ~trice** /avjatœr, -tris/ *n.m., f.* aviator.

aviation /avjasjɔ̃/ *n.f.* flying; (*industrie aviation*); (*mil.*) air force. **d'**~, air.

avid|**e** /avid/ *a.* greedy (**de**, for); (*anxieux*) eager (**de**, for). ~**e de faire**, eager to do. ~**ité** *n.f.* greed; eagerness.

avilir /avilir/ *v.t.* degrade.

avion /avjɔ̃/ *n.m.* plane, aeroplane, aircraft; (*Amer.*) airplane. ~ **à réaction**, jet.

aviron /avirɔ̃/ *n.m.* oar. **l'**~, (*sport*) rowing.

avis /avi/ *n.m.* opinion; (*renseignement*) notification; (*comm.*)

advice. **à mon ~**, in my opinion. **changer d'~**, change one's mind. **être d'~ que**, be of the opinion that.

avisé /avize/ *a.* sensible. **bien/mal ~ de**, well-/ill-advised to do.

aviser /avize/ *v.t.* notice; (*informer*) advise. —*v.i.* decide what to do (**à**, about). **s'~ de**, suddenly realize. **s'~ de faire**, take it into one's head to do.

aviver /avive/ *v.t.* revive.

avocat[1] /~e /avɔka, -t/ *n.m., f.* barrister; (*Amer.*) attorney; (*fig.*) advocate. **~ de la défense**, counsel for the defence.

avocat[2] /avɔka/ *n.m.* (*fruit*) avocado (pear).

avoine /avwan/ *n.f.* oats.

avoir† /avwar/ *v. aux.* have. —*v.t.* have; (*obtenir*) get; (*duper: fam.*) take in. —*n.m.* assets. **je n'ai pas de café**, I haven't (got) any coffee; (*Amer.*) I don't have any coffee. **est-ce que tu as du café?**, have you (got) any coffee?; (*Amer.*) do you have any coffee? **~ à faire**, have to do. **tu n'as qu'à l'appeler**, all you have to do is call her. **~ chaud/faim**/*etc.*, be hot/hungry/*etc.* **~ dix**/*etc.* **ans**, be ten/*etc.* years old. **~ lieu**, take place. **~ lieu de**, have good reason to. **en ~ contre qn.**, have a grudge against s.o. **en ~ assez**, have had enough. **en ~ pour une minute**/*etc.*, be busy for a minute/*etc.* **il en a pour cent francs**, it will cost him one hundred francs. **qu'est-ce que vous avez?**, what is the matter with you? **on m'a eu!**, I've been had.

avoisin|er /avwazine/ *v.t.* border on. **~ant**, **~ante** *a.* neighbouring.

avort|er /avɔrte/ *v.i.* miscarry. **(se faire) ~er**, have an abortion. **~é** *a.*

abortive. **~ement** *n.m.* (*méd.*) abortion.

avouer /avwe/ *v.t.* confess (to). —*v.i.* confess. **~é a.** avowed; *n.m.* solicitor; (*Amer.*) attorney.

avril /avril/ *n.m.* April.

axe /aks/ *n.m.* axis; (*essieu*) axle; (*d'une politique*) main line(s), basis. **~ (routier)**, main road.

axer /akse/ *v.t.* centre.

axiome /aksjom/ *n.m.* axiom.

ayant /ɛjɑ̃/ *voir* **avoir**.

azimuts /azimyt/ *n.m. pl.* **dans tous les ~**, (*fam.*) all over the place.

azote /azɔt/ *n.m.* nitrogen.

azur /azyr/ *n.m.* sky-blue.

B

ba-ba /beaba/ *n.m.* **le ~ (de)**, the basics (of).

baba /baba/ *n.m.* **~ (au rhum)**, rum baba. **en rester ~**, (*fam.*) be flabbergasted.

babil /babi(l)/ *n.m.* babble. **~ler** /-ije/ *v.i.* babble.

babines /babin/ *n.f. pl.* **se lécher les ~**, lick one's chops.

babiole /babjɔl/ *n.f.* knick-knack.

bâbord /babɔr/ *n.m.* port (side).

babouin /babwɛ̃/ *n.m.* baboon.

baby-foot /babifut/ *n.m. invar.* table football.

baby-sitt|er /bebisitœr/ *n.m./f.* baby-sitter. **~ing** *n.m.* **faire du ~ing**, babysit.

bac[1] /bak/ *n.m.* = **baccalauréat**.

bac[2] /bak/ *n.m.* (*bateau*) ferry; (*récipient*) tub; (*plus petit*) tray.

baccalauréat /bakalɔrea/ *n.m.* school leaving certificate.

bâch|e /baʃ/ *n.f.* tarpaulin. **~er** *v.t.* cover (with a tarpaulin).

bachel|ier, **~ière** /baʃəlje, -jɛr/ *n.m., f.* holder of the *baccalauréat*.

bachot /baʃo/ *n.m.* (*fam.*) = **baccalauréat**. ~**er** /-ɔte/ *v.i.* cram (for an exam).

bâcler /bɑkle/ *v.t.* botch (up).

bactérie /bakteri/ *n.f.* bacterium.

badaud, ~**e** /bado, -d/ *n.m., f.* (*péj.*) onlooker.

badigeon /badiʒɔ̃/ *n.m.* white-wash. ~**ner** /-ɔne/ *v.t.* white-wash; (*barbouiller*) daub.

badin, ~**e** /badɛ̃, -in/ *a.* light-hearted.

badiner /badine/ *v.i.* joke (**sur**, **avec**, about).

badminton /badmintɔn/ *n.m.* bad-minton.

baffe /baf/ *n.f.* (*fam.*) slap.

baffle /bafl/ *n.m.* speaker.

bafouer /bafwe/ *v.t.* scoff at.

bafouiller /bafuje/ *v.t./i.* stam-mer.

bâfrer /bɑfre/ *v.i.* (*fam.*) gobble. se ~ *v.pr.* stuff o.s.

bagage /bagaʒ/ *n.m.* bag; (*fig.*) (store of knowledge. ~**s**, (*lug-gage, baggage. ~**s à main**, hand luggage.

bagarr|**e** /bagar/ *n.f.* fight. ~**er** *v.i.*, se ~**er** *v. pr.* fight.

bagatelle /bagatɛl/ *n.f.* trifle; (*somme*) trifling amount.

bagnard /baɲar/ *n.m.* convict.

bagnole /baɲol/ *n.f.* (*fam.*) car.

bagou(t) /bagu/ *n.m.* avoir du ~, have the gift of the gab. .

bagu|**e** /bag/ *n.f.* (*anneau*) ring. ~**er** *v.t.* ring.

baguette /bagɛt/ *n.f.* stick; (*de chef d'orchestre*) baton; (*chinoise*) chopstick; (*magique*) wand; (*pain*) stick of bread. ~ **de tambour**, drumstick.

baie /bɛ/ *n.f.* (*géog.*) bay; (*fruit*) berry. ~ (**vitrée**), picture win-dow.

baign|**er** /beɲe/ *v.t.* bathe; (*enfant*) bath. —*v.i.* ~**er dans**, soak in; (*être enveloppé dans*) be steeped in. se ~**er** *v. pr.* go swimming

(*ou*) bathing. ~**é de**, bathed in; (*sang*) soaked in. ~**ade** /beɲad/ *n.f.* bathing, swimming. ~**eur**, ~**euse** /beɲœr, -øz/ *n.m., f.* bather.

baignoire /beɲwar/ *n.f.* bath (-tub).

bail (*pl.* **baux**) /baj, bo/ *n.m.* lease.

bâill|**er** /baje/ *v.i.* yawn; (*être ouvert*) gape. ~**ement** *n.m.* yawn.

bailleur /bajœr/ *n.m.* ~ **de fonds**, (*comm.*) backer.

bâillon /bajɔ̃/ *n.m.* gag. ~**ner** /bajɔne/ *v.t.* gag.

bain /bɛ̃/ *n.m.* bath; (*de mer*) bathe. ~(**s**) **de soleil**, sunbathing. ~-**marie** (*pl.* ~**s-marie**) *n.m.* double boiler. ~ **de bouche**, mouthwash. **mettre qn. dans le** ~, (*compromettre*) drop s.o. in it; (*au courant*) put s.o. in the picture. **se remettre dans le** ~, get back into the swim of things. **prendre un** ~ **de foule**, mingle with the crowd.

baiser /beze/ *n.m.* kiss. —*v.t.* (*main*) kiss; (*fam.*) screw.

baisse /bes/ *n.f.* fall, drop. **en** ~, falling.

baisser /bese/ *v.t.* lower; (*radio, lampe, etc.*) turn down. —*v.i.* go down, fall; (*santé, forces*) fail. se ~ *v. pr.* bend down.

bajoues /baʒu/ *n.f. pl.* chops.

bakchich /bakʃiʃ/ *n.m.* (*fam.*) bribe.

bal (*pl.* ~**s**) /bal/ *n.m.* dance; (*habillé*) ball; (*lieu*) dance-hall. ~ **costumé**, fancy-dress ball.

balad|**e** /balad/ *n.f.* stroll; (*en auto*) drive. ~**er** *v.t.* take for a stroll. se ~**er** *v. pr.* (go for a) stroll; (*excursionner*) wander around. se ~**er** (**en auto**), go for a drive.

baladeur /baladœr/ *n.m.* personal stereo.

balafr|**e** /balafr/ *n.f.* gash; (*cicatrice*) scar. ~**er** *v.t.* gash.

balai /balɛ/ *n.m.* broom. **~-brosse** *n.m.* garden broom.

balance /balɑ̃s/ *n.f.* scales. **la B~**, Libra.

balancer /balɑ̃se/ *v.t.* swing; (*doucement*) sway; (*lancer: fam.*) chuck; (*se débarrasser de: fam.*) chuck out. —*v.i.*, **se ~** *v. pr.* swing; sway. **se ~ de**, (*fam.*) not care about.

balancier /balɑ̃sje/ *n.m.* (*d'horloge*) pendulum; (*d'équilibriste*) pole.

balançoire /balɑ̃swar/ *n.f.* swing; (*bascule*) see-saw.

balayer /baleje/ *v.t.* sweep (up); (*chasser*) sweep away; (*se débarrasser de*) sweep aside. **~age** *n.m.* sweeping; (*cheveux*) highlights. **~eur, ~euse** *n.m., f.* road sweeper.

balbutier /balbysje/ *v.t./i.* stammer. **~iement** *n.m.* stammering.

balcon /balkɔ̃/ *n.m.* balcony; (*théâtre*) dress circle.

baleine /balɛn/ *n.f.* whale.

balise /baliz/ *n.f.* beacon; (*bouée*) buoy; (*auto.*) (road) sign. **~er** *v.t.* mark out with beacons; (*route*) signpost.

balistique /balistik/ *a.* ballistic.

balivernes /balivern/ *n.f. pl.* balderdash.

ballade /balad/ *n.f.* ballad.

ballant, ~e /balɑ̃, -t/ *a.* dangling.

ballast /balast/ *n.m.* ballast.

balle /bal/ *n.f.* (*projectile*) bullet; (*sport*) ball; (*paquet*) bale.

ballerine /balrin/ *n.f.* ballerina.

ballet /balɛ/ *n.m.* ballet.

ballon /balɔ̃/ *n.m.* balloon; (*sport*) ball. **~ de football**, football.

ballonné /balɔne/ *a.* bloated.

ballot /balo/ *n.m.* bundle; (*nigaud: fam.*) idiot.

ballottage /balɔtaʒ/ *n.m.* second ballot (*due to indecisive result*).

ballotter /balɔte/ *v.t./i.* shake about, toss.

balnéaire /balneɛr/ *a.* seaside.

balourd, ~e /balur, -d/ *n.m., f.* oaf. —*a.* oafish.

balustrade /balystrad/ *n.f.* railing(s).

bambin /bɑ̃bɛ̃/ *n.m.* tot.

bambou /bɑ̃bu/ *n.m.* bamboo.

ban /bɑ̃/ *n.m.* round of applause. **~s**, (*de mariage*) banns. **mettre au ~ de**, cast out from. **publier les ~s**, have the banns called.

banal (*m. pl.* **~s**) /banal/ *a.* commonplace, banal. **~ité** *n.f.* banality.

banane /banan/ *n.f.* banana.

banc /bɑ̃/ *n.m.* bench; (*de poissons*) shoal. **~ des accusés**, dock. **~ d'essai**, test bed; (*fig.*) testing-ground.

bancaire /bɑ̃kɛr/ *a.* banking; (*chèque*) bank.

bancal (*m. pl.* **~s**) /bɑ̃kal/ *a.* wobbly; (*raisonnement*) shaky.

bandage /bɑ̃daʒ/ *n.m.* bandage. **~ herniaire**, truss.

bande[1] /bɑ̃d/ *n.f.* (*de papier etc.*) strip; (*rayure*) stripe; (*de film*) reel; (*radio*) band; (*pansement*) bandage. **~ (magnétique)**, tape. **~ dessinée**, comic strip. **~ sonore**, sound-track. **par la ~**, indirectly.

bande[2] /bɑ̃d/ *n.f.* (*groupe*) bunch, band, gang.

bandeau (*pl.* **~x**) /bɑ̃do/ *n.m.* headband; (*sur les yeux*) blindfold.

bander /bɑ̃de/ *v.t.* bandage; (*muscle*) tense. **~ les yeux à**, blindfold.

banderole /bɑ̃drɔl/ *n.f.* banner.

bandit /bɑ̃di/ *n.m.* bandit. **~isme** /-tism/ *n.m.* crime.

bandoulière (en) /(ɑ̃)bɑ̃duljɛr/ *adv.* across one's shoulder.

banjo /bɑ̃(d)ʒo/ *n.m.* banjo.

banlieue /bɑ̃ljø/ *n.f.* suburbs. **ɢe**

~e, suburban. **~sard**, **~sarde** /-zar, -zard/ *n.m.*, *f.* (suburban) commuter.

bannière /banjɛr/ *n.f.* banner.

bannir /banir/ *v.t.* banish.

banque /bɑ̃k/ *n.f.* bank; (*activité*) banking. **~ d'affaires**, merchant bank.

banqueroute/bɑ̃krut/*n.f.*(fraudulent) bankruptcy.

banquet /bɑ̃kɛ/ *n.m.* dinner; (*fastueux*) banquet.

banquette /bɑ̃kɛt/ *n.f.* seat.

banquier /bɑ̃kje/ *n.m.* banker.

bapt|ème /batɛm/ *n.m.* baptism; christening. **~iser** *v.t.* baptize, christen; (*appeler*) christen.

baquet /bakɛ/ *n.m.* tub.

bar /bar/ *n.m.* (*lieu*) bar.

baragouin /baragwɛ̃/ *n.m.* gibberish, gabble. **~er** /-wine/ *v.t./i.* gabble; (*langue*) speak a few words of.

baraque /barak/ *n.f.* hut, shed; (*boutique*) stall; (*maison: fam.*) house. **~ments** *n.m. pl.* huts.

baratin /baratɛ̃/ *n.m.* (*fam.*) sweet *ou* smooth talk. **~er** /-ine/ *v.t.* (*fam.*) chat up; (*Amer.*) sweet-talk.

barbar|e /barbar/ *a.* barbaric. **—**n.m./f. barbarian. **~ie** *n.f.* (*cruauté*) barbarity.

barbe /barb/ *n.f.* beard. **~ à papa**, candy-floss; (*Amer.*) cotton candy. **la ~!**, (*fam.*) blast (it)! **quelle ~!**, (*fam.*) what a bore!

barbecue /barbəkju/ *n.m.* barbecue.

barbelé /barbəle/ *a.* **fil ~**, barbed wire.

barber /barbe/ *v.t.* (*fam.*) bore.

barbiche /barbiʃ/ *n.f.* goatee.

barbiturique /barbityrik/ *n.m.* barbiturate.

barboter¹ /barbote/ *v.i.* paddle, splash.

barboter² /barbote/ *v.t.* (*voler: fam.*) pinch.

barbouill|er /barbuje/ *v.t.* (*peindre*) daub; (*souiller*) smear; (*griffonner*) scribble. **avoir l'estomac ~é** ou **se sentir ~é** feel liverish.

barbu /barby/ *a.* bearded.

barda /barda/ *n.m.* (*fam.*) gear.

barder /barde/ *v.i.* **ça va ~**, (*fam.*) sparks will fly.

barème /barɛm/ *n.m.* list, table; (*échelle*) scale.

baril /bari(l)/ *n.m.* barrel; (*de poudre*) keg.

bariolé /barjole/ *a.* motley.

barman /barman/ *n.m.* barman; (*Amer.*) bartender.

baromètre /barɔmɛtr/ *n.m.* barometer.

baron, **~ne** /barɔ̃, -ɔn/ *n.m.*, *f.* baron, baroness.

baroque /barɔk/ *a.* (*fig.*) weird; (*archit., art*) baroque.

baroud /barud/ *n.m.* **~ d'honneur**, gallant last fight.

barque /bark/ *n.f.* (small) boat.

barrage /baraʒ/ *n.m.* dam; (*sur route*) road-block.

barre /bar/ *n.f.* bar; (*trait*) line, stroke; (*naut.*) helm.

barreau (*pl.* **~x**) /baro/ *n.m.* bar; (*d'échelle*) rung. **le ~**, (*jurid.*) the bar.

barrer /bare/ *v.t.* block; (*porte*) bar; (*rayer*) cross out; (*naut.*) steer. **se ~** *v. pr.* (*fam.*) hop it.

barrette /barɛt/ *n.f.* (*hair-*)slide.

barricad|e /barikad/ *n.f.* barricade. **~er** *v.t.* barricade. **se ~er** *v. pr.* barricade o.s.

barrière /barjɛr/ *n.f.* (*porte*) gate; (*clôture*) fence; (*obstacle*) barrier.

barrique /barik/ *n.f.* barrel.

baryton /baritɔ̃/ *n.m.* baritone.

bas, **basse** /bɑ, bɑs/ *a.* low; (*action*) base. **—***n.m.* bottom; (*chaussette*) stocking. **—***n.f.* (*mus.*) bass. **—***adv.* low. **à ~**, down with. **au ~ mot**, at the lowest estimate. **en ~**, down below; (*dans une maison*) downstairs. **en ~ âge,** young. **en ~ de,** at the bottom of. **plus ~,** further *ou* lower down. **~-côté** *n.m.* (*de route*) verge; (*Amer.*) shoulder. **~ de casse** *n.m. invar.* lower case. **~ de laine,** nest-egg. **~-fonds** *n.m. pl.* (*eau*) shallows; (*fig.*) dregs. **~morceaux,** (*viande*) cheap cuts. **~-relief** *n.m.* low relief. **~ventre** *n.m.* lower abdomen. **mettre ~,** give birth (to).

basané /bazane/ *a.* tanned.

bascule /baskyl/ *n.f.* (*balance*) scales. **cheval/fauteuil à ~,** rocking-horse/-chair.

basculer /baskyle/ *v.t./i.* topple over; (*benne*) tip up.

base /baz/ *n.f.* base; (*fondement*) basis; (*pol.*) rank and file. **de ~,** basic.

baser /baze/ *v.t.* base. **se ~ sur,** base o.s. on.

basilic /bazilik/ *n.m.* basil.

basilique /bazilik/ *n.f.* basilica.

basket(-ball) /basket(bol)/ *n.m.* basketball.

basque /bask/ *a. & n.m./f.* Basque.

basse /bas/ *voir* **bas**.

basse-cour (*pl.* **basses-cours**) /baskur/ *n.f.* farmyard.

bassement /basmã/ *adv.* basely.

bassesse /bases/ *n.f.* baseness; (*action*) base act.

bassin /basɛ̃/ *n.m.* bowl; (*pièce d'eau*) pond; (*rade*) dock; (*géog.*) basin; (*anat.*) pelvis. **~ houiller,** coalfield.

basson /basɔ̃/ *n.m.* bassoon.

bastion /bastjɔ̃/ *n.m.* bastion.

bat /ba/ *voir* **battre**.

bât /ba/ *n.m.* **là où le ~ blesse,** where the shoe pinches.

bataill|e /bataj/ *n.f.* battle; (*fig.*) fight. **~er** *v.i.* fight.

bataillon /batajɔ̃/ *n.m.* battalion.

bâtard, ~e /batar, -d/ *n.m., f.* bastard. —*a.* (*solution*) hybrid.

bateau (*pl.* **~x**) /bato/ *n.m.* boat. **~-mouche** (*pl.* **~x-mouches**) *n.m.* sightseeing boat.

bâti /bati/ *a.* **bien ~,** well-built.

batifoler /batifole/ *v.i.* fool about.

bâtiment /batimã/ *n.m.* building; (*navire*) vessel; (*industrie*) building trade.

bâtir /batir/ *v.t.* build; (*coudre*) baste.

bâtisse /batis/ *n.f.* (*péj.*) building.

bâton /batɔ̃/ *n.m.* stick. **à ~s rompus,** jumping from subject to subject. **~ de rouge,** lipstick.

battage /bataʒ/ *n.m.* (*publicité: fam.*) (hard) plugging.

battant /batã/ *n.m.* (*vantail*) flap. **porte à deux ~s,** double door.

battement /batmã/ *n.m.* (*de cœur*) beat(ing); (*temps*) interval.

batterie /batri/ *n.f.* (*mil., électr.*) battery; (*mus.*) drums. **~ de cuisine,** pots and pans.

batteur /batœr/ *n.m.* (*mus.*) drummer; (*culin.*) whisk.

battre† /batr/ *v.t./i.* beat; (*blé*) thresh; (*cartes*) shuffle; (*parcourir*) scour; (*faire du bruit*) bang. **se ~** *v. pr.* fight. **~ des ailes,** flap its wings. **~ des mains,** clap. **~ en retraite,** beat a retreat. **~ la semelle,** stamp one's feet. **~ pavillon britannique/etc.,** fly the British/*etc.* flag. **~ son plein,** be in full swing.

battue /baty/ *n.f.* (*chasse*) beat; (*de police*) search.

baume /bom/ *n.m.* balm.

bavard, ~e /bavar, -d/ *a.* talkative. —*n.m., f.* chatterbox.

bavard|er /bavarde/ *v.i.* chat; (*jacasser*) chatter, gossip. **~age** *n.m.* chatter, gossip.

bav|e /bav/ *n.f.* dribble, slobber; (*de limace*) slime. **~er** *v.i.* dribble, slobber. **~eux, ~euse** *a.* dribbling; (*omelette*) runny.

bav|ette /bavɛt/ *n.f.,* **~oir** *n.m.*

bib. **tailler une ~ette**, (*fam.*) have a chat.

bavure /bavyr/ *n.f.* smudge; (*erreur*) mistake. **~ policière**, (*fam.*) police cock-up. **sans ~**, flawless(ly).

bazar /bazar/ *n.m.* bazaar; (*objets: fam.*) clutter.

bazarder /bazarde/ *v.t.* (*vendre: fam.*) get rid of, flog.

BCBG *abrév.* (*bon chic bon genre*) posh.

BD *abrév.* (*bande dessinée*) comic strip.

béant, ~e /beã, -t/ *a.* gaping.

béat, ~e /bea, -t/ *a.* (*hum.*) blissful; (*péj.*) smug. **~itude** /-tityd/ *n.f.* (*hum.*) bliss.

beau *ou* **bel*, belle** (*m. pl. ~x*) /bo, bɛl/ *a.* fine, beautiful; (*femme*) beautiful; (*homme*) handsome; (*grand*) big. —*n.f.* beauty; (*sport*) deciding game. **au ~ milieu**, right in the middle. **bel et bien**, well and truly. **de plus belle**, more than ever. **faire le ~**, sit up and beg. **on a ~ essayer/insister/etc.**, however much one tries/insists/*etc.*, it is no use trying/insisting/*etc.* **~x-arts** *n.m. pl.* fine arts. **~-fils** (*pl.* **~x-fils**) *n.m.* son-in-law; (*re-mariage*) stepson. **~frère** (*pl.* **~x-frères**) *n.m.* brother-in-law. **~père** (*pl.* **~x-pères**) *n.m.* father-in-law; stepfather. **~x-parents** *n.m. pl.* parents-in-law.

beaucoup /boku/ *adv.* a lot, very much. —*pron.* many (people). **~ de**, (*nombre*) many; (*quantité*) a lot of. **pas ~ (de)**, not many; (*quantité*) not much. **~ plus/etc.**, much more/*etc.* **~ trop**, much too much. **de ~**, by far.

beauté /bote/ *n.f.* beauty. **en ~**, magnificently. **tu es en ~**, you are looking good.

bébé /bebe/ *n.m.* baby. **~-éprouvette**, test-tube baby.

bec /bɛk/ *n.m.* beak; (*de plume*) nib; (*de bouilloire*) spout; (*de casserole*) lip; (*bouche: fam.*) mouth. **~-de-cane** (*pl.* **~s-de-cane**) door-handle. **~ de gaz**, gas lamp (*in street*).

bécane /bekan/ *n.f.* (*fam.*) bike.

bécasse /bekas/ *n.f.* woodcock.

bêche /bɛʃ/ *n.f.* spade.

bêcher /beʃe/ *v.t.* dig.

bécoter /bekɔte/ *v.t.*, **se ~** *v. pr.* (*fam.*) kiss.

becquée /beke/ *n.f.* **donner la ~ à**, (*oiseau*) feed; (*fig.*) spoon-feed.

bedaine /bədɛn/ *n.f.* paunch.

bedeau (*pl.* **~x**) /bədo/ *n.m.* beadle.

bedonnant, ~e /bədɔnã, -t/ *a.* paunchy.

beffroi /befrwa/ *n.m.* belfry.

bégayer /begeje/ *v.t./i.* stammer.

bègue /bɛg/ *n.m./f.* stammerer. **être ~**, stammer.

bégueule /begœl/ *a.* prudish.

béguin /begɛ̃/ *n.m.* **avoir le ~ pour**, (*fam.*) have a crush on.

beige /bɛʒ/ *a.* & *n.m.* beige.

beignet /bɛɲɛ/ *n.m.* fritter.

bel /bɛl/ *voir* **beau**.

bêler /bele/ *v.i.* bleat.

belette /bəlɛt/ *n.f.* weasel.

belge /bɛlʒ/ *a.* & *n.m./f.* Belgian.

Belgique /bɛlʒik/ *n.f.* Belgium.

bélier /belje/ *n.m.* ram. **le B~**, Aries.

belle /bɛl/ *voir* **beau**.

belle-fille (*pl.* **~s-filles**) /bɛlfij/ *n.f.* daughter-in-law; (*remariage*) stepdaughter. **~-mère** (*pl.* **~s-mères**) *n.f.* mother-in-law; stepmother. **~-sœur** (*pl.* **~s-sœurs**) *n.f.* sister-in-law.

belligérant, ~e /beliʒerã, -t/ *a.* & *n.m.* belligerent.

belliqueu|x, ~se /belikø, -z/ *a.* warlike.

belote /bəlɔt/ *n.f.* belote (*card game*).

belvédère /bɛlvedɛr/ n.m. (*lieu*) viewing spot, viewpoint.

bémol /bemɔl/ n.m. (*mus.*) flat.

bénédiction /benediksjɔ̃/ n.f. blessing.

bénéfice /benefis/ n.m. (*gain*) profit; (*avantage*) benefit.

bénéficiaire /benefisjɛr/ n.m./f. beneficiary.

bénéficier /benefisje/ v.i. ~ **de**, benefit from; (*jouir de*) enjoy, have.

bénéfique /benefik/ a. beneficial.

Bénélux /benelyks/ n.m. Benelux.

benêt /bənɛ/ n.m. simpleton.

bénévole /benevɔl/ a. voluntary.

bén|in, ~igne /benɛ̃, -iɲ/ a. mild, slight; (*tumeur*) benign.

bén|ir /benir/ v.t. bless. **~it, ~ite** a. (*eau*) holy; (*pain*) consecrated.

bénitier /benitje/ n.m. stoup.

benjamin, ~e /bɛ̃ʒamɛ̃, -in/ n.m., f. youngest child.

benne /bɛn/ n.f. (*de grue*) scoop; (*amovible*) skip. ~ **(basculante)**, dump truck.

benzine /bɛ̃zin/ n.f. benzine.

béotien, ~ne /beɔsjɛ̃, -jɛn/ n.m., f. philistine.

béquille /bekij/ n.f. crutch; (*de moto*) stand.

bercail /bɛrkaj/ n.m. fold.

berceau (pl. ~x) /bɛrso/ n.m. cradle.

bercer /bɛrse/ v.t. (*balancer*) rock; (*apaiser*) lull; (*leurrer*) delude.

berceuse /bɛrsøz/ n.f. lullaby.

béret /berɛ/ n.m. beret.

berge /bɛrʒ/ n.f. (*bord*) bank.

berg|er, ~ère /bɛrʒe, -ɛr/ n.m., f. shepherd, shepherdess. **~erie** n.f. sheep-fold.

berlingot /bɛrlɛ̃go/ n.m. boiled sweet; (*emballage*) carton.

berne (en) /(ɑ̃)bɛrn/ adv. at half-mast.

berner /bɛrne/ v.t. hoodwink.

besogne /bəzɔɲ/ n.f. task, job, chore.

besoin /bəzwɛ̃/ n.m. need. **avoir ~ de**, need. **au ~**, if need be.

bestial (m. pl. ~iaux) /bɛstjal, -jo/ a. bestial.

bestiaux /bɛstjo/ n.m. pl. livestock.

bestiole /bɛstjɔl/ n.f. creepy-crawly.

bétail /betaj/ n.m. farm animals.

bête[1] /bɛt/ n.f. animal. **~ noire**, pet hate, pet peeve. **~ sauvage**, wild beast. **chercher la petite ~**, be overfussy.

bête[2] /bɛt/ a. stupid. **~ment** adv. stupidly.

bêtise /betiz/ n.f. stupidity; (*action*) stupid thing.

béton /betɔ̃/ n.m. concrete. **~ armé**, reinforced concrete. **~nière** /-ɔnjɛr/ n.f. cement-mixer, concrete-mixer.

betterave /bɛtrav/ n.f. beetroot. **~ sucrière**, sugar-beet.

beugler /bøgle/ v.i. bellow, low; (*radio*) blare.

beur /bœr/ n.m./f. & a. (*fam.*) young French North African.

beurr|e /bœr/ n.m. butter. **~er** v.t. butter. **~ier** n.m. butter-dish. **~é** a. buttered; (*fam.*) drunk.

bévue /bevy/ n.f. blunder.

biais /bjɛ/ n.m. (*fig.*) expedient; (*côté*) angle. **de ~**, **en ~**, at an angle. **de ~**, (*fig.*) indirectly.

biaiser /bjeze/ v.i. hedge.

bibelot /biblo/ n.m. curio.

biberon /bibrɔ̃/ n.m. (*feeding-*) bottle. **nourrir au ~**, bottle-feed.

bible /bibl/ n.f. bible. **la B~**, the Bible.

bibliographie /biblijɔgrafi/ n.f. bibliography.

bibliophile /biblijɔfil/ n.m./f. book-lover.

biblioth|èque /biblijɔtɛk/ n.f. library; (*meuble*) bookcase; **~écaire** n.m./f. librarian.

biblique /biblik/ *a.* biblical.

bic /bik/ *n.m.* (P.) biro (P.).

bicarbonate /bikarbɔnat/ *n.m.* ~ **(de soude)**, bicarbonate (of soda).

biceps /bisɛps/ *n.m.* biceps.

biche /biʃ/ *n.f.* doe.

bichonner /biʃɔne/ *v.t.* doll up.

bicoque /bikɔk/ *n.f.* shack.

bicyclette /bisiklɛt/ *n.f.* bicycle.

bide /bid/ *n.m.* (*ventre: fam.*) belly; (*théâtre: fam.*) flop.

bidet /bidɛ/ *n.m.* bidet.

bidon /bidɔ̃/ *n.m.* can. —*a. invar.* (*fam.*) phoney. **c'est pas du** ~, (*fam.*) it's the truth, it's for real.

bidonville /bidɔ̃vil/ *n.f.* shanty town.

bidule /bidyl/ *n.m.* (*fam.*) thing.

bielle /bjɛl/ *n.f.* connecting rod.

bien /bjɛ̃/ *adv.* well; (*très*) quite, very. —*n.m.* good; (*patrimoine*) possession. —*a. invar.* good; (*passable*) all right; (*en forme*) well; (*à l'aise*) comfortable; (*beau*) attractive; (*respectable*) nice, respectable. —*conj.* ~ **que**, (al)though. ~ **que ce soit/que ça ait**, although it is/it has. ~ **du**, (*quantité*) a lot of, much. ~ **des**, (*nombre*) many. **il l'a ~ fait**, (*intensif*) he did do it. **ce n'est pas ~ de**, it is not right to. ~ **sûr**, of course. ~**s de consommation**, consumer goods. ~**-aimé**, ~**-aimée** *a. & n.m.,f.* beloved. ~**-être** *n.m.* well-being. ~**-fondé** *n.m.* soundness. ~**-pensant**, ~**-pensante** *a. & n.m.,f.* (*péj.*) right-thinking.

bienfaisan|t, **-te** /bjɛ̃fəzɑ̃, -t/ *a.* beneficial. ~**ce** *n.f.* charity. **fête de** ~**ce**, fête.

bienfait /bjɛ̃fɛ/ *n.m.* (kind) favour; (*avantage*) benefit.

bienfai|teur, ~**trice** /bjɛ̃fɛtœr, -tris/ *n.m., f.* benefactor.

bienheureu|x, ~**se** /bjɛ̃nœrø, -z/ *a.* happy, blessed.

bienséan|t, ~**te** /bjɛ̃seɑ̃, -t/ *a.* proper. ~**ce** *n.f.* propriety.

bientôt /bjɛ̃to/ *adv.* soon. à ~, see you soon.

bienveillan|t, ~**te** /bjɛ̃vɛjɑ̃, -t/ *a.* kind(ly). ~**ce** *n.f.* kind(li)ness.

bienvenu, ~**e** /bjɛ̃vny/ *a.* welcome. —*n.f.* welcome. —*n.m.* être le ~, être la ~**e**, be welcome. **souhaiter la** ~ **à**, welcome.

bière /bjɛr/ *n.f.* beer; (*cercueil*) coffin. ~ **blonde**, lager. ~ **brune**, stout, brown ale. ~ **pression**, draught beer.

biffer /bife/ *v.t.* cross out.

bifteck /biftɛk/ *n.m.* steak.

bifur|quer /bifyrke/ *v.i.* branch off, fork. ~**cation** *n.f.* fork, junction.

bigam|e /bigam/ *a.* bigamous. —*n.m.,f.* bigamist. ~**ie** *n.f.* bigamy.

bigarré /bigare/ *a.* motley.

big-bang /bigbãg/ *n.m.* big bang.

bigot, ~**e** /bigo, -ɔt/ *n.m., f.* religious fanatic. —*a.* over-pious.

bigoudi /bigudi/ *n.m.* curler.

bijou (*pl.* ~**x**) /biʒu/ *n.m.* jewel. ~**terie** *n.f.* (*boutique*) jeweller's shop; (*comm.*) jewellery. ~**tier**, ~**tière** *n.m., f.* jeweller.

bikini /bikini/ *n.m.* bikini.

bilan /bilɑ̃/ *n.m.* outcome; (*d'une catastrophe*) (casualty) toll; (*comm.*) balance sheet. **faire le** ~ **de**, assess. ~ **de santé**, check-up.

bile /bil/ *n.f.* bile. **se faire de la** ~, (*fam.*) worry.

bilieu|x, ~**se** /biljø, -z/ *a.* bilious; (*fig.*) irascible.

bilingue /bilɛ̃g/ *a.* bilingual.

billard /bijar/ *n.m.* billiards; (*table*) billiard-table.

bille /bij/ *n.f.* (*d'enfant*) marble; (*de billard*) billiard-ball.

billet /bijɛ/ *n.m.* ticket; (*lettre*) note; (*article*) column. ~ **(de banque)**, (bank)note. ~ **d'aller**

et retour, return ticket; (*Amer.*) round trip ticket. ～ de faveur, complimentary ticket. ～ aller simple, single ticket; (*Amer.*) one-way ticket.

billetterie /bijɛtri/ *n.f.* cash dispenser.

billion /biljɔ̃/ *n.m.* billion (= 10¹²); (*Amer.*) trillion.

billot /bijo/ *n.m.* block.

bimensuel, ～le /bimɑ̃sɥɛl/ *a.* fortnightly, bimonthly.

bin|er /bine/ *v.t.* hoe. ～ette *n.f.* hoe; (*fam.*) face.

biochimie /bjoʃimi/ *n.f.* biochemistry.

biodégradable /bjodegradabl/ *a.* biodegradable.

biograph|ie /bjografi/ *n.f.* biography. ～e *n.m./f.* biographer.

biolog|ie /bjɔlɔʒi/ *n.f.* biology. ～ique *a.* biological. ～iste *n.m./f.* biologist.

bipède /biped/ *n.m.* biped.

bis¹, **bise** /bi, biz/ *a.* greyish brown.

bis² /bis/ *a.invar.* (*numéro*) A, *a.* —*n.m. & int.* encore.

bisbille (en) /(ɑ̃)bisbij/ *adv.* (*fam.*) at loggerheads (**avec,** with).

biscornu /biskɔrny/ *a.* crooked; (*bizarre*) weird.

biscotte /biskɔt/ *n.f.* rusk.

biscuit /biskɥi/ *n.m.* (*salé*) biscuit; (*Amer.*) cracker; (*sucré*) biscuit; (*Amer.*) cookie. ～ de Savoie, sponge-cake.

bise¹ /biz/ *n.f.* (*fam.*) kiss.

bise² /biz/ *n.f.* (*vent*) north wind.

bison /bizɔ̃/ *n.m.* (American) buffalo, bison.

bisou /bizu/ *n.m.* (*fam.*) kiss.

bisser /bise/ *v.t.* encore.

bistouri /bisturi/ *n.m.* lancet.

bistre /bistr/ *a. & n.m.* dark brown.

bistro(t) /bistro/ *n.m.* café, bar.

bit /bit/ *n.m.* (*comput.*) bit.

bitume /bitym/ *n.m.* asphalt.

bizarre /bizar/ *a.* odd, peculiar.

～ment *adv.* oddly. ～rie *n.f.* peculiarity.

blafard, ～e /blafar, -d/ *a.* pale.

blagu|e /blag/ *n.f.* joke. ～e à tabac, tobacco-pouch. ～er *v.i.* joke; *v.t.* tease. ～eur, ～euse *n.m., f.* joker; *a.* jokey.

blaireau (*pl.* ～x) /blɛro/ *n.m.* shaving-brush; (*animal*) badger.

blâm|e /blɑm/ *n.m.* rebuke, blame. ～able *a.* blameworthy. ～er *v.t.* rebuke, blame.

blanc, **blanche** /blɑ̃, blɑ̃ʃ/ *a.* white; (*papier, page*) blank. —*n.m.* white; (*espace*) blank. —*n.m., f.* white man, white woman. —*n.f.* (*mus.*) minim. ～ (**de poulet**), breast, white meat (of the chicken). **le ～,** (*linge*) whites. **laisser en ～,** leave blank.

blancheur /blɑ̃ʃœr/ *n.f.* whiteness.

blanch|ir /blɑ̃ʃir/ *v.t.* whiten; (*linge*) launder; (*personne: fig.*) clear; (*culin.*) blanch. —*v.i.* turn white. ～issage *n.m.* laundering. ～isserie *n.f.* laundry. ～isseur, ～isseuse *n.m., f.* laundryman, laundress.

blasé /blaze/ *a.* blasé.

blason /blazɔ̃/ *n.m.* coat of arms.

blasph|ème /blasfɛm/ *n.m.* blasphemy. ～ématoire *a.* blasphemous. ～émer *v.t./i.* blaspheme.

blatte /blat/ *n.f.* cockroach.

blazer /blɛzœr/ *n.m.* blazer.

blé /ble/ *n.m.* wheat.

bled /blɛd/ *n.m.* (*fam.*) dump, hole.

blême /blɛm/ *a.* (sickly) pale.

bless|er /blese/ *v.t.* injure, hurt; (*par balle*) wound; (*offenser*) hurt, wound. **se ～** *v. pr.* injure *ou* hurt o.s. ～ant, ～ante /blɛsɑ̃, -t/ *a.* hurtful. ～é, ～ée *n.m., f.* casualty, injured person.

blessure /blesyr/ *n.f.* wound.

blet, **~te** /blɛ, blɛt/ *a.* over-ripe.

bleu /blø/ *a.* blue; (*culin.*) very rare. **—marine**, navy blue. **—***n.m.* blue; (*contusion*) bruise. **~(s)**, (*vêtement*) overalls. **~ir** *v.t./i.* turn blue.

bleuet /bløɛ/ *n.m.* cornflower.

bleuté /bløte/ *a.* slightly blue.

blind|er /blɛ̃de/ *v.t.* armour (-plate); (*fig.*) harden. **~é** *a.* armoured; (*fig.*) immune (**contre**, to); *n.m.* armoured car, tank.

blizzard /blizar/ *n.m.* blizzard.

bloc /blɔk/ *n.m.* block; (*de papier*) pad; (*système*) unit; (*pol.*) bloc. à **~**, hard, tight. **en ~**, all together. **~-notes** (*pl.* **~s-notes**) *n.m.* note-pad.

blocage /blɔkaʒ/ *n.m.* (*des prix*) freeze, freezing; (*des roues*) locking; (*psych.*) block.

blocus /blɔkys/ *n.m.* blockade.

blond, **~e** /blɔ̃, -d/ *a.* fair, blond. **—***n.m.*, *f.* fair-haired *ou* blond man *ou* woman. **~eur** /-dœr/ *n.f.* fairness.

bloquer /blɔke/ *v.t.* block; (*porte, machine*) jam; (*freins*) slam on; (*roues*) lock; (*prix, crédits*) freeze; (*grouper*) put together. **se ~** *v. pr.* jam; (*roues*) lock.

blottir (se) /(sə)blɔtir/ *v. pr.* snuggle, huddle.

blouse /bluz/ *n.f.* smock.

blouson /bluzɔ̃/ *n.m.* lumber-jacket; (*Amer.*) windbreaker.

blue-jean /bludʒin/ *n.m.* jeans.

bluff /blœf/ *n.m.* bluff. **~er** *v.t./i.* bluff.

blush /blœʃ/ *n.m.* blusher.

boa /bɔa/ *n.m.* boa.

bobard /bɔbar/ *n.m.* (*fam.*) fib.

bobine /bɔbin/ *n.f.* reel; (*sur machine*) spool; (*électr.*) coil.

bobo /bɔbo/ *n.m.* (*fam.*) sore, cut. **avoir ~**, have a pain.

bocage /bɔkaʒ/ *n.m.* grove.

boc|al (*pl.* **~aux**) /bɔkal, -o/ *n.m.* jar.

bock /bɔk/ *n.m.* beer glass; (*contenu*) glass of beer.

body /bɔdi/ *n.m.* leotard.

bœuf (*pl.* **~s**) /bœf, bø/ *n.m.* ox; (*viande*) beef. **~s**, oxen.

bogue /bɔg/ *n.m.* (*comput.*) bug.

bohème /bɔɛm/ *a. & n.m./f.* unconventional.

boire† /bwar/ *v.t./i.* drink; (*absorber*) soak up. **~ un coup**, have a drink.

bois¹ /bwa/ *voir* **boire**.

bois² /bwa/ *n.m.* (*matériau, forêt*) wood. **de ~**, **en ~**, wooden.

boisé /bwaze/ *a.* wooded.

bois|er /bwaze/ *v.t.* (*chambre*) panel. **~eries** *n.f. pl.* panelling.

boisson /bwasɔ̃/ *n.f.* drink.

boit /bwa/ *voir* **boire**.

boîte /bwat/ *n.f.* box; (*de conserves*) tin, can; (*firme: fam.*) firm. **~ à gants**, glove compartment. **~ aux lettres**, letter-box. **~ de nuit**, night-club. **~ postale**, post-office box. **~ de vitesses**, gear box.

boiter /bwate/ *v.i.* limp; (*meuble*) wobble.

boiteu|x, **~se** /bwatø, -z/ *a.* lame; (*meuble*) wobbly; (*raisonnement*) shaky.

boîtier /bwatje/ *n.m.* case.

bol /bɔl/ *n.m.* bowl. **un ~ d'air**, a breath of fresh air. **avoir du ~**, (*fam.*) be lucky.

bolide /bɔlid/ *n.m.* racing car.

Bolivie /bɔlivi/ *n.f.* Bolivia.

bolivien, **~ne** /bɔlivjɛ̃, -jɛn/ *a. & n.m.*, *f.* Bolivian.

bombance /bɔ̃bɑ̃s/ *n.f.* **faire ~**, (*fam.*) revel.

bombard|er /bɔ̃barde/ *v.t.* bomb; (*par obus*) shell; (*nommer: fam.*) appoint unexpectedly (as). **~er qn. de**, (*fig.*) bombard s.o. with. **~ement** *n.m.* bombing; shelling. **~ier** *n.m.* (*aviat.*) bomber.

bombe /bɔ̃b/ *n.f.* bomb; (*atomiseur*) spray, aerosol.

bombé /bɔ̃be/ a. rounded; (*route*) cambered.

bomber /bɔ̃be/ v.t. ~ **la poitrine**, throw out one's chest.

bon, bonne /bɔ̃, bɔn/ a. good; (*qui convient*) right; (*prudent*) wise. ~ **à/pour**, (*approprié*) fit to/for. **tenir** ~, stand firm. (*billet*) voucher, coupon; (*comm.*) bond. **du** ~, some good. **pour de** ~, for good. **à quoi** ~?, what's the good *ou* point? **bonne année**, happy New Year. ~ **anniversaire**, happy birthday. ~ **appétit/voyage**, enjoy your meal/trip. **bonne chance/nuit**, good luck/night. **bonne femme**, (*péj.*) woman. **bonne-maman** (*pl.* **bonnes-mamans**) *n.f.* (*fam.*) granny. ~-**papa** (*pl.* ~**s-papas**) *n.m.* (*fam.*) grand-dad. ~ **sens**, common sense. ~ **vivant**, bon viveur. **de bonne heure**, early.

bonbon /bɔ̃bɔ̃/ *n.m.* sweet; (*Amer.*) candy. ~**nière** /-ɔnjɛr/ *n.f.* sweet box; (*Amer.*) candy box.

bonbonne /bɔ̃bɔn/ *n.f.* demijohn; (*de gaz*) canister.

bond /bɔ̃/ *n.m.* leap. **faire un** ~, leap in the air; (*de surprise*) jump.

bonde /bɔ̃d/ *n.f.* plug; (*trou*) plughole.

bondé /bɔ̃de/ a. packed.

bondir /bɔ̃dir/ v.i. leap; (*de surprise*) jump.

bonheur /bɔnœr/ *n.m.* happiness; (*chance*) (good) luck. **au petit** ~, haphazardly. **par** ~, luckily.

bonhomme¹ (*pl.* **bonshommes**) /bɔnɔm, bɔ̃zɔm/ *n.m.* fellow. ~ **de neige**, snowman.

bonhom|me² /bɔnɔm/ a. invar. good-hearted. ~**ie** *n.f.* good-heartedness.

bonifier (se) /(sə)bɔnifje/ v. pr. improve.

boniment /bɔnimɑ̃/ *n.m.* smooth talk.

bonjour /bɔ̃ʒur/ *n.m. & int.* hallo, hello, good morning *ou* afternoon.

bon marché /bɔ̃marʃe/ a. invar. cheap. —*adv.* cheap(ly).

bonne¹ /bɔn/ a.f. voir **bon**.

bonne² /bɔn/ *n.f.* (*domestique*) maid. ~ **d'enfants**, nanny.

bonnement /bɔnmɑ̃/ adv. **tout** ~, quite simply.

bonnet /bɔnɛ/ *n.m.* hat; (*de soutien-gorge*) cup. ~ **de bain**, swimming cap.

bonneterie /bɔnɛtri/ *n.f.* hosiery.

bonsoir /bɔ̃swar/ *n.m. & int.* good evening; (*en se couchant*) good night.

bonté /bɔ̃te/ *n.f.* kindness.

bonus /bɔnys/ *n.m.* (*auto.*) no claims bonus.

boom /bum/ *n.m.* (*comm.*) boom.

boots /buts/ *n.m. pl.* ankle boots.

bord /bɔr/ *n.m.* edge; (*rive*) bank. **à** ~ (**de**), on board. **au** ~ **de la mer**, at the seaside. **au** ~ **des larmes**, on the verge of tears. ~ **de la route**, roadside. ~ **du trottoir**, kerb; (*Amer.*) curb.

bordeaux /bɔrdo/ *n.m. invar.* Bordeaux (wine), claret. —*a. invar.* maroon.

bordée /bɔrde/ *n.f.* ~ **d'injures**, torrent of abuse.

bordel /bɔrdɛl/ *n.m.* brothel; (*désordre: fam.*) shambles.

border /bɔrde/ v.t. line, border; (*tissu*) edge; (*personne, lit*) tuck in.

bordereau (*pl.* ~**x**) /bɔrdəro/ *n.m.* (*liste*) note, slip; (*facture*) invoice.

bordure /bɔrdyr/ *n.f.* border. **en** ~ **de**, on the edge of.

borgne /bɔrɲ/ a. one-eyed; (*fig.*) shady.

borne /bɔrn/ *n.f.* boundary marker. ~ (**kilométrique**), (*approx.*) milestone. ~**s**, limits.

borné /bɔrne/ a. narrow; (*personne*) narrow-minded.

borner /bɔrne/ *v.t.* confine. **se ~** *v. pr.* confine o.s. (à, to).

bosquet /bɔskɛ/ *n.m.* grove.

bosse /bos/ *n.f.* bump; (*de chameau*) hump. **avoir la ~ de**, (*fam.*) have a gift for. **avoir roulé sa ~**, have been around.

bosseler /bosle/ *v.t.* emboss; (*endommager*) dent.

bosser /bose/ *v.i.* (*fam.*) work (hard). —*v.t.* (*fam.*) work (hard) at.

bossu, ~e /bosy/ *n.m., f.* hunchback.

botani|que /bɔtanik/ *n.f.* botany. —*a.* botanical. **~ste** *n.m./f.* botanist.

bott|e /bɔt/ *n.f.* boot; (*de fleurs, légumes*) bunch; (*de paille*) bundle, bale. **~es de caoutchouc**, wellingtons. **~ier** *n.m.* boot-maker.

botter /bɔte/ *v.t.* (*fam.*) **ça me botte**, I like the idea.

Bottin /bɔtɛ̃/ *n.m.* (P.) phone book.

bouc /buk/ *n.m.* (billy-)goat; (*barbe*) goatee. **~ émissaire**, scapegoat.

boucan /bukɑ̃/ *n.m.* (*fam.*) din.

bouche /buʃ/ *n.f.* mouth. **~ bée**, open-mouthed. **~ d'égout**, manhole. **~ d'incendie**, (fire) hydrant. **~ de métro**, entrance to the underground or subway (*Amer.*). **~-à-bouche** *n.m.* mouth-to-mouth resuscitation.

bouché /buʃe/ *a.* **c'est ~**, (*profession, avenir*) it's a dead end.

bouchée /buʃe/ *n.f.* mouthful.

boucher /buʃe/ *v.t.* block; (*bouteille*) cork. **se ~** *v. pr.* get blocked. **se ~ le nez**, hold one's nose.

bouch|er², **~ère** /buʃe, -ɛr/ *n.m., f.* butcher. **~erie** *n.f.* butcher's (shop); (*carnage*) butchery.

bouche-trou /buʃtru/ *n.m.* stop-gap.

bouchon /buʃɔ̃/ *n.m.* stopper; (*en liège*) cork; (*de bidon, tube*) cap; (*de pêcheur*) float; (*de circulation, fig.*) hold-up.

boucle /bukl/ *n.f.* (*de ceinture*) buckle; (*forme*) loop; (*de cheveux*) curl. **~ d'oreille**, ear-ring.

boucl|er /bukle/ *v.t.* fasten; (*terminer*) finish off; (*enfermer: fam.*) shut up; (*encercler*) seal off; (*budget*) balance. —*v.i.* curl. **~é** *a.* (*cheveux*) curly.

bouclier /buklije/ *n.m.* shield.

bouddhiste /budist/ *a. & n.m./f.* Buddhist.

boud|er /bude/ *v.i.* sulk. —*v.t.* steer clear of. **~erie** *n.f.* sulkiness. **~eur, ~euse** *a. & n.m., f.* sulky (person).

boudin /budɛ̃/ *n.m.* black pudding.

boudoir /budwar/ *n.m.* boudoir.

boue /bu/ *n.f.* mud.

bouée /bwe/ *n.f.* buoy. **~ de sauvetage**, lifebuoy.

boueu|x, ~se /bwø, -z/ *a.* muddy. —*n.m.* dustman; (*Amer.*) garbage collector.

bouff|e /buf/ *n.f.* (*fam.*) food, grub. **~er** *v.t./i.* (*fam.*) eat; (*bâfrer*) gobble.

bouffée /bufe/ *n.f.* puff, whiff; (*méd.*) flush; (*d'orgueil*) fit.

bouffi /bufi/ *a.* bloated.

bouffon, ~ne /bufɔ̃, -ɔn/ *a.* farcical. —*n.m.* buffoon.

bouge /buʒ/ *n.m.* hovel; (*bar*) dive.

bougeoir /buʒwar/ *n.m.* candlestick.

bougeotte /buʒɔt/ *n.f.* **la ~**, (*fam.*) the fidgets.

bouger /buʒe/ *v.t./i.* move; (*agir*) stir. **se ~** *v. pr.* (*fam.*) move.

bougie /buʒi/ *n.f.* candle; (*auto.*) spark(ing)-plug.

bougon, ~ne /bugɔ̃, -ɔn/ *a.* grumpy. **~ner** /-ɔne/ *v.i.* grumble.

bouillabaisse /bujabɛs/ *n.f.* bouillabaisse.

bouillie /buji/ *n.f.* porridge; (*pour bébé*) baby food; (*péj.*) mush. **en ∼**, crushed, mushy.

bouill|ir† /bujir/ *v.i.* boil. —*v.t.* (**faire**) **∼ir**, boil. **∼ant, ∼ante** *a.* boiling; (*très chaud*) boiling hot.

bouilloire /bujwar/ *n.f.* kettle.

bouillon /bujɔ̃/ *n.m.* (*aliment*) stock. **∼ cube**, stock cube. **∼ner** /-jɔne/ *v.i.* bubble.

bouillotte /bujɔt/ *n.f.* hot-water bottle.

boulang|er, ∼ère /bulɑ̃ʒe, -ɛr/ *n.m., f.* baker. **∼erie** *n.f.* bakery. **∼erie-pâtisserie** *n.f.* baker's and confectioner's shop.

boule /bul/ *n.f.* ball; (*de machine à écrire*) golf ball. **∼s**, (*jeu*) bowls. **jouer aux ∼s**, play bowls. **une ∼ dans la gorge**, lump in one's throat. **∼ de neige**, snowball. **faire ∼ de neige**, snowball.

bouleau (*pl.* **∼x**) /bulo/ *n.m.* (silver) birch.

bouledogue /buldɔg/ *n.m.* bull-dog.

boulet /bulɛ/ *n.m.* (*de canon*) cannon-ball; (*de forçat: fig.*) ball and chain.

boulette /bulɛt/ *n.f.* (*de papier*) pellet; (*aliment*) meat ball.

boulevard /bulvar/ *n.m.* boulevard.

boulevers|er /bulvɛrse/ *v.t.* turn upside down; (*pays, plans*) disrupt; (*émouvoir*) distress, upset. **∼ant, ante** *a.* deeply moving. **∼ement** *n.m.* upheaval.

boulier /bulje/ *n.m.* abacus.

boulimie /bulimi/ *n.f.* compulsive eating; (*méd.*) bulimia.

boulon /bulɔ̃/ *n.m.* bolt.

boulot¹ /bulo/ *n.m.* (*travail: fam.*) work.

boulot², ∼te /bulo, -ɔt/ *a.* (*rond: fam.*) dumpy.

boum /bum/ *n.m. & int.* bang. —*n.f.* (*réunion: fam.*) party.

bouquet /bukɛ/ *n.m.* (*de fleurs*) bunch, bouquet; (*d'arbres*) clump. **c'est le ∼!**, (*fam.*) that's the last straw!

bouquin /bukɛ̃/ *n.m.* (*fam.*) book. **∼er** /-ine/ *v.t./i.* (*fam.*) read. **∼iste** /-inist/ *n.m./f.* second-hand bookseller.

bourbeu|x, ∼se /burbø, -z/ *a.* muddy.

bourbier /burbje/ *n.m.* mire.

bourde /burd/ *n.f.* blunder.

bourdon /burdɔ̃/ *n.m.* bumble-bee.

bourdonn|er /burdɔne/ *v.i.* buzz. **∼ement** *n.m.* buzzing.

bourg /bur/ *n.m.* (market) town.

bourgade /burgad/ *n.f.* village.

bourgeois, ∼e /burʒwa, -z/ *a. & n.m., f.* middle-class (person); (*péj.*) bourgeois. **∼ie** /-zi/ *n.f.* middle class(es).

bourgeon /burʒɔ̃/ *n.m.* bud. **∼ner** /-ɔne/ *v.i.* bud.

bourgogne /burgɔɲ/ *n.m.* burgundy. —*n.f.* **la B∼**, Burgundy.

bourlinguer /burlɛ̃ge/ *v.i.* (*fam.*) travel about.

bourrade /burad/ *n.f.* prod.

bourrage /buraʒ/ *n.m.* **∼ de crâne**, brainwashing.

bourrasque /burask/ *n.f.* squall.

bourrati|f, ∼ve /buratif, -v/ *a.* filling, stodgy.

bourreau (*pl.* **∼x**) /buro/ *n.m.* executioner. **∼ de travail**, workaholic.

bourrelet /burlɛ/ *n.m.* weather-strip, draught excluder; (*de chair*) roll of fat.

bourrer /bure/ *v.t.* cram (**de**, with); (*pipe*) fill. **∼ de**, (*nourriture*) stuff with. **∼ de coups**, thrash. **∼ le crâne à qn.**, fill s.o.'s head with nonsense.

bourrique /burik/ *n.f.* ass.

bourru /bury/ *a.* surly.

bours|e /burs/ *n.f.* purse; (*subvention*) grant. **la B∼e**, the Stock Exchange. **∼ier, ∼ière** *a.* Stock

Exchange; *n.m., f.* holder of a grant.

boursoufler /bursufle/ *v.t.*, **se** ~ *v. pr.* puff up, swell.

bousculer /buskyle/ *v.t.* (*pousser*) jostle; (*presser*) rush; (*renverser*) knock over. ~**ade** *n.f.* rush; (*cohue*) crush.

bouse /buz/ *n.f.* (cow) dung.

bousiller /buzije/ *v.t.* (*fam.*) mess up.

boussole /busɔl/ *n.f.* compass.

bout /bu/ *n.m.* end; (*de langue, bâton*) tip; (*morceau*) bit. à ~, exhausted. à ~ **de souffle**, out of breath. à ~ **portant**, point-blank. **au** ~ **de**, (*après*) after. ~ **filtre**, filter-tip. **venir à** ~ **de**, (*finir*) manage to finish.

boutade /butad/ *n.f.* jest; (*caprice*) whim.

boute-en-train /butɑ̃trɛ̃/ *n.m. invar.* joker, live wire.

bouteille /butej/ *n.f.* bottle.

boutique /butik/ *n.f.* shop; (*de mode*) boutique.

bouton /butɔ̃/ *n.m.* button; (*pustule*) pimple; (*pousse*) bud; (*de porte, radio, etc.*) knob. ~ **de manchette**, cuff-link. ~**-d'or** *n.m.* (*pl.* ~**s-d'or**) buttercup. ~**ner** /-ɔne/ *v.t.* button (up). ~**nière** /-ɔnjɛr/ *n.f.* buttonhole. ~**-pression** (*pl.* ~**s-pression**) *n.m.* press-stud; (*Amer.*) snap.

boutonneu|x, ~se /butɔnø, -z/ *a.* pimply.

bouture /butyr/ *n.f.* (*plante*) cutting.

bovin, ~e /bɔvɛ̃, -in/ *a.* bovine. ~**s** *n.m. pl.* cattle.

bowling /boliŋ/ *n.m.* bowling; (*salle*) bowling-alley.

box (*pl.* ~ **ou boxes**) /bɔks/ *n.m.* lock-up garage; (*de dortoir*) cubicle; (*d'écurie*) (loose) box; (*jurid.*) dock.

box|e /bɔks/ *n.f.* boxing. ~**er** *v.t./i.* box. ~**eur** *n.m.* boxer.

boyau (*pl.* ~**x**) /bwajo/ *n.m.* gut; (*corde*) catgut; (*galerie*) gallery; (*de bicyclette*) tyre; (*Amer.*) tire.

boycott|er /bɔjkɔte/ *v.t.* boycott. ~**age** *n.m.* boycott.

BP *abrév.* (*boîte postale*) PO Box.

bracelet /braslɛ/ *n.m.* bracelet; (*de montre*) strap.

braconn|er /brakɔne/ *v.i.* poach. ~**ier** *n.m.* poacher.

brad|er /brade/ *v.t.* sell off. ~**erie** *n.f.* open-air sale.

braguette /bragɛt/ *n.f.* fly.

braille /braj/ *n.m. & a.* Braille.

brailler /braje/ *v.t./i.* bawl.

braire /brɛr/ *v.i.* bray.

braise /brɛz/ *n.f.* embers.

braiser /brɛze/ *v.t.* braise.

brancard /brɑ̃kar/ *n.m.* stretcher; (*bras*) shaft. ~**ier** /-dje/ *n.m.* stretcher-bearer.

branch|e /brɑ̃ʃ/ *n.f.* branch. ~**ages** *n.m. pl.* (cut) branches.

branché /brɑ̃ʃe/ *a.* (*fam.*) trendy.

branch|er /brɑ̃ʃe/ *v.t.* connect; (*électr.*) plug in. ~**ement** *n.m.* connection.

branchies /brɑ̃ʃi/ *n.f. pl.* gills.

brandir /brɑ̃dir/ *v.t.* brandish.

branle /brɑ̃l/ *n.m.* mettre en ~, set in motion. se mettre en ~, get started. ~**bas** (**de combat**) *n.m. invar.* bustle.

branler /brɑ̃le/ *v.i.* be shaky. —*v.t.* shake.

braquer /brake/ *v.t.* aim; (*regard*) fix; (*roue*) turn; (*banque: fam.*) hold up. ~ **qn. contre**, turn s.o. against. —*v.i.* (*auto.*) turn (the wheel). —*v. pr.* **se** ~, dig one's heels in.

bras /brɑ/ *n.m.* arm. ~ (*fig.*) labour, hands. à ~**-le-corps** *adv.* round the waist. ~ **dessus bras dessous**, arm in arm. ~ **droit**, (*fig.*) right-hand man. **en** ~ **de chemise**, in one's shirtsleeves.

brasier /brɑzje/ n.m. blaze.

brassard /brasar/ n.m. arm-band.

brasse /bras/ n.f. (breast-)stroke; (mesure) fathom.

brassée /brase/ n.f. armful.

brass|er /brase/ v.t. mix; (bière) brew; (affaires) handle a lot of. ~age n.m. mixing; brewing. ~erie n.f. brewery; (café) brasserie. ~eur n.m. brewer. ~eur d'affaires, big businessman.

brassière /brasjer/ n.f. (baby's) vest.

bravache /bravaʃ/ n.m. braggart.

bravade /bravad/ n.f. par ~, out of bravado.

brave /brav/ a. brave; (bon) good. ~ment adv. bravely.

braver /brave/ v.t. defy.

bravo /bravo/ int. bravo. —n.m. cheer.

bravoure /bravur/ n.f. bravery.

break /brɛk/ n.m. estate car; (Amer.) station-wagon.

brebis /brəbi/ n.f. ewe. ~ galeuse, black sheep.

brèche /brɛʃ/ n.f. gap, breach. être sur la ~, be on the go.

bredouille /brəduj/ a. empty-handed.

bredouiller /brəduje/ v.t./i. mumble.

bref, brève /brɛf, -v/ a. short, brief. —adv. in short. en ~, in short.

Brésil /brezil/ n.m. Brazil.

brésilien, ~ne /breziljɛ̃, -jɛn/ a. & n.m., f. Brazilian.

Bretagne /brətaɲ/ n.f. Brittany.

bretelle /brətɛl/ n.f. (shoulder-) strap; (d'autoroute) access road. ~s, (pour pantalon) braces; (Amer.) suspenders.

breton, ~ne /brətɔ̃, -ɔn/ a. & n.m., f. Breton.

breuvage /brœvaʒ/ n.m. beverage.

brève /brɛv/ voir bref.

brevet /brəvɛ/ n.m. diploma. ~ (d'invention), patent.

brevet|er /brəvte/ v.t. patent. ~é a. patented.

bribes /brib/ n.f. pl. scraps.

bric-à-brac /brikabrak/ n.m. invar. bric-à-brac.

bricole /brikɔl/ n.f. trifle.

bricol|er /brikɔle/ v.i. do odd (do-it-yourself) jobs. —v.t. fix (up). ~age n.m. do-it-yourself (jobs). ~eur, ~euse n.m., f. handyman, handywoman.

brid|e /brid/ n.f. bridle. tenir en ~e, keep in check. ~er v.t. (cheval) bridle; (fig.) keep in check, (culin.) truss.

bridé /bride/ a. yeux ~s, slit eyes.

bridge /bridʒ/ n.m. (cartes) bridge.

briève|ment /brijɛvmɑ̃/ adv. briefly. ~té n.f. brevity.

brigad|e /brigad/ n.f. (de police) squad; (mil.) brigade; (fig.) team. ~ier n.m. (de police) sergeant.

brigand /brigɑ̃/ n.m. robber. ~age /-daʒ/ n.m. robbery.

briguer /brige/ v.t. seek (after).

brill|ant, ~ante /brijɑ̃, -t/ a. (couleur) bright; (luisant) shiny; (remarquable) brilliant. —n.m. (éclat) shine; (diamant) diamond. ~amment adv. brilliantly.

briller /brije/ v.i. shine.

brim|er /brime/ v.t. bully, harass. se sentir brimé, feel put down. ~ade n.f. vexation.

brin /brɛ̃/ n.m. (de corde) strand; (de muguet) sprig. ~ d'herbe, blade of grass. un ~ de, a bit of.

brindille /brɛ̃dij/ n.f. twig.

bringuebaler /brɛ̃gbale/ v.i. (fam.) wobble about.

brio /brijo/ n.m. brilliance. avec ~, brilliantly.

brioche /brijɔʃ/ n.f. brioche (small round sweet cake); (ventre: fam.) paunch.

brique /brik/ n.f. brick.

briquer /brike/ v.t. polish.

briquet /brikɛ/ n.m. (cigarette-) lighter.

brisant /brizɑ̃/ *n.m.* reef.

brise /briz/ *n.f.* breeze.

bris|er /brize/ *v.t.* break. **se ~er** *v. pr.* break. **~e-lames** *n.m. invar.* breakwater. **~eur de grève** *n.m.* strikebreaker.

britannique /britanik/ *a.* British. —*n.m./f.* Briton. **les B~s**, the British.

broc /bro/ *n.m.* pitcher.

brocant|e /brokɑ̃t/ *n.f.* second-hand goods. **~eur, ~euse** *n.m.,f.* second-hand goods dealer.

broche /brɔʃ/ *n.f.* brooch; (*culin.*) spit. **à la ~**, spit-roasted.

broché /brɔʃe/ *a.* paperback(ed).

brochet /brɔʃɛ/ *n.m.* (*poisson*) pike.

brochette /brɔʃɛt/ *n.f.* skewer.

brochure /brɔʃyr/ *n.f.* brochure, booklet.

brod|er /brɔde/ *v.t.* embroider. —*v.i.* (*fig.*) embroider the truth. **~erie** *n.f.* embroidery.

broncher /brɔ̃ʃe/ *v.i.* **sans ~**, without turning a hair.

bronch|es /brɔ̃ʃ/ *n.f. pl.* bronchial tubes. **~ite** *n.f.* bronchitis.

bronze /brɔ̃z/ *n.m.* bronze.

bronz|er /brɔ̃ze/ *v.t.* **~er** *v. pr.* get a (sun-)tan. **~age** *n.m.* (sun-)tan. **~é** *a.* (sun-)tanned.

brosse /brɔs/ *n.f.* brush. **~ à dents**, toothbrush. **~ à habits**, clothes-brush. **en ~**, (*coiffure*) in a crew cut.

brosser /brɔse/ *v.t.* brush; (*fig.*) paint. **se ~ les dents/les cheveux**, brush one's teeth/hair.

brouette /bruɛt/ *n.f.* wheelbarrow.

brouhaha /bruaa/ *n.m.* hubbub.

brouillard /brujar/ *n.m.* fog.

brouille /bruj/ *n.f.* quarrel.

brouill|er /bruje/ *v.t.* mix up; (*vue*) blur; (*œufs*) scramble; (*radio*) jam; (*amis*) set at odds. **se ~** *v. pr.* become confused; (*ciel*) cloud over; (*amis*) fall out. **~on¹**, **~onne** *a.* untidy.

brouillon² /brujɔ̃/ *n.m.* (rough) draft.

broussailles /brusaj/ *n.f. pl.* undergrowth.

brousse /brus/ *n.f.* **la ~**, the bush.

brouter /brute/ *v.t./i.* graze.

broutille /brutij/ *n.f.* trifle.

broyer /brwaje/ *v.t.* crush; (*moudre*) grind.

bru /bry/ *n.f.* daughter-in-law.

bruin|e /brɥin/ *n.f.* drizzle. **~er** *v.i.* drizzle.

bruire /brɥir/ *v.i.* rustle.

bruissement /brɥismɑ̃/ *n.m.* rustling.

bruit /brɥi/ *n.m.* noise; (*fig.*) rumour.

bruitage /brɥitaʒ/ *n.m.* sound effects.

brûlant, **~e** /brylɑ̃, -t/ *a.* burning (hot); (*sujet*) red-hot; (*ardent*) fiery.

brûlé /bryle/ *a.* (*démasqué: fam.*) blown. —*n.m.* burning. **ça sent le ~**, I can smell sth. burning.

brûle-pourpoint (à) /(a)brylpurpwɛ̃/ *adv.* point-blank.

brûl|er /bryle/ *v.t./i.* burn; (*essence*) use (up); (*signal*) go through ou past (without stopping); (*dévorer: fig.*) consume. **se ~er** *v. pr.* burn o.s. **~eur** *n.m.* burner.

brûlure /brylyr/ *n.f.* burn. **~s d'estomac**, heartburn.

brum|e /brym/ *n.f.* mist. **~eux**, **~euse** *a.* misty; (*idées*) hazy.

brun, **~e** /brœ̃, bryn/ *a.* brown, dark. —*n.m.* brown. —*n.m.,f.* dark-haired person. **~ir** /brynir/ *v.i.* turn brown; (*se bronzer*) get a tan.

brunch /brœnʃ/ *n.m.* brunch.

brushing /brœʃiŋ/ *n.m.* blow-dry.

brusque /brysk/ *a.* (*soudain*) sudden, abrupt; (*rude*) abrupt. **~ment** /-əmɑ̃/ *adv.* suddenly, abruptly.

brusquer /bryske/ *v.t.* rush.

brut /bryt/ *a.* (*diamant*) rough; (*soie*) raw; (*pétrole*) crude; (*comm.*) gross.

brut|al (*m. pl.* ~**aux**) /brytal, -o/ *a.* brutal. ~**aliser** *v.t.* treat roughly *ou* violently, manhandle. ~**alité** *n.f.* brutality.

brute /bryt/ *n.f.* brute.

Bruxelles /brysɛl/ *n.m./f.* Brussels.

bruy|ant, ~ante /brɥijã -t/ *a.* noisy. ~**amment** *adv.* noisily.

bruyère /brɥjɛr/ *n.f.* heather.

bu /by/ *voir* **boire**.

bûche /byʃ/ *n.f.* log. ~ **de Noël,** Christmas log. **(se) ramasser une** ~, (*fam.*) come a cropper.

bûcher[1] /byʃe/ *n.m.* (*supplice*) stake.

bûch|er[2] /byʃe/ *v.t./i.* (*fam.*) slog away (at). ~**eur, ~euse** *n.m., f.* (*fam.*) slogger.

bûcheron /byʃrɔ̃/ *n.m.* woodcutter.

budg|et /bydʒɛ/ *n.m.* budget. ~**étaire** *a.* budgetary.

buée /bɥe/ *n.f.* mist, condensation.

buffet /byfɛ/ *n.m.* sideboard; (*réception, restaurant*) buffet.

buffle /byfl/ *n.m.* buffalo.

buis /bɥi/ *n.m.* (*arbre, bois*) box.

buisson /bɥisɔ̃/ *n.m.* bush.

buissonnière /bɥisɔnjɛr/ *a.f.* **faire l'école** ~, play truant.

bulbe /bylb/ *n.m.* bulb.

bulgare /bylgar/ *a. & n.m./f.* Bulgarian.

Bulgarie /bylgari/ *n.f.* Bulgaria.

bulldozer /byldozɛr/ *n.m.* bulldozer.

bulle /byl/ *n.f.* bubble.

bulletin /byltɛ̃/ *n.m.* bulletin, report; (*scol.*) report; (*billet*) ticket. ~ **d'information,** news bulletin. ~ **météorologique,** weather report. ~ **(de vote),** ballot-paper. ~ **de salaire,** payslip. ~-**réponse** *n.m.* (*pl.* ~**s-réponses**) reply slip.

buraliste /byralist/ *n.m./f.* tobacconist; (*à la poste*) clerk.

bureau (*pl.* ~**x**) /byro/ *n.m.* office; (*meuble*) desk; (*comité*) board. ~ **de location,** booking-office; (*théâtre*) box-office. ~ **de poste,** post office. ~ **de tabac,** tobacconist's (shop). ~ **de vote,** polling station.

bureaucrate /byrokrat/ *n.m./f.* bureaucrat.

bureaucrat|ie /byrokrasi/ *n.f.* bureaucracy. ~**ique** /-tik/ *a.* bureaucratic.

bureautique /byrotik/ *n.f.* office automation.

burette /byrɛt/ *n.f.* (*de graissage*) oilcan.

burin /byrɛ̃/ *n.m.* (cold) chisel.

burlesque /byrlɛsk/ *a.* ludicrous; (*théâtre*) burlesque.

bus /bys/ *n.m.* bus.

busqué /byske/ *a.* hooked.

buste /byst/ *n.m.* bust.

but /by(t)/ *n.m.* target; (*dessein*) aim, goal; (*football*) goal. **avoir pour** ~ **de,** aim to. **de** ~ **en blanc,** point-blank. **dans le** ~ **de,** with the intention of.

butane /bytan/ *n.f.* butane, Calor gas (P.).

buté /byte/ *a.* obstinate.

buter /byte/ *v.i.* ~ **contre,** knock against; (*problème*) come up against. —*v.t.* antagonize. **se** ~ *v. pr.* (*s'entêter*) become obstinate.

buteur /bytœr/ *n.m.* striker.

butin /bytɛ̃/ *n.m.* booty, loot.

butiner /bytine/ *v.i.* gather nectar.

butoir /bytwar/ *n.m.* ~ **(de porte),** doorstop.

butor /bytɔr/ *n.m.* (*péj.*) lout.

butte /byt/ *n.f.* mound. **en** ~ **à,** exposed to.

buvard /byvar/ *n.m.* blotting-paper.

buvette /byvɛt/ *n.f.* (*refreshment*) bar.

buveu|r, **~se** /byvœr, -øz/ *n.m., f.* drinker.

C

c' /s/ *voir* **ce**[1].

ça /sa/ *pron.* it, that; (*pour désigner* that; (*plus près*) this. **ça va?**, (*fam.*) how's it going? **ça va!**, (*fam.*) all right! **où ça?**, (*fam.*) where? **quand ça?**, (*fam.*) when? **c'est ça**, that's right.

çà /sa/ *adv.* **çà et là**, here and there.

caban|e /kaban/ *n.f.* hut; (*à outils*) shed. **~on** *n.m.* hut; (*en Provence*) cottage.

cabaret /kabarɛ/ *n.m.* night-club.

cabas /kaba/ *n.m.* shopping bag.

cabillaud /kabijo/ *n.m.* cod.

cabine /kabin/ *n.f.* (*à la piscine*) cubicle; (*à la plage*) (beach) hut; (*de bateau*) cabin; (*de pilotage*) cockpit; (*de camion*) cab; (*d'ascenseur*) cage. **~ (téléphonique)**, phone-booth, phone-box.

cabinet /kabinɛ/ *n.m.* (*de médecin*) surgery; (*Amer.*) office; (*d'avocat*) office; (*clientèle*) practice; (*pol.*) Cabinet; (*pièce*) room. **~s**, (*toilettes*) toilet. **~ de toilette**, toilet.

câble /kɑbl/ *n.m.* cable; (*corde*) rope.

câbler /kɑble/ *v.t.* cable.

cabosser /kabɔse/ *v.t.* dent.

cabot|age /kabɔtaʒ/ *n.m.* coastal navigation. **~eur** *n.m.* coaster.

cabotin, **~e** /kabɔtɛ̃, -in/ *n.m., f.* (*théâtre*) ham; (*fig.*) play-actor. **~age** /-inaʒ/ *n.m.* ham acting; (*fig.*) play-acting.

cabrer /kabre/ *v.t.*, **se ~** *v. pr.* (*cheval*) rear up. **se ~ contre**, rebel against.

cabri /kabri/ *n.m.* kid.

cabriole /kabrijɔl/ *n.f.* (*culbute*)

somersault. **faire des ~s**, caper about.

cacahuète /kakaɥɛt/ *n.f.* peanut.

cacao /kakao/ *n.m.* cocoa.

cachalot /kaʃalo/ *n.m.* sperm whale.

cache /kaʃ/ *n.m.* mask; (*photo.*) lens cover.

cachemire /kaʃmir/ *n.m.* cashmere.

cach|er /kaʃe/ *v.t.* hide, conceal (**à**, from). **se ~er** *v. pr.* hide; (*se trouver caché*) be hidden. **~e-cache** *n.m. invar.* hide-and-seek. **~e-nez** *n.m. invar.* scarf. **~e-pot** *n.m.* cache-pot.

cachet /kaʃɛ/ *n.m.* seal; (*de la poste*) postmark; (*comprimé*) tablet; (*d'artiste*) fee; (*fig.*) style.

cacheter /kaʃte/ *v.t.* seal.

cachette /kaʃɛt/ *n.f.* hiding-place. **en ~**, in secret.

cachot /kaʃo/ *n.m.* dungeon.

cachott|eries /kaʃɔtri/ *n.f. pl.* secrecy. **faire des ~eries**, be secretive. **~ier**, **~ière** *a.* secretive.

cacophonie /kakɔfɔni/ *n.f.* cacophony.

cactus /kaktys/ *n.m.* cactus.

cadavérique /kadaverik/ *a.* (*teint*) deathly pale.

cadavre /kadavr/ *n.m.* corpse.

caddie /kadi/ *n.m.* trolley.

cadeau (*pl.* **~x**) /kado/ *n.m.* present, gift. **faire un ~ à qn.**, give s.o. a present.

cadenas /kadna/ *n.m.* padlock. **~ser** /-ase/ *v.t.* padlock.

cadenc|e /kadɑ̃s/ *n.f.* rhythm, cadence; (*de travail*) rate. **en ~e**, in time. **~é a** rhythmic(al).

cadet, **~te** /kadɛ, -t/ *a.* youngest; (*entre deux*) younger. **—n.m.**, *f.* youngest (child); younger (child).

cadran /kadrɑ̃/ *n.m.* dial. **~ solaire**, sundial.

cadre /kadr/ *n.m.* frame; (*milieu*)

surroundings; (*limites*) scope; (*contexte*: *comm.*) framework. —*n.m./f.* (*personne*: *comm.*) executive. **les ~s,** (*comm.*) the managerial staff.

cadrer /kadre/ *v.i.* **~ avec,** tally with. —*v.t.* (*photo*) centre.

caduc, ~que /kadyk/ *a.* obsolete.

cafard /kafar/ *n.m.* (*insecte*) cockroach. **avoir le ~,** (*fam.*) be feeling low. **~er** /-de/ *v.i.* (*fam.*) tell tales.

café /kafe/ *n.m.* coffee; (*bar*) café. **~é au lait,** white coffee. **~etière** *n.f.* coffee-pot.

caféine /kafein/ *n.f.* caffeine.

cafouiller /kafuje/ *v.i.* (*fam.*) bumble, flounder.

cage /kaʒ/ *n.f.* cage; (*d'escalier*) well; (*d'ascenseur*) shaft.

cageot /kaʒo/ *n.m.* crate.

cagibi /kaʒibi/ *n.m.* storage room.

cagneu|x, ~se /kaɲø, -z/ *a.* knock-kneed.

cagnotte /kaɲɔt/ *n.f.* kitty.

cagoule /kagul/ *n.f.* hood.

cahier /kaje/ *n.m.* notebook; (*scol.*) exercise-book.

cahin-caha /kaɛ̃kaa/ *adv.* aller **~,** (*fam.*) jog along.

cahot /kao/ *n.m.* bump, jolt. **~er** /kaote/ *v.t./i.* bump, jolt. **~eux, ~euse** /kaote, -z/ *a.* bumpy.

caïd /kaid/ *n.m.* (*fam.*) big shot.

caille /kaj/ *n.f.* quail.

cailler /kaje/ *v.t./i.,* **se ~** *v. pr.* (*sang*) clot; (*lait*) curdle.

caillot /kajo/ *n.m.* (blood) clot.

caillou (*pl.* **~x**) /kaju/ *n.m.* stone; (*galet*) pebble. **~teux, ~teuse** *a.* stony. **~tis** *n.m.* gravel.

caisse /kɛs/ *n.f.* crate, case; (*tiroir, machine*) till; (*guichet*) pay-desk; (*bureau*) office; (*mus.*) drum. **~ enregistreuse,** cash register. **~ d'épargne,** savings bank. **~ de retraite,** pension fund.

caiss|ier, ~ière /kesje, -jɛr/ *n.m.,f.* cashier.

cajol|er /kaʒɔle/ *v.t.* coax. **~eries** *n.f. pl.* coaxing.

cake /kɛk/ *n.m.* fruit-cake.

calamité /kalamite/ *n.f.* calamity.

calandre /kalɑ̃dr/ *n.f.* radiator grill.

calanque /kalɑ̃k/ *n.f.* creek.

calcaire /kalkɛr/ *a.* (*sol*) chalky; (*eau*) hard.

calciné /kalsine/ *a.* charred.

calcium /kalsjɔm/ *n.m.* calcium.

calcul /kalkyl/ *n.m.* calculation; (*scol.*) arithmetic; (*différentiel*) calculus. **~ biliaire,** gallstone.

calcul|er /kalkyle/ *v.t.* calculate. **~ateur** *n.m.* (*ordinateur*) computer, calculator. **~atrice** *n.f.* (*ordinateur*) calculator. **~ette** *n.f.* (pocket) calculator.

cale /kal/ *n.f.* wedge; (*de navire*) hold. **~ sèche,** dry dock.

calé /kale/ *a.* (*fam.*) clever.

caleçon /kalsɔ̃/ *n.m.* underpants; (*de femme*) leggings. **~ de bain,** (bathing) trunks.

calembour /kalɑ̃bur/ *n.m.* pun.

calendrier /kalɑ̃drije/ *n.m.* calendar; (*fig.*) timetable.

calepin /kalpɛ̃/ *n.m.* notebook.

caler /kale/ *v.t.* wedge; (*moteur*) stall. —*v.i.* stall.

calfeutrer /kalføtre/ *v.t.* stop up the cracks of.

calibr|e /kalibr/ *n.m.* calibre; (*d'un œuf, fruit*) grade. **~er** *v.t.* grade.

calice /kalis/ *n.m.* (*relig.*) chalice; (*bot.*) calyx.

califourchon (**à**) /(a)kalifurʃɔ̃/ *adv.* astride. —*prép.* **à ~ sur,** astride.

câlin|e /kɑlɛ̃, -in/ *a.* endearing, cuddly. **~er** /-ine/ *v.t.* cuddle.

calmant /kalmɑ̃/ *n.m.* sedative.

calm|e /kalm/ *a.* calm —*n.m.* calm(ness). **du ~e!,** calm down! **~er** *v.t.,* **se ~er** *v. pr.* (*personne*) calm (down); (*diminuer*) ease.

calomn|ie /kalɔmni/ *n.f.* slander; (*écrite*) libel. ~**ier** *v.t.* slander; libel. ~**ieux**, ~**ieuse** *a.* slanderous; libellous.

calorie /kalɔri/ *n.f.* calorie.

calorifuge /kalɔrifyʒ/ *a.* (heat-) insulating. —*n.m.* lagging.

calot /kalo/ *n.m.* (*mil.*) forage-cap.

calotte /kalɔt/ *n.f.* (*relig.*) skullcap; (*tape: fam.*) slap.

calqu|e /kalk/ *n.m.* tracing; (*fig.*) exact copy. ~**er** *v.t.* trace; (*fig.*) copy. ~**er sur**, model on.

calvaire /kalvɛr/ *n.m.* (*croix*) calvary; (*fig.*) suffering.

calvitie /kalvisi/ *n.f.* baldness.

camarade /kamarad/ *n.m./f.* friend; (*pol.*) comrade. ~ **de jeu**, playmate. ~**rie** *n.f.* good companionship.

cambiste /kãbist/ *n.m./f.* foreign exchange dealer.

cambouis /kãbwi/ *n.m.* (engine) oil.

cambrer /kãbre/ *v.t.* arch. **se** ~ *v. pr.* arch one's back.

cambriol|er /kãbrijɔle/ *v.t.* burgle. ~**age** *n.m.* burglary. ~**eur**, ~**euse** *n.m./f.* burglar.

cambrure /kãbryr/ *n.f.* curve.

came /kam/ *n.f.* **arbe à** ~**s**, camshaft.

camée /kame/ *n.m.* cameo.

camelot /kamlo/ *n.m.* street vendor.

camelote /kamlɔt/ *n.f.* junk.

camembert /kamãbɛr/ *n.m.* Camembert (cheese).

caméra /kamera/ *n.f.* (*cinéma, télévision*) camera.

caméra|man (*pl.* ~**men**) /kameraman, -mɛn/ *n.m.* cameraman.

camion /kamjɔ̃/ *n.m.* lorry, truck. ~**-citerne** *n.m.* tanker. ~**nage** /-jɔnaʒ/ *n.m.* haulage. ~**nette** /-jɔnɛt/ *n.f.* van. ~**neur** /-jɔnœr/ *n.m.* lorry *ou* truck

driver; (*entrepreneur*) haulage contractor.

camisole /kamizɔl/ *n.f.* ~ (**de force**), strait-jacket.

camoufl|er /kamufle/ *v.t.* camouflage. ~**age** *n.m.* camouflage.

camp /kã/ *n.m.* camp; (*sport*) side.

campagn|e /kãpaɲ/ *n.f.* country (side); (*mil., pol.*) campaign. ~**ard**, ~**arde** *a.* country; *n.m., f.* countryman, countrywoman.

campanile /kãpanil/ *n.m.* bell-tower.

camp|er /kãpe/ *v.i.* camp. —*v.t.* plant boldly; (*esquisser*) sketch. **se** ~**er** *v. pr.* plant o.s. ~**ement** *n.m.* encampment. ~**eur**, ~**euse** *n.m., f.* camper.

camphre /kãfr/ *n.m.* camphor.

camping /kãpiŋ/ *n.m.* camping. **faire du** ~, go camping. ~**car** *n.m.* camper-van; (*Amer.*) motor-home. ~**-gaz** *n.m. invar.* (P.) camping-gaz. (**terrain de**) ~, campsite.

campus /kãpys/ *n.m.* campus.

Canada /kanada/ *n.m.* Canada.

canadien, ~**ne** /kanadjɛ̃, -jɛn/ *a. & n.m., f.* Canadian. —*n.f.* fur-lined jacket.

canaille /kanaj/ *n.f.* rogue.

can|al (*pl.* ~**aux**) /kanal, -o/ *n.m.* (*artificiel*) canal; (*bras de mer*) channel; (*techn., TV*) channel. **par le** ~**al de**, through.

canalisation /kanalizasjɔ̃/ *n.f.* (*tuyaux*) main(s).

canaliser /kanalize/ *v.t.* (*eau*) canalize; (*fig.*) channel.

canapé /kanape/ *n.m.* sofa.

canard /kanar/ *n.m.* duck; (*journal: fam.*) rag.

canari /kanari/ *n.m.* canary.

cancans /kãkã/ *n.m. pl.* malicious gossip.

canc|er /kãser/ *n.m.* cancer. **le** **C~er**, Cancer. ~**éreux**, ~**éreuse** *a.* cancerous. ~**érigène** *a.* carcinogenic.

cancre /kɑ̃kr/ *n.m.* dunce.

cancrelat /kɑ̃krəla/ *n.m.* cockroach.

candélabre /kɑ̃delabr/ *n.m.* candelabrum.

candeur /kɑ̃dœr/ *n.f.* naïvety.

candidat, ~e /kɑ̃dida, -t/ *n.m., f.* candidate; (à un poste) applicant, candidate (à, for). **~ure** /-tyr/ *n.f.* application; (pol.) candidacy. **poser sa ~ pour,** apply for.

candide /kɑ̃did/ *a.* naïve.

cane /kan/ *n.f.* (female) duck. **~ton** *n.m.* duckling.

canette /kanɛt/ *n.f.* (de bière) bottle.

canevas /kanva/ *n.m.* canvas; (plan) framework, outline.

caniche /kaniʃ/ *n.m.* poodle.

canicule /kanikyl/ *n.f.* hot summer days.

canif /kanif/ *n.m.* penknife.

canin, ~e /kanɛ̃, -in/ *a.* canine. —*n.f.* canine (tooth).

caniveau (pl. ~x) /kanivo/ *n.m.* gutter.

cannabis /kanabis/ *n.m.* cannabis.

canne /kan/ *n.f.* (walking-)stick. **~ à-pêche,** fishing-rod. **~ à sucre,** sugar-cane.

cannelle /kanɛl/ *n.f.* cinnamon.

cannibale /kanibal/ *a. & n.m./f.* cannibal.

canoë /kanɔe/ *n.m.* canoe; (sport) canoeing.

canon /kanɔ̃/ *n.m.* (big) gun; (d'une arme) barrel; (principe, règle) canon. **~nade** /-ɔnad/ *n.f.* gunfire. **~nier** /-ɔnje/ *n.m.* gunner.

canot /kano/ *n.m.* boat. **~ de sauvetage,** lifeboat. **~ pneumatique,** rubber dinghy.

canot|er /kanɔte/ *v.i.* boat. **~age** *n.m.* boating. **~ier** *n.m.* boater.

cantate /kɑ̃tat/ *n.f.* cantata.

cantatrice /kɑ̃tatris/ *n.f.* opera singer.

cantine /kɑ̃tin/ *n.f.* canteen.

cantique /kɑ̃tik/ *n.m.* hymn.

canton /kɑ̃tɔ̃/ *n.m.* (en France) district; (en Suisse) canton.

cantonade (à la) /(ala)kɑ̃tɔnad/ *adv.* for all to hear.

cantonner /kɑ̃tɔne/ *v.t.* (mil.) billet. **se ~ dans,** confine o.s. to.

cantonnier /kɑ̃tɔnje/ *n.m.* roadman, road mender.

canular /kanylar/ *n.m.* hoax.

caoutchou|c /kautʃu/ *n.m.* rubber; (élastique) rubber band. **~c mousse,** foam rubber. **~té** *a.* rubberized. **~teux, ~teuse** *a.* rubbery.

cap /kap/ *n.m.* cape, headland; (direction) course. **doubler ou franchir le ~ de,** go beyond (the point of). **mettre le ~ sur,** steer a course for.

capable /kapabl/ *a.* able, capable. **~ de qch.,** capable of sth. **~ de faire,** able to do, capable of doing.

capacité /kapasite/ *n.f.* ability; (contenance) capacity.

cape /kap/ *n.f.* cape. **rire sous ~,** laugh up one's sleeve.

capillaire /kapilɛr/ *a.* (lotion, soins) hair. (vaisseau) ~, capillary.

capilotade (en) /(ɑ̃)kapilɔtad/ *adv.* (fam.) reduced to a pulp.

capitaine /kapitɛn/ *n.m.* captain.

capit|al, ~ale (m. pl. **~aux**) /kapital, -o/ *a.* major, fundamental; (peine, lettre) capital. —*n.m.* (pl. **~aux**) (comm.) capital; (fig.) stock. **~aux,** (comm.) capital. —*n.f.* (ville, lettre) capital.

capitalis|te /kapitalist/ *a. & n.m./f.* capitalist. **~me** *n.m.* capitalism.

capiteu|x, ~se /kapitø, -z/ *a.* heady.

capitonné /kapitɔne/ *a.* padded.

capitul|er /kapityle/ *v.i.* capitulate. **~ation** *n.f.* capitulation.

capor|al (*pl.* **~aux**) /kapɔral, -o/ *n.m.* corporal.

capot /kapo/ *n.m.* (*auto.*) bonnet; (*auto.*, *Amer.*) hood.

capote /kapɔt/ *n.f.* (*auto.*) hood; (*auto.*, *Amer.*) (convertible) top; (*fam.*) condom.

capoter /kapɔte/ *v.i.* overturn.

câpre /kɑpr/ *n.f.* (*culin.*) caper.

capric|e /kapris/ *n.m.* whim, caprice. **~ieux, ~ieuse** *a.* capricious; (*appareil*) temperamental.

Capricorne /kaprikɔrn/ *n.m.* le **~**, Capricorn.

capsule /kapsyl/ *n.f.* capsule; (*de bouteille*) cap.

capter /kapte/ *v.t.* (*eau*) tap; (*émission*) pick up; (*fig.*) win, capture.

capti|f, ~ve /kaptif, -v/ *a.* & *n.m.,f.* captive.

captiver /kaptive/ *v.t.* captivate.

captivité /kaptivite/ *n.f.* captivity.

captur|e /kaptyr/ *n.f.* capture. **~er** *v.t.* capture.

capuch|e /kakɔf/ *n.f.* hood. **~on** *n.m.* hood; (*de stylo*) cap.

caquet /kakɛ/ *n.m.* **rabattre le ~ à qn.**, take s.o. down a peg or two.

caquet|er /kakte/ *v.i.* cackle. **~age** *n.m.* cackle.

car¹ /kar/ *conj.* because, for.

car² /kar/ *n.m.* coach; (*Amer.*) bus.

carabine /karabin/ *n.f.* rifle.

caracoler /karakɔle/ *v.i.* prance.

caract|ère /karaktɛr/ *n.m.* (*nature, lettre*) character. **~ères d'imprimerie**, block letters. **~ériel, ~érielle** *a.* character; *n.m.,f.* disturbed child.

caractérisé /karakterize/ *a.* well-defined.

caractéris|er /karakterize/ *v.t.* characterize. **se ~ par**, be characterized by.

caractéristique /karakteristik/ *a.* & *n.f.* characteristic.

carafe /karaf/ *n.f.* carafe; (*pour le vin*) decanter.

caraïbe /karaib/ *a.* Caribbean. **les C~s**, the Caribbean.

carambol|er (se) /(sə)karɑ̃bɔle/ *v. pr.* (*voitures*) smash into each other. **~age** *n.m.* multiple smash-up.

caramel /karamɛl/ *n.m.* caramel. **~iser** *v.t./i.* caramelize.

carapace /karapas/ *n.f.* shell.

carat /kara/ *n.m.* carat.

caravane /karavan/ *n.f.* (*auto.*) caravan; (*auto.*, *Amer.*) trailer; (*convoi*) caravan.

carbone /karbɔn/ *n.m.* carbon; (*double*) carbon (copy). **(papier) ~**, carbon (paper).

carboniser /karbɔnize/ *v.t.* burn (to ashes).

carburant /karbyrɑ̃/ *n.m.* (*motor*) fuel.

carburateur /karbyratœr/ *n.m.* carburettor; (*Amer.*) carburetor.

carcan /karkɑ̃/ *n.m.* (*contrainte*) yoke.

carcasse /karkas/ *n.f.* carcass; (*d'immeuble, de voiture*) frame.

cardiaque /kardjak/ *a.* heart. **—** *n.m./f.* heart patient.

cardigan /kardigɑ̃/ *n.m.* cardigan.

cardin|al (*pl.* **~aux**) /kardinal, -o/ *a.* cardinal. **—** *n.m.* (*pl.* **~aux**) cardinal.

Carême /karɛm/ *n.m.* Lent.

carence /karɑ̃s/ *n.f.* inadequacy; (*manque*) deficiency.

caressant, ~e /karesɑ̃, -t/ *a.* endearing.

caress|e /karɛs/ *n.f.* caress. **~er** /-ese/ *v.t.* caress, stroke; (*espoir*) cherish.

cargaison /kargɛzɔ̃/ *n.f.* cargo.

cargo /kargo/ *n.m.* cargo boat.

caricatur|e /karikatyr/ *n.f.* caricature. **~al** (*m. pl.* **~aux**) *a.* caricature-like.

car|ie /kari/ *n.f.* cavity. **la ~ie** (*dentaire*), tooth decay. **~ié** *a.* (*dent*) decayed.

carillon /karijɔ̃/ *n.m.* chimes;

(*horloge*) chiming clock. **∼ner** /-jɔne/ *v.i.* chime, peal.

caritati|f /karitatif, -v/ *a.* **association ∼ve,** charity.

carlingue /karlɛ̃g/ *n.f.* (*d'avion*) cabin.

carnage /karnaʒ/ *n.m.* carnage.

carnass|ier, ∼ière /karnasje, -jɛr/ *a.* flesh-eating.

carnaval (*pl.* **∼s**) /karnaval/ *n.m.* carnival.

carnet /karnɛ/ *n.m.* notebook; (*de tickets etc.*) book. **∼ de chèques,** cheque-book. **∼ de notes,** school report.

carotte /karɔt/ *n.f.* carrot.

carotter /karɔte/ *v.t.* (*argot*) swindle. **∼ qch. à qn.,** (*argot*) wangle sth. from s.o.

carpe /karp/ *n.f.* carp.

carpette /karpɛt/ *n.f.* rug.

carré /kare/ *a.* (*forme, mesure*) square; (*fig.*) straightforward. —*n.m.* square; (*de terrain*) patch.

carreau (*pl.* **∼x**) /karo/ *n.m.* (*window*) pane; (*par terre, au mur*) tile; (*dessin*) check; (*cartes*) diamonds. **à ∼x,** check(ed).

carrefour /karfur/ *n.m.* crossroads.

carrel|er /karle/ *v.t.* tile. **∼age** *n.m.* tiling; (*sol*) tiles.

carrelet /karlɛ/ *n.m.* (*poisson*) plaice.

carrément /karemɑ̃/ *adv.* straight; (*dire*) straight out.

carrer (se) /(sə)kare/ *v. pr.* settle firmly (**dans,** in).

carrière /karjɛr/ *n.f.* career; (*terrain*) quarry.

carrossable /karɔsabl/ *a.* suitable for vehicles.

carrosse /karɔs/ *n.m.* (*horse-drawn*) coach.

carross|erie /karɔsri/ *n.f.* (*auto.*) body(work). **∼ier** *n.m.* (*auto.*) body-builder.

carrure /karyr/ *n.f.* build; (*fig.*) calibre.

cartable /kartabl/ *n.m.* satchel.

carte /kart/ *n.f.* card; (*géog.*) map; (*naut.*) chart; (*au restaurant*) menu. **∼s,** (*jeu*) cards. **à la ∼,** (*manger*) à la carte. **∼ blanche,** a free hand. **∼ de crédit,** credit card. **∼ des vins,** wine list. **∼ de visite,** (business) card. **∼ grise,** (car) registration card. **∼ postale,** postcard.

cartel /kartɛl/ *n.m.* cartel.

cartilage /kartilaʒ/ *n.m.* cartilage.

carton /kartɔ̃/ *n.m.* cardboard; (*boîte*) (cardboard) box. **∼ à dessin,** portfolio. **faire un ∼,** (*fam.*) take a pot-shot. **∼nage** /-ɔnaʒ/ *n.m.* cardboard packing. **∼-pâte** *n.m.* pasteboard. **en ∼-pâte,** cardboard.

cartonné /kartɔne/ *a.* (*livre*) hardback.

cartouch|e /kartuʃ/ *n.f.* cartridge; (*de cigarettes*) carton. **∼ière** *n.f.* cartridge-belt.

cas /ka/ *n.m.* case. **au ∼ où,** in case. **∼ urgent,** emergency. **en aucun ∼,** on no account. **en ∼ de,** in the event of, in case of. **en tout ∼,** in any case. **faire ∼ de,** set great store by. **∼ de conscience** matter of conscience.

casan|ier, ∼ière /kazanje, -jɛr/ *a.* home-loving.

casaque /kazak/ *n.f.* (*de jockey*) shirt.

cascade /kaskad/ *n.f.* waterfall; (*fig.*) spate.

cascad|eur, ∼euse /kaskadœr, -øz/ *n.m.*, *f.* stuntman, stuntgirl.

case /kaz/ *n.f.* hut; (*compartiment*) pigeon-hole; (*sur papier*) square.

caser /kaze/ *v.t.* (*mettre*) put; (*loger*) put up; (*dans un travail*) find a job for; (*marier: péj.*) marry off.

caserne /kazɛrn/ *n.f.* barracks.

cash /kaʃ/ *adv.* **payer ∼,** pay (in) cash.

casier /kɑzje/ n.m. pigeon-hole, compartment; (meuble) cabinet; (à bouteilles) rack. ~ **judiciaire**, criminal record.

casino /kazino/ n.m. casino.

casque /kask/ n.m. helmet; (chez le coiffeur) (hair-)drier. ~**e** (à écouteurs), headphones. ~**é** a. wearing a helmet.

casquette /kasket/ n.f. cap.

cassant, ~**e** /kɑsɑ̃, -t/ a. brittle; (brusque) curt.

cassation /kasasjɔ̃/ n.f. **cour de** ~, appeal court.

casse /kɑs/ n.f. (objets) breakages. **mettre à la** ~, scrap.

cass|er /kɑse/ v.t./i. break; (annuler) annul. **se** ~**er** v. pr. break. ~**er la tête à**, (fam.) give a headache to. ~**e-cou** n.m. invar. daredevil. ~**e-croûte** n.m. invar. snack. ~**e-noisettes** ou ~**e-noix** n.m. invar. nutcrackers. ~**e-pieds** n.m./f. invar. (fam.) pain (in the neck). ~**e-tête** n.m. invar. (problème) headache; (jeu) brain teaser.

casserole /kasrɔl/ n.f. saucepan.

cassette /kaset/ n.f. casket; (de magnétophone) cassette; (de video) video tape.

cassis[1] /kasis/ n.m. black currant.

cassis[2] /kasi/ n.m. (auto.) dip.

cassoulet /kasulɛ/ n.m. stew (of beans and meat).

cassure /kɑsyr/ n.f. break.

caste /kast/ n.f. caste.

castor /kastɔr/ n.m. beaver.

castr|er /kastre/ v.t. castrate. ~**ation** n.f. castration.

cataclysme /kataklism/ n.m. cataclysm.

catalogu|e /katalɔg/ n.m. catalogue. ~**er** v.t. catalogue; (personne: péj.) label.

catalyseur /katalizœr/ n.m. catalyst.

cataphote /katafɔt/ n.m. reflector.

cataplasme /kataplasm/ n.m. poultice.

catapult|e /katapylt/ n.f. catapult. ~**er** v.t. catapult.

cataracte /katarakt/ n.f. cataract.

catastroph|e /katastrɔf/ n.f. disaster, catastrophe. ~**ique** a. catastrophic.

catch /katʃ/ n.m. (all-in) wrestling. ~**eur**, ~**euse** n.m., f. (all-in) wrestler.

catéchisme /kateʃism/ n.m. catechism.

catégorie /kategɔri/ n.f. category.

catégorique /kategɔrik/ a. categorical.

cathédrale /katedral/ n.f. cathedral.

catholi|que /katɔlik/ a. Catholic. ~**cisme** n.m. Catholicism. **pas très** ~**que**, a bit fishy.

catimini (en) /(ɑ̃)katimini/ adv. on the sly.

cauchemar /koʃmar/ n.m. nightmare.

cause /koz/ n.f. cause; (jurid.) case. **à** ~ **de**, because of. **en** ~, (en jeu, concerné) involved. **pour** ~ **de**, on account of.

caus|er /koze/ v.t. cause. —v.i. chat. ~**erie** n.f. talk. ~**ette** n.f. **faire la** ~**ette**, have a chat.

caustique /kostik/ a. caustic.

caution /kosjɔ̃/ n.f. surety; (jurid.) bail; (appui) backing; (garantie) deposit. **sous** ~, on bail.

cautionn|er /kosjɔne/ v.t. guarantee; (soutenir) back.

cavalcade /kavalkad/ n.f. (fam.) stampede, rush.

cavalerie /kavalri/ n.f. (mil.) cavalry; (au cirque) horses.

caval|ier, ~**ière** /kavalje, -jɛr/ a. offhand. —n.m., f. rider; (pour danser) partner. —n.m. (échecs) knight.

cave[1] /kav/ n.f. cellar.

cave[2] /kav/ a. sunken.

caveau (pl. ~**x**) /kavo/ n.m. vault.

caverne /kavɛrn/ n.f. cave.

caviar /kavjar/ n.m. caviare.

cavité /kavite/ n.f. cavity.

CD (abrév.) (compact disc) CD.

ce¹, c'* /sə, s/ pron. it, that. **c'est, il** ou that is. **ce sont, they are. c'est moi,** it's me. **c'est un chanteur/une chanteuse/etc.,** he/she is a singer/etc. **ce qui, ce que,** what. **ce que c'est bon/etc.!,** how good/etc. it is! **tout ce qui, tout ce que,** everything that.

ce² ou **cet*, cette** (pl. **ces**) /sə, sɛt, se/ a. that; (proximité) this. **ces,** those; (proximité) these.

CE abrév. (Communauté européenne) EC.

ceci /səsi/ pron. this.

cécité /sesite/ n.f. blindness.

céder /sede/ v.t. give up. —v.i. (se rompre) give way; (se soumettre) give in.

cédille /sedij/ n.f. cedilla.

cèdre /sɛdr/ n.m. cedar.

CEE abrév. (Communauté économique européenne) EEC.

ceinture /sɛ̃tyr/ n.f. belt; (taille) waist; (de bus, métro) circle (line). **~ de sauvetage,** lifebelt. **~ de sécurité,** seat-belt.

ceinturer /sɛ̃tyre/ v.t. seize round the waist; (entourer) surround.

cela /səla/ pron. it, that; (pour désigner) that. **~ va de soi,** it is obvious.

célèbre /selɛbr/ a. famous.

célébr|er /selebre/ v.t. celebrate. **~ation** n.f. celebration (de, of).

célébrité /selebrite/ n.f. fame; (personne) celebrity.

céleri /sɛlri/ n.m. (en branches) celery. **~(-rave),** celeriac.

céleste /selɛst/ a. celestial.

célibat /seliba/ n.m. celibacy.

célibataire /selibatɛr/ a. unmarried. —n.m. bachelor. —n.f. unmarried woman.

celle, celles /sɛl/ voir **celui.**

cellier /selje/ n.m. store-room (for wine).

cellophane /selɔfan/ n.f. (P.) Cellophane (P.).

cellul|e /selyl/ n.f. cell. **~aire** a. cell. **fourgon** ou **voiture ~aire,** prison van.

celui, celle (pl. **ceux, celles**) /səlɥi, sɛl, sø/ pron. the one. **~ de mon ami,** my friend's. **~-ci,** this (one). **~-là,** that (one). **ceux-ci,** these (ones). **ceux-là,** those (ones).

cendr|e /sɑ̃dr/ n.f. ash. **~é** a. (couleur) ashen. **blond ~é,** ash blond.

cendrier /sɑ̃drije/ n.m. ashtray.

censé /sɑ̃se/ a. être **~ faire,** be supposed to do.

censeur /sɑ̃sœr/ n.m. censor; (scol.) assistant headmaster.

censur|e /sɑ̃syr/ n.f. censorship. **~er** v.t. censor; (critiquer) censure.

cent (pl. **~s**) /sɑ̃/ (generally /sɑ̃t/ pl. /sɑ̃z/ before vowel) a. & n.m. (a) hundred. **~ un** /sɑ̃œ̃/ a hundred and one.

centaine /sɑ̃tɛn/ n.f. hundred. **une ~ (de),** (about) a hundred.

centenaire /sɑ̃tnɛr/ n.m. (anniversaire) centenary.

centième /sɑ̃tjɛm/ a. & n.m./f. hundredth.

centigrade /sɑ̃tigrad/ a. centigrade.

centilitre /sɑ̃tilitr/ n.m. centilitre.

centime /sɑ̃tim/ n.m. centime.

centimètre /sɑ̃timɛtr/ n.m. centimetre; (ruban) tape-measure.

centr|al, ~ale (m. pl. **~aux**) /sɑ̃tral, -o/ a. central. —n.m. (pl. **~aux**). **~al** (téléphonique), (telephone) exchange. —n.f. power-station. **~aliser** v.t. centralize.

centr|e /sɑ̃tr/ n.m. centre. **~e-ville** n.m. town centre. **~er** v.t. centre.

centuple /sãtypl/ *n.m.* **le ~ (de),** a hundredfold. **au ~,** a hundredfold.

cep /sɛp/ *n.m.* vine stock.

cépage /sepaʒ/ *n.m.* (variety of) vine.

cèpe /sɛp/ *n.m.* (edible) boletus.

cependant /səpãdã/ *adv.* however.

céramique /seramik/ *n.f.* ceramic; (*art*) ceramics.

cerceau (*pl.* ~x) /sɛrso/ *n.m.* hoop.

cercle /sɛrkl/ *n.m.* circle; (*cerceau*) hoop. ~ **vicieux,** vicious circle.

cercueil /sɛrkœj/ *n.m.* coffin.

céréale /sereal/ *n.f.* cereal.

cérébr|al (*m. pl.* ~aux) /serebral, -o/ *a.* cerebral.

cérémonial (*pl.* ~s) /seremɔnjal/ *n.m.* ceremonial.

cérémon|ie /seremɔni/ *n.f.* ceremony. ~**ie(s),** (*façons*) fuss. ~**ieux, ~ieuse** *a.* ceremonious.

cerf /sɛr/ *n.m.* stag.

cerfeuil /sɛrfœj/ *n.m.* chervil.

cerf-volant (*pl.* **cerfs-volants**) /sɛrvɔlã/ *n.m.* kite.

ceris|e /sriz/ *n.f.* cherry. ~**ier** *n.m.* cherry tree.

cerne /sɛrn/ *n.m.* ring.

cern|er /sɛrne/ *v.t.* surround; (*question*) define. **les yeux ~és,** with rings under one's eyes.

certain, ~**e** /sɛrtɛ̃, -ɛn/ *a.* certain; (*sûr*) certain, sure (**de,** of; **que,** that). —*pron.* ~**s,** certain people. **d'un ~ âge,** past one's prime. **un ~ temps,** some time.

certainement /sɛrtɛnmã/ *adv.* certainly.

certes /sɛrt/ *adv.* indeed.

certificat /sɛrtifika/ *n.m.* certificate.

certifi|er /sɛrtifje/ *v.t.* certify. ~**ier qch. à qn.,** assure s.o. of sth. ~**ié** *a.* (*professeur*) qualified.

certitude /sɛrtityd/ *n.f.* certainty.

cerveau (*pl.* ~x) /sɛrvo/ *n.m.* brain.

cervelas /sɛrvəla/ *n.m.* saveloy.

cervelle /sɛrvɛl/ *n.f.* (*anat.*) brain; (*culin.*) brains.

ces /se/ *voir* **ce².**

césarienne /sezarjɛn/ *n.f.* Caesarean (section).

cessation /sesasjɔ̃/ *n.f.* suspension.

cesse /sɛs/ *n.f.* **n'avoir de ~ que,** have no rest until. **sans ~,** incessantly.

cesser /sese/ *v.t./i.* stop. ~ **de faire,** stop doing.

cessez-le-feu /seselfø/ *n.m. invar.* cease-fire.

cession /sesjɔ̃/ *n.f.* transfer.

c'est-à-dire /sɛtadir/ *conj.* that is (to say).

cet, cette /sɛt/ *voir* **ce².**

ceux /sø/ *voir* **celui.**

chacal (*pl.* ~s) /ʃakal/ *n.m.* jackal.

chacun, ~**e** /ʃakœ̃, -yn/ *pron.* each (one), every one; (*tout le monde*) everyone.

chagrin /ʃagrɛ̃/ *n.m.* sorrow. **avoir du ~,** be distressed. ~**er** /-ine/ *v.t.* distress.

chahut /ʃay/ *n.m.* row, din. ~**er** /-te/ *v.i.* make a row; *v.t.* **rowdy with.** ~**eur, ~euse** /-tœr, -tøz/ *n.m.,f.* rowdy.

chaîn|e /ʃɛn/ *n.f.* chain; (*de télévision*) channel. ~**e de montagnes,** mountain range. ~**e de montage/fabrication,** assembly/production line. ~**e hi-fi,** hi fi system. **en ~e,** (*accidents*) multiple. ~**ette** *n.f.* (small) chain. ~**on** *n.m.* link.

chair /ʃɛr/ *n.f.* flesh. **bien en ~,** plump. **en ~ et en os,** in the flesh. ~ **à saucisses,** sausage meat. **la ~ de poule,** goose-flesh. —*a. invar.* (**couleur**) ~, flesh-coloured.

chaire /ʃɛr/ *n.f.* (*d'église*) pulpit; (*univ.*) chair.

chaise /ʃɛz/ n.f. chair. ～ **longue,**
deck-chair.

chaland /ʃalɑ̃/ n.m. barge.

châle /ʃal/ n.m. shawl.

chalet /ʃalɛ/ n.m. chalet.

chaleur /ʃalœr/ n.f. heat; (moins
intense) warmth; (d'un accueil,
d'une couleur) warmth. ～**eux,**
～**euse** a. warm.

challenge /ʃalɑ̃ʒ/ n.m. contest.

chaloupe /ʃalup/ n.f. launch,
boat.

chalumeau (pl. ～**x**) /ʃalymo/
n.m. blowlamp; (Amer.) blowtorch.

chalut /ʃaly/ n.m. trawl-net ～**ier**
/-tje/ n.m. trawler.

chamailler (se) /(sə)ʃamaje/ v. pr.
squabble.

chambarder /ʃɑ̃barde/ v.t. (fam.)
turn upside down.

chambre /ʃɑ̃br/ n.f. (bed)room;
(pol., jurid.) chamber. **faire ～ à
part,** sleep in different rooms. ～
à air, inner tube. ～ **d'amis,**
spare ou guest room. ～ **à
coucher,** bedroom. ～ **à un
lit/deux lits,** single/double
room. ～ **forte,** strong-room.

chambrer /ʃɑ̃bre/ v.t. (vin) bring
to room temperature.

chameau (pl. ～**x**) /ʃamo/ n.m.
camel.

chamois /ʃamwa/ n.m. chamois.
peau de ～, chamois leather.

champ /ʃɑ̃/ n.m. field. ～ **de
bataille,** battlefield. ～ **de
courses,** racecourse.

champagne /ʃɑ̃paɲ/ n.m. champagne.

champêtre /ʃɑ̃pɛtr/ a. rural.

champignon /ʃɑ̃piɲɔ̃/ n.m. mushroom; (moisissure) fungus. ～ **de
Paris,** button mushroom.

champion, ～**ne** /ʃɑ̃pjɔ̃, -jɔn/
n.m., f. champion. ～**nat** /-jɔna/
n.m. championship.

chance /ʃɑ̃s/ n.f. (good) luck;
(possibilité) chance. **avoir de la**

～, be lucky. **quelle ～!,** what
luck!

chanceler /ʃɑ̃sle/ v.i. stagger;
(fig.) falter.

chancelier /ʃɑ̃səlje/ n.m. chancellor.

chanceu|x, ～**se** /ʃɑ̃sø, -z/ a.
lucky.

chancre /ʃɑ̃kr/ n.m. canker.

chandail /ʃɑ̃daj/ n.m. sweater.

chandelier /ʃɑ̃dəlje/ n.m. candlestick.

chandelle /ʃɑ̃dɛl/ n.f. candle.
dîner aux ～s, candlelight dinner.

change /ʃɑ̃ʒ/ n.m. (foreign) exchange.

changeant, ～**e** /ʃɑ̃ʒɑ̃, -t/ a.
changeable.

changement /ʃɑ̃ʒmɑ̃/ n.m.
change. ～ **de vitesses** (dispositif) gears.

changer /ʃɑ̃ʒe/ v.t./i. change. **se ～**
v. pr. change (one's clothes). ～ **de
nom/voiture,** change one's
name/car. ～ **de place/train,**
change places/trains. ～ **de
direction,** change direction. ～
d'avis ou **d'idée,** change one's
mind. ～ **de vitesses,** change
gear.

changeur /ʃɑ̃ʒœr/ n.m. ～
automatique, (money) change
machine.

chanoine /ʃanwan/ n.m. canon.

chanson /ʃɑ̃sɔ̃/ n.f. song.

chant /ʃɑ̃/ n.m. singing; (chanson)
song; (religieux) hymn.

chantage /ʃɑ̃taʒ/ n.m. blackmail.
～ **psychologique,** emotional
blackmail.

chant|er /ʃɑ̃te/ v.t./i. sing. **si cela
vous ～e,** (fam.) if you feel
like it. **faire ～,** (délit) blackmail. ～**eur,** ～**euse** n.m., f.
singer.

chantier /ʃɑ̃tje/ n.m. building site.
～ **naval,** shipyard. **mettre en
～,** get under way, start.

chantonner /ʃɑ̃tɔne/ *v.t./i.* hum.

chanvre /ʃɑ̃vr/ *n.m.* hemp.

chao|s /kao/ *n.m.* chaos. **~tique** /kaɔtik/ *a.* chaotic.

chaparder /ʃaparde/ *v.t.* (*fam.*) filch.

chapeau (*pl.* **~x**) /ʃapo/ *n.m.* hat. **~!**, well done!

chapelet /ʃaplɛ/ *n.m.* rosary; (*fig.*) string.

chapelle /ʃapɛl/ *n.f.* chapel. **~ ardente,** chapel of rest.

chapelure /ʃaplyr/ *n.f.* breadcrumbs.

chaperon /ʃaprɔ̃/ *n.m.* chaperon. **~ner** /-ɔne/ *v.t.* chaperon.

chapiteau (*pl.* **~x**) /ʃapito/ *n.m.* (*de cirque*) big top; (*de colonne*) capital.

chapitre /ʃapitr/ *n.m.* chapter; (*fig.*) subject.

chapitrer /ʃapitre/ *v.t.* reprimand.

chaque /ʃak/ *a.* every, each.

char /ʃar/ *n.m.* (*mil.*) tank; (*de carnaval*) float; (*charrette*) cart; (*dans l'antiquité*) chariot.

charabia /ʃarabja/ *n.m.* (*fam.*) gibberish.

charade /ʃarad/ *n.f.* riddle.

charbon /ʃarbɔ̃/ *n.m.* coal. **~ de bois,** charcoal. **~nages** /-ɔnaʒ/ *n.m. pl.* coal-mines.

charcut|erie /ʃarkytri/ *n.f.* pork-butcher's shop; (*aliments*) (cooked) pork meats. **~ier,** **~ière** *n.m., f.* pork-butcher.

chardon /ʃardɔ̃/ *n.m.* thistle.

charge /ʃarʒ/ *n.f.* load, burden; (*mil., électr., jurid.*) charge; (*mission*) responsibility. **~s,** expenses; (*de locataire*) service charges. **être à la ~ de,** be the responsibility of. **~s sociales,** social security contributions. **prendre en ~,** take charge of; (*transporter*) give a ride to.

chargé /ʃarʒe/ *a.* (*journée*) busy; (*langue*) coated. —*n.m., f.* **~ de**

mission. head of mission. **~ d'affaires,** chargé d'affaires. **~ de cours,** lecturer.

charger /ʃarʒe/ *v.t.* load; (*attaquer*) charge; (*batterie*) charge. —*v.i.* (*attaquer*) charge. **se ~ de,** take charge *ou* care of. **~ qn. de,** weigh. s.o. down with; (*tâche*) entrust s.o. with. **~ qn. de faire,** instruct s.o. to do. **chargement** /-əmɑ̃/ *n.m.* loading; (*objets*) load.

chariot /ʃarjo/ *n.m.* (*à roulettes*) trolley; (*charrette*) cart.

charitable /ʃaritabl/ *a.* charitable.

charité /ʃarite/ *n.f.* charity, **faire la ~,** give to charity. **faire la ~ à,** give to.

charlatan /ʃarlatɑ̃/ *n.m.* charlatan.

charmant, ~e /ʃarmɑ̃, -t/ *a.* charming.

charm|e /ʃarm/ *n.m.* charm. **~er** *v.t.* charm. **~eur, ~euse** *n.m., f.* charmer.

charnel, ~le /ʃarnɛl/ *a.* carnal.

charnier /ʃarnje/ *n.m.* mass grave.

charnière /ʃarnjɛr/ *n.f.* hinge. **à la ~ de,** at the meeting point between.

charnu /ʃarny/ *a.* fleshy.

charpent|e /ʃarpɑ̃t/ *n.f.* framework; (*carrure*) build. **~é** *a.* built.

charpentier /ʃarpɑ̃tje/ *n.m.* carpenter.

charpie (en) /(ɑ̃)ʃarpi/ *adv.* in(to) shreds.

charretier /ʃartje/ *n.m.* carter.

charrette /ʃarɛt/ *n.f.* cart.

charrier /ʃarje/ *v.t.* carry.

charrue /ʃary/ *n.f.* plough.

charte /ʃart/ *n.f.* charter.

charter /ʃarter/ *n.m.* charter flight.

chasse /ʃas/ *n.f.* hunting; (*au fusil*) shooting; (*poursuite*) chase; (*recherche*) hunt. **~ (d'eau),** (toilet) flush. **~ sous-marine,** underwater fishing.

châsse /ʃɑs/ *n.f.* shrine, reliquary.

chass|er /ʃase/ *v.t./i.* hunt; (*faire partir*) chase away; (*odeur, employé*) get rid of. ~**e-neige** *n.m. invar.* snow-plough. ~**eur, ~euse** *n.m.,f.* hunter; *n.m.* pageboy; (*avion*) fighter.

châssis /ʃasi/ *n.m.* frame; (*auto.*) chassis.

chaste /ʃast/ *a.* chaste. ~**té** /-əte/ *n.f.* chastity.

chat, ~te /ʃa, ʃat/ *n.m.,f.* cat.

châtaigne /ʃatɛɲ/ *n.f.* chestnut.

châtaignier /ʃatɛɲe/ *n.m.* chestnut tree.

châtain /ʃatɛ̃/ *a. invar.* chestnut (brown).

château (*pl.* ~**x**) /ʃato/ *n.m.* castle; (*manoir*) manor. ~ **d'eau**, water-tower. ~ **fort**, fortified castle.

châtelain, ~e /ʃatlɛ̃, -ɛn/ *n.m., f.* lord of the manor, lady of the manor.

châtier /ʃatje/ *v.t.* chastise; (*style*) refine.

châtiment /ʃatimɑ̃/ *n.m.* punishment.

chaton /ʃatɔ̃/ *n.m.* (*chat*) kitten.

chatouill|er /ʃatuje/ *v.t.* tickle. ~**ement** *n.m.* tickling.

chatouilleux|x, ~se /ʃatujø, -z/ *a.* ticklish; (*susceptible*) touchy.

chatoyer /ʃatwaje/ *v.i.* glitter.

châtrer /ʃatre/ *v.t.* castrate.

chatte /ʃat/ *voir* **chat**.

chaud, ~e /ʃo, ʃod/ *a.* warm; (*brûlant*) hot; (*vif: fig.*) warm. —*n.m.* heat. **au** ~, in the warm(th). **avoir** ~, be warm; be hot. **il fait** ~, it is warm; it is hot. **pour te tenir** ~, to keep you warm. ~**ement** /-dmɑ̃/ *adv.* warmly; (*disputé*) hotly.

chaudière /ʃodjɛr/ *n.f.* boiler.

chaudron /ʃodrɔ̃/ *n.m.* cauldron.

chauffage /ʃofaʒ/ *n.m.* heating. ~ **central**, central heating.

chauffard /ʃofar/ *n.m.* (*péj.*) reckless driver.

chauff|er /ʃofe/ *v.t./i.* heat (up). **se** ~**er** *v. pr.* warm o.s. (up). ~**eau** *n.m. invar.* water-heater.

chauffeur /ʃofœr/ *n.m.* driver; (*aux gages de qn.*) chauffeur.

chaum|e /ʃom/ *n.m.* (*de toit*) thatch.

chaussée /ʃose/ *n.f.* road(way).

chauss|er /ʃose/ *v.t.* (*chaussures*) put on; (*enfant*) put shoes on (to). **se** ~**er** *v. pr.* put one's shoes on. ~**er bien**, (*aller*) fit well. ~**er du 35**/*etc.*, take a size 35/*etc.* shoe. ~**e-pied** *n.m.* shoehorn. ~**eur** *n.m.* shoemaker.

chaussette /ʃosɛt/ *n.f.* sock.

chausson /ʃosɔ̃/ *n.m.* slipper; (*de bébé*) bootee. ~ **(aux pommes)**, (apple) turnover.

chaussure /ʃosyr/ *n.f.* shoe. ~**s de ski**, ski boots. ~**s de marche**, hiking boots.

chauve /ʃov/ *a.* bald.

chauve-souris (*pl.* **chauves-souris**) /ʃovsuri/ *n.f.* bat.

chauvin, ~e /ʃovɛ̃, -in/ *a.* chauvinistic. —*n.m., f.* chauvinist. ~**isme** /-inism/ *n.m.* chauvinism.

chaux /ʃo/ *n.f.* lime.

chavirer /ʃavire/ *v.t./i.* (*bateau*) capsize.

chef /ʃɛf/ *n.m.* leader, head; (*culin.*) chef; (*de tribu*) chief. ~ **d'accusation**, (*jurid.*) charge. ~ **d'équipe**, foreman; (*sport*) captain. ~ **d'État**, head of State. ~ **de famille**, head of the family. . ~ **de file**, (*pol.*) leader. ~ **de gare**, station-master. ~ **d'orchestre**, conductor. ~ **de service**, department head. ~**lieu** (*pl.* ~**s-lieux**) *n.m.* county town.

chef-d'œuvre (*pl.* **chefs-d'œuvre**) /ʃɛdœvr/ *n.m.* masterpiece.

cheik /ʃɛk/ n.m. sheikh.

chemin /ʃmɛ̃/ n.m. path, road; (direction, trajet) way. **beaucoup de ~ à faire,** a long way to go. **~ de fer,** railway. **en** ou **par ~ de fer,** by rail. **~ de halage,** towpath. **~ vicinal,** by-road. **se mettre en ~,** start out.

cheminée /ʃmine/ n.f. chimney; (intérieure) fireplace; (encadrement) mantelpiece; (de bateau) funnel.

chemin|er /ʃmine/ v.i. plod; (fig.) progress. **~ement** n.m. progress.

cheminot /ʃmino/ n.m. railwayman; (Amer.) railroad man.

chemis|e /ʃmiz/ n.f. shirt; (dossier) folder; (de livre) jacket. **~e de nuit,** night-dress. **~ette** n.f. short-sleeved shirt.

chemisier /ʃmizje/ n.m. blouse.

chen|al (pl. **~aux**) /ʃənal, -o/ n.m. channel.

chêne /ʃɛn/ n.m. oak.

chenil /ʃni(l)/ n.m. kennels.

chenille /ʃnij/ n.f. caterpillar.

chenillette /ʃnijɛt/ n.f. tracked vehicle.

cheptel /ʃɛptɛl/ n.m. livestock.

chèque /ʃɛk/ n.m. cheque. **~ de voyage,** traveller's cheque.

chéquier /ʃekje/ n.m. chequebook.

cher, chère /ʃɛr/ a. (coûteux) dear, expensive; (aimé) dear. —adv. (coûter, payer) a lot (of money). —n.m., f. **mon ~, ma chère,** my dear.

chercher /ʃɛrʃe/ v.t. look for; (aide, paix, gloire) seek. **aller ~,** go and get ou fetch. **go for. ~ à faire,** attempt to do. **~ la petite bête,** be finicky.

chercheu|r, ~se /ʃɛrʃœr, -øz/ n.m., f. research worker.

chèrement /ʃɛrmɑ̃/ adv. dearly.

chéri, ~e /ʃeri/ a. beloved. —n.m., f. darling.

chérir /ʃerir/ v.t. cherish.

cherté /ʃɛrte/ n.f. high cost.

chéti|f, ~ve /ʃetif, -v/ a. puny.

chev|al (pl. **~aux**) /ʃəval, -o/ n.m. horse. **~al (vapeur),** horsepower. **à ~al,** on horseback. **à ~al sur,** straddling. **faire du ~al,** ride (a horse). **~al-d'arçons** n.m. invar. (gymnastique) horse.

chevaleresque /ʃvalrɛsk/ a. chivalrous.

chevalerie /ʃvalri/ n.f. chivalry.

chevalet /ʃvalɛ/ n.m. easel.

chevalier /ʃvalje/ n.m. knight.

chevalière /ʃvaljɛr/ n.f. signet ring.

chevalin, ~e /ʃvalɛ̃, -in/ a. (boucherie) horse; (espèce) equine.

chevauchée /ʃvoʃe/ n.f. (horse) ride.

chevaucher /ʃvoʃe/ v.t. straddle. —v.i., **se ~** v. pr. overlap.

chevelu, ~e /ʃəvly/ a. hairy.

chevelure /ʃəvlyr/ n.f. hair.

chevet /ʃvɛ/ n.m. **au ~ de,** at the bedside of.

cheveu (pl. **~x**) /ʃvø/ n.m. (poil) hair. **~x,** (chevelure) hair. **avoir les ~x longs,** have long hair.

cheville /ʃvij/ n.f. ankle; (fiche) peg, pin; (pour mur) (wall) plug.

chèvre /ʃɛvr/ n.f. goat.

chevreau (pl. **~x**) /ʃəvro/ n.m. kid.

chevreuil /ʃəvrœj/ n.m. roe (-deer); (culin.) venison.

chevron /ʃəvrɔ̃/ n.m. (poutre) rafter. **à ~s,** herring-bone.

chevronné, ~e /ʃəvrɔne/ a. experienced, seasoned.

chevrotant, ~e /ʃəvrɔtɑ̃, -t/ a. quavering.

chewing-gum /ʃwiŋgɔm/ n.m. chewing-gum.

chez /ʃe/ prép. **at** ou **to the house of;** (parmi) among; (dans le caractère ou l'œuvre de) in. **~ le boucher/etc.,** at the butcher's/

etc. ~ **soi**, at home; (*avec direction*) home. **~-soi** *n.m. invar.* home.

chic /ʃik/ *a. invar.* smart; (*gentil*) kind. **sois** ~, do me a favour. —*n.m.* style. **avoir le** ~ **pour**, have the knack of. ~ (**alors**)!, great!

chicane /ʃikan/ *n.f.* zigzag. **chercher** ~ **à qn**, needle s.o.

chiche /ʃiʃ/ *a.* mean (**de**, with). ~ (**que je le fais**)!, (*fam.*) I bet you I will, can, *etc.*

chichis /ʃiʃi/ *n.m. pl.* (*fam.*) fuss.

chicorée /ʃikɔre/ *n.f.* (*frisée*) endive; (*à café*) chicory.

chien, **~ne** /ʃjɛ̃, ʃjɛn/ *n.m.* dog. —*n.f.* dog, bitch. ~ **de garde**, watch-dog. **~-loup** *n.m.* (*pl.* **~s-loups**) wolfhound.

chiffon /ʃifɔ̃/ *n.m.* rag.

chiffonner /ʃifone/ *v.t.* crumple; (*préoccuper: fam.*) bother.

chiffonnier /ʃifonje/ *n.m.* rag-and-bone man.

chiffre /ʃifr/ *n.m.* figure; (*code*) code. **~s arabes/romains**, Arabic/Roman numerals. ~ **d'affaires**, turnover.

chiffrer /ʃifre/ *v.t.* set a figure to, assess; (*texte*) encode. **se** ~ **à**, amount to.

chignon /ʃiɲɔ̃/ *n.m.* bun, chignon.

Chili /ʃili/ *n.m.* Chile.

chilien, **~ne** /ʃiljɛ̃, -jɛn/ *a.* & *n.m.*, *f.* Chilean.

chimère /ʃimɛr/ *n.f.* fantasy. **~érique** *a.* fanciful.

chim|ie /ʃimi/ *n.f.* chemistry. **~ique** *a.* chemical. **~iste** *n.m./f.* chemist.

chimpanzé /ʃɛ̃pɑ̃ze/ *n.m.* chimpanzee.

Chine /ʃin/ *n.f.* China.

chinois, **~e** /ʃinwa, -z/ *a.* & *n.m.*, *f.* Chinese. —*n.m.* (*lang.*) Chinese.

chiot /ʃjo/ *n.m.* pup(py).

chiper /ʃipe/ *v.t.* (*fam.*) swipe.

chipoter /ʃipote/ *v.i.* (*manger*) nibble; (*discuter*) quibble.

chips /ʃips/ *n.m. pl.* crisps; (*Amer.*) chips.

chiquenaude /ʃiknod/ *n.f.* flick.

chiromanc|ie /kirɔmɑ̃si/ *n.f.* palmistry. **~ien**, **~ienne** *n.m.*, *f.* palmist.

chirurgic|al (*m. pl.* **~aux**) /ʃiryrʒikal, -o/ *a.* surgical.

chirurg|ie /ʃiryrʒi/ *n.f.* surgery. **~ie esthétique**, plastic surgery. **~ien** *n.m.* surgeon.

chlore /klɔr/ *n.m.* chlorine.

choc /ʃɔk/ *n.m.* (*heurt*) impact, shock; (*émotion*) shock; (*collision*) crash; (*affrontement*) clash; (*méd.*) shock.

chocolat /ʃɔkɔla/ *n.m.* chocolate; (*à boire*) drinking chocolate. ~ **au lait**, milk chocolate. ~ **chaud**, hot chocolat.

chœur /kœr/ *n.m.* (*antique*) chorus; (*chanteurs, nef*) choir. **en** ~, in chorus.

chois|ir /ʃwazir/ *v.t.* choose, select. **~i** *a.* carefully chosen; (*passage*) selected.

choix /ʃwa/ *n.m.* choice, selection. **au** ~, according to preference. **de** ~, choice. **de premier** ~, top quality.

choléra /kɔlera/ *n.m.* cholera.

chômage /ʃomaʒ/ *n.m.* unemployment. **en** ~, unemployed. **mettre en** ~ **technique**, lay off.

chôm|er /ʃome/ *v.i.* be unemployed; (*usine*) lie idle. **~eur**, **~euse** *n.m.*, *f.* unemployed person. **les ~eurs**, the unemployed.

chope /ʃɔp/ *n.f.* tankard.

choper /ʃope/ *v.t.* (*fam.*) catch.

choquer /ʃoke/ *v.t.* shock; (*commotionner*) shake.

choral, **~e** (*m. pl.* **~s**) /kɔral/ *a.* choral. —*n.f.* choir, choral society.

chorégraph|ie /kɔregrafi/ n.f. choreography. **~e** n.m./f. choreographer.

choriste /kɔrist/ n.m./f. (à l'église) chorister; (opéra, etc.) member of the chorus ou choir.

chose /ʃoz/ n.f. thing. **(très) peu de ~,** nothing much.

chou (pl. **~x**) /ʃu/ n.m. cabbage. **~ (à la crème),** cream puff. **~x de Bruxelles,** Brussels sprouts. **mon petit ~,** (fam.) my little dear.

choucas /ʃuka/ n.m. jackdaw.

chouchou, ~te /ʃuʃu, -t/ n.m., f. pet, darling. **le ~ du prof.,** the teacher's pet.

choucroute /ʃukrut/ n.f. sauerkraut.

chouette[1] /ʃwɛt/ n.f. owl.

chouette[2] /ʃwɛt/ a. (fam.) super.

chou-fleur (pl. **choux-fleurs**) /ʃuflœr/ n.m. cauliflower.

choyer /ʃwaje/ v.t. pamper.

chrétien, ~ne /kretjɛ̃, -jɛn/ a. & n.m., f. Christian.

Christ /krist/ n.m. **le ~,** Christ.

christianisme /kristjanism/ n.m. Christianity.

chrom|e /krom/ n.m. chromium, chrome. **~é** a. chromium-plated.

chromosome /krɔmozom/ n.m. chromosome.

chroniqu|e /krɔnik/ a. chronic. —n.f. (rubrique) column; (nouvelles) news; (annales) chronicle. **~eur** n.m. columnist; (historien) chronicler.

chronolog|ie /krɔnɔlɔʒi/ n.f. chronology. **~ique** a. chronological.

chronom|ètre /krɔnɔmɛtr/ n.m. stop-watch. **~étrer** v.t. time.

chrysanthème /krizɑ̃tɛm/ n.m. chrysanthemum.

chuchot|er /ʃyʃɔte/ v.t./i. whisper. **~ement** n.m. whisper(ing).

chuinter /ʃwɛ̃te/ v.i. hiss.

chut /ʃyt/ int. shush.

chute /ʃyt/ n.f. fall; (déchet) scrap. **~ (d'eau),** waterfall. **~ du jour,** nightfall. **~ de pluie,** rainfall. **la ~ des cheveux,** hair loss.

chuter /ʃyte/ v.i. fall.

Chypre /ʃipr/ n.f. Cyprus.

-ci /si/ adv. (après un nom précédé de ce, cette, etc.) **cet homme-ci,** this man. **ces maisons-ci,** these houses.

ci /si/ adv. here. **ci-après,** hereafter. **ci-contre,** opposite. **ci-dessous,** below. **ci-dessus,** above. **ci-gît,** here lies. **ci-inclus, ci-incluse, ci-joint, ci-jointe,** enclosed.

cible /sibl/ n.f. target.

ciboul|e /sibul/ n.f., **~ette** n.f. chive(s).

cicatrice /sikatris/ n.f. scar.

cicatriser /sikatrize/ v.t., **se ~** v. pr. heal (up).

cidre /sidr/ n.m. cider.

ciel (pl. **cieux, ciels**) /sjɛl, sjø/ n.m. sky; (relig.) heaven. **cieux,** (relig.) heaven.

cierge /sjɛrʒ/ n.m. candle.

cigale /sigal/ n.f. cicada.

cigare /sigar/ n.m. cigar.

cigarette /sigarɛt/ n.f. cigarette.

cigogne /sigɔɲ/ n.f. stork.

cil /sil/ n.m. (eye)lash.

ciller /sije/ v.i. blink.

cime /sim/ n.f. peak, tip.

ciment /simɑ̃/ n.m. cement. **~er** /-te/ v.t. cement.

cimetière /simtjɛr/ n.m. cemetery. **~ de voitures,** breaker's yard.

cinéaste /sineast/ n.m./f. filmmaker.

ciné-club /sineklœb/ n.m. film society.

cinéma /sinema/ n.m. cinema. **~tographique** a. cinematographic.

cinémathèque /sinematɛk/ n.f. film library; (salle) film theatre.

cinéphile /sinefil/ n.m./f. film lover.

cinétique /sinetik/ *a.* kinetic.
cinglant, ~e /sɛ̃glɑ̃, -t/ *a.* biting.
cinglé /sɛ̃gle/ *a.* (*fam.*) crazy.
cingler /sɛ̃gle/ *v.t.* lash.
cinq /sɛ̃k/ *a.* & *n.m.* five. ~ième *a.* & *n.m./f.* fifth.
cinquantaine /sɛ̃kɑ̃tɛn/ *n.f.* une ~ (de), about fifty.
cinquant|**e** /sɛ̃kɑ̃t/ *a.* & *n.m.* fifty. ~ième *a.* & *n.m./f.* fiftieth.
cintre /sɛ̃tr/ *n.m.* coat-hanger; (*archit.*) curve.
cintré /sɛ̃tre/ *a.* (*chemise*) fitted.
cirage /siraʒ/ *n.m.* (wax) polish.
circoncision /sirkɔ̃sizjɔ̃/ *n.f.* circumcision.
circonférence /sirkɔ̃ferɑ̃s/ *n.f.* circumference.
circonflexe /sirkɔ̃flɛks/ *a.* circumflex.
circonscription /sirkɔ̃skripsjɔ̃/ *n.f.* district. ~ (**électorale**), constituency.
circonscrire /sirkɔ̃skrir/ *v.t.* confine; (*sujet*) define.
circonspect /sirkɔ̃spɛkt/ *a.* circumspect.
circonstance /sirkɔ̃stɑ̃s/ *n.f.* circumstance; (*occasion*) occasion. ~s atténuantes, mitigating circumstances.
circonstancié /sirkɔ̃stɑ̃sje/ *a.* detailed.
circonvenir /sirkɔ̃vnir/ *v.t.* circumvent.
circuit /sirkɥi/ *n.m.* circuit; (*trajet*) tour, trip.
circulaire /sirkylɛr/ *a.* & *n.f.* circular.
circul|**er** /sirkyle/ *v.i.* circulate; (*train, automobile, etc.*) travel; (*piéton*) walk. **faire** ~**er,** (*badauds*) move on. ~**ation** *n.f.* circulation; (*de véhicules*) traffic.
cire /sir/ *n.f.* wax.
ciré /sire/ *n.m.* oilskin; waterproof.
cir|**er** /sire/ *v.t.* polish, wax. ~**euse** *n.f.* (*appareil*) floor-polisher.

cirque /sirk/ *n.m.* circus; (*arène*) amphitheatre; (*désordre:* *fig.*) chaos.
cirrhose /siroz/ *n.f.* cirrhosis.
cisaille(s) /sizaj/ *n.f.* (*pl.*) shears.
ciseau (*pl.* ~**x**) /sizo/ *n.m.* chisel. ~**x,** scissors.
ciseler /sizle/ *v.t.* chisel.
citadelle /sitadɛl/ *n.f.* citadel.
citadin, ~**e** /sitadɛ̃, -in/ *n.m., f.* city dweller. —*a.* city.
cité /site/ *n.f.* city. ~ **ouvrière,** (workers') housing estate. ~ **universitaire,** (university) halls of residence. ~**-dortoir** *n.f.* (*pl.* ~**s-dortoirs**) dormitory town.
cit|**er** /site/ *v.t.* quote, cite; (*jurid.*) summon. ~**ation** *n.f.* quotation; (*jurid.*) summons.
citerne /sitɛrn/ *n.f.* tank.
cithare /sitar/ *n.f.* zither.
citoyen, ~**ne** /sitwajɛ̃, -jɛn/ *n.m., f.* citizen. ~**neté** /-jɛnte/ *n.f.* citizenship.
citron /sitrɔ̃/ *n.m.* lemon. ~ **vert,** lime. ~**nade** /-ɔnad/ *n.f.* lemon squash *ou* drink, (still) lemonade.
citrouille /sitruj/ *n.f.* pumpkin.
civet /sivɛ/ *n.m.* stew. ~ **de lièvre/lapin,** jugged hare/rabbit.
civette /sivɛt/ *n.f.* (*culin.*) chive(s).
civière /sivjɛr/ *n.f.* stretcher.
civil /sivil/ *a.* civil; (*non militaire*) civilian; (*poli*) civil. —*n.m.* civilian. **dans le** ~**,** in civilian life. **en** ~**,** in plain clothes.
civilisation /sivilizasjɔ̃/ *n.f.* civilization.
civiliser /sivilize/ *v.t.* civilize. **se** ~ *v. pr.* become civilized.
civi|**que** /sivik/ *a.* civic. ~**sme** *n.m.* civic sense.
clair /klɛr/ *a.* clear; (*éclairé*) light, bright; (*couleur*) light; (*liquide*) thin. —*adv.* clearly. —*n.m.* ~ **de lune,** moonlight. **le plus** ~ **de,** most of. ~**ement** *adv.* clearly.
claire-voie (à) /(a)klɛrvwa/ *adv.* with slits to let the light through.

clairière /klɛrjɛr/ *n.f.* clearing.

clairon /klɛrɔ̃/ *n.m.* bugle. **~ner** /-ɔne/ *v.t.* trumpet (forth).

clairsemé /klɛrsəme/ *a.* sparse.

clairvoyant, **~e** /klɛrvwajɑ̃, -t/ *a.* clear-sighted.

clamer /klame/ *v.t.* utter aloud.

clameur /klamœr/ *n.f.* clamour.

clan /klɑ̃/ *n.m.* clan.

clandestin, **~e** /klɑ̃dɛstɛ̃, -in/ *a.* secret; (*journal*) underground. **passager ~,** stowaway.

clapet /klapɛ/ *n.m.* valve.

clapier /klapje/ *n.m.* (rabbit) hutch.

clapot|er /klapote/ *v.i.* lap. **~is** *n.m.* lapping.

claquage /klakaʒ/ *n.m.* strained muscle.

claque /klak/ *n.f.* slap. **en avoir sa ~ (de),** (*fam.*) be fed up (with).

claqu|er /klake/ *v.i.* bang; (*porte*) slam, bang; (*fouet*) snap, crack; (*se casser: fam.*) conk out; (*mourir: fam.*) snuff it. —*v.t.* (*porte*) slam, bang; (*dépenser: fam.*) blow; (*fatiguer: fam.*) tire out. **~er des doigts,** snap one's fingers. **~er des mains,** clap one's hands. **il claque des dents,** his teeth are chattering. **~ement** *n.m.* bang(ing); slam(ming); snap(ping).

claquettes /klakɛt/ *n.f. pl.* tap-dancing.

clarifier /klarifje/ *v.t.* clarify.

clarinette /klarinɛt/ *n.f.* clarinet.

clarté /klarte/ *n.f.* light, brightness; (*netteté*) clarity.

classe /klɑs/ *n.f.* class; (*salle: scol.*) class(-room). **~,** go to school. **~ ouvrière/moyenne,** working/middle class. **faire la ~,** teach.

class|er /klɑse/ *v.t.* classify; (*par mérite*) grade; (*papiers*) file; (*affaire*) close. **se ~er premier/ dernier,** come first/last. **~e- ment** *n.m.* classification; grading;

filing; (*rang*) place, grade; (*de coureur*) placing.

classeur /klɑsœr/ *n.m.* filing cabinet; (*chemise*) file.

classif|ier /klasifje/ *v.t.* classify. **~ication** *n.f.* classification.

classique /klasik/ *a.* classical; (*de qualité*) classic(al); (*habituel*) classic. —*n.m.* classic; (*auteur*) classical author.

clause /kloz/ *n.f.* clause.

claustration /klostrasjɔ̃/ *n.f.* confinement.

claustrophobie /klostrɔfɔbi/ *n.f.* claustrophobia.

clavecin /klavsɛ̃/ *n.m.* harpsichord.

clavicule /klavikyl/ *n.f.* collarbone.

clavier /klavje/ *n.m.* keyboard.

claviste /klavist/ *n.m./f.* keyboarder.

clé, clef /kle/ *n.f.* key; (*outil*) spanner; (*mus.*) clef. —*a. invar.* key. **~ anglaise,** (monkey-) wrench. **~ de contact,** ignition key. **~ de voûte,** keystone. **prix ~s en main,** (*voiture*) on-the-road price.

clémen|t, **~te** /klemɑ̃, -t/ *a.* (*doux*) mild; (*indulgent*) lenient. **~ce** *n.f.* mildness; leniency.

clémentine /klemɑ̃tin/ *n.f.* clementine.

clerc /klɛr/ *n.m.* (d'avoué etc.) clerk; (*relig.*) cleric.

clergé /klɛrʒe/ *n.m.* clergy.

cléric|al (*m. pl.* **~aux**) /klerikal, -o/ *a.* clerical.

cliché /kliʃe/ *n.m.* cliché; (*photo.*) negative.

client, **~e** /klijɑ̃, -t/ *n.m., f.* customer; (*d'un avocat*) client; (*d'un médecin*) patient; (*d'hôtel*) guest. **~èle** /-tɛl/ *n.f.* customers, clientele; (*d'un avocat*) clientele, clients, practice; (*d'un médecin*) practice, patients; (*soutien*) custom.

cligner /kliɲe/ v.i. ~ **des yeux,** blink. ~ **de l'œil,** wink.

clignoter /kliɲɔte/ v.i. blink; (*lumière*) flicker; (*comme signal*) flash. ~**ant** n.m. (*auto.*) indicator; (*auto., Amer.*) directional signal.

climat /klima/ n.m. climate. ~**ique** /-tik/ a. climatic.

climatisation /klimatizasjɔ̃/ n.f. air-conditioning. ~**é** a. air-conditioned.

clin d'œil /klɛ̃dœj/ n.m. wink. **en un** ~, in a flash.

clinique /klinik/ a. clinical. —n.f. (*private*) clinic.

clinquant, ~e /klɛ̃kɑ̃, -t/ a. showy.

clip /klip/ n.m. video.

clique /klik/ n.f. clique; (*mus., mil.*) band.

cliqueter /klikte/ v.i. clink. ~**is** n.m. clink(ing).

clitoris /klitoris/ n.m. clitoris.

clivage /klivaʒ/ n.m. cleavage.

clochard, ~e /klɔʃar, -d/ n.m., f. tramp.

cloche¹ /klɔʃ/ n.f. bell; (*fam.*) idiot. ~ **à fromage,** cheese-cover. ~**ette** n.f. bell.

cloche² /klɔʃ/ n.f. (*fam.*) idiot.

cloche-pied (à) /(a)klɔʃpje/ adv. hopping on one foot.

clocher¹ /klɔʃe/ n.m. bell-tower; (*pointu*) steeple. **de** ~, parochial.

clocher² /klɔʃe/ v.i. (*fam.*) be wrong.

cloison /klwazɔ̃/ n.f. partition; (*fig.*) barrier. ~**ner** /-ɔne/ v.t. partition; (*personne*) cut off.

cloître /klwatr/ n.m. cloister.

cloîtrer (se) /(sə)klwatre/ v. pr. shut o.s. away.

clopin-clopant /klɔpɛ̃klɔpɑ̃/ adv. hobbling.

cloque /klɔk/ n.f. blister.

clore /klɔr/ v.t. close.

clos, ~e /klo, -z/ a. closed.

clôture /klotyr/ n.f. fence; (*fermeture*) closure. ~**er** v.t. enclose; (*festival, séance, etc.*) close.

clou /klu/ n.m. nail; (*furoncle*) boil; (*de spectacle*) star attraction. ~ **de girofle,** clove. **les** ~**s,** (*passage*) zebra ou pedestrian crossing. ~**er** v.t. nail down; (*fig.*) pin down. **être cloué au lit,** be confined to one's bed. ~**er le bec à qn.,** shut s.o. up.

clouté /klute/ a. studded.

clown /klun/ n.m. clown.

club /klœb/ n.m. club.

coaguler /kɔagyle/ v.t./i., **se** ~ v. pr. coagulate.

coaliser (se) /(sə)kɔalize/ v. pr. join forces.

coalition /kɔalisjɔ̃/ n.f. coalition.

coasser /kɔase/ v.i. croak.

cobaye /kɔbaj/ n.m. guinea-pig.

coca /kɔka/ n.m. (P.) Coke.

cocagne /kɔkaɲ/ n.f. **pays de** ~, land of plenty.

cocaïne /kɔkain/ n.f. cocaine.

cocarde /kɔkard/ n.f. rosette.

cocardier, ~ière /kɔkardje, -jɛr/ a. chauvinistic.

cocasse /kɔkas/ a. comical.

coccinelle /kɔksinɛl/ n.f. ladybird; (*Amer.*) ladybug; (*voiture*) beetle.

cocher¹ /kɔʃe/ v.t. tick (off), check.

cocher² /kɔʃe/ n.m. coachman.

cochon, ~ne /kɔʃɔ̃, -ɔn/ n.m. pig. —n.m., f. (*personne: fam.*) pig. —a. (*fam.*) filthy. ~**nerie** /-ɔnri/ n.f. (*saleté: fam.*) filth; (*marchandise: fam.*) rubbish.

cocktail /kɔktɛl/ n.m. cocktail; (*réunion*) cocktail party.

cocon /kɔkɔ̃/ n.m. cocoon.

cocorico /kɔkɔriko/ n.m. cock-a-doodle-doo.

cocotier /kɔkɔtje/ n.m. coconut palm.

cocotte /kɔkɔt/ n.f. (*marmite*) casserole. ~ **minute,** (P.)

pressure-cooker. **ma** ~, (fam.) my sweet, my dear.

cocu /kɔky/ n.m. (fam.) cuckold.

code /kɔd/ n.m. code. ~**s, phares** ~, dipped headlights. ~ **de la route,** Highway Code. **se mettre en** ~, dip one's headlights.

coder /kɔde/ v.t. code.

codifier /kɔdifje/ v.t. codify.

coéquip|ier, ~**ière** /kɔekipje, -jɛr/ n.m., f. team-mate.

cœur /kœr/ n.m. heart; (cartes) hearts. ~ **d'artichaut,** artichoke heart. ~ **de palmier,** heart of palm. **à** ~ **ouvert,** (opération) open-heart; (parler) freely. **avoir bon** ~, be kindhearted. **de bon** ~, with a good heart. **par** ~, by heart. **avoir mal au** ~, feel sick. **je veux en avoir le** ~ **net,** I want to be clear in my own mind (about it).

coexist|er /kɔɛgziste/ v.i. coexist. ~**ence** n.f. coexistence.

coffre /kɔfr/ n.m. chest; (pour argent) safe; (auto.) boot; (auto., Amer.) trunk. ~**-fort** (pl. ~**s-forts**) n.m. safe.

coffrer /kɔfre/ v.t. (fam.) lock up.

coffret /kɔfrɛ/ n.m. casket, box.

cognac /kɔɲak/ n.m. cognac.

cogner /kɔɲe/ v.t./i. knock. **se** ~ v. pr. knock o.s.

cohabit|er /kɔabite/ v.i. live together. ~**ation** n.f. living together.

cohérent, ~**e** /kɔerɑ̃, -t/ a. coherent.

cohésion /kɔezjɔ̃/ n.f. cohesion.

cohorte /kɔɔrt/ n.f. troop.

cohue /kɔy/ n.f. crowd.

coi, coite /kwa, -t/ a. silent.

coiffe /kwaf/ n.f. head-dress.

coiff|er /kwafe/ v.t. do the hair of; (chapeau) put on; (surmonter) cap. ~**er qn. d'un chapeau,** put a hat on s.o. **se** ~**er** v. pr. do one's hair. ~**é de,** wearing. **bien/mal**

~**é,** with tidy/untidy hair. ~**eur,** ~**euse** n.m., f. hairdresser; n.f. dressing-table.

coiffure /kwafyr/ n.f. hairstyle; (chapeau) hat; (métier) hairdressing.

coin /kwɛ̃/ n.m. corner; (endroit) spot; (cale) wedge; (pour graver) die. **au** ~ **du feu,** by the fireside. **dans le** ~, locally. **du** ~, local. **le boulanger du** ~, the local baker.

coincer /kwɛ̃se/ v.t. jam; (caler) wedge; (attraper. fam.) catch. **se** ~ v. pr. get jammed.

coïncid|er /kɔɛ̃side/ v.i. coincide. ~**ence** n.f. coincidence.

coing /kwɛ̃/ n.m. quince.

coït /kɔit/ n.m. intercourse.

coite /kwat/ voir **coi.**

coke /kɔk/ n.m. coke.

col /kɔl/ n.m. collar; (de bouteille) neck; (de montagne) pass. ~ **roulé,** polo-neck; (Amer.) turtleneck. ~ **de l'utérus,** cervix.

coléoptère /kɔleɔptɛr/ n.m. beetle.

colère /kɔlɛr/ n.f. anger; (accès) fit of anger. **en** ~, angry. **se mettre en** ~, lose one's temper.

colér|eux, ~**euse** /kɔlerø, -z/, ~**ique** adj.s. quick-tempered.

colibri /kɔlibri/ n.m. hummingbird.

colifichet /kɔlifiʃɛ/ n.m. trinket.

colimaçon (en) /(ɑ̃)kɔlimasɔ̃/ adv. spiral.

colin /kɔlɛ̃/ n.m. (poisson) hake.

colin-maillard /kɔlɛ̃majar/ n.m. **jouer à** ~, play blind man's buff.

colique /kɔlik/ n.f. diarrhoea; (méd.) colic.

colis /kɔli/ n.m. parcel.

collabor|er /kɔlabɔre/ v.i. collaborate (**à,** on). ~**er à,** (journal) contribute to. ~**ateur,** ~**atrice** n.m., f. collaborator; contributor. ~**ation** n.f. collaboration (**à,** on); contribution (**à,** to).

collant /kɔlɑ̃/ ~e /-t/ a. skin-tight; (*poisseux*) sticky. —n.m. (*bas*) tights; (*de danseur*) leotard.

collation /kɔlasjɔ̃/ n.f. light meal.

colle /kɔl/ n.f. glue; (*en pâte*) paste; (*problème: fam.*) poser; (*scol., argot*) detention.

collect|**e** /kɔlɛkt/ n.f. collection. **~er** v.t. collect.

collecteur /kɔlɛktœr/ n.m. (*égout*) main sewer.

collecti|**f**, **~ve** /kɔlɛktif, -v/ a. collective; (*billet, voyage*) group. **~vement** adv. collectively.

collection /kɔlɛksjɔ̃/ n.f. collection.

collectionn|**er** /kɔlɛksjɔne/ v.t. collect. **~eur**, **~euse** n.m., f. collector.

collectivité /kɔlɛktivite/ n.f. community.

coll|**ège** /kɔlɛʒ/ n.m. (secondary) school; (*assemblée*) college. **~égien**, **~égienne** n.m., f. schoolboy, schoolgirl.

collègue /kɔlɛg/ n.m./f. colleague.

coll|**er** /kɔle/ v.t. stick; (*avec colle liquide*) glue; (*affiche*) stick up; (*mettre: fam.*) stick; (*question: scol., argot*) keep in; (*par une question: fam.*) stump. —v.i. stick (à, to); (*être collant*) be sticky. **~er à**, (*convenir à*) fit, correspond to. **être ~é à**, (*examen: fam.*) fail.

collet /kɔlɛ/ n.m. (*piège*) snare. **~ monté**, prim and proper. **prendre qn. au ~**, collar s.o.

collier /kɔlje/ n.m. necklace; (*de chien*) collar.

colline /kɔlin/ n.f. hill.

collision /kɔlizjɔ̃/ n.f. (*choc*) collision; (*lutte*) clash. **entrer en ~** (**avec**), collide (with).

colloque /kɔlɔk/ n.m. symposium.

collyre /kɔlir/ n.m. eye drops.

colmater /kɔlmate/ v.t. seal; (*trou*) fill in.

colombe /kɔlɔ̃b/ n.f. dove.

Colombie /kɔlɔ̃bi/ n.f. Colombia.

colon /kɔlɔ̃/ n.m. settler.

colonel /kɔlɔnɛl/ n.m. colonel.

colon|**ial**, **~iale** (*m. pl.* **~iaux**) /kɔlɔnjal, -jo/ a. colonial.

colonie /kɔlɔni/ n.f. colony. **~ de vacances**, children's holiday camp.

coloniser /kɔlɔnize/ v.t. colonize.

colonne /kɔlɔn/ n.f. column. **~ vertébrale**, spine. **en ~ par deux**, in double file.

color|**er** /kɔlɔre/ v.t. colour; (*bois*) stain. **~ant** n.m. colouring. **~ation** n.f. (*couleur*) colour(ing).

colorier /kɔlɔrje/ v.t. colour (in).

coloris /kɔlɔri/ n.m. colour.

coloss|**al** (*m. pl.* **~aux**) /kɔlɔsal, -o/ a. colossal.

colosse /kɔlɔs/ n.m. giant.

colport|**er** /kɔlpɔrte/ v.t. hawk. **~eur**, **~euse** n.m., f. hawker.

colza /kɔlza/ n.m. rape(-seed).

coma /kɔma/ n.m. coma. **dans le ~**, in a coma.

combat /kɔ̃ba/ n.m. fight; (*sport*) match. **~s**, fighting.

combati|**f**, **~ve** /kɔ̃batif, -v/ a. eager to fight; (*esprit*) fighting.

combatt|**re†** /kɔ̃batr/ v.t./i. fight. **~ant**, **~ante** n.m., f. fighter; (*mil.*) combatant.

combien /kɔ̃bjɛ̃/ adv. **~ (de)**, (*quantité*) how much; (*nombre*) how many; (*temps*) how long. **~ il a changé**, (*comme*) how he has changed! **~ y a-t-il d'ici à . . .?**, how far is it to . . .?

combinaison /kɔ̃binɛzɔ̃/ n.f. combination; (*manigance*) scheme; (*de femme*) slip; (*bleu de travail*) boiler suit; (*Amer.*) overalls; (*de plongée*) wetsuit. **~ d'aviateur**, flying-suit.

combine /kɔ̃bin/ n.f. trick; (*fraude*) fiddle.

combiné /kɔ̃bine/ n.m. (*de téléphone*) receiver.

combiner /kɔ̃bine/ v.t. (*réunir*) combine; (*calculer*) devise.

comble¹ /kɔ̃bl/ a. packed.

comble² /kɔ̃bl/ n.m. height. **~s**, (mansarde) attic, loft. **c'est le ~!**, that's the (absolute) limit!

combler /kɔ̃ble/ v.t. fill; (perte, déficit) make good; (désir) fulfil; (personne) gratify. **~ qn. de cadeaux**/etc., lavish gifts/etc. on s.o.

combustible /kɔ̃bystibl/ n.m. fuel.

combustion /kɔ̃bystjɔ̃/ n.f. combustion.

comédie /kɔmedi/ n.f. comedy. **~ musicale**, musical. **jouer la ~**, put on an act.

comédien, ~ne /kɔmedjɛ̃, -jɛn/ n.m., f. actor, actress.

comestible /kɔmɛstibl/ a. edible. **~s** n.m. pl. foodstuffs.

comète /kɔmɛt/ n.f. comet.

comique /kɔmik/ a. comical; (genre) comic. —n.m. (acteur) comic; (comédie) comedy; (côté drôle) comical aspect.

comité /kɔmite/ n.m. committee.

commandant /kɔmɑ̃dɑ̃/ n.m. commander; (armée de terre) major. **~ (de bord)**, captain. **~ en chef**, Commander-in-Chief.

commande /kɔmɑ̃d/ n.f. (comm.) order. **~s**, (d'avion etc.) controls.

command|er /kɔmɑ̃de/ v.t. command; (acheter) order. —v.i. be in command. **~er à**, (maîtriser) control. **~er à qn. de**, command s.o. to. **~ement** n.m. command; (relig.) commandment.

commando /kɔmɑ̃do/ n.m. commando.

comme /kɔm/ conj. as. —prép. like. —adv. (exclamation) how. **~ ci comme ça**, so-so. **~ d'habitude, ~ à l'ordinaire**, as usual. **~ il faut**, proper(ly). **~ pour faire**, as if to do. **~ quoi**, to the effect that. **qu'avez-vous ~ amis**/etc.?, what have you in the way of friends/etc.? **~ c'est bon!**, it's so

good! **~ il est mignon!** isn't he sweet!

commémor|er /kɔmemɔre/ v.t. commemorate. **~ation** n.f. commemoration.

commenc|er /kɔmɑ̃se/ v.t./i. begin, start. **~er à faire**, begin ou start to do. **~ement** n.m. beginning, start.

comment /kɔmɑ̃/ adv. how. **~?**, (répétition) pardon?; (surprise) what? **~ est-il?**, what is he like? **le ~ et le pourquoi**, the whys and wherefores.

commentaire /kɔmɑ̃tɛr/ n.m. comment; (d'un texte) commentary.

comment|er /kɔmɑ̃te/ v.t. comment on. **~ateur, ~atrice** n.m., f. commentator.

commérages /kɔmeraʒ/ n.m. pl. gossip.

commerçant, ~e /kɔmɛrsɑ̃, -t/ a. (rue) shopping; (personne) business-minded. —n.m., f. shopkeeper.

commerce /kɔmɛrs/ n.m. trade, commerce; (magasin) business. **faire du ~**, trade.

commercial (m. pl. **~iaux**) /kɔmɛrsjal, -jo/ a. commercial. **~ialiser** v.t. market. **~ialisable** a. marketable.

commère /kɔmɛr/ n.f. gossip.

commettre /kɔmɛtr/ v.t. commit.

commis /kɔmi/ n.m. (de magasin) assistant; (de bureau) clerk.

commissaire /kɔmisɛr/ n.m. (sport) steward. **~ (de police)**, (police) superintendent. **~priseur** (pl. **~s-priseurs**) n.m. auctioneer.

commissariat /kɔmisarja/ n.m. **(de police)**, police station.

commission /kɔmisjɔ̃/ n.f. commission; (course) errand; (message) message. **~s**, shopping. **~naire** /-jɔnɛr/ n.m. errand-boy.

commod|e /kɔmɔd/ a. handy; (*facile*) easy. **pas ~e**, (*personne*) a difficult customer. **—n.f.** chest (of drawers). **~ité** n.f. convenience.

commotion /kɔmosjɔ̃/ n.f. **~ (cérébrale)**, concussion. **~né** /-jɔne/ a. shaken.

commuer /kɔmɥe/ v.t. commute.

commun, ~e /kɔmœ̃, -yn/ a. common; (*effort, action*) joint; (*frais, pièce*) shared. —n.f. (*circonscription*) commune. **~s** n.m. pl. outhouses, outbuildings. **avoir** ou **mettre en ~**, share. **le ~ des mortels**, ordinary mortals. **~al** (m. pl. **~aux**) /-ynal, -o/ a. of the commune, local. **~ément** /-ynemã/ adv. commonly.

communauté /kɔmynote/ n.f. community. **~ des biens** (*entre époux*) shared estate.

commune /kɔmyn/ voir **commun**.

communiant, ~e /kɔmynjã, -t/ n.m., f. (*relig.*) communicant.

communicati|f, ~ve /kɔmynikatif, -v/ a. communicative.

communication /kɔmynikasjɔ̃/ n.f. communication; (*téléphonique*) call. **~ interurbaine**, long-distance call.

commun|ier /kɔmynje/ v.i. (*relig.*) receive communion; (*fig.*) commune. **~ion** n.f. communion.

communiqué /kɔmynike/ n.m. communiqué.

communiquer /kɔmynike/ v.t. pass on, communicate; (*mouvement*) impart. —v.i. communicate. **se ~**, spread to.

communis|te /kɔmynist/ a. & n.m./f. communist. **~me** n.m. communism.

commutateur /kɔmytatœr/ n.m. (*électr.*) switch.

compact /kɔ̃pakt/ a. dense; (*voiture*) compact.

compact disc /kɔ̃paktdisk/ n.m. (P.) compact disc.

compagne /kɔ̃paɲ/ n.f. companion.

compagnie /kɔ̃paɲi/ n.f. company. **tenir ~ à**, keep company.

compagnon /kɔ̃paɲɔ̃/ n.m. companion; (*ouvrier*) workman. **~ de jeu**, playmate.

comparaître /kɔ̃parɛtr/ v.i. (*jurid.*) appear (**devant**, before).

compar|er /kɔ̃pare/ v.t. compare. **~er qch./qn. à** ou **et** compare sth./s.o. with ou and; **se ~er** v. pr. be compared. **~able** a. comparable. **~aison** n.f. comparison; (*littéraire*) simile. **~atif, ~ative** a. & n.m. comparative. **~é a.** comparative.

comparse /kɔ̃pars/ n.m./f. (*péj.*) stooge.

compartiment /kɔ̃partimã/ n.m. compartment. **~er** /-te/ v.t. divide up.

comparution /kɔ̃parysjɔ̃/ n.f. (*jurid.*) appearance.

compas /kɔ̃pa/ n.m. (pair of) compasses; (*boussole*) compass.

compassé /kɔ̃pase/ a. stilted.

compassion /kɔ̃pɑsjɔ̃/ n.f. compassion.

compatible /kɔ̃patibl/ a. compatible.

compatir /kɔ̃patir/ v.i. sympathize. **~ à**, share in.

compatriote /kɔ̃patrijɔt/ n.m./f. compatriot.

compens|er /kɔ̃pãse/ v.t. compensate for, make up for. **~ation** n.f. compensation.

compère /kɔ̃pɛr/ n.m. accomplice.

compéten|t, ~te /kɔ̃petã, -t/ a. competent. **~ce** n.f. competence.

compétiti|f, ~ve /kɔ̃petitif, -v/ a. competitive.

compétition /kɔ̃petisjɔ̃/ n.f. competition; (*sportive*) event. **de ~**, competitive.

complainte /kõplɛ̃t/ *n.f.* lament.

complaire (se) /(sə)kõplɛr/ *v. pr.* **se ~ dans**, delight in.

complaisan|t, ~te /kõplɛzã, -t/ *a.* kind; (*indulgent*) indulgent. **~ce** *n.f.* kindness; indulgence.

complément /kõplemã/ *n.m.* complement; (*reste*) rest. **~ (d'objet)**, (*gram.*) object. **~ d'information**, further information. **~aire** /-tɛr/ *a.* complementary; (*renseignements*) supplementary.

compl|et¹, ~ète /kõplɛ, -t/ *a.* complete; (*train, hôtel, etc.*) full. **~ètement** *adv.* completely.

complet² /kõplɛ/ *n.m.* suit.

compléter /kõplete/ *v.t.* complete; (*agrémenter*) complement. **se ~** *v. pr.* complement each other.

complexe¹ /kõplɛks/ *a.* complex. **~ité** *n.f.* complexity.

complex|e² /kõplɛks/ *n.m.* (*sentiment, bâtiments*) complex. **~é a.** hung-up.

complication /kõplikasjõ/ *n.f.* complication; (*complexité*) complexity.

complic|e /kõplis/ *n.m.* accomplice. **~ité** *n.f.* complicity.

compliment /kõplimã/ *n.m.* compliment. **~s**, (*félicitations*) congratulations. **~er** /-te/ *v.t.* compliment.

compliqu|er /kõplike/ *v.t.* complicate. **se ~er** *v. pr.* become complicated. **~é a.** complicated.

complot /kõplo/ *n.m.* plot. **~er** /-ɔte/ *v.t./i.* plot.

comporter¹ /kõpɔrte/ *v.t.* contain; (*impliquer*) involve.

comport|er² (se) /(sə)kõpɔrte/ *v. pr.* behave; (*joueur*) perform. **~ement** *n.m.* behaviour; (*de joueur*) performance.

composé /kõpoze/ *a.* compound; (*guindé*) affected. **—n.m.** compound.

compos|er /kõpoze/ *v.t.* make up,

compose; (*chanson, visage*) compose; (*numéro*) dial. **—v.i.** (*scol.*) take an exam; (*transiger*) compromise. **se ~er de**, be made up of. **~ant** *n.m.*, **~ante** *n.f.* component.

composi|teur, ~trice /kõpozitœr, -tris/ *n.m., f.* (*mus.*) composer.

composition /kõpozisjõ/ *n.f.* composition; (*examen*) test, exam.

composter /kõpɔste/ *v.t.* (*billet*) punch.

compot|e /kõpɔt/ *n.f.* stewed fruit. **~e de pommes**, stewed apples. **~ier** *n.m.* fruit dish.

compréhensible /kõpreãsibl/ *a.* understandable.

compréhensi|f, ~ve /kõpreãsif, -v/ *a.* understanding.

compréhension /kõpreãsjõ/ *n.f.* understanding, comprehension.

comprendre† /kõprãdr/ *v.t.* understand; (*comporter*) comprise. **ça se comprend**, that is understandable.

compresse /kõprɛs/ *n.f.* compress.

compression /kõprɛsjõ/ *n.f.* (*physique*) compression, (*réduction*) reduction. **~ de personnel**, staff cuts.

comprimé /kõprime/ *n.m.* tablet.

comprimer /kõprime/ *v.t.* compress; (*réduire*) reduce.

compris, ~e /kõpri, -z/ *a.* included; (*d'accord*) agreed. **~ entre**, (contained) between. **service (non) ~**, service (not) included, (not) including service. **tout ~**, (all) inclusive. **y ~**, including.

compromettre /kõprɔmɛtr/ *v.t.* compromise.

compromis /kõprɔmi/ *n.m.* compromise.

comptab|le /kõtabl/ *a.* accounting. **—n.m.** accountant. **~ilité** *n.f.* accountancy; (*comptes*) accounts; (*service*) accounts department.

comptant /kɔ̃tɑ̃/ *adv.* (payer) (in) cash; (acheter) for cash.

compte /kɔ̃t/ *n.m.* count; (facture, à la banque, comptabilité) account; (nombre exact) right number. **demander/rendre des ~s,** ask for/give an explanation. **à bon ~,** cheaply. **s'en tirer à bon ~,** get off lightly. **à son ~,** (travailler) for o.s., on one's own. **faire le ~ de,** count. **pour le ~ de,** on behalf of. **sur le ~ de,** about. **~ à rebours,** countdown. **~-gouttes** *n.m. invar.* (méd.) dropper. **au ~-gouttes,** (fig.) in dribs and drabs. **~ rendu,** report; (de film, livre) review. **~-tours** *n.m. invar.* rev counter.

compter /kɔ̃te/ *v.t.* count; (prévoir) reckon; (facturer) charge for; (avoir) have; (classer) consider. —*v.i.* (calculer, importer) count. **~ avec,** reckon with. **~ faire,** expect to do. **~ parmi,** (figurer) be considered among. **~ sur,** rely on.

compteur /kɔ̃tœr/ *n.m.* meter. **~ de vitesse,** speedometer.

comptine /kɔ̃tin/ *n.f.* nursery rhyme.

comptoir /kɔ̃twar/ *n.m.* counter; (de café) bar.

compulser /kɔ̃pylse/ *v.t.* examine.

comt|e, **~esse** /kɔ̃t, -ɛs/ *n.m., f.* count, countess.

comté /kɔ̃te/ *n.m.* county.

con, conne /kɔ̃, kɔn/ *a.* (argot) bloody foolish. —*n.m., f.* (argot) bloody fool.

concave /kɔ̃kav/ *a.* concave.

concéder /kɔ̃sede/ *v.t.* grant, concede.

concentr|er /kɔ̃sɑ̃tre/ *v.t.,* **se ~er** *v. pr.* concentrate. **~ation** *n.f.* concentration. **~é** *a.* concentrated; (lait) condensed; (personne) absorbed; —*n.m.* concentrate.

concept /kɔ̃sɛpt/ *n.m.* concept.

conception /kɔ̃sɛpsjɔ̃/ *n.f.* conception.

concerner /kɔ̃sɛrne/ *v.t.* concern. **en ce qui me concerne,** as far as I am concerned.

concert /kɔ̃sɛr/ *n.m.* concert. **de ~,** in unison.

concert|er /kɔ̃sɛrte/ *v.t.* organize, prepare. **se ~er** *v. pr.* confer. **~é** *a.* (plan etc.) concerted.

concerto /kɔ̃sɛrto/ *n.m.* concerto.

concession /kɔ̃sesjɔ̃/ *n.f.* concession; (terrain) plot.

concessionnaire /kɔ̃sesjɔnɛr/ *n.m./f.* (authorized) dealer.

concevoir† /kɔ̃svwar/ *v.t.* (imaginer, engendrer) conceive; (comprendre) understand.

concierge /kɔ̃sjɛrʒ/ *n.m./f.* caretaker.

concile /kɔ̃sil/ *n.m.* council.

concil|ier /kɔ̃silje/ *v.t.* reconcile. **se ~ier** *v. pr.* (s'attirer) win (over). **~iation** *n.f.* conciliation.

concis, ~e /kɔ̃si, -z/ *a.* concise. **~ion** -zjɔ̃/ *n.f.* concision.

concitoyen, ~ne /kɔ̃sitwajɛ̃, -jɛn/ *n.m., f.* fellow citizen.

conclu|re† /kɔ̃klyr/ *v.t./i.* conclude. **~ure à,** conclude in favour of. **~uant, ~uante** *a.* conclusive. **~usion** *n.f.* conclusion.

concocter /kɔ̃kɔkte/ *v.t.* (fam.) cook up.

concombre /kɔ̃kɔ̃br/ *n.m.* cucumber.

concorde /kɔ̃kɔrd/ *n.f.* concord.

concord|er /kɔ̃kɔrde/ *v.i.* agree. **~ance** *n.f.* agreement; (analogie) similarity. **~ant, ~ante** *a.* in agreement.

concourir /kɔ̃kurir/ *v.i.* compete. **~ à,** contribute towards.

concours /kɔ̃kur/ *n.m.* competition; (examen) competitive examination; (aide) aid; (de circonstances) combination.

concr|et, ~ète /kɔ̃krɛ, -t/ *a.*

concrete. **~ètement** *adv.* in concrete terms.

concrétiser /kɔ̃kretize/ *v.t.* give concrete form to. **se ~** *v. pr.* materialize.

conçu /kɔ̃sy/ *a.* **bien/mal ~,** (*appartement etc.*) well/badly planned.

concubinage /kɔ̃kybinaʒ/ *n.m.* cohabitation.

concurrenc|e /kɔ̃kyrɑ̃s/ *n.f.* competition. **faire ~ e à,** compete with. **jusqu'à ~ e de,** up to. **~er** *v.t.* compete with.

concurrent, ~e /kɔ̃kyrɑ̃, -t/ *n.m., f.* competitor; (*scol.*) candidate. **—a.** competing.

condamn|er /kɔ̃dane/ *v.t.* (*censurer, obliger*) condemn; (*jurid.*) sentence; (*porte*) block up. **~ation** *n.f.* condemnation; (*peine*) sentence. **~é à** (*fichu*) without hope, doomed.

condens|er /kɔ̃dɑ̃se/ *v.t.,* **se ~er** *v. pr.* condense. **~ation** *n.f.* condensation.

condescendre /kɔ̃desɑ̃dr/ *v.i.* condescend (**à,** to).

condiment /kɔ̃dimɑ̃/ *n.m.* condiment.

condisciple /kɔ̃disipl/ *n.m.* classmate, schoolfellow.

condition /kɔ̃disjɔ̃/ *n.f.* condition. **~s,** (*prix*) terms. **à ~ de ou que,** provided (that). **sans ~,** unconditional(ly). **sous ~,** conditionally. **~nel, ~nelle** /-jɔnɛl/ *a.* conditional. **~nel** *n.m.* conditional (tense).

conditionnement /kɔ̃disjɔnmɑ̃/ *n.m.* conditioning; (*emballage*) packaging.

conditionner /kɔ̃disjɔne/ *v.t.* condition; (*emballer*) package.

condoléances /kɔ̃dɔleɑ̃s/ *n.f. pl.* condolences.

conduc|teur, ~trice /kɔ̃dyktœr, -tris/ *n.m., f.* driver.

conduire† /kɔ̃dyir/ *v.t.* lead;

(*auto.*) drive; (*affaire*) conduct. **—v.i.** drive. **se ~** *v. pr.* behave. **~ à,** (*accompagner à*) take to.

conduit /kɔ̃dyi/ *n.m.* (*anat.*) duct.

conduite /kɔ̃dyit/ *n.f.* conduct; (*auto.*) driving; (*tuyau*) main. **~à droite,** (*place*) right-hand drive.

cône /kon/ *n.m.* cone.

confection /kɔ̃fɛksjɔ̃/ *n.f.* making. **de ~,** ready-made. **la ~,** the clothing industry. **~ner** /-jɔne/ *v.t.* make.

confédération /kɔ̃federasjɔ̃/ *n.f.* confederation.

conférenc|e /kɔ̃ferɑ̃s/ *n.f.* conference; (*exposé*) lecture. **~e au sommet,** summit conference. **~ier, ~ière** *n.m., f.* lecturer.

conférer /kɔ̃fere/ *v.t.* give; (*décerner*) confer.

confess|er /kɔ̃fese/ *v.t.,* **se ~er** *v. pr.* confess. **~eur** *n.m.* confessor. **~ion** *n.f.* confession; (*religion*) denomination. **~ionnal** (*pl.* **~ionnaux**) *n.m.* confessional. **~ionnel, ~ionnelle** *a.* denominational.

confettis /kɔ̃feti/ *n.m. pl.* confetti.

confiance /kɔ̃fjɑ̃s/ *n.f.* trust. **avoir ~ en,** trust.

confiant, ~e /kɔ̃fjɑ̃, -t/ *a.* (*assuré*) confident; (*sans défiance*) trusting. **~ en ou dans,** confident in.

confiden|t, ~te /kɔ̃fidɑ̃, -t/ *n.m., f.* confidant, confidante. **~ce** *n.f.* confidence.

confidentiel, ~le /kɔ̃fidɑ̃sjɛl/ *a.* confidential.

confier /kɔ̃fje/ *v.t.* **à qn.,** entrust s.o. with; (*secret*) confide to s.o. **se ~ à,** confide in.

configuration /kɔ̃figyrasjɔ̃/ *n.f.* configuration.

confiner /kɔ̃fine/ *v.t.* confine. **—v.i. ~ à,** border on. **se ~** *v. pr.* confine o.s. (**à, dans,** to).

confins /kɔ̃fɛ̃/ *n.m. pl.* confines.

confirm|er /kɔ̃firme/ *v.t.* confirm. **~ation** *n.f.* confirmation.

confis|erie /kɔ̃fizri/ n.f. sweet shop. **~eries,** confectionery. **~eur, ~euse** n.m., f. confectioner.

confis|quer /kɔ̃fiske/ v.t. confiscate. **~cation** n.f. confiscation.

confit, ~e /kɔ̃fi, -t/ a. (culin.) candied. **fruits ~s,** crystallized fruits. —n.m. **~ d'oie,** goose liver conserve.

confiture /kɔ̃fityr/ n.f. jam.

conflit /kɔ̃fli/ n.m. conflict.

confondre /kɔ̃fɔ̃dr/ v.t. confuse, mix up; (consterner, étonner) confound. **se ~** v. pr. merge. **se ~ en excuses,** apologize profusely.

confondu /kɔ̃fɔ̃dy/ a. (déconcerté) overwhelmed, confounded.

conforme /kɔ̃fɔrm/ a. **~ à,** in accordance with.

conformémé|ment /kɔ̃fɔrmemã/ adv. **~ à,** in accordance with.

conform|er /kɔ̃fɔrme/ v.t. adapt. **se ~er à,** conform to. **~ité** n.f. conformity.

conformis|te /kɔ̃fɔrmist/ a. & n.m./f. conformist. **~me** n.m. conformism.

confort /kɔ̃fɔr/ n.m. comfort. **tout ~,** with all mod cons. **~able** /-tabl/ a. comfortable.

confrère /kɔ̃frɛr/ n.m. colleague.

confrérie /kɔ̃freri/ n.f. brotherhood.

confront|er /kɔ̃frɔ̃te/ v.t. confront; (textes) compare. **se ~er à** v. pr. confront. **~ation** n.f. confrontation.

confus, ~e /kɔ̃fy, -z/ a. confused; (gêné) embarrassed.

confusion /kɔ̃fyzjɔ̃/ n.f. confusion; (gêné) embarrassment.

congé /kɔ̃ʒe/ n.m. holiday; (arrêt momentané) time off; (mil.) leave; (avis de départ) notice. **~ de maladie,** sick-leave. **~ de maternité,** maternity leave. **jour de ~,** day off. **prendre ~ de,** take one's leave of.

congédier /kɔ̃ʒedje/ v.t. dismiss.

congel|er /kɔ̃ʒle/ v.t. freeze. **les ~elés,** frozen food. **~élateur** n.m. freezer.

congénère /kɔ̃ʒenɛr/ n.m./f. fellow creature.

congénit|al (m. pl. **~aux**) /kɔ̃ʒenital, -o/ a. congenital.

congère /kɔ̃ʒɛr/ n.f. snow-drift.

congestion /kɔ̃ʒɛstjɔ̃/ n.f. congestion. **~ cérébrale,** stroke, cerebral haemorrhage. **~ner** /-jɔne/ v.t. congest; (visage) flush.

congrégation /kɔ̃gregasjɔ̃/ n.f. congregation.

congrès /kɔ̃grɛ/ n.m. congress.

conifère /kɔnifɛr/ n.m. conifer.

conique /kɔnik/ a. conic(al).

conjectur|e /kɔ̃ʒɛktyr/ n.f. conjecture. **~er** v.t./i. conjecture.

conjoint, ~e¹ /kɔ̃ʒwɛ̃, -t/ n.m., f. spouse.

conjoint, ~e² /kɔ̃ʒwɛ̃, -t/ a. joint. **~ement** /-tmã/ adv. jointly.

conjonction /kɔ̃ʒɔ̃ksjɔ̃/ n.f. conjunction.

conjonctivite /kɔ̃ʒɔ̃ktivit/ n.f. conjunctivitis.

conjoncture /kɔ̃ʒɔ̃ktyr/ n.f. circumstances; (économique) economic climate.

conjugaison /kɔ̃ʒygɛzɔ̃/ n.f. conjugation.

conjug|al (m. pl. **~aux**) /kɔ̃ʒygal, -o/ a. conjugal.

conjug|uer /kɔ̃ʒyge/ v.t. (gram.) conjugate; (efforts) combine. **se ~** v. pr. (gram.) be conjugated.

conjur|er /kɔ̃ʒyre/ v.t. (éviter) avert; (implorer) entreat. **~ation** n.f. conspiracy. **~é, ~ée** n.m., f. conspirator.

connaissance /kɔnɛsãs/ n.f. knowledge; (personne) acquaintance. **~s,** (science) knowledge. **faire la ~ de,** meet; (personne connue) get to know. **perdre ~,** lose consciousness. **sans ~,** unconscious.

connaisseur /kɔnɛsœr/ *n.m.* connoisseur.

connaître† /kɔnɛtr/ *v.t.* know; (*avoir*) have. se ~ *v. pr.* (*se rencontrer*) meet. **faire** ~, make known. **s'y** ~ **à** *ou* **en**, know (all) about.

conne|cter /kɔnɛkte/ *v.t.* connect. ~**xion** *n.f.* connection.

connerie /kɔnri/ *n.f.* (*argot*) (*remarque*) rubbish. **faire une** ~, do sth. stupid. **dire une** ~, talk rubbish. **quelle** ~!, how stupid!

connivence /kɔnivɑ̃s/ *n.f.* connivance.

connotation /kɔnɔtasjɔ̃/ *n.f.* connotation.

connu /kɔny/ *a.* well-known.

conquér|ir /kɔ̃kerir/ *v.t.* conquer. ~**ant**, ~**ante** *n.m.*, *f.* conqueror.

conquête /kɔ̃kɛt/ *n.f.* conquest.

consacrer /kɔ̃sakre/ *v.t.* devote; (*relig.*) consecrate; (*sanctionner*) establish. se ~ *v. pr.* devote o.s. (**à**, to).

consciemment /kɔ̃sjamɑ̃/ *adv.* consciously.

conscience /kɔ̃sjɑ̃s/ *n.f.* conscience; (*perception*) consciousness. **avoir/prendre** ~ **de**, be/become aware of. **perdre** ~, lose consciousness. **avoir bonne/mauvaise** ~, have a clear/guilty conscience.

consciencieu|x, ~**se** /kɔ̃sjɑ̃sjø, -z/ *a.* conscientious.

conscient, ~**e** /kɔ̃sjɑ̃, -t/ *a.* conscious. ~ **de**, aware *ou* conscious of.

conscrit /kɔ̃skri/ *n.m.* conscript.

consécration /kɔ̃sekrasjɔ̃/ *n.f.* consecration.

consécuti|f, ~**ve** /kɔ̃sekytif, -v/ *a.* consecutive. ~**f à**, following upon. ~**vement** *adv.* consecutively.

conseil /kɔ̃sɛj/ *n.m.* (piece of) advice; (*assemblée*) council, committee; (*séance*) meeting; (*personne*) consultant. ~ **d'administration**, board of directors. ~ **des ministres**, Cabinet. ~ **municipal**, town council.

conseiller[1] /kɔ̃seje/ *v.t.* advise. ~ **à qn. de**, advise s.o. to. ~ **qch. à qn.**, recommend sth. to s.o.

conseill|er[2], ~**ère** /kɔ̃seje, -ɛjɛr/ *n.m.*, *f.* adviser, counsellor. ~**er municipal**, town councillor.

consent|ir /kɔ̃sɑ̃tir/ *v.i.* agree (**à**, to). —*v.t.* grant. ~**ement** *n.m.* consent.

conséquence /kɔ̃sekɑ̃s/ *n.f.* consequence. **en** ~, consequently; (*comme il convient*) accordingly.

conséquent, ~**e** /kɔ̃sekɑ̃, -t/ *a.* logical; (*important: fam.*) sizeable. **par** ~, consequently.

conserva|teur, ~**trice** /kɔ̃sɛrvatœr, -tris/ *a.* conservative. —*n.m.*, *f.* (*pol.*) conservative. —*n.m.* (*de musée*) curator. ~**tisme** *n.m.* conservatism.

conservatoire /kɔ̃sɛrvatwar/ *n.m.* academy.

conserve /kɔ̃sɛrv/ *n.f.* tinned *ou* canned food. **en** ~, tinned, canned.

conserv|er /kɔ̃sɛrve/ *v.t.* keep; (*en bon état*) preserve; (*culin.*) preserve. se ~**er** *v. pr.* (*culin.*) keep. ~**ation** *n.f.* preservation.

considérable /kɔ̃siderabl/ *a.* considerable.

considération /kɔ̃siderasjɔ̃/ *n.f.* consideration; (*respect*) regard. **prendre en** ~, take into consideration.

considérer /kɔ̃sidere/ *v.t.* consider; (*respecter*) esteem. ~ **comme**, consider to be.

consigne /kɔ̃siɲ/ *n.f.* (*de gare*) left luggage (office); (*Amer.*) (baggage) checkroom; (*scol.*) detention; (*somme*) deposit; (*ordres*) orders. **~ automatique,** (left-luggage) lockers; (*Amer.*) (baggage) lockers.

consigner /kɔ̃siɲe/ *v.t.* (*comm.*) charge a deposit on; (*écrire*) record; (*élève*) keep in; (*soldat*) confine.

consistan|t, **~te** /kɔ̃sistɑ̃, -t/ *a.* solid; (*épais*) thick. **~ce** *n.f.* consistency; (*fig.*) solidity.

consister /kɔ̃siste/ *v.i.* **~ en/dans,** consist of/in. **~ à faire,** consist in doing.

consœur /kɔ̃sœr/ *n.f.* colleague; fellow member.

consol|er /kɔ̃sɔle/ *v.t.* console. **se ~er** *v. pr.* be consoled (**de,** for). **~ation** *n.f.* consolation.

consolider /kɔ̃sɔlide/ *v.t.* strengthen; (*fig.*) consolidate.

consomma|teur, ~trice /kɔ̃sɔmatœr, -tris/ *n.m., f.* (*comm.*) consumer; (*dans un café*) customer.

consommé[1] /kɔ̃sɔme/ *a.* consummate.

consommé[2] /kɔ̃sɔme/ *n.m.* (*bouillon*) consommé.

consomm|er /kɔ̃sɔme/ *v.t.* consume; (*user*) use, consume; (*mariage*) consummate. —*v.i.* drink. **~ation** *n.f.* consumption; consummation; (*boisson*) drink. **de ~ation,** (*comm.*) consumer.

consonne /kɔ̃sɔn/ *n.f.* consonant.

consortium /kɔ̃sɔrsjɔm/ *n.m.* consortium.

conspir|er /kɔ̃spire/ *v.i.* conspire. **~ateur, ~atrice** *n.m., f.* conspirator. **~ation** *n.f.* conspiracy.

conspuer /kɔ̃spɥe/ *v.t.* boo.

const|ant, ~ante /kɔ̃stɑ̃, -t/ *a.* constant. —*n.f.* constant. **~amment** /-amɑ̃/ *adv.* constantly. **~ance** *n.f.* constancy.

constat /kɔ̃sta/ *n.m.* (official) report.

constat|er /kɔ̃state/ *v.t.* note;

(*certifier*) certify. **~ation** *n.f.* observation, statement of fact.

constellation /kɔ̃stelasjɔ̃/ *n.f.* constellation.

constellé /kɔ̃stele/ *a.* **~ de,** studded with.

constern|er /kɔ̃sterne/ *v.t.* dismay. **~ation** *n.f.* dismay.

constip|é /kɔ̃stipe/ *a.* constipated; (*fig.*) stilted. **~ation** *n.f.* constipation.

constitu|er /kɔ̃stitɥe/ *v.t.* make up, constitute; (*organiser*) form; (*être*) constitute. **se ~er prisonnier,** give o.s. up. **~é de,** made up of.

constituti|f, ~ve /kɔ̃stitytif, -v/ *a.* constituent.

constitution /kɔ̃stitysjɔ̃/ *n.f.* formation; (*d'une équipe*) composition; (*pol., méd.*) constitution. **~nel, ~nelle** /-jɔnel/ *a.* constitutional.

constructeur /kɔ̃stryktœr/ *n.m.* manufacturer.

constructi|f, ~ve /kɔ̃stryktif, -v/ *a.* constructive.

constr|uire /kɔ̃strɥir/ *v.t.* build; (*système, phrase, etc.*) construct. **~uction** *n.f.* building; (*structure*) construction.

consul /kɔ̃syl/ *n.m.* consul. **~aire** *a.* consular. **~at** *n.m.* consulate.

consult|er /kɔ̃sylte/ *v.t.* consult. —*v.i.* (*médecin*) hold surgery; (*Amer.*) hold office hours. **se ~er** *v. pr.* confer. **~ation** *n.f.* consultation; (*réception: méd.*) surgery; (*Amer.*) office.

consumer /kɔ̃syme/ *v.t.* consume. **se ~** *v. pr.* be consumed.

contact /kɔ̃takt/ *n.m.* contact; (*toucher*) touch. **au ~ de,** on contact with; (*personne*) by contact with, by seeing. **mettre/couper le ~,** (*auto.*) switch on/off the ignition. **prendre ~ avec,** get in touch with. **~er** *v.t.* contact.

contag|ieux, **∼ieuse** /kɔ̃taʒjø, -z/ *a.* contagious. **∼ion** *n.f.* contagion.

container /kɔ̃tɛnɛr/ *n.m.* container.

contamin|er /kɔ̃tamine/ *v.t.* contaminate. **∼ation** *n.f.* contamination.

conte /kɔ̃t/ *n.m.* tale. **∼ de fées**, fairy tale.

contempl|er /kɔ̃tɑ̃ple/ *v.t.* contemplate. **∼ation** *n.f.* contemplation.

contemporain, **∼e** /kɔ̃tɑ̃pɔrɛ̃, -ɛn/ *a. & n.m., f.* contemporary.

contenance /kɔ̃tnɑ̃s/ *n.f.* (*contenu*) capacity; (*allure*) bearing; (*sangfroid*) composure.

conteneur /kɔ̃tnœr/ *n.m.* container.

contenir† /kɔ̃tnir/ *v.t.* contain; (*avoir une capacité de*) hold. **se ∼** *v. pr.* contain o.s.

content, **∼e** /kɔ̃tã, -t/ *a.* pleased (**de**, with). **∼ de faire**, pleased to do.

content|er /kɔ̃tɑ̃te/ *v.t.* satisfy. **se ∼er de**, content o.s. with. **∼ement** *n.m.* contentment.

contentieux /kɔ̃tɑ̃sjø/ *n.m.* matters in dispute; (*service*) legal department.

contenu /kɔ̃tny/ *n.m.* (*de contenant*) contents; (*de texte*) content.

conter /kɔ̃te/ *v.t.* tell, relate.

contestataire /kɔ̃tɛstatɛr/ *n.m./f.* protester.

conteste (sans) /(sɑ̃)kɔ̃tɛst/ *adv.* indisputably.

contest|er /kɔ̃tɛste/ *v.t.* dispute; (*s'opposer*) protest against. —*v.i.* protest. **∼able** *a.* debatable. **∼ation** *n.f.* dispute; (*opposition*) protest.

conteu|r, **∼se** /kɔ̃tœr, -øz/ *n.m., f.* story-teller.

contexte /kɔ̃tɛkst/ *n.m.* context.

contigu, **∼ë** /kɔ̃tigy/ *a.* adjacent (**à**, to).

continent /kɔ̃tinã/ *n.m.* continent. **∼al** (*m. pl.* **∼aux**) /-tal, -to/ *a.* continental.

contingences /kɔ̃tɛ̃ʒɑ̃s/ *n.f. pl.* contingencies.

contingent /kɔ̃tɛ̃ʒɑ̃/ *n.m.* (*mil.*) contingent; (*comm.*) quota.

continu /kɔ̃tiny/ *a.* continuous.

continuel, **∼le** /kɔ̃tinɥɛl/ *a.* continual. **∼lement** *adv.* continually.

contin|uer /kɔ̃tinɥe/ *v.t.* continue. —*v.i.* continue, go on. **∼uer à** *ou* **de faire**, carry on *ou* go on *ou* continue doing. **∼uation** *n.f.* continuation.

continuité /kɔ̃tinɥite/ *n.f.* continuity.

contorsion /kɔ̃tɔrsjɔ̃/ *n.f.* contortion. **se ∼ner** *v. pr.* wriggle.

contour /kɔ̃tur/ *n.m.* outline, contour. **∼s**, (*d'une route etc.*) twists and turns, bends.

contourner /kɔ̃turne/ *v.t.* go round; (*difficulté*) get round.

contracepti|f, **∼ve** /kɔ̃trasɛptif, -v/ *a. & n.m.* contraceptive.

contraception /kɔ̃trasɛpsjɔ̃/ *n.f.* contraception.

contract|er /kɔ̃trakte/ *v.t.* (*maladie, dette*) contract; (*muscle*) tense, contract; (*assurance*) take out. **se ∼er** *v. pr.* contract. **∼é a.** tense. **∼ion** -ksjɔ̃/ *n.f.* contraction.

contractuel, **∼le** /kɔ̃traktɥɛl/ *n.m., f.* (*agent*) traffic warden.

contradiction /kɔ̃tradiksjɔ̃/ *n.f.* contradiction.

contradictoire /kɔ̃tradiktwar/ *a.* contradictory; (*débat*) devon.

contraignant, **∼e** /kɔ̃trɛɲɑ̃, -t/ *a.* restricting.

contraindre† /kɔ̃trɛ̃dr/ *v.t.* compel.

contraint, **∼e** /kɔ̃trɛ̃, -t/ *a.* constrained. —*n.f.* constraint.

contraire /kɔ̃trɛr/ a. & n.m. opposite. **~ à**, contrary to. **au ~**, on the contrary. **~ment** adv. **~ment à**, contrary to.

contralto /kɔ̃tralto/ n.m. contralto.

contrar|ier /kɔ̃trarje/ v.t. annoy; (action) frustrate. **~iété** n.f. annoyance.

contrast|e /kɔ̃trast/ n.m. contrast. **~er** v.i. contrast.

contrat /kɔ̃tra/ n.m. contract.

contravention /kɔ̃travɑ̃sjɔ̃/ n.f. (parking-)ticket. **en ~**, in contravention (à, of).

contre /kɔ̃tr(ə)/ prép. against; (en échange de) for. **par ~**, on the other hand. **tout ~**, close by. **~-attaque** n.f. **~attaquer** v.t. counter-attack. **~-balancer** v.t. counterbalance. **~-courant** n.m. aller à **~-courant de**, swim against the current of. **~indiqué** a. (méd.) contra-indicated; (déconseillé) not recommended. **à ~-jour** adv. against the (sun)light. **~-offensive** n.f. counter-offensive. **prendre le ~-pied**, do the opposite; (opinion) take the opposite view. **à ~-pied** adv. (sport) on the wrong foot. **~-plaqué** n.m. plywood. **~-révolution** n.f. counter-revolution. **~-torpilleur** n.m. destroyer.

contreband|e /kɔ̃trəbɑ̃d/ n.f. contraband. faire la **~e de**, passer en **~e**, smuggle. **~ier** n.m. smuggler.

contrebas (en) /(ɑ̃)kɔ̃trəba/ adv. & prép. en **~ (de)**, below.

contrebasse /kɔ̃trəbas/ n.f. double-bass.

contrecarrer /kɔ̃trəkare/ v.t. thwart.

contrecœur (à) /(a)kɔ̃trəkœr/ adv. reluctantly.

contrecoup /kɔ̃trəku/ n.m. consequence.

contredire† /kɔ̃trədir/ v.t. contradict. se **~** v. pr. contradict o.s.

contrée /kɔ̃tre/ n.f. region, land.

contrefaçon /kɔ̃trəfasɔ̃/ n.f. (objet imité, action) forgery.

contrefaire /kɔ̃trəfɛr/ v.t. (falsifier) forge; (parodier) mimic; (déguiser) disguise.

contrefait, ~e /kɔ̃trəfɛ, -t/ a. deformed.

contreforts /kɔ̃trəfɔr/ n.m. pl. foothills.

contremaître /kɔ̃trəmɛtr/ n.m. foreman.

contrepartie /kɔ̃trəparti/ n.f. compensation. **en ~**, in exchange, in return.

contrepoids /kɔ̃trəpwa/ n.m. counterbalance.

contrer /kɔ̃tre/ v.t. counter.

contresens /kɔ̃trəsɑ̃s/ n.m. misinterpretation; (absurdité) nonsense. **à ~**, the wrong way.

contresigner /kɔ̃trəsiɲe/ v.t. countersign.

contretemps /kɔ̃trətɑ̃/ n.m. hitch. **à ~**, at the wrong time.

contrevenir /kɔ̃trəvnir/ v.i. **~ à**, contravene.

contribuable /kɔ̃tribɥabl/ n.m./f. taxpayer.

contribuer /kɔ̃tribɥe/ v.t. contribute (à, to, towards).

contribution /kɔ̃tribysjɔ̃/ n.f. contribution. **~s**, (impôts) taxes; (administration) tax office.

contrit, ~e /kɔ̃tri, -t/ a. contrite.

contrôl|e /kɔ̃trol/ n.m. check; (des prix, d'un véhicule) control; (poinçon) hallmark; (scol.) test. **~e continu**, continuous assessment. **~e de soi-même**, self-control. **~e des changes**, exchange control. **~e des naissances** birth-control. **~er** v.t. check; (surveiller, maîtriser) control. se **~er** v. pr. control o.s.

contrôleu|r, **~se** /kõtrolœr, -øz/ *n.m., f.* (bus) conductor *ou* conductress; (*de train*) (ticket) inspector.

contrordre /kõtrɔrdr/ *n.m.* change of orders.

controvers|e /kõtrovɛrs/ *n.f.* controversy. **~é** *a.* controversial.

contumace (par) /(par)kõtymas/ *adv.* in one's absence.

contusion /kõtyzjõ/ *n.f.* bruise. **~né** /-jɔne/ *a.* bruised.

convaincre† /kõvɛ̃kr/ *v.t.* convince. **~ qn. de faire**, persuade s.o. to do.

convalescen|t, ~te /kõvalesã, -t/ *a. et n.m., f.* convalescent. **~ce** *n.f.* convalescence. **être en ~ce**, convalesce.

convenable /kõvnabl/ *a.* (correct) decent, proper; (*approprié*) suitable.

convenance /kõvnãs/ *n.f.* **à sa ~**, to one's satisfaction. **les ~s**, the proprieties.

convenir† /kõvnir/ *v.i.* be suitable. **~ à** suit. **~ de/que**, (*avouer*) admit (to)/that. **~ de qch.**, (*s'accorder sur*) agree on sth. **~ de faire**, agree to do. **il convient de**, it is advisable to; (*selon les bienséances*) it would be right to.

convention /kõvãsjõ/ *n.f.* convention. **~s**, (*convenances*) conventional. **~ collective**, industrial agreement. **~né** *a.* (*prix*) official; (*médecin*) health service (*not private*). **~nel, ~nelle** /-jɔnel/ *a.* conventional.

convenu /kõvny/ *a.* agreed.

converger /kõvɛrʒe/ *v.i.* converge.

convers|er /kõvɛrse/ *v.i.* converse. **~ation** *n.f.* conversation.

conver|tir /kõvɛrtir/ *v.t.* convert (à, to; en, into). **se ~tir** *v. pr.* be converted, convert. **~sion** *n.f.* conversion. **~tible** *a.* convertible.

convexe /kõvɛks/ *a.* convex.

conviction /kõviksjõ/ *n.f.* conviction.

convier /kõvje/ *v.t.* invite.

convive /kõviv/ *n.m./f.* guest.

convivi|al (*m. pl.* **~iaux**) /kõvivjal, -jo/ *a.* convivial; (*comput.*) user-friendly.

convocation /kõvɔkasjõ/ *n.f.* summons to attend; (*d'une assemblée*) convening; (*document*) notification to attend.

convoi /kõvwa/ *n.m.* convoy; (*train*) train. **~ (funèbre)**, funeral procession.

convoit|er /kõvwate/ *v.t.* desire, covet, envy. **~ise** *n.f.* desire, envy.

convoquer /kõvɔke/ *v.t.* (*assemblée*) convene; (*personne*) summon.

convoy|er /kõvwaje/ *v.t.* escort. **~eur** *n.m.* escort ship. **~eur de fonds**, security guard.

convulsion /kõvylsjõ/ *n.f.* convulsion.

cool /kul/ *a. invar.* cool, laid-back.

coopérati|f, ~ve /kɔɔperatif, -v/ *a.* co-operative. —*n.f.* co-operative (society).

coopér|er /kɔɔpere/ *v.i.* co-operate (à, in). **~ation** *n.f.* co-operation. **la C~ation**, civilian national service.

coopter /kɔɔpte/ *v.t.* co-opt.

coordination /kɔɔrdinasjõ/ *n.f.* co-ordination.

coordonn|er /kɔɔrdɔne/ *v.t.* co-ordinate. **~ées** *n.f. pl.* co-ordinates; (*adresse: fam.*) particulars.

copain /kɔpɛ̃/ *n.m.* (*fam.*) pal; (*petit ami*) boyfriend.

copeau (*pl.* **~x**) /kɔpo/ *n.m.* (*lamelle de bois*) shaving.

cop|ie /kɔpi/ *n.f.* copy; (*scol.*) paper. **~ier** *v.t./i.* copy. **~ier sur**, (*scol.*) copy *ou* crib from.

copieu|x, **~se** /kɔpjø, -z/ a. copious.

copine /kɔpin/ n.f. (fam.) pal; (petite amie) girlfriend.

copiste /kɔpist/ n.m./f. copyist.

coproduction /kɔprɔdyksjɔ̃/ n.f. coproduction.

copropriété /kɔprɔprijete/ n.f. co-ownership.

copulation /kɔpylasjɔ̃/ n.f. copulation.

coq /kɔk/ n.m. cock. **~-à-l'âne** n.m. invar. abrupt change of subject.

coque /kɔk/ n.f. shell; (de bateau) hull.

coquelicot /kɔkliko/ n.m. poppy.

coqueluche /kɔklyʃ/ n.f. whooping cough.

coquet, **~te** /kɔkɛ, -t/ a. flirtatious; (élégant) pretty; (somme, fam.) tidy. **~terie** /-tri/ n.f. flirtatiousness.

coquetier /kɔktje/ n.m. egg-cup.

coquillage /kɔkijaʒ/ n.m. shellfish; (coquille) shell.

coquille /kɔkij/ n.f. shell; (faute) misprint. **~ Saint-Jacques**, scallop.

coquin, **~e** /kɔkɛ̃, -in/ a. naughty. —n.m., f. rascal.

cor /kɔr/ n.m. (mus.) horn; (au pied) corn.

cor|ail (pl. **~aux**) /kɔraj, -o/ n.m. coral.

Coran /kɔrɑ̃/ n.m. Koran.

corbeau (pl. **~x**) /kɔrbo/ n.m. (oiseau) crow.

corbeille /kɔrbɛj/ n.f. basket. **~ à papier**, waste-paper basket.

corbillard /kɔrbijar/ n.m. hearse.

cordage /kɔrdaʒ/ n.m. rope. **~s**, (naut.) rigging.

corde /kɔrd/ n.f. rope; (d'arc, de violon, etc.) string. **~ à sauter**, skipping-rope. **~ raide**, tightrope. **~s vocales**, vocal cords.

cordée /kɔrde/ n.f. roped party.

cord|ial (m. pl. **~iaux**) /kɔrdjal, -jo/ a. warm, cordial. **~ialité** n.f. warmth.

cordon /kɔrdɔ̃/ n.m. string, cord. **~-bleu** (pl. **~s-bleus**) n.m. first-rate cook. **~ de police**, police cordon.

cordonnier /kɔrdɔnje/ n.m. shoe mender.

Corée /kɔre/ n.f. Korea.

coreligionnaire /kɔrəliʒjɔnɛr/ n.m./f. person of the same religion.

coriace /kɔrjas/ a. (aliment) tough. —a. & n.m. tenacious and tough (person).

corne /kɔrn/ n.f. horn.

cornée /kɔrne/ n.f. cornea.

corneille /kɔrnɛj/ n.f. crow.

cornemuse /kɔrnəmyz/ n.f. bagpipes.

corner[1] /kɔrne/ v.t. (page) make dog-eared. —v.i. (auto.) hoot; (auto., Amer.) honk.

corner[2] /kɔrnɛr/ n.m. (football) corner.

cornet /kɔrnɛ/ n.m. (paper) cone; (crème glacée) cornet, cone.

corniaud /kɔrnjo/ n.m. (fam.) nitwit.

corniche /kɔrniʃ/ n.f. cornice; (route) cliff road.

cornichon /kɔrniʃɔ̃/ n.m. gherkin.

corollaire /kɔrɔlɛr/ n.m. corollary.

corporation /kɔrpɔrasjɔ̃/ n.f. professional body.

corporel, **~le** /kɔrpɔrɛl/ a. bodily; (châtiment) corporal.

corps /kɔr/ n.m. body; (mil., pol.) corps. **~ à corps**, hand to hand. **~ électoral**, electorate. **~ enseignant**, teaching profession. **faire ~ avec**, form part of.

corpulen|t, **~te** /kɔrpylɑ̃, -t/ a. stout. **~ce** n.f. stoutness.

correct /kɔrɛkt/ a. proper, correct; (exact) correct; (tenue) decent. **~ement** adv. properly; correctly; decently.

correc|teur, ~trice /kɔrɛk-
tœr, -tris/ *n.m., f.* (*d'épreuves*)
proof-reader; (*scol.*) examiner.
~teur d'orthographe, spelling
checker.

correction /kɔrɛksjɔ̃/ *n.f.* correction; (*punition*) beating.

corrélation /kɔrelasjɔ̃/ *n.f.* cor-
relation.

correspondan|t, ~te /kɔrɛspɔ̃dɑ̃,
-t/ *a.* corresponding. —*n.m., f.*
correspondent; (*au téléphone*)
caller. **~ce** *n.f.* correspondence;
(*de train, d'autobus*) connection.
vente par ~ce, mail order.

correspondre /kɔrɛspɔ̃dr/ *v.i.*
(*s'accorder, écrire*) correspond;
(*chambres*) communicate.

corrida /kɔrida/ *n.f.* bullfight.

corridor /kɔridɔr/ *n.m.* corridor.

corri|ger /kɔriʒe/ *v.t.* correct;
(*devoir*) mark, correct; (*punir*)
beat; (*guérir*) cure. **se ~er de**,
cure o.s. of. **~é** *n.m.* (*scol.*) correct
version, model answer.

corroborer /kɔrɔbɔre/ *v.t.* corroborate.

corro|der /kɔrɔde/ *v.t.* corrode.
~sion /-ozjɔ̃/ *n.f.* corrosion.

corrom|pre† /kɔrɔ̃pr/ *v.t.* corrupt;
(*soudoyer*) bribe. **~u** *a.* corrupt.

corrosi|f, ~ve /kɔrozif, -v/ *a.*
corrosive.

corruption /kɔrypsjɔ̃/ *n.f.* corruption.

corsage /kɔrsaʒ/ *n.m.* bodice;
(*chemisier*) blouse.

corsaire /kɔrsɛr/ *n.m.* pirate.

Corse /kɔrs/ *n.f.* Corsica.

corse /kɔrs/ *a. & n.m./f.* Corsican.

corsé /kɔrse/ *a.* (*vin*) full-bodied;
(*scabreux*) spicy.

corset /kɔrsɛ/ *n.m.* corset.

cortège /kɔrtɛʒ/ *n.m.* procession.

cortisone /kɔrtizon/ *n.f.* cortisone.

corvée /kɔrve/ *n.f.* chore.

cosaque /kɔzak/ *n.m.* Cossack.

cosmétique /kɔsmetik/ *a.* cosmetic.

cosmique /kɔsmik/ *a.* cosmic.

cosmonaute /kɔsmɔnot/ *n.m./f.*
cosmonaut.

cosmopolite /kɔsmɔpɔlit/ *a.* cosmopolitan.

cosmos /kɔsmɔs/ *n.m.* (*espace*)
(outer) space; (*univers*) cosmos.

cosse /kɔs/ *n.f.* (*de pois*) pod.

cossu /kɔsy/ *a.* (*gens*) well-to-do;
(*demeure*) opulent.

costaud, ~e /kɔsto, -d/ *a.* (*fam.*)
strong. —*n.m.* (*fam.*) strong man.

costum|e /kɔstym/ *n.m.* suit;
(*théâtre*) costume. **~é** *a.* dressed
up.

cote /kɔt/ *n.f.* (classification)
mark; (*en Bourse*) quotation; (*de
cheval*) odds (**de**, on); (*de candidat, acteur*) rating. **~ d'alerte**,
danger level.

côte /kot/ *n.f.* (*littoral*) coast;
(*pente*) hill; (*anat.*) rib; (*de porc*)
chop. **~ à côte**, side by side.
la C~ d'Azur, the (French)
Riviera.

côté /kote/ *n.m.* side; (*direction*)
way. **à ~**, nearby; (*voisin*)
nextdoor. **à ~ de**, next to;
(*comparé à*) compared to; (*cible*)
wide of. **aux ~s de**, by the side of
de ~, aside; (*regarder*) sideways.
mettre de ~, put aside. **de ce ~**,
this way. **de chaque ~**, on each
side. **de tous les ~s**, on every
side; (*partout*) everywhere. **du ~
de**, towards; (*proximité*) near;
(*provenance*) from.

coteau (*pl.* **~x**) /kɔto/ *n.m.* hill.

côtelette /kotlɛt/ *n.f.* chop.

coter /kɔte/ *v.t.* (*comm.*) quote;
(*apprécier, noter*) rate.

coterie /kɔtri/ *n.f.* clique.

côt|ier, ~ière /kotje, -jɛr/ *a.*
coastal.

cotis|er /kɔtize/ *v.i.* pay one's
contributions (**à**, to); (*à un club*)
pay one's subscription. **se ~er** *v.
pr.* club together. **~ation** *n.f.*
contribution(s); subscription.

coton /kɔtɔ̃/ *n.m.* cotton. ∼ **hydrophile**, cotton wool.

côtoyer /kotwaje/ *v.t.* skirt, run along; (*fréquenter*) rub shoulders with; (*fig.*) verge on.

cotte /kɔt/ *n.f.* (*d'ouvrier*) overalls.

cou /ku/ *n.m.* neck.

couchage /kuʃaʒ/ *n.m.* sleeping arrangements.

couchant /kuʃɑ̃/ *n.m.* sunset.

couche /kuʃ/ *n.f.* layer; (*de peinture*) coat; (*de bébé*) nappy. ∼**s**, (*méd.*) childbirth. ∼**s sociales**, social strata.

coucher /kuʃe/ *n.m.* ∼ (**du soleil**), sunset. —*v.t.* put to bed; (*loger*) put up; (*étendre*) lay down. ∼ (**par écrit**), set down. —*v.i.* sleep. **se** ∼ *v. pr.* go to bed; (*s'étendre*) lie down; (*soleil*) set. **couché** *a.* in bed; (*étendu*) lying down.

couchette /kuʃɛt/ *n.f.* (*rail.*) couchette; (*naut.*) bunk.

coucou /kuku/ *n.m.* cuckoo.

coude /kud/ *n.m.* elbow; (*de rivière etc.*) bend. ∼ **à coude**, side by side.

cou-de-pied (*pl.* **cous-de-pied**) /kudpje/ *n.m.* instep.

coudoyer /kudwaje/ *v.t.* rub shoulders with.

coudre† /kudr/ *v.t./i.* sew.

couenne /kwan/ *n.f.* (*de porc*) rind.

couette /kwɛt/ *n.f.* duvet, continental quilt.

couffin /kufɛ̃/ *n.m.* Moses basket.

couiner /kwine/ *v.i.* squeak.

coulant, ∼**e** /kulɑ̃, -t/ *a.* (*indulgent*) easy-going; (*fromage*) runny.

coulée /kule/ *n.f.* ∼ **de lave**, lava flow.

couler¹ /kule/ *v.i.* flow, run; (*fromage, nez*) run; (*fuir*) leak. —*v.t.* (*sculpture, métal*) cast; (*vie*) pass, lead. **se** ∼ *v. pr.* (*se glisser*) slip.

couler² /kule/ *v.t./i.* (*bateau*) sink.

couleur /kulœr/ *n.f.* colour;

(*peinture*) paint; (*cartes*) suit. ∼**s**, (*teint*) colour. **de** ∼, (*homme, femme*) coloured. **en** ∼**s**, (*télévision, film*) colour.

couleuvre /kulœvr/ *n.f.* (grass *ou* smooth) snake.

coulis /kuli/ *n.m.* (*culin.*) coulis.

coulisse /kulis/ *n.f.* (*de tiroir etc.*) runner. ∼**es**, (*théâtre*) wings. **à** ∼**e**, (*porte, fenêtre*) sliding. ∼**er** *v.i.* slide.

couloir /kulwar/ *n.m.* corridor; (*de bus*) gangway; (*sport*) lane.

coup /ku/ *n.m.* blow; (*choc*) knock; (*sport*) stroke; (*de crayon, chance, cloche*) stroke; (*de fusil, pistolet*) shot; (*fois*) time; (*aux échecs*) move. **à** ∼ **sûr**, definitely. **après** ∼, after the event. **boire un** ∼, have a drink. ∼ **de chiffon**, wipe (with a rag). ∼ **de coude**, nudge. ∼ **de couteau**, stab. ∼ **d'envoi**, kick-off. ∼ **d'état** (*pol.*) coup. ∼ **de feu**, shot. ∼ **de fil**, phone call. ∼ **de filet**, haul. ∼ **de frein**, sudden braking. ∼ **de grâce**, coup de grâce. ∼ **de main**, helping hand. **avoir le** ∼ **de main**, have the knack. ∼ **d'œil**, glance. ∼ **de pied**, kick. ∼ **de poing**, punch. ∼ **de sang**, (*méd.*) stroke. ∼ **de soleil**, sunburn. ∼ **de sonnette**, ring (on a bell). ∼ **de téléphone**, (tele)phone call. ∼ **de tête**, wild impulse. ∼ **de théâtre**, dramatic event. ∼ **de tonnerre**, thunderclap. ∼ **de vent**, gust of wind. ∼ **franc**, free kick. ∼ **sur coup**, in rapid succession. **d'un seul** ∼, in one go. **du premier** ∼, first go. **sale** ∼, dirty trick. **sous le** ∼ **de**, under the influence of. **sur le** ∼, immediately. **tenir le coup**, take it. —*n.m./f.* culprit.

coupe¹ /kup/ *n.f.* cup; (*de champagne*) goblet; (*à fruits*) dish.

coupe² /kup/ *n.f.* (*de vêtement etc.*)

cut; (*dessin*) section. **~ de cheveux**, haircut.

coupé /kupe/ *n.m.* (*voiture*) coupé.

coup|er /kupe/ *v.t./i.* cut; (*arbre*) cut down; (*arrêter*) cut off; (*voyage*) break; (*appétit*) take away; (*vin*) water down. **~er par**, take a short cut via. **se ~er** *v. pr.* cut o.s.; (*routes*) intersect. **~er la parole à**, cut short. **~e-papier** *n.m. invar.* paper-knife.

couperosé /kuproze/ *a.* blotchy.

couple /kupl/ *n.m.* couple.

coupler /kuple/ *v.t.* couple.

couplet /kuplɛ/ *n.m.* verse.

coupole /kupɔl/ *n.f.* dome.

coupon /kupɔ̃/ *n.m.* (*étoffe*) remnant; (*billet, titre*) coupon.

coupure /kupyr/ *n.f.* cut; (*billet de banque*) note; (*de presse*) cutting. **~ de courant**, power cut.

cour /kur/ *n.f.* (*court*)yard; (*de roi*) court; (*tribunal*) court. **~ de récréation**, playground. **~ martiale**, court martial. **faire la ~ à**, court.

courag|e /kuraʒ/ *n.m.* courage. **~eux, ~euse** *a.* courageous.

couramment /kuramã/ *adv.* frequently; (*parler*) fluently.

courant¹, **~e** /kurã, -t/ *a.* standard, ordinary; (*en cours*) current.

courant² /kurã/ *n.m.* current; (*de mode, d'idées*) trend. **~ d'air**, draught. **dans le ~ de**, in the course of. **être/mettre au ~ de**, know/tell about; (*à jour*) be/bring up to date on.

courbatur|e /kurbatyr/ *n.f.* ache. **~é** *a.* aching.

courbe /kurb/ *n.f.* curve. —*a.* curved.

courber /kurbe/ *v.t./i., se ~* *v. pr.* bend.

coureu|r, ~se /kurœr, -øz/ *n.m., f.* (*sport*) runner. **~r automobile**, racing driver. —*n.m.* womanizer.

courge /kurʒ/ *n.f.* marrow; (*Amer.*) squash.

courgette /kurʒɛt/ *n.f.* courgette; (*Amer.*) zucchini.

courir† /kurir/ *v.i.* run; (*se hâter*) rush; (*nouvelles etc.*) go round. —*v.t.* (*risque*) run; (*danger*) face; (*épreuve sportive*) run *ou* compete in; (*fréquenter*) do the rounds of; (*filles*) chase.

couronne /kurɔn/ *n.f.* crown; (*de fleurs*) wreath.

couronn|er /kurɔne/ *v.t.* crown. **~ement** *n.m.* coronation, crowning; (*fig.*) crowning achievement.

courrier /kurje/ *n.m.* post, mail; (*à écrire*) letters; (*de journal*) column.

courroie /kurwa/ *n.f.* strap; (*techn.*) belt.

courroux /kuru/ *n.m.* wrath.

cours /kur/ *n.m.* (*leçon*) class; (*série de leçons*) course; (*prix*) price; (*cote*) rate; (*déroulement d'une rivière*) course; (*allée*) avenue. **au ~ de**, (*monnaie*) be legal tender; (*fig.*) be current; (*scol.*) have a lesson. **~ d'eau**, river, stream. **~ du soir**, evening class. **~ magistral**, (*univ.*) lecture. **en ~**, current; (*travail*) in progress. **en ~ de route**, on the way.

course /kurs/ *n.f.* run(ning); (*épreuve de vitesse*) race; (*entre rivaux*) race; (*de projectile*) flight; (*voyage*) journey; (*commission*) errand. **~s**, (*achats*) shopping; (*de chevaux*) races.

cours|ier, ~ère /kursje, -jɛr/ *n.m., f.* messenger.

court¹, **~e** /kur, -t/ *a.* short. —*adv.* short. **à ~ de**, short of. **pris de ~**, caught unawares. **~-circuit** (*pl.* **~s-circuits**) *n.m.* short circuit.

court² /kur/ *n.m.* **~ (de tennis)**, (tennis) court.

court|ier, **∼ière** /kurtje, -jɛr/ *n.m., f.* broker.

courtisan /kurtizɑ̃/ *n.m.* courtier.

courtisane /kurtizan/ *n.f.* courtesan.

courtiser /kurtize/ *v.t.* court.

courtois, **∼e** /kurtwa, -z/ *a.* courteous. **∼ie** /-zi/ *n.f.* courtesy.

couscous /kuskus/ *n.m.* couscous.

cousin, **∼e** /kuzɛ̃, -in/ *n.m., f.* cousin. **∼ germain**, first cousin.

coussin /kusɛ̃/ *n.m.* cushion.

coût /ku/ *n.m.* cost.

couteau (*pl.* **∼x**) /kuto/ *n.m.* knife. **∼ à cran d'arrêt**, flick-knife.

coutellerie /kutɛlri/ *n.f.* (*magasin*) cutlery shop.

coût|er /kute/ *v.t./i.* cost. **∼e que coûte**, at all costs. **au prix ∼ant**, at cost (price). **∼eux**, **∼euse** *a.* costly.

coutum|e /kutym/ *n.f.* custom. **∼ier**, **∼ière** *a.* customary.

coutur|e /kutyr/ *n.f.* sewing; (*métier*) dressmaking; (*points*) seam. **∼ier** *n.m.* fashion designer. **∼ière** *n.f.* dressmaker.

couvée /kuve/ *n.f.* brood.

couvent /kuvɑ̃/ *n.m.* convent; (*de moines*) monastery.

couver /kuve/ *v.t.* (*œufs*) hatch; (*personne*) pamper; (*maladie*) be coming down with, be sickening for. —*v.i.* (*feu*) smoulder; (*mal*) be brewing.

couvercle /kuvɛrkl/ *n.m.* (*de marmite, boîte*) lid; (*d'objet allongé*) top.

couvert[1] /kuvɛr/ *a.* covered (**de**, with); (*habillé*) covered up; (*ciel*) overcast. —*n.m.* (*abri*) cover. **à ∼ de**, (*mil.*) under cover. **à ∼ de**, (*fig.*) safe from.

couvert[2] /kuvɛr/ *n.m.* (*à table*) place-setting; (*prix*) cover charge. **∼s**, (*couteaux etc.*) cutlery. **mettre le ∼**, lay the table.

couverture /kuvɛrtyr/ *n.f.* cover;

(*de lit*) blanket; (*toit*) roofing. **∼ chauffante**, electric blanket.

couveuse /kuvøz/ *n.f.* **∼ (artificielle)**, incubator.

couvreur /kuvrœr/ *n.m.* roofer.

couvr|ir† /kuvrir/ *v.t.* cover. **se ∼ir** *v. pr.* (*s'habiller*) cover up; (*se coiffer*) put one's hat on; (*ciel*) become overcast. **∼e-chef** *n.m.* hat. **∼e-feu** (*pl.* **∼e-feux**) *n.m.* curfew. **∼e-lit** *n.m.* bedspread.

cow-boy /koboj/ *n.m.* cowboy.

crabe /krab/ *n.m.* crab.

crachat /kraʃa/ *n.m.* spit(tle).

cracher /kraʃe/ *v.i.* spit; (*radio*) crackle. —*v.t.* spit (out).

crachin /kraʃɛ̃/ *n.m.* drizzle.

crack /krak/ *n.m.* (*fam.*) wizard, ace, prodigy.

craie /krɛ/ *n.f.* chalk.

craindre† /krɛdr/ *v.t.* be afraid of, fear; (*être sensible à*) be easily damaged by.

crainte /krɛ̃t/ *n.f.* fear. **de ∼ de/que**, for fear of/that.

crainti|f, **∼ve** /krɛ̃tif, -v/ *a.* timid.

cramoisi /kramwazi/ *a.* crimson.

crampe /krɑ̃p/ *n.f.* cramp.

crampon /krɑ̃pɔ̃/ *n.m.* (*de chaussure*) stud.

cramponner (se) /(sə)krɑ̃pɔne/ *v. pr.* **se ∼ à**, cling to.

cran /krɑ̃/ *n.m.* (*entaille*) notch; (*trou*) hole; (*courage: fam.*) pluck.

crâne /krɑn/ *n.m.* skull.

crâner /krɑne/ *v.i.* (*fam.*) swank.

crapaud /krapo/ *n.m.* toad.

crapul|e /krapyl/ *n.f.* villain. **∼eux**, **∼euse** *a.* sordid, foul.

craqu|er /krake/ *v.i.* crack, snap; (*plancher*) creak; (*couture*) split; (*fig.*) break down; (*céder*) give in. —*v.t.* **∼er une allumette**, strike a match. **∼ement** *n.m.* crack (-ing), snap(ping), creak(ing); striking.

crasse /kras/ *n.f.* grime. **∼eux**, **∼euse** *a.* grimy.

cratère /kratɛr/ n.m. crater.

cravache /kravaʃ/ n.f. horsewhip.

cravate /kravat/ n.f. tie.

crawl /krol/ n.m. (*nage*) crawl.

crayeu|x, ~se /krɛjø, -z/ a. chalky.

crayon /krɛjɔ̃/ n.m. pencil. **~ (de couleur)**, crayon. **~ à bille**, ball-point pen. **~ optique**, light pen.

créanc|ier, ~ière /kreɑ̃sje, -jɛr/ n.m., f. creditor.

créa|teur, ~trice /kreatœr, -tris/ a. creative. —n.m., f. creator.

création /kreasjɔ̃/ n.f. creation; (*comm.*) product.

créature /kreatyr/ n.f. creature.

crèche /krɛʃ/ n.f. day nursery; (*relig.*) crib.

crédibilité /kredibilite/ n.f. credibility.

crédit /kredi/ n.m. credit; (*banque*) bank. **~s**, funds. **à ~**, on credit. **faire ~**, give credit (**à**, to). **~er** /-te/ v.t. credit. **~eur, ~euse** /-tœr, -tøz/ a. in credit.

credo /kredo/ n.m. creed.

crédule /kredyl/ a. credulous.

créer /kree/ v.t. create.

crémation /kremasjɔ̃/ n.f. cremation.

crème /krɛm/ n.f. cream; (*dessert*) cream dessert. —a. invar. cream. —n.m. (*café*) **~**, white coffee. **~ anglaise**, fresh custard. **~ à raser**, shaving-cream.

crémeu|x, ~se /kremø, -z/ a. creamy.

crém|ier, ~ière /kremje, -jɛr/ n.m., f. dairyman, dairywoman. **~erie** /kremri/ n.f. dairy.

créneau (pl. **~x**) /kreno/ n.m. (*trou, moment*) slot; (*dans le marché*) gap; **faire un ~**, park between two cars.

créole /kreɔl/ n.m./f. Creole.

crêpe¹ /krɛp/ n.f. (*galette*) pancake. **~rie** n.f. pancake shop.

crêpe² /krɛp/ n.m. (*tissu*) crêpe; (*matière*) crêpe (rubber).

crépit|er /krepite/ v.i. crackle. **~ement** n.m. crackling.

crépu /krepy/ a. frizzy.

crépuscule /krepyskyl/ n.m. twilight, dusk.

crescendo /kreʃɛndo/ adv. & n.m. invar. crescendo.

cresson /kresɔ̃/ n.m. (water)cress.

crête /krɛt/ n.f. crest; (*de coq*) comb.

crétin, ~e /kretɛ̃, -in/ n.m., f. cretin.

creuser /krøze/ v.t. dig; (*évider*) hollow out; (*fig.*) go deeply into. **se ~ (la cervelle)**, (*fam.*) rack one's brains.

creuset /krøzɛ/ n.m. (*lieu*) melting-pot.

creu|x, ~se /krø, -z/ a. hollow; (*heures*) off-peak. —n.m. hollow; (*de l'estomac*) pit.

crevaison /krəvɛzɔ̃/ n.f. puncture.

crevasse /krəvas/ n.f. crack; (*de glacier*) crevasse; (*de la peau*) chap.

crevé /krəve/ a. (*fam.*) worn out.

crève-cœur /krɛvkœr/ n.m. invar. heart-break.

crever /krəve/ v.t./i. burst; (*pneu*) puncture burst; (*exténuer. fam.*) exhaust; (*mourir. fam.*) die; (*œil*) put out.

crevette /krəvɛt/ n.f. **~ (grise)**, shrimp. **~ (rose)**, prawn.

cri /kri/ n.m. cry; (*de douleur*) scream, cry.

criant, ~e /krijɑ̃, -t/ a. glaring.

criard, ~e /krijar, -d/ a. (*couleur*) garish; (*voix*) bawling.

crible /kribl/ n.m. sieve, riddle.

criblé /krible/ a. **~ de**, riddled with.

cric /krik/ n.m. (*auto.*) jack.

crier /krije/ v.i. (*fort*) shout, cry (out); (*de douleur*) scream; (*grincer*) creak. —v.t. (*ordre*) shout (out).

crim|e /krim/ *n.m.* crime; (*meurtre*) murder. **~inalité** *n.f.* crime. **~inel, ~inelle** *a.* criminal; *n.m., f.* criminal; (*assassin*) murderer.

crin /krɛ̃/ *n.m.* horsehair.

crinière /krinjɛr/ *n.f.* mane.

crique /krik/ *n.f.* creek.

criquet /krikɛ/ *n.m.* locust.

crise /kriz/ *n.f.* crisis; (*méd.*) attack; (*de colère*) fit. **~ cardiaque,** heart attack. **~ de foie,** bilious attack.

crisp|er /krispe/ *v.t.,* se **~er** *v. pr.* tense; (*poings*) clench. **~ation** *n.f.* tenseness; (*spasme*) twitch. **~é a.** tense.

crisser /krise/ *v.i.* crunch; (*pneu*) screech.

crist|al (*pl.* **~aux**) /kristal, -o/ *n.m.* crystal.

cristallin /kristalɛ̃, -in/ *a.* (*limpide*) crystal-clear.

cristalliser /kristalize/ *v.t./i.,* se **~** *v. pr.* crystallize.

critère /kritɛr/ *n.m.* criterion.

critique /kritik/ *a.* critical. —*n.f.* criticism; (*article*) review. —*n.m.* critic. **la ~,** (*personnes*) the critics.

critiquer /kritike/ *v.t.* criticize.

croasser /krɔase/ *v.i.* caw.

croc /kro/ *n.m.* (*dent*) fang; (*crochet*) hook.

croc-en-jambe (*pl.* **crocs-en-jambe**) /krɔkɑ̃ʒɑ̃b/ *n.m.* = **croche-pied.**

croche /krɔʃ/ *n.f.* quaver. **double ~,** semiquaver.

croche-pied /krɔʃpje/ *n.m.* **faire un ~ à,** trip up.

crochet /krɔʃɛ/ *n.m.* hook; (*détour*) detour; (*signe*) (square) bracket; (*tricot*) crochet. **faire au ~,** crochet.

crochu /krɔʃy/ *a.* hooked.

crocodile /krɔkɔdil/ *n.m.* crocodile.

crocus /krɔkys/ *n.m.* crocus.

croire† /krwar/ *v.t./i.* believe (à, en, in); (*estimer*) think, believe (que, that).

croisade /krwazad/ *n.f.* crusade.

croisé /krwaze/ *a.* (*veston*) double-breasted. —*n.m.* crusader.

croisée /krwaze/ *n.f.* window. **~ des chemins,** crossroads.

crois|er¹ /krwaze/ *v.t.,* se **~er** *v. pr.* cross; (*passant, véhicule*) pass (each other). **(se) ~er les bras,** fold one's arms. **(se) ~er les jambes,** cross one's legs. **~ement** *n.m.* crossing; passing; (*carrefour*) crossroads.

crois|er² /krwaze/ *v.i.* (*bateau*) cruise. **~eur** *n.m.* cruiser. **~ière** *n.f.* cruise.

croissan|t¹, ~te /krwasɑ̃, -t/ *a.* growing. **~ce** *n.f.* growth.

croissant² /krwasɑ̃/ *n.m.* crescent; (*pâtisserie*) croissant.

croître† /krwatr/ *v.i.* grow; (*lune*) wax.

croix /krwa/ *n.f.* cross. **~ gammée,** swastika. **C~-Rouge,** Red Cross.

croque-monsieur /krɔkməsjø/ *n.m. invar.* toasted ham and cheese sandwich.

croque-mort /krɔkmɔr/ *n.m.* undertaker's assistant.

croqu|er /krɔke/ *v.t./i.* crunch; (*dessiner*) sketch. **chocolat à ~er,** plain chocolate. **~ant, ~ante** *a.* crunchy.

croquet /krɔkɛ/ *n.m.* croquet.

croquette /krɔkɛt/ *n.f.* croquette.

croquis /krɔki/ *n.m.* sketch.

crosse /krɔs/ *n.f.* (*de fusil*) butt; (*d'évêque*) crook.

crotte /krɔt/ *n.f.* droppings.

crotté /krɔte/ *a.* muddy.

crottin /krɔtɛ̃/ *n.m.* (*horse*) dung.

crouler /krule/ *v.i.* collapse; (*être en ruines*) crumble.

croupe /krup/ *n.f.* rump; (*de colline*) brow. **en ~,** pillion.

croupier /krupje/ *n.m.* croupier.

croupir /krupir/ *v.i.* stagnate.

croustill|er /krustije/ *v.i.* be crusty. **~ant, ~ante** *a.* crusty; (*fig.*) spicy.

croûte /krut/ *n.f.* crust; (*de fromage*) rind; (*de plaie*) scab. **en ~,** (*culin.*) en croûte.

croûton /krutɔ̃/ *n.m.* (*bout de pain*) crust; (*avec potage*) croûton.

croyable /krwajabl/ *a.* credible.

croyan|t, ~te /krwajɑ̃, -t/ *n.m., f.* believer. **~ce** *n.f.* belief.

CRS *abrév.* (*Compagnies républicaines de sécurité*) French state security police.

cru¹ /kry/ *voir* **croire.**

cru² /kry/ *a.* raw; (*lumière*) harsh; (*propos*) crude. —*n.m.* vineyard; (*vin*) wine.

crû /kry/ *voir* **croître.**

cruauté /kryote/ *n.f.* cruelty.

cruche /kryʃ/ *n.f.* pitcher.

cruc|ial (*m. pl.* **~iaux**) /krysjal, -jo/ *a.* crucial.

crucif|ier /krysifje/ *v.t.* crucify. **~ixion** *n.f.* crucifixion.

crucifix /krysifi/ *n.m.* crucifix.

crudité /krydite/ *n.f.* (*de langage*) crudeness. **~s,** (*culin.*) raw vegetables.

crue /kry/ *n.f.* rise in water level. **en ~,** in spate.

cruel, ~le /kryɛl/ *a.* cruel.

crûment /krymɑ̃/ *adv.* crudely.

crustacés /krystase/ *n.m. pl.* shellfish.

crypte /kript/ *n.f.* crypt.

Cuba /kyba/ *n.m.* Cuba.

cubain, ~e /kybɛ̃, -ɛn/ *a. & n.m., f.* Cuban.

cub|e /kyb/ *n.m.* cube. —*a.* (*mètre etc.*) cubic. **~ique** *a.* cubic.

cueillir|t /kœjir/ *v.t.* pick, gather; (*personne: fam.*) pick up. **~ette** *n.f.* picking, gathering.

cuill|er, ~ère /kɥijɛr/ *n.f.* spoon. **~er à soupe,** soup-spoon; (*mesure*) tablespoonful. **~erée** *n.f.* spoonful.

cuir /kɥir/ *n.m.* leather. **~ chevelu,** scalp.

cuirassé /kɥirase/ *n.m.* battleship.

cuire /kɥir/ *v.t./i.* cook; (*picoter*) smart. **~ (au four),** bake. **faire ~,** cook.

cuisine /kɥizin/ *n.f.* kitchen; (*art*) cookery, cooking; (*aliments*) cooking. **faire la ~,** cook.

cuisin|er /kɥizine/ *v.t./i.* cook; (*interroger: fam.*) grill. **~ier, ~ière** *n.m., f.* cook; *n.f.* (*appareil*) cooker, stove.

cuisse /kɥis/ *n.f.* thigh; (*de poulet, mouton*) leg.

cuisson /kɥisɔ̃/ *n.m.* cooking.

cuit, ~e /kɥi, -t/ *a.* cooked. **bien ~,** well done *ou* cooked. **trop ~,** overdone.

cuivr|e /kɥivr/ *n.m.* copper. **~e (jaune),** brass. **~es,** (*mus.*) brass. **~é** *a.* coppery.

cul /ky/ *n.m.* (*derrière: fam.*) backside, bum.

culasse /kylas/ *n.f.* (*auto.*) cylinder head; (*arme*) breech.

culbut|e /kylbyt/ *n.f.* somersault; (*chute*) tumble. **~er** *v.i.* tumble; *v.t.* knock over.

cul-de-sac (*pl.* **culs-de-sac**) /kydsak/ *n.m.* cul-de-sac.

culinaire /kylinɛr/ *a.* culinary; (*recette*) cooking.

culminer /kylmine/ *v.i.* reach the highest point.

culot¹ /kylo/ *n.m.* (*audace: fam.*) nerve, cheek.

culot² /kylo/ *n.m.* (*fond: techn.*) base.

culotte /kylot/ *n.f.* (*de femme*) knickers; (*Amer.*) panties. **~ (de cheval),** (*riding*) breeches. **~ courte,** short trousers.

culpabilité /kylpabilite/ *n.f.* guilt.

culte /kylt/ *n.m.* cult, worship; (*religion*) religion; (*protestant*) service.

cultivé /kyltive/ *a.* cultured.

cultiv|er /kyltive/ *v.t.* cultivate;

(*plantes*) grow. **~ateur**, **~atrice** *n.m.*, *f.* farmer.

culture /kyltyr/ *n.f.* cultivation; (*de plantes*) growing; (*agriculture*) farming; (*éducation*) culture. **~s**, (*terrains*) lands under cultivation. **~ physique**, physical training.

culturel, **~le** /kyltyrɛl/ *a.* cultural.

cumuler /kymyle/ *v.t.* (*fonctions*) hold simultaneously.

cupide /kypid/ *a.* grasping.

cure /kyr/ *n.f.* (course of) treatment, cure.

curé /kyre/ *n.m.* (parish) priest.

cur|er /kyre/ *v.t.* clean. **se ~er les dents/ongles**, clean one's teeth/nails. **~e-dent** *n.m.* toothpick. **~e-pipe** *n.m.* pipe-cleaner.

curieu|x, **~se** /kyrjø, -z/ *a.* curious. **—**, *n.m.*, *f.* (*badaud*) onlooker. **~sement** *adv.* curiously.

curiosité /kyrjozite/ *n.f.* curiosity; (*objet*) curio; (*spectacle*) unusual sight.

curriculum vitae /kyrikylɔm vite/ *n.m. invar.* curriculum vitae.

curseur /kyrsœr/ *n.m.* cursor.

cutané /kytane/ *a.* skin.

cuve /kyv/ *n.f.* tank.

cuvée /kyve/ *n.f.* (*de vin*) vintage.

cuvette /kyvɛt/ *n.f.* bowl; (*de lavabo*) (wash-)basin; (*des cabinets*) pan, bowl.

CV /seve/ *n.m.* CV.

cyanure /sjanyr/ *n.m.* cyanide.

cybernétique /sibɛrnetik/ *n.f.* cybernetics.

cycl|e /sikl/ *n.m.* cycle. **~ique** *a.* cyclic(al).

cyclis|te /siklist/ *n.m./f.* cyclist. **—***a.* cycle. **~me** *n.m.* cycling.

cyclomoteur /syklɔmɔtœr/ *n.m.* moped.

cyclone /syklon/ *n.m.* cyclone.

cygne /siɲ/ *n.m.* swan.

cylindr|e /silɛdr/ *n.m.* cylinder. **~ique** *a.* cylindrical.

cylindrée /silɛdre/ *n.f.* (*de moteur*) capacity.

cymbale /sɛbal/ *n.f.* cymbal.

cyni|que /sinik/ *a.* cynical. **—***n.m.* cynic. **~sme** *n.m.* cynicism.

cyprès /siprɛ/ *n.m.* cypress.

cypriote /siprijɔt/ *a.* & *n.m./f.* Cypriot.

cystite /sistit/ *n.f.* cystitis.

D

d' /d/ *voir* de.

d'abord /dabɔr/ *adv.* first; (*au début*) at first.

dactylo /daktilo/ *n.f.* typist. **~(graphie)** *n.f.* typing. **~graphe** *n.f.* typist. **~graphier** *v.t.* type.

dada /dada/ *n.m.* hobby-horse.

dahlia /dalja/ *n.m.* dahlia.

daigner /deɲe/ *v.t.* deign.

daim /dɛ̃/ *n.m.* (fallow) deer; (*cuir*) suede.

dalle /dal/ *n.f.* paving stone, slab. **~age** *n.m.* paving.

daltonien, **~ne** /daltɔnjɛ̃, -jɛn/ *a.* colour-blind.

dame /dam/ *n.f.* lady; (*cartes*, *échecs*) queen. **~s**, (*jeu*) draughts; (*jeu*: *Amer.*) checkers.

damier /damje/ *n.m.* draughtboard; (*Amer.*) checker-board. **à ~**, chequered.

damn|er /dane/ *v.t.* damn. **~ation** *n.f.* damnation.

dancing /dɑ̃siŋ/ *n.m.* dance-hall.

dandiner (se) /(sə)dɑ̃dine/ *v. pr.* waddle.

Danemark /danmark/ *n.m.* Denmark.

danger /dɑ̃ʒe/ *n.m.* danger. **en ~**, in danger. **mettre en ~**, endanger.

dangereu|x, **~se** /dɑ̃ʒrø, -z/ *a.* dangerous.

danois, ~e /danwa, -z/ a. Danish. —n.m., f. Dane. —n.m. (lang.) Danish.

dans /dɑ̃/ prép. in; (mouvement) into; (à l'intérieur de) inside, in; (approximation) about. ~ dix jours, in ten days' time. prendre/boire/etc. ~, take/drink/etc. out of or from.

dans|e /dɑ̃s/ n.f. dance; (art) dancing. ~er v.t./i. dance. ~eur, ~euse n.m., f. dancer.

dard /dar/ n.m. (d'animal) sting.

darne /darn/ n.f. steak (of fish).

dat|e /dat/ n.f. date. ~e limite, deadline; ~e limite de vente, sell-by date; ~e de péremption, expiry date. ~er v.t./i. date. à ~er de, as from.

datt|e /dat/ n.f. (fruit) date. ~ier n.m. date-palm.

daube /dob/ n.f. casserole.

dauphin /dofɛ̃/ n.m. (animal) dolphin.

davantage /davɑ̃taʒ/ adv. more; (plus longtemps) longer. ~ de, more. ~ que, more than; longer than.

de, d'* /də, d/ prép. (de + le = du, de + les = des) of; (provenance) from; (moyen, manière) from; (agent) by. —article some; (interrogation) any, some. le livre de mon ami, my friend's book. un pont de fer, an iron bridge. dix mètres de haut, ten metres high. du pain, (some) bread; une tranche de pain, a slice of bread. des fleurs, (some) flowers.

dé /de/ n.m. (à jouer) dice; (à coudre) thimble. dés, (jeu) dice.

dealer /dilər/ n.m. (drug) dealer.

débâcle /debɑkl/ n.f. (mil.) rout.

déball|er /debale/ v.t. unpack; (montrer, péj.) spill out. ~age n.m. unpacking.

débarbouiller /debarbuje/ v.t. wash the face of. se ~ v. pr. wash one's face.

débarcadère /debarkadɛr/ n.m. landing-stage.

débardeur /debardœr/ n.m. docker; (vêtement) tank top.

débarqu|er /debarke/ v.t./i. disembark, land; (arriver. fam.) turn up. ~ement n.m. disembarkation.

débarras /debara/ n.m. junk room. bon ~!, good riddance!

débarrasser /debarase/ v.t. clear (de, of). ~ qn. de, take from s.o.; (défaut, ennemi) rid s.o. of. se ~ de, get rid of, rid o.s. of.

débat /deba/ n.m. debate.

débattre†¹ /debatr/ v.t. debate. —v.i. ~ de, discuss.

débattre†² (se) /(sə)debatr/ v. pr. struggle (to get free).

débauch|e /debof/ n.f. debauchery; (fig.) profusion. ~er¹ v.t. debauch.

débaucher² /debofe/ v.t. (licencier) lay off.

débile /debil/ a. weak; (fam.) stupid. —n.m./f. moron.

débit /debi/ n.m. (rate of) flow; (de magasin) turnover; (élocution) delivery; (de compte) debit. ~ de tabac, tobacconist's shop; ~ de boissons, licensed premises.

débit|er /debite/ v.t. cut up; (fournir) produce; (vendre) sell; (dire. péj.) spout; (compte) debit. ~teur, ~trice n.m., f. debtor; a. (compte) in debit.

débl|ayer /debleje/ v.t. clear. ~aiement, ~ayage n.m. clearing.

débloquer /debloke/ v.t. (prix, salaires) free. ~cage n.m. freeing.

déboires /debwar/ n.m. pl. disappointments.

déboiser /debwaze/ v.t. clear (of trees).

déboîter /debwate/ v.i. (*véhicule*) pull out. —v.t. (*membre*) dislocate.

débord|er /deborde/ v.i. overflow. —v.t. (*dépasser*) extend beyond. **~er de,** (*joie etc.*) be overflowing with. **~é á** snowed under (de, with). **~ement** n.m. overflowing.

débouché /debuʃe/ n.m. opening; (*carrière*) prospect; (*comm.*) outlet; (*sortie*) exit.

débouch|er /debuʃe/ v.t. (*bouteille*) uncork; (*évier*) unblock. —v.i. emerge (de, from). **~ sur,** (*rue*) lead into.

débourser /deburse/ v.t. pay out.

déboussolé /debusole/ a. (*fam.*) disorientated, disoriented.

debout /dabu/ adv. standing; (*levé, éveillé*) up. **être ~, se tenir ~,** be standing, stand. **se mettre ~,** stand up.

déboutonner /debutone/ v.t. unbutton. **se ~** v. pr. unbutton o.s.; (*vêtement*) come undone.

débraillé /debraje/ a. slovenly.

débrancher /debrãʃe/ v.t. unplug, disconnect.

débray|er /debreje/ v.i. (*auto.*) declutch; (*faire grève*) stop work. **~age** /debrejaʒ/ n.m. (*pédale*) clutch; (*grève*) stoppage.

débris /debri/ n.m. pl. fragments; (*détritus*) rubbish, debris.

débrouill|er /debruje/ v.t. disentangle; (*problème*) sort out. **se ~er** v. pr. manage. **~ard, ~arde** a. (*fam.*) resourceful.

débroussailler /debrusaje/ v.t. clear (of brushwood).

début /deby/ n.m. beginning. **faire ses ~s,** (*en public*) make one's début.

début|er /debyte/ v.i. begin; (*dans un métier etc.*) start out. **~ant, ~ante** n.m., f. beginner.

déca /deka/ n.m. decaffeinated coffee.

décaféiné /dekafeine/ a. decaffeinated. —n.m. du **~,** decaffeinated coffee.

deçà (en) /(ã)dəsa/ adv. this side. —*prép.* **en ~ de,** this side of.

décacheter /dekaʃte/ v.t. open.

décade /dekad/ n.f. ten days; (*décennie*) decade.

décaden|t, /dekadɑ̃, -t/ a. decadent. **~ce** n.f. decadence.

décalcomanie /dekalkɔmani/ n.f. transfer; (*Amer.*) decal.

décal|er /dekale/ v.t. shift. **~age** n.m. (*écart*) gap. **~age horaire,** time difference.

décalquer /dekalke/ v.t. trace.

décamper /dekɑ̃pe/ v.i. clear off.

décanter /dekɑ̃te/ v.t. allow to settle. **se ~** v. pr. settle.

décap|er /dekape/ v.t. scrape down; (*surface peinte*) strip. **~ant** n.m. chemical agent; (*pour peinture*) paint stripper.

décapotable /dekapotabl/ a. convertible.

décapsul|er /dekapsyle/ v.t. take the cap off. **~eur** n.m. bottle-opener.

décarcasser (se) /(sə)dekarkase/ v. pr. (*fam.*) work o.s. to death.

décathlon /dekatlɔ̃/ n.m. decathlon.

décéd|er /desede/ v.i. die. **~é á** deceased.

décel|er /desle/ v.t. detect; (*démontrer*) reveal. **~able** a. detectable.

décembre /desɑ̃br/ n.m. December.

décennie /deseni/ n.f. decade.

décen|t, ~ente /desɑ̃, -t/ a. decent. **~emment** /-amɑ̃/ adv. decently. **~ence** n.f. decency.

décentralis|er /desɑ̃tralize/ v.t. decentralize. **~ation** n.f. decentralization.

déception /desɛpsjɔ̃/ n.f. disappointment.

décerner /deserne/ v.t. award.

décès /dese/ *n.m.* death.

décev|oir† /dɛsvwar/ *v.t.* disappoint. **~ant,** *e a.* disappointing.

déchaîn|er /deʃene/ *v.t.* (*violence etc.*) unleash; (*enthousiasme etc.*) arouse a good deal of. **se ~er** *v. pr.* erupt. **~ement** /-ɛnmɑ̃/ *n.m.* (*de passions*) outburst.

décharge /deʃarʒ/ *n.f.* (*salve*) volley of shots. **~** (*électrique*), electrical discharge. **~** (*publique*), rubbish tip.

décharg|er /deʃarʒe/ *v.t.* unload; (*arme,accusé*) discharge. **~er de,** release from. **se ~er** *v. pr.* (*batterie, pile*) go flat. **~ement** *n.m.* unloading.

décharné /deʃarne/ *a.* bony.

déchausser (se) /(sə)deʃose/ *v. pr.* take off one's shoes; (*dent*) work loose.

dèche /dɛʃ/ *n.f.* **dans la ~,** broke.

déchéance /deʃeɑ̃s/ *n.f.* decay.

déchet /deʃɛ/ *n.m.* (*reste*) scrap; (*perte*) waste. **~s,** (*ordures*) refuse.

déchiffrer /deʃifre/ *v.t.* decipher.

déchiqueter /deʃikte/ *v.t.* tear to shreds.

déchir|ant, **~ante** /deʃirɑ̃, -t/ *a.* heart-breaking. **~ement** *n.m.* heart-break; (*conflit*) split.

déchir|er /deʃire/ *v.t.* tear; (*lacérer*) tear up; (*arracher*) tear off *ou* out; (*diviser*) tear apart; (*oreilles: fig.*) split. **se ~er** *v. pr.* tear. **~ure** *n.f.* tear.

déch|oir /deʃwar/ *v.i.* demean o.s. **~oir de,** (*rang*) lose, fall from. **~u a.** fallen.

décibel /desibɛl/ *n.m.* decibel.

décid|er /deside/ *v.t.* decide on; (*persuader*) persuade. **~er que/ de,** decide that/to. **—***v.i.* decide. **~er de qch.,** decide on sth. **se ~er** *v. pr.* make up one's mind (**à,** to). **~é a.** (*résolu*) determined; (*fixé, marqué*) decided. **~ément** *adv.* really.

décim|al, **~ale** (*m. pl.* **~aux**) /desimal, -o/ *a.* & *n.f.* decimal.

décimètre /desimɛtr/ *n.m.* decimetre.

décisi|f, **~ve** /desizif,. -v/ *a.* decisive.

décision /desizjɔ̃/ *n.f.* decision.

déclar|er /deklare/ *v.t.* declare; (*naissance*) register. **se ~er** *v. pr.* (*feu*) break out. **~er forfait,** (*sport*) withdraw. **~ation** *n.f.* declaration; (*commentaire politique*) statement. **~ation d'impôts,** tax return.

déclasser /deklose/ *v.t.* (*coureur*) relegate; (*hôtel*) downgrade.

déclench|er /deklɑ̃ʃe/ *v.t.* (*techn.*) release, set off; (*lancer*) launch; (*provoquer*) trigger off. **se ~er** *v. pr.* (*techn.*) go off. **~eur** *n.m.* (*photo.*) trigger.

déclic /deklik/ *n.m.* click; (*techn.*) trigger mechanism.

déclin /deklɛ̃/ *n.m.* decline.

déclin|er[1] /dekline/ *v.i.* decline. **~aison** *n.f.* (*lang.*) declension.

décliner[2] /dekline/ *v.t.* (*refuser*) decline; (*dire*) state.

déclivité /deklivite/ *n.f.* slope.

décocher /dekɔʃe/ *v.t.(coup*) fling; (*regard*) shoot.

décoder /dekɔde/ *v.t.* decode.

décoiffer /dekwafe/ *v.t.* (*ébouriffer*) disarrange the hair of.

décoincer /dekwɛ̃se/ *v.t.* free.

décoll|er[1] /dekɔle/ *v.i.* (*avion*) take off. **~age** *n.m.* take-off.

décoller[2] /dekɔle/ *v.t.* unstick.

décolleté /dekɔlte/ *a.* low-cut. **—***n.m.* low neckline.

décolor|er /dekɔlore/ *v.t.* fade; (*cheveux*) bleach. **se ~er** *v. pr.* fade. **~ation** *n.f.* bleaching.

décombres /dekɔ̃br/ *n.m. pl.* rubble.

décommander /dekɔmɑ̃de/ *v.t.* cancel.

décompos|er /dekɔ̃poze/ *v.t.*

break up; (*substance*) decompose; (*visage*) contort. se ⁓er *v. pr.* (*pourrir*) decompose. ⁓ition *n.f.* decomposition.

decompt|e /dekɔ̃t/ *n.m.* deduction; (*détail*) breakdown. ⁓er *v.t.* deduct.

déconcerter /dekɔ̃sɛrte/ *v.t.* disconcert.

décongel|er /dekɔ̃ʒle/ *v.t.* thaw. ⁓ation *n.f.* thawing.

décongestionner /dekɔ̃ʒɛstjɔne/ *v.t.* relieve congestion in.

déconseill|er /dekɔ̃seje/ *v.t.* ⁓er qch. à qn., advise s.o. against sth. ⁓é *a.* not advisable, inadvisable.

décontenancer /dekɔ̃tnɑ̃se/ *v.t.* disconcert.

décontract|er /dekɔ̃trakte/ *v.t.*, se ⁓ *v. pr.* relax. ⁓é *a.* relaxed.

déconvenue /dekɔ̃vny/ *n.f.* disappointment.

décor /dekɔr/ *n.m.* (*paysage, théâtre*) scenery; (*cinéma*) set; (*cadre*) setting; (*de maison*) décor.

décorati|f, ⁓ve /dekɔratif, -v/ *a.* decorative.

décor|er /dekɔre/ *v.t.* decorate. ⁓ateur, ⁓atrice *n.m., f.* (*interior*) decorator. ⁓ation *n.f.* decoration.

décortiquer /dekɔrtike/ *v.t.* shell; (*fig.*) dissect.

découdre (se) /(sə)dekudr/ *v. pr.* come unstitched.

découler /dekule/ *v.i.* ⁓ de, follow from.

découp|er /dekupe/ *v.t.* cut up; (*viande*) carve; (*détacher*) cut out. se ⁓er sur, stand out against. ⁓age *n.m.* (*image*) cut-out.

décourag|er /dekuraʒe/ *v.t.* discourage. se ⁓er *v. pr.* become discouraged. ⁓ement *n.m.* discouragement. ⁓é *a.* discouraged.

décousu /dekuzy/ *a.* (*vêtement*) falling apart; (*idées etc.*) disjointed.

découvert, ⁓e /dekuvɛr, -t/ *a.*

(*tête etc.*) bare; (*terrain*) open. —*n.m.* (*de compte*) overdraft. —*n.f.* discovery. à ⁓, exposed; (*fig.*) openly. à la ⁓e de, in search of.

découvrir† /dekuvrir/ *v.t.* discover; (*enlever ce qui couvre*) uncover; (*voir*) see; (*montrer*) reveal. se ⁓ *v. pr.* uncover o.s.; (*se décoiffer*) take one's hat off; (*ciel*) clear.

décrasser /dekrase/ *v.t.* clean.

décrépit, ⁓e /dekrepi, -t/ *a.* decrepit. ⁓ude *n.f.* decay.

décret /dekrɛ/ *n.m.* decree. ⁓er /-ete/ *v.t.* decree.

décrié /dekrije/ *v.t.* decried.

décrire† /dekrir/ *v.t.* describe.

décrisp|er (se) /(sə)dekrispe/ *v. pr.* become less tense. ⁓ation *n.f.* lessening of tension.

décroch|er /dekrɔʃe/ *v.t.* unhook; (*obtenir: fam.*) get. —*v.i.* (*abandonner: fam.*) give up. ⁓er (le téléphone), pick up the phone. ⁓é *a.* (*téléphone*) off the hook.

décroître /dekrwatr/ *v.i.* decrease.

décrue /dekry/ *n.f.* going down (of river water).

déçu /desy/ *a.* disappointed.

décupl|e /dekypl/ *n.m.* au ⁓, tenfold. le ⁓e de, ten times. ⁓er *v.t./i.* increase tenfold.

dédaign|er /dedeɲe/ *v.t.* scorn. ⁓er de faire, consider it beneath one to do. ⁓eux, ⁓euse /dedeɲø, -z/ *a.* scornful.

dédain /dedɛ̃/ *n.m.* scorn.

dédale /dedal/ *n.m.* maze.

dedans /dədɑ̃/ *adv. & n.m.* inside. au ⁓ (de), inside. en ⁓, on the inside.

dédicac|e /dedikas/ *n.f.* dedication, inscription. ⁓er *v.t.* dedicate, inscribe.

dédier /dedje/ *v.t.* dedicate.

dédommag|er /dedɔmaʒe/ *v.t.* compensate (**de**, for). ⁓ement *n.m.* compensation.

dédouaner /dedwane/ v.t. clear through customs.

dédoubler /deduble/ v.t. split into two. ~ **un train**, put on a relief train.

déd|uire† /dedɥir/ v.t. deduct; (conclure) deduce. ~**uction** n.f. deduction; ~**uction d'impôts** tax deduction.

déesse /deɛs/ n.f. goddess.

défaillance /defajɑ̃s/ n.f. weakness; (évanouissement) black-out; (panne) failure.

défaill|ir /defajir/ v.i. faint; (forces etc.) fail. ~**ant,** ~**ante** a. (personne) faint; (candidat) defaulting.

défaire† /defɛr/ v.t. undo; (valise) unpack; (démonter) take down; (débarrasser) rid. **se** ~ v. pr. come undone. **se** ~ **de**, rid o.s. of.

défait, ~**e¹** /defɛ, -t/ a. (cheveux) ruffled; (visage) haggard.

défaite² /defɛt/ n.f. defeat.

défaitisme /defetizm/ n.m. defeatism.

défaitiste /defetist/ a. & n.m./f. defeatist.

défalquer /defalke/ v.t. (somme) deduct.

défaut /defo/ n.m. fault, defect; (d'un verre, diamant, etc.) flaw; (carence) lack; (pénurie) shortage. **à** ~ **de**, for lack of. **en** ~, at fault. **faire** ~, (argent etc.) be lacking. **par** ~, (jurid.) in one's absence.

défav|eur /defavœr/ n.f. disfavour. ~**orable** a. unfavourable.

défavoriser /defavɔrize/ v.t. put at a disadvantage.

défection /defɛksjɔ̃/ n.f. desertion. **faire** ~, desert.

défect|ueux, ~**ueuse** /defɛktɥø, -z/ a. faulty, defective. ~**uosité** n.f. faultiness; (défaut) fault.

défendre /defɑ̃dr/ v.t. defend; (interdire) forbid. ~ **à qn. de,**

forbid s.o. to. **se** ~ v. pr. defend o.s.; (se débrouiller) manage; (se protéger) protect o.s. **se** ~ **de,** (refuser) refrain from.

défense /defɑ̃s/ n.f. defence; (d'éléphant) tusk. ~ **de fumer,** etc., no smoking/etc.

défenseur /defɑ̃sœr/ n.m. defender.

défensi|f, ~**ve** /defɑ̃sif, -v/ a. & n.f. defensive.

déféren|t, ~**te** /deferɑ̃, -t/ a. deferential. ~**ce** n.f. deference.

déférer /defere/ v.t. (jurid.) refer. —v.i. ~ **à,** (avis etc.) defer to.

déferler /defɛrle/ v.i. (vagues) break; (violence etc.) erupt.

défi /defi/ n.m. challenge; (refus) defiance. **mettre au** ~, challenge.

déficeler /defisle/ v.t. untie.

déficience /defisjɑ̃s/ n.f. deficiency.

déficient /defisjɑ̃/ a. deficient.

déficit /defisit/ n.m. deficit. ~**aire** a. in deficit.

défier /defje/ v.t. challenge; (braver) defy. **se** ~ **de,** mistrust.

défilé¹ /defile/ n.m. procession; (mil.) parade; (fig.) (continual) stream. ~ **de mode,** fashion parade.

défilé² /defile/ n.m. (géog.) gorge.

défiler /defile/ v.i. march (past); (visiteurs) stream; (images) flash by. **se** ~ v. pr. (fam.) sneak off.

défini /defini/ a. definite.

définir /definir/ v.t. define.

définissable /definisabl/ a. definable.

définiti|f, ~**ve** /definitif, -v/ a. final; (permanent) definitive. **en** ~**ve,** in the final analysis. ~**vement** adv. definitively, permanently.

définition /definisjɔ̃/ n.f. definition; (de mots croisés) clue.

déflagration /deflagrasjɔ̃/ n.f. explosion.

déflation /deflɑsjɔ̃/ n.f. deflation. **~niste** /-jɔnist/ a. deflationary.

défoncer /defɔ̃se/ v.t. (porte etc.) break down; (route, terrain) dig up; (lit) break the springs of. **se ~** v. pr. (fam.) work like mad; (drogué) get high.

déform|er /deforme/ v.t. put out of shape; (membre) deform; (faits, pensée) distort. **~ation** n.f. loss of shape; deformation; distortion.

défouler (se) /(sə)defule/ v. pr. let off steam.

défraîchir (se) /(sə)defreʃir/ v. pr. become faded.

défrayer /defreje/ v.t. (payer) pay the expenses of.

défricher /defriʃe/ v.t. clear (for cultivation).

défroisser /defrwase/ v.t. smooth out.

défunt, ~e /defœ̃, -t/ a. (mort) late. —n.m.,f. deceased.

dégagé /degaʒe/ a. clear; (ton) free and easy.

dégag|er /degaʒe/ v.t. (exhaler) give off; (désencombrer) clear; (délivrer) free; (faire ressortir) bring out. —v.i. (football) kick the ball (down the pitch ou field). **se ~er** v. pr. free o.s.; (ciel, rue) clear; (odeur etc.) emanate. **~ement** n.m. giving off; clearing; freeing; (espace) clearing; (football) clearance.

dégaîner /degene/ v.t./i. draw.

dégarnir /degarnir/ v.t. clear, empty. **se ~** v. pr. clear, empty; (crâne) go bald.

dégâts /degɑ/ n.m. pl. damage.

dégel /deʒɛl/ n.m. thaw. **~er** /deʒle/ v.t./i. thaw (out). **(faire) ~er,** (culin.) thaw.

dégénér|er /deʒenere/ v.i. degenerate. **~é, ~ée** a. & n.m., f. degenerate.

dégingandé /deʒɛ̃gɑ̃de/ a. gangling.

dégivrer /deʒivre/ v.t. (auto.) de-ice; (frigo) defrost.

déglacer /deglase/ v.t. (culin.) deglaze.

dégling|uer /deglɛ̃ge/ (fam.) v.t. knock about. **se ~er** v. pr. fall to bits. **~é** adj. falling to bits.

dégonfl|er /degɔ̃fle/ v.t. let down, deflate. **se ~er** v. pr. (fam.) get cold feet. **~é** a. (pneu) flat; (lâche: fam.) yellow.

dégorger /degorʒe/ v.i. faire ~, (culin.) soak.

dégouliner /deguline/ v.i. trickle.

dégourdi /degurdi/ a. smart.

dégourdir /degurdir/ v.t. (membre, liquide) warm up. **se ~ les jambes,** stretch one's legs.

dégoût /degu/ n.m. disgust.

dégoût|er /degute/ v.t. disgust. **~er qn. de qch.,** put s.o. off sth. **~ant, ~ante** a. disgusting. **~é** a. disgusted. **~é de,** sick of. **faire le ~é,** look disgusted.

dégradant /degradɑ̃/ a. degrading.

dégrader /degrade/ v.t. degrade; (abîmer) damage. **se ~** v. pr. (se détériorer) deteriorate.

dégrafer /degrafe/ v.t. unhook.

degré /dəgre/ n.m. degree; (d'escalier) step.

dégressi|f /degresif/ ~**ve** /degresif, -v/ a. gradually lower.

dégrèvement /degrɛvmɑ̃/ n.m. ~ **fiscal** ou **d'impôts,** tax reduction.

dégrever /degrəve/ v.t. reduce the tax on.

dégringol|er /degrɛ̃gole/ v.i. tumble (down). —v.t. rush down. **~ade** n.f. tumble.

dégrossir /degrosir/ v.t. (bois) trim; (projet) rough out.

déguerpir /degerpir/ v.i. clear off.

dégueulasse /degœlas/ a. (argot) disgusting, lousy.

dégueuler /degœle/ v.t. (argot) throw up.

déguis|er /degize/ v.t. disguise. se **~er** v. pr. disguise o.s.; (au carnaval etc.) dress up. **~ement** n.m. disguise; (de carnaval etc.) fancy dress.

dégust|er /degyste/ v.t. taste, sample; (savourer) enjoy. **~ation** n.f. tasting, sampling.

déhancher (se) /(sə)deɑ̃ʃe/ v. pr. sway one's hips.

dehors /dəɔr/ adv. & n.m. outside. —n.m. pl. (aspect de qn.) exterior. au **~** (de), outside. en **~** de, outside; (hormis) apart from. jeter/mettre/etc. **~**, throw/put/ etc. out.

déjà /deʒa/ adv. already; (avant) before, already.

déjà-vu /deʒavy/ n.m. inv. déjà vu.

déjeuner /deʒœne/ v.i. (have) lunch; (le matin) (have) breakfast. —n.m. lunch. (petit) **~**, breakfast.

déjouer /deʒwe/ v.t. thwart.

delà /dəla/ adv. & prép. au **~** (de), en **~** (de), par **~**, beyond.

délabrer (se) /(sə)delɑbre/ v.t. become dilapidated.

délacer /delase/ v.t. undo.

délai /delɛ/ n.m. time-limit; (attente) wait; (sursis) extension (of time). sans **~**, without delay. dans les plus brefs **~s**, as soon as possible.

délaisser /delese/ v.t. desert.

délass|er /delase/ v.t., se **~er** v. pr. relax. **~ement** n.m. relaxation.

délation /delasjɔ̃/ n.f. informing.

délavé /delave/ a. faded.

délayer /deleje/ v.t. mix (with liquid); (idée) drag out.

delco /dɛlko/ n.m. (P., auto.) distributor.

délecter /(sə)delɛkte/ v. pr. se **~ de**, delight in.

délégation /delegasjɔ̃/ n.f. delegation.

délégu|er /delege/ v.t. delegate. **~é**, **~ée** n.m., f. delegate.

délibéré /delibere/ a. deliberate; (résolu) determined. **~ment** adv. deliberately.

délibér|er /delibere/ v.i. deliberate. **~ation** n.f. deliberation.

délicat, **~e** /delika, -t/ a. delicate; (plein de tact) tactful; (exigeant) particular. **~ement** /-tmɑ̃/ adv. delicately; tactfully. **~esse** /-tɛs/ n.f. delicacy; tact. **~esses** /-tɛs/ n.f. pl. (kind) attentions.

délice /delis/ n.m. delight. **~s** n.f. pl. delights.

délicieu|x, **~se** /delisjø, -z/ a. (au goût) delicious; (charmant) delightful.

délié /delje/ a. fine, slender; (agile) nimble.

délier /delje/ v.t. untie; (délivrer) free. se **~** v. pr. come untied.

délimit|er /delimite/ v.t. determine, demarcate. **~ation** n.f. demarcation.

délinquan|t, **~te** /delɛ̃kɑ̃, -t/ a. & n.m., f. delinquent. **~ce** n.f. delinquency.

délire /delir/ n.m. delirium; (fig.) frenzy.

délir|er /delire/ v.i. be delirious (de, with); (déraisonner) rave. **~ant**, **~ante** a. delirious; (frénétique) frenzied; (fam.) wild.

délit /deli/ n.m. offence, crime.

délivr|er /delivre/ v.t. free, release; (pays) deliver; (remettre) issue. **~ance** n.f. release; deliverance; issue.

déloger /deloʒe/ v.t. force out.

déloy|al, (m. pl. **~aux**) /delwajal, -jo/ a. disloyal; (procédé) unfair.

delta /dɛlta/ n.m. delta.

deltaplane /dɛltaplan/ n.m. hang-glider.

déluge /delyʒ/ n.m. flood; (pluie) downpour.

démagogie /demaɔʒi/ *n.m.* demagogy.

démagogue /demagɔg/ *n.m./f.* demagogue.

demain /dmɛ̃/ *adv.* tomorrow.

demande /dmɑ̃d/ *n.f.* request; (*d'emploi*) application; (*exigence*) demand. ～ **en mariage**, proposal (of marriage).

demandé /dmɑ̃de/ *a.* in demand.

demander /dmɑ̃de/ *v.t.* ask for; (*chemin, heure*) ask; (*emploi*) apply for; (*nécessiter*) require. ～ **que/si**, ask that/if. ～ **qch. à qn.**, ask s.o. for sth. ～ **à qn. de**, ask s.o. to. ～ **en mariage**, propose to. **se** ～ **si/où/etc.**, wonder if/where/etc.

demandeu|r, ～se /dmɑ̃dœr, -øz/ *n.m., f.* **les ～rs d'emploi** job seekers.

démang|er /demɑ̃ʒe/ *v.t./i.* itch. **～eaison** *n.f.* itch(ing).

démanteler /demɑ̃tle/ *v.t.* break up.

démaquill|er (se) /(sə)demakije/ *v. pr.* remove one's make-up. **～ant** *n.m.* make-up remover.

démarcation /demarkasjɔ̃/ *n.f.* demarcation.

démarchage /demarʃaʒ/ *n.m.* door-to-door selling.

démarche /demarʃ/ *n.f.* walk, gait; (*procédé*) step. **faire des ～s auprès de**, make approaches to.

démarcheu|r, ～se /demarʃœr, -øz/ *n.m., f.* (door-to-door) canvasser.

démarr|er /demare/ *v.i.* (*moteur*) start (up); (*partir*) move off; (*fig.*) get moving. —*v.t.* (*fam.*) get moving. **～age** *n.m.* start. **～eur** *n.m.* starter.

démasquer /demaske/ *v.t.* unmask.

démêlant /demɛlɑ̃/ *n.m.* conditioner.

démêler /demele/ *v.t.* disentangle.

démêlés /demele/ *n.m. pl.* trouble.

déménag|er /demenaʒe/ *v.i.* move (house). —*v.t.* (*meubles*) remove. **～ement** *n.m.* move; (*de meubles*) removal. **～eur** *n.m.* removal man; (*Amer.*) furniture mover.

démener (se) /(sə)demne/ *v. pr.* move about wildly; (*fig.*) exert o.s.

démen|t, ～te /demɑ̃, -t/ *a.* insane. —*n.m., f.* lunatic. **～ce** *n.f.* insanity.

démenti /demɑ̃ti/ *n.m.* denial.

démentir /demɑ̃tir/ *v.t.* refute; (*ne pas être conforme à*) belie. **～ que**, deny that.

démerder (se) /(sə)demɛrde/ (*fam.*) manage.

démesuré /deməzyre/ *a.* inordinate.

démettre /demɛtr/ *v.t.* (*poignet etc.*) dislocate. **～ qn. de**, dismiss s.o. from. **se ～ v. pr.** resign (de, from).

demeure /dəmœr/ *n.f.* residence. **mettre en ～ de**, order to.

demeurer /dəmœre/ *v.i.* live; (*rester*) remain.

demi, ～e /dmi/ *a.* half(-). —*n.m., f.* half. —*n.m.* (*bière*) (half-pint) glass of beer; (*football*) half-back. —*n.f.* (*à l'horloge*) half-hour. —*adv.* **à ～**, half; (*ouvrir, fermer*) half-way. **à la ～e**, at half-past. **une heure et ～e**, an hour and a half; (*à l'horloge*) half past one. **une ～-journée/-livre/etc.**, half a day/pound/etc., a half-day/-pound/etc. **～-cercle** *n.m.* semicircle. **～-finale** *n.f.* semifinal. **～-frère** *n.m.* stepbrother. **～-heure** *n.f.* half-hour, half an hour. **～-jour** *n.m.* half-light. **～-mesure** *n.f.* half-measure. **à ～-mot** *adv.* without having to express every word. **～-pension** *n.f.* half-board. **～-pensionnaire** *n.m./f.* day-boarder. **～-sel** *a. invar.* slightly salted. **～-sœur** *n.f.* stepsister. **～-tarif** *n.m.* half-fare. **～-tour** *n.m.* about turn;

(*auto.*) U-turn. **faire ~-tour,** turn back.

démis, ~e /demi, -z/ *a.* dislocated. **~ de ses fonctions,** removed from his post.

démission /demisjɔ̃/ *n.f.* resignation. **~ner** /-jɔne/ *v.i.* resign.

démobiliser /demɔbilize/ *v.t.* demobilize.

démocrate /demɔkrat/ *n.m./f.* democrat. —*a.* democratic.

démocrat|ie /demɔkrasi/ *n.f.* democracy. **~ique** /-atik/ *a.* democratic.

démodé /demɔde/ *a.* old-fashioned.

démographi|e /demɔgrafi/ *n.f.* demography. **~que** *a.* demographic.

demoiselle /dəmwazɛl/ *n.f.* young lady; (*célibataire*) spinster. **~ d'honneur,** bridesmaid.

démol|ir /demɔlir/ *v.t.* demolish. **~ition** *n.f.* demolition.

démon /demɔ̃/ *n.m.* demon. **le D~,** the Devil.

démoniaque /demɔnjak/ *a.* fiendish.

démonstra|teur, ~trice /demɔ̃strater, -tris/ *n.m., f.* demonstrator. **~tion** /-asjɔ̃/ *n.f.* demonstration; (*de force*) show.

démonstrati|f, ~ve /demɔ̃stratif, -v/ *a.* demonstrative.

démonter /demɔ̃te/ *v.t.* take apart, dismantle; (*installation*) take down; (*fig.*) disconcert. **se ~** *v. pr.* come apart.

démontrer /demɔ̃tre/ *v.t.* show, demonstrate.

démoraliser /demɔralize/ *v.t.* demoralize.

démuni /demyni/ *a.* impoverished. **~ de,** without.

démunir /demynir/ *v.t.* **~ de,** deprive of. **se ~ de,** part with.

démystifier /demistifje/ *v.t.* enlighten.

dénaturer /denatyre/ *v.t.* (*faits etc.*) distort.

dénégation /denegasjɔ̃/ *n.f.* denial.

dénicher /deniʃe/ *v.t.* (*trouver*) dig up; (*faire sortir*) flush out.

dénigr|er /denigre/ *v.t.* denigrate. **~ement** *n.m.* denigration.

dénivellation /denivelasjɔ̃/ *n.f.* (*pente*) slope.

dénombrer /denɔ̃bre/ *v.t.* count; (*énumérer*) enumerate.

dénomination /denɔminasjɔ̃/ *n.f.* designation.

dénommé, ~e /denɔme/ *n. m., f.* **le ~ X,** the said X.

dénonc|er /denɔ̃se/ *v.t.* denounce; (*scol.*) tell on. **se ~er** *v. pr.* give o.s. up. **~iateur, ~iatrice** *n.m., f.* informer; (*scol.*) tell-tale. **~iation** *n.f.* denunciation.

dénoter /denɔte/ *v.t.* denote.

dénouement /denumɑ̃/ *n.m.* outcome; (*théâtre*) dénouement.

dénouer /denwe/ *v.t.* unknot, undo. **se ~** *v. pr.* (*nœud*) come undone.

dénoyauter /denwajote/ *v.t.* stone; (*Amer.*) pit.

denrée /dɑ̃re/ *n.f.* foodstuff.

dens|e /dɑ̃s/ *a.* dense. **~ité** *n.f.* density.

dent /dɑ̃/ *n.f.* tooth; (*de roue*) cog. **faire ses ~s,** teethe. **~aire** /-tɛr/ *a.* dental.

dentelé /dɑ̃tle/ *a.* jagged.

dentelle /dɑ̃tɛl/ *n.f.* lace.

dentier /dɑ̃tje/ *n.m.* denture.

dentifrice /dɑ̃tifris/ *n.m.* toothpaste.

dentiste /dɑ̃tist/ *n.m./f.* dentist.

dentition /dɑ̃tisjɔ̃/ *n.f.* teeth.

dénud|er /denyde/ *v.t.* bare. **~é** *a.* bare.

dénué /denɥe/ *a.* **~ de,** devoid of.

dénuement /denymɑ̃/ *n.m.* destitution.

déodorant /deɔdɔrɑ̃/ *a.m. & n.m.* **(produit) ~,** deodorant.

déontologi|e /deɔ̃tɔlɔʒi/ n.f. code of practice. **~que** a. ethical.

dépann|er /depane/ v.t. repair; (fig.) help out. **~age** n.m. repair. **de ~age**, (service etc.) breakdown. **~euse** n.f. breakdown lorry; (Amer.) wrecker.

dépareillé /depareje/ a. odd, not matching.

départ /depar/ n.m. departure; (sport) start. **au ~**, at the outset.

départager /departaʒe/ v.t. settle the matter between.

département /departəmɑ̃/ n.m. department.

dépassé /depase/ a. outdated.

dépass|er /depase/ v.t. go past, pass; (véhicule) overtake; (excéder) exceed; (rival) surpass; (dérouter: fam.) be beyond. —v.i. stick out; (véhicule) overtake. **~ement** n.m. overtaking.

dépays|er /depeize/ v.t. disorientate, disorient. **~ant**, **~e** a. disorientating. **~ement** n.m. disorientation; (changement) change of scenery.

dépêch|e /depeʃ/ n.f. dispatch. **~er¹** /-eʃe/ v.t. dispatch.

dépêcher² (se) /(sə)depeʃe/ v. pr. hurry (up).

dépeindre /depɛ̃dr/ v.t. depict.

dépendance /depɑ̃dɑ̃s/ n.f. dependence; (bâtiment) outbuilding.

dépendre /depɑ̃dr/ v.t. take down. —v.i. depend (de, on). **~ de**, (appartenir à) belong to.

dépens (aux) /(o)depɑ̃/ prép. **~ de**, at the expense of.

dépens|e /depɑ̃s/ n.f. expense; expenditure. **~er** v.t./i. spend; (énergie etc.) expend. se **~er** v. pr. exert o.s.

dépens|ier, **~ière** /depɑ̃sje, -jɛr/ a. **être ~ier**, be a spendthrift.

dépérir /deperir/ v.i. wither.

dépêtrer (se) /(sə)depetre/ v. pr. get o.s. out (de, of).

dépeupler /depœple/ v.t. depopulate. se **~** v. pr. become depopulated.

déphasé /defaze/ a. (fam.) out of touch.

dépilatoire /depilatwar/ a. & n.m. depilatory.

dépist|er /depiste/ v.t. detect; (criminel) track down; (poursuivant) throw off the scent. **~age** n.m. detection.

dépit /depi/ n.m. resentment. **en ~ de**, despite. **en ~ du bon sens**, against all common sense. **~é** /-te/ a. vexed.

déplacé /deplase/ a. out of place.

déplac|er /deplase/ v.t. move. se **~er** v. pr. move; (voyager) travel. **~ement** n.m. moving; travel (-ling).

déplaire /deplɛr/ v.i. **~ à**, (irriter) displease. **ça me déplaît**, I dislike that.

déplaisant, **~e** /deplɛzɑ̃, -t/ a. unpleasant, disagreeable.

déplaisir /deplezir/ n.m. displeasure.

dépliant /deplijɑ̃/ n.m. leaflet.

déplier /deplije/ v.t. unfold.

déplor|er /deplore/ v.t. (trouver regrettable) deplore; (mort) lament. **~able** a. deplorable.

dépl|oyer /deplwaje/ v.t. (ailes, carte) spread; (courage) display; (armée) deploy. **~oiement** n.m. display; deployment.

déport|er /deporte/ v.t. (exiler) deport; (dévier) carry off course. **~ation** n.f. deportation.

dépos|er /depoze/ v.t. put down; (laisser) leave; (passager) drop; (argent) deposit; (installation) dismantle; (plainte) lodge; (armes) lay down; (roi) depose. —v.i. (jurid.) testify. se **~** v. pr. settle.

dépositaire /depozitɛr/ n.m./f. (comm.) agent.

déposition /depozisjɔ̃/ *n.f.* (*jurid.*) statement.

dépôt /depo/ *n.m.* (*garantie, lie*) deposit; (*entrepôt*) warehouse; (*d'autobus*) depot; (*d'ordures*) dump. **laisser en** ~, give for safe keeping.

dépotoir /depotwar/ *n.m.* rubbish dump.

dépouille /depuj/ *n.f.* skin, hide. ~ (**mortelle**), mortal remains. ~s, (*butin*) spoils.

dépouiller /depuje/ *v.t.* go through; (*votes*) count; (*écorcher*) skin. ~ **de**, strip of.

dépourvu /depurvy/ *a.* ~ **de**, devoid of. **prendre au** ~, catch unawares.

dépréc|ier /depresje/ *v.t., se* ~**ier** *v. pr.* depreciate. ~**iation** *n.f.* depreciation.

déprédations /depredasjɔ̃/ *n.f. pl.* damage.

dépr|imer /deprime/ *v.t.* depress. ~**ession** *n.f.* depression. ~**ession nerveuse**, nervous breakdown.

depuis /dəpɥi/ *prép.* since; (*durée*) for; (*à partir de*) from. —*adv.* (*ever*) since. ~ **que**, since. ~ **quand attendez-vous?**, how long have you been waiting?

députation /depytasjɔ̃/ *n.f.* deputation.

député, ~**e** /depyte/ *n.m.*, *f.* Member of Parliament.

déraciné, ~**e** /derasine/ *a. & n.m.*, *f.* rootless (person).

déraciner /derasine/ *v.t.* uproot.

déraill|er /deraje/ *v.i.* be derailed; (*fig., fam.*) be talking nonsense. **faire** ~**er**, derail. ~**ement** *n.m.* derailment. ~**eur** *n.m.* (*de vélo*) gear mechanism, *dérailleur*.

déraisonnable /derezɔnabl/ *a.* unreasonable.

dérang|er /derɑ̃ʒe/ *v.t.* (*gêner*) bother, disturb; (*dérégler*) upset, disrupt. **se** ~**er** *v. pr.* put o.s. out.

ça vous ~**e si . . .?**, do you mind if . . .? ~**ement** *n.m.* bother; (*désordre*) disorder, upset. **en** ~**ement**, out of order.

dérap|er /derape/ *v.i.* skid; (*fig.*) get out of control. ~**age** *n.m.* skid.

déréglé /deregle/ *a.* (*vie*) dissolute; (*estomac*) upset; (*pendule*) (that is) not running properly.

dérégler /deregle/ *v.t.* put out of order. **se** ~ *v. pr.* go wrong.

dérision /derizjɔ̃/ *n.f.* mockery. **par** ~, derisively. **tourner en** ~, mock.

dérisoire /derizwar/ *a.* derisory.

dérivatif /derivatif/ *n.m.* distraction.

dériv|e /deriv/ *n.f.* **aller à la** ~**e**, drift. ~**er**[1] *v.i.* (*bateau*) drift; (*détourner*) divert.

dériv|er[2] /derive/ *v.i.* ~**er de**, derive from. ~**é** *a.* derived; *n.m.* derivative; (*techn.*) by-product.

dermatolo|gie /dermatɔlɔʒi/ *n.f.* dermatology. ~**gue** /-g/ *n.m./f.* dermatologist.

dern|ier, ~**ière** /dernje, -jɛr/ *a.* last; (*nouvelles, mode*) latest; (*étage*) top. —*n.m.*, *f.* last (one). **ce** ~**ier**, the latter. **en** ~**ier**, last. **le** ~**ier cri**, the latest fashion.

dernièrement /dernjɛrmɑ̃/ *adv.* recently.

dérobé, ~**e** /derɔbe/ *a.* hidden. **à la** ~**e**, stealthily.

dérober /derɔbe/ *v.t.* steal; (*cacher*) hide (**à**, from). **se** ~ *v. pr.* slip away. **se** ~ **à**, (*obligation*) shy away from; (*se cacher à*) hide from.

dérogation /derɔgasjɔ̃/ *n.f.* exemption.

déroger /derɔʒe/ *v.i.* ~ **à**, go against.

dérouiller (se) /(sə)deruje/ *v. pr.* **se** ~ **les jambes** to stretch one's legs.

déroul|er /derule/ v.t. (*fil etc.*) unwind. **se ~er** v. pr. unwind; (*avoir lieu*) take place; (*récit, paysage*) unfold. **~ement** n.m. (*d'une action*) development.

déroute /derut/ n.f. (*mil.*) rout.

dérouter /derute/ v.t. disconcert.

derrière /dɛrjɛr/ prép. & adv. behind. —n.m. back, rear; (*postérieur*) behind. **de ~,** back, rear; (*pattes*) hind. **par ~,** (from) behind, at the back *ou* rear.

des /de/ *voir* **de.**

dès /dɛ/ prép. (right) from, from the time of. **~ lors,** from then on. **~ que,** as soon as.

désabusé /dezabyze/ a. disillusioned.

désaccord /dezakɔr/ n.m. disagreement. **~é** /-de/ a. out of tune.

désaffecté /dezafɛkte/ a. disused.

désaffection /dezafɛksjɔ̃/ n.f. alienation (**pour,** from).

désagréable /dezagreabl/ a. unpleasant.

désagréger (se) /(sə)dezagreʒe/ v. pr. disintegrate.

désagrément /dezagremã/ n.m. annoyance.

désaltérant /dezalterã/ a. thirst-quenching, refreshing.

désaltérer /dezaltere/ v.i., **se ~** v. pr. quench one's thirst.

désamorcer /dezamɔrse/ v.t. (*situation, obus*) defuse.

désappr|ouver /dezapruve/ v.t. disapprove of. **~obation** n.f. disapproval.

désarçonner /dezarsɔne/ v.t. disconcert, throw; (*jockey*) unseat, throw.

désarmant /dezarmã/ a. disarming.

désarm|er /dezarme/ v.t./i. disarm. **~ement** n.m. (*pol.*) disarmament.

désarroi /dezarwa/ n.m. confusion.

désarticulé /dezartikyle/ a. dislocated.

désastr|e /dezastr/ n.m. disaster. **~eux, ~euse** a. disastrous.

désavantage /dezavãtaʒ/ n.m. disadvantage. **~er** v.t. put at a disadvantage. **~eux, ~euse** a. disadvantageous.

désaveu (*pl.* **~x**) /dezavø/ n.m. repudiation.

désavouer /dezavwe/ v.t. repudiate.

désaxé, ~e /dezakse/ a. & n.m., f. unbalanced (person).

descendan|t, ~te /desãdã, -t/ n.m., f. descendant. **~ce** n.f. descent; (*enfants*) descendants.

descendre /desãdr/ v.i. (*aux. être*) go down; (*venir*) come down; (*passager*) get off *ou* out; (*nuit*) fall. **~ de,** (*être issu de*) be descended from. **~ à l'hôtel,** go to a hotel. —v.t. (*aux. avoir*) (*escalier etc.*) go *ou* come down; (*objet*) take down; (*abattre, fam.*) shoot down.

descente /desãt/ n.f. descent; (*pente*) (downward) slope; (*raid*) raid. **~ de lit,** bedside rug.

descripti|f, ~ve /dɛskriptif, -v/ a. descriptive.

description /dɛskripsjɔ̃/ n.f. description.

désemparé /dezãpare/ a. distraught.

désemplir /dezãplir/ v.i. **ne pas ~,** be always crowded.

désendettement /dezãdɛtmã/ n.m. getting out of debt.

désenfler /dezãfle/ v.i. go down.

déséquilibre /dezekilibr/ n.m. imbalance. **en ~,** unsteady.

déséquilibr|er /dezekilibre/ v.t. throw off balance. **~é, ~ée** a. & n.m., f. unbalanced (person).

désert[1] **~e** /dezɛr, -t/ a. deserted.

désert[2] /dezɛr/ n.m. desert. **~ique** /-tik/ a. desert.

déserter /dezɛrte/ v.t./i. desert.

~eur *n.m.* deserter. ~ion /-ɛrsjɔ̃/ *n.f.* desertion.

désespér|er /dezɛspere/ *v.i.*, se ~er *v. pr.* despair. ~er de, despair of. ~ant, ~ante *a.* utterly disheartening. ~é *a.* in despair; (*état, cas*) hopeless; (*effort*) desperate. ~ément *adv.* desperately.

désespoir /dezɛspwar/ *n.m.* despair. au ~, in despair. en ~ de cause, as a last resort.

déshabill|er /dezabije/ *v.t.* se ~ *v. pr.* undress, get undressed. ~é *a.* undressed; *n.m.* négligée.

déshabituer (se) /(sə)dezabitɥe/ *v. pr.* se ~ de, get out of the habit of.

désherb|er /dezɛrbe/ *v.t.* weed. ~ant *n.m.* weed-killer.

déshérit|er /dezerite/ *v.t.* disinherit. ~é *a.* (*région*) deprived. les ~és *n.m. pl.* the underprivileged.

déshonneur /dezɔnœr/ *n.m.* dishonour.

déshonor|er /dezɔnɔre/ *v.t.* dishonour. ~ant, ~ante *a.* dishonourable.

déshydrater /dezidrate/ *v.t.*, se ~ *v. pr.* dehydrate.

désigner /dezine/ *v.t.* (*montrer*) point to *ou* out; (*élire*) appoint; (*signifier*) indicate.

désillusion /dezilyzjɔ̃/ *n.f.* disillusionment.

désincrust|er /dezɛ̃kryste/ *v. pr.* (*chaudière*) descale; (*peau*) exfoliate. ~ant *a.* produit ~ant, (*skin*) scrub.

désinence /dezinɑ̃s/ *n.f.* (*gram.*) ending.

désinfect|er /dezɛ̃fɛkte/ *v.t.* disinfect. ~ant *n.m.* disinfectant.

désinfection /dezɛ̃fɛksjɔ̃/ *n.f.* disinfection.

désintégrer /dezɛ̃tegre/ *v.t.*, se ~ *v. pr.* disintegrate.

désintéressé /dezɛ̃terese/ *a.* disinterested.

désintéresser (se) /(sə)dezɛ̃terese/ *v. pr.* se ~ de, lose interest in.

désintoxication /dezɛ̃tɔksikasjɔ̃/ *n.f.* detoxication. cure de ~, detoxification course.

désintoxiquer /dezɛ̃tɔksike/ *v.t.* cure of an addiction; (*régime*) purify.

désinvolt|e /dezɛ̃vɔlt/ *a.* casual. ~ure *n.f.* casualness.

désir /dezir/ *n.m.* wish, desire; (*convoitise*) desire.

désirer /dezire/ *v.t.* want; (*convoiter*) desire. ~ faire, want *ou* wish to do.

désireu|x, ~se /dezirø, -z/ *a.* ~x, anxious to.

désist|er (se) /(sə)deziste/ *v. pr.* withdraw. ~ement *n.m.* withdrawal.

désobéir /dezɔbeir/ *v.i.* ~ (à), disobey.

désobéissan|t, ~te /dezɔbeisã, -t/ *a.* disobedient. ~ce *n.f.* disobedience.

désobligeant, ~e /dezɔbliʒã, -t/ *a.* disagreeable, unkind.

désodé /desɔde/ *a.* sodium-free.

désodorisant /dezɔdɔrizã/ *n.m.* air freshener.

désœuvr|é /dezœvre/ *a.* idle. ~ement *n.m.* idleness.

désol|er /dezɔle/ *v.t.* distress. être ~é, (*regretter*) be sorry. ~ation *n.f.* distress.

désopilant, ~e /dezɔpilã, -t/ *a.* hilarious.

désordonné /dezɔrdɔne/ *a.* untidy; (*mouvements*) uncoordinated.

désordre /dezɔrdr/ *n.m.* disorder; (*de vêtements, cheveux*) untidiness. mettre en ~, make untidy.

désorganiser /dezɔrganize/ *v.t.* disorganize.

désorienté /dezɔrjãte/ *a.* disorientated.

désorienter /dezɔrjãte/ *v.t.* disorientate, disorient.

désormais /dezɔrmɛ/ adv. from now on.

désosser /dezose/ v.t. bone.

despote /dɛspɔt/ n.m. despot.

desquels, desquelles /dekɛl/ voir **lequel**.

dessécher /deseʃe/ v.t., **se ~** v. pr. dry out ou up.

dessein /desɛ̃/ n.m. intention. **à ~**, intentionally.

desserrer /desere/ v.t. loosen. **sans ~ les dents**, without opening his/her mouth. **se ~** v. pr. come loose.

dessert /desɛr/ n.m. dessert.

desserte /desɛrt/ n.f. (transports) service, servicing.

desservir /desɛrvir/ v.t./i. clear away; (autobus) provide a service to, serve.

dessin /desɛ̃/ n.m. drawing; (motif) design; (contour) outline. **~ animé**, (cinéma) cartoon. **~ humoristique**, cartoon.

dessin|er /desine/ v.t./i. draw; (fig.) outline. **se ~er** v. pr. appear, take shape. **~ateur, ~atrice** n.m., f. artist; (industriel) draughtsman.

dessoûler /desule/ v.t./i. sober up.

dessous /dsu/ adv. underneath. —n.m. under-side, underneath. —n.m. pl. underclothes. **du ~**, bottom; (voisins) downstairs. **en ~, par ~**, underneath. **~-de-plat** n.m. invar. (heat-resistant) table-mat. **~-de-table** n.m. invar. backhander.

dessus /dsy/ adv. on top (of it), on it. —n.m. top. **du ~**, top; (voisins) upstairs. **en ~**, above. **par ~**, over (it). **avoir le ~**, get the upper hand. **~-de-lit** n.m. invar. bedspread.

destabilis|er /destabilize/ v.t. destabilize. **~ation** n.f. destabilization.

destin /dɛstɛ̃/ n.m. (sort) fate; (avenir) destiny.

destinataire /dɛstinatɛr/ n.m./f. addressee.

destination /dɛstinasjɔ̃/ n.f. destination; (emploi) purpose. **à ~ de**, (going) to.

destinée /dɛstine/ n.f. (sort) fate; (avenir) destiny.

destin|er /dɛstine/ v.t. **~er à**, intend for; (vouer) destine for; (affecter) earmark for. **être ~é à faire**, be intended to do; (condamné, obligé) be destined to do. **se ~er à**, (carrière) intend to take up.

destit|uer /dɛstitɥe/ v.t. dismiss (from office). **~ution** n.f. dismissal.

destruc|teur, ~trice /dɛstryktœr, -tris/ a. destructive.

destruction /dɛstryksjɔ̃/ n.f. destruction.

dés|uet, ~uète /desɥɛ, -ɛt/ a. outdated.

désunir /dezynir/ v.t. divide.

détachant /detaʃɑ̃/ n.m. stain-remover.

détach|é /detaʃe/ a. detached. **~ement** n.m. detachment.

détacher /detaʃe/ v.t. untie; (déléguer) send (on assignment ou secondment). **se ~** v. pr. come off, break away; (nœud etc.) come undone; (ressortir) stand out.

détail /detaj/ n.m. detail; (de compte) breakdown; (comm.) retail. **au ~**, (vendre etc.) retail. **de ~**, (prix etc.) retail. **en ~**, in detail.

détaillé /detaje/ a. detailed.

détaill|er /detaje/ v.t. (articles) sell in small quantities, split up. **~ant, ~ante** n.m., f. retailer.

détaler /detale/ v.i. (fam.) make tracks, run off.

détartrant /detartrɑ̃/ n.m. descaler.

détaxer /detakse/ v.t. reduce the tax on.

détect|er /detɛkte/ v.t. detect.
~eur n.m. detector. **~ion**
/-ksjɔ̃/ n.f. detection.

détective /detɛktiv/ n.m. detective.

déteindre /detɛ̃dr/ v.i. (couleur)
run (**sur**, on to). **~ sur**, (fig.) rub
off on.

détend|re /detɑ̃dr/ v.t. slacken;
(ressort) release; (personne) relax.
se ~re v. pr. become slack,
slacken; be released; relax. **~u** a.
(calme) relaxed.

détenir† /detnir/ v.t. hold; (secret,
fortune) possess.

détente /detɑ̃t/ n.f. relaxation;
(pol.) détente; (saut) spring;
(gâchette) trigger; (relâchement)
release.

déten|teur, ~trice /detɑ̃tœr,
-tris/ n.m., f. holder.

détention /detɑ̃sjɔ̃/ n.f. **~
préventive**, custody.

détenu, ~e /detny/ n.m., f.
prisoner.

détergent /detɛrʒɑ̃/ n.m. detergent.

détérior|er /deterjɔre/ v.t. dam-
age. **se ~er** v. pr. deteriorate.
~ation n.f. damaging; deteri-
oration.

détermin|er /detɛrmine/ v.t. deter-
mine. **se ~er** v. pr. make up one's
mind (**à**, to). **~ation** n.f. deter-
mination. **~é** a. (résolu) determined; (précis) definite.

déterrer /detere/ v.t. dig up.

détersif /detɛrsif/ n.m. detergent.

détestable /detɛstabl/ a. foul.

détester /detɛste/ v.t. hate. **se ~** v.
pr. hate each other.

déton|er /detɔne/ v.i. explode,
detonate. **~ateur** n.m. detonator.
~ation n.f. explosion, detona-
tion.

détonner /detɔne/ v.i. clash.

détour /detur/ n.m. bend; (crochet)
detour; (fig.) roundabout means.

détourné /deturne/ a. roundabout.

détourn|er /deturne/ v.t. divert;
(tête, yeux) turn away; (avion)
hijack; (argent) embezzle. **se ~er**
de, stray from. **~ement** n.m.
hijack(ing); embezzlement.

détrac|teur, ~trice /detraktœr,
-tris/ n.m., f. critic.

détraquer /detrake/ v.t. break, put
out of order; (estomac) upset. **se**
~ v. pr. (machine) go wrong.

détresse /detrɛs/ n.f. distress.

détriment /detrimɑ̃/ n.m. detriment.

détritus /detritys/ n.m. pl. rubbish.

détroit /detrwa/ n.m. strait.

détromper /detrɔ̃pe/ v.t. un-
deceive, enlighten.

détruire† /detrɥir/ v.t. destroy.

dette /dɛt/ n.f. debt.

deuil /dœj/ n.m. mourning; (perte)
bereavement. **porter le ~**, be in
mourning.

deux /dø/ a. & n.m. two. **~ fois**,
twice. **tous (les) ~**, both. **~-**
pièces n.m. invar. (vêtement) two-
piece; (logement) two-room flat or
apartment. **~-points** n.m. invar.
(gram.) colon. **~-roues** n.m.
invar. two-wheeled vehicle.

deuxième /døzjɛm/ a. & n.m./f.
second. **~ment** adv. secondly.

dévaler /devale/ v.t./i. hurtle
down.

dévaliser /devalize/ v.t. rob, clean
out.

dévaloriser /devalɔrize/ v.t., **se**
v. pr. reduce in value.

dévalorisant, ~e /devalɔrizɑ̃, -t/
a. demeaning.

déval|uer /devalɥe/ v.t., **se ~uer**
v. pr. devalue. **~uation** n.f.
devaluation.

devancer /dəvɑ̃se/ v.t. be ou go
ahead of; (arriver) arrive ahead
of; (prévenir) anticipate.

devant /dvɑ̃/ prép. in front of;

(*distance*) ahead of; (*avec mouve-ment*) past; (*en présence de*) before; (*face à*) in the face of. —*adv.* in front; (*à distance*) ahead. —*n.m.* front. **prendre les ~s**, take the initiative. **de ~**, front. **par ~**, at ou from the front, in front. **aller au ~ de qn.**, go to meet sb. **aller au ~ des désirs de qn.**, anticipate sb.'s wishes.

devanture /dəvɑ̃tyr/ *n.f.* shop front; (*étalage*) shop-window.

dévaster /devaste/ *v.t.* devastate.

déveine /deven/ *n.f.* bad luck.

développ|er /devlɔpe/ *v.t.*, **se ~er** *v. pr.* develop. **~ement** *n.m.* development; (*de photos*) developing.

devenir† /dəvnir/ *v.i.* (*aux. être*) become. **qu'est-il devenu?**, what has become of him?

dévergondé /devɛrgɔ̃de/ *a.* shame-less.

déverser /devɛrse/ *v.t.*, **se ~** *v. pr.* empty out, pour out.

dévêtir /devetir/ *v.t.*, **se ~** *v. pr.* undress.

déviation /devjɑsjɔ̃/ *n.f.* diversion.

dévier /devje/ *v.t.* divert; (*coup*) deflect. —*v.i.* (*ballon, balle*) veer; (*personne*) deviate.

devin /dəvɛ̃/ *n.m.* fortune-teller.

deviner /dvine/ *v.t.* guess; (*apercevoir*) distinguish.

devinette /dvinɛt/ *n.f.* riddle.

devis /dvi/ *n.m.* estimate.

dévisager /devizaʒe/ *v.t.* stare at.

devise /dviz/ *n.f.* motto. **~s**, (*monnaie*) (foreign) currency.

dévisser /devise/ *v.t.* unscrew.

dévitaliser /devitalize/ *v.t.* (*dent*) kill the nerve in.

dévoiler /devwale/ *v.t.* reveal.

devoir[1] /dvwar/ *n.m.* duty; (*scol.*) homework; (*fait en classe*) exer-cise.

devoir†[2] /dvwar/ *v.t.* owe. —*v. aux.* **~ faire**, (*nécessité*) must do, have (got) to do; (*intention*) must

to do. **~ être**, (*probabilité*) must be. **vous devriez**, you should. **il aurait dû**, he should have.

dévolu /devɔly/ *n.m.* **jeter son ~ sur**, set one's heart on. —*a.* **~ à**, allotted to.

dévorer /devɔre/ *v.t.* devour.

dévot, ~e /devo, -ɔt/ *a.* devout.

dévotion /devɔsjɔ̃/ *n.f.* (*relig.*) devotion.

dévou|er (se) /(sə)devwe/ *v. pr.* devote o.s. (**à**, to); (*se sacrifier*) sacrifice o.s. **~é** *a.* devoted. **~ement** /-vumɑ̃/ *n.m.* devotion.

dextérité /dɛksterite/ *n.f.* skill.

diab|ète /djabɛt/ *n.m.* diabetes. **~étique** *a.* & *n.m./f.* diabetic.

diab|le /djabl/ *n.m.* devil. **~olique** *a.* diabolical.

diagnostic /djagnɔstik/ *n.m.* diag-nosis. **~quer** *v.t.* diagnose.

diagon|al, ~ale (*m. pl.* **~aux**) /djagɔnal, -o/ *a.* & *n.f.* diagonal. **en ~ale**, diagonally.

diagramme /djagram/ *n.m.* dia-gram; (*graphique*) graph.

dialecte /djalɛkt/ *n.m.* dialect.

dialogu|e /djalɔg/ *n.m.* dialogue. **~er** *v.i.* (*pol.*) have a dialogue.

diamant /djamɑ̃/ *n.m.* diamond.

diamètre /djamɛtr/ *n.m.* diameter.

diapason /djapazɔ̃/ *n.m.* tuning-fork.

diaphragme /djafragm/ *n.m.* diaphragm.

diapo /djapo/ *n.f.* (colour) slide.

diapositive /djapozitiv/ *n.f.* (colour) slide.

diarrhée /djare/ *n.f.* diarrhoea.

dictat|eur /diktatœr/ *n.m.* dic-tator. **~ure** *n.f.* dictatorship.

dict|er /dikte/ *v.t.* dictate. **~ée** *n.f.* dictation.

diction /diksjɔ̃/ *n.f.* diction.

dictionnaire /diksjɔnɛr/ *n.m.* dic-tionary.

dicton /diktɔ̃/ *n.m.* saying.

dièse /djɛz/ *n.m.* (*mus.*) sharp.

diesel /djezɛl/ *n.m. & a. invar.* diesel.

diète /djɛt/ *n.f.* (*régime*) diet.

diététicien, **~ne** /djetetisjɛ̃, -jɛn/ *n.m., f.* dietician.

diététique /djetetik/ *n.f.* dietetics. —*a.* **produit** *ou* **aliment ~,** dietary product.

dieu (*pl.* **~x**) /djø/ *n.m.* god. **D~,** God.

diffamatoire /difamatwar/ *a.* defamatory.

diffam|er /difame/ *v.t.* slander; (*par écrit*) libel. **~ation** *n.f.* slander; libel.

différé (en) /(ɑ̃)difere/ *adv.* (*émission*) recorded.

différemment /diferamɑ̃/ *adv.* differently.

différence /diferɑ̃s/ *n.f.* difference. **à la ~ de,** unlike.

différencier /diferɑ̃sje/ *v.t.* differentiate. **se ~ de,** (*différer de*) differ from.

différend /diferɑ̃/ *n.m.* difference (of opinion).

différent, ~e /diferɑ̃, -t/ *a.* different (**de,** from).

différentiel, ~le /diferɑ̃sjɛl/ *a. & n.m.* differential.

différer[1] /difere/ *v.t.* postpone.

différer[2] /difere/ *v.i.* differ (**de,** from).

difficile /difisil/ *a.* difficult. **~ment** *adv.* with difficulty.

difficulté /difikylte/ *n.f.* difficulty.

difform|e /diform/ *a.* deformed. **~ité** *n.f.* deformity.

diffus, ~e /dify, -z/ *a.* diffuse.

diffus|er /difyze/ *v.t.* broadcast; (*lumière, chaleur*) diffuse. **~ion** *n.f.* broadcasting; diffusion.

dig|érer /diʒere/ *v.t.* digest; (*endurer: fam.*) stomach. **~este, ~estible** *adjs.* digestible. **~estion** *n.f.* digestion.

digestif, ~ve /diʒɛstif, -v/ *a.* digestive. —*n.m.* after-dinner liqueur.

digit|al (*m. pl.* **~aux**) /diʒital, -o/ *a.* digital.

digne /diɲ/ *a.* (*noble*) dignified; (*honnête*) worthy. **~ de,** worthy of. **~ de foi,** trustworthy.

dignité /diɲite/ *n.f.* dignity.

digression /digresjɔ̃/ *n.f.* digression.

digue /dig/ *n.f.* dike.

diktat /diktat/ *n.m.* diktat.

dilapider /dilapide/ *v.t.* squander.

dilat|er /dilate/ *v.t.,* **se ~** *v. pr.* dilate. **~ation** /-asjɔ̃/ *n.f.* dilation.

dilemme /dilɛm/ *n.m.* dilemma.

dilettante /diletɑ̃t/ *n.m., f.* amateur.

diluant /dilɥɑ̃/ *n.m.* thinner.

diluer /dilɥe/ *v.t.* dilute.

diluvien, ~ne /dilyvjɛ̃, -ɛn/ *a.* (*pluie*) torrential.

dimanche /dimɑ̃ʃ/ *n.m.* Sunday.

dimension /dimɑ̃sjɔ̃/ *n.f.* (*taille*) size; (*mesure*) dimension.

dimin|uer /diminɥe/ *v.t.* reduce, decrease; (*plaisir, courage, etc.*) lessen; (*dénigrer*) lessen. —*v.i.* decrease. **~ution** *n.f.* decrease (**de,** in).

diminutif /diminytif/ *n.m.* diminutive; (*surnom*) pet name *ou* form.

dinde /dɛ̃d/ *n.f.* turkey.

dindon /dɛ̃dɔ̃/ *n.m.* turkey.

dîn|er /dine/ *n.m.* dinner. —*v.i.* have dinner. **~eur, ~euse** *n.m., f.* diner.

dingue /dɛ̃g/ *a.* (*fam.*) crazy.

dinosaure /dinozɔr/ *n.m.* dinosaur.

diocèse /djosɛz/ *n.m.* diocese.

diphtérie /difteri/ *n.f.* diphtheria.

diphtongue /diftɔ̃g/ *n.f.* diphthong.

diplomate /diplɔmat/ *n.m.* diplomat. —*a.* diplomatic.

diplomat|ie /diplɔmasi/ *n.f.* diplomacy. **~ique** /-atik/ *a.* diplomatic.

diplôm|e /diplom/ *n.m.* certificate, diploma; (*univ.*) degree. **~é** *a.* qualified.

dire† /dir/ *v.t.* say; (*secret, vérité, heure*) tell; (*penser*) think. **~ que,** say that. **~ à qn. que/de,** tell s.o. that/to. **se ~** *v. pr.* (*mot*) be said; (*fatigué etc.*) say that one is. **ça me/vous/***etc.* **dit de faire,** I/you/*etc.* feel like doing. **on dirait que,** it would seem that, it seems that. **dis/dites donc!,** hey! **—n.m. au ~ de, selon les ~s de,** according to.

direct /dirɛkt/ *a.* direct. **en ~,** (*émission*) live. **~ement** *adv.* directly.

direc|teur, **~trice** /dirɛktœr, -tris/ *n.m., f.* director; (*chef de service*) manager, manageress; (*d'école*) headmaster, headmistress.

direction /dirɛksjɔ̃/ *n.f.* (*sens*) direction; (*de société etc.*) management; (*auto.*) steering. **en ~ de,** (going) to.

directive /dirɛktiv/ *n.f.* instruction.

dirigeant, **~e** /diriʒɑ̃, -t/ *n.m., f.* (*pol.*) leader; (*comm.*) manager. **—a.** (*classe*) ruling.

diriger /diriʒe/ *v.t.* run, manage, direct; (*véhicule*) steer; (*orchestre*) conduct; (*braquer*) aim; (*tourner*) turn. **se ~** *v. pr.* guide o.s. **se ~ vers,** make one's way to.

dirigisme /diriʒism/ *n.m.* interventionism. **~te** /-ist/ *a. & n.m./f.* interventionist.

dis /di/ *voir* **dire.**

discern|er /disɛrne/ *v.t.* discern. **~ement** *n.m.* discernment.

disciple /disipl/ *n.m.* disciple.

disciplin|e /disiplin/ *n.f.* discipline. **~aire** *a.* disciplinary. **~er** *v.t.* discipline.

discontinu /diskɔ̃tiny/ *a.* intermittent.

discontinuer /diskɔ̃tinɥe/ *v.i.* **sans ~,** without stopping.

discordant, **~e** /diskɔrdɑ̃, -t/ *a.* discordant.

discorde /diskɔrd/ *n.f.* discord.

discothèque /diskɔtɛk/ *n.f.* record library; (*club*) disco(thèque).

discount /diskunt/ *n.m.* discount.

discourir /diskurir/ *v.i.* (*péj.*) hold forth, ramble on.

discours /diskur/ *n.m.* speech.

discréditer /diskredite/ *v.t.* discredit.

discr|et, **~ète** /diskre, -t/ *a.* discreet. **~ètement** *adv.* discreetly.

discrétion /diskresjɔ̃/ *n.f.* discretion. **à ~,** as much as one desires.

discrimination /diskriminasjɔ̃/ *n.f.* discrimination.

discriminatoire /diskriminatwar/ *a.* discriminatory.

disculper /diskylpe/ *v.t.* exonerate. **se ~** *v. pr.* prove o.s. innocent.

discussion /diskysjɔ̃/ *n.f.* discussion; (*querelle*) argument.

discuté /diskyte/ *a.* controversial.

discut|er /diskyte/ *v.t.* discuss; (*contester*) question. **—v.i.** (*parler*) talk; (*répliquer*) argue. **~er de,** discuss. **~able** *a.* debatable.

disette /dizɛt/ *n.f.* (*food*) shortage.

diseuse /dizøz/ *n.f.* **~ de bonne aventure,** fortune-teller.

disgrâce /disgras/ *n.f.* disgrace.

disgracieu|x, **~se** /disgrasjø, -z/ *a.* ungainly.

disjoindre /disʒwɛ̃dr/ *v.t.* take apart. **se ~** *v. pr.* come apart.

dislo|quer /disləke/ *v.t.* (*membre*) dislocate; (*machine etc.*) break (apart). **se ~quer** *v. pr.* (*parti, cortège*) break up; (*meuble*) come apart. **~cation** *n.f.* (*anat.*) dislocation.

dispar|aître† /disparɛtr/ *v.i.* disappear; (*mourir*) die. **faire ~aître,** get rid of. **~ition** *n.f.*

disappearance; (*mort*) death. **~u, ~ue ea**. (*soldat etc*.) missing; *n.m., f.* missing person; (*mort*) dead person.

disparate /disparat/ *a.* ill-assorted.

disparité /disparite/ *n.f.* disparity.

dispensaire /dispᾶsɛr/ *n.m.* clinic.

dispense /dispᾶs/ *n.f.* exemption.

dispenser /dispᾶse/ *v.t.* exempt (**de**, from). **se ~ de** (**faire**), avoid (doing).

disperser /dispɛrse/ *v.t.* (*éparpiller*) scatter; (*répartir*) disperse. **se ~** *v. pr.* disperse.

disponible /disponibl/ *a.* available. **~ilité e** /-lite/ *n.f.* availability.

dispos, ~e /dispo, -z/ *a.* **frais et ~**, fresh and alert.

disposé /dispoze/ *a.* **bien/mal ~**, in a good/bad mood. **~ à**, prepared to. **~ envers**, disposed towards.

disposer /dispoze/ *v.t.* arrange. **~ à**, (*engager à*) incline to. **—v.i. de**, have at one's disposal. **se ~ à**, prepare to.

dispositif /dispozitif/ *n.m.* device; (*plan*) plan of action. **~ antiparasite**, suppressor.

disposition /dispozisjᴐ̃/ *n.f.* arrangement; (*humeur*) mood; (*tendance*) tendency. **~s**, (*préparatifs*) arrangements; (*aptitude*) aptitude. **à la ~ de**, at the disposal of.

disproportionné /disproporsjone/ *a.* disproportionate.

dispute /dispyt/ *n.f.* quarrel.

disputer /dispyte/ *v.t.* (*match*) play; (*course*) run in; (*prix*) fight for; (*gronder: fam.*) tell off. **se ~** *v. pr.* quarrel; (*se battre pour*) fight over; (*match*) be played.

disquaire /diskɛr/ *n.m./f.* record dealer.

disqualifier /diskalifje/ *v.t.* disqualify. **~ication** /-ikasjᴐ̃/ *n.f.* disqualification.

disque /disk/ *n.m.* (*mus*.) record; (*sport*) discus; (*cercle*) disc, disk. **~ dur**, hard disk.

disquette /diskɛt/ *n.f.* (floppy) disk.

dissection /disɛksjᴐ̃/ *n.f.* dissection.

dissemblable /disᾶblabl/ *a.* dissimilar.

disséminer /disemine/ *v.t.* scatter.

disséquer /diseke/ *v.t.* dissect.

dissertation /disɛrtasjᴐ̃/ *n.f.* (*scol.*) essay.

disserter /disɛrte/ *v.i.* **~ sur**, comment upon.

dissiden|t, ~te /disidᾶ, -t/ *a. & n.m., f.* dissident. **~ce** *n.f.* dissidence.

dissimul|er /disimyle/ *v.t.* conceal (**à**, from). **se ~er** *v. pr.* conceal o.s. **~ation** *n.f.* concealment; (*fig*.) deceit.

dissipé /disipe/ *a.* (*élève*) unruly.

dissip|er /disipe/ *v.t.* (*fumée, crainte*) dispel; (*fortune*) squander; (*personne*) lead into bad ways. **s. ~er** *v. pr.* disappear. **~ation** *n.f.* squandering; (*indiscipline*) misbehaviour.

dissolution /disᴐlysjᴐ̃/ *n.f.* dissolution.

dissolvant /disᴐlvᾶ/ *n.m.* solvent; (*pour ongles*) nail polish remover.

dissonant, ~e /disonᾶ, -t/ *a.* discordant.

dissoudre† /disudr/ *v.t.*, **se ~** *v. pr.* dissolve.

dissua|der /disɥade/ *v.t.* dissuade (**de**, from). **~sion** /-ɥazjᴐ̃/ *n.f.* dissuasion. **force de ~sion**, deterrent force.

dissuasi|f, ~ve /disɥazif, -v/ *a.* dissuasive.

distance /distᾶs/ *n.f.* distance; (*écart*) gap. **à ~**, at *ou* from a distance.

distancer /distᾶse/ *v.t.* leave behind.

distant, ~e /distᾶ, -t/ *a.* distant.

distendre /distɑ̃dr/ v.t., **se** ~ v. pr. distend.

distill|er /distile/ v.t. distil. ~**ation** n.f. distillation.

distillerie /distilri/ n.f. distillery.

distinct, ~**e** /distɛ̃(kt), -ɛ̃kt/ a. distinct. ~**ement** /-ɛ̃ktəmɑ̃/ adv. distinctly.

distincti|f, ~**ve** /distɛ̃ktif, -v/ a. distinctive.

distinction /distɛ̃ksjɔ̃/ n.f. distinction.

distingué /distɛ̃ge/ a. distinguished.

distinguer /distɛ̃ge/ v.t. distinguish.

distraction /distraksjɔ̃/ n.f. absent-mindedness; (oubli) lapse; (passe-temps) distraction.

distraire† /distrɛr/ v.t. amuse; (rendre inattentif) distract. **se** ~ v. pr. amuse o.s.

distrait, ~**e** /distrɛ, -t/ a. absent-minded. ~**ement** a. absent-mindedly.

distrayant, ~**e** /distrɛjɑ̃, -t/ a. entertaining.

distrib|uer /distribɥe/ v.t. hand out, distribute; (répartir, amener) distribute; (courrier) deliver. ~**uteur** n.m. (auto., comm.) distributor. ~**uteur** (automatique), vending-machine; (de billets) (cash) dispenser. ~**ution** n.f. distribution; (du courrier) delivery; (acteurs) cast.

district /distrikt/ n.m. district.

dit¹, dites /di, dit/ voir **dire**.

dit², ~**e** /di, dit/ a. (décidé) agreed; (surnommé) called.

diurétique /djyretik/ a. & n.m. diuretic.

diurne /djyrn/ a. diurnal.

divag|uer /divage/ v.i. rave. ~**ations** n.f. pl. ravings.

divan /divɑ̃/ n.m. divan.

divergen|t, ~**te** /divɛrʒɑ̃, -t/ a. divergent. ~**ce** n.f. divergence.

diverger /divɛrʒe/ v.i. diverge.

divers, ~**e** /divɛr, -s/ a. (varié) diverse; (différent) various. ~**ement** /-səmɑ̃/ adv. variously.

diversifier /divɛrsifje/ v.t. diversify.

diversion /divɛrsjɔ̃/ n.f. diversion.

diversité /divɛrsite/ n.f. diversity.

divert|ir /divɛrtir/ v.t. amuse. **se** ~**ir** v. pr. amuse o.s. ~**issement** n.m. amusement.

dividende /dividɑ̃d/ n.m. dividend.

divin, ~**e** /divɛ̃, -in/ a. divine.

divinité /divinite/ n.f. divinity.

divis|er /divize/ v.t., **se** ~**er** v. pr. divide. ~**ion** n.f. division.

divorc|e /divɔrs/ n.m. divorce. ~**é** ~**ée** a. divorced; n.m.,f. divorcee. ~**er** v.i. ~**er (d'avec)** divorce.

divulguer /divylge/ v.t. divulge.

dix /dis/ (/di/ before consonant, /diz/ before vowel) a. & n.m. ten. ~**ième** /dizjɛm/ a. & n.m./f. tenth.

dix-huit /dizɥit/ a. & n.m. eighteen. ~**ième** a. & n.m./f. eighteenth.

dix-neu|f /diznœf/ a. & n.m. nineteen. ~**vième** a. & n.m./f. nineteenth.

dix-sept /disɛt/ a. & n.m. seventeen. ~**ième** a. & n.m./f. seventeenth.

dizaine /dizɛn/ n.f. (about) ten.

docile /dɔsil/ a. docile.

docilité /dɔsilite/ n.f. docility.

dock /dɔk/ n.m. dock.

docker /dɔkɛr/ n.m. docker.

doct|eur /dɔktɛr/ n.m. doctor. ~**oresse** n.f. (fam.) lady doctor.

doctorat /dɔktɔra/ n.m. doctorate.

doctrin|e /dɔktrin/ n.f. doctrine. ~**aire** a. doctrinaire.

document /dɔkymɑ̃/ n.m. document. ~**aire** a. & n.m. documentary.

documentaliste /dɔkymɑ̃talist/ n.m./f. information officer.

document|er /dɔkymɑ̃te/ v.t. document. se ∼er v. pr. collect information. ∼ation n.f. information, literature. ∼é a. well-documented.

dodo /dodo/ n.m. faire ∼, (langage enfantin) go to byebyes.

dodu /dody/ a. plump.

dogm|e /dɔgm/ n.m. dogma. ∼atique a. dogmatic.

doigt /dwa/ n.m. finger. un ∼ de, a drop of. à deux ∼s de, a hair's breadth away from. ∼ de pied, toe.

doigté /dwate/ n.m. (mus.) fingering, touch; (adresse) tact.

dois, doit /dwa/ voir **devoir**[2].

Dolby /dɔlbi/ n.m. & a. (P.) Dolby (P.).

doléances /dɔleɑ̃s/ n.f. pl. grievances.

dollar /dɔlar/ n.m. dollar.

domaine /dɔmɛn/ n.m. estate, domain; (fig.) domain.

dôme /dom/ n.m. dome.

domestique /dɔmɛstik/ a. domestic. —n.m./f. servant.

domestiquer /dɔmɛstike/ v.t. domesticate.

domicile /dɔmisil/ n.m. home. à ∼, at home; (livrer) to the home.

domicilié /dɔmisilje/ a. resident.

domin|er /dɔmine/ v.t./i. dominate; (surplomber) tower over, dominate; (équipe) dictate the game (to). ∼ant, ∼ante a. dominant; n.f. dominant feature. ∼ation n.f. domination.

domino /dɔmino/ n.m. domino.

dommage /dɔmaʒ/ n.m. (tort) harm. ∼(s), (dégâts) damage. c'est ∼, it's a pity. quel ∼, what a shame. ∼s-intérêts n.m. pl. (jurid.) damages.

dompt|er /dɔ̃te/ v.t. tame. ∼eur, ∼euse n.m., f. tamer.

don /dɔ̃/ n.m. (cadeau, aptitude) gift.

dona|teur, ∼**trice** /dɔnatœr, -tris/ n.m., f. donor.

donation /dɔnasjɔ̃/ n.f. donation.

donc /dɔ̃(k)/ conj. so, then; (par conséquent) so, therefore.

donjon /dɔ̃ʒɔ̃/ n.m. (tour) keep.

donné /dɔne/ a. (fixé) given; (pas cher, fam.) dirt cheap. étant ∼ que, given that.

données /dɔne/ n.f. pl. (de science) data; (de problème) facts.

donner /dɔne/ v.t. give; (vieilles affaires) give away; (distribuer) give out; (récolte etc.) produce; (film) show; (pièce) put on. —v.i. ∼ sur, look out on to. ∼ dans, (piège) fall into. ça donne soif/faim, it makes one thirsty/hungry. ∼ à réparer/etc., take to be repaired/etc. ∼ lieu à, give rise to. se ∼ à, devote o.s. to. se ∼ du mal, go to a lot of trouble (pour faire, to do).

donneu|r, ∼**se** /dɔnœr, -øz/ n.m., f. (de sang) donor.

dont /dɔ̃/ pron. rel. (chose) whose, of which; (personne) whose; (partie d'un tout) of whom; (chose) of which; (provenance) from which; (manière) in which. le père ∼ la fille, the father whose daughter. ce ∼, what. ∼ il a besoin, which he needs. l'enfant ∼ il est fier, the child he is proud of. trois enfants ∼ deux sont jumeaux, three children, two of whom are twins.

dopage /dɔpaʒ/ n.m. doping.

doper /dɔpe/ v.t. dope. se ∼ v. pr. take dope.

doré /dɔre/ a. (couleur d'or) golden; (avec dorure) gold. la bourgeoisie ∼e the affluent middle class.

dorénavant /dɔrenavɑ̃/ adv. henceforth.

dorer /dɔre/ v.t. gild; (culin.) brown.

dorloter /dɔʀlɔte/ v.t. pamper.

dorm|ir /dɔʀmiʀ/ v.i. sleep; (*être endormi*) be asleep. **~eur, ~euse** n.m., f. sleeper. **il dort debout**, he can't keep awake. **une histoire à ~ir debout**, a cock-and-bull story.

dortoir /dɔʀtwaʀ/ n.m. dormitory.

dorure /dɔʀyʀ/ n.f. gilding.

dos /do/ n.m. back; (*de livre*) spine. **à ~ de**, riding on. **de ~**, from behind. **~ crawlé**, backstroke.

dos|e /doz/ n.f. dose. **~age** n.m. (*mélange*) mixture. **faire le ~age de**, measure out; balance. **~er** v.t. measure out; (*équilibrer*) balance.

dossard /dɔsaʀ/ n.m. (*sport*) number.

dossier /dɔsje/ n.m. (*documents*) file; (*de chaise*) back.

dot /dɔt/ n.f. dowry.

doter /dɔte/ v.t. **~ de**, equip with.

douan|e /dwan/ n.f. customs. **~ier, ~ière** a. customs; n.m., f. customs officer.

double /dubl/ a. & adv. double. —n.m. (*copie*) duplicate; (*sosie*) double. **le ~e (de)**, twice as much ou as many as.) **le ~e messieurs**, the men's doubles. **~e décimètre**, ruler. **~ement**[1] adv. doubly.

doubl|er /duble/ v.t./i. double; (*dépasser*) overtake; (*vêtement*) line; (*film*) dub; (*classe*) repeat; (*cap*) round. **~ement**[2] n.m. doubling. **~ure** n.f. (*étoffe*) lining; (*acteur*) understudy.

douce /dus/ voir **doux**.

douceâtre /dusatʀ/ a. sickly sweet.

doucement /dusmã/ adv. gently.

douceur /dusœʀ/ n.f. (*mollesse*) softness; (*de climat*) mildness; (*de personne*) gentleness; (*joie, plaisir*) sweetness. **~s**, (*friandises*) sweet things. **en ~**, smoothly.

douch|e /duʃ/ n.f. shower. **~er** v.t.

give a shower to. **se ~er** v. pr. (have ou take a) shower.

doudoune /dudun/ n.f. (*fam.*) anorak.

doué /dwe/ a. gifted. **~ de**, endowed with.

douille /duj/ n.f. (*électr.*) socket.

douillet, ~te /duja, -t/ a. cosy, comfortable; (*personne: péj.*) soft.

doul|eur /dulœʀ/ n.f. pain; (*chagrin*) grief. **~oureux, ~oureuse** a. painful; (*plaie*) **~oureuse** n.f. the bill.

doute /dut/ n.m. doubt. **sans ~**, no doubt. **sans aucun ~**, without doubt.

douter /dute/ v.i. **~ de**, doubt. **se ~ de**, suspect.

douteu|x, ~se /dutø, -z/ a. doubtful.

Douvres /duvʀ/ n.m./f. Dover.

doux, douce /du, dus/ a. (*moelleux*) soft; (*sucré*) sweet; (*clément, pas fort*) mild; (*pas brusque, bienveillant*) gentle.

douzaine /duzɛn/ n.f. about twelve; (*douze*) dozen. **une ~ d'œufs/etc.**, a dozen eggs/etc.

douz|e /duz/ a. & n.m. twelve. **~ième** a. & n.m./f. twelfth.

doyen, ~ne /dwajɛ̃, -jɛn/ n.m., f. dean; (*en âge*) most senior person.

dragée /draʒe/ n.f. sugared almond.

dragon /dragɔ̃/ n.m. dragon.

dragu|e /drag/ n.f. (*bateau*) dredger. **~er** v.t. (*rivière*) dredge; (*filles: fam.*) chat up, try to pick up.

drain /drɛ̃/ n.m. drain.

drainer /dʀene/ v.t. drain.

dramatique /dramatik/ a. dramatic; (*tragique*) tragic. —n.f. (television) drama.

dramatiser /dramatize/ v.t. dramatize.

dramaturge /dramatyʀʒ/ n.m./f. dramatist.

drame /dram/ n.m. drama.

drap /dra/ n.m. sheet; (tissu) (woollen) cloth. **~-housse** /draus/ n.m. fitted sheet.

drapeau (pl. **~x**) /drapo/ n.m. flag.

draper /drape/ v.t. drape.

dress|er /drese/ v.t. put up, erect; (tête) raise; (animal) train; (liste etc.) draw up. **se ~er** v. pr. (bâtiment etc.) stand; (personne) draw o.s. up. **~er l'oreille**, prick up one's ears. **~age** /drɛsaʒ/ n.m. training. **~eur, ~euse** /drɛsœr, -øz/ n.m., f. trainer.

dribbler /drible/ v.t./i. (sport) dribble.

drille /drij/ n.m. **un joyeux ~**, a cheery character.

drive /drajv/ n.m. (comput.) drive.

drogue /drɔg/ n.f. drug. la **~**, drugs.

drogu|er /drɔge/ v.t. (malade) drug heavily, dose up; (victime) drug. **se ~er** v. pr. take drugs. **~é, ~ée** n.m., f. drug addict.

drogu|erie /drɔgri/ n.f. hardware and chemist's shop; (Amer.) drugstore. **~iste** n.m./f. owner of a droguerie.

droit[1], **~e** /drwa, -t/ a. (non courbe) straight; (loyal) upright; (angle) right. **—adv.** straight. **—n.f.** straight line.

droit[2] **~e** /drwa, -t/ a. (contraire de gauche) right. **à ~e**, on the right; (direction) (to the) right. **la ~e**, the right (side); (pol.) the right (wing). **~ier, ~ière** /-tje, -tjɛr/ a. & n.m., f. right-handed (person).

droit[3] /drwa/ n.m. right. **~(s)** (taxe) duty; (d'inscription) fees. le **~**, (jurid.) law. avoir **~ à**, be entitled to. avoir le **~ de**, be allowed to. être dans son **~**, be in the right. **~ d'auteur**, copyright. **~s d'auteur**, royalties.

drôle /drol/ a. funny. **~ d'air**, funny look. **~ment** adv. funnily; (extrêmement; fam.) dreadfully.

dromadaire /drɔmadɛr/ n.m. dromedary.

dru /dry/ a. thick. **tomber ~**, fall thick and fast.

drugstore /drœgstɔr/ n.m. drugstore.

du /dy/ voir **de**.

dû, due /dy/ voir devoir[2]. **—a.** due. **—n.m.** due; (argent) dues. **dû à**, due to.

duc, duchesse /dyk, dyʃɛs/ n.m., f. duke, duchess.

duel /dyɛl/ n.m. duel.

dune /dyn/ n.f. dune.

duo /dyo/ n.m. (mus.) duet; (fig.) duo.

dup|e /dyp/ n.f. dupe. **~er** v.t. dupe.

duplex /dyplɛks/ n.m. split-level apartment; (Amer.) duplex; (émission) link-up.

duplicata /dyplikata/ n.m. invar. duplicate.

duplicité /dyplisite/ n.f. duplicity.

duquel /dykɛl/ voir lequel.

dur /dyr/ a. hard; (sévère) harsh, hard; (viande) tough, hard; (col, brosse) stiff. **—adv.** hard. **~ d'oreille**, hard of hearing.

durable /dyrabl/ a. lasting.

durant /dyrɑ̃/ prép. during; (mesure de temps) for.

durc|ir /dyrsir/ v.t./i, **se ~ir** v. pr. harden. **~issement** n.m. hardening.

dure /dyr/ n.f. **à la ~**, the hard way.

durée /dyre/ n.f. length; (période) duration.

durement /dyrmɑ̃/ adv. harshly.

durer /dyre/ v.i. last.

dureté /dyrte/ n.f. hardness; (sévérité) harshness.

duvet /dyvɛ/ n.m. down; (sac) (down-filled) sleeping-bag.

dynami|que /dinamik/ *a.* dynamic. **~sme** *n.m.* dynamism.

dynamit|e /dinamit/ *n.f.* dynamite. **~er** *v.t.* dynamite.

dynamo /dinamo/ *n.f.* dynamo.

dynastie /dinasti/ *n.f.* dynasty.

dysenterie /disɑ̃tri/ *n.f.* dysentery.

E

eau (*pl.* **~x**) /o/ *n.f.* water. **~ courante/dormante,** running/still water. **~ de Cologne,** eau-de-Cologne. **~ dentifrice,** mouthwash. **~ de toilette,** toilet water. **~-de-vie** (*pl.* **~x-de-vie**) *n.f.* brandy. **~ douce/salée,** fresh/salt water. **~-forte** (*pl.* **~x-fortes**) *n.f.* etching. **~ de Javel,** bleach. **~ minérale,** mineral water. **~ gazeuse,** fizzy water. **~ plate,** still water. **~x usées,** dirty water. **tomber à l'~** (*fig.*) fall through. **prendre l'~,** take in water.

ébahi /ebai/ *a.* dumbfounded.

ébattre (s') /(s)ebatr/ *v. pr.* frolic.

ébauch|e /eboʃ/ *n.f.* outline. **~er** *v.t.* outline. **s'~er** *v. pr.* form.

ébène /eben/ *n.f.* ebony.

ébéniste /ebenist/ *n.m.* cabinet-maker.

éberlué /eberlɥe/ *a.* flabbergasted.

éblou|ir /ebluir/ *v.t.* dazzle. **~issement** *n.m.* dazzle, dazzling; (*malaise*) dizzy turn.

éboueur /ebwœr/ *n.m.* dustman; (*Amer.*) garbage collector.

ébouillanter /ebujɑ̃te/ *v.t.* scald.

éboul|er (s') /(s)ebule/ *v. pr.* crumble, collapse. **~ement** *n.m.* landslide. **~is** *n.m. pl.* fallen rocks and earth.

ébouriffé /eburife/ *a.* dishevelled.

ébranler /ebrɑ̃le/ *v.t.* shake. **s'~** *v. pr.* move off.

ébrécher /ebreʃe/ *v.t.* chip.

ébriété /ebrijete/ *n.f.* intoxication.

ébrouer (s') /(s)ebrue/ *v. pr.* shake o.s.

ébruiter /ebrɥite/ *v.t.* spread about.

ébullition /ebylisjɔ̃/ *n.f.* boiling. **en ~,** boiling.

écaille /ekaj/ *n.f.* (*de poisson*) scale; (*de peinture, roc*) flake; (*matière*) tortoiseshell.

écailler /ekaje/ *v.t.* (*poisson*) scale. **s'~** *v. pr.* flake (off).

écarlate /ekarlat/ *a. & n.f.* scarlet.

écarquiller /ekarkije/ *v.t.* **~ les yeux,** open one's eyes wide.

écart /ekar/ *n.m.* gap; (*de prix etc.*) difference; (*embardée*) swerve; (*de conduite*) lapse (de, in). **à l'~,** out of the way. **tenir à l'~,** (*participant*) keep out of things. **à l'~ de,** away from.

écarté /ekarte/ *a.* (*lieu*) remote. **les jambes ~es,** (with) legs apart. **les bras ~s,** with one's arms out.

écartement /ekartəmɑ̃/ *n.m.* gap.

écarter /ekarte/ *v.t.* (*objets*) move apart; (*ouvrir*) open; (*éliminer*) dismiss. **~ qch. de,** move sth. away from. **~ qn. de,** keep s.o. away from. **s'~** *v. pr.* (*s'éloigner*) move away; (*quitter son chemin*) move aside. **s'~ de,** stray from.

ecchymose /ekimoz/ *n.f.* bruise.

ecclésiastique /eklezjastik/ *a.* ecclesiastical. *—n.m.* clergyman.

écervelé, ~e /eservəle/ *a.* scatter-brained. *—n.m., f.* scatter-brain.

échafaud|age /eʃafodaʒ/ *n.m.* scaffolding; (*amas*) heap. **~er** *v.t.* (*projets*) construct.

échalote /eʃalot/ *n.f.* shallot.

échang|e /eʃɑ̃ʒ/ *n.m.* exchange. **en ~ (de),** in exchange (for). **~er** *v.t.* exchange (**contre,** for).

échangeur /eʃɑ̃ʒœr/ *n.m.* (*auto.*) interchange.

échantillon /eʃɑ̃tijɔ̃/ *n.m.* sample. **~nage** /-jonaʒ/ *n.m.* range of samples.

échappatoire /eʃapatwar/ *n.f.* (clever) way out.

échappée /eʃape/ *n.f.* (*sport*) break-away.

échappement /eʃapmɑ̃/ *n.m.* exhaust.

échapper /eʃape/ *v.i.* ~ à, escape; (*en fuyant*) escape (from). **s'**~ *v. pr.* escape. ~ **des mains de** *ou* à, slip out of the hands of. **l'**~ **belle**, have a narrow *ou* lucky escape.

écharde /eʃard/ *n.f.* splinter.

écharpe /eʃarp/ *n.f.* scarf; (*de maire*) sash. **en** ~, (*bras*) in a sling.

échasse /eʃas/ *n.f.* stilt.

échassier /eʃasje/ *n.m.* wader.

échaud|er /eʃode/ *v.t.* **se faire** ~**er, être** ~**é**, get one's fingers burnt.

échauffer /eʃofe/ *v.t.* heat; (*fig.*) excite. **s'**~ *v. pr.* warm up.

échauffourée /eʃofure/ *n.f.* (*mil.*) skirmish; (*bagarre*) scuffle.

échéance /eʃeɑ̃s/ *n.f.* due date (for payment); (*délai*) deadline; (*obligation*) (financial) commitment.

échéant (le cas) /(ləkaz)eʃeɑ̃/ *adv.* if the occasion arises, possibly.

échec /eʃɛk/ *n.m.* failure. ~**s**, (*jeu*) chess. ~ **et mat**, checkmate. **en** ~, in check.

échelle /eʃɛl/ *n.f.* ladder; (*dimension*) scale.

échelon /eʃlɔ̃/ *n.m.* rung; (*de fonctionnaire*) grade; (*niveau*) level.

échelonner /eʃlɔne/ *v.t.* spread out, space out.

échevelé /eʃəvle/ *a.* dishevelled.

échine /eʃin/ *n.f.* backbone.

échiquier /eʃikje/ *n.m.* chessboard.

écho /eko/ *n.m.* echo. ~**s**, (*dans la presse*) gossip.

échographie /ekografi/ *n.f.* ultrasound (scan).

échoir /eʃwar/ *v.i.* (*dette*) fall due; (*délai*) expire.

échoppe /eʃɔp/ *n.f.* stall.

échouer[1] /eʃwe/ *v.i.* fail.

échouer[2] /eʃwe/ *v.t.* (*bateau*) ground. —*v.i.*, **s'**~ *v. pr.* run aground.

échu /eʃy/ *a.* (*delai*) expired.

éclabouss|er /eklabuse/ *v.t.* splash. ~**ure** *n.f.* splash.

éclair /eklɛr/ *n.m.* (flash of) lightning; (*fig.*) flash; (*gâteau*) éclair. —*a. invar.* lightning.

éclairage /eklɛraʒ/ *n.m.* lighting; (*point de vue*) light. ~**iste** /-aʒist/ *n.* lighting technician.

éclaircie /eklɛrsi/ *n.f.* sunny interval.

éclairc|ir /eklɛrsir/ *v.t.* make lighter; (*mystère*) clear up. **s'**~**ir** *v. pr.* (*ciel*) clear; (*mystère*) become clearer. ~**issement** *n.m.* clarification.

éclairer /eklere/ *v.t.* light (up); (*personne*) give some light to; (*fig.*) enlighten; (*situation*) throw light on. —*v.i.* give light. **s'**~ *v. pr.* become clearer. **s'**~ **à la bougie**, use candle-light.

éclaireu|r, ~se /eklɛrœr, -øz/ *n.m., f.* (boy) scout, (girl) guide. —*n.m.* (*mil.*) scout.

éclat /ekla/ *n.m.* fragment; (*de lumière*) brightness; (*de rire*) (out)burst; (*splendeur*) brilliance.

éclatant, ~e /eklatɑ̃, -t/ *a.* brilliant.

éclat|er /eklate/ *v.i.* burst; (*exploser*) go off; (*verre*) shatter; (*guerre*) break out; (*groupe*) split up. ~**er de rire**, burst out laughing. ~**ement** *n.m.* bursting; (*de bombe*) explosion; (*scission*) split.

éclipse /eklips/ *n.f.* eclipse. **s'**~ *v. pr.* slip away.

éclo|re /eklɔr/ *v.i.* (*œuf*) hatch; (*fleur*) open. ~**sion** *n.f.* hatching; opening.

écluse /eklyz/ *n.f.* (*de canal*) lock.

écœurant, ~e /ekœrã, -t/ *a.* (*gâteau*) sickly; (*fig.*) disgusting.

écœurer /ekœre/ *v.t.* sicken.

école /ekɔl/ *n.f.* school. ~ **maternelle / primaire / secondaire,** nursery / primary / secondary school. ~ **normale,** teachers' training college.

écol|ier, ~ière /ekɔlje, -jɛr/ *n.m., f.* schoolboy, schoolgirl.

écolo /ekɔlo/ *a. & n.m./f.* green.

écolog|ie /ekɔlɔʒi/ *n.f.* ecology. ~**ique** *a.* ecological, green.

écologiste /ekɔlɔʒist/ *n.m./f.* ecologist.

éconduire /ekɔ̃dɥir/ *v.t.* dismiss.

économat /ekɔnɔma/ *n.m.* bursary.

économe /ekɔnɔm/ *a.* thrifty. —*n.m./f.* bursar.

économ|ie /ekɔnɔmi/ *n.f.* economy. ~**ies,** (*argent*) savings. **une ~ie de,** (*gain*) a saving of. ~**ie politique,** economics. ~**ique** *a.* economic; (*bon marché*) economical. ~**iser** *v.t./i.* save. ~**iste** *n.m./f.* economist.

écoper /ekɔpe/ *v.t.* bail out. ~ (**de**), (*fam.*) get.

écorce /ekɔrs/ *n.f.* bark; (*de fruit*) peel.

écorch|er /ekɔrʃe/ *v.t.* graze; (*animal*) skin. **s'~er** *v. pr.* graze o.s. ~**ure** *n.f.* graze.

écossais, ~e /ekɔsɛ, -z/ *a.* Scottish. —*n.m., f.* Scot.

Écosse /ekɔs/ *n.f.* Scotland.

écosser /ekɔse/ *v.t.* shell.

écosystème /ekɔsistɛm/ *n.m.* ecosystem.

écouler[1] /ekule/ *v.t.* dispose of, sell.

écoul|er[2] (**s'**) /(s)ekule/ *v. pr.* flow (out), run (off); (*temps*) pass. ~**ement** *n.m.* flow.

écourter /ekurte/ *v.t.* shorten.

écoute /ekut/ *n.f.* listening. **à l'~**

(**de**), listening in (to). **aux ~s,** attentive. **heures de grande ~,** peak time. **~s téléphoniques,** phone tapping.

écout|er /ekute/ *v.t.* listen to; (*radio*) listen (in) to. —*v.i.* listen. ~**eur** *n.m.* earphones; (*de téléphone*) receiver.

écran /ekrã/ *n.m.* screen. ~ **total,** sun-block.

écrasant, ~e /ekrazã, -t/ *a.* overwhelming.

écraser /ekraze/ *v.t.* crush; (*piéton*) run over. **s'~** *v. pr.* crash (**contre**, into).

écrémé /ekreme/ *a.* **lait ~,** skimmed milk. **lait demi-~,** semi-skimmed milk.

écrevisse /ekrəvis/ *n.f.* crayfish.

écrier (s') /(s)ekrije/ *v. pr.* exclaim.

écrin /ekrɛ̃/ *n.m.* case.

écrire† /ekrir/ *v.t./i.* write; (*orthographier*) spell. **s'~** *v. pr.* (*mot*) be spelt.

écrit /ekri/ *n.m.* document; (*examen*) written paper. **par ~,** in writing.

écriteau (*pl.* ~**x**) /ekrito/ *n.m.* notice.

écriture /ekrityr/ *n.f.* writing. ~**s,** (*comm.*) accounts. **l'É-~ (sainte),** the Scriptures.

écrivain /ekrivɛ̃/ *n.m.* writer.

écrou /ekru/ *n.m.* nut.

écrouer /ekrue/ *v.t.* imprison.

écrouler (s') /(s)ekrule/ *v. pr.* collapse.

écru /ekry/ *a.* (*couleur*) natural; (*tissu*) raw.

Écu /eky/ *n.m. invar.* ecu.

écueil /ekœj/ *n.m.* reef; (*fig.*) danger.

éculé /ekyle/ *a.* (*soulier*) worn at the heel; (*fig.*) well-worn.

écume /ekym/ *n.f.* foam; (*culin.*) scum.

écum|er /ekyme/ *v.t.* skim; (*piller*) plunder. —*v.i.* foam. ~**oire** *n.f.* skimmer.

écureuil /ekyrœj/ *n.m.* squirrel.

écurie /ekyri/ *n.f.* stable.

écuy|er, **~ère** /ekɥije. -jer/ *n.m.,
f.* (horse) rider.

eczéma /ɛgzema/ *n.m.* eczema.

édenté /edɑ̃te/ *a.* toothless.

édifice /edifis/ *n.m.* building.

édif|ier /edifje/ *v.t.* construct;
(*porter à la vertu, éclairer*) edify.
~ication *n.f.* construction;
edification.

édit /edi/ *n.m.* edict.

édi|ter /edite/ *v.t.* publish;
(*annoter*) edit. **~teur**, **~trice**
n.m., f. publisher; editor.

édition /edisjɔ̃/ *n.f.* edition;
(*industrie*) publishing.

éditor|ial (*pl.* **~iaux**) /editɔrjal.
-jo/ *n.m.* editorial.

édredon /edrədɔ̃/ *n.m.* eiderdown.

éducateur, **~trice** /edykatœr.
-tris/ *n.m., f.* teacher.

éducati|f, **~ve** /edykatif. -v/ *a.*
educational.

éducation /edykasjɔ̃/ *n.f.* education; (*dans la famille*) upbringing;
(*manières*) manners. **~ physique**, physical education.

édulcorant /edylkɔrɑ̃/ *n.m. & a.*
(*produit*) **~**, sweetener.

éduquer /edyke/ *v.t.* educate; (*à la
maison*) bring up.

effac|é /efase/ *a.* (*modeste*) unas-
suming. **~ement** *n.m.* unassuming manner; (*suppression*) eras-
ure.

effacer /efase/ *v.t.* (*gommer*) rub
out; (*par lavage*) wash out;
(*souvenir etc.*) erase. **s'~** *v. pr.*
fade; (*s'écarter*) step aside.

effar|er /efare/ *v.t.* alarm.
~ement *n.m.* alarm.

effaroucher /efaruʃe/ *v.t.* scare
away.

effecti|f[1], **~ve** /efɛktif. -v/ *a.*
effective. **~vement** *adv.* effec-
tively; (*en effet*) indeed.

effectif[2] /efɛktif/ *n.m.* size,
strength. **~s**, numbers.

effectuer /efɛktɥe/ *v.t.* carry out,
make.

effervescen|t, **~te** /efɛrvesɑ̃. -t/
a. **comprimé ~t**, effervescent
tablet. **~ce** *n.f.* excitement.

effet /efɛ/ *n.m.* effect; (*impression*)
impression. **~s**, (*habits*) clothes,
things. **en ~**, indeed. **faire de
l'~**, have an effect, be effective.
faire bon/mauvais ~, make a
good/bad impression.

efficac|e /efikas/ *a.* effective;
(*personne*) efficient. **~ité** *n.f.*
effectiveness; efficiency.

effigie /efiʒi/ *n.f.* effigy.

effilocher (s') /(s)efiloʃe/ *v. pr.*
fray.

efflanqué /eflɑ̃ke/ *a.* emaciated.

effleurer /eflœre/ *v.t.* touch
lightly; (*sujet*) touch on; (*se
présenter à*) occur to.

effluves /eflyv/ *n.m. pl.* exhala-
tions.

effondr|er (s') /(s)efɔ̃dre/ *v. pr.*
collapse. **~ement** *n.m.* collapse.

efforcer (s') /(s)efɔrse/ *v. pr.* try
(*hard*) (de, to).

effort /efɔr/ *n.m.* effort.

effraction /efraksjɔ̃/ *n.f.* entrer
par ~, break in.

effray|er /efreje/ *v.t.* frighten;
(*décourager*) put off. **s'~er** *v. pr.*
be frightened. **~ant**, **~ante** *a.*
frightening; (*fig.*) frightful.

effréné /efrene/ *a.* wild.

effriter (s') /(s)efrite/ *v. pr.*
crumble.

effroi /efrwa/ *n.m.* dread.

effronté /efrɔ̃te/ *a.* impudent.

effroyable /efrwajabl/ *a.* dreadful.

effusion /efyzjɔ̃/ *n.f.* **~ de sang**,
bloodshed.

égal, **~ale** (*m. pl.* **~aux**) /egal.
-o/ *a.* equal; (*surface, vitesse*)
even. **~**, **~**, *f.* equal. **ça
m'est/lui est ~al**, it is all the
same to me/him. **sans égal**,

matchless. **d'~ à égal,** between equals.

également /egalmã/ *adv.* equally; *(aussi)* as well.

égaler /egale/ *v.t.* equal.

égaliser /egalize/ *v.t./i. (sport)* equalize; *(niveler)* level out; *(cheveux)* trim.

égalit|é /egalite/ *n.f.* equality; *(de surface, d'humeur)* evenness. **à ~é (de points),** equal. **~aire** *a.* egalitarian.

égard /egar/ *n.m.* regard. **~s,** consideration. **à cet ~,** in this respect. **à l'~ de,** with regard to; *(envers)* towards. **eu ~ à,** in view of.

égar|er /egare/ *v.t.* mislay; *(tromper)* lead astray. **s'~er** *v. pr.* get lost; *(se tromper)* go astray. **~ement** *n.m.* loss; *(affolement)* confusion.

égayer /egeje/ *v.t. (personne)* cheer up; *(pièce)* brighten up.

égide /eʒid/ *n.f.* aegis.

églantier /eglãtje/ *n.m.* wild rose (-bush).

églefin /egləfɛ̃/ *n.m.* haddock.

église /egliz/ *n.f.* church.

égoïs|te /egoist/ *a.* selfish. —*n.m./f.* egoist. **~me** *n.m.* selfishness, egoism.

égorger /egorʒe/ *v.t.* slit the throat of.

égosiller (s') /(s)egozije/ *v. pr.* shout one's head off.

égout /egu/ *n.m.* sewer.

égoutt|er /egute/ *v.t./i.,* **s'~er** *v. pr. (vaisselle)* drain. **~oir** *n.m.* draining-board; *(panier)* dish drainer.

égratign|er /egratiɲe/ *v.t.* scratch. **~ure** *n.f.* scratch.

égrener /egrəne/ *v.t. (raisins)* pick off; *(notes)* sound one by one.

Égypte /eʒipt/ *n.f.* Egypt.

égyptien, ~ne /eʒipsjɛ̃, -jɛn/ *a. & n.m.,f.* Egyptian.

eh /e/ *int.* hey. **eh bien,** well.

éjacul|er /eʒakyle/ *v.i.* ejaculate. **~ation** *n.f.* ejaculation.

éjectable /eʒɛktabl/ *a.* **siège ~,** ejector seat.

éjecter /eʒɛkte/ *v.t.* eject.

élabor|er /elabore/ *v.t.* elaborate. **~ation** *n.f.* elaboration.

élaguer /elage/ *v.t.* prune.

élan[1] /elã/ *n.m. (sport)* run-up; *(vitesse)* momentum; *(fig.)* surge.

élan[2] /elã/ *n.m. (animal)* moose.

élancé /elãse/ *a.* slender.

élancement /elãsmã/ *n.m.* twinge.

élancer (s') /(s)elãse/ *v. pr.* leap forward, dash; *(se dresser)* soar.

élarg|ir /elarʒir/ *v.t.,* **s'~ir** *v. pr.* widen. **~issement** *n.m.* widening.

élasti|que /elastik/ *a.* elastic. —*n.m.* elastic band; *(tissu)* elastic. **~cité** *n.f.* elasticity.

élec|teur, ~trice /elɛktœr, -tris/ *n.m., f.* voter, elector.

élection /elɛksjɔ̃/ *n.f.* election.

élector|al *(m. pl. ~aux)* /elɛktoral, -o/ *a. (réunion etc.)* election; *(collège)* electoral.

électorat /elɛktora/ *n.m.* electorate, voters.

électricien /elɛktrisjɛ̃/ *n.m.* electrician.

électricité /elɛktrisite/ *n.f.* electricity.

électrifier /elɛktrifje/ *v.t.* electrify.

électrique /elɛktrik/ *a.* electric(al).

électrocuter /elɛktrokyte/ *v.t.* electrocute.

électroménager /elɛktromenaʒe/ *n.m.* l'**~,** household appliances.

électron /elɛktrɔ̃/ *n.m.* electron.

électronique /elɛktronik/ *a.* electronic. —*n.f.* electronics.

électrophone /elɛktrofon/ *n.m.* record-player.

élég|ant, ~ante /elegã, -t/ *a.* elegant. **~amment** *adv.* elegantly. **~ance** *n.f.* elegance.

élément /elemã/ *n.m.* element;

(*meuble*) unit. **~aire** /-tɛr/ *a.* elementary.

éléphant /elefɑ̃/ *n.m.* elephant.

élevage /elvaʒ/ *n.m.* (stock-) breeding.

élévation /elevasjɔ̃/ *n.f.* raising; (*hausse*) rise; (*plan*) elevation.

élève /elɛv/ *n.m./f.* pupil.

élevé /elve/ *a.* high; (*noble*) elevated. **bien ~**, well-mannered.

élever /elve/ *v.t.* raise; (*enfants*) bring up; (*animal*) breed. **s'~** *v. pr.* rise; (*dans le ciel*) soar up. **s'~ à**, amount to.

éleveu|r, ~se /elvœr, -øz/ *n.m., f.* (stock-)breeder.

éligible /eliʒibl/ *a.* eligible.

élimé /elime/ *a.* worn thin.

élimin|er /elimine/ *v.t.* eliminate. **~ation** *n.f.* elimination. **~atoire** *a.* eliminating; *n.f.* (*sport*) heat.

élire† /elir/ *v.t.* elect.

élite /elit/ *n.f.* élite.

elle /ɛl/ *pron.* she; (*complément*) her; (*chose*) it. **~-même** *pron.* herself; itself.

elles /ɛl/ *pron.* they; (*complément*) them. **~-mêmes** *pron.* themselves.

ellip|se /elips/ *n.f.* ellipse. **~tique** *a.* elliptical.

élocution /elɔkysjɔ̃/ *n.f.* diction.

élog|e /elɔʒ/ *n.m.* praise. **faire l'~e de**, praise. **~ieux, ~ieuse** *a.* laudatory.

éloigné /elwaɲe/ *a.* distant. **~ de**, far away from. **parent ~**, distant relative.

éloign|er /elwaɲe/ *v.t.* take away *ou* remove (**de**, from); (*personne aimée*) estrange (**de**, from); (*danger*) ward off; (*visite*) put off. **s'~er** *v. pr.* go *ou* move away (**de**, from); (*affectivement*) become estranged (**de**, from). **~ement** *n.m.* removal; (*distance*) distance; (*oubli*) estrangement.

élongation /elɔ̃gasjɔ̃/ *n.f.* strained muscle.

éloquen|t, ~te /elɔkɑ̃, -t/ *a.* eloquent. **~ce** *n.f.* eloquence.

élu, ~e /ely/ *a.* elected. —*n.m., f.* (*pol.*) elected representative.

élucider /elyside/ *v.t.* elucidate.

éluder /elyde/ *v.t.* elude.

émacié /emasje/ *a.* emaciated.

ém|ail (*pl.* **~aux**) /emaj, -o/ *n.m.* enamel.

émaillé /emaje/ *a.* enamelled. **~ de**, studded with.

émancip|er /emɑ̃sipe/ *v.t.* emancipate. **s'~er** *v. pr.* become emancipated. **~ation** *n.f.* emancipation.

éman|er /emane/ *v.i.* emanate. **~ation** *n.f.* emanation.

émarger /emarʒe/ *v.t.* initial.

emball|er /ɑ̃bale/ *v.t.* pack, wrap; (*personne. fam.*) enthuse. **s'~er** *v. pr.* (*moteur*) race; (*cheval*) bolt; (*personne*) get carried away. **~age** *n.m.* package, wrapping.

embarcadère /ɑ̃barkadɛr/ *n.m.* landing-stage.

embarcation /ɑ̃barkasjɔ̃/ *n.f.* boat.

embardée /ɑ̃barde/ *n.f.* swerve.

embargo /ɑ̃bargo/ *n.m.* embargo.

embarqu|er /ɑ̃barke/ *v.t.* embark; (*charger*) load; (*emporter. fam.*) cart off. —*v.i., v. pr.* embark. **s'~er dans**, embark upon. **~ement** *n.m.* embarkation; loading.

embarras /ɑ̃bara/ *n.m.* obstacle; (*gêne*) embarrassment; (*difficulté*) difficulty.

embarrass|er /ɑ̃barase/ *v.t.* clutter (up); (*gêner dans les mouvements*) hinder; (*fig.*) embarrass. **s'~ de**, burden o.s. with.

embauch|e /ɑ̃boʃ/ *n.f.* hiring; (*emploi*) employment. **~er** *v.t.* hire, take on.

embauchoir /ɑ̃boʃwar/ *n.m.* shoe tree.

embaumer /ãbome/ v.t./i. (make) smell fragrant; (cadavre) embalm.

embellir /ãbelir/ v.t. brighten up; (récit) embellish.

embêt|er /ãbete/ v.t. (fam.) annoy. **s'~er** v. pr. (fam.) get bored. **~ant, ~ante** a. (fam.) annoying. **~ement** /ãbɛtmã/ n.m. (fam.) annoyance.

emblée (d') /(d)ãble/ adv right away.

emblème /ãblɛm/ n.m. emblem.

embobiner /ãbɔbine/ v.t. (fam.) get round.

emboît|er /ãbwate/ v.t., **s'~** v. pr. fit together. **(s')~ dans**, fit into. **~ le pas à qn.**, (imiter) follow suit.

embonpoint /ãbɔ̃pwɛ̃/ n.m. stoutness.

embouchure /ãbuʃyr/ n.f. (de fleuve) mouth; (mus.) mouthpiece.

embourber (s') /(s)ãburbe/ v. pr. get bogged down.

embourgeoiser (s') /(s)ãbur-ʒwaze/ v. pr. become middle-class.

embout /ãbu/ n.m. tip.

embouteillage /ãbutejaʒ/ n.m. traffic jam.

emboutir /ãbutir/ v.t. (heurter) crash into.

embranchement /ãbrãʃmã/ n.m. (de routes) junction.

embras|er /ãbraze/ v.t. set on fire, fire. **s'~** v. pr. flare up.

embrass|er /ãbrase/ v.t. kiss; (adopter, contenir) embrace. **s'~er** v. pr. kiss. **~ades** n.f. pl. kissing.

embrasure /ãbrazyr/ n.f. opening.

embray|er /ãbreje/ v.i. let in the clutch. **~age** /ãbrejaʒ/ n.m. clutch.

embrigader /ãbrigade/ v.t. enrol.

embrocher /ãbrɔʃe/ v.t. (viande) spit.

embrouiller /ãbruje/ v.t. mix up;

(fils) tangle. **s'~** v. pr. get mixed up.

embroussaillé /ãbrusaje/ a. (poils, chemin) bushy.

embryon /ãbrijɔ̃/ n.m. embryo. **~naire** /-jɔnɛr/ a. embryonic.

embûches /ãbyʃ/ n.f. pl. traps.

embuer /ãbɥe/ v.t. mist up.

embuscade /ãbyskad/ n.f. ambush.

embusquer (s') /(s)ãbyske/ v. pr. lie in ambush.

éméché /emeʃe/ a. tipsy.

émeraude /emrod/ n.f. emerald.

émerger /emɛrʒe/ v.i. emerge; (fig.) stand out.

émeri /emri/ n.m. emery.

émerveill|er /emɛrveje/ v.t. amaze. **s'~er de**, marvel at, be amazed at. **~ement** /-vejmã/ n.m. amazement, wonder.

émett|re† /emɛtr/ v.t. give out; (message) transmit; (timbre, billet) issue; (opinion) express. **~eur** n.m. transmitter.

émeut|e /emøt/ n.f. riot. **~ier, ~ière** n.m., f. rioter.

émietter /emjete/ v.t., **s'~** v. pr. crumble.

émigrant, ~e /emigrã, -t/ n.m., f. emigrant.

émigr|er /emigre/ v.i. emigrate. **~ation** n.f. emigration.

émincer /emɛ̃se/ v.t. cut into thin slices.

émin|ent, ~ente /eminã, -t/ a. eminent. **~emment** /-amã/ adv. eminently. **~ence** n.f. eminence; (colline) hill. **~ence grise**, éminence grise.

émissaire /emisɛr/ n.m. emissary.

émission /emisjɔ̃/ n.f. emission; (de message) transmission; (de timbre) issue; (programme) broadcast.

emmagasiner /ãmagazine/ v.t. store.

emmanchure /ãmãʃyr/ n.f. armhole.

emmêler /ɑ̃mele/ v.t. tangle. **s'~** v. pr. get mixed up.

emménager /ɑ̃menaʒe/ v.i. move in. **~ dans,** move into.

emmener /ɑ̃mne/ v.t. take; *(comme prisonnier)* take away.

emmerder /ɑ̃mɛrde/ v.t. *(argot)* bother. **s'~** v. pr. *(argot)* get bored.

emmitoufler /ɑ̃mitufle/ v.t., **s'~** v. pr. wrap up (warmly).

émoi /emwa/ n.m. excitement.

émoluments /emolymɑ̃/ n.m. pl. remuneration.

émonder /emɔ̃de/ v.t. prune.

émoti|f, **~ve** /emɔtif, -v/ a. emotional.

émotion /emosjɔ̃/ n.f. emotion; *(peur)* fright. **~nel,** **~nelle** /-jɔnɛl/ a. emotional.

émousser /emuse/ v.t. blunt.

émouv|oir /emuvwar/ v.t. move. **s'~oir** v. pr. be moved. **~ant,** **~ante** a. moving.

empailler /ɑ̃paje/ v.t. stuff.

empaqueter /ɑ̃pakte/ v.t. package.

emparer (s') /(s)ɑ̃pare/ v. pr. **s'~ de,** seize.

empâter (s') /(s)ɑ̃pate/ v. pr. fill out, grow fatter.

empêchement /ɑ̃pɛʃmɑ̃/ n.m. hitch, difficulty.

empêcher /ɑ̃pɛʃe/ v.t. prevent. **~ de faire,** prevent ou stop (from) doing. **il ne peut pas s'~ de penser,** he cannot help thinking. **(il) n'empêche que,** still.

empeigne /ɑ̃pɛɲ/ n.f. upper.

empereur /ɑ̃prœr/ n.m. emperor.

empeser /ɑ̃paze/ v.t. starch.

empester /ɑ̃pɛste/ v.t. make stink, stink out; *(essence etc.)* stink of. —v.i. stink.

empêtrer (s') /(s)ɑ̃petre/ v. pr. become entangled.

emphase /ɑ̃faz/ n.f. pomposity.

empiéter /ɑ̃pjete/ v.i. **~ sur,** encroach upon.

empiffrer (s') /(s)ɑ̃pifre/ v. pr. *(fam.)* gorge o.s.

empiler /ɑ̃pile/ v.t., **s'~** v. pr. pile (up).

empire /ɑ̃pir/ n.m. empire; *(fig.)* control.

empirer /ɑ̃pire/ v.i. worsen.

empirique /ɑ̃pirik/ a. empirical.

emplacement /ɑ̃plasmɑ̃/ n.m. site.

emplâtre /ɑ̃plɑtr/ n.m. *(méd.)* plaster.

emplettes /ɑ̃plɛt/ n.f. pl. purchase. **faire des ~,** do one's shopping.

emplir /ɑ̃plir/ v.t., **s'~** v. pr. fill.

emploi /ɑ̃plwa/ n.m. use; *(travail)* job. **~ du temps,** timetable. **l'~,** *(pol.)* employment.

employ|er /ɑ̃plwaje/ v.t. use; *(personne)* employ. **s'~er** v. pr. be used. **s'~er à,** devote o.s. to. **~é,** **~ée** n.m., f. employee. **~eur,** **~euse** n.m., f. employer.

empocher /ɑ̃pɔʃe/ v.t. pocket.

empoigner /ɑ̃pwaɲe/ v.t. grab. **s'~** v. pr. come to blows.

empoisonn|er /ɑ̃pwazɔne/ v.t. poison; *(empuantir)* stink out; *(embêter: fam.)* annoy. **~ement** n.m. poisoning.

emport|é /ɑ̃pɔrte/ a. quick-tempered. **~ement** n.m. anger.

emporter /ɑ̃pɔrte/ v.t. take (away); *(entraîner)* carry away; *(prix)* carry off; *(arracher)* tear off. **~ un chapeau/etc.,** *(vent)* blow off a hat/etc. **s'~** v. pr. lose one's temper. **l'~,** get the upper hand (sur, of). **plat à ~,** take-away.

empourpré /ɑ̃purpre/ a. crimson.

empreint|e /ɑ̃prɛ̃, -t/ a. **~e de,** marked with. —n.f. mark. **~e (digitale),** fingerprint. **~e de pas,** footprint.

empresser (s') /(s)ɑ̃prese/ v. pr. **s'~er auprès de,** be attentive to.

s'**~er de**, hasten to. **~é** a. eager, attentive. **~ement** /ãprəsmã/ n.m. eagerness.

emprise /ãpriz/ n.f. influence.

emprisonn|er /ãprizɔne/ v.t. imprison. **~ement** n.m. imprisonment.

emprunt /ãprœ̃/ n.m. loan. **faire un ~**, take out a loan.

emprunté /ãprœ̃te/ a. awkward.

emprunt|er /ãprœ̃te/ v.t. borrow (**à**, from); (route) take; (fig.) assume. **~eur, ~euse** n.m., f. borrower.

ému /emy/ a. moved; (apeuré) nervous; (joyeux) excited.

émulation /emylasjɔ̃/ n.f. emulation.

émule /emyl/ n.m./f. imitator.

émulsion /emylsjɔ̃/ n.f. emulsion.

en[1] /ã/ prép. in; (avec direction) to; (manière, état) in, on; (moyen de transport); (composition) made of. **en cadeau/médecin**/etc., as a present/doctor/etc. **en guerre**, at war. **en faisant**, by ou on ou while doing.

en[2] /ã/ pron. of it, of them; (moyen) with it; (cause) from it; (lieu) from there. **en avoir/vouloir**/etc., have/want/etc. some. **ne pas en avoir/vouloir**/etc., not have/want/etc. any. **où en êtes-vous?**, where are you up to, how far have you got? **j'en ai assez**, I've had enough. **en êtes-vous sûr?**, are you sure?

encadr|er /ãkadre/ v.t. frame; (entourer d'un trait) circle; (entourer) surround. **~ement** n.m. framing; (de porte) frame.

encaiss|er /ãkese/ v.t. (argent) collect; (chèque) cash; (coups: fam.) take. **~eur** /ãkesœr/ n.m. debt-collector.

encart /ãkar/ n.m. **~ publicitaire**, (advertising) insert.

en-cas /ãka/ n.m. (stand-by) snack.

encastré /ãkastre/ a. built-in.

encaustiqu|e /ãkostik/ n.f. wax polish. **~er** v.t. wax.

enceinte[1] /ãsɛ̃t/ a.f. pregnant. **~ de 3 mois**, 3 months pregnant.

enceinte[2] /ãsɛ̃t/ n.f. enclosure. **~ (acoustique)**, loudspeaker.

encens /ãsã/ n.m. incense.

encercler /ãserkle/ v.t. surround.

enchaîn|er /ãʃene/ v.t. chain (up); (coordonner) link (up). —v.i. continue. **s'~er** v. pr. be linked (up). **~ement** /ãʃenmã/ n.m. (suite) chain; (liaison) link(ing).

enchant|er /ãʃãte/ v.t. delight; (ensorceler) enchant. **~é** a. (ravi) delighted. **~ement** n.m. delight; (magie) enchantment.

enchâsser /ãʃase/ v.t. set.

enchère /ãʃer/ n.f. bid. **mettre ou vendre aux ~s**, sell by auction.

enchevêtr|er /ãʃvetre/ v.t. tangle. **s'~** v. pr. become tangled.

enclave /ãklav/ n.f. enclave.

enclencher /ãklãʃe/ v.t. engage.

enclin, ~e /ãklɛ̃, -in/ a. **~ à**, inclined to.

enclore /ãklɔr/ v.t. enclose.

enclos /ãklo/ n.m. enclosure.

enclume /ãklym/ n.f. anvil.

encoche /ãkɔʃ/ n.f. notch.

encoignure /ãkɔɲyr/ n.f. corner.

encoller /ãkɔle/ v.t. paste.

encolure /ãkɔlyr/ n.f. neck.

encombre n.m. **sans ~**, without any problems.

encombr|er /ãkɔ̃bre/ v.t. clutter (up); (gêner) hamper. **s'~er de**, burden o.s. with. **~ant, ~ante** a. cumbersome. **~ement** n.m. congestion; (auto.) traffic jam; (volume) bulk.

encontre (à l') /(al)ãkɔ̃trədə/ prép. against.

encore /ãkɔr/ adv. (toujours) still; (de nouveau) again; (de plus) more; (aussi) also. **~ mieux/plus grand**/etc., even better/larger/etc. **~ une heure/un**

café/*etc.*, another hour/coffee/ *etc.* **pas ~**, not yet. **si ~**, if only.

encourag|er /ākuraʒe/ *v.t.* encourage. **~ement** *n.m.* encouragement.

encourir /ākurir/ *v.t.* incur.

encrasser /ākrase/ *v.t.* clog up (with dirt).

encr|e /ākr/ *n.f.* ink. **~er** *v.t.* ink.

encrier /ākrije/ *n.m.* ink-well.

encroûter (s') /(s)ākrute/ *v. pr.* become doggedly set in one's ways. **s'~ dans**, sink into.

encyclopéd|ie /āsiklopedi/ *n.f.* encyclopaedia. **~ique** *a.* encyclopaedic.

endetter /ādete/ *v.t.*, **s'~** *v. pr.* get into debt.

endeuiller /ādœje/ *v.t.* plunge into mourning.

endiablé /ādjable/ *a.* wild.

endiguer /ādige/ *v.t.* dam; (*fig.*) check.

endimanché /ādimāʃe/ *a.* in one's Sunday best.

endive /ādiv/ *n.f.* chicory.

endocrinolo|gie /ādɔkrinɔlɔʒi/ *n.f.* endocrinology. **~gue** *n.m./f.* endocrinologist.

endoctrin|er /ādɔktrine/ *v.t.* indoctrinate. **~ement** *n.m.* indoctrination.

endommager /ādɔmaʒe/ *v.t.* damage.

endorm|ir /ādɔrmir/ *v.t.* send to sleep; (*atténuer*) allay. **s'~ir** *v. pr.* fall asleep. **~i** *a.* asleep; (*apathique*) sleepy.

endosser /ādose/ *v.t.* (*vêtement*) put on; (*assumer*) assume; (*comm.*) endorse.

endroit /ādrwa/ *n.m.* place; (*de tissu*) right side. **à l'~**, the right way round, right side out.

end|uire /āduir/ *v.t.* coat. **~uit** *n.m.* coating.

endurance /ādyrās/ *n.f.* endurance.

endurant, ~e /ādyrā, -t/ *a.* tough.

endurci /ādyrsi/ *a.* **célibataire ~**, confirmed bachelor.

endurcir /ādyrsir/ *v.t.* harden. **s'~** *v. pr.* become hard(ened).

endurer /ādyre/ *v.t.* endure.

énerg|ie /enɛrʒi/ *n.f.* energy; (*techn.*) power. **~étique** *a.* energy. **~ique** *a.* energetic.

énervant, ~e /enɛrvā, -t/ *a.* irritating, annoying.

énerver /enɛrve/ *v.t.* irritate. **s'~** *v. pr.* get worked up.

enfance /āfās/ *n.f.* childhood. **la petite ~**, infancy.

enfant /āfā/ *n.m./f.* child. **~ en bas âge**, infant. **~illage** /-tijaʒ/ *n.m.* childishness. **~in, ~ine** /-tɛ̃, -tin/ *a.* childlike; (*puéril*) childish; (*jeu, langage*) children's.

enfanter /āfāte/ *v.t./i.* give birth (to).

enfer /āfɛr/ *n.m.* hell.

enfermer /āfɛrme/ *v.t.* shut up. **s'~** *v. pr.* shut o.s. up.

enferrer (s') /(s)āfɛre/ *v. pr.* become entangled.

enfiévré /āfjevre/ *a.* feverish.

enfilade /āfilad/ *n.f.* string, row.

enfiler /āfile/ *v.t.* (*aiguille*) thread; (*anneaux*) string; (*vêtement*) slip on; (*rue*) take; (*insérer*) insert.

enfin /āfɛ̃/ *adv.* at last, finally; (*en dernier lieu*) finally; (*somme toute*) after all; (*résignation, conclusion*) well.

enflammer /āflame/ *v.t.* set fire to; (*méd.*) inflame. **s'~** *v. pr.* catch fire.

enfl|er /āfle/ *v.t./i.*, **s'~er** *v. pr.* swell. **~é** *a.* swollen. **~ure** *n.f.* swelling.

enfoncer /āfɔse/ *v.t.* (*épingle etc.*) push *ou* drive in; (*chapeau*) push down; (*porte*) break down; (*mettre*) thrust, put. —*v.i.*, **s'~** *v. pr.* sink (**dans**, into).

enfouir /ãfwir/ v.t. bury.

enfourcher /ãfurʃe/ v.t. mount.

enfourner /ãfurne/ v.t. put in the oven.

enfreindre /ãfrɛ̃dr/ v.t. infringe.

enfuir† (s') /(s)ãfyir/ v. pr. run off.

enfumer /ãfyme/ v.t. fill with smoke.

engagé /ãgaʒe/ a. committed.

engageant, ~e /ãgaʒɑ̃, -t/ a. attractive.

engag|er /ãgaʒe/ v.t. (lier) bind, commit; (embaucher) take on; (commencer) start; (introduire) insert; (entraîner) involve; (encourager) urge; (investir) invest. **s'~er** de (promettre) commit o.s.; (commencer) start; (soldat) enlist; (concurrent) enter. **s'~er dans,** (voie) enter. **~ement** n.m. (promesse) promise; (pol., comm.) commitment; (début) start; (inscription: sport) entry.

engelure /ãʒlyr/ n.f. chilblain.

engendrer /ãʒãdre/ v.t. beget; (causer) generate.

engin /ãʒɛ̃/ n.m. machine; (outil) instrument; (projectile) missile. **~ explosif,** explosive device.

englober /ãglɔbe/ v.t. include.

engloutir /ãglutir/ v.t. swallow (up). **s'~** v. pr. (navire) be engulfed.

engorger /ãgɔrʒe/ v.t. block.

engouer (s') /(s)ãgwe/ v. pr. **s'~er de,** become infatuated with. **~ement** /-umã/ n.m. infatuation.

engouffrer /ãgufre/ v.t. devour. **s'~ dans,** rush into (with force).

engourd|ir /ãgurdir/ v.t. numb. **s'~ir** v. pr. go numb. **~ia.** numb.

engrais /ãgrɛ/ n.m. manure; (chimique) fertilizer.

engraisser /ãgrese/ v.t. fatten. **s'~** v. pr. get fat.

engrenage /ãgrənaʒ/ n.m. gears; (fig.) chain (of events).

engueuler /ãgœle/ v.t. (argot) curse, swear at, hurl abuse at.

enhardir (s') /(s)ãardir/ v. pr. become bolder.

énième /ɛnjɛm/ a. (fam.) umpteenth.

énigm|e /enigm/ n.f. riddle, enigma. **~atique** a. enigmatic.

enivrer /ãnivre/ v.t. intoxicate. **s'~** v. pr. get drunk.

enjamb|er /ãʒãbe/ v.t. step over; (pont) span. **~ée** n.f. stride.

enjeu (pl. **~x**) /ãʒø/ n.m. stake(s).

enjôler /ãʒole/ v.t. wheedle.

enjoliver /ãʒolive/ v.t. embellish.

enjoliveur /ãʒolivœr/ n.m. hubcap.

enjoué /ãʒwe/ a. cheerful.

enlacer /ãlase/ v.t. entwine.

enlaidir /ãledir/ v.t. make ugly. **—v.i.** grow ugly.

enlèvement /ãlɛvmã/ n.m. removal; (rapt) kidnapping.

enlever /ãlve/ v.t. (emporter) take (away), remove (à, from); (vêtement) take off, remove; (tache, organe) take out, remove; (kidnapper) kidnap; (gagner) win.

enliser (s') /(s)ãlize/ v. pr. get bogged down.

enluminure /ãlyminyr/ n.f. illumination.

enneig|é /ãneʒe/ a. snow-covered. **~ement** /ãneʒmã/ n.m. snow conditions.

ennemi /ɛnmi/ n.m. & a. enemy. **~ de,** (fig.) hostile to. **l'~ public numéro un,** public enemy number one.

ennui /ãnɥi/ n.m. boredom; (tracas) trouble, worry. **il a des ~s,** he's got problems.

ennuyer /ãnɥije/ v.t. bore; (irriter) annoy; (préoccuper) worry. **s'~** v. pr. get bored.

ennuyeu|x, ~se /ãnɥijø, -z/ a. boring; (fâcheux) annoying.

énoncé /enɔ̃se/ n.m. wording, text; (gram.) utterance.

énoncer /enɔ̃se/ v.t. express, state.

enorgueillir (s') /(s)ãnɔrgœjir/ v. pr. **s'~ de**, pride o.s. on.

énorm|e /enɔrm/ a. enormous. **~ément** adv. enormously. **~ément de**, an enormous amount of. **~ité** n.f. enormous size; (atrocité) enormity; (bévue) enormous blunder.

enquérir (s') /(s)ãkerir/ v. pr. **s'~ de**, enquire about.

* **enquêt|e** /ãkɛt/ n.f. investigation; (jurid.) inquiry; (sondage) survey. **mener l'~e**, lead the inquiry. **~er** /-ete/ v.i. **~er (sur)**, investigate. **~eur, ~euse** n.m., f. investigator.

enquiquin|er /ãkikine/ v.t. (fam.) bother. **~ant, ~ante** a. irritating. **c'est ~ant**, it's a nuisance.

enraciné /ãrasine/ a. deep-rooted.

enrag|er /ãraʒe/ v.i. be furious. **faire ~er**, annoy. **~é** a. furious; (chien) mad; (fig.) fanatical. **~eant, ~eante** a. infuriating.

enrayer /ãreje/ v.t. check.

enregistr|er /ãrʒistre/ v.t. note, record; (mus.) record. **(faire) ~er**, (bagages) register, check in. **~ement** n.m. recording; (des bagages) registration.

enrhumer (s') /(s)ãryme/ v. pr. catch a cold.

enrich|ir /ãriʃir/v.t. enrich. **s'~ir** v. pr. grow rich(er). **~issement** n.m. enrichment.

enrober /ãrɔbe/ v.t. coat (de, with).

enrôl|er /ãrole/ v.t., **s'~** v. pr. enlist, enrol.

enrou|er (s') /(s)ãrwe/ v. pr. become hoarse. **~é** a. hoarse.

enrouler /ãrule/ v.t., **s'~** v. pr. wind. **s'~ dans une couverture**, roll o.s. up in a blanket.

ensabler (s') /ãsable/ v.t., **s'~** v. pr. (port) silt up.

ensanglanté /ãsãglãte/ a. blood-stained.

enseignant, ~e /ãsɛɲã, -t/ n.m., f. teacher. —a. teaching.

enseigne /ãsɛɲ/ n.f. sign.

enseignement /ãsɛɲmã/ n.m. teaching; (instruction) education.

enseigner /ãsɛɲe/ v.t./i. teach. **~ qch. à qn.**, teach s.o. sth.

ensemble /ãsãbl/ adv. together. —n.m. unity; (d'objets) set; (mus.) ensemble; (vêtements) outfit. **dans l'~**, on the whole. **d'~**, (idée etc.) general. **l'~ de**, (totalité) all of, the whole of.

ensemencer /ãsmãse/ v.t. sow.

enserrer /ãsere/ v.t. grip (tightly).

ensevelir /ãsəvlir/ v.t. bury.

ensoleill|é /ãsoleje/ a. sunny. **~ement** /ãsɔlɛjmã/ n.m. (period of) sunshine.

ensommeillé /ãsɔmeje/ a. sleepy.

ensorceler /ãsɔrsəle/ v.t. bewitch.

ensuite /ãsɥit/ adv. next, then; (plus tard) later.

ensuivre (s') /(s)ãsɥivr/ v. pr. follow. **et tout ce qui s'ensuit**, and so on.

entaill|e /ãtaj/ n.f. notch; (blessure) gash. **~er** v.t. notch; gash.

entamer /ãtame/ v.t. start; (inciser) cut into; (ébranler) shake.

entass|er /ãtase/ v.t., **s'~er** v. pr. pile up. **(s')~er dans**, cram (together) into. **~ement** n.m. (tas) pile.

entendement /ãtãdmã/ n.m. understanding. **ça dépasse l'~**, it defies one's understanding.

entendre /ãtãdr/ v.t. hear; (comprendre) understand; (vouloir) intend, mean; (vouloir dire) mean. **s'~** v. pr. (être d'accord) agree. **~ dire que**, hear that. **~ parler de**, hear of. **s'~ (bien)**, get on (avec, with). **(cela) s'entend**, of course.

entendu /ātãdy/ a. (convenu) agreed; (sourire, air) knowing.
bien ∼, of course. (c'est) ∼! all right!

entente /ātãt/ n.f. understanding. **à double ∼,** with a double meaning.

entériner /āterine/ v.t. ratify.

enterr|er /ātere/ v.t. bury. **∼ement** /ātermã/ n.m. burial, funeral.

entêtant, ∼e /ātetã, -t/ a. heady.

en-tête /ātɛt/ n.m. heading. **à ∼,** headed.

entêt|é /ātete/ a. stubborn. **∼ement** /ātetmã/ n.m. stubbornness.

entêter (s') /(s)ātete/ v. pr. persist (à, dans, in).

enthousias|me /ātuzjasm/ n.m. enthusiasm. **∼mer** v.t. enthuse. **s'∼mer pour,** enthuse over. **∼te** a. enthusiastic.

enticher (s') /(s)ātiʃe/ v. pr. **s'∼ de,** become infatuated with.

ent|ier, ∼ière /ātje, -jɛr/ a. whole; (absolu) absolute; (entêté) unyielding. —n.m. whole. **en ∼ier,** entirely. **∼ièrement** adv. entirely.

entité /ātite/ n.f. entity.

entonner /ātɔne/ v.t. start singing.

entonnoir /ātɔnwar/ n.m. funnel; (trou) crater.

entorse /ātɔrs/ n.f. sprain. **∼ à,** (loi) infringement of.

entortiller /ātɔrtije/ v.t. wrap (up); (enrouler) wind, wrap; (duper) deceive.

entourage /āturaʒ/ n.m. circle of family and friends; (bordure) surround.

entourer /āture/ v.t. surround (de, with); (réconforter) rally round. **∼ de,** (écharpe etc.) wrap round.

entracte /ātrakt/ n.m. interval.

entraide /ātrɛd/ n.f. mutual aid.

entraider (s') /(s)ātrede/ v. pr. help each other.

entrailles /ātraj/ n.f. pl. entrails.

entrain /ātrɛ̃/ n.m. zest, spirit.

entraînant, ∼e /ātrenā, -t/ a. rousing.

entraînement /ātrɛnmã/ n.m. (sport) training.

entraîn|er /ātrene/ v.t. carry away ou along; (emmener, influencer) lead; (impliquer) entail; (sport) train; (roue) drive. **∼eur** /ātrɛnœr/ n.m. trainer.

entrav|e /ātrav/ n.f. hindrance. **∼er** v.t. hinder.

entre /ātr(ə)/ prép. between; (parmi) among(st). **∼ autres,** among other things. **l'un d'∼ nous/vous/eux,** one of us/you/them.

entrebâillé /ātrəbaje/ a. ajar.

entrechoquer (s') /(s)ātrəʃɔke/ v. pr. knock against each other.

entrecôte /ātrəkot/ n.f. rib steak.

entrecouper /ātrəkupe/ v.t. **∼ de,** intersperse with.

entrecroiser (s') /(s)ātrəkrwaze/ v. pr. (routes) intersect.

entrée /ātre/ n.f. entrance; (accès) admission, entry; (billet) ticket; (culin.) first course; (de données, techn.) input. **∼ interdite,** no entry.

entrefaites (sur ces) /(syrsez)-ātrəfɛt/ adv. at that moment.

entrefilet /ātrəfile/ n.m. paragraph.

entrejambe /ātrəʒãb/ n.m. crotch.

entrelacer /ātrəlase/ v.t., **s'∼** v. pr. intertwine.

entremêler /ātrəmele/ v.t., **s'∼** v. pr. (inter)mingle.

entremets /ātrəmɛ/ n.m. dessert.

entremetteu|r, ∼se /ātrəmɛtœr, -øz/ n.m., f. (péj.) go-between.

entre|mettre (s') /(s)ātrəmɛtr/ v. pr. intervene. **∼mise** n.f. intervention. **par l'∼mise de,** through.

entreposer /ɑ̃trəpoze/ v.t. store.
entrepôt /ɑ̃trəpo/ n.m. warehouse.
entreprenant, **~e** /ɑ̃trəprənɑ̃, -t/ a. (actif) enterprising; (séducteur) forward.
entreprendre† /ɑ̃trəprɑ̃dr/ v.t. start on; (personne) buttonhole. **~ de faire**, undertake to do.
entrepreneur /ɑ̃trəprənœr/ n.m. **~ (de bâtiments)**, (building) contractor.
entreprise /ɑ̃trəpriz/ n.f. undertaking; (société) firm.
entrer /ɑ̃tre/ v.i. (aux. être) go in, enter; (venir) come in, enter. **~ dans**, go ou come into, enter; (club) join. **~ en collision**, collide (avec, with). **faire ~**, (personne) show in. **laisser ~**, let in.
entresol /ɑ̃trəsɔl/ n.m. mezzanine.
entre-temps /ɑ̃trətɑ̃/ adv. meanwhile.
entretenir† /ɑ̃trətnir/ v.t. maintain; (faire durer) keep alive. **~ qn. de**, converse with s.o. about. **s'~** v. pr. speak (de, about; avec, to).
entretien /ɑ̃trətjɛ̃/ n.m. maintenance; (discussion) talk; (audience, pour un emploi) interview.
entrevoir /ɑ̃trəvwar/ v.t. make out; (brièvement) glimpse.
entrevue /ɑ̃trəvy/ n.f. interview.
entrouvrir /ɑ̃truvrir/ v.t. halfopen.
énumér|er /enymere/ v.t. enumerate. **~ation** n.f. enumeration.
envah|ir /ɑ̃vair/ v.t. invade, overrun; (douleur, peur) overcome. **~isseur** n.m. invader.
enveloppe /ɑ̃vlɔp/ n.f. envelope; (emballage) covering; (techn.) casing.

envelopper /ɑ̃vlope/ v.t. wrap (up); (fig.) envelop.
envenimer /ɑ̃vnime/ v.t. embitter. **s'~** v. pr. become embittered.
envergure /ɑ̃vɛrgyr/ n.f. wingspan; (importance) scope; (qualité) calibre.
envers /ɑ̃vɛr/ prép. toward(s), to. **—n.m.** (de tissu) wrong side. **à l'~**, upside down; (pantalon) back to front; (chaussette) inside out.
enviable /ɑ̃vjabl/ a. enviable. **peu ~**, unenviable.
envie /ɑ̃vi/ n.f. desire, wish; (jalousie) envy. **avoir ~ de**, want, feel like. **avoir ~ de faire**, want to do, feel like doing.
envier /ɑ̃vje/ v.t. envy.
envieu|x, **~se** /ɑ̃vjø, -z/ a. & n.m., f. envious (person).
environ /ɑ̃virɔ̃/ adv. (round) about. **~s** n.m. pl. surroundings. **aux ~s de**, round about.
environnement /ɑ̃virɔnmɑ̃/ n.m. environment.
environn|er /ɑ̃virɔne/ v.t. surround. **~ant**, **~ante** a. surrounding.
envisager /ɑ̃vizaʒe/ v.t. consider. **~ de faire**, consider doing.
envoi /ɑ̃vwa/ n.m. dispatch; (paquet) consignment.
envol /ɑ̃vɔl/ n.m. flight; (d'avion) take-off.
envoler (s') /(s)ɑ̃vɔle/ v. pr. fly away; (avion) take off; (papiers) blow away.
envoûter /ɑ̃vute/ v.t. bewitch.
envoyé, **~e** /ɑ̃vwaje/ n.m., f. envoy; (de journal) correspondent.
envoyer† /ɑ̃vwaje/ v.t. send; (lancer) throw. **~ promener qn.**, give s.o. the brush-off.
enzyme /ɑ̃zim/ n.m. enzyme.
épagneul, **~e** /epaɲœl/ n.m., f. spaniel.

épais, ~se /epɛ, -s/ a. thick.
~seur /-sœr/ n.f. thickness.

épaissir /epesir/ v.t./i., **s'~** v. pr. thicken.

épanch|er (s') /(s)epɑ̃ʃe/ v. pr. pour out one's feelings; (liquide) pour out. **~ement** n.m. outpouring.

épanoui /epanwi/ a. (joyeux) beaming, radiant.

épan|ouir (s') /(s)epanwir/ v. pr. (fleur) open out; (visage) beam; (personne) blossom. **~ouissement** n.m. (éclat) blossoming, full bloom.

épargne /eparɲ/ n.f. saving; (somme) savings. **caisse d'~,** savings bank.

épargn|er /eparɲe/ v.t./i. save; (ne pas tuer) spare. **~er qch. à qn.,** spare s.o. sth. **~ant, ~ante** n.m., f. saver.

éparpiller /eparpije/ v.t. scatter. **s'~** v. pr. scatter; (fig.) dissipate one's efforts.

épars, ~e /epar, -s/ a. scattered.

épat|er /epate/ v.t. (fam.) amaze. **~ant, ~ante** a. (fam.) amazing.

épaule /epol/ n.f. shoulder.

épauler /epole/ v.t. (arme) raise; (aider) support.

épave /epav/ n.f. wreck.

épée /epe/ n.f. sword.

épeler /eple/ v.t. spell.

éperdu /eperdy/ a. wild, frantic. **~ment** adv. wildly, frantically.

éperon /eprɔ̃/ n.m. spur. **~ner** /-one/ v.t. spur (on).

épervier /epɛrvje/ n.m. sparrow-hawk.

éphémère /efemɛr/ a. ephemeral.

éphéméride /efemerid/ n.f. tear-off calendar.

épi /epi/ n.m. (de blé) ear. **~ de cheveux,** tuft of hair.

épic|e /epis/ n.f. spice. **~é** a. spicy. **~er** v.t. spice.

épic|ier, ~ière /episje, -jɛr/ n.m.,

f. grocer. **~erie** n.f. grocery shop; (produits) groceries.

épidémie /epidemi/ n.f. epidemic.

épiderme /epidɛrm/ n.m. skin.

épier /epje/ v.t. spy on.

épilep|sie /epilɛpsi/ n.f. epilepsy. **~tique** a. & n.m./f. epileptic.

épiler /epile/ v.t. remove unwanted hair from; (sourcils) pluck.

épilogue /epilɔg/ n.m. epilogue; (fig.) outcome.

épinard /epinar/ n.m. (plante) spinach. **~s,** (nourriture) spinach.

épin|e /epin/ n.f. thorn, prickle; (d'animal) prickle, spine. **~e dorsale,** backbone. **~eux, ~euse** a. thorn.f.

épingle /epɛ̃gl/ n.f. pin. **~e de nourrice,** **~e de sûreté,** safety-pin. **~er** v.t. pin; (arrêter: fam.) nab.

épique /epik/ a. epic.

épisod|e /epizɔd/ n.m. episode. **à ~es,** serialized. **~ique** a. occasional.

épitaphe /epitaf/ n.f. epitaph.

épithète /epitɛt/ n.f. epithet.

épître /epitr/ n.f. epistle.

éploré /eplore/ a. tearful.

épluche-légumes /eplyʃlegym/ n.m. invar. (potato) peeler.

épluch|er /eplyʃe/ v.t. peel; (examiner: fig.) scrutinize. **~age** n.m. peeling; (fig.) scrutiny. **~ure** n.f. piece of peel ou peeling. **~ures** n.f. pl. peelings.

épong|e /epɔ̃ʒ/ n.f. sponge. **~er** v.t. (liquide) sponge up; (surface) sponge (down); (front) mop; (dettes) wipe out.

épopée /epope/ n.f. epic.

époque /epɔk/ n.f. time, period. **à l'~,** at the time. **d'~,** period.

épouse /epuz/ n.f. wife.

épouser[1] /epuze/ v.t. marry.

épouser[2] /epuze/ v.t. (forme, idée) assume, embrace, adopt.

épousseter /epuste/ *v.t.* dust.

époustouflant, ~e /epustuflɑ̃, -t/ *a.* (*fam.*) staggering.

épouvantable /epuvɑ̃tabl/ *a.* appalling.

épouvantail /epuvɑ̃taj/ *n.m.* scarecrow.

épouvant|e /epuvɑ̃t/ *n.f.* terror. **~er** *v.t.* terrify.

époux /epu/ *n.m.* husband. **les ~,** the married couple.

éprendre (s') /(s)eprɑ̃dr/ *v. pr.* **s'~ de,** fall in love with.

épreuve /eprœv/ *n.f.* test; (*sport*) event; (*malheur*) ordeal; (*photo.*) print; (*d'imprimerie*) proof. **mettre à l'~,** put to the test.

éprouvé /epruve/ *a.* (well-)proven.

éprouv|er /epruve/ *v.t.* test; (*ressentir*) experience; (*affliger*) distress. **~ant, ~ante** *a.* testing.

éprouvette /epruvɛt/ *n.f.* test-tube. **bébé-~,** test-tube baby.

épuis|er /epɥize/ *v.t.* (*fatiguer, user*) exhaust. **s'~er** *v. pr.* become exhausted. **~é** *a.* exhausted; (*livre*) out of print. **~ement** *n.m.* exhaustion.

épuisette /epɥizɛt/ *n.f.* fishing-net.

épur|er /epyre/ *v.t.* purify; (*pol.*) purge. **~ation** *n.f.* purification; (*pol.*) purge.

équat|eur /ekwatœr/ *n.m.* equator. **~orial** (*m. pl.* **~oriaux**) *a.* equatorial.

équation /ekwɑsjɔ̃/ *n.f.* equation.

équerre /ekɛr/ *n.f.* (set) square. **d'~,** square.

équilibr|e /ekilibr/ *n.m.* balance. **être** *ou* **se tenir en ~e,** (*personne*) balance; (*objet*) be balanced. **~é** *a.* well-balanced. **~er** *v.t.* balance. **s'~er** *v. pr.* (*forces etc.*) counterbalance each other.

équilibriste /ekilibrist/ *n.m./f.* tightrope walker.

équinoxe /ekinɔks/ *n.m.* equinox.

équipage /ekipaʒ/ *n.m.* crew.

équipe /ekip/ *n.f.* team. **~ de nuit/jour,** night/day shift.

équipé /ekipe/ *a.* **bien/mal ~,** well/poorly equipped.

équipée /ekipe/ *n.f.* escapade.

équipement /ekipmɑ̃/ *n.m.* equipment. **~s,** (*installations*) amenities, facilities.

équiper /ekipe/ *v.t.* equip (**de,** with). **s'~** *v. pr.* equip o.s.

équip|ier, ~ière /ekipje, -jɛr/ *n.m., f.* team member.

équitable /ekitabl/ *a.* fair. **~ment** /-əmɑ̃/ *adv.* fairly.

équitation /ekitɑsjɔ̃/ *n.f.* (horse-)riding.

équité /ekite/ *n.f.* equity.

équivalen|t, ~te /ekivalɑ̃, -t/ *a.* equivalent. **~ce** *n.f.* equivalence.

équivaloir /ekivalwar/ *v.i.* **~ à,** be equivalent to.

équivoque /ekivɔk/ *a.* equivocal; (*louche*) questionable. —*n.f.* ambiguity.

érable /erabl/ *n.m.* maple.

éraf|ler /erafle/ *v.t.* scratch. **~ure** *n.f.* scratch.

éraillé /eraje/ *a.* (*voix*) raucous.

ère /ɛr/ *n.f.* era.

érection /erɛksjɔ̃/ *n.f.* erection.

éreinter /erɛ̃te/ *v.t.* exhaust; (*fig.*) criticize severely.

ergoter /ɛrgote/ *v.i.* quibble.

ériger /eriʒe/ *v.t.* erect. **(s')~ en,** set (o.s.) up as.

ermite /ɛrmit/ *n.m.* hermit.

éroder /erode/ *v.t.* erode.

érosion /erozjɔ̃/ *n.f.* erosion.

éroti|que /erotik/ *a.* erotic. **~sme** *n.m.* eroticism.

errer /ɛre/ *v.i.* wander.

erreur /ɛrœr/ *n.f.* mistake, error. **dans l'~,** mistaken. **par ~,** by mistake. **~ judiciaire,** miscarriage of justice.

erroné /ɛrone/ *a.* erroneous.

ersatz /ɛrzats/ *n.m.* ersatz.

érudit, ~e /erydi, -t/ *a.* scholarly. —*n.m.*, *f.* scholar. **∼ion** /-sjɔ̃/ *n.f.* scholarship.

éruption /erypsjɔ/ *n.f.* eruption; (*méd.*) rash.

es /ɛ/ *voir* **être**.

escabeau (*pl.* **∼x**) /ɛskabo/ *n.m.* step-ladder; (*tabouret*) stool.

escadre /ɛskadr/ *n.f.* (*naut.*) squadron.

escadrille /ɛskadrij/ *n.f.* (*aviat.*) flight, squadron.

escadron /ɛskadrɔ̃/ *n.m.* (*mil.*) squadron.

escalad|e /ɛskalad/ *n.f.* climbing; (*pol.*, *comm.*) escalation. **∼er** *v.t.* climb.

escalator /ɛskalatɔr/ *n.m.* (P.) escalator.

escale /ɛskal/ *n.f.* (*d'avion*) stopover; (*port*) port of call. **faire ∼ à**, (*avion*, *passager*) stop over at; (*navire*, *passager*) put in at.

escalier /ɛskalje/ *n.m.* stairs. **∼ mécanique** *ou* **roulant**, escalator.

escalope /ɛskalɔp/ *n.f.* escalope.

escamotable /ɛskamɔtabl/ *a.* (*techn.*) retractable.

escamoter /ɛskamɔte/ *v.t.* make vanish; (*éviter*) dodge.

escargot /ɛskargo/ *n.m.* snail.

escarmouche /ɛskarmuʃ/ *n.f.* skirmish.

escarpé /ɛskarpe/ *a.* steep.

escarpin /ɛskarpɛ̃/ *n.m.* pump.

escient /ɛsjã/ *n.m.* **à bon ∼**, with good reason.

esclaffer (s') /(s)ɛsklafe/ *v. pr.* guffaw, burst out laughing.

esclandre /ɛsklɑ̃dr/ *n.m.* scene.

esclav|e /ɛsklav/ *n.m./f.* slave. **∼age** *n.m.* slavery.

escompte /ɛskɔ̃t/ *n.m.* discount.

escompter /ɛskɔ̃te/ *v.t.* expect; (*comm.*) discount.

escort|e /ɛskɔrt/ *n.f.* escort. **∼er** *v.t.* escort. **∼eur** *n.m.* escort (ship).

escouade /ɛskwad/ *n.f.* squad.

escrim|e /ɛskrim/ *n.f.* fencing. **∼eur, ∼euse** *n.m.*, *f.* fencer.

escrimer (s') /(s)ɛskrime/ *v. pr.* struggle.

escroc /ɛskro/ *n.m.* swindler.

escroqu|er /ɛskrɔke/ *v.t.* swindle. **∼er qch. à qn.**, swindle s.o. out of sth. **∼erie** *n.f.* swindle.

espace /ɛspas/ *n.m.* space. **∼s verts**, gardens, parks.

espacer /ɛspase/ *v.t.* space out. **s'∼** *v. pr.* become less frequent.

espadrille /ɛspadrij/ *n.f.* rope sandals.

Espagne /ɛspaɲ/ *n.f.* Spain.

espagnol, ∼e /ɛspaɲɔl/ *a.* Spanish. —*n.m.*, *f.* Spaniard. —*n.m.* (*lang.*) Spanish.

espagnolette /ɛspaɲɔlɛt/ *n.f.* (window) catch.

espèce /ɛspɛs/ *n.f.* kind, sort; (*race*) species. **∼s**, (*argent*) cash. **∼ d'idiot/de brute/etc.!**, you idiot/brute/*etc.*!

espérance /ɛsperɑ̃s/ *n.f.* hope.

espérer /ɛspere/ *v.t.* hope for. **∼ faire/que**, hope to do/that. —*v.i.* hope. **∼ en**, have faith in.

espiègle /ɛspjɛgl/ *a.* mischievous.

espion, ∼ne /ɛspjɔ̃, -jɔn/ *n.m.*, *f.* spy.

espionn|er /ɛspjɔne/ *v.t./i.* spy (on). **∼age** *n.m.* espionage, spying.

esplanade /ɛsplanad/ *n.f.* esplanade.

espoir /ɛspwar/ *n.m.* hope.

esprit /ɛspri/ *n.m.* spirit; (*intellect*) mind; (*humour*) wit. **perdre l'∼**, lose one's mind. **reprendre ses ∼s**, come to. **vouloir faire de l'∼**, try to be witty.

Esquimau, ∼de (*m. pl.* **∼x**) /ɛskimo, -d/ *n.m.*, *f.* Eskimo.

esquinter /ɛskɛ̃te/ *v.t.* (*fam.*) ruin.

esquiss|e /ɛskis/ *n.f.* sketch; (*fig.*) suggestion. **∼er** *v.t.* sketch; (*geste etc.*) make an attempt at.

esquiv|e /ɛskiv/ *n.f.* (*sport*) dodge.

~er *v.t.* dodge. s'~er *v. pr.* slip away.

essai /ese/ *n.m.* testing; (*épreuve*) test, trial; (*tentative*) try; (*article*) essay. à l'~, on trial.

essaim /esɛ̃/ *n.m.* swarm. ~er /eseme/ *v.i.* swarm; (*fig.*) spread.

essayage /esɛjaʒ/ *n.m.* (*de vêtement*) fitting. **salon d'~**, fitting room.

essayer /eseje/ *v.t./i.* try; (*vêtement*) try (on); (*voiture etc.*) try (out). ~ **de faire**, try to do.

essence[1] /esɑ̃s/ *n.f.* (*carburant*) petrol; (*Amer.*) gas.

essence[2] /esɑ̃s/ *n.f.* (*nature, extrait*) essence.

essentiel, ~le /esɑ̃sjɛl/ *a.* essential.—*n.m.* l'~, the main thing; (*quantité*) the main part. ~**lement** *adv.* essentially.

essieu (*pl.* ~x) /esjø/ *n.m.* axle.

essor /esɔr/ *n.m.* expansion. **prendre son ~**, expand.

essor|er /esɔre/ *v.t.* (*linge*) spin-dry; (*en tordant*) wring. ~**euse** *n.f.* spin-drier.

essouffler *v.t.* make breathless. s'~ *v. pr.* get out of breath.

essuyer[1] /esɥije/ *v.t.* wipe. s'~**uyer** *v. pr.* dry *ou* wipe o.s. ~**uie-glace** *n.m. invar.* windscreen wiper; (*Amer.*) windshield wiper. ~**uie-mains** *n.m. invar.* hand-towel.

essuyer[2] /esɥije/ *v.t.* (*subir*) suffer.

est[1] /ɛ/ *voir* **être**.

est[2] /ɛst/ *n.m.* east.—*a. invar.* east; (*partie*) eastern; (*direction*) easterly.

estampe /estɑ̃p/ *n.f.* print.

estampille /estɑ̃pij/ *n.f.* stamp.

esthète /ɛstɛt/ *n.m./f.* aesthete.

esthéticienne /ɛstetisjɛn/ *n.f.* beautician.

esthétique /ɛstetik/ *a.* aesthetic.

estimable /ɛstimabl/ *a.* worthy.

estimation /ɛstimasjɔ̃/ *n.f.* valuation.

estime /ɛstim/ *n.f.* esteem.

estim|er /ɛstime/ *v.t.* (*objet*) value; (*calculer*) estimate; (*respecter*) esteem; (*considérer*) consider. ~**ation** *n.f.* valuation; (*calcul*) estimation.

estomac /ɛstɔma/ *n.m.* stomach.

estomaqué /ɛstɔmake/ *a.* (*fam.*) stunned.

estomper (s') /(s)ɛstɔ̃pe/ *v. pr.* become blurred.

estrade /ɛstrad/ *n.f.* platform.

estragon /ɛstragɔ̃/ *n.m.* tarragon.

estropi|er /ɛstrɔpje/ *v.t.* cripple; (*fig.*) mangle. ~**ié, ~iée** *n.m., f.* cripple.

estuaire /ɛstɥɛr/ *n.m.* estuary.

estudiantin, ~e /ɛstydjɑ̃tɛ̃, -in/a. student.

esturgeon /ɛstyrʒɔ̃/ *n.m.* sturgeon.

et /e/ *conj.* and. **et moi/lui/***etc.***?**, what about me/him/*etc.*?

étable /etabl/ *n.f.* cow-shed.

établi[1] /etabli/ *a.* established. **un fait bien ~**, a well-established fact.

établi[2] /etabli/ *n.m.* work-bench.

établir /etablir/ *v.t.* establish; (*liste, facture*) draw up; (*personne, camp, record*) set up. s'~ *v. pr.* (*personne*) establish o.s. s'~ **épicier/***etc.***, set (o.s.) up as a grocer/*etc.* s'~ **à son compte**, set up on one's own.

établissement /etablismɑ̃/ *n.m.* (*bâtiment, institution*) establishment.

étage /etaʒ/ *n.m.* floor, storey; (*de fusée*) stage. à l'~, upstairs. **au premier ~**, on the first floor.

étager (s') /(s)etaʒe/ *v. pr.* rise at different levels.

étagère /etaʒɛr/ *n.f.* shelf; (*meuble*) shelving unit.

étai /etɛ/ *n.m.* prop, buttress.

étain /etɛ̃/ *n.m.* pewter.

étais, était /etɛ/ *voir* **être**.

étal (*pl.* **~s**) /etal/ *n.m.* stall.

étal|age /etalaʒ/ *n.m.* display; (*vitrine*) shop-window. **faire ~e de**, show off **~iste** *n.m./f.* window-dresser.

étaler /etale/ *v.t.* display; (*journal*) spread (out); (*vacances*) stagger; (*exposer*) display. **s'~** *v. pr.* (*s'étendre*) stretch out; (*tomber, fam.*) fall flat. **s'~ sur,** (*paiement*) be spread over.

étalon /etalɔ̃/ *n.m.* (*cheval*) stallion; (*modèle*) standard.

étanche /etɑ̃ʃ/ *a.* watertight; (*montre*) waterproof.

étanch|er /etɑ̃ʃe/ *v.t.* (*soif*) quench; (*sang*) stem.

étang /etɑ̃/ *n.m.* pond.

étant /etɑ̃/ *voir* **être**.

étape /etap/ *n.f.* stage; (*lieu d'arrêt*) stopover.

état /eta/ *n.m.* state; (*liste*) statement; (*métier*) profession; (*nation*) State. **en bon/mauvais ~,** in good/bad condition. **en ~ de,** in a position to. **hors d'~ de,** not in a position to. **en ~ de marche,** in working order. **~ civil,** civil status. **~-major** (*pl.* **~s-majors**) *n.m.* (*officiers*) staff. **faire ~ de,** (*citer*) mention. **être dans tous ses ~s,** be in a state. **~ des lieux,** inventory.

étatisé /etatize/ *a.* State-controlled.

États-Unis /etazyni/ *n.m. pl.* **~ (d'Amérique),** United States (of America).

étau (*pl.* **~x**) /eto/ *n.m.* vice.

étayer /eteje/ *v.t.* prop up.

été[1] /ete/ *voir* **être**.

été[2] /ete/ *n.m.* summer.

étein|dre /etɛ̃dr/ *v.t.* put out, extinguish; (*lumière, radio*) turn off. **s'~dre** *v. pr.* go out; (*mourir*) die. **~t, ~te** /etɛ̃, -t/ *a.* (*feu*) out; (*volcan*) extinct.

étendard /etɑ̃dar/ *n.m.* standard.

étendre /etɑ̃dr/ *v.t.* spread; (*journal, nappe*) spread out; (*bras, jambes*) stretch (out); (*linge*) hang out; (*agrandir*) extend. **s'~** *v. pr.* (*s'allonger*) stretch out; (*se propager*) spread; (*plaine etc.*) stretch. **s'~ sur,** (*sujet*) dwell on.

étendu /etɑ̃dy/ *a.* extensive. **—n.f.** area; (*d'eau*) stretch; (*importance*) extent.

étern|el, ~le /etɛrnel/ *a.* eternal. **~lement** *adv.* eternally.

éterniser (s') /(s)etɛrnize/ *v. pr.* (*durer*) drag on.

éternité /etɛrnite/ *n.f.* eternity.

étern|uer /etɛrnɥe/ *v.i.* sneeze. **~uement** /-ymɑ̃/ *n.m.* sneeze.

êtes /ɛt/ *voir* **être**.

éthique /etik/ *a.* ethical. **—n.f.** ethics.

ethn|ie /ɛtni/ *n.f.* ethnic group. **~ique** *a.* ethnic.

éthylisme /etilism/ *n.m.* alcoholism.

étinceler /etɛ̃sle/ *v.i.* sparkle.

étincelle /etɛ̃sel/ *n.f.* spark.

étioler (s') /(s)etjole/ *v. pr.* wilt.

étiqueter /etikte/ *v.t.* label.

étiquette /etikɛt/ *n.f.* label; (*protocole*) etiquette.

étirer /etire/ *v.t.*, **s'~** *v. pr.* stretch.

étoffe /etɔf/ *n.f.* fabric.

étoffer /etɔfe/ *v.t.*, **s'~** *v. pr.* fill out.

étoil|e /etwal/ *n.f.* star. **à la belle ~e,** in the open. **~e de mer,** starfish. **~é** *a.* starry.

étonn|er /etɔne/ *v.t.* amaze. **s'~** *v. pr.* be amazed (**de, at**). **~ant, ~ante** *a.* amazing. **~ement** *n.m.* amazement.

étouffée /etufe/ *n.f.* **cuire à l'~,** braise.

étouff|er /etufe/ *v.t./i.* suffocate; (*sentiment, révolte*) stifle; (*feu*) smother; (*bruit*) muffle. **on ~e,** it is stifling. **s'~er** *v. pr.* suffocate;

(en mangeant) choke. ～ant, ～ante a. stifling.

étourdir, ～ie /eturdi/ a. unthinking, scatter-brained. —n.m., f. scatter-brain. ～erie n.f. thoughtlessness; (acte) thoughtless act.

étourdir /eturdir/ v.t. stun; (griser) make dizzy. ～issant, ～issante a. stunning. ～issement n.m. (syncope) dizzy spell.

étourneau (pl. ～x) /eturno/ n.m. starling.

étrange /ētrã3/ a. strange. ～ment adv. strangely. ～té n.f. strangeness.

étranger, ～ère /etrã3e, -er/ a. strange, unfamiliar; (d'un autre pays) foreign. —n.m., f. foreigner; (inconnu) stranger. à l'～er, abroad. de l'～er, from abroad.

étrangler /etrãgle/ v.t. strangle; (col) stifle. s'～ v. pr. choke.

être† /etr/ v.i. be. —v. aux. (avec aller, sortir, etc.) have. ～ donné/fait par, (passif) be given/done by. —n.m. (personne, créature) being. ～ humain, human being ～ médecin/tailleur/etc., be a doctor/a tailor/etc. ～ à qn., be s.o.'s. c'est à faire, it needs to be ou should be done. est-ce qu'il travaille?, is he working?, does he work? vous travaillez, n'est-ce pas?, you are working, aren't you?, you work, don't you? il est deux heures/etc., it is two o'clock/etc. nous sommes le six mai, it is the sixth of May.

étrein|dre /etrēdr/ v.t. grasp; (ami) embrace. ～te /-ēt/ n.f. grasp; embrace.

étrenner /etrene/ v.t. use for the first time.

étrennes /etren/ n.f. pl. (cadeau) New Year's gift.

étrier /etrije/ n.m. stirrup.

étriqué /etrike/ a. tight; (fig.) small-minded.

étroit, ～e /etrwa, -t/ a. narrow; (vêtement) tight; (liens, surveillance) close. à l'～, cramped. ～ement /-tmã/ adv. closely. ～esse /-tes/ n.f. narrowness.

étude /etyd/ n.f. study; (bureau) office. (salle d')～, (scol.) prep room; (scol., Amer.) study hall. à l'～, under consideration. faire des ～s (de), study.

étudiant, ～e /etydjã, -t/ n.m., f. student.

étudier /etydje/ v.t./i. study.

étui /etyi/ n.m. case.

étuve /etyv/ n.f. steamroom. quelle étuve!, it's like a hothouse in here.

étuvée /etyve/ n.f. cuire à l'～, braise.

étymologie /etimɔlɔʒi/ n.f. etymology.

eu, eue /y/ voir avoir.

eucalyptus /økaliptys/ n.m. eucalyptus.

euphémisme /øfemism/ n.m. euphemism.

euphorie /øfɔri/ n.f. euphoria.

Europe /ørɔp/ n.f. Europe.

européen, ～ne /ørɔpeẽ, -eɛn/ a. & n.m., f. European.

euthanasie /øtanazi/ n.f. euthanasia.

eux /ø/ pron. they; (complément) them. ～mêmes pron. themselves.

évac|uer /evakɥe/ v.t. evacuate. ～uation n.f. evacuation.

évad|er (s') /(s)evade/ v. pr. escape. ～é, ～ée a. escaped; n.m., f. escaped prisoner.

éval|uer /evalɥe/ v.t. assess. ～uation n.f. assessment.

évang|ile /evãʒil/ n.m. gospel. l'Évangile, the Gospel. ～élique a. evangelical.

évan|ouir (s') /(s)evanwir/ v. pr. faint; (disparaître) vanish. ～ouissement n.m. (syncope) fainting fit.

évapor|er /evapɔre/ *v.t.*, **s'~er** *v. pr.* evaporate. **~ation** *n.f.* evaporation.

évasi|f, **~ve** /evazif, -v/ *a.* evasive.

évasion /evazjɔ̃/ *n.f.* escape; (*par le rêve etc.*) escapism.

éveil /evɛj/ *n.m.* awakening. **donner l'~ à**, arouse the suspicions of. **en ~**, alert.

éveill|er /eveje/ *v.t.* awake(n); (*susciter*) arouse. **s'~er** *v. pr.* awake(n); be aroused. **~é a.** awake; (*intelligent*) alert.

événement /evɛnmã/ *n.m.* event.

éventail /evãtaj/ *n.m.* fan; (*gamme*) range.

éventaire /evãtɛr/ *n.m.* stall, stand.

éventé /evãte/ *a.* (*gâté*) stale.

éventrer /evãtre/ *v.t.* (*sac etc.*) rip open.

éventualité /evãtɥalite/ *n.f.* possibility. **dans cette ~**, in that event.

éventuel, **~le** /evãtɥɛl/ *a.* possible. **~lement** *adv.* possibly.

évêque /evɛk/ *n.m.* bishop.

évertuer (s') /(s)evɛrtɥe/ *v. pr.* **s'~ à**, struggle hard to.

éviction /eviksjɔ̃/ *n.f.* eviction.

évidemment /evidamã/ *adv.* obviously; (*bien sûr*) of course.

évidence /evidãs/ *n.f.* obviousness; (*fait*) obvious fact. **être en ~**, be conspicuous. **mettre en ~**, (*fait*) highlight.

évident, **~e** /evidã, -t/ *a.* obvious, evident.

évider /evide/ *v.t.* hollow out.

évier /evje/ *n.m.* sink.

évincer /evɛ̃se/ *v.t.* oust.

éviter /evite/ *v.t.* avoid (**de faire**, doing). **~ à qn.**, (*dérangement etc.*) spare s.o.

évoca|teur, **~trice** /evɔkatœr, -tris/ *a.* evocative.

évocation /evɔkasjɔ̃/ *n.f.* evocation.

évolué /evɔlɥe/ *a.* highly developed.

évol|uer /evɔlɥe/ *v.i.* develop; (*se déplacer*) move, manœuvre; (*Amer.*) maneuver. **~ution** *n.f.* development; (*d'une espèce*) evolution; (*déplacement*) movement.

évoquer /evɔke/ *v.t.* call to mind, evoke.

ex- /ɛks/ *préf.* ex-.

exacerber /ɛgzasɛrbe/ *v.t.* exacerbate.

exact, **~e** /ɛgza(kt), -akt/ *a.* exact, accurate; (*correct*) correct; (*personne*) punctual. **~ement** /-ktamã/ *adv.* exactly. **~itude** /-ktityd/ *n.f.* exactness; punctuality.

ex aequo /ɛgzeko/ *adv.* (*classer*) equal. **être ~**, be equally placed.

exagéré /ɛgzaʒere/ *a.* excessive.

exagér|er /ɛgzaʒere/ *v.t./i.* exaggerate; (*abuser*) go too far. **~ation** *n.f.* exaggeration.

exaltation /ɛgzaltasjɔ̃/ *n.f.* elation.

exalté, **~e** /ɛgzalte/ *n.m.*, *f.* fanatic.

exalter /ɛgzalte/ *v.t.* excite; (*glorifier*) exalt.

examen /ɛgzamɛ̃/ *n.m.* examination; (*scol.*) exam(ination).

examin|er /ɛgzamine/ *v.t.* examine. **~ateur**, **~atrice** *n.m.*, *f.* examiner.

exaspér|er /ɛgzaspere/ *v.t.* exasperate. **~ation** *n.f.* exasperation.

exaucer /ɛgzose/ *v.t.* grant; (*personne*) grant the wish(es) of.

excavateur /ɛkskavatœr/ *n.m.* digger.

excavation /ɛkskavasjɔ̃/ *n.f.* excavation.

excédent /ɛksedã/ *n.m.* surplus. **~ de bagages**, excess luggage. **~ de la balance commerciale**, trade surplus. **~aire** /-tɛr/ *a.* excess, surplus.

excéder[1] /ɛksede/ v.t. (*dépasser*) exceed.

excéder[2] /ɛksede/ v.t. (*agacer*) irritate.

excellen|t /ɛksɛlɑ̃/ ~**te** /ɛksɛlɑ̃t, -t/ a. excellent. ~**ce** n.f. excellence.

exceller /ɛksele/ v.i. excel (**dans**, in).

excentri|que /ɛksɑ̃trik/ a. & n.m./f. eccentric. ~**cité** n.f. eccentricity.

excepté /ɛksɛpte/ a. & prép. except.

excepter /ɛksɛpte/ v.t. except.

exception /ɛksɛpsjɔ̃/ n.f. exception. **à l'**~ **de**, except for. **d'**~, exceptional. **faire** ~, be an exception. ~**nel, **~**nelle** /-jɔnɛl/ a. exceptional. ~**nellement** /-jɔnɛlmɑ̃/ adv. exceptionally.

excès /ɛksɛ/ n.m. excess. ~ **de vitesse**, speeding.

excessi|f, ~**ve** /ɛksesif, -v/ a. excessive. ~**vement** adv. excessively.

excitant /ɛksitɑ̃/ n.m. stimulant.

excit|er /ɛksite/ v.t. excite; (*encourager*) exhort (**à**, to); (*irriter. fam.*) annoy. ~**ation** n.f. excitement.

exclam|er (s') /(s)ɛksklame/ v. pr. exclaim. ~**ation** n.f. exclamation.

exclu|re† /ɛksklyr/ v.t. exclude; (*expulser*) expel; (*empêcher*) preclude. ~**sion** n.f. exclusion.

exclusi|f, ~**ve** /ɛksklyzif, -v/ a. exclusive. ~**vement** adv. exclusively. ~**vité** n.f. (*comm.*) exclusive rights. **en** ~**vité à**, (*film*) (showing) exclusively at.

excrément(s) /ɛkskremɑ̃/ n.m. (*pl.*). excrement.

excroissance /ɛkskrwasɑ̃s/ n.f. (out)growth, excrescence.

excursion /ɛkskyrsjɔ̃/ n.f. excursion; (*à pied*) hike.

excuse /ɛkskyz/ n.f. excuse. ~**s**, apology. **faire des** ~**s**, apologize.

excuser /ɛkskyze/ v.t. excuse. **s'**~ v. pr. apologize (**de**, for). **je m'excuse**, (*fam.*) excuse me.

exécrable /ɛgzekrabl/ a. abominable.

exécrer /ɛgzekre/ v.t. loathe.

exécut|er /ɛgzekyte/ v.t. carry out, execute; (*mus.*) perform; (*tuer*) execute. ~**ion** /-sjɔ̃/ n.f. execution; (*mus.*) performance.

exécuti|f, ~**ve** /ɛgzekytif, -v/ a. & n.m. (*pol.*) executive.

exemplaire /ɛgzɑ̃plɛr/ a. exemplary. —n.m. copy.

exemple /ɛgzɑ̃pl/ n.m. example. **par** ~, for example. **donner l'**~, set an example.

exempt, ~**e** /ɛgzɑ̃, -t/ a. ~ **de**, exempt from.

exempt|er /ɛgzɑ̃te/ v.t. exempt (**de**, from). ~**ion** /-psjɔ̃/ n.f. exemption.

exercer /ɛgzɛrse/ v.t. exercise; (*influence*, *contrôle*) exert; (*métier*) work at; (*former*) train, exercise. **s'**~ (**à**), practise.

exercice /ɛgzɛrsis/ n.m. exercise; (*mil.*) drill; (*de métier*) practice. **en** ~, in office; (*médecin*) in practice.

exhaler /ɛgzale/ v.t. emit.

exhausti|f, ~**ve** /ɛgzostif, -v/ a. exhaustive.

exhiber /ɛgzibe/ v.t. exhibit.

exhibitionniste /ɛgzibisjɔnist/ n.m./f. exhibitionist.

exhorter /ɛgzɔrte/ v.t. exhort (**à**, to).

exigence /ɛgziʒɑ̃s/ n.f. demand.

exig|er /ɛgziʒe/ v.t. demand. ~**eant**, ~**eante** a. demanding.

exigu, ~**ë** /ɛgzigy/ a. tiny.

exil /ɛgzil/ n.m. exile. ~**é**, ~**ée** n.m., f. exile. **s'**~**er** v. pr. exile. **s'**~**er** v. pr. go into exile.

existence /ɛgzistɑ̃s/ n.f. existence.

exist|er /ɛgziste/ v.i. exist. ~**ant**, ~**ante** a. existing.

exode /ɛgzɔd/ n.m. exodus.

exonér|er /ɛgzɔnere/ v.t. exempt (**de**, from). **~ation** n.f. exemption.

exorbitant, ~e /ɛgzɔrbitɑ̃, -t/ a. exorbitant.

exorciser /ɛgzɔrsize/ v.t. exorcize.

exotique /ɛgzɔtik/ a. exotic.

expansi|f, ~ve /ɛkspɑ̃sif, -v/ a. expansive.

expansion /ɛkspɑ̃sjɔ̃/ n.f. expansion.

expatri|er (s') /(s)ɛkspatrije/ v. pr. leave one's country. **~ié, ~iée** n.m., f. expatriate.

expectative /ɛkspɛktativ/ n.f. **dans l'~**, still waiting.

expédient, ~e /ɛkspedjɑ̃, -t/ a. & n.m. expedient. **vivre d'~s**, live by one's wits. **user d'~s**, resort to expedients.

expéd|ier /ɛkspedje/ v.t. send, dispatch; (tâche: péj.) dispatch. **~iteur, ~itrice** n.m., f. sender. **~ition** n.f. dispatch; (voyage) expedition.

expéditi|f, ~ve /ɛkspeditif, -v/ a. quick.

expérience /ɛksperjɑ̃s/ n.f. experience; (scientifique) experiment.

expérimenté /ɛksperimɑ̃te/ a. experienced.

expériment|er /ɛksperimɑ̃te/ v.t. test, experiment with. **~al** (m. pl. **~aux**) a. experimental. **~ation** n.f. experimentation.

expert, ~e /ɛkspɛr, -t/ a. expert. —n.m. expert; (d'assurances) valuer; (Amer.) appraiser. **~-comptable** (pl. **~s-comptables**) n.m. accountant.

expertise /ɛkspɛrtiz/ n.f. expert appraisal. **~er** v.t. appraise.

expier /ɛkspje/ v.t. atone for.

expir|er /ɛkspire/ v.i. breathe out; (finir, mourir) expire. **~ation** n.f. expiry.

explicati|f, ~ve /ɛksplikatif, -v/ a. explanatory.

explication /ɛksplikɑsjɔ̃/ n.f. explanation; (fig.) discussion; (scol.) commentary. **~ de texte**, (scol.) literary commentary.

explicite /ɛksplisit/ a. explicit.

expliquer /ɛksplike/ v.t. explain. **s'~** v. pr. explain o.s.; (discuter) discuss things; (être compréhensible) be understandable.

exploit /ɛksplwa/ n.m. exploit.

exploitant /ɛksplwatɑ̃/ n.m. **~ (agricole)**, farmer.

exploit|er /ɛksplwate/ v.t. (personne) exploit; (ferme) run; (champs) work. **~ation** n.f. exploitation; running; working; (affaire) concern. **~eur, ~euse** n.m., f. exploiter.

explor|er /ɛksplɔre/ v.t. explore. **~ateur, ~atrice** n.m., f. explorer. **~ation** n.f. exploration.

explos|er /ɛksplɔze/ v.i. explode. **faire ~er**, explode; (bâtiment) blow up. **~ion** n.f. explosion.

explosi|f, ~ve /ɛksplozif, -v/ a. & n.m. explosive.

export|er /ɛkspɔrte/ v.t. export. **~ateur, ~atrice** n.m., f. exporter; a. exporting. **~ation** n.f. export.

exposant, ~e /ɛkspozɑ̃, -t/ n.m., f. exhibitor.

exposé /ɛkspoze/ n.m. talk (**sur**, on); (d'une action) account. **faire l'~ de la situation**, give an account of the situation.

expos|er /ɛkspoze/ v.t. display, show; (expliquer) explain; (soumettre, mettre en danger) expose (**à**, to); (vie) endanger. **~é au nord/etc.**, facing north/etc. **s'~er à**, expose o.s. to.

exposition /ɛkspozisjɔ̃/ n.f. display; (salon) exhibition. **~ à**, exposure to.

exprès[1] /ɛksprɛ/ adv. specially; (délibérément) on purpose.

exprès² **~esse** /ɛkspres/ a. express. **~essément** adv. expressly.

exprès³ /ɛkspres/ a. invar. & n.m. **lettre ~**, express letter. **(par) ~**, sent special delivery.

express /ɛkspres/ a. & n.m. invar. **(café) ~**, espresso. **(train) ~**, fast train.

expressi|f, **~ve** /ɛkspresif, -v/ a. expressive.

expression /ɛkspresjɔ̃/ n.f. expression. **~ corporelle**, physical expression.

exprimer /ɛksprime/ v.t. express. **s'~** v. pr. express o.s.

expuls|er /ɛkspylse/ v.t. expel; (locataire) evict; (Joueur) send off. **~ion** n.f. (expulsion); eviction.

expurger /ɛkspyrʒe/ v.t. expurgate.

exquis, **~e** /ɛkski, -z/ a. exquisite.

extase /ɛkstaz/ n.f. ecstasy.

extasier (s') /(s)ɛkstazje/ v. pr. **s'~ sur**, be ecstatic about.

extensible /ɛkstɑ̃sibl/ a. expandable, extendible. **tissu ~**, stretch fabric.

extensi|f, **~ve** /ɛkstɑ̃sif, -v/ a. extensive.

extension /ɛkstɑ̃sjɔ̃/ n.f. extension; (expansion) expansion.

exténuer /ɛkstenye/ v.t. exhaust.

extérieur /ɛksterjœr/ a. outside; (signe, gaieté) outward; (politique) foreign. —n.m. outside, exterior; (de personne) exterior. **à l'~ (de)**, outside. **~ement** adv. outwardly.

extérioriser /ɛksterjɔrize/ v.t. show, externalize.

extermin|er /ɛkstɛrmine/ v.t. exterminate. **~ation** n.f. extermination.

externe /ɛkstɛrn/ a. external. —n.m./f. (scol.) day pupil.

extincteur /ɛkstɛ̃ktœr/ n.m. fire extinguisher.

extinction /ɛkstɛ̃ksjɔ̃/ n.f. extinction. **~ de voix**, loss of voice.

extirper /ɛkstirpe/ v.t. eradicate.

extor|quer /ɛkstɔrke/ v.t. extort. **~sion** n.f. extortion.

extra /ɛkstra/ a. invar. first-rate. —n.m. invar. (repas) (special) treat.

extra- /ɛkstra/ préf. extra-.

extrad|er /ɛkstrade/ v.t. extradite. **~ition** n.f. extradition.

extr|aire† /ɛkstrer/ v.t. extract. **~action** n.f. extraction.

extrait /ɛkstre/ n.m. extract.

extraordinaire /ɛkstraɔrdinɛr/ a. extraordinary.

extravagan|t, **~te** /ɛkstravagɑ̃, -t/ a. extravagant. **~ce** n.f. extravagance.

extraverti, **~e** /ɛkstravɛrti/ n.m., f. extrovert.

extrême /ɛkstrɛm/ a. & n.m. extreme. **E~-Orient** n.m. Far East. **~ment** adv. extremely.

extrémiste /ɛkstremist/ n.m., f. extremist.

extrémité /ɛkstremite/ n.f. extremity, end; (misère) dire straits. **~s**, (excès) extremes.

exubéran|t, **~te** /ɛgzyberɑ̃, -t/ a. exuberant. **~ce** n.f. exuberance.

exulter /ɛgzylte/ v.i. exult.

exutoire /ɛgzytwar/ n.m. outlet.

F

F abrév. (franc, francs) franc, francs.

fable /fabl/ n.f. fable.

fabrique /fabrik/ n.f. factory.

fabri|quer /fabrike/ v.t. make; (industriellement) manufacture; (fig.) make up. **~cant**, **~cante**

n.m., f. manufacturer. **~cation** *n.f.* making; manufacture.

fabul|er /fabyle/ *v.i.* fantasize. **~ation** *n.f.* fantasizing.

fabuleu|x, ~se /fabylø, -z/ *a.* fabulous.

fac /fak/ *n.f.* (*fam.*) university.

façade /fasad/ *n.f.* front; (*fig.*) façade.

face /fas/ *n.f.* face; (*d'un objet*) side. **en ~ (de), d'en ~,** opposite. **en ~ de,** (*fig.*) faced with. **~ à,** facing; (*fig.*) faced with. **faire ~ à,** face.

facétie /fasesi/ *n.f.* joke.

facette /faset/ *n.f.* facet.

fâch|er /faʃe/ *v.t.* anger. **se ~er** *v. pr.* get angry; (*se brouiller*) fall out. **~é** *a.* angry; (*désolé*) sorry.

fâcheu|x, ~se /faʃø, -z/ *a.* unfortunate.

facil|e /fasil/ *a.* easy; (*caractère*) easygoing. **~ement** *adv.* easily. **~ité** *n.f.* easiness; (*aisance*) ease; (*aptitude*) ability; (*possibilité*) facility. **~ités de paiement,** easy terms.

faciliter /fasilite/ *v.t.* facilitate.

façon /fasɔ̃/ *n.f.* way; (*de vêtement*) cut. **~s,** (*chichis*) fuss. **de cette ~,** in this way. **de ~ à,** so as to. **de toute ~,** anyway.

façonner /fasɔne/ *v.t.* shape; (*faire*) make.

facteur¹ /faktœr/ *n.m.* postman.

facteur² /faktœr/ *n.m.* (*élément*) factor.

factice /faktis/ *a.* artificial.

faction /faksjɔ̃/ *n.f.* faction. **de ~,** (*mil.*) on guard.

factur|e /faktyr/ *n.f.* bill; (*comm.*) invoice. **~er** *v.t.* invoice.

facultati|f, ~ve /fakyltatif, -v/ *a.* optional.

faculté /fakylte/ *n.f.* faculty; (*possibilité*) power; (*univ.*) faculty.

fade /fad/ *a.* insipid.

fagot /fago/ *n.m.* bundle of firewood.

fagoter /fagɔte/ *v.t.* (*fam.*) rig out.

faibl|e /fɛbl/ *a.* weak; (*espoir, quantité, écart*) slight; (*revenu, intensité*) low. —*n.m.* weakling (*penchant, défaut*) weakness. **~e d'esprit,** feeble-minded. **~esse** *n.f.* weakness. **~ir** *v.i.* weaken.

faïence /fajɑ̃s/ *n.f.* earthenware.

faille /faj/ *n.f.* (*géog.*) fault; (*fig.*) flaw.

faillir /fajir/ *v.i.* **j'ai failli acheter**/*etc.*, I almost bought/*etc.*

faillite /fajit/ *n.f.* bankruptcy; (*fig.*) collapse.

faim /fɛ̃/ *n.f.* hunger. **avoir ~,** be hungry.

fainéant, ~e /feneɑ̃, -t/ *a.* idle. —*n.m., f.* idler.

faire† /fɛr/ *v.t.* make; (*activité*) do; (*rêve, chute, etc.*) have; (*dire*) say. **ça fait 20 F,** that's 20 F. **ça fait 3 ans,** it's been 3 years. —*v.i.* do; (*paraître*) look. **se ~,** *v. pr.* (*petit etc.*) make o.s.; (*amis, argent etc.*) make; (*illusions*) have; (*devenir*) become. **~ du rugby/du violon**/*etc.*, play rugby/the violin/*etc.* **~ construire/punir**/*etc.*, have *ou* get built/punished/*etc.* **~ pleurer/tomber**/*etc.*, make cry/fall/*etc.* **se ~ tuer**/*etc.*, get killed/*etc.* **se ~ couper les cheveux,** have one's hair cut. **il fait beau/chaud**/*etc.*, it is fine/hot/*etc.* **~ l'idiot,** play the fool. **ne ~ que pleurer**/*etc.*, (*faire continuellement*) do nothing but cry/*etc.* **ça ne fait rien,** it doesn't matter. **se ~ à,** get used to. **s'en ~,** worry. **ça se fait,** that is done. **~-part** *n.m. invar.* announcement.

fais, fait¹ /fɛ/ *voir* faire.

faisable /fəzabl/ *a.* feasible.

faisan /fəzɑ̃/ *n.m.* pheasant.

faisandé /fəzɑ̃de/ *a.* high.

faisceau (pl. ~x) /fɛso/ n.m. (rayon) beam; (fagot) bundle.

fait², ~e /fɛ, fɛt/ a. done; (fromage) ripe. ~ pour, made for. **tout** ~, ready made. **c'est bien** ~ **pour toi**, it serves you right.

fait³ /fɛ/ n.m. fact; (événement) event. **au** ~ **(de)**, informed (of). **de ce** ~, therefore. **du** ~ **de**, on account of. ~ **divers**, (trivial) news item. ~ **nouveau**, new development. **sur le** ~, in the act.

faîte /fɛt/ n.m. top; (fig.) peak.

faites /fɛt/ voir **faire**.

faitout /fɛtu/ n.m. stew-pot.

falaise /falɛz/ n.f. cliff.

falloir† /falwar/ v.i. **il faut qch./qn.**, we, you, etc. need sth./so. **il lui faut du pain**, he needs bread. **il faut rester**, we, you, etc. have to ou must stay. **il faut que j'y aille**, I have to ou must go. **il faudrait que tu partes**, you should leave. **il aurait fallu le faire**, we, you, etc. should have done it. **il s'en faut de beaucoup que je sois**, I am far from being. **comme il faut**, a proper.

falot, ~e /falo, falɔt/ a. grey.

falsifier /falsifje/ v.t. falsify.

famélique /famelik/ a. starving.

fameu|x, ~se /famø, -z/ a. famous; (excellent: fam.) first-rate. ~sement adv. (fam.) extremely.

famil|ial (m. pl. ~iaux) /familjal, -jo/ a. family.

familiar|iser /familjarize/ v.t. familiarize (avec, with). **se** ~iser v. pr. familiarize o.s. ~isé a. familiar. ~ité n.f. familiarity.

famil|ier, ~ière /familje, -jɛr/ a. familiar; (amical) informal. —n.m. regular visitor. ~ièrement adv. informally.

famille /famij/ n.f. family. **en** ~, with one's family.

famine /famin/ n.f. famine.

fanati|que /fanatik/ a. fanatical. —n.m./f. fanatic. ~sme n.m. fanaticism.

faner (se) /(sə)fane/ v. pr. fade.

fanfare /fɑ̃far/ n.f. brass band; (musique) fanfare.

fanfaron, ~ne /fɑ̃farɔ̃, -ɔn/ a. boastful. —n.m., f. boaster.

fanion /fanjɔ̃/ n.m. pennant.

fantaisie /fɑ̃tezi/ n.f. imagination, fantasy; (caprice) whim. **(de)** ~, (boutons etc.) fancy.

fantaisiste /fɑ̃tezist/ a. unorthodox.

fantasme /fɑ̃tasm/ n.m. fantasy.

fantasque /fɑ̃task/ a. whimsical.

fantastique /fɑ̃tastik/ a. fantastic.

fantoche /fɑ̃tɔʃ/ a. puppet.

fantôme /fɑ̃tom/ n.m. ghost. —a. (péj.) bogus.

faon /fɑ̃/ n.m. fawn.

faramineux, ~se /faraminø, -z/ a. astronomical.

farce¹ /fars/ n.f. (practical) joke; (théâtre) farce. ~eur, ~euse n.m., f. joker.

farce² /fars/ n.f. (hachis) stuffing. ~ir v.t. stuff.

fard /far/ n.m. make-up. **piquer un** ~, blush. ~er /-de/ v.t., **se** ~er v. pr. make up.

fardeau (pl. ~x) /fardo/ n.m. burden.

farfelu, ~e /farfəly/ a. & n.m., f. eccentric.

farin|e /farin/ n.f. flour. ~eux, ~euse a. floury. **les** ~eux n.m. pl. starchy food.

farouche /faruʃ/ a. shy; (peu sociable) unsociable; (violent) fierce. ~ment adv. fiercely.

fascicule /fasikyl/ n.m. volume.

fascin|er /fasine/ v.t. fascinate. ~ation n.f. fascination.

fasc|isme /faʃism/ n.m. fascism.

fascis|te /faʃist/ a. & n.m./f. fascist. ~me n.m. fascism.

fasse /fas/ voir **faire**.

faste /fast/ n.m. splendour.

fast-food /fastfud/ *n.m.* fast-food place.

fastidieu|x, **~se** /fastidjø, -z/ *a.* tedious.

fat|al (*m. pl.* **~als**) /fatal/ *a.* inevitable; (*mortel*) fatal. **~alement** *adv.* inevitably. **~alité** *n.f.* (*destin*) fate.

fataliste /fatalist/ *n.m./f.* fatalist.

fatidique /fatidik/ *a.* fateful.

fatigant, **~e** /fatigã, -t/ *a.* tiring; (*ennuyeux*) tiresome.

fatigue /fatig/ *n.f.* fatigue, tiredness.

fatigu|er /fatige/ *v.t.* tire; (*yeux, moteur*) strain. —*v.i.* (*moteur*) labour. **se ~er** *v. pr.* get tired, tire (*de, of*). **~é** *a.* tired.

fatras /fatra/ *n.m.* jumble.

faubourg /fobur/ *n.m.* suburb.

fauché /fofe/ *a.* (*fam.*) broke.

faucher /fofe/ *v.t.* (*herbe*) mow; (*voler: fam.*) pinch. **~ qn.**, (*véhicule, tir*) mow s.o. down.

faucille /fosij/ *n.f.* sickle.

faucon /fokõ/ *n.m.* falcon, hawk.

faudra, **faudrait** /fodra, fodrɛ/ *voir* **falloir**.

faufiler (se) /(sə)fofile/ *v. pr.* edge one's way.

faune /fon/ *n.f.* wildlife, fauna.

faussaire /fosɛr/ *n.m.* forger.

fausse /fos/ *voir* **faux²**.

faussement /fosmã/ *adv.* falsely, wrongly.

fausser /fose/ *v.t.* buckle; (*fig.*) distort. **~ compagnie à**, sneak away from.

fausseté /foste/ *n.f.* falseness.

faut /fo/ *voir* **falloir**.

faute /fot/ *n.f.* mistake; (*responsabilité*) fault; (*délit*) offence; (*péché*) sin. **en ~**, at fault. **~ de**, for want of. **~ de quoi**, failing which. **sans faute**, without fail. **~ de frappe**, typing error. **~ de goût**, bad taste. **~ professionelle**, professional misconduct.

fauteuil /fotœj/ *n.m.* armchair; (*de président*) chair; (*théâtre*) seat. **~ roulant**, wheelchair.

fauti|f, **~ve** /fotif, -v/ *a.* guilty; (*faux*) faulty. —*n.m., f.* guilty party.

fauve /fov/ *a.* (*couleur*) fawn. —*n.m.* wild cat.

faux¹ /fo/ *n.f.* scythe.

faux², **fausse** /fo, fos/ *a.* false; (*falsifié*) fake, forged; (*numéro, calcul*) wrong; (*voix*) out of tune. **c'est ~!**, that is wrong! **~ témoignage**, perjury. **faire ~ bond à qn.**, stand s.o. up. —*adv.* (*chanter*) out of tune. —*n.m.* forgery. **fausse alerte**, false alarm. **fausse couche**, miscarriage. **~-filet** *n.m.* sirloin. **frais**, **~ n.m. pl.** incidental expenses. **~-monnayeur** *n.m.* forger.

faveur /favœr/ *n.f.* favour. **de ~**, (*régime*) preferential. **en ~ de**, in favour of.

favorable /favorabl/ *a.* favourable.

favori, **~te** /favori, -t/ *a.* & *n.m., f.* favourite. **~tisme** *n.m.* favouritism.

favoriser /favorize/ *v.t.* favour.

fax /faks/ *n.m.* fax. **~er** *v.t.* fax.

fébrile /febril/ *a.* feverish.

fécond, **~e** /fekõ, -d/ *a.* fertile. **~er** /-de/ *v.t.* fertilize. **~ité** /-dite/ *n.f.* fertility.

fédér|al (*m. pl.* **~aux**) /federal, -o/ *a.* federal.

fédération /federasjõ/ *n.f.* federation.

fée /fe/ *n.f.* fairy.

féer|ie /feri/ *n.f.* magical spectacle. **~ique** *a.* magical.

feindre† /fɛdr/ *v.t.* feign. **~ de**, pretend to.

feinte /fɛt/ *n.f.* feint.

fêler /fele/ *v.t.*, **se ~** *v. pr.* crack.

félicit|er /felisite/ *v.t.* congratulate (*de, on*). **~ations** *n.f. pl.* congratulations (*pour, on*).

félin, ～e /felɛ̃, -in/ *a. & n.m.* feline.

fêlure /felyr/ *n.f.* crack.

femelle /fəmɛl/ *a. & n.f.* female.

fémin|in, ～**ine** /feminɛ̃, -in/ *a.* feminine; (*sexe*) female; (*mode, équipe*) women's. —*n.m.* feminine. ～**ité** *n.f.* femininity.

féministe /feminist/ *n.m./f.* feminist.

femme /fam/ *n.f.* woman; (*épouse*) wife. ～ **au foyer**, housewife. ～ **de chambre**, chambermaid. ～ **de ménage**, cleaning lady.

fémur /femyr/ *n.m.* thigh-bone.

fendiller /fãdije/ *v.t.*, **se** ～ *v. pr.* crack.

fendre /fãdr/ *v.t.* (*couper*) split; (*fissurer*) crack; (*foule*) push through. **se** ～ *v. pr.* crack.

fenêtre /fənɛtr/ *n.f.* window.

fenouil /fənuj/ *n.m.* fennel.

fente /fãt/ *n.f.* (*ouverture*) slit, slot; (*fissure*) crack.

féod|al (*m. pl.* ～**aux**) /feɔdal, -o/ *a.* feudal.

fer /fɛr/ *n.m.* iron. ～ (**à repasser**), iron. ～ **à cheval**, horseshoe. ～-**blanc** (*pl.* ～**s-blancs**) /-blã/ tinplate. ～ **de lance**, spearhead. ～ **forgé**, wrought iron.

fera, ferait /fəra, fərɛ/ *voir* **faire**.

férié /ferje/ *a.* **jour** ～, public holiday.

ferme[1] /fɛrm/ *a.* firm. —*adv.* (*travailler*) hard. ～**ment** /-əmã/ *adv.* firmly.

ferme[2] /fɛrm/ *n.f.* farm; (*maison*) farm(house).

fermé /fɛrme/ *a.* closed; (*gaz, radio, etc.*) off.

ferment /fɛrmã/ *n.m.* ferment.

fermenter /fɛrmãte/ *v.i.* ferment. ～**ation** *n.f.* fermentation.

fermer /fɛrme/ *v.t./i.* close, shut; (*cesser d'exploiter*) close down; (*gaz, robinet*) turn off. **se** ～ *v. pr.* close, shut.

fermeté /fɛrməte/ *n.f.* firmness.

fermeture /fɛrmətyr/ *n.f.* closing; (*dispositif*) catch. ～ **annuelle,** annual closure. ～ **éclair,** (P.) zip(-fastener); (*Amer.*) zipper.

ferm|ier, ～**ière** /fɛrmje, -jɛr/ *n.m.* farmer. —*n.f.* farmer's wife. —*a.* farm.

fermoir /fɛrmwar/ *n.m.* clasp.

féroc|e /ferɔs/ *a.* ferocious. ～**ité** *n.f.* ferocity.

ferraille /fɛraj/ *n.f.* scrap-iron.

ferré /fɛre/ *a.* (*canne*) steel-tipped.

ferrer /fɛre/ *v.t.* (*cheval*) shoe.

ferronnerie /fɛrɔnri/ *n.f.* iron-work.

ferroviaire /fɛrɔvjɛr/ *a.* rail(way).

ferry(-boat) /feri(bot)/ *n.m.* ferry.

fertile /fɛrtil/ *a.* fertile. ～ **en** (*fig.*) rich in. ～**iser** *v.t.* fertilize. ～**ité** *n.f.* fertility.

féru, ～**e** /fery/ *a.* ～ **de,** passionate about.

ferv|ent, ～**ente** /fɛrvã, -t/ *a.* fervent. —*n.m.*, *f.* enthusiast (de, of). ～**eur** *n.f.* fervour.

fesse /fɛs/ *n.f.* buttock.

fessée /fese/ *n.f.* spanking.

festin /fɛstɛ̃/ *n.m.* feast.

festival (*pl.* ～**s**) /fɛstival/ *n.m.* festival.

festivités /fɛstivite/ *n.f. pl.* festivities.

festoyer /fɛstwaje/ *v.i.* feast.

fêtard /fɛtar/ *n.m.* merry-maker.

fête /fɛt/ *n.f.* holiday; (*religieuse*) feast; (*du nom*) name-day; (*réception*) party; (*en famille*) celebration; (*foire*) fair; (*folklorique*) festival. ～ **des Mères,** Mother's Day. ～ **foraine,** funfair. **faire la** ～, make merry. **les** ～**s** (**de fin d'année**), the Christmas season.

fêter /fete/ *v.t.* celebrate; (*personne*) give a celebration for.

fétiche /fetiʃ/ *n.m.* fetish; (*fig.*) mascot.

fétide /fetid/ *a.* fetid.

feu[1] (*pl.* ∼**x**) /fø/ *n.m.* fire; (*lumière*) light; (*de réchaud*) burner. ∼**x** (**rouges**), (traffic) lights. **à** ∼ **doux/vif**, on a low/ high heat. **du** ∼, (*pour cigarette*) a light, have ∼!, fire! ∼ **d'artifice**, firework display. ∼ **de joie**, bonfire. ∼ **rouge/vert/orange**, red/green/amber *ou* yellow (*Amer.*). ∼ **de position**, sidelight. **mettre le** ∼ **à**, set fire to. **prendre** ∼, catch fire. **jouer avec le** ∼, play with fire. **ne pas faire long** ∼, not last.

feuillage /fœjaʒ/ *n.m.* foliage.

feuille /fœj/ *n.f.* leaf; (*de papier, bois, etc.*) sheet; (*formulaire*) form.

feuillet /fœjɛ/ *n.m.* leaf.

feuilleter /fœjte/ *v.t.* leaf through.

feuilleton /fœjtɔ̃/ *n.m.* (*à suivre*) serial; (*histoire complète*) series.

feuillu /fœjy/ *a.* leafy.

feutre /føtr/ *n.m.* felt; (*chapeau*) felt hat; (*crayon*) felt-tip (pen).

feutré /føtre/ *a.* (*bruit*) muffled.

fève /fɛv/ *n.f.* broad bean.

février /fevrije/ *n.m.* February.

fiable /fjabl/ *a.* reliable.

fiançailles /fjɑ̃saj/ *n.f. pl.* engagement.

fiancer (se) /(sə)fjɑ̃se/ *v. pr.* become engaged (**avec**, to). ∼**é**, ∼**ée** *a.* engaged; *n.m.* fiancé; *n.f.* fiancée.

fiasco /fjasko/ *n.m.* fiasco.

fibre /fibr/ *n.f.* fibre. ∼ **de verre**, fibreglass.

ficeler /fisle/ *v.t.* tie up.

ficelle /fisɛl/ *n.f.* string.

fiche /fiʃ/ *n.f.* (index) card; (*formulaire*) form, slip; (*électr.*) plug.

ficher[1] /fiʃe/ *v.t.* (*enfoncer*) drive (**dans**, into).

ficher[2] /fiʃe/ *v.t.* (*faire: fam.*) do; (*donner: fam.*) give; (*mettre: fam.*) put. **se** ∼ **de**, (*fam.*) make fun of.

∼ **le camp**, (*fam.*) clear off. **il s'en fiche**, (*fam.*) he couldn't care less.

fichier /fiʃje/ *n.m.* file.

fichu /fiʃy/ *a.* (*mauvais: fam.*) rotten; (*raté: fam.*) done for. **mal** ∼, (*fam.*) terrible.

fictif, ∼**ve** /fiktif, -v/ *a.* fictitious.

fiction /fiksjɔ̃/ *n.f.* fiction.

fidèle /fidɛl/ *a.* faithful. ∼ (*client*) regular; (*relig.*) believer. ∼**s**, (*à l'église*) congregation. ∼**ment** *adv.* faithfully.

fidélité /fidelite/ *n.f.* fidelity.

fier[1], **fière** /fjɛr/ *a.* proud (**de**, of). **fièrement** *adv.* proudly. ∼**té** *n.f.* pride.

fier[2] **(se)** /(sə)fje/ *v. pr.* **se** ∼ **à**, trust.

fièvre /fjɛvr/ *n.f.* fever.

fiévreu|x, ∼**se** /fjevrø, -z/ *a.* feverish.

figé /fiʒe/ *a.* fixed, set; (*manières*) stiff.

figer /fiʒe/ *v.t./i.* ∼, **se** ∼ *v. pr.* congeal. ∼ **sur place**, petrify.

fignoler /fiɲɔle/ *v.t.* refine (upon), finish off meticulously.

figu|e /fig/ *n.f.* fig. ∼**ier** *n.m.* fig-tree.

figurant, ∼**e** /figyrã, -t/ *n.m.*, *f.* (*cinéma*) extra.

figure /figyr/ *n.f.* face; (*forme, personnage*) figure; (*illustration*) picture.

figuré /figyre/ *a.* (*sens*) figurative. **au** ∼, figuratively.

figurer /figyre/ *v.i.* appear. —*v.t.* represent. **se** ∼ *v. pr.* imagine.

fil /fil/ *n.m.* thread; (*métallique, électrique*) wire; (*de couteau*) edge; (*à coudre*) cotton. **au** ∼ **de**, with the passing of. **au** ∼ **de l'eau**, with the current. ∼ **de fer**, wire. **au bout du** ∼, on the phone.

filament /filamɑ̃/ *n.m.* filament.

filature /filatyr/ *n.f.* (*textile*) mill; (*surveillance*) shadowing.

file /fil/ *n.f.* line; (*voie: auto.*) lane.

~ (d'attente), queue; (*Amer.*) line. **en ~ indienne,** in single file. **se mettre en ~,** line up.

filer /file/ *v.t.* spin; (*suivre*) shadow. **~ qch. à qn.,** (*fam.*) slip s.o. sth. —*v.i.* (*bas*) ladder, run; (*liquide*) run; (*aller vite*: *fam.*) speed along, fly by; (*partir*: *fam.*) dash off. **~ doux,** do as one's told. **~ à l'anglaise,** take French leave.

filet /file/ *n.m.* net; (*d'eau*) trickle; (*de viande*) fillet. **~ (à bagages),** (luggage) rack. **~ à provisions,** string bag (*for shopping*).

fil|ial, **~iale** (*m. pl.* **~iaux**) /filjal, -jo/ *a.* filial. —*n.f.* subsidiary (company).

filière /filjɛr/ *n.f.* (official) channels; (*de trafiquants*) network. **passer par ou suivre la ~,** (*employé*) work one's way up.

filigrane /filigran/ *n.m.* watermark. **en ~,** between the lines.

filin /filɛ̃/ *n.m.* rope.

fille /fij/ *n.f.* girl; (*opposé à fils*) daughter. **~-mère** (*pl.* **~s-mères**) *n.f.* (*péj.*) unmarried mother.

fillette /fijɛt/ *n.f.* little girl.

filleul /fijœl/ *n.m.* godson. **~e** *n.f.* god-daughter.

film /film/ *n.m.* film. **~ d'épouvante / muet / parlant,** horror/silent/talking film. **~ dramatique,** drama. **~er** *v.t.* film.

filon /filɔ̃/ *n.m.* (*géol.*) seam; (*situation*) source of wealth.

filou /filu/ *n.m.* crook.

fils /fis/ *n.m.* son.

filtr|e /filtr/ *n.m.* filter. **~er** *v.t./i.* filter; (*personne*) screen.

fin¹ /fɛ̃/ *n.f.* end. **à la ~,** finally. **en ~ de compte,** all things considered. **~ de semaine,** weekend. **mettre ~ à,** put an end to. **prendre ~,** come to an end.

fin², fine /fɛ̃, fin/ *a.* fine; (*tranche,*

couche) thin; (*taille*) slim; (*plat*) exquisite; (*esprit, vue*) sharp. —*adv.* (*couper*) finely. **~es herbes,** herbs.

fin|al, ~ale (*m. pl.* **~aux** *ou* **~als**) /final, -o/ *a.* final. —*n.f.* (*sport*) final; (*gram.*) final syllable. —*n.m.* (*pl.* **~aux** *ou* **~als**) (*mus.*) finale. **~alement** *adv.* finally; (*somme toute*) after all.

finaliste /finalist/ *n.m./f.* finalist.

financ|e /finɑ̃s/ *n.f.* finance. **~er** *v.t.* finance. **~ier, ~ière** *a.* financial; *n.m.* financier.

finesse /finɛs/ *n.f.* fineness; (*de taille*) slimness; (*acuité*) sharpness. **~s,** (*de langue*) niceties.

fini /fini/ *a.* finished; (*espace*) finite. —*n.m.* finish.

finir /finir/ *v.t./i.* finish, end; (*arrêter*) stop; (*manger*) finish (up). **en ~ avec,** have done with. **~ par faire,** end up doing. **ça va mal ~,** it will turn out badly.

finition /finisjɔ̃/ *n.f.* finish.

finland|ais, ~e /fɛ̃lɑ̃dɛ, -z/ *a.* Finnish. —*n.m., f.* Finn.

finlande /fɛ̃lɑ̃d/ *n.f.* Finland.

finnois, ~e /finwa, -z/ *a.* Finnish. —*n.m.* (*lang.*) Finnish.

fiole /fjɔl/ *n.f.* phial.

firme /firm/ *n.f.* firm.

fisc /fisk/ *n.m.* tax authorities. **~al** (*m. pl.* **~aux**) *a.* tax, fiscal. **~alité** *n.f.* tax system.

fission /fisjɔ̃/ *n.f.* fission.

fissur|e /fisyr/ *n.f.* crack. **~er** *v.t.*, **se ~er** *v. pr.* crack.

fiston /fistɔ̃/ *n.m.* (*fam.*) son.

fixation /fiksasjɔ̃/ *n.f.* fixing; (*complexe*) fixation.

fixe /fiks/ *a.* fixed; (*stable*) steady. **à heure ~,** at a set time. **menu à prix ~,** set menu.

fix|er /fikse/ *v.t.* fix. **~er** (*du regard*), stare at. **se ~er** *v. pr.* (*s'installer*) settle down. **être ~é,** (*personne*) have made up one's mind.

flacon /flakõ/ *n.m.* bottle.

flageolet /flaʒɔlɛ/ *n.m.* (*haricot*) (dwarf) kidney bean.

flagrant, **~e** /flagrã, -t/ *a.* flagrant. **en ~ délit,** in the act.

flair /flɛr/ *n.m.* (sense of) smell; (*fig.*) intuition. **~er** /flɛre/ *v.t.* sniff at; (*fig.*) sense.

flamand, **~e** /flamã, -d/ *a.* Flemish. —*n.m.* (*lang.*) Flemish. —*n.m., f.* Fleming.

flamant /flamã/ *n.m.* flamingo.

flambant /flãbã/ *adv.* **~ neuf,** brand-new.

flambé, **~e** /flãbe/ *a.* (*culin.*) flambé.

flambeau (*pl.* **~x**) /flãbo/ *n.m.* torch.

flambée /flãbe/ *n.f.* blaze; (*fig.*) explosion.

flamber /flãbe/ *v.i.* blaze; (*prix*) shoot up. —*v.t.* (*aiguille*) sterilize; (*volaille*) singe.

flamboyer /flãbwaje/ *v.i.* blaze.

flamme /flam/ *n.f.* flame; (*fig.*) ardour. **en ~s,** ablaze.

flan /flã/ *n.m.* custard-pie.

flanc /flã/ *n.m.* side; (*d'animal, d'armée*) flank.

flancher /flãʃe/ *v.i.* (*fam.*) give in.

Flandre(s) /flãdr/ *n.f.* (*pl.*) Flanders.

flanelle /flanɛl/ *n.f.* flannel.

flân|er /flane/ *v.i.* stroll. **~erie** *n.f.* stroll.

flanquer /flãke/ *v.t.* flank; (*jeter: fam.*) chuck; (*donner: fam.*) give. **~ à la porte,** kick out.

flaque /flak/ *n.f.* (*d'eau*) puddle; (*de sang*) pool.

flash (*pl.* **~es**) /flaʃ/ *n.m.* (*photo.*) flash; (*information*) news flash.

flasque /flask/ *a.* flabby.

flatt|er /flate/ *v.t.* flatter. **se ~er de,** pride o.s. on. **~erie** *n.f.* flattery. **~eur, ~euse** *a.* flattering; *n.m., f.* flatterer.

fléau (*pl.* **~x**) /fleo/ *n.m.* (*désastre*) scourge; (*personne*) bane.

flèche /flɛʃ/ *n.f.* arrow; (*de clocher*) spire. **monter en ~,** spiral. **partir en ~,** shoot off.

flécher /fleʃe/ *v.t.* mark *ou* signpost (with arrows).

fléchette /fleʃɛt/ *n.f.* dart.

fléchir /fleʃir/ *v.t.* bend; (*personne*) move. —*v.i.* (*faiblir*) weaken; (*poutre*) sag, bend.

flegmatique /flɛgmatik/ *a.* phlegmatic.

flemm|e /flɛm/ *n.f.* (*fam.*) laziness. **j'ai la ~e de faire,** I can't be bothered doing. **~ard, ~arde** *a.* (*fam.*) lazy; *n.m., f.* (*fam.*) lazybones.

flétrir /fletrir/ *v.t., se ~ v. pr.* wither.

fleur /flœr/ *n.f.* flower. **à ~ de terre/d'eau,** just above the ground/water. **à ~s,** flowery. **~ de l'âge,** prime of life. **en ~s,** in flower.

fleur|ir /flœrir/ *v.i.* flower; (*arbre*) blossom; (*fig.*) flourish. —*v.t.* adorn with flowers. **~i** *a.* flowery.

fleuriste /flœrist/ *n.m./f.* florist.

fleuve /flœv/ *n.m.* river.

flexible /flɛksibl/ *a.* flexible.

flexion /flɛksjõ/ *n.f.* (*anat.*) flexing.

flic /flik/ *n.m.* (*fam.*) cop.

flipper /flipœr/ *n.m.* pinball (machine).

flirter /flœrte/ *v.i.* flirt.

flocon /flɔkõ/ *n.m.* flake.

flopée /flɔpe/ *n.f.* (*fam.*) **une ~ de,** masses of.

floraison /flɔrɛzõ/ *n.f.* flowering.

flore /flɔr/ *n.f.* flora.

florissant, **~e** /flɔrisã, -t/ *a.* flourishing.

flot /flo/ *n.m.* flood, stream. **être à ~,** be afloat. **les ~s,** the waves.

flottant, **~e** /flɔtã, -t/ *a.* (*vêtement*) loose; (*indécis*) indecisive.

flotte /flɔt/ n.f. fleet; (pluie: fam.) rain; (eau: fam.) water.

flottement /flɔtmã/ n.m. (incertitude) indecision.

flott|er /flɔte/ v.i. float; (drapeau) flutter; (nuage, parfum, pensées) drift; (pleuvoir: fam.) rain. **~eur** n.m. float.

flou /flu/ a. out of focus; (fig.) vague.

fluctu|er /flyktɥe/ v.i. fluctuate. **~ation** n.f. fluctuation.

fluet, ~te /flɥɛ, -t/ a. thin.

fluid|e /flɥid/ a. & n.m. fluid. **~ité** n.f. fluidity.

fluor /flyɔr/ n.m. (pour les dents) fluoride.

fluorescent, ~e /flyɔresã, -t/ a. fluorescent.

flût|e /flyt/ n.f. flute; (verre) champagne glass. **~iste** n.m./f. flautist; (Amer.) flutist.

fluvial (m. pl. **~iaux**) /flyvjal, -jo/ a. river.

flux /fly/ n.m. flow. **~ et reflux**, ebb and flow.

FM /ɛfɛm/ abrév. f. FM.

foc /fɔk/ n.m. jib.

fœtus /fetys/ n.m. foetus.

foi /fwa/ n.f. faith. **être de bonne/mauvaise ~**, be acting in good/bad faith. **ma ~!**, well (indeed)! **digne de ~**, reliable.

foie /fwa/ n.m. liver. **~ gras**, foie gras.

foin /fwɛ̃/ n.m. hay. **faire tout un ~**, (fam.) make a fuss.

foire /fwar/ n.f. fair. **faire la ~**, (fam.) make merry.

fois /fwa/ n.f. time. **une ~**, once. **deux ~**, twice. **à la ~**, at the same time. **des ~**, (parfois) sometimes. **une ~ pour toutes**, once and for all.

foison /fwazɔ̃/ n.f. abundance. **à ~**, in abundance. **~ner** /-ɔne/ v.i. abound (**de**, in).

fol /fɔl/ voir **fou**.

folâtrer /fɔlɑtre/ v.i. frolic.

folichon, ~ne /fɔliʃɔ̃, -ɔn/ a. **pas ~**, (fam.) not much fun.

folie /fɔli/ n.f. madness; (bêtise) foolish thing, folly.

folklor|e /fɔlklɔr/ n.m. folklore. **~ique** a. folk; (fam.) picturesque.

folle /fɔl/ voir **fou**.

follement /fɔlmã/ adv. madly.

fomenter /fɔmãte/ v.t. foment.

fonc|er¹ /fɔ̃se/ v.t./i. darken. **~é** a. dark.

foncer² /fɔ̃se/ v.i. (fam.) dash along. **~ sur**, (fam.) charge at.

fonc|ier, ~ière /fɔ̃sje, -jɛr/ a. fundamental; (comm.) real estate. **~ièrement** adv. fundamentally.

fonction /fɔ̃ksjɔ̃/ n.f. function; (emploi) position. **~s**, (obligations) duties. **en ~ de**, according to. **~ publique**, civil service. **voiture de ~**, company car.

fonctionnaire /fɔ̃ksjɔnɛr/ n.m./f. civil servant.

fonctionnel, ~le /fɔ̃ksjɔnɛl/ a. functional.

fonctionn|er /fɔ̃ksjɔne/ v.i. work. **faire ~er**, work. **~ement** n.m. working.

fond /fɔ̃/ n.m. bottom; (de salle, magasin, etc.) back; (essentiel) basis; (contenu) content; (plan) background. **à ~**, thoroughly. **au ~**, basically. **de ~**, (bruit) background; (sport) long-distance. **de ~ en comble**, from top to bottom. **au ou dans le ~**, really.

fondament|al (m. pl. **~aux**) /fɔ̃damãtal, -o/ a. fundamental.

fondation /fɔ̃dasjɔ̃/ n.f. foundation.

fond|er /fɔ̃de/ v.t. found (baser) base (**sur**, on). **(bien) ~é**, well-founded. **~é** à, justified in. **se ~er sur**, be guided by, place one's reliance on. **~ateur** n.m., **~atrice** n.m., f. founder.

fonderie /fɔ̃dri/ n.f. foundry.

fondre /fɔ̃dr/ v.t./i. melt; (dans l'eau) dissolve; (mélanger) merge. **se ~** v. pr. merge. **faire ~,** melt; dissolve. **~ en larmes,** burst into tears. **~ sur,** swoop on.

fondrière /fɔ̃drijɛr/ n.f. pot-hole.

fonds /fɔ̃/ n.m. fund. —n.m. pl. (capitaux) funds. **~ de commerce,** business.

fondu /fɔ̃dy/ a. melted; (métal) molten.

font /fɔ̃/ voir **faire.**

fontaine /fɔ̃tɛn/ n.f. fountain; (source) spring.

fonte /fɔ̃t/ n.f. melting; (fer) cast iron. **~ des neiges,** thaw.

foot /fut/ n.m. (fam.) football.

football /futbal/ n.m. football. **~eur** n.m. footballer.

footing /futiŋ/ n.m. fast walking.

forage /fɔraʒ/ n.m. drilling.

forain /fɔrɛ̃/ n.m. fairground entertainer. **(marchand) ~,** stall-holder (at a fair or market).

forçat /fɔrsa/ n.m. convict.

force /fɔrs/ n.f. force; (physique) strength; (hydraulique etc.) power. **~s,** (physiques) strength. **à ~ de,** by sheer force of. **de ~, par la ~,** by force. **~ de dissuasion,** deterrent. **~ de frappe,** strike force, deterrent. **~ de l'âge,** prime of life. **~s de l'ordre,** police (force).

forcé /fɔrse/ a. forced; (inévitable) inevitable.

forcément /fɔrsemɑ̃/ adv. necessarily; (évidemment) obviously.

forcené, ~e /fɔrsəne/ a. frenzied. —n.m., f. maniac.

forceps /fɔrsɛps/ n.m. forceps.

forcer /fɔrse/ v.t. force (à faire, to do); (voix) strain. —v.i. (exagérer) overdo it. **se ~** v. pr. force o.s.

forcir /fɔrsir/ v.i. fill out.

forer /fɔre/ v.t. drill.

forest|ier, ~ière /fɔrɛstje, -jɛr/ a. forest.

foret /fɔrɛ/ n.m. drill.

forêt /fɔrɛ/ n.f. forest.

forfait /fɔrfɛ/ n.m. (comm.) inclusive price. **~aire** /-tɛr/ a. (prix) inclusive.

forge /fɔrʒ/ n.f. forge.

forger /fɔrʒe/ v.t. forge; (inventer) make up.

forgeron /fɔrʒərɔ̃/ n.m. blacksmith.

formaliser (se) /(sə)fɔrmalize/ v. pr. take offence (de, at).

formalité /fɔrmalite/ n.f. formality.

format /fɔrma/ n.m. format.

formater /fɔrmate/ v.t. (comput.) format.

formation /fɔrmasjɔ̃/ n.f. formation; (de médecin etc.) training; (culture) education. **~ permanente ou continue,** continuing education. **~ professionnelle,** professional training.

forme /fɔrm/ n.f. (contour) shape, form. **~s,** (de femme) figure. **en ~,** (sport) in good shape, on form. **en ~ de,** in the shape of. **en bonne et due ~,** in due form.

formel, ~le /fɔrmɛl/ a. formal; (catégorique) positive. **~lement** adv. positively.

former /fɔrme/ v.t. form; (instruire) train. **se ~** v. pr. form.

formidable /fɔrmidabl/ a. fantastic.

formulaire /fɔrmylɛr/ n.m. form.

formul|e /fɔrmyl/ n.f. formula; (expression) expression; (feuille) form. **~e de politesse,** polite phrase, letter ending. **~er** v.t. formulate.

fort¹, ~e /fɔr, -t/ a. strong; (grand) big; (pluie) heavy; (bruit) loud; (pente) steep; (élève) clever. —adv. (frapper) hard; (parler) loud; (très) very; (beaucoup) very much. —n.m. strong point. **au plus ~ de,** at the height of. **c'est une ~ tête,** she/he's headstrong.

fort² /fɔr/ *n.m.* (*mil.*) fort.

forteresse /fɔrtərɛs/ *n.f.* fortress.

fortifiant /fɔrtifjɑ̃/ *n.m.* tonic.

fortifi|er /fɔrtifje/ *v.t.* fortify. **~ication** *n.f.* fortification.

fortiori /fɔrsjɔri/ **a ~,** even more so.

fortuit, **~e** /fɔrtɥi, -t/ *a.* fortuitous.

fortune /fɔrtyn/ *n.f.* fortune. **de ~,** (*improvisé*) makeshift. **faire ~,** make one's fortune.

fortuné /fɔrtyne/ *a.* wealthy.

fosse /fos/ *n.f.* pit; (*tombe*) grave. **~ d'aisances,** cesspool. **~ d'orchestre,** orchestral pit. **~ septique,** septic tank.

fossé /fose/ *n.m.* ditch; (*fig.*) gulf.

fossette /fosɛt/ *n.f.* dimple.

fossile /fosil/ *n.m.* fossil.

fossoyeur /foswajœr/ *n.m.* gravedigger.

fou *ou* **fol*,** **fole** /fu, fɔl/ *a.* mad; (*course, regard*) wild; (*énorme: fam.*) tremendous. **~ de,** crazy about. —*n.m.* madman; (*bouffon*) jester. —*n.f.* madwoman; (*fam.*) gay. **le ~ rire,** the giggles.

foudre /fudr/ *n.f.* lightning.

foudroy|er /fudrwaje/ *v.t.* strike by lightning; (*maladie etc.*) strike down; (*atterrer*) stagger. **~ant,** **~ante** *a.* staggering; (*mort, maladie*) violent.

fouet /fwɛ/ *n.m.* whip; (*culin.*) whisk.

fouetter /fwete/ *v.t.* whip; (*crème etc.*) whisk.

fougère /fuʒɛr/ *n.f.* fern.

fougu|e /fug/ *n.f.* ardour. **~eux,** **~euse** *a.* ardent.

fouill|e /fuj/ *n.f.* search; (*archéol.*) excavation. **~er** *v.t./i.* search; (*creuser*) dig. **~er dans,** (*tiroir*) rummage through.

fouillis /fuji/ *n.m.* jumble.

fouine /fwin/ *n.f.* beech-marten.

fouiner /fwine/ *v.i.* nose about.

foulard /fular/ *n.m.* scarf.

foule /ful/ *n.f.* crowd. **une ~ de,** (*fig.*) a mass of.

foulée /fule/ *n.f.* stride. **il l'a fait dans la ~,** he did it while he was at it.

fouler /fule/ *v.t.* press; (*sol*) tread. **se ~ le poignet/le pied** sprain one's wrist/foot. **ne pas se ~,** (*fam.*) not strain o.s.

foulure /fulyr/ *n.f.* sprain.

four /fur/ *n.m.* oven; (*de potier*) kiln; (*théâtre*) flop. **~ à micro-ondes,** microwave oven. **~ crématoire,** crematorium.

fourbe /furb/ *a.* deceitful.

fourbu /furby/ *a.* exhausted.

fourche /furʃ/ *n.f.* fork; (*à foin*) pitchfork.

fourchette /furʃɛt/ *n.f.* fork; (*comm.*) margin.

fourchu /furʃy/ *a.* forked.

fourgon /furgɔ̃/ *n.m.* van; (*wagon*) wagon. **~ mortuaire,** hearse.

fourgonnette /furgɔnɛt/ *n.f.* (small) van.

fourmi /furmi/ *n.f.* ant. **avoir des ~s,** have pins and needles.

fourmiller /furmije/ *v.i.* swarm (**de,** with).

fournaise /furnɛz/ *n.f.* (*feu, endroit*) furnace.

fourneau (*pl.* **~x**) /furno/ *n.m.* stove.

fournée /furne/ *n.f.* batch.

fourni /furni/ *a.* (*épais*) thick.

fourn|ir /furnir/ *v.t.* supply, provide; (*client*) supply; (*effort*) put in. **~ir à qn.,** supply s.o. with. **se ~ir chez,** shop at. **~isseur** *n.m.* supplier. **~iture** *n.f.* supply.

fourrage /furaʒ/ *n.m.* fodder.

fourré¹ /fure/ *n.m.* thicket.

fourré² /fure/ *a.* (*vêtement*) fur-lined; (*gâteau etc.*) filled (*with jam, cream, etc.*).

fourreau (*pl.* **~x**) /furo/ *n.m.* sheath.

fourr|er /fure/ *v.t.* (*mettre: fam.*)

stick. **~e-tout** *n.m. invar.* (*sac*) holdall.

fourreur /furœr/ *n.m.* furrier.

fourrière /furjɛr/ *n.f.* (*lieu*) pound.

fourrure /furyr/ *n.f.* fur.

fourvoyer (se) /(sə)furvwaje/ *v. pr.* go astray.

foutaise /futez/ *n.f.* (*argot*) rubbish.

foutre /futr/ *v.t.* (*argot*) = **ficher²**.

foutu, **~e** /futy/ *a.* (*argot*) = **fichu.**

foyer /fwaje/ *n.m.* home; (*être*) hearth; (*club*) club; (*d'étudiants*) hostel; (*théâtre*) foyer; (*photo.*) focus; (*centre*) centre.

fracas /fraka/ *n.m.* din; (*de train*) roar; (*d'objet qui tombe*) crash.

fracass|er /frakase/ *v.t.*, **se ~er** *v. pr.* smash. **~ant, ~ante** *a.* (*bruyant, violent*) shattering.

fraction /fraksjɔ̃/ *n.f.* fraction. **~ner** /-jone/ *v.t.*, **se ~ner** *v. pr.* split (up).

fracture /fraktyr/ *n.f.* fracture. **~er** *v.t.* (*os*) fracture; (*porte etc.*) break open.

fragil|e /fraʒil/ *a.* fragile. **~ité** *n.f.* fragility.

fragment /fragmã/ *n.m.* bit, fragment. **~aire** /-tɛr/ *a.* fragmentary. **~er** /-te/ *v.t.* split, fragment.

fraîche /frɛʃ/ *voir* **frais¹.**

fraîchement /frɛʃmã/ *adv.* (*récemment*) freshly; (*avec froideur*) coolly.

fraîcheur /frɛʃœr/ *n.f.* coolness; (*nouveauté*) freshness.

fraîchir /freʃir/ *v.i.* freshen.

frais¹, fraîche /frɛ, -ʃ/ *a.* fresh; (*temps, accueil*) cool; (*peinture*) wet. —*n.m.* (*récemment*) newly. —*n.m.* **mettre au ~,** put in a cool place. **prendre le ~,** take a breath of cool air. **~ et dispos,** fresh. **il fait ~,** it is cool.

frais² /frɛ/ *n.m. pl.* expenses; (*droits*) fees. **~ généraux,**

(*comm.*) overheads, running expenses. **~ de scolarité,** school fees.

frais|e /frez/ *n.f.* strawberry. **~ier** *n.m.* strawberry plant.

frambois|e /frãbwaz/ *n.f.* raspberry. **~ier** *n.m.* raspberry bush.

fran|c¹, ~che /frã, -ʃ/ *a.* frank; (*regard*) open; (*net*) clear; (*cassure*) clean; (*libre*) free; (*véritable*) downright. **~c-ma-çon** (*pl.* **~cs-maçons**) *n.m.* Freemason. **~c-maçonnerie** *n.f.* Freemasonry. **~-parler** *n.m. inv.* outspokenness.

franc² /frã/ *n.m.* franc.

français, ~e /frãsɛ, -z/ *a.* French. —*n.m., f.* Frenchman, Frenchwoman. —*n.m.* (*lang.*) French.

France /frãs/ *n.f.* France.

franche /frãʃ/ *voir* **franc¹.**

franchement /frãʃmã/ *adv.* frankly; (*nettement*) clearly; (*tout à fait*) really.

franchir /frãʃir/ *v.t.* (*obstacle*) get over; (*traverser*) cross; (*distance*) cover; (*limite*) exceed.

franchise /frãʃiz/ *n.f.* frankness; (*douanière*) exemption (from duties).

franco /frãko/ *adv.* postage paid.

franco- /frãko/ *préf.* Franco-.

francophone /frãkɔfɔn/ *a.* French-speaking. —*n.m./f.* French speaker.

frange /frãʒ/ *n.f.* fringe.

franquette (à la bonne) /(alabɔn)frãkɛt/ *adv.* informally.

frappant, ~e /frapã, -t/ *a.* striking.

frappe /frap/ *n.f.* (*de courrier etc.*) typing; (*de dactylo*) touch.

frappé, ~e /frape/ *a.* chilled.

frapp|er /frape/ *v.t./i.* strike; (*battre*) hit, strike; (*monnaie*) mint; (*à la porte*) knock, bang. **~é de panique,** panic-stricken.

frasque /frask/ *n.f.* escapade.

fratern|el, ~elle /fratɛrnɛl/ *a.*

brotherly. **~iser** v.i. frater*n*ize. **~ité** n.f. brotherhood.

fraude /frod/ n.f. fraud; (à un examen) cheating.

frauder /frode/ v.t./i. cheat.

frauduleu|x /frodylø/ a. **~se** -z/ a. fraudulent.

frayer /freje/ v.t. open up. **se ~ un passage**, force one's way (**dans**, through).

frayeur /frejœr/ n.f. fright.

fredonner /frədɔne/ v.t. hum.

free-lance /frilɑ̃s/ a. & n.m./f. freelance.

freezer /frizœr/ n.m. freezer.

frégate /fregat/ n.f. frigate.

frein /frɛ̃/ n.m. brake. **mettre un ~ à**, curb. **~ à main**, hand brake.

frein|er /frene/ v.t. slow down; (modérer, enrayer) curb. —v.i. (auto.) brake. **~age** /frenaʒ/ n.m. braking.

frelaté /frəlate/ a. adulterated.

frêle /frɛl/ a. frail.

frelon /frəlɔ̃/ n.m. hornet.

freluquet /frəlyke/ n.m. (fam.) weed.

frémir /fremir/ v.i. shudder, shake; (feuille, eau) quiver.

frêne /frɛn/ n.m. ash.

frénésie /frenezi/ n.f. frenzy. **~tique** a. frenzied.

fréquent, ~ente /frekɑ̃, -t/ a. frequent. **~emment** -amɑ̃/ adv. frequently. **~ence** n.f. frequency.

fréquenté /frekɑ̃te/ a. crowded.

fréquent|er /frekɑ̃te/ v.t. frequent; (école) attend; (personne) see. **~ation** n.f. frequenting. **~ations** n.f. pl. acquaintances.

frère /frɛr/ n.m. brother.

fresque /frɛsk/ n.f. fresco.

fret /frɛ/ n.m. freight.

frétiller /fretije/ v.i. wriggle.

fretin /frətɛ̃/ n.m. menu **~**, small fry.

friable /frijabl/ a. crumbly.

friand, ~e /frijɑ̃, -d/ a. **~ de**, fond of.

friandise /frijɑ̃diz/ n.f. sweet; (Amer.) candy; (gâteau) cake.

fric /frik/ n.m. (fam.) money.

fricassée /frikase/ n.f. casserole.

friche (en) /(ɑ̃)friʃ/ adv. fallow. être en **~**, lie fallow.

friction /friksjɔ̃/ n.f. friction; (massage) rub-down. **~ner** /-jɔne/ v.t. rub (down).

frigidaire /friʒider/ n.m. (P.) refrigerator.

frigid|e /friʒid/ a. frigid. **~ité** n.f. frigidity.

frigo /frigo/ n.m. (fam.) fridge.

frigorifi|er /frigɔrifje/ v.t. refrigerate. **~que** a. (vitrine etc.) refrigerated.

frileu|x /frilø/ a. **~se** /frilø, -z/ a. sensitive to cold.

frime /frim/ n.f. (fam.) show off. **~r** v.i. (fam.) putting on a show.

frimousse /frimus/ n.f. (sweet) face.

fringale /frɛ̃gal/ n.f. (fam.) ravenous appetite.

fringant, ~e /frɛ̃gɑ̃, -t/ a. dashing.

fringues /frɛ̃g/ n.f. pl. (fam.) togs.

friper /fripe/ v.t., **se ~** v. crumple.

fripon, ~ne /fripɔ̃, -ɔn/ n.m., f. rascal. —a. rascally.

fripouille /fripuj/ n.f. rogue.

frire /frir/ v.t./i. fry. **faire ~**, fry.

frise /friz/ n.f. frieze.

fris|er /frize/ v.t./i. (cheveux) curl; (personne) curl the hair of. **~é a.** curly.

frisquet /friske/ a.m. (fam.) chilly.

frisson /frisɔ̃/ n.m. (de froid) shiver; (de peur) shudder. **~ner** /-ɔne/ v.i. shiver; shudder.

frit, ~e /fri, -t/ a. fried. **~e** n.f. chip. **avoir la ~e**, (fam.) feel good.

friteuse /fritøz/ n.f. (deep)fryer.

friture /frityr/ n.f. fried fish; (huile) (frying) oil ou fat.

frivol|e /frivɔl/ *a.* frivolous. **∼ité** *n.f.* frivolity.

froid, ∼e /frwa, -d/ *a. & n.m.* cold. **avoir/prendre ∼**, be/catch cold. **il fait ∼**, it is cold. **∼ement** /-dmã/ *adv.* coldly; (*calculer*) coolly. **∼eur** /-dœr/ *n.f.* coldness.

froisser /frwase/ *v.t.* crumple; (*fig.*) offend. **se ∼** *v. pr.* crumple; (*fig.*) take offence. **se ∼ un muscle**, strain a muscle.

frôler /frole/ *v.t.* brush against, skim; (*fig.*) come close to.

fromag|e /frɔmaʒ/ *n.m.* cheese. **∼er, ∼ère** *a.* cheese; *n.m., f.* cheese maker; (*marchand*) cheesemonger.

froment /frɔmã/ *n.m.* wheat.

froncer /frõse/ *v.t.* gather. **∼ les sourcils**, frown.

fronde /frõd/ *n.f.* sling; (*fig.*) revolt.

front /frõ/ *n.m.* forehead; (*mil., pol.*) front. **de ∼**, at the same time; (*de face*) head-on; (*côte à côte*) abreast. **faire ∼ à**, face up to. **∼al** (*m. pl.* **∼aux**) /-tal, -to/ *a.* frontal.

frontali|er, ère /frõtalje, -ɛr/ *a.* border. (**travailleur**) **∼er**, commuter from across the border.

frontière /frõtjɛr/ *n.f.* border, frontier.

frott|er /frɔte/ *v.t./i.* rub; (*allumette*) strike. **∼ement** *n.m.* rubbing.

frottis /frɔti/ *n.m.* **∼ vaginal**, smear test.

frouss|e /frus/ *n.f.* (*fam.*) fear. **avoir la ∼e**, (*fam.*) be scared. **∼ard, ∼arde** *n.m., f.* (*fam.*) coward.

fructifier /fryktifje/ *v.i.* **faire ∼**, put to work.

fructueu|x, ∼se /fryktɥø, -z/ *a.* fruitful.

frug|al (*m. pl.* **∼aux**) /frygal, -o/ *a.* frugal. **∼alité** *n.f.* frugality.

fruit /frɥi/ *n.m.* fruit. **des ∼s**, (some) fruit. **∼s de mer**, seafood. **∼é** /-te/ *a.* fruity. **∼ier, ∼ière** /-tje, -tjɛr/ *a.* fruit; *n.m., f.* fruiterer.

fruste /fryst/ *a.* coarse.

frustr|er /frystre/ *v.t.* frustrate. **∼ant, ∼ante** *a.* frustrating. **∼ation** *n.f.* frustration.

fuel /fjul/ *n.m.* fuel oil.

fugitif, ∼ve /fyʒitif, -v/ *a.* (*passager*) fleeting. —*n.m., f.* fugitive.

fugue /fyg/ *n.f.* (*mus.*) fugue. **faire une ∼**, run away.

fuir† /fɥir/ *v.i.* flee, run away; (*eau, robinet, etc.*) leak. —*v.t.* (*éviter*) shun.

fuite /fɥit/ *n.f.* flight; (*de liquide, d'une nouvelle*) leak. **en ∼**, on the run. **mettre en ∼**, put to flight. **prendre la ∼**, take (to) flight.

fulgurant, ∼e /fylgyrã, -t/ *a.* (*vitesse*) lightning.

fumée /fyme/ *n.f.* smoke; (*vapeur*) steam.

fum|er /fyme/ *v.t./i.* smoke. **∼e-cigarette** *n.m. invar.* cigaretteholder. **∼é a** (*poisson, verre*) smoked. **∼eur, ∼euse** *n.m., f.* smoker.

fumet /fymɛ/ *n.m.* aroma.

fumeu|x, ∼se /fymø, -z/ *a.* (*confus*) hazy.

fumier /fymje/ *n.m.* manure.

fumiste /fymist/ *n.m./f.* (*fam.*) shirker.

funambule /fynãbyl/ *n.m./f.* tightrope walker.

funèbre /fynɛbr/ *a.* funeral; (*fig.*) gloomy.

funérailles /fyneraj/ *n.f. pl.* funeral.

funéraire /fynerɛr/ *a.* funeral.

funeste /fynɛst/ *a.* fatal.

funiculaire /fynikylɛr/ *n.m.* funicular.

fur /fyr/ *n.m.* **au ∼ et à mesure**,

as one goes along, progressively.
au ∼ et à mesure que, as.

furet /fyrɛ/ *n.m.* ferret.

fureter /fyrte/ *v.i.* nose (about).

fureur /fyrœr/ *n.f.* fury; (*passion*) passion. **avec ∼,** furiously; passionately. **mettre ∼,** infuriate. **faire ∼,** be all the rage.

furibond, ∼e /furibɔ̃, -d/ *a.* furious.

furie /fyri/ *n.f.* fury; (*femme*) shrew.

furieu|x, ∼se /fyrjø, -z/ *a.* furious.

furoncle /fyrɔ̃kl/ *n.m.* boil.

furti|f, ∼ve /fyrtif, -v/ *a.* furtive.

fusain /fyzɛ̃/ *n.m.* (*crayon*) charcoal; (*arbre*) spindle-tree.

fuseau (*pl.* ∼**x**) /fyzo/ *n.m.* ski trousers; (*pour filer*) spindle. **∼ horaire,** time zone.

fusée /fyze/ *n.f.* rocket.

fuselage /fyzlaʒ/ *n.m.* fuselage.

fuselé /fyzle/ *a.* slender.

fuser /fyze/ *v.i.* issue forth.

fusible /fyzibl/ *n.m.* fuse.

fusil /fyzi/ *n.m.* rifle, gun; (*de chasse*) shotgun. **∼ mitrailleur,** machine-gun.

fusill|er /fyzije/ *v.t.* shoot. **∼ade** *n.f.* shooting.

fusion /fyzjɔ̃/ *n.f.* fusion; (*comm.*) merger. **∼ner** /-jɔne/ *v.t./i.* merge.

fut /fy/ *voir* **être.**

fût /fy/ *n.m.* (*tonneau*) barrel; (*d'arbre*) trunk.

futé /fyte/ *a.* cunning.

futil|e /fytil/ *a.* futile. **∼ité** *n.f.* futility.

futur, ∼e /fytyr/ *a. & n.m.* future. **∼ femme/maman,** wife-/mother-to-be.

fuyant, ∼e /fɥijɑ̃, -t/ *a.* (*front, ligne*) receding; (*personne*) evasive.

fuyard, ∼e /fɥijar, -d/ *n.m., f.* runaway.

G

gabardine /gabardin/ *n.f.* gabardine; raincoat.

gabarit /gabari/ *n.m.* dimension; (*patron*) template; (*fig.*) calibre.

gâcher /gaʃe/ *v.t.* (*gâter*) spoil; (*gaspiller*) waste.

gâchette /gaʃɛt/ *n.f.* trigger.

gâchis /gaʃi/ *n.m.* waste.

gadoue /gadu/ *n.f.* sludge.

gaffe /gaf/ *n.f.* blunder. **faire ∼e,** (*fam.*) be careful (à, of). **∼er** *v.i.* blunder.

gag /gag/ *n.m.* gag.

gage /gaʒ/ *n.m.* pledge; (*de jeu*) forfeit. **∼s,** (*salaire*) wages. **en ∼ de,** as a token of. **mettre en ∼,** pawn.

gageure /gaʒyr/ *n.f.* wager (against all the odds).

gagn|er /gaɲe/ *v.t.* (*match, prix, etc.*) win; (*argent, pain*) earn; (*temps, terrain*) gain; (*atteindre*) reach; (*convaincre*) win over. —*v.i.* win; (*fig.*) gain. **∼er sa vie,** earn one's living. **∼ant, ∼ante,** *a.* winning; *n.m., f.* winner. **∼e-pain** *n.m. invar.* job.

gai /ge/ *a.* cheerful; (*ivre*) merry. **∼ement** *adv.* cheerfully. **∼eté** *n.f.* cheerfulness. **∼etés** *n.f. pl.* delights.

gaillard, ∼e /gajar, -d/ *a.* hale and hearty; (*grivois*) coarse. —*n.m.* hale and hearty fellow; (*type: fam.*) fellow.

gain /gɛ̃/ *n.m.* (*salaire*) earnings; (*avantage*) gain; (*économie*) saving. **∼s,** (*comm.*) profits; (*au jeu*) winnings.

gaine /gɛn/ *n.f.* (*corset*) girdle; (*étui*) sheath.

gala /gala/ *n.m.* gala.

galant, ∼e /galɑ̃, -t/ *a.* courteous; (*scène, humeur*) romantic.

galaxie /galaksi/ *n.f.* galaxy.

galb|e /galb/ *n.m.* curve. **∼é** *a.* shapely.

gale /gal/ *n.f.* (*de chat etc.*) mange.

galéjade /galeʒad/ *n.f.* (*fam.*) tall tale.

galère /galɛr/ *n.f.* (*navire*) galley. **c'est la ∼!**, (*fam.*) what an ordeal!

galérer /galere/ *v.i.* (*fam.*) have a hard time.

galerie /galri/ *n.f.* gallery. (*théâtre*) circle; (*de voiture*) roofrack.

galet /galɛ/ *n.m.* pebble.

galette /galɛt/ *n.f.* flat cake.

galeu|x, ∼se /galø, -z/ *a.* (*animal*) mangy.

galipette /galipɛt/ *n.f.* somersault.

Galles /gal/ *n.f. pl.* **le pays de ∼**, Wales.

gallois, ∼e /galwa, -z/ *a.* Welsh. —*n.m., f.* Welshman, Welshwoman. —*n.m.* (*lang.*) Welsh.

galon /galɔ̃/ *n.m.* braid; (*mil.*) stripe. **prendre du ∼**, be promoted.

galop /galo/ *n.m.* gallop. **aller au ∼**, gallop. **∼ d'essai**, trial run. **∼er** /-ɔpe/ *v.i.* (*cheval*) gallop; (*personne*) run.

galopade /galɔpad/ *n.f.* wild rush.

galopin /galɔpɛ̃/ *n.m.* (*fam.*) rascal.

galvaudé /galvode/ *a.* worthless.

gambad|e /gɑ̃bad/ *n.f.* leap. **∼er** *v.i.* leap about.

gamelle /gamɛl/ *n.f.* (*de soldat*) mess bowl *ou* tin; (*d'ouvrier*) foodbox.

gamin, ∼e /gamɛ̃, -in/ *a.* playful. —*n.m., f.* (*fam.*) kid.

gamme /gam/ *n.f.* (*mus.*) scale; (*série*) range. **haut de ∼**, upmarket, top of the range. **bas de ∼**, down-market, bottom of the range.

gang /gɑ̃g/ *n.m.* gang.

ganglion /gɑ̃glijɔ̃/ *n.m.* swelling.

gangrène /gɑ̃grɛn/ *n.f.* gangrene.

gangster /gɑ̃gstɛr/ *n.m.* gangster; (*escroc*) crook.

gant /gɑ̃/ *n.m.* glove. **∼ de toilette**, face-flannel, face-cloth. **∼é** /gɑ̃te/ *a.* (*personne*) wearing gloves.

garag|e /garaʒ/ *n.m.* garage. **∼iste** *n.m.* garage owner; (*employé*) garage mechanic.

garant, ∼e /garɑ̃, -t/ *n.m., f.* guarantor. —*n.m.* guarantee. **se porter ∼ de**, guarantee, vouch for.

garant|ie /garɑ̃ti/ *n.f.* guarantee; (*protection*) safeguard. **∼ies**, (*de police d'assurance*) cover. **∼ir** *v.t.* guarantee; (*protéger*) protect (**de**, from).

garce /gars/ *n.f.* (*fam.*) bitch.

garçon /garsɔ̃/ *n.m.* boy; (*célibataire*) bachelor. **∼ (de café)**, waiter. **∼ d'honneur**, best man.

garçonnière /garsɔnjɛr/ *n.f.* bachelor flat.

garde[1] /gard/ *n.f.* guard; (*d'enfants, de bagages*) care; (*service*) guard (duty); (*infirmière*) nurse. **de ∼**, on duty. **à ∼ vue**, (*police*) custody. **mettre en ∼**, warn. **prendre ∼**, be careful (**à**, of). **(droit de) ∼**, custody (**de**, of).

garde[2] /gard/ *n.m.* guard; (*de propriété, parc*) warden. **∼ champêtre**, village policeman. **∼ du corps**, bodyguard.

gard|er /garde/ *v.t.* (*conserver, maintenir*) keep; (*vêtement*) keep on; (*surveiller*) look after; (*défendre*) guard. **se ∼er** *v. pr.* (*denrée*) keep. **∼er le lit**, stay in bed. **se ∼er de**, be careful not to do. **∼e-à-vous** *int.* (*mil.*) attention. **∼e-boue** *n.m. invar.* mudguard. **∼e-chasse** (*pl.* **∼e-chasses**) *n.m.* gamekeeper. **∼e-fou** *n.m.* railing. **∼e-manger**

n.m. invar. (food) safe; (*placard*) larder. **~e-robe** *n.f.* wardrobe.

garderie /gardəri/ *n.f.* crèche.

gardien, **~ne** /gardjɛ̃, -jɛn/ *n.m.*, *f.* (*de prison, réserve*) warden; (*d'immeuble*) caretaker; (*de musée*) attendant; (*garde*) guard. **~ de but**, goalkeeper. **~ de la paix**, policeman. **~ de nuit**, night watchman. **~ne d'enfants**, child-minder.

gare[1] /gar/ *n.f.* (*rail.*) station. **~ routière**, coach station; (*Amer.*) bus station.

gare[2] /gar/ *int.* **~ (à toi)**, watch out!

garer /gare/ *v.t.*, **se ~** *v. pr.* park.

gargariser (se) /(sə)gargarize/ *v. pr.* gargle.

gargarisme /gargarism/ *n.m.* gargle.

gargouille /garguj/ *n.f.* (water-)spout; (*sculptée*) gargoyle.

gargouiller /garguje/ *v.i.* gurgle.

garnement /garnəmɑ̃/ *n.m.* rascal.

garn|ir /garnir/ *v.t.* fill; (*décorer*) decorate; (*couvrir*) cover; (*doubler*) line; (*culin.*) garnish. **~i** *a.* (*plat*) served with vegetables. **bien ~i**, (*rempli*) well-filled.

garnison /garnizɔ̃/ *n.f.* garrison.

garniture /garnityr/ *n.f.* (*légumes*) vegetables; (*ornement*) trimming; (*de voiture*) trim.

garrot /garo/ *n.m.* (*méd.*) tourniquet.

gars /ga/ *n.m.* (*fam.*) fellow.

gas-oil /gazɔjl/ *n.m.* diesel oil.

gaspill|er /gaspije/ *v.t.* waste. **~age** *n.m.* waste.

gastrique /gastrik/ *a.* gastric.

gastronom|e /gastronom/ *n.m./f.* gourmet. **~ie** *n.f.* gastronomy.

gâteau (*pl.* **~x**) /gato/ *n.m.* cake. **~ sec**, biscuit; (*Amer.*) cookie. **un papa ~**, a doting dad.

gâter /gate/ *v.t.* spoil. **se ~** *v. pr.* (*dent, viande*) go bad; (*temps*) get worse.

gâterie /gatri/ *n.f.* little treat.

gâteu|x, **~se** /gatø, -z/ *a.* senile.

gauche[1] /goʃ/ *a.* left. **à ~e**, on the left; (*direction*) (to the) left. **la ~e**, the left (side); (*pol.*) the left (wing). **~er**, **~ère** *a. & n.m., f.* left-handed (person). **~iste** *a. & n.m./f.* (*pol.*) leftist.

gauche[2] /goʃ/ *a.* (*maladroit*) awkward. **~rie** *n.f.* awkwardness.

gaufre /gofr/ *n.f.* waffle.

gaufrette /gofret/ *n.f.* wafer.

gaulois, **~e** /golwa, -z/ *a.* Gallic; (*fig.*) bawdy. **~e**, *n.m., f.* Gaul.

gausser (se) /(sə)gose/ *v. pr.* **se ~ de**, deride, scoff at.

gaver /gave/ *v.t.* force-feed; (*fig.*) cram. **se ~ de**, gorge o.s. with.

gaz /gaz/ *n.m. invar.* gas. **~ lacrymogène**, tear-gas.

gaze /gaz/ *n.f.* gauze.

gazelle /gazɛl/ *n.f.* gazelle.

gaz|er /gaze/ *v.i.* (*fam.*) **ça ~e**, it's going all right.

gazette /gazɛt/ *n.f.* newspaper.

gazeu|x, **~se** /gazø, -z/ *a.* (*boisson*) fizzy.

gazoduc /gazodyk/ *n.m.* gas pipeline.

gazomètre /gazomɛtr/ *n.m.* gasometer.

gazon /gazɔ̃/ *n.m.* lawn, grass.

gazouiller /gazuje/ *v.i.* (*oiseau*) chirp; (*bébé*) babble.

geai /ʒɛ/ *n.m.* jay.

géant, **~e** /ʒeɑ̃, -t/ *a. & n.m., f.* giant.

geindre /ʒɛ̃dr/ *v.i.* groan.

gel /ʒɛl/ *n.m.* frost; (*pâte*) gel; (*comm.*) freezing.

gélatine /ʒelatin/ *n.f.* gelatine.

gel|er /ʒəle/ *v.t./i.* freeze. **on gèle**, it's freezing. **~é** *a.* frozen; (*membre abîmé*) frost-bitten.

~ée *n.f.* frost; (*culin.*) jelly. ~ée blanche, hoar-frost.

gélule /ʒelyl/ *n.f.* (*méd.*) capsule.

Gémeaux /ʒemo/ *n.m. pl.* Gemini.

gém|ir /ʒemir/ *v.i.* groan. ~issement *n.m.* groan(ing).

gênant, ~e /ʒɛnɑ̃, -t/ *a.* embarrassing; (*irritant*) annoying.

gencive /ʒɑ̃siv/ *n.f.* gum.

gendarme /ʒɑ̃darm/ *n.m.* policeman, gendarme. ~rie /-əri/ *n.f.* police force; (*local*) police station.

gendre /ʒɑ̃dr/ *n.m.* son-in-law.

gène /ʒɛn/ *n.m.* gene.

gêne /ʒɛn/ *n.f.* discomfort; (*confusion*) embarrassment; (*dérangement*) trouble. **dans la ~,** in financial straits.

généalogie /ʒe, nealɔʒi/ *n.f.* genealogy.

gên|er /ʒene/ *v.t.* bother, disturb; (*troubler*) embarrass; (*encombrer*) hamper; (*bloquer*) block. ~é *a.* embarrassed.

génér|al (*m. pl.* ~aux) /ʒeneral, -o/ *a.* general. —*n.m.* (*pl.* ~aux) general. **en ~al,** in general. ~alement *adv.* generally.

généralis|er /ʒeneralize/ *v.t./i.* generalize. **se ~er** *v. pr.* become general. ~ation /-zasjɔ̃/ *n.f.* generalization.

généraliste /ʒeneralist/ *n.m./f.* general practitioner, GP.

généralité /ʒeneralite/ *n.f.* majority. ~s, general points.

génération /ʒenerasjɔ̃/ *n.f.* generation.

génératrice /ʒeneratris/ *n.f.* generator.

généreu|x, ~se /ʒenerø, -z/ *a.* generous. ~sement *adv.* generously.

générique /ʒenerik/ *n.m.* (*cinéma*) credits. —*a.* generic.

générosité /ʒenerozite/ *n.f.* generosity.

genêt /ʒənɛ/ *n.m.* (*plante*) broom.

génétique /ʒenetik/ *a.* genetic. —*n.f.* genetics.

Genève /ʒənɛv/ *n.m./f.* Geneva.

gén|ial (*m. pl.* ~iaux) /ʒenjal, -jo/ *a.* brilliant; (*fam.*) fantastic.

génie /ʒeni/ *n.m.* genius. ~ **civil,** civil engineering.

genièvre /ʒənjɛvr/ *n.m.* juniper.

génisse /ʒenis/ *n.f.* heifer.

génit|al (*m. pl.* ~aux) /ʒenital, -o/ *a.* genital.

génocide /ʒenɔsid/ *n.m.* genocide.

génoise /ʒenwaz/ *n.f.* sponge (cake).

genou (*pl.* ~x) /ʒnu/ *n.m.* knee. **à ~x,** kneeling. **se mettre à ~x,** kneel.

genre /ʒɑ̃r/ *n.m.* sort, kind; (*attitude*) manner; (*gram.*) gender. ~ **de vie,** life-style.

gens /ʒɑ̃/ *n.m. pl.* people.

gentil, ~le /ʒɑ̃ti, -j/ *a.* kind, nice; (*agréable*) nice; (*sage*) good. ~**lesse** /-jes/ *n.f.* kindness. ~**ment** *adv.* kindly.

géographie /ʒeɔgrafi/ *n.f.* geography. ~e *n.m./f.* geographer. ~**ique** *a.* geographical.

geôl|ier, ~ière /ʒolje, -jɛr/ *n.m./f.* gaoler, jailer.

géolog|ie /ʒeɔlɔʒi/ *n.f.* geology. ~**ique** *a.* geological. ~**gue** *n.m./f.* geologist.

géomètre /ʒeɔmɛtr/ *n.m.* surveyor.

géométr|ie /ʒeɔmetri/ *n.f.* geometry. ~**ique** *a.* geometric.

géranium /ʒeranjɔm/ *n.m.* geranium.

géran|t, ~te /ʒerɑ̃, -t/ *n.m., f.* manager, manageress. ~**t d'immeuble,** landlord's agent. ~**ce** *n.f.* management.

gerbe /ʒɛrb/ *n.f.* (*de fleurs, d'eau*) spray; (*de blé*) sheaf.

gercé /ʒɛrse/ *a.* chapped.

ger|cer /ʒɛrse/ *v.t./i.*, **se ~cer** *v. pr.* chap. ~**çure** *n.f.* chap.

gérer /ʒere/ *v.t.* manage.

germain, ~e /ʒɛrmɛ̃, -ɛn/ a. cousin ~, first cousin.

germanique /ʒɛrmanik/ a. Germanic.

germe /ʒɛrm/ n.m. germ. ~er v.i. germinate.

gésier /ʒezje/ n.m. gizzard.

gestation /ʒɛstasjɔ̃/ n.f. gestation.

geste /ʒɛst/ n.m. gesture.

gesticuler /ʒɛstikyle/ v.i. gesticulate. ~ation n.f. gesticulation.

gestion /ʒɛstjɔ̃/ n.f. management.

geyser /ʒezɛr/ n.m. geyser.

ghetto /ɡeto/ n.m. ghetto.

gibecière /ʒibsjɛr/ n.f. shoulderbag.

gibet /ʒibɛ/ n.m. gallows.

gibier /ʒibje/ n.m. (animaux) game.

giboulée /ʒibule/ n.f. shower.

gicler /ʒikle/ v.i. squirt. faire ~er, squirt. ~ée n.f. squirt.

gifle /ʒifl/ n.f. slap (in the face). ~er v.t. slap.

gigantesque /ʒiɡɑ̃tɛsk/ a. gigantic.

gigot /ʒiɡo/ n.m. leg (of lamb).

gigoter /ʒiɡɔte/ v.i. (fam.) wriggle.

gilet /ʒilɛ/ n.m. waistcoat; (cardigan) cardigan. ~ de sauvetage, life-jacket.

gin /dʒin/ n.m. gin.

gingembre /ʒɛ̃ʒɑ̃br/ n.m. ginger.

gingivite /ʒɛ̃ʒivit/ n.f. gum infection.

girafe /ʒiraf/ n.f. giraffe.

giratoire /ʒiratwar/ a. sens ~, roundabout.

giroflée /ʒirɔfle/ n.f. wallflower.

girouette /ʒirwɛt/ n.f. weathercock, weather-vane.

gisement /ʒizmɑ̃/ n.m. deposit.

gitan, ~e /ʒitɑ̃, -an/ n.m., f. gypsy.

gîte /ʒit/ n.m. (maison) home; (abri) shelter. ~ rural, holiday cottage.

givre /ʒivr/ n.m. (hoar-)frost. ~er v.t., se ~er v. pr. frost (up).

givré /ʒivre/ a. (fam.) nuts.

glace /ɡlas/ n.f. ice; (crème) ice-cream; (vitre) window; (miroir) mirror; (verre) glass.

glacer /ɡlase/ v.t. freeze; (gâteau, boisson) ice; (papier) glaze; (pétrifier) chill. se ~er v. pr. freeze. ~é a. (vent, accueil) icy.

glacial (m. pl. ~iaux) /ɡlasjal, -jo/ a. icy.

glacier /ɡlasje/ n.m. (géog.) glacier; (vendeur) ice-cream man.

glacière /ɡlasjɛr/ n.f. icebox.

glaçon /ɡlasɔ̃/ n.m. (pour boisson) ice-cube; (péj.) cold fish.

glaïeul /ɡlajœl/ n.m. gladiolus.

glaise /ɡlɛz/ n.f. clay.

gland /ɡlɑ̃/ n.m. acorn; (ornement) tassel.

glande /ɡlɑ̃d/ n.f. gland.

glander /ɡlɑ̃de/ v.i. (fam.) laze around.

glaner /ɡlane/ v.t. glean.

glapir /ɡlapir/ v.i. yelp.

glas /ɡlɑ/ n.m. knell.

glauque /ɡlok/ a. (fig.) gloomy.

glissant, ~e /ɡlisɑ̃, -t/ a. slippery.

glisser /ɡlise/ v.i. slide; (sur l'eau) glide; (déraper) slip; (véhicule) skid. —v.t., se ~er v. pr. slip (dans, into). ~ade n.f. sliding; (endroit) slide. ~ement n.m. sliding; gliding; (fig.) shift. ~ement de terrain, landslide.

glissière /ɡlisjɛr/ n.f. groove. à ~, (porte, système) sliding.

global (m. pl. ~aux) /ɡlɔbal, -o/ a. (entier, général) overall. ~alement adv. as a whole.

globe /ɡlɔb/ n.m. globe. ~ oculaire, eyeball. ~ terrestre, globe.

globule /ɡlɔbyl/ n.m. (du sang) corpuscle.

gloire /ɡlwar/ n.f. glory.

glorieu|x, ~se /ɡlɔrjø, -z/ a. glorious. ~sement adv. gloriously.

glorifier /ɡlɔrifje/ v.t. glorify.

glose /ɡloz/ n.f. gloss.

glossaire /glɔsɛr/ n.m. glossary.

glousser /gluse/ v.i. chuckle; (poule) cluck. ~ement n.m. chuckle; cluck.

glouton, ~ne /glutɔ̃, -ɔn/ a. gluttonous. —n.m., f. glutton.

gluant, ~e /glyɑ̃, -t/ a. sticky.

glucose /glykoz/ n.m. glucose.

glycérine /gliserin/ n.f. glycerine.

glycine /glisin/ n.f. wisteria.

gnome /gnom/ n.m. gnome.

go /go/ **tout de go,** straight out.

GO (abrév. **grandes ondes**) long wave.

goal /gol/ n.m. goalkeeper.

gobelet /gɔblɛ/ n.m. tumbler, mug.

gober /gɔbe/ v.t. swallow (whole). **je ne peux pas le ~,** (fam.) I can't stand him.

godasse /gɔdas/ n.f. (fam.) shoe.

godet /gɔdɛ/ n.m. (small) pot.

goéland /gɔelɑ̃/ n.m. (sea)gull.

goélette /gɔelɛt/ n.f. schooner.

gogo (à) /(a)gɔgo/ adv. (fam.) galore, in abundance.

goguenard, ~e /gɔgnar, -d/ a. mocking.

goguette (en) /(ɑ̃)gɔgɛt/ adv. (fam.) having a binge ou spree.

goinfre /gwɛ̃fr/ n.m. (glouton: fam.) pig. **se ~er** v. pr. (fam.) stuff o.s. like a pig (**de,** with).

golf /gɔlf/ n.m. golf; golf course.

golfe /gɔlf/ n.m. gulf.

gomme /gɔm/ n.f. rubber; (Amer.) eraser; (résine) gum. ~er v.t. rub out.

gond /gɔ̃/ n.m. hinge. **sortir de ses ~s,** go mad.

gondole /gɔ̃dɔl/ n.f. gondola. ~ier n.m. gondolier.

gondoler (se) /(sə)gɔ̃dɔle/ v. pr. warp; (rire: fam.) split one's sides.

gonfler /gɔ̃fle/ v.t./i. swell; (ballon, pneu) pump up, blow up; (exagérer) inflate. **se ~er** v. pr. swell. ~é a. swollen. **il est ~é,** (fam.) he's got a nerve. ~ement n.m. swelling.

gorge /gɔrʒ/ n.f. throat; (poitrine) breast; (vallée) gorge.

gorgée /gɔrʒe/ n.f. sip, gulp.

gorger /gɔrʒe/ v.t. fill (**de,** with). **se ~** v. pr. gorge o.s. (**de,** with). ~é **de,** full of.

gorille /gɔrij/ n.m. gorilla; (garde: fam.) bodyguard.

gosier /gozje/ n.m. throat.

gosse /gɔs/ n.m./f. (fam.) kid.

gothique /gɔtik/ a. Gothic.

goudron /gudrɔ̃/ n.m. tar. ~ner /-ɔne/ v.t. tar; (route) surface. **à faible teneur en ~,** low tar.

gouffre /gufr/ n.m. gulf, abyss.

goujat /guʒa/ n.m. lout, boor.

goulot /gulo/ n.m. neck. **boire au ~,** drink from the bottle.

goulu, ~e /guly/ a. gluttonous. —n.m., f. glutton.

gourde /gurd/ n.f. (à eau) flask; (idiot: fam.) chump.

gourdin /gurdɛ̃/ n.m. club, cudgel.

gourer (se) /(sə)gure/ v. pr. (fam.) make a mistake.

gourmand, ~e /gurmɑ̃, -d/ a. greedy. —n.m., f. glutton. ~ise /-diz/ n.f. greed; (mets) delicacy.

gourmet /gurmɛ/ n.m. gourmet.

gourmette /gurmɛt/ n.f. chain bracelet.

gousse /gus/ n.f. ~ **d'ail,** clove of garlic.

goût /gu/ n.m. taste.

goûter /gute/ v.t. taste; (apprécier) enjoy. —v.i. have tea. —n.m. tea, snack. ~ **à** ou **de,** taste.

goutte /gut/ n.f. drop; (méd.) gout. ~er v.i. drip.

goutte-à-goutte /gutagut/ n.m. drip.

gouttelette /gutlɛt/ n.f. droplet.

gouttière /gutjɛr/ n.f. gutter.

gouvernail /guvɛrnaj/ n.m. rudder; (barre) helm.

gouvernante /guvɛrnɑ̃t/ n.f. governess.

gouvernement /guvɛrnəmɑ̃/ n.m.

government. **~al** (*m. pl.* **~aux**) /-tal, -to/ *a.* government.

gouvern|er /guvɛrne/ *v.t./i.* govern. **~eur** *n.m.* governor.

grâce /grɑs/ *n.f.* (*charme*) grace; (*faveur*) favour; (*jurid.*) pardon; (*relig.*) grace. **~ à**, thanks to.

gracier /grasje/ *v.t.* pardon.

gracieu|x, ~se /grasjø, -z/ *a.* graceful; (*gratuit*) free. **~sement** *adv.* gracefully; free (of charge).

gradation /gradasjɔ̃/ *n.f.* gradation.

grade /grad/ *n.m.* rank. **monter en ~**, be promoted.

gradé /grade/ *n.m.* non-commissioned officer.

gradin /gradɛ̃/ *n.m.* tier, step. **en ~s**, terraced.

gradué /gradye/ *a.* graded, graduated.

graduel, ~le /gradɥɛl/ *a.* gradual.

gradu|er /gradɥe/ *v.t.* increase gradually. **~uation** *n.f.* graduation.

graffiti /grafiti/ *n.m. pl.* graffiti.

grain /grɛ̃/ *n.m.* grain; (*naut.*) squall; (*de café*) bean; (*de poivre*) pepper corn. **~ de beauté**, beauty spot. **~ de raisin**, grape.

graine /grɛn/ *n.f.* seed.

graissage /grɛsaʒ/ *n.m.* lubrication.

graiss|e /grɛs/ *n.f.* fat; (*lubrifiant*) grease. **~er** *v.t.* grease. **~eux, ~euse** *a.* greasy.

gramm|aire /gramɛr/ *n.f.* grammar. **~atical** (*m. pl.* **~aticaux**) *a.* grammatical.

gramme /gram/ *n.m.* gram.

grand, ~e /grɑ̃, -d/ *a.* big, large; (*haut*) tall; (*mérite, distance, ami*) great; (*bruit*) loud; (*plus âgé*) big. —*adv.* (*ouvrir*) wide. **~ ouvert**, wide open. **voir ~**, think big. —*n.m., f.* (*adulte*) grown-up; (*enfant*) older child. **au ~**, in the open air. **au ~ jour**, in broad daylight; (*fig.*) in the open. **de ~e**

envergure, large-scale. **en ~e partie**, largely. **~-angle**, *n.m.* wide angle. **~e banlieue**, outer suburbs. **G~e-Bretagne** *n.f.* Great Britain. **pas ~-chose**, not much. **~ ensemble**, housing estate. **~es lignes**, (*rail.*) main lines. **~ magasin**, department store. **~-mère** (*pl.* **~s-mères**) *n.f.* grandmother. **~s-parents** *n.m. pl.* grandparents. **~-père** (*pl.* **~s-pères**) *n.m.* grandfather. **~e personne**, grown-up. **~ public**, general public. **~-rue** *n.f.* high street. **~e surface**, hypermarket. **~es vacances**, summer holidays.

grandeur /grɑ̃dœr/ *n.f.* greatness; (*dimension*) size. **folie des ~s**, delusions of grandeur.

grandiose /grɑ̃djoz/ *a.* grandiose.

grandir /grɑ̃dir/ *v.i.* grow; (*bruit*) grow louder. —*v.t.* make taller.

grange /grɑ̃ʒ/ *n.f.* barn.

granit /granit/ *n.m.* granite.

granulé /granyle/ *n.m.* granule.

graphique /grafik/ *a.* graphic. —*n.m.* graph.

graphologie /grafɔlɔʒi/ *n.f.* graphology.

grappe /grap/ *n.f.* cluster. **~ de raisin**, bunch of grapes.

grappin /grapɛ̃/ *n.m.* **mettre le ~ sur**, get one's claws into.

gras, ~se /grɑ, -s/ *a.* fat; (*aliment*) fatty; (*surface*) greasy; (*épais*) thick; (*caractères*) bold. —*n.m.* (*culin.*) fat. **faire la ~se matinée**, sleep late. **~sement** *adv.* highly paid.

gratification /gratifikasjɔ̃/ *n.f.* bonus, satisfaction.

gratifi|er /gratifje/ *v.t.* favour, reward (**de**, with). **~ant, ~ante** *a.* rewarding.

gratin /gratɛ̃/ *n.m.* baked dish with cheese topping; (*élite: fam.*) upper crust.

gratis /gratis/ *adv.* free.

gratitude /gratityd/ *n.f.* gratitude.
gratt|er /grate/ *v.t./i.* scratch; (*avec un outil*) scrape. **se ~er** *v. pr.* scratch o.s. **ça me ~e,** (*fam.*) it itches. **~e-ciel** *n.m. invar.* skyscraper. **~-papier** *n.m. invar.* (*péj.*) pen pusher.
gratuit, **~e** /gratɥi, -t/ *a.* free; (*acte*) gratuitous. **~ement** /-tmɑ̃/ *adv.* free (of charge).
gravats /grava/ *n.m. pl.* rubble.
grave /grav/ *a.* serious; (*solennel*) grave; (*voix*) deep; (*accent*) grave. **~ment** *adv.* seriously; gravely.
grav|er /grave/ *v.t.* engrave; (*sur bois*) carve. **~eur** *n.m.* engraver.
gravier /gravje/ *n.m.* gravel.
gravir /gravir/ *v.t.* climb.
gravitation /gravitasjɔ̃/ *n.f.* gravitation.
gravité /gravite/ *n.f.* gravity.
graviter /gravite/ *v.i.* revolve.
gravure /gravyr/ *n.f.* engraving; (*de tableau, photo*) print, plate.
gré /gre/ *n.m.* (*volonté*) will; (*goût*) taste. **à son ~,** (*agir*) as one likes. **de bon ~,** willingly. **bon ~ mal gré,** like it or not. **je vous en saurais ~,** I'll be grateful for that.
grec, ~que /grɛk/ *a. & n.m., f.* Greek. —*n.m.* (*lang.*) Greek.
Grèce /grɛs/ *n.f.* Greece.
greff|e /grɛf/ *n.f.* graft; (*d'organe*) transplant. **~er** /grefe/ *v.t.* graft; transplant.
greffier /grefje/ *n.m.* clerk of the court.
grégaire /greger/ *a.* gregarious.
grêle¹ /grɛl/ *a.* (*maigre*) spindly; (*voix*) shrill.
grêl|e² /grɛl/ *n.f.* hail. **~er** /grele/ *v.i.* hail. **~on** *n.m.* hailstone.
grelot /grəlo/ *n.m.* (little) bell.
grelotter /grəlɔte/ *v.i.* shiver.
grenade¹ /grənad/ *n.f.* (*fruit*) pomegranate.
grenade² /grənad/ *n.f.* (*explosif*) grenade.

grenat /grəna/ *a. invar.* dark red.
grenier /grənje/ *n.m.* attic; (*pour grain*) loft.
grenouille /grənuj/ *n.f.* frog.
grès /grɛ/ *n.m.* sandstone; (*poterie*) stoneware.
grésiller /grezije/ *v.i.* sizzle; (*radio*) crackle.
grève¹ /grɛv/ *n.f.* strike. **se mettre en ~,** go on strike. **~ du zèle,** work-to-rule; (*Amer.*) rule-book slow-down. **~ de la faim,** hunger strike. **~ sauvage,** wildcat strike.
grève² /grɛv/ *n.f.* (*rivage*) shore.
gréviste /grevist/ *n.m./f.* striker.
gribouill|er /gribuje/ *v.t./i.* scribble. **~is** /-ji/ *n.m.* scribble.
grief /grijɛf/ *n.m.* grievance.
grièvement /grijɛvmɑ̃/ *adv.* seriously.
griff|e /grif/ *n.f.* claw; (*de couturier*) label. **~er** *v.t.* scratch, claw.
griffonner /grifɔne/ *v.t./i.* scrawl.
grignoter /griɲɔte/ *v.t./i.* nibble.
gril /gril/ *n.m.* grill, grid(iron).
grillade /grijad/ *n.f.* (*viande*) grill.
grillage /grijaʒ/ *n.m.* wire netting.
grille /grij/ *n.f.* railings; (*portail*) (metal) gate; (*de fenêtre*) bars; (*de cheminée*) grate; (*fig.*) grid.
grill|er /grije/ *v.t./i.* burn; (*ampoule*) blow; (*feu rouge*) go through. (**faire**) **~er,** (*pain*) toast; (*viande*) grill; (*café*) roast. **~e-pain** *n.m. invar.* toaster.
grillon /grijɔ̃/ *n.m.* cricket.
grimace /grimas/ *n.f.* (*funny*) face; (*de douleur, dégoût*) grimace.
grimer /grime/ *v.t.,* **se ~** *v. pr.* make up.
grimper /grɛ̃pe/ *v.t./i.* climb.
grinc|er /grɛ̃se/ *v.i.* creak. **~er des dents,** grind one's teeth. **~ement** *n.m.* creak(ing).
grincheu|x, ~se /grɛ̃ʃø, -z/ *a.* grumpy.

gripp|e /grip/ *n.f.* influenza, flu. **être ~é**, have (the) flu; *(mécanisme)* be seized up *ou* jammed.

gris, ~e /gri, -z/ *a.* grey; *(saoul)* tipsy.

grisaille /grizaj/ *n.f.* greyness, gloom.

grisonner /grizɔne/ *v.i.* go grey.

grisou /grizu/ *n.m.* **coup de ~**, firedamp explosion.

grive /griv/ *n.f.* *(oiseau)* thrush.

grivois, ~e /grivwa, -z/ *a.* bawdy.

grog /grɔg/ *n.m.* grog.

grogn|er /grɔne/ *v.i.* growl; *(fig.)* grumble. **~ement** *n.m.* growl; grumble.

grognon, ~ne /grɔɲɔ̃, -ɔn/ *a.* grumpy.

groin /grwɛ̃/ *n.m.* snout.

grommeler /grɔmle/ *v.t./i.* mutter.

grond|er /grɔ̃de/ *v.i.* rumble; *(chien)* growl; *(conflit etc.)* be brewing. *—v.t.* scold. **~ement** *n.m.* rumbling; growling.

groom /grum/ *n.m.* page(-boy).

gros, ~se /gro, -s/ *a.* big, large; *(gras)* fat; *(important)* great; *(épais)* thick; *(lourd)* heavy. *—n.m., f.* fat man, fat woman. *—n.m.* **le ~ de**, the bulk of. **de ~**, *(comm.)* wholesale. **en ~**, roughly; *(comm.)* wholesale. **~ bonnet**, *(fam.)* bigwig. **~ lot**, jackpot. **~ mot**, rude word. **~ plan**, close-up. **~ titre**, headline. **~se caisse**, big drum.

groseille /grozɛj/ *n.f.* (red *ou* white) currant. **~ à maquereau**, gooseberry.

grosse /gros/ *voir* **gros**.

grossesse /grosɛs/ *n.f.* pregnancy.

grosseur /grosœr/ *n.f.* *(volume)* size; *(enflure)* lump.

gross|ier, ~ière /grosje, -jɛr/ *a.* coarse, rough; *(imitation, instrument)* crude; *(vulgaire)* coarse; *(insolent)* rude; *(erreur)*

gross. ~ièrement *adv.* *(sommairement)* roughly; *(vulgairement)* coarsely. **~ièreté** *n.f.* coarseness; crudeness; rudeness; *(mot)* rude word.

grossir /grosir/ *v.t./i.* swell; *(personne)* put on weight; *(au microscope)* magnify; *(augmenter)* grow; *(exagérer)* magnify.

grossiste /grosist/ *n.m./f.* wholesaler.

grosso modo /grosomɔdo/ *adv.* roughly.

grotesque /grotɛsk/ *a.* grotesque; *(ridicule)* ludicrous.

grotte /grɔt/ *n.f.* cave, grotto.

grouill|er /gruje/ *v.i.* be swarming **(de**, with). **~ant, ~ante** *a.* swarming.

groupe /grup/ *n.m.* group; *(mus.)* band. **~ électrogène**, generating set. **~ scolaire**, school block.

group|er /grupe/ *v.t.*, **se ~er** *v. pr.* group (together). **~ement** *n.m.* grouping.

grue /gry/ *n.f.* *(machine, oiseau)* crane.

grumeau *(pl. ~x)* /grymo/ *n.m.* lump.

gruyère /gryjɛr/ *n.m.* gruyère *(cheese)*.

gué /ge/ *n.m.* ford. **passer** *ou* **traverser à ~**, ford.

guenon /gənɔ̃/ *n.f.* female monkey.

guépard /gepar/ *n.m.* cheetah.

guêp|e /gɛp/ *n.f.* wasp. **~ier** /gepje/ *n.m.* wasp's nest; *(fig.)* trap.

guère /gɛr/ *adv.* **(ne) ~**, hardly. **il n'y a ~ d'espoir**, there is no hope.

guéridon /geridɔ̃/ *n.m.* pedestal table.

guérill|a /gerija/ *n.f.* guerrilla warfare. **~ero** /-jero/ *n.m.* guerrilla.

guér|ir /gerir/ *v.t.* *(personne, maladie, mal)* cure **(de**, of); *(plaie,* *membre)* heal. —*v.i.* get better; (*blessure)* heal. **~ir de,** recover from. **~ison** *n.f.* curing; healing; (*de personne)* recovery. **~isseur, ~isseuse** *n.m., f.* healer.

guérite /gerit/ *n.f.* (*mil.*) sentry-box.

guerre /gɛr/ *n.f.* war. **en ~,** at war. **faire la ~,** wage war (à, against). **~ civile,** civil war. **~ d'usure,** war of attrition.

guerr|ier, ~ière /gɛrje, -jɛr/ *a.* warlike. —*n.m., f.* warrior.

guet /gɛ/ *n.m.* watch. **faire le ~,** be on the watch. **~apens** /gɛtapɑ̃/ *n.m. invar.* ambush.

guetter /gete/ *v.t.* watch; (*attendre)* watch out for.

gueule /gœl/ *n.f.* mouth; (*figure: fam.*) face. **ta ~!,** (*fam.*) shut up!

gueuler /gœle/ *v.i.* (*fam.*) bawl.

gueuleton /gœltɔ̃/ *n.m.* (*repas: fam.*) blow-out, slap-up meal.

gui /gi/ *n.m.* mistletoe.

guichet /giʃɛ/ *n.m.* window, counter; (*de gare)* ticket-office (window); (*de théâtre)* box-office (window).

guide /gid/ *n.m.* guide. —*n.f.* (*fille scout)* girl guide. **~s** *n.f. pl.* (*rênes)* reins.

guider /gide/ *v.t.* guide.

guidon /gidɔ̃/ *n.m.* handlebars.

guignol /giɲɔl/ *n.m.* puppet; (*personne)* clown; (*spectacle)* puppet-show.

guili-guili /giligili/ *n.m.* (*fam.*) tickle. **faire ~ à,** tickle.

guillemets /gijmɛ/ *n.m. pl.* quotation marks, inverted commas. **entre ~,** in inverted commas.

guilleret, ~te /gijrɛ, -t/ *a.* sprightly, jaunty.

guillotin|e /gijɔtin/ *n.f.* guillotine. **~er** *v.t.* guillotine.

guimauve /gimov/ *n.f.* marshmallow. **c'est de la ~,** (*fam.*) it's mush.

guindé /gɛ̃de/ *a.* stilted.

guirlande /girlɑ̃d/ *n.f.* garland.

guise /giz/ *n.f.* **à sa ~,** as one pleases. **en ~ de,** by way of.

guitar|e /gitar/ *n.f.* guitar. **~iste** *n.m./f.* guitarist.

gus /gys/ *n.m.* (*fam.*) bloke.

guttur|al (*m. pl.* **~aux**) /gytyral, -o/ *a.* guttural.

gym /ʒim/ *n.f.* gym.

gymnas|e /ʒimnaz/ *n.m.* gym(nasium). **~te** /-ast/ *n.m./f.* gymnast. **~tique** /-astik/ *n.f.* gymnastics.

gynécolo|gie /ʒinekɔlɔʒi/ *n.f.* gynaecology. **~gique** *a.* gynaecological. **~gue** *n.m./f.* gynaecologist.

gypse /ʒips/ *n.m.* gypsum.

H

habile /abil/ *a.* skilful, clever. **~té** *n.f.* skill.

habilité /abilite/ *a.* **~ à faire,** entitled to do.

habill|er /abije/ *v.t.* dress (**de,** in); (*équiper)* clothe; (*recouvrir)* cover (**de,** with). **s'~er** *v. pr.* dress (o.s.), get dressed; (*se déguiser)* dress up. **~é** *a.* (*costume)* dressy. **~ement** *n.m.* clothing.

habit /abi/ *n.m.* dress, outfit; (*de cérémonie)* tails. **~s,** clothes.

habitable /abitabl/ *a.* (in)habitable.

habitant, ~e /abitɑ̃, -t/ *n.m., f.* (*de maison)* occupant; (*de pays)* inhabitant.

habitat /abita/ *n.m.* housing conditions; (*d'animal)* habitat.

habitation /abitasjɔ̃/ *n.f.* living; (*logement)* house.

habit|er /abite/ *v.i.* live. —*v.t.* live in; (*planète, zone)* inhabit. **~é** *a.* (*terre)* inhabited.

habitude /abityd/ *n.f.* habit. **avoir l'~ de faire,** be used to doing.

d'∼, usually. **comme d'∼**, as usual.

habitué, ∼e /abitɥe/ n.m., f. regular visitor; (*client*) regular.

habituel, ∼le /abitɥɛl/ a. usual. ∼lement adv. usually.

habituer /abitɥe/ v.t. ∼ à, accustom to. **s'∼ à**, get used to.

hache /'aʃ/ n.f. axe.

haché /'aʃe/ a. (*viande*) minced; (*phrases*) jerky.

hacher /'aʃe/ v.t. mince; (*au couteau*) chop.

hachette /'aʃɛt/ n.f. hatchet.

hachis /'aʃi/ n.m. minced meat; (*Amer.*) ground meat.

hachisch /'aʃiʃ/ n.m. hashish.

hachoir /'aʃwar/ n.m. (*appareil*) mincer; (*couteau*) chopper; (*planche*) chopping board.

hagard, ∼e /'agar, -d/ a. wild(-looking).

haie /'ɛ/ n.f. hedge; (*rangée*) row. **course de ∼s**, hurdle race.

haillon /'ɑjɔ̃/ n.m. rag.

hain|e /'ɛn/ n.f. hatred. ∼eux, ∼euse a. full of hatred.

haïr /'air/ v.t. hate.

hâl|e /'al/ n.m. (sun-)tan. ∼é a. (sun-)tanned.

haleine /alɛn/ n.f. breath. **hors d'∼**, out of breath. **travail de longue ∼**, long job.

hal|er /'ale/ v.t. tow. ∼age n.m. towing.

haleter /'alte/ v.i. pant.

hall /'ɔl/ n.m. hall; (*de gare*) concourse.

halle /'al/ n.f. (covered) market. ∼s, (main) food market.

hallucination /alysinɑsjɔ̃/ n.f. hallucination.

halo /'alo/ n.m. halo.

halte /'alt/ n.f. stop; (*repos*) break; (*escale*) stopping place. ∼ !, int. stop; (*mil.*) halt. **faire ∼**, stop.

halt|ère /altɛr/ n.m. dumb-bell. ∼érophilie n.f. weight-lifting.

hamac /'amak/ n.m. hammock.

hamburger /ãburgœr/ n.m. hamburger.

hameau (*pl.* ∼x) /'amo/ n.m. hamlet.

hameçon /amsɔ̃/ n.m. (fish-)hook.

hanche /'ɑ̃ʃ/ n.f. hip.

hand-ball /'ɑ̃dbal/ n.m. handball.

handicap /'ɑ̃dikap/ n.m. handicap. ∼é, ∼ée a. & n.m., f. handicapped (person). ∼er v.t. handicap.

hangar /'ɑ̃gar/ n.m. shed; (*pour avions*) hangar.

hanneton /'antɔ̃/ n.m. May-bug.

hanter /'ɑ̃te/ v.t. haunt.

hantise /'ɑ̃tiz/ n.f. obsession (**de**, with).

happer /'ape/ v.t. snatch, catch.

haras /'ara/ n.m. stud-farm.

harasser /'arase/ v.t. exhaust.

harcèlement /arsɛlmɑ̃/ n.m. ∼ **sexuel**, sexual harassment.

harceler /'arsəle/ v.t. harass.

hardi /'ardi/ a. bold. ∼**esse** /-djɛs/ n.f. boldness. ∼**ment** adv. boldly.

hareng /'arɑ̃/ n.m. herring.

hargn|e /'arɲ/ n.f. (aggressive) bad temper. ∼**eux**, ∼**euse** a. bad-tempered.

haricot /'ariko/ n.m. bean. ∼ **vert**, French ou string bean; (*Amer.*) green bean.

harmonica /armɔnika/ n.m. harmonica.

harmoni|e /armɔni/ n.f. harmony. ∼**eux**, ∼**ieuse** a. harmonious.

harmoniser /armɔnize/ v.t., s'∼ v. pr. harmonize.

harnacher /'arnaʃe/ v.t. harness.

harnais /'arnɛ/ n.m. harness.

harp|e /'arp/ n.f. harp. ∼**iste** n.m./f. harpist.

harpon /'arpɔ̃/ n.m. harpoon. ∼**ner** /-ɔne/ v.t. harpoon; (*arrêter: fam.*) detain.

hasard /'azar/ n.m. chance; (*coïncidence*) coincidence. ∼**s**, (*risques*) hazards. **au ∼**, (*choisir* *etc.*) at random; (*flâner*) aimlessly. ~**eux**, ~**euse** /-dø, -z/ *a.* risky.

hasarder /'azarde/ *v.t.* risk; (*remarque*) venture. se ~ **dans**, risk going into. se ~ **à faire**, risk doing.

hâte /'at/ *n.f.* haste. **à la** ~, **en** ~, hurriedly. **avoir** ~ **de**, be eager to.

hâter /'ate/ *v.t.* hasten. se ~ *v. pr.* hurry (**de**, to).

hâtif, ~**ve** /'atif, -v/ *a.* hasty; (*précoce*) early.

hauss|**e** /'os/ *n.f.* rise (**de**, in). ~**e des prix**, price rises. **en** ~**e**, rising. ~**er** *v.t.* raise; (*épaules*) shrug. se ~**er** *v. pr.* stand up, raise o.s. up.

haut, ~**e** /'o, 'ot/ *a.* high; (*de taille*) tall. —*adv.* high; (*parler*) loud(ly); (*lire*) aloud. —*n.m.* top. **à** ~**e voix**, aloud. **des** ~**s et des bas**, ups and downs. **en** ~, (*regarder*, *jeter*) up; (*dans une maison*) upstairs. **en** ~ (**de**), at the top (of). ~ **en couleur**, colourful. **plus** ~, further up, higher up; (*dans un texte*) above. **en** ~ **lieu**, in high places. ~**de-forme** (*pl.* ~**s-de-forme**) *n.m.* top hat. ~**fourneau** (*pl.* ~**s-fourneaux**) *n.m.* blast-furnace. ~**le-cœur** *n.m. invar.* nausea. ~**parleur** *n.m.* loudspeaker.

hautain, ~**e** /'otɛ̃, -ɛn/ *a.* haughty.

hautbois /'obwa/ *n.m.* oboe.

hautement /'otmã/ *adv.* highly.

hauteur /'otœr/ *n.f.* height; (*colline*) hill; (*arrogance*) haughtiness. **à la** ~, (*fam.*) up to it. **à la** ~ **de**, level with; (*tâche*, *situation*) equal to.

hâve /'av/ *a.* gaunt.

havre /'avr/ *n.m.* haven.

Haye (La) /(la)'ɛ/ *n.f.* The Hague.

hayon /'ɛjɔ̃/ *n.m.* (*auto.*) rear opening, tail-gate.

hebdo /ɛbdɔ/ *n.m.* (*fam.*) weekly.

hebdomadaire /ɛbdɔmadɛr/ *a.* & *n.m.* weekly.

héberg|**er** /ebɛrʒe/ *v.t.* accommodate, take in. ~**ement** *n.m.* accommodation.

hébété /ebete/ *a.* dazed.

hébraïque /ebraik/ *a.* Hebrew.

hébreu (*pl.* ~**x**) /ebrø/ *a.m.* Hebrew. —*n.m.* (*lang.*) Hebrew. **c'est de l'**~**!**, it's double Dutch.

hécatombe /ekatɔ̃b/ *n.f.* slaughter.

hectare /ɛktar/ *n.m.* hectare (= 10,000 square metres).

hégémonie /eʒemɔni/ *n.f.* hegemony.

hein /'ɛ̃/ *int.* (*fam.*) eh.

hélas /'elas/ *int.* alas. —*adv.* sadly.

héler /'ele/ *v.t.* hail.

hélice /elis/ *n.f.* propeller.

hélicoptère /elikɔptɛr/ *n.m.* helicopter.

helvétique /ɛlvetik/ *a.* Swiss.

hématome /ematom/ *n.m.* bruise.

hémisphère /emisfɛr/ *n.m.* hemisphere.

hémorragie /emɔraʒi/ *n.f.* haemorrhage.

hémorroïdes /emɔrɔid/ *n.f. pl.* piles, haemorrhoids.

henn|**ir** /'enir/ *v.i.* neigh. ~**issement** *n.m.* neigh.

hépatite /epatit/ *n.f.* hepatitis.

herbage /ɛrbaʒ/ *n.m.* pasture.

herb|**e** /ɛrb/ *n.f.* grass; (*méd.*, *culin.*) herb. **en** ~**e**, green; (*fig.*) budding. ~**eux**, ~**euse** *a.* grassy.

herbicide /ɛrbisid/ *n.m.* weed-killer.

hérédit|**é** /eredite/ *n.f.* heredity. ~**aire** *a.* hereditary.

héré|**sie** /erezi/ *n.f.* heresy. ~**tique** *a.* heretical; *n.m./f.* heretic.

héris|**ser** /'erise/ *v.t.*, se ~**er** *v. pr.* bristle. ~**er qn.**, ruffle s.o. ~**é** *a.* bristling (**de**, with).

hérisson /'erisɔ̃/ *n.m.* hedgehog.

héritage /eritaʒ/ *n.m.* inheritance; (*spirituel etc.*) heritage.

hérit|er /erite/ *v.t./i.* inherit (**de**, from). **~er de qch.**, inherit sth. **~ier**, **~ière** *n.m.*, *f.* heir, heiress.

hermétique /ɛrmetik/ *a.* airtight; (*fig.*) unfathomable. **~ment** *adv.* hermetically.

hermine /ɛrmin/ *n.f.* ermine.

hernie /'ɛrni/ *n.f.* hernia.

héroïne¹ /erɔin/ *n.f.* (*femme*) heroine.

héroïne² /erɔin/ *n.f.* (*drogue*) heroin.

héroï|que /erɔik/ *a.* heroic. **~sme** *n.m.* heroism.

héron /erõ/ *n.m.* heron.

héros /'ero/ *n.m.* hero.

hésit|er /ezite/ *v.i.* hesitate (**à**, to). **en ~ant**, hesitantly. **~ant** *a.* hesitant. **~ation** *n.f.* hesitation.

hétéro /etero/ *n.m.* & *a.* (*fam.*) straight.

hétéroclite /eterɔklit/ *a.* heterogeneous.

hétérogène /eterɔʒɛn/ *a.* heterogeneous.

hétérosexuel, **~le** /eterɔseksyɛl/ *n.m.*, *f.* & *a.* heterosexual.

hêtre /'ɛtr/ *n.m.* beech.

heure /œr/ *n.f.* time; (*mesure de durée*) hour; (*scol.*) period. **quelle ~ est-il?**, what time is it? **il est dix/etc. ~s**, it is ten/etc. o'clock. **à l'~**, (*venir*, *être*) on time. **d'~ en heure**, hourly. **~ avancée**, late hour. **~ d'affluence**, **~ de pointe**, rush-hour. **~ indue**, ungodly hour. **~s creuses**, off-peak periods. **~s supplémentaires**, overtime.

heureusement /œrøzmã/ *adv.* fortunately, luckily.

heureu|x, **~se** /œrø, -z/ *a.* happy; (*chanceux*) lucky, fortunate.

heurt /'œr/ *n.m.* collision; (*conflit*) clash.

heurter /'œrte/ *v.t.* (*cogner*) hit; (*mur etc.*) bump into, hit; (*choquer*) offend. **se ~ à**, bump into, hit; (*fig.*) come up against.

hexagone /ɛgzagɔn/ *n.m.* hexagon. **l'~**, France.

hiberner /iberne/ *v.i.* hibernate.

hibou (*pl.* **~x**) /'ibu/ *n.m.* owl.

hideu|x, **~se** /'idø, -z/ *a.* hideous.

hier /jɛr/ *adv.* yesterday. **~ soir**, last night, yesterday evening.

hiérarch|ie /'jerarʃi/ *n.f.* hierarchy. **~ique** *a.* hierarchical.

hi-fi /'ifi/ *a. invar.* & *n.f.* (*fam.*) hi-fi.

hilare /ilar/ *a.* merry.

hilarité /ilarite/ *n.f.* laughter.

hindou, **~e** /ɛ̃du/ *a.* & *n.m.*, *f.* Hindu.

hippi|que /ipik/ *a.* horse, equestrian. **~sme** *n.m.* horse-riding.

hippodrome /ipodrom/ *n.m.* racecourse.

hippopotame /ipopotam/ *n.m.* hippopotamus.

hirondelle /irõdɛl/ *n.f.* swallow.

hirsute /irsyt/ *a.* shaggy.

hisser /'ise/ *v.t.* hoist, haul. **se ~** *v. pr.* raise o.s.

histoire /istwar/ *n.f.* (*récit*, *mensonge*) story; (*étude*) history; (*affaire*) business. **~(s)**, (*chichis*) fuss. **~s**, (*ennuis*) trouble.

historien, **~ne** /istɔrjɛ̃, -jɛn/ *n.m.*, *f.* historian.

historique /istɔrik/ *a.* historical.

hiver /iver/ *n.m.* winter. **~nal** (*m. pl.* **~naux**) *a.* winter; (*glacial*) wintry. **~ner** *v.i.* winter.

H.L.M. /'aʃɛlɛm/ *n.m./f.* (= *habitation à loyer modéré*) block of council flats; (*Amer.*) (government-sponsored) low-cost apartment building.

hocher /'ɔʃe/ *v.t.* **~ la tête**, (*pour dire oui*) nod; (*pour dire non*) shake one's head.

hochet /'ɔʃɛ/ n.m. rattle.

hockey /'ɔkɛ/ n.m. hockey. ~ sur glace, ice hockey.

hold-up /'ɔldœp/ n.m. invar. (attaque) hold-up.

hollandais, ~e /'ɔlɑ̃dɛ, -z/ a. Dutch. —n.m., f. Dutchman, Dutchwoman. —n.m. (lang.) Dutch.

Hollande /'ɔlɑ̃d/ n.f. Holland.

hologramme /ɔlɔgram/ n.m. hologram.

homard /'ɔmar/ n.m. lobster.

homéopathie /ɔmeɔpati/ n.f. homoeopathy.

homicide /ɔmisid/ n.m. homicide. ~ involontaire, manslaughter.

hommage /ɔmaʒ/ n.m. tribute. ~s, (salutations) respects. rendre ~ à, pay tribute.

homme /ɔm/ n.m. man; (espèce) man(kind). ~ d'affaires, businessman. ~ de la rue, man in the street. ~ d'État, statesman. ~ de paille, stooge. ~grenouille (pl. ~s-grenouilles), n.m. frogman. ~ politique, politician.

homogène /ɔmɔʒɛn/ a. homogeneous. ~énéité n.f. homogeneity.

homologue /ɔmɔlɔg/ n.m./f. counterpart.

homologué /ɔmɔlɔge/ a. (record) officially recognized; (tarif) official.

homologuer /ɔmɔlɔge/ v.t. recognize (officially), validate.

homonyme /ɔmɔnim/ n.m. (personne) namesake.

homosex|uel, ~uelle /ɔmɔsɛksɥɛl/ a. & n.m., f. homosexual. ~ualité n.f. homosexuality.

Hongrie /'ɔ̃gri/ n.f. Hungary.

hongrois, ~e /'ɔ̃grwa, -z/ a. & n.m., f. Hungarian.

honnête /ɔnɛt/ a. honest; (satisfaisant) fair. ~ment adv. honestly; fairly. ~té n.f. honesty.

honneur /ɔnœr/ n.m. honour; (mérite) credit. d'~, (invité, place) of honour; (membre) honorary. en l'~ de, in honour of. en quel ~?, (fam.) why?

honorable /ɔnɔrabl/ a. honourable; (convenable) respectable. ~ment adv. honourably; respectably.

honoraire /ɔnɔrɛr/ a. honorary. ~s n.m. pl. fees.

honorer /ɔnɔre/ v.t. honour; (faire honneur à) do credit to. s'~ de, pride o.s. on.

honorifique /ɔnɔrifik/ a. honorary.

hont|e /'ɔ̃t/ n.f. shame. avoir ~e, be ashamed (de, of). faire ~e à, make ashamed. ~eux, ~euse a. (personne) ashamed (de, of); (action) shameful. ~eusement adv. shamefully.

hôpit|al (pl. ~aux) /ɔpital, -o/ n.m. hospital.

hoquet /'ɔkɛ/ n.m. hiccup. le ~, (the) hiccups.

horaire /ɔrɛr/ a. hourly. —n.m. timetable. ~ flexible, flexitime.

horizon /ɔrizɔ̃/ n.m. horizon; (perspective) view.

horizont|al (m. pl. ~aux) /ɔrizɔ̃tal, -o/ a. horizontal. ~alement adv. horizontally.

horloge /ɔrlɔʒ/ n.f. clock.

horlog|er, ~ère /ɔrlɔʒe, -ɛr/ n.m., f. watchmaker.

hormis /'ɔrmi/ prép. save.

hormon|al (m. pl. ~aux) /ɔrmɔnal, -no/ a. hormonal, hormone.

hormone /ɔrmɔn/ n.f. hormone.

horoscope /ɔrɔskɔp/ n.m. horoscope.

horreur /ɔrœr/ n.f. horror. avoir ~ de, detest.

horrible /ɔribl/ a. horrible. ~ment /-əmɑ̃/ adv. horribly.

horrifier /ɔrifje/ v.t. horrify.

hors /ˈɔr/ *prép.* ~ **de**, out of; (*à l'extérieur de*) outside. ~**bord** *n.m. invar.* speedboat. ~ **d'atteinte**, out of reach. ~ **d'haleine**, out of breath. ~ **d'œuvre** *n.m. invar.* hors-d'œuvre. ~ **de prix**, exorbitant. ~ **de soi**, beside o.s. ~**jeu** *a. invar.* offside. ~**la-loi** *n.m. invar.* outlaw. ~**pair**, outstanding. ~**taxe** *a. invar.* duty-free.

hortensia /ɔrtɑ̃sja/ *n.m.* hydrangea.

horticulture /ɔrtikyltyr/ *n.f.* horticulture.

hospice /ɔspis/ *n.m.* home.

hospital|ier, ~ière[1] /ɔspitalje, -jɛr/ *a.* hospitable. ~**ité** *n.f.* hospitality.

hospital|ier, ~ière[2] /ɔspitalje, -jɛr/ *a.* (*méd.*) hospital. ~**iser** *v.t.* take to hospital.

hostie /ɔsti/ *n.f.* (*relig.*) host.

hostil|e /ɔstil/ *a.* hostile. ~**ité** *n.f.* hostility.

hosto /ɔstɔ/ *n.m.* (*fam.*) hospital.

hôte /ot/ *n.m.* (*maître*) host; (*invité*) guest.

hôtel /otɛl/ *n.m.* hotel. ~ (**particulier**), (private) mansion. ~ **de ville**, town hall. ~**ier, ~ière** /otɛlje, -jɛr/ *a.* hotel; *n.m., f.* hotelier. ~**lerie** *n.f.* hotel business; (*auberge*) country hotel.

hôtesse /otɛs/ *n.f.* hostess. ~ **de l'air**, air hostess.

hotte /ɔt/ *n.f.* basket; (*de cuisinière*) hood.

houblon /ublɔ̃/ *n.m.* le ~, hops.

houille /uj/ *n.f.* coal. ~ **blanche**, hydroelectric power. ~**er, ~ère** /uje, -jɛr/ *a.* coal; *n.f.* coalmine.

houl|e /ul/ *n.f.* (*de mer*) swell. ~**eux, ~euse** *a.* stormy.

houligan /uligan/ *n.m.* hooligan.

houppette /upɛt/ *n.f.* powderpuff.

hourra /ura/ *n.m. & int.* hurrah.

housse /us/ *n.f.* dust-cover.

houx /u/ *n.m.* holly.

hovercraft /ɔverkraft/ *n.m.* hovercraft.

hublot /yblo/ *n.m.* porthole.

huche /yʃ/ *n.f.* ~ **à pain**, bread bin.

huer /ɥe/ *v.t.* boo. **huées** *n.f. pl.* boos.

huil|e /ɥil/ *n.f.* oil; (*personne: fam.*) bigwig. ~**er** *v.t.* oil. ~**eux, ~euse** *a.* oily.

huis /ɥi/ *n.m.* à ~ **clos**, in camera.

huissier /ɥisje/ *n.m.* (*appariteur*) usher; (*jurid.*) bailiff.

huit /ɥi(t)/ *a.* eight. —*n.m.* eight. ~ **jours**, a week. **lundi en** ~, a week on Monday. ~**aine** /ɥitɛn/ *n.f.* (*semaine*) week. ~**ième** /ɥitjɛm/ *a. & n.m./f.* eighth.

huître /ɥitr/ *n.f.* oyster.

humain, ~e /ymɛ̃, ymɛn/ *a.* human; (*compatissant*) humane. ~**ement** /ymɛnmɑ̃/ *adv.* humanly; humanely.

humanitaire /ymanitɛr/ *a.* humanitarian.

humanité /ymanite/ *n.f.* humanity.

humble /œbl/ *a.* humble.

humecter /ymɛkte/ *v.t.* moisten.

humer /yme/ *v.t.* smell.

humeur /ymœr/ *n.f.* mood; (*tempérament*) temper. **de bonne/mauvaise** ~, in a good/bad mood.

humide /ymid/ *a.* damp; (*chaleur, climat*) humid; (*lèvres, yeux*) moist. ~**ité** *n.f.* humidity.

humili|er /ymilje/ *v.t.* humiliate. ~**ation** *n.f.* humiliation.

humilité /ymilite/ *n.f.* humility.

humorist|e /ymɔrist/ *n.m./f.* humorist. ~**ique** *a.* humorous.

humour /ymur/ *n.m.* humour; (*sens*) sense of humour.

huppé /ype/ *a.* (*fam.*) high-class.

hurl|er /yrle/ *v.t./i.* howl. ~**ement** *n.m.* howl(ing).

hurluberlu /yrlybɛrly/ *n.m.* scatter-brain.

hutte /'yt/ *n.f.* hut.
hybride /ibrid/ *a.* & *n.m.* hybrid.
hydratant, /idratã, -t/ *a.* (*lotion*) moisturizing.
hydrate /idrat/ *n.m.* **~ de carbone,** carbohydrate.
hydraulique /idrolik/ *a.* hydraulic.
hydravion /idravjõ/ *n.m.* seaplane.
hydro-electrique /idroɛlɛktrik/ *a.* hydroelectric.
hydrogène /idroʒɛn/ *n.m.* hydrogen.
hyène /jɛn/ *n.f.* hyena.
hygiène /iʒjɛn/ *n.f.* hygiene. **~iénique** /iʒjenik/ *a.* hygienic.
hymne /imn/ *n.m.* hymn. **~ national,** national anthem.
hyper- /iper/ *préf.* hyper-.
hypermarché /ipermarʃe/ *n.m.* (*supermarché*) hypermarket.
hypermétrope /ipermetrop/ *a.* long-sighted.
hypertension /ipertãsjõ/ *n.f.* high blood-pressure.
hypno|se /ipnoz/ *n.f.* hypnosis. **~tique** /-ɔtik/ *a.* hypnotic. **~tisme** /-ɔtism/ *n.m.* hypnotism.
hypnotis|er /ipnotize/ *v.t.* hypnotize. **~eur** *n.m.* hypnotist.
hypocrisie /ipokrizi/ *n.f.* hypocrisy.
hypocrite /ipokrit/ *a.* hypocritical. *—n.m./f.* hypocrite.
hypoth|èque /ipotɛk/ *n.f.* mortgage. **~équer** *v.t.* mortgage.
hypoth|èse /ipotɛz/ *n.f.* hypothesis. **~étique** *a.* hypothetical.
hystér|ie /isteri/ *n.f.* hysteria. **~ique** *a.* hysterical.

I

iceberg /isbɛrg/ *n.m.* iceberg.
ici /isi/ *adv.* (*espace*) here; (*temps*)

now. **d'~ demain,** by tomorrow. **d'~ là,** in the meantime. **d'~ peu,** shortly. **~ même,** in this very place.
icône /ikon/ *n.f.* icon.
idéal (*m. pl.* **~aux**) /ideal, -o/ *a.* ideal. *—n.m.* (*pl.* **~aux**) ideal. **~aliser** *v.t.* idealize.
idéalis|te /idealist/ *a.* idealistic. *—n.m./f.* idealist. **~me** *n.m.* idealism.
idée /ide/ *n.f.* idea; (*esprit*) mind. **~ fixe,** obsession. **~ reçue,** conventional opinion.
identifi|er /idãtifje/ *v.t.,* **s'~ier** *v. pr.* identify (**à,** with). **~cation** *n.f.* identification.
identique /idãtik/ *a.* identical.
identité /idãtite/ *n.f.* identity.
idéolog|ie /ideɔlɔʒi/ *n.f.* ideology. **~ique** *a.* ideological.
idiom|e /idjom/ *n.m.* idiom. **~atique** /idjomatik/ *a.* idiomatic.
idiot, ~e /idjo, idjɔt/ *a.* idiotic. *—n.m., f.* idiot. **~ie** /idjosi/ *n.f.* idiocy; (*acte, parole*) idiotic thing.
idiotisme /idjotism/ *n.m.* idiom.
idolâtrer /idolatre/ *v.t.* idolize.
idole /idol/ *n.f.* idol.
idyll|e /idil/ *n.f.* idyll. **~ique** *a.* idyllic.
if /if/ *n.m.* (*arbre*) yew.
igloo /iglu/ *n.m.* igloo.
ignare /iɲar/ *a.* ignorant. *—n.m./f.* ignoramus.
ignifugé /iɲifyʒe/ *a.* fireproof.
ignoble /iɲɔbl/ *a.* vile.
ignoran|t, ~te /iɲorã, -t/ *a.* ignorant. *—n.m., f.* ignoramus. **~ce** *n.f.* ignorance.
ignorer /iɲore/ *v.t.* not know; (*personne*) ignore.
il /il/ *pron.* he; (*chose*) it. **il est vrai/***etc.* **que,** it is true/*etc.* that. **il neige/pleut/***etc.***,** it is snowing/raining/*etc.* **il y a,** there is; (*pluriel*) there are; (*temps*) ago; (*durée*) for. **il y a 2 ans,** 2 years

ago. **il y a plus d'une heure que j'attends,** I've been waiting for over an hour.

île /il/ *n.f.* island. **~ déserte,** desert island. **~ anglo-normandes,** Channel Islands. **~s Britanniques,** British Isles.

illégal (*m. pl.* **~aux**) /ilegal, -o/ *a.* illegal. **~alité** *n.f.* illegality.

illégitim|e /ileʒitim/ *a.* illegitimate. **~ité** *n.f.* illegitimacy.

illettré, ~e /iletre/ *a. & n.m., f.* illiterate.

illicite /ilisit/ *a.* illicit.

illimité /ilimite/ *a.* unlimited.

illisible /ilizibl/ *a.* illegible; (*livre*) unreadable.

illogique /ilɔʒik/ *a.* illogical.

illumin|er /ilymine/ *v.t.,* **s'~er** *v. pr.* light up. **~ation** *n.f.* illumination. **~é** *a.* (*monument*) floodlit.

illusion /ilyzjɔ̃/ *n.f.* illusion. **se faire des ~s,** delude o.s. **~ner** /-jɔne/ *v.t.* delude. **~niste** /-jɔnist/ *n.m./f.* conjuror.

illusoire /ilyzwar/ *a.* illusory.

illustre /ilystr/ *a.* illustrious.

illustr|er /ilystre/ *v.t.* illustrate. **s'~er** *v. pr.* become famous. **~ation** *n.f.* illustration. **~é** *a.* illustrated; *n.m.* illustrated magazine.

îlot /ilo/ *n.m.* island; (*de maisons*) block.

ils /il/ *pron.* they.

imag|e /imaʒ/ *n.f.* picture; (*métaphore*) image; (*reflet*) reflection. **~é** *a.* full of imagery.

imaginaire /imaʒiner/ *a.* imaginary.

imaginati|f, ~ve /imaʒinatif, -v/ *a.* imaginative.

imagin|er /imaʒine/ *v.t.* imagine; (*inventer*) think up. **s'~er** *v. pr.* imagine (**que,** that). **~ation** *n.f.* imagination.

imbattable /ɛ̃batabl/ *a.* unbeatable.

imbécil|e /ɛ̃besil/ *a.* idiotic. **—***n.m./f.* idiot. **~lité** *n.f.* idiocy; (*action*) idiotic thing.

imbib|er /ɛ̃bibe/ *v.t.* soak (**de,** with). **être ~é,** (*fam.*) be sozzled. **s'~er** *v. pr.* become soaked.

imbriqué /ɛ̃brike/ *a.* (*lié*) linked.

imbroglio /ɛ̃brɔglijo/ *n.m.* imbroglio.

imbu /ɛ̃by/ *a.* **~ de,** full of.

imbuvable /ɛ̃byvabl/ *a.* undrinkable; (*personne: fam.*) insufferable.

imit|er /imite/ *v.t.* imitate; (*personnage*) impersonate; (*faire comme*) do the same as; (*document*) copy. **~ateur, ~atrice** *n.m., f.* imitator; impersonator. **~ation** *n.f.* imitation; impersonation.

immaculé /imakyle/ *a.* spotless.

immangeable /ɛ̃mɑ̃ʒabl/ *a.* inedible.

immatricul|er /imatrikyle/ *v.t.* register. **(se) faire ~er,** register. **~ation** *n.f.* registration.

immature /imatyr/ *a.* immature.

immédiat, ~e /imedja, -t/ *a.* immediate. **—***n.m.* **dans l'~,** for the moment. **~ement** /-tmã/ *adv.* immediately.

immens|e /imãs/ *a.* immense. **~ément** *adv.* immensely. **~ité** *n.f.* immensity.

immer|ger /imerʒe/ *v.t.* immerse. **s'~ger** *v. pr.* submerge. **~sion** *n.f.* immersion.

immeuble /imœbl/ *n.m.* block of flats, building. **~ (de bureaux),** (office) building *ou* block.

immigr|er /imigre/ *v.i.* immigrate. **~ant, ~ante** *a. & n.m., f.* immigrant. **~ation** *n.f.* immigration. **~é, ~ée** *a. & n.m., f.* immigrant.

imminen|t, ~te /iminã, -t/ *a.* imminent. **~ce** *n.f.* imminence.

immiscer (s') /(s)imise/ *v. pr.* interfere (**dans,** in).

immobil|e /imɔbil/ a. still, motionless. ~**ité** n.f. stillness; (*inaction*) immobility.

immobil|ier, ~**ière** /imɔbilje, -jɛr/ a. property. **agence** ~**ière,** estate agent's office; (*Amer.*) real estate office. **agent** ~**ier,** estate agent; (*Amer.*) real estate agent. **l'**~**ier,** property; (*Amer.*) real estate.

immobilis|er /imɔbilize/ v.t. immobilize; (*stopper*) stop. **s'**~**er** v. pr. stop. ~**ation** n.f. immobilization.

immodéré /imɔdere/ a. immoderate.

immoler /imɔle/ v.t. sacrifice.

immonde /imɔ̃d/ a. filthy.

immondices /imɔ̃dis/ n.f. pl. refuse.

immor|al (*m. pl.* ~**aux**) /imɔral, -o/ a. immoral. ~**alité** n.f. immorality.

immortaliser /imɔrtalize/ v.t. immortalize.

immort|el, ~**elle** /imɔrtɛl/ a. immortal. ~**alité** n.f. immortality.

immuable /imɥabl/ a. unchanging.

immunis|er /imynize/ v.t. immunize. ~**é contre,** (*à l'abri de*) immune to.

immunité /imynite/ n.f. immunity.

impact /ɛ̃pakt/ n.m. impact.

impair[1] /ɛ̃pɛr/ a. (*numéro*) odd.

impair[2] /ɛ̃pɛr/ n.m. blunder.

impardonnable /ɛ̃pardɔnabl/ a. unforgivable.

imparfait, ~**e** /ɛ̃parfɛ, -t/ a. & n.m. imperfect.

impart|ial (*m. pl.* ~**iaux**) /ɛ̃parsjal, -jo/ a. impartial. ~**ialité** n.f. impartiality.

impasse /ɛ̃pas/ n.f. (*rue*) dead end; (*situation*) deadlock.

impassible /ɛ̃pasibl/ a. impassive.

impat|ient, ~**iente** /ɛ̃pasjɑ̃, -t/ a. impatient. ~**iemment** /-jamɑ̃/ adv. impatiently. ~**ience** n.f. impatience.

impatienter /ɛ̃pasjɑ̃te/ v.t. annoy. **s'**~ v. pr. lose patience (**contre,** with).

impayable /ɛ̃pɛjabl/ a. (killingly) funny, hilarious.

impayé /ɛ̃pɛje/ a. unpaid.

impeccable /ɛ̃pekabl/ a. impeccable.

impénétrable /ɛ̃penetrabl/ a. impenetrable.

impensable /ɛ̃pɑ̃sabl/ a. unthinkable.

impérati|f, ~**ve** /ɛ̃peratif, -v/ a. imperative. —*n.m.* requirement; (*gram.*) imperative.

impératrice /ɛ̃peratris/ n.f. empress.

imperceptible /ɛ̃persɛptibl/ a. imperceptible.

imperfection /ɛ̃pɛrfɛksjɔ̃/ n.f. imperfection.

impér|ial (*m. pl.* ~**iaux**) /ɛ̃perjal, -jo/ a. imperial. ~**ialisme** n.m. imperialism.

impériale /ɛ̃perjal/ n.f. upper deck.

impérieu|x, ~**se** /ɛ̃perjø, -z/ a. imperious; (*pressant*) pressing.

impérissable /ɛ̃perisabl/ a. undying.

imperméable /ɛ̃pɛrmeabl/ a. impervious (**à,** to); (*manteau, tissu*) waterproof. —*n.m.* raincoat.

impersonnel, ~**le** /ɛ̃pɛrsɔnɛl/ a. impersonal.

impertin|ent, ~**te** /ɛ̃pɛrtinɑ̃, -t/ a. impertinent. ~**ce** n.f. impertinence.

imperturbable /ɛ̃pɛrtyrbabl/ a. unshakeable.

impét|ueux, ~**ueuse** /ɛ̃petɥø, -z/ a. impetuous. ~**uosité** n.f. impetuosity.

impitoyable /ɛ̃pitwajabl/ a. merciless.

implacable /ɛ̃plakabl/ a. implacable.

implant /ɛ̃plɑ̃/ n.m. implant.

implant|er /ɛ̃plɑ̃te/ v.t. establish. **s'~er** v. pr. become established. **~ation** n.f. establishment.

implication /ɛ̃plikasjɔ̃/ n.f. implication.

implicite /ɛ̃plisit/ a. implicit.

impliquer /ɛ̃plike/ v.t. imply (**que**, that). **~ dans**, implicate in.

implorer /ɛ̃plɔre/ v.t. implore.

impoli /ɛ̃pɔli/ a. impolite. **~tesse** n.f. impoliteness; (*remarque*) impolite remark.

impondérable /ɛ̃pɔ̃derabl/ a. & n.m. imponderable.

impopulaire /ɛ̃pɔpylɛr/ a. unpopular.

importance /ɛ̃pɔrtɑ̃s/ n.f. importance; (*taille*) size; (*ampleur*) extent. **sans ~**, unimportant.

important, ~e /ɛ̃pɔrtɑ̃, -t/ a. important; (*en quantité*) considerable, sizeable, big. —n.m. **l'~**, the important thing.

import|er¹ /ɛ̃pɔrte/ v.t. (*comm.*) import. **~ateur, ~atrice** n.m., f. importer; a. importing. **~ation** n.f. import.

import|er² /ɛ̃pɔrte/ v.i. matter, be important (**à**, to). **il ~e que**, it is important that. **n'~e**, **peu ~e**, it does not matter. **n'~e comment**, anyhow. **n'~e où**, anywhere. **n'~e qui**, anybody. **n'~e quoi**, anything.

importun, ~e /ɛ̃pɔrtœ̃, -yn/ a. troublesome. —n.m., f. nuisance. **~er** /-yne/ v.t. trouble.

imposant, ~e /ɛ̃pozɑ̃, -t/ a. imposing.

imposer /ɛ̃poze/ v.t. impose (**à**, on); (*taxer*) tax. **s'~** v. pr. (*action*) be essential; (*se faire reconnaître*) stand out. **en ~ à qn.**, impress s.o.

imposition /ɛ̃pozisjɔ̃/ n.f. taxation. **~ des mains**, laying-on of hands.

impossibilité /ɛ̃posibilite/ n.f. possibility. **dans l'~ de**, unable to.

impossible /ɛ̃posibl/ a. impossible. **faire l'~**, do the impossible.

imposteur /ɛ̃postœr/ n.m. impostor. **~ure** n.f. imposture.

impôt /ɛ̃po/ n.m. tax. **~s**, (*contributions*) tax(ation), taxes. **~ sur le revenu**, income tax.

impotent, ~e /ɛ̃pɔtɑ̃, -t/ a. crippled. —n.m., f. cripple.

impraticable /ɛ̃pratikabl/ a. (*route*) impassable.

imprécis, ~e /ɛ̃presi, -z/ a. imprecise. **~ion** /-zjɔ̃/ n.f. imprecision.

imprégner /ɛ̃preɲe/ v.t. fill (de, with); (*imbiber*) impregnate (de, with). **s'~ de**, become filled with; (*s'imbiber*) become impregnated with.

imprenable /ɛ̃prǝnabl/ a. impregnable.

impresario /ɛ̃presarjo/ n.m. manager.

impression /ɛ̃presjɔ̃/ n.f. impression; (*de livre*) printing.

impressionn|er /ɛ̃presjɔne/ v.t. impress. **~able** a. impressionable. **~ant, ~ante** a. impressive.

imprévisible /ɛ̃previzibl/ a. unpredictable.

imprévoyant, ~e /ɛ̃prevwajɑ̃, -t/ a. improvident.

imprévu /ɛ̃prevy/ a. unexpected. —n.m. unexpected incident.

imprim|er /ɛ̃prime/ v.t. print; (*marquer*) imprint; (*transmettre*) impart. **~ante** n.f. (*d'un ordinateur*) printer. **~é** a. printed; n.m. (*formulaire*) printed form. **~erie** n.f. (*art*) printing; (*lieu*) printing works. **~eur** n.m. printer.

improbable /ɛprɔbabl/ a. unlikely, improbable.

impromptu /ɛprɔ̃pty/ a. & adv. impromptu.

impropr|e /ɛprɔpr/ a. incorrect. **~e à**, unfit for. **~iété**, n.f. incorrectness; (*erreur*) error.

improvis|er /ɛprɔvize/ v.t./i. improvise. **~ation** n.f. improvisation.

improviste (à l') /(al)ɛprɔvist/ adv. unexpectedly.

imprud|ent, ~ente /ɛprydã, -t/ a. careless. **il est ~ent de**, it is unwise to. **~emment** /-amã/ adv. carelessly. **~ence** n.f. carelessness; (*acte*) careless action.

impuden|t, ~te /ɛpydã, -t/ a. impudent. **~ce** n.f. impudence.

impudique /ɛpydik/ a. immodest.

impuissan|t, ~te /ɛpɥisã, -t/ a. helpless; (*méd.*) impotent. **~t à**, powerless to. **~ce** n.f. helplessness; (*méd.*) impotence.

impuls|if, ~ve /ɛpylsif, -v/ a. impulsive.

impulsion /ɛpylsjɔ̃/ n.f. (*poussée, influence*) impetus; (*instinct, mouvement*) impulse.

impunément /ɛpynemã/ adv. with impunity.

impuni /ɛpyni/ a. unpunished.

impunité /ɛpynite/ n.f. impunity.

impur /ɛpyr/ a. impure. **~eté** n.f. impurity.

imput|er /ɛpyte/ v.t. **~ à**, impute to. **~able** a. ascribable (à, to).

inabordable /inabɔrdabl/ a. (*prix*) prohibitive.

inacceptable /inakseptabl/ a. unacceptable; (*scandaleux*) outrageous.

inaccessible /inaksesibl/ a. inaccessible.

inaccoutumé /inakutyme/ a. unaccustomed.

inachevé /inaʃve/ a. unfinished.

inact|if, ~ve /inaktif, -v/ a. inactive.

inaction /inaksjɔ̃/ n.f. inactivity.

inadapté, ~e /inadapte/ n.m., f. (*psych.*) maladjusted person.

inadéquat, ~e /inadekwa, -t/ a. inadequate.

inadmissible /inadmisibl/ a. unacceptable.

inadvertance /inadvɛrtãs/ n.f. **par ~**, by mistake.

inaltérable /inalterabl/ a. stable, that does not deteriorate; (*sentiment*) unfailing.

inanimé /inanime/ a. (*évanoui*) unconscious; (*mort*) lifeless; (*matière*) inanimate.

inaperçu /inapɛrsy/ a. unnoticed.

inappréciable /inapresjabl/ a. invaluable.

inapte /inapt/ a. unsuited (à, to). **~ à faire**, incapable of doing.

inarticulé /inartikyle/ a. inarticulate.

inassouvi /inasuvi/ a. unsatisfied.

inattendu /inatãdy/ a. unexpected.

inattent|if, ~ve /inatãtif, -v/ a. inattentive (à, to).

inattention /inatãsjɔ̃/ n.f. inattention.

inaugur|er /inɔgyre/ v.t. inaugurate. **~ation** n.f. inauguration.

inaugur|al (m. pl. **~aux**) /inɔgyral, -o/ a. inaugural.

incalculable /ɛkalkylabl/ a. incalculable.

incapable /ɛkapabl/ a. incapable (de qch., of sth.). **~ de faire**, unable to do, incapable of doing. **—n.m./f.** incompetent.

incapacité /ɛkapasite/ n.f. incapacity. **dans l'~ de**, unable to.

incarcérer /ɛkarsere/ v.t. incarcerate.

incarn|er /ɛkarne/ v.t. embody. **~ation** n.f. embodiment, incarnation. **~é a.** (*ongle*) ingrowing.

incartade /ɛkartad/ n.f. indiscretion, misdeed, prank.

incassable /ɛ̃kasabl/ *a.* unbreakable.

incendiaire /ɛ̃sɑ̃djɛr/ *a.* incendiary, (*propos*) inflammatory. —*n.m./f.* arsonist.

incend|ie /ɛ̃sɑ̃di/ *n.m.* fire. **~ie criminel,** arson. **~ier** *v.t.* set fire to.

incert|ain, **~aine** /ɛ̃sɛrtɛ̃, -ɛn/ *a.* uncertain; (*contour*) vague. **~itude** *n.f.* uncertainty.

incessamment /ɛ̃sɛsamɑ̃/ *adv.* shortly.

incessant, **~e** /ɛ̃sɛsɑ̃, -t/ *a.* incessant.

incest|e /ɛ̃sɛst/ *n.m.* incest. **~ueux,** **~ueuse** *a.* incestuous.

inchangé /ɛ̃ʃɑ̃ʒe/ *a.* unchanged.

incidence /ɛ̃sidɑ̃s/ *n.f.* effect.

incident /ɛ̃sidɑ̃/ *n.m.* incident. **~ technique,** technical hitch.

incinér|er /ɛ̃sinere/ *v.t.* incinerate; (*mort*) cremate. **~ateur** *n.m.* incinerator.

incis|er /ɛ̃size/ *v.t.* (*abcès etc.*) lance. **~ion** *n.f.* lancing; (*entaille*) incision.

incisif, **~ve** /ɛ̃sizif, -v/ *a.* incisive.

incit|er /ɛ̃site/ *v.t.* incite (à, to). **~ation** *n.f.* incitement.

inclinaison /ɛ̃klinɛzɔ̃/ *n.f.* incline; (*de la tête*) tilt.

inclination[1] /ɛ̃klinasjɔ̃/ *n.f.* (*penchant*) inclination.

inclin|er /ɛ̃kline/ *v.t.* tilt, lean; (*courber*) bend; (*inciter*) encourage (à, to). —*v.i.* **~er à,** be inclined to. **s'~er** *v. pr.* (*se courber*) bow down; (*céder*) give in; (*chemin*) slope. **~er la tête,** (*approuver*) nod; (*révérence*) bow. **~ation**[2] *n.f.* (*de la tête*) nod; (*du buste*) bow.

incl|ure /ɛ̃klyr/ *v.t.* include; (*enfermer*) enclose. **jusqu'au lundi ~us,** up to and including Monday. **~usion** *n.f.* inclusion.

incognito /ɛ̃kɔɲito/ *adv.* incognito.

incohéren|t, **~te** /ɛ̃kɔerɑ̃, -t/ *a.* incoherent. **~ce** *n.f.* incoherence.

incollable /ɛ̃kɔlabl/ *a.* **il est ~,** he can't be stumped.

incolore /ɛ̃kɔlɔr/ *a.* colourless; (*crème, verre*) clear.

incomber /ɛ̃kɔ̃be/ *v.i.* **il vous/***etc.* **incombe de,** it is your/*etc.* responsibility to.

incombustible /ɛ̃kɔ̃bystibl/ *a.* incombustible.

incommode /ɛ̃kɔmɔd/ *a.* awkward.

incommoder /ɛ̃kɔmɔde/ *v.t.* inconvenience.

incomparable /ɛ̃kɔ̃parabl/ *a.* incomparable.

incompatib|le /ɛ̃kɔ̃patibl/ *a.* incompatible. **~ilité** *n.f.* incompatibility.

incompéten|t, **~te** /ɛ̃kɔ̃petɑ̃, -t/ *a.* incompetent. **~ce** *n.f.* incompetence.

incompl|et, **~ète** /ɛ̃kɔ̃plɛ, -t/ *a.* incomplete.

incompréhensible /ɛ̃kɔ̃preɑ̃sibl/ *a.* incomprehensible.

incompréhension /ɛ̃kɔ̃preɑ̃sjɔ̃/ *n.f.* lack of understanding.

incompris, **~e** /ɛ̃kɔ̃pri, -z/ *a.* misunderstood.

inconcevable /ɛ̃kɔ̃svabl/ *a.* inconceivable.

inconciliable /ɛ̃kɔ̃siljabl/ *a.* irreconcilable.

inconditionnel, **~le** /ɛ̃kɔ̃disjɔnɛl/ *a.* unconditional.

inconduite /ɛ̃kɔ̃dɥit/ *n.f.* loose behaviour.

inconfort /ɛ̃kɔ̃fɔr/ *n.m.* discomfort. **~able** /-tabl/ *a.* uncomfortable.

incongru /ɛ̃kɔ̃gry/ *a.* unseemly.

inconnu, **~e** /ɛ̃kɔny/ *a.* unknown (à, to). —*n.m., f.* stranger. —*n.m.* **l'~,** the unknown. —*n.f.* unknown (quantity).

inconsc|ient, ~iente /ɛ̃kɔ̃sjã, -t/ *a.* unconscious (**de**, of); (*fou*) mad. —*n.m.* (*psych.*) subconscious. ~iemment /-jamã/ *adv.* unconsciously. ~ience *n.f.* unconsciousness; (*folie*) madness.

inconsidéré /ɛ̃kɔ̃sidere/ *a.* thoughtless.

inconsistant, ~e /ɛ̃kɔ̃sistã, -t/ *a.* (*fig.*) flimsy.

inconsolable /ɛ̃kɔ̃sɔlabl/ *a.* inconsolable.

inconstan|t, ~te /ɛ̃kɔ̃stã, -t/ *a.* fickle. ~ce *n.f.* fickleness.

incontest|able /ɛ̃kɔ̃tɛstabl/ *a.* indisputable. ~é *a.* undisputed.

incontinen|t, ~te /ɛ̃kɔ̃tinã, -t/ *a.* incontinent. ~ce *n.f.* incontinence.

incontrôlable /ɛ̃kɔ̃trolabl/ *a.* unverifiable.

inconvenan|t, ~te /ɛ̃kɔ̃vnã, -t/ *a.* improper. ~ce *n.f.* impropriety.

inconvénient /ɛ̃kɔ̃venjã/ *n.m.* disadvantage; (*risque*) risk; (*objection*) objection.

incorpor|er /ɛ̃kɔrpore/ *v.t.* incorporate; (*mil.*) enlist. ~ation *n.f.* incorporation; (*mil.*) enlistment.

incorrect /ɛ̃kɔrɛkt/ *a.* (*faux*) incorrect; (*malséant*) improper; (*impoli*) impolite.

incorrigible /ɛ̃kɔriʒibl/ *a.* incorrigible.

incrédul|e /ɛ̃kredyl/ *a.* incredulous. ~ité *n.f.* incredulity.

increvable /ɛ̃krəvabl/ *a.* (*fam.*) tireless.

incriminer /ɛ̃krimine/ *v.t.* incriminate.

incroyable /ɛ̃krwajabl/ *a.* incredible.

incroyant, ~e /ɛ̃krwajã, -t/ *n.m., f.* non-believer.

incrust|er /ɛ̃kryste/ *v.t.* (*décorer*) inlay (**de**, with). s'~er (*invité*; *péj.*) take root. ~ation *n.f.* inlay.

incubateur /ɛ̃kybatœr/ *n.m.* incubator.

inculp|er /ɛ̃kylpe/ *v.t.* charge (**de**, with). ~ation *n.f.* charge. ~é, ~ée *n.m., f.* accused.

inculquer /ɛ̃kylke/ *v.t.* instil (**à**, into).

inculte /ɛ̃kylt/ *a.* uncultivated; (*personne*) uneducated.

incurable /ɛ̃kyrabl/ *a.* incurable.

incursion /ɛ̃kyrsjɔ̃/ *n.f.* incursion.

incurver /ɛ̃kyrve/ *v.t.*, s'~ *v. pr.* curve.

Inde /ɛ̃d/ *n.f.* India.

indécen|t, ~te /ɛ̃desã, -t/ *a.* indecent. ~ce *n.f.* indecency.

indéchiffrable /ɛ̃deʃifrabl/ *a.* indecipherable.

indécis, ~e /ɛ̃desi, -z/ *a.* indecisive; (*qui n'a pas encore pris de décision*) undecided. ~ion /-izjɔ̃/ *n.f.* indecision.

indéfendable /ɛ̃defãdabl/ *a.* indefensible.

indéfini /ɛ̃defini/ *a.* indefinite; (*vague*) undefined. ~ment *adv.* indefinitely. ~ssable *a.* indefinable.

indélébile /ɛ̃delebil/ *a.* indelible.

indélicat, ~e /ɛ̃delika, -t/ *a.* (*malhonnête*) unscrupulous.

indemne /ɛ̃dɛmn/ *a.* unharmed.

indemniser /ɛ̃dɛmnize/ *v.t.* compensate (**de**, for).

indemnité /ɛ̃dɛmnite/ *n.f.* indemnity; (*allocation*) allowance. ~s de licenciement, redundancy payment.

indéniable /ɛ̃denjabl/ *a.* undeniable.

indépend|ant, ~ante /ɛ̃depãdã, -t/ *a.* independent. ~amment *adv.* independently. ~amment de, apart from. ~ance *n.f.* independence.

indescriptible /ɛ̃dɛskriptibl/ *a.* indescribable.

indésirable /ɛ̃dezirabl/ *a.* & *n.m./f.* undesirable.

indestructible /ɛ̃dɛstryktibl/ a. indestructible.

indétermination /ɛ̃detɛrminɑsjɔ̃/ n.f. indecision.

indéterminé /ɛ̃detɛrmine/ a. unspecified.

index /ɛ̃dɛks/ n.m. forefinger; (liste) index. **~er** v.t. index.

indic /ɛ̃dik/ (fam.) grass.

indica|teur, ~trice /ɛ̃dikatœr, -tris/ n.m., f. (police) informer. —n.m. (livre) guide; (techn.) indicator. **~teur des chemins de fer**, railway timetable. **~teur des rues**, street directory.

indicati|f, ~ve /ɛ̃dikatif, -v/ a. indicative (de, of). —n.m. (radio) signature tune; (téléphonique) dialling code; (gram.) indicative.

indication /ɛ̃dikɑsjɔ̃/ n.f. indication; (renseignement) information; (directive) instruction.

indice /ɛ̃dis/ n.m. sign; (dans une enquête) clue; (des prix) index; (de salaire) rating.

indien, ~ne /ɛ̃djɛ̃, -jɛn/ a. & n.m., f. Indian.

indifféremment /ɛ̃diferamɑ̃/ adv. equally.

indifféren|t, ~te /ɛ̃diferɑ̃, -t/ a. indifferent (à, to). **ça m'est ~t**, it makes no difference to me. **~ce** n.f. indifference.

indigène /ɛ̃diʒɛn/ a. & n.m./f. native.

indigen|t, ~te /ɛ̃diʒɑ̃, -t/ a. poor **~ce** n.f. poverty.

indigest|e /ɛ̃diʒɛst/ a. indigestible. **~ion** n.f. indigestion.

indignation /ɛ̃diɲɑsjɔ̃/ n.f. indignation.

indign|e /ɛ̃diɲ/ a. unworthy (de, of); (acte) vile. **~ité** n.f. unworthiness; (acte) vile act.

indigner (s'~ /ɛ̃diɲe/ s'~ v. pr. become indignant (de, at).

indiqu|er /ɛ̃dike/ v.t. show, indicate; (renseigner sur) point out,

tell; (déterminer) give, state, appoint. **~er du doigt**, point to ou out ou at. **~é a.** (heure) appointed; (opportun) appropriate; (conseillé) recommended.

indirect /ɛ̃dirɛkt/ a. indirect.

indiscipliné /ɛ̃disipline/ a. unruly.

indiscr|et, ~ète /ɛ̃diskrɛ, -ɛt/ a. inquisitive. **~étion** n.f. indiscretion; inquisitiveness.

indiscutable /ɛ̃diskytabl/ a. unquestionable.

indispensable /ɛ̃dispɑ̃sabl/ a. indispensable. **il est ~ qu'il vienne**, it is essential that he comes.

indispos|er /ɛ̃dispoze/ v.t. make unwell. **~er** (mécontenter) antagonize. **~é a.** unwell. **~ition** n.f. indisposition.

indistinct, ~e /ɛ̃distɛ̃(kt), -ɛkt/ a. indistinct. **~ement** /-ɛ̃ktəmɑ̃/ adv. indistinctly; (également) without distinction.

individu /ɛ̃dividy/ n.m. individual. **~aliste** n.m./f. individualist.

individuel, ~le /ɛ̃dividɥɛl/ a. individual; (opinion) personal. **chambre ~le**, single room. **maison ~le**, private house. **~lement** adv. individually.

indivisible /ɛ̃divizibl/ a. indivisible.

indolen|t, ~te /ɛ̃dɔlɑ̃, -t/ a. indolent. **~ce** n.f. indolence.

indolore /ɛ̃dɔlɔr/ a. painless.

Indonésie /ɛ̃dɔnezi/ n.f. Indonesia.

Indonésien, ~ne /ɛ̃dɔnezjɛ̃, -jɛn/ a. & n.m., f. Indonesian.

indu, ~e /ɛ̃dy/ a. **à une heure ~e**, at some ungodly hour.

induire /ɛ̃dɥir/ v.t. infer (de, from). **~ en erreur**, mislead.

indulgen|t, ~te /ɛ̃dylʒɑ̃, -t/ a. indulgent; (clément) lenient. **~ce** n.f. indulgence; leniency.

industr|ie /ɛ̃dystri/ n.f. industry. **~ialisé** a. industrialized.

industriel, ∼le /ɛ̃dystrijɛl/ a. industrial. —n.m. industrialist. ∼lement adv. industrially.

inébranlable /inebrɑ̃labl/ a. unshakeable.

inédit, ∼e /inedi, -t/ a. unpublished; (fig.) original.

inefficace /inefikas/ a. ineffective.

inég|al (m. pl. ∼aux) /inegal, -o/ a. unequal; (irrégulier) uneven. ∼alé a. unequalled. ∼alement a. matchless. ∼alité n.f. (injustice) inequality; (irrégularité) unevenness; (différence) difference (de, between).

inéluctable /inelyktabl/ a. inescapable.

inept|e /inɛpt/ a. inept, absurd. ∼ie /inɛpsi/ n.f. ineptitude.

inépuisable /inepɥizabl/ a. inexhaustible.

inert|e /inɛrt/ a. inert; (mort) lifeless. ∼ie /inɛrsi/ n.f. inertia.

inespéré /inɛspere/ a. unhoped for.

inestimable /inɛstimabl/ a. priceless.

inévitable /inevitabl/ a. inevitable.

inexact, ∼e /inɛgza(kt), -akt/ a. (imprécis) inaccurate; (incorrect) incorrect.

inexcusable /inɛkskyzabl/ a. unforgivable.

inexistant, ∼e /inɛgzistɑ̃, -t/ a. non-existent.

inexorable /inɛgzɔrabl/ a. inexorable.

inexpérience /inɛksperjɑ̃s/ n.f. inexperience.

inexpli|cable /inɛksplikabl/ a. inexplicable. ∼qué a. unexplained.

in extremis /inɛkstremis/ adv. (par nécessité) (taken/done etc.) as a last resort; (au dernier moment) (at the) last minute.

inextricable /inɛkstrikabl/ a. inextricable.

infaillible /ɛ̃fajibl/ a. infallible.

infâme /ɛ̃fɑm/ a. vile.

infamie /ɛ̃fami/ n.f. infamy; (action) vile action.

infanterie /ɛ̃fɑ̃tri/ n.f. infantry.

infantile /ɛ̃fɑ̃til/ a. infantile.

infantilisme /ɛ̃fɑ̃tilism/ n.m. infantilism. **faire de l'**∼, be childish.

infarctus /ɛ̃farktys/ n.m. coronary (thrombosis).

infatigable /ɛ̃fatigabl/ a. tireless.

infatué /ɛ̃fatɥe/ a. ∼ **de sa personne,** full of himself.

infect /ɛ̃fɛkt/ a. revolting.

infect|er /ɛ̃fɛkte/ v.t. infect. **s'**∼**er** v. pr. become infected. ∼**ion** /-ksjɔ̃/ n.f. infection.

infectieu|x, ∼**se** /ɛ̃fɛksjø, -z/ a. infectious.

inférieur, ∼e /ɛ̃ferjœr/ a. (plus bas) lower; (moins bon) inferior (à, to). —n.m., f. inferior. ∼ à, (plus petit que) smaller than.

infériorité /ɛ̃ferjorite/ n.f. inferiority.

infern|al (m. pl. ∼aux) /ɛ̃fɛrnal, -o/ a. infernal.

infester /ɛ̃fɛste/ v.t. infest.

infid|èle /ɛ̃fidɛl/ a. unfaithful. ∼**élité** n.f. unfaithfulness; (acte) infidelity.

infiltr|er (s') /(s)ɛ̃filtre/ v. pr. **s'**∼**er (dans),** (personnes, idées, etc.) infiltrate; (liquide) percolate. ∼**ation** n.f. infiltration.

infime /ɛ̃fim/ a. tiny, minute.

infini /ɛ̃fini/ a. infinite. —n.m. infinity. **à l'**∼, endlessly. ∼**ment** adv. infinitely.

infinité /ɛ̃finite/ n.f. **une** ∼ **de,** an infinite amount of.

infinitésimal /ɛ̃finitezimal/ a. infinitesimal.

infinitif /ɛ̃finitif/ n.m. infinitive.

infirm|e /ɛ̃firm/ a. & n.m./f. disabled (person). ∼**ité** n.f. disability.

infirmer /ɛ̃firme/ v.t. invalidate.

infirm|erie /ɛ̃firməri/ n.f. sickbay, infirmary. ∼ier n.m. (male) nurse. ∼ière n.f. nurse. ∼ière-chef, sister.

inflammable /ɛ̃flamabl/ a. (in)flammable.

inflammation /ɛ̃flamasjɔ̃/ n.f. inflammation.

inflation /ɛ̃flasjɔ̃/ n.f. inflation.

inflexible /ɛ̃flɛksibl/ a. inflexible.

inflexion /ɛ̃flɛksjɔ̃/ n.f. inflexion.

infliger /ɛ̃fliʒe/ v.t. inflict; (sanction) impose.

influen|ce /ɛ̃flyɑ̃s/ n.f. influence. ∼çable a. easily influenced. ∼cer v.t. influence.

influent, ∼e /ɛ̃flyɑ̃, -t/ a. influential.

influer /ɛ̃flye/ v.i. ∼ sur, influence.

info /ɛ̃fo/ n.f. (some) news. les ∼s, the news.

informa|teur, ∼trice /ɛ̃fɔrmatœr, -tris/ n.m., f. informant.

informaticien, ∼ne /ɛ̃fɔrmatisjɛ̃, -jɛn/ n.m., f. computer scientist.

information /ɛ̃fɔrmasjɔ̃/ n.f. information; (jurid.) inquiry. une ∼, (some) information; (nouvelle) (some) news. les ∼s, the news.

informati|que /ɛ̃fɔrmatik/ n.f. computer science; (techniques) data processing. ∼ser v.t. computerize.

informe /ɛ̃fɔrm/ a. shapeless.

informer /ɛ̃fɔrme/ v.t. inform (de, about, of). s'∼ v. pr. enquire (de, about).

infortune /ɛ̃fɔrtyn/ n.f. misfortune.

infraction /ɛ̃fraksjɔ̃/ n.f. offence. ∼ à, breach of.

infranchissable /ɛ̃frɑ̃ʃisabl/ a. impassable; (fig.) insuperable.

infrarouge /ɛ̃fraruʒ/ a. infrared.

infrastructure /ɛ̃frastryktyr/ n.f. infrastructure.

infructueu|x, ∼se /ɛ̃fryktɥø, -z/ a. fruitless.

infus|er /ɛ̃fyze/ v.t./i. infuse, brew. ∼ion n.f. herb-tea, infusion.

ingénier (s') /(s)ɛ̃ʒenje/ v. pr. s'∼ à, strive to.

ingénieur /ɛ̃ʒenjœr/ n.m. engineer.

ingén|ieux, ∼ieuse /ɛ̃ʒenjø, -z/ a. ingenious. ∼iosité n.f. ingenuity.

ingénu /ɛ̃ʒeny/ a. naïve.

ingér|er (s') /(s)ɛ̃ʒere/ v. pr. s'∼er dans, interfere in. ∼ence n.f. interference.

ingrat, ∼e /ɛ̃gra, -t/ a. ungrateful; (pénible) thankless; (disgracieux) unattractive. ∼itude /-tityd/ n.f. ingratitude.

ingrédient /ɛ̃gredjɑ̃/ n.m. ingredient.

ingurgiter /ɛ̃gyrʒite/ v.t. swallow.

inhabité /inabite/ a. uninhabited.

inhabituel, ∼le /inabitɥel/ a. unusual.

inhalation /inalasjɔ̃/ n.f. inhaling.

inhérent, ∼e /inerɑ̃, -t/ a. inherent (à, in).

inhibition /inibisjɔ̃/ n.f. inhibition.

inhospital|ier, ∼ière /inɔspitalje, -jɛr/ a. inhospitable.

inhumain, ∼e /inymɛ̃, -ɛn/ a. inhuman.

inhum|er /inyme/ v.t. bury. ∼ation n.f. burial.

inimaginable /inimaʒinabl/ a. unimaginable.

inimitié /inimitje/ n.f. enmity.

ininterrompu /inɛ̃terɔ̃py/ a. continuous, uninterrupted.

iniqu|e /inik/ a. iniquitous. ∼ité n.f. iniquity.

init|ial (m. pl. ∼iaux) /inisjal, -jo/ a. initial. ∼ialement adv. initially.

initiale /inisjal/ n.f. initial.

initialis|er /inisjalize/ (comput.) format. ∼ation n.f. formatting.

initiative /inisjativ/ *n.f.* initiative.

init|ier /inisje/ *v.t.* initiate (à, into). **s'~ier** *v. pr.* become initiated (à, into). **~iateur, ~iatrice** *n.m., f.* initiator. **~iation** *n.f.* initiation.

inject|er /ɛ̃ʒɛkte/*v.t.* inject. **~é de sang**, bloodshot. **~ion** /-ksjɔ̃/ *n.f.* injection.

injur|e /ɛ̃ʒyr/ *n.f.* insult. **~ier** *v.t.* insult. **~ieux, ~ieuse** *a.* insulting.

injust|e /ɛ̃ʒyst/ *a.* unjust, unfair. **~ice** *n.f.* injustice.

inlassable /ɛ̃lasabl/ *a.* tireless.

inné /ine/ *a.* innate, inborn.

innocen|t, ~te /inɔsɑ̃, -t/ *a. & n.m.* innocent. **~ce** *n.f.* innocence.

innocenter /inɔsɑ̃te/ *v.t.* (*disculper*) clear, prove innocent.

innombrable /inɔ̃brabl/ *a.* countless.

innov|er /inɔve/ *v.i.* innovate. **~ateur, ~atrice** *n.m., f.* innovator. **~ation** *n.f.* innovation.

inoccupé /inɔkype/ *a.* unoccupied.

inoculer /inɔkyle/ *v.t.* inoculate.

inodore /inɔdɔr/ *a.* odourless.

inoffensi|f, ~ve /inɔfɑ̃sif, -v/ *a.* harmless.

inond|er /inɔ̃de/ *v.t.* flood; (*mouiller*) soak; (*envahir*) inundate (de, with). **~é de soleil**, bathed in sunlight. **~ation** *n.f.* flood; (*action*) flooding.

inopérant, ~e /inɔperɑ̃, -t/ *a.* inoperative.

inopiné /inɔpine/ *a.* unexpected.

inopportun, ~e /inɔpɔrtɛ̃, -yn/ *a.* inopportune.

inoubliable /inublijabl/ *a.* unforgettable.

inouï /inwi/ *a.* incredible.

inox /inɔks/ *n.m.* (P.) stainless steel.

inoxydable /inɔksidabl/ *a.* **acier ~**, stainless steel.

inqualifiable /ɛ̃kalifjabl/ *a.* unspeakable.

inqu|iet, ~iète /ɛ̃kjɛ, -ɛ̃kjɛt/ *a.* worried. **~iéter** *v.t.* worry. **s'~ier** worry (de, about). **~ant, ~ante** *a.* worrying.

inquiétude /ɛ̃kjetyd/ *n.f.* anxiety, worry.

inquisition /ɛ̃kizisjɔ̃/ *n.f.* inquisition.

insaisissable /ɛ̃sezisabl/ *a.* indefinable.

insalubre /ɛ̃salybr/ *a.* unhealthy.

insanité /ɛ̃sanite/ *n.f.* insanity.

insatiable /ɛ̃sasjabl/ *a.* insatiable.

insatisfaisant, ~e /ɛ̃satisfəzɑ̃, -t/ *a.* unsatisfactory.

insatisfait, ~e /ɛ̃satisfɛ, -t/ *a.* (*mécontent*) dissatisfied; (*frustré*) unfulfilled.

inscription /ɛ̃skripsjɔ̃/ *n.f.* inscription; (*immatriculation*) enrolment.

inscrire† /ɛ̃skrir/ *v.t.* write (down); (*graver, tracer*) inscribe; (*personne*) enrol; (*sur une liste*) put down. **s'~** *v. pr.* put one's name down. **s'~ à**, (*école*) enrol at; (*club, parti*) join; (*examen*) enter for. **s'~ dans le cadre de**, come within the framework of.

insecte /ɛ̃sɛkt/ *n.m.* insect.

insecticide /ɛ̃sɛktisid/ *n.m.* insecticide.

insécurité /ɛ̃sekyrite/ *n.f.* insecurity.

insensé /ɛ̃sɑ̃se/ *a.* mad.

insensib|le /ɛ̃sɑ̃sibl/ *a.* insensitive (à, to); (*graduel*) imperceptible. **~ilité** *n.f.* insensitivity.

inséparable /ɛ̃separabl/ *a.* inseparable.

insérer /ɛ̃sere/ *v.t.* insert. **s'~ dans**, be part of.

insidieu|x, ~se /ɛ̃sidjø, -z/ *a.* insidious.

insigne /ɛ̃siɲ/ *n.m.* badge. **~(s)**, (*d'une fonction*) insignia.

insignifian|t, **∼te** /ɛ̃siɲifjã, -t/ a. insignificant. **∼ce** n.f. insignificance.

insinuation /ɛ̃sinɥasjɔ̃/ n.f. insinuation.

insinuer /ɛ̃sinɥe/ v.t. insinuate. **s'∼ dans**, penetrate.

insipide /ɛ̃sipid/ a. insipid.

insistan|t, **∼te** /ɛ̃sistã, -t/ a. insistent. **∼ce** n.f. insistence.

insister /ɛ̃siste/ v.i. insist (**pour faire**, on doing). **∼ sur**, stress.

insolation /ɛ̃sɔlasjɔ̃/ n.f. (méd.) sunstroke.

insolen|t, **∼te** /ɛ̃sɔlã, -t/ a. insolent. **∼ce** n.f. insolence.

insolite /ɛ̃sɔlit/ a. unusual.

insoluble /ɛ̃sɔlybl/ a. insoluble.

insolvable /ɛ̃sɔlvabl/ a. insolvent.

insomnie /ɛ̃sɔmni/ n.f. insomnia.

insonoriser /ɛ̃sɔnɔrize/ v.t. soundproof.

insoucian|t, **∼te** /ɛ̃susjã, -t/ a. carefree. **∼ce** n.f. unconcern.

insoumission /ɛ̃sumisjɔ̃/ n.f. rebelliousness.

insoupçonnable /ɛ̃supsɔnabl/ a. undetectable.

insoutenable /ɛ̃sutnabl/ a. unbearable; (argument) untenable.

inspec|ter /ɛ̃spɛkte/ v.t. inspect. **∼teur**, **∼trice** n.m., f. inspector. **∼tion** /-ksjɔ̃/ n.f. inspection.

inspir|er /ɛ̃spire/ v.t. inspire. —v.i. breathe in. **∼er à qn.**, inspire s.o. with. **s'∼er de**, be inspired by. **∼ation** n.f. inspiration; (respiration) breath.

instab|le /ɛ̃stabl/ a. unstable; (temps) unsettled; (meuble, équilibre) unsteady. **∼ilité** n.f. instability; unsteadiness.

install|er /ɛ̃stale/ v.t. install; (gaz, meuble) put in; (étagère) put up; (équiper) fit out. **s'∼er** v. pr. settle (down); (emménager) settle in. **s'∼er comme**, set o.s. up as. **∼ation** n.f. installation; (de local) fitting out; (de locataire) settling in. **∼ations** n.f. pl. (appareils) fittings.

instance /ɛ̃stɑ̃s/ n.f. authority; (prière) entreaty. **avec ∼**, with insistence. **en ∼**, pending. **en ∼ de**, in the course of, on the point of.

instant /ɛ̃stɑ̃/ n.m. moment, instant. **à l'∼**, this instant.

instantané /ɛ̃stɑ̃tane/ a. instantaneous; (café) instant.

instar /ɛ̃star/ n.m. **à l'∼ de**, like.

instaur|er /ɛ̃stɔre/ v.t. institute. **∼ation** n.f. institution.

instiga|teur, **∼trice** /ɛ̃stigatœr, -tris/ n.m., f. instigator. **∼tion** /-asjɔ̃/ n.f. instigation.

instinct /ɛ̃stɛ̃/ n.m. instinct. **d'∼**, instinctively.

instinctif, **∼ve** /ɛ̃stɛ̃ktif, -v/ a. instinctive. **∼vement** adv. instinctively.

instit /ɛ̃stit/ n.m./f. (fam.) teacher.

instituer /ɛ̃stitɥe/ v.t. establish.

institut /ɛ̃stity/ n.m. institute. **∼ de beauté**, beauty parlour. **∼ universitaire de technologie**, polytechnic, technical college.

institu|teur, **∼trice** /ɛ̃stitytœr, -tris/ n.m., f. primary-school teacher.

institution /ɛ̃stitysjɔ̃/ n.f. institution; (école) private school.

instructif, **∼ve** /ɛ̃stryktif, -v/ a. instructive.

instruction /ɛ̃stryksjɔ̃/ n.f. education; (document) directive. **∼s**, (ordres, mode d'emploi) instructions.

instruire† /ɛ̃strɥir/ v.t. teach, educate. **∼ de**, inform of. **s'∼ v. pr.** educate o.s. **s'∼ de**, enquire about.

instruit, **∼e** /ɛ̃strɥi, -t/ a. educated.

instrument /ɛ̃strymã/ n.m. instrument; (outil) implement.

insu /ɛ̃sy/ n.m. à l'~ de, without the knowledge of.

insubordination /ɛ̃sybɔrdinasjɔ̃/ n.f. insubordination.

insuffisan|t, ~te /ɛ̃syfizɑ̃, -t/ a. inadequate; (en nombre) insufficient. ~ce n.f. inadequacy.

insulaire /ɛ̃sylɛr/ a. island. —n.m./f. islander.

insuline /ɛ̃sylin/ n.f. insulin.

insult|e /ɛ̃sylt/ n.f. insult. ~er v.t. insult.

insupportable /ɛ̃syportabl/ a. unbearable.

insurg|er (s') /(s)ɛ̃syrʒe/ v. pr. rebel. ~é, ~ée a. & n.m., f. rebel.

insurmontable /ɛ̃syrmɔ̃tabl/ a. insurmountable.

insurrection /ɛ̃syrɛksjɔ̃/ n.f. insurrection.

intact /ɛ̃takt/ a. intact.

intangible /ɛ̃tɑ̃ʒibl/ a. intangible.

intarissable /ɛ̃tarisabl/ a. inexhaustible.

intégr|al (m. pl. ~aux) /ɛ̃tegral, -o/ a. complete; (édition) unabridged. ~alement adv. in full. ~alité n.f. whole. dans son ~alité, in full.

intégrant, ~e /ɛ̃tegrɑ̃, -t/ a. faire partie ~e de, be part and parcel of.

intègre /ɛ̃tegr/ a. upright.

intégr|er /ɛ̃tegre/ v.t., s'~er v. pr. integrate. ~ation n.f. integration.

intégri|ste /ɛ̃tegrist/ a. fundamentalist. ~sme /-sm/ n.m. fundamentalism.

intégrité /ɛ̃tegrite/ n.f. integrity.

intellect /ɛ̃telɛkt/ n.m. intellect. ~uel, ~uelle a. & n.m., f. intellectual.

intelligence /ɛ̃teliʒɑ̃s/ n.f. intelligence; (compréhension) understanding; (complicité) complicity.

intelligent, ~ente /ɛ̃teliʒɑ̃, -t/ a. intelligent. ~emment /-amɑ̃/ adv. intelligently.

intelligible /ɛ̃teliʒibl/ a. intelligible.

intempéries /ɛ̃tɑ̃peri/ n.f. pl. severe weather.

intempesti|f, ~ve /ɛ̃tɑ̃pestif, -v/ a. untimely.

intenable /ɛ̃tnabl/ a. unbearable; (enfant) impossible.

intendan|t, ~te /ɛ̃tɑ̃dɑ̃, -t/ n.m. (mil.) quartermaster. —n.m., f. (scol.) bursar. ~ce n.f. (scol.) bursar's office.

intens|e /ɛ̃tɑ̃s/ a. intense; (circulation) heavy. ~ément adv. intensely. ~ifier v., s'~ifier v. pr. intensify. ~ité n.f. intensity.

intensi|f, ~ve /ɛ̃tɑ̃sif, -v/ a. intensive.

intenter /ɛ̃tɑ̃te/ v.t. ~ un procès ou une action, institute proceedings (à, contre, against).

intention /ɛ̃tɑ̃sjɔ̃/ n.f. intention (de faire, of doing). à l'~ de qn., for s.o. ~né /-jɔne/ a. bien/mal ~né, well-/ill-intentioned.

intentionnel, ~le /ɛ̃tɑ̃sjɔnɛl/ a. intentional.

inter- /ɛ̃tɛr/ préf. inter-.

interaction /ɛ̃tɛraksjɔ̃/ n.f. interaction.

intercaler /ɛ̃tɛrkale/ v.t. insert.

intercéder /ɛ̃tɛrsede/ v.i. intercede (en faveur de, on behalf of).

intercept|er /ɛ̃tɛrsɛpte/ v.t. intercept. ~ion /-psjɔ̃/ n.f. interception.

interchangeable /ɛ̃tɛrʃɑ̃ʒabl/ a. interchangeable.

interdiction /ɛ̃tɛrdiksjɔ̃/ n.f. ban. ~ de fumer, no smoking.

interdire† /ɛ̃tɛrdir/ v.t. forbid; (officiellement) ban, prohibit. ~ à qn. de faire, forbid s.o. to do.

interdit, ~e /ɛ̃tɛrdi, -t/ a. (étonné) nonplussed.

intéressant, ~e /ɛ̃teresɑ̃, -t/ a. interesting; (avantageux) attractive.

intéressé, ~e /ɛ̃terese/ a. (*en cause*) concerned; (*pour profiter*) self-interested. —*n.m., f.* person concerned.

intéresser /ɛ̃terese/ v.t. interest; (*concerner*) concern. **s'~ à**, be interested in.

intérêt /ɛ̃terɛ/ n.m. interest; (*égoïsme*) self-interest. ~(s), (*comm.*) interest. **vous avez ~ à**, it is in your interest to.

interférence /ɛ̃terferɑ̃s/ n.f. interference.

intérieur /ɛ̃terjœr/ a. inner, inside; (*vol, politique*) domestic; (*vie, calme*) inner. —*n.m.* interior; (*de boîte, tiroir*) inside; **à l'~ (de)**, inside; (*fig.*) within. **~ement** adv. inwardly.

intérim /ɛ̃terim/ n.m. interim. **assurer l'~**, deputize (**de, for**). **par ~**, acting. **faire de l'~**, temp. **~aire** a. temporary, interim.

interjection /ɛ̃tɛrʒɛksjɔ̃/ n.f. interjection.

interlocu|teur, ~**trice** /ɛ̃tɛrlɔkytœr, -tris/ n.m., f. **son ~teur**, the person one is speaking to.

interloqué /ɛ̃tɛrlɔke/ a. **être ~**, be taken aback.

intermède /ɛ̃tɛrmɛd/ n.m. interlude.

intermédiaire /ɛ̃tɛrmedjɛr/ a. intermediate. —*n.m./f.* intermediary.

interminable /ɛ̃tɛrminabl/ a. endless.

intermittence /ɛ̃tɛrmitɑ̃s/ n.f. **par ~**, intermittently.

intermittent, ~e /ɛ̃tɛrmitɑ̃, -t/ a. intermittent.

internat /ɛ̃terna/ n.m. boarding-school.

internation|al (*m. pl.* ~**aux**) /ɛ̃tɛrnasjɔnal, -o/ a. international.

interne /ɛ̃tɛrn/ a. internal. —*n.m./f.* (*scol.*) boarder.

intern|er /ɛ̃tɛrne/ v.t. (*pol.*) intern; (*méd.*) confine. **~ement** n.m. (*pol.*) internment.

interpell|er /ɛ̃tɛrpɔle/ v.t. shout to; (*apostropher*) shout at; (*interroger*) question. **~ation** n.f. (*pol.*) questioning.

interphone /ɛ̃tɛrfɔn/ n.m. intercom.

interposer (s') /(s)ɛ̃tɛrpoze/ v. pr. intervene.

interpr|ète /ɛ̃tɛrprɛt/ n.m./f. interpreter; (*artiste*) performer. **~étariat** n.m. interpreting.

interpr|éter /ɛ̃tɛrprete/ v.t. interpret; (*jouer*) play; (*chanter*) sing. **~ation** n.f. interpretation; (*d'artiste*) performance.

interroga|teur, ~**trice** /ɛ̃tɛrɔgatœr, -tris/ a. questioning.

interrogati|f, ~**ve** /ɛ̃tɛrɔgatif, -v/ a. interrogative.

interrogatoire /ɛ̃tɛrɔgatwar/ n.m. interrogation.

interro|ger /ɛ̃terɔʒe/ v.t. question; (*élève*) test. **~gateur**, ~**gatrice** a. questioning. **~gation** n.f. question; (*action*) questioning; (*épreuve*) test.

interr|ompre /ɛ̃tɛrɔ̃pr/ v.t. break off, interrupt; (*personne*) interrupt. **s'~ompre** v. pr. break off. **~upteur** n.m. switch. **~uption** n.f. interruption; (*arrêt*) break.

intersection /ɛ̃tɛrsɛksjɔ̃/ n.f. intersection.

interstice /ɛ̃tɛrstis/ n.m. crack.

interurbain /ɛ̃tɛryrbɛ̃/ n.m. long-distance telephone service.

intervalle /ɛ̃tɛrval/ n.m. space; (*temps*) interval. **dans l'~**, in the meantime.

interven|ir /ɛ̃tɛrvənir/ v.i. intervene; (*survenir*) occur; (*méd.*) operate. **~tion** /-vɑ̃sjɔ̃/ n.f. intervention; (*méd.*) operation.

intervertir /ɛ̃tɛrvɛrtir/ v.t. invert.

interview /ɛ̃tɛrvju/ n.f. interview. **~er** /-ve/ v.t. interview.

intestin /ɛ̃tɛstɛ̃/ n.m. intestine.

intim|e /ɛ̃tim/ a. intimate; (*fête, vie*) private; (*dîner*) quiet. —n.m./f. intimate friend. **~ement** adv. intimately. **~ité** n.f. intimacy; (*vie privée*) privacy.

intimid|er /ɛ̃timide/ v.t. intimidate. **~ation** n.f. intimidation.

intituler /ɛ̃tityle/ v.t. entitle. **s'~** v. pr. be entitled.

intolérable /ɛ̃tɔlerabl/ a. intolerable.

intoléran|t, ~te /ɛ̃tɔlerɑ̃, -t/ a. intolerant. **~ce** n.f. intolerance.

intonation /ɛ̃tɔnasjɔ̃/ n.f. intonation.

intox /ɛ̃tɔks/ n.m. (*fam.*) brainwashing.

intoxi|quer /ɛ̃tɔksike/ v.t. poison; (*pol.*) brainwash. **~cation** n.f. poisoning; (*pol.*) brainwashing.

intraduisible /ɛ̃tradɥizibl/ a. untranslatable.

intraitable /ɛ̃trɛtabl/ a. inflexible.

intransigean|t, ~te /ɛ̃trɑ̃siʒɑ̃, -t/ a. intransigent. **~ce** n.f. intransigence.

intransiti|f, ~ve /ɛ̃trɑ̃zitif, -v/ a. intransitive.

intraveineu|x, ~se /ɛ̃travɛnø, -z/ a. intravenous.

intrépide /ɛ̃trepid/ a. fearless.

intrigu|e /ɛ̃trig/ n.f. intrigue; (*théâtre*) plot. **~er** v.t./i. intrigue.

intrinsèque /ɛ̃trɛ̃sɛk/ a. intrinsic.

introduction /ɛ̃trɔdyksjɔ̃/ n.f. introduction.

introduire† /ɛ̃trɔdɥir/ v.t. introduce, bring in; (*insérer*) put in, insert. **~ qn.**, show s.o. in. **s'~ dans**, get into, enter.

introspecti|f, ~ve /ɛ̃trɔspektif, -v/ a. introspective.

introuvable /ɛ̃truvabl/ a. that cannot be found.

introverti, ~e /ɛ̃trɔverti/ n.m., f. introvert. —a. introverted.

intrus, ~e /ɛ̃try, -z/ n.m., f.

intruder. **~ion** /-zjɔ̃/ n.f. intrusion.

intuiti|f, ~ve /ɛ̃tɥitif, -v/ a. intuitive.

intuition /ɛ̃tɥisjɔ̃/ n.f. intuition.

inusable /inyzabl/ a. hard-wearing.

inusité /inyzite/ a. little used.

inutil|e /inytil/ a. useless; (*vain*) needless. **~ement** adv. needlessly. **~ité** n.f. uselessness.

inutilisable /inytilizabl/ a. unusable.

invalid|e /ɛ̃valid/ a. & n.m./f. disabled (person). **~ité** n.f. disablement.

invariable /ɛ̃varjabl/ a. invariable.

invasion /ɛ̃vazjɔ̃/ n.f. invasion.

invectiv|e /ɛ̃vɛktiv/ n.f. invective. **~er** v.t. abuse.

invendable /ɛ̃vɑ̃dabl/ a. unsaleable. **~u** a. unsold.

inventaire /ɛ̃vɑ̃ter/ n.m. inventory. **faire l'~ de**, take stock of.

invent|er /ɛ̃vɑ̃te/ v.t. invent. **~eur** n.m. inventor. **~ion** /ɛ̃vɑ̃sjɔ̃/ n.f. invention.

inventi|f, ~ve /ɛ̃vɑ̃tif, -v/ a. inventive.

inverse /ɛ̃vers/ a. opposite; (*ordre*) reverse. —n.m. reverse. **~ment** /-əmɑ̃/ adv. conversely.

invers|er /ɛ̃verse/ v.t. reverse, invert. **~ion** n.f. inversion.

investigation /ɛ̃vestigasjɔ̃/ n.f. investigation.

invest|ir /ɛ̃vestir/ v.t. invest. **~issement** n.m. (*comm.*) investment.

investiture /ɛ̃vestityr/ n.f. nomination.

invétéré /ɛ̃vetere/ a. inveterate.

invincible /ɛ̃vɛ̃sibl/ a. invincible.

invisible /ɛ̃vizibl/ a. invisible.

invit|er /ɛ̃vite/ v.t. invite (à, to). **~ation** n.f. invitation. **~é, ~ée** n.m., f. guest.

invivable /ɛ̃vivabl/ a. unbearable.

involontaire /ɛ̃vɔlɔ̃tɛr/ a. involuntary.

invoquer /ɛ̃vɔke/ v.t. call upon, invoke; (*alléguer*) plead.

invraisembl|able /ɛ̃vrɛsɑ̃blabl/ a. improbable; (*incroyable*) incredible. **∼ance** n.f. improbability.

invulnérable /ɛ̃vylnerabl/ a. invulnerable.

iode /jɔd/ n.m. iodine.

ion /jɔ̃/ n.m. ion.

ira, irait /ira, irɛ/ *voir* **aller**[1].

Irak /irak/ n.m. Iraq. **∼ien, ∼ienne** a. & n.m., f. Iraqi.

Iran /irɑ̃/ n.m. Iran. **∼ien, ∼ienne** /iranjɛ̃, -jɛn/ a. & n.m., f. Iranian.

irascible /irasibl/ a. irascible.

iris /iris/ n.m. iris.

irlandais, ∼e /irlɑ̃dɛ, -z/ a. Irish. —n.m., f. Irishman, Irishwoman.

Irlande /irlɑ̃d/ n.f. Ireland.

iron|ie /irɔni/ n.f. irony. **∼ique** a. ironic(al).

irraisonné /irɛzɔne/ a. irrational.

irrationnel, ∼le /irasjɔnɛl/ a. irrational.

irréalisable /irealizabl/ a. (*projet*) unworkable.

irrécupérable /irekyperabl/ a. irretrievable, beyond recall.

irréel, ∼le /ireel/ a. unreal.

irréfléchi /irefleʃi/ a. thoughtless.

irréfutable /irefytabl/ a. irrefutable.

irrégul|ier, ∼ière /iregylje, -jɛr/ a. irregular. **∼arité** n.f. irregularity.

irrémédiable /iremedjabl/ a. irreparable.

irremplaçable /irɑ̃plasabl/ a. irreplaceable.

irréparable /ireparabl/ a. beyond repair.

irréprochable /ireproʃabl/ a. flawless.

irrésistible /irezistibl/ a. irresistible; (*drôle*) hilarious.

irrésolu /irezɔly/ a. indecisive.

irrespirable /irɛspirabl/ a. stifling.

irresponsable /irɛspɔ̃sabl/ a. irresponsible.

irréversible /irevɛrsibl/ a. irreversible.

irrévocable /irevɔkabl/ a. irrevocable.

irrigation /irigasjɔ̃/ n.f. irrigation.

irriguer /irige/ v.t. irrigate.

irrit|er /irite/ v.t. irritate. **s'∼er de**, be annoyed at. **∼able** a. irritable. **∼ation** n.f. irritation.

irruption /irypsjɔ̃/ n.f. faire **∼ dans**, burst into.

Islam /islam/ n.m. Islam.

islamique /islamik/ a. Islamic.

islandais, ∼e /islɑ̃dɛ, -z/ a. Icelandic. —n.m., f. Icelander. —n.m. (*lang.*) Icelandic.

Islande /islɑ̃d/ n.f. Iceland.

isolé /izɔle/ a. isolated. **∼ment** adv. in isolation.

isol|er /izɔle/ v.t. isolate; (*électr.*) insulate. **s'∼er** v. pr. isolate o.s. **∼ant** n.m. insulating material. **∼ation** n.f. insulation. **∼ement** n.m. isolation.

isoloir /izɔlwar/ n.m. polling booth.

Isorel /izɔrɛl/ n.m. (P.) hardboard.

isotope /izɔtɔp/ n.m. isotope.

Israël /israɛl/ n.m. Israel.

israélien, ∼ne /israeljɛ̃, -jɛn/ a. & n.m., f. Israeli.

israélite /israelit/ a. Jewish. —n.m./f. Jew, Jewess.

issu /isy/ a. **être ∼ de**, come from.

issue /isy/ n.f. exit; (*résultat*) outcome; (*fig.*) solution. **à l'∼ de**, at the conclusion of. **rue** *ou* **voie sans ∼**, dead end.

isthme /ism/ n.m. isthmus.

Italie /itali/ n.f. Italy.

italien, ∼ne /italjɛ̃, -jɛn/ a. & n.m., f. Italian. —n.m. (*lang.*) Italian.

italique /italik/ *n.m.* italics.

itinéraire /itinerɛr/ *n.m.* itinerary, route.

itinérant, ~e /itinerɑ̃, -t/ *a.* itinerant.

I.U.T. /iyte/ *n.m.* (*abrév.*) polytechnic.

I.V.G. /iveʒe/ *n.f.* (*abrév.*) abortion.

ivoire /ivwar/ *n.m.* ivory.

ivr|e /ivr/ *a.* drunk. **~esse** *n.f.* drunkenness. **~ogne** *n.m.* drunk(ard).

J

j' /ʒ/ *voir* **je**.

jacasser /ʒakase/ *v.i.* chatter.

jachère (en) /(ɑ̃)ʒaʃɛr/ *adv.* fallow.

jacinthe /ʒasɛ̃t/ *n.f.* hyacinth.

jade /ʒad/ *n.m.* jade.

jadis /ʒadis/ *adv.* long ago.

jaillir /ʒajir/ *v.i.* (*liquide*) spurt (out); (*lumière*) stream out; (*apparaître, fuser*) burst forth.

jais /ʒɛ/ *n.m.* (**noir de ~**, jet-black.

jalon /ʒalɔ̃/ *n.m.* (*piquet*) marker. **~ner** /-ɔne/ *v.t.* mark (out).

jalou|x, ~se /ʒalu, -z/ *a.* jealous. **~ser** *v.t.* be jealous of. **~sie** *n.f.* jealousy; (*store*) (venetian) blind.

jamais /ʒamɛ/ *adv.* ever. (**ne**) **~**, never. **il ne boit ~**, he never drinks. **à ~**, for ever. **si ~**, if ever.

jambe /ʒɑ̃b/ *n.f.* leg.

jambon /ʒɑ̃bɔ̃/ *n.m.* ham. **~neau** (*pl.* **~neaux**) /-ɔno/ *n.m.* knuckle of ham.

jante /ʒɑ̃t/ *n.f.* rim.

janvier /ʒɑ̃vje/ *n.m.* January.

Japon /ʒapɔ̃/ *n.m.* Japan.

japonais, ~e /ʒaponɛ, -z/ *a. & n.m., f.* Japanese. —*n.m.* (*lang.*) Japanese.

japper /ʒape/ *v.i.* yelp.

jaquette /ʒakɛt/ *n.f.* (*de livre, femme*) jacket; (*d'homme*) morning coat.

jardin /ʒardɛ̃/ *n.m.* garden. **~ d'enfants**, nursery (school). **~ public**, public park.

jardin|er /ʒardine/ *v.i.* garden. **~age** *n.m.* gardening. **~ier, ~ière** *n.m., f.* gardener; *n.f.* (*meuble*) plant-stand. **~ière de légumes**, mixed vegetables.

jargon /ʒargɔ̃/ *n.m.* jargon.

jarret /ʒarɛ/ *n.m.* back of the knee.

jarretelle /ʒartɛl/ *n.f.* suspender; (*Amer.*) garter.

jarretière /ʒartjɛr/ *n.f.* garter.

jaser /ʒaze/ *v.i.* jabber.

jasmin /ʒasmɛ̃/ *n.m.* jasmine.

jatte /ʒat/ *n.f.* bowl.

jaug|e /ʒoʒ/ *n.f.* capacity; (*de navire*) tonnage; (*compteur*) gauge. **~er** *v.t.* gauge.

jaun|e /ʒon/ *a. & n.m.* yellow; (*péj.*) scab. **~ d'œuf**, (egg) yolk. **rire ~e**, laugh on the other side of one's face. **~ir** *v.t./i.* turn yellow. **~isse** /ʒonis/ *n.f.* jaundice.

javelot /ʒavlo/ *n.m.* javelin.

jazz /dʒaz/ *n.m.* jazz.

J.C. /ʒezykri/ *n.m.* (*abrév.*) **500 avant/après ~**, 500 B.C./A.D.

je, j'* /ʒə, ʒ/ *pron.* I.

jean /dʒin/ *n.m.* jeans.

jeep /(d)ʒip/ *n.f.* jeep.

jerrycan /(d)ʒerikan/ *n.m.* jerrycan.

jersey /ʒɛrze/ *n.m.* jersey.

Jersey /ʒɛrze/ *n.f.* Jersey.

Jésus /ʒezy/ *n.m.* Jesus.

jet¹ /ʒɛ/ *n.m.* throw; (*de liquide, vapeur*) jet. **~ d'eau**, fountain.

jet² /dʒɛt/ *n.m.* (*avion*) jet.

jetable /ʒətabl/ *a.* disposable.

jetée /ʒte/ *n.f.* pier.

jeter /ʒte/ *v.t.* throw; (*au rebut*) throw away; (*regard, ancre, lumière*) cast; (*cri*) utter; (*bases*) lay. **~ un coup d'œil**, have or take a look (**à**, at). **se ~ contre,**

(*heurter*) bash into. **se ~ dans**, (*fleuve*) flow into. **se ~ sur**, (*se ruer sur*) rush at.

jeton /ʒtɔ̃/ *n.m.* token; (*pour compter*) counter.

jeu (*pl.* **~x**) /ʒø/ *n.m.* game; (*amusement*) play; (*au casino etc.*) gambling; (*théâtre*) acting; (*série*) set; (*de lumière, ressort*) play. **en ~**, (*honneur*) at stake; (*forces*) at work. **~ de cartes**, (*paquet*) pack of cards. **~ d'échecs**, (*boîte*) chess set. **~ de mots**, pun. **~ télévisé**, television quiz.

jeudi /ʒødi/ *n.m.* Thursday.

jeun (à) /(a)ʒœ̃/ *adv.* **être/rester à ~**, be/stay without food; **comprimé à prendre à ~**, tablet to be taken on an empty stomach.

jeune /ʒœn/ *a.* young. —*n.m./f.* young person. **~ fille**, girl. **~s mariés**, newlyweds. **les ~s**, young people.

jeunesse /ʒœnɛs/ *n.f.* youth; (*apparence*) youthfulness. **la ~**, (*jeunes*) the young.

joaill|ier, **~ière** /ʒɔaje, -jɛr/ *n.m., f.* jeweller. **~erie** *n.f.* jewellery; (*magasin*) jeweller's shop.

job /dʒɔb/ *n.m.* (*fam.*) job.

jockey /ʒɔkɛ/ *n.m.* jockey.

joie /ʒwa/ *n.f.* joy.

joindre† /ʒwɛ̃dr/ *v.t.* join (à, to); (*contacter*) contact; (*mains, pieds*) put together; (*efforts*) combine; (*dans une enveloppe*) enclose. **se ~ à**, join.

joint, **~e** /ʒwɛ̃, -t/ *a.* (*efforts*) joint; (*pieds*) together. —*n.m.* joint; (*ligne*) join; (*de robinet*) washer. **~ure** /-tyr/ *n.f.* joint; (*ligne*) join.

joker /ʒɔkɛr/ *n.m.* (*carte*) joker.

joli /ʒɔli/ *a.* pretty, nice; (*somme, profit*) nice. **c'est du ~!**, (*ironique*) charming! **c'est bien ~ mais**, that is all very well but.

~ment *adv.* prettily; (*très: fam.*) awfully.

jonc /ʒɔ̃/ *n.m.* (bul)rush.

jonch|er /ʒɔ̃ʃe/ *v.t.*, **~é de**, littered with.

jonction /ʒɔ̃ksjɔ̃/ *n.f.* junction.

jongl|er /ʒɔ̃gle/ *v.i.* juggle. **~eur**, **~euse** *n.m., f.* juggler.

jonquille /ʒɔ̃kij/ *n.f.* daffodil.

Jordanie /ʒɔrdani/ *n.f.* Jordan.

joue /ʒu/ *n.f.* cheek.

jou|er /ʒwe/ *v.t./i.* play; (*théâtre*) act; (*au casino etc.*) gamble; (*fonctionner*) work; (*film, pièce*) put on; (*cheval*) back. **~er à ou de**, play. **~er la comédie**, put on an act. **bien ~é!**, well done!

jouet /ʒwɛ/ *n.m.* toy; (*personne, fig.*) plaything; (*victime*) victim.

joueu|r, **~se** /ʒwœr, -øz/ *n.m., f.* player; (*parieur*) gambler.

joufflu /ʒufly/ *a.* chubby-cheeked; (*visage*) chubby.

joug /ʒu/ *n.m.* yoke.

jouir /ʒwir/ *v.i.* (*sexe*) come. **~ de**, enjoy.

jouissance /ʒwisɑ̃s/ *n.f.* pleasure; (*usage*) use (**de qch.**, of sth.).

joujou (*pl.* **~x**) /ʒuʒu/ *n.m.* (*fam.*) toy.

jour /ʒur/ *n.m.* day; (*opposé à nuit*) day(time); (*lumière*) daylight; (*aspect*) light; (*ouverture*) gap. **de nos ~s**, nowadays. **du ~ au lendemain**, overnight. **il fait ~**, it is (day)light. **~ chômé ou férié**, public holiday. **~ de fête**, holiday. **~ ouvrable**, (*vendre*) day. **~ de travail**, working day. **mettre à ~**, update. **mettre au ~**, uncover. **au grand ~**, in the open. **donner le ~**, give birth. **voir le ~**, be born. **vivre au ~ le jour**, live from day to day.

journ|al (*pl.* **~aux**) /ʒurnal, -o/ *n.m.* (news)paper; (*spécialisé*) journal; (*intime*) diary; (*radio*) news. **~al de bord**, log-book.

journal|ier, **~ière** /ʒurnalje, -jɛr/ *a.* daily.

journalis|te /ʒurnalist/ *n.m./f.* journalist. **~me** *n.m.* journalism.

journée /ʒurne/ *n.f.* day.

journellement /ʒurnɛlmã/ *adv.* daily.

jov|ial (*m. pl.* **~iaux**) /ʒɔvjal, -jo/ *a.* jovial.

joyau (*pl.* **~x**) /ʒwajo/ *n.m.* gem.

joyeu|x, **~se** /ʒwajø, -z/ *a.* merry, joyful. **~x anniversaire**, happy birthday. **~sement** *adv.* merrily.

jubilé /ʒybile/ *n.m.* jubilee.

jubil|er /ʒybile/ *v.i.* be jubilant. **~ation** *n.f.* jubilation.

jucher /ʒyʃe/ *v.t.*, **se** ~ *v. pr.* perch.

judaï|que /ʒydaik/ *a.* Jewish. **~sme** *n.m.* Judaism.

judas /ʒyda/ *n.m.* peep-hole.

judiciaire /ʒydisjɛr/ *a.* judicial.

judicieu|x, **~se** /ʒydisjø, -z/ *a.* judicious.

judo /ʒydo/ *n.m.* judo.

juge /ʒyʒ/ *n.m.* judge; (*arbitre*) referee. ~ **de paix**, Justice of the Peace. ~ **de touche**, linesman.

jugé (au) /(o)ʒyʒe/ *adv.* by guesswork.

jugement /ʒyʒmã/ *n.m.* judgement; (*criminel*) sentence.

jugeote /ʒyʒɔt/ *n.f.* (*fam.*) gumption, common sense.

juger /ʒyʒe/ *v.t./i.* judge; (*estimer*) consider (**que**, that). ~ **de**, judge.

juguler /ʒygyle/ *v.t.* stifle, check.

jui|f, **~ve** /ʒɥif, -v/ *a.* Jewish. **~n.m., f.** Jew, Jewess.

juillet /ʒɥijɛ/ *n.m.* July.

juin /ʒɥɛ̃/ *n.m.* June.

jules /ʒyl/ *n.m.* (*fam.*) guy.

jum|eau, **~elle** (*m. pl.* **~eaux**) /ʒymo, -ɛl/ *a. & n.m., f.* twin. **~elage** *n.m.* twinning. **~eler** *v.t.* (*villes*) twin.

jumelles /ʒymɛl/ *n.f. pl.* binoculars.

jument /ʒymã/ *n.f.* mare.

jungle /ʒœɡl/ *n.f.* jungle.

junior /ʒynjɔr/ *n.m./f. & a.* junior.

junte /ʒœt/ *n.f.* junta.

jupe /ʒyp/ *n.f.* skirt.

jupon /ʒypɔ̃/ *n.m.* slip, petticoat.

juré, **~e** /ʒyre/ *n.m., f.* juror. **—a.** sworn.

jurer /ʒyre/ *v.t.* swear (**que**, that). **—v.i.** (*pester*) swear; (*contraster*) clash (**avec**, with). ~ **de qch./de faire**, swear to sth./to do.

juridiction /ʒyridiksjɔ̃/ *n.f.* jurisdiction; (*tribunal*) court of law.

juridique /ʒyridik/ *a.* legal.

juriste /ʒyrist/ *n.m./f.* legal expert.

juron /ʒyrɔ̃/ *n.m.* swear-word.

jury /ʒyri/ *n.m.* jury.

jus /ʒy/ *n.m.* juice; (*de viande*) gravy. ~ **de fruit**, fruit juice.

jusque /ʒysk(ə)/ *prép.* **jusqu'à**, (up) to, as far as; (*temps*) until, till; (*limite*) up to; (*y compris*) even. **jusqu'à ce que**, until **jusqu'à présent**, until now. **jusqu'en**, until. **jusqu'ou?**, how far? ~ **dans**, ~ **sur**, as far as.

juste /ʒyst/ *a.* fair, just; (*légitime*) just; (*correct, exact*) right; (*vrai*) true; (*vêtement*) tight; (*quantité*) on the short side. **le** ~ **milieu**, the happy medium. **—adv.** rightly, correctly; (*chanter*) in tune; (*seulement, exactement*) just. **(un peu)** ~, (*calculer, mesurer*) a bit fine *ou* close. **au** ~, exactly. **c'était** ~, (*presque raté*) it was a close thing.

justement /ʒystəmã/ *adv.* just; (*avec justice ou justesse*) justly.

justesse /ʒystɛs/ *n.f.* accuracy. **de** ~, just, narrowly.

justice /ʒystis/ *n.f.* justice; (*autorités*) law; (*tribunal*) court.

justifi|er /ʒystifje/ *v.t.* justify. **—v.i.** ne pas, de, prove. **se ~ier** *v. pr.* justify o.s. **~iable** *a.* justifiable. **~ication** *n.f.* justification.

juteu|x, **~se** /ʒytø, -z/ *a.* juicy.

juvénile /ʒyvenil/ *a.* youthful.

juxtaposer /ʒykstapoze/ v.t. juxtapose.

kyste /kist/ n.m. cyst.

K

kaki /kaki/ a. invar. & n.m. khaki.

kaléidoscope /kaleidɔskɔp/ n.m. kaleidoscope.

kangourou /kãguru/ n.m. kangaroo.

karaté /karate/ n.m. karate.

kart /kart/ n.m. go-cart.

kascher /kaʃɛr/ a. invar. kosher.

képi /kepi/ n.m. kepi.

kermesse /kɛrmɛs/ n.f. fair; (de charité) fête.

kérosène /kerozɛn/ n.m. kerosene, aviation fuel.

kibboutz /kibuts/ n.m. kibbutz.

kidnapp|er /kidnape/ v.t. kidnap. **~eur, ~euse** n.m., f. kidnapper.

kilo /kilo/ n.m. kilo.

kilogramme /kilɔgram/ n.m. kilogram.

kilohertz /kilɔɛrts/ n.m. kilohertz.

kilom|ètre /kilɔmɛtr/ n.m. kilometre. **~étrage** n.m. (approx.) mileage.

kilowatt /kilɔwat/ n.m. kilowatt.

kinésithérapie /kineziterapi/ n.f. physiotherapy.

kiosque /kjɔsk/ n.m. kiosk. **~ à musique,** bandstand.

kit /kit/ n.m. **meubles en ~,** flat-pack furniture.

kiwi /kiwi/ n.m. kiwi (fruit, bird).

klaxon /klaksɔn/ n.m. (P.) (auto.) horn. **~ner** /-e/ v.i. sound one's horn.

knock-out /nɔkawt/ n.m. knock-out.

ko /kao/ n.m. (comput.) k.

K.O. /kao/ a. invar. (knocked) out.

k-way /kawe/ n.m. invar. (P.) cagoule.

L

l', la /l, la/ voir le.

là /la/ adv. there; (ici) here; (chez soi) in; (temps) then. **c'est là que,** this is where. **là où,** where. **là-bas** adv. over there. **là-dedans** adv. inside, in there. **là-dessous** adv. underneath, under there. **là-dessus** adv. on there. **là-haut** adv. up there; (à l'étage) upstairs.

-là /la/ adv. (après un nom précédé de ce, cette, etc.) **cet homme-là,** that man. **ces maisons-là,** those houses.

label /label/ n.m. (comm.) seal.

labeur /labœr/ n.m. toil.

labo /labo/ n.m. (fam.) lab.

laboratoire /labɔratwar/ n.m. laboratory.

laborieu|x, ~se /labɔrjø, -z/ a. laborious; (personne) industrious; (dur) heavy going. **classes/masses ~ses,** working classes/masses.

labour /labur/ n.m. ploughing; (Amer.) plowing. **~er** v.t./i. plough; (Amer.) plow; (déchirer) rip at. **~eur** n.m. ploughman; (Amer.) plowman.

labyrinthe /labirɛ̃t/ n.m. maze.

lac /lak/ n.m. lake.

lacer /lase/ v.t. lace up.

lacérer /lasere/ v.t. tear (up).

lacet /lasɛ/ n.m. (shoe-)lace; (de route) sharp bend, zigzag.

lâche /laʃ/ a. cowardly; (détendu) loose. —n.m./f. coward. **~ment** adv. in a cowardly way.

lâcher /laʃe/ v.t. let go of; (abandonner) give up; (laisser) leave; (libérer) release; (parole) utter; (desserrer) loosen. —v.i. give way. **~ prise,** let go.

lâcheté /laʃte/ n.f. cowardice.

laconique /lakɔnik/ a. laconic.

lacrymogène /lakrimɔʒɛn/ a. gaz ∼, tear gas. **grenade** ∼, tear gas grenade.

lacté /lakte/ a. milk.

lacune /lakyn/ n.f. gap.

ladite /ladit/ voir **ledit**.

lagune /lagyn/ n.f. lagoon.

laïc /laik/ n.m. layman.

laid, ∼**e** /lɛ, lɛd/ a. ugly; (action) vile. —**eur** /lɛdœr/ n.f. ugliness.

lain|**e** /lɛn/ n.f. wool. **de** ∼**e**, woollen. ∼**age** n.m. woollen garment.

laïque /laik/ a. secular; (habit, personne) lay. —n.m./f. layman, laywoman.

laisse /lɛs/ n.f. lead, leash.

laisser /lese/ v.t. leave. ∼ **qn. faire**, let s.o. do. ∼ **qch. à qn.**, let s.o. have sth, leave s.o. sth. ∼ **tomber**, drop. **se** ∼ **aller**, let o.s. go. ∼-**aller** n.m. invar. carelessness.

laissez-passer n.m. invar. pass.

lait /lɛ/ n.m. milk. **frère/sœur de** ∼, foster-brother/-sister. ∼**age** /letaʒ/ n.m. milk product. ∼**eux**, ∼**euse** /lɛtø, -z/ a. milky.

lait|**ier**, ∼**ière** /letje, lɛtjɛr/ a. dairy. —n.m., f. dairyman, dairywoman. —n.m. (livreur) milkman. ∼**erie** /lɛtri/ n.f. dairy.

laiton /lɛtɔ̃/ n.m. brass.

laitue /lety/ n.f. lettuce.

laïus /lajys/ n.m. (péj.) big speech.

lama /lama/ n.m. llama.

lambeau (pl. ∼**x**) /lɑ̃bo/ n.m. shred. **en** ∼**x**, in shreds.

lambris /lɑ̃bri/ n.m. panelling.

lame /lam/ n.f. blade; (lamelle) strip; (vague) wave. ∼ **de fond**, ground swell.

lamelle /lamɛl/ n.f. (thin) strip.

lamentable /lamɑ̃tabl/ a. deplorable.

lament|**er (se)** /(sə)lamɑ̃te/ v. pr. moan. ∼**ation(s)** n.f. (pl.) moaning.

laminé /lamine/ a. laminated.

lampadaire /lɑ̃padɛr/ n.m. standard lamp; (de rue) street lamp.

lampe /lɑ̃p/ n.f. lamp; (de radio) valve; (Amer.) vacuum tube. ∼ **(de poche)**, torch; (Amer.) flashlight. ∼ **de chevet**, bedside lamp.

lampion /lɑ̃pjɔ̃/ n.m. (Chinese) lantern.

lance /lɑ̃s/ n.f. spear; (de tournoi) lance; (tuyau) hose. ∼ **d'incendie**, fire hose.

lancée /lɑ̃se/ n.f. **continuer sur sa** ∼, keep going.

lanc|**er** /lɑ̃se/ v.t. throw; (avec force) hurl; (navire, idée, personne) launch; (émettre) give out; (regard) cast; (moteur) start. **se** ∼**er** v. pr. (sport) gain momentum; (se précipiter) rush. **se** ∼**er dans**, launch into. —n.m. throw; (action) throwing. ∼**ement** n.m. throwing; (de navire) launching. ∼**e-missiles** n.m. invar. missile launcher. ∼**e-pierres** n.m. invar. catapult.

lancinant, ∼**e** /lɑ̃sinɑ̃, -t/ a. haunting; (douleur) throbbing.

landau /lɑ̃do/ n.m. pram; (Amer.) baby carriage.

lande /lɑ̃d/ n.f. heath, moor.

langage /lɑ̃gaʒ/ n.m. language.

langoureu|**x**, ∼**se** /lɑ̃gurø, -z/ a. languid.

langoust|**e** /lɑ̃gust/ n.f. (spiny) lobster. ∼**ine** n.f. (Norway) lobster.

langue /lɑ̃g/ n.f. tongue; (idiome) language. **il m'a tiré la** ∼, he stuck his tongue out at me. **de** ∼ **anglaise/française**, English/French-speaking. ∼ **maternelle**, mother tongue.

languette /lɑ̃gɛt/ n.f. tongue.

langueur /lɑ̃gœr/ n.f. languor.

langu|**ir** /lɑ̃gir/ v.i. languish; (conversation) flag. **faire** ∼**ir qn.**, keep s.o. waiting. **se** ∼**ir de**, miss. ∼**issant**, ∼**issante** a. languid.

lanière /lanjɛr/ n.f. strap.

lanterne /lɑ̃tɛrn/ *n.f.* lantern; (*électrique*) lamp; (*de voiture*) sidelight.

laper /lape/ *v.t./i.* lap.

lapider /lapide/ *v.t.* stone.

lapin /lapɛ̃/ *n.m.* rabbit. **poser un ~ à qn.**, stand s.o. up.

laps /laps/ *n.m.* **~ de temps**, lapse of time.

lapsus /lapsys/ *n.m.* slip (of the tongue).

laquais /lakɛ/ *n.m.* lackey.

laqu|e /lak/ *n.f.* lacquer. **~er** *v.t.* lacquer.

laquelle /lakɛl/ *voir* **lequel**.

larcin /larsɛ̃/ *n.m.* theft.

lard /lar/ *n.m.* (pig's) fat; (*viande*) bacon.

large /larʒ/ *a.* wide, broad; (*grand*) large; (*non borné*) broad; (*généreux*) generous. —*adv.* (*mesurer*) broadly; (*voir*) big. —*n.m.* **de ~**, (*mesure*) wide. **le ~**, (*mer*) the open sea. **au ~ de**, (*en face de:naut.*) off. **~ d'esprit**, broad-minded. **~ment** /-əmɑ̃/ *adv.* widely; (*ouvrir*) wide; (*amplement*) amply; (*généreusement*) generously; (*au moins*) easily.

largesse /larʒɛs/ *n.f.* generosity.

largeur /larʒœr/ *n.f.* width, breadth; (*fig.*) breadth.

larguer /large/ *v.t.* drop. **~ les amarres**, cast off.

larme /larm/ *n.f.* tear; (*goutte: fam.*) drop.

larmoyant, **~e** /larmwajɑ̃, -t/ *a.* tearful.

larron /larɔ̃/ *n.m.* thief.

larve /larv/ *n.f.* larva.

larvé /larve/ *a.* latent.

laryngite /larɛ̃ʒit/ *n.f.* laryngitis.

larynx /larɛ̃ks/ *n.m.* larynx.

las, **~se** /lɑ, lɑs/ *a.* weary.

lasagnes /lazaɲ/ *n.f.pl.* lasagne.

lasci|f, **~ve** /lasif, -v/ *a.* lascivious.

laser /lazɛr/ *n.m.* laser.

lasse /lɑs/ *voir* **las**.

lasser /lase/ *v.t.* weary. **se ~** *v. pr.* weary (**de**, of).

lassitude /lasityd/ *n.f.* weariness.

lasso /laso/ *n.m.* lasso.

latent, **~e** /latɑ̃, -t/ *a.* latent.

latér|al (*m. pl.* **~aux**) /lateral, -o/ *a.* lateral.

latex /latɛks/ *n.m.* latex.

latin, **~e** /latɛ̃, -in/ *a. & n.m., f.* Latin. —*n.m.* (*lang.*) Latin.

latitude /latityd/ *n.f.* latitude.

latrines /latrin/ *n.f.pl.* latrine(s).

latte /lat/ *n.f.* lath; (*de plancher*) board.

lauréat, **~e** /lɔrea, -t/ *a.* prizewinning. —*n.m.,f.* prize-winner.

laurier /lorje/ *n.m.* laurel; (*culin.*) bay-leaves.

lavable /lavabl/ *a.* washable.

lavabo /lavabo/ *n.m.* wash-basin. **~s**, toilet(s).

lavage /lavaʒ/ *n.m.* washing. **~ de cerveau**, brainwashing.

lavande /lavɑ̃d/ *n.f.* lavender.

lave /lav/ *n.f.* lava.

lav|er /lave/ *v.t.* wash; (*injure etc.*) avenge. **se ~er** *v. pr.* wash (o.s.). **(se) ~er de**, clear (o.s.) of. **~e-glace** *n.m.* windscreen washer. **~eur de carreaux**, window-cleaner. **~e-vaisselle** *n.m.* invar. dishwasher.

laverie /lavri/ *n.f.* **~ (automatique)**, launderette; (*Amer.*) laundromat.

lavette /lavɛt/ *n.f.* dishcloth; (*péj.*) wimp.

lavoir /lavwar/ *n.m.* wash-house.

laxati|f, **~ve** /laksatif, -v/ *a. & n.m.* laxative.

laxisme /laksism/ *n.m.* laxity.

layette /lɛjɛt/ *n.f.* baby clothes.

le ou **l'***, **la** ou **l'*** (*pl.* **les**) /lə, l/, /la, le/ *article* the; (*mesure*) a, per. —*pron.* (*homme*) him; (*femme*) her; (*chose, animal*) it. **les** *pron.* them. **aimer le thé/la France**, like tea/France. **le**

matin, in the morning. **il sort le mardi**, he goes out on Tuesdays. **levez le bras**, raise your arm. **je le connais**, I know him. **je le sais**, I know (it).

lécher /leʃe/ v.t. lick.

lèche-vitrines /lɛʃvitrin/ n.m. **faire du ~**, go window-shopping.

leçon /ləsɔ̃/ n.f. lesson. **faire la ~ à**, lecture.

lec|teur, ~trice /lɛktœr, -tris/ n.m., f. reader; (univ.) foreign language assistant. **~teur de cassettes**, cassette player. **~teur de disquettes**, (disk) drive.

lecture /lɛktyr/ n.f. reading.

ledit, ladite (pl. **lesdit(e)s**) /lədi, ladit, ledi(t)/ a. the aforesaid.

lég|al (m. pl. **~aux**) /legal, -o/ a. legal. **~alement** adv. legally. **~aliser** v.t. legalize. **~alité** n.f. legality; (loi) law.

légation /legasjɔ̃/ n.f. legation.

légend|e /leʒɑ̃d/ n.f. (histoire, inscription) legend. **~aire** a. legendary.

lég|er, ~ère /leʒe, -ɛr/ a. light; (bruit, faute, maladie) slight; (café, argument) weak; (imprudent) thoughtless; (frivole) fickle. **à la ~ère**, thoughtlessly. **~èrement** /-ɛrmɑ̃/ adv. lightly; (agir) thoughtlessly; (un peu) slightly. **~èreté** /-ɛrte/ n.f. lightness; thoughtlessness.

légion /leʒjɔ̃/ n.f. legion. **une ~ de**, a crowd of. **~naire** /-jɔnɛr/ n.m. (mil.) legionnaire.

législati|f, ~ve /leʒislatif, -v/ a. legislative.

législation /leʒislasjɔ̃/ n.f. legislation.

legislature /leʒislatyr/ n.f. term of office.

légitim|e /leʒitim/ a. legitimate. **en état de ~e défense**, acting in self-defence. **~ité** n.f. legitimacy.

legs /lɛg/ n.m. legacy.

léguer /lege/ v.t. bequeath.

légume /legym/ n.m. vegetable.

lendemain /lɑ̃dmɛ̃/ n.m. **le ~**, the next day, the day after; (fig.) the future. **le ~ de**, the day after. **le ~ matin/soir**, the next morning/evening.

lent, ~e /lɑ̃, lɑ̃t/ a. slow. **~ement** /lɑ̃tmɑ̃/ adv. slowly. **~eur** /lɑ̃tœr/ n.f. slowness.

lentille¹ /lɑ̃tij/ n.f. (plante) lentil.

lentille² /lɑ̃tij/ n.f. (verre) lens; **~s de contact**, (contact) lenses.

léopard /leɔpar/ n.m. leopard.

lèpre /lɛpr/ n.f. leprosy.

lequel, laquelle (pl. **lesquel(le)s**) /ləkɛl, lakɛl, lekɛl/ pron. (à + lequel = auquel, à + lesquel(le)s = auxquel(le)s, de + lequel = duquel, de + lesquel(le)s = desquel(le)s) which (one); (personne) who; (complément indirect) whom.

les /le/ voir **le**.

lesbienne /lɛsbjɛn/ n.f. lesbian.

léser /leze/ v.t. wrong.

lésiner /lezine/ v.i. **ne pas ~ sur**, not stint on.

lésion /lezjɔ̃/ n.f. lesion.

lesquels, lesquelles /lekɛl/ voir **lequel**.

lessive /lesiv/ n.f. washing-powder; (linge, action) washing.

lest /lɛst/ n.m. ballast. **jeter du ~**, (fig.) climb down. **~er** v.t. ballast.

leste /lɛst/ a. nimble; (grivois) coarse.

léthargie /letarʒi/ n.f. lethargy. **~ique** a. lethargic.

lettre /lɛtr/ n.f. letter. **à la ~**, literally. **en toutes ~s**, in full. **~ exprès**, express letter. **les ~s**, (univ.) (the) arts.

lettré /letre/ a. well-read.

leucémie /løsemi/ n.f. leukaemia.

leur /lœr/ a. (f. invar.) their. **—pron.** (to) them. **le ~, la ~, les ~s**, theirs.

leurr|e /lœr/ *n.m.* illusion; (*duperie*) deception. **~er** *v.t.* delude.

levain /ləvɛ̃/ *n.m.* leaven.

levé /ləve/ *a.* (*debout*) up.

levée /ləve/ *n.f.* lifting; (*de courrier*) collection; (*de troupes, d'impôts*) levying.

lever /ləve/ *v.t.* lift (up); raise; (*interdiction*) lift; (*séance*) close; (*armée, impôts*) levy. —*v.i.* (*pâte*) rise. **se ~** *v. pr.* get up; (*soleil, rideau*) rise; (*jour*) break. —*n.m.* **au ~**, on getting up. **~ du jour**, daybreak. **~ du rideau**, (*théâtre*) curtain (up). **~ du soleil**, sunrise.

levier /ləvje/ *n.m.* lever.

lèvre /lɛvr/ *n.f.* lip.

lévrier /levrije/ *n.m.* greyhound.

levure /ləvyr/ *n.f.* yeast. **~ alsacienne** *ou* **chimique**, baking powder.

lexicographie /lɛksikɔgrafi/ *n.f.* lexicography.

lexique /lɛksik/ *n.m.* vocabulary; (*glossaire*) lexicon.

lézard /lezar/ *n.m.* lizard.

lézard|e /lezard/ *n.f.* crack. **se ~er** *v. pr.* crack.

liaison /ljɛzɔ̃/ *n.f.* connection; (*transport*) link; (*contact*) contact; (*gram., mil.*) liaison; (*amoureuse*) affair.

liane /ljan/ *n.f.* creeper.

liasse /ljas/ *n.f.* bundle, wad.

Liban /libã/ *n.m.* Lebanon.

libanais, ~e /libanɛ, -z/ *a. & n.m., f.* Lebanese.

libell|er /libele/ *v.t.* (*chèque*) write; (*lettre*) draw up. **~é à l'ordre de**, made out to.

libellule /libelyl/ *n.f.* dragonfly.

libér|al (*m. pl.* **~aux**) /liberal, -o/ *a.* liberal. **les professions ~ales** the professions. **~alement** *adv.* liberally. **~alisme** *n.m.* liberalism. **~alité** *n.f.* liberality.

libér|er /libere/ *v.t.* (*personne*) free, release; (*pays*) liberate, free. **se ~er** *v. pr.* free o.s. **~ateur, ~atrice** *a.* liberating; *n.m., f.* liberator. **~ation** *n.f.* release; (*de pays*) liberation.

liberté /liberte/ *n.f.* freedom, liberty; (*loisir*) free time. **en ~ provisoire**, on bail. **être/mettre en ~**, be/set free.

libertin, -in /libertɛ̃, -in/ *a. & n.m., f.* libertine.

librair|e /librer/ *n.m./f.* bookseller. **~ie** /-eri/ *n.f.* bookshop.

libre /libr/ *a.* free; (*place, pièce*) vacant, free; (*passage*) clear; (*école*) private (*usually religious*). **~ de qch./de faire**, free from sth./to do. **~-échange** *n.m.* free trade. **~ment** /-əmã/ *adv.* freely. **~-service** (*pl.* **~s-services**) *n.m.* self-service.

Libye /libi/ *n.f.* Libya.

libyen, ~ne /libjɛ̃, -jɛn/ *a. & n.m., f.* Libyan.

licence /lisãs/ *n.f.* licence; (*univ.*) degree.

licencié, ~e /lisãsje/ *n.m., f.* **~ ès lettres/sciences**, Bachelor of Arts/Science.

licenc|ier /lisãsje/ *v.t.* make redundant, (*pour faute*) dismiss. **~iements** *n.m. pl.* redundancies.

licencieu|x, ~se /lisãsjø, -z/ *a.* licentious, lascivious.

lichen /likɛn/ *n.m.* lichen.

licite /lisit/ *a.* lawful.

licorne /likɔrn/ *n.f.* unicorn.

lie /li/ *n.f.* dregs.

liège /ljɛʒ/ *n.m.* cork.

lien /ljɛ̃/ *n.m.* (*rapport*) link; (*attache*) bond, tie; (*corde*) rope.

lier /lje/ *v.t.* tie (up), bind; (*relier*) link; (*engager, unir*) bind. **~ conversation**, strike up a conversation. **se ~ avec**, make friends with. **ils sont très liés**, they are very close.

lierre /ljɛr/ *n.m.* ivy.

lieu (pl. ∼x) /ljø/ n.m. place. ∼x, (locaux) premises; (d'un accident) scene. **au** ∼ **de**, instead of. **avoir** ∼, take place. **tenir** ∼ **de**, serve as. **en premier** ∼, firstly. **en dernier** ∼, lastly. ∼ **commun**, commonplace.

lieutenant /ljøtnā/ n.m. lieutenant.

lièvre /ljɛvr/ n.m. hare.

ligament /ligamā/ n.m. ligament.

ligne /liɲ/ n.f. line; (trajet) route; (formes) lines; (de femme) figure. **en** ∼, (joueurs etc.) lined up; (personne au téléphone) on the phone.

lignée /liɲe/ n.f. ancestry, line.

ligoter /ligɔte/ v.t. tie up.

ligue /lig/ n.f. league. **se** ∼**er** v. pr. form a league (contre, against).

lilas /lila/ n.m. & a. invar. lilac.

limace /limas/ n.f. slug.

limande /limɑ̃d/ n.f. (poisson) dab.

lime /lim/ n.f. file. ∼ **à ongles**, nail file. ∼**er** v.t. file.

limier /limje/ n.m. bloodhound; (policier) sleuth.

limitation /limitasjɔ̃/ n.f. limitation. ∼ **de vitesse**, speed limit.

limite /limit/ n.f. limit; (de jardin, champ) boundary. —a. (vitesse, âge) maximum. **cas** ∼**e**, borderline case. **date** ∼**e**, deadline. ∼**er** v.t. limit; (délimiter) form the border of.

limoger /limɔʒe/ v.t. dismiss.

limon /limɔ̃/ n.m. stilt.

limonade /limɔnad/ n.f. lemonade.

limpid|e /lɛ̃pid/ a. limpid, clear. ∼**ité** n.f. clearness.

lin /lɛ̃/ n.m. (tissu) linen.

linceul /lɛ̃sœl/ n.m. shroud.

linéaire /lineɛr/ a. linear.

linge /lɛ̃ʒ/ n.m. linen; (lessive) washing; (torchon) cloth. ∼ **(de corps)**, underwear. ∼**rie** n.f. underwear.

lingot /lɛ̃go/ n.m. ingot.

linguiste /lɛ̃gɥist/ n.m./f. linguist.

linguistique /lɛ̃gɥistik/ a. linguistic. —n.f. linguistics.

lino /lino/ n.m. lino.

linoléum /linɔleɔm/ n.m. linoleum.

lion, ∼**ne** /ljɔ̃, ljɔn/ n.m., f. lion, lioness. **le L**∼, Leo.

lionceau (pl. ∼x) /ljɔ̃so/ n.m. lion cub.

liquéfier /likefje/ v.t., **se** ∼ v. pr. liquefy.

liqueur /likœr/ n.f. liqueur.

liquide /likid/ a. & n.m. liquid. (argent) ∼, ready money. **payer en** ∼, pay cash.

liquid|er /likide/ v.t. liquidate; (vendre) sell. ∼**ation** n.f. liquidation; (vente) (clearance) sale.

lire[1] /lir/ v.t./i. read.

lire[2] /lir/ n.f. lira.

lis[1] /li/ voir **lire**[1].

lis[2] /lis/ n.m. (fleur) lily.

lisible /lizibl/ a. legible; (roman etc.) readable.

lisière /lizjɛr/ n.f. edge.

liss|e /lis/ a. smooth. ∼**er** v.t. smooth.

liste /list/ n.f. list. ∼ **électorale**, register of voters.

listing /listiŋ/ n.m. printout.

lit[1] /li/ voir **lire**[1].

lit[2] /li/ n.m. (de personne, fleuve) bed. **se mettre au** ∼, get into bed. ∼ **de camp**, camp-bed. ∼ **d'enfant**, cot. ∼ **d'une personne**, single bed.

litanie /litani/ n.f. litany.

litchi /litʃi/ n.m. litchi.

literie /litri/ n.f. bedding.

litière /litjɛr/ n.f. (paille) litter.

litige /litiʒ/ n.m. dispute.

litre /litr/ n.m. litre.

littéraire /literɛr/ a. literary.

littér|al (m. pl. ∼**aux**) /literal, -o/ a. literal. ∼**alement** adv. literally.

littérature /literatyr/ n.f. literature.

littor|al (pl. ~aux) /litɔral, -o/ n.m. coast.

liturg|ie /lityrʒi/ n.f. liturgy. ~ique a. liturgical.

livide /livid/ a. (blême) pallid.

livraison /livrɛzɔ̃/ n.f. delivery.

livre[1] /livr/ n.m. book. ~ de bord, log-book. ~ de compte, books. ~ de poche, paperback.

livre[2] /livr/ n.f. (monnaie, poids) pound.

livrée /livre/ n.f. livery.

livr|er /livre/ v.t. deliver; (abandonner) give over (à, to); (secret) give away. ~é à soi-même, left to o.s. se ~er à, give o.s. over to; (actes, boisson) indulge in; (se confier à) confide in; (effectuer) carry out.

livret /livrɛ/ n.m. book; (mus.) libretto. ~ scolaire, school report (book).

livreu|r, ~se /livrœr, -øz/ n.m., f. delivery boy ou girl.

lobe /lɔb/ n.m. lobe.

loc|al[1] (m. pl. ~aux) /lɔkal, -o/ a. local. ~alement adv. locally.

loc|al[2] (pl. ~aux) /lɔkal, -o/ n.m. premises. ~aux, premises.

localisé /lɔkalize/ a. localized.

localité /lɔkalite/ n.f. locality.

locataire /lɔkatɛr/ n.m./f. tenant; (de chambre, d'hôtel) lodger.

location /lɔkasjɔ̃/ n.f. (de maison) renting; (de voiture) renting; (de place) booking, reservation; (guichet) booking office; (théâtre) box office; (par propriétaire) renting out; hiring out. en ~, (voiture) on hire, rented.

lock-out /lɔkawt/ n.m. invar. lock-out.

locomotion /lɔkɔmosjɔ̃/ n.f. locomotion.

locomotive /lɔkɔmɔtiv/ n.f. engine, locomotive.

locution /lɔkysjɔ̃/ n.f. phrase.

logarithme /lɔgaritm/ n.m. logarithm.

loge /lɔʒ/ n.f. (de concierge) lodge; (d'acteur) dressing-room; (de spectateur) box.

logement /lɔʒmã/ n.m. accommodation; (appartement) flat; (habitat) housing.

log|er /lɔʒe/ v.t. accommodate. —v.i., se ~er v. pr. live. trouver à se ~er, find accommodation. être ~é, live. se ~er dans, (balle) lodge itself in.

logeu|r, ~se /lɔʒœr, -øz/ n.m., f. landlord, landlady.

logiciel /lɔʒisjɛl/ n.m. software.

logique /lɔʒik/ a. logical. —n.f. logic. ~ment adv. logically.

logis /lɔʒi/ n.m. dwelling.

logistique /lɔʒistik/ n.f. logistics.

logo /lɔgo/ n.m. logo.

loi /lwa/ n.f. law.

loin /lwɛ̃/ adv. far (away). au ~, far away. de ~, from far away; (de beaucoup) by far. ~ de là, far from it. plus ~, further. il revient de ~, (fig.) he had a close shave.

lointain, ~e /lwɛ̃tɛ̃, -ɛn/ a. distant. —n.m. distance.

loir /lwar/ n.m. dormouse.

loisir /lwazir/ n.m. (spare) time. ~s, spare time; (distractions) spare time activities. à ~, at one's leisure.

londonien, ~ne /lɔ̃dɔnjɛ̃, -jɛn/ a. London. —n.m., f. Londoner.

Londres /lɔ̃dr/ n.m./f. London.

long, ~ue /lɔ̃, lɔ̃g/ a. long. —n.m. de ~, (mesure) long. à la ~ue, in the end. à ~ terme, long-term. de ~ en large, back and forth. à ~ faire, a long time doing. (tout) le ~ de, (all) along.

longer /lɔ̃ʒe/ v.t. go along; (limiter) border.

longévité /lɔ̃ʒevite/ n.f. longevity.

longiligne /lɔ̃ʒiliɲ/ a. tall and slender.

longitude /lɔ̃ʒityd/ n.f. longitude.

longtemps /lɔ̃tɑ̃/ adv. a long time. **avant ∼**, before long. **trop ∼**, too long. **ça prendra ∼**, it will take a long time.

longue /lɔ̃g/ voir **long**.

longuement /lɔ̃gmɑ̃/ adv. at length.

longueur /lɔ̃gœr/ n.f. length. **∼s**, (de texte etc.) over-long parts. **à ∼ de journée**, all day long. **∼ d'onde**, wavelength.

longue-vue /lɔ̃gvy/ n.f. telescope.

look /luk/ n.m. (fam.) look, image.

lopin /lɔpɛ̃/ n.m. **∼ de terre**, patch of land.

loquace /lɔkas/ a. talkative.

loque /lɔk/ n.f. **∼s**, rags. **∼ (humaine)**, (human) wreck.

loquet /lɔkɛ/ n.m. latch.

lorgner /lɔrɲe/ v.t. eye.

lors de /lɔrdə/ prép. at the time of.

lorsque /lɔrsk(ə)/ conj. when.

losange /lɔzɑ̃ʒ/ n.m. diamond.

lot /lo/ n.m. prize; (portion, destin) lot.

loterie /lɔtri/ n.f. lottery.

lotion /losjɔ̃/ n.f. lotion.

lotissement /lɔtismɑ̃/ n.m. (à construire) building plot; (construit) (housing) development.

louable /lwabl/ a. praiseworthy.

louange /lwɑ̃ʒ/ n.f. praise.

louche[1] /luʃ/ a. shady, dubious.

louche[2] /luʃ/ n.f. ladle.

loucher /luʃe/ v.i. squint.

louer[1] /lwe/ v.t. (maison) rent; (voiture) hire, rent; (place) book, reserve; (propriétaire) rent out; hire out. **à ∼**, to let, for rent (Amer.).

louer[2] /lwe/ v.t. (approuver) praise (de, for). **se ∼ de**, congratulate o.s. on.

loufoque /lufɔk/ a. (fam.) crazy.

loup /lu/ n.m. wolf.

loupe /lup/ n.f. magnifying glass.

louper /lupe/ v.t. (fam.) miss.

lourd /lur/, **∼e** /lur, -d/ a. heavy; (chaleur) close; (faute) gross. **∼**

de conséquences, with dire consequences. **∼ement** /-dəmɑ̃/ adv. heavily. **∼eur** /-dœr/ n.f. heaviness.

lourdaud /lurdo/, **∼e** /lurdo, -d/ a. loutish. —n.m., f. lout, oaf.

loutre /lutr/ n.f. otter.

louve /luv/ n.f. she-wolf.

louveteau (pl. **∼x**) /luvto/ n.m. wolf cub; (scout) Cub (Scout).

louvoyer /luvwaje/ v.i. (fig.) sidestep the issue; (naut.) tack.

loyal (m. pl. **∼aux**) /lwajal, -o/ a. loyal; (honnête) fair. **∼alement** adv. loyally; fairly. **∼auté** n.f. loyalty; fairness.

loyer /lwaje/ n.m. rent.

lu /ly/ voir **lire**[1].

lubie /lybi/ n.f. whim.

lubrifier /lybrifje/ v.t. lubricate. **∼iant** n.m. lubricant.

lubrique /lybrik/ a. lewd.

lucarne /lykarn/ n.f. skylight.

lucide /lysid/ a. lucid. **∼ité** n.f. lucidity.

lucratif, **∼ve** /lykratif, -v/ a. lucrative. **à but non ∼f**, non-profit-making.

lueur /lɥœr/ n.f. (faint) light, glimmer; (fig.) glimmer, gleam.

luge /lyʒ/ n.f. toboggan.

lugubre /lygybr/ a. gloomy.

lui /lɥi/ pron. him; (sujet) he; (chose) it; (objet indirect) (to) him; (femme) (to) her; (chose) (to) it. **∼-même** pron. himself; itself.

luire† /lɥir/ v.i. shine; (reflet humide) glisten; (reflet chaud, faible) glow.

lumbago /lɔ̃bago/ n.m. lumbago.

lumière /lymjɛr/ n.f. light. **∼s**, (connaissances) knowledge. **faire (toute) la ∼ sur**, clear up.

luminaire /lyminɛr/ n.m. lamp.

lumineu|x, **∼se** /lyminø, -z/ a. luminous; (éclairé) illuminated; (source, rayon) (of) light; (vif) bright.

lunaire /lynɛr/ a. lunar.

lunatique /lynatik/ *a.* temperamental.

lunch /lœntʃ/ *n.m.* buffet lunch.

lundi /lœdi/ *n.m.* Monday.

lune /lyn/ *n.f.* moon. ～ **de miel,** honeymoon.

lunette /lynɛt/ *n.f.* ～s, glasses; (*de protection*) goggles. ～ **arrière,** (*auto.*) rear window. ～s **de soleil,** sun-glasses.

luron /lyrɔ̃/ *n.m.* gai *ou* joyeux ～, (*fam.*) quite a lad.

lustre /lystr/ *n.m.* (*éclat*) lustre; (*objet*) chandelier.

lustré /lystre/ *a.* shiny.

luth /lyt/ *n.m.* lute.

lutin /lytɛ̃/ *n.m.* goblin.

lutrin /lytrɛ̃/ *n.m.* lectern.

lutt|e /lyt/ *n.f.* fight; struggle; (*sport*) wrestling. ～**er** *v.i.* fight, struggle; (*sport*) wrestle. ～**eur,** ～**euse** *n.m., f.* fighter; (*sport*) wrestler.

luxe /lyks/ *n.m.* luxury. **de ～,** luxury; (*produit*) de luxe.

Luxembourg /lyksɑ̃bur/ *n.m.* Luxemburg.

lux|er /lykse/ *v.t.* **se ～er le genou,** dislocate one's knee. ～**ation** *n.f.* dislocation.

luxueu|x, ～**se** /lyksɥø, -z/ *a.* luxurious.

luxure /lyksyr/ *n.f.* lust.

luxuriant, ～**e** /lyksyrjɑ̃, -t/ *a.* luxuriant.

luzerne /lyzɛrn/ *n.f.* (*plante*) lucerne, alfalfa.

lycée /lise/ *n.m.* (secondary) school. ～**n,** ～**nne** /-ɛ̃, -ɛn/ *n.m., f.* pupil (at secondary school).

lynch|er /lɛ̃ʃe/ *v.t.* lynch. ～**age** *n.m.* lynching.

lynx /lɛ̃ks/ *n.m.* lynx.

lyophilis|er /ljɔfilize/ *v.t.* freeze-dry. ～**é** *a.* freeze-dried.

lyre /lir/ *n.f.* lyre.

lyri|que /lirik/ *a.* (*poésie*) lyric; (*passionné*) lyrical. **artiste**/

théâtre ～**que,** opera singer/-house. ～**sme** *n.m.* lyricism.

lys /lis/ *n.m.* lily.

M

m' /m/ *voir* me.

ma /ma/ *voir* mon.

maboul /mabul/ *a.* (*fam.*) mad.

macabre /makabr/ *a.* gruesome, macabre.

macadam /makadam/ *n.m.* (*goudronné*) Tarmac (P.).

macaron /makarɔ̃/ *n.m.* (*gâteau*) macaroon; (*insigne*) badge.

macaronis /makarɔni/ *n.m. pl.* macaroni.

macédoine /masedwan/ *n.f.* mixed vegetables. ～ **de fruits,** fruit salad.

macérer /masere/ *v.t./i.* soak; (*dans du vinaigre*) pickle.

mâchefer /maʃfɛr/ *n.m.* clinker.

mâcher /maʃe/ *v.t.* chew. **ne pas ～ ses mots,** not mince one's words.

machiavélique /makjavelik/ *a.* machiavellian.

machin /maʃɛ̃/ *n.m.* (*chose: fam.*) thing; (*personne: fam.*) what's-his-name.

machin|al (*m. pl.* ～**aux**) /maʃinal, -o/ *a.* automatic. ～**alement** *adv.* automatically.

machinations /maʃinasjɔ̃/ *n.f. pl.* machinations.

machine /maʃin/ *n.f.* machine; (*d'un train, navire*) engine. ～ **à écrire,** typewriter. ～ **à laver/coudre,** washing-/sewing-machine. ～ **à sous,** fruit machine; (*Amer.*) slot-machine. ～**-outil** (*pl.* ～**s-outils**) *n.f.* machine tool. ～**rie** *n.f.* machinery.

machiner /maʃine/ *v.t.* plot.

machiniste /maʃinist/ n.m. (théâtre) stage-hand; (conducteur) driver.

macho /ma(t)ʃo/ n.m. (fam.) macho.

mâchoire /maʃwar/ n.f. jaw.

mâchonner /maʃone/ v.t. chew at.

maçon /masɔ̃/ n.m. builder; (poseur de briques) bricklayer. **~nerie** /-ɔnri/ n.f. brickwork; (pierres) stonework, masonry.

maçonnique /masɔnik/ a. Masonic.

macrobiotique /makrɔbjɔtik/ a. macrobiotic.

maculer /makyle/ v.t. stain.

Madagascar /madagaskar/ n.f. Madagascar.

madame (pl. **mesdames**)/ madam, medam/ n.f. madam. **M~** ou **Mme Dupont**, Mrs Dupont. **bonsoir, mesdames**, good evening, ladies.

madeleine /madlɛn/ n.f. madeleine (small shell-shaped sponge-cake).

mademoiselle (pl. **mesdemoiselles**) /madmwazɛl, medmwazɛl/ n.f. miss. **M~** ou **Mlle Dupont**, Miss Dupont. **bonsoir, mesdemoiselles**, good evening, ladies.

madère /madɛr/ n.m. (vin) Madeira.

madone /madɔn/ n.f. madonna.

madrig|al (pl. **~aux**) /madrigal, -o/ n.m. madrigal.

maestro /maɛstro/ n.m. maestro.

maf(f)ia /mafja/ n.f. Mafia.

magasin /magazɛ̃/ n.m. shop, store; (entrepôt) warehouse; (d'une arme etc.) magazine.

magazine /magazin/ n.m. magazine; (émission) programme.

Maghreb /magrɛb/ n.m. North Africa. **~in, ~ine** a. & n.m., f. North African.

magicien, ~ne /maʒisjɛ̃, -jɛn/ n.m., f. magician.

magie /maʒi/ n.f. magic.

magique /maʒik/ a. magic; (mystérieux) magical.

magistr|al (m. pl. **~aux**) /maʒistral, -o/ a. masterly; (grand: hum.) colossal. **~alement** adv. in a masterly fashion.

magistrat /maʒistra/ n.m. magistrate.

magistrature /maʒistratyr/ n.f. judiciary.

magnanim|e /maɲanim/ a. magnanimous. **~ité** n.f. magnanimity.

magnat /magna/ n.m. tycoon, magnate.

magner (se) /(sə)maɲe/ v. pr. (argot) hurry.

magnésie /maɲezi/ n.f. magnesia.

magnéti|que /maɲetik/ a. magnetic. **~ser** v.t. magnetize. **~sme** n.m. magnetism.

magnétophone /maɲetɔfɔn/ n.m. tape recorder. **~ à cassettes**, cassette recorder.

magnétoscope /maɲetɔskɔp/ n.m. video-recorder.

magnifi|que /maɲifik/ a. magnificent. **~cence** n.f. magnificence.

magnolia /maɲɔlja/ n.m. magnolia.

magot /mago/ n.m. (fam.) hoard (of money).

magouill|er /maguje/ v.i. (fam.) scheming. **~eur, ~euse** n.m., f. (fam.) schemer. **~e** n.f. (fam.) scheming.

magret /magrɛ/ n.m. **~ de canard**, steaklet of duck.

mai /mɛ/ n.m. May.

maigr|e /mɛgr/ a. thin; (viande) lean; (yaourt) low-fat; (fig.) poor, meagre. **faire ~e**, abstain from meat. **~ement** adv. poorly. **~eur** n.f. thinness; leanness; (fig.) meagreness.

maigrir /megrir/ v.i. get thin(ner);

(en suivant un régime) slim. —*v.t.* make thin(ner).

maille /maj/ *n.f.* stitch; *(de filet)* mesh. ~ **filée,** ladder, run.

maillet /majɛ/ *n.m.* mallet.

maillon /majɔ̃/ *n.m.* link.

maillot /majo/ *n.m. (de sport)* jersey. ~ **(de corps),** vest. ~ **(de bain),** (swimming) costume.

main /mɛ̃/ *n.f.* hand. **avoir la ~ heureuse,** be lucky. **donner la ~ à qn.,** hold s.o.'s hand. **en ~s propres,** in person. **en bonnes ~,** in good hands. **~ courante,** handrail. **~-d'œuvre** *(pl.* ~**s-d'œuvre)** *n.f.* labour; *(ensemble d'ouvriers)* labour force. **~-forte** *n.f. invar.* assistance. **se faire la ~,** get the hang of it. **perdre la ~,** lose one's touch. **sous la ~,** to hand. **vol/attaque à ~ armée,** armed robbery/attack.

mainmise /mɛ̃miz/ *n.f.* ~ **sur,** complete hold on.

maint, ~**e** /mɛ̃, mɛ̃t/ *a.* many a. ~**s,** many. **à ~es reprises,** on many occasions.

maintenant† /mɛ̃tnɑ̃/ *adv.* now; *(de nos jours)* nowadays.

maintenir† /mɛ̃tnir/ *v.t.* keep, maintain; *(soutenir)* hold up; *(affirmer)* maintain. **se ~** *v. pr. (continuer)* persist; *(rester)* remain.

maintien /mɛ̃tjɛ̃/ *n.m. (attitude)* bearing; *(conservation)* maintenance.

maire /mɛr/ *n.m.* mayor.

mairie /meri/ *n.f.* town hall; *(administration)* town council.

mais /mɛ/ *conj.* but. ~ **oui,** ~ **si,** of course. ~ **non,** definitely not.

maïs /mais/ *n.m. (à cultiver)* maize; *(culin.)* sweet corn; *(Amer.)* corn.

maison /mɛzɔ̃/ *n.f.* house; *(foyer)* home; *(immeuble)* building. ~ **(de commerce),** firm. —*a. invar. (culin.)* home-made. **à la ~,** at home. **rentrer** *ou* **aller à la ~,**

go home. ~ **des jeunes,** youth centre. ~ **de repos,** ~ **de convalescence,** convalescent home. ~ **de retraite,** old people's home. ~ **mère,** parent company.

maisonnée /mɛzɔne/ *n.f.* household.

maisonnette /mɛzɔnɛt/ *n.f.* small house, cottage.

maître /mɛtr/ *n.m.* master. ~ **(d'école),** schoolmaster. ~ **de,** in control of. **se rendre ~ de,** gain control of; *(incendie)* bring under control. ~ **assistant/de conférences,** junior/senior lecturer. ~ **chanteur,** blackmailer. ~ **d'hôtel,** head waiter; *(domestique)* butler. ~ **nageur,** swimming instructor.

maîtresse /mɛtrɛs/ *n.f.* mistress. ~ **(d'école),** schoolmistress. —*a.f. (idée, poutre, qualité)* main. ~ **de,** in control of.

maîtrise /metriz/ *n.f.* mastery; *(univ.)* master's degree. ~**e (de soi),** self-control. ~**er** *v.t.* master; *(incendie)* control; *(personne)* subdue. **se ~er** *v. pr.* control o.s.

maïzena /maizena/ *n.f.* (P.) cornflour.

majesté /maʒɛste/ *n.f.* majesty.

majestueu|x, ~**se** /maʒɛstɥø, -z/ *a.* majestic. ~**sement** *adv.* majestically.

majeur /maʒœr/ *a.* major; *(jurid.)* of age. —*n.m.* middle finger. **en ~e partie,** mostly. **la ~e partie de,** most of.

major|er /maʒɔre/ *v.t.* increase. ~**ation** *n.f.* increase (de, in).

majorit|é /maʒɔrite/ *n.f.* majority. **en ~é,** chiefly. ~**aire** *a.* majority. **être ~aire,** be in the majority.

Majorque /maʒɔrk/ *n.f.* Majorca.

majuscule /maʒyskyl/ *a.* capital. —*n.f.* capital letter.

mal¹ /mal/ *adv.* badly; *(incorrectement)* wrong(ly). ~ **(à l'aise),**

uncomfortable. aller ~, (*malade*) be bad. c'est ~ de, it is wrong *ou* bad to. ~ entendre/comprendre, not hear/understand properly. ~ famé, of ill repute. ~ fichu, (*personne: fam.*) feeling lousy. ~ en point, in a bad state. pas ~, not bad; quite a lot.

mal² (*pl. maux*) /mal, mo/ *n.m.* evil; (*douleur*) pain, ache; (*maladie*) disease; (*effort*) trouble; (*dommage*) harm; (*malheur*) misfortune. avoir ~ à la tête/aux dents/à la gorge, have a headache/a toothache/a sore throat. avoir le ~ de mer/du pays, be seasick/homesick. faire du ~ à, hurt, harm. se donner du ~ pour faire qch., go to a lot of trouble to do sth.

malade /malad/ *a.* sick, ill; (*bras, gorge*) bad; (*plante*) diseased. tu es complètement ~l, (*fam.*) you're mad. —*n.m./f.* sick person; (*d'un médecin*) patient.

maladie /maladi/ *n.f.* illness, disease.

maladi|f, ~ve /maladif, -v/ *a.* sickly; (*peur*) morbid.

maladresse /maladres/ *n.f.* clumsiness; (*erreur*) blunder.

maladroit, ~e /maladrwa, -t/*a.* & *n.m., f.* clumsy (person).

malais, ~e¹ /malɛ, -z/ *a.* & *n.m., f.* Malay.

malaise² /malɛz/ *n.m.* feeling of faintness *ou* dizziness; (*fig.*) uneasiness, malaise.

malaisé /malɛze/ *a.* difficult.

malaria /malarja/ *n.f.* malaria.

Malaysia /malɛzja/ *n.f.* Malaysia.

malaxer /malakse/ *v.t.* (*pétrir*) knead; (*mêler*) mix.

malchanc|e /malʃɑ̃s/ *n.f.* misfortune. ~eux, ~euse *a.* unlucky.

malcommode /malkɔmɔd/ *a.* awkward.

mâle /mɑl/ *a.* male; (*viril*) manly. —*n.m.* male.

malédiction /malediksjɔ̃/ *n.f.* curse.

maléfice /malefis/ *n.m.* evil spell.

maléfique /malefik/*a.* evil.

malencontreu|x, ~se /malɑ̃-kɔ̃trø, -z/ *a.* unfortunate.

malentendant, ~e *a.* & *n.m., f.* hard of hearing.

malentendu /malɑ̃tɑ̃dy/ *n.m.* misunderstanding.

malfaçon /malfasɔ̃/ *n.f.* fault.

malfaisant, ~e /malfəzɑ̃, -t/ *a.* harmful.

malfaiteur /malfɛtœr/ *n.m.* criminal.

malformation /malfɔrmasjɔ̃/ *n.f.* malformation.

malgache /malgaʃ/ *a.* & *n.m./f.* Malagasy.

malgré /malgre/ *prép.* in spite of, despite. ~ tout, after all.

malhabile /malabil/ *a.* clumsy.

malheur /malœr/ *n.m.* misfortune; (*accident*) accident. faire un ~, be a big hit.

malheureu|x, ~se /malœrø, -z/ *a.* unhappy; (*regrettable*) unfortunate; (*sans succès*) unlucky; (*insignifiant*) wretched. —*n.m., f.* (*poor*) wretch. ~sement *adv.* unfortunately.

malhonnête /malɔnɛt/ *a.* dishonest. ~té *n.f.* dishonesty; (*action*) dishonest action.

malic|e /malis/ *n.f.* mischievousness; (*méchanceté*) malice. ~ieux, ~ieuse *a.* mischievous.

malin, ~igne /malɛ̃, -iɲ/ *a.* clever, smart; (*méchant*) malicious; (*tumeur*) malignant; (*difficile: fam.*) difficult. ~ignité *n.f.* malignancy.

malingre /malɛ̃gr/ *a.* puny.

malintentionné /malɛ̃tɑ̃sjɔne/ *a.* malicious.

malle /mal/ *n.f.* (*valise*) trunk;

(*auto.*) boot; (*auto.*, *Amer.*) trunk.

malléable /maleabl/ *a.* malleable.

mallette /malɛt/ *n.f.* (small) suit-case.

malmener /malməne/ *v.t.* man-handle, handle roughly.

malnutrition /malnytrisjɔ̃/ *n.f.* malnutrition.

malodorant, ∼e /malɔdɔrɑ̃, -t/ *a.* smelly, foul-smelling.

malotru /malɔtry/ *n.m.* boor.

malpoli /malpɔli/ *a.* impolite.

malpropre /malprɔpr/ *a.* dirty. ∼té /-əte/ *n.f.* dirtiness.

malsain, ∼e /malsɛ̃, -ɛn/ *a.* unhealthy.

malt /malt/ *n.m.* malt.

maltais, ∼e /maltɛ, -z/ *a.* & *n.m.*, *f.* Maltese.

Malte /malt/ *n.f.* Malta.

maltraiter /maltrete/ *v.t.* ill-treat.

malveillan|t, ∼te /malvɛjɑ̃, -t/ *a.* malevolent. ∼ce *n.f.* malevo-lence.

maman /mamɑ̃/ *n.f.* mum(my), mother.

mamelle /mamɛl/ *n.f.* teat.

mamelon /mamlɔ̃/ *n.m.* (*anat.*) nipple; (*colline*) hillock.

mamie /mami/ *n.f.* (*fam.*) granny.

mammifère /mamifɛr/ *n.m.* mam-mal.

mammouth /mamut/ *n.m.* mam-moth.

manche[1] /mɑ̃ʃ/ *n.f.* sleeve; (*sport*, *pol.*) round. **la M**∼, the Channel.

manche[2] /mɑ̃ʃ/ *n.m.* (*d'un instru-ment*) handle. ∼ **à balai,** broomstick.

manchette /mɑ̃ʃɛt/ *n.f.* cuff; (*de journal*) headline.

manchot[1] /mɑ̃ʃo, -ɔt/ *a.* & *n.m.*, *f.* one-armed (person); (*sans bras*) armless (person).

manchot[2] /mɑ̃ʃo/ *n.m.* (*oiseau*) penguin.

mandarin /mɑ̃darɛ̃/ *n.m.* (*fonc-tionnaire*) mandarin.

mandarine /mɑ̃darin/ *n.f.* tan-gerine, mandarin (orange).

mandat /mɑ̃da/ *n.m.* (*postal*) money order; (*pol.*) mandate; (*procuration*) proxy; (*de police*) warrant. ∼**aire** /-tɛr/ *n.m.* (*représentant*) representative. ∼**er** /-te/ *v.t.* (*pol.*) delegate.

manège /manɛʒ/ *n.m.* riding-school; (*à la foire*) merry-go-round; (*manœuvre*) wiles, ploy.

manette /manɛt/ *n.f.* lever; (*comput.*) joystick.

mangeable /mɑ̃ʒabl/ *a.* edible.

mangeoire /mɑ̃ʒwar/ *n.f.* trough.

mang|er /mɑ̃ʒe/ *v.t./i.* eat; (*fortune*) go through; (*ronger*) eat into. —*n.m.* food. **donner à** ∼**er à,** feed. ∼**eur,** ∼**euse** *n.m.*, *f.* eater.

mangue /mɑ̃g/ *n.f.* mango.

maniable /manjabl/ *a.* easy to handle.

maniaque /manjak/ *a.* fussy. —*n.m./f.* fuss-pot; (*fou*) maniac. **un** ∼ **de,** a maniac for.

manie /mani/ *n.f.* habit; obses-sion.

man|ier /manje/ *v.t.* handle. ∼**iement** *n.m.* handling.

manière /manjɛr/ *n.f.* way, man-ner. ∼**s,** (*politesse*) manners; (*chichis*) fuss. **de cette** ∼, in this way. **de** ∼ **à,** so as to. **de toute** ∼, anyway, in any case.

maniéré /manjere/ *a.* affected.

manif /manif/ *n.f.* (*fam.*) demo.

manifestant, ∼e /manifɛstɑ̃, -t/ *n.m.*, *f.* demonstrator.

manifeste /manifɛst/ *a.* obvious. —*n.m.* manifesto.

manifest|er[1] /manifɛste/ *v.t.* show, manifest. **se** ∼**er** *v. pr.* (*sentiment*) show itself; (*apparaître*) appear. ∼**ation**[1] *n.f.* expression, demonstration, mani-festation; (*de maladie*) ap-pearance.

manifest|er[2] /manifɛste/ *v.i.* (*pol.*)

demonstrate. ~ation² /n.f. (*pol.*)
demonstration; (*événement*) event.

maniganc|e /manigɑ̃s/ *n.f.* little
plot. **~er** *v.t.* plot.

manipul|er /manipyle/ *v.t.* handle;
(*péj.*) manipulate. **~ation** *n.f.*
handling; (*péj.*) manipulation.

manivelle /manivɛl/ *n.f.* crank.

manne /man/ *n.f.* (*aubaine*) godsend.

mannequin /mankɛ̃/ *n.m.* (*personne*) model; (*statue*) dummy.

manœuvre¹ /manœvr/ *n.f.* manœuvre. **~er** *v.t./i.* manœuvre;
(*machine*) operate.

manœuvre² /manœvr/ *n.m.* (*ouvrier*) labourer.

manoir /manwar/ *n.m.* manor.

manque /mɑ̃k/ *n.m.* lack (**de**, of);
(*vide*) gap. **~s**, (*défauts*) faults. **~
à gagner**, loss of profit. **en (état
de) ~**, having withdrawal
symptoms.

manqué /mɑ̃ke/ *a.* (*écrivain etc.*)
failed. **garçon ~,** tomboy.

manquement /mɑ̃kmɑ̃/ *n.m.* **~ à,**
breach of.

manquer /mɑ̃ke/ *v.t.* miss;
(*gâcher*) spoil; (*examen*) fail.
—*v.i.* be lacking; (*absent*)
be absent; (*en moins, disparu*) be
missing; (*échouer*) fail. **~ à,**
(*devoir*) fail in. **~ de,** be short of,
lack. **il/ça lui manque,** he
misses him/it. **~ (de) faire,**
(*faillir*) nearly do. **ne pas ~ de,**
not fail to.

mansarde /mɑ̃sard/ *n.f.* attic.

manteau (*pl.* **~x**) /mɑ̃to/ *n.m.*
coat.

manucur|e /manykyr/ *n.m./f.*
manicurist. **~er** *v.t.* manicure.

manuel /manɥɛl/ *a.* manual.
—*n.m.* (*livre*) manual. **~lement**
adv. manually.

manufactur|e /manyfaktyr/ *n.f.*
factory. **~é** *a.* manufactured.

manuscrit, ~e /manyskri, -t/ *a.*
handwritten. —*n.m.* manuscript.

manutention /manytɑ̃sjɔ̃/ *n.f.*
handling.

mappemonde /mapmɔ̃d/ *n.f.*
world map; (*sphère*) globe.

maquereau (*pl.* **~x**) /makro/
n.m. (*poisson*) mackerel; (*fam.*)
pimp.

maquette /makɛt/ *n.f.* (*scale*)
model; (*mise en page*) paste-up.

maquill|er /makije/ *v.t.* make up;
(*truquer*) fake. **se ~er** *v.pr.* make
(o.s.) up. **~age** *n.m.* make-up.

maquis /maki/ *n.m.* (*paysage*)
scrub; (*mil.*) Maquis, underground.

maraîch|er, ~ère /mareʃe,
-ɛʃɛr/ *n.m., f.* market gardener;
(*Amer.*) truck farmer. **cultures
~ères,** market gardening.

marais /marɛ/ *n.m.* marsh.

marasme /marasm/ *n.m.* slump.

marathon /maratɔ̃/ *n.m.* marathon.

marbre /marbr/ *n.m.* marble.

marc /mar/ *n.m.* (*eau-de-vie*) marc.
~ de café, coffee-grounds.

marchand, ~e /marʃɑ̃, -d/ *n.m., f.*
trader; (*de charbon, vins*) merchant. —*a.* (*valeur*) market. **~ de
couleurs,** ironmonger; **~ de
journaux,** newsagent. **~ de
légumes,** greengrocer. **~ de
poissons,** fishmonger.

marchand|er /marʃɑ̃de/ *v.t.*
haggle over. —*v.i.* haggle. **~age**
n.m. haggling.

marchandise /marʃɑ̃diz/ *n.f.* goods.

marche /marʃ/ *n.f.* (*démarche,
trajet*) walk; (*rythme*) pace; (*mil.,
mus.*) march; (*d'escalier*) step;
(*sport*) walking; (*de machine*)
working; (*de véhicule*) running.
en ~, (*train etc.*) moving. **faire
~ arrière,** (*véhicule*) reverse.
mettre en ~, start (up). **se
mettre en ~,** start moving.

marché /marʃe/ *n.m.* market;
(*contrat*) deal. **faire son ~,** do

one's shopping. **~ aux puces,** flea market. **M~ commun,** Common Market. **~ noir,** black market.

marchepied /marʃəpje/ *n.m.* (*de train, camion*) step.

march|er /marʃe/ *v.i.* walk; (*aller*) go; (*fonctionner*) work, run; (*prospérer*) go well; (*consentir, fam.*) agree. **~er (au pas),** (*mil.*) march. **faire ~er qn.,** pull s.o.'s leg. **~eur, ~euse** *n.m., f.* walker.

mardi /mardi/ *n.m.* Tuesday. **M~ gras,** Shrove Tuesday.

mare /mar/ *n.f.* (*étang*) pond; (*flaque*) pool.

marécag|e /mareka3/ *n.m.* marsh. **~eux, ~euse** *a.* marshy.

maréch|al (*pl.* **~aux**) /mareʃal, -o/ *n.m.* marshal. **~al-ferrant** (*pl.* **~aux-ferrants**) blacksmith.

marée /mare/ *n.f.* tide; (*poissons*) fresh fish. **~ haute/basse,** high/low tide. **~ noire,** oil-slick.

marelle /marɛl/ *n.f.* hopscotch.

margarine /margarin/ *n.f.* margarine.

marge /mar3/ *n.f.* margin. **en ~ de,** (*à l'écart de*) on the fringes of. **~ bénéficiaire,** profit margin.

margin|al, ~ale (*m. pl.* **~aux**) /marginal, -o/ *a.* marginal. —*n.m., f.* drop-out.

marguerite /margərit/ *n.f.* daisy; (*qui imprime*) daisy-wheel.

mari /mari/ *n.m.* husband.

mariage /marja3/ *n.m.* marriage; (*cérémonie*) wedding.

mari|é, ~e /marje/ *a.* married. —*n.m.* (bride)groom. —*n.f.* bride. **les ~s,** the bride and groom.

marier /marje/ *v.t.* marry. **se ~,** *v. pr.* get married, marry. **se ~ avec,** marry, get married to.

marin, ~e /marɛ̃, -in/ *a.* sea. —*n.m.* sailor. —*n.f.* navy. **~e marchande,** merchant navy.

mariner /marine/ *v.t./i.* marinate. **faire ~,** (*fam.*) keep hanging around.

marionnette /marjɔnɛt/ *n.f.* puppet; (*à fils*) marionette.

maritalement /maritalmɑ̃/ *adv.* as husband and wife.

maritime /maritim/ *a.* maritime, coastal; (*droit, agent*) shipping.

mark /mark/ *n.m.* mark.

marmaille /marmaj/ *n.f.* (*enfants: fam.*) brats.

marmelade /marməlad/ *n.f.* stewed fruit. **~ (d'oranges),** marmelade.

marmite /marmit/ *n.f.* (cooking-) pot.

marmonner /marmɔne/ *v.t./i.* mumble.

marmot /marmo/ *n.m.* (*fam.*) kid.

marmotter /marmɔte/ *v.t./i.* mumble.

Maroc /marɔk/ *n.m.* Morocco.

marocain, ~e /marɔkɛ̃, -ɛn/ *a.* & *n.m., f.* Moroccan.

maroquinerie /marɔkinri/ *n.f.* (*magasin*) leather goods shop.

marotte /marɔt/ *n.f.* fad, craze.

marquant, ~e /markã, -t/ *a.* (*remarquable*) outstanding; (*qu'on n'oublie pas*) significant.

marque /mark/ *n.f.* mark; (*de produits*) brand, make. **à vos ~s!,** (*sport*) on your marks! de **~,** (*comm.*) brand-name; (*fig.*) important. **~ de fabrique,** trade mark. **~ déposée,** registered trade mark.

marqué /marke/ *a.* marked.

marquer /marke/ *v.t.* mark; (*indiquer*) show; (*écrire*) note down; (*point, but*) score; (*joueur*) mark; (*animal*) brand. —*v.i.* (*trace*) leave a mark; (*événement*) stand out.

marqueterie /markɛtri/ *n.f.* marquetry.

marquis, ~e¹ /marki, -z/ *n.m., f.* marquis, marchioness.

marquise[2] /markiz/ *n.f.* (*auvent*) glass awning.

marraine /marɛn/ *n.f.* godmother.

marrant, ~e /marɑ̃, -t/ *a.* (*fam.*) funny.

marre /mar/ *adv.* **en avoir ~,** (*fam.*) be fed up (**de,** with).

marrer (se) /(sə)mare/ *v. pr.* (*fam.*) laugh, have a (good) laugh.

marron /marɔ̃/ *n.m.* chestnut; (*couleur*) brown; (*coup: fam.*) thump. *—a. invar.* brown. **~ d'Inde,** horse-chestnut.

mars /mars/ *n.m.* March.

marsouin /marswɛ̃/ *n.m.* porpoise.

marteau (*pl.* **~x**) /marto/ *n.m.* hammer. **~ (de porte),** (*door*) knocker. **~ piqueur** *ou* **pneumatique,** pneumatic drill. **être ~,** (*fam.*) mad.

marteler /martəle/ *v.t.* hammer.

mart|ial (*m. pl.* **~iaux**) /marsjal, -jo/ *a.* martial.

martien, ~ne /marsjɛ̃, -jɛn/ *a. & n.m.,f.* Martian.

martyr, ~e[1] /martir/ *n.m.,f.* martyr. *—a.* martyred. **~iser** *v.t.* martyr; (*fig.*) batter.

martyre[2] /martir/ *n.m.* (*souffrance*) martyrdom.

marxis|te /marksist/ *a. & n.m./f.* Marxist. **~me** *n.m.* Marxism.

mascara /maskara/ *n.m.* mascara.

mascarade /maskarad/ *n.f.* masquerade.

mascotte /maskɔt/ *n.f.* mascot.

masculin, ~e /maskylɛ̃, -in/ *a.* masculine; (*sexe*) male; (*mode, équipe*) men's. *—n.m.* masculine. **~ité** /-inite/ *n.f.* masculinity.

maso /mazo/ *n.m./f.* (*fam.*) masochist. *—a. invar.* masochistic.

masochis|te /mazoʃist/ *n.m./f.* masochist. *—a.* masochistic. **~me** *n.m.* masochism.

masqu|e /mask/ *n.m.* mask. **~er** *v.t.* (*cacher*) hide, conceal (**à,** from); (*lumière*) block (off).

massacr|e /masakr/ *n.m.* massacre. **~er** *v.t.* massacre; (*abîmer: fam.*) spoil.

massage /masaʒ/ *n.m.* massage.

masse /mas/ *n.f.* (*volume*) mass; (*gros morceau*) lump, mass; (*outil*) sledge-hammer. **en ~,** (*vendre*) in bulk; (*venir*) in force; (*production*) mass. **la ~,** (*foule*) the masses. **une ~ de,** (*fam.*) masses of.

masser[1] /mase/ *v.t.,* **se ~** *v. pr.* (*gens, foule*) mass.

mass|er[2] /mase/ *v.t.* (*pétrir*) massage. **~eur, ~euse** *n.m., f.* masseur, masseuse.

massif, ~ve /masif, -v/ *a.* massive; (*or, argent*) solid. *—n.m.* (*de fleurs*) clump; (*géog.*) massif. **~vement** *adv.* (*en masse*) in large numbers.

massue /masy/ *n.f.* club, bludgeon.

mastic /mastik/ *n.m.* putty.

mastiquer /mastike/ *v.t.* (*mâcher*) chew.

masturb|er (se) /(sə)mastyrbe/ *v. pr.* masturbate. **~ation** *n.f.* masturbation.

masure /mazyr/ *n.f.* hovel.

mat /mat/ *a.* (*couleur*) matt; (*bruit*) dull. **être ~,** (*aux échecs*) be checkmate.

mât /mo/ *n.m.* mast; (*pylône*) pole.

match /matʃ/ *n.m.* match; (*Amer.*) game. **(faire) ~ nul,** tie, draw. **~ aller,** first leg. **~ retour,** return match.

matelas /matla/ *n.m.* mattress. **~ pneumatique,** air mattress.

matelassé /matlase/ *a.* padded; (*tissu*) quilted.

matelot /matlo/ *n.m.* sailor.

mater /mate/ *v.t.* (*personne*) subdue; (*réprimer*) stifle.

matérialiser (se) /(sə)materjalize/ *v. pr.* materialize.

matérialiste /materjalist/ *a.* materialistic. *—n.m./f.* materialist.

matériaux /materjo/ *n.m. pl.* materials.

matériel, ∼le /materjɛl/ *a.* material. —*n.m.* equipment, materials; (*d'un ordinateur*) hardware.

maternel, ∼le /matɛrnɛl/ *a.* motherly, maternal; (*rapport de parenté*) maternal. —*n.f.* nursery school.

maternité /matɛrnite/ *n.f.* maternity hospital; (*état de mère*) motherhood.

mathémati|que /matematik/ *a.* mathematical. —*n.f. pl.* mathematics. **∼cien, ∼cienne** *n.m., f.* mathematician.

maths /mat/ *n.f. pl.* (*fam.*) maths.

matière /matjɛr/ *n.f.* matter; (*produit*) material; (*sujet*) subject. **en ∼ de,** as regards. **∼ plastique,** plastic. **∼s grasses,** fat. **à 0% de ∼s grasses,** fat free. **∼s premières,** raw materials.

matin /matɛ̃/ *n.m.* morning. **de bon ∼,** early in the morning.

matin|al (*m. pl.* **∼aux**) /matinal, -o/ *a.* morning; (*de bonne heure*) early. **être ∼,** be up early.

matinée /matine/ *n.f.* morning; (*spectacle*) matinée.

matou /matu/ *n.m.* tom-cat.

matraqu|e /matrak/ *n.f.* (*de police*) truncheon; (*Amer.*) billy (club). **∼er** *v.t.* club, beat; (*message*) plug.

matrice /matris/ *n.f.* (*techn.*) matrix.

matrimon|ial (*m. pl.* **∼iaux**) /matrimɔnjal, -jo/ *a.* matrimonial.

maturité /matyrite/ *n.f.* maturity.

maudire† /modir/ *v.t.* curse.

maudit, ∼e /modi, -t/ *a.* (*fam.*) damned.

maugréer /mogree/ *v.i.* grumble.

mausolée /mozɔle/ *n.m.* mausoleum.

maussade /mosad/ *a.* gloomy.

mauvais, ∼e /mɔvɛ, -z/ *a.* bad; (*erroné*) wrong; (*malveillant*) evil; (*désagréable*) nasty, bad; (*mer*) rough. —*n.m.* **il fait ∼,** the weather is bad. **le ∼ moment,** the wrong time. **∼e herbe,** weed. **∼e langue,** gossip. **∼ passe,** tight spot. **∼ traitements,** ill-treatment.

mauve /mov/ *a.* & *n.m.* mauve.

mauviette /movjɛt/ *n.f.* weakling.

maux /mo/ *voir* **mal².**

maxim|al (*m. pl.* **∼aux**) /maksimal, -o/ *a.* maximum.

maxime /maksim/ *n.f.* maxim.

maximum /maksimɔm/ *a.* & *n.m.* maximum. **au ∼,** as much as possible; (*tout au plus*) at most.

mayonnaise /majɔnɛz/ *n.f.* mayonnaise.

mazout /mazut/ *n.m.* (fuel) oil.

me, m'* /mə, m/ *pron.* me; (*indirect*) (to) me; (*réfléchi*) myself.

méandre /meɑ̃dr/ *n.m.* meander.

mec /mek/ *n.m.* (*fam.*) bloke, guy.

mécanicien /mekanisjɛ̃/ *n.m.* mechanic; (*rail.*) train driver.

mécani|que /mekanik/ *a.* mechanical; (*jouet*) clockwork. **problème ∼que,** engine trouble. —*n.f.* mechanics; (*mécanisme*) mechanism. **∼ser** *v.t.* mechanize.

mécanisme /mekanism/ *n.m.* mechanism.

méch|ant, ∼ante /meʃɑ̃, -t/ *a.* (*cruel*) wicked; (*désagréable*) nasty; (*enfant*) naughty; (*chien*) vicious; (*sensationnel: fam.*) terrific. —*n.m., f.* (*enfant*) naughty child. **∼amment** *adv.* wickedly. **∼anceté** *n.f.* wickedness; (*action*) wicked action.

mèche /mɛʃ/ *n.f.* (*de cheveux*) lock; (*de bougie*) wick; (*d'explosif*) fuse. **de ∼ avec,** in league with.

méconnaissable /mekɔnɛsabl/ a. unrecognizable.

méconn|aître /mekɔnɛtr/ v.t. be ignorant of; (*mésestimer*) under-estimate. **~aissance** n.f. ignorance. **~u** a. unrecognized.

mécontent, **~e** /mekɔ̃tɑ̃, -t/ a. dissatisfied (de, with); (*irrité*) annoyed (de, at, with). **~ement** /-tmɑ̃/ n.m. dissatisfaction; annoyance. **~er** /-te/ v.t. dissatisfy; (*irriter*) annoy.

médaill|e /medaj/ n.f. medal; (*insigne*) badge; (*bijou*) medallion. **~é**, **~ée** n.m., f. medal holder.

médaillon /medajɔ̃/ n.m. medallion; (*bijou*) locket.

médecin /medsɛ̃/ n.m. doctor.

médecine /medsin/ n.f. medicine.

média /medja/ n.m. medium. **les ~s**, the media.

média|teur, **~trice** /medjatœr, -tris/ n.m., f. mediator.

médiation /medjasjɔ̃/ n.f. mediation.

médiatique /medjatik/ a. **événement/personnalité ~**, media event/personality.

médic|al (m. pl. **~aux**) /medikal, -o/ a. medical.

médicament /medikamɑ̃/ n.m. medicine.

médicin|al (m. pl. **~aux**) /medisinal, -o/ a. medicinal.

médico-lég|al (m. pl. **~aux**) /medikolegal, -o/ a. forensic.

médiév|al (m. pl. **~aux**) /medjeval, -o/ a. medieval.

médiocr|e /medjɔkr/ a. mediocre, poor. **~ement** adv. (*peu*) not very; (*mal*) in a mediocre way. **~ité** n.f. mediocrity.

médire /medir/ v.i. **~ de**, speak ill of.

médisance /medizɑ̃s/ n.f. **~(s)**, malicious gossip.

méditati|f, **~ve** /meditatif, -v/ a. (*pensif*) thoughtful.

médit|er /medite/ v.t./i. meditate. **~er de**, plan to. **~ation** n.f. meditation.

Méditerranée /mediterane/ n.f. **la ~**, the Mediterranean.

méditerranéen, **~ne** /mediteraneɛ̃, -ɛn/ a. Mediterranean.

médium /medjɔm/ n.m. (*personne*) medium.

méduse /medyz/ n.f. jellyfish.

meeting /mitiŋ/ n.m. meeting.

méfait /mefɛ/ n.m. misdeed. **les ~s de**, (*conséquences*) the ravages of.

méfian|t, **~e** /mefjɑ̃, -t/ a. distrustful. **~ce** n.f. distrust.

méfier (se) /(s)mefje/ v. pr. be wary ou careful. **se ~ de**, distrust, be wary of.

mégarde (par) /(par)megard/ adv. by accident, accidentally.

mégère /meʒɛr/ n.f. (*femme*) shrew.

mégot /mego/ n.m. (*fam.*) cigarette-end.

meilleur, **~e** /mɛjœr/ a. & adv. better (que, than). **le ~ livre/etc.**, the best book/etc. **mon ~ ami/etc.**, my best friend/etc. **~ marché**, cheaper. —n.m., f. **le ~/la ~e**, the best (one).

mélancoli|e /melɑ̃kɔli/ n.f. melancholy. **~que** a. melancholy.

mélang|e /melɑ̃ʒ/ n.m. mixture, blend. **~er** v.t., **se ~er** v.pr. mix, blend; (*embrouiller*) mix up.

mélasse /melas/ n.f. treacle; (*Amer.*) molasses.

mêlée /mele/ n.f. scuffle; (*rugby*) scrum.

mêler /mele/ v.t. mix (à, with); (*qualités*) combine; (*embrouiller*) mix up. **~ à**, (*impliquer dans*) involve in. **se ~** v. pr. mix; combine. **se ~ à**, (*se joindre à*) join. **se ~ de**, meddle in. **mêle-toi de ce qui te regarde**, mind your own business.

méli-mélo /melimelo/ *n.m.* (*pl.* **mélis-mélos**) jumble.

mélo /melo/ (*fam.*) *n.m.* melodrama. —*a. invar.* melodramatic.

mélodie /melɔdi/ *n.f.* melody. **~ieux, ~ieuse** *a.* melodious. **~ique** *a.* melodic.

mélodrame /melɔdram/ *n.m.* melodrama. **~atique** *a.* melodramatic.

mélomane /melɔman/ *n.m./f.* music lover.

melon /məlɔ̃/ *n.m.* melon. (**chapeau**) **~**, bowler (hat).

membrane /mãbran/ *n.f.* membrane.

membre[1] /mãbr/ *n.m.* limb.

membre[2] /mãbr/ *n.m.* (*adhérent*) member.

même /mɛm/ *a.* same. **ce livre**/*etc.* **~**, this very book/*etc.* **la bonté**/*etc.* **~**, kindness/*etc.* itself. —*pron.* **le ~/la ~**, the same (one). —*adv.* even. **à ~, (sur)** directly on. **à ~ de**, in a position to. **de ~, (aussi)** too; (*de la même façon*) likewise. **de ~ que**, just as. **en ~ temps**, at the same time.

mémé /meme/ *n.f.* (*fam.*) granny.

mémo /memo/ *n.m.* memo.

mémoire /memwar/ *n.f.* memory. —*n.m.* (*requête*) memorandum; (*univ.*) dissertation. **~s**, (*souvenirs écrits*) memoirs. **à la ~ de**, to the memory of. **de ~**, from memory. **~ morte/vive, (comput.)** ROM/RAM.

mémorable /memɔrabl/ *a.* memorable.

mémorandum /memɔrãdɔm/ *n.m.* memorandum.

menace /mənas/ *n.f.* threat. **~er** *v.t.* threaten (**de faire**, to do).

ménage /menaʒ/ *n.m.* (*married*) couple; (*travail*) housework. **se mettre en ~**, set up house. **scène de ~**, scene. **dépenses du ~**, household expenditure.

ménagement /menaʒmã/ *n.m.* care and consideration.

ménager[1], **~ère** /menaʒe, -ɛr/ *a.* household, domestic. **travaux ~ers**, housework. —*n.f.* housewife.

ménager[2] /menaʒe/ *v.t.* treat with tact; (*utiliser*) be sparing in the use of; (*organiser*) prepare (carefully).

ménagerie /menaʒri/ *n.f.* menagerie.

mendiant, ~e /mãdjã, -t/ *n.m., f.* beggar.

mendicité /mãdisite/ *n.f.* begging.

mendier /mãdje/ *v.t.* beg for. —*v.i.* beg.

menées /məne/ *n.f. pl.* schemings.

mener /məne/ *v.t.* lead; (*entreprise, pays*) run. —*v.i.* lead. **~ à, (accompagner à)** take to. **~ à bien**, see through.

meneur /mənœr/ *n.m.* (*chef*) (ring)leader. **~ de jeu**, compère; (*Amer.*) master of ceremonies.

méningite /menɛʒit/ *n.f.* meningitis.

ménopause /menɔpoz/ *n.f.* menopause.

menotte /mənɔt/ *n.f.* (*fam.*) hand. **~s**, handcuffs.

mensonge /mãsɔ̃ʒ/ *n.m.* lie; (*action*) lying. **~er, ~ère** *a.* untrue.

menstruation /mãstryɑsjɔ̃/ *n.f.* menstruation.

mensualité /mãsɥalite/ *n.f.* monthly payment.

mensuel, ~le /mãsɥɛl/ *a. & n.m.* monthly. **~lement** *adv.* monthly.

mensurations /mãsyrɑsjɔ̃/ *n.f. pl.* measurements.

mental, (m. pl. ~aux) /mãtal, -o/ *a.* mental.

mentalité /mãtalite/ *n.f.* mentality.

menteur, ~se /mãtœr, -øz/ *n.m., f.* liar. —*a.* untruthful.

menthe /mãt/ *n.f.* mint.

mention /mãsjõ/ *n.f.* mention; (*annotation*) note; (*scol.*) grade. ~ **bien**, (*scol.*) distinction. ~**ner** /-jone/ *v.t.* mention.

mentir† /mãtir/ *v.i.* lie.

menton /mãtõ/ *n.m.* chin.

mentor /mɛ̃tɔr/ *n.m.* mentor.

menu[1] /məny/ *n.m.* (*carte*) menu; (*repas*) meal.

menu[2] /məny/ *a.* (*petit*) tiny; (*fin*) fine; (*insignifiant*) minor. —*adv.* (*couper*) fine.

menuis|ier /mənɥizje/ *n.m.* carpenter, joiner. ~**erie** *n.f.* carpentry, joinery.

méprendre (se) /(sə)meprãdr/ *v. pr.* **se** ~ **sur**, be mistaken about.

mépris /mepri/ *n.m.* contempt, scorn (**de**, for). **au** ~ **de**, in defiance of.

méprisable /meprizabl/ *a.* despicable.

méprise /mepriz/ *n.f.* mistake.

mépris|er /meprize/ *v.t.* scorn, despise. ~**ant**, ~**ante** *a.* scornful.

mer /mɛr/ *n.f.* sea; (*marée*) tide. **en haute** ~, on the open sea.

mercenaire /mɛrsəner/ *n.m. & a.* mercenary.

merci /mɛrsi/ *int.* thank you, thanks (**de, pour**, for). —*n.f.* mercy. ~ **beaucoup** ~ **bien**, thank you very much.

merc|ier, ~**ière** /mɛrsje, -jɛr/ *n.m., f.* haberdasher; (*Amer.*) notions merchant. ~**erie** *n.f.* haberdashery; (*Amer.*) notions store.

mercredi /mɛrkrədi/ *n.m.* Wednesday. ~ **des Cendres**, Ash Wednesday.

mercure /mɛrkyr/ *n.m.* mercury.

merde /mɛrd/ *n.f.* (*fam.*) shit. **être dans la** ~, be in a mess.

mère /mɛr/ *n.f.* mother. ~ **de famille**, mother.

méridien /meridjɛ̃/ *n.m.* meridian.

méridion|al /meridjɔnal/ *a.* (*m. pl.* ~**aux**) /meridjɔnal, -o/ *a.* southern. —*n.m., f.* southerner.

meringue /mərɛ̃g/ *n.f.* meringue.

mérite /merit/ *n.m.* merit. **il n'a aucun** ~, that's as it should be. **il a du** ~, it's very much to his credit.

mérit|er /merite/ *v.t.* deserve. ~**ant**, ~**ante** *a.* deserving.

méritoire /meritwar/ *a.* commendable.

merlan /mɛrlã/ *n.m.* whiting.

merle /mɛrl/ *n.m.* blackbird.

merveille /mɛrvɛj/ *n.f.* wonder, marvel. **à** ~, wonderfully. **faire des** ~**s**, work wonders.

merveilleu|x, ~**se** /mɛrvɛjø, -z/ *a.* wonderful, marvellous. ~**sement** *adv.* wonderfully.

mes /me/ *voir* **mon**.

mésange /mezãʒ/ *n.f.* tit(mouse).

mésaventure /mezavãtyr/ *n.f.* misadventure.

mesdames /medam/ *voir* **madame**.

mesdemoiselles /medmwazɛl/ *voir* **mademoiselle**.

mésentente /mezãtãt/ *n.f.* disagreement.

mesquin, ~**e** /mɛskɛ̃, -in/ *a.* mean. ~**erie** /-inri/ *n.f.* meanness.

mess /mɛs/ *n.m.* (*mil.*) mess.

messag|e /mesaʒ/ *n.m.* message. ~**er**, ~**ère** *n.m., f.* messenger.

messe /mɛs/ *n.f.* (*relig.*) mass.

Messie /mesi/ *n.m.* Messiah.

messieurs /mesjø/ *voir* **monsieur**.

mesure /məzyr/ *n.f.* measurement; (*quantité, étalon*) measure; (*disposition*) measure, step; (*cadence*) time; (*modération*) moderation. **à** ~ **que**, as. **dans la** ~ **où**, in so far as. **dans une certaine** ~, to some extent. **en** ~ **de**, in a position to.

mesuré /məzyre/ a. measured; (*personne*) moderate.

mesurer /məzyre/ v.t. measure; (*juger*) assess; (*argent*, *temps*) ration. se ~ avec, pit o.s. against.

met /mɛ/ *voir* **mettre**.

métabolisme /metabolism/ n.m. metabolism.

mét|al (*pl.* ~aux) /metal, -o/ n.m. metal. ~allique a. (*objet*) metal; (*éclat etc.*) metallic.

métallurg|ie /metalyrʒi/ n.f. (*industrie*) steel *ou* metal industry. ~iste n.m. steel *ou* metal worker.

métamorphos|e /metamɔrfoz/ n.f. metamorphosis. ~er v.t., se ~er v. pr. transform.

métaphore /metafɔr/ n.f. metaphor. ~ique a. metaphorical.

météo /meteo/ n.f. (*bulletin*) weather forecast.

météore /meteɔr/ n.m. meteor.

météorolog|ie /meteɔrɔlɔʒi/ n.f. meteorology; (*service*) weather bureau. ~ique a. weather; (*études etc.*) meteorological.

méthod|e /metɔd/ n.f. method; (*ouvrage*) course, manual. ~ique a. methodical.

méticuleu|x, ~se /metikylø, -z/ a. meticulous.

métier /metje/ n.m. job; (*manuel*) trade; (*intellectuel*) profession; (*expérience*) skill. ~ (à tisser), loom. remettre sur le ~, keep going back to the drawing-board.

métis, ~se /metis/ a. & n.m., f. half-caste.

métrage /metraʒ/ n.m. length. court ~, short film. long ~, full-length film.

mètre /mɛtr/ n.m. metre; (*règle*) rule. ~ ruban, tape-measure.

métreur /metrœr/ n.m. quantity surveyor.

métrique /metrik/ a. metric.

métro /metro/ n.m. underground; (*à Paris*) Métro.

métropol|e /metrɔpɔl/ n.f. metropolis; (*pays*) mother country. ~itain, ~itaine a. metropolitan.

mets¹ /mɛ/ n.m. dish.

mets² /mɛ/ *voir* **mettre**.

mettable /mɛtabl/ a. wearable.

metteur /mɛtœr/ n.m. ~ en scène, (*théâtre*) producer; (*cinéma*) director.

mettre† /mɛtr/ v.t. put; (*vêtement*) put on; (*radio, chauffage, etc.*) put *ou* switch on; (*table*) lay; (*pendule*) set; (*temps*) take; (*installer*) put in; (*supposer*) suppose. se ~ v. pr. put o.s.; (*objet*) go; (*porter*) wear. ~ bas, give birth. ~ qn. en boîte, pull s.o.'s leg. ~ en cause *ou* en question, question. ~ en colère, make angry. ~ en valeur, highlight; (*un bien*) exploit. se ~ à, (*entrer dans*) get *ou* go into. se ~ à faire, start doing. se ~ à l'aise, make o.s. comfortable. se ~ à table, sit down at the table. se ~ au travail, set to work. (se) ~ en ligne, line up. se ~ dans tous ses états, get into a state. se ~ du sable dans les yeux, get sand in one's eyes.

meuble /mœbl/ n.m. piece of furniture. ~s, furniture.

meublé /mœble/ n.m. furnished flatlet.

meubler /mœble/ v.t. furnish; (*fig.*) fill. se ~ v. pr. buy furniture.

meugl|er /møgle/ v.i. moo. ~ement(s) n.m. (*pl.*) mooing.

meule /møl/ n.f. (*de foin*) haystack; (*à moudre*) millstone.

meun|ier, ~ière /mønje, -jɛr/ n.m., f. miller.

meurs, **meurt** /mœr/ *voir* **mourir**.

meurtr|e /mœrtr/ n.m. murder. ~ier, ~ière a. deadly; n.m. murderer; n.f. murderess.

meurtr|ir /mœrtrir/ v.t. bruise.
~issure n.f. bruise.
meute /møt/ n.f. (troupe) pack.
mexicain, ~e /mɛksikɛ̃, -ɛn/ a.
& n.m., f. Mexican.
Mexique /mɛksik/ n.m. Mexico.
mi- /mi/ préf. mid-, half-. **à mi-
chemin**, half-way. **à mi-côte**,
half-way up the hill. **la mi-
juin/**etc., mid-June/etc.
miaou /mjau/ n.m. mew.
miaul|er /mjole/ v.i. mew.
~ement n.m. mew.
miche /miʃ/ n.f. round loaf.
micro /mikro/ n.m. microphone,
mike; (comput.) micro.
micro- /mikro/ préf. micro-.
microbe /mikrɔb/ n.m. germ.
microfilm /mikrɔfilm/ n.m. microfilm.
micro-onde /mikrɔ̃d/ n.f. microwave. **un (four à) ~s**,
microwave (oven).
microphone /mikrɔfɔn/ n.m.
microphone.
microplaquette /mikrɔplakɛt/ n.f.
(micro)chip.
microprocesseur /mikrɔprɔ-
sɛsœr/ n.m. microprocessor.
microscop|e /mikrɔskɔp/ n.m.
microscope. **~ique** a. micro-
scopic.
microsillon /mikrɔsijɔ̃/ n.m. long-
playing record.
midi /midi/ n.m. twelve o'clock,
midday, noon; (déjeuner) lunch-
time; (sud) south. **le M~**, the
South of France.
mie /mi/ n.f. soft part of the (loaf).
un pain de ~, a sandwich loaf.
miel /mjɛl/ n.m. honey.
mielleu|x, ~se /mjelø, -z/ a.
unctuous.
mien, ~ne /mjɛ̃, mjɛn/ pron. **le
~, la ~ne, les (~ne)s**, mine.
miette /mjɛt/ n.f. crumb; (fig.)
scrap. **en ~s**, in pieces.
mieux /mjø/ adv. & a. invar. better
(que, than). **le ou la ou les ~**,

(the) best. —n.m. best; (progrès)
improvement. **faire de son ~**, do
one's best. **tu ferais ~ de faire**,
you would be better off doing. **le
~ serait de**, the best thing
would be to.
mièvre /mjɛvr/ a. genteel and
insipid.
mignon, ~ne /miɲɔ̃, -ɔn/ a.
pretty.
migraine /migrɛn/ n.f. headache.
migration /migrasjɔ̃/ n.f. migration.
mijoter /miʒɔte/ v.t./i. simmer;
(tramer: fam.) cook up.
mil /mil/ n.m. a thousand.
milic|e /milis/ n.f. militia. **~ien**
n.m. militiaman.
milieu (pl. **~x**) /miljø/ n.m.
middle; (environnement) environment; (groupe) circle; (voie)
middle way; (criminel) underworld. **au ~ de**, in the middle of.
en plein ou au beau ~ de, right
in the middle (of).
militaire /militɛr/ a. military.
—n.m. soldier.
milit|er /milite/ v.i. be a militant.
~er pour, militate in favour of.
~ant, ~ante n.m., f. militant.
milk-shake /milkʃɛk/ n.m. milk
shake.
mille[1] /mil/ a. & n.m. invar. a
thousand. **deux ~**, two thous-
and. **dans le ~**, bang on target.
mille[2] /mil/ n.m. **~ (marin)**,
(nautical) mile.
millénaire /milenɛr/ n.m. millennium.
mille-pattes /milpat/ n.m. invar.
centipede.
millésime /milezim/ n.m. year.
millésimé /milezime/ a. **vin ~**,
vintage wine.
millet /mijɛ/ n.m. millet.
milliard /miljar/ n.m. thousand
million, billion. **~aire** /-dɛr/
n.m./f. multimillionaire.

millier /milje/ *n.m.* thousand. **un ~ (de)**, about a thousand.

millimètre /milimɛtr/ *n.m.* millimetre.

million /miljɔ̃/ *n.m.* million. **deux ~s (de)**, two million. **~naire** /-jɔnɛr/ *n.m./f.* millionaire.

mim|e /mim/ *n.m./f.* (*personne*) mime. —*n.m.* (*art*) mime. **~er** *v.t.* mime; (*singer*) mimic.

mimique /mimik/ *n.f.* (expressive) gestures.

mimosa /mimoza/ *n.m.* mimosa.

minable /minabl/ *a.* shabby.

minaret /minarɛ/ *n.m.* minaret.

minauder /minode/ *v.i.* simper.

minc|e /mɛ̃s/ *a.* thin; (*svelte, insignifiant*) slim. —*int.* dash (it). **~ir** *v.i.* get slimmer. **ça te ~it**, it makes you look slimmer. **~eur** *n.f.* thinness; slimness.

mine[1] /min/ *n.f.* expression; (*allure*) appearance. **avoir bonne ~**, look well. **faire ~ de**, make as if to.

mine[2] /min/ *n.f.* (*exploitation, explosif*) mine; (*de crayon*) lead. **~ de charbon**, coal-mine.

miner /mine/ *v.t.* (*saper*) undermine; (*garnir d'explosifs*) mine.

mineral /minɛr/ *n.m.* ore.

minér|al /mineral/ (*m. pl.* **~aux**) /mineral, -o/ *a.* mineral. —*n.m.* (*pl.* **~aux**) mineral.

minéralogique /mineralɔʒik/ *a.* **plaque ~**, number/license (*Amer.*) plate.

minet|, ~te /minɛ, -t/ *n.m., f.* (*chat: fam.*) puss(y).

mineur[1]**, ~e** /minœr/ *a.* minor; (*jurid.*) under age. —*n.m., f.* (*jurid.*) minor.

mineur[2] /minœr/ *n.m.* (*ouvrier*) miner.

mini- /mini/ *préf.* mini-.

miniature /minjatyr/ *n.f. & a.* miniature.

minibus /minibys/ *n.m.* minibus.

min|ier, ~ière /minje, -jɛr/ *a.* mining.

minim|al (*m. pl.* **~aux**) /minimal, -o/ *a.* minimum.

minime /minim/ *a.* minor. —*n.m./f.* (*sport*) junior.

minimiser /minimize/ *v.t.* minimize.

minimum /minimɔm/ *a. & n.m.* minimum. **au ~**, (*pour le moins*) at the very least.

mini-ordinateur /miniɔrdinatœr/ *n.m.* minicomputer.

minist|ère /ministɛr/ *n.m.* ministry; (*gouvernement*) government. **~ère de l'Intérieur**, Home Office; (*Amer.*) Department of the Interior. **~ériel, ~érielle** *a.* ministerial, government.

ministre /ministr/ *n.m.* minister. **~ de l'Intérieur**, Home Secretary; (*Amer.*) Secretary of the Interior.

Minitel /minitɛl/ *n.m.* (P.) Minitel (*telephone videotext system*).

minorer /minore/ *v.t.* reduce.

minorit|é /minorite/ *n.f.* minority. **~aire** *a.* minority. **être ~aire**, be in the minority.

minuit /minɥi/ *n.m.* midnight.

minuscule /minyskyl/ *a.* minute. —*n.f.* (*lettre*) **~**, small letter.

minut|e /minyt/ *n.f.* minute. **~er** *v.t.* time (to the minute).

minuterie /minytri/ *n.f.* time-switch.

minutie /minysi/ *n.f.* meticulousness.

minutieu|x, ~se /minysjø, -z/ *a.* meticulous. **~sement** *adv.* meticulously.

mioche /mjoʃ/ *n.m., f.* (*fam.*) youngster, kid.

mirabelle /mirabɛl/ *n.f.* (mirabelle) plum.

miracle /mirakl/ *n.m.* miracle.

miraculeu|x, ~se /mirakylø, -z/ *a.* miraculous. **~sement** *adv.* miraculously.

mirage /miraʒ/ *n.m.* mirage.

mire /mir/ *n.f.* (*fig.*) centre of attraction; (TV) test card.

miro /miro/ *a. invar.* (*fam.*) short-sighted.

mirobolant, ~e /mirobolã, -t/ *a.* (*fam.*) marvellous.

miroir /mirwar/ *n.m.* mirror.

miroiter /mirwate/ *v.i.* gleam, shimmer.

mis, ~e[1] /mi, miz/ *voir* mettre. —*a.* **bien ~**, well-dressed.

misanthrope /mizãtrɔp/ *n.m.* misanthropist. —*a.* misanthropic.

mise[2] /miz/ *n.f.* (*argent*) stake; (*tenue*) attire. **~ à feu**, blast-off. **~ au point**, adjustment; (*fig.*) clarification. **~ de fonds**, capital outlay. **~ en garde**, warning. **~ en scène**, (*théâtre*) production; (*cinéma*) direction.

miser /mize/ *v.t.* (*argent*) bet, stake (sur, on). **~ sur**, (*compter sur:* *fam.*) bank on.

misérable /mizerabl/ *a.* miserable, wretched; (*indigent*) poverty-stricken; (*minable*) seedy. —*n.m./f.* wretch.

misère /mizɛr/ *n.f.* (grinding) poverty; (*malheur*) misery. **~eux, ~euse** *n.m., f.* pauper.

miséricorde /mizerikɔrd/ *n.f.* mercy.

missel /misɛl/ *n.m.* missal.

missile /misil/ *n.m.* missile.

mission /misjɔ̃/ *n.f.* mission. **~naire** /-jɔnɛr/ *n.m./f.* missionary.

missive /misiv/ *n.f.* missive.

mistral /mistral/ *n.m. invar.* (*vent*) mistral.

mitaine /mitɛn/ *n.f.* mitten.

mit|e /mit/ *n.f.* (clothes-)moth. **~é** *a.* moth-eaten.

mi-temps /mitã/ *n.f. invar.* (*repos: sport*) half-time; (*période: sport*) half. **à ~**, part time.

miteu|x, ~se /mitø, -z/ *a.* shabby.

mitigé /mitiʒe/ *a.* (*modéré*) lukewarm.

mitonner /mitone/ *v.t.* cook slowly with care; (*fig.*) cook up.

mitoyen, ~ne /mitwajɛ̃, -ɛn/ *a.* **mur ~**, party wall.

mitrailler /mitraje/ *v.t.* machine-gun; (*fig.*) bombard.

mitraill|ette /mitrajɛt/ *n.f.* sub-machine-gun. **~euse** *n.f.* machine-gun.

mi-voix (à) /(a)mivwa/ *adv.* in an undertone.

mixeur /miksœr/ *n.m.* liquidizer, blender.

mixte /mikst/ *a.* mixed; (*usage*) dual; (*tribunal*) joint; (*école*) co-educational.

mixture /mikstyr/ *n.f.* (*péj.*) mixture.

mobile[1] /mɔbil/ *a.* mobile; (*pièce*) moving; (*feuillet*) loose. —*n.m.* (*art*) mobile.

mobile[2] /mɔbil/ *n.m.* (*raison*) motive.

mobilier /mɔbilje/ *n.m.* furniture.

mobilis|er /mɔbilize/ *v.t.* mobilize. **~ation** *n.f.* mobilization.

mobilité /mɔbilite/ *n.f.* mobility.

mobylette /mɔbilɛt/ *n.f.* (P.) moped.

mocassin /mɔkasɛ̃/ *n.m.* moccasin.

moche /mɔʃ/ *a.* (*laid: fam.*) ugly; (*mauvais: fam.*) lousy.

modalité /mɔdalite/ *n.f.* mode.

mode[1] /mɔd/ *n.f.* fashion; (*coutume*) custom. **à la ~**, fashionable.

mode[2] /mɔd/ *n.m.* method, mode; (*genre*) way. **~ d'emploi**, directions (for use).

modèle /mɔdɛl/ *n.m. & a.* model. **~ réduit**, (small-scale) model.

modeler /mɔdle/ *v.t.* model (sur, on). **se ~ sur**, model o.s. on.

modem /mɔdɛm/ *n.m.* modem.

modéré, ∼e /mɔdere/ a. & n.m., f. moderate. ∼ment adv. moderately.

modér|er /mɔdere/ v.t. moderate. se ∼er v. pr. restrain o.s. ∼ateur, ∼atrice a. moderating. ∼ation n.f. moderation.

modern|e /mɔdɛrn/ a. modern. —n.m. modern style. ∼iser v.t. modernize.

modest|e /mɔdɛst/ a. modest. ∼ement adv. modestly. ∼ie n.f. modesty.

modif|ier /mɔdifje/ v.t. modify. se ∼ier v. pr. alter. ∼ication n.f. modification.

modique /mɔdik/ a. low.

modiste /mɔdist/ n.f. milliner.

module /mɔdyl/ n.m. module.

modul|er /mɔdyle/ v.t./i. modulate. ∼ation n.f. modulation.

moelle /mwal/ n.f. marrow. ∼ épinière, spinal cord.

moelleu|x, ∼se /mwalø, -z/ a. soft; (onctueux) smooth.

mœurs /mœr(s)/ n.f. pl. (morale) morals; (habitudes) customs; (manières) ways.

moi /mwa/ pron. me; (indirect) (to) me; (sujet) I. —n.m. self. ∼-même pron. myself.

moignon /mwaɲɔ̃/ n.m. stump.

moindre /mwɛ̃dr/ a. (moins grand) less(er). le ou la ∼, les ∼s, the slightest, the least.

moine /mwan/ n.m. monk.

moineau (pl. ∼x) /mwano/ n.m. sparrow.

moins /mwɛ̃/ adv. less (que, than). —prép. (soustraction) minus. ∼ de, (quantité) less, not so much (que, as); (objets, personnes) fewer, not so many (que, as). ∼ de dix francs/d'une livre/etc., less than ten francs/one pound/ etc. le ou la ou les ∼, the least. le ∼ grand/haut, the smallest/lowest. au ∼, du ∼, at least. de ∼, less. en ∼, less;

(manquant) missing. une heure ∼ dix, ten to one. à ∼ que, unless. de ∼ en moins, less and less.

mois /mwa/ n.m. month.

moise /mwaz/ n.m. moses basket.

mois|i /mwazi/ a. mouldy. —n.m. mould. de ∼i, (odeur, goût) musty. ∼ir v.i. go mouldy. ∼issure n.f. mould.

moisson /mwasɔ̃/ n.f. harvest.

moissonn|er /mwasɔne/ v.t. harvest, reap. ∼eur, ∼euse n.m., f. harvester. ∼euse-batteuse (pl. ∼euses-batteuses) n.f. combine harvester.

moit|e /mwat/ a. sticky, clammy. ∼eur n.f. stickiness.

moitié /mwatje/ n.f. half; (milieu) half-way mark. à ∼, half-way. à ∼ vide/fermé/etc., half empty/ closed/etc. à ∼ prix, (at) half-price. la ∼ de, half (of). ∼ ∼, moitié, half-and-half.

moka /mɔka/ n.m. (gâteau) coffee cream cake.

mol /mɔl/ voir mou.

molaire /mɔlɛr/ n.f. molar.

molécule /mɔlekyl/ n.f. molecule.

molester /mɔlɛste/ v.t. manhandle, rough up.

molle /mɔl/ voir mou.

moll|ement /mɔlmɑ̃/ adv. softly; (faiblement) feebly. ∼esse n.f. softness; (faiblesse, indolence) feebleness.

mollet /mɔlɛ/ n.m. (de jambe) calf.

molletonné /mɔltɔne/ a. (fleece-) lined.

mollir /mɔlir/ v.i. soften; (céder) yield.

mollusque /mɔlysk/ n.m. mollusc.

môme /mom/ n.m./f. (fam.) kid.

moment /mɔmɑ̃/ n.m. moment; (période) time. (petit) ∼, short while. au ∼ où, when. par ∼s, now and then. du ∼ où ou que, seeing that. en ce ∼, at the moment.

momentané /mɔmɑ̃tane/ a. momentary. **~ment** adv. momentarily; (*en ce moment*) at present.

momie /mɔmi/ n.f. mummy.

mon, ma ou **mon*** (pl. **mes**) /mɔ̃, ma, mɔ̃, me/ a. my.

Monaco /mɔnako/ n.f. Monaco.

monarchie /mɔnaʀʃi/ n.f. monarchy.

monarque /mɔnaʀk/ n.m. monarque.

monastère /mɔnastɛʀ/ n.m. monastery.

monceau (pl. **~x**) /mɔ̃so/ n.m. heap, pile.

mondain /mɔ̃dɛ̃/, **~e** /mɔ̃dɛ̃, -ɛn/ a. society, social.

monde /mɔ̃d/ n.m. world. **du ~,** (a lot of) people; (*quelqu'un*) somebody. **le** (**grand**) **~,** (high) society. **se faire un ~ de qch.,** make a great deal of fuss about sth.

mondial (m. pl. **~iaux**) /mɔ̃djal, -jo/ a. world; (*influence*) world-wide. **~ialement** adv. the world over.

monégasque /mɔnegask/ a. & n.m./f. Monegasque.

monétaire /mɔnetɛʀ/ a. monetary.

moni|teur, ~trice /mɔnitœʀ, -tʀis/ n.m., f. instructor, instructress; (*de colonie de vacances*) supervisor; (*Amer.*) (camp) counselor.

monnaie /mɔnɛ/ n.f. currency; (*pièce*) coin; (*appoint*) change. **faire la ~ de,** get change for. **faire ~ de qn. la ~,** give s.o. change for. **menue** ou **petite ~,** small change.

monnayer /mɔneje/ v.t. convert into cash.

mono /mɔno/ a. invar. mono.

monocle /mɔnɔkl/ n.m. monocle.

monocorde /mɔnɔkɔʀd/ a. monotonous.

monogramme /mɔnɔgʀam/ n.m. monogram.

monologue /mɔnɔlɔg/ n.m. monologue.

monopol|e /mɔnɔpɔl/ n.m. monopoly. **~iser** v.t. monopolize.

monosyllabe /mɔnɔsilab/ n.m. monosyllable.

monoton|e /mɔnɔtɔn/ a. monotonous. **~ie** n.f. monotony.

monseigneur /mɔ̃sɛɲœʀ/ n.m. Your ou His Grace.

monsieur (pl. **messieurs**) /məsjø, mesjø/ n.m. gentleman. **M~** ou **M. Dupont,** Mr Dupont. **Messieurs** ou **MM. Dupont,** Messrs Dupont. oui **~,** yes; (*avec déférence*) yes, sir.

monstre /mɔ̃stʀ/ n.m. monster. —a. (*fam.*) colossal.

monstr|ueux, ~ueuse /mɔ̃stʀyø, -z/ a. monstrous. **~uosité** n.f. monstrosity.

mont /mɔ̃/ n.m. mount. **par ~s et par vaux,** up hill and down dale.

montage /mɔ̃taʒ/ n.m. (*assemblage*) assembly; (*cinéma*) editing.

montagn|e /mɔ̃taɲ/ n.f. mountain; (*région*) mountains. **~es russes,** roller-coaster. **~ard, ~arde** n.m., f. mountain dweller. **~eux, ~euse** a. mountainous.

montant¹, ~e /mɔ̃tɑ̃, -t/ a. rising; (*col*) high-necked.

montant² /mɔ̃tɑ̃/ n.m. amount; (*pièce de bois*) upright.

mont-de-piété (pl. **monts-de-piété**) /mɔ̃dpjete/ n.m. pawnshop.

monte-charge /mɔ̃tʃaʀʒ/ n.m. invar. service lift; (*Amer.*) dumb waiter.

montée /mɔ̃te/ n.f. ascent, climb; (*de prix*) rise; (*côte*) hill. **au milieu de la ~,** halfway up. **à la ~ de lait,** when the milk comes.

monter /mɔ̃te/ v.i. (aux. être) go ou come up; (*grimper*) climb; (*prix, mer*) rise. **~ à,** (*cheval*) mount. **~**

dans, (train, avion) get on to; (voiture) get into. ～ sur, (colline) climb up; (trône) ascend. —v.t. (aux. avoir) go ou come up; (objet) take ou bring up; (cheval, garde) mount; (société) start up. ～ à cheval, (sport) ride. ～ en flèche, soar. ～ en graine, go to seed.

monteu|r /mɔ̃tœr, -øz/ n.m., f. (techn.) fitter; (cinéma) editor.

monticule /mɔ̃tikyl/ n.m. mound.

montre /mɔ̃tr/ n.f. watch. ～-bracelet (pl. ～s-bracelets) n.f. wrist-watch. faire ～ de, show.

montrer /mɔ̃tre/ v.t. show (à, to). se ～ v. pr. show o.s.; (être) be; (s'avérer) prove to be. ～ du doigt, point to.

monture /mɔ̃tyr/ n.f. (cheval) mount; (de lunettes) frame; (de bijou) setting.

monument /mɔnymɑ̃/ n.m. monument. ～ aux morts, war memorial. ～al (m. pl. ～aux) /-tal, -to/ a. monumental.

moqu|er (se) /(sə)mɔke/ v. pr. se ～er de, make fun of. je m'en ～e, (fam.) I couldn't care less. ～erie n.f. mockery. ～eur, ～euse a. mocking.

moquette /mɔkɛt/ n.f. fitted carpet; (Amer.) wall-to-wall carpeting.

mor|al, ～ale (m. pl. ～aux) /mɔral, -o/ a. moral. —n.m. (pl. ～aux) morale. —n.f. moral code; (mœurs) morals; (de fable) moral. avoir le ～al, be on form. ça m'a remonté le ～al, it gave me a boost. faire la ～ale à, lecture. ～alement adv. morally. ～alité n.f. morality; (de fable) moral.

moralisa|teur, ～trice /mɔralizatœr, -tris/ a. moralizing.

morbide /mɔrbid/ a. morbid.

morceau (pl. ～x) /mɔrso/ n.m. piece, bit; (de sucre) lump; (de

viande) cut; (passage) passage.

manger un ～, have a bite to eat.

mettre en ～x, smash ou tear etc. to bits.

morceler /mɔrsəle/ v.t. fragment.

mordant, ～e /mɔrdɑ̃, -t/ a. scathing; (froid) biting. —n.m. (énergie) vigour, punch.

mordiller /mɔrdije/ v.t. nibble at.

mord|re /mɔrdr/ v.t./i. bite. ～re sur, overlap into. ～re à l'hameçon, bite. ～u, ～ue n.m., f. (fam.) fan; a. bitten. ～u de, (fam.) crazy about.

morfondre (se) /(sə)mɔrfɔ̃dr/ v. pr. mope, wait anxiously.

morgue[1] /mɔrg/ n.f. morgue, mortuary.

morgue[2] /mɔrg/ n.f. (attitude) haughtiness.

moribond, ～e /mɔribɔ̃, -d/ a. dying.

morne /mɔrn/ a. dull.

morose /mɔroz/ a. morose.

morphine /mɔrfin/ n.f. morphine.

mors /mɔr/ n.m. (de cheval) bit.

morse[1] /mɔrs/ n.m. walrus.

morse[2] /mɔrs/ n.m. (code) Morse code.

morsure /mɔrsyr/ n.f. bite.

mort[1] /mɔr/ n.f. death.

mort[2], ～e /mɔr, -t/ a. dead. —n.m., f. dead man, dead woman. les ～s, the dead. ～ de fatigue, dead tired. ～-né a. stillborn.

mortadelle /mɔrtadɛl/ n.f. mortadella.

mortalité /mɔrtalite/ n.f. death rate.

mortel, ～le /mɔrtɛl/ a. mortal; (accident) fatal; (poison, silence) deadly. —n.m., f. mortal. ～lement adv. mortally.

mortier /mɔrtje/ n.m. mortar.

mortifié /mɔrtifje/ a. mortified.

mortuaire /mɔrtɥɛr/ a. (cérémonie) funeral; (avis) death.

morue /mɔry/ n.f. cod.

mosaïque /mɔzaik/ n.f. mosaic.

Moscou /mɔsku/ n.m./f. Moscow.

mosquée /mɔske/ n.f. mosque.

mot /mo/ n.m. word; (*lettre*, *message*) line, note. **~ d'ordre**, watchword. **~ de passe**, password. **~s croisés**, cross-word (puzzle).

motard /mɔtar/ n.m. biker; (*policier*) police motorcyclist.

motel /mɔtɛl/ n.m. motel.

moteur¹ /mɔtœr/ n.m. engine, motor. **barque à ~**, motor launch.

mo|teur², **~trice** /mɔtœr, -tris/ a. (*nerf*) motor; (*force*) driving. **à 4 roues motrices**, 4-wheel drive.

motif /mɔtif/ n.m. reason; (*jurid.*) motive; (*dessin*) pattern.

motion /mɔsjɔ̃/ n.f. motion.

motiv|er /mɔtive/ v.t. motivate; (*justifier*) justify. **~ation** n.f. motivation.

moto /mɔto/ n.f. motor cycle. **~cycliste** n.m./f. motorcyclist.

motorisé /mɔtorize/ a. motorized.

motrice /mɔtris/ *voir* **moteur²**.

motte /mɔt/ n.f. lump; (*de beurre*) slab; (*de terre*) clod. **~ de gazon**, turf.

mou *ou* **mol***, **molle** /mu, mɔl/ a. soft; (*péj.*) flabby; (*faible*, *indolent*) feeble. —n.m. **du ~**, slack. **avoir du ~**, be slack.

mouchard /muʃar/ n.m. (*fam.*) informer; (*scol.*) sneak. **~er** /-de/ v.t. (*fam.*) inform on.

mouche /muʃ/ n.f. fly.

moucher (se) /(sə)muʃe/ v. pr. blow one's nose.

moucheron /muʃrɔ̃/ n.m. midge.

moucheté /muʃte/ a. speckled.

mouchoir /muʃwar/ n.m. hanky; handkerchief; (*en papier*) tissue.

moudre /mudr/ v.t. grind.

moue /mu/ n.f. long face. **faire la ~**, pull a long face.

mouette /mwɛt/ n.f. (sea)gull.

moufle /mufl/ n.f. (*gant*) mitten.

mouill|er /muje/ v.t. wet, make

wet. **se ~** v. pr. get (o.s.) wet. **~er (l'ancre)**, anchor. **~é** a. wet.

moulage /mulaʒ/ n.m. cast.

moul|e¹ /mul/ n.m. mould. **~er** v.t. mould; (*statue*) cast. **~e à gâteau**, cake tin. **~e à tarte**, flan dish.

moule² /mul/ n.f. (*coquillage*) mussel.

moulin /mulɛ̃/ n.m. mill; (*moteur*: *fam.*) engine. **~ à vent**, windmill.

moulinet /mulinɛ/ n.m. (*de canne à pêche*) reel. **faire des ~s avec qch.**, twirl sth. around.

moulinette /mulinɛt/ n.f. (P.) purée maker.

moulu /muly/ a. ground; (*fatigué*: *fam.*) dead beat.

moulure /mulyr/ n.f. moulding.

mourant, **~e** /murã, -t/ a. dying. —n.m., f. dying person.

mourir† /murir/ v.i. (*aux. être*) die. **~ d'envie de**, be dying to. **~ de faim**, be starving. **~ d'ennui**, be dead bored.

mousquetaire /muskətɛr/ n.m. musketeer.

mousse¹ /mus/ n.f. moss; (*écume*) froth, foam; (*de savon*) lather; (*dessert*) mousse. **~ à raser**, shaving cream.

mousse² /mus/ n.m. ship's boy.

mousseline /muslin/ n.f. muslin; (*de soie*) chiffon.

mousser /muse/ v.i. froth, foam; (*savon*) lather.

mousseu|x, **~se** /musø, -z/ a. frothy. —n.m. sparkling wine.

mousson /musɔ̃/ n.f. monsoon.

moustach|e /mustaʃ/ n.f. moustache. **~es**, (*d'animal*) whiskers. **~u** a. wearing a moustache.

moustiquaire /mustikɛr/ n.f. mosquito-net.

moustique /mustik/ n.m. mosquito.

moutarde /mutard/ n.f. mustard.

mouton /mutɔ̃/ *n.m.* sheep; (*peau*) sheepskin; (*viande*) mutton.

mouvant, **~e** /muvɑ̃, -t/ *a.* changing; (*terrain*) shifting.

mouvement /muvmɑ̃/ *n.m.* movement; (*agitation*) bustle; (*en gymnastique*) exercise; (*impulsion*) impulse; (*tendance*) tendency. **en ~,** in motion.

mouvementé /muvmɑ̃te/ *a.* eventful.

mouvoir† /muvwar/ *v.t.* (*membre*) move. **se ~** *v. pr.* move.

moyen¹, **~ne** /mwajɛ̃, -jɛn/ *a.* average; (*médiocre*) average; (*scol.*) pass-mark. **de taille ~ne,** medium-sized. **~ âge,** Middle Ages. **~ne d'âge,** average age. **M~-Orient** /mɔ-/ *n.m.* Middle East. **~nement** /-jɛnmɑ̃/ *adv.* moderately.

moyen² /mwajɛ̃/ *n.m.* means, way. **~s,** means; (*dons*) abilities. **au ~ de,** by means of. **il n'y a pas ~ de,** it is not possible to.

moyennant /mwajɛnɑ̃/ *prép.* (*pour*) for; (*grâce à*) with.

moyeu (*pl.* **~x**) /mwajø/ *n.m.* hub.

mû, mue¹ /my/ *a.* driven (**par,** by).

mucoviscidose /mykɔvisidoz/ *n.f.* cystic fibrosis.

mue² /my/ *n.f.* moulting; (*de voix*) breaking of the voice.

muer /mɥe/ *v.i.* moult; (*voix*) break. **se ~ en,** change into.

muesli /mysli/ *n.m.* muesli.

muet, **~te** /mɥɛ, -t/ *a.* (*personne*) dumb; (*fig.*) speechless (**de,** with); (*silencieux*) silent. *—n.m., f.* dumb person.

mufle /myfl/ *n.m.* nose, muzzle; (*personne: fam.*) boor, lout.

mugir /myʒir/ *v.i.* (*vache*) moo; (*bœuf*) bellow; (*fig.*) howl.

muguet /mygɛ/ *n.m.* lily of the valley.

mule /myl/ *n.f.* (she-)mule; (*pantoufle*) mule.

mulet /mylɛ/ *n.m.* (he-)mule.

multi- /mylti/ *préf.* multi-.

multicolore /myltikɔlɔr/ *a.* multi-coloured.

multinational, **~ale** (*m. pl.* **~aux**) /myltinasjɔnal, -o/ *a. & n.f.* multinational.

multiple /myltipl/ *a. & n.m.* multiple.

multiplicité /myltiplisite/ *n.f.* multiplicity, abundance.

multiplier /myltiplije/ *v.t.,* **se ~ier** *v. pr.* multiply. **~ication** *n.f.* multiplication.

multitude /myltityd/ *n.f.* multitude, mass.

municipal (*m. pl.* **~aux**) /mynisipal, -o/ *a.* municipal; (*conseil*) town. **~alité** *n.f.* (*ville*) municipality; (*conseil*) town council.

munir /mynir/ *v.t.* **~ de,** provide with. **se ~ de,** provide o.s. with.

munitions /mynisjɔ̃/ *n.f. pl.* ammunition.

mur /myr/ *n.m.* wall. **~ du son,** sound barrier.

mûr /myr/ *a.* ripe; (*personne*) mature.

muraille /myraj/ *n.f.* (high) wall.

mural, **~al** (*m. pl.* **~aux**) /myral, -o/ *a.* wall; (*tableau*) mural.

mûre /myr/ *n.f.* blackberry.

muret /myrɛ/ *n.m.* low wall.

mûrir /myrir/ *v.t./i.* ripen; (*abcès*) come to a head; (*personne, projet*) mature.

murmur|e /myrmyr/ *n.m.* murmur. **~er** *v.t./i.* murmur.

musc /mysk/ *n.m.* musk.

muscade /myskad/ *n.f.* **noix (de ~,** nutmeg.

muscl|e /myskl/ *n.m.* muscle. **~é** *a.* muscular, brawny.

muscul|aire /myskylɛr/ *a.* muscular. **~ature** *n.f.* muscles.

museau (*pl.* **~x**) /myzo/ *n.m.* muzzle; (*de porc*) snout.

musée /myze/ *n.m.* museum; (*de peinture*) art gallery.

museler /myzle/ *v.t.* muzzle.

muselière /myzəljɛr/ *n.f.* muzzle.

musette /myzɛt/ *n.f.* haver-sack.

muséum /myzeɔm/ *n.m.* (natural history) museum.

music|**al** (*m. pl.* **~aux**) /myzikal, -o/ *a.* musical.

music-hall /myzikol/ *n.m.* variety theatre.

musicien, ~ne /myzisjɛ̃, -jɛn/ *a.* musical. —*n.m., f.* musician.

musique /myzik/ *n.f.* music; (*orchestre*) band.

musulman, ~e /myzylmɑ̃, -an/ *a.* & *n.m., f.* Muslim.

mutation /mytasjɔ̃/ *n.f.* change; (*biologique*) mutation.

muter /myte/ *v.t.* transfer.

mutil|**er** /mytile/ *v.t.* mutilate. **~ation** /-si/ *n.f.* mutilation. **~é, ée** *a. & n.m., f.* disabled (person).

mutin, ~e /mytɛ̃, -in/ *a.* saucy. —*n.m., f.* rebel.

mutin|**er (se)** /(sə)mytine/ *v. pr.* mutiny. **~é** *a.* mutinous. **~erie** *n.f.* mutiny.

mutisme /mytism/ *n.m.* silence.

mutuel, ~le /mytɥɛl/ *a.* mutual. —*n.f.* Friendly Society; (*Amer.*) benefit society. **~lement** *adv.* mutually; (*l'un l'autre*) each other.

myop|**e** /mjɔp/ *a.* short-sighted. **~ie** *n.f.* short-sightedness.

myosotis /mjozotis/ *n.m.* forget-me-not.

myriade /mirjad/ *n.f.* myriad.

myrtille /mirtij/ *n.f.* bilberry; (*Amer.*) blueberry.

mystère /mistɛr/ *n.m.* mystery.

mystérieu|**x, ~se** /misterjø, -z/ *a.* mysterious.

mystif|**ier** /mistifje/ *v.t.* deceive, hoax. **~ication** *n.f.* hoax.

mysti|**que** /mistik/ *a.* mystic(al). —*n.m./f.* mystic. —*n.f.* (*puissance*) mystique. **~cisme** *n.m.* mysticism.

myth|**e** /mit/ *n.m.* myth. **~ique** *a.* mythical.

mytholog|**ie** /mitoloʒi/ *n.f.* mythology. **~ique** *a.* mythological.

mythomane /mitɔman/ *n.m./f.* compulsive liar (and fantasizer).

N

n' /n/ *voir* ne.

nacre /nakr/ *n.f.* mother-of-pearl. **~é** *a.* pearly.

nage /naʒ/ *n.f.* swimming; (*manière*) (swimming) stroke. **à la ~**, by swimming. **traverser à la ~**, swim across. **en ~**, sweating.

nageoire /naʒwar/ *n.f.* fin.

nag|**er** /naʒe/ *v.t./i.* swim. **~eur, ~euse** *n.m., f.* swimmer.

naguère /nagɛr/ *adv.* some time ago.

naï|**f, ~ve** /naif, -v/ *a.* naïve.

nain, ~e /nɛ̃, nɛn/ *n.m., f.* & *a.* dwarf.

naissance /nɛsɑ̃s/ *n.f.* birth. **donner ~ à**, give birth to, (*fig.*) give rise to.

naître /nɛtr/ *v.i.* be born; (*résulter*) arise (**de**, from). **faire ~**, (*susciter*) give rise to.

naïveté /naivte/ *n.f.* naïvety.

nana /nana/ *n.f.* (*fam.*) girl.

nanti /nɑ̃ti/ *a.* **les ~s**, the affluent.

nantir /nɑ̃tir/ *v.t.* **~ de**, provide with.

naphtaline /naftalin/ *n.f.* moth-balls.

nappe /nap/ *n.f.* table-cloth; (*de pétrole, gaz*) layer. **~ phréatique**, ground water.

napperon /naprɔ̃/ *n.m.* (cloth) table-mat.

narcotique /narkɔtik/ *a. & n.m.* narcotic.

narguer /narge/ *v.t.* mock.

narine /narin/ *n.f.* nostril.

narquois, **~e** /narkwa, -z/ *a.* derisive.

narr|er /nare/ *v.t.* narrate. **~ateur**, **~atrice** *n.m.*, *f.* narrator. **~ation** *n.f.* narrative; (*action*) narration; (*scol.*) composition.

nas|al (*m. pl.* **~aux**) /nazal, -o/ *a.* nasal.

naseau (*pl.* **~x**) /nazo/ *n.m.* nostril.

nasiller /nazije/ *v.i.* have a nasal twang.

nat|al (*m. pl.* **~als**) /natal/ *a.* native.

natalité /natalite/ *n.f.* birth rate.

natation /natasjɔ̃/ *n.f.* swimming.

nati|f, **~ve** /natif, -v/ *a.* native.

nation /nasjɔ̃/ *n.f.* nation.

nation|al, **~ale** (*m. pl.* **~aux**) /nasjonal, -o/ *a.* national. —*n.f.* A road; (*Amer.*) highway. **~aliser** *v.t.* nationalize. **~alisme** *n.m.* nationalism.

nationalité /nasjonalite/ *n.f.* nationality.

Nativité /nativite/ *n.f.* **la ~**, the Nativity.

natte /nat/ *n.f.* (*de cheveux*) plait; (*tapis de paille*) mat.

naturaliser /natyralize/ *v.t.* naturalize.

nature /natyr/ *n.f.* nature. —*a. invar.* (*eau, omelette, etc.*) plain. **de ~** à, likely to. **payer en ~**, pay in kind. **~ morte**, still life.

naturel, **~le** /natyrɛl/ *a.* natural. —*n.m.* nature; (*simplicité*) naturalness. **~lement** *adv.* naturally.

naufrag|e /nofraʒ/ *n.m.* (ship)-wreck. **faire ~e**, be ship-wrecked; (*bateau*) be wrecked. **~é**, **~ée** *a.* & *n.m.*, *f.* shipwrecked (person).

nauséabond, **~e** /nozeabɔ̃, -d/ *a.* nauseating.

nausée /noze/ *n.f.* nausea.

nautique /notik/ *a.* nautical; (*sports*) aquatic.

naval (*m. pl.* **~s**) /naval/ *a.* naval.

navet /navɛ/ *n.m.* turnip; (*film, tableau*) dud.

navette /navɛt/ *n.f.* shuttle (service). **faire la ~**, shuttle back and forth.

navigable /navigabl/ *a.* navigable.

navig|uer /navige/ *v.i.* sail; (*piloter*) navigate. **~ateur** *n.m.* seafarer; (*d'avion*) navigator. **~ation** *n.f.* navigation; (*trafic*) shipping.

navire /navir/ *n.m.* ship.

navré /navre/ *a.* sorry (de, to).

navrer /navre/ *v.t.* upset.

ne, **n'** /na, n/ *adv.* **ne pas**, not. **ne jamais**, never. **ne plus**, (*temps*) no longer, not any more. **ne que**, only. **je crains qu'il ne parte**, (*sans valeur négative*) I am afraid he will leave.

né, **née** /ne/ *voir* **naître**. —*a.* & *n.m.*, *f.* born. **il est né**, he was born. **premier-/dernier-né**, first-/last-born. **née Martin**, née Martin.

néanmoins /neɑ̃mwɛ̃/ *adv.* nevertheless.

néant /neɑ̃/ *n.m.* nothingness; (*aucun*) none.

nébuleu|x, **~se** /nebylø, -z/ *a.* nebulous.

nécessaire /nesesɛr/ *a.* necessary. —*n.m.* (*sac*) bag; (*trousse*) kit. **le ~**, (*l'indispensable*) the necessities. **faire le ~**, do what is necessary. **~ment** *adv.* necessarily.

nécessité /nesesite/ *n.f.* necessity.

nécessiter /nesesite/ *v.t.* necessitate.

nécrologie /nekrɔlɔʒi/ *n.f.* obituary.

néerlandais, **~e** /neɛrlɑ̃dɛ, -z/ *a.* Dutch. —*n.m.*, *f.* Dutchman, Dutchwoman. **~**, (*lang.*) Dutch.

nef /nɛf/ *n.f.* nave.

néfaste /nefast/ *a.* harmful (à, to); (*funeste*) ill-fated.

négati|f, ~ve /negatif, -v/ *a. & n.m., f.* negative.

négation /negɑsjɔ̃/ *n.f.* negation.

négligé /negliʒe/ *a.* (*tenue, travail*) slovenly. —*n.m.* (*tenue*) négligé.

négligeable /negliʒabl/ *a.* negligible, insignificant.

néglig|ent, ~te /negliʒɑ̃, -t/ *a.* careless, negligent. **~ce** *n.f.* carelessness, negligence; (*erreur*) omission.

négliger /negliʒe/ *v.t.* neglect; (*ne pas tenir compte de*) disregard. **se ~** *v. pr.* neglect o.s.

négoce /negɔs/ *n.m.* business. **~iant, ~iante** *n.m., f.* merchant.

négoc|ier /negɔsje/ *v.t./i.* negotiate. **~iable** *a.* negotiable. **~iateur, ~iatrice** *n.m., f.* negotiator. **~iation** *n.f.* negotiation.

nègre[1] /nɛgr/ *a.* (*musique etc.*) Negro.

nègre[2] /nɛgr/ *n.m.* (*écrivain*) ghost writer.

neige /nɛʒ/ *n.f.* snow. **~eux, ~euse** *a.* snowy.

neiger /neʒe/ *v.i.* snow.

nénuphar /nenyfar/ *n.m.* water-lily.

néologisme /neɔlɔʒism/ *n.m.* neologism.

néon /neɔ̃/ *n.m.* neon.

néo-zélandais, ~e /neozelɑ̃dɛ, -z/ *a.* New Zealand. —*n.m., f.* New Zealander.

nerf /nɛr/ *n.m.* nerve; (*vigueur: fam.*) stamina.

nerv|eux, ~euse /nɛrvø, -z/ *a.* nervous; (*irritable*) nervy; (*centre, cellule*) nerve-; (*voiture*) responsive. **~eusement** *adv.* nervously. **~osité** *n.f.* nervousness; (*irritabilité*) touchiness.

nervure /nɛrvyr/ *n.f.* (*bot.*) vein.

net, ~te /nɛt/ *a.* (*clair, distinct*) clear; (*propre*) clean; (*soigné*) neat; (*prix, poids*) net. —*adv.* (*s'arrêter*) dead; (*refuser*) flatly; (*parler*) plainly; (*se casser*) clean. **~tement** *adv.* clearly; (*certainement*) definitely.

netteté /nɛtte/ *n.f.* clearness.

nettoyer /nɛtwaje/ *v.t.* clean. **~age** *n.m.* cleaning. **~age à sec,** dry-cleaning.

neuf[1] /nœf/ (/nœv/ *before heures, ans*) *a. & n.m.* nine.

neu|f[2], **~ve** /nœf, -v/ *a. & n.m.* new. **remettre à ~f,** brighten up. **du ~f,** (*fait nouveau*) some new development.

neutr|e /nøtr/ *a.* neutral; (*gram.*) neuter. —*n.m.* (*gram.*) neuter. **~alité** *n.f.* neutrality.

neutron /nøtrɔ̃/ *n.m.* neutron.

neuve /nœv/ *voir* **neuf**[2].

neuvième /nœvjɛm/ *a. & n.m./f.* ninth.

neveu (*pl.* **~x**) /nəvø/ *n.m.* nephew.

névros|e /nevroz/ *n.f.* neurosis. **~é, ~ée** *a. & n.m., f.* neurotic.

nez /ne/ *n.m.* nose. **~ à nez,** face to face. **~ épaté,** flat nose. **~ retroussé,** turned-up nose. **avoir du ~,** have flair.

ni /ni/ *conj.* neither, nor. **ni grand ni petit,** neither big nor small. **ni l'un ni l'autre ne fument,** neither (one nor the other) smokes.

niais, ~e /njɛ, -z/ *a.* silly. —*n.m., f.* simpleton. **~erie** /-zri/ *n.f.* silliness.

niche /niʃ/ *n.f.* (*de chien*) kennel; (*cavité*) niche; (*farce*) trick.

nichée /niʃe/ *n.f.* brood.

nicher /niʃe/ *v.i.* nest. **se ~** *v. pr.* nest; (*se cacher*) hide.

nickel /nikɛl/ *n.m.* nickel. **c'est ~!,** (*fam.*) it's spotless.

nicotine /nikɔtin/ *n.f.* nicotine.
nid /ni/ *n.m.* nest. ~ **de poule**, pothole.
nièce /njɛs/ *n.f.* niece.
nier /nje/ *v.t.* deny.
nigaud, ~e /nigo, -d/ *a.* silly. —*n.m., f.* silly idiot.
nippon, ~e /nipɔ̃, -ɔn/ *a. & n.m., f.* Japanese.
niveau (*pl.* ~x) /nivo/ *n.m.* level; (*compétence*) standard. **au** ~, up to standard. **à bulle**, spirit-level. ~ **de vie**, standard of living.
nivel|**er** /nivle/ *v.t.* level. ~**ement** /-ɛlmɑ̃/ *n.m.* levelling.
noble /nɔbl/ *a.* noble. —*n.m./f.* nobleman, noblewoman.
noblesse /nɔblɛs/ *n.f.* nobility.
noce /nɔs/ *n.f.* wedding; (*personnes*) wedding guests. ~**s**, wedding. **faire la** ~, (*fam.*) make merry.
noci|**f**, ~**ve** /nɔsif, -v/ *a.* harmful.
noctambule /nɔktɑ̃byl/ *n.m./f.* night-owl, late-night reveller.
nocturne /nɔktyrn/ *a.* nocturnal.
Noël /nɔɛl/ *n.m.* Christmas.
nœud[1] /nø/ *n.m.* knot; (*ornemental*) bow. ~**s**, (*fig.*) ties. ~ **coulant**, noose. ~ **papillon**, bow-tie.
nœud[2] /nø/ *n.m.* (*naut.*) knot.
noir, ~e /nwar/ *a.* black; (*obscur*, *sombre*) dark; (*triste*) gloomy. —*n.m.* black; (*obscurité*) dark. **travail au** ~, moonlighting. —*n.m., f.* (*personne*) Black. —*n.f.* (*mus.*) crotchet. ~**ceur** /-kœr/ *n.f.* blackness; (*indignité*) vileness.
noircir /nwarsir/ *v.t./i.,* **se** ~ *v. pr.* blacken.
nois|**ette** /nwazɛt/ *n.f.* hazel-nut; (*de beurre*) knob. ~**etier** *n.m.* hazel tree.
noix /nwa/ *n.f.* nut; (*du noyer*) walnut; (*de beurre*) knob. ~ **de**

cajou, cashew nut. ~ **de coco**, coconut. **à la** ~, (*fam.*) useless.
nom /nɔ̃/ *n.m.* name; (*gram.*) noun. **au** ~ **de**, on behalf of. ~ **de famille**, surname. ~ **de jeune fille**, maiden name. ~ **propre**, proper noun.
nomade /nɔmad/ *a.* nomadic. —*n.m./f.* nomad.
no man's land /nomanslɑ̃d/ *n.m. invar.* no man's land.
nombre /nɔ̃br/ *n.m.* number. **au** ~ **de**, (*parmi*) among; (*l'un de*) one of. **en** (**grand**) ~, in large numbers.
nombreu|**x**, ~**se** /nɔ̃brø, -z/ *a.* numerous; (*important*) large.
nombril /nɔ̃bri/ *n.m.* navel.
nomin|**al** (*m. pl.* ~**aux**) /nɔminal, -o/ *a.* nominal.
nomination /nɔminasjɔ̃/ *n.f.* appointment.
nommément /nɔmemɑ̃/ *adv.* by name.
nommer /nɔme/ *v.t.* name; (*élire*) appoint. **se** ~ *v. pr.* (*s'appeler*) be called.
non /nɔ̃/ *adv.* no; (*pas*) not. —*n.m. invar.* no. ~ (**pas**) **que**, not that. **il vient**, ~?, he is coming, isn't he? **moi** ~ **plus**, neither am, do, can, *etc.* I.
non- /nɔ̃/ *préf.* non-. ~**fumeur**, non-smoker.
nonante /nɔnɑ̃t/ *a. & n.m.* ninety.
nonchalance /nɔ̃ʃalɑ̃s/ *n.f.* nonchalance.
non-sens /nɔ̃sɑ̃s/ *n.m.* absurdity.
non-stop /nɔnstɔp/ *a. invar.* non-stop.
nord /nɔr/ *n.m.* north. —*a. invar.* north; (*partie*) northern; (*direction*) northerly. **au** ~ **de**, to the north of. ~**africain**, ~**africaine** *a. & n.m., f.* North African. ~**est** *n.m.* north-east. ~**ouest** *n.m.* north-west.
nordique /nɔrdik/ *a. & n.m./f.* Scandinavian.

norm|al, **~ale** (*m. pl.* **~aux**) /nɔrmal, -o/ *a.* normal. —*n.f.* normality; (*norme*) norm; (*moyenne*) average. **~alement** *adv.* normally.

normand, **~e** /nɔrmɑ̃, -d/ *a. & n.m.*, *f.* Norman.

Normandie /nɔrmɑ̃di/ *n.f.* Normandy.

norme /nɔrm/ *n.f.* norm; (*de production*) standard.

Norvège /nɔrvɛʒ/ *n.f.* Norway.

norvégien, **~ne** /nɔrveʒjɛ̃, -jɛn/ *a. & n.m.*, *f.* Norwegian.

nos /no/ *voir* notre.

nostalg|ie /nɔstalʒi/ *n.f.* nostalgia. **~ique** *a.* nostalgic.

notable /nɔtabl/ *a. & n.m.* notable.

notaire /nɔtɛr/ *n.m.* notary.

notamment /nɔtamɑ̃/ *adv.* notably.

notation /nɔtasjɔ̃/ *n.f.* notation; (*remarque*) remark.

note /nɔt/ *n.f.* (*remarque*) note; (*chiffrée*) mark; (*facture*) bill; (*mus.*) note. **~** (**de service**), memorandum. **prendre ~ de**, take note of.

not|er /nɔte/ *v.t.* note, notice; (*écrire*) note (down); (*devoir*) mark. **bien/mal ~é**, (*employé etc.*) highly/poorly rated.

notice /nɔtis/ *n.f.* note; (*mode d'emploi*) directions.

notif|ier /nɔtifje/ *v.t.* notify (à, to). **~ication** *n.f.* notification.

notion /nɔsjɔ̃/ *n.f.* notion.

notoire /nɔtwar/ *a.* well-known; (*criminel*) notorious.

notre (*pl.* **nos**) /nɔtr, no/ *a.* our.

nôtre /notr/ *pron.* **le** *ou* **la ~**, **les ~s**, ours.

nouer /nwe/ *v.t.* tie, knot; (*relations*) strike up.

noueu|x, **~se** /nwø, -z/ *a.* gnarled.

nougat /nuga/ *n.m.* nougat.

nouille /nuj/ *n.f.* (*idiot. fam.*) idiot.

nouilles /nuj/ *n.f. pl.* noodles.

nounours /nunurs/ *n.m.* teddy bear.

nourri /nuri/ *a.* (*fig.*) intense. **logé ~**, bed and board. **~ au sein**, breastfed.

nourr|ir /nurir/ *v.t.* feed; (*faire vivre*) feed, provide for; (*sentiment: fig.*) nourish. —*v.i.* be nourishing. **se ~ir** *v. pr.* eat. **se ~ir de**, feed on. **~issant**, **~issante** *a.* nourishing.

nourrisson /nurisɔ̃/ *n.m.* infant.

nourriture /nurityr/ *n.f.* food.

nous /nu/ *pron. we*; (*complément*) us; (*indirect*) (to) us; (*réfléchi*) ourselves; (*l'un l'autre*) each other. **~-mêmes** *pron.* ourselves.

nouveau *ou* **nouvel***, **nouvelle**[1] (*m. pl.* **~x**) /nuvo, nuvɛl/ *a. & n.m.* new. —*n.m.*, *f.* (*élève*) new boy, new girl. **de ~**, **à ~**, again. **du ~**, (*fait nouveau*) some new development. **nouvel an**, new year. **~x mariés**, newly-weds. **~-né**, **~-née** *a.* new-born; *n.m.*, *f.* newborn baby. **~ venu**, **nouvelle venue**, newcomer. **Nouvelle Zélande**, New Zealand.

nouveauté /nuvote/ *n.f.* novelty; (*chose*) new thing.

nouvelle[2] /nuvɛl/ *n.f.* (*piece of*) news; (*récit*) short story. **~s**, news.

nouvellement /nuvɛlmɑ̃/ *adv.* newly, recently.

novembre /nɔvɑ̃br/ *n.m.* November.

novice /nɔvis/ *a.* inexperienced. —*n.m./f.* novice.

noyade /nwajad/ *n.f.* drowning.

noyau (*pl.* **~x**) /nwajo/ *n.m.* (*de fruit*) stone; (*de cellule*) nucleus; (*groupe*) group; (*centre: fig.*) core.

noyauter /nwajote/ *v.t.* (*organisation*) infiltrate.

noy|er[1] /nwaje/ *v.t.* drown; (*inonder*) flood. **se ~er** *v. pr.* drown; (*volontairement*) drown o.s. **se ~er dans un verre d'eau**, make a mountain out of a molehill. **~é**, **~ée** *n.m.*, *f.* drowning person; (*mort*) drowned person.

noyer[2] /nwaje/ *n.m.* (*arbre*) walnut-tree.

nu /ny/ *a.* naked; (*mains, mur, fil*) bare. —*n.m.* nude. **se mettre à nu**, (*fig.*) bare one's heart. **mettre à nu**, lay bare. **nu-pieds** *adv.* barefoot; *n.m. pl.* beach shoes. **nu-tête** *adv.* bareheaded. **à l'oeil nu**, to the naked eye.

nuag|e /nɥaʒ/ *n.m.* cloud. **~eux**, **~euse** *a.* cloudy.

nuance /nɥɑ̃s/ *n.f.* shade; (*de sens*) nuance; (*différence*) difference.

nuancer /nɥɑ̃se/ *v.t.* (*opinion*) qualify.

nucléaire /nyklɛɛr/ *a.* nuclear.

nudis|te /nydist/ *n.m./f.* nudist. **~me** *n.m.* nudism.

nudité /nydite/ *n.f.* (*de personne*) nudity; (*de chambre etc.*) bareness.

nuée /nɥe/ *n.f.* (*foule*) host.

nues /ny/ *n.f. pl.* **tomber des ~**, be amazed. **porter aux ~**, extol.

nuire† /nɥir/ *v.i.* **~ à**, harm.

nuisible /nɥizibl/ *a.* harmful.

nuit /nɥi/ *n.f.* night; **cette ~**, tonight; (*hier*) last night. **il fait ~**, it is dark. **~ blanche**, sleepless night. **la ~**, **de ~**, at night. **~ de noces**, wedding night.

nul /nyl/ *a.* (*aucun*) no; (*non valable*) null. **match ~**, draw. **~ en**, no good at. —*pron.* no one. **autre**, no one else. **no le part**, nowhere. **~lement** *adv.* not at all. **~lité** *n.f.* uselessness; (*personne*) useless person.

numéraire /nymerɛr/ *n.m.* cash.

numér|al (*pl.* **~aux**) /nymeral, -o/ *n.m.* numeral.

numérique /nymerik/ *a.* numerical; (*montre, horloge*) digital.

numéro /nymero/ *n.m.* number; (*de journal*) issue; (*spectacle*) act. **~ter** /-ɔte/ *v.t.* number.

nuque /nyk/ *n.f.* nape (of the neck).

nurse /nœrs/ *n.f.* (children's) nurse.

nutriti|f, **~ve** /nytritif, -v/ *a.* nutritious; (*valeur*) nutritional.

nutrition /nytrisjɔ̃/ *n.f.* nutrition.

nylon /nilɔ̃/ *n.m.* nylon.

nymphe /nɛ̃f/ *n.f.* nymph.

O

oasis /ɔazis/ *n.f.* oasis.

obéir /ɔbeir/ *v.i.* obey. **~ à**, obey. **être obéi**, be obeyed.

obéissan|t, **~te** /ɔbeisɑ̃, -t/ *a.* obedient. **~ce** *n.f.* obedience.

obèse /ɔbɛz/ *a.* obese.

obésité /ɔbezite/ *n.f.* obesity.

object|er /ɔbʒɛkte/ *v.t.* put forward (as an excuse). **~er que**, object that. **~ion** /-ksjɔ̃/ *n.f.* objection.

objecteur /ɔbʒɛktœr/ *n.m.* **~ de conscience**, conscientious objector.

objecti|f, **~ve** /ɔbʒɛktif, -v/ *a.* objective. —*n.m.* objective; (*photo.*) lens. **~vement** *adv.* objectively. **~vité** *n.f.* objectivity.

objet /ɔbʒɛ/ *n.m.* object; (*sujet*) subject. **être** *ou* **faire l'~ de**, be the subject of; (*recevoir*) receive. **~ d'art**, objet d'art. **~s de toilette**, toilet requisites. **~s trouvés**, lost property; (*Amer.*) lost and found.

obligation /ɔbligasjɔ̃/ *n.f.* obligation; (*comm.*) bond. **être dans l'~ de**, be under obligation to.

obligatoire /ɔbligatwar/ *a.* compulsory. ∼**ment** *adv.* of necessity; (*fam.*) inevitably.

obligean|t, ∼te /ɔbliʒã, -t/ *a.* obliging, kind. ∼**ce** *n.f.* kindness.

oblig|er /ɔbliʒe/ *v.t.* compel, oblige (**à faire**, to do); (*aider*) oblige. **être ∼é de**, have to. ∼**é à qn.**, obliged to s.o. (**de**, for).

oblique /ɔblik/ *a.* oblique. **regard ∼**, sidelong glance. **en ∼**, at an angle.

obliquer /ɔblike/ *v.i.* turn off (**vers**, towards).

oblitérer /ɔblitere/ *v.t.* (*timbre*) cancel.

oblong, ∼ue /ɔblɔ̃, -g/ *a.* oblong.

obnubilé, ∼e /ɔbnybile/ *a.* obsessed.

obsc|ène /ɔpsɛn/ *a.* obscene. ∼**énité** *n.f.* obscenity.

obscur /ɔpskyr/ *a.* dark; (*confus, humble*) obscure.

obscurantisme /ɔpskyrãtizm/ *n.m.* obscurantism.

obscurcir /ɔpskyrsir/ *v.t.* darken; (*fig.*) obscure. **s'∼** *v. pr.* (*ciel etc.*) darken.

obscurité /ɔpskyrite/ *n.f.* dark(-ness); (*passage, situation*) obscurity.

obséd|er /ɔpsede/ *v.t.* obsess. ∼**ant, ∼ante** *a.* obsessive. ∼**é, ∼ée** *n.m., f.* maniac.

obsèques /ɔpsɛk/ *n.f. pl.* funeral.

observation /ɔpsɛrvasjɔ̃/ *n.f.* observation; (*reproche*) criticism; (*obéissance*) observance. **en ∼**, under observation.

observatoire /ɔpsɛrvatwar/ *n.m.* observatory; (*mil.*) observation post.

observ|er /ɔpsɛrve/ *v.t.* observe; (*surveiller*) watch, observe. **faire ∼er qch.**, point sth. out (**à**, to). ∼**ateur, ∼atrice** *a.* observant; *n.m., f.* observer.

obsession /ɔpsesjɔ̃/ *n.f.* obsession.

obstacle /ɔpstakl/ *n.m.* obstacle; (*cheval*) jump; (*athlète*) hurdle. **faire ∼ à**, stand in the way of.

obstétrique /ɔpstetrik/ *n.f.* obstetrics.

obstin|é /ɔpstine/ *a.* obstinate. ∼**ation** *n.f.* obstinacy.

obstiner (s') /(s)ɔpstine/ *v. pr.* persist (**à**, in).

obstruction /ɔpstryksjɔ̃/ *n.f.* obstruction. **faire de l'∼**, obstruct.

obstruer /ɔpstrye/ *v.t.* obstruct.

obten|ir /ɔptanir/ *v.t.* get, obtain. ∼**tion** /-ãsjɔ̃/ *n.f.* obtaining.

obturateur /ɔptyratœr/ *n.m.* (*photo.*) shutter.

obtus, ∼e /ɔpty, -z/ *a.* obtuse.

obus /ɔby/ *n.m.* shell.

occasion /ɔkazjɔ̃/ *n.f.* opportunity (**de faire**, of doing); (*circonstance*) occasion; (*achat*) bargain; (*article non neuf*) second-hand buy. **à l'∼**, sometimes. **d'∼**, second-hand. ∼**nel, ∼nelle** /-jɔnɛl/ *a.* occasional.

occasionner /ɔkazjɔne/ *v.t.* cause.

occident /ɔksidã/ *n.m.* west. ∼**al, ∼ale** (*m. pl.* ∼**aux**) /-tal, -to/ *a.* western. —*n.m., f.* westerner.

occulte /ɔkylt/ *a.* occult.

occupant, ∼e /ɔkypã, -t/ *n.m., f.* occupant. —*n.m.* (*mil.*) forces of occupation.

occupation /ɔkypasjɔ̃/ *n.f.* occupation.

occupé /ɔkype/ *a.* busy; (*place, pays*) occupied; (*téléphone*) engaged; (*Amer.*) busy.

occuper /ɔkype/ *v.t.* occupy; (*poste*) hold. **s'∼** *v. pr.* (*s'affairer*) keep busy (**à faire**, doing). **s'∼ de**, (*personne, problème*) take care of; (*bureau, firme*) be in charge of.

occurrence (en l') /(ãl)ɔkyrãs/ *adv.* in this case.

océan /ɔseã/ *n.m.* ocean.

ocre /ɔkr/ *a. invar.* ochre.

octane /ɔktan/ *n.m.* octane.

octante /ɔktɑ̃t/ *a.* (*régional*) eighty.

octave /ɔktav/ *n.f.* (*mus.*) octave.

octet /ɔktɛ/ *n.m.* byte.

octobre /ɔktɔbr/ *n.m.* October.

octogone /ɔktɔgɔn/ *n.m.* octagon.

octroyer /ɔktrwaje/ *v.t.* grant.

oculaire /ɔkylɛr/ *a.* ocular.

oculiste /ɔkylist/ *n.m./f.* eye-specialist.

ode /ɔd/ *n.f.* ode.

odeur /ɔdœr/ *n.f.* smell.

odieu|x, ∼se /ɔdjø, -z/ *a.* odious.

odorant, ∼e /ɔdɔrɑ̃, -t/ *a.* sweet-smelling.

odorat /ɔdɔra/ *n.m.* (sense of) smell.

œcuménique /ekymenik/ *a.* ecumenical.

œil (*pl.* **yeux**) /œj, jø/ *n.m.* eye. à l'∼, (*fam.*) free. à mes yeux, in my view. **faire de l'∼ à**, make eyes at. **faire les gros yeux à**, scowl at. **ouvrir l'∼,** keep one's eye open. **fermer l'∼,** shut one's eyes. ∼ **poché**, black eye. **yeux bridés**, slit eyes.

œillade /œjad/ *n.f.* wink.

œillères /œjɛr/ *n.f. pl.* blinkers.

œillet /œjɛ/ *n.m.* (*plante*) carnation; (*trou*) eyelet.

œuf (*pl.* ∼**s**) /œf, ø/ *n.m.* egg. ∼ **à la coque/dur/sur le plat**, boiled/hard-boiled/fried egg.

œuvre /œvr/ *n.f.* (*ouvrage, travail*) work. ∼ **d'art**, work of art. ∼ (**de bienfaisance**), charity. **être à l'∼**, be at work. **mettre en ∼**, (*moyens*) implement.

œuvrer /œvre/ *v.i.* work.

off /ɔf/ *a. invar.* **voix** ∼, voice off.

offense /ɔfɑ̃s/ *n.f.* insult; (*péché*) offence.

offens|er /ɔfɑ̃se/ *v.t.* offend. **s'∼er de**, take offence at. ∼**ant**, ∼**ante** *a.* offensive.

offensi|f, ∼ve /ɔfɑ̃sif, -v/ *a.* & *n.f.* offensive.

offert, ∼e /ɔfɛr, -t/ *voir* **offrir**.

office /ɔfis/ *n.m.* office; (*relig.*) service; (*de cuisine*) pantry. **d'∼**, automatically.

officiel, ∼le /ɔfisjɛl/ *a. & n.m., f.* official. ∼**lement** *adv.* officially.

officier¹ /ɔfisje/ *n.m.* officer.

officier² /ɔfisje/ *v.i.* (*relig.*) officiate.

officieu|x, ∼se /ɔfisjø, -z/ *a.* unofficial. ∼**sement** *adv.* unofficially.

offrande /ɔfrɑ̃d/ *n.f.* offering.

offrant /ɔfrɑ̃/ *n.m.* **au plus ∼**, to the highest bidder.

offre /ɔfr/ *n.f.* offer; (*aux enchères*) bid. l'∼ **et la demande**, supply and demand. ∼**s d'emploi**, jobs advertised; (*rubrique*) situations vacant.

offr|ir /ɔfrir/ *v.t.* offer (**de faire**, to do); (*cadeau*) give; (*acheter*) buy. **s'∼** *v. pr.* offer o.s. (**comme**, as); (*spectacle*) present itself; (*s'acheter*) treat o.s. to. ∼ **à boire à**, (*chez soi*) give a drink to; (*au café*) buy a drink for.

offusquer /ɔfyske/ *v.t.* offend.

ogive /ɔʒiv/ *n.f.* (*atomique etc.*) warhead.

ogre /ɔgr/ *n.m.* ogre.

oh /o/ *int.* oh.

oie /wa/ *n.f.* goose.

oignon /ɔɲɔ̃/ *n.m.* (*légume*) onion; (*de tulipe etc.*) bulb.

oiseau (*pl.* ∼**x**) /wazo/ *n.m.* bird.

oisi|f, ∼ve /wazif, -v/ *a.* idle. ∼**veté** *n.f.* idleness.

O.K. /oke/ *int.* O.K.

oléoduc /ɔleɔdyk/ *n.m.* oil pipeline.

oliv|e /ɔliv/ *n.f. & a. invar.* olive. ∼**ier** *n.m.* olive-tree.

olympique /ɔlɛ̃pik/ *a.* Olympic.

ombrag|e /ɔ̃braʒ/ *n.m.* shade. **prendre ∼e de**, take offence at.

~é a. shady. ~eux, ~euse a. easily offended.

ombre /5br/ n.f. (pénombre) shade; (contour) shadow; (soupçon: fig.) hint, shadow. dans l'~, (secret) in the dark. faire de l'~ à qn., be in s.o.'s light.

ombrelle /5brɛl/ n.f. parasol.

omelette /5mlɛt/ n.f. omelette.

omettre† /5mɛtr/ v.t. omit.

omission /5misjɔ̃/ n.f. omission.

omnibus /5mnibys/ n.m. stopping train.

omoplate /5moplat/ n.f. shoulder-blade.

on /5/ pron. we, you, one; (les gens) people, they; (quelqu'un) someone. on dit, people say, they say, it is said (que, that).

once /5s/ n.f. ounce.

oncle /5kl/ n.m. uncle.

onctueu|x, ~se /ɔ̃ktɥø, -z/ a. smooth.

onde /5d/ n.f. wave. ~s courtes/longues, short/long wave. sur les ~s, on the radio.

ondée /5de/ n.f. shower.

on-dit /5di/ n.m. invar. les ~, rumour.

ondul|er /5dyle/ v.i. undulate; (cheveux) be wavy. ~ation n.f. wave, undulation. ~é a. (cheve-lure) wavy.

onéreu|x, ~se /5nerø, -z/ a. costly.

ongle /5gl/ n.m. (finger-)nail. se faire les ~s, do one's nails.

ont /5/ voir avoir.

ONU abrév. (Organisation des nations unies) UN.

onyx /5niks/ n.m. onyx.

onz|e /5z/ a. & n.m. eleven. ~ième a. & n.m./f. eleventh.

opale /5pal/ n.f. opal.

opa|que /5pak/ a. opaque. ~cité n.f. opaqueness.

open /5pɛn/ n.m. open (champion-ship).

opéra /5pera/ n.m. opera; (édifice) opera-house. ~-comique (pl. ~s-comiques) n.m. light opera.

opérateur /5peratœr/ n.m. (camé-raman) cameraman.

opération /5perasjɔ̃/ n.f. opera-tion; (comm.) deal.

opérationnel, ~le /5perasjɔnɛl/ a. operational.

opératoire /5peratwar/ a. (méd.) surgical. bloc ~, operating suite.

opérer /5pere/ v.t. (personne) operate on; (kyste etc.) remove; (exécuter) carry out, make. se faire ~, have an operation. —v.i. (méd.) operate; (faire effet) work. s'~ v. pr. (se produire) occur.

opérette /5peret/ n.f. operetta.

opiner /5pine/ v.i. nod.

opiniâtre /5pinjɑtr/ a. obstinate.

opinion /5pinjɔ̃/ n.f. opinion.

opium /5pjɔm/ n.m. opium.

opportun, ~e /5pɔrtœ̃, -yn/ a. opportune. ~ité /-ynite/ n.f. opportuneness.

opposant, ~e /5pozɑ̃, -t/ n.m., f. opponent.

opposé /5poze/ a. (sens, angle, etc.) opposite; (factions) opposing; (intérêts) conflicting. —n.m. op-posite. à l'~, (opinion etc.) contrary (de, to). être ~ à, be opposed to.

opposer /5poze/ v.t. (objets) place opposite each other; (personnes) oppose; (contraster) contrast; (résistance, argument) put up. s'~ v. pr. (personnes) confront each other; (styles) contrast. s'~ à, oppose.

opposition /5pozisjɔ̃/ n.f. opposi-tion. par ~ à, in contrast with. entrer en ~ avec, come into conflict with. faire ~ à un chèque, stop a cheque.

oppress|er /5prese/ v.t. oppress. ~ant, ~ante a. oppressive. ~eur n.m. oppressor. ~ion n.f. oppression.

opprimer /ɔprime/ *v.t.* oppress.

opter /ɔpte/ *v.i.* ~ **pour**, opt for.

opticien, ~ne /ɔptisjɛ̃, -jɛn/ *n.m., f.* optician.

optimis|te /ɔptimist/ *n.m./f.* optimist. —*a.* optimistic. ~**me** *n.m.* optimism.

optimum /ɔptimɔm/ *a. & n.m.* optimum.

option /ɔpsjɔ̃/ *n.f.* option.

optique /ɔptik/ *a.* (*verre*) optical. —*n.f.* (*perspective*) perspective.

opulen|t, ~te /ɔpylɑ̃, -t/ *a.* opulent. ~**ce** *n.f.* opulence.

or[1] /ɔr/ *n.m.* gold. **d'or**, golden. **en or**, gold; (*occasion*) golden.

or[2] /ɔr/ *conj.* now, well.

oracle /ɔrakl/ *n.m.* oracle.

orag|e /ɔraʒ/ *n.m.* (thunder)storm. ~**eux, ~euse** *a.* stormy.

oraison /ɔrezɔ̃/ *n.f.* prayer.

or|al (*m. pl.* ~**aux**) /ɔral, -o/ *a.* oral. —*n.m.* (*pl.* ~**aux**) oral.

orang|e /ɔrɑ̃ʒ/ *n.f. & a. invar.* orange. ~**é** *a.* orange-coloured. ~**er** *n.m.* orange-tree.

orangeade /ɔrɑ̃ʒad/ *n.f.* orangeade.

orateur /ɔratœr/ *n.m.* speaker.

oratorio /ɔratɔrjo/ *n.m.* oratorio.

orbite /ɔrbit/ *n.f.* orbit; (*d'œil*) socket.

orchestr|e /ɔrkɛstr/ *n.m.* orchestra; (*de jazz*) band; (*parterre*) stalls. ~**er** *v.t.* orchestrate.

orchidée /ɔrkide/ *n.f.* orchid.

ordinaire /ɔrdinɛr/ *a.* ordinary; (*habituel*) usual; (*qualité*) standard. —*n.m.* **l'~**, the ordinary; (*nourriture*) the standard fare. **d'~, à l'~**, usually. ~**ment** *adv.* usually.

ordinateur /ɔrdinatœr/ *n.m.* computer.

ordination /ɔrdinasjɔ̃/ *n.f.* (*relig.*) ordination.

ordonnance /ɔrdɔnɑ̃s/ *n.f.* (*ordre, décret*) order; (*de médecin*) prescription; (*soldat*) orderly.

ordonné /ɔrdɔne/ *a.* tidy.

ordonner /ɔrdɔne/ *v.t.* order (**à qn. de**, s.o. to); (*agencer*) arrange; (*méd.*) prescribe; (*prêtre*) ordain.

ordre /ɔrdr/ *n.m.* order; (*propreté*) tidiness. **aux ~s de qn.**, at s.o.'s disposal. **avoir de l'~**, be tidy. **de premier ~**, first-rate. **l'~ du jour**, (*programme*) agenda. **mettre en ~**, tidy (up). **de premier ~**, first rate. **jusqu'à nouvel ~**, until further notice. **un ~ de grandeur**, an approximate idea.

ordure /ɔrdyr/ *n.f.* filth. ~**s**, (*détritus*) rubbish; (*Amer.*) garbage. ~**s ménagères**, household refuse.

oreille /ɔrɛj/ *n.f.* ear.

oreiller /ɔreje/ *n.m.* pillow.

oreillons /ɔrejɔ̃/ *n.m. pl.* mumps.

orfèvr|e /ɔrfɛvr/ *n.m.* goldsmith, silversmith. ~**erie** *n.f.* goldsmith's *ou* silversmith's trade.

organe /ɔrgan/ *n.m.* organ; (*porteparole*) mouthpiece.

organigramme /ɔrganigram/ *n.m.* flow chart.

organique /ɔrganik/ *a.* organic.

organisation /ɔrganizasjɔ̃/ *n.f.* organization.

organis|er /ɔrganize/ *v.t.* organize. **s'~er** *v. pr.* organize o.s. ~**ateur, ~atrice** *n.m., f.* organizer.

organisme /ɔrganism/ *n.m.* body, organism.

organiste /ɔrganist/ *n.m./f.* organist.

orgasme /ɔrgasm/ *n.m.* orgasm.

orge /ɔrʒ/ *n.f.* barley.

orgelet /ɔrʒəlɛ/ *n.m.* (*furoncle*) sty.

orgie /ɔrʒi/ *n.f.* orgy.

orgue /ɔrg/ *n.m.* organ. ~**s** *n.f. pl.* organ. ~ **de Barbarie**, barrel-organ.

orgueil /ɔrgœj/ *n.m.* pride.

orgueilleu|x, ~se /ɔrgœjø, -z/ *a.* proud.

Orient /ɔrjɑ̃/ *n.m.* **l'~**, the Orient.

orientable /ɔrjɑ̃tabl/ a. adjustable.

orient|al, ~ale (m. pl. **~aux**) /ɔrjɑ̃tal, -o/ a. eastern; (de l'Orient) oriental. —n.m., f. Oriental.

orientation /ɔrjɑ̃tasjɔ̃/ n.f. direction; (d'une politique) course; (de maison) aspect. **~ professionnelle**, careers advisory service.

orienté /ɔrjɑ̃te/ a. (partial) slanted, tendentious.

orienter /ɔrjɑ̃te/ v.t. position; (personne) direct. **s'~** v. pr. (se repérer) find one's bearings. **s'~ vers**, turn towards.

orifice /ɔrifis/ n.m. orifice.

origan /ɔrigɑ̃/ n.m. oregano.

originaire /ɔriʒinɛr/ a. **être ~ de**, be a native of.

origin|al, ~ale (m. pl. **~aux**) /ɔriʒinal, -o/ a. original; (curieux) eccentric. —n.m., f. eccentric. **~alité** n.f. originality; eccentricity.

origine /ɔriʒin/ n.f. origin. **à l'~**, originally. **d'~**, (pièce, pneu) original.

originel, ~le /ɔriʒinɛl/ a. original.

orme /ɔrm/ n.m. elm.

ornement /ɔrnəmɑ̃/ n.m. ornament. **~al** (m. pl. **~aux**) /-tal, -to/ a. ornamental.

orner /ɔrne/ v.t. decorate.

ornière /ɔrnjɛr/ n.f. rut.

ornithologie /ɔrnitɔlɔʒi/ n.f. ornithology.

orphelin, ~e /ɔrfəlɛ̃, -in/ n.m., f. orphan. **~é** a. orphaned. **~at** /-ina/ n.m. orphanage.

orteil /ɔrtɛj/ n.m. toe.

orthodoxe /ɔrtɔdɔks/ a. orthodox. **~ie** n.f. orthodoxy.

orthograph|e /ɔrtɔgraf/ n.f. spelling. **~ier** v.t. spell.

orthopédique /ɔrtɔpedik/ a. orthopaedic.

ortie /ɔrti/ n.f. nettle.

os (pl. **os**) /ɔs, o/ n.m. bone.

OS abrév. voir **ouvrier spécialisé**.

oscar /ɔskar/ n.m. award; (au cinéma) oscar.

oscill|er /ɔsile/ v.i. sway; (techn.) oscillate; (hésiter) waver, fluctuate. **~ation** n.f. (techn.) oscillation; (variation) fluctuation.

oseille /ozɛj/ n.f. (plante) sorrel.

os|er /oze/ v.t./i. dare. **~é** a. daring.

osier /ozje/ n.m. wicker.

ossature /ɔsatyr/ n.f. frame.

ossements /ɔsmɑ̃/ n.m. pl. bones.

osseu|x, ~se /ɔsø, -z/ a. bony; (tissu) bone.

ostensible /ɔstɑ̃sibl/ a. conspicuous, obvious.

ostentation /ɔstɑ̃tasjɔ̃/ n.f. ostentation.

ostéopathe /ɔsteɔpat/ n.m./f. osteopath.

otage /ɔtaʒ/ n.m. hostage.

otarie /ɔtari/ n.f. sea-lion.

ôter /ote/ v.t. remove (à qn., from s.o.); (déduire) take away.

otite /ɔtit/ n.f. ear infection.

ou /u/ conj. or. **ou bien**, or else. **vous ou moi**, either you or me.

où /u/ adv. & pron. where; (dans lequel) in which; (sur lequel) on which; (auquel) at which. **d'où**, from which; (pour cette raison) hence. **d'où?**, from where? **par où**, through which. **par où?**, which way? **où qu'il soit**, wherever he may be. **au prix où c'est**, at those prices. **le jour où**, the day when.

ouate /wat/ n.f. cotton wool; (Amer.) absorbent cotton.

oubli /ubli/ n.m. forgetfulness; (trou de mémoire) lapse of memory; (négligence) oversight. **l'~**, (tomber dans, sauver de) oblivion.

oublier /ublije/ v.t. forget. **s'~** v. pr. forget o.s.; (chose) be forgotten.

oublieu|x, ~se /ublijø, -z/ a. forgetful (**de**, of).

ouest /wɛst/ n.m. west. —a. invar. west; (*partie*) western; (*direction*) westerly.

ouf /uf/ int. phew.

oui /wi/ adv. yes.

oui-dire (par) /(par)widir/ adv. by hearsay.

ouïe /wi/ n.f. hearing.

ouïes /wi/ n.f. pl. gills.

ouille /uj/ int. ouch.

ouïr /wir/ v.t. hear.

ouragan /uragã/ n.m. hurricane.

ourler /urle/ v.t. hem.

ourlet /urlɛ/ n.m. hem.

ours /urs/ n.m. bear. **~ blanc**, polar bear. **~ en peluche**, teddy bear. **~ mal léché**, boor.

ouste /ust/ int. (*fam.*) scram.

outil /uti/ n.m. tool.

outillage /utijaʒ/ n.m. tools; (*d'une usine*) equipment.

outiller /utije/ v.t. equip.

outrage /utraʒ/ n.m. (grave) insult.

outrag|er /utraʒe/ v.t. offend. **~eant, ~eante** a. offensive.

outrance /utrãs/ n.f. excess. **à ~e**, to excess; (*guerre*) all-out. **~ier, ~ière** a. excessive.

outre /utr/ prép. besides. **en ~**, besides. **~-mer** adv. overseas. **~ mesure**, excessively.

outrepasser /utrəpase/ v.t. exceed.

outrer /utre/ v.t. exaggerate; (*indigner*) incense.

outsider /awtsajdœr/ n.m. outsider.

ouvert, ~e /uvɛr, -t/ voir **ouvrir**. —a. open; (*gaz, radio, etc.*) on. **~ement** /-təmã/ adv. openly.

ouverture /uvɛrtyr/ n.f. opening; (*mus.*) overture; (*photo.*) aperture. **~s**, (*offres*) overtures. **~ d'esprit**, open-mindedness.

ouvrable /uvrabl/ a. **jour ~**, working day.

ouvrage /uvraʒ/ n.m. (*travail, livre*) work; (*couture*) needlework. **~é** a. finely worked.

ouvreuse /uvrøz/ n.f. usherette.

ouvr|ier, ~ière /uvrije, -jɛr/ n.m., f. worker. —a. workingclass; (*conflit*) industrial; (*syndicat*) workers'. **~ier qualifié/spécialisé**, skilled/unskilled worker.

ouvr|ir† /uvrir/ v.t. open (up); (*gaz, robinet, etc.*) turn ou switch on. —v.i. open (up). **s'~ir** v. pr. open (up). **s'~ir à qn.**, open one's heart to s.o. **~e-boîte(s)** n.m. tinopener. **~e-bouteille(s)** n.m. bottle-opener.

ovaire /ɔvɛr/ n.m. ovary.

ovale /ɔval/ a. & n.m. oval.

ovation /ɔvasjɔ̃/ n.f. ovation.

overdose /ɔvɛrdoz/ n.f. overdose.

ovni /ɔvni/ n.m. (*abrév.*) UFO.

ovule /ɔvyl/ n.f. (*à féconder*) egg; (*gynécologique*) pessary.

oxyder (s') /(s)ɔkside/ v. pr. become oxidized.

oxygène /ɔksiʒɛn/ n.m. oxygen.

oxygéner (s') /(s)ɔksiʒene/ v. pr. (*fam.*) get some fresh air.

ozone /ozon/ n.f. ozone. **la couche d'~**, the ozone layer.

P

pacemaker /pesmekœr/ n.m. pacemaker.

pachyderme /paʃidɛrm/ n.m. elephant.

pacifier /pasifje/ v.t. pacify.

pacifique /pasifik/ a. peaceful; (*personne*) peaceable; (*géog.*) Pacific. —n.m. **P~**, Pacific (Ocean).

pacifiste /pasifist/ n.m./f. pacifist.

pacotille /pakɔtij/ *n.f.* trash.

pacte /pakt/ *n.m.* pact.

pactiser /paktize/ *v.i.* **∼ avec,** be in league *ou* agreement with.

paddock /padɔk/ *n.m.* paddock.

pagaie /pagɛ/ *n.f.* paddle. **∼ayer** *v.i.* paddle.

pagaille /pagaj/ *n.f.* mess, shambles.

page /paʒ/ *n.f.* page. **être à la ∼,** be up to date.

pagode /pagɔd/ *n.f.* pagoda.

paie /pɛ/ *n.f.* pay.

paiement /pemã/ *n.m.* payment.

païen, ∼ne /pajɛ̃, -jɛn/ *a. & n.m., f.* pagan.

paillasse /pajas/ *n.f.* straw mattress; *(dans un laboratoire)* draining-board.

paillasson /pajasɔ̃/ *n.m.* doormat.

paille /paj/ *n.f.* straw; *(défaut)* flaw.

paillette /pajɛt/ *n.f.* *(sur robe)* sequin; *(de savon)* flake. **∼s d'or,** gold-dust.

pain /pɛ̃/ *n.m.* bread; *(unité)* loaf (of bread); *(de savon etc.)* bar. **∼ d'épice,** gingerbread. **∼ grillé,** toast.

pair[1] /pɛr/ *a. (nombre)* even.

pair[2] /pɛr/ *n.m. (personne)* peer. **au ∼,** *(jeune fille etc.)* au pair. **aller de ∼,** go together **(avec,** with).

paire /pɛr/ *n.f.* pair.

paisible /pezibl/ *a.* peaceful.

paître /pɛtr/ *v.i. (brouter)* graze.

paix /pɛ/ *n.f.* peace; *(papier)* peace treaty.

Pakistan /pakistɑ̃/ *n.m.* Pakistan.

pakistanais, ∼e /pakistanɛ, -z/ *a. & n.m., f.* Pakistani.

palace /palas/ *n.m.* luxury hotel.

palais[1] /palɛ/ *n.m.* palace. **P∼ de Justice,** Law Courts. **∼ des sports,** sports stadium.

palais[2] /palɛ/ *n.m. (anat.)* palate.

palan /palɑ̃/ *n.m.* hoist.

pâle /pɑl/ *a.* pale.

Palestine /palestin/ *n.f.* Palestine.

palestinien, ∼ne /palestinjɛ̃, -jɛn/ *a. & n.m., f.* Palestinian.

palet /palɛ/ *n.m. (hockey)* puck.

paletot /palto/ *n.m.* thick jacket.

palette /palɛt/ *n.f.* palette.

pâleur /palœr/ *n.f.* paleness.

palier /palje/ *n.m. (d'escalier)* landing; *(étape)* stage; *(de route)* level stretch.

pâlir /palir/ *v.t./i.* (turn) pale.

palissade /palisad/ *n.f.* fence.

pallier /palje/ *v.t.* alleviate.

palmarès /palmares/ *n.m.* list of prize-winners.

palm|e /palm/ *n.f.* palm leaf; *(symbole)* palm; *(de nageur)* flipper. **∼ier** *n.m.* palm(-tree).

palmé /palme/ *a. (patte)* webbed.

pâlot, ∼te /palo, -ɔt/ *a.* pale.

palourde /palurd/ *n.f.* clam.

palper /palpe/ *v.t.* feel.

palpit|er /palpite/ *v.i. (battre)* pound, palpitate; *(frémir)* quiver. **∼ations** *n.f. pl.* palpitations. **∼ant, ∼ante** *a.* thrilling.

paludisme /palydism/ *n.m.* malaria.

pâmer (se) /(sə)pame/ *v. pr.* swoon.

pamphlet /pɑ̃flɛ/ *n.m.* satirical pamphlet.

pamplemousse /pɑ̃pləmus/ *n.m.* grapefruit.

pan[1] /pɑ̃/ *n.m.* piece; *(de chemise)* tail.

pan[2] /pɑ̃/ *int.* bang.

panacée /panase/ *n.f.* panacea.

panache /panaʃ/ *n.m.* plume; *(bravoure)* gallantry; *(allure)* panache.

panaché /panaʃe/ *a. (bariolé, mélangé)* motley. **glace ∼e,** mixed-flavour ice cream. —*n.m.* shandy. **bière ∼e, demi ∼,** shandy.

pancarte /pɑ̃kart/ *n.f.* sign; *(de manifestant)* placard.

pancréas /pãkreas/ *n.m.* pancreas.

pané /pane/ *a.* breaded.

panier /panje/ *n.m.* basket. ~ à provisions, shopping basket. ~ à salade, (*fam.*) police van.

paniqu|e /panik/ *n.f.* panic. (*fam.*) ~er *v.i.* panic.

panne /pan/ *n.f.* breakdown. être en ~, have broken down. être en ~ sèche, have run out of petrol *ou* gas (*Amer.*). ~ d'électricité *ou* de courant, power failure.

panneau (*pl.* ~x) /pano/ *n.m.* sign; (*publicitaire*) hoarding; (*de porte etc.*) panel. ~ (d'affichage), notice-board. ~ (de signalisation), road sign.

panoplie /panɔpli/ *n.f.* (*jouet*) outfit; (*gamme*) range.

panoram|a /panɔrama/ *n.m.* panorama. ~ique *a.* panoramic.

panse /pãs/ *n.f.* paunch.

pans|er /pãse/ *v.t.* (*plaie*) dress; (*personne*) dress the wound/s of; (*cheval*) groom. ~ement *n.m.* dressing. ~ement adhésif, sticking-plaster.

pantalon /pãtalɔ̃/ *n.m.* (pair of) trousers. ~s, trousers.

panthère /pãtɛr/ *n.f.* panther.

pantin /pãtɛ̃/ *n.m.* puppet.

pantomime /pãtɔmim/ *n.f.* mime; (*spectacle*) mime show.

pantoufle /pãtufl/ *n.f.* slipper.

paon /pã/ *n.m.* peacock.

papa /papa/ *n.m.* dad(dy). de ~, (*fam.*) old-time.

papauté /papote/ *n.f.* papacy.

pape /pap/ *n.m.* pope.

paperass|e /papras/ *n.f.* ~e(s), (*péj.*) papers; (*tracasserie*) red tape.

papet|ier, ~ière /paptje, -jɛr/ *n.m., f.* stationer. ~erie /papetri/ *n.f.* (*magasin*) stationer's shop.

papier /papje/ *n.m.* paper; (*formulaire*) form. ~s (d'identité), (identity) papers. ~ à

lettres, writing-paper. ~ aluminium, tin foil. ~ buvard, blotting-paper. ~ calque, tracing-paper. ~ carbone, carbon paper. ~ collant, sticky paper. ~ de verre, sandpaper. ~ hygiénique, toilet-paper. ~ journal, newspaper. ~ mâché, papier mâché. ~ peint, wallpaper.

papillon /papijɔ̃/ *n.m.* butterfly; (*contravention*) parking-ticket. ~ (de nuit), moth.

papot|er /papote/ *v.i.* prattle. ~age *n.m.* prattle.

paprika /paprika/ *n.m.* paprika.

Pâque /pak/ *n.f.* Passover.

paquebot /pakbo/ *n.m.* liner.

pâquerette /pakrɛt/ *n.f.* daisy.

Pâques /pak/ *n.f. pl. & n.m.* Easter.

paquet /pakɛ/ *n.m.* packet; (*de cartes*) pack; (*colis*) parcel. un ~ de, (*tas*) a mass of.

par /par/ *prép.* by; (*à travers*) through; (*motif*) out of, from; (*provenance*) from. commencer/finir ~ qch., begin/end with sth. commencer/finir ~ faire, begin by/end up (by) doing. ~ an/mois/*etc.*, a *ou* per year/month/*etc.* ~ avion, (*lettre*) (by) airmail. ~ci, par-là, here and there. ~ contre, on the other hand. ~ hasard, by chance. ~ ici/là, this/that way. ~ inadvertence, inadvertently. ~ intermittence, intermittently. ~ l'intermédiaire de, through. ~ jour, a day. ~ malheur *ou* malchance, unfortunately. ~ miracle, miraculously. ~ moments, at times. ~ opposition à, as opposed to. ~ personne, each, per person.

parabole /parabɔl/ *n.f.* (*relig.*) parable; (*maths*) parabola.

paracétamol /parasetamɔl/ *n.m.* paracetamol.

parachever /paraʃve/ *v.t.* perfect.

parachut|e /paraʃyt/ *n.m.* parachute. ∼**er** *v.t.* parachute. ∼**iste** *n.m./f.* parachutist; (*mil.*) parachutist; (*mil.*) paratrooper.

parad|e /parad/ *n.f.* parade; (*sport*) parry; (*réplique*) reply. ∼**er** *v.i.* show off.

paradis /paradi/ *n.m.* paradise. ∼ **fiscal,** tax haven.

paradox|e /paradɔks/ *n.m.* paradox. ∼**al** (*m. pl.* ∼**aux**) *a.* paradoxical.

paraffine /parafin/ *n.f.* paraffin wax.

parages /paraʒ/ *n.m. pl.* area, vicinity.

paragraphe /paragraf/ *n.m.* paragraph.

paraître† /parɛtr/ *v.i.* appear; (*sembler*) seem, appear; (*ouvrage*) be published, come out. **faire** ∼, (*ouvrage*) bring out.

parallèle /paralɛl/ *a.* parallel; (*illégal*) unofficial. —*n.m.* parallel. **faire un** ∼ **entre,** draw a parallel between. **faire le** ∼, make a connection. —*n.f.* parallel (line). ∼**ment** *adv.* parallel (à, to).

paraly|ser /paralize/ *v.t.* paralyse. ∼**sie** *n.f.* paralysis. ∼**tique** *a.* & *n.m./f.* paralytic.

paramètre /paramɛtr/ *n.m.* parameter.

paranoïa /paranɔja/ *n.f.* paranoia.

parapet /parapɛ/ *n.m.* parapet.

paraphe /paraf/ *n.m.* signature.

paraphrase /parafraz/ *n.f.* paraphrase.

parapluie /paraplɥi/ *n.m.* umbrella.

parasite /parazit/ *n.m.* parasite. ∼**s,** (*radio*) interference.

parasol /parasɔl/ *n.m.* sunshade.

paratonnerre /paratɔnɛr/ *n.m.* lightning-conductor *ou* -rod.

paravent /paravɑ̃/ *n.m.* screen.

parc /park/ *n.m.* park; (*de bétail*) pen; (*de bébé*) play-pen; (*entrepôt*) depot. ∼ **de stationnement,** car-park.

parcelle /parsɛl/ *n.f.* fragment; (*de terre*) plot.

parce que /parsk(ə)/ *conj.* because.

parchemin /parʃəmɛ̃/ *n.m.* parchment.

parcimon|ie /parsimɔni/ *n.f.* **avec** ∼**ie,** parsimoniously. ∼**ieux,** ∼**ieuse** *a.* parsimonious.

parcmètre /parkmɛtr/ *n.m.* parking-meter.

parcourir† /parkurir/ *v.t.* travel *ou* go through; (*distance*) travel; (*des yeux*) glance at *ou* over.

parcours /parkur/ *n.m.* route; (*voyage*) journey.

par-delà /pardəla/ *prép. & adv.* beyond.

par-derrière /pardɛrjɛr/ *prép. & adv.* behind, at the back *ou* rear (of).

par-dessous /pardəsu/ *prép. & adv.* under(neath).

pardessus /pardəsy/ *n.m.* overcoat.

par-dessus /pardəsy/ *prép. & adv.* over. ∼ **bord,** overboard. ∼ **le marché,** into the bargain. ∼ **tout,** above all.

par-devant /pardvɑ̃/ *adv.* at *ou* from the front, in front.

pardon /pardɔ̃/ *n.m.* forgiveness. **(je vous demande)** ∼**!,** (I am) sorry!; (*pour demander qch.*) excuse me!

pardonn|er /pardɔne/ *v.t.* forgive. ∼**er qch. à qn.,** forgive s.o. for sth. ∼**able** *a.* forgivable.

paré /pare/ *a.* ready.

pare-balles /parbal/ *a. invar.* bullet-proof.

pare-brise /parbriz/ *n.m. invar.* windscreen; (*Amer.*) windshield.

pare-chocs /parʃɔk/ *n.m. invar.* bumper.

pareil, ⁓le /parɛj/ a. similar (à to); (tel) such (a). —n.m., f. equal. —adv. (fam.) the same. **c'est ⁓**, it is the same. **vos ⁓s**, (péj.) those of your type, those like you. **⁓lement** adv. the same.

parement /parmã/ n.m. facing.

parent, ⁓e /parã, -t/ a. related (de, to). —n.m., f. relative, relation. ⁓s (père et mère) n.m.pl. parents. **⁓ seul**, single parent.

parenté /parãte/ n.f. relationship.

parenthèse /parãtɛz/ n.f. bracket, parenthesis; (fig.) digression.

parer[1] /pare/ v.t. (coup) parry. —v.i. **⁓ à**, deal with. **⁓ au plus pressé**, tackle the most urgent things first.

parer[2] /pare/ v.t. (orner) adorn.

paress|e /parɛs/ n.f. laziness. **⁓er** /-ese/ v.i. laze (about). **⁓eux**, **⁓euse** a. lazy; n.m., f. lazybones.

parfaire /parfɛr/ v.t. perfect.

parfait, ⁓e /parfɛ, -t/ a. perfect. **⁓ement** /-tmã/ adv. perfectly; (bien sûr) certainly.

parfois /parfwa/ adv. sometimes.

parfum /parfœ̃/ n.m. scent; (substance) perfume, scent; (goût) flavour.

parfum|er /parfyme/ v.t. perfume; (gâteau) flavour. **se ⁓er** v.pr. put on one's perfume. **⁓é a**. fragrant; (savon) scented. **⁓erie** n.f. (produits) perfumes; (boutique) perfume shop.

pari /pari/ n.m. bet.

par|ier /parje/ v.t. bet. **⁓ieur**, **⁓ieuse** n.m., f. punter, better.

Paris /pari/ n.m./f. Paris.

parisien, ⁓ne /parizjɛ̃, -jɛn/ a. Paris, Parisian. —n.m., f. Paris, Parisian.

parit|é /parite/ n.f. parity. **⁓aire** a. (commission) joint.

parjure /parʒyr/ n.m. perjury. —n.m./f. perjurer. **se ⁓er** v.pr. perjure o.s.

parking /parkiŋ/ n.m. car-park; (Amer.) parking-lot; (stationnement) parking.

parlement /parləmã/ n.m. parliament. **⁓aire** /-tɛr/ a. parliamentary; n.m./f. Member of Parliament; (fig.) negotiator. **⁓er** /-te/ v.i. negotiate.

parl|er /parle/ v.i. talk, speak (à, to). —v.t. (langue) speak; (politique, affaires, etc.) talk. **se ⁓er** v.pr. (langue) be spoken. —n.m. speech; (dialecte) dialect. **⁓ant**, **⁓ante** a. (film) talking; (fig.) eloquent. **⁓eur**, **⁓euse** n.m., f. talker.

parloir /parlwar/ n.m. visiting room.

parmi /parmi/ prép. among(st).

parod|ie /parɔdi/ n.f. parody. **⁓ier** v.t. parody.

paroi /parwa/ n.f. wall; (cloison) partition (wall). **⁓ rocheuse**, rock face.

paroiss|e /parwas/ n.f. parish. **⁓ial** (m. pl. **⁓iaux**) a. parish. **⁓ien**, **⁓ienne** n.m., f. parishioner.

parole /parɔl/ n.f. (mot, promesse) word; (langage) speech. **demander la ⁓**, ask to speak. **prendre la ⁓**, (begin to) speak. **tenir ⁓**, keep one's word. **croire qn. sur ⁓**, take s.o.'s word for it.

paroxysme /parɔksism/ n.m. height, highest point.

parquer /parke/ v.t., **se ⁓** v.pr. (auto.) park. **⁓ des réfugiés**, pen up refugees.

parquet /parkɛ/ n.m. floor; (jurid.) public prosecutor's department.

parrain /parɛ̃/ n.m. godfather; (fig.) sponsor. **⁓er** /-ene/ v.t. sponsor.

pars, part[1] /par/ voir **partir**.

parsemer /parsəme/ v.t. strew (de, with).

part[2] /par/ n.f. share, part. **à ⁓**, (de côté) aside; (séparément) apart;

(*excepté*) apart from. **d'autre** ~, on the other hand; (*de plus*) moreover. **de la** ~ **de**, from. **de toutes** ~**s**, from all sides. **de** ~ **et d'autre**, on both sides. **d'une** ~, on the one hand. **faire** ~ **à qn.**, inform s.o. (**de**, of). **faire la** ~ **des choses**, make allowances. **prendre** ~ **à**, take part in. (*joie, douleur*) share. **pour ma** ~, as for me.

partag|e /partaʒ/ *n.m.* dividing; sharing out; (*part*) share. ~**er** *v.t.* divide; (*distribuer*) share out; (*avoir en commun*) share. **se** ~**er qch.**, share sth.

partance (en) /(ã)partãs/ *adv.* about to depart.

partant /partã/ *n.m.* (*sport*) starter.

partenaire /partǝnɛr/ *n.m./f.* partner.

parterre /partɛr/ *n.m.* flower-bed; (*théâtre*) stalls.

parti /parti/ *n.m.* (*pol.*) party; (*en mariage*) match; (*décision*) decision. ~ **pris**, prejudice. **prendre** ~ **pour**, side with. **j'en prends mon** ~, I've come to terms with that.

part|ial (*m. pl.* ~**iaux**) /parsjal, -jo/ *a.* biased. ~**ialité** *n.f.* bias.

participe /partisip/ *n.m.* (*gram.*) participle.

particip|er /partisipe/ *v.i.* ~**er à**, take part in, participate in; (*profits, frais*) share; (*spectacle*) appear in. ~**ant**, ~**ante** *n.m.,f.* participant (**à**, in); (*à un concours*) entrant. ~**ation** *n.f.* participation; sharing; (*comm.*) interest. (*d'un artiste*) appearance.

particularité /partikylarite/ *n.f.* particularity.

particule /partikyl/ *n.f.* particle.

particul|ier, ~**ière** /partikylje, -jer/ *a.* (*spécifique*) particular; (*bizarre*) peculiar; (*privé*) private. —*n.m.* private an-

dividual. **en** ~**ier**, in particular; (*en privé*) in private. ~**ier à**, peculiar to. ~**ièrement** *adv.* particularly.

partie /parti/ *n.f.* part; (*cartes, sport*) game; (*jurid.*) party; (*sortie*) outing, party. **une** ~ **de pêche**, a fishing trip. **en** ~, partly. **faire** ~ **de**, be part of; (*adhérer à*) belong to. **en grande** ~, largely. ~ **intégrante**, integral part.

partiel, ~**le** /parsjɛl/ *a.* partial. —*n.m.* (*univ.*) class examination. ~**lement** *adv.* partially, partly.

partir† /partir/ *v.i.* (*aux. être*) go; (*quitter un lieu*) leave, go; (*tache*) come out; (*bouton*) come off; (*coup de feu*) go off; (*commencer*) start. **à** ~ **de**, from.

partisan, ~**e** /partizã, -an/ *n.m., f.* supporter. —*n.m.* (*mil.*) partisan. **être** ~ **de**, be in favour of.

partition /partisjɔ̃/ *n.f.* (*mus.*) score.

partout /partu/ *adv.* everywhere. ~ **où**, wherever.

paru /pary/ *voir* **paraître**.

parure /paryr/ *n.f.* adornment; (*bijoux*) jewellery; (*de draps*) set.

parution /parysjɔ̃/ *n.f.* publication.

parvenir† /parvǝnir/ *v.i.* (*aux. être*) ~ **à**, reach; (*résultat*) achieve. ~ **à faire**, manage to do. **faire** ~, send.

parvenu, ~**e** /parvǝny/ *n.m., f.* upstart.

parvis /parvi/ *n.m.* (*place*) square.

pas¹ /pa/ *adv.* not. (**ne**) ~, not. **je ne sais** ~, I do not know. ~ **de sucre/livres/etc.**, no sugar/books/*etc.* ~ **du tout**, not at all. ~ **encore**, not yet. ~ **mal**, not bad; (*beaucoup*) quite a lot (**de**, of). ~ **vrai?**, (*fam.*) isn't that so?

pas² /pa/ *n.m.* step; (*bruit*)

footstep; (*trace*) footprint; (*vitesse*) pace; (*de vis*) thread. **à deux ~ (de)**, close by. **au ~**, at a walking pace; (*véhicule*) very slowly. **au ~ (cadencé)**, in step. **à ~ de loup**, stealthily. **faire les cent ~**, walk up and down. **faire les premiers ~**, take the first steps. **sur le ~ de la porte**, on the doorstep.

passable /pɑsabl/ *a.* tolerable. **mention ~**, pass mark.

passage /pɑsaʒ/ *n.m.* passing, passage; (*traversée*) crossing; (*visite*) visit; (*chemin*) way, passage; (*d'une œuvre*) passage. **de ~**, (*voyageur*) visiting; (*amant*) casual. **~ à niveau**, level crossing. **~ clouté**, pedestrian crossing. **~ interdit**, (*panneau*) no thoroughfare. **~ souterrain**, subway; (*Amer.*) underpass.

passag|er, ~ère /pɑsaʒe, -ɛr/ *a.* temporary. —*n.m.*, *f.* passenger. **~er clandestin**, stowaway.

passant, ~e /pɑsɑ̃, -t/ *a.* (*rue*) busy. —*n.m.*, *f.* passer-by. —*n.m.* (*anneau*) loop.

passe /pɑs/ *n.f.* pass. **bonne/ mauvaise ~**, good/bad patch. **en ~ de**, on the road to. **~-droit**, *n.m.* special privilege. **~-montagne** *n.m.* Balaclava. **~-partout** *n.m. invar.* master-key; *a. invar.* for all occasions. **~-temps** *n.m. invar.* pastime.

passé /pɑse/ *a.* (*révolu*) past; (*dernier*) last; (*fini*) over; (*fané*) faded. —*prép.* after. —*n.m.* past. **~ de mode**, out of fashion.

passeport /pɑspɔr/ *n.m.* passport.

passer /pɑse/ *v.i.* (*aux. être ou avoir*) pass; (*aller*) go; (*venir*) come; (*temps*) pass (by), go by; (*film*) be shown; (*couleur*) fade. —*v.t.* (*aux. avoir*) pass, cross; (*donner*) pass, hand; (*mettre*) put; (*oublier*) overlook; (*enfiler*) slip

on; (*dépasser*) go beyond; (*temps*) spend, pass; (*film*) show; (*examen*) take; (*commande*) place; (*soupe*) strain. **se ~** *v. pr.* happen, take place. **laisser ~**, let through; (*occasion*) miss. **~ à tabac**, (*fam.*) beat up. **~ devant**, (*édifice*) go past. **~ en fraude**, smuggle. **~ outre**, take no notice (**à**, of). **~ par**, go through. **~ pour**, (*riche etc.*) be taken to be. **~ sur**, (*détail*) pass over. **~ l'aspirateur**, hoover, vacuum. **~ un coup de fil à qn.**, give s.o. a ring. **je vous passe Mme X**, (*par le standard*) I'm putting you through to Mrs X; (*en donnant l'appareil*) I'll hand you over to Mrs X. **se ~ de**, go ou do without.

passerelle /pɑsrɛl/ *n.f.* footbridge; (*pour accéder à un avion, à un navire*) gangway.

passeur, ~euse /pɑsœr, œz/ *n.m.*, *f.* smuggler.

passible /pɑsibl/ *a.* **~ de**, liable to.

passif, ~ve /pɑsif, -v/ *a.* passive. —*n.m.* (*comm.*) liabilities. **~vité** *n.f.* passiveness.

passion /pɑsjɔ̃/ *n.f.* passion.

passionn|er /pɑsjɔne/ *v.t.* fascinate. **se ~er pour**, have a passion for. **~é** *a.* passionate. **être ~é de**, have a passion for. **~ément** *adv.* passionately.

passoire /pɑswar/ *n.f.* (*à thé*) strainer; (*à légumes*) colander.

pastel /pɑstɛl/ *n.m.* & *a. invar.* pastel.

pastèque /pɑstɛk/ *n.f.* watermelon.

pasteur /pɑstœr/ *n.m.* (*relig.*) minister.

pasteurisé /pɑstœrize/ *a.* pasteurized.

pastiche /pɑstiʃ/ *n.m.* pastiche.

pastille /pɑstij/ *n.f.* (*bonbon*) pastille, lozenge.

pastis /pɑstis/ *n.m.* aniseed liqueur.

patate /patat/ *n.f.* (*fam.*) potato. ~ **(douce),** sweet potato.

patauger /patoʒe/ *v.i.* splash about.

pâte /pɑt/ *n.f.* paste; (*farine*) dough; (*à tarte*) pastry; (*à frire*) batter. ~**s (alimentaires),** pasta. ~ **à modeler,** Plasticine (P.). ~ **dentifrice,** toothpaste.

pâté /pate/ *n.m.* (*culin.*) pâté; (*d'encre*) ink-blot. ~ **de maisons,** block of houses; (*de sable*) sand-pie. ~ **en croûte,** meat pie.

pâtée /pɑte/ *n.f.* feed, mash.

patelin /patlɛ̃/ *n.m.* (*fam.*) village.

patent, ~e[1] /patɑ̃, -t/ *a.* patent.

patent|e[2] /patɑ̃t/ *n.f.* trade licence. ~**é** *a.* licensed.

patère /patɛr/ *n.f.* (coat) peg.

patern|el, ~elle /patɛrnɛl/ *a.* paternal. ~**ité** *n.f.* paternity.

pâteu|x, ~se /pɑtø, -z/ *a.* pasty; (*langue*) coated.

pathétique /patetik/ *a.* moving. —*n.m.* pathos.

patholog|ie /patɔlɔʒi/ *n.f.* pathology. ~**ique** *a.* pathological.

pat|ient, ~iente /pasjɑ̃, -t/ *a. & n.m. & f.* patient. ~**iemment** /-jamɑ̃/ *adv.* patiently. ~**ience** *n.f.* patience.

patienter /pasjɑ̃te/ *v.i.* wait.

patin /patɛ̃/ *n.m.* skate. ~ **à roulettes,** roller-skate.

patin|er /patine/ *v.i.* skate; (*voiture*) spin. ~**age** *n.m.* skating. ~**eur, ~euse** *n.m., f.* skater.

patinoire /patinwar/ *n.f.* skating-rink.

pâtir /pɑtir/ *v.i.* suffer (**de,** from).

pâtiss|ier, ~ière /pɑtisje, -jɛr/ *n.m., f.* pastry-cook, cake shop owner. ~**erie** *n.f.* cake shop; (*gâteau*) pastry; (*art*) cake making.

patois /patwa/ *n.m.* patois.

patraque /patrak/ *a.* (*fam.*) peaky, out of sorts.

patrie /patri/ *n.f.* homeland.

patrimoine /patrimwan/ *n.m.* heritage.

patriot|e /patrijɔt/ *a.* patriotic. —*n.m./f.* patriot. ~**ique** *a.* patriotic. ~**isme** *n.m.* patriotism.

patron[1], **~ne** /patrɔ̃, -ɔn/ *n.m., f.* employer, boss; (*propriétaire*) owner, boss; (*saint*) patron saint. ~**al** (*m. pl.* ~**aux**) /-ɔnal, -o/ *a.* employers'. ~**at** /-ɔna/ *n.m.* employers.

patron[2] /patrɔ̃/ *n.m.* (*couture*) pattern.

patronage /patrɔnaʒ/ *n.m.* patronage; (*foyer*) youth club.

patronner /patrɔne/ *v.t.* support.

patrouill|e /patruj/ *n.f.* patrol. ~**er** *v.i.* patrol.

patte /pat/ *n.f.* leg; (*pied*) foot; (*de chat*) paw. ~**s,** (*favoris*) side-burns.

pâturage /pɑtyraʒ/ *n.m.* pasture.

pâture /pɑtyr/ *n.f.* food.

paume /pom/ *n.f.* (*de main*) palm.

paumé, ~e /pome/ *n.m., f.* (*fam.*) wretch, loser.

paumer /pome/ *v.t.* (*fam.*) lose.

paupière /popjɛr/ *n.f.* eyelid.

pause /poz/ *n.f.* pause; (*halte*) break.

pauvre /povr/ *a.* poor. —*n.m./f.* poor man, poor woman. ~**ment** /-əmɑ̃/ *adv.* poorly. ~**té** /-əte/ *n.f.* poverty.

pavaner (se) /(sə)pavane/ *v. pr.* strut.

pav|er /pave/ *v.t.* pave; (*chaussée*) cobble. ~**é** *n.m.* paving-stone; cobble(-stone).

pavillon[1] /pavijɔ̃/ *n.m.* house; (*de gardien*) lodge.

pavillon[2] /pavijɔ̃/ *n.m.* (*drapeau*) flag.

pavoiser /pavwaze/ *v.t.* deck with flags. —*v.i.* put out the flags.

pavot /pavo/ *n.m.* poppy.

payant, ~e /pɛjɑ̃, -t/ a. (billet) for which a charge is made; (spectateur) (fee-)paying; (rentable) profitable.

payer /peje/ v.t./i. pay; (service, travail, etc.) pay for; (acheter) buy (à, for). se ~ v. pr. (s'acheter) buy o.s. faire ~ à, (cent francs etc.) charge s.o. (pour, for). se la tête de, make fun of. il me le paiera!, he'll pay for this.

pays /pei/ n.m. country; (région) region; (village) village. du ~, local. les P~-Bas, the Netherlands. le ~ de Galles, Wales.

paysage /peizaʒ/ n.m. landscape.

paysan, ~ne /peizɑ̃, -an/ n.m., f. farmer, country person; (péj.) peasant. —a. (agricole) farming; (rural) country.

PCV (en) /(ɑ̃)peseve/ adv. appeler ou téléphoner en ~, reverse the charges; (Amer.) collect.

PDG abrév. voir président directeur général.

péage /peaʒ/ n.m. toll; (lieu) tollgate.

peau (pl. ~x) /po/ n.f. skin; (cuir) hide. ~ de chamois, chamois (-leather). ~ de mouton, sheepskin. être bien/mal dans sa ~, be/not be at ease with oneself.

pêche¹ /pɛʃ/ n.f. peach.

pêche² /pɛʃ/ n.f. (activité) fishing; (poissons) catch. ~ à la ligne, angling.

péché /peʃe/ n.m. sin.

péch|er /peʃe/ v.i. sin. ~er par timidité/etc., be too timid/etc. ~eur, ~eresse n.m., f. sinner.

pêch|er /peʃe/ v.t. (poisson) catch; (dénicher: fam.) dig up. —v.i. fish. ~eur n.m. fisherman; (à la ligne) angler.

pécule /pekyl/ n.m. (économies) savings.

pécuniaire /pekynjɛr/ a. financial.

pédago|gie /pedagɔʒi/ n.f. education. ~gique a. educational. ~gue n.m./f. teacher.

pédale /pedal/ n.f. pedal. ~er v.i. pedal.

pédalo /pedalo/ n.m. pedal boat.

pédant, ~e /pedɑ̃, -t/ a. pedantic.

pédé /pede/ n.m. (argot) queer, fag (Amer.).

pédestre /pedɛstr/ a. faire de la randonnée ~, go walking ou hiking.

pédiatre /pedjatr/ n.m./f. paediatrician.

pédicure /pedikyr/ n.m./f. chiropodist.

pedigree /pedigri/ n.m. pedigree.

pègre /pɛgr/ n.f. underworld.

peign|e /pɛɲ/ n.m. comb. ~er /peɲe/ v.t. comb; (personne) comb the hair of. se ~er v. pr. comb one's hair.

peignoir /pɛɲwar/ n.m. dressing-gown.

peindre† /pɛ̃dr/ v.t. paint.

peine /pɛn/ n.f. sadness, sorrow; (effort, difficulté) trouble; (punition) punishment; (jurid.) sentence. avoir de la ~, feel sad. faire de la ~ à, hurt. ce n'est pas la ~ de faire, it is not worth (while) doing. se donner ou prendre la ~ de faire, go to the trouble of doing. ~ de mort death penalty.

peine (à) /(a)pɛn/ adv. hardly.

peiner /pene/ v.i. struggle. —v.t. sadden.

peintre /pɛ̃tr/ n.m. painter. ~ en bâtiment, house painter.

peinture /pɛ̃tyr/ n.f. painting; (matière) paint. ~ à l'huile, oil-painting.

péjoratif, ~ve /peʒɔratif, -v/ a. pejorative.

pelage /pəlaʒ/ n.m. coat, fur.

pêle-mêle /pɛlmɛl/ adv. in a jumble.

peler /pəle/ v.t./i. peel.

pèlerin /pɛlrɛ̃/ n.m. pilgrim. ~**age** /-inaʒ/ n.m. pilgrimage.

pèlerine /pɛlrin/ n.f. cape.

pélican /pelikɑ̃/ n.m. pelican.

pelle /pɛl/ n.f. shovel; (*d'enfant*) spade. ~**tée** n.f. shovelful.

pellicule /pelikyl/ n.f. film. ~**s,** (*cheveux*) dandruff.

pelote /pələt/ n.f. ball; (*d'épingles*) pincushion.

peloton /plətɔ̃/ n.m. troop, squad; (*sport*) pack. ~ **d'exécution,** firing-squad.

pelotonner (se) /(sə)plətɔne/ v. pr. curl up.

pelouse /pluz/ n.f. lawn.

peluche /plyʃ/ n.f. (*tissu*) plush; (*jouet*) cuddly toy. en ~, (*lapin, chien*) fluffy, furry.

pelure /plyr/ n.f. peeling.

pén|al (m. pl. ~**aux**) /penal, -o/ a. penal. ~**aliser** v.t. penalize. ~**alité** n.f. penalty.

penalt|y (pl. ~**ies**) /penalti/ n.m. penalty (kick).

penaud, ~**e** /pəno, -d/ a. sheepish.

penchant /pɑ̃ʃɑ̃/ n.m. inclination; (*goût*) liking (pour, for).

pench|er /pɑ̃ʃe/ v.t. tilt. —v.i. lean (over), tilt. se ~**er** v. pr. lean (forward). ~**er pour,** favour. se ~**er sur,** (*problème etc.*) examine.

pendaison /pɑ̃dɛzɔ̃/ n.f. hanging.

pendant[1] /pɑ̃dɑ̃/ prép. (*au cours de*) during; (*durée*) for. ~ **que,** while.

pendant[2], ~**e** /pɑ̃dɑ̃, -t/ a. hanging; (*question etc.*) pending. —n.m. (*contrepartie*) matching piece (de, to). faire ~ **à,** match. ~ **d'oreille,** drop ear-ring.

pendentif /pɑ̃dɑ̃tif/ n.m. pendant.

penderie /pɑ̃dri/ n.f. wardrobe.

pend|re /pɑ̃dr/ v.t./i. hang v. pr. hang (à, from); (*se tuer*) hang o.s. ~**re la crémaillère,** have a house-warming. ~**u,** ~**ue** a. hanging (à, from); n.m., f. hanged man, hanged woman.

pendul|e /pɑ̃dyl/ n.f. clock. —n.m. pendulum. ~**ette** n.f. (travelling) clock.

pénétr|er /penetre/ v.i. ~**er (dans),** enter. —v.t. penetrate. se ~**er de,** become convinced of. ~**ant,** ~**ante** a. penetrating.

pénible /penibl/ a. difficult; (*douloureux*) painful; (*fatigant*) tiresome. ~**ment** /-əmɑ̃/ adv. with difficulty; (*cruellement*) painfully.

péniche /peniʃ/ n.f. barge.

pénicilline /penisilin/ n.f. penicillin.

péninsule /penɛ̃syl/ n.f. peninsula.

pénis /penis/ n.m. penis.

pénitence /penitɑ̃s/ n.f. (*peine*) penance; (*regret*) penitence; (*fig.*) punishment. faire ~, repent.

péniten|cier /penitɑ̃sje/ n.m. penitentiary. ~**tiaire** /-sjɛr/ a. prison.

pénombre /penɔ̃br/ n.f. half-light.

pensée[1] /pɑ̃se/ n.f. thought.

pensée[2] /pɑ̃se/ n.f. (*fleur*) pansy.

pens|er /pɑ̃se/ v.t./i. think. ~**er à,** (*réfléchir à*) think about; (*se souvenir de, prévoir*) think of. ~**er faire,** think of doing. faire ~**er à,** remind one of. ~**eur** n.m. thinker.

pensi|f, ~**ve** /pɑ̃sif, -v/ a. pensive.

pension /pɑ̃sjɔ̃/ n.f. (*scol.*) boarding-school; (*repas, somme*) board; (*allocation*) pension. ~ **(de famille),** guest-house. ~ **alimentaire,** (*jurid.*) alimony. ~**naire** /-jɔnɛr/ n.m./f. boarder; (*d'hôtel*) guest. ~**nat** /-jɔna/ n.m. boarding-school.

pente /pɑ̃t/ n.f. slope. en ~, sloping.

Pentecôte /pãtkot/ *n.f.* la ~, Whitsun.

pénurie /penyri/ *n.f.* shortage.

pépé /pepe/ *n.m.* (*fam.*) grandad.

pépier /pepje/ *v.i.* chirp.

pépin /pepɛ̃/ *n.m.* (*graine*) pip; (*ennui: fam.*) hitch; (*parapluie: fam.*) brolly.

pépinière /pepinjɛr/ *n.f.* (tree) nursery.

perçant, ~e /pɛrsã, -t/ *a.* (*froid*) piercing; (*regard*) keen.

percée /pɛrse/ *n.f.* opening; (*attaque*) breakthrough.

perce-neige /pɛrsənɛʒ/ *n.m./f. invar.* snowdrop.

percepteur /pɛrsɛptœr/ *n.m.* tax-collector.

perceptible /pɛrsɛptibl/ *a.* perceptible.

perception /pɛrsɛpsjɔ̃/ *n.f.* perception; (*d'impôts*) collection.

percer /pɛrse/ *v.t.* pierce; (*avec perceuse*) drill; (*mystère*) penetrate. —*v.i.* break through; (*dent*) come through.

perceuse /pɛrsøz/ *n.f.* drill.

percevoir† /pɛrsəvwar/ *v.t.* perceive; (*impôt*) collect.

perche /pɛrʃ/ *n.f.* (*bâton*) pole.

percher /pɛrʃe/ *v.t./i.*, se ~er *v. pr.* perch. ~oir *n.m.* perch.

percolateur /pɛrkɔlatœr/ *n.m.* percolator.

percussion /pɛrkysjɔ̃/ *n.f.* percussion.

percuter /pɛrkyte/ *v.t.* strike; (*véhicule*) crash into.

perd|re /pɛrdr/ *v.t./i.* lose; (*gaspiller*) waste; (*ruiner*) ruin. se ~re *v. pr.* get lost; (*rester inutilisé*) go to waste. ~ant, ~ante *a.* losing; *n.m., f.* loser. ~u *a.* (*endroit*) isolated; (*moments*) spare; (*malade*) finished.

perdreau (*pl.* ~x) /pɛrdro/ *n.m.* (young) partridge.

perdrix /pɛrdri/ *n.f.* partridge.

père /pɛr/ *n.m.* father. ~ de famille, father, family man. ~ spirituel, father figure. le ~ Noël, Father Christmas, Santa Claus.

péremptoire /perãptwar/ *a.* peremptory.

perfection /pɛrfɛksjɔ̃/ *n.f.* perfection.

perfectionn|er /pɛrfɛksjɔne/ *v.t.* improve. se ~er en anglais/*etc.*, improve one's English/*etc.* ~é *a.* sophisticated. ~ement *n.m.* improvement.

perfectionniste /pɛrfɛksjɔnist/ *n.m./f.* perfectionist.

perfid|e /pɛrfid/ *a.* perfidious, treacherous. ~ie *n.f.* perfidy.

perfor|er /pɛrfɔre/ *v.t.* perforate; (*billet, bande*) punch. ~ateur *n.m.* (*appareil*) punch. ~ation *n.f.* perforation; (*trou*) hole.

performan|ce /pɛrfɔrmãs/ *n.f.* performance. ~t, ~te *a.* high-performance, successful.

perfusion /pɛrfyzjɔ̃/ *n.f.* drip. mettre qn. sous ~, put s.o. on a drip.

péricliter /periklite/ *v.i.* decline, be in rapid decline.

péridural /peridyral/ *a.* (**anesthésie**) ~e, epidural.

péril /peril/ *n.m.* peril.

périlleu|x, ~se /perijø, -z/ *a.* perilous.

périmé /perime/ *a.* expired; (*désuet*) outdated.

périmètre /perimɛtr/ *n.m.* perimeter.

périod|e /perjɔd/ *n.f.* period. ~ique *a.* periodic(al). ~ique *n.m.* (*journal*) periodical.

péripétie /peripesi/ *n.f.* (unexpected) event, adventure.

périphér|ie /periferi/ *n.f.* periphery; (*banlieue*) outskirts. ~ique *a.* peripheral; (*boulevard*) ~ique, ring road.

périple /peripl/ *n.m.* journey.

pér|ir /perir/ *v.i.* perish, die. **~issable** *a.* perishable.

périscope /periskɔp/ *n.m.* periscope.

perle /pɛrl/ *n.f.* (*bijou*) pearl; (*boule, de sueur*) bead.

permanence /pɛrmanɑ̃s/ *n.f.* permanence; (*bureau*) study office; (*scol.*) study room. **de ~**, on duty. **en ~**, permanently. **assurer une ~**, keep the office open.

permanent, **~e** /pɛrmanɑ̃, -t/ *a.* permanent; (*spectacle*) continuous; (*comité*) standing. —*n.f.* (*coiffure*) perm.

perméable /pɛrmeabl/ *a.* permeable; (*personne*) susceptible (à, to).

permettre† /pɛrmɛtr/ *v.t.* allow, permit. **~ à qn. de**, allow *ou* permit s.o. to. **se ~ de**, take the liberty to.

permis, **~e** /pɛrmi, -z/ *a.* allowed. —*n.m.* licence, permit. **~ (de conduire)**, driving-licence.

permission /pɛrmisjɔ̃/ *n.f.* permission. **en ~**, (*mil.*) on leave.

permut|er /pɛrmyte/ *v.t.* change round. **~ation** *n.f.* permutation.

pernicieu|x, **~se** /pɛrnisjø, -z/ *a.* pernicious.

Pérou /peru/ *n.m.* Peru.

perpendiculaire /pɛrpɑ̃dikylɛr/ *a.* & *n.f.* perpendicular.

perpétrer /pɛrpetre/ *v.t.* perpetrate.

perpétuel, **~le** /pɛrpetɥɛl/ *a.* perpetual.

perpétuer /pɛrpetɥe/ *v.t.* perpetuate.

perpétuité (à) /(a)pɛrpetɥite/ *adv.* for life.

perplex|e /pɛrplɛks/ *a.* perplexed. **~ité** *n.f.* perplexity.

perquisition /pɛrkizisjɔ̃/ *n.f.* (police) search. **~ner** /-jɔne/ *v.t./i.* search.

perron /pɛrɔ̃/ *n.m.* (front) steps.

perroquet /pɛrɔkɛ/ *n.m.* parrot.

perruche /perys/ *n.f.* budgerigar.

perruque /peryk/ *n.f.* wig.

persan, **~e** /pɛrsɑ̃, -an/ *a.* & *n.m.* (*lang.*) Persian.

persécut|er /pɛrsekyte/ *v.t.* persecute. **~ion** /-ysjɔ̃/ *n.f.* persecution.

persévér|er /pɛrsevere/ *v.i.* persevere. **~ance** *n.f.* perseverance.

persienne /pɛrsjɛn/ *n.f.* (outside) shutter.

persil /pɛrsi/ *n.m.* parsley.

persistan|t, **~te** /pɛrsistɑ̃, -t/ *a.* persistent; (*feuillage*) evergreen. **~ce** *n.f.* persistence.

persister /pɛrsiste/ *v.i.* persist (à faire, in doing).

personnage /pɛrsɔnaʒ/ *n.m.* character; (*important*) personality.

personnalité /pɛrsɔnalite/ *n.f.* personality.

personne /pɛrsɔn/ *n.f.* person. **~s**, people. —*pron.* (*quelqu'un*) anybody. **(ne) ~**, nobody.

personnel, **~le** /pɛrsɔnɛl/ *a.* personal; (*égoïste*) selfish. —*n.m.* staff. **~lement** *adv.* personally.

personnifier /pɛrsɔnifje/ *v.t.* personify.

perspective /pɛrspɛktiv/ *n.f.* (*art*) perspective; (*vue*) view; (*possibilité*) prospect; (*point de vue*) viewpoint, perspective.

perspicac|e /pɛrspikas/ *a.* shrewd. **~ité** *n.f.* shrewdness.

persua|der /pɛrsɥade/ *v.t.* persuade (de faire, to do). **~sion** /-qazjɔ̃/ *n.f.* persuasion.

persuasi|f, **~ve** /pɛrsɥazif, -v/ *a.* persuasive.

perte /pɛrt/ *n.f.* loss; (*ruine*) ruin. **à ~ de vue**, as far as the eye can see. **~ de**, (*temps, argent*) waste of. **~ sèche**, total loss. **~s**, (*méd.*) discharge.

pertinen|t, **~te** /pɛrtinɑ̃, -t/ *a.* pertinent; (*esprit*) judicious. **~ce** *n.f.* pertinence.

perturb|er /pɛrtyrbe/ *v.t.* disrupt;

(*personne*) perturb. ~**ateur,** ~**atrice** *a.* disruptive; *n.m., f.* disruptive element. ~**ation** *n.f.* disruption.

pervenche /pɛrvɑ̃ʃ/ *n.f.* periwinkle; (*fam.*) traffic warden.

pervers, ~**e** /pɛrvɛr, -s/ *a.* perverse; (*dépravé*) perverted. ~**ion** /-sjɔ̃/ *n.f.* perversion.

pervert|ir /pɛrvɛrtir/ *v.t.* pervert. ~**i,** ~**ie** *n.m., f.* pervert.

pes|ant, ~**ante** /pəzɑ̃, -t/ *a.* heavy. ~**amment** *adv.* heavily. ~**anteur** *n.f.* heaviness. **la** ~**anteur,** (*force*) gravity.

pèse-personne /pɛzpɛrsɔn/ *n.m.* (bathroom) scales.

pes|er /pəze/ *v.t./i.* weigh. ~**er sur,** bear upon. ~**ée** *n.f.* weighing; (*effort*) pressure.

peseta /pezeta/ *n.f.* peseta.

pessimis|te /pesimist/ *a.* pessimistic. —*n.m.* pessimist. ~**me** *n.m.* pessimism.

peste /pɛst/ *n.f.* plague; (*personne*) pest.

pester /pɛste/ *v.i.* ~ (**contre**), curse.

pestilentiel, ~**le** /pɛstilɑ̃sjɛl/ *a.* fetid, stinking.

pet /pɛ/ *n.m.* fart.

pétale /petal/ *n.m.* petal.

pétanque /petɑ̃k/ *n.f.* bowls.

pétarader /petarade/ *v.i.* backfire.

pétard /petar/ *n.m.* banger.

péter /pete/ *v.i.* fart; (*fam.*) go bang; (*casser: fam.*) snap.

pétill|er /petije/ *v.i.* (*feu*) crackle; (*champagne, yeux*) sparkle. ~**er d'intelligence,** sparkle with intelligence. ~**ant,** ~**ante** *a.* (*gazeux*) fizzy.

petit, ~**e** /pti, -t/ *a.* small; (*avec nuance affective*) little; (*jeune*) young, small; (*mesquin*) petty. —*n.m., f.* little child; (*scol.*) junior. ~**s,** (*de chat*) kittens; (*de chien*) pups. **en** ~, in miniature. ~ **ami,** boy-friend.

~**e amie,** girl-friend. **à petit,** little by little. ~**es annonces,** small ads. ~**e cuiller,** teaspoon. ~ **déjeuner,** breakfast. **le** ~ **écran,** the small screen, television. ~**-enfant** (*pl.* ~**s-enfants**) *n.m.* grandchild. ~**e-fille** (*pl.* ~**es-filles**) *n.f.* granddaughter. ~**-fils** (*pl.* ~**s-fils**) *n.m.* grandson. ~ **pain,** roll. ~**-pois** (*pl.* ~**s-pois**) *n.m.* garden pea.

petitesse /ptites/ *n.f.* smallness; (*péj.*) meanness.

pétition /petisjɔ̃/ *n.f.* petition.

pétrifier /petrifje/ *v.t.* petrify.

pétrin /petrɛ̃/ *n.m.* (*situation: fam.*) **dans le** ~, in a fix.

pétrir /petrir/ *v.t.* knead.

pétrole /petrol/ *n.m.* (*brut*) oil; (*pour lampe etc.*) paraffin. **lampe à** ~**e,** oil lamp. ~**ier,** ~**ière** *a.* oil; (*navire*) oil-tanker.

pétulant, ~**e** /petylɑ̃, -t/ *a.* exuberant, full of high spirits.

peu /pø/ *adv.* ~ (**de**), (*quantité*) little, not much; (*nombre*) few, not many. ~ **intéressant**/*etc.*, not very interesting/*etc.* —*pron.* few. —*n.m.* little. **un** ~ (**de**), a little. **à** ~ **près,** more or less. **de** ~, only just. ~ **à peu,** gradually. ~ **après/avant,** shortly after/before. ~ **de chose,** not much. ~ **nombreux,** few. ~ **souvent,** seldom. **pour** ~ **que,** as long as.

peuplade /pœplad/ *n.f.* tribe.

peuple /pœpl/ *n.m.* people.

peupler /pœple/ *v.t.* populate.

peuplier /pøplije/ *n.m.* poplar.

peur /pœr/ *n.f.* fear. **avoir** ~, be afraid (**de,** of). **de** ~ **de,** for fear of. **faire** ~ **à,** frighten. ~**eux,** ~**euse** *a.* fearful, timid.

peut /pø/ *voir* **pouvoir**[1].

peut-être /pøtɛtr/ *adv.* perhaps, maybe. ~ **que,** perhaps, maybe.

peux /pø/ *voir* **pouvoir**[1].

pèze /pɛz/ *n.m.* (*fam.*) **du** ~, money, dough.

phallique /falik/ a. phallic.

phantasme /fɑ̃tasm/ n.m. fantasy.

phare /far/ n.m. (tour) lighthouse; (de véhicule) headlight. ~ **anti-brouillard,** fog lamp.

pharmaceutique /farmasøtik/ a. pharmaceutical.

pharmac|ie /farmasi/ n.f. (magasin) chemist's (shop); (Amer.) pharmacy; (science) pharmacy; (armoire) medicine cabinet. ~**ien, ~ienne** n.m., f. chemist, pharmacist.

pharyngite /farɛ̃ʒit/ n.f. pharyngitis.

phase /faz/ n.f. phase.

phénomène /fenɔmɛn/ n.m. phenomenon; (original: fam.) eccentric.

philanthrop|e /filɑ̃trɔp/ n.m./f. philanthropist. ~**ique** a. philanthropic.

philatél|ie /filateli/ n.f. philately. ~**iste** n.m./f. philatelist.

philharmonique /filarmɔnik/ a. philharmonic.

Philippines /filipin/ n.f. pl. **les ~,** the Philippines.

philosoph|e /filozɔf/ n.m./f. philosopher. —a. philosophical. ~**ie** n.f. philosophy. ~**ique** a. philosophical.

phobie /fɔbi/ n.f. phobia.

phonétique /fɔnetik/ a. phonetic.

phoque /fɔk/ n.m. (animal) seal.

phosphate /fɔsfat/ n.m. phosphate.

phosphore /fɔsfɔr/ n.m. phosphorus.

photo /fɔto/ n.f. photo; (art) photography. **prendre en ~,** take a photo of. ~ **d'identité,** passport photograph.

photocop|ie /fɔtɔkɔpi/ n.f. photocopy. ~**ier** v.t. photocopy. ~**ieuse** n.f. photocopier.

photogénique /fɔtɔʒenik/ a. photogenic.

photograph|e /fɔtɔgraf/ n.m./f. photographer. ~**ie** n.f. photograph; (art) photography. ~**ier** v.t. take a photo of. ~**ique** a. photographic.

phrase /fraz/ n.f. sentence.

physicien, ~ne /fizisjɛ̃, -jɛn/ n.m., f. physicist.

physiologie /fizjɔlɔʒi/ n.f. physiology.

physionomie /fizjɔnɔmi/ n.f. face.

physique¹ /fizik/ a. physical. —n.m. physique. **au ~,** physically. ~**ment** adv. physically.

physique² /fizik/ n.f. physics.

piailler /pjaje/ v.i. squeal, squawk.

piano /pjano/ n.m. piano. ~**iste** n.m./f. pianist.

pianoter /pjanɔte/ v.t. (air) tap out. —v.i. (sur, on) (ordinateur) tap away; (table) tap one's fingers.

pic /pik/ n.m. (outil) pickaxe; (sommet) peak; (oiseau) woodpecker. à ~, (verticalement) sheer; (couler) straight to the bottom; (arriver) just at the right time.

pichenette /piʃnɛt/ n.f. flick.

pichet /piʃɛ/ n.m. jug.

pickpocket /pikpɔkɛt/ n.m. pickpocket.

pick-up /pikœp/ n.m. invar. record-player.

picorer /pikɔre/ v.t./i. peck.

picot|er /pikɔte/ v.t. prick; (yeux) make smart. ~**ement** n.m. pricking; smarting.

pie /pi/ n.f. magpie.

pièce /pjɛs/ n.f. piece; (chambre) room; (pour raccommoder) patch; (écrit) document. ~ (de monnaie), coin. ~ (de théâtre), play. **dix francs/etc. (la) ~,** ten francs/etc. each. ~ **de rechange,** spare part. ~ **détachée,** part. ~ **d'identité,** identity paper. ~ **montée,** tiered cake. ~**s justificatives,** supporting documents. **deux/trois** etc. ~**s,**

two-/three-/*etc.* room flat *ou* apartment (*Amer.*).

pied /pje/ *n.m.* foot; (*de meuble*) leg; (*de lampe*) base; (*de salade*) plant. **à ~**, on foot. **au ~ de la lettre**, literally. **avoir ~**, have a footing. **avoir les ~s plats**, have flat feet. **comme un ~**, (*fam.*) terribly. **mettre sur ~**, set up. **~ bot**, club-foot. **sur un ~ d'égalité**, on an equal footing. **mettre les ~s dans le plat**, put one's foot in it. **c'est le ~!**, (*fam.*) it's great!

piédest|al (*pl.* **~aux**) /pjedɛstal, -o/ *n.m.* pedestal.

piège /pjɛʒ/ *n.m.* trap.

piég|er /pjeʒe/ *v.t.* trap; (*avec explosifs*) booby-trap. **lettre/voiture ~ée**, letter-/car-bomb.

pierr|e /pjɛr/ *n.f.* stone. **~e d'achoppement**, stumbling-block. **~e de touche**, touch-stone. **~e précieuse**, precious stone. **~e tombale**, tombstone. **~eux, ~euse** *a.* stony.

piété /pjete/ *n.f.* piety.

piétiner /pjetine/ *v.i.* stamp one's feet; (*ne pas avancer: fig.*) mark time. —*v.t.* trample on.

piéton /pjetɔ̃/ *n.m.* pedestrian. **~nier, ~nière** /-ɔnje, -jɛr/ *a.* pedestrian.

piètre /pjɛtr/ *a.* wretched.

pieu (*pl.* **~x**) /pjø/ *n.m.* post, stake.

pieuvre /pjœvr/ *n.f.* octopus.

pieu|x, ~se /pjø, -z/ *a.* pious.

pif /pif/ *n.m.* (*fam.*) nose.

pigeon /piʒɔ̃/ *n.m.* pigeon.

piger /piʒe/ *v.t./i.* (*fam.*) understand, get (it).

pigment /pigmɑ̃/ *n.m.* pigment.

pignon /piɲɔ̃/ *n.m.* (*de maison*) gable.

pile /pil/ *n.f.* (*tas, pilier*) pile; (*électr.*) battery; (*atomique*) pile. —*adv.* (*s'arrêter: fam.*) dead. **à dix heures ~**, (*fam.*) at ten on

the dot. **~ ou face?**, heads or tails?

piler /pile/ *v.t.* pound.

pilier /pilje/ *n.m.* pillar.

pill|er /pije/ *v.t.* loot. **~age** *n.m.* looting. **~ard, ~arde** *n.m., f.* looter.

pilonner /pilone/ *v.t.* pound.

pilori /pilori/ *n.m.* **mettre** *ou* **clouer au ~**, pillory.

pilot|e /pilot/ *n.m.* pilot; (*auto.*) driver. —*a.* pilot. **~er** *v.t.* (*aviat., naut.*) pilot; (*auto.*) drive; (*fig.*) guide.

pilule /pilyl/ *n.f.* pill. **la ~**, the pill.

piment /pimɑ̃/ *n.m.* pepper, pimento; (*fig.*) spice. **~é** /-te/ *a.* spicy.

pimpant, ~e /pɛ̃pɑ̃, -t/ *a.* spruce.

pin /pɛ̃/ *n.m.* pine.

pinard /pinar/ *n.m.* (*vin: fam.*) plonk, cheap wine.

pince /pɛ̃s/ *n.f.* (*outil*) pliers; (*levier*) crowbar; (*de crabe*) pincer; (*à sucre*) tongs. **~ (à épiler)**, tweezers. **~ (à linge)**, (clothes-)peg.

pinceau (*pl.* **~x**) /pɛ̃so/ *n.m.* paintbrush.

pinc|er /pɛ̃se/ *v.t.* pinch; (*arrêter: fam.*) pinch. **se ~er le doigt**, catch one's finger. **~é a.** (*ton, air*) stiff. **~ée** *n.f.* pinch (de, of).

pince-sans-rire /pɛ̃sɑ̃rir/ *a. invar.* po-faced. **c'est un ~**, he's po-faced.

pincettes /pɛ̃sɛt/ *n.f. pl.* (fire) tongs.

pinède /pinɛd/ *n.f.* pine forest.

pingouin /pɛ̃gwɛ̃/ *n.m.* penguin.

ping-pong /piɲpɔ̃g/ *n.m.* table tennis, ping-pong.

pingre /pɛ̃gr/ *a.* miserly.

pinson /pɛ̃sɔ̃/ *n.m.* chaffinch.

pintade /pɛ̃tad/ *n.f.* guinea-fowl.

pioch|e /pjɔʃ/ *n.f.* pick(axe). **~er** *v.t./i.* dig; (*étudier: fam.*) study hard, slog away (at).

pion /pjɔ̃/ n.m. (de jeu) piece; (échecs) pawn; (scol., fam.) supervisor.

pionnier /pjɔnje/ n.m. pioneer.

pipe /pip/ n.f. pipe. **fumer la ~,** smoke a pipe.

pipe-line /piplin/ n.m. pipeline.

piquant, ~e /pikã, -t/ a. (barbe etc.) prickly; (goût) pungent; (détail etc.) spicy. —n.m. prickle; (de hérisson) spine, prickle; (fig.) piquancy.

pique[1] /pik/ n.f. (arme) pike.

pique[2] /pik/ n.m. (cartes) spades.

pique-nique /piknik/ n.m. picnic. **~er** v.i. picnic.

piquer /pike/ v.t. prick; (langue) burn, sting; (abeille etc.) sting; (serpent etc.) bite; (enfoncer) stick; (coudre) (machine-)stitch; (curiosité) excite; (crise) have; (voler: fam.) pinch. —v.i. (avion) dive; (goût) be hot. **~ une tête,** plunge headlong. **se ~ de,** pride o.s. on.

piquet /pike/ n.m. stake; (de tente) peg. **au ~,** (scol.) in the corner. **~ de grève,** (strike) picket.

piqûre /pikyr/ n.f. prick; (d'abeille etc.) sting; (de serpent etc.) bite; (point) stitch; (méd.) injection, shot (Amer.) **faire une ~ à qn.,** give s.o. an injection.

pirate /pirat/ n.m. pirate. **~ de l'air,** hijacker. **~rie** n.f. piracy.

pire /pir/ a. worse (que, than). **le ~ livre/etc.,** the worst book/etc. —n.m. **le ~,** the worst (thing). **au ~,** at worst.

pirogue /pirɔg/ n.f. canoe, dug-out.

pirouette /pirwɛt/ n.f. pirouette.

pis[1] /pi/ n.m. (de vache) udder.

pis[2] /pi/ a. invar. & adv. worse. **aller de mal en ~,** go from bad to worse.

pis-aller /pizale/ n.m. invar. stopgap, temporary expedient.

piscine /pisin/ n.f. swimming-pool. **~ couverte,** indoor swimmingpool.

pissenlit /pisãli/ n.m. dandelion.

pistache /pistaʃ/ n.f. pistachio.

piste /pist/ n.f. track; (de personne, d'animal) track, trail; (aviat.) runway; (de cirque) ring; (de ski) run; (de patinage) rink; (de danse) floor; (sport) race-track. **~ cyclable,** cycle-track; (Amer.) bicycle path.

pistolet /pistɔlɛ/ n.m. gun, pistol; (de peintre) spray-gun.

piston /pistɔ̃/ n.m. (techn.) piston. **il a un ~,** (fam.) somebody is pulling strings for him.

pistonner /pistɔne/ v.t. (fam.) recommend, pull strings for.

piteu|x, ~se /pitø, -z/ a. pitiful.

pitié /pitje/ n.f. pity. **il me fait ~, j'ai ~ de lui,** I pity him.

piton /pitɔ̃/ n.m. (à crochet) hook; (sommet pointu) peak.

pitoyable /pitwajabl/ a. pitiful.

pitre /pitr/ n.m. clown. **faire le ~,** clown around.

pittoresque /pitɔrɛsk/ a. picturesque.

pivot /pivo/ n.m. pivot. **~er** /-ɔte/ v.i. revolve; (personne) swing round.

pizza /pidza/ n.f. pizza.

placage /plakaʒ/ n.m. (en bois) veneer; (sur un mur) facing.

placard /plakar/ n.m. cupboard; (affiche) poster. **~er** /-de/ v.t. (affiche) post up; (mur) cover with posters.

place /plas/ n.f. place; (espace libre) room, space; (siège) seat, place; (prix d'un trajet) fare; (esplanade) square; (emploi) position; (de parking) space. **à la ~ de,** instead of. **en ~, à sa ~,** in its place. **faire ~ à,** give way to. **sur ~,** on the spot. **remettre qn. à sa ~,** put s.o. in his place. **ça prend de la ~,** it takes up a lot of room. **se mettre à la ~ de qn.** put oneself in s.o.'s shoes ou place.

placebo /plasebo/ *n.m.* placebo.

placenta /plasẽta/ *n.m.* placenta.

plac|er /plase/ *v.t.* place; (*invité, spectateur*) seat; (*argent*) invest. se ∼er *v. pr.* (*personne*) take up a position; (*troisième etc.*: *sport*) come (in); (*à un endroit*) to go and stand (à, in). ∼é a. (*sport*) placed. bien ∼é pour, in a position to. ∼ement *n.m.* (*d'argent*) investment.

placide /plasid/ a. placid.

plafond /plafɔ̃/ *n.m.* ceiling.

plage /plaʒ/ *n.f.* beach; (*station*) (seaside) resort; (*aire*) area.

plagiat /plaʒja/ *n.m.* plagiarism.

plaid /plɛd/ *n.m.* travelling-rug.

plaid|er /plede/ *v.t./i.* plead. ∼oirie /plɛdwari/ *n.f.* (*defence*) speech. ∼oyer *n.m.* plea.

plaie /plɛ/ *n.f.* wound; (*personne*: *fam.*) nuisance.

plaignant, ∼e /plɛɲɑ̃, -t/ *n.m.*, *f.* plaintiff.

plaindre† /plɛ̃dr/ *v.t.* pity. se ∼ *v. pr.* complain (de, about). se ∼ de, (*souffrir de*) complain of.

plaine /plɛn/ *n.f.* plain.

plaint|e /plɛ̃t/ *n.f.* complaint; (*gémissement*) groan. ∼if, ∼ive a. plaintive.

plaire† /plɛr/ *v.i.* ∼ à, please. ça lui plaît, he likes it. elle lui plaît, he likes her. ça me plaît de faire, I like ou enjoy doing. s'il vous plaît, please. se ∼ *v. pr.* (à Londres etc.) like ou enjoy it.

plaisance /plɛzɑ̃s/ *n.f.* la (navigation de) ∼, yachting.

plaisant, ∼e /plɛzɑ̃, -t/ a. pleasant; (*drôle*) amusing.

plaisant|er /plɛzɑ̃te/ *v.i.* joke. ∼erie *n.f.* joke. ∼in *n.m.* joker.

plaisir /plɛzir/ *n.m.* pleasure. faire ∼ à, please. pour le ∼, for fun ou pleasure.

plan¹ /plɑ̃/ *n.m.* plan; (*de ville*) map; (*surface, niveau*) plane. ∼

d'eau, expanse of water.

premier ∼, foreground.

dernier ∼, background.

plan², ∼e /plɑ̃, -an/ a. flat.

planche /plɑ̃ʃ/ *n.f.* board, plank; (*gravure*) plate; (*de potager*) bed. ∼ à repasser, ironing-board. à ∼ voile, sailboard; (*sport*) windsurfing.

plancher /plɑ̃ʃe/ *n.m.* floor.

plancton /plɑ̃ktɔ̃/ *n.m.* plankton.

plan|er /plane/ *v.i.* glide. ∼er sur, (*mystère, danger*) hang over. ∼eur *n.m.* (*avion*) glider.

planète /planɛt/ *n.f.* planet.

planifi|er /planifje/ *v.t.* plan. ∼ication *n.f.* planning.

planqu|e /plɑ̃k/ *n.f.* (*fam.*) hideout; (*emploi*: *fam.*) cushy job. ∼er *v.t.*, se ∼er *v. pr.* hide.

plant /plɑ̃/ *n.m.* seedling; (*de légumes*) bed.

plante /plɑ̃t/ *n.f.* plant. ∼ des pieds, sole (of the foot).

plant|er /plɑ̃te/ *v.t.* (*plante etc.*) plant; (*enfoncer*) drive in; (*installer*) put up; (*mettre*) put. rester ∼é, stand still, remain standing. ∼ation *n.f.* planting; (*de tabac etc.*) plantation.

plantureu|x, ∼se /plɑ̃tyrø, -z/ a. abundant; (*femme*) buxom.

plaque /plak/ *n.f.* plate; (*de marbre*) slab; (*insigne*) badge; (*commémorative*) plaque. ∼ chauffante, hotplate. ∼ minéralogique, number-plate.

plaqu|er /plake/ *v.t.* (*bois*) veneer; (*aplatir*) flatten; (*rugby*) tackle; (*abandonner*: *fam.*) ditch. ∼er qch. sur ou contre, make sth. stick to. ∼age n.m. (*rugby*) tackle.

plasma /plasma/ *n.m.* plasma.

plastic /plastik/ *n.m.* plastic explosive.

plastique /plastik/ a. & *n.m.* plastic. en ∼, plastic.

plastiquer /plastike/ *v.t.* blow up.

plat¹, ∼e /pla, -t/ a. flat. —*n.m.*

(de la main) flat. **à ~** *adv. (poser)*
flat; *a. (batterie, pneu)* flat. **à ~
ventre,** flat on one's face.

plat² /pla/ *n.m. (culin.)* dish;
(partie de repas) course.

platane /platan/ *n.m.* plane-tree.

plateau *(pl. ~x)* /plato/ *n.m.* tray;
(d'électrophone) turntable, deck;
(de balance) pan; *(géog.)* plateau.
~ de fromages, cheeseboard.

plateau-repas *(pl. plateaux-
repas)* *n.m.* tray meal.

plate-bande *(pl. plates-bandes)*
/platbɑ̃d/ *n.f.* flower-bed.

plate-forme *(pl. plates-formes)*
/platform/ *n.f.* platform.

platine¹ /platin/ *n.m.* platinum.

platine² /platin/ *n.f. (de tourne-
disque)* turntable.

platitude /platityd/ *n.f.* platitude.

platonique /platɔnik/ *a.* platonic.

plâtr|e /plɑtr/ *n.m.* plaster; *(méd.)*
(plaster) cast. **~er** *v.t.* plaster;
(membre) put in plaster.

plausible /plozibl/ *a.* plausible.

plébiscite /plebisit/ *n.m.* plebiscite.

plein, ~e /plɛ̃, plɛn/ *a.* full *(de,
of)*; *(total)* complete. —*n.m.* **faire
le ~ (d'essence),** fill up *(the
tank)*. **à ~,** to the full. **à ~ temps,**
full-time. **en ~ air,** in the open
air. **en ~ milieu/visage,** right
in the middle/the face. **en ~e
nuit/etc.,** in the middle of the
night/etc. **~ les mains,** all over
one's hands.

pleinement /plɛnmɑ̃/ *adv.* fully.

pléthore /pletɔr/ *n.f.* over-abun-
dance, plethora.

pleurer /plœre/ *v.i.* cry, weep *(sur,
over)*; *(yeux)* water. —*v.t.* mourn.

pleurésie /plœrezi/ *n.f.* pleurisy.

pleurnicher /plœrniʃe/ *v.i. (fam.)*
snivel.

pleurs (en) /(ɑ̃)plœr/ *adv.* in tears.

pleuvoir† /pløvwar/ *v.i.* rain;
(fig.) rain *ou* shower down. **il
pleut,** it is raining. **il pleut à**

verse *ou* à torrents, it is
pouring.

pli /pli/ *n.m.* fold; *(de jupe)* pleat;
(de pantalon) crease; *(enveloppe)*
cover; *(habitude)* habit. **(faux)
~,** crease.

pliant, ~e /plijɑ̃, -t/ *a.* folding;
(parapluie) telescopic. —*n.m.*
folding stool, camp-stool.

plier /plije/ *v.t.* fold; *(courber)*
bend; *(personne)* submit *(à, to)*.
—*v.i.* bend; *(personne)* submit. **se
~ à,** submit to.

plinthe /plɛ̃t/ *n.f.* skirting-board;
(Amer.) baseboard.

plisser /plise/ *v.t.* crease; *(yeux)*
screw up; *(jupe)* pleat.

plomb /plɔ̃/ *n.m.* lead; *(fusible)*
fuse. **~s,** *(de chasse)* lead shot. **de
ou en ~,** lead. **de ~,** *(ciel)* leaden.

plomb|er /plɔ̃be/ *v.t. (dent)* fill.
~age *n.m.* filling.

plomb|ier /plɔ̃bje/ *n.m.* plumber.
~erie *n.f.* plumbing.

plongeant, ~e /plɔ̃ʒɑ̃, -t/ *a.
(vue)* from above; *(décolleté)*
plunging.

plongeoir /plɔ̃ʒwar/ *n.m.* diving-
board.

plongeon /plɔ̃ʒɔ̃/ *n.m.* dive.

plong|er /plɔ̃ʒe/ *v.i.* dive; *(route)*
plunge. —*v.t.* plunge. **se ~er** *v.
pr.* plunge *(dans, into)*. **~é dans,**
(lecture) immersed in. **~ée** *n.f.*
diving. **en ~ée** *(sous-marin)*
submerged. **~eur, ~euse** *n.m.,
f.* diver; *(employé)* dishwasher.

plouf /pluf/ *n.m. & int.* splash.

ployer /plwaje/ *v.t./i.* bend.

plu /ply/ *voir* **plaire, pleuvoir.**

pluie /plɥi/ *n.f.* rain; *(averse)*
shower. **~ battante/diluvien-
ne,** driving/torrential rain.

plumage /plymaʒ/ *n.m.* plumage.

plume /plym/ *n.f.* feather; *(stylo)*
pen; *(pointe)* nib.

plumeau *(pl. ~x)* /plymo/ *n.m.*
feather duster.

plumer /plyme/ *v.t.* pluck.

plumier /plymje/ *n.m.* pencil box.

plupart /plypar/ *n.f.* most. **la ~ des,** (*gens, cas, etc.*) most. **la ~ du temps,** most of the time. **pour la ~,** for the most part.

pluriel, ~le /plyrjɛl/ *a. & n.m.* plural. **au ~,** (*nom*) plural.

plus¹ /ply/ *adv. de négation.* (**ne**) **~,** (*temps*) no longer, not any more. (**ne**) **~ de,** (*quantité*) no more. **je n'y vais ~,** I do not go there any longer *ou* any more. (**il n'y a**) **~ de pain,** (there is) no more bread.

plus² /ply/ (/plyz/ *before vowel,* /plys/ *in final position*) *adv.* (*que,* than). **~ âgé/tard/etc.,** older/later/*etc.* **~ beau/etc.,** more beautiful/*etc.* **le ~ beau/etc.,** the most. **le ~ beau/etc.,** the most beautiful; (*de deux*) the more beautiful. **le ~ de,** (*gens etc.*) most. **~ de,** (*pain etc.*) more; (*dix jours etc.*) more than. **il est ~ de huit heures/etc.** it is after eight/*etc.* o'clock. **de ~,** more (*que,* than); (*en outre*) moreover. (**âgés) de ~ de** (*huit ans etc.*) over, more than. **de ~ en plus,** more and more. **en ~,** extra. **en ~ de,** in addition to. **~ ou moins,** more or less.

plus³ /plys/ *conj.* plus.

plusieurs /plyzjœr/ *a. & pron.* several.

plus-value /plyvaly/ *n.f.* (*bénéfice*) profit.

plutôt /plyto/ *adv.* rather (*que,* than).

pluvieu|x, ~se /plyvjø, -z/ *a.* rainy.

pneu (*pl.* **~s**) /pnø/ *n.m.* tyre; (*lettre*) express letter. **~matique** *a.* inflatable.

pneumonie /pnømɔni/ *n.f.* pneumonia.

poche /pɔʃ/ *n.f.* pocket; (*sac*) bag. **~s,** (*sous les yeux*) bags.

pocher /pɔʃe/ *v.t.* (*œuf*) poach.

pochette /pɔʃɛt/ *n.f.* pack(et), envelope; (*sac*) bag, pouch; (*d'allumettes*) book; (*de disque*) sleeve; (*mouchoir*) pocket hand-kerchief. **~ surprise,** lucky bag.

podium /pɔdjɔm/ *n.m.* rostrum.

poêle¹ /pwal/ *n.f.* **~ (à frire),** frying-pan.

poêle² /pwal/ *n.m.* stove.

poème /pɔɛm/ *n.m.* poem.

poésie /pɔezi/ *n.f.* poetry; (*poème*) poem.

poète /pɔɛt/ *n.m.* poet.

poétique /pɔetik/ *a.* poetic.

poids /pwa/ *n.m.* weight. **~ coq/lourd/plume,** bantamweight/heavyweight / featherweight. **~ lourd,** (*camion*) lorry, jugger-naut; (*Amer.*) truck.

poignant, ~e /pwaɲɑ̃, -t/ *a.* poignant.

poignard /pwaɲar/ *n.m.* dagger. **~er** /-de/ *v.t.* stab.

poigne /pwaɲ/ *n.f.* grip. **avoir de la ~,** have an iron fist.

poignée /pwaɲe/ *n.f.* handle; (*quantité*) handful. **~ de main,** handshake.

poignet /pwaɲɛ/ *n.m.* wrist; (*de chemise*) cuff.

poil /pwal/ *n.m.* hair; (*pelage*) fur; (*de brosse*) bristle. **~s,** (*de tapis*) pile. **à ~,** (*fam.*) naked. **~u** *a.* hairy.

poinçon /pwɛ̃sɔ̃/ *n.m.* awl; (*marque*) hallmark. **~ner** /-ɔne/ *v.t.* (*billet*) punch. **~neuse** /-ɔnøz/ *n.f.* punch.

poing /pwɛ̃/ *n.m.* fist.

point¹ /pwɛ̃/ *n.m.* point; (*note: scol.*) mark; (*tache*) spot, dot; (*de couture*) stitch. **~ (final),** full stop, period. **à ~,** (*culin.*) medium; (*arriver*) at the right time. **faire le ~,** take stock. **mettre au ~,** (*photo.*) focus; (*technique*) perfect; (*fig.*) clear up. **deux ~s,** colon. **~ culminant,**

peak. **~ de repère,** landmark.
~s de suspension, suspension
points. **~ de suture,** (*méd.*)
stitch. **~ de vente,** retail outlet.
~ de vue, point of view. **~
d'interrogation / d'exclamation,** question/exclamation
mark. **~ du jour,** daybreak. **~
mort,** (*auto.*) neutral. **~ virgule,** semicolon. **sur le ~ de,**
about to.

point² /pwɛ̃/ *adv.* (**ne**) **~,** not.

pointe /pwɛ̃t/ *n.f.* point, tip; (*clou*)
tack; (*de grille*) spike; (*fig.*) touch
(**de,** of). **de ~,** (*industrie*) highly
advanced. **en ~,** pointed. **heure
de ~,** peak hour. **sur la ~ des
pieds,** on tiptoe.

pointer¹ /pwɛ̃te/ *v.t.* (*cocher*) tick
off. —*v.i.* (*employé*) clock in ou
out. **se ~** *v. pr.* (*fam.*) turn up.

pointer² /pwɛ̃te/ *v.t.* (*diriger*)
point, aim.

pointillé /pwɛ̃tije/ *n.m.* dotted
line. —*a.* dotted.

pointilleu|x, **~se** /pwɛ̃tijø, -z/
a. fastidious, particular.

pointu /pwɛ̃ty/ *a.* pointed;
(*aiguisé*) sharp.

pointure /pwɛ̃tyr/ *n.f.* size.

poire /pwar/ *n.f.* pear.

poireau (*pl.* **~x**) /pwaro/ *n.m.*
leek.

poireauter /pwarote/ *v.i.* (*fam.*)
hang about.

poirier /pwarje/ *n.m.* pear-tree.

pois /pwa/ *n.m.* pea; (*dessin*) dot.

poison /pwazɔ̃/ *n.m.* poison.

poisseu|x, **~se** /pwaso, -z/ *a.*
sticky.

poisson /pwasɔ̃/ *n.m.* fish. **~
rouge,** goldfish. **~ d'avril,** April
fool. **les P~s,** Pisces.

poissonn|ier, **~ière** /pwasɔnje,
-jɛr/ *n.m., f.* fishmonger. **~erie**
n.f. fish shop.

poitrail /pwatraj/ *n.m.* breast.

poitrine /pwatrin/ *n.f.* chest;
(*seins*) bosom; (*culin.*) breast.

poivr|e /pwavr/ *n.m.* pepper. **~é·a.**
peppery. **~ière** *n.f.* pepper-pot.

poivron /pwavrɔ̃/ *n.m.* pepper,
capsicum.

poivrot, **~e** /pwavro, -ɔt/ *n.m.,
f.* (*fam.*) drunkard.

poker /pɔkɛr/ *n.m.* poker.

polaire /pɔlɛr/ *a.* polar.

polariser /pɔlarize/ *v.t.* polarize.

polaroïd /pɔlarɔid/ *n.m.* (P.)
Polaroid (P.).

pôle /pol/ *n.m.* pole.

polémique /pɔlemik/ *n.f.* argument. —*a.* controversial.

poli /pɔli/ *a.* (*personne*) polite.
~ment *adv.* politely.

police¹ /pɔlis/ *n.f.* police; (*discipline*) (law and) order. **~ier,**
~ière *a.* (*roman*) detective; *n.m.* policeman.

police² /pɔlis/ *n.f.* (*d'assurance*)
policy.

polio(myélite) /pɔljɔ(mjelit)/ *n.f.*
polio(myelitis).

polir /pɔlir/ *v.t.* polish.

polisson, **~ne** /pɔlisɔ̃, -ɔn/ *a.*
naughty. —*n.m., f.* rascal.

politesse /pɔlitɛs/ *n.f.* politeness;
(*parole*) polite remark.

politicien, **~ne** /pɔlitisjɛ̃, -jɛn/
n.m., f. (*péj.*) politician.

politi|que /pɔlitik/ *a.* political.
—*n.f.* politics; (*ligne de conduite*)
policy. **~ser** *v.t.* politicize.

pollen /pɔlɛn/ *n.m.* pollen.

polluant, **~e** /pɔlɥɑ̃, -t/ *a.*
polluting. —*n.m.* pollutant.

poll|uer /pɔlɥe/ *v.t.* pollute.
~ution *n.f.* pollution.

polo /pɔlo/ *n.m.* polo; (*vêtement*)
sports shirt, tennis shirt.

Pologne /pɔlɔɲ/ *n.f.* Poland.

polonais, **~e** /pɔlɔnɛ, -z/ *a.*
Polish. —*n.m., f.* Pole. —*n.m.*
(*lang.*) Polish.

poltron, **~ne** /pɔltrɔ̃, -ɔn/ *a.*
cowardly. —*n.m., f.* coward.

polycopier /pɔlikɔpje/ *v.t.* duplicate, stencil.

polygamie /pɔligami/ n.f. polygamy.

polyglotte /pɔliglɔt/ n.m./f. polyglot.

polyvalent, ~e /pɔlivalɑ̃, -t/ a. varied; (*personne*) versatile.

pommade /pɔmad/ n.f. ointment.

pomme /pɔm/ n.f. apple; (*d'arrosoir*) rose. **~ d'Adam,** Adam's apple. **~ de pin,** pine cone. **~ de terre,** potato. **~s frites,** chips; (*Amer.*) French fries. **tomber dans les ~s,** (*fam.*) pass out.

pommeau (*pl.* **~x**) /pɔmo/ n.m. (*de canne*) knob.

pommette /pɔmɛt/ n.f. cheekbone.

pommier /pɔmje/ n.m. apple-tree.

pompe /pɔ̃p/ n.f. pump; (*splendeur*) pomp. **~ à incendie,** fireengine. **~s funèbres,** undertaker's.

pomper /pɔ̃pe/ v.t. pump; (*copier; fam.*) copy, crib. **~ l'air à qn.,** (*fam.*) get on s.o.'s nerves.

pompeu|x, ~se /pɔ̃pø, -z/ a. pompous.

pompier /pɔ̃pje/ n.m. fireman.

pompiste /pɔ̃pist/ n.m./f. petrol pump attendant; (*Amer.*) gas station attendant.

pompon /pɔ̃pɔ̃/ n.m. pompon.

pomponner /pɔ̃pɔne/ v.t. deck out.

poncer /pɔ̃se/ v.t. rub down.

ponctuation /pɔ̃ktɥasjɔ̃/ n.f. punctuation.

ponct|uel, ~uelle /pɔ̃ktɥɛl/ a. punctual. **~ualité** n.f. punctuality.

ponctuer /pɔ̃ktɥe/ v.t. punctuate.

pondéré /pɔ̃dere/ a. level-headed.

pondre /pɔ̃dr/ v.t./i. lay.

poney /pɔnɛ/ n.m. pony.

pont /pɔ̃/ n.m. bridge; (*de navire*) deck; (*de graissage*) ramp. **faire le ~,** take the extra day(s) off (*between holidays*). **~ aérien,** airlift. **~-levis** (*pl.* **~s-levis**) n.m. drawbridge.

ponte /pɔ̃t/ n.f. laying (of eggs).

pontife /pɔ̃tif/ n.m. (**souverain) ~,** pope.

pontific|al (*m. pl.* **~aux**) /pɔ̃tifikal, -o/ a. papal.

pop /pɔp/ n.m. & a. invar. (*mus.*) pop.

popote /pɔpɔt/ n.f. (*fam.*) cooking.

populace /pɔpylas/ n.f. (*péj.*) rabble.

popul|aire /pɔpylɛr/ a. popular; (*expression*) colloquial; (*quartier, origine*) working-class. **~arité** n.f. popularity.

population /pɔpylasjɔ̃/ n.f. population.

populeu|x, ~se /pɔpylø, -z/ a. populous.

porc /pɔr/ n.m. pig; (*viande*) pork.

porcelaine /pɔrsəlɛn/ n.f. china, porcelain.

porc-épic (*pl.* **porcs-épics**) /pɔrkepik/ n.m. porcupine.

porche /pɔrʃ/ n.m. porch.

porcherie /pɔrʃəri/ n.f. pigsty.

por|e /pɔr/ n.m. pore. **~eux, ~euse** a. porous.

pornograph|ie /pɔrnɔgrafi/ n.f. pornography. **~ique** a. pornographic.

port[1] /pɔr/ n.m. port, harbour. **à bon ~,** safely. **~ maritime,** seaport.

port[2] /pɔr/ n.m. (*transport*) carriage; (*d'armes*) carrying; (*de barbe*) wearing.

portail /pɔrtaj/ n.m. portal.

portant, ~e /pɔrtɑ̃, -t/ a. **bien/mal ~,** in good/bad health.

portati|f, ~ve /pɔrtatif, -v/ a. portable.

porte /pɔrt/ n.f. door; (*passage*) doorway; (*de jardin, d'embarquement*) gate. **mettre à la ~,** throw out. **~ d'entrée,** front door. **~-fenêtre** (*pl.* **~s-fenêtres**) n.f. French window.

porté /pɔrte/ a. ~ **à**, inclined to. ~ **sur**, fond of.

portée /pɔrte/ n.f. (d'une arme) range; (de voûte) span; (d'animaux) litter; (impact) significance; (mus.) stave. **à** ~, within reach of. **à** ~ **de (la) main**, within (arm's) reach. **hors de** ~ **(de)**, out of reach (of). **à la** ~ **de qn.** at s.o.'s level.

portefeuille /pɔrtəfœj/ n.m. wallet; (de ministre) portfolio.

portemanteau (pl. ~**x**) /pɔrtmɑ̃to/ n.m. coat ou hat stand.

port|er /pɔrte/ v.t. carry; (vêtement, bague) wear; (fruits, responsabilité, nom) bear; (coup) strike; (amener) bring; (inscrire) enter. —v.i. (bruit) carry; (coup) hit home. ~**er sur**, rest on; (concerner) bear on. **se** ~**er bien**, be ou feel well. **se** ~**er candidat**, stand as a candidate. ~**er aux nues**, praise to the skies. ~**-avions** n.m. invar. aircraft-carrier. ~**e-bagages** n.m. invar. luggage rack. ~**e-bonheur** n.m. invar. (objet) charm. ~**e-clefs** n.m. invar. key-ring. ~**e-documents** n.m. invar. attaché case, document wallet. ~**e-monnaie** n.m. invar. purse. ~**e-parole** n.m. invar. spokesman. ~**e-voix** n.m. invar. megaphone.

porteu|r, ~se /pɔrtœr, -øz/ n.m., f. (de nouvelles) bearer; (méd.) carrier. —n.m. (rail.) porter.

portier /pɔrtje/ n.m. door-man.

portière /pɔrtjɛr/ n.f. door.

portillon /pɔrtijɔ̃/ n.m. gate.

portion /pɔrsjɔ̃/ n.f. portion.

portique /pɔrtik/ n.m. portico; (sport) crossbar.

porto /pɔrto/ n.m. port (wine).

portrait /pɔrtre/ n.m. portrait. ~**-robot** (pl. ~**s-robots**) n.m. identikit, photofit.

portuaire /pɔrtɥɛr/ a. port.

portugais, ~e /pɔrtɥgɛ, -z/ a. & n.m., f. Portuguese. —n.m. (lang.) Portuguese.

Portugal /pɔrtɥgal/ n.m. Portugal.

pose /poz/ n.f. installation; (attitude) pose; (photo.) exposure.

posé /poze/ a. calm, serious.

poser /poze/ v.t. put (down); (installer) install, put in; (fondations) lay; (question) ask; (problème) pose. —v.i. (modèle) pose. **se** ~ v. pr. (avion, oiseau) land; (regard) alight; (se présenter) arise. ~ **sa candidature**, apply (à, for).

positi|f, ~ve /pozitif, -v/ a. positive.

position /pozisjɔ̃/ n.f. position; (banque) balance (of account). **prendre** ~, take a stand.

posologie /pozɔlɔʒi/ n.f. directions for use.

poss|éder /pɔsede/ v.t. possess; (propriété) own, possess. ~**esseur** n.m. possessor; owner.

possessi|f, ~ve /pɔsesif, -v/ a. possessive.

possession /pɔsesjɔ̃/ n.f. possession. **prendre** ~ **de**, take possession of

possibilité /pɔsibilite/ n.f. possibility.

possible /pɔsibl/ a. possible. —n.m. **le** ~, what is possible. **dès que** ~, as soon as possible. **faire son** ~, do one's utmost. **le plus tard** /etc., as late /etc. as possible. **pas** ~, impossible; (int.) really!

post- /pɔst/ préf. post-

post|al (m. pl. ~**aux**) /pɔstal, -o/ a. postal.

poste[1] /pɔst/ n.f. (service) post; (bureau) post office. ~ **aérienne**, airmail. **mettre à la** ~, post. ~ **restante**, poste restante.

poste[2] /pɔst/ n.m. (lieu, emploi) post; (de radio, télévision) set; (téléphone) extension (number).

~ **d'essence**, petrol *ou* gas (*Amer.*) station. ~ **d'incendie**, fire point. ~ **de pilotage**, cockpit. ~ **de police**, police station. ~ **de secours**, first-aid post.

poster[1] /poste/ *v.t.* (*lettre, personne*) post.

poster[2] /poster/ *n.m.* poster.

postérieur /posterjœr/ *a.* later; (*partie*) back. ~ **à**, after. —*n.m.* (*fam.*) posterior.

postérité /posterite/ *n.f.* posterity.

posthume /postym/ *a.* posthumous.

postiche /postiʃ/ *a.* false.

post|ier, ~**ière** /postje, -jɛr/ *n.m., f.* postal worker.

post-scriptum /postskriptɔm/ *n.m. invar.* postscript.

postul|er /postyle/ *v.t./i.* apply (à *ou* pour, for); (*principe*) postulate. ~**ant**, ~**ante** *n.m., f.* applicant.

posture /postyr/ *n.f.* posture.

pot /po/ *n.m.* pot; (*en carton*) carton; (*en verre*) jar; (*chance: fam.*) luck; (*boisson: fam.*) drink. ~**-au-feu** /potofø/ *n.m. invar.* (*plat*) stew. ~**-d'échappement**, exhaust-pipe. ~**-de-vin** (*pl.* ~**s-de-vin**) *n.m.* bribe. ~**-pourri**, (*pl.* ~**s-pourris**) *n.m.* pot pourri.

potable /potabl/ *a.* drinkable. **eau** ~, drinking water.

potage /potaʒ/ *n.m.* soup.

potag|er, ~**ère** /potaʒe, -ɛr/ *a.* vegetable. —*n.m.* vegetable garden.

pote /pot/ *n.m.* (*fam.*) chum.

poteau (*pl.* ~**x**) /poto/ *n.m.* post; (*télégraphique*) pole. ~ **indicateur**, signpost.

potelé /potle/ *a.* plump.

potence /potɑ̃s/ *n.f.* gallows.

potentiel, ~**le** /potɑ̃sjɛl/ *a. & n.m.* potential.

pot|erie /potri/ *n.f.* pottery; (*objet*) piece of pottery. ~**ier** *n.m.* potter.

potins /potɛ̃/ *n.m. pl.* gossip.

potion /posjɔ̃/ *n.f.* potion.

potiron /potirɔ̃/ *n.m.* pumpkin.

pou (*pl.* ~**x**) /pu/ *n.m.* louse.

poubelle /pubɛl/ *n.f.* dustbin; (*Amer.*) garbage can.

pouce /pus/ *n.m.* thumb; (*de pied*) big toe; (*mesure*) inch.

poudr|e /pudr/ *n.f.* powder. ~**e** (à canon), gunpowder. **en** ~**e**, (*lait*) powdered; (*chocolat*) drinking. ~**er** *v.t.* powder. ~**eux**, ~**euse** *a.* powdery.

poudrier /pudrije/ *n.m.* (powder) compact.

poudrière /pudrijɛr/ *n.f.* (*région: fig.*) powder-keg.

pouf /puf/ *n.m.* pouffe.

pouffer /pufe/ *v.i.* guffaw.

pouilleu|x, ~**se** /pujø, -z/ *a.* filthy.

poulailler /pulaje/ *n.m.* (hen-)coop.

poulain /pulɛ̃/ *n.m.* foal; (*protégé*) protégé.

poule /pul/ *n.f.* hen; (*culin.*) fowl; (*femme: fam.*) tart; (*rugby*) group.

poulet /pulɛ/ *n.m.* chicken.

pouliche /puliʃ/ *n.f.* filly.

poulie /puli/ *n.f.* pulley.

pouls /pu/ *n.m.* pulse.

poumon /pumɔ̃/ *n.m.* lung.

poupe /pup/ *n.f.* stern.

poupée /pupe/ *n.f.* doll.

poupon /pupɔ̃/ *n.m.* baby. ~**nière** /-ɔnjɛr/ *n.f.* crèche, day nursery.

pour /pur/ *prép.* for; (*envers*) to; (à *la place de*) on behalf of; (*comme*) as. ~ **cela**, for that reason. ~ **cent**, per cent. ~ **de bon**, for good. ~ **faire**, (in order) to do. ~ **que**, so that. ~ **moi**, as for me. **petit**/*etc.* **qu'il soit**, however small/*etc.* he may be. **trop poli**/*etc.* ~, too polite/*etc.* to. **le** ~ **et le contre**, the pros and cons. ~ **ce qui est de**, as for.

pourboire /purbwar/ *n.m.* tip.

pourcentage /pursɑ̃taʒ/ *n.m.* percentage.

pourchasser /purʃase/ *v.t.* pursue.

pourparlers /purparle/ *n.m. pl.* talks.

pourpre /purpr/ *a. & n.m.* crimson; (*violet*) purple.

pourquoi /purkwa/ *conj. & adv.* why. —*n.m. invar.* reason.

pourra, pourrait /pura, purɛ/ *voir* **pouvoir**[1].

pourr|ir /purir/ *v.t./i.* rot. ~**i** *a.* rotten. ~**iture** *n.f.* rot.

poursuite /pursɥit/ *n.f.* pursuit (**de**, of). ~**s**, (*jurid.*) legal action.

poursuiv|re† /pursɥivr/ *v.t.* pursue; (*continuer*) continue; (*en justice*), (*au criminel*) prosecute; (*au civil*) sue. —*v.i.*, se ~**re** *v. pr.* continue. ~**ant**, ~**ante** *n.m., f.* pursuer.

pourtant /purtɑ̃/ *adv.* yet.

pourtour /purtur/ *n.m.* perimeter.

pourv|oir† /purvwar/ *v.t.* ~**oir de**, provide with. —*v.i.* ~**oir à**, provide for. —*v. pr.* se ~**oir** **de** (*argent*) provide o.s. with. ~**oyeur**, ~**oyeuse** *n.m., f.* supplier.

pourvu que /purvykə/ *conj.* (*condition*) provided (that); (*souhait*) let us hope (that). **pourvu qu'il ne soit rien arrivé**, I hope nothing's happened.

pousse /pus/ *n.f.* growth; (*bourgeon*) shoot.

poussé /puse/ *a.* (*études*) advanced.

poussée /puse/ *n.f.* pressure; (*coup*) push; (*de prix*) upsurge; (*méd.*) outbreak.

pousser /puse/ *v.t.* push; (*du coude*) nudge; (*cri*) let out; (*soupir*) heave; (*continuer*) continue; (*exhorter*) urge (**à**, to); (*forcer*) drive (**à**, to); (*amener*) bring (**à**, to). —*v.i.* push;

(*grandir*) grow. **faire** ~ (*cheveux*) let grow; (*plante*) grow. **se** ~ *v. pr.* move over *ou* up.

poussette /pusɛt/ *n.f.* push-chair; (*Amer.*) (baby) stroller.

pouss|ière /pusjɛr/ *n.f.* dust. ~**iéreux**, ~**iéreuse** *a.* dusty.

poussif, ~**ve** /pusif, -v/ *a.* short-winded, wheezing.

poussin /pusɛ̃/ *n.m.* chick.

poutre /putr/ *n.f.* beam; (*en métal*) girder.

pouvoir†[1] /puvwar/ *v. aux.* (*possibilité*) can, be able; (*permission, éventualité*) may, can. **il peut/pouvait/pourrait venir**, he can/could/might come. **je n'ai pas pu**, I could not. **j'ai pu faire**, (*réussi à*) I managed to do. **je n'en peux plus**, I am exhausted. **il se peut que**, it may be that.

pouvoir[2] /puvwar/ *n.m.* power; (*gouvernement*) government. **au** ~, in power. ~**s publics**, authorities.

prairie /preri/ *n.f.* meadow.

praline /pralin/ *n.f.* sugared almond.

praticable /pratikabl/ *a.* practicable.

praticien, ~**ne** /pratisjɛ̃, -jɛn/ *n.m., f.* practitioner.

pratiquant, ~**e** /pratikɑ̃, -t/ *a.* practising. —*n.m., f.* churchgoer.

pratique /pratik/ *a.* practical. —*n.f.* practice; (*expérience*) experience. **la** ~ **du golf/du cheval**, golfing/riding. ~**ment** *adv.* in practice; (*presque*) practically.

pratiquer /pratike/ *v.t./i.* practise; (*sport*) play; (*faire*) make.

pré /pre/ *n.m.* meadow.

pré- /pre/ *préf.* pre-.

préalable /prealabl/ *a.* preliminary, prior. —*n.m.* precondition. **au** ~, first.

préambule /preɑ̃byl/ *n.m.* preamble.

préau (*pl.* ~x) /preo/ *n.m.* (*scol.*) playground shelter.

préavis /preavi/ *n.m.* (advance) notice.

précaire /preker/ *a.* precarious.

précaution /prekosjɔ̃/ *n.f.* (*mesure*) precaution; (*prudence*) caution.

précéd|ent, ~ente /preseda, -t/ *a.* previous. —*n.m.* precedent. **~emment** /-amɑ̃/ *adv.* previously.

précéder /presede/ *v.t./i.* precede.

précepte /presept/ *n.m.* precept.

précep|teur, ~trice /preseptœr, -tris/ *n.m., f.* tutor.

prêcher /preʃe/ *v.t./i.* preach.

précieu|x, ~se /presjø, -z/ *a.* precious.

précipice /presipis/ *n.m.* abyss, chasm.

précipit|é /presipite/ *a.* hasty. **~amment** *adv.* hastily. **~ation** *n.f.* haste.

précipiter /presipite/ *v.t.* throw, precipitate; (*hâter*) hasten. **se** ~ *v. pr.* rush (sur, at, on to); (*se jeter*) throw o.s; (*s'accélérer*) speed up.

précis, ~e /presi, -z/ *a.* precise; (*mécanisme*) accurate. —*n.m.* summary. **dix heures** /*etc.* ~, ten o'clock/*etc.* sharp. **~ément** /-zemɑ̃/ *adv.* precisely.

préciser /presize/ *v.t./i.* specify; (*pensée*) be more specific about. **se** ~ *v. pr.* become clear(er).

précision /presizjɔ̃/ *n.f.* precision; (*détail*) detail.

précoc|e /prekos/ *a.* early; (*enfant*) precocious. **~ité** *n.f.* earliness; precociousness.

préconçu /prekɔ̃sy/ *a.* preconceived.

préconiser /prekɔnize/ *v.t.* advocate.

précurseur /prekyrsœr/ *n.m.* forerunner.

prédécesseur /predesesœr/ *n.m.* predecessor.

prédicateur /predikatœr/ *n.m.* preacher.

prédilection /predileksjɔ̃/ *n.f.* preference.

prédi|re† /predir/ *v.t.* predict. **~ction** *n.f.* prediction.

prédisposer /predispoze/ *v.t.* predispose.

prédomin|ant, ~e /predominɑ̃, -t/ *a.* predominant.

prédominer /predomine/ *v.i.* predominate.

préfabriqué /prefabrike/ *a.* prefabricated.

préface /prefas/ *n.f.* preface.

préfecture /prefektyr/ *n.f.* prefecture. ~ **de police,** police headquarters.

préférence /preferɑ̃s/ *n.f.* preference. **de ~,** preferably. **de ~ à,** in preference to.

préférentiel, ~le /preferɑ̃sjel/ *a.* preferential.

préfér|er /prefere/ *v.t.* prefer (à, to). **je ne préfère pas,** I'd rather not. ~ **er faire,** prefer to do. **~able** *a.* preferable. **~é, ~ée** *a.* & *n.m., f.* favourite.

préfet /prefɛ/ *n.m.* prefect. ~ **de police,** prefect ou chief of police.

préfixe /prefiks/ *n.m.* prefix.

préhistorique /preistorik/ *a.* prehistoric.

préjudic|e /preʒydis/ *n.m.* harm, prejudice. **porter ~e à,** harm. **~iable** *a.* harmful.

préjugé /preʒyʒe/ *n.m.* prejudice. **avoir un ~ contre,** be prejudiced against. **sans ~s,** without prejudices.

préjuger /preʒyʒe/ *v.i.* ~ **de,** prejudge.

prélasser (se) /(sə)prelase/ *v. pr.* loll (about).

prél|ever /prelve/ *v.t.* deduct (sur, from); (*sang*) take. **~èvement** *n.m.* deduction. **~èvement de sang,** blood sample.

préliminaire /preliminer/ *a.* &

n.m. preliminary. **~s**, (*sexuels*) foreplay.

prélude /prelyd/ *n.m.* prelude.

prématuré /prematyre/ *a.* premature. —*n.m.* premature baby.

prémédit|er /premedite/ *v.t.* premeditate. **~ation** *n.f.* premeditation.

prem|ier, ~ière /prəmje, -jɛr/ *a.* first; (*rang*) front, first; (*enfance*) early; (*nécessité, souci*) prime; (*qualité*) top, prime; (*état*) original. —*n.m., f.* first (one). —*n.m.* (*date*) first; (*étage*) first floor. —*n.f.* (*rail.*) first class; (*exploit jamais vu*) first; (*cinéma, théâtre*) première. **de ~ier ordre**, first-rate. **en ~ier**, first. **~ier jet**, first draft. **~ier ministre**, Prime Minister.

premièrement /prəmjɛrmɑ̃/ *adv.* firstly.

prémisse /premis/ *n.f.* premiss.

prémonition /premɔnisjɔ̃/ *n.f.* premonition.

prémunir /premynir/ *v.t.* protect (**contre**, against).

prenant, ~e /prənɑ̃, -t/ *a.* (*activité*) engrossing; (*enfant*) demanding.

prénatal (*m. pl.* **~s**) /prenatal/ *a.* antenatal; (*Amer.*) prenatal.

prendre† /prɑ̃dr/ *v.t.* take; (*attraper*) catch, get; (*acheter*) get; (*repas*) have; (*engager, adopter*) take on; (*poids*) put on; (*chercher*) pick up; (*panique, colère*) take hold of. —*v.i.* (*liquide*) set; (*feu*) catch; (*vaccin*) take. **se ~ pour**, think one is. **s'en ~ à**, attack; (*rendre responsable*) blame. **s'y ~**, set about (it).

preneu|r, ~se /prənœr, -øz/ *n.m., f.* buyer. **être ~r**, be willing to buy. **trouver ~r**, find a buyer.

prénom /prenɔ̃/ *n.m.* first name. **~mer** /-ɔme/ *v.t.* call. **se ~mer** *v. pr.* be called.

préoccup|er /preɔkype/ *v.t.* worry;

(*absorber*) preoccupy. **se ~er de**, be worried about; be preoccupied about. **~ation** *n.f.* worry; (*idée fixe*) preoccupation.

préparatifs /preparatif/ *n.m. pl.* preparations.

préparatoire /preparatwar/ *a.* preparatory.

prépar|er /prepare/ *v.t.* prepare; (*repas, café*) make. **se ~er** *v. pr.* prepare o.s.; (*être proche*) be brewing. **~er à qn.**, (*surprise*) have (got) in store for s.o. **~ation** *n.f.* preparation.

prépondéran|t, ~te /prepɔ̃derɑ̃, -t/ *a.* dominant. **~ce** *n.f.* dominance.

prépos|er /prepoze/ *v.t.* put in charge (**à**, of). **~é, ~ée** *n.m., f.* employee; (*des postes*) postman, postwoman.

préposition /prepozisjɔ̃/ *n.f.* preposition.

préretraite /prerətrɛt/ *n.f.* early retirement.

prérogative /prerɔgativ/ *n.f.* prerogative.

près /prɛ/ *adv.* near, close. **~ de**, near (to); close to; (*presque*) nearly. **à cela ~**, apart from that. **de ~**, closely.

présag|e /prezaʒ/ *n.m.* foreboding, omen. **~er** *v.t.* forebode.

presbyte /prɛsbit/ *a.* long-sighted, far-sighted.

presbytère /prɛsbitɛr/ *n.m.* presbytery.

prescr|ire† /prɛskrir/ *v.t.* prescribe. **~iption** *n.f.* prescription.

préséance /preseɑ̃s/ *n.f.* precedence.

présence /prezɑ̃s/ *n.f.* presence; (*scol.*) attendance.

présent, ~e /prezɑ̃, -t/ *a.* present. —*n.m.* (*temps, cadeau*) present. **à ~**, now.

présent|er /prezɑ̃te/ *v.t.* present; (*personne*) introduce (**à**, to); (*montrer*) show. **se ~er** *v. pr.*

introduce o.s. (**à**, to); (*aller*) go; (*apparaître*) appear; (*candidat*) come forward; (*occasion etc.*) arise. **~er bien**, have a pleasing appearance. se **~er à**, (*examen*) sit for; (*élection*) stand for. se **~er bien**, look good. **~able** *a.* presentable. **~ateur, ~atrice** *n.m., f.* presenter. **~ation** *n.f.* presentation; introduction.

préservatif /prezɛrvatif/ *n.m.* condom.

préserv|er /prezɛrve/ *v.t.* protect. **~ation** *n.f.* protection, preservation.

présiden|t, ~te /prezidã, -t/ *n.m., f.* president; (*de firme, comité*) chairman, chairwoman. **~t directeur général,** managing director. **~ce** *n.f.* presidency; chairmanship.

présidentiel, ~le /prezidãsjɛl/ *a.* presidential.

présider /prezide/ *v.t.* preside over. —*v.i.* preside.

présomption /prezɔ̃psjɔ̃/ *n.f.* presumption.

présomptueu|x, ~se /prezɔ̃ptɥø, -z/ *a.* presumptuous.

presque /prɛsk(ə)/ *adv.* almost, nearly. **~ jamais,** hardly ever. **~ rien,** hardly anything. **~ pas (de),** hardly any.

presqu'île /prɛskil/ *n.f.* peninsula.

pressant, ~e /prɛsã, -t/ *a.* pressing, urgent.

presse /prɛs/ *n.f.* (*journaux, appareil*) press.

pressent|ir /presãtir/ *v.t.* sense. **~iment** *n.m.* presentiment.

press|er /prese/ *v.t.* squeeze, press; (*appuyer sur, harceler*) press; (*hâter*) hasten; (*vouloir*) urge (de, to). —*v.i.* (*temps*) press; (*affaire*) be pressing. se **~er** *v. pr.* (*se hâter*) hurry; (*se grouper*) crowd. **~é** *a.* in a hurry; (*orange, citron*) freshly squeezed. **~e-papiers** *n.m. invar.* paperweight.

pressing /presiŋ/ *n.m.* (*magasin*) dry-cleaner's.

pression /presjɔ̃/ *n.f.* pressure. —*n.m./f.* (*bouton*) press-stud; (*Amer.*) snap.

pressuriser /presyrize/ *v.t.* pressurize.

prestance /prɛstãs/ *n.f.* (*imposing*) presence.

prestation /prɛstasjɔ̃/ *n.f.* allowance; (*d'artiste etc.*) performance.

prestidigita|teur, ~trice /prɛstidiʒitatœr, -tris/ *n.m., f.* conjuror. **~tion** /-asjɔ̃/ *n.f.* conjuring.

prestig|e /prɛstiʒ/ *n.m.* prestige. **~ieux, ~ieuse** *a.* prestigious.

présumer /prezyme/ *v.t.* presume. **~ que,** assume that. **~ de,** overrate.

prêt[1], **~e** /prɛ, -t/ *a.* ready (**à qch.**, for sth., **à faire**, to do). **~-à-porter** /prɛ(t)aporte/ *n.m. invar.* ready-to-wear clothes.

prêt[2] /prɛ/ *n.m.* loan.

prétendant /pretãdã/ *n.m.* (*amoureux*) suitor.

prétend|re /pretãdr/ *v.t.* claim (**que,** that); (*vouloir*) intend. **~re qn. riche/**etc., claim that s.o. is rich/etc. **~u** *a.* so-called. **~ument** *adv.* supposedly, allegedly.

prétent|ieux, ~ieuse /pretãsjø, -z/ *a.* pretentious. **~ion** *n.f.* pretentiousness; (*exigence*) claim.

prêt|er /prete/ *v.t.* lend (**à**, to); (*attribuer*) attribute. —*v.i.* **~er à**, lead to. **~er attention,** pay attention. **~er serment,** take an oath. **~eur, ~euse** /pretœr, -øz/ *n.m., f.* (money-)lender. **~eur sur gages,** pawnbroker.

prétext|e /pretɛkst/ *n.m.* pretext, excuse. **~er** *v.t.* plead.

prêtre /prɛtr/ *n.m.* priest.

prêtrise /pretriz/ *n.f.* priesthood.

preuve /prœv/ *n.f.* proof. **faire ∼**
de, show. **faire ses ∼s,** prove
one's *ou* its worth.

prévaloir /prevalwar/ *v.i.* prevail.

prévenan|t, ∼te /prevnã, -t/ *a.*
thoughtful. **∼ce(s)** *n.f.* (*pl.*)
thoughtfulness.

prévenir† /prevnir/ *v.t.* (*menacer*)
warn; (*informer*) tell; (*éviter,*
anticiper) forestall.

préventi|f, ∼ve /prevãtif, -v/ *a.*
preventive.

prévention /prevãsjõ/ *n.f.* preven-
tion; (*préjugé*) prejudice. **∼**
routière, road safety.

prévenu, ∼e /prevny/ *n.m., f.*
defendant.

prév|oir† /prevwar/ *v.t.* foresee;
(*temps*) forecast; (*organiser*) plan
(for), provide for; (*envisager*)
allow (for). **∼u pour,** (*jouet etc.*)
designed for. **∼isible** *a.* foresee-
able. **∼ision** *n.f.* prediction;
(*météorologique*) forecast.

prévoyan|t, ∼te /prevwajã, -t/
a. showing foresight. **∼ce** *n.f.*
foresight.

prier /prije/ *v.i.* pray. —*v.t.* pray to;
(*implorer*) beg (**de,** to); (*demander*
à) ask (**de,** to). **je vous en prie,**
please; (*il n'y a pas de quoi*) don't
mention it.

prière /prijer/ *n.f.* prayer;
(*demande*) request. **∼ de,** (*vous*
êtes prié de) will you please.

primaire /primer/ *a.* primary.

primauté /primote/ *n.f.* primacy.

prime /prim/ *n.f.* free gift;
(*d'employé*) bonus; (*subvention*)
subsidy; (*d'assurance*) premium.

primé /prime/ *a.* prize-winning.

primer /prime/ *v.t./i.* excel.

primeurs /primœr/ *n.f. pl.* early
fruit and vegetables.

primevère /primver/ *n.f.* primrose.

primiti|f, ∼ve /primitif, -v/ *a.*

primitive; (*originel*) original.
—*n.m., f.* primitive.

primordial (*m. pl.* **∼iaux**)
/primordjal, -jo/ *a.* essential.

princ|e /prɛ̃s/ *n.m.* prince. **∼esse**
n.f. princess. **∼ier, ∼ière** *a.*
princely.

principal (*m. pl.* **∼aux**)
/prɛ̃sipal, -o/ *a.* main, principal. —*n.m.* (*pl.* **∼aux**) headmaster; (*chose*) main thing.
∼alement *adv.* mainly.

principauté /prɛ̃sipote/ *n.f.* prin-
cipality.

principe /prɛ̃sip/ *n.m.* principle. **en ∼,** theoretically; (*d'habitude*)
as a rule.

printan|ier, ∼ière /prɛ̃tanje, -jer/ *a.*
spring(-like).

printemps /prɛ̃tɑ̃/ *n.m.* spring.

priorit|é /prijorite/ *n.f.* priority;
(*auto.*) right of way. **∼aire** *a.*
priority. **être ∼aire,** have
priority.

pris, ∼e¹ /pri, -z/ *voir* **prendre.**
—*a.* (*place*) taken; (*personne,*
journée) busy; (*gorge*) infected. **∼**
de, (*peur, fièvre, etc.*) stricken
with. **∼ de panique,** panic-
stricken.

prise² /priz/ *n.f.* hold, grip;
(*animal etc. attrapé*) catch; (*mil.*)
capture. **∼ (de courant),** (*mâle*)
plug; (*femelle*) socket. **aux ∼s**
avec, at grips with. **∼ de**
conscience, awareness. **∼ de**
contact, first contact, initial
meeting. **∼ de position,** stand.
∼ de sang, blood test.

priser /prize/ *v.t.* (*estimer*) prize.

prisme /prism/ *n.m.* prism.

prison /prizõ/ *n.f.* prison, gaol,
jail; (*réclusion*) imprisonment.
∼nier, ∼nière /-onje, -jer/ *n.m.,*
f. prisoner.

privé /prive/ *a.* private. —*n.m.*
(*comm.*) private sector. **en ∼,**
dans le ∼, in private.

priv|er /prive/ *v.t.* **∼er de,**

deprive of. **se ∼er de,** go without. **∼ation** n.f. deprivation; (sacrifice) hardship.

privil|ège /privilɛʒ/ n.m. privilege. **∼égié, ∼égiée** a. & n.m., f. privileged (person).

prix /pri/ n.m. price; (récompense) prize. **à tout ∼,** at all costs. **au ∼ de,** (fig.) at the expense of. **∼ coûtant, ∼ de revient,** cost price. **à ∼ fixe,** set price.

pro- /pro/ préf. pro-.

probab|le /prɔbabl/ a. probable, likely. **∼ilité** n.f. probability. **∼lement** adv. probably.

probant, ∼e /prɔbɑ̃, -t/ a. convincing, conclusive.

probité /prɔbite/ n.f. integrity.

problème /prɔblɛm/ n.m. problem.

procéd|er /prɔsede/ v.i. proceed. **∼er à,** carry out. **∼é** n.m. process; (conduite) behaviour.

procédure /prɔsedyr/ n.f. procedure.

procès /prɔsɛ/ n.m. (criminel) trial; (civil) lawsuit, proceedings. **∼verbal** (pl. **∼-verbaux**) n.m. report; (contravention) ticket.

procession /prɔsesjɔ̃/ n.f. procession.

processus /prɔsesys/ n.m. process.

prochain, ∼e /prɔʃɛ̃, -ɛn/ a. (suivant) next; (proche) imminent; (avenir) near. **je descends à la ∼e,** I'm getting off at the next stop. —n.m. fellow. **∼ement** /-ɛnmɑ̃/ adv. soon.

proche /prɔʃ/ a. near, close; (avoisinant) neighbouring; (parent, ami) close. **∼ de,** close ou near to. **de ∼ en proche,** gradually. **dans un ∼ avenir,** in the near future. **être ∼,** (imminent) be approaching. **∼s** n.m. pl. close relations. **P-Orient** n.m. Near East.

proclam|er /prɔklame/ v.t. declare, proclaim. **∼ation** n.f. declaration, proclamation.

procréation /prɔkreasjɔ̃/ n.f. procreation.

procuration /prɔkyrasjɔ̃/ n.f. proxy.

procurer /prɔkyre/ v.t. bring (à, to). **se ∼,** obtain.

procureur /prɔkyrœr/ n.m. public prosecutor.

prodig|e /prɔdiʒ/ n.m. marvel; (personne) prodigy. **enfant/musicien ∼e,** child/musical prodigy. **∼ieux, ∼ieuse** a. tremendous, prodigious.

prodigu|e /prɔdig/ a. wasteful. **fils ∼e,** prodigal son. **∼er** v.t. **∼er à,** lavish on.

producti|f, ∼ve /prɔdyktif, -v/ a. productive. **∼vité** n.f. productivity.

prod|uire† /prɔdɥir/ v.t. produce. **se ∼uire** v. pr. (survenir) happen; (acteur) perform. **∼ucteur, ∼uctrice** a. producing; n.m., f. producer. **∼uction** n.f. production; (produit) product.

produit /prɔdɥi/ n.m. product. **∼s,** (de la terre) produce. **∼s chimique,** chemical. **∼s alimentaires,** foodstuffs. **∼ de consommation,** consumer goods. **∼ national brut,** gross national product.

proéminent, ∼e /prɔeminɑ̃, -t/ a. prominent.

prof /prɔf/ n.m. (fam.) teacher.

profane /prɔfan/ a. secular. —n.m./f. lay person.

profaner /prɔfane/ v.t. desecrate.

proférer /prɔfere/ v.t. utter.

professer¹ /prɔfese/ v.t. (déclarer) profess.

professer² /prɔfese/ v.t./i. (enseigner) teach.

professeur /prɔfesœr/ n.m. teacher; (univ.) lecturer; (avec chaire) professor.

profession /prɔfesjɔ̃/ n.f. occupation; (intellectuelle) profession.

~**nel**, ~**nelle** /-jɔnɛl/ *a*. professional; (*école*) vocational; *n.m.*, *f.* professional.

professorat /prɔfɛsɔra/ *n.m.* teaching.

profil /prɔfil/ *n.m.* profile.

profiler (se) /(sə)prɔfile/ *v. pr.* be outlined.

profit /prɔfi/ *n.m.* profit. **au ~ de**, in aid of. **~able** /-tabl/ *a.* profitable.

profiter /prɔfite/ *v.i.* ~ **à**, benefit. ~ **de**, take advantage of.

profond, ~**e** /prɔfɔ̃, -d/ *a.* deep; (*sentiment, intérêt*) profound; (*causes*) underlying. **au plus ~ de**, in the depths of. ~**ément** /-demã/ *adv.* deeply; (*différent, triste*) profoundly; (*dormir*) soundly. ~**eur** /-dœr/ *n.f.* depth.

profusion /prɔfyzjɔ̃/ *n.f.* profusion.

progéniture /prɔʒenityr/ *n.f.* offspring.

programmation /prɔgramasjɔ̃/ *n.f.* programming.

programm|e /prɔgram/ *n.m.* programme; (*matières: scol.*) syllabus; (*informatique*) program. ~**e(d'études)**, curriculum. ~**er** *v.t.* (*ordinateur, appareil*) program; (*émission*) schedule. ~**eur**, ~**euse** *n.m.*, *f.* computer programmer.

progrès /prɔgrɛ/ *n.m. & n.m. pl.* progress. **faire des ~**, make progress.

progress|er /prɔgrese/ *v.i.* progress. ~**ion** /-ɛsjɔ̃/ *n.f.* progression.

progressi|f, ~**ve** /prɔgresif, -v/ *a.* progressive. ~**vement** *adv.* progressively.

progressiste /prɔgresist/ *a.* progressive.

prohib|er /prɔibe/ *v.t.* prohibit. ~**ition** *n.f.* prohibition.

prohibiti|f, ~**ve** /prɔibitif, -v/ *a.* prohibitive.

proie /prwa/ *n.f.* prey. **en ~ à**, tormented by.

projecteur /prɔʒɛktœr/ *n.m.* floodlight; (*mil.*) searchlight; (*cinéma*) projector.

projectile /prɔʒɛktil/ *n.m.* missile.

projection /prɔʒɛksjɔ̃/ *n.f.* projection; (*séance*) show.

projet /prɔʒɛ/ *n.m.* plan; (*ébauche*) draft. ~ **de loi**, bill.

projeter /prɔʒte/ *v.t.* plan (**de**, to); (*film*) project, show; (*jeter*) hurl, project.

prolét|aire /prɔleter/ *n.m./f.* proletarian. ~**ariat** /-arja/ *n.m.* proletariat. ~**arien**, ~**arienne** *a.* proletarian.

prolifér|er /prɔlifere/ *v.i.* proliferate. ~**ation** /-rasjɔ̃/ *n.f.* proliferation.

prolifique /prɔlifik/ *a.* prolific.

prologue /prɔlɔg/ *n.m.* prologue.

prolongation /prɔlɔ̃gasjɔ̃/ *n.f.* extension. ~**s**, (*football*) extra time.

prolong|er /prɔlɔ̃ʒe/ *v.t.* prolong. **se ~er** *v. pr.* continue, extend. ~**é** *a.* prolonged. ~**ement** *n.m.* extension.

promenade /prɔmnad/ *n.f.* walk; (*à bicyclette, à cheval*) ride; (*en auto*) drive, ride. **faire une ~**, go for a walk.

promen|er /prɔmne/ *v.t.* take for a walk. ~**er sur qch.**, (*main, regard*) run over sth. **se ~er** *v. pr.* walk. (**aller**) **se ~er**, go for a walk. ~**eur**, ~**euse** *n.m.*, *f.* walker.

promesse /prɔmɛs/ *n.f.* promise.

promett|re|† /prɔmɛtr/ *v.t./i.* promise. ~ **re (beaucoup)**, be promising. **se ~re de**, resolve to. ~**eur**, ~**euse** *a.* promising.

promontoire /prɔmɔ̃twar/ *n.m.* headland.

promoteur /prɔmɔtœr/ *n.m.* (*immobilier*) property developer.

prom|ouvoir /prɔmuvwar/ *v.t.* promote. **être ~u**, be promoted.

~**otion** *n.f.* promotion; (*univ.*) year; (*comm.*) special offer.

prompt, ~**e** /prɔ̃, -t/ *a.* swift.

prôner /prone/ *v.t.* extol; (*préconiser*) preach, advocate.

pronom /prɔnɔ̃/ *n.m.* pronoun. ~**inal** (*m. pl.* ~**inaux**) /-ɔminal, -o/ *a.* pronominal.

prononc|er /prɔnɔ̃se/ *v.t.* pronounce; (*discours*) make. **se** ~**er** *v. pr.* (*mot*) be pronounced; (*personne*) make a decision (**pour**, in favour of). ~**é** *a.* pronounced. ~**iation** /-jasjɔ̃/ *n.f.* pronunciation.

pronosti|c /prɔnɔstik/ *n.m.* forecast; (*méd.*) prognosis. ~**quer** *v.t.* forecast.

propagande /prɔpagɑ̃d/ *n.f.* propaganda.

propag|er /prɔpaʒe/ *v.t.*, **se** ~**er** *v. pr.* spread. ~**ation** /-gasjɔ̃/ *n.f.* spread(ing).

proph|ète /prɔfɛt/ *n.m.* prophet. ~**étie** /-esi/ *n.f.* prophecy. ~**étique** *a.* prophetic. ~**étiser** *v.t./i.* prophesy.

propice /prɔpis/ *a.* favourable.

proportion /prɔpɔrsjɔ̃/ *n.f.* proportion; (*en mathématiques*) ratio. **toutes** ~**s gardées**, making appropriate allowances. ~**né** /-jone/ *a.* proportionate (**à**, to). ~**nel**, ~**nelle** /-jonɛl/ *a.* proportional. ~**ner** /-jone/ *v.t.* proportion.

propos /prɔpo/ *n.m.* intention; (*sujet*) subject. —*n.m. pl.* (*paroles*) remarks. **à** ~, at the right time; (*dans un dialogue*) by the way. **à** ~ **de**, about. **à tout** ~, at every possible occasion.

propos|er /prɔpoze/ *v.t.* propose; (*offrir*) offer. **se** ~**er** *v. pr.* volunteer (**pour**, to); (*but*) set o.s. **se** ~**er de faire**, propose to do. ~**ition** *n.f.* proposal; (*affirmation*) proposition; (*gram.*) clause.

propre[1] /prɔpr/ *a.* clean; (*soigné*) neat; (*honnête*) decent. **mettre au** ~, write out again neatly. **c'est du** ~**!** (*ironique*) well done! ~**ment**[1] /-əmɑ̃/ *adv.* cleanly; neatly; decently.

propre[2] /prɔpr/ *a.* (*à soi*) own; (*sens*) literal. ~**à**, (*qui convient*) suited to; (*spécifique*) peculiar to. ~**à-rien** *n.m./f.* good-for-nothing. ~**ment**[2] /-əmɑ̃/ *adv.* strictly. **le bureau**/*etc.* ~**ment dit**, the office/*etc.* itself.

propreté /prɔprəte/ *n.f.* cleanliness; (*netteté*) neatness.

propriétaire /prɔprijetɛr/ *n.m./f.* owner; (*comm.*) proprietor; (*qui loue*) landlord, landlady.

propriété /prɔprijete/ *n.f.* property; (*droit*) ownership.

propuls|er /prɔpylse/ *v.t.* propel. ~**ion** *n.f.* propulsion.

prorata /prɔrata/ *n.m. invar.* **au** ~ **de**, in proportion to.

proroger /prɔrɔʒe/ *v.t.* (*contrat*) defer; (*passeport*) extend.

prosaïque /prɔzaik/ *a.* prosaic.

proscr|ire /prɔskrir/ *v.t.* proscribe. ~**it**, ~**ite** *a.* proscribed; *n.m., f.* (*exilé*) exile.

prose /proz/ *n.f.* prose.

prospec|ter /prɔspɛkte/ *v.t.* prospect. ~**teur**, ~**trice** *n.m., f.* prospector. ~**tion** /-ksjɔ̃/ *n.f.* prospecting.

prospectus /prɔspɛktys/ *n.m.* leaflet.

prosp|ère /prɔspɛr/ *a.* flourishing, thriving, prosperous. ~**érer** *v.i.* thrive, prosper. ~**érité** *n.f.* prosperity.

prostern|er (se) /(sə)prɔstɛrne/ *v. pr.* bow down. ~**é** *a.* prostrate.

prostitu|ée /prɔstitɥe/ *n.f.* prostitute. ~**ution** *n.f.* prostitution.

prostré /prɔstre/ *a.* prostrate.

protagoniste /prɔtagɔnist/ *n.m.* protagonist.

protec|teur, ~**trice** /prɔtɛktœr,

-tris/ *n.m.,* *f.* protector. —*a.* protective.

protection /prɔtɛksjɔ̃/ *n.f.* protection; (*fig.*) patronage.

protég|er /prɔteʒe/ *v.t.* protect; (*fig.*) patronize. **se ~er** *v. pr.* protect o.s. **~é** *n.m.* protégé. **~ée** *n.f.* protégée.

protéine /prɔtein/ *n.f.* protein.

protestant, **~e** /prɔtɛstɑ̃, -t/ *a.* & *n.m.,* *f.* Protestant.

protest|er /prɔtɛste/ *v.t./i.* protest. **~ation** *n.f.* protest.

protocole /prɔtɔkɔl/ *n.m.* protocol.

prototype /prɔtɔtip/ *n.m.* prototype.

protubéran|t, **~te** /prɔtyberɑ̃, -t/ *a.* bulging. **~ce,** *n.f.* protuberance.

proue /pru/ *n.f.* bow, prow.

prouesse /prues/ *n.f.* feat, exploit.

prouver /pruve/ *v.t.* prove.

provenance /prɔvnɑ̃s/ *n.f.* origin. **en ~ de,** from.

provenç|al, **~ale** /prɔvɑ̃sal, -o/ *a.* & *n.m.,* *f.* (*m. pl.* **~aux**) Provençal.

Provence /prɔvɑ̃s/ *n.f.* Provence.

provenir† /prɔvnir/ *v.i.* **~ de,** come from.

proverb|e /prɔvɛrb/ *n.m.* proverb. **~ial** (*m. pl.* **~iaux**) *a.* proverbial.

providence /prɔvidɑ̃s/ *n.f.* providence.

provinc|e /prɔvɛ̃s/ *n.f.* province. **de ~e,** provincial. **la ~e,** the provinces. **~ial,** **~iale** (*m. pl.* **~iaux**) *a.* & *n.m.,* *f.* provincial.

proviseur /prɔvizœr/ *n.m.* headmaster, principal.

provision /prɔvizjɔ̃/ *n.f.* supply, store; (*dans un compte*) funds; (*acompte*) deposit. **~s,** (*vivres*) provisions. **panier à ~s,** shopping basket.

provisoire /prɔvizwar/ *a.* temporary. **~ment** *adv.* temporarily.

provo|quer /prɔvɔke/ *v.t.* cause; (*exciter*) arouse; (*défier*) provoke. **~cant,** **~cante** *a.* provocative. **~cation** *n.f.* provocation.

proximité /prɔksimite/ *n.f.* proximity. **à ~ de,** close to.

prude /pryd/ *a.* prudish. —*n.f.* prude.

prud|ent, **~ente** /prydɑ̃, -t/ *a.* cautious; (*sage*) wise. **soyez ~ent,** be careful. **~emment** /-amɑ̃/ *adv.* cautiously; wisely. **~ence** *n.f.* caution; wisdom.

prune /pryn/ *n.f.* plum.

pruneau (*pl.* **~x**) /pryno/ *n.m.* prune.

prunelle¹ /prynɛl/ *n.f.* (*pupille*) pupil.

prunelle² /prynɛl/ *n.f.* (*fruit*) sloe.

psaume /psom/ *n.m.* psalm.

pseudo- /psødo/ *préf.* pseudo-.

pseudonyme /psødɔnim/ *n.m.* pseudonym.

psychanalys|e /psikanaliz/ *n.f.* psychoanalysis. **~er** *v.t.* psychoanalyse. **~te** /-st/ *n.m./f.* psychoanalyst.

psychiatr|e /psikjatr/ *n.m./f.* psychiatrist. **~ie** *n.f.* psychiatry. **~ique** *a.* psychiatric.

psychique /psiʃik/ *a.* mental, psychological.

psycholo|gie /psikɔlɔʒi/ *n.f.* psychology. **~gique** *a.* psychological. **~gue** *n.m./f.* psychologist.

psychosomatique /psikɔsɔmatik/ *a.* psychosomatic.

psychothérapie /psikɔterapi/ *n.f.* psychotherapy.

PTT *abrév.* (*Postes, Télécommunications et Télédiffusion*) Post Office.

pu /py/ *voir* **pouvoir¹**.

puant, **~e** /pɥɑ̃, -t/ *a.* stinking. **~eur** /-tœr/ *n.f.* stink.

pub /pyb/ *n.f.* **la ~,** advertising. **une ~,** an advert.

puberté /pybɛrte/ *n.f.* puberty.

publi|c, **~que** /pyblik/ *a.* public.

—n.m. public; (assistance) audience. en ~c, in public.

publicit|é /pyblisite/ n.f. publicity, advertising; (annonce) advertisement. ~aire n.f. publicity.

publ|ier /pyblije/ v.t. publish. ~ication n.f. publication.

publiquement /pyblikmã/ adv. publicly.

puce¹ /pys/ n.f. flea. **marché aux ~s**, flea market.

puce² /pys/ n.f. (électronique) chip.

pud|eur /pydœr/ n.f. modesty. ~ique a. modest.

pudibond /pydibɔ̃, -d/ a. prudish.

puer /pɥe/ v.i. stink. —v.t. stink of.

puéricultrice /pɥerikyltris/ n.f. children's nurse.

puéril /pɥeril/ a. puerile.

pugilat /pyʒila/ n.m. fight.

puis /pɥi/ adv. then.

puiser /pɥize/ v.t. draw (**qch. dans**, sth. from). —v.i. ~ **dans qch.**, dip into sth.

puisque /pɥisk(ə)/ conj. since, as.

puissance /pɥisɑ̃s/ n.f. power. **en ~**, potential; adv. potentially.

puiss|ant, ~ante /pɥisɑ̃, -t/ a. powerful. ~**amment** adv. powerfully.

puits /pɥi/ n.m. well; (de mine) shaft.

pull(-over) /pyl(ɔvɛr)/ n.m. pullover, jumper.

pulpe /pylp/ n.f. pulp.

pulsation /pylsasjɔ̃/ n.f. (heart)beat.

pulvéris|er /pylverize/ v.t. pulverize; (liquide) spray. ~**ateur** n.m. spray.

punaise /pynɛz/ n.f. (insecte) bug; (clou) drawing-pin; (Amer.) thumbtack.

punch¹ /pɔ̃ʃ/ n.m. punch.

punch² /pœnʃ/ n.m. **avoir du ~**, have drive.

pun|ir /pynir/ v.t. punish. ~**ition** n.f. punishment.

punk /pœnk/ a. invar. punk.

pupille¹ /pypij/ n.f. (de l'œil) pupil.

pupille² /pypij/ n.m./f. (enfant) ward.

pupitre /pypitr/ n.m. (scol.) desk. **~ à musique**, music stand.

pur /pyr/ a. pure; (whisky) neat. ~**ement** adv. purely. ~**eté** n.f. purity. ~**-sang** n.m. invar. (cheval) thoroughbred.

purée /pyre/ n.f. purée; (de pommes de terre) mashed potatoes.

purgatoire /pyrgatwar/ n.m. purgatory.

purg|e /pyrʒ/ n.f. purge. ~**er** v.t. (pol., méd.) purge; (peine: jurid.) serve.

purif|ier /pyrifje/ v.t. purify. ~**ication** n.f. purification.

purin /pyrɛ̃/ n.m. (liquid) manure.

puritain, ~e /pyritɛ̃, -ɛn/ n.m., f. puritan. —a. puritanical.

pus /py/ n.m. pus.

pustule /pystyl/ n.f. pimple.

putain /pytɛ̃/ n.f. (fam.) whore.

putréfier (se) /(sə)pytrefje/ v. pr. putrefy.

putsch /putʃ/ n.m. putsch.

puzzle /pœzl/ n.m. jigsaw (puzzle).

P-V abrév. (procès-verbal) ticket, traffic fine.

pygmée /pigme/ n.m. pygmy.

pyjama /piʒama/ n.m. pyjamas. **un ~**, a pair of pyjamas.

pylône /pilon/ n.m. pylon.

pyramide /piramid/ n.f. pyramid.

Pyrénées /pirene/ n.f. pl. **les ~**, the Pyrenees.

pyromane /pirɔman/ n.m./f. arsonist.

Q

QG abrév. (quartier général) HQ.

QI abrév. (quotient intellectuel) IQ.

qu' /k/ voir que.

quadrill|er /kadrije/ v.t. (zone) comb, control. ~**age** n.m. (mil.) control. ~**é** a. (papier) squared.

quadrupède . /kadrypɛd/ n.m. quadruped.

quadrupl|e /kadrypl/ a. & n.m. quadruple. ~**er** v.t./i. quadruple. ~**és**, ~**ées** n.m., f. pl. quadruplets.

quai /ke/ n.m. (de gare) platform; (de port) quay; (de rivière) embankment.

qualificatif /kalifikatif/ n.m. (épithète) term.

qualif|ier /kalifje/ v.t. qualify; (décrire) describe (de, as). se ~**ier** v. tr. qualify (pour, for). ~**ication** n.f. qualification; description. ~**ié** a. qualified; (main d'œuvre) skilled.

qualit|é /kalite/ n.f. quality; occupation. en ~**é de**, in one's capacity as. ~**atif**, ~**ative** a. qualitative.

quand /kɑ̃/ conj. & adv. when. ~ **même**, all the same. ~ (bien) **même**, even if.

quant (à) /kɑ̃t(a)/ prép. as for.

quant-à-soi /kɑ̃taswa/ n.m. rester sur son ~, stand aloof.

quantit|é /kɑ̃tite/ n.f. quantity. une ~ **de**, a lot of. des ~**és**, masses. ~**atif**, ~**ative** a. quantitative.

quarantaine /karɑ̃tɛn/ n.f. (méd.) quarantine. une ~ (de), about forty.

quarant|e /karɑ̃t/ a. & n.m. forty. ~**ième** a. & n.m./f. fortieth.

quart /kar/ n.m. quarter (naut.) watch. ~ (de litre), quarter litre. ~ **de finale**, quarter-final. ~ **d'heure**, quarter of an hour.

quartier /kartje/ n.m. neighbourhood, district; (de lune, bœuf) quarter; (de fruit) segment. ~**s**, (mil.) quarters. **de** ~, **du** ~, local. ~ **général**, headquarters. **avoir** ~ **libre**, be free.

quartz /kwarts/ n.m. quartz.

quasi- /kazi/ préf. quasi-.

quasiment /kazimɑ̃/ adv. almost.

quatorz|e /katɔrz/ a. & n.m. fourteen. ~**ième** a. & n.m./f. fourteenth.

quatre /katr(ə)/ a. & n.m. four. ~-**vingt(s)** a. & n.m. eighty. ~-**vingt-dix** a. & n.m. ninety.

quatrième /katrijɛm/ a. & n.m./f. fourth. ~**ment** adv. fourthly.

quatuor /kwatɥɔr/ n.m. quartet.

que, qu' /k(ə), k/ conj. that; (comparaison) than. **qu'il vienne**, let him come. **qu'il vienne ou non**, whether he comes or not. **ne faire** ~ **demander**/etc., only ask/etc. —adv. (ce) ~ **tu es bête**, **qu'est-ce** ~ **tu es bête**, how silly you are. ~ **de**, what a lot of. —pron. rel. (personne) that; whom; (chose) that, which; (temps, moment) when; (interrogatif) what. **un jour**/etc. ~, one day/etc. when. ~ **faites-vous?**, **qu'est-ce** ~ **vous faites?**, what are you doing?

Québec /kebɛk/ n.m. Quebec.

quel, ~**le** /kɛl/ a. what; (interrogatif) which, what; (qui) who. —pron. which. ~ **dommage**, what a pity. ~ **qu'il soit**, (chose) whatever ou whichever it may be; (personne) whoever he may be.

quelconque /kɛlkɔ̃k/ a. any, some; (banal) ordinary; (médiocre) poor.

quelque /kɛlkə/ a. some. ~**s**, a few, some. ~ (environ) some. **et** ~, (fam.) and a bit. ~ **chose**, something; (partie) anything. ~ **part**, somewhere. ~ **peu**, somewhat.

quelquefois /kɛlkəfwa/ adv. sometimes.

quelques|-uns, ~**-unes** /kɛlkəzœ̃, -yn/ pron. some, a few.

quelqu'un /kɛlkœ̃/ *pron.* someone, somebody; (*interrogation*) anyone, anybody.

quémander /kemɑ̃de/ *v.t.* beg for.

qu'en-dira-t-on /kɑ̃diratɔ̃/ *invar.* le ~, gossip.

querell|e /kɔrɛl/ *n.f.* quarrel. **~eur, ~euse** *a.* quarrelsome.

quereller (se) /(sə)kɑrele/ *v. pr.* quarrel.

question /kɛstjɔ̃/ *n.f.* question; (*affaire*) matter, question. **en ~**, in question; (*en jeu*) at stake. **il est ~ de**, (*cela concerne*) it is about; (*on parle de*) there is talk of. **il n'en est pas ~**, it is out of the question. **~ner** /-jɔne/ *v.t.* question.

questionnaire /kɛstjɔnɛr/ *n.m.* questionnaire.

quêt|e /kɛt/ *n.f.* (*relig.*) collection. **en ~e de**, in search of. **~er** /kete/ *v.i.* collect money; *v.t.* seek.

quetsche /kwɛtʃ/ *n.f.* (sort of dark red) plum.

queue /kø/ *n.f.* tail; (*de poêle*) handle; (*de fruit*) stalk; (*de fleur*) stem; (*file*) queue; (*file: Amer.*) line; (*de train*) rear. **faire la ~**, queue (up); (*Amer.*) line up. **~ de cheval**, pony-tail.

qui /ki/ *pron. rel.* (*personne*) who; (*chose*) which, that; (*interrogatif*) who; (*après prép.*) whom; (*quiconque*) whoever. **à ~ est ce stylo/etc.?**, whose pen/etc. is this? **qu'est-ce ~?**, what? **~ est-ce qui?**, who? **~ que ce soit**, anyone.

quiche /kiʃ/ *n.f.* quiche.

quiconque /kikɔ̃k/ *pron.* whoever; (*n'importe qui*) anyone.

quiétude /kjetyd/ *n.f.* quiet.

quignon /kiɲɔ̃/ *n.m.* ~ de pain, chunk of bread.

quille¹ /kij/ *n.f.* (*de bateau*) keel.

quille² /kij/ *n.f.* (*jouet*) skittle.

quincaill|ier, ~ière /kɛ̃kaje, -jɛr/ *n.m., f.* hardware dealer. **~erie** *n.f.* hardware; (*magasin*) hardware shop.

quinine /kinin/ *n.f.* quinine.

quinquenn|al (*m. pl.* ~**aux**) /kɛ̃kenal, -o/ *a.* five-year.

quint|al (*pl.* ~**aux**) /kɛ̃tal, -o/ *n.m.* quintal (= *100 kg.*).

quinte /kɛ̃t/ *n.f.* ~ de toux, coughing fit.

quintette /kɛ̃tɛt/ *n.m.* quintet.

quintupl|e /kɛ̃typl/ *a.* fivefold. —*n.m.* quintuple. **~er** *v.t./i.* increase fivefold. **~és, ~ées**, *n.m., f. pl.* quintuplets.

quinzaine /kɛ̃zɛn/ *n.f.* une ~ (de), about fifteen.

quinz|e /kɛ̃z/ *a. & n.m.* fifteen. **~e jours**, two weeks. **~ième** *a. & n.m./f.* fifteenth.

quiproquo /kiprɔko/ *n.m.* misunderstanding.

quittance /kitɑ̃s/ *n.f.* receipt.

quitte /kit/ *a.* quits (**envers**, with). **~ à faire**, even if it means doing.

quitter /kite/ *v.t.* leave; (*vêtement*) take off. se ~ *v. pr.* part.

quoi /kwa/ *pron.* what; (*après prép.*) which. **de ~ vivre/manger/etc.**, (*assez*) enough to live on/for eat/etc. **de ~ écrire**, sth. to write with, what is necessary to write with. **~ que**, whatever. **~ que ce soit**, anything.

quoique /kwak(ə)/ *conj.* (al)though.

quolibet /kɔlibɛ/ *n.m.* gibe.

quorum /kɔrɔm/ *n.m.* quorum.

quota /kɔta/ *n.m.* quota.

quote-part (*pl.* **quotes-parts**) /kɔtpar/ *n.f.* share.

quotidien, ~ne /kɔtidjɛ̃, -jɛn/ *a.* daily; (*banal*) everyday. —*n.m.* daily (paper). **~nement** /-jɛnmɑ̃/ *adv.* daily.

quotient /kɔsjɑ̃/ *n.m.* quotient.

R

rab /rab/ *n.m.* (*fam.*) extra. **il y en a en ~**, there's some over.

rabâcher /rabaʃe/ *v.t.* keep repeating.

rabais /rabɛ/ *n.m.* (price) reduction.

rabaisser /rabese/ *v.t.* (*déprécier*) belittle; (*réduire*) reduce.

rabat /raba/ *n.m.* flap. **~-joie** *n.m. invar.* killjoy.

rabattre /rabatr/ *v.t.* pull ou put down; (*diminuer*) reduce; (*déduire*) take off. **se ~** *v. pr.* (*se refermer*) close; (*véhicule*) cut in, turn sharply. **se ~ sur**, fall back on.

rabbin /rabɛ̃/ *n.m.* rabbi.

rabibocher /rabiboʃe/ *v.t.* (*fam.*) reconcile.

rabiot /rabjo/ *n.m.* (*fam.*) = **rab**.

râblé /rɑble/ *a.* stocky, sturdy.

rabot /rabo/ *n.m.* plane. **~er** /-ɔte/ *v.t.* plane.

raboteu|x, **~se** /rabotø, -z/ *a.* uneven.

rabougri /rabugri/ *a.* stunted.

rabrouer /rabrue/ *v.t.* snub.

racaille /rakaj/ *n.f.* rabble.

raccommoder /rakɔmɔde/ *v.t.* mend; (*personnes: fam.*) reconcile.

raccompagner /rakɔ̃paɲe/ *v.t.* see ou take back (home).

raccord /rakɔr/ *n.m.* link; (*de papier peint*) join. **~ (de peinture)**, touch-up.

raccord|er /rakɔrde/ *v.t.* connect, join. **~ement** *n.m.* connection.

raccourci /rakursi/ *n.m.* short cut. **en ~**, in brief.

raccourcir /rakursir/ *v.t.* shorten. —*v.i.* get shorter.

raccrocher /rakroʃe/ *v.t.* hang back up; (*personne*) grab hold of; (*relier*) connect. **~ (le récepteur)**, hang up. **se ~ à**, cling to;

(*se relier à*) be connected to ou with.

rac|e /ras/ *n.f.* race; (*animale*) breed. **de ~e**, pure-bred. **~ial** (*m. pl.* **~iaux**) *a.* racial.

rachat /raʃa/ *n.m.* buying (back); (*de pécheur*) redemption.

racheter /raʃte/ *v.t.* buy (back); (*davantage*) buy more; (*nouvel objet*) buy another; (*pécheur*) redeem. **se ~** *v. pr.* make amends.

racine /rasin/ *n.f.* root. **~ carrée/cubique**, square/cube root.

racis|te /rasist/ *a. & n.m./f.* racist. **~me** *n.m.* racism.

racket /raket/ *n.m.* racketeering.

raclée /rɑkle/ *n.f.* (*fam.*) thrashing.

racler /rɑkle/ *v.t.* scrape. **se ~ la gorge**, clear one's throat.

racol|er /rakɔle/ *v.t.* solicit; (*marchand, parti*) drum up. **~age** *n.m.* soliciting.

racontars /rakɔ̃tar/ *n.m. pl.* (*fam.*) gossip, stories.

raconter /rakɔ̃te/ *v.t.* (*histoire*) tell, relate; (*vacances etc.*) tell about. **~ à qn. que**, tell s.o. that, say to s.o. that.

racorni /rakɔrni/ *a.* hard(ened).

radar /radar/ *n.m.* radar.

rade /rad/ *n.f.* harbour. **en ~**, (*personne: fam.*) stranded, behind.

radeau (*pl.* **~x**) /rado/ *n.m.* raft.

radiateur /radjatœr/ *n.m.* radiator; (*électrique*) heater.

radiation /radjasjɔ̃/ *n.f.* (*énergie*) radiation.

radic|al (*m. pl.* **~aux**) /radikal, -o/ *a.* radical. —*n.m.* (*pl.* **~aux**) radical.

radier /radje/ *v.t.* cross off.

radieu|x, **~se** /radjø, -z/ *a.* radiant.

radin, **~e** /radɛ̃, -in/ *a.* (*fam.*) stingy.

radio /radjo/ n.f. radio; (radio-
graphie) X-ray.

radioacti|f,~ve /radjoaktif,-v/ a.
radioactive. **~vité** n.f. radio-
activity.

radiocassette /radjokasɛt/ n.f.
radiocassette-player.

radiodiffus|er /radjodifyze/ v.t.
broadcast. **~ion** n.f. broadcast-
ing.

radiograph|ie /radjografi/ n.f.
(photographie) X-ray. **~ier** v.t.
X-ray. **~ique** a. X-ray.

radiologue /radjolog/ n.m./f.
radiographer.

radiophonique /radjofonik/ a.
radio.

radis /radi/ n.m. radish. **ne pas
avoir un ~,** be broke.

radoter /radɔte/ v.i. (fam.) talk
drivel.

radoucir (se) /(sə)radusir/ v. pr.
calm down; (temps) become
milder.

rafale /rafal/ n.f. (de vent) gust;
(tir) burst of gunfire.

raffermir /rafɛrmir/ v.t.
strengthen. **se ~** v. pr. become
stronger.

raffin|é /rafine/ a. refined.
~ement n.m. refinement.

raffin|er /rafine/ v.t. refine. **~age**
n.m. refining. **~erie** n.f. re-
finery.

raffoler /rafɔle/ v.i. **~ de,** be
extremely fond of.

raffut /rafy/ n.m. (fam.) din.

rafiot /rafjo/ n.m. (fam.) boat.

rafistoler /rafistɔle/ v.t. (fam.)
patch up.

rafle /rafl/ n.f. (police) raid.

rafler /rafle/ v.t. grab, swipe.

rafraîch|ir /rafreʃir/ v.t. cool
(down); (raviver) brighten up;
(personne, mémoire) refresh. **se
~ir** v. pr. (se laver) freshen up;
(boire) refresh o.s.; (temps) get
cooler. **~issant, ~issante** a.
refreshing.

rafraîchissement /rafreʃismã/
n.m. (boisson) cold drink. **~s,**
(fruits etc.) refreshments.

ragaillardir /ragajardir/ v.t.
(fam.) buck up. **se ~** v. pr. buck
up.

rag|e /raʒ/ n.f. rage; (maladie)
rabies. **faire ~e,** rage. **~e de
dents,** raging toothache. **~er** v.i.
rage. **~eur, ~euse** a. ill-
tempered. **~eant, ~eante** a.
maddening.

ragot(s) /rago/ n.m. (pl.) (fam.)
gossip.

ragoût /ragu/ n.m. stew.

raid /rɛd/ n.m. (mil.) raid; (sport)
rally.

raid|e /rɛd/ a. stiff; (côte) steep;
(corde) tight; (cheveux) straight.
—adv. (en pente) steeply. **~eur**
n.f. stiffness; steepness.

raidir /redir/ v.t., **se ~** v. pr.
stiffen; (position) harden; (corde)
tighten.

raie¹ /rɛ/ n.f. line; (bande) strip;
(de cheveux) parting.

raie² /rɛ/ n.f. (poisson) skate.

raifort /refor/ n.m. horse-radish.

rail /raj/ n.m. (barre) rail. **le ~,**
(transport) rail.

raill|er /raje/ v.t. mock (at). **~erie**
n.f. mocking remark. **~eur,
~euse** a. mocking.

rainure /renyr/ n.f. groove.

raisin /rezɛ̃/ n.m. **~(s),** grapes.
~ sec, raisin.

raison /rezɔ̃/ n.f. reason. **à ~ de,**
at the rate of. **avec ~,** rightly.
avoir ~, be right (de faire, to
do). **avoir ~ de qn.,** get the
better of s.o. **donner ~ à,** prove
right. **en ~ de,** (cause) because
of. **~ de plus,** all the more
reason. **perdre la ~,** lose one's
mind.

raisonnable /rezɔnabl/ a. reasonable, sensible.

raisonn|er /rezɔne/ v.i. reason.
—v.t. (personne) reason with.

~**ement** *n.m.* reasoning; (*propositions*) argument.

rajeunir /raʒœnir/ *v.t.* make (look) younger; (*moderniser*) modernize; (*méd.*) rejuvenate. —*v.i.* look younger.

rajout /raʒu/ *n.m.* addition. ~**er** /-te/ *v.t.* add.

rajust|er /raʒyste/ *v.t.* straighten; (*salaires*) (re)adjust. ~**ement** *n.m.* (re)adjustment.

râl|e /rɑl/ *n.m.* (*de blessé*) groan. ~**er** *v.i.* groan; (*protester: fam.*) moan.

ralent|ir /ralɑ̃tir/ *v.t./i.*, **se** ~**ir** *v. pr.* slow down. ~**i** *a.* slow; (*cinéma*) slow motion. **être** *ou* **tourner au** ~**i**, tick over, idle.

rall|ier /ralje/ *v.t.* rally; (*rejoindre*) rejoin. **se** ~**ier** *v. pr.* rally. **se** ~**ier à**, (*avis*) come over to. ~**iement** *n.m.* rallying.

rallonge /ralɔ̃ʒ/ *n.f.* (*de table*) extension. ~ **de**, (*supplément de*) extra.

rallonger /ralɔ̃ʒe/ *v.t.* lengthen.

rallumer /ralyme/ *v.t.* light (up) again; (*lampe*) switch on again; (*ranimer: fig.*) revive.

rallye /rali/ *n.m.* rally.

ramadan /ramadɑ̃/ *n.m.* Ramadan.

ramassé /ramase/ *a.* squat; (*concis*) concise.

ramass|er /ramase/ *v.t.* pick up; (*récolter*) gather; (*recueillir*) collect. **se** ~**er** *v. pr.* draw up together, curl up. ~**age** *n.m.* (*cueillette*) gathering. ~**age scolaire**, school bus service.

rambarde /rɑ̃bard/ *n.f.* guardrail.

rame /ram/ *n.f.* (*aviron*) oar; (*train*) train; (*perche*) stake.

rameau (*pl.* ~**x**) /ramo/ *n.m.* branch.

ramener /ramne/ *v.t.* bring back. ~ **à**, (*réduire à*) reduce to. **se** ~ *v. pr.* (*fam.*) turn up. **se** ~ **à**, (*problème*) come down to.

ram|er /rame/ *v.i.* row. ~**eur, ~euse** *n.m., f.* rower.

ramif|ier (**se**) /(s)ramifje/ *v. pr.* ramify. ~**ication** *n.f.* ramification.

ramollir /ramɔlir/ *v.t.*, **se** ~ *v. pr.* soften.

ramon|er /ramɔne/ *v.t.* sweep. ~**eur** *n.m.* (chimney-)sweep.

rampe /rɑ̃p/ *n.f.* banisters; (*pente*) ramp. ~ **de lancement**, launching pad.

ramper /rɑ̃pe/ *v.i.* crawl.

rancard /rɑ̃kar/ *n.m.* (*fam.*) appointment.

rancart /rɑ̃kar/ *n.m.* **mettre** *ou* **jeter au** ~, (*fam.*) scrap.

ranc|e /rɑ̃s/ *a.* rancid. ~**ir** *v.i.* go *ou* turn rancid.

rancœur /rɑ̃kœr/ *n.f.* resentment.

rançon /rɑ̃sɔ̃/ *n.f.* ransom. ~**ner** /-ɔne/ *v.t.* hold to ransom.

rancun|e /rɑ̃kyn/ *n.f.* grudge. **sans** ~**!**, no hard feelings. ~**ier, ~ière** *a.* vindictive.

randonnée /rɑ̃dɔne/ *n.f.* walk; (*en auto, vélo*) ride.

rang /rɑ̃/ *n.m.* row; (*hiérarchie, condition*) rank. **se mettre en** ~, line up. **au premier** ~, in the first row; (*fig.*) at the forefront. **de second** ~, (*péj.*) second-rate.

rangée /rɑ̃ʒe/ *n.f.* row.

rang|er /rɑ̃ʒe/ *v.t.* put away; (*chambre etc.*) tidy (up); (*disposer*) place; (*véhicule*) park. **se** ~**er** *v. pr.* (*véhicule*) park; (*s'écarter*) stand aside; (*s'assagir*) settle down. **se** ~**er à**, (*avis*) accept. ~**ement** *n.m.* (*de chambre*) tidying (up); (*espace*) storage space.

ranimer /ranime/ *v.t.*, **se** ~ *v. pr.* revive.

rapace¹ /rapas/ *n.m.* bird of prey.

rapace² /rapas/ *a.* grasping.

rapatr|ier /rapatrije/ *v.t.* repatriate. ~**iement** *n.m.* repatriation.

râpe /rap/ *n.f.* (*culin.*) grater; (*lime*) rasp. **~er** *v.t.* grate; (*bois*) rasp.

râpé /rape/ *a.* threadbare. **c'est ~!**, (*fam.*) that's right out!

rapetisser /raptise/ *v.t.* make smaller. **—v.i.** get smaller.

râpeu|x, ~se /rapø, -z/ *a.* rough.

rapid|e /rapid/ *a.* fast. rapid. **—n.m.** (*train*) express (train); (*cours d'eau*) rapids *pl.* **~ement** *adv.* fast, rapidly. **~ité** *n.f.* speed.

rapiécer /rapjese/ *v.t.* patch.

rappel /rapel/ *n.m.* recall; (*deuxième avis*) reminder; (*de salaire*) back pay; (*méd.*) booster.

rappeler /raple/ *v.t.* call back; (*diplomate, réserviste*) recall; (*évoquer*) remind, **~ qch. à qn.**, (*redire*) remind s.o. of sth. **se ~** *v. pr.* remember, recall.

rapport /rapor/ *n.m.* connection; (*compte rendu*) report; (*profit*) yield. **~s**, (*relations*) relations. **en ~ avec**, (*accord*) in keeping with. **mettre/se mettre en ~ avec**, put/get in touch with. **par ~ à**, in relation to. **~s** (*sexuels*), intercourse.

rapport|er /raporte/ *v.t.* bring back; (*profit*) bring in; (*dire, répéter*) report. **—v.i.** (*comm.*) bring in a good return; (*mouchard: fam.*) tell. **se ~er à**, relate to. **s'en ~er à**, rely on. **~eur**, **~euse** *n.m., f.* (*mouchard*) tell-tale; *n.m.* (*instrument*) protractor.

rapproch|er /raproʃe/ *v.t.* bring closer (**de**, to); (*réconcilier*) bring together; (*comparer*) compare. **se ~er** *v. pr.* get ou come closer (**de**, to); (*personnes, pays*) come together; (*s'apparenter*) be close (**de**, to). **~é** *a.* close. **~ement** *n.m.* reconciliation; (*rapport*) connection; (*comparaison*) parallel.

rapt /rapt/ *n.m.* abduction.

raquette /raket/ *n.f.* (*de tennis*) racket; (*de ping-pong*) bat.

rare /rar/ *a.* rare; (*insuffisant*) scarce. **~ment** *adv.* rarely, seldom. **~té** *n.f.* rarity; scarcity; (*objet*) rarity.

raréfier (se) /(sə)rarefje/ *v. pr.* (*nourriture etc.*) become scarce.

ras /rɑ, rɑ/ *a.* (*herbe, poil*) short. **à ~ de**, very close to. **en avoir ~ le bol**, (*fam.*) be really fed up. **~ campagne**, open country. **coupé à ~**, cut short. **à ~ bord**, to the brim. **pull ~ du cou**, round-neck pull-over. **~-le-bol** *n.m.* (*fam.*) anger. **en avoir ~ le bol**, be fed-up.

ras|er /raze/ *v.t.* shave; (*cheveux, barbe*) shave off; (*frôler*) skim; (*abattre*) raze; (*ennuyer: fam.*) bore. **se ~er** *v. pr.* shave. **~age** *n.m.* shaving. **~eur**, **~euse** *n.m., f.* (*fam.*) bore.

rasoir /rɑzwar/ *n.m.* razor.

rassas|ier /rasazje/ *v.t.* satisfy. **être ~ié de**, have had enough of.

rassembl|er /rɑsɑble/ *v.t.* gather; (*courage*) muster. **se ~er** *v. pr.* gather. **~ement** *n.m.* gathering.

rasseoir (se) /(sə)raswar/ *v. pr.* sit down again.

rass|is, **~ise** *ou* **~ie** /rasi, -z/ *a.* (*pain*) stale.

rassurer /rasyre/ *v.t.* reassure.

rat /ra/ *n.m.* rat.

ratatiner (se) /(sə)ratatine/ *v. pr.* shrivel up.

rate /rat/ *n.f.* spleen.

râteau (*pl.* **~x**) /rɑto/ *n.m.* rake.

râtelier /rɑtəlje/ *n.m.*; (*fam.*) dentures.

rat|er /rate/ *v.t./i.* miss; (*gâcher*) spoil; (*échouer*) fail. **c'est ~é**, that's right out. **~é**, **~ée** *n.m., f.* (*personne*) failure. **avoir des ~és**, (*auto.*) backfire.

ratifier /ratifje/ *v.t.* ratify. **~ication** *n.f.* ratification.

ratio /rasjo/ *n.m.* ratio.

ration /rasjɔ̃/ *n.f.* ration.

rationaliser /rasjonalize/ *v.t.* rationalize.

rationnel, ~le /rasjonɛl/ *a.* rational.

rationn|er /rasjone/ *v.t.* ration. **~ement** *n.m.* rationing.

ratisser /ratise/ *v.t.* rake; (*fouiller*) comb.

rattacher /rataʃe/ *v.t.* tie up again; (*relier*) link; (*incorporer*) join.

rattrapage /ratrapaʒ/ *n.m.* ~ scolaire, remedial classes.

rattraper /ratrape/ *v.t.* catch; (*rejoindre*) catch up with; (*retard, erreur*) make up for. se ~ *v. pr.* catch up; (*se dédommager*) make up for it. se ~ à, catch hold of.

ratur|e /ratyr/ *n.f.* deletion. **~er** *v.t.* delete.

rauque /rok/ *a.* raucous, harsh.

ravager /ravaʒe/ *v.t.* devastate, ravage.

ravages /ravaʒ/ *n.m. pl.* faire des ~, wreak havoc.

raval|er /ravale/ *v.t.* (*façade etc.*) clean; (*humilier*) lower (à, down to). **~ement** *n.m.* cleaning.

ravi /ravi/ *a.* delighted (**que**, that).

ravier /ravje/ *n.m.* hors-d'œuvre dish.

ravigoter /ravigote/ *v.t.* (*fam.*) buck up.

ravin /ravɛ̃/ *n.m.* ravine.

ravioli /ravjoli/ *n.m. pl.* ravioli.

ravir /ravir/ *v.t.* delight. **~ à qn.**, (*enlever*) rob s.o. of.

raviser (se) /(sə)ravize/ *v. pr.* change one's mind.

ravissant, ~e /ravisɑ̃, -t/ *a.* beautiful.

ravisseu|r, ~se /ravisœr, -øz/ *n.m., f.* kidnapper.

ravitaill|er /ravitaje/ *v.t.* provide with supplies; (*avion*) refuel. se ~er *v. pr.* stock up. **~ement** *n.m.* provision of supplies (**de**, to), refuelling; (*denrées*) supplies.

raviver /ravive/ *v.t.* revive.

rayé /reje/ *a.* striped.

rayer /reje/ *v.t.* scratch; (*biffer*) cross out.

rayon /rɛjɔ̃/ *n.m.* ray; (*planche*) shelf; (*de magasin*) department; (*de roue*) spoke; (*de cercle*) radius. ~ d'action, range. ~ de miel, honeycomb. ~ X, X-ray. en connaître un ~, (*fam.*) know one's stuff.

rayonner /rɛjone/ *v.i.* radiate; (*de joie*) beam; (*se déplacer*) tour around (*from a central point*). **~ement** *n.m.* (*éclat*) radiance; (*influence*) influence; (*radiations*) radiation.

rayure /rɛjyr/ *n.f.* scratch; (*dessin*) stripe. à ~s, striped.

raz-de-marée /radmare/ *n.m. invar.* tidal wave. ~ électoral, landslide.

re- /rə/ *préf.* re-.

ré- /re/ *préf.* re-.

réacteur /reaktœr/ *n.m.* jet engine; (*nucléaire*) reactor.

réaction /reaksjɔ̃/ *n.f.* reaction. ~ en chaîne, chain reaction. **~naire** /-jonɛr/ *a. & n.m./f.* reactionary.

réadapter /readapte/ *v.t.*, se ~ *v. pr.* readjust (à, to).

réaffirmer /reafirme/ *v.t.* reaffirm.

réagir /reaʒir/ *v.i.* react.

réalis|er /realize/ *v.t.* carry out; (*effort, bénéfice, achat*) make; (*rêve*) fulfil; (*film*) produce, direct; (*capital*) realize; (*se rendre compte de*) realize. se ~er *v. pr.* materialize. **~ateur, ~atrice** *n.m., f.* (*cinéma*) director; (*TV*) producer. **~ation** *n.f.* realization; (*œuvre*) achievement.

réalis|te /realist/ *a.* realistic. **~me** *n.m./f.* realist. **~me** *n.m.* realism.

réalité /realite/ *n.f.* reality.

réanim|er /reanime/ v.t. resuscitate. **~ation** n.f. resuscitation. **service de ~ation,** intensive care.

réapparaître /reaparɛtr/ v.i. reappear.

réarm|er (se) /(sə)rearme/ v. pr. rearm. **~ement** n.m. rearmament.

rébarbati|f, ~ve /rebarbatif, -v/ a. forbidding, off-putting.

rebâtir /rəbatir/ v.t. rebuild.

rebelle /rəbɛl/ a. rebellious; (soldat) rebel. —n.m./f. rebel.

rebeller (se) /(sə)rəbele/ v. pr. rebel, hit back defiantly.

rébellion /rebeljɔ̃/ n.f. rebellion.

rebiffer (se) /(sə)rəbife/ v. pr. (fam.) rebel.

rebond /rəbɔ̃/ n.m. bounce; (par ricochet) rebound. **~ir** /-dir/ v.i. bounce; rebound.

rebondi /rəbɔ̃di/ a. chubby.

rebondissement /rəbɔ̃dismɑ̃/ n.m. (new) development.

rebord /rəbɔr/ n.m. edge. **~ de la fenêtre,** window-ledge.

rebours (à) /(a)rəbur/ adv. the wrong way.

rebrousse-poil (à) /(a)rəbruspwal/ adv. (fig.) prendre qn. **~,** rub s.o. up the wrong way.

rebrousser /rəbruse/ v.t. **~ chemin,** turn back.

rebuffade /rəbyfad/ n.f. rebuff.

rébus /rebys/ n.m. rebus.

rebut /rəby/ n.m. mettre ou jeter au **~,** scrap.

rebut|er /rəbyte/ v.t. put off. **~ant, ~ante** a. off-putting.

récalcitrant, ~e /rekalsitrɑ̃, -t/ a. stubborn.

recal|er /rəkale/ v.t. (fam.) fail. **se faire ~er** ou **être ~é,** fail.

récapitul|er /rekapityle/ v.t./i. recapitulate. **~ation** n.f. recapitulation.

recel /rəsɛl/ n.m. receiving. **~er**

/rəs(ə)le/ v.t. (objet volé) receive; (cacher) conceal.

récemment /resamɑ̃/ adv. recently.

recens|er /rəsɑ̃se/ v.t. (population) take a census of; (objets) list. **~ement** n.m. census; list.

récent, ~e /resɑ̃, -t/ a. recent.

récépissé /resepise/ n.m. receipt.

récepteur /reseptœr/ n.m. receiver.

récepti|f, ~ve /reseptif, -v/ a. receptive.

réception /resɛpsjɔ̃/ n.f. reception. **~ de,** (lettre etc.) receipt of. **~niste** /-jɔnist/ n.m./f. receptionist.

récession /resesjɔ̃/ n.f. recession.

recette /rəsɛt/ n.f. (culin.) recipe; (argent) takings. **~s,** (comm.) receipts.

receveu|r, ~se /rəsvœr, -øz/ n.m., f. (des impôts) tax collector.

recevoir† /rəsvwar/ v.t. receive; (client, malade) see; (obtenir) get, receive. **être reçu** (à), pass. —v.i. (médecin) receive patients. **se ~** v. pr. (tomber) land.

rechange (de) /(də)rəʃɑ̃ʒ/ a. (roue, vêtements, etc.) spare; (solution etc.) alternative.

réchapper /reʃape/ v.i. **~ de** ou **à,** come through, survive.

recharge /rəʃarʒ/ n.f. (de stylo) refill. **~er** v.t. refill; (batterie) recharge.

réchaud /reʃo/ n.m. stove.

réchauff|er /reʃofe/ v.t. warm up. **se ~** v. pr. warm o.s. up; (temps) get warmer. **~ement** n.m. (de température) rise (de, in).

rêche /rɛʃ/ a. rough.

recherche /rəʃɛrʃ/ n.f. search (de, for); (raffinement) elegance. **~(s),** (univ.) research. **~s,** (enquête) investigations.

recherch|er /rəʃɛrʃe/ v.t. search for. **~é** a. in great demand;

(*élégant*) elegant. **~é pour meurtre**, wanted for murder.

rechigner /rəʃiɲe/ *v.i.* **~ à**, balk at.

rechute /rəʃyt/ *n.f.* (*méd.*) relapse. **~er** *v.i.* relapse.

récidiv|e /residiv/ *n.f.* second offence. **~er** *v.i.* commit a second offence.

récif /resif/ *n.m.* reef.

récipient /resipjã/ *n.m.* container.

réciproque /resiprɔk/ *a.* mutual, reciprocal. **~ment** *adv.* each other; (*inversement*) conversely.

récit /resi/ *n.m.* (*compte rendu*) account, story; (*histoire*) story.

récital (*pl.* **~s**) /resital/ *n.m.* recital.

récit|er /resite/ *v.t.* recite. **~ation** *n.f.* recitation.

réclame /reklam/ *n.f.* **faire de la ~**, advertise. **en ~**, on offer.

réclam|er /reklame/ *v.t.* call for, demand; (*revendiquer*) claim. **—***v.i.* complain. **~ation** *n.f.* complaint.

reclus, ~e /rəkly, -z/ *n.m., f.* recluse. **—***a.* cloistered.

réclusion /reklyzjɔ̃/ *n.f.* imprisonment.

recoin /rəkwɛ̃/ *n.m.* nook.

récolt|e /rekɔlt/ *n.f.* (*action*) harvest; (*produits*) crop, harvest; (*fig.*) crop. **~er** *v.t.* harvest, gather; (*fig.*) collect.

recommand|er /rəkɔmɑ̃de/ *v.t.* recommend; (*lettre*) register. **envoyer en ~é**, send registered. **~ation** *n.f.* recommendation.

recommenc|er /rəkɔmɑ̃se/ *v.t./i.* (*reprendre*) begin *ou* start again; (*refaire*) repeat. **ne ~ pas**, don't do it again.

récompens|e /rekɔ̃pɑ̃s/ *n.f.* reward; (*prix*) award. **~er** *v.t.* reward (**de**, for).

réconcil|ier /rekɔ̃silje/ *v.t.* reconcile. **se ~ier** *v. pr.* become

reconciled (**avec**, with). **~iation** *n.f.* reconciliation.

reconduire† /rəkɔ̃dɥir/ *v.t.* see home; (*à la porte*) show out; (*renouveler*) renew.

réconfort /rekɔ̃fɔr/ *n.m.* comfort. **~er** /-te/ *v.t.* comfort.

reconnaissable /rəkɔnɛsabl/ *a.* recognizable.

reconnaissan|t, ~te /rəkɔnɛsɑ̃, -t/ *a.* grateful (**de**, for). **~ce** *n.f.* gratitude; (*fait de reconnaître*) recognition; (*mil.*) reconnaissance.

reconnaître† /rəkɔnɛtr/ *v.t.* recognize; (*admettre*) admit (**que**, that); (*mil.*) reconnoitre; (*enfant, tort*) acknowledge.

reconstituant /rəkɔ̃stitɥɑ̃/ *n.m.* tonic.

reconstituer /rəkɔ̃stitɥe/ *v.t.* reconstitute; (*crime*) reconstruct.

reconstr|uire† /rəkɔ̃strɥir/ *v.t.* rebuild. **~uction** *n.f.* rebuilding.

reconversion /rəkɔ̃vɛrsjɔ̃/ *n.f.* (*de main-d'œuvre*) redeployment.

recopier /rəkɔpje/ *v.t.* copy out.

record /rəkɔr/ *n.m. & a. invar.* record.

recoup|er /rəkupe/ *v.t.* confirm. **se ~** *v. pr.* check, tally, match up. **par ~ment**, by making connections.

recourbé /rəkurbe/ *a.* curved; (*nez*) hooked.

recourir /rəkurir/ *v.i.* **~ à**, resort to.

recours /rəkur/ *n.m.* resort. **avoir ~ à**, have recourse to, resort to.

recouvrer /rəkuvre/ *v.t.* recover.

recouvrir† /rəkuvrir/ *v.t.* cover.

récréation /rekreasjɔ̃/ *n.f.* recreation; (*scol.*) playtime.

récrier (se) /(sə)rekrije/ *v. pr.* cry out.

récrimination /rekriminasjɔ̃/ *n.f.* recrimination.

recroqueviller (se) /(sə)rəkrɔkvije/ *v. pr.* curl up.

recrudescence /rəkrydesɑ̃s/ *n.f.* new outbreak.

recrue /rəkry/ *n.f.* recruit.

recrut|er /rəkryte/ *v.t.* recruit. **~ement** *n.m.* recruitment.

rectang|le /rɛktɑ̃gl/ *n.m.* rectangle. **~ulaire** *a.* rectangular.

rectif|ier /rɛktifje/ *v.t.* correct, rectify. **~ication** *n.f.* correction.

recto /rɛkto/ *n.m.* front of the page.

reçu /rəsy/ *voir* **recevoir.** —*n.m.* receipt. —*a.* accepted; (*candidat*) successful.

recueil /rəkœj/ *n.m.* collection.

recueill|ir† /rəkœjir/ *v.t.* collect; (*prendre chez soi*) take in. **se ~ir** *v. pr.* meditate. **~ement** *n.m.* meditation. **~i** *a.* meditative.

recul /rəkyl/ *n.m.* retreat; (*éloignement*) distance; (*déclin*) decline. **(mouvement de) ~,** backward movement. **~ade** *n.f.* retreat.

reculé /rəkyle/ *a.* (*région*) remote.

reculer /rəkyle/ *v.t./i.* move back; (*véhicule*) reverse; (*armée*) retreat; (*diminuer*) decline; (*différer*) postpone. **~ devant,** (*fig.*) shrink from.

reculons (à) /(a)rəkylɔ̃/ *adv.* backwards.

récupér|er /rekypere/ *v.t./i.* recover; (*vieux objets*) salvage. **~ation** *n.f.* recovery; salvage.

récurer /rekyre/ *v.t.* scour. **poudre à ~,** scouring powder.

récuser /rekyze/ *v.t.* challenge. **se ~** *v. pr.* state that one is not qualified to judge.

recycl|er /rəsikle/ *v.t.* (*personne*) retrain; (*chose*) recycle. **se ~er** *v. pr.* retrain. **~age** *n.m.* retraining; recycling.

rédac|teur, ~trice /redaktœr, -tris/ *n.m., f.* writer, editor. **le ~teur en chef,** the editor (in chief).

rédaction /redaksjɔ̃/ *n.f.* writing;

(*scol.*) composition; (*personnel*) editorial staff.

reddition /redisjɔ̃/ *n.f.* surrender.

redemander /rədmɑ̃de/ *v.t.* ask again for; ask for more of.

redevable /rədvabl/ *a.* **être ~ à qn. de,** (*argent*) owe sb; (*fig.*) be indebted to s.o. for.

redevance /rədvɑ̃s/ *n.f.* (*de télévision*) licence fee.

rédiger /rediʒe/ *v.t.* write; (*contrat*) draw up.

redire† /rədir/ *v.t.* repeat. **avoir ou trouver à ~ à,** find fault with.

redondant, ~e /rədɔ̃dɑ̃, -t/ *a.* superfluous.

redonner /rədɔne/ *v.t.* give back; (*davantage*) give more.

redoubl|er /rəduble/ *v.t./i.* increase; (*classe scol.*) repeat. **~er de prudence/etc.,** be more careful/etc. **~ement** *n.m.* (*accroissement*) increase (**de,** in).

redouter /rədute/ *v.t.* dread. **~able** *a.* formidable.

redoux /rədu/ *n.m.* milder weather.

redress|er /rədrese/ *v.t.* straighten (out ou up); (*situation*) right, redress. **se ~er** *v. pr.* (*personne*) straighten (o.s.) up; (*se remettre debout*) stand up; (*pays, économie*) recover. **~ement** /rədrɛsmɑ̃/ *n.m.* (*relèvement*) recovery.

réduction /redyksjɔ̃/ *n.f.* reduction.

réduire† /reduir/ *v.t.* reduce (**à,** to). **se ~ à,** (*revenir à*) come down to.

réduit¹, ~e /redɥi, -t/ *a.* (*objet*) small-scale; (*limité*) limited.

réduit² /redɥi/ *n.m.* recess.

rééduqu|er /reedyke/ *v.t.* (*personne*) rehabilitate; (*membre*) re-educate. **~cation** *n.f.* rehabilitation; re-education.

réel, ~le /reɛl/ *a.* real. —*n.m.* reality. **~lement** *adv.* really.

réexpédier /reɛkspedje/ v.t. forward; (retourner) send back.

refaire† /rəfɛr/ v.t. do again; (erreur, voyage) make again; (réparer) do up, redo.

réfection /refɛksjɔ̃/ n.f. repair.

réfectoire /refɛktwar/ n.m. refectory.

référence /referɑ̃s/ n.f. reference.

référendum /referɛ̃dɔm/ n.m. referendum.

référer /refere/ v.i. en ~ à, refer the matter to. se ~ à, refer to.

refermer /rəfɛrme/ v.t., se ~, v. pr. close (again).

refiler /rəfile/ v.t. (fam.) palm off (à, on).

réfléchir /refleʃir/ v.i. think (à, about). —v.t. reflect. se ~ir v. pr. be reflected. ~i a. (personne) thoughtful; (verbe) reflexive.

reflet /rəflɛ/ n.m. reflection; (lumière) light. ~éter /-ete/ v.t. reflect. se ~éter v. pr. be reflected.

réflexe /reflɛks/ a. & n.m. reflex.

réflexion /reflɛksjɔ̃/ n.f. reflection; (pensée) thought, reflection. à la ~, on second thoughts.

refluer /rəflye/ v.i. flow back; (foule) retreat.

reflux /rəfly/ n.m. (de marée) ebb.

refondre /rəfɔ̃dr/ v.t. recast.

réforme /refɔrm/ n.f. reform. ~ateur, ~atrice n.m., f. reformer. ~er v.t. reform; (soldat) invalid (out of the army).

refouler /rəfule/ v.t. (larmes) force back; (désir) repress. ~é a. repressed. ~ement n.m. repression.

réfractaire /refraktɛr/ a. être ~ à, resist.

refrain /rəfrɛ̃/ n.m. chorus. le même ~, the same old story.

refréner /rəfrene/ v.t. curb, check.

réfrigér|er /refriʒere/ v.t. refrigerate. ~ateur n.m. refrigerator.

refroid|ir /rəfrwadir/ v.t./i. cool (down). se ~ir v. pr. (personne, temps) get cold; (ardeur) cool (off). ~issement n.m. cooling; (rhume) chill.

refuge /rəfyʒ/ n.m. refuge; (chalet) mountain hut.

réfugier (se) /(sə)refyʒje/ v. pr. take refuge. ~ié, ~iée n.m., f. refugee.

refus /rəfy/ n.m. refusal. ce n'est pas de ~, I wouldn't say no. ~er /-ze/ v.t. refuse (de, to); (recaler) fail. se ~er à, (évidence etc.) reject.

réfuter /refyte/ v.t. refute.

regagner /rəgaɲe/ v.t. regain; (revenir à) get back to.

regain /rəgɛ̃/ n.m. ~ de, renewal of.

régal (pl. ~s) /regal/ n.m. treat. ~er v.t. treat (de, to). se ~er v. pr. treat o.s. (de, to).

regard /rəgar/ n.m. (expression, coup d'œil) look; (fixe) stare; (vue, œil) eye. au ~ de, in regard to. en ~ de, compared with.

regardant, ~e /rəgardɑ̃, -t/ a. careful (with money). peu ~ (sur), not fussy (about).

regarder /rəgarde/ v.t. look at; (observer) watch; (considérer) consider; (concerner) concern. ~ (fixement), stare at. —v.i. look. ~ à, (qualité etc.) pay attention to. ~ vers, (maison) face. se ~ v. pr. (personnes) look at each other.

régates /regat/ n.f. pl. regatta.

régénérer /reʒenere/ v.t. regenerate.

régen|t, ~te /reʒɑ̃, -t/ n.m., f. regent. ~ce n.f. regency.

régenter /reʒɑ̃te/ v.t. rule.

reggae /rege/ n.m. reggae.

régie /reʒi/ n.f. (entreprise) public corporation; (radio, TV) control room; (cinéma, théâtre) production.

regimber /rəʒɛ̃be/ v.i. balk.

régime /reʒim/ n.m. (organisation) system; (pol.) regime; (méd.) diet; (de moteur) speed; (de bananes) bunch. se mettre au ~, go on a diet.

régiment /reʒimɑ̃/ n.m. regiment.

région /reʒjɔ̃/ n.f. region. ~al (m. pl. ~aux) /-jɔnal, -o/ a. regional.

régir /reʒir/ v.t. govern.

régisseur /reʒisœr/ n.m. (théâtre) stage-manager; (cinéma, TV) assistant director.

registre /rəʒistr/ n.m. register.

réglage /reglaʒ/ n.m. adjustment.

règle /regl/ n.f. rule; (instrument) ruler. ~s, (de femme) period. en ~, in order. ~ à calculer, slide-rule.

réglé /regle/ a. (vie) ordered; (arrangé) settled.

règlement /reglamɑ̃/ n.m. regulation; (règles) regulations; (solution, paiement) settlement. ~aire /-tɛr/ a. (uniforme) regulation.

réglement|er /reglamɑ̃te/ v.t. regulate. ~ation n.f. regulation.

régler /regle/ v.t. settle; (machine) adjust; (programmer) set; (facture) settle; (personne) settle up with; (papier) rule. ~ son compte à, settle a score with.

réglisse /reglis/ n.f. liquorice.

règne /rɛɲ/ n.m. reign; (végétal, animal, minéral) kingdom.

régner /reɲe/ v.i. reign.

regorger /rəgɔrʒe/ v.i. ~ de, be overflowing with.

regret /rəgrɛ/ n.m. regret. à ~, with regret.

regrett|er /rəgrete/ v.t. regret; (personne) miss. ~able a. regrettable.

regrouper /rəgrupe/ v.t., group together. se ~ v. pr. gather (together).

régulariser /regylarize/ v.t. regularize.

régulation /regylasjɔ̃/ n.f. regulation.

régul|ier, **~ière** /regylje, -jɛr/ a. regular; (qualité, vitesse) steady, even; (ligne, paysage) even; (légal) legal; (honnête) honest. ~arité n.f. regularity; steadiness; evenness. ~ièrement adv. regularly; (d'ordinaire) normally.

réhabilit|er /reabilte/ n.f. rehabilitate. ~ation n.f. rehabilitation.

rehausser /roose/ v.t. raise; (faire valoir) enhance.

rein /rɛ̃/ n.m. kidney. ~s, (dos) back.

réincarnation /reɛ̃karnasjɔ̃/ n.f. reincarnation.

reine /rɛn/ n.f. queen. ~-claude n.f. greengage.

réinsertion /reɛ̃sɛrsjɔ̃/ n.f. reintegration, rehabilitation.

réintégrer /reɛ̃tegre/ v.t. (lieu) return to; (jurid.) reinstate.

réitérer /reitere/ v.t. repeat.

rejaillir /rəʒajir/ v.i. ~ sur, rebound on.

rejet /rəʒɛ/ n.m. rejection.

rejeter /rəʒte/ v.t. throw back; (refuser) reject; (vomir) bring up; (déverser) discharge. ~ une faute/etc. sur qn., shift the blame for a mistake/etc. on to s.o.

rejeton(s) /rəʒtɔ̃/ n.m. (pl.) (fam.) offspring.

rejoindre† /rəʒwɛ̃dr/ v.t. go back to, rejoin; (rattraper) catch up with; (rencontrer) join, meet. se ~ v. pr. (personnes) meet; (routes) join, meet.

réjoui /reʒwi/ a. joyful.

réjou|ir /reʒwir/ v.t. delight. se ~ir v. pr. be delighted (de qch., at sth.). ~issances n.f. pl. festivities. ~issant, ~issante a. cheering.

relâche /rəlaʃ/ n.m. (repos) respite. faire ~, (théâtre) close.

relâché /rəlaʃe/ a. lax.

relâch|er /rəlaʃe/ v.t. slacken;

(*personne*) release; (*discipline*) relax. se ~er v. pr. slacken. ~ement n.m. slackening.

relais /rəlɛ/ n.m. relay. ~ (routier), roadside café.

relancle /rəlɑ̃s/ n.f. boost. ~er v.t. boost, revive; (*renvoyer*) throw back.

relatilf, ~ve /rəlatif, -v/ a. relative.

relation /rəlasjɔ̃/ n.f. relation(ship); (*ami*) acquaintance; (*récit*) account. ~s, relation. en ~ avec qn., in touch with s.o.

relativement /rəlativmɑ̃/ adv. relatively. ~ à, in relation to.

relativité /rəlativite/ n.f. relativity.

relaxler (se) /(sə)rəlakse/ v. pr. relax. ~ation.n.f. relaxation. ~e a. (*fam.*) laid-back.

relayer /rəleje/ v.t. relieve; (*émission*) relay. se ~ v. pr. take over from one another.

reléguer /rəlege/ v.t. relegate.

relent /rəlɑ̃/ n.m. stink.

relève /rəlɛv/ n.f. relief. prendre ou assurer la ~, take over (de, from).

relevé /rəlve/ n.m. list; (*de compte*) statement; (*de compteur*) reading. —a. spicy.

relever /rəlve/ v.t. pick up; (*personne tombée*) help up; (*remonter*) raise; (*col*) turn up; (*manches*) roll up; (*sauce*) season; (*goût*) bring out; (*compteur*) read; (*défi*) accept; (*relayer*) relieve; (*remarquer, noter*) note; (*rebâtir*) rebuild. —v.i. — de, (*dépendre de*) be the concern of; (*méd.*) recover from. se ~ v. pr. (*personne*) get up (again); (*pays, économie*) recover.

relief /rəljɛf/ n.m. relief. mettre en ~, highlight.

relier /rəlje/ v.t. link (à, to); (*ensemble*) link together; (*livre*) bind.

religieulx, ~se /rəliʒjø, -z/ a.

religious. —n.m. monk. —n.f. nun; (*culin.*) choux bun.

religion /rəliʒjɔ̃/ n.f. religion.

reliquat /rəlika/ n.m. residue.

relique /rəlik/ n.f. relic.

reliure /rəljyr/ n.f. binding.

reluire /rəlɥir/ v.i. shine. faire ~, shine.

reluisant, ~e /rəlɥizɑ̃, -t/ a. peu ou pas ~, not brilliant.

remanler /rəmanje/ v.t. revise; (*ministère*) reshuffle. ~iement n.m. revision; reshuffle.

remarier (se) /(sə)rəmarje/ v. pr. remarry.

remarquable /rəmarkabl/ a. remarkable.

remarque /rəmark/ n.f. remark; (*par écrit*) note.

remarquer /rəmarke/ v.t. notice; (*dire*) say. faire ~, point out (à, to). se faire ~, attract attention. remarque(z), mind you.

remblai /rɑ̃blɛ/ n.m. embankment.

rembourrer /rɑ̃bure/ v.t. pad.

remboursler /rɑ̃burse/ v.t. repay; (*billet, frais*) refund. ~ement n.m. repayment; refund.

remède /rəmɛd/ n.m. remedy; (*médicament*) medicine.

remédier /rəmedje/ v.i. ~ à, remedy.

remémorer (se) /(sə)rəmemɔre/ v. pr. recall.

remercler /rəmɛrsje/ v.t. thank (de, for); (*licencier*) dismiss. ~iements n.m. pl. thanks.

remettret /rəmɛtr/ v.t. put back; (*vêtement*) put back on; (*donner*) hand (over); (*devoir, démission*) hand in; (*restituer*) give back; (*différer*) put off; (*ajouter*) add; (*se rappeler*) remember; (*peine*) remit. se ~ v. pr. (*guérir*) recover. se ~ à, go back to. se ~ à faire, start doing again. s'en ~ à, leave it to. ~ en cause ou en question, call into question.

réminiscence /reminisɑ̃s/ *n.f.* reminiscence.

remise[1] /rəmiz/ *n.f.* (*abri*) shed.

remise[2] /rəmiz/ *n.f.* (*rabais*) discount; (*livraison*) delivery; (*ajournement*) postponement. ∼ **en cause** *ou* **en question,** calling into question.

remiser /rəmize/ *v.t.* put away.

rémission /remisjɔ̃/ *n.f.* remission.

remontant /rəmɔ̃tɑ̃/ *n.m.* tonic.

remontée /rəmɔ̃te/ *n.f.* ascent; (*d'eau, de prix*) rise. ∼ **mécanique,** ski-lift.

remont|er /rəmɔ̃te/ *v.i. go ou* come (back) up; (*prix, niveau*) rise (again); (*revenir*) go back. —*v.t.* (*rue etc.*) *go ou* come (back) up; (*relever*) raise; (*montre*) wind up; (*objet démonté*) put together again; (*personne*) buck up. ∼**e-pente** *n.m.* ski-lift.

remontoir /rəmɔ̃twar/ *n.m.* winder.

remontrer /rəmɔ̃tre/ *v.t.* show again. **en** ∼ **à qn.,** go one up on s.o.

remords /rəmɔr/ *n.m.* remorse. **avoir un** *ou* **des** ∼, feel remorse.

remorqu|e /rəmɔrk/ *n.f.* (*véhicule*) trailer. **en** ∼**e,** on tow. ∼**er** *v.t.* tow.

remorqueur /rəmɔrkœr/ *n.m.* tug.

remous /rəmu/ *n.m.* eddy; (*de bateau*) backwash; (*fig.*) turmoil.

rempart /rɑ̃par/ *n.m.* rampart.

remplaçant, ∼**e** /rɑ̃plasɑ̃, -t/ *n.m., f.* replacement; (*joueur*) reserve.

remplac|er /rɑ̃plase/ *v.t.* replace. ∼**ement** *n.m.* replacement.

rempli /rɑ̃pli/ *a.* full (**de,** of).

rempl|ir /rɑ̃plir/ *v.t.* fill (up); (*formulaire*) fill (in *ou* out); (*tâche, condition*) fulfil. **se** ∼**ir** *v. pr.* fill (up). ∼**issage** *n.m.* filling; (*de texte*) padding.

remporter /rɑ̃pɔrte/ *v.t.* take back; (*victoire*) win.

remuant, ∼**e** /rəmɥɑ̃, -t/ *a.* restless.

remue-ménage /rəmymena$ʒ$/ *n.m. invar.* commotion, bustle.

remuer /rəmɥe/ *v.t./i.* move; (*thé, café*) stir; (*gigoter*) fidget. **se** ∼ *v. pr.* move.

rémunér|er /remynere/ *v.t.* pay. ∼**ation** *n.f.* payment.

renâcler /rənɑkle/ *v.i.* snort. ∼ **à,** balk at, jib at.

ren|aître /rənɛtr/ *v.i.* be reborn; (*sentiment*) be revived. ∼**aissance** *n.f.* rebirth.

renard /rənar/ *n.m.* fox.

renchérir /rɑ̃ʃerir/ *v.i.* become dearer. ∼ **sur,** go one better than.

rencontr|e /rɑ̃kɔ̃tr/ *n.f.* meeting; (*de routes*) junction; (*mil.*) encounter; (*match*) match; (*Amer.*) game. ∼**er** *v.t.* meet; (*heurter*) strike; (*trouver*) find. **se** ∼ *v. pr.* meet.

rendement /rɑ̃dmɑ̃/ *n.m.* yield; (*travail*) output.

rendez-vous /rɑ̃devu/ *n.m.* appointment; (*d'amoureux*) date; (*lieu*) meeting-place. **prendre** ∼ (**avec**), make an appointment (with).

rendormir (se) /(sə)rɑ̃dɔrmir/ *v. pr.* go back to sleep.

rendre /rɑ̃dr/ *v.t.* give back, return; (*donner en retour*) return; (*monnaie*) give; (*hommage*) pay; (*justice*) dispense; (*jugement*) pronounce. ∼ **heureux/possible/etc.,** make happy/possible/etc. —*v.i.* (*terres*) yield; (*vomir*) vomit. **se** ∼ *v. pr.* (*capituler*) surrender; (*aller*) go (**à,** to); (*ridicule, utile, etc.*) make o.s. ∼ **compte de,** report on. ∼ **des comptes à,** be accountable to. ∼ **justice à qn.,** do s.o. justice. ∼ **service (à),** help. ∼ **visite à,** visit. **se** ∼ **compte de,** realize.

rendu /rɑ̃dy/ *a.* **être** ∼, (*arrivé*) have arrived.

rêne /rɛn/ *n.f.* rein.

renégat, **~e** /ʀɔnega, -t/ *n.m.*, *f.* renegade.

renfermé /ʀɑ̃fɛʀme/ *n.m.* stale smell. **sentir le ~**, smell stale. —*a.* withdrawn.

renfermer /ʀɑ̃fɛʀme/ *v.t.* contain. **se ~ (en soi-même)**, withdraw (into o.s.).

renfl|**é** /ʀɑ̃fle/ *a.* bulging. **~ement** *n.m.* bulge.

renflouer /ʀɑ̃flue/ *v.t.* refloat.

renfoncement /ʀɑ̃fɔ̃smɑ̃/ *n.m.* recess.

renforcer /ʀɑ̃fɔʀse/ *v.t.* reinforce.

renfort /ʀɑ̃fɔʀ/ *n.m.* reinforcement. **de ~**, (*armée, personnel*) back-up. **à grand ~ de**, with a great deal of.

renfrogn|**er (se)** /(sɔ)ʀɑ̃fʀɔɲe/ *v. pr.* scowl. **~é** *a.* surly, sullen.

rengaine /ʀɑ̃gɛn/ *n.f.* (*péj.*). **la même ~**, the same old story.

renier /ʀɔnje/ *v.t.* (*personne, pays*) disown, deny; (*foi*) renounce.

renifler /ʀɔnifle/ *v.t./i.* sniff.

renne /ʀɛn/ *n.m.* reindeer.

renom /ʀɔnɔ̃/ *n.m.* renown; (*réputation*) reputation. **~mé** /-ɔme/ *a.* famous. **~mée** /-ɔme/ *n.f.* fame; reputation.

renonc|**er** /ʀɔnɔ̃se/ *v.i.* **~er à**, (*habitude, ami, etc.*) give up, renounce. **~er à faire**, give up (all thought of) doing. **~ement** *n.m.*, **~iation** *n.f.* renunciation.

renouer /ʀɔnwe/ *v.t.* tie up (again); (*reprendre*) renew. —*v.i.* **avec**, start up again with.

renouveau (*pl.* **~x**) /ʀɔnuvo/ *n.m.* revival.

renouvel|**er** /ʀɔnuvle/ *v.t.* renew; (*réitérer*) repeat. **se ~er** *v. pr.* be renewed; be repeated. **~lement** /-vɛlmɑ̃/ *n.m.* renewal.

rénov|**er** /ʀenɔve/ *v.t.* (*édifice*) renovate; (*institution*) reform. **~ation** *n.f.* renovation; reform.

renseignement /ʀɑ̃sɛɲmɑ̃/ *n.m.* **~(s)**, information. **(bureau des) ~s**, information desk.

renseigner /ʀɑ̃sɛɲe/ *v.t.* inform, give information to. **se ~** *v. pr.* enquire, make enquiries, find out.

rentab|**le** /ʀɑ̃tabl/ *a.* profitable. **~ilité** *n.f.* profitability.

rent|**e** /ʀɑ̃t/ *n.f.* (private) income; (*pension*) pension, annuity. **~ier**, **~ière** *n.m.*, *f.* person of private means.

rentrée /ʀɑ̃tʀe/ *n.f.* return; **la ~ parlementaire**, the reopening of Parliament; (*scol.*) start of the new year.

rentrer /ʀɑ̃tʀe/ (*aux. être*) *v.i.* go ou come back home, return home; (*entrer*) go ou come in; (*entrer à nouveau*) go ou come back in; (*revenu*) come in; (*élèves*) go back. **~ dans**, (*heurter*) smash into. —*v.t.* (*aux. avoir*) bring in; (*griffes*) draw in; (*vêtement*) tuck in. **~ dans l'ordre**, be back to normal. **~ dans ses frais**, break even.

renverse (à la) /(ala)ʀɑ̃vɛʀs/ *adv.* backwards.

renvers|**er** /ʀɑ̃vɛʀse/ *v.t.* knock over ou down; (*piéton*) knock down; (*liquide*) upset, spill; (*mettre à l'envers*) turn upside down; (*gouvernement*) overturn; (*inverser*) reverse. **se ~er** *v. pr.* (*véhicule*) overturn; (*verre, vase*) fall over. **~ement** *n.m.* (*pol.*) overthrow.

renv|**oi** /ʀɑ̃vwa/ *n.m.* return; dismissal; expulsion; postponement; reference; (*rot*) belch. **~oyer†** *v.t.* send back, return; (*employé*) dismiss; (*élève*) expel; (*ajourner*) postpone; (*référer*) refer; (*réfléchir*) reflect.

réorganiser /ʀeɔʀɡanize/ *v.t.* reorganize.

réouverture /ʀeuvɛʀtyʀ/ *n.f.* reopening.

repaire /rəpɛr/ *n.m.* den.

répandre /repɑ̃dr/ *v.t.* (*liquide*) spill; (*étendre, diffuser*) spread; (*lumière, sang*) shed; (*odeur*) give off. **se ~** *v. pr.* spread; (*liquide*) spill. **se ~ en,** (*injures etc.*) pour forth, launch forth into.

répandu /repɑ̃dy/ *a.* (*courant*) widespread.

réparer /repare/ *v.t.* repair, mend; (*faute*) make amends for; (*remédier à*) put right. **~ateur** *n.m.* repairer. **~ation** *n.f.* repair; (*compensation*) compensation.

repartie /rəparti/ *n.f.* retort. **avoir (le sens) de la ~,** be good at repartee.

repartir† /rəpartir/ *v.i.* start (up) again; (*voyageur*) set off again; (*s'en retourner*) go back.

répart|ir /rəpartir/ *v.t.* distribute; (*partager*) share out; (*étaler*) spread. **~ition** *n.f.* distribution.

repas /rəpɑ/ *n.m.* meal.

repass|er /rəpase/ *v.i.* come ou go back. —*v.t.* (*linge*) iron; (*leçon*) go over; (*examen*) retake, (*film*) show again. **~age** *n.m.* ironing.

repêcher /rəpeʃe/ *v.t.* fish out; (*candidat*) allow to pass.

repentir /rəpɑ̃tir/ *n.m.* repentance. **se ~** *v. pr.* (*relig.*) repent (**de,** of). **se ~ de,** (*regretter*) regret.

répercu|ter /repɛrkyte/ *v.t.* (*bruit*) echo. **se ~ter** *v. pr.* echo. **se ~ter sur,** have repercussions on. **~ssion** *n.f.* repercussion.

repère /rəpɛr/ *n.m.* mark; (*jalon*) marker; (*fig.*) landmark.

repérer /rəpere/ *v.t.* locate, spot. **se ~** *v. pr.* find one's bearings.

répert|oire /repɛrtwar/ *n.m.* index; (*artistique*) repertoire. **~orier** *v.t.* index.

répéter /repete/ *v.t.* repeat. —*v.t./i.* (*théâtre*) rehearse. **se ~** *v. pr.* be repeated; (*personne*) repeat o.s.

répétition /repetisjɔ̃/ *n.f.* repetition; (*théâtre*) rehearsal.

repiquer /rəpike/ *v.t.* (*plante*) plant out.

répit /repi/ *n.m.* rest, respite.

replacer /rəplase/ *v.t.* replace.

repl|i /rəpli/ *n.m.* fold; (*retrait*) withdrawal. **~ier** *v.t.* fold (up); (*ailes, jambes*) tuck in. **se ~ier** *v. pr.* withdraw (**sur soi-même,** into o.s.).

répliqu|e /replik/ *n.f.* reply; (*riposte*) retort; (*discussion*) objection; (*théâtre*) line(s); (*copie*) replica. **~er** *v.t./i.* reply; (*riposter*) retort; (*objecter*) answer back.

répondant, ~e /repɔ̃dɑ̃, -t/ *n.m., f.* guarantor. **avoir du ~,** have money behind one.

répondeur /repɔ̃dœr/ *n.m.* answering machine.

répondre /repɔ̃dr/ *v.t.* (*remarque etc.*) reply with. **~ que,** answer ou reply that. —*v.i.* answer, reply; (*être insolent*) answer back; (*réagir*) respond (**à,** to). **~ à,** answer. **~ de,** answer for.

réponse /repɔ̃s/ *n.f.* answer, reply; (*fig.*) response.

report /rəpɔr/ *n.m.* (*transcription*) transfer; (*renvoi*) postponement.

reportage /rəpɔrtaʒ/ *n.m.* report; (*en direct*) commentary; (*par écrit*) article.

reporter¹ /rəpɔrte/ *v.t.* take back; (*ajourner*) put off; (*transcrire*) transfer. **se ~ à,** refer to.

reporter² /rəpɔrtɛr/ *n.m.* reporter.

repos /rəpo/ *n.m.* rest; (*paix*) peace; (*tranquillité*) peace and quiet; (*moral*) peace of mind.

repos|er /rəpoze/ *v.t.* put down again; (*délasser*) rest. —*v.i.* rest (**sur,** on). **se ~er** *v. pr.* rest. **se ~er sur,** rely on. **~ant, ~ante** *a.* restful. **laisser ~er,** (*pâte*) leave to stand.

repoussant /ʀəpusɑ̃/, **~e** /ʀəpusɑ̃, -t/ *a.* repulsive.

repousser /ʀəpuse/ *v.t.* push back; (*écarter*) push away; (*dégoûter*) repel; (*décliner*) reject; (*ajourner*) put back. —*v.i.* grow again.

répréhensible /ʀepʀeɑ̃sibl/ *a.* blameworthy.

reprendre† /ʀəpʀɑ̃dʀ/ *v.t.* take back; (*retrouver*) regain; (*évadé*) recapture; (*recommencer*) resume; (*redire*) repeat; (*modifier*) alter; (*blâmer*) reprimand. **~ du pain**/*etc.*, take some more bread/*etc.* —*v.i.* (*recommencer*) resume; (*affaires*) pick up. **se ~** *v. pr.* (*se ressaisir*) pull o.s. together; (*se corriger*) correct o.s. **on ne m'y reprendra pas,** I won't be caught out again.

représailles /ʀəpʀezaj/ *n.f. pl.* reprisals.

représentati|f, **~ve** /ʀəpʀezɑ̃tatif, -v/ *a.* representative.

représent|er /ʀəpʀezɑ̃te/ *v.t.* represent; (*théâtre*) perform. **se ~er** *v. pr.* (*s'imaginer*) imagine. **~ant,** **~ante** *n.m., f.* representative. **~ation** *n.f.* representation; (*théâtre*) performance.

réprimand|e /ʀepʀimɑ̃d/ *n.f.* reprimand. **~er** *v.t.* reprimand.

réprim|er /ʀepʀime/ *v.t.* repress; (*sentiment*) suppress. **~ession** *n.f.* repression.

repris /ʀəpʀi/ *n.m.* **~ de justice,** ex-convict.

reprise /ʀəpʀiz/ *n.f.* resumption; (*théâtre*) revival; (*télévision*) repeat; (*de tissu*) darn, mend; (*essor*) recovery; (*comm.*) part-exchange, trade-in. **à plusieurs ~s,** on several occasions.

repriser /ʀəpʀize/ *v.t.* darn, mend.

réprobation /ʀepʀɔbasjɔ̃/ *n.f.* condemnation.

reproch|e /ʀəpʀɔʃ/ *n.m.* reproach, blame. **~er** *v.t.* **~er qch. à qn.,** reproach *ou* blame s.o. for sth.

reprodui|re† /ʀəpʀɔdɥiʀ/ *v.t.* reproduce. **se ~uire** *v. pr.* reproduce; (*arriver*) recur. **~uc-teur, ~uctrice** *a.* reproductive. **~uction** *n.f.* reproduction.

réprouver /ʀepʀuve/ *v.t.* condemn.

reptile /ʀeptil/ *n.m.* reptile.

repu /ʀəpy/ *a.* satiated.

républi|que /ʀepyblik/ *n.f.* republic. **~que populaire,** people's republic. **~cain, ~caine** *a. & n.m., f.* republican.

répudier /ʀepydje/ *v.t.* repudiate.

répugnance /ʀepyɲɑ̃s/ *n.f.* repugnance; (*hésitation*) reluctance.

répugn|er /ʀepyɲe/ *v.i.* **~er à,** be repugnant to. **~er à faire,** be reluctant to do. **~ant, ~ante** *a.* repulsive.

répulsion /ʀepylsjɔ̃/ *n.f.* repulsion.

réputation /ʀepytasjɔ̃/ *n.f.* reputation.

réputé /ʀepyte/ *a.* renowned (**pour,** for). **~ pour être,** reputed to be.

requérir /ʀəkeʀiʀ/ *v.t.* require, demand.

requête /ʀəkɛt/ *n.f.* request; (*jurid.*) petition.

requiem /ʀekɥijɛm/ *n.m. invar.* requiem.

requin /ʀəkɛ̃/ *n.m.* shark.

requis, ~e /ʀəki, -z/ *a.* required.

réquisition /ʀekizisjɔ̃/ *n.f.* requisition. **~ner** /-jɔne/ *v.t.* requisition.

rescapé, ~e /ʀeskape/ *n.m., f.* survivor. —*a.* surviving.

rescousse /ʀeskus/ *n.f.* **à la ~,** to the rescue.

réseau (*pl.* **~x**) /ʀezo/ *n.m.* network.

réservation /ʀezɛʀvasjɔ̃/ *n.f.* reservation. **bureau de ~,** booking office.

réserve /ʀezɛʀv/ *n.f.* reserve; (*restriction*) reservation, reserve; (*indienne*) reservation; (*entrepôt*) store-room. **en ~,** in reserve. **les ~s,** (mil.) the reserves.

réserv|er /rezɛrve/ v.t. reserve; (place) book, reserve. **se ~er le droit de,** reserve the right to. **—é** a. (personne, place) reserved.

réserviste /rezɛrvist/ n.m. reservist.

réservoir /rezɛrvwar/ n.m. tank; (lac) reservoir.

résidence /rezidɑ̃s/ n.f. residence.

résiden|t, ~te /rezidɑ̃, -t/ n.m., f. resident foreigner. **~iel, ~ielle** /-sjɛl/ a. residential.

résider /rezide/ v.i. reside.

résidu /rezidy/ n.m. residue.

résign|er (se) /(sə)rezine/ v. pr. **se ~er à faire,** resign o.s. to doing. **~ation** n.f. resignation.

résilier /rezilje/ v.t. terminate.

résille /rezij/ n.f. (hair-)net.

résine /rezin/ n.f. resin.

résistance /rezistɑ̃s/ n.f. resistance; (fil électrique) element.

résistant, ~e /rezistɑ̃, -t/ a. tough.

résister /reziste/ v.i. resist. **~ à,** resist; (examen, chaleur) stand up to.

résolu /rezɔly/ voir **résoudre. —**a. resolute. **~, à,** resolved to. **~ment** adv. resolutely.

résolution /rezɔlysjɔ̃/ n.f. (fermeté) resolution; (d'un problème) solving.

résonance /rezɔnɑ̃s/ n.f. resonance.

résonner /rezɔne/ v.i. resound.

résor|ber /rezɔrbe/ v.t. reduce. **se ~ber** v. pr. be reduced. **~ption** n.f. reduction.

résoudre† /rezudr/ v.t. solve; (décider) decide on. **se ~ à,** resolve to.

respect /rɛspɛ/ n.m. respect.

respectab|le /rɛspɛktabl/ a. respectable. **~ilité** n.f. respectability.

respecter /rɛspɛkte/ v.t. respect. **faire ~,** (loi, décision) enforce.

respecti|f, ~ve /rɛspɛktif, -v/ a. respective. **~vement** adv. respectively.

respectueu|x, ~se /rɛspɛktɥø, -z/ a. respectful.

respir|er /rɛspire/ v.i. breathe; (se reposer) get one's breath. **—**v.t. breathe; (exprimer) radiate. **~ation** n.f. breathing; (haleine) breath. **~atoire** a. breathing.

resplend|ir /rɛsplɑ̃dir/ v.i. shine (de, with). **~issant, ~issante** a. radiant.

responsabilité /rɛspɔ̃sabilite/ n.f. responsibility; (légale) liability.

responsable /rɛspɔ̃sabl/ a. responsible (de, for). **~ de,** (chargé de) in charge of. **—**n.m./f. person in charge; (coupable) person responsible.

resquiller /rɛskije/ v.i. (fam.) get in without paying; (dans la queue) jump the queue.

ressaisir (se) /(sə)rəsezir/ v. pr. pull o.s. together.

ressasser /rəsase/ v.t. keep going over.

ressembl|er /rəsɑ̃ble/ v.i. **~er à,** resemble, look like. **se ~er** v. pr. look alike. **~ance** n.f. resemblance. **~ant, ~ante** a. (portrait) true to life; (pareil) alike.

ressemeler /rəsəmle/ v.t. sole.

ressentiment /rəsɑ̃timɑ̃/ n.m. resentment.

ressentir /rəsɑ̃tir/ v.t. feel. **se ~ de,** feel the effects of.

resserre /rəsɛr/ n.f. shed.

resserrer /rəsere/ v.t. tighten; (contracter) contract. **se ~** v. pr. tighten; contract; (route etc.) narrow.

resservir /rəsɛrvir/ v.i. come in useful (again).

ressort /rəsɔr/ n.m. (objet) spring; (fig.) energy. **du ~ de,** within the jurisdiction ou scope of. **en dernier ~,** in the last resort.

ressortir† /rəsɔrtir/ *v.i.* go *ou* come back out; (*se voir*) stand out. **faire** ~, bring out. ~ **de**, (*résulter*) result *ou* emerge from.

ressortissant, ~**e** /rəsɔrtisɑ̃, -t/ *n.m., f.* national.

ressource /rəsurs/ *n.f.* resource. ~**s**, resources.

ressusciter /resysite/ *v.i.* come back to life.

restant, ~**e** /rɛstɑ̃, -t/ *a.* remaining. —*n.m.* remainder.

restaur|ant, ~**ateur**, ~**atrice** /rɛstɔrɑ̃, -atœr, -atris/ *n.m.* restaurant. ~**ateur**, ~**atrice** *n.m., f.* restaurant owner.

restaur|er /rɛstɔre/ *v.t.* restore. **se** ~**er** *v. pr.* eat. ~**ation** *n.f.* restoration; (*hôtellerie*) catering.

reste /rɛst/ *n.m.* rest; (*d'une soustraction*) remainder. ~**s**, remains (**de**, of); (*nourriture*) leftovers. **un** ~ **de pain/***etc.*, some left-over bread/*etc.* **au** ~, **du** ~, moreover, besides.

rest|er /rɛste/ *v.i.* (*aux. être*) stay, remain; (*subsister*) be left, remain. **il** ~**e du pain/***etc.*, there is some bread/*etc.* left (over). **il me** ~**e du pain**, I have some bread left (over). **il me** ~**e à**, it remains for me to. **en** ~**er à**, go no further than. **en** ~**er là**, stop there.

restitu|er /rɛstitɥe/ *v.t.* (*rendre*) return, restore; (*son*) reproduce. ~**tion** *n.f.* return.

restreindre† /rɛstrɛ̃dr/ *v.t.* restrict. **se** ~ *v. pr.* (*dans les dépenses*) cut down.

restricti|f, ~**ve** /rɛstriktif, -v/ *a.* restrictive.

restriction /rɛstriksjɔ̃/ *n.f.* restriction.

résultat /rezylta/ *n.m.* result.

résulter /rezylte/ *v.i.* ~ **de**, result from.

résum|er /rezyme/ *v.t.*, **se** ~ *v. pr.* summarize. ~**é** *n.m.* summary. **en** ~**é**, in short.

résurrection /rezyrɛksjɔ̃/ *n.f.* resurrection; (*renouveau*) revival.

rétabl|ir /retablir/ *v.t.* restore; (*personne*) restore to health. **se** ~**ir** *v. pr.* be restored; (*guérir*) recover. ~**issement** *n.m.* restoring; (*méd.*) recovery.

retaper /rətape/ *v.t.* (*maison etc.*) do up. **se** ~ *v. pr.* (*guérir*) get back on one's feet.

retard /rətar/ *n.m.* lateness; (*sur un programme*) delay; (*infériorité*) backwardness. **avoir du** ~, be late; (*montre*) be slow. **en** ~, late; (*retardé*) backward. **en** ~ **sur**, behind. **rattraper** *ou* **combler son** ~, catch up.

retardataire /rətardatɛr/ *n.m./f.* latecomer. —*a.* (*arrivant*) late.

retardé /rətarde/ *a.* backward.

retardement (à) /(a)rətardəmɑ̃/ *a.* (*bombe etc.*) delayed-action.

retarder /rətarde/ *v.t.* delay; (*sur un programme*) set back; (*montre*) put back. —*v.i.* (*montre*) be slow; (*fam.*) be out of touch.

retenir† /rətnir/ *v.t.* hold back; (*souffle, attention, prisonnier*) hold; (*eau, chaleur*) retain, hold; (*larmes*) hold back; (*garder*) keep; (*retarder*) detain; (*réserver*) book; (*se rappeler*) remember; (*déduire*) deduct; (*accepter*) accept. **se** ~ *v. pr.* (*se contenir*) restrain o.s. **se** ~ **à**, hold on to. **se** ~ **de**, stop o.s. from.

rétention /retɑ̃sjɔ̃/ *n.f.* retention.

retent|ir /rətɑ̃tir/ *v.i.* ring out (**de**, with). ~**issant**, ~**issante** *a.* resounding. ~**issement** *n.m.* (*effet, répercussion*) effect.

retenue /rətny/ *n.f.* restraint; (*somme*) deduction; (*scol.*) detention.

réticen|t, ~**te** /retisɑ̃, -t/ *a.* (*hésitant*) reluctant; (*réservé*) reticent. ~**ce** *n.f.* reluctance; reticence.

rétif, **~ve** /retif, -v/ *a.* restive, recalcitrant.

rétine /retin/ *n.f.* retina.

retiré /ʀ(ə)tire/ *a.* (*vie*) secluded; (*lieu*) remote.

retirer /ʀ(ə)tire/ *v.t.* (*sortir*) take out; (*ôter*) take off; (*argent, candidature*) withdraw; (*avantage*) derive. **~ à qn.**, take away from s.o. **se ~** *v. pr.* withdraw, retire.

retombées /ʀ(ə)tɔ̃be/ *n.f. pl.* fall-out.

retomber /ʀ(ə)tɔ̃be/ *v.i.* fall; (*à nouveau*) fall again. **~ dans**, (*erreur etc.*) fall back into.

rétorquer /retɔrke/ *v.t.* retort.

rétorsion /retɔrsjɔ̃/ *n.f.* **mesures de ~**, retaliation.

retouch|e /ʀ(ə)tuʃ/ *n.f.* touch-up; alteration. **~er** *v.t.* touch up; (*vêtement*) alter.

retour /ʀ(ə)tur/ *n.m.* return. **être de ~**, be back (**de**, from). **~ en arrière**, flashback. **par ~ du courrier**, by return of post. **en ~**, in return.

retourner /ʀ(ə)turne/ *v.t.* (*aux. avoir*) turn over; (*lettre, compliment*) return; (*émouvoir: fam.*) upset. —*v.i.* (*aux. être*) go back, return. **se ~** *v. pr.* turn round; (*dans son lit*) twist and turn. **s'en ~**, go back. **se ~ contre**, turn against.

retracer /ʀ(ə)trase/ *v.t.* retrace.

rétracter /retrakte/ *v.t.*, **se ~** *v. pr.* retract.

retrait /ʀ(ə)trɛ/ *n.m.* withdrawal; (*des eaux*) ebb, receding. **être** (**situé**) **en ~**, be set back.

retraite /ʀ(ə)trɛt/ *n.f.* retirement; (*pension*) (retirement) pension; (*fuite, refuge*) retreat. **mettre à la ~**, pension off. **prendre sa ~**, retire.

retraité, **~e** /ʀ(ə)trete/ *a.* retired. —*n.m.*, *f.* (old-age) pensioner, senior citizen.

retrancher /ʀ(ə)trɑ̃ʃe/ *v.t.* remove; (*soustraire*) deduct. **se ~** *v. pr.*

(*mil.*) entrench o.s. **se ~ derrière/dans**, take refuge behind/in.

retransm|ettre /ʀ(ə)trɑ̃smɛtr/ *v.t.* broadcast. **~ission** *n.f.* broadcast.

rétrécir /retresir/ *v.t.* narrow; (*vêtement*) take in. —*v.i.* (*tissu*) shrink. **se ~**, (*rue*) narrow.

rétribu|er /retribɥe/ *v.t.* pay. **~ution** *n.f.* payment.

rétroacti|f, **~ve** /retrɔaktif, -v/ *a.* retrospective. **augmentation à effet ~f**, backdated pay rise.

rétrograd|e /retrɔgrad/ *a.* retrograde. **~er** *v.i.* (*reculer*) fall back, recede; *v.t.* demote.

rétrospectivement /retrɔspɛktivmɑ̃/ *adv.* in retrospect.

retrousser /ʀ(ə)truse/ *v.t.* pull up.

retrouvailles /ʀ(ə)truvaj/ *n.f. pl.* reunion.

retrouver /ʀ(ə)truve/ *v.t.* find (again); (*rejoindre*) meet (again); (*forces, calme*) regain; (*se rappeler*) remember. **se ~** *v. pr.* find o.s. (back); (*se réunir*) meet (again). **s'y ~**, (*s'orienter, comprendre*) find one's way; (*rentrer dans ses frais*) break even.

rétroviseur /retrɔvizœr/ *n.m.* (*auto.*) (rear-view) mirror.

réunion /reynjɔ̃/ *n.f.* meeting; (*d'objets*) collection.

réunir /reynir/ *v.t.* gather, collect; (*rapprocher*) bring together; (*convoquer*) call together; (*raccorder*) join; (*qualités*) combine. **se ~** *v. pr.* meet.

réussi /reysi/ *a.* successful.

réussir /reysir/ *v.i.* succeed, be successful (**à faire, in doing**). **~ à qn.**, work well for s.o.; (*climat etc.*) agree with s.o. —*v.t.* make a success of.

réussite /reysit/ *n.f.* success; (*jeu*) patience.

revaloir /ʀ(ə)valwar/ *v.t.* **je vous**

revaudrai cela, (en mal) I'll pay you back for this; (en bien) I'll repay you some day.

revaloriser /rəvalɔrize/ v.t. (monnaie) revalue; (salaires) raise.

revanche /rəvɑ̃ʃ/ n.f. revenge. (sport) return ou revenge match. **en ～**, on the other hand.

revasser /revase/ v.i. day-dream.

rêve /rɛv/ n.m. dream. **faire un ～**, have a dream.

revêche /rəvɛʃ/ a. ill-tempered.

réveil /revɛj/ n.m. waking up, (fig.) awakening; (pendule) alarm-clock.

réveill|er /reveje/ v.t. **se ～er** v. pr. wake (up); (fig.) awaken. **～é** a. awake. **～e-matin** n.m. invar. alarm-clock.

réveillon /revejɔ̃/ n.m. (Noël) Christmas Eve; (nouvel an) New Year's Eve. **～ner** /-jɔne/ v.i. celebrate the réveillon.

révél|er /revele/ v.t. reveal. **se ～er** v. pr. be revealed. se **～er facile**/etc., prove easy/etc. **～ateur, ～atrice** a. revealing. —n.m. (photo) developer. **～ation** n.f. revelation.

revenant /rəvnɑ̃/ n.m. ghost.

revendi|quer /rəvɑ̃dike/ v.t. claim. **～catif, ～cative** a. (mouvement etc.) in support of one's claims. **～cation** n.f. claim; (action) claiming.

revend|re /rəvɑ̃dr/ v.t. sell (again). **～eur, ～euse** n.m., f. dealer.

revenir† /rəvnir/ v.i. (aux. être) come back, return (à, to). **～ à**, (activité) go back to; (se résumer à) come down to; (échoir à) fall to; (coûter) cost. **～ de**, (maladie, surprise) get over. **～ sur ses pas**, retrace one's steps. **faire ～**, (culin.) brown. **ça me revient**, it comes back to me.

revente /rəvɑ̃t/ n.f. resale.

revenu /rəvny/ n.m. income; (d'un état) revenue.

rêver /reve/ v.t./i. dream (à ou de, of).

réverbération /reverberasjɔ̃/ n.f. reflection, reverberation.

réverbère /reverber/ n.m. street lamp.

révérenc|e /reverɑ̃s/ n.f. reverence; (salut d'homme) bow; (salut de femme) curtsy. **～ieuse** a. reverent.

révérend, ～e /reverɑ̃, -d/ a. & n.m. reverend.

rêverie /revri/ n.f. day-dream; (activité) day-dreaming.

revers /rəver/ n.m. reverse; (de main) back; (d'étoffe) wrong side; (de veste) lapel; (tennis) backhand; (fig.) set-back.

réversible /reversibl/ a. reversible.

revêt|ir† /rəvetir/ v.t. cover; (habit) put on; (prendre, avoir) assume. **～ement** /-vetmɑ̃/ n.m. covering; (de route) surface.

rêveu|r, ～se /revœr, -øz/ a. dreamy. —n.m., f. dreamer.

revigorer /rəvigɔre/ v.t. revive.

revirement /rəvirmɑ̃/ n.m. sudden change.

révis|er /revize/ v.t. revise; (véhicule) overhaul. **～ion** n.f. revision; overhaul.

revivre† /rəvivr/ v.i. live again. —v.t. relive. **faire ～**, revive.

révocation /revɔkasjɔ̃/ n.f. repeal; (d'un fonctionnaire) dismissal.

revoir† /rəvwar/ v.t. see (again); (réviser) revise. **au ～**, goodbye.

révolte /revɔlt/ n.f. revolt.

révolt|er /revɔlte/ v.t., **se ～er** v. pr. revolt. **～ant, ～ante** a. revolting. **～é, ～ée** n.m., f. rebel.

révolu /revɔly/ a. past.

révolution /revɔlysjɔ̃/ n.f. revolution. **～naire** /-jɔner/ a. & n.m./f. revolutionary. **～ner** /-jɔne/ v.t. revolutionize.

revolver /revɔlver/ n.m. revolver, gun.

révoquer /revɔke/ *v.t.* repeal; *(fonctionnaire)* dismiss.

revue /rəvy/ *n.f.* *(examen, défilé)* review; *(magazine)* magazine; *(spectacle)* variety show.

rez-de-chaussée /redʃose/ *n.m. invar.* ground floor; *(Amer.)* first floor.

RF *abrév.* *(République Française)* French Republic.

rhabiller (se) /(sə)rabije/ *v. pr.* get dressed (again), dress (again).

rhapsodie /rapsɔdi/ *n.f.* rhapsody.

rhétorique /retɔrik/ *n.f.* rhetoric. —*a.* rhetorical.

rhinocéros /rinɔserɔs/ *n.m.* rhinoceros.

rhubarbe /rybarb/ *n.f.* rhubarb.

rhum /rɔm/ *n.m.* rum.

rhumatis|me /rymatism/ *n.m.* rheumatism. ~ant, ~ante /-zã, -t/ *a.* rheumatic.

rhume /rym/ *n.m.* cold. ~ des foins, hay fever.

ri /ri/ *voir* rire.

riant, ~e /rjã, -t/ *a.* cheerful.

ricaner /rikane/ *v.i.* snigger, giggle.

riche /riʃ/ *a.* rich (en, in). —*n.m./f.* rich person. ~ment *adv.* richly.

richesse /riʃes/ *n.f.* wealth; *(de sol, décor)* richness. ~s, wealth.

ricoch|er /rikɔʃe/ *v.i.* rebound, ricochet. ~et, *n.m.* rebound, ricochet. par ~et, indirectly.

rictus /riktys/ *n.m.* grin, rictus.

rid|e /rid/ *n.f.* wrinkle; *(sur l'eau)* ripple. ~er *v.t.* wrinkle; *(eau)* ripple.

rideau *(pl.* ~x) /rido/ *n.m.* curtain; *(métallique)* shutter; *(fig.)* screen. ~ de fer, *(pol.)* Iron Curtain.

ridicul|e /ridikyl/ *a.* ridiculous. —*n.m.* absurdity. le ~e, ridicule. ~iser *v.t.* ridicule.

rien /rjɛ̃/ *pron.* (ne) ~, nothing. —*n.m.* trifle. de ~!, don't mention it! ~ d'autre/de plus,

nothing else/more. ~ du tout, nothing at all. ~ que, just, only. trois fois ~, next to nothing. il n'y est pour ~, he has nothing to do with it. en un ~ de temps, in next to no time. ~ à faire, it's no good!

rieu|r, ~se /rjœr, rjøz/ *a.* merry.

rigid|e /riʒid/ *a.* rigid; *(muscle)* stiff. ~ité *n.f.* rigidity; stiffness.

rigole /rigɔl/ *n.f.* channel.

rigol|er /rigɔle/ *v.i.* laugh; *(s'amuser)* have some fun; *(plaisanter)* joke. ~ade *n.f.* fun.

rigolo, ~te /rigɔlo, -ɔt/ *a. (fam.)* funny. —*n.m., f. (fam.)* joker.

rigoureu|x, ~se /rigurø, -z/ *a.* rigorous; *(hiver)* harsh. ~sement *adv.* rigorously.

rigueur /rigœr/ *n.f.* rigour. à la ~, at a pinch. être de ~, be the rule. tenir ~ à qn. de qch., hold sth. against s.o.

rim|e /rim/ *n.f.* rhyme. ~er *v.i.* rhyme (avec, with). cela ne ~e à rien, it makes no sense.

rin|cer /rɛ̃se/ *v.t.* rinse. ~çage *n.m.* rinse; *(action)* rinsing. ~ce-doigts *n.m. invar.* finger-bowl.

ring /riŋ/ *n.m.* boxing ring.

ripost|e /ripɔst/ *n.f.* retort; *(mil.)* reprisal. ~er *v.i.* retaliate; *v.t.* retort *(que,* that). ~er à, *(attaque)* counter; *(insulte etc.)* reply to.

rire† /rir/ *v.i.* laugh (de, at); *(plaisanter)* joke; *(s'amuser)* have fun. c'était pour ~, it was a joke. —*n.m.* laugh. ~s, le ~, laughter.

risée /rize/ *n.f.* la ~ de, the laughing-stock of.

risible /rizibl/ *a.* laughable.

risqu|e /risk/ *n.m.* risk. ~é *a.* risky; *(osé)* daring. ~er *v.t.* risk. ~er de faire, stand a good chance of doing. se ~er à/dans, venture to/into.

rissoler /risɔle/ *v.t./i.* brown. (faire) ~, brown.

ristourne /risturn/ *n.f.* discount.

rite /rit/ *n.m.* rite; (*habitude*) ritual.

rituel, ∼le /rityɛl/ *a. & n.m.* ritual.

rivage /rivaʒ/ *n.m.* shore.

riv|al, ∼ale (*m. pl.* ∼aux) /rival, -o/ *n.m.*, *f.* rival. —*a.* rival. ∼aliser *v.i.* compete (avec, with). ∼alité *n.f.* rivalry.

rive /riv/ *n.f.* (*de fleuve*) bank; (*de lac*) shore.

riv|er /rive/ *v.t.* rivet. ∼er son clou à qn., shut s.o. up. ∼et *n.m.* rivet.

riverain, ∼e /rivrɛ̃, -ɛn/ *a.* riverside. —*n.m.*, *f.* riverside resident; (*d'une rue*) resident.

rivière /rivjɛr/ *n.f.* river.

rixe /riks/ *n.f.* brawl.

riz /ri/ *n.m.* rice. ∼ière /rizjɛr/ *n.f.* paddy(-field), rice field.

robe /rɔb/ *n.f.* (*de femme*) dress; (*de juge*) robe; (*de cheval*) coat. ∼ de chambre, dressing-gown.

robinet /rɔbinɛ/ *n.m.* tap; (*Amer.*) faucet.

robot /rɔbo/ *n.m.* robot.

robuste /rɔbyst/ *a.* robust. ∼sse /-ɛs/ *n.f.* robustness.

roc /rɔk/ *n.m.* rock.

rocaill|e /rɔkaj/ *n.f.* rocky ground; (*de jardin*) rockery. ∼eux, ∼euse *a.* (*terrain*) rocky.

roch|e /rɔʃ/ *n.f.* rock. ∼eux, ∼euse *a.* rocky.

rocher /rɔʃe/ *n.m.* rock.

rock /rɔk/ *n.m.* (*mus.*) rock.

rod|er /rɔde/ *v.t.* (*auto.*) run in (*auto.*, *Amer.*) break in. être ∼é, (*personne*) be broken in. ∼age *n.m.* running in; breaking in.

rôd|er /rɔde/ *v.i.* roam; (*suspect*) prowl. ∼eur, ∼euse *n.m.*, *f.* prowler.

rogne /rɔɲ/ *n.f.* (*fam.*) anger.

rogner /rɔɲe/ *v.t.* trim; (*réduire*) cut. ∼ sur, cut down on.

rognon /rɔɲɔ̃/ *n.m.* (*culin.*) kidney.

rognures /rɔɲyr/ *n.f. pl.* scraps.

roi /rwa/ *n.m.* king. les Rois mages, the Magi. la fête des Rois, Twelfth Night.

roitelet /rwatlɛ/ *n.m.* wren.

rôle /rol/ *n.m.* role, part.

romain, ∼e /rɔmɛ̃, -ɛn/ *a. & n.m.*, *f.* Roman. —*f.* (*laitue*) cos.

roman /rɔmɑ̃/ *n.m.* novel; (*fig.*) story; (*genre*) fiction.

romance /rɔmɑ̃s/ *n.f.* sentimental ballad.

romanc|ier, ∼ière /rɔmɑ̃sje, -jɛr/ *n.m.*, *f.* novelist.

romanesque /rɔmanɛsk/ *a.* romantic (*fantastique*) fantastic. œuvres ∼s, novels, fiction.

romanichel, ∼le /rɔmaniʃɛl/ *n.m.*, *f.* gypsy.

romanti|que /rɔmɑ̃tik/ *a. & n.m./f.* romantic. ∼sme *n.m.* romanticism.

romp|re† /rɔ̃pr/ *v.t./i.* break; (*relations*) break off; (*fiancés*) break it off. se ∼ *v. pr.* break.

rompu /rɔ̃py/ *a.* (*exténué*) exhausted.

ronces /rɔ̃s/ *n.f. pl.* brambles.

ronchonner /rɔ̃ʃɔne/ *v.i.* (*fam.*) grumble.

rond, ∼e¹ /rɔ̃, rɔ̃d/ *a.* round; (*gras*) plump; (*ivre: fam.*) tight. —*n.m.* (*cercle*) ring; (*tranche*) slice. il n'a pas un ∼, (*fam.*) he hasn't got a penny. en ∼, in a circle. ∼ement /rɔ̃dmɑ̃/ *adv.* briskly; (*franchement*) straight. ∼eur /rɔ̃dœr/ *n.f.* roundness; (*franchise*) frankness; (*embonpoint*) plumpness. ∼-point (*pl.* ∼s-points) *n.m.* roundabout; (*Amer.*) traffic circle.

ronde² /rɔ̃d/ *n.f.* round(s); (*de policier*) beat; (*mus.*) semibreve.

rondelet, ∼te /rɔ̃dlɛ, -t/ *a.* chubby.

rondelle /rɔ̃dɛl/ *n.f.* (*techn.*) washer; (*tranche*) slice.

rondin /rɔ̃dɛ̃/ *n.m.* log.

ronfl|er /rɔ̃fle/ v.i. snore; (*moteur*) hum. **~ement(s)** n.m. (pl.) snoring; humming.

rong|er /rɔ̃ʒe/ v.t. gnaw (at); (*vers, acide*) eat into; (*personne: fig.*) consume. **se ~er les ongles**, bite one's nails. **~eur** n.m. rodent.

ronronn|er /rɔ̃rɔne/ v.i. purr. **~ement** n.m. purr(ing).

roquette /rɔkɛt/ n.f. rocket.

rosace /rozas/ n.f. (*d'église*) rose window.

rosaire /rozɛr/ n.m. rosary.

rosbif /rɔsbif/ n.m. roast beef.

rose /roz/ n.f. rose. —a. pink; (*situation, teint*) rosy. —n.m. pink.

rosé /roze/ a. pinkish; (*vin*) rosé. —n.m. rosé.

roseau (pl. **~x**) /rozo/ n.m. reed.

rosée /roze/ n.f. dew.

roseraie /rozrɛ/ n.f. rose garden.

rosette /rozɛt/ n.f. rosette.

rosier /rozje/ n.m. rose-bush, rose tree.

rosse /rɔs/ a. (*fam.*) nasty.

rosser /rɔse/ v.t. thrash.

rossignol /rɔsiɲɔl/ n.m. nightingale.

rot /ro/ n.m. (*fam.*) burp.

rotati|f, ~ve /rɔtatif, -v/ a. rotary.

rotation /rɔtasjɔ̃/ n.f. rotation.

roter /rɔte/ v.i. (*fam.*) burp.

rotin /rɔtɛ̃/ n.m. (rattan) cane.

rôt|ir /rotir/ v.t./i. **se ~ir** v. pr. roast. **~i** n.m. roasting meat; (*cuit*) roast. **~i de porc**, roast pork.

rôtisserie /rotisri/ n.f. grill-room.

rôtissoire /rotiswar/ n.f. (roasting) spit.

rotule /rɔtyl/ n.f. kneecap.

roturi|er, ère /rɔtyrje, -ɛr/ n.m., f. commoner.

rouage /rwaʒ/ n.m. (*techn.*) (working) part. **~s**, (*d'une organisation: fig.*) wheels.

roucouler /rukule/ v.i. coo.

roue /ru/ n.f. wheel. **~ (dentée)**, cog(-wheel). **~ de secours**, spare wheel.

roué /rwe/ a. wily, calculating.

rouer /rwe/ v.t. **~ de coups**, thrash.

rouet /rwɛ/ n.m. spinning-wheel.

rouge /ruʒ/ a. red; (*fer*) red-hot. —n.m. red; (*vin*) red wine; (*fard*) rouge. **~ (à lèvres)**, lipstick. —n.m./f. (*pol.*) red. **~-gorge** (pl. **~s-gorges**) n.m. robin.

rougeole /ruʒɔl/ n.f. measles.

rougeoyer /ruʒwaje/ v.i. glow (red).

rouget /ruʒɛ/ n.m. red mullet.

rougeur /ruʒœr/ n.f. redness; (*tache*) red blotch; (*gêne, honte*) red face.

rougir /ruʒir/ v.t./i. turn red; (*de honte*) blush.

rouille /ruj/ n.f. rust. **~é a.** rusty. **~er** v.i., **se ~er** v. pr. get rusty, rust.

roulant, ~e /rulɑ̃, -t/ a. (*meuble*) on wheels; (*escalier*) moving.

rouleau (pl. **~x**) /rulo/ n.m. roll; (*outil, vague*) roller. **~ à pâtisserie**, rolling-pin. **~ compresseur**, steamroller.

roulement /rulmɑ̃/ n.m. rotation; (*bruit*) rumble; (*succession de personnes*) turnover; (*de tambour*) roll. **~ à billes**, ball-bearing. **par ~**, in rotation.

rouler /rule/ v.t./i. roll; (*ficelle, manches*) roll up; (*duper: fam.*) cheat; (*véhicule, train*) go, travel; (*conducteur*) drive. **se ~ dans** v. pr. roll (over) in.

roulette /rulɛt/ n.f. (*de meuble*) castor; (*de dentiste*) drill; (*jeu*) roulette. **comme sur des ~s**, very smoothly.

roulis /ruli/ n.m. roll.

roulotte /rulɔt/ n.f. caravan.

roumain, ~e /rumɛ̃, -ɛn/ a. & n.m., f. Romanian.

Roumanie /rumani/ n.f. Romania.

roupiller /rupije/ v.i. (*fam.*) sleep.

rouquin, **~e** /rukɛ̃, -in/ a. (fam.) red-haired. —n.m., f. (fam.) redhead.

rouspéter /ruspete/ v.i. (fam.) grumble, moan, complain.

rousse /rus/ voir **roux**.

roussir /rusir/ v.t. scorch. —v.i. turn brown.

route /rut/ n.f. road; (naut., aviat.) route; (direction) way; (voyage) journey; (chemin: fig.) path. **en ~**, on the way. **en ~!**, let's go! **mettre en ~**, start. **~ nationale**, trunk road, main road. **se mettre en ~**, set out.

rout|ier, **~ière** /rutje, -jɛr/ a. road. —n.m. long-distance lorry driver ou truck driver (Amer.); (restaurant) roadside café.

routine /rutin/ n.f. routine.

rouvrir /ruvrir/ v.t., **se ~ir** v.pr. reopen, open again.

roux, **~sse** /ru, rus/ a. red, reddish-brown; (personne) red-haired. —n.m., f. redhead.

roy|al (m. pl. **~aux**) /rwajal, -jo/ a. royal; (total: fam.) thorough. **~alement** adv. royally.

royaume /rwajom/ n.m. kingdom. **R~-Uni** n.m. United Kingdom.

royauté /rwajote/ n.f. royalty.

ruade /rɥad, rɥad/ n.f. kick.

ruban /rybɑ̃/ n.m. ribbon; (de magnétophone) tape; (de chapeau) band. **~ adhésif**, sticky tape.

rubéole /rybeɔl/ n.f. German measles.

rubis /rybi/ n.m. ruby; (de montre) jewel.

rubrique /rybrik/ n.f. heading; (article) column.

ruche /ryʃ/ n.f. beehive.

rude /ryd/ a. rough; (pénible) tough; (grossier) crude; (fameux: fam.) tremendous. **~ment** adv. (frapper etc.) hard; (traiter) harshly; (très: fam.) awfully.

rudiment|s /rydimɑ̃/ n.m. pl. rudiments. **~aire** /-tɛr/ a. rudimentary.

rudoyer /rydwaje/ v.t. treat harshly.

rue /ry/ n.f. street.

ruée /rɥe/ n.f. rush.

ruelle /rɥɛl/ n.f. alley.

ruer /rɥe/ v.i. (cheval) kick. **se ~ dans/vers**, rush into/towards. **se ~ sur**, pounce on.

rugby /rygbi/ n.m. Rugby.

rugby|man (pl. **~men**) /rygbiman, -men/ n.m. Rugby player.

rug|ir /ryʒir/ v.i. roar. **~issement** n.m. roar.

rugueu|x, **~se** /rygø, -z/ a. rough.

ruin|e /rɥin/ n.f. ruin. **en ~e(s)**, in ruins. **~er** v.t. ruin.

ruineu|x, **~se** /rɥinø, -z/ a. ruinous.

ruisseau (pl. **~x**) /rɥiso/ n.m. stream; (rigole) gutter.

ruisseler /rɥisle/ v.i. stream.

rumeur /rymœr/ n.f. (nouvelle) rumour; (son) murmur, hum; (protestation) rumblings.

ruminer /rymine/ v.t./i. (herbe) ruminate; (méditer) meditate.

rupture /ryptyr/ n.f. break; (action) breaking; (de contrat) breach; (de pourparlers) breakdown.

rur|al (m. pl. **~aux**) /ryral, -o/ a. rural.

rus|e /ryz/ n.f. cunning; (perfidie) trickery. **une ~e**, a trick, a ruse. **~é** a. cunning.

russe /rys/ a. & n.m./f. Russian. —n.m. (lang.) Russian.

Russie /rysi/ n.f. Russia.

rustique /rystik/ a. rustic.

rustre /rystr/ n.m. lout, boor.

rutilant /rytilɑ̃, -t/ a. sparkling, gleaming.

rythm|e /ritm/ n.m. rhythm; (vitesse) rate; (de la vie) pace. **~é**, **~ique** adjs. rhythmical.

S

s' /s/ *voir* se.
sa /sa/ *voir* son[1].
SA *abrév.* (*société anonyme*) PLC.
sabbat /saba/ *n.m.* sabbath.
~**ique** *a.* année ~ique, sabbatical year.
sable /sabl/ *n.m.* sand. ~**es mouvants**, quicksands. ~**er** *v.t.* sand. ~**er le champagne**, drink champagne. ~**eux**, ~**euse**, ~**onneux**, ~**onneuse** *adjs.* sandy.
sablier /sablije/ *n.m.* (*culin.*) egg-timer.
saborder /saborde/ *v.t.* (*navire, projet*) scuttle.
sabot /sabo/ *n.m.* (*de cheval etc.*) hoof; (*chaussure*) clog; (*de frein etc.*) shoe. ~ **de Denver**, (wheel) clamp.
sabot|er /sabote/ *v.t.* sabotage; (*bâcler*) botch. ~**age** *n.m.* sabotage; (*acte*) act of sabotage. ~**eur**, ~**euse** *n.m., f.* saboteur.
sabre /sabr/ *n.m.* sabre.
sac /sak/ *n.m.* bag; (*grand, en toile*) sack. **mettre à** ~, (*maison*) ransack; (*ville*) sack. ~ **à dos**, rucksack. ~ **à main**, handbag. ~ **de couchage**, sleeping-bag. **mettre dans le même** ~, lump together.
saccad|e /sakad/ *n.f.* jerk. ~**é** *a.* jerky.
saccager /sakaʒe/ *v.t.* (*ville, pays*) sack; (*maison*) ransack; (*ravager*) wreck.
saccharine /sakarin/ *n.f.* saccharin.
sacerdoce /saserdɔs/ *n.m.* priesthood; (*fig.*) vocation.
sachet /saʃɛ/ *n.m.* (small) bag; (*de médicament etc.*) sachet. ~ **de thé**, tea-bag.
sacoche /sakɔʃ/ *n.f.* bag; (*d'élève*) satchel; (*de moto*) saddle-bag.

sacquer /sake/ *v.t.* (*fam.*) sack. **je ne peux pas le** ~, I can't stand him.
sacr|e /sakr/ *n.m.* (*de roi*) coronation; (*d'évêque*) consecration. ~**er** *v.t.* crown; consecrate.
sacré /sakre/ *a.* sacred; (*maudit: fam.*) damned.
sacrement /sakrəmɑ̃/ *n.m.* sacrament.
sacrifice /sakrifis/ *n.m.* sacrifice.
sacrifier /sakrifje/ *v.t.* sacrifice. ~ **à**, conform to. **se** ~ *v. pr.* sacrifice o.s.
sacrilège /sakrilɛʒ/ *n.m.* sacrilege. ~ *a.* sacrilegious.
sacristain /sakristɛ̃/ *n.m.* sexton.
sacristie /sakristi/ *n.f.* (*protestante*) vestry; (*catholique*) sacristy.
sacro-saint, ~**e** /sakrosɛ̃, -t/ *a.* sacrosanct.
sadi|que /sadik/ *a.* sadistic. ~ *n.m./f.* sadist. ~**sme** *n.m.* sadism.
safari /safari/ *n.m.* safari.
sagace /sagas/ *a.* shrewd.
sage /saʒ/ *a.* wise; (*docile*) good. ~ *n.m.* wise man. ~**-femme** (*pl.* ~**s-femmes**) *n.f.* midwife. ~**ment** *adv.* wisely; (*docilement*) quietly. ~**sse** /-ɛs/ *n.f.* wisdom.
Sagittaire /saʒiter/ *n.m.* **le** ~, Sagittarius.
Sahara /saara/ *n.m.* **le** ~, the Sahara (desert).
saignant, ~**e** /sɛɲɑ̃, -t/ *a.* (*culin.*) rare.
saign|er /seɲe/ *v.t./i.* bleed. ~**er du nez**, have a nosebleed. ~**ée** *n.f.* bleeding. ~**ement** *n.m.* bleeding. ~**ement de nez**, nosebleed.
saillie /saji/ *n.f.* projection. **faire** ~**ie**, project. ~**ant**, ~**ante** *a.* projecting; (*remarquable*) salient.
sain, ~**e** /sɛ̃, sɛn/ *a.* healthy; (*moralement*) sane. ~ **et sauf**,

safe and sound. **∼ement** /sɛ̃nmɑ̃/ *adv.* healthily; (*juger*) sanely.

saindoux /sɛ̃du/ *n.m.* lard.

saint, ∼e /sɛ̃, sɛ̃t/ *a.* holy; (*bon, juste*) saintly. —*n.m., f.* saint. **S∼e-Esprit** *n.m.* Holy Spirit. **S∼-Siège** *n.m.* Holy See. **S∼-Sylvestre** *n.f.* New Year's Eve. **S∼e Vierge,** Blessed Virgin.

sainteté /sɛ̃tte/ *n.f.* holiness; (*d'un lieu*) sanctity.

sais /sɛ/ *voir* **savoir.**

saisie /sezi/ *n.f.* (*jurid.*) seizure; (*comput.*) keyboarding. **∼ de données,** data capture.

sais|ir /sezir/ *v.t.* grab (hold of), seize; (*occasion, biens*) seize; (*comprendre*) grasp; (*frapper*) strike; (*comput.*) keyboard, capture. **∼i de,** (*peur*) stricken by, overcome by. **se ∼ir de,** seize. **∼issant, ∼issante** *a.* (*spectacle*) gripping.

saison /sɛzɔ̃/ *n.f.* season. **la morte ∼,** the off season. **∼nier, ∼nière** /-ɔnje, -jɛr/ *a.* seasonal.

sait /sɛ/ *voir* **savoir.**

salad|e /salad/ *n.f.* salad; (*laitue*) lettuce; (*désordre: fam.*) mess. **∼ier** *n.m.* salad bowl.

salaire /salɛr/ *n.m.* wages, salary.

salami /salami/ *n.m.* salami.

salarié, ∼e /salarje/ *a.* wage-earning. —*n.m., f.* wage-earner.

salaud /salo/ *n.m.* (*argot*) bastard.

sale /sal/ *a.* dirty, filthy; (*mauvais*) nasty.

sal|er /sale/ *v.t.* salt. **∼é a.** (*goût*) salty; (*plat*) salted; (*viande, poisson*) salt; (*grivois: fam.*) spicy; (*excessif: fam.*) steep.

saleté /salte/ *n.f.* dirtiness; (*crasse*) dirt; (*action*) dirty trick; (*obscénité*) obscenity. **∼(s),** (*camelote*) rubbish. **∼s,** (*détritus*) mess.

salière /saljɛr/ *n.f.* salt-cellar.

salin, ∼e /salɛ̃, -in/ *a.* saline.

sal|ir /salir/ *v.t.* (make) dirty; (*réputation*) tarnish. **se ∼ir** *v. pr.*

get dirty. **∼issant, ∼issante** *a.* dirty; (*étoffe*) easily dirtied.

salive /saliv/ *n.f.* saliva.

salle /sal/ *n.f.* room; (*grande, publique*) hall; (*d'hôpital*) ward; (*théâtre, cinéma*) auditorium. **∼ à manger,** dining-room. **∼ d'attente,** waiting-room. **∼ de bains,** bathroom. **∼ de séjour,** living-room. **∼ de classe,** classroom. **∼ d'embarquement,** departure lounge. **∼ d'opération,** operating theatre. **∼ des ventes,** saleroom.

salon /salɔ̃/ *n.m.* lounge; (*de coiffure, beauté*) salon; (*exposition*) show. **∼ de thé,** tea-room.

salope /salɔp/ *n.f.* (*argot*) bitch.

saloperie /salɔpri/ *n.f.* (*fam.*) (*action*) dirty trick; (*chose de mauvaise qualité*) rubbish.

salopette /salɔpɛt/ *n.f.* dungarees; (*d'ouvrier*) overalls.

salsifis /salsifi/ *n.m.* salsify.

saltimbanque /saltɛ̃bɑ̃k/ *n.m./f.* (*street ou* fairground) acrobat.

salubre /salybr/ *a.* healthy.

saluer /salɥe/ *v.t.* greet; (*en partant*) take one's leave of; (*de la tête*) nod to; (*de la main*) wave to; (*mil.*) salute.

salut /saly/ *n.m.* greeting; (*de la tête*) nod; (*de la main*) wave; (*mil.*) salute; (*sauvegarde, rachat*) salvation. —*int.* (*bonjour: fam.*) hallo; (*au revoir: fam.*) bye-bye.

salutaire /salytɛr/ *a.* salutary.

salutation /salytasjɔ̃/ *n.f.* greeting. **veuillez agréer, Monsieur, mes ∼s distingués,** yours faithfully.

salve /salv/ *n.f.* salvo.

samedi /samdi/ *n.m.* Saturday.

sanatorium /sanatɔrjɔm/ *n.m.* sanatorium.

sanctifier /sɑ̃ktifje/ *v.t.* sanctify.

sanction /sɑ̃ksjɔ̃/ *n.f.* sanction. **∼ner** /-jɔne/ *v.t.* sanction; (*punir*) punish.

sanctuaire /sɑ̃ktɥɛr/ *n.m.* sanctuary.

sandale /sɑ̃dal/ *n.f.* sandal.

sandwich /sɑ̃dwitʃ/ *n.m.* sandwich.

sang /sɑ̃/ *n.m.* blood. **~-froid** *n.m. invar.* calm, self-control. **se faire du mauvais ~** *ou* **un ~ d'encre** be worried stiff.

sanglant, ~e /sɑ̃glɑ̃, -t/ *a.* bloody.

sangl|e /sɑ̃gl/ *n.f.* strap. **~er** *v.t.* strap.

sanglier /sɑ̃glije/ *n.m.* wild boar.

sanglot /sɑ̃glo/ *n.m.* sob. **~er** /-ɔte/ *v.i.* sob.

sangsue /sɑ̃sy/ *n.f.* leech.

sanguin, ~e /sɑ̃gɛ̃, -in/ *a.* (*groupe etc.*) blood; (*caractère*) fiery.

sanguinaire /sɑ̃ginɛr/ *a.* bloodthirsty.

sanitaire /sanitɛr/ *a.* health; (*conditions*) sanitary; (*appareils, installations*) bathroom, sanitary. **~s** *n.m. pl.* bathroom.

sans /sɑ̃/ *prép.* without. **~ que vous le sachiez**, without your knowing. **~-abri** /sɑ̃zabri/ *n.m./f. invar.* homeless person. **~ ça, ~ quoi**, otherwise. **~ arrêt**, nonstop. **~ encombre/faute/tarder**, without incident/fail/delay. **~fin/goût/limite**, endless/tasteless/limitless. **~-gêne** *a. invar.* inconsiderate, thoughtless; *n.m. invar.* thoughtlessness. **~ importance / pareil / précédent / travail**, unimportant / unparalleled / unprecedented / unemployed. **~ plus**, but no more than that, but nothing more.

santé /sɑ̃te/ *n.f.* health. **à ta** *ou* **votre santé**, cheers!

saoul, ~e /su, su/ *voir* **soûl**.

saper /sape/ *v.t.* undermine.

sapeur /sapœr/ *n.m.* (*mil.*) sapper. **~-pompier** (*pl.* **~s-pompiers**) *n.m.* fireman.

saphir /safir/ *n.m.* sapphire.

sapin /sapɛ̃/ *n.m.* fir(-tree). **~ de Noël**, Christmas tree.

sarbacane /sarbakan/ *n.f.* (*jouet*) pea-shooter.

sarcas|me /sarkasm/ *n.m.* sarcasm. **~tique** *a.* sarcastic.

sarcler /sarkle/ *v.t.* weed.

sardine /sardin/ *n.f.* sardine.

sardonique /sardɔnik/ *a.* sardonic.

sarment /sarmɑ̃/ *n.m.* vine shoot.

sas /sa(s)/ *n.m.* (*naut., aviat.*) airlock.

satané /satane/ *a.* (*fam.*) blasted.

satanique /satanik/ *a.* satanic.

satellite /satelit/ *n.m.* satellite.

satin /satɛ̃/ *n.m.* satin.

satir|e /satir/ *n.f.* satire. **~ique** *a.* satirical.

satisfaction /satisfaksjɔ̃/ *n.f.* satisfaction.

satis|faire† /satisfɛr/ *v.t.* satisfy. **—v.i. ~faire à**, satisfy. **~faisant, ~faisante** *a.* (*acceptable*) satisfactory. **~fait, ~faite** *a.* satisfied (**de**, with).

satur|er /satyre/ *v.t.* saturate. **~ation** *n.f.* saturation.

sauc|e /sos/ *n.f.* sauce; (*jus de viande*) gravy. **~er** *v.t.* (*plat*) wipe. **se faire ~er** (*fam.*) get soaked. **~e tartare**, tartar sauce. **~ière** *n.f.* sauce-boat.

saucisse /sosis/ *n.f.* sausage.

saucisson /sosisɔ̃/ *n.m.* (*slicing*) sausage.

sauf¹ /sof/ *prép.* except. **~ erreur/imprévu**, barring error/the unforeseen. **~ avis contraire**, unless you hear otherwise.

sau|f², ~ve /sof, sov/ *a.* safe, unharmed. **~f-conduit** *n.m.* safe conduct.

sauge /soʒ/ *n.f.* (*culin.*) sage.

saugrenu /sogrəny/ *a.* preposterous, ludicrous.

saule /sol/ *n.m.* willow. ~ **pleureur,** weeping willow.

saumon /somɔ̃/ *n.m.* salmon. —*a. invar.* salmon-pink.

saumure /somyr/ *n.f.* brine.

sauna /sona/ *n.m.* sauna.

saupoudrer /sopudre/ *v.t.* sprinkle (**de,** with).

saut /so/ *n.m.* jump, leap. **faire un** ~ **chez qn.,** pop round to s.o.'s (place). **le** ~, (*sport*) jumping. ~ **en hauteur/longueur,** high/ long jump. ~ **périlleux,** somersault. **au** ~ **du lit,** on getting up.

sauté /sote/ *a. & n.m.* (*culin.*) sauté.

saut|er /sote/ *v.i.* jump, leap; (*exploser*) blow up; (*fusible*) blow; (*se détacher*) come off. —*v.t.* jump (over); (*page, classe*) skip. **faire** ~**er,** (*détruire*) blow up; (*fusible*) blow; (*casser*) break; (*culin.*) sauté; (*renvoyer: fam.*) kick out. ~**er à la corde,** skip. ~**er aux yeux,** be obvious. ~**e-mouton** *n.m.* leap-frog. ~**er au cou de qn.,** fling one's arms round s.o. ~**er sur une occasion,** jump at an opportunity.

sauterelle /sotrɛl/ *n.f.* grasshopper.

sautiller /sotije/ *v.i.* hop.

sauvage /sovaʒ/ *a.* wild; (*primitif, cruel*) savage; (*farouche*) unsociable; (*illégal*) unauthorized. —*n.m./f.* unsociable person; (*brute*) savage. ~**rie** *n.f.* savagery.

sauve /sov/ *voir* **sauf²**.

sauvegard|e /sovgard/ *n.f.* safeguard; (*comput.*) backup. ~**er** *v.t.* safeguard; (*comput.*) save.

sauv|er /sove/ *v.t.* save; (*d'un danger*) rescue; (*matériel*) salvage. **se** ~**er** *v. pr.* (*fuir*) run away; (*partir: fam.*) be off. ~**e- qui-peut** *n.m. invar.* stampede. ~**etage** *n.m.* rescue; salvage.

~**eteur** *n.m.* rescuer. ~**eur** *n.m.* saviour.

sauvette (à la) /(ala)sovɛt/ *adv.* hastily; (*vendre*) illicitly.

savamment /savamɑ̃/ *adv.* learnedly; (*avec habileté*) skilfully.

savan|t, /savɑ̃, -t/ *a.* learned; (*habile*) skilful. —*n.m.* scientist.

saveur /savœr/ *n.f.* flavour; (*fig.*) savour.

savoir† /savwar/ *v.t.* know; (*apprendre*) hear. **elle sait conduire/nager,** she can drive/ swim. —*n.m.* learning. **à** ~, namely. **faire** ~ **à qn. que,** inform s.o. that. **je ne saurais pas,** I could not, I cannot. (**pas**) **que je sache,** (not) as far as I know.

savon /savɔ̃/ *n.m.* soap. **passer un** ~ **à qn.,** (*fam.*) give s.o. a dressing down. ~**ner** /-ɔne/ *v.t.* soap. ~**nette** /-ɔnɛt/ *n.f.* bar of soap. ~**neux,** ~**neuse** /-ɔnø, -z/ *a.* soapy.

savour|er /savure/ *v.t.* savour. ~**eux,** ~**euse** *a.* tasty; (*fig.*) spicy.

saxo(phone) /saksɔ(fɔn)/ *n.m.* sax(ophone).

scabreu|x, ~**se** /skabrø, -z/ *a.* risky; (*indécent*) obscene.

scandal|e /skɑ̃dal/ *n.m.* scandal; (*tapage*) uproar; (*en public*) noisy scene. **faire** ~**e,** shock people. **faire un** ~**e,** make a scene. ~**eux,** ~**euse** *a.* scandalous. ~**iser** *v.t.* scandalize, shock.

scander /skɑ̃de/ *v.t.* (*vers*) scan; (*slogan*) chant.

scandinave /skɑ̃dinav/ *a. & n.m./f.* Scandinavian.

Scandinavie /skɑ̃dinavi/ *n.f.* Scandinavia.

scarabée /skarabe/ *n.m.* beetle.

scarlatine /skarlatin/ *n.f.* scarlet fever.

scarole /skarɔl/ *n.f.* endive.

sceau (*pl.* ~**x**) /so/ *n.m.* seal.

scélérat /selera/ *n.m.* scoundrel.

scell|er /sele/ *v.t.* seal; (*fixer*) cement. ~és *n.m. pl.* seals.

scénario /senarjo/ *n.m.* scenario.

scène /sɛn/ *n.f.* scene; (*estrade, art dramatique*) stage. mettre en ~, (*pièce*) stage. ~ de ménage, domestic scene.

scepti|que /sɛptik/ *a.* sceptical. —*n.m./f.* sceptic. ~cisme *n.m.* scepticism.

sceptre /sɛptr/ *n.m.* sceptre.

schéma /ʃema/ *n.m.* diagram. ~tique *a.* diagrammatic; (*sommaire*) sketchy.

schisme /ʃism/ *n.m.* schism.

schizophrène /skizɔfrɛn/ *a.* & *n.m./f.* schizophrenic.

sciatique /sjatik/ *n.f.* sciatica.

scie /si/ *n.f.* saw.

sciemment /sjamɑ̃/ *adv.* knowingly.

scien|ce /sjɑ̃s/ *n.f.* science; (*savoir*) knowledge. ~ce-fiction *n.f.* science fiction. ~tifique *a.* scientific; *n.m./f.* scientist.

scier /sje/ *v.t.* saw.

scinder /sɛ̃de/ *v.t.*, se ~ *v. pr.* split.

scintill|er /sɛ̃tije/ *v.i.* glitter; (*étoile*) twinkle. ~ement *n.m.* glittering; twinkling.

scission /sisjɔ̃/ *n.f.* split.

sciure /sjyr/ *n.f.* sawdust.

sclérose /skleroz/ *n.f.* sclerosis. ~ en plaques, multiple sclerosis.

scol|aire /skɔlɛr/ *a.* school. ~arisation *n.f.*, ~arité *n.f.* schooling. ~arisé *a.* provided with schooling.

scorbut /skɔrbyt/ *n.m.* scurvy.

score /skɔr/ *n.m.* score.

scories /skɔri/ *n.f. pl.* slag.

scorpion /skɔrpjɔ̃/ *n.m.* scorpion. le S~, Scorpio.

scotch¹ /skɔtʃ/ *n.m.* (*boisson*) Scotch (whisky).

scotch² /skɔtʃ/ *n.m.* (P.) Sellotape (P.); (*Amer.*) Scotch (tape) (P.).

scout, ~e /skut/ *n.m.* & *a.* scout.

script /skript/ *n.m.* (*cinéma*) script; (*écriture*) printing. ~-girl, continuity girl.

scrupul|e /skrypyl/ *n.m.* scruple. ~eusement *adv.* scrupulously. ~eux, ~euse *a.* scrupulous.

scruter /skryte/ *v.t.* examine, scrutinize.

scrutin /skrytɛ̃/ *n.m.* (*vote*) ballot; (*opération électorale*) poll.

sculpt|er /skylte/ *v.t.* sculpture. (*bois*) carve (dans, out of). ~eur *n.m.* sculptor. ~ure *n.f.* sculpture.

se, s'* /sə, s/ *pron.* himself; (*femelle*) herself; (*indéfini*) oneself; (*non humain*) itself; (*pl.*) themselves; (*réciproque*) each other, one another. se parler, (*à soi-même*) talk to o.s.; (*réciproque*) talk to each other. se faire, (*passif*) be done. se laver les mains, (*possessif*) wash one's hands.

séance /seɑ̃s/ *n.f.* session; (*cinéma, théâtre*) show. ~ de pose, sitting. ~ tenante, forthwith.

seau (*pl.* ~x) /so/ *n.m.* bucket, pail.

sec, sèche /sɛk, sɛʃ/ *a.* dry; (*fruits*) dried; (*coup, bruit*) sharp; (*cœur*) hard; (*whisky*) neat; (*Amer.*) straight. —*n.m.* à ~, (*sans eau*) dry; (*sans argent*) broke. au ~, in a dry place. —*n.f.* (*fam.*) (*cigarette*) fag.

sécateur /sekatœr/ *n.m.* (*pour les haies*) shears; (*petit*) secateurs.

sécession /sesesjɔ̃/ *n.f.* secession. faire ~, secede.

sèche /sɛʃ/ *voir* sec. ~ment *adv.* drily.

sèche-cheveux /sɛʃʃəvø/ *n.m.* invar. hair-drier.

sécher /seʃe/ *v.t./i.* dry; (*cours: fam.*) skip; (*ne pas savoir: fam.*) be stumped. se ~ *v. pr.* dry o.s.

sécheresse /seʃrɛs/ *n.f.* dryness; (*temps sec*) drought.

séchoir /seʃwar/ *n.m.* drier.

second, ∼e[1] /sgɔ̃, -d/ *a.* & *n.m.,* *f.* second. —*n.m.* (*adjoint*) second in command; (*étage*) second floor, (*Amer.*) third floor. —*n.f.* (*transport*) second class.

secondaire /sgɔ̃dɛr/ *a.* secondary.

seconde[2] /sgɔ̃d/ *n.f.* (*instant*) second.

seconder /sgɔ̃de/ *v.t.* assist.

secouer /skwe/ *v.t.* shake; (*poussière, torpeur*) shake off. **se** ∼, (*fam.*) (*se dépêcher*) get a move on; (*réagir*) shake o.s. up.

secour|ir /skurir/ *v.t.* assist, help. ∼**able** *a.* helpful. ∼**iste** *n.m./f.* first-aid worker.

secours /skur/ *n.m.* assistance, help. —*n.m.* (*méd.*) first aid. **au** ∼**!,** help! **de** ∼, emergency; (*équipe, opération*) rescue.

secousse /skus/ *n.f.* jolt, jerk; (*électrique*) shock; (*séisme*) tremor.

secr|et, ∼ète /sɔkrɛ, -t/ *a.* secret. —*n.m.* secret; (*discrétion*) secrecy. **le** ∼**et professionnel,** professional secrecy. ∼**et de Polichinelle,** open secret. **en** ∼**et,** in secret, secretly.

secrétaire /skretɛr/ *n.m./f.* secretary. ∼ **de direction,** executive secretary. —*n.m.* (*meuble*) writing-desk. ∼ **d'État,** junior minister.

secrétariat /skretarja/ *n.m.* secretarial work; (*bureau*) secretary's office; (*d'un organisme*) secretariat.

sécrét|er /sekrete/ *v.t.* secrete. ∼**ion** /-sjɔ̃/ *n.f.* secretion.

sect|e /sɛkt/ *n.f.* sect. ∼**aire** *a.* sectarian.

secteur /sɛktœr/ *n.m.* area; (*mil., comm.*) sector; (*circuit: électr.*) mains. ∼ **primaire/secondaire/tertiaire,** primary/secondary/tertiary industry.

section /sɛksjɔ̃/ *n.f.* section; (*transports publics*) fare stage; (*mil.*) platoon. ∼**ner** /-jɔne/ *v.t.* sever.

sécu /seky/ *n.f.* (*fam.*) **la** ∼, the social security services.

séculaire /sekylɛr/ *a.* age-old.

sécul|ier, ∼ière /sekylje, -jɛr/ *a.* secular.

sécuriser /sekyrize/ *v.t.* reassure.

sécurité /sekyrite/ *n.f.* security; (*absence de danger*) safety. **en** ∼, safe, secure. **S∼ sociale,** social services, social security services.

sédatif /sedatif/ *n.m.* sedative.

sédentaire /sedɑ̃tɛr/ *a.* sedentary.

sédiment /sedimɑ̃/ *n.m.* sediment.

séditieu|x, ∼se /sedisjø, -z/ *a.* seditious.

sédition /sedisjɔ̃/ *n.f.* sedition.

séd|uire /sedɥir/ *v.t.* charm; (*plaire à*) appeal to; (*abuser de*) seduce. ∼**ucteur,** *n.m.,* **∼uctrice** *a.* seducer. ∼**uction** *n.f.* seduction; (*charme*) charm. ∼**uisant, ∼uisante** *a.* attractive.

segment /sɛgmɑ̃/ *n.m.* segment.

ségrégation /segregasjɔ̃/ *n.f.* segregation.

seigle /sɛgl/ *n.m.* rye.

seigneur /sɛɲœr/ *n.m.* lord. **le S∼,** the Lord.

sein /sɛ̃/ *n.m.* breast; (*fig.*) bosom. **au** ∼ **de,** in the midst of.

Seine /sɛn/ *n.f.* Seine.

séisme /seism/ *n.m.* earthquake.

seize /sɛz/ *a.* & *n.m.* sixteen. ∼**ième** *a.* & *n.m./f.* sixteenth.

séjour /seʒur/ *n.m.* stay; (*pièce*) living-room. ∼**ner** *v.i.* stay.

sel /sɛl/ *n.m.* salt; (*piquant*) spice.

sélect /selɛkt/ *a.* select.

sélecti|f, ∼ve /selɛktif, -v/ *a.* selective.

sélection /selɛksjɔ̃/ *n.f.* selection. ∼**ner** /-jɔne/ *v.t.* select.

self-service /sɛlfsɛrvis/ *n.m.* self-service.

selle /sɛl/ *n.f.* saddle.
seller /sele/ *v.t.* saddle.
sellette /selɛt/ *n.f.* **sur le ~**, (*question*) under examination; (*personne*) in the hot seat.
selon /slɔ̃/ *prép.* according to (**que**, whether).
semaine /smɛn/ *n.f.* week. **en ~**, in the week.
sémantique /semɑ̃tik/ *a.* semantic. —*n.f.* semantics.
sémaphore /semafɔr/ *n.m.* (*appareil*) semaphore.
semblable /sɑ̃blabl/ *a.* similar (**à**, to). **de ~s propos**/*etc.*, (*tels*) such remarks/*etc.* —*n.m.* fellow (creature).
semblant /sɑ̃blɑ̃/ *n.m.* **faire ~ de**, pretend to. **un ~ de**, a semblance of.
sembl|er /sɑ̃ble/ *v.i.* seem (**à**, to; **que**, that). **il me ~e que**, it seems to me that.
semelle /smɛl/ *n.f.* sole.
semence /smɑ̃s/ *n.f.* seed; (*clou*) tack. **~s**, (*graines*) seed.
sem|er /sme/ *v.t.* sow; (*jeter, parsemer*) strew; (*répandre*) spread; (*personne: fam.*) lose. **~eur, ~euse** *n.m., f.* sower.
semestr|e /smɛstr/ *n.m.* half-year; (*univ.*) semester. **~iel, ~ielle** *a.* half-yearly.
semi- /səmi/ *préf.* semi-.
séminaire /seminɛr/ *n.m.* (*relig.*) seminary; (*univ.*) seminar.
semi-remorque /səmirəmɔrk/ *n.m.* articulated lorry; (*Amer.*) semi(-trailer).
semis /smi/ *n.m.* (*terrain*) seedbed; (*plant*) seedling.
sémit|e /semit/ *a.* Semitic. —*n.m./f.* Semite. **~ique** *a.* Semitic.
semonce /səmɔ̃s/ *n.f.* reprimand. **coup de ~**, warning shot.
semoule /smul/ *n.f.* semolina.
sénat /sena/ *n.m.* senate. **~eur** /-tœr/ *n.m.* senator.

sénil|e /senil/ *a.* senile. **~ité** *n.f.* senility.
sens /sɑ̃s/ *n.m.* sense; (*signification*) meaning, sense; (*direction*) direction. **à mon ~**, to my mind. **à ~ unique**, (*rue etc.*) one-way. **ça n'a pas de ~**, that does not make sense. **~ commun**, common sense. **~ giratoire**, roundabout; (*Amer.*) rotary. **~ interdit**, no entry; (*rue*) one-way street. **dans le ~ des aiguilles d'une montre**, clockwise. **~ dessus dessous**, upside down.
sensation /sɑ̃sasjɔ̃/ *n.f.* feeling, sensation. **faire ~**, create a sensation. **~nel, ~nelle** /-jɔnɛl/ *a.* sensational.
sensé /sɑ̃se/ *a.* sensible.
sensibiliser /sɑ̃sibilize/ *v.t.* **~ à**, make sensitive to.
sensib|le /sɑ̃sibl/ *a.* sensitive (**à**, to); (*appréciable*) noticeable. **~ilité** *n.f.* sensitivity. **~lement** *adv.* noticeably; (*à peu près*) more or less.
sensoriel, ~le /sɑ̃sɔrjɛl/ *a.* sensory.
sens|uel, ~uelle /sɑ̃sɥɛl/ *a.* sensuous; (*sexuel*) sensual. **~ualité** *n.f.* sensuousness; sensuality.
sentenc|e /sɑ̃tɑ̃s/ *n.f.* sentence. **~ieux, ~ieuse** *a.* sententious.
senteur /sɑ̃tœr/ *n.f.* scent.
sentier /sɑ̃tje/ *n.m.* path.
sentiment /sɑ̃timɑ̃/ *n.m.* feeling. **avoir le ~ de**, be aware of.
sentiment|al (*m. pl.* **~aux**) /sɑ̃timɑ̃tal, -o/ *a.* sentimental. **~alité** *n.f.* sentimentality.
sentinelle /sɑ̃tinɛl/ *n.f.* sentry.
sentir† /sɑ̃tir/ *v.t.* feel; (*odeur*) smell; (*goût*) taste; (*pressentir*) sense. **~ la lavande**/*etc.*, smell of lavender/*etc.* —*v.i.* smell. **je ne peux pas le ~**, (*fam.*) I can't stand him. **se ~ fier/mieux**/*etc.*, feel proud/better/*etc.*

séparatiste /separatist/ *a.* & *n.m./f.* separatist.

séparé /separe/ *a.* separate; (*conjoints*) separated. **~ment** *adv.* separately.

sépar|er /separe/ *v.t.* separate; (*en deux*) split. **se ~er** *v. pr.* separate, part (**de,** from); (*se détacher*) split. **se ~er de,** (*se défaire de*) part with. **~ation** *n.f.* separation.

sept /sɛt/ *a.* & *n.m.* seven.

septante /sɛptɑ̃t/ *a.* & *n.m.* (*en Belgique, Suisse*) seventy.

septembre /sɛptɑ̃br/ *n.m.* September.

septentrion|al (*m. pl.* **~aux**) /sɛptɑ̃trijɔnal, -o/ *a.* northern.

septième /sɛtjɛm/ *a.* & *n.m./f.* seventh.

sépulcre /sepylkr/ *n.m.* (*relig.*) sepulchre.

sépulture /sepyltyr/ *n.f.* burial; (*lieu*) burial place.

séquelles /sekɛl/ *n.f. pl.* (*maladie*) after-effects; (*fig.*) aftermath.

séquence /sekɑ̃s/ *n.f.* sequence.

séquestrer /sekɛstre/ *v.t.* confine (*illegally*); (*biens*) impound.

sera, serait /sra, srɛ/ *voir* **être**.

serein, ~e /sarɛ̃, -ɛn/ *a.* serene.

sérénade /serenad/ *n.f.* serenade.

sérénité /serenite/ *n.f.* serenity.

sergent /sɛrʒɑ̃/ *n.m.* sergeant.

série /seri/ *n.f.* series; (*d'objets*) set. **de ~,** (*véhicule etc.*) standard. **fabrication** *ou* **production en ~,** mass production.

sérieu|x, ~se /serjø, -z/ *a.* serious; (*digne de foi*) reliable; (*chances, raison*) good. **—** *n.m.* seriousness. **garder/perdre son ~x,** keep/be unable to keep a straight face. **prendre au ~x,** take seriously. **~sement** *adv.* seriously.

serin /srɛ̃/ *n.m.* canary.

seringue /srɛ̃g/ *n.f.* syringe.

serment /sɛrmɑ̃/ *n.m.* oath; (*promesse*) pledge.

sermon /sɛrmɔ̃/ *n.m.* sermon. **~ner** /-ɔne/ *v.t.* (*fam.*) lecture.

séropositi|f, ~ve /seropozitif, -v/ *a.* HIV-positive.

serpe /sɛrp/ *n.f.* bill(hook).

serpent /sɛrpɑ̃/ *n.m.* snake. **~ à sonnettes,** rattlesnake.

serpenter /sɛrpɑ̃te/ *v.i.* meander.

serpentin /sɛrpɑ̃tɛ̃/ *n.m.* streamer.

serpillière /sɛrpijɛr/ *n.f.* floor-cloth.

serre[1] /sɛr/ *n.f.* (*local*) green-house.

serre[2] /sɛr/ *n.f.* (*griffe*) claw.

serré /sere/ *a.* (*habit, nœud, programme*) tight; (*personnes*) packed, crowded; (*lutte, mailles*) close; (*cœur*) heavy.

serrer /sere/ *v.t.* (*saisir*) grip; (*presser*) squeeze; (*vis, corde, ceinture*) tighten; (*poing, dents*) clench; (*pieds*) pinch. **~ qn.** **dans ses bras,** hug. **~ les rangs,** close ranks. **~ qn.,** (*vêtement*) be tight on s.o. **—***i.v.* **~ à droite,** keep over to the right. **se ~** *v. pr.* (*se rapprocher*) squeeze (up) (**contre,** against). **~ de près,** follow closely. **~ la main à,** shake hands with.

serrur|e /seryr/ *n.f.* lock. **~ier** *n.m.* locksmith.

sertir /sertir/ *v.t.* (*bijou*) set.

sérum /serɔm/ *n.m.* serum.

servante /sɛrvɑ̃t/ *n.f.* (*maid*)servant.

serveu|r, ~se /sɛrvœr, -øz/ *n.m., f.* waiter, waitress; (*au bar*) barman, barmaid.

serviable /sɛrvjabl/ *a.* helpful.

service /sɛrvis/ *n.m.* service; (*fonction, temps de travail*) duty; (*pourboire*) service (charge). **(non) compris,** service (not) included. **être de ~,** be on duty. **pendant le ~,** (when) on duty. **rendre un ~/mauvais ~ à qn.,** do s.o. a favour/disservice. **~ d'ordre,** (*policiers*) police. **~**

après-vente, after-sales service. **∼ militaire**, military service.

serviette /sɛrvjɛt/ *n.f.* (*de toilette*) towel; (*sac*) briefcase. **∼ (de table)**, serviette; (*Amer.*) napkin. **∼ hygiénique**, sanitary towel.

servile /sɛrvil/ *a.* servile.

servir† /sɛrvir/ *v.t./i.* serve; (*être utile*) be of use, serve. **∼ qn.** (à table), wait on s.o. **ça sert à**, (*outil, récipient, etc.*) it is used for. **ça me sert à/de**, I use it for/as. **∼ de**, serve as, be used as. **∼ à qn. de guide**/*etc.*, act as a guide/etc. for s.o. **se ∼** *v. pr.* (à table) help o.s. (**de**, to). **se ∼ de**, use.

serviteur /sɛrvitœr/ *n.m.* servant.

servitude /sɛrvityd/ *n.f.* servitude.

ses /se/ *voir* **son**[1].

session /sesjɔ̃/ *n.f.* session.

seuil /sœj/ *n.m.* doorstep; (*entrée*) doorway; (*fig.*) threshold.

seul, ∼e /sœl/ *a.* alone, on one's own; (*unique*) only. **un ∼ travail**/*etc.*, only one job/etc. **pas un ∼ ami**/*etc.*, not a single friend/etc. **parler tout ∼**, talk to o.s. **faire qch. tout ∼**, do sth. on one's own. **—***n.m., f.* **le ∼, la ∼e**, the only one. **un ∼, une ∼e**, only one. **pas un ∼**, not a (single) one.

seulement /sœlmɑ̃/ *adv.* only.

sève /sɛv/ *n.f.* sap.

sév|ère /sevɛr/ *a.* severe. **∼èrement** *adv.* severely. **∼érité** /-erite/ *n.f.* severity.

sévices /sevis/ *n.m. pl.* cruelty.

sévir /sevir/ *v.i.* (*fléau*) rage. **∼ contre**, punish.

sevrer /səvre/ *v.t.* wean.

sex|e /sɛks/ *n.m.* sex; (*organes*) sex organs. **∼isme** *n.m.* sexism. **∼iste** *a.* sexist.

sex|uel, ∼uelle /sɛksɥɛl/ *a.* sexual. **∼ualité** *n.f.* sexuality.

seyant, ∼e /sejɑ̃, -t/ *a.* becoming.

shampooing /ʃɑ̃pwɛ̃/ *n.m.* shampoo.

shérif /ʃerif/ *n.m.* sheriff.

short /ʃɔrt/ *n.m.* (pair of) shorts.

si[1] (**s'** before **il, ils**) /si, s/ *conj.* if; (*interrogation indirecte*) if, whether. **si on partait?**, (*suggestion*) what about going? **s'il vous ou te plaît**, please. **si oui**, if so. **si seulement**, if only.

si[2] /si/ *adv.* (*tellement*) so; (*oui*) yes. **un si bon repas**, such a good meal. **pas si riche que**, not as rich as. **si habile qu'il soit**, however skilful he may be. **si bien que**, with the result that.

siamois, ∼e /sjamwa, -z/ *a.* Siamese.

Sicile /sisil/ *n.f.* Sicily.

sida /sida/ *n.m.* (*méd.*) AIDS.

sidéré /sidere/ *a.* staggered.

sidérurgie /sideryrʒi/ *n.f.* iron and steel industry.

siècle /sjɛkl/ *n.m.* century; (*époque*) age.

siège /sjɛʒ/ *n.m.* seat; (*mil.*) siege. **∼ éjectable**, ejector seat. **∼ social**, head office, headquarters.

siéger /sjeʒe/ *v.i.* (*assemblée*) sit.

sien, ∼ne /sjɛ̃, sjɛn/ *pron.* **le ∼, la ∼ne, les ∼(ne)s**, his; (*femme*) hers; (*chose*) its. **les ∼s**, (*famille*) one's family.

sieste /sjɛst/ *n.f.* nap; (*en Espagne*) siesta. **faire la ∼**, have an afternoon nap.

siffl|er /sifle/ *v.i.* whistle; (*avec un sifflet*) blow one's whistle; (*serpent, gaz*) hiss. **—***v.t.* (*air*) whistle; (*chien*) whistle to ou for; (*acteur*) hiss; (*signaler*) blow one's whistle for. **∼ement** *n.m.* whistling. **un ∼ement**, a whistle.

sifflet /siflɛ/ *n.m.* whistle. **∼s**, (*huées*) boos.

siffloter /siflote/ *v.t./i.* whistle.

sigle /sigl/ *n.m.* abbreviation, acronym.

sign|al (*pl.* **∼aux**) /siɲal, -o/

signaler /siɲale/ *v.t.* indicate; (*par une sonnerie, un écriteau*) signal; (*dénoncer, mentionner*) report; (*faire remarquer*) point out. **se ~er par**, distinguish o.s. by. **~ement** *n.m.* description.

signalisation /siɲalizasjɔ̃/ *n.f.* signalling, signposting; (*signaux*) signals.

signataire /siɲatɛr/ *n.m./f.* signatory.

signature /siɲatyr/ *n.f.* signature; (*action*) signing.

signe /siɲ/ *n.m.* sign; (*de ponctuation*) mark. **faire ~ à**, beckon (**de**, to); (*contacter*) contact. **faire ~ que non**, shake one's head. **faire ~ que oui**, nod.

signer /siɲe/ *v.t.* sign. **se ~er** *v. pr.* (*relig.*) cross o.s.

signet /siɲɛ/ *m.* bookmark.

significatif, **~ve** /siɲifikatif, -v/ *a.* significant.

signification /siɲifikasjɔ̃/ *n.f.* meaning.

signifier /siɲifje/ *v.t.* mean, signify; (*faire connaître*) make known (**à**, to).

silence /silɑ̃s/ *n.m.* silence; (*mus.*) rest. **garder le ~e**, keep silent. **~ieux**, **~ieuse** *a.* silent; *n.m.* (*auto.*) silencer; (*auto., Amer.*) muffler.

silex /silɛks/ *n.m.* flint.

silhouette /silwɛt/ *n.f.* outline, silhouette.

silicium /silisjɔm/ *n.m.* silicon.

sillage /sijaʒ/ *n.m.* (*trace d'eau*) wake.

sillon /sijɔ̃/ *n.m.* furrow; (*de disque*) groove.

sillonner /sijɔne/ *v.t.* criss-cross.

silo /silo/ *n.m.* silo.

simagrées /simagre/ *n.f. pl.* fuss, pretence.

similaire /similɛr/ *a.* similar. **~itude** *n.f.* similarity.

simple /sɛ̃pl/ *a.* simple; (*non double*) single. —*n.m.* (*tennis*) singles. **~ d'esprit** *n.m./f.* simpleton. **~ soldat**, private. **~ment** /-əmɑ̃/ *adv.* simply.

simplicité /sɛ̃plisite/ *n.f.* simplicity; (*naïveté*) simpleness.

simplifier /sɛ̃plifje/ *v.t.* simplify. **~ication** *n.f.* simplification.

simpliste /sɛ̃plist/ *a.* simplistic.

simulacre /simylakr/ *n.m.* pretence, sham.

simuler /simyle/ *v.t.* simulate. **~ateur** *m.* (*appareil*) simulator. **~ation** *n.f.* simulation.

simultané /simyltane/ *a.* simultaneous. **~ment** *adv.* simultaneously.

sincère /sɛ̃sɛr/ *a.* sincere. **~rement** *adv.* sincerely. **~érité** *n.f.* sincerity.

singe /sɛ̃ʒ/ *n.m.* monkey, ape.

singer /sɛ̃ʒe/ *v.t.* mimic, ape.

singeries /sɛ̃ʒri/ *n.f. pl.* antics.

singulariser (se) /(sə)sɛ̃gylarize/ *v. pr.* make o.s. conspicuous.

singulier, **~ière** /sɛ̃gylje, -jɛr/ *a.* peculiar, remarkable; (*gram.*) singular. —*n.m.* (*gram.*) singular. **~arité** *n.f.* peculiarity. **~ièrement** *adv.* peculiarly; (*beaucoup*) remarkably.

sinistre[1] /sinistr/ *a.* sinister.

sinistre[2] /sinistr/ *n.m.* disaster; (*incendie*) blaze; (*dommages*) damage. **~é** *a.* disaster-stricken; *n.m.*, *f.* disaster victim.

sinon /sinɔ̃/ *conj.* (*autrement*) otherwise; (*sauf*) except (**que**, that); (*si ce n'est*) if not.

sinueu|**x**, **~se** /sinɥø, -z/ *a.* winding; (*fig.*) tortuous.

sinus /sinys/ *n.m.* (*anat.*) sinus.

sionisme /sjɔnism/ *n.m.* Zionism.

siphon /sifɔ̃/ *n.m.* siphon; (*de WC*) U-bend.

sirène[1] /sirɛn/ *n.f.* (*appareil*) siren.

sirène[2] /sirɛn/ *n.f.* (*femme*) mermaid.

sirop /siro/ *n.m.* syrup; *(boisson)* cordial.

siroter /sirɔte/ *v.t.* sip.

sirupeu|x, **~se** /sirypø, -z/ *a.* syrupy.

sis, **~e** /si, siz/ *a.* situated.

sismique /sismik/ *a.* seismic.

site /sit/ *n.m.* setting; *(pittoresque)* beauty site; *(emplacement)* site; *(monument etc.)* place of interest.

sitôt /sito/ *adv.* **~ entré/etc.**, immediately after coming in/etc. **~ que**, as soon as. **pas de ~**, not for a while.

situation /situɑsjɔ̃/ *n.f.* situation, position. **~ de famille**, marital status.

situer /situe/ *v.t.* situate, locate. **se ~er** *v. pr.* (se trouver) be situated. **~é** *a.* situated.

six /sis/ (/si *before consonant*, /siz/ *before vowel*) *a.* & *n.m.* six. **~ième** /sizjɛm/ *a.* & *n.m./f.* sixth.

sketch (*pl.* **~es**) /skɛtʃ/ *n.m.* (théâtre) sketch.

ski /ski/ *n.m.* (patin) ski; *(sport)* skiing. **faire du ~**, ski. **~ de fond**, cross-country skiing. **~ nautique**, water-skiing.

sk|ier /skje/ *v.i.* ski. **~ieur**, **~ieuse** *n.m., f.* skier.

slalom /slalɔm/ *n.m.* slalom.

slave /slav/ *a.* Slav; *(lang.)* Slavonic. —*n.m./f.* Slav.

slip /slip/ *n.m.* (d'homme) (under-)pants; *(de femme)* knickers; *(Amer.)* panties. **~ de bain**, (swimming) trunks; *(du bikini)* briefs.

slogan /slɔgɑ̃/ *n.m.* slogan.

smoking /smɔkiŋ/ *n.m.* evening ou dinner suit, dinner-jacket.

snack(-bar) /snak(bar)/ *n.m.* snack-bar.

snob /snɔb/ *n.m./f.* snob. —*a.* snobbish. **~isme** *n.m.* snobbery.

sobr|e /sɔbr/ *a.* sober. **~iété** *n.f.* sobriety.

sobriquet /sɔbrikɛ/ *n.m.* nickname.

sociable /sɔsjabl/ *a.* sociable.

soc|ial (*m. pl.* **~iaux**) /sɔsjal, -jo/ *a.* social.

socialis|te /sɔsjalist/ *n.m./f.* socialist. **~me** *n.m.* socialism.

société /sɔsjete/ *n.f.* society; *(compagnie, firme)* company.

sociolo|gie /sɔsjɔlɔʒi/ *n.f.* sociology. **~gique** *a.* sociological. **~gue** *n.m./f.* sociologist.

socle /sɔkl/ *n.m.* (de colonne, statue) plinth; *(de lampe)* base.

socquette /sɔkɛt/ *n.f.* ankle sock.

soda /sɔda/ *n.m.* (fizzy) drink.

sodium /sɔdjɔm/ *n.m.* sodium.

sœur /sœr/ *n.f.* sister.

sofa /sɔfa/ *n.m.* sofa.

soi /swa/ *pron.* oneself. **en ~**, in itself. **~-disant** *a. invar.* so-called; *(qui se veut tel)* self-styled; *adv.* supposedly.

soie /swa/ *n.f.* silk.

soif /swaf/ *n.f.* thirst. **avoir ~**, be thirsty. **donner ~ à**, make thirsty.

soigné /swaɲe/ *a.* tidy, neat; *(bien fait)* careful.

soigner /swaɲe/ *v.t.* look after, take care of; *(tenue, style)* take care over; *(maladie)* treat. **se ~** *v. pr.* look after o.s.

soigneu|x, **~se** /swaɲø, -z/ *a.* careful (de, about); *(ordonné)* tidy. **~sement** *adv.* carefully.

soi-même /swamɛm/ *pron.* oneself.

soin /swɛ̃/ *n.m.* care; *(ordre)* tidiness. **~s**, care; *(méd.)* treatment. **avoir ou prendre ~ de qn./de faire**, take care of s.o./to do. **premiers ~s**, first aid.

soir /swar/ *n.m.* evening.

soirée /sware/ *n.f.* evening; *(réception)* party. **~ dansante**, dance.

soit /swa/ *voir* **être**. —*conj.* (à

savoir) that is to say. **~ ... soit**, either . . . or.

soixantaine /swasɑ̃tɛn/ *n.f.* **une ~ (de)**, about sixty.

soixant|e /swasɑ̃t/ *a.* & *n.m.* sixty. **~e-dix** *a.* & *n.m.* seventy. **~e-dixième** *a.* & *n.m./f.* seventieth. **~ième** *a.* & *n.m./f.* sixtieth.

soja /sɔʒa/ *n.m.* (*graines*) soya beans; (*plante*) soya.

sol /sɔl/ *n.m.* ground; (*de maison*) floor; (*terrain agricole*) soil.

solaire /sɔlɛr/ *a.* solar; (*huile, filtre*) sun. **les rayons ~s**, the sun's rays.

soldat /sɔlda/ *n.m.* soldier.

solde[1] /sɔld/ *n.f.* (*salaire*) pay.

solde[2] /sɔld/ *n.m.* (*comm.*) balance. **~s**, (*articles*) sale goods. **en ~**, (*acheter etc.*) at sale price. **les ~s**, the sales.

solder /sɔlde/ *v.t.* reduce; (*liquider*) sell off at sale price; (*compte*) settle. **se ~ par**, (*aboutir à*) end in.

sole /sɔl/ *n.f.* (*poisson*) sole.

soleil /sɔlɛj/ *n.m.* sun; (*chaleur*) sunshine; (*fleur*) sunflower. **il y a du ~**, it is sunny.

solennel /sɔlanɛl/ *a.* solemn.

solennité /sɔlanite/ *n.f.* solemnity.

solex /sɔlɛks/ *n.m.* (P.) moped.

solfège /sɔlfɛʒ/ *n.m.* elementary musical theory.

solid|aire /sɔlidɛr/ *a.* (*mécanismes*) interdependent; (*couple*) (mutually) supportive; (*ouvriers*) who show solidarity. **~arité** *n.f.* solidarity.

solidariser (se) /(sə)sɔlidarize/ *v. pr.* show solidarity (**avec**, with).

solid|e /sɔlid/ *a.* solid. —*n.m.* (*objet*) solid; (*corps*) sturdy. **~ement** *adv.* solidly. **~ité** *n.f.* solidity.

solidifier /sɔlidifje/ *v.t.*, **se ~** *v. pr.* solidify.

soliste /sɔlist/ *n.m./f.* soloist.

solitaire /sɔlitɛr/ *a.* solitary. —*n.m./f.* (*ermite*) hermit; (*personne insociable*) loner.

solitude /sɔlityd/ *n.f.* solitude.

solive /sɔliv/ *n.f.* joist.

sollicit|er /sɔlisite/ *v.t.* request; (*attirer, pousser*) prompt; (*tenter*) tempt; (*faire travailler*) make demands on. **~ation** *n.f.* earnest request.

sollicitude /sɔlisityd/ *n.f.* concern.

solo /sɔlo/ *n.m.* & *a. invar.* (*mus.*) solo.

solstice /sɔlstis/ *n.m.* solstice.

soluble /sɔlybl/ *a.* soluble.

solution /sɔlysjɔ̃/ *n.f.* solution.

solvable /sɔlvabl/ *a.* solvent.

solvant /sɔlvɑ̃/ *n.m.* solvent.

sombre /sɔ̃br/ *a.* dark; (*triste*) sombre.

sombrer /sɔ̃bre/ *v.i.* sink (**dans**, into).

sommaire /sɔmɛr/ *a.* summary; (*tenue, repas*) scant. —*n.m.* summary.

sommation /sɔmasjɔ̃/ *n.f.* (*mil.*) warning; (*jurid.*) summons.

somme[1] /sɔm/ *n.f.* sum. **en ~, ~ toute**, in short. **faire la ~ de**, add (up), total (up).

somme[2] /sɔm/ *n.m.* (*sommeil*) nap.

sommeil /sɔmɛj/ *n.m.* sleep; (*besoin de dormir*) drowsiness. **avoir ~**, be ou feel sleepy. **~ler** /-meje/ *v.i.* doze; (*fig.*) lie dormant.

sommelier /sɔməlje/ *n.m.* wine waiter.

sommer /sɔme/ *v.t.* summon.

sommes /sɔm/ *voir* **être**.

sommet /sɔmɛ/ *n.m.* top; (*de montagne*) summit; (*de triangle*) apex; (*gloire*) height.

sommier /sɔmje/ *n.m.* base (of bed).

somnambule /sɔmnɑ̃byl/ *n.m.* sleep-walker.

somnifère /sɔmnifɛr/ *n.m.* sleeping-pill.

somnolen|t, **~te** /sɔmnɔlɑ̃, -t/ *a.* drowsy. **~ce** *n.f.* drowsiness.

somnoler /sɔmnɔle/ *v.i.* doze.

sompt|ueux, **~ueuse** /sɔ̃ptɥø, -z/ *a.* sumptuous. **~uosité** *n.f.* sumptuousness.

son¹, **sa** *ou* **son*** (*pl.* **ses**) /sɔ̃, sa, sɔ̃, se/ *a.* his; (*femme*) her; (*chose*) its; (*indéfini*) one's.

son² /sɔ̃/ *n.m.* (*bruit*) sound.

son³ /sɔ̃/ *n.m.* (*de blé*) bran.

sonar /sɔnar/ *n.* Sonar.

sonate /sɔnat/ *n.f.* sonata.

sonde /sɔ̃d/ *n.f.* (*pour les forages*) drill; (*méd.*) probe.

sond|er /sɔ̃de/ *v.t.* sound; (*terrain*) drill; (*personne*) sound out. **~age** *n.m.* sounding; drilling. **~age (d'opinion)** opinion poll.

song|e /sɔ̃ʒ/ *n.m.* dream. **~er** *v.i.* dream; (*v.t.*) **~er que**, think that. **~er à**, think about. **~eur**, **~euse** *a.* pensive.

sonnantes /sɔnɑ̃t/ *a.f.pl.* **à six/***etc.* **heures ~**, on the stroke of six/*etc.*

sonné /sɔne/ *a.* (*fam.*) crazy; (*fatigué*) knocked out.

sonn|er /sɔne/ *v.t./i.* ring; (*clairon*, *glas*) sound; (*heure*) strike; (*domestique*) ring for. **midi ~é**, well past noon. **~er de** *(clairon etc.*) sound, blow.

sonnerie /sɔnri/ *n.f.* ringing; (*de clairon*) sound; (*mécanisme*) bell.

sonnet /sɔnɛ/ *n.m.* sonnet.

sonnette /sɔnɛt/ *n.f.* bell.

sonor|e /sɔnɔr/ *a.* resonant; (*onde*, *effets, etc.*) sound. **~ité** *n.f.* resonance; (*d'un instrument*) tone.

sonoris|er /sɔnɔrize/ *v.t.* (*salle*) wire for sound. **~ation** *n.f.* (*matériel*) sound equipment.

sont /sɔ̃/ *voir* **être**.

sophistiqué /sɔfistike/ *a.* sophisticated.

soporifique /sɔpɔrifik/ *a.* soporific.

sorbet /sɔrbɛ/ *n.m.* sorbet.

sorcellerie /sɔrsɛlri/ *n.f.* witchcraft.

sorc|ier /sɔrsje/ *n.m.* sorcerer. **~ière** *n.f.* witch.

sordide /sɔrdid/ *a.* sordid; (*lieu*) squalid.

sort /sɔr/ *n.m.* (*destin, hasard*) fate; (*condition*) lot; (*maléfice*) spell. **tirer (qch.) au ~**, draw lots (for sth.).

sortant, **~e** /sɔrtɑ̃, -t/ *a.* (*président etc.*) outgoing.

sorte /sɔrt/ *n.f.* sort, kind. **de ~ que**, so that. **en quelque ~**, in a way. **faire en ~ que**, see to it that.

sortie /sɔrti/ *n.f.* departure, exit; (*porte*) exit; (*promenade, dîner*) outing; (*invective*) outburst; (*parution*) appearance; (*de disque, gaz*) release; (*d'un ordinateur*) output. **~s**, (*argent*) outgoings.

sortilège /sɔrtilɛʒ/ *n.m.* (*magic*) spell.

sortir† /sɔrtir/ *v.i.* (*aux. être*) go out, leave; (*venir*) come out; (*aller au spectacle etc.*) go out; (*livre, film*) come out; (*plante*) come up. **~ de**, (*pièce*) leave; (*milieu social*) come from; (*limites*) go beyond. —*v.t.* (*aux. avoir*) take out; (*livre, modèle*) bring out; (*dire: fam.*) come out with. **~ d'affaire**, **(s')en ~**, get out of an awkward situation. **~ du commun** *ou* **de l'ordinaire**, be out of the ordinary.

sosie /sɔzi/ *n.m.* double.

sot, **~te** /so, sɔt/ *a.* foolish.

sottise /sɔtiz/ *n.f.* foolishness; (*action, remarque*) foolish thing.

sou /su/ *n.m.* **~s**, money. **pas un ~**, not a penny. **sans le ~**, without a penny. **près de ses ~s**, tight-fisted.

soubresaut /subrəso/ *n.m.* (sudden) start.

souche /suʃ/ *n.f.* (*d'arbre*) stump; (*de famille, vigne*) stock; (*de carnet*) counterfoil. **planté comme une ~,** standing like an idiot.

souci[1] /susi/ *n.m.* (*inquiétude*) worry; (*préoccupation*) concern. **se faire du ~,** worry.

souci[2] /susi/ *n.m.* (*plante*) marigold.

soucier (se) /(sə)susje/ *v. pr.* **se ~ de,** be concerned about.

soucieu|x, ~se /susjø, -z/ *a.* concerned (**de,** about).

soucoupe /sukup/ *n.f.* saucer. **~ volante,** flying saucer.

soudain, ~e /sudɛ̃, -ɛn/ *a.* sudden. —*adv.* suddenly. **~ement** /-ɛnmã/ *adv.* suddenly. **~eté** /-ɛnte/ *n.f.* suddenness.

soude /sud/ *n.f.* soda.

soud|er /sude/ *v.t.* solder, (*à la flamme*) weld. **se ~er** *v. pr.* (*os*) knit (together). **~ure** *n.f.* soldering, welding; (*substance*) solder.

soudoyer /sudwaje/ *v.t.* bribe.

souffle /sufl/ *n.m.* blow, puff; (*haleine*) breath; (*respiration*) breathing; (*explosion*) blast; (*vent*) breath of air.

soufflé /sufle/ *n.m.* (*culin.*) soufflé.

souffl|er /sufle/ *v.i.* blow; (*haleter*) puff. —*v.t.* (*bougie*) blow out; (*poussière, fumée*) blow; (*par explosion*) destroy; (*chuchoter*) whisper. **~er son rôle à,** prompt. **~eur, ~euse** *n.m., f.* (*théâtre*) prompter.

soufflet /suflɛ/ *n.m.* (*instrument*) bellows.

souffrance /sufrãs/ *n.f.* suffering. **en ~,** (*affaire*) pending.

souffr|ir† /sufrir/ *v.i.* suffer (**de,** from). —*v.t.* (*endurer*) suffer; (*admettre*) admit of. **il ne peut pas le ~ir,** he cannot stand *ou* bear him. **~ant, ~ante** *a.* unwell.

soufre /sufr/ *n.m.* sulphur.

souhait /swɛ/ *n.m.* wish. **nos ~s de,** (*vœux*) good wishes for. **à vos ~s!,** bless you!

souhait|er /swete/ *v.t.* (*bonheur etc.*) wish for. **~er qch. à qn.,** wish s.o. sth. **~er que/faire,** hope that/to do. **~able** /swetabl/ *a.* desirable.

souiller /suje/ *v.t.* soil.

soûl, ~e /su, sul/ *a.* drunk. —*n.m.* **tout son ~,** as much as one can.

soulag|er /sulaʒe/ *v.t.* relieve. **~ement** *n.m.* relief.

soûler /sule/ *v.t.* make drunk. **se ~** *v. pr.* get drunk.

soulèvement /sulɛvmã/ *n.m.* uprising.

soulever /sulve/ *v.t.* lift, raise; (*exciter*) stir; (*question, poussière*) raise. **se ~** *v. pr.* lift *ou* raise o.s. up; (*se révolter*) rise up.

soulier /sulje/ *n.m.* shoe.

souligner /suliɲe/ *v.t.* underline; (*taille, yeux*) emphasize.

soum|ettre† /sumɛtr/ *v.t.* (*dompter, assujettir*) subject (**à,** to); (*présenter*) submit (**à,** to). **se ~ettre** *v. pr.* submit (**à,** to). **~is, ~ise** *a.* submissive. **~ission** *n.f.* submission.

soupape /supap/ *n.f.* valve.

soupçon /supsɔ̃/ *n.m.* suspicion. **un ~ de,** (*fig.*) a touch of. **~ner** /-ɔne/ *v.t.* suspect. **~neux, ~neuse** /-ɔnø, -z/ *a.* suspicious.

soupe /sup/ *n.f.* soup.

souper /supe/ *n.m.* supper. —*v.i.* have supper.

soupeser /supəze/ *v.t.* judge the weight of; (*fig.*) weigh up.

soupière /supjɛr/ *n.f.* (*soup*) tureen.

soupir /supir/ *n.m.* sigh. **pousser un ~,** heave a sigh. **~er** *v.i.* sigh.

soupir|ail (*pl.* **~aux**) /supiraj, -o/ *n.m.* small basement window.

soupirant /supirã/ *n.m.* suitor.

souple /supl/ *a.* supple; (*règlement, caractère*) flexible. **~sse** /-ɛs/ *n.f.* suppleness; flexibility.

source /surs/ *n.f.* source; (*eau*) spring. **de ~ sûre**, from a reliable source. **~ thermale**, hot springs.

sourcil /sursi/ *n.m.* eyebrow.

sourciller /sursije/ *v.i.* **sans ~**, without batting an eyelid.

sourd, ~e /sur, -d/ *a.* deaf; (*bruit, douleur*) dull; (*inquiétude, conflit*) silent, hidden. —*n.m., f.* deaf person. **faire la ~e oreille**, turn a deaf ear. **~-muet** (*pl.* **~s-muets**), **~e-muette** (*pl.* **~es-muettes**) *a.* deaf and dumb; *n.m., f.* deaf mute.

sourdine /surdin/ *n.f.* (*mus.*) mute. **en ~**, quietly.

souricière /surisjɛr/ *n.f.* mousetrap; (*fig.*) trap.

sourire /surir/ *n.m.* smile. **garder le ~**, keep smiling. —*v.i.* smile (**à, at**). **~ à**, (*fortune*) smile on.

souris /suri/ *n.f.* mouse.

sournois, ~e /surnwa, -z/ *a.* sly, underhand. **~ement** /-zmã/ *adv.* slyly.

sous /su/ *prép.* under, beneath. **~ la main**, handy. **~ la pluie**, in the rain. **~ peu**, shortly. **~ terre**, underground.

sous- /su/ *préf.* (*subordination*) sub-; (*insuffisance*) under-.

sous-alimenté /suzalimãte/ *a.* undernourished.

sous-bois /subwa/ *n.m. invar.* undergrowth.

souscr|ire /suskrir/ *v.i.* **~ire à**, subscribe to. **~iption** /-ipsjɔ̃/ *n.f.* subscription.

sous-direct|eur /sudirɛktœr, -ris/ *n.m., f.* assistant manager.

sous-entend|re /suzãtãdr/ *v.t.* imply. **~u** *n.m.* insinuation.

sous-estimer /suzɛstime/ *v.t.* underestimate.

sous-jacent, ~e /suʒasã, -t/ *a.* underlying.

sous-marin, ~e /sumarɛ̃, -in/ *a.* underwater. —*n.m.* submarine.

sous-officier /suzɔfisje/ *n.m.* non-commissioned officer.

sous-préfecture /suprefɛktyr/ *n.f.* sub-prefecture.

sous-produit /suprɔdɥi/ *n.m.* by-product.

sous-programme /suprɔgram/ *n.m.* subroutine.

soussigné, ~e /susiɲe/ *a. & n.m.* f. undersigned.

sous-sol /susɔl/ *n.m.* (*cave*) basement.

sous-titr|e /sutitr/ *n.m.* subtitle. **~er** *v.t.* subtitle.

soustr|aire† /sustrer/ *v.t.* remove; (*déduire*) subtract. **se ~aire à**, escape from. **~action** *n.f.* (*déduction*) subtraction.

sous-trait|er /sutrete/ *v.t.* subcontract. **~ant** *n.m.* subcontractor.

sous-verre /suver/ *n.m. invar.* picture frame, glass mount.

sous-vêtement /suvɛtmã/ *n.m.* undergarment. **~s**, underwear.

soutane /sutan/ *n.f.* cassock.

soute /sut/ *n.f.* (*de bateau*) hold. **~ à charbon**, coal-bunker.

soutenir† /sutnir/ *v.t.* support; (*fortifier, faire durer*) sustain; (*résister à*) withstand. **~ que**, maintain that. **se ~** *v. pr.* (*se tenir debout*) support o.s.

soutenu, ~e *a.* (*constant*) sustained; (*style*) lofty.

souterrain, ~e /suterɛ̃, -ɛn/ *a.* underground. —*n.m.* underground passage, subway.

soutien /sutjɛ̃/ *n.m.* support. **~-gorge** (*pl.* **~s-gorge**) *n.m.* bra.

soutirer /sutire/ *v.t.* **~ à qn.**, extract from s.o.

souvenir¹ /suvnir/ *n.m.* memory, recollection; (*objet*) memento;

(cadeau) souvenir. **en ~ de**, in memory of.

souvenir²† (se) /(sə)suvniːr/ *v. pr.* se ~ **de**, remember. se ~ **que**, remember that.

souvent /suvɑ̃/ *adv.* often.

souverain, ~e /suvrɛ̃, -ɛn/ *a.* sovereign; *(extrême: péj.)* supreme. —*n.m., f.* sovereign. ~**eté** /-ɛnte/ *n.f.* sovereignty.

soviétique /sɔvjetik/ *a.* Soviet. —*n.m./f.* Soviet citizen.

soyeu|x, ~**se** /swajø, -z/ *a.* silky.

spacieu|x, ~**se** /spasjø, -z/ *a.* spacious.

spaghetti /spageti/ *n.m. pl.* spaghetti.

sparadrap /sparadra/ *n.m.* sticking-plaster; *(Amer.)* adhesive tape *ou* bandage.

spasm|e /spasm/ *n.m.* spasm. ~**odique** *a.* spasmodic.

spat|ial *(m. pl.* ~**iaux)** /spasjal, -jo/ *a.* space.

spatule /spatyl/ *n.f.* spatula.

speaker, ~**ine** /spikœr, -rin/ *n.m., f.* announcer.

spéc|ial *(m. pl.* ~**iaux)** /spesjal, -jo/ *a.* special; *(singulier)* peculiar. ~**ialement** *adv.* especially; *(exprès)* specially.

spécialis|er (se) /(sə)spesjalize/ *v. pr.* specialize **(dans**, in). ~**ation** *n.f.* specialization.

spécialiste /spesjalist/ *n.m./f.* specialist.

spécialité /spesjalite/ *n.f.* speciality; *(Amer.)* specialty.

spécif|ier /spesifje/ *v.t.* specify. ~**ication** *n.f.* specification.

spécifique /spesifik/ *a.* specific.

spécimen /spesimɛn/ *n.m.* specimen.

spectacle /spɛktakl/ *n.m.* sight, spectacle; *(représentation)* show.

spectaculaire /spɛktakylɛr/ *a.* spectacular.

specta|teur, ~**trice** /spɛktatœr, -tris/ *n.m., f.* onlooker; *(sport)*

spectator. **les** ~**teurs**, *(théâtre)* the audience.

spectre /spɛktr/ *n.m.* *(revenant)* spectre; *(images)* spectrum.

spécul|er /spekyle/ *v.i.* speculate. ~**ateur**, ~**atrice** *n.m., f.* speculator. ~**ation** *n.f.* speculation.

spéléologie /speleɔlɔʒi/ *n.f.* cave exploration, pot-holing; *(Amer.)* spelunking.

sperme /spɛrm/ *n.m.* sperm.

sph|ère /sfɛr/ *n.f.* sphere. ~**érique** *a.* spherical.

sphinx /sfɛ̃ks/ *n.m.* sphinx.

spirale /spiral/ *n.f.* spiral.

spirite /spirit/ *n.m./f.* spiritualist.

spirit|uel, ~**le** /spirituɛl/ *a.* spiritual; *(amusant)* witty.

spiritueux /spirituø/ *n.m.* *(alcool)* spirit.

splend|ide /splɑ̃did/ *a.* splendid. ~**eur** *n.f.* splendour.

spongieu|x, ~**se** /spɔ̃ʒjø, -z/ *a.* spongy.

sponsor /spɔ̃sɔr/ *n.m.* sponsor. ~**iser** *v.t.* sponsor.

spontané /spɔ̃tane/ *a.* spontaneous. ~**ité** *n.f.* spontaneity. ~**ment** *adv.* spontaneously.

sporadique /spɔradik/ *a.* sporadic.

sport /spɔr/ *n.m.* sport. —*a. invar.* *(vêtements)* casual. **veste/voiture de** ~, sports jacket/car.

sport|if, ~**ve** /spɔrtif, -v/ *a.* sporting; *(physique)* athletic; *(résultats)* sports. —*n.m.* sportsman. —*n.f.* sportswoman.

spot /spɔt/ *n.m.* spotlight; *(publicitaire)* ad.

spray /sprɛ/ *n.m.* spray; *(méd.)* inhaler.

sprint /sprint/ *n.m.* sprint. ~**er** *v.i.* sprint; *n.m.* /-œr/ sprinter.

square /skwar/ *n.m.* (public) garden.

squash /skwaʃ/ *n.m.* squash.

squatter /skwatœr/ *n.m.* squatter. ~**iser** *v.t.* squat in.

squelett|e /skəlɛt/ *n.m.* skeleton.

~**ique** /-etik/ a. skeletal;
(*maigre*) all skin and bone.

stabiliser /stabilize/ v.t. stabilize.

stab|le /stabl/ a. stable. ~**ilité** n.f.
stability.

stade[1] /stad/ n.m. (*sport*) stadium.

stade[2] /stad/ n.m. (*phase*) stage.

stag|e /staʒ/ n.m. course. ~**iaire**
a. & n.m./f. course member;
(*apprenti*) trainee.

stagn|er /stagne/ v.i. stagnate.
~**ant**, ~**ante** a. stagnant.
~**ation** n.f. stagnation.

stand /stɑ̃d/ n.m. stand, stall. ~ **de
tir**, (shooting-)range.

standard[1] /stɑ̃dar/ n.m. switchboard. ~**iste** /-dist/ n.m./f.
switchboard operator.

standard[2] /stɑ̃dar/ a. invar. standard. ~**iser** /-dize/ v.t. standardize.

standing /stɑ̃diŋ/ n.m. status,
standing. **de** ~, (*hôtel etc.*)
luxury.

star /star/ n.f. (*actrice*) star.

starter /starter/ n.m. (*auto.*)
choke.

station /stasjɔ̃/ n.f. station; (*halte*)
stop. ~ **balnéaire**, seaside
resort. ~ **debout**, standing position. ~ **de taxis**, taxi rank;
(*Amer.*) taxi stand. ~**service**
(*pl.* ~**s-service**) n.f. service
station. ~ **thermale**, spa.

stationnaire /stasjɔnɛr/ a. stationary.

stationn|er /stasjɔne/ v.i. park.
~**ement** n.m. parking.

statique /statik/ a. static.

statistique /statistik/ n.f. statistic;
(*science*) statistics. —a. statisti-
cal.

statue /staty/ n.f. statue.

statuer /statɥe/ v.i. ~ **sur**, rule
on.

statu quo /statykwo/ n.m. status
quo.

stature /statyr/ n.f. stature.

statut /staty/ n.m. status. ~**s**,

(*règles*) statutes. ~**aire** /-tɛr/ a.
statutory.

steak /stɛk/ n.m. steak.

stencil /stɛnsil/ n.m. stencil.

sténo /steno/ n.f. (*personne*)
stenographer; (*sténographie*)
shorthand.

sténodactylo /stenodaktilo/ n.f.
shorthand typist; (*Amer.*) stenographer.

sténographie /stenografi/ n.f.
shorthand.

stéréo /stereo/ n.f. & a. invar.
stereo. ~**phonique** /-ɔfɔnik/ a.
stereophonic.

stéréotyp|e /stereotip/ n.m. stereo-
type. ~**é** a. stereotyped.

stéril|e /steril/ a. sterile. ~**ité** n.f.
sterility.

stérilet /sterilɛ/ n.m. coil, IUD.

stérilis|er /sterilize/ v.t. sterilize.
~**ation** n.f. sterilization.

stéroïde /steroid/ a. & n.m. steroid.

stéthoscope /stetɔskɔp/ n.m.
stethoscope.

stigmat|e /stigmat/ n.m. mark,
stigma. ~**iser** v.t. stigmatize.

stimul|er /stimyle/ v.t. stimulate.
~**ant** n.m. stimulus; (*médicament*) stimulant. ~**ateur cardiaque**, pacemaker. ~**ation** n.f.
stimulation.

stipul|er /stipyle/ v.t. stipulate.
~**ation** n.f. stipulation.

stock /stɔk/ n.m. stock. ~**er** v.t.
stock. ~**iste** n.m. stockist;
(*Amer.*) dealer.

stoïque /stɔik/ a. stoical. —n.m./f.
stoic.

stop /stɔp/ int. stop. —n.m. stop
sign; (*feu arrière*) brake light.
faire du ~, (*fam.*) hitch-hike.

stopper /stɔpe/ v.t./i. stop;
(*vêtement*) mend, reweave.

store /stɔr/ n.m. blind; (*Amer.*)
shade; (*de magasin*) awning.

strabisme /strabism/ n.m. squint.

strapontin /strapɔ̃tɛ̃/ n.m. folding
seat, jump seat.

stratagème /strataʒɛm/ n.m. stratagem.

stratégie /strateʒi/ n.f. strategy. **~ique** a. strategic.

stress /strɛs/ n. stress, **~ant** a. stressful. **~er** v.t. put under stress.

strict /strikt/ a. strict; (tenue, vérité) plain. **le ~ minimum**, the absolute minimum. **~ement** adv. strictly.

strident, **~e** /stridɑ̃, -t/ a. shrill.

strie /stri/ n.f. streak. **~ier** v.t. streak.

strip-tease /striptiz/ n.m. strip-tease.

strophe /strɔf/ n.f. stanza, verse.

structure /stryktyr/ n.f. structure. **~al** (m. pl. **~aux**) a. structural. **~er** v.t. structure.

studieu/x, **~se** /stydjø, -z/ a. studious; (période) devoted to study.

studio /stydjo/ n.m. (d'artiste, de télévision, etc.) studio; (logement) studio flat, bed-sitter.

stupéfait, **~aite** /stypefɛ, -t/ a. amazed. **~action** n.f. amazement.

stupéfier /stypefje/ v.t. amaze. **~iant,** **~iante** a. amazing; n.m. drug, narcotic.

stupeur /stypœr/ n.f. amazement; (méd.) stupor.

stupide /stypid/ a. stupid. **~ité** n.f. stupidity.

style /stil/ n.m. style. **~isé** a. stylized.

stylé /stile/ a. well-trained.

styliste /stilist/ n.m./f. fashion designer.

stylo /stilo/ n.m. pen. **~ (à) bille,** ball-point pen. **~ (à) encre,** fountain-pen.

su /sy/ voir **savoir**.

suave /sɥav/ a. sweet.

subalterne /sybaltɛrn/ a. & n.m./f. subordinate.

subconscient, **~e** /sypkɔ̃sjɑ̃, -t/ a. & n.m. subconscious.

subdiviser /sybdivize/ v.t. subdivide.

subir /sybir/ v.t. suffer; (traitement, expériences) undergo.

subit, **~e** /sybi, -t/ a. sudden. **~ement** /-tmɑ̃/ adv. suddenly.

subjecti/f, **~ve** /sybʒɛktif, -v/ a. subjective. **~vité** n.f. subjectivity.

subjonctif /sybʒɔ̃ktif/ a. & n.m. subjunctive.

subjuguer /sybʒyge/ v.t. (charmer) captivate.

sublime /syblim/ a. sublime.

submer/ger /sybmɛrʒe/ v.t. submerge; (fig.) overwhelm. **~sion** n.f. submersion.

subordonné, **~e** /sybɔrdɔne/ a. & n.m., f. subordinate.

subordonner /sybɔrdɔne/ v.t. subordinate (à, to). **~ination** n.f. subordination.

subreptice /sybrɛptis/ a. surreptitious.

subside /sybzid/ n.m. grant.

subsidiaire /sypsidjɛr/ a. subsidiary.

subsister /sybziste/ v.i. subsist; (durer, persister) exist. **~ance** n.f. subsistence.

substance /sypstɑ̃s/ n.f. substance.

substantiel, **~le** /sypstɑ̃sjɛl/ a. substantial.

substantif /sypstɑ̃tif/ n.m. noun.

substit/uer /sypstitɥe/ v.t. substitute (à, for). **se ~uer à,** (remplacer) substitute for; (évincer) take over from. **~ut** n.m. substitute; (jurid.) deputy public prosecutor. **~ution** n.f. substitution.

subterfuge /sypterfyʒ/ n.m. subterfuge.

subtil /syptil/ a. subtle. **~ité** n.f. subtlety.

subtiliser /syptilize/ *v.t* ~ **qch. (à qn.),** spirit sth. away (from s.o.).

subvenir /sybvənir/ *v.i.* ~ **à,** provide for.

subvention /sybvãsjɔ̃/ *n.f.* subsidy. **~ner** /-jone/ *v.t.* subsidize.

subversi|f, **~ve** /sybvɛrsif, -v/ *a.* subversive.

subversion /sybvɛrsjɔ̃/ *n.f.* subversion.

suc /syk/ *n.m.* juice.

succédané /syksedane/ *n.m.* substitute (**de,** for).

succéder /syksede/ *v.i.* ~ **à,** succeed. **se ~** *v. pr.* succeed one another.

succès /syksɛ/ *n.m.* success. **à ~,** (*film, livre, etc.*) successful. **avoir du ~,** be a success.

successeur /syksesœr/ *n.m.* successor.

successi|f, **~ve** /syksesif, -v/ *a.* successive. **~vement** *adv.* successively.

succession /syksesjɔ̃/ *n.f.* succession; (*jurid.*) inheritance.

succinct, **~e** /syksɛ̃, -t/ *a.* succinct.

succomber /sykɔ̃be/ *v.i.* die. **~ à,** succumb to.

succulent, **~e** /sykylã, -t/ *a.* succulent.

succursale /sykyrsal/ *n.f.* (*comm.*) branch.

sucer /syse/ *v.t.* suck.

sucette /sysɛt/ *n.f.* (*bonbon*) lollipop; (*tétine*) dummy; (*Amer.*) pacifier.

sucr|e /sykr/ *n.m.* sugar. **~e d'orge,** barley sugar. **~e en poudre,** caster sugar; (*Amer.*) finely ground sugar. **~e glace,** icing sugar. **~e roux,** brown sugar. **~ier,** **~ière** *a.* sugar; *n.m.* (*récipient*) sugar-bowl.

sucr|er /sykre/ *v.t.* sugar, sweeten. **~é a.** sweet; (*additionné de sucre*) sweetened.

sucreries /sykrəri/ *n.f. pl.* sweets.

sud /syd/ *n.m.* south. —*a. invar.* south; (*partie*) southern; (*direction*) southerly. **~africain,** **~africaine** *a. & n.m., f.* South African. **~est** *n.m.* south-east. **~ouest** *n.m.* south-west.

Suède /suɛd/ *n.f.* Sweden.

suédois, **~e** /suedwa, -z/ *a.* Swedish. —*n.m., f.* Swede. —*n.m.* (*lang.*) Swedish.

suer /sue/ *v.t./i.* sweat. **faire ~ qn.,** (*fam.*) get on s.o.'s nerves.

sueur /suœr/ *n.f.* sweat. **en ~,** sweating.

suffi|re† /syfir/ *v.i.* be enough (**à qn.,** for s.o.). **il ~it de faire,** one only has to do. **il ~it d'une goutte pour,** a drop is enough to. **~ire à, (besoin)** satisfy. **se ~ire à soi-même,** be self-sufficient.

suffis|ant, **~ante** /syfizã, -t/ *a.* sufficient; (*vaniteux*) conceited. **~amment** *adv.* sufficiently. **~amment de,** sufficient. **~ance** *n.f.* (*vanité*) conceit.

suffixe /syfiks/ *n.m.* suffix.

suffoquer /syfoke/ *v.t./i.* choke, suffocate.

suffrage /syfraʒ/ *n.m.* (*voix: pol.*) vote; (*modalité*) suffrage.

sugg|érer /sygʒere/ *v.t.* suggest. **~estion** /-ʒɛstjɔ̃/ *n.f.* suggestion.

suggesti|f, **~ve** /sygʒɛstif, -v/ *a.* suggestive.

suicid|e /suisid/ *n.m.* suicide. **~aire** *a.* suicidal.

suicid|er (se) /(sə)suiside/ *v. pr.* commit suicide. **~é,** **~ée** *n.m., f.* suicide.

suie /sui/ *n.f.* soot.

suint|er /suɛ̃te/ *v.i.* ooze. **~ement** *n.m.* oozing.

suis /sui/ *voir* **être, suivre.**

Suisse /suis/ *n.f.* Switzerland.

suisse /suis/ *a. & n.m.* Swiss. **~sse** /-ɛs/ *n.f.* Swiss (woman).

suite /sɥit/ n.f. continuation, rest; (d'un film) sequel; (série) series; (appartement, escorte) suite; (résultat) consequence; (cohérence) order. **~s**, (de maladie) after-effects. **à la ~, de ~**, (successivement) in succession. **la ~ de**, (derrière) behind. **à la ~ de, par ~ de**, as a result of. **faire ~ (à)**, follow. **par ~ de**, afterwards. **à votre lettre du,** further to your letter of the.

suivant[1], **~e** /sɥivɑ̃, -t/ a. following, next. —n.m., f. following ou next person.

suivant[2] /sɥivɑ̃/ prép. (selon) according to.

suivi /sɥivi/ a. steady, sustained; (cohérent) consistent. **peu/très ~**, (cours) poorly-/well-attended.

suivre† /sɥivr/ v.t./i. follow; (comprendre) keep up (with), follow. **se ~** v. pr. follow each other. **faire ~**, (courrier etc.) forward.

sujet[1], **~te** /syʒɛ, -t/ a. **~ à**, liable ou subject to. —n.m., f. (gouverné) subject.

sujet[2] /syʒɛ/ n.m. (matière, individu) subject; (motif) cause; (gram.) subject. **au ~ de**, about.

sulfurique /sylfyrik/ a. sulphuric.

sultan /syltɑ̃/ n.m. sultan.

summum /sɔmɔm/ n.m. height.

super /sypɛr/ n.m. (essence) fourstar, premium (Amer.). —a. invar. (fam.) great. —adv. (fam.) ultra, fantastically.

superbe /sypɛrb/ a. superb.

supercherie /sypɛrʃəri/ n.f. trickery.

supérette /sypɛrɛt/ n.f. minimarket.

superficie /sypɛrfisi/ n.f. area.

superficiel, ~le /sypɛrfisjɛl/ a. superficial.

superflu /sypɛrfly/ a. superfluous. —n.m. (excédent) surplus.

supérieur, ~e /sypɛrjœr/ a. (plus haut) upper; (quantité, nombre) greater (à, than); (études, principe) higher (à, than); (meilleur, hautain) superior (à, to). —n.m., f. superior.

supériorité /sypɛrjɔrite/ n.f. superiority.

superlatif, ~ve /sypɛrlatif, -v/ a. & n.m. superlative.

supermarché /sypɛrmarʃe/ n.m. supermarket.

superposer /sypɛrpoze/ v.t. superimpose.

superproduction /sypɛrprɔdyksjɔ̃/ n.f. (film) spectacular.

superpuissance /sypɛrpɥisɑ̃s/ n.f. superpower.

supersonique /sypɛrsɔnik/ a. supersonic.

superstit|ion /sypɛrstisjɔ̃/ n.f. superstition. **~ieux, ~ieuse** a. superstitious.

superviser /sypɛrvize/ v.t. supervise.

supplanter /syplɑ̃te/ v.t. supplant.

suppléan|t, ~te /sypleɑ̃, -t/ n.m., f. & a. (professeur) **~t**, supply teacher; (juge) **~t**, deputy (judge). **~ce** n.f. (fonction) temporary appointment.

suppléer /syplee/ v.t. (remplacer) replace; (ajouter) supply. —v.i. **~ à**, (compenser) make up for.

supplément /syplemɑ̃/ n.m. (argent) extra charge; (de frites, légumes) extra portion. **en ~**, extra. **un ~ de**, (travail etc.) extra. **payer pour un ~ de bagages**, pay extra for excess luggage. **~aire** /-tɛr/ a. extra, additional.

supplic|e /syplis/ n.m. torture. **~ier** v.t. torture.

supplier /syplije/ v.t. beg, beseech (de, to).

support /sypɔr/ n.m. support; (publicitaire: fig.) medium.

support|er[1] /sypɔrte/ v.t. (endurer) bear; (subir) suffer;

(*soutenir*) support; (*résister, à*) withstand. ~**able** *a.* bearable.

supporter² /syportɛr/ *n.m.* (*sport*) supporter.

suppos|er /sypoze/ *v.t.* suppose; (*impliquer*) imply. **à ~er que**, supposing that. ~**ition** *n.f.* supposition.

suppositoire /sypozitwar/ *n.m.* suppository.

suppr|imer /syprime/ *v.t.* get rid of, remove; (*annuler*) cancel; (*mot*) delete. ~**imer à qn.**, (*enlever*) take away from s.o. ~**ession** *n.f.* removal; cancellation; deletion.

suprématie /sypremasi/ *n.f.* supremacy.

suprême /syprɛm/ *a.* supreme.

sur /syr/ *prép.* on, upon; (*pardessus*) over; (*au sujet de*) about, on; (*proportion*) out of; (*mesure*) by. **aller/tourner/etc. ~**, go/turn/etc. towards. **mettre/jeter/etc. ~**, put/throw/etc. on to. ~**-le-champ** *adv.* immediately. ~ **le qui-vive**, on the alert. ~ **mesure**, made to measure. ~ **place**, on the spot. ~**ce**, hereupon.

sur- /syr/ *préf.* over-.

sûr /syr/ *a.* certain, sure; (*sans danger*) safe; (*digne de confiance*) reliable; (*main*) steady; (*jugement*) sound.

surabondance /syrabɔ̃dɑ̃s/ *n.f.* superabundance.

suranné /syrane/ *a.* outmoded.

surcharg|e /syrʃarʒ/ *n.f.* overloading; (*poids*) extra load. ~**er** *v.t.* overload; (*texte*) alter.

surchauffer /syrʃofe/ *v.t.* overheat.

surchoix /syrʃwa/ *a. invar.* of finest quality.

surclasser /syrklase/ *v.t.* outclass.

surcroît /syrkrwa/ *n.m.* increase (**de**, in), additional amount (**de**, of). **de ~**, in addition.

surdité /syrdite/ *n.f.* deafness.

sureau (*pl.* ~**x**) /syro/ *n.m.* (*arbre*) elder.

surélever /syrelve/ *v.t.* raise.

sûrement /syrmɑ̃/ *adv.* certainly; (*sans danger*) safely.

surenchè|re /syrɑ̃ʃɛr/ *n.f.* higher bid. ~**rir** *v.i.* bid higher (**sur**, than).

surestimer /syrɛstime/ *v.t.* overestimate.

sûreté /syrte/ *n.f.* safety; (*garantie*) surety; (*d'un geste*) steadiness. **être en ~**, be safe. **S~ (nationale)**, division of French Ministère de l'Intérieur in charge of police.

surexcité /syrɛksite/ *a.* very excited.

surf /syrf/ *n.m.* surfing.

surface /syrfas/ *n.f.* surface. **faire ~**, (*sous-marin etc.*) surface. **en ~**, (*fig.*) superficially.

surfait, ~e /syrfɛ, -t/ *a.* overrated.

surgelé /syrʒəle/ *a.* (deep-)frozen. (*aliments*) ~**s**, frozen food.

surgir /syrʒir/ *v.i.* appear (suddenly); (*difficulté*) arise.

surhomme /syrɔm/ *n.m.* superman.

surhumain, ~e /syrymɛ̃, -ɛn/ *a.* superhuman.

surlendemain /syrlɑ̃dmɛ̃/ *n.m.* **le ~**, two days later. **le ~ de**, two days after.

surligneur /syrliɲœr/ *n.m.* highlighter (pen).

surmen|er /syrməne/ *v.t.*, **se ~er** *v. pr.* overwork. ~**age** *n.m.* overworking; (*méd.*) overwork.

surmonter /syrmɔ̃te/ *v.t.* (*vaincre*) overcome, surmount; (*être audessus de*) surmount, top.

surnager /syrnaʒe/ *v.i.* float.

surnaturel, ~le /syrnatyrɛl/ *a.* supernatural.

surnom /syrnɔ̃/ *n.m.* nickname. ~**mer** /-ɔme/ *v.t.* nickname.

surnombre (en) /(ɑ̃)syrnɔ̃br/ *adv.*

too many. **il est en ~,** he is one too many.

surpasser /syrpɑse/ *v.t.* surpass.

surpeuplé /syrpœple/ *a.* overpopulated.

surplomb /syrplɔ̃/ *n.m.* **en ~,** overhanging. **~er** /-be/ *v.t./i.* overhang.

surplus /syrply/ *n.m.* surplus.

surpr|endre† /syrprɑ̃dr/ *v.t.* (*étonner*) surprise; (*prendre au dépourvu*) catch, surprise; (*entendre*) overhear. **~enant, ~enante** *a.* surprising. **~is, ~ise** *a.* surprised (**de,** at).

surprise /syrpriz/ *n.f.* surprise. **~-partie** (*pl.* **~s-parties**) *n.f.* party.

surréalisme /syrrealism/ *n.m.* surrealism.

sursaut /syrso/ *n.m.* start, jump. **en ~,** with a start. **~ de,** (*regain*) burst of. **~er** /-te/ *v.i.* start, jump.

sursis /syrsi/ *n.m.* reprieve; (*mil.*) deferment. **deux ans (de prison) avec ~,** a two-year suspended sentence.

surtaxe /syrtaks/ *n.f.* surcharge.

surtout /syrtu/ *adv.* especially, mainly; (*avant tout*) above all. **~ pas,** certainly not.

surveillant, ~e /syrvejɑ̃, -t/ *n.m., f.* (*de prison*) warder; (*au lycée*) supervisor (in charge of discipline).

surveill|er /syrveje/ *v.t.* watch; (*travaux, élèves*) supervise. **~ance** *n.f.* watch; supervision; (*de la police*) surveillance.

survenir /syrvənir/ *v.i.* occur, come about; (*personne*) turn up; (*événement*) take place.

survêtement /syrvɛtmɑ̃/ *n.m.* (*sport*) track suit.

survie /syrvi/ *n.f.* survival.

survivance /syrvivɑ̃s/ *n.f.* survival.

surviv|re† /syrvivr/ *v.i.* survive

~re à, (*conflit etc.*) survive; (*personne*) outlive. **~ant, ~ante** *a.* surviving; *n.m., f.* survivor.

survol /syrvɔl/ *n.m.* **le ~ de,** flying over. **~er** *v.t.* fly over; (*livre*) skim through.

survolté /syrvɔlte/ *a.* (*surexcité*) worked up.

susceptib|le /syseptibl/ *a.* touchy. **~le de faire,** (*possibilité*) liable to do; (*capacité*) able to do. **~ilité** *n.f.* susceptibility.

susciter /sysite/ *v.t.* (*éveiller*) arouse; (*occasionner*) create.

suspect, ~e /syspɛ, -ɛkt/ *a.* (*témoignage*) suspect; (*individu*) suspicious. **~ de,** suspected of. *—n.m., f.* suspect. **~er** /-ɛkte/ *v.t.* suspect.

suspend|re /syspɑ̃dr/ *v.t.* (*arrêter, différer, destituer*) suspend; (*accrocher*) hang (up). **se ~re à,** hang from. **~u à,** hanging from.

suspens (en) /(ɑ̃)syspɑ̃/ *adv.* (*affaire*) in abeyance; (*dans l'indécision*) in suspense.

suspense /syspɑ̃s/ *n.m.* suspense.

suspension /syspɑ̃sjɔ̃/ *n.f.* suspension; (*lustre*) chandelier.

suspicion /syspisjɔ̃/ *n.f.* suspicion.

susurrer /sysyre/ *v.t./i.* murmur.

suture /sytyr/ *n.f.* **point de ~,** stitch.

svelte /svɛlt/ *a.* slender.

S.V.P. *abrév. voir* **s'il vous plaît.**

sweat-shirt /switʃœrt/ *n.m.* sweatshirt.

syllabe /silab/ *n.f.* syllable.

symbol|e /sɛ̃bɔl/ *n.m.* symbol. **~ique** *a.* symbolic(al). **~iser** *v.t.* symbolize.

symétr|ie /simetri/ *n.f.* symmetry. **~ique** *a.* symmetrical.

sympa /sɛ̃pa/ *a. invar.* (*fam.*) nice. **sois ~,** be a pal.

sympath|ie /sɛ̃pati/ *n.f.* (*goût*) liking; (*affinité*) affinity; (*condoléances*) sympathy. **~ique** *a.* nice, pleasant.

sympathis|er /sɛpatize/ *v.i.* get on well (**avec**, with). **~ant**, **~ante** *n.m.*, *f.* sympathizer.

symphon|ie /sɛ̃fɔni/ *n.f.* symphony. **~ique** *a.* symphonic; (*orchestre*) symphony.

symposium /sɛ̃pozjɔm/ *n.m.* symposium.

sympt|ôme /sɛ̃ptom/ *n.m.* symptom. **~omatique** /-ɔma-tik/*a.* symptomatic.

synagogue /sinagɔg/ *n.f.* synagogue.

synchroniser /sɛ̃krɔnize/ *v.t.* synchronize.

syncope /sɛ̃kɔp/ *n.f.* (*méd.*) black-out.

syncoper /sɛ̃kɔpe/ *v.t.* syncopate.

syndic /sɛ̃dik/ *n.m.* **~ (d'immeuble)**, managing agent.

syndic|at /sɛ̃dika/ *n.m.* (trade) union. **~at d'initiative**, tourist office. **~al** (*m. pl.* **~aux**) *a.* (trade-)union. **~aliste** *n.m./f.* (trade-)unionist; *a.* (trade-)union.

syndiqué, **~e** /sɛ̃dike/ *n.m.*, *f.* (trade-)union member.

syndrome /sɛ̃drom/ *n.m.* syndrome.

synonyme /sinɔnim/ *a.* synonymous. —*n.m.* synonym.

syntaxe /sɛ̃taks/ *n.f.* syntax.

synthèse /sɛ̃tɛz/ *n.f.* synthesis.

synthétique /sɛ̃tetik/ *a.* synthetic.

synthé(tiseur) /sɛ̃te(tizœr)/ *n.m.* synthesizer.

syphilis /sifilis/ *n.f.* syphilis.

Syrie /siri/ *n.f.* Syria.

syrien, **~ne** /sirjɛ̃, -jɛn/ *a. & n.m.*, *f.* Syrian.

systématique /sistematik/ *a.* systematic. **~ment** *adv.* systematically.

système /sistɛm/ *n.m.* system. **le ~ D**, coping with problems.

T

t' /t/ *voir* **te**.

ta /ta/ *voir* **ton**[1].

tabac /taba/ *n.m.* tobacco; (*magasin*) tobacconist's shop. —*a. invar.* buff. **~ à priser**, snuff.

tabasser /tabase/ *v.t.* (*fam.*) beat up.

table /tabl/ *n.f.* table. **à ~!**, come and eat! **faire ~ rase**, make a clean sweep (**de**, of). **~ de nuit**, bedside table. **~ des matières**, table of contents. **~ roulante**, (tea-)trolley; (*Amer.*) (serving) cart.

tableau (*pl.* **~x**) /tablo/ *n.m.* picture; (*peinture*) painting; (*panneau*) board; (*graphique*) chart; (*liste*) list. **~ (noir)**, blackboard. **~ d'affichage**, notice-board. **~ de bord**, dashboard.

tabler /table/ *v.i.* **~ sur**, count on.

tablette /tablɛt/ *n.f.* shelf. **~ de chocolat**, bar of chocolate.

tablier /tablije/ *n.m.* apron; (*de pont*) platform; (*de magasin*) shutter.

tabloïd(e) /tabloid/ *a. & n.m.* tabloïd.

tabou /tabu/ *n.m. & a.* taboo.

tabouret /taburɛ/ *n.m.* stool.

tabulateur /tabylatœr/ *n.m.* tabulator.

tac /tak/ *n.m.* **du ~ au tac**, tit for tat.

tache /taʃ/ *n.f.* mark, spot; (*salissure*) stain. **faire ~ d'huile**, spread. **~ de rousseur**, freckle.

tâche /taʃ/ *n.f.* task, job.

tacher /taʃe/ *v.t.* stain. **se ~** *v. pr.* (*personne*) get stains on one's clothes.

tâcher /taʃe/ *v.i.* **~ de faire**, try to do.

tacheté /taʃte/ *a.* spotted.

tacite /tasit/ *a.* tacit.

taciturne /tasityrn/ *a.* taciturn.

tact /takt/ *n.m.* tact.

tactile /taktil/ *a.* tactile.

tactique /taktik/ *a.* tactical. —*n.f.* tactics. **une ~,** a tactic.

taie /tɛ/ *n.f.* **~ d'oreiller,** pillow-case.

taillader /tajade/ *v.t.* gash, slash.

taille[1] /taj/ *n.f.* (*milieu du corps*) waist; (*hauteur*) height; (*grandeur*) size. **de ~ à faire,** be up to doing. **être de ~ à faire,** be up to doing.

taille[2] /taj/ *n.f.* cutting; pruning; (*forme*) cut. **~er** *v.t.* cut; (*arbre*) prune; (*crayon*) sharpen; (*vêtement*) cut out. **se ~er** *v. pr.* (*argot*) clear off. **~e-crayon(s)** *n.m. invar.* pencil-sharpener.

tailleur /tajœr/ *n.m.* tailor; (*costume*) lady's suit. **en ~,** cross-legged.

taillis /taji/ *n.m.* copse.

taire† /tɛr/ *v.t.* say nothing about. **se ~** *v. pr.* be silent *ou* quiet; (*devenir silencieux*) fall silent. **faire ~,** silence.

talc /talk/ *n.m.* talcum powder.

talent /talɑ̃/ *n.m.* talent. **~ueux, ~ueuse** /-tɥø, -z/ *a.* talented.

taloche /talɔʃ/ *n.f.* (*fam.*) slap.

talon /talɔ̃/ *n.m.* heel; (*de chèque*) stub.

talonner /talɔne/ *v.t.* follow hard on the heels of.

talus /taly/ *n.m.* embankment.

tambour /tɑ̃bur/ *n.m.* drum; (*personne*) drummer; (*porte*) revolving door.

tambourin /tɑ̃burɛ̃/ *n.m.* tambourine.

tambouriner /tɑ̃burine/ *v.t./i.* drum (**sur,** on).

tamis /tami/ *n.m.* sieve. **~er** /-ze/ *v.t.* sieve.

Tamise /tamiz/ *n.f.* Thames.

tamisé /tamize/ *a.* (*lumière*) subdued.

tampon /tɑ̃pɔ̃/ *n.m.* (*pour boucher*) plug; (*ouate*) wad, pad; (*timbre*) stamp; (*de train*) buffer. **~ (hygiénique),** tampon.

tamponner /tɑ̃pɔne/ *v.t.* crash into; (*timbre*) stamp; (*plaie*) dab; (*mur*) plug. **se ~** *v. pr.* (*véhicules*) crash into each other.

tandem /tɑ̃dɛm/ *n.m.* (*bicyclette*) tandem; (*personnes: fig.*) duo.

tandis que /tɑ̃dik(ə)/ *conj.* while.

tangage /tɑ̃gaʒ/ *n.m.* pitching.

tangente /tɑ̃ʒɑ̃t/ *n.f.* tangent.

tangible /tɑ̃ʒibl/ *a.* tangible.

tango /tɑ̃go/ *n.m.* tango.

tanguer /tɑ̃ge/ *v.i.* pitch.

tanière /tanjɛr/ *n.f.* den.

tank /tɑ̃k/ *n.m.* tank.

tann|er /tane/ *v.t.* tan. **~é** *a.* (*visage*) tanned, weather-beaten.

tant /tɑ̃/ *adv.* (*travailler, manger, etc.*) so much; (*quantité*) so much; (*nombre*) so many. **~ que,** as long as; (*autant que*) as much as. **en ~ que,** (*comme*) as. **~ mieux!, fine!,** all the better! **~ pis!,** too bad!

tante /tɑ̃t/ *n.f.* aunt.

tantôt /tɑ̃to/ *adv.* sometimes; (*cet après-midi*) this afternoon.

tapage /tapaʒ/ *n.m.* din. **~eur, ~euse** *a.* rowdy; (*tape-à-l'œil*) flashy.

tapant, ~e /tapɑ̃, -t/ *a.* **à deux/trois/etc. heures ~es** at exactly two/three/etc. o'clock.

tape /tap/ *n.f.* slap. **~-à-l'œil** *a. invar.* flashy, tawdry.

taper /tape/ *v.t.* bang; (*enfant*) slap; (*emprunter. fam.*) touch for money. **~ (à la machine),** type. **—***v.i.* (*cogner*) bang; (*soleil*) beat down. **~ dans,** (*puiser dans*) dig into. **~ sur,** thump; (*critiquer. fam.*) knock. **se ~** *v. pr.* (*repas: fam.*) put away; (*corvée. fam.*) do.

tap|ir (se) /(sə)tapir/ *v. pr.* crouch. **~i** *a.* crouching.

tapis /tapi/ *n.m.* carpet; (*petit*) rug;

(aux cartes) baize. **∼ de bain,** bath mat. **∼-brosse** n.m. doormat. **∼ de sol,** groundsheet. **∼ roulant,** (pour objets) conveyor belt.

tapiss|er /tapise/ v.t. (wall)paper; (fig.) cover (de, with). **∼erie** n.f. tapestry; (papier peint) wallpaper. **∼ier, ∼ière** n.m., f. (décorateur) interior decorator; (qui recouvre un siège) upholsterer.

tapoter /tapɔte/ v.t. tap, pat.

taquin, ∼e /takɛ̃, -in/ a. fond of teasing. —n.m., f. tease(r). **∼er** /-ine/ v.t. tease. **∼erie(s)** /-inri/ n.f. (pl.) teasing.

tarabiscoté /tarabiskɔte/ a. overelaborate.

tard /tar/ adv. late. **au plus ∼,** at the latest. **plus ∼,** later. **sur le ∼,** late in life.

tard|er /tarde/ v.i. (être lent à venir) be a long time coming. **∼er (à faire)** take a long time (doing), delay (doing). **sans (plus) ∼er,** without (further) delay. **il me ∼e de,** I long to.

tardi|f, ∼ve /tardif, -v/ a. late; (regrets) belated.

tare /tar/ n.f. (défaut) defect.

taré /tare/ a. cretin.

targette /tarʒɛt/ n.f. bolt.

targuer (se) /(sə)targe/ v. pr. **se ∼ de,** boast about.

tarif /tarif/ n.m. tariff; (de train, taxi) fare. **∼s postaux,** postage ou postal rates. **∼aire** a. tariff.

tarir /tarir/ v.t./i., **se ∼** v. pr. dry up.

tartare /tartar/ a. (culin.) tartar.

tarte /tart/ n.f. tart; (Amer.) (open) pie. —a. invar. (sot. fam.) stupid; (laid: fam.) ugly.

tartin|e /tartin/ n.f. slice of bread. **∼e beurrée,** slice of bread and butter. **∼er** v.t. spread.

tartre /tartr/ n.m. (bouilloire) fur, calcium deposit; (dents) tartar.

tas /ta/ n.m. pile, heap. **un** ou **des ∼ de,** (fam.) lots of.

tasse /tas/ n.f. cup. **∼ à thé,** teacup.

tasser /tase/ v.t. pack, squeeze; (terre) pack down. **se ∼** v. pr. (terrain) sink; (se serrer) squeeze up.

tâter /tate/ v.t. feel; (fig.) sound out. —v.i. **∼ de,** try out.

tatillon, ∼ne /tatijɔ̃, -jɔn/ a. finicky.

tâtonn|er /tatɔne/ v.i. grope about. **∼ements** n.m. pl. (essais) trial and error.

tâtons (à) /(a)tatɔ̃/ adv. **avancer** ou **marcher à ∼,** grope one's way along.

tatou|er /tatwe/ v.t. tattoo. **∼age** n.m. (dessin) tattoo.

taudis /todi/ n.m. hovel.

taule /tol/ n.f. (fam.) prison.

taup|e /top/ n.f. mole. **∼inière** n.f. molehill.

taureau (pl. **∼x**) /tɔro/ n.m. bull. **le T∼,** Taurus.

taux /to/ n.m. rate.

taverne /tavɛrn/ n.f. tavern.

tax|e /taks/ n.f. tax. **∼e sur la valeur ajoutée,** value added tax. **∼er** v.t. tax; (produit) fix the price of. **∼er qn. de,** accuse s.o. of.

taxi /taksi/ n.m. taxi(-cab); (personne: fam.) taxi-driver.

taxiphone /taksifɔn/ n.m. pay phone.

Tchécoslovaquie /tʃekɔslɔvaki/ n.f. Czechoslovakia.

tchèque /tʃɛk/ a. & n.m./f. Czech.

te, t' /tə, t/ pron. you; (indirect) (to) you; (réfléchi) yourself.

technicien, ∼ne /tɛknisjɛ̃, -jɛn/ n.m., f. technician.

technique /tɛknik/ a. technical. —n.f. technique. **∼ment** adv. technically.

technolog|ie /tɛknɔlɔʒi/ n.f. technology. **∼ique** a. technological.

teck /tɛk/ *n.m.* teak.

tee-shirt /tiʃœrt/ *n.m.* tee-shirt.

teindre† /tɛ̃dr/ *v.t.* dye. se **~ les cheveux** /tɛ̃dr/ *v.t.* dye one's hair.

teint /tɛ̃/ *n.m.* complexion.

teinte /tɛ̃t/ *n.f.* shade, tint. **une ~e de**, *(fig.)* a tinge of. **~er** *v.t. (papier, verre, etc.)* tint; *(bois)* stain.

teintur|e /tɛ̃tyr/ *n.f.* dyeing; *(produit)* dye. **~erie** *n.f. (boutique)* dry-cleaner's. **~ier, ~ière** *n.m., f.* dry-cleaner.

tel, ~le /tɛl/ *a.* such. un **~ livre/etc.**, such a book/etc. un **~ chagrin/etc.**, such sorrow/etc. **~ que**, such as, like; *(ainsi que)* (just) as. **~ ou tel**, such-and-such. **~ quel**, (just) as it is.

télé /tele/ *n.f. (fam.)* TV.

télécommande /telekɔmɑ̃d/ *n.f.* remote control.

télécommunications /telekɔmynikasjɔ̃/ *n.f. pl.* telecommunications.

télécopi|e /telekɔpi/ *n.f.* tele(fax). **~eur** *n.m.* fax machine.

téléfilm /telefilm/ *n.m.* (tele)film.

télégramme /telegram/ *n.m.* telegram.

télégraph|e /telegraf/ *n.m.* telegraph. **~ier** *v.t./i.* **~ier (à)**, cable. **~ique** *a.* telegraphic; *(fil, poteau)* telegraph.

téléguid|er /telegide/ *v.t.* control by radio. **~é** *a.* radio-controlled.

télématique /telematik/ *n.f.* computer communications.

télépathe /telepat/ *a. & n.m., f.* psychic.

télépathie /telepati/ *n.f.* telepathy.

téléphérique /teleferik/ *n.m.* cable-car.

téléphon|e /telefɔn/ *n.m.* (tele)phone. **~e rouge**, *(pol.)* hot line. **~er** *v.t./i.* **~er (à)**, (tele)phone. **~ique** *a.* (tele)phone. **~iste** *n.m./f.* operator.

téléscope /teleskɔp/ *n.m.* telescope. **~ique** *a.* telescopic.

télescoper /teleskɔpe/ *v.t.* smash into. se **~** *v. pr. (véhicules)* smash into each other.

télésiege /telesjɛʒ/ *n.m.* chair-lift.

téléski /teleski/ *n.m.* ski tow.

téléspecta|teur, ~trice /telespektatœr, -tris/ *n.m., f.* (television) viewer.

télévente /televɑ̃t/ *n.f.* telesales.

télévis|é /televize/ *a.* **émission ~ée**, television programme. **~eur** *n.m.* television set.

télévision /televizjɔ̃/ *n.f.* television.

télex /telɛks/ *n.m.* telex.

télexer /telɛkse/ *v.t.* telex.

telle /tɛl/ *voir* tel.

tellement /tɛlmɑ̃/ *adv. (tant)* so much; *(si)* so. **~ de**, *(quantité)* so much; *(nombre)* so many.

témér|aire /temerɛr/ *a.* rash. **~ité** *n.f.* rashness.

témoignage /temwaɲaʒ/ *n.m.* testimony, evidence; *(récit)* account. **~ de**, *(sentiment)* token of.

témoigner /temwaɲe/ *v.i.* testify *(de, to).* —*v.t.* show. **~ que**, testify that.

témoin /temwɛ̃/ *n.m.* witness; *(sport)* baton. **être ~ de**, witness. **~ oculaire**, eyewitness.

tempe /tɑ̃p/ *n.f. (anat.)* temple.

tempérament /tɑ̃peramɑ̃/ *n.m.* temperament; *(physique)* constitution. **à ~**, *(acheter)* on hire-purchase; *(Amer.)* on the instalment plan.

température /tɑ̃peratyr/ *n.f.* temperature.

tempér|er /tɑ̃pere/ *v.t.* temper. **~é** *a. (climat)* temperate.

tempête /tɑ̃pɛt/ *n.f.* storm. **~ de neige**, snowstorm.

tempêter /tɑ̃pɛte/ *v.i. (crier)* rage.

temple /tɑ̃pl/ *n.m.* temple; *(protestant)* church.

temporaire /tɑ̃pɔrɛr/ a. temporary. **~ment** adv. temporarily.

temporel, ~le /tɑ̃pɔrɛl/ a. temporal.

temporiser /tɑ̃pɔrize/ v.i. play for time.

temps¹ /tɑ̃/ n.m. time; (gram.) tense; (étape) stage. à **~** partiel/plein, part-/full-time. ces derniers **~**, lately. dans le **~**, at one time. dans quelque **~**, in a while. de **~** en temps, from time to time. **~** d'arrêt, pause. avoir tout son **~**, have plenty of time.

temps² /tɑ̃/ n.m. (atmosphère) weather. **~** de chien, filthy weather. quel **~** fait-il?, what's the weather like?

tenace /tənas/ a. stubborn.

ténacité /tenasite/ n.f. stubbornness.

tenaille(s) /tənɑj/ n.f. (pl.) pincers.

tenanc|ier, -ière /tənɑ̃sje, -jɛr/ n.m., f. keeper (de, of).

tenant /tənɑ̃/ n.m. (partisan) supporter; (d'un titre) holder.

tendance /tɑ̃dɑ̃s/ n.f. tendency; (opinions) leanings; (évolution) trend. avoir **~** à, have a tendency to, tend to.

tendon /tɑ̃dɔ̃/ n.m. tendon.

tendre¹ /tɑ̃dr/ v.t. stretch; (piège) set; (bras) stretch out; (main) hold out; (cou) crane; (tapisserie) hang. **~** à qn., hold out to s.o. —v.i. **~** à, tend to. **~** l'oreille, prick up one's ears.

tendre² /tɑ̃dr/ a. tender; (couleur, bois) soft. **~ment** /-əmɑ̃/ adv. tenderly. **~sse** /-ɛs/ n.f. tenderness.

tendu /tɑ̃dy/ a. (corde) tight; (personne, situation) tense; (main) outstretched.

tén|èbres /tenɛbr/ n.f. pl. darkness. **~ébreux, ~ébreuse** a. dark.

teneur /tənœr/ n.f. content.

tenir† /tənir/ v.t. hold; (pari, promesse, hôtel) keep; (place) take up; (propos) utter; (rôle) play. **~** de, (avoir reçu de) have got from. **~** pour, regard as. **~** propre/chaud**/**etc., keep clean/warm/ etc. **~** à, be attached to. **~** à faire, be anxious to do. **~** dans, fit into. **~** de qn., take after s.o. se **~** v. pr. (rester) remain; (debout) stand; (avoir lieu) be held. se **~** à, hold on to. se **~** bien, behave o.s. s'en **~** à, (se limiter à) confine o.s. to. **~** bon, stand firm. **~** compte de, take into account. **le ~** coup, hold out. **~** tête à, stand up to. tiens!, (surprise) hey!

tennis /tenis/ n.m. tennis; (terrain) tennis-court. —n.m. pl. (chaussures) sneakers. **~** de table, table tennis.

ténor /tenɔr/ n.m. tenor.

tension /tɑ̃sjɔ̃/ n.f. tension. avoir de la **~**, have high blood-pressure.

tentacule /tɑ̃takyl/ n.m. tentacle.

tentative /tɑ̃tativ/ n.f. attempt.

tente /tɑ̃t/ n.f. tent.

tenter¹ /tɑ̃te/ v.t. try (de faire, to do).

tent|er² /tɑ̃te/ v.t. (allécher) tempt. **~é de**, tempted to. **~ation** n.f. temptation.

tenture /tɑ̃tyr/ n.f. (wall) hanging. **~s**, drapery.

tenu /təny/ voir tenir. —a. bien **~**, well-kept. **~** de, obliged to.

ténu /teny/ a. (fil etc.) fine; (cause, nuance) tenuous.

tenue /təny/ n.f. (habillement) dress; (de sport) clothes; (de maison) upkeep; (conduite) (good) behaviour; (maintien) posture. **~** de soirée, evening dress.

tér|ebenthine /terebɑ̃tin/ n.f. turpentine.

tergiverser /tɛrʒiverse/ v.i. procrastinate.

terme /tɛrm/ n.m. (mot) term; (date limite) time-limit; (fin) end; (date de loyer) term. **à long/court ～**, long-/short-term. **en bons ～s**, on good terms (**avec**, with).

termin|al, ～ale (m. pl. **～aux**) /terminal, -o/ a. terminal. (classe) **～ale**, sixth form; (Amer.) twelfth grade. **—n.** (pl. **～aux**) terminal.

termin|er /tɛrmine/ v.t./i. finish; (soirée, débat) end, finish. **se ～** v. pr. end (**par**, with). **～aison** n.f. (gram.) ending.

terminologie /tɛrminɔlɔʒi/ n.f. terminology.

terminus /tɛrminys/ n.m. terminus.

terne /tɛrn/ a. dull, drab.

ternir /tɛrnir/ v.t./i., **se ～** v. pr. tarnish.

terrain /tɛrɛ̃/ n.m. ground; (parcelle) piece of land; (à bâtir) plot. **～ d'aviation**, airfield. **～ de camping**, campsite. **～ de golf**, golf-course. **～ de jeu**, playground. **～ vague**, waste ground; (Amer.) vacant lot.

terrasse /tɛras/ n.f. terrace; (de café) pavement area.

terrassement /tɛrasmɑ̃/ n.m. excavation.

terrasser /tɛrase/ v.t. (adversaire) floor; (maladie) strike down.

terrassier /tɛrasje/ n.m. navvy, labourer, ditch-digger.

terre /tɛr/ n.f. (planète, matière) earth; (étendue, pays) land; (sol) ground; (domaine) estate. **à ～** (naut.) ashore. **par ～**, (tomber, jeter) to the ground; (s'asseoir, poser) on the ground. **la ～** (cuite), terracotta. **～-à-terre** a. invar. matter-of-fact, down-to-earth. **～-plein** n.m. platform, (auto.) central reservation. **la ～ ferme**, dry land. **～ glaise**, clay.

terreau /tɛro/ n.m. invar. compost.

terrer (se) /(sə)tɛre/ v.pr. hide o.s., dig o.s. in.

terrestre /tɛrɛstr/ a. land; (de notre planète) earth's; (fig.) earthly.

terreur /tɛrœr/ n.f. terror.

terreu|x, ～se /tɛrø, -z/ a. earthy; (sale) grubby.

terrible /tɛribl/ a. terrible; (formidable: fam.) terrific.

terrien, ～ne /tɛrjɛ̃, -jɛn/ n.m., f. earth-dweller.

terrier /tɛrje/ n.m. (trou de lapin etc.) burrow; (chien) terrier.

terrifier /tɛrifje/ v.t. terrify.

terrine /tɛrin/ n.f. (culin.) terrine.

territ|oire /tɛritwar/ n.m. territory. **～orial** (m. pl. **～oriaux**) a. territorial.

terroir /tɛrwar/ n.m. (sol) soil; (région) region. **du ～**, country.

terroriser /tɛrɔrize/ v.t. terrorize.

terroris|te /tɛrɔrist/ n.m./f. terrorist. **～me** n.m. terrorism.

tertre /tɛrtr/ n.m. mound.

tes /te/ voir **ton¹**.

tesson /tɛsɔ̃/ n.m. **～ de bouteille**, piece of broken bottle.

test /tɛst/ n.m. test. **～er** v.t. test.

testament /tɛstamɑ̃/ n.m. (jurid.) will; (politique, artistique) testament. **Ancien/Nouveau T～**, Old/New Testament.

testicule /tɛstikyl/ n.m. testicle.

tétanos /tetanos/ n.m. tetanus.

têtard /tɛtar/ n.m. tadpole.

tête /tɛt/ n.f. head; (figure) face; (cheveux) hair; (cerveau) brain. **à la ～ de**, at the head of. **à ～ reposée**, in a leisurely moment. **de ～**, (calculer) in one's head. **en ～**, (sport) in the lead. **faire la ～**, sulk. **faire une ～**, (football) head the ball. **tenir ～ à qn.**, stand up to s.o. **une forte ～**, a rebel. **la ～ la première**, head first. **il n'en fait qu'à sa ～**, he does just as he pleases. **de la ~ aux pieds**, from head to toe. **~-à-queue** n.m. invar. (auto.) spin. **~-à-tête** n.m. invar. tête-à-tête. **en ~-à-tête**, in private.

tétée /tete/ n.f. feed.

téter /tete/ v.t./i. suck.

tétine /tetin/ n.f. (de biberon) teat; (sucette) dummy; (Amer.) pacifier.

têtu /tety/ a. stubborn.

texte /tɛkst/ n.m. text; (de leçon) subject; (morceau choisi) passage.

textile /tɛkstil/ n.m. & a. textile.

textuel, ~le /tɛkstɥɛl/ a. literal.

texture /tɛkstyr/ n.f. texture.

thaïlandais, ~e /tailɑ̃dɛ, -z/ a. & n.m., f. Thai.

Thaïlande /tailɑ̃d/ n.f. Thailand.

thé /te/ n.m. tea.

théâtral (m. pl. **~aux**) /teatral, -o/ a. theatrical.

théâtre /teatr/ n.m. theatre; (jeu forcé) play-acting; (d'un crime) scene. **faire du ~**, act.

théière /tejɛr/ n.f. teapot.

thème /tɛm/ n.m. theme; (traduction: scol.) prose.

théologie /teɔlɔʒi/ n.f. theology. **~ien** n.m. theologian. **~ique** a. theological.

théorème /teɔrɛm/ n.m. theorem.

théorie /teɔri/ n.f. theory. **~icien, ~icienne** n.m., f. theorist. **~ique** a. theoretical. **~iquement**, adv. theoretically.

thérapie /terapi/ n.f. therapy. **~eutique** a. therapeutic.

thermique /tɛrmik/ a. thermal.

thermomètre /tɛrmɔmɛtr/ n.m. thermometer.

thermonucléaire /tɛrmɔnykleɛr/ a. thermonuclear.

thermos /tɛrmɔs/ n.m./f. (P.) Thermos (P.) (flask).

thermostat /tɛrmɔsta/ n.m. thermostat.

thésauriser /tezɔrize/ v.t./i. hoard.

thèse /tɛz/ n.f. thesis.

thon /tɔ̃/ n.m. (poisson) tuna.

thrombose /trɔ̃boz/ n.f. thrombosis.

thym /tɛ̃/ n.m. thyme.

thyroïde /tiroid/ n.f. thyroid.

tibia /tibja/ n.m. shin-bone.

tic /tik/ n.m. (contraction) twitch; (manie) mannerism.

ticket /tikɛ/ n.m. ticket.

tic-tac /tiktak/ n.m. invar. (de pendule) ticking. **faire ~**, go tick tock.

tiède /tjɛd/ a. lukewarm; (atmosphère) mild. **tiédeur** /tjedœr/ n.f. lukewarmness; mildness.

tiédir /tjedir/ v.t./i. (faire) ~, warm slightly.

tien, ~ne /tjɛ̃, tjɛn/ pron. le ~, la ~ne, les ~(ne)s, yours. **à la ~ne!**, cheers!

tiens, tient /tjɛ̃/ voir tenir.

tiercé /tjɛrse/ n.m. place-betting.

tier|s, ~ce /tjɛr, -s/ a. third. **—n.m.** (fraction) third; (personne) third party. **T~s-Monde** n.m. Third World.

tifs /tif/ n.m. pl. (fam.) hair.

tige /tiʒ/ n.f. (bot.) stem, stalk; (en métal) shaft.

tignasse /tiɲas/ n.f. mop of hair.

tigre /tigr/ n.m. tiger. **~sse** /-ɛs/ n.f. tigress.

tigré /tigre/ a. (rayé) striped; (chat) tabby.

tilleul /tijœl/ n.m. lime(-tree), linden(-tree); (infusion) lime tea.

timbale /tɛ̃bal/ n.f. (gobelet) (metal) tumbler.

timbr|e /tɛ̃br/ n.m. stamp; (sonnette) bell; (de voix) tone. **~e-poste** (pl. **~es-poste**) n.m. postage stamp. **~er** v.t. stamp.

timbré /tɛ̃bre/ a. (fam.) crazy.

timid|e /timid/ a. timid. **~ité** n.f. timidity.

timoré /timɔre/ a. timorous.

tintamarre /tɛ̃tamar/ n.m. din.

tint|er /tɛ̃te/ v.i. ring; (clefs) jingle. **~ement** n.m. ringing; jingling.

tique /tik/ *n.f.* (*insecte*) tick.

tir /tir/ *n.m.* (*sport*) shooting; (*action de tirer*) firing; (*feu, rafale*) fire. **~à l'arc**, archery. **~ forain**, shooting-gallery.

tirade /tirad/ *n.f.* soliloquy.

tirage /tiraʒ/ *n.m.* (*de photo*) printing; (*de journal*) circulation; (*de livre*) edition; (*de loterie*) draw; (*de cheminée*) draught. **~ au sort**, drawing lots.

tiraill|er /tiraje/ *v.t.* pull (away) at; (*harceler*) plague. **~é entre**, (*possibilités etc.*) torn between. **~ement** *n.m.* (*douleur*) gnawing pain; (*conflit*) conflict.

tiré /tire/ *a.* (*traits*) drawn.

tire-bouchon /tirbuʃɔ̃/ *n.m.* corkscrew.

tire-lait /tirlɛ/ *n.m.* breastpump.

tirelire /tirlir/ *n.f.* money-box; (*Amer.*) coin-bank.

tirer /tire/ *v.t.* pull; (*navire*) tow, tug; (*langue*) stick out; (*conclusion, trait, rideaux*) draw; (*coup de feu*) fire; (*gibier*) shoot; (*photo*) print. **~ de**, (*sortir*) take ou get out of; (*extraire*) extract from; (*plaisir, nom*) derive from. —*v.i.* shoot, fire (**sur**, at). **~ sur**, (*couleur*) verge on; (*corde*) pull at. **se ~** *v. pr.* (*fam.*) clear off. **se ~ de**, get out of. **s'en ~**, (*en réchapper*) pull through; (*réussir: fam.*) cope. **~ à sa fin**, be drawing to a close. **~ au clair**, clarify. **~ au sort**, draw lots (for). **~ parti de**, take advantage of. **~ profit de**, profit from.

tiret /tire/ *n.m.* dash.

tireur /tirœr/ *n.m.* gunman. **~ d'élite**, marksman. **~ isolé**, sniper.

tiroir /tirwar/ *n.m.* drawer. **~-caisse** (*pl.* **~s-caisses**) *n.m.* till.

tisane /tizan/ *n.f.* herb-tea.

tison /tizɔ̃/ *n.m.* ember.

tisonnier /tizɔnje/ *n.m.* poker.

tiss|er /tise/ *v.t.* weave. **~age** *n.m.* weaving. **~erand** /tisrã/ *n.m.* weaver.

tissu /tisy/ *n.m.* fabric, material; (*biologique*) tissue. **un ~ de**, (*fig.*) a web of. **~-éponge** (*pl.* **~s-éponge**) *n.m.* towelling.

titre /titr/ *n.m.* title; (*diplôme*) qualification; (*comm.*) bond. **~s**, (*droits*) claims. (*gros*) **~s**, headlines. **à ce ~**, (*pour cette qualité*) as such. **à ~ d'exemple**, as an example. **à juste ~**, rightly. **à ~ privé**, in a private capacity. **~ de propriété**, title-deed.

titré /titre/ *a.* titled.

titrer /titre/ *v.t.* (*journal*) give as a headline.

tituber /titybe/ *v.i.* stagger.

titul|aire /titylɛr/ *a.* **être ~aire**, have tenure. **être ~aire de**, hold. —*n.m./f.* (*de permis etc.*) holder. **~ariser** *v.t.* give tenure to.

toast /tost/ *n.m.* piece of toast; (*allocution*) toast.

toboggan /tɔbɔgã/ *n.m.* (*traîneau*) toboggan; (*glissière*) slide; (*auto.*) flyover; (*auto., Amer.*) overpass.

toc /tɔk/ *int.* **~ toc!** knock knock!

tocsin /tɔksɛ̃/ *n.m.* alarm (bell).

toge /tɔʒ/ *n.f.* (*de juge etc.*) gown.

tohu-bohu /tɔyboy/ *n.m.* hubbub.

toi /twa/ *pron.* you; (*réfléchi*) yourself. **lève-~**, stand up.

toile /twal/ *n.f.* cloth; (*sac, tableau*) canvas; (*coton*) cotton. **~ d'araignée**, (spider's) web; (*délabrée*) cobweb. **~ de fond**, backdrop, backcloth.

toilette /twalɛt/ *n.f.* washing; (*habillement*) clothes, dress. **~s**, (*cabinets*) toilet(s). **de ~**, (*articles, savon, etc.*) toilet. **faire sa ~**, wash (and get ready).

toi-même /twamɛm/ *pron.* yourself.

toiser /twaze/ *v.t.* **~ qn.**, look s.o. up and down.

toison /twazɔ̃/ *n.f.* (*laine*) fleece.

toit /twa/ *n.m.* roof. ~ **ouvrant,** (*auto.*) sun-roof.

toiture /twatyr/ *n.f.* roof.

tôle /tol/ *n.f.* (*plaque*) iron sheet. ~ **ondulée,** corrugated iron.

tolérable /tolerabl/ *a.* tolerable.

toléran|t, ~**te** /tolerɑ̃, -t/ *a.* tolerant. ~**ce** *n.f.* tolerance; (*importations: comm.*) allowance.

tolérer /tolere/ *v.t.* tolerate; (*importations: comm.*) allow.

tollé /tole/ *n.m.* hue and cry.

tomate /tomat/ *n.f.* tomato.

tombe /tɔ̃b/ *n.f.* grave; (*avec monument*) tomb.

tombeau (*pl.* ~**x**) /tɔ̃bo/ *n.m.* tomb.

tombée /tɔ̃be/ *n.f.* ~ **de la nuit,** nightfall.

tomber /tɔ̃be/ *v.i.* (*aux. être*) fall; (*fièvre, vent*) drop; (*enthousiasme*) die down. **faire** ~, knock over; (*gouvernement*) bring down. **laisser** ~, drop; (*abandonner*) let down. **laisse** ~!, forget it! ~ **à l'eau,** (*projet*) fall through. ~ **bien** *ou* **à point,** come at the right time. ~ **en panne,** break down. ~ **en syncope,** faint. ~ **sur,** (*trouver*) run across.

tombola /tɔ̃bola/ *n.f.* tombola; (*Amer.*) lottery.

tome /tom/ *n.m.* volume.

ton¹, ta *ou* **ton*** (*pl.* **tes**) /tɔ̃, ta, tɔ̃n, te/ *a.* your.

ton² /tɔ̃/ *n.m.* tone; (*gamme: mus.*) key; (*hauteur de la voix*) pitch. **de bon** ~, in good taste.

tonalité /tonalite/ *n.f.* tone; (*téléphone*) dialling tone; (*téléphone: Amer.*) dial tone.

tond|re /tɔ̃dr/ *v.t.* (*herbe*) mow; (*mouton*) shear; (*cheveux*) clip. ~**euse** *n.f.* shears; clippers. ~**euse** (*à gazon*), (lawn-)mower.

tongs /tɔ̃g/ *n.f. pl.* flip-flops.

tonifier /tonifje/ *v.t.* tone up.

tonique /tonik/ *a.* & *n.m.* tonic.

tonne /ton/ *n.f.* ton(ne).

tonneau (*pl.* ~**x**) /tono/ *n.m.* (*récipient*) barrel; (*naut.*) ton; (*culbute*) somersault.

tonnelle /tonɛl/ *n.f.* bower.

tonner /tone/ *v.i.* thunder.

tonnerre /tonɛr/ *n.m.* thunder.

tonte /tɔ̃t/ *n.f.* (*de gazon*) mowing; (*de moutons*) shearing.

tonton /tɔ̃tɔ̃/ *n.m.* (*fam.*) uncle.

tonus /tonys/ *n.m.* energy.

top /top/ *n.m.* (*signal pour marquer un instant précis*) stroke.

topo /topo/ *n.m.* (*fam.*) talk, oral report.

toquade /tokad/ *n.f.* craze; (*pour une personne*) infatuation.

toque /tok/ *n.f.* (*fur*) hat; (*de jockey*) cap; (*de cuisinier*) hat.

toqué /toke/ *a.* (*fam.*) crazy.

torche /torʃ/ *n.f.* torch.

torcher /torʃe/ *v.t.* (*fam.*) wipe.

torchon /torʃɔ̃/ *n.m.* cloth, duster; (*pour la vaisselle*) tea-towel; (*Amer.*) dish-towel.

tord|re /tordr/ *v.t.* twist; (*linge*) wring. **se** ~ *v. pr.* twist, bend; (*de douleur*) writhe. **se** ~ (*de rire*), split one's sides.

tordu /tordy/ *a.* twisted, bent; (*esprit*) warped.

tornade /tornad/ *n.f.* tornado.

torpeur /torpœr/ *n.f.* lethargy.

torpill|e /torpij/ *n.f.* torpedo. ~**er** *v.t.* torpedo.

torréfier /torefje/ *v.t.* roast.

torren|t /torɑ̃/ *n.m.* torrent. ~**iel,** ~**ielle** /-sjɛl/ *a.* torrential.

torride /torid/ *a.* torrid.

torsade /torsad/ *n.f.* twist.

torse /tors/ *n.m.* chest; (*sculpture*) torso.

tort /tor/ *n.m.* wrong. **à** ~, wrongly. **à** ~ **et à travers,** without thinking. **avoir** ~, be wrong (**de faire,** to do). **donner** ~ **à,** prove wrong. **être dans son** ~, be in the wrong. **faire (du)** ~ **à,** harm.

torticolis /tɔrtikɔli/ *n.m.* stiff neck.

tortiller /tɔrtije/ *v.t.* twist, twirl. **se ~** *v. pr.* wriggle, wiggle.

tortionnaire /tɔrsjɔnɛr/ *n.m.* torturer.

tortue /tɔrty/ *n.f.* tortoise; (*de mer*) turtle.

tortueu|x, ~se /tɔrtɥø, -z/ *a.* (*explication*) tortuous; (*chemin*) twisting.

tortur|e(s) /tɔrtyr/ *n.f.* (*pl.*) torture. **~er** *v.t.* torture.

tôt /to/ *adv.* early. **plus ~,** earlier. **au plus ~,** at the earliest. **le plus ~ possible,** as soon as possible. **~ ou tard,** sooner or later.

tot|al (*m. pl.* **~aux**) /tɔtal, -o/ *a.* total. —*n.m.* (*pl.* **~aux**) total. —*adv.* (*fam.*) to conclude, in short. **au ~al,** all in all. **~alement** *adv.* totally. **~aliser** *v.t.* total.

totalitaire /tɔtalitɛr/ *a.* totalitarian.

totalité /tɔtalite/ *n.f.* entirety. **la ~ de,** all of.

toubib /tubib/ *n.m.* (*fam.*) doctor.

touchant, ~e /tuʃɑ̃, -t/ *a.* (*émouvant*) touching.

touche /tuʃ/ *n.f.* (*de piano*) key; (*de peintre*) touch; (*ligne de*) **~,** touch-line. **une ~ de,** a touch of.

toucher[1] /tuʃe/ *v.t.* touch; (*émouvoir*) move, touch; (*contacter*) get in touch with; (*cible*) hit; (*argent*) draw; (*chèque*) cash; (*concerner*) affect. —*v.i.* **~ à,** touch; (*question*) touch on; (*fin, but*) approach. **je vais lui en un mot,** I'll talk to him about it. **se ~** *v. pr.* (*lignes*) touch.

toucher[2] /tuʃe/ *n.m.* (*sens*) touch.

touffe /tuf/ *n.f.* (*de poils, d'herbe*) tuft; (*de plantes*) clump.

touffu /tufy/ *a.* thick, bushy; (*fig.*) complex.

toujours /tuʒur/ *adv.* always; (*encore*) still; (*en tout cas*) anyhow. **pour ~,** for ever.

toupet /tupɛ/ *n.m.* (*culot: fam.*) cheek, nerve.

toupie /tupi/ *n.f.* (*jouet*) top.

tour[1] /tur/ *n.f.* tower; (*immeuble*) tower block; (*échecs*) rook.

tour[2] /tur/ *n.m.* (*mouvement, succession, tournure*) turn; (*excursion*) trip; (*à pied*) walk; (*en auto*) drive; (*artifice*) trick; (*circonférence*) circumference; (*techn.*) lathe. **~ (de piste),** lap. **à ~ de rôle,** in turn. **à mon/etc.~,** when it is my/*etc.* turn. **c'est mon/etc. de,** it is my/*etc.* turn to. **faire le ~ de,** go round; (*question*) survey. **~ de contrôle,** control tower. **~ d'horizon,** survey. **~ de passe-passe,** sleight of hand. **~ de taille,** waist measurement; (*ligne*) waistline.

tourbe /turb/ *n.f.* peat.

tourbillon /turbijɔ̃/ *n.m.* whirlwind; (*d'eau*) whirlpool; (*fig.*) whirl, swirl. **~ner** /-jɔne/ *v.i.* whirl, swirl.

tourelle /turɛl/ *n.f.* turret.

tourisme /turism/ *n.m.* tourism. **faire du ~,** do some sightseeing.

tourist|e /turist/ *n.m./f.* tourist. **~ique** *a.* touristic; (*route*) scenic.

tourment /turmɑ̃/ *n.m.* torment. **~er** /-te/ *v.t.* torment. **se ~er** *v. pr.* worry.

tournage /turnaʒ/ *n.m.* (*cinéma*) shooting.

tournant[1], **~e** /turnɑ̃, -t/ *a.* (*qui pivote*) revolving.

tournant[2] /turnɑ̃/ *n.m.* bend; (*fig.*) turning-point.

tourne-disque /turnədisk/ *n.m.* record-player.

tournée /turne/ *n.f.* (*voyage, consommations*) round; (*théâtre*) tour. **faire la ~,** make the rounds (de, of). **je paye ou j'offre la ~,** I'll buy this round.

tourner /turne/ *v.t.* turn; (*film*) shoot, make. —*v.i.* turn; (*toupie, tête*) spin; (*moteur, usine*) run. **se**

~ *v. pr.* turn. ~ **au froid,** turn cold. ~ **autour de,** go round; (*personne, maison*) hang around; (*terre*) revolve round; (*question*) centre on. ~ **de l'œil,** (*fam.*) faint. ~ **en dérision,** mock. ~ **en ridicule,** ridicule. ~ **le dos à,** turn one's back on. ~ **mal,** turn out badly.

tournesol /turnəsɔl/ *n.m.* sunflower.

tournevis /turnəvis/ *n.m.* screwdriver.

tourniquet /turnikɛ/ *n.m.* (*barrière*) turnstile.

tournoi /turnwa/ *n.m.* tournament.

tournoyer /turnwaje/ *v.i.* whirl.

tournure /turnyr/ *n.f.* turn; (*locution*) turn of phrase.

tourte /turt/ *n.f.* pie.

tourterelle /turtərɛl/ *n.f.* turtledove.

Toussaint /tusɛ̃/ *n.f.* **la ~,** All Saints' Day.

tousser /tuse/ *v.i.* cough.

tout¹ /, ~**e** (*pl.* **tous, toutes** /tu, tut/ *a.* all; (*n'importe quel*) any; (*tout à fait*) entirely. ~ **le pays/etc.,** the whole country/*etc.,* all the country/*etc.* ~**e la nuit/journée,** the whole night/day. ~ **un paquet,** a whole pack. **tous les jours/mois/etc.,** every day/month/*etc.* —*pron.* everything, all. **tous** /tus/, **toutes,** all. **prendre ~,** take everything, take it all. ~ **ce que,** all that. ~ **le monde,** everyone. **tous les deux, toutes les deux,** both of them. **tous les trois,** all three (of them). —*adv.* (*très*) very; (*tout à fait*) quite. ~ **au bout/début/etc.,** right at the end/beginning/*etc.* **le ~ premier,** the very first. ~ **en chantant/marchant/etc.,** while singing/walking/*etc.* ~ **à coup,** all of a sudden. ~ **à fait,** quite,

completely. ~ **à l'heure,** in a moment; (*passé*) a moment ago. ~ **au ou le long de,** throughout. ~ **au plus/moins,** at most/least. ~ **de même,** all the same. ~ **de suite,** straight away. ~ **entier,** whole. ~ **le contraire,** quite the opposite. ~ **neuf,** brand-new. ~ **nu,** stark naked. ~ **près,** nearby. ~**-puissant,** ~**e-puissante** *a.* omnipotent. ~ **seul,** alone. **terrain à ~ terrain,** all terrain.

tout² /tu/ *n.m.* (*ensemble*) whole. **en ~,** in all. **pas du ~!,** not at all!

tout-à-l'égout /tutalegu/ *n.m.* main drainage.

toutefois /tutfwa/ *adv.* however.

toux /tu/ *n.f.* cough.

toxicomane /tɔksikɔman/ *n.m./f.* drug addict.

toxine /tɔksin/ *n.f.* toxin.

toxique /tɔksik/ *a.* toxic.

trac /trak/ *n.m.* **le ~,** nerves; (*théâtre*) stage fright.

tracas /traka/ *n.m.* worry. ~**ser** /-se/ *v.t.,* **se ~ser** *v. pr.* worry.

trace /tras/ *n.f.* trace, mark; (*d'animal, de pneu*) tracks; (*vestige*) trace. **sur la ~ de,** on the track of. ~**s de pas,** footprints.

tracé /trase/ *n.m.* (*ligne*) line; (*plan*) layout.

tracer /trase/ *v.t.* draw, trace; (*écrire*) write; (*route*) mark out.

trachée(-artère) /traʃe(artɛr)/ *n.f.* windpipe.

tract /trakt/ *n.m.* leaflet.

tractations /traktasjɔ̃/ *n.f. pl.* dealings.

tracteur /traktœr/ *n.m.* tractor.

traction /traksjɔ̃/ *n.f.* (*sport*) press-up, push-up.

tradition /tradisjɔ̃/ *n.f.* tradition. ~**nel,** ~**nelle** /-jɔnɛl/ *a.* traditional.

tradu|ire† /traduir/ *v.t.* translate; (*sentiment*) express. ~**ire en justice,** take to court. ~**ucteur,**

~uctrice *n.m., f.* translator. ~uction *n.f.* translation.

trafic /trafik/ *n.m. (commerce, circulation)* traffic.

trafiqu|er /trafike/ *v.i.* traffic. —*v.t. (fam.) (vin)* doctor; *(moteur)* fiddle with. ~ant, ~ante *n.m., f.* trafficker; *(d'armes, de drogues)* dealer.

tragédie /traʒedi/ *n.f.* tragedy.

tragique /traʒik/ *a.* tragic. ~ment *adv.* tragically.

trah|ir /trair/ *v.t.* betray. ~ison *n.f.* betrayal; *(crime)* treason.

train /trɛ̃/ *n.m. (rail.)* train; *(allure)* pace. en ~, *(en forme)* in shape. en ~ de faire, *(busy)* doing. mettre en ~, start up. ~ d'atterrissage, undercarriage. ~ électrique, *(jouet)* electric train set. ~ de vie, lifestyle.

traînard, ~e /trenar, -d/ *n.m., f.* slowcoach; *(Amer.)* slowpoke; *(en marchant)* straggler.

traîne /trɛn/ *n.f. (de robe)* train. à la ~, lagging behind; *(en remorque)* in tow.

traîneau *(pl. ~x)* /trɛno/ *n.m.* sledge.

traînée /trene/ *n.f. (trace)* trail; *(bande)* streak; *(femme: péj.)* slut.

traîner /trene/ *v.t.* drag (along); *(véhicule)* pull. —*v.i. (pendre)* trail; *(rester en arrière)* trail behind; *(flâner)* hang about; *(papiers, affaires)* lie around. ~ *(en longueur)*, drag on. se ~ *v. pr. (par terre)* crawl. (faire) ~ en longueur, drag out. ~ les pieds, drag one's feet. ça n'a pas traîné!, that didn't take long.

train-train /trɛ̃trɛ̃/ *n.m.* routine.

traire† /trɛr/ *v.t.* milk.

trait /trɛ/ *n.m.* line; *(en dessinant)* stroke; *(caractéristique)* feature, trait; *(acte)* act. ~s, *(du visage)* features. avoir ~ à, relate to. d'un ~, *(boire)* in one gulp. ~ d'union, hyphen; *(fig.)* link.

traite /trɛt/ *n.f. (de vache)* milking; *(comm.)* draft. d'une *(seule)* ~, in one go, at a stretch.

traité /trete/ *n.m. (pacte)* treaty; *(ouvrage)* treatise.

traitement /trɛtmã/ *n.m.* treatment; *(salaire)* salary. ~ de données, data processing. ~ de texte, word processing.

traiter /trete/ *v.t.* treat; *(affaire)* deal with; *(données, produit)* process. ~ qn. de lâche/*etc.*, call s.o. a coward/*etc.* —*v.i.* deal *(avec, with).* ~ de, *(sujet)* deal with.

traiteur /trɛtœr/ *n.m.* caterer; *(boutique)* delicatessen.

traître, ~sse /trɛtr, -ɛs/ *a.* treacherous. —*n.m./f.* traitor.

trajectoire /traʒɛktwar/ *n.f.* path.

trajet /traʒɛ/ *n.m. (à parcourir)* distance; *(voyage)* journey; *(itinéraire)* route.

trame /tram/ *n.f. (de tissu)* weft; *(de récit etc.)* framework. usé jusqu'à la ~, threadbare.

tram|er /trame/ *v.t.* plot; *(complot)* hatch. qu'est ce qui se ~?, what's brewing?

tramway /tramwɛ/ *n.m.* tram; *(Amer.)* streetcar.

tranchant, ~e /trãʃã, -t/ *a.* sharp; *(fig.)* cutting. *n.m.* cutting edge. à double ~, two-edged.

tranche /trãʃ/ *n.f. (rondelle)* slice; *(bord)* edge; *(partie)* portion.

tranchée /trãʃe/ *n.f.* trench.

tranch|er¹ /trãʃe/ *v.t.* cut; *(question)* decide. —*v.i. (décider)* decide. ~é *a. (net)* clear-cut.

trancher² /trãʃe/ *v.i. (contraster)* contrast *(sur, with).*

tranquille /trãkil/ *a.* quiet; *(esprit)* at rest; *(conscience)* clear. être/laisser ~e, be/leave in peace. ~ement *adv.* quietly. ~ité *n.f.* (peace and) quiet; *(d'esprit)* peace of mind.

tranquillisant /trãkiliză/ *n.m.* tranquillizer.

tranquilliser /trãkilize/ *v.t.* reassure.

transaction /trãzaksjɔ̃/ *n.f.* transaction.

transat /trãzat/ *n.m.* (*fam.*) deckchair.

transatlantique /trãzatlãtik/ *n.m.* transatlantic liner. —*a.* transatlantic.

transborder /trãsbɔrde/ *v.t.* transfer, transship.

transcend|er /trãsãde/ *v.t.* transcend. **~ant, ~ante** *a.* transcendent.

transcr|ire /trãskrir/ *v.t.* transcribe. **~iption** *n.f.* transcription; (*copie*) transcript.

transe /trãs/ *n.f.* **en ~**, in a trance; (*fig.*) very excited.

transférer /trãsfere/ *v.t.* transfer.

transfert /trãsfɛr/ *n.m.* transfer.

transform|er /trãsfɔrme/ *v.t.* change; (*radicalement*) transform; (*vêtement*) alter. **se ~er** *v. pr.* change; be transformed. (**se**) **~er en**, turn into. **~ateur** *n.m.* transformer. **~ation** *n.f.* change; transformation.

transfuge /trãsfyʒ/ *n.m.* renegade.

transfusion /trãsfyzjɔ̃/ *n.f.* transfusion.

transgresser /trãsgrese/ *v.t.* disobey.

transiger /trãziʒe/ *v.i.* compromise. **ne pas ~ sur**, not compromise on.

transi /trãzi/ *a.* chilled to the bone.

transistor /trãzistɔr/ *n.m.* (*dispositif, poste de radio*) transistor.

transit /trãzit/ *n.m.* transit. **~er** *v.t./i.* pass in transit.

transiti|f, ~ve /trãzitif, -v/ *a.* transitive.

transi|tion /trãzisjɔ̃/ *n.f.* transition. **~toire** *a.* (*provisoire*) transitional.

translucide /trãslysid/ *a.* translucent.

transm|ettre† /trãsmɛtr/ *v.t.* pass on; (*techn.*) transmit; (*radio*) broadcast. **~ission** *n.f.* transmission; (*radio*) broadcasting.

transparaître /trãsparɛtr/ *v.i.* show (through).

transparen|t, ~te /trãsparã, -t/ *a.* transparent. **~ce** *n.f.* transparency.

transpercer /trãspɛrse/ *v.t.* pierce.

transpir|er /trãspire/ *v.i.* perspire. **~ation** *n.f.* perspiration.

transplant|er /trãsplãte/ *v.t.* (*bot., méd.*) transplant. **~ation** *n.f.* (*bot.*) transplantation; (*méd.*) transplant.

transport /trãspɔr/ *n.m.* transport(ation); (*sentiment*) rapture. **les ~s**, transport. **les ~s en commun**, public transport.

transport|er /trãspɔrte/ *v.t.* transport; (*à la main*) carry. **se ~er** *v. pr.* take o.s. (**à**, to). **~eur** *n.m.* haulier; (*Amer.*) trucker.

transposer /trãspoze/ *v.t.* transpose.

transvaser /trãsvaze/ *v.t.* decant.

transvers|al (*m. pl.* **~aux**) /trãvɛrsal, -o/ *a.* cross, transverse.

trap|èze /trapɛz/ *n.m.* (*sport*) trapeze. **~éziste** /-ezist/ *n.m./f.* trapeze artist.

trappe /trap/ *n.f.* trapdoor.

trappeur /trapœr/ *n.m.* trapper.

trapu /trapy/ *a.* stocky.

traquenard /traknar/ *n.m.* trap.

traquer /trake/ *v.t.* track down.

traumatis|me /tromatism/ *n.m.* trauma. **~ant, ~ante** /-zã, -t/ *a.* traumatic. **~er** /-ze/ *v.t.* traumatize.

trav|ail (*pl.* **~aux**) /travaj, -o/ *n.m.* work; (*emploi, poste*) job; (*façonnage*) working. **~aux**, work. **en ~ail**, (*femme*) in labour. **~ail à la chaîne**, production line work. **~ail à la pièce** *ou* **à la tâche**, piece-work. **~ail au noir**, (*fam.*) moonlighting. **~aux forcés**, hard labour. **~aux manuels**, handicrafts. **~aux ménagers**, housework.

travaill|er /travaje/ *v.i.* work; (*se déformer*) warp. **~er à**, (*livre etc.*) work on. —*v.t.* (*façonner*) work; (*étudier*) work at or on; (*tourmenter*) worry. **~eur, ~euse** *n.m., f.* worker; *a.* hardworking.

travailliste /travajist/ *a.* Labour. —*n.m./f.* Labour party member.

travers /traver/ *n.m.* (*défaut*) failing. **à ~**, through. **au ~ (de)**, through. **de ~**, (*chapeau, nez*) crooked; (*mal*) badly, the wrong way; (*regarder*) askance. **en ~ (de)**, across.

traverse /travers/ *n.f.* (*rail.*) sleeper; (*rail., Amer.*) tie.

traversée /traverse/ *n.f.* crossing.

traverser /traverse/ *v.t.* cross; (*transpercer*) go (right) through; (*période, forêt*) go *ou* pass through.

traversin /traversɛ̃/ *n.m.* bolster.

travesti /travesti/ *n.m.* transvestite.

travestir /travestir/ *v.t.* disguise; (*vérité*) misrepresent.

trébucher /trebyʃe/ *v.i.* stumble, trip (over). **faire ~**, trip (up).

trèfle /trɛfl/ *n.m.* (*plante*) clover; (*cartes*) clubs.

treillage /trɛjaʒ/ *n.m.* trellis.

treillis¹ /treji/ *n.m.* trellis; (*en métal*) wire mesh.

treillis² /treji/ *n.m.* (*tenue militaire*) combat uniform.

treize /trɛz/ *a. & n.m.* thirteen. **~ième** *a. & n.m./f.* thirteenth.

tréma /trema/ *n.m.* diaeresis.

trembl|er /trɑ̃ble/ *v.i.* shake, tremble; (*lumière, voix*) quiver. **~ement** *n.m.* shaking; (*frisson*) shiver. **~ement de terre**, earthquake.

trembloter /trɑ̃blote/ *v.i.* quiver.

trémousser (se) /(sə)tremuse/ *v. pr.* wriggle, wiggle.

trempe /trɑ̃p/ *n.f.* (*caractère*) calibre.

tremper /trɑ̃pe/ *v.t./i.* soak; (*plonger*) dip; (*acier*) temper. **mettre à ~** *ou* **faire ~**, soak. **~ dans**, (*fig.*) be involved in. **se ~** *v. pr.* (*se baigner*) have a dip.

trempette /trɑ̃pɛt/ *n.f.* **faire ~**, have a little dip.

tremplin /trɑ̃plɛ̃/ *n.m.* springboard.

trentaine /trɑ̃tɛn/ *n.f.* **une ~ (de)**, about thirty. **il a la ~**, he's about thirty.

trent|e /trɑ̃t/ *a. & n.m.* thirty. **~ième** *a. & n.m./f.* thirtieth. **se mettre sur son ~ et un**, put on one's Sunday best. **tous les ~-six du mois**, once in a blue moon.

trépider /trepide/ *v.i.* vibrate.

trépied /trepje/ *n.m.* tripod.

trépigner /trepiɲe/ *v.i.* stamp one's feet.

très /trɛ/ (/trɛz/ *before vowel*) *adv.* very. **~ aimé/estimé**, much liked/esteemed.

trésor /trezɔr/ *n.m.* treasure; (*ressources: comm.*) finances. **le T~**, the revenue department.

trésorerie /trezɔrri/ *n.f.* (*bureaux*) accounts department; (*du Trésor*) revenue office; (*argent*) finances; (*gestion*) accounts.

trésor|ier, ~ière /trezɔrje, -jɛr/ *n.m., f.* treasurer.

tressaill|ir /tresajir/ *v.i.* shake, quiver; (*sursauter*) start. **~ement** *n.m.* quiver; start.

tressauter /tresote/ *v.i.* (*sursauter*) start, jump.

tresse /trɛs/ *n.f.* braid, plait.

tresser /trese/ *v.t.* braid, plait.

tréteau (*pl.* **~x**) /treto/ *n.m.* trestle. **~x**, (*théâtre*) stage.

treuil /trœj/ *n.m.* winch.

trêve /trɛv/ *n.f.* truce; *(fig.)* respite. **~ de plaisanteries**, enough of this joking.

tri /tri/ *n.m. (classement)* sorting; *(sélection)* selection. **faire le ~ de**, select; sort. **~age** /-jaʒ/ *n.m.* sorting.

triangle /trijɑ̃gl/ *n.m.* triangle. **~ulaire** *a.* triangular.

trib|al *(m. pl. ~aux)* /tribal, -o/ *a.* tribal.

tribord /tribɔr/ *n.m.* starboard.

tribu /triby/ *n.f.* tribe.

tribulations /tribylasjɔ̃/ *n.f. pl.* tribulations.

tribun|al *(m. pl. ~aux)* /tribynal, -o/ *n.m.* court. **~al d'instance**, magistrates' court.

tribune /tribyn/ *n.f.* (public) gallery; *(dans un stade)* grandstand; *(d'orateur)* rostrum; *(débat)* forum.

tribut /triby/ *n.m.* tribute.

tributaire /tribytɛr/ *a.* **~ de**, dependent on.

trich|er /triʃe/ *v.i.* cheat. **~erie** *n.f.* cheating. **une ~erie**, piece of trickery. **~eur, ~euse** *n.m., f.* cheat.

tricolore /trikɔlɔr/ *a.* three-coloured; *(français)* red, white and blue; *(français: fig.)* French.

tricot /triko/ *n.m.* knitting; *(pull)* sweater, en ~, knitted. **~ de corps**, vest; *(Amer.)* undershirt. **~er** /-ɔte/ *v.t./i.* knit.

trictrac /triktrak/ *n.m.* backgammon.

tricycle /trisikl/ *n.m.* tricycle.

trier /trije/ *v.t. (classer)* sort; *(choisir)* select.

trilogie /trilɔʒi/ *n.f.* trilogy.

trimbaler /trɛ̃bale/ *v.t./i.* **se ~** *v. pr. (fam.)* trail around.

trimer /trime/ *v.i. (fam.)* slave.

trimestr|e /trimɛstr/ *n.m.* quarter; *(scol.)* term. **~iel, ~ielle** *a.* quarterly; *(bulletin)* end-of-term.

tringle /trɛ̃gl/ *n.f.* rod.

Trinité /trinite/ *n.f.* **la ~**, *(dogme)* the Trinity; *(fête)* Trinity.

trinquer /trɛ̃ke/ *v.i.* clink glasses.

trio /trijo/ *n.m.* trio.

triomph|e /trijɔ̃f/ *n.m.* triumph. **~al** *(m. pl. ~aux)* *a.* triumphant.

triomph|er /trijɔ̃fe/ *v.i.* triumph *(de, over)*; *(jubiler)* be triumphant. **~ant, ~ante** *a.* triumphant.

trip|es /trip/ *n.f. pl. (mets)* tripe; *(entrailles: fam.)* guts.

triple /tripl/ *a.* triple, treble. **—n.m. le ~**, three times as much *(de, as).* **~ment** /-əmɑ̃/ *adv.* trebly.

tripl|er /triple/ *v.t./i.* triple, treble. **~és, ~ées** *n.m., f. pl.* triplets.

tripot /tripo/ *n.m.* gambling den.

tripoter /tripote/ *v.t. (fam.)* fiddle with. **—v.i. (fam.)** fiddle about.

trique /trik/ *n.f.* cudgel.

trisomique /trizomik/ *a.* **enfant ~**, Down's (syndrome) child.

triste /trist/ *a.* sad; *(rue, temps, couleur)* gloomy; *(lamentable)* wretched, dreadful. **~ment** /-əmɑ̃/ *adv.* sadly. **~sse** /-ɛs/ *n.f.* sadness; gloominess.

trivi|al *(m. pl. ~iaux)* /trivjal, -jo/ *a.* coarse. **~ialité** *n.f.* coarseness.

troc /trɔk/ *n.m.* exchange; *(comm.)* barter.

troène /trɔɛn/ *n.m. (bot.)* privet.

trognon /trɔɲɔ̃/ *n.m. (de pomme)* core.

trois /trwa/ *a. & n.m.* three. **hôtel ~-étoiles**, three-star hotel. **~ième** /-zjɛm/ *a. & n.m./f.* third. **~ièmement** /-zjɛmmɑ̃/ *adv.* thirdly.

trombe /trɔ̃b/ *n.f.* **~ d'eau**, downpour.

trombone /trɔ̃bɔn/ *n.m. (mus.)* trombone; *(agrafe)* paper-clip.

trompe /trɔ̃p/ *n.f. (d'éléphant)* trunk; *(mus.)* horn.

tromp|er /trɔ̃pe/ v.t. deceive, mislead; *(déjouer)* elude. **se ~er** v.pr. be mistaken. **se ~er de route/train/**etc., take the wrong road/train/etc. **~erie** n.f. deception. **~eur, ~euse** a. *(personne)* deceitful; *(chose)* deceptive.

trompette /trɔ̃pet/ n.f. trumpet.

tronc /trɔ̃/ n.m. trunk *(boîte)* collection box.

tronçon /trɔ̃sɔ̃/ n.m. section. **~ner** /-ɔne/ v.t. cut into sections.

trône /tron/ n.m. throne. **~er** v.i. occupy the place of honour.

tronquer /trɔ̃ke/ v.t. truncate.

trop /tro/ adv. *(grand, loin, etc.)* too; *(boire, marcher, etc.)* too much. **~ (de)**, *(quantité)* too much; *(nombre)* too many. **c'est ~ chauffé**, it's overheated. **de ~, en ~**, too much; too many, **il a bu un verre de ~**, he's had one too many. **de ~**, *(intrus)* in the way. **~plein** n.m. excess; *(dispositif)* overflow.

trophée /trɔfe/ n.m. trophy.

tropic|al (m. pl. **~aux**) /trɔpikal, -o/ a. tropical.

tropique /trɔpik/ n.m. tropic. **~s**, tropics.

troquer /trɔke/ v.t. exchange; *(comm.)* barter **(contre**, for).

trot /tro/ n.m. trot. **aller au ~**, trot. **au ~**, *(fam.)* on the double.

trotter /trɔte/ v.i. trot.

trotteuse /trɔtøz/ n.f. *(aiguille de montre)* second hand.

trottiner /trɔtine/ v.i. patter along.

trottinette /trɔtinɛt/ n.f. *(jouet)* scooter.

trottoir /trɔtwar/ n.m. pavement; *(Amer.)* sidewalk. **~ roulant**, moving walkway.

trou /tru/ n.m. hole; *(moment)* gap; *(lieu:* péj.*)* dump. **~ (de mémoire)**, lapse (of memory). **~ de la serrure**, keyhole. **faire son ~**, carve one's niche.

trouble /trubl/ a. *(eau, image)* unclear; *(louche)* shady. —n.m. agitation. **~s**, *(pol.)* disturbances; *(méd.)* trouble.

troubl|er /truble/ v.t. disturb; *(eau)* make cloudy; *(inquiéter)* trouble. **~ant, ~ante** a. disturbing. **se ~er** v. pr. *(personne)* become flustered. **~e-fête** n.m./ f. invar. killjoy.

trouée /true/ n.f. gap, open space; *(mil.)* breach **(dans**, in).

trouer /true/ v.t. make a hole ou holes in. **mes chaussures se sont trouées**, my shoes have got holes in them.

trouille /truj/ n.f. **avoir la ~**, *(fam.)* be scared.

troupe /trup/ n.f. troop; *(d'acteurs)* troupe. **~s**, *(mil.)* troops.

troupeau (pl. **~x**) /trupo/ n.m. herd; *(de moutons)* flock.

trousse /trus/ n.f. case, bag; *(de réparations)* kit. **aux ~s de**, on the tail of. **~ de toilette**, toilet bag.

trousseau (pl. **~x**) /truso/ n.m. *(de clefs)* bunch; *(de mariée)* trousseau.

trouvaille /truvaj/ n.f. find.

trouver /truve/ v.t. find; *(penser)* think. **aller/venir ~**, *(rendre visite à)* go/come and see. **se ~** v. pr. find o.s.; *(être)* be; *(se sentir)* feel. **il se trouve que**, it happens that. **se ~ mal**, faint.

truand /tryɑ̃/ n.m. gangster.

truc /tryk/ n.m. *(moyen)* way; *(artifice)* trick; *(chose:* fam.*)* thing. **~age** n.m. = **truquage**.

truchement /tryʃmɑ̃/ n.m. **par le ~ de**, through.

truculent, ~e /trykylɑ̃, -t/ a. colourful.

truelle /tryɛl/ n.f. trowel.

truffe /tryf/ n.f. *(champignon, chocolat)* truffle; *(nez)* nose.

truffer /tryfe/ v.t. *(fam.)* fill, pack **(de**, with).

truie /trɥi/ n.f. (animal) sow.

truite /trɥit/ n.f. trout.

truqu|er /tryke/ v.t. fix, rig; (photo, texte) fake. **~age** n.m. fixing; faking; (cinéma) special effect.

trust /trœst/ n.m. (comm.) trust.

tsar /tsar/ n.m. tsar, czar.

tsigane /tsigan/ a. & n.m./f. (Hungarian) gypsy.

tu¹ /ty/ pron. (parent, ami, enfant, etc.) you.

tu² /ty/ voir taire.

tuba /tyba/ n.m. (mus.) tuba; (sport) snorkel.

tube /tyb/ n.m. tube.

tubercul|eux, ~euse /tyberkløˈ-z/ a. être **~eux,** have tuberculosis. **~ose** n.f. tuberculosis.

tubulaire /tybyler/ a. tubular.

tubulure /tybylyr/ n.f. tubing.

tu|er /tɥe/ v.t. kill; (d'une balle) shoot, kill; (épuiser) exhaust. se **~er** v. pr. kill o.s.; (accident) be killed. **~ant, ~ante,** a. exhausting. **~é, ~ée** n.m., f. person killed. **~eur, ~euse** n.m., f. killer.

tuerie /tyri/ n.f. slaughter.

tue-tête (à) /a(tytet/ adv. at the top of one's voice.

tuile /tɥil/ n.f. tile; (malchance: fam.) (stroke of) bad luck.

tulipe /tylip/ n.f. tulip.

tuméfié /tymefje/ a. swollen.

tumeur /tymœr/ n.f. tumour.

tumult|e /tymylt/ n.m. commotion; (désordre) turmoil. **~ueux, ~ueuse** a. turbulent.

tunique /tynik/ n.f. tunic.

Tunisie /tynizi/ n.f. Tunisia.

tunisien, ~ne /tynizjɛ̃, -jɛn/ a. & n.m., f. Tunisian.

tunnel /tynɛl/ n.m. tunnel.

turban /tyrbɑ̃/ n.m. turban.

turbine /tyrbin/ n.f. turbine.

turbo /tyrbo/ a. turbo. n.f. (voiture) turbo.

turbulen|t, ~te /tyrbylɑ̃, -t/ a.

boisterous, turbulent. **~ce** n.f. turbulence.

tur|c, ~que /tyrk/ a. Turkish. **~n.m., f.** Turk. **n.m.** (lang.) Turkish.

turf /tyrf/ n.m. le **~,** the turf. **~iste** n.m./f. racegoer.

Turquie /tyrki/ n.f. Turkey.

turquoise /tyrkwaz/ a. invar. turquoise.

tutelle /tytɛl/ n.f. (jurid.) guardianship; (fig.) protection.

tu|teur, ~trice /tytœr, -tris/ n.m., f. (jurid.) guardian. **n.m.** (bâton) stake.

tutoyer /tytwaje/ v.t. address familiarly (using tu). **~oiement** n.m. use of (familiar) tu.

tuyau (pl. **~x**) /tɥijo/ n.m. pipe; (conseil: fam.) tip. **~d'arrosage,** hose-pipe. **~ter** v.t. (fam.) give a tip to. **~terie** n.f. piping.

TVA abrév. (taxe sur la valeur ajoutée) VAT.

tympan /tɛ̃pɑ̃/ n.m. ear-drum.

type /tip/ n.m. (modèle) type; (traits) features; (individu: fam.) bloke, guy. —a. invar. typical. le **~même de,** a classic example of.

typhoïde /tifoid/ n.f. typhoid (fever).

typhon /tifɔ̃/ n.m. typhoon.

typhus /tifys/ n.m. typhus.

typique /tipik/ a. typical. **~ment** adv. typically.

tyran /tirɑ̃/ n.m. tyrant.

tyrann|ie /tirani/ n.f. tyranny. **~ique** a. tyrannical. **~iser** v.t. oppress, tyrannize.

U

ulcère /ylsɛr/ n.m. ulcer.

ulcérer /ylsere/ v.t. (vexer) embitter, gall.

ULM abrév. m. (ultraléger motorisé) microlight.

ultérieur /ylterjœr/ *a.,* **~ement** *adv.* later.

ultimatum /yltimatɔm/ *n.m.* ultimatum.

ultime /yltim/ *a.* final.

ultra /yltra/ *n.m./f.* hardliner.

ultra- /yltra/ *préf.* ultra-.

un, une /œ̃, yn/ *a.* one; (*indéfini*) a, an. **un enfant,** /œ̃nɑ̃fɑ̃/ a child. —*pron. & n.m., f.* one. **l'un,** one. **les uns,** some. **l'un et l'autre,** both. **l'un l'autre, les uns les autres,** each other. **l'un ou l'autre,** either. **la une,** (*de journal*) front page. **un autre,** another. **un par un,** one by one.

unanim|e /ynanim/ *a.* unanimous. **~ité** *n.f.* unanimity. **à l'~ité,** unanimously.

uni /yni/ *a.* united; (*couple*) close; (*surface*) smooth; (*sans dessins*) plain.

unième /ynjɛm/ *a.* -first. **vingt et ~,** twenty-first. **cent ~,** one hundred and first.

unifi|er /ynifje/ *v.t.* unify. **~ication** *n.f.* unification.

uniform|e /yniform/ *n.m.* uniform. —*a.* uniform. **~ément** *adv.* uniformly. **~iser** *v.t.* standardize. **~ité** *n.f.* uniformity.

unilatér|al (*m. pl.* **~aux**) /ynilateral, -o/ *a.* unilateral.

union /ynjɔ̃/ *n.f.* union. **l'U~ soviétique,** the Soviet Union.

unique /ynik/ *a.* (*seul*) only; (*prix, voie*) one; (*incomparable*) unique. **enfant ~,** only child. **sens ~,** one-way street. **~ment** *adv.* only, solely.

unir /ynir/ *v.t.,* **s'~** *v. pr.* unite, join.

unisson (à l') /(al)ynisɔ̃/ *adv.* in unison.

unité /ynite/ *n.f.* unit; (*harmonie*) unity.

univers /yniver/ *n.m.* universe.

universel, **~le** /yniversɛl/ *a.* universal.

universit|é /yniversite/ *n.f.* university. **~aire** *a.* university; *n.m./f.* academic.

uranium /yranjɔm/ *n.m.* uranium.

urbain, **~e** /yrbɛ̃, -ɛn/ *a.* urban.

urbanisme /yrbanism/ *n.m.* town planning; (*Amer.*) city planning.

urgence /yrʒɑ̃s/ *n.f.* (*cas*) emergency; (*de situation, tâche, etc.*) urgency. **d'~** *a.* emergency; *adv.* urgently.

urgent, **~e** /yrʒɑ̃, -t/ *a.* urgent. **urger** /yrʒe/ *v.i.* **ça urge!,** (*fam.*) it's getting urgent.

urin|e /yrin/ *n.f.* urine. **~er** *v.i.* urinate.

urinoir /yrinwar/ *n.m.* urinal.

urne /yrn/ *n.f.* (*électorale*) ballotbox; (*vase*) urn. **aller aux ~s,** go to the polls.

URSS *abrév.* (*Union des Républiques Socialistes Soviétiques*) USSR.

urticaire /yrtiker/ *n.f.* **une crise d'~,** nettle rash.

us /ys/ *n.m. pl.* **les us et coutumes,** habits and customs.

usage /yzaʒ/ *n.m.* use; (*coutume*) custom; (*de langage*) usage. **à l'~ de,** for. **d'~,** (*habituel*) customary. **faire ~ de,** make use of.

usagé /yzaʒe/ *a.* worn.

usager /yzaʒe/ *n.m.* user.

usé /yze/ *a.* worn (out); (*banal*) trite.

user /yze/ *v.t.* wear (out); (*consommer*) use (up). —*v.i.* **~ de,** use. **s'~** *v. pr.* (*tissu etc.*) wear (out).

usine /yzin/ *n.f.* factory; (*de métallurgie*) works.

usité /yzite/ *a.* common.

ustensile /ystɑ̃sil/ *n.m.* utensil.

usuel, **~le** /yzɥɛl/ *a.* ordinary, everyday.

usufruit /yzyfrɥi/ *n.m.* usufruct.

usure /yzyr/ *n.f.* (*détérioration*) wear (and tear).

usurper /yzyrpe/ *v.t.* usurp.

utérus /yterys/ *n.m.* womb, uterus.

utile /ytil/ *a.* useful. **~ment** *adv.* usefully.

utilis|er /ytilize/ *v.t.* use. **~able** *a.* usable. **~ation** *n.f.* use.

utilitaire /ytiliter/ *a.* utilitarian.

utilité /ytilite/ *n.f.* use(fulness).

utop|ie /ytɔpi/ *n.f.* Utopia; (*idée*) Utopian idea. **~ique** *a.* Utopian.

UV *abrév. f.* (*unité de valeur*) (*scol.*) credit.

V

va /va/ *voir* aller¹.

vacanc|e /vakɑ̃s/ *n.f.* (*poste*) vacancy. **~es**, holiday(s); (*Amer.*) vacation. **en ~es**, on holiday. **~ier**, **~ière** *n.m.*, *f.* holiday-maker; (*Amer.*) vacationer.

vacant, **~e** /vakɑ̃, -t/ *a.* vacant.

vacarme /vakarm/ *n.m.* uproar.

vaccin /vaksɛ̃/ *n.m.* vaccine; (*inoculation*) vaccination.

vaccin|er /vaksine/ *v.t.* vaccinate. **~ation** *n.f.* vaccination.

vache /vaʃ/ *n.f.* cow. **—a.** (*méchant*: *fam.*) nasty. **~ment** *adv.* (*très*: *fam.*) damned; (*pleuvoir, manger, etc.*: *fam.*) a hell of a lot. **~rie** /-ri/ *n.f.* (*fam.*) nastiness; (*chose*: *fam.*) nasty thing.

vacill|er /vasije/ *v.i.* sway, wobble; (*lumière*) flicker; (*fig.*) falter. **~ant**, **~ante** *a.* (*mémoire, démarche*) shaky.

vadrouiller /vadruje/ *v.i.* (*fam.*) wander about.

va-et-vient /vaevjɛ̃/ *n.m. invar.* to and fro (motion); (*de personnes*) comings and goings.

vagabond, **~e** /vagabɔ̃, -d/ *n.m.*, *f.* (*péj.*) vagrant, vagabond. **~er** /-de/ *v.i.* wander.

vagin /vaʒɛ̃/ *n.m.* vagina.

vagir /vaʒir/ *v.i.* cry.

vague¹ /vag/ *a.* vague. **—n.m.** vagueness. **il est resté dans le ~**, he was vague about it. **~ment** *adv.* vaguely.

vague² /vag/ *n.f.* wave. **~ de fond**, ground swell. **~ de froid**, cold spell. **~ de chaleur**, hot spell.

vaill|ant, **~ante** /vajɑ̃, -t/ *a.* brave; (*vigoureux*) healthy. **~amment** /-amɑ̃/ *adv.* bravely.

vaille /vaj/ *voir* valoir.

vain, **~e** /vɛ̃, vɛn/ *a.* vain. **en ~**, in vain. **~ement** /vɛnmɑ̃/ *adv.* vainly.

vain|cre† /vɛ̃kr/ *v.t.* defeat; (*surmonter*) overcome. **~cu**, **~cue** *n.m.*, *f.* (*sport*) loser. **~queur** *n.m.* victor; (*sport*) winner.

vais /vɛ/ *voir* aller¹.

vaisseau (*pl.* **~x**) /veso/ *n.m.* ship; (*veine*) vessel. **~ spatial**, spaceship.

vaisselle /vesɛl/ *n.f.* crockery; (*à laver*) dishes. **faire la ~**, do the washing-up, wash the dishes. **produit pour la ~**, washing-up liquid.

val (*pl.* **~s** *ou* **vaux**) /val, vo/ *n.m.* valley.

valable /valabl/ *a.* valid; (*de qualité*) worthwhile.

valet /valɛ/ *n.m.* (*cartes*) jack. **~ (de chambre)**, manservant. **~ de ferme**, farm-hand.

valeur /valœr/ *n.f.* value; (*mérite*) worth, value. **~s**, (*comm.*) stocks and shares. **avoir de la ~**, be valuable.

valid|e /valid/ *a.* (*personne*) fit; (*billet*) valid. **~er** *v.t.* validate. **~ité** *n.f.* validity.

valise /valiz/ *n.f.* (suit)case. **faire ses ~s**, pack (one's bags).

vallée /vale/ *n.f.* valley.

vallon /valɔ̃/ *n.m.* (small) valley. **~né** /-ɔne/ *a.* undulating.

valoir† /valwar/ *v.i.* be worth; (*s'appliquer*) apply. ~ **qch.**, be worth sth.; (*être aussi bon que*) be as good as sth. —*v.t.* ~ **qch. à qn.**, brings.o. sth. **se** ~ *v.pr.* (*être équivalents*) be as good as each other. **faire** ~, put forward to advantage; (*droit*) assert. ~ **la peine**, ~ **le coup**, be worth it. **ça ne vaut rien**, it is no good. **il vaudrait mieux faire**, we'd better do. **ça ne me dit rien qui vaille**, I don't think much of it.

valoriser /valɔrize/ *v.t.* add value to. **se sentir valorisé**, feel valued.

vals|e /vals/ *n.f.* waltz. ~**er** *v.i.* waltz.

valve /valv/ *n.f.* valve.

vampire /vɑ̃pir/ *n.m.* vampire.

van /vɑ̃/ *n.m.* van.

vandal|e /vɑ̃dal/ *n.m./f.* vandal. ~**isme** *n.m.* vandalism.

vanille /vanij/ *n.f.* vanilla.

vanit|é /vanite/ *n.f.* vanity. ~**eux,** ~**euse** *a.* vain, conceited.

vanne /van/ *n.f.* (*d'écluse*) sluice (-gate); (*fam.*) joke.

vant|ail (*pl.* ~**aux**) /vɑ̃taj, -o/ *n.m.* door, flap.

vantard, ~**e** /vɑ̃tar, -d/ *a.* boastful; *n.m.,* *f.* boaster. ~**ise** /-diz/ *n.f.* boastfulness; (*acte*) boast.

vanter /vɑ̃te/ *v.t.* praise. **se** ~ *v.pr.* boast (**de**, about).

va-nu-pieds /vanypje/ *n.m./f. invar.* vagabond, beggar.

vapeur¹ /vapœr/ *n.f.* (*eau*) steam; (*brume, émanation*) vapour.

vapeur² /vapœr/ *n.m.* (*bateau*) steamer.

vaporeu|x, ~**se** /vapɔrø, -z/ *a.* hazy; (*léger*) filmy, flimsy.

vaporis|er /vapɔrize/ *v.t.* spray. ~**ateur** *n.m.* spray.

vaquer /vake/ *v.i.* ~ **à**, attend to.

varappe /varap/ *n.f.* rock climbing.

vareuse /varøz/ *n.f.* (*d'uniforme*) tunic.

variable /varjabl/ *a.* variable; (*temps*) changeable.

variante /varjɑ̃t/ *n.f.* variant.

varicelle /varisɛl/ *n.f.* chickenpox.

varices /varis/ *n.f. pl.* varicose veins.

var|ier /varje/ *v.t./i.* vary. ~**iation** *n.f.* variation. ~**ié** *a.* (*non monotone, étendu*) varied; (*divers*) various.

variété /varjete/ *n.f.* variety. ~**s,** (*spectacle*) variety.

variole /varjɔl/ *n.f.* smallpox.

vase¹ /vaz/ *n.m.* vase.

vase² /vaz/ *n.f.* (*boue*) silt, mud.

vaseu|x, ~**se** /vazø, -z/ *a.* (*confus: fam.*) woolly, hazy.

vasistas /vazistas/ *n.m.* fanlight, hinged panel (*in door or window*).

vaste /vast/ *a.* vast, huge.

vaudeville /vodvil/ *n.m.* vaudeville, light comedy.

vau-l'eau (à) /(a)volo/ *adv.* downhill.

vaurien, ~**ne** /vorjɛ̃, -jɛn/ *n.m.,* *f.* good-for-nothing.

vautour /votur/ *n.m.* vulture.

vautrer (se) /(sə)votre/ *v.pr.* sprawl. **se** ~ **dans,** (*vice, boue*) wallow in.

va-vite (à la) /(ala)vavit/ *adv.* (*fam.*) in a hurry.

veau (*pl.* ~**x**) /vo/ *n.m.* calf; (*viande*) veal; (*cuir*) calfskin.

vécu /veky/ *voir* **vivre.** —*a.* (*réel*) true, real.

vedette¹ /vədɛt/ *n.f.* (*artiste*) star. **en** ~, (*objet*) in a prominent position; (*personne*) in the limelight.

vedette² /vədɛt/ *n.f.* (*bateau*) launch.

végét|al (*m. pl.* ~**aux**) /veʒetal, -o/ *a.* plant. —*n.m.* (*pl.* ~**aux**) plant.

végétalien, ~ne /veʒetaljɛ̃, -jɛn/ *n.m., f.* & *a.* vegan.

végétarien, ~ne /veʒetarjɛ̃, -jɛn/ *a.* & *n.m., f.* vegetarian.

végétation /veʒetɑsjɔ̃/ *n.f.* vegetation. ~s, (*méd.*) adenoids.

végéter /veʒete/ *v.i.* vegetate.

véhémen|t, ~te /veemɑ̃, -t/ *a.* vehement. ~ce *n.f.* vehemence.

véhicul|e /veikyl/ *n.m.* vehicle. ~er *v.t.* convey.

veille¹ /vɛj/ *n.f.* la ~ (de), the day before. la ~ de Noël, Christmas Eve. à la ~ de, on the eve of.

veille² /vɛj/ *n.f.* wakefulness.

veillée /veje/ *n.f.* evening (gathering); (*mortuaire*) vigil, wake.

veiller /veje/ *v.i.* stay up *ou* awake. ~ à, attend to. ~ sur, watch over. —*v.t.* (*malade*) watch over.

veilleur /vɛjœr/ *n.m.* ~ de nuit, night-watchman.

veilleuse /vɛjøz/ *n.f.* night-light; (*de véhicule*) sidelight; (*de réchaud*) pilot-light. mettre qch. en ~, put sth. on the back burner.

veinard, ~e /vɛnar, -d/ *n.m., f.* (*fam.*) lucky devil.

veine¹ /vɛn/ *n.f.* (*anat.*) vein; (*nervure, filon*) vein.

veine² /vɛn/ *n.f.* (*chance: fam.*) luck. avoir de la ~, (*fam.*) be lucky.

velcro /vɛlkro/ *n.m.* (P.) velcro.

véliplanchiste /veliplɑ̃ʃist/ *n.m./f.* windsurfer.

vélo /velo/ *n.m.* bicycle; bike; (*activité*) cycling.

vélodrome /velodrom/ *n.m.* velodrome, cycle-racing track.

vélomoteur /velomotœr/ *n.m.* moped.

velours /vlur/ *n.m.* velvet. ~ côtelé, ~ à côtes, corduroy.

velouté /vəlute/ *a.* smooth. —*n.m.* smoothness.

velu /vəly/ *a.* hairy.

venaison /vənɛzɔ̃/ *n.f.* venison.

vendang|es /vɑ̃dɑ̃ʒ/ *n.f. pl.* grape harvest. ~er *v.i.* pick the grapes. ~eur, ~euse *n.m., f.* grape-picker.

vendetta /vɑ̃deta/ *n.f.* vendetta.

vendeu|r, ~se /vɑ̃dœr, -øz/ *n.m., f.* shop assistant; (*marchand*) salesman, saleswoman; (*jurid.*) vendor, seller.

vendre /vɑ̃dr/ *v.t.*, se ~ *v. pr.* sell. à ~, for sale.

vendredi /vɑ̃drədi/ *n.m.* Friday. V~ saint, Good Friday.

vénéneu|x, ~se /venenø, -z/ *a.* poisonous.

vénérable /venerabl/ *a.* venerable.

vénérer /venere/ *v.t.* revere.

vénérien, ~ne /venerjɛ̃, -jɛn/ *a.* venereal.

vengeance /vɑ̃ʒɑ̃s/ *n.f.* revenge, vengeance.

veng|er /vɑ̃ʒe/ *v.t.* avenge. se ~er *v. pr.* take (one's) revenge (de, for). ~eur, ~eresse *a.* vengeful; *n.m., f.* avenger.

venin /vənɛ̃/ *n.m.* venom. ~imeux, ~imeuse *a.* poisonous, venomous.

venir† /vənir/ *v.i.* (*aux. être*) come (de, from). ~ faire, come to do. venez faire, come and do. ~ de faire, to have just done. il vient/venait d'arriver, he has/had just arrived. en ~ à, (*question, conclusion, etc.*) come to. en ~ aux mains, come to blows. faire ~, send for. il m'est venu à l'esprit *ou* à l'idée que, it occurred to me that.

vent /vɑ̃/ *n.m.* wind. être dans le ~, (*fam.*) be with it. il fait du ~, it is windy.

vente /vɑ̃t/ *n.f.* sale. ~ (aux enchères), auction. en *ou* à ~ for sale. ~ de charité, (charity) bazaar.

ventil|er /vɑ̃tile/ *v.t.* ventilate. ~ateur *n.m.* fan, ventilator. ~ation *n.f.* ventilation.

ventouse /vãtuz/ *n.f.* (*dispositif*) suction pad; (*pour déboucher l'évier etc.*) plunger.

ventre /vãtr/ *n.m.* belly, stomach; (*utérus*) womb. **avoir/prendre du ~,** have/develop a paunch.

ventriloque /vãtrilɔk/ *n.m./f.* ventriloquist.

ventru /vãtry/ *a.* pot-bellied.

venu /vəny/ *voir* **venir.** —*a.* **bien ~,** (*à propos*) timely. **mal ~,** untimely. **être mal ~ de faire,** have no grounds for doing.

venue /vəny/ *n.f.* coming.

vêpres /vɛpr/ *n.f. pl.* vespers.

ver /vɛr/ *n.m.* worm; (*des fruits, de la viande*) maggot; (*du bois*) woodworm. **~ luisant,** glow-worm. **~ à soie,** silkworm. **~ solitaire,** tapeworm. **~ de terre,** earthworm.

véranda /verãda/ *n.f.* veranda.

verb|e /vɛrb/ *n.m.* (*gram.*) verb. **~al** (*m. pl.* **~aux**) *a.* verbal.

verdâtre /vɛrdatr/ *a.* greenish.

verdict /vɛrdikt/ *n.m.* verdict.

verdir /vɛrdir/ *v.i.* turn green.

verdoyant, ~e /vɛrdwajã, -t/ *a.* green, verdant.

verdure /vɛrdyr/ *n.f.* greenery.

véreu|x, ~se /verø, -z/ *a.* maggoty, wormy; (*malhonnête: fig.*) shady.

verger /vɛrʒe/ *n.m.* orchard.

vergla|s /vɛrgla/ *n.m.* (black) ice; (*Amer.*) sleet. **~cé** *a.* icy.

vergogne (sans) /(sã)vɛrgɔɲ/ *a.* shameless. —*adv.* shamelessly.

véridique /veridik/ *a.* truthful.

vérif|ier /verifje/ *v.t.* check, verify; (*compte*) audit; (*confirmer*) confirm. **~ication** *n.f.* check(ing), verification.

véritable /veritabl/ *a.* true, real; (*authentique*) real. **~ment** /-əmã/ *adv.* really.

vérité /verite/ *n.f.* truth; (*de tableau, roman*) trueness to life. **en ~,** in fact.

vermeil, ~le /vɛrmɛj/ *a.* bright red.

vermicelle(s) /vɛrmisɛl/ *n.m. (pl.)* vermicelli.

vermine /vɛrmin/ *n.f.* vermin.

vermoulu /vɛrmuly/ *a.* worm-eaten.

vermouth /vɛrmut/ *n.m.* (*apéritif*) vermouth.

verni /vɛrni/ *a.* (*fam.*) lucky. **chaussures ~es,** patent (leather) shoes.

vernir /vɛrnir/ *v.t.* varnish.

vernis /vɛrni/ *n.m.* varnish; (*de poterie*) glaze. **~ à ongles,** nail polish *ou* varnish.

vernissage /vɛrnisaʒ/ *n.m.* (*exposition*) preview.

vernisser /vɛrnise/ *v.t.* glaze.

verra, verrait /vɛra, vɛrɛ/ *voir* **voir.**

verre /vɛr/ *n.m.* glass. **prendre** *ou* **boire un ~,** have a drink. **~ de contact,** contact lens. **~ dépoli/grossissant,** frosted/magnifying glass. **~rie** *n.f.* (*objets*) glassware.

verrière /vɛrjɛr/ *n.f.* (*toit*) glass roof; (*paroi*) glass wall.

verrou /vɛru/ *n.m.* bolt. **sous les ~s,** behind bars.

verrouiller /vɛruje/ *v.t.* bolt.

verrue /vɛry/ *n.f.* wart.

vers[1] /vɛr/ *prép.* towards; (*temps*) about.

vers[2] /vɛr/ *n.m.* (*ligne*) line. **les ~,** (*poésie*) verse.

versant /vɛrsã/ *n.m.* slope, side.

versatile /vɛrsatil/ *a.* fickle.

verse (à) /(a)vɛrs/ *adv.* in torrents.

versé /vɛrse/ *a.* **~ dans,** versed in.

Verseau /vɛrso/ *n.m.* **le ~,** Aquarius.

vers|er /vɛrse/ *v.t./i.* pour; (*larmes, sang*) shed; (*basculer*) overturn; (*payer*) pay. **~ement** *n.m.* payment.

verset /vɛrsɛ/ *n.m.* (*relig.*) verse.

version /vɛrsjɔ̃/ n.f. version; (*traduction*) translation.

verso /vɛrso/ n.m. back (of the page).

vert, ~e /vɛr, -t/ a. green; (*vieillard*) sprightly. —n.m. green.

vertèbre /vɛrtɛbr/ n.f. vertebra.

vertement /vɛrtəmɑ̃/ adv. sharply.

vertic|al, ~ale (m. pl. ~aux) /vɛrtikal, -o/ a. & n.f. vertical. **à la ~ale, ~alement** adv. vertically.

vertig|e /vɛrtiʒ/ n.m. dizziness. **~es,** dizzy spells. **avoir le ou un ~e,** feel dizzy. **~ineux, ~ineuse** a. dizzy; (*très grand*) staggering.

vertu /vɛrty/ n.f. virtue. **en ~ de,** by virtue of. **~eux, ~euse** /-tɥø, -z/ a. virtuous.

verve /vɛrv/ n.f. spirit, wit.

verveine /vɛrvɛn/ n.f. verbena.

vésicule /vezikyl/ n.f. **~ biliaire,** gall-bladder.

vessie /vesi/ n.f. bladder.

veste /vɛst/ n.f. jacket.

vestiaire /vɛstjɛr/ n.m. cloakroom; (*sport*) changing-room.

vestibule /vɛstibyl/ n.m. hall.

vestige /vɛstiʒ/ n.m. (*objet*) relic; (*trace*) vestige.

veston /vɛstɔ̃/ n.m. jacket.

vêtement /vɛtmɑ̃/ n.m. article of clothing. **~s,** clothes.

vétéran /veterɑ̃/ n.m. veteran.

vétérinaire /veterinɛr/ n.m./f. vet, veterinary surgeon, (*Amer.*) veterinarian.

vétille /vetij/ n.f. trifle.

vêt|ir /vetir/ v.t., **se ~ir** v. pr. dress. **~u** a. dressed (**de,** in).

veto /veto/ n.m. invar. veto.

vétuste /vetyst/ a. dilapidated.

veu|f, ~ve /vœf, -v/ a. widowed. —n.m. widower. —n.f. widow.

veuille /vœj/ voir **vouloir**.

veule /vøl/ a. feeble.

veut, veux /vø/ voir **vouloir**.

vexation /vɛksasjɔ̃/ n.f. humiliation.

vex|er /vɛkse/ v.t. upset, hurt. **se ~er** v. pr. be upset, be hurt. **~ant, ~ante** a. upsetting.

via /vja/ prép. via.

viable /vjabl/ a. viable.

viaduc /vjadyk/ n.m. viaduct.

viande /vjɑ̃d/ n.f. meat.

vibr|er /vibre/ v.i. vibrate; (*être ému*) thrill. **~ant, ~ante** a. (*émouvant*) vibrant. **~ation** n.f. vibration.

vicaire /vikɛr/ n.m. curate.

vice /vis/ n.m. (*moral*) vice; (*défectuosité*) defect.

vice- /vis/ préf. vice-.

vice versa /vis(e)vɛrsa/ adv. vice versa.

vicier /visje/ v.t. taint.

vicieu|x, ~se /visjø, -z/ a. depraved. —n.m., f. pervert.

vicin|al (pl. ~aux) /visinal, -o/ a.m. **chemin ~al,** by-road, minor road.

vicomte /vikɔ̃t/ n.m. viscount.

victime /viktim/ n.f. victim; (*d'un accident*) casualty.

vict|oire /viktwar/ n.f. victory; (*sport*) win. **~orieux, ~orieuse** a. victorious; (*équipe*) winning.

victuailles /viktɥaj/ n.f. pl. provisions.

vidang|e /vidɑ̃ʒ/ n.f. emptying; (*auto.*) oil change; (*dispositif*) waste pipe. **~er** v.t. empty.

vide /vid/ a. empty. —n.m. emptiness, void; (*trou, manque*) gap; (*espace sans air*) vacuum. **à ~,** empty.

vidéo /video/ a. invar. video. **jeu ~,** video game. **~cassette** n.f. **~thèque** n.f. video library.

vide-ordures /vidɔrdyr/ n.m. invar. (rubbish) chute.

vider /vide/ v.t. empty; (*poisson*) gut; (*expulser: fam.*) throw out. **~**

les lieux, vacate the premises. **se ~ v.** *pr.* empty.

videur /vidœr/ *n.m.* bouncer.

vie /vi/ *n.f.* life; (*durée*) lifetime. **à ~, pour la ~,** for life. **donner la ~ à,** give birth to. **en ~,** alive. **~ chère,** high cost of living.

vieil /vjɛj/ *voir* **vieux.**

vieillard /vjɛjar/ *n.m.* old man.

vieille /vjɛj/ *voir* **vieux.**

vieillesse /vjɛjɛs/ *n.f.* old age.

vieill|ir /vjejir/ *v.i.* grow old, age; (*mot, idée*) become old-fashioned. —*v.t.* age. **~issement** *n.m.* ageing.

viens, vient /vjɛ̃/ *voir* **venir.**

vierge /vjɛrʒ/ *n.f.* virgin. **la V~,** Virgo. —*a.* virgin; (*feuille, film*) blank.

vieux *ou* **vieil***, **vieille** (*m. pl.* **vieux** /vjø, vjɛj/ *a.* old. —*n.m.* old man. —*n.f.* old woman. **les ~,** old people. **mon ~,** (*fam.*) old man *ou* boy. **ma vieille,** (*fam.*) old girl, dear. **vieille fille,** (*péj.*) spinster. **~ garçon,** bachelor. **jeu** *a. invar.* old-fashioned.

vif, vive /vif, viv/ *a.* lively; (*émotion, vent*) keen; (*froid*) biting;(*lumière*) bright; (*douleur, parole*) sharp; (*souvenir, style, teint*) vivid; (*succès, impatience*) great. **brûler/enterrer ~,** burn/bury alive. **de vive voix,** personally. **avoir les nerfs à ~,** be on edge.

vigie /viʒi/ *n.f.* look-out.

vigilan|t, ~te /viʒilɑ̃, -t/ *a.* vigilant. **~ce** *n.f.* vigilance.

vigne /viɲ/ *n.f.* (*plante*) vine; (*vignoble*) vineyard.

vigneron, ~ne /viɲrɔ̃, -ɔn/ *n.m.,f.* wine-grower.

vignette /viɲɛt/ *n.f.* (*étiquette*) label; (*auto.*) road tax sticker.

vignoble /viɲɔbl/ *n.m.* vineyard.

vigoureu|x, ~se /viguro, -z/ *a.* vigorous, sturdy.

vigueur /vigœr/ *n.f.* vigour.

être/entrer en ~, (*loi*) be/come into force. **en ~,** (*terme*) in use.

VIH *abrév.* (*virus d'immuno-déficience humaine*) HIV.

vil /vil/ *a.* vile, base.

vilain, ~e /vilɛ̃, -ɛn/ *a.* (*mauvais*) nasty; (*laid*) ugly.

villa /villa/ *n.f.* (detached) house.

village /vilaʒ/ *n.m.* village.

villageois, ~e /vilaʒwa, -z/ *a.* village. —*n.m.,f.* villager.

ville /vil/ *n.f.* town; (*importante*) city. **~ d'eaux,** spa.

vin /vɛ̃/ *n.m.* wine. **~ d'honneur,** reception. **~ ordinaire,** table wine.

vinaigre /vinɛgr/ *n.m.* vinegar.

vinaigrette /vinɛgrɛt/ *n.f.* oil and vinegar dressing, vinaigrette.

vindicati|f, ~ve /vɛ̃dikatif, -v/ *a.* vindictive.

vingt /vɛ̃/ /vɛ̃t/ *before vowel and in numbers 22–29*) *a.* & *n.m.* twenty. **~ième** *a.* & *n.m./f.* twentieth.

vingtaine /vɛ̃tɛn/ *n.f.* une **~ (de),** about twenty.

vinicole /vinikɔl/ *a.* wine(-growing).

vinyle /vinil/ *n.m.* vinyl.

viol /vjɔl/ *n.m.* (*de femme*) rape; (*de lieu, loi*) violation.

violacé /vjɔlase/ *a.* purplish.

viol|ent, ~ente /vjɔlɑ̃, -t/ *a.* violent. **~emment** /-amɑ̃/ *adv.* violently. **~ence** *n.f.* violence; (*acte*) act of violence.

viol|er /vjɔle/ *v.t.* rape; (*lieu, loi*) violate. **~ation** *n.f.* violation.

violet, ~te /vjɔlɛ, -t/ *a.* & *n.m.* purple. —*n.f.* violet.

violon /vjɔlɔ̃/ *n.m.* violin. **~iste** /-ɔnist/ *n.m./f.* violinist. **d'Ingres,** hobby.

violoncelle /vjɔlɔ̃sɛl/ *n.m.* cello. **~iste** /-elist/ *n.m./f.* cellist.

vipère /vipɛr/ *n.f.* viper, adder.

virage /viraʒ/ *n.m.* bend; (*de véhicule*) turn; (*changement d'attitude: fig.*) change of course.

virée /vire/ n.f. (fam.) trip, outing.

vir|er /vire/ v.i. turn. **~er de bord**, tack. **~er au rouge**/etc., turn red/etc. —v.t. (argent) transfer; (expulser: fam.) throw out. **~ement** n.m. (comm.) (credit) transfer.

virevolter /virvɔlte/ v.i. spin round, swing round.

virginité /virʒinite/ n.f. virginity.

virgule /virgyl/ n.f. comma; (dans un nombre) (decimal) point.

viril /viril/ a. manly, virile. **~ité** n.f. manliness, virility.

virtuel, **~le** /virtɥɛl/ a. virtual. **~lement** adv. virtually.

virtuos|e /virtɥoz/ n.m./f. virtuoso. **~ité** n.f. virtuosity.

virulen|t, **~te** /virylɑ̃, -t/ a. virulent. **~ce** n.f. virulence.

virus /virys/ n.m. virus.

vis¹ /vi/ voir **vivre**, **voir**.

vis² /vis/ n.f. screw.

visa /viza/ n.m. visa.

visage /vizaʒ/ n.m. face.

vis-à-vis /vizavi/ adv. face to face, opposite. **~ de**, opposite; (à l'égard de) with respect to. —n.m. invar. (personne) person opposite.

viscères /viser/ n.m. pl. intestines.

visées /vize/ n.f. pl. aim. **avoir des ~ sur**, have designs on.

vis|er /vize/ v.t. aim at; (concerner) be aimed at; (timbrer) stamp. —v.i. aim. **~ à**, aim at; (mesure, propos) be aimed at.

visib|le /vizibl/ a. visible. **~ilité** n.f. visibility. **~lement** adv. visibly.

visière /vizjɛr/ n.f. (de casquette) peak; (de casque) visor.

vision /vizjɔ̃/ n.f. vision.

visionnaire /vizjɔnɛr/ a. & n.m./f. visionary.

visionn|er /vizjɔne/ v.t. view. **~euse** n.f. (appareil) viewer.

visite /vizit/ n.f. visit; (examen) examination; (personne) visitor.

heures de ~, visiting hours. **~ guidée**, guided tour. **rendre ~ à**, visit. **être en ~ (chez qn.)**, be visiting (s.o.).

visit|er /vizite/ v.t. visit; (examiner) examine. **~eur**, **~euse** n.m., f. visitor.

vison /vizɔ̃/ n.m. mink.

visqueu|x, **~se** /viskø, -z/ a. viscous.

visser /vise/ v.t. screw (on).

visuel, **~le** /vizɥɛl/ a. visual.

vit|al (m. pl. **~aux**) /vital, -o/ a. vital. **~alité** n.f. vitality.

vitamine /vitamin/ n.f. vitamin.

vite /vit/ adv. fast, quickly; (tôt) soon. **~!**, quick! **faire ~**, be quick.

vitesse /vites/ n.f. speed; (régime: auto.) gear. **à toute ~**, at top speed. **en ~**, in a hurry, quickly.

vitic|ole /vitikɔl/ a. wine. **~ulteur** n.m. wine-grower. **~ulture** n.f. wine-growing.

vitrage /vitraʒ/ n.m. (vitres) windows. **double ~**, double glazing.

vitr|ail (pl. **~aux**) /vitraj, -o/ n.m. stained-glass window.

vitr|e /vitr/ n.f. (window) pane; (de véhicule) window. **~é a** glass, glazed. **~er** v.t. glaze.

vitrine /vitrin/ n.f. (shop) window; (meuble) display cabinet.

vivable /vivabl/ a. ce n'est pas ~, it's unbearable.

vivace /vivas/ a. (plante, sentiment) perennial.

vivacité /vivasite/ n.f. liveliness; (agilité) quickness; (d'émotion, de l'air) keenness; (de souvenir, style, teint) vividness.

vivant, **~e** /vivã, -t/ a. (doué de vie, en usage) living (en vie) alive, living; (actif, vif) lively. —n.m. un **bon ~**, bon viveur. **de son ~**, in one's lifetime. **les ~s**, the living.

vivats /viva/ n.m. pl. cheers.

vive[1] /viv/ *voir* **vif.**

vive[2] /viv/ *int.* ~ **le roi/président**/*etc.*!, long live the king/president/*etc.*!

vivement /vivmɑ̃/ *adv.* (*vite*, *sèchement*) sharply; (*avec éclat*) vividly; (*beaucoup*) greatly. ~ **la fin!**, roll on the end, I'll be glad when it's the end!

vivier /vivje/ *n.m.* fish-pond.

vivifier /vivifje/ *v.t.* invigorate.

vivisection /visisɛksjɔ̃/ *n.f.* vivisection.

vivoter /vivɔte/ *v.i.* plod on, get by.

vivre† /vivr/ *v.i.* live. ~ **de,** (*nourriture*) live on. —*v.t.* (*vie*) live; (*période, aventure*) live through. —**s** *n.m. pl.* supplies. **faire** ~, (*famille etc.*) support. ~ **encore,** be still alive.

vlan /vlɑ̃/ *int.* bang.

vocabulaire /vɔkabylɛr/ *n.m.* vocabulary.

voc|al (*m. pl.* ~**aux**) /vɔkal, -o/ *a.* vocal.

vocalise /vɔkaliz/ *n.f.* voice exercise.

vocation /vɔkasjɔ̃/ *n.f.* vocation.

vociférer /vɔsifere/ *v.t./i.* scream.

vodka /vɔdka/ *n.f.* vodka.

vœu (*pl.* ~**x**) /vø/ *n.m.* (*souhait*) wish; (*promesse*) vow.

vogue /vɔg/ *n.f.* fashion, vogue.

voguer /vɔge/ *v.i.* sail.

voici /vwasi/ *prép.* here is, this is; (*au pluriel*) here are, these are. **me** ~, here I am. ~ **un an,** (*temps passé*) a year ago. ~ **un an que,** it is a year since.

voie /vwa/ *n.f.* (*route*) road; (*chemin*) way; (*moyen*) means, way; (*partie de route*) lane; (*rails*) track; (*quai*) platform. **en** ~ **de développement,** (*pays*) developing. **par la** ~ **des airs,** by air. ~ **de dégagement,** slip-road. ~ **ferrée,** railway; (*Amer.*) railroad. ~ **lactée,** Milky Way. ~

navigable, waterway. ~ **publique,** public highway. ~ **sans issue,** cul-de-sac, dead end. **sur la bonne** ~, (*fig.*) well under way. **mettre sur une** ~ **de garage,** (*fig.*) sideline.

voilà /vwala/ *prép.* there is, that is; (*au pluriel*) there are, those are; (*voici*) here is; here are. **le** ~, there he is. ~!, right!; (*en offrant qch.*) there you are! ~ **un an,** (*temps passé*) a year ago. ~ **un an que,** it is a year since.

voilage /vwalaʒ/ *n.m.* net curtain.

voile[1] /vwal/ *n.f.* (*de bateau*) sail; (*sport*) sailing.

voile[2] /vwal/ *n.m.* veil; (*tissu léger et fin*) net.

voil|er[1] /vwale/ *v.t.* veil. **se** ~**er** *v. pr.* (*devenir flou*) become hazy. ~**é** *a.* (*terme, femme*) veiled; (*flou*) hazy.

voiler[2] /vwale/ *v.t.*, **se** ~ *v. pr.* (*roue etc.*) buckle.

voilier /vwalje/ *n.m.* sailing-ship.

voilure /vwalyr/ *n.f.* sails.

voir† /vwar/ *v.t./i.* see. **se** ~ *v. pr.* (*être visible*) show; (*se produire*) be seen; (*se trouver*) find o.s.; (*se fréquenter*) see each other. **ça n'a rien à** ~ **avec,** that has nothing to do with. **faire** ~, **laisser** ~, show. **je ne peux pas le** ~, (*fam.*) I cannot stand him. ~ **trouble,** have blurred vision. **voyons!,** (*irritation*) come on!

voire /vwar/ *adv.* indeed.

voirie /vwari/ *n.f.* (*service*) highway maintenance. **travaux de** ~, road-works.

voisin, ~**e** /vwazɛ̃, -in/ *a.* (*proche*) neighbouring; (*adjacent*) next (de, to); (*semblable*) similar (de, to). —*n.m., f.* neighbour. **le** ~, the man next door.

voisinage /vwazinaʒ/ *n.m.* neighbourhood; (*proximité*) proximity.

voiture /vwatyr/ *n.f.* (motor) car; (*wagon*) coach, carriage. **en** ~!, all aboard! **~ à cheval**, horse-drawn carriage. **~ de course**, racing-car. **~ d'enfant**, pram; (*Amer.*) baby carriage. **~ de tourisme**, private car.

voix /vwa/ *n.f.* voice; (*suffrage*) vote. **à ~ basse**, in a whisper.

vol[1] /vɔl/ *n.m.* (*d'avion, d'oiseau*) flight; (*groupe d'oiseaux etc.*) flock, flight. **à ~ d'oiseau**, as the crow flies. **~ libre**, hang-gliding. **~ plané**, gliding.

vol[2] /vɔl/ *n.m.* (*délit*) theft; (*hold-up*) robbery. **~ à la tire**, pickpocketing.

volage /vɔlaʒ/ *a.* fickle.

volaille /vɔlɑj/ *n.f.* **la ~**, (*poules etc.*) poultry. **une ~**, a fowl.

volant /vɔlɑ̃/ *n.m.* (steering-)wheel; (*de jupe*) flounce.

volcan /vɔlkɑ̃/ *n.m.* volcano. **~ique** /-anik/ *a.* volcanic.

volée /vɔle/ *n.f.* flight; (*oiseaux*) flight, flock; (*de coups, d'obus*) volley. **à toute ~**, with full force. **de ~, à la ~**, in flight.

voler[1] /vɔle/ *v.i.* (*oiseau etc.*) fly.

vol|er[2] /vɔle/ *v.t./i.* steal (**à**, from). **il ne l'a pas ~é**, he deserved it. **~er qn.**, rob s.o. **~eur, ~euse** *n.m., f.* thief; *a.* thieving.

volet /vɔlɛ/ *n.m.* (*de fenêtre*) shutter; (*de document*) (folded *ou* tear-off) section. **trié sur le ~**, hand-picked.

voleter /vɔlte/ *v.i.* flutter.

volière /vɔljɛr/ *n.f.* aviary.

volontaire /vɔlɔ̃tɛr/ *a.* voluntary; (*personne*) determined. —*n.m./f.* volunteer. **~ment** *adv.* voluntarily; (*exprès*) intentionally.

volonté /vɔlɔ̃te/ *n.f.* (*faculté, intention*) will; (*souhait*) wish; (*énergie*) will-power. **à ~**, (*à son gré*) at will. **bonne ~**, goodwill. **mauvaise ~**, ill will. **faire ses quatre ~s**, do exactly as one pleases.

volontiers /vɔlɔ̃tje/ *adv.* (*de bon gré*) with pleasure, willingly, gladly; (*ordinairement*) readily.

volt /vɔlt/ *n.m.* volt. **~age** *n.m.* voltage.

volte-face /vɔltəfas/ *n.f. invar.* about-face. **faire ~**, turn round.

voltige /vɔltiʒ/ *n.f.* acrobatics.

voltiger /vɔltiʒe/ *v.i.* flutter.

voluble /vɔlybl/ *a.* voluble.

volume /vɔlym/ *n.m.* volume.

volumineu|x, ~se /vɔlyminø, -z/ *a.* bulky.

volupt|é /vɔlypte/ *n.f.* sensual pleasure. **~ueux, ~ueuse** *a.* voluptuous.

vom|ir /vɔmir/ *v.t./i.* vomit. **~i** *n.m.* vomit. **~issement(s)** *n.m.* (*pl.*) vomiting.

vont /vɔ̃/ *voir* **aller**[1].

vorace /vɔras/ *a.* voracious.

vos /vo/ *voir* **votre**.

vote /vɔt/ *n.m.* (*action*) voting; (*d'une loi*) passing; (*suffrage*) vote.

vot|er /vɔte/ *v.i.* vote. —*v.t.* vote for; (*adopter*) pass; (*crédits*) vote. **~ant, ~ante** *n.m., f.* voter.

votre (*pl.* **vos**) /vɔtr, vo/ *a.* your.

vôtre /votr/ *pron.* **le** *ou* **la ~**, **les ~s**, yours.

vou|er /vwe/ *v.t.* dedicate (**à**, to); (*promettre*) vow. **~é à l'échec**, doomed to failure.

vouloir† /vulwar/ *v.t.* want (**faire**, to do). **ça ne veut pas bouger**/*etc.*, it will not move/*etc.* **je voudrais**/**voudrais bien venir**/*etc.*, I should *ou* would like/really like to come/*etc.* **je veux bien venir**/*etc.*, I am happy to come/*etc.* **voulez-vous attendre**/*etc.***?**, will you wait/*etc.***?** **veuillez attendre**/*etc.*, kindly wait/*etc.* **~ absolument faire**, insist on doing. **comme** *ou* **si vous voulez**, if you like *ou* wish. **en ~ à qn.**, have a grudge against s.o.; (*être en colère contre*) be annoyed with s.o. **qu'est ce qu'il me veut?**, what does he want with me? **ne pas ~ de qch./qn.**, not want sth./s.o. **~ dire**, mean. **~ du bien à**, wish well.

voulu /vuly/ *a.* (*délibéré*) intentional; (*requis*) required.

vous /vu/ *pron.* (*sujet, complément*) you; (*indirect*) (to) you; (*réfléchi*) yourself; (*pl.*) yourselves; (*l'un l'autre*) each other. **~-même** *pron.* yourself. **~-mêmes** *pron.* yourselves.

voûte /vut/ *n.f.* (*plafond*) vault; (*porche*) archway.

voûté /vute/ *a.* bent, stooped. **il a le dos ~**, he's stooped.

vouv|oyer /vuvwaje/ *v.t.* address politely (using *vous*). **~oiement** *n.m.* use of (polite) *vous*.

voyage /vwajaʒ/ *n.m.* journey, trip; (*par mer*) voyage. **~(s)**, (*action*) travelling. **~ d'affaires**, business trip. **~ de noces**, honeymoon. **~ organisé**, (package) tour.

voyag|er /vwajaʒe/ *v.i.* travel. **~eur, ~euse** *n.m., f.* traveller.

voyant¹ /vwajã, -t/ *a.* gaudy. —*n.f.* (*femme*) clairvoyant.

voyant² /vwajã/ *n.m.* (*signal*) (warning) light.

voyelle /vwajɛl/ *n.f.* vowel.

voyeur /vwajœr/ *n.m.* voyeur.

voyou /vwaju/ *n.m.* hooligan.

vrac (en) /(ã)vrak/ *adv.* in disorder; (*sans emballage, au poids*) loose, in bulk.

vrai /vrɛ/ *a.* true; (*réel*) real. —*n.m.* truth. **à ~ dire**, to tell the truth.

vraiment /vrɛmã/ *adv.* really.

vraisembl|able /vrɛsɑ̃blabl/ *a.* likely. **~ablement** *adv.* very likely. **~ance** *n.f.* likelihood, plausibility.

vrille /vrij/ *n.f.* (*aviat.*) spin.

vromb|ir /vrɔ̃bir/ *v.i.* hum. **~issement** *n.m.* humming.

VRP *abrév. m.* (*voyageur représentant placier*) rep.

vu /vy/ *voir* voir. —*a.* **bien/mal ~**, well/not well thought of. —*prép.* in view of. **~ que**, seeing that.

vue /vy/ *n.f.* (*spectacle*) sight; (*sens*) (eye)sight; (*panorama, idée*) view. **avoir en ~**, have in mind. **à ~**, (*tirer, payable*) at sight. **de ~**, by sight. **perdre de ~**, lose sight of. **en ~**, (*proche*) in sight; (*célèbre*) in the public eye. **en ~ de faire**, with a view to doing.

vulg|aire /vylgɛr/ *a.* (*grossier*) vulgar; (*ordinaire*) common. **~arité** *n.f.* vulgarity.

vulgariser /vylgarize/ *v.t.* popularize.

vulnérab|le /vylnerabl/ *a.* vulnerable. **~ilité** *n.f.* vulnerability.

vulve /vylv/ *n.f.* vulva.

W

wagon /vagɔ̃/ *n.m.* (*de voyageurs*) carriage; (*Amer.*) car; (*de marchandises*) (*Amer.*) freight car. **~-lit** (*pl.* **~s-lits**) *n.m.* sleeping-car, sleeper. **~-restaurant** (*pl.* **~s-restaurants**) *n.m.* dining-car.

walkman /wɔkman/ *n.m.* (P.) walkman.

wallon, ~ne /walɔ̃, -ɔn/ *a. & n.m., f.* Walloon.

waters /watɛr/ *n.m. pl.* toilet.

watt /wat/ *n.m.* watt.

w.-c. /(dubl)vese/ *n.m. pl.* toilet.

week-end /wikɛnd/ *n.m.* weekend.

western /wɛstɛrn/ *n.m.* western.

whisk|y (*pl.* **~ies**) /wiski/ *n.m.* whisky.

X

xénophob|e /ksenɔfɔb/ a. xenophobic. —n.m./f. xenophobe. ~**ie** n.f. xenophobia.

xérès /kseres/ n.m. sherry.

xylophone /ksilɔfɔn/ n.m. xylophone.

Y

y /i/ adv. & pron. there; (dessus) on it; (pl.) on them; (dedans) in it; (pl.) in them. **s'y habituer**, (à cela) get used to it. **s'y attendre**, expect it. **y penser**, think of it. **il y entra**, (dans cela) he entered it. **j'y vais**, I'm on my way. **ça y est**, that is it. **y être pour qch.**, have sth. to do with it.

yacht /jɔt/ n.m. yacht.

yaourt /jaur(t)/ n.m. yoghurt. ~**ière** /-tjɛr/ n.f. yoghurt maker.

yeux /jø/ voir œil.

yiddish /(j)idiʃ/ n.m. Yiddish.

yoga /jɔga/ n.m. yoga.

yougoslave /jugɔslav/ a. & n.m./f. Yugoslav.

Yougoslavie /jugɔslavi/ n.f. Yugoslavia.

yo-yo /jojo/ n.m. invar. (P.) yo-yo (P.).

yuppie /jøpi/ n.m./f. yuppie.

Z

zèbre /zɛbr/ n.m. zebra.

zébré /zebre/ a. striped.

zèle /zɛl/ n.m. zeal.

zélé /zele/ a. zealous.

zénith /zenit/ n.m. zenith.

zéro /zero/ n.m. nought, zero; (température) zero; (dans un numéro) 0; (football) nil; (football: Amer.) zero; (personne) nonentity. **(re)partir de ~**, start from scratch.

zeste /zɛst/ n.m. peel. **un ~ de**, (fig.) a pinch of.

zézayer /zezeje/ v.i. lisp.

zigzag /zigzag/ n.m. zigzag. **en ~**, zigzag. ~**uer** /-e/ v.i. zigzag.

zinc /zɛ̃g/ n.m. (métal) zinc; (comptoir: fam.) bar.

zizanie /zizani/ n.f. **semer la ~**, put the cat among the pigeons.

zizi /zizi/ n.m. (fam.) willy.

zodiaque /zɔdjak/ n.m. zodiac.

zona /zona/ n.m. (méd.) shingles.

zone /zon/ n.f. zone, area; (faubourgs) shanty town. **~ bleue**, restricted parking zone.

zoo /zo(o)/ n.m. zoo.

zoolog|ie /zɔɔlɔʒi/ n.f. zoology. ~**ique** a. zoological. ~**iste** n.m./f. zoologist.

zoom /zum/ n.m. zoom lens.

zut /zyt/ int. blast (it), (oh) hell.

ANGLAIS–FRANÇAIS
ENGLISH–FRENCH

A

a /eɪ, *unstressed* ə/ *a.* (*before vowel* **an** /æn, ən/) un(e). **I'm a painter,** je suis peintre. **ten pence a kilo,** dix pence le kilo. **once a year,** une fois par an.

aback /ə'bæk/ *adv.* **taken ~,** déconcerté, interdit.

abandon /ə'bændən/ *v.t.* abandonner. —*n.* désinvolture *f.* **~ed** *a.* (*behaviour*) débauché. **~ment** *n.* abandon *m.*

abashed /ə'bæʃt/ *a.* confus.

abate /ə'beɪt/ *v.i.* se calmer. —*v.t.* diminuer. **~ment** *n.* diminution *f.*

abattoir /'æbətwɑ:(r)/ *n.* abattoir *m.*

abbey /'æbɪ/ *n.* abbaye *f.*

abb|**ot** /'æbət/ *n.* abbé *m.* **~ess** *n.* abbesse *f.*

abbreviat|**e** /ə'bri:vɪeɪt/ *v.t.* abréger. **~ion** /-'eɪʃn/ *n.* abréviation *f.*

abdicat|**e** /'æbdɪkeɪt/ *v.t./i.* abdiquer. **~ion** /-'keɪʃn/ *n.* abdication *f.*

abdom|**en** /'æbdəmən/ *n.* abdomen *m.* **~inal** /-'dɒmɪnl/ *a.* abdominal.

abduct /æb'dʌkt/ *v.t.* enlever. **~ion** -kʃn/ *n.* rapt *m.* **~or** *n.* ravisseur|r, -se *m., f.*

aberration /æbə'reɪʃn/ *n.* aberration *f.*

abet /ə'bet/ *v.t.* (*p.t.* **abetted**) (*jurid.*) encourager.

abeyance /ə'beɪəns/ *n.* **in ~,** (*matter*) en suspens; (*custom*) en désuétude.

abhor /əb'hɔ:(r)/ *v.t.* (*p.t.* **abhorred**) exécrer. **~rence** /-'hɒrəns/ *n.* horreur *f.* **~rent** /-'hɒrənt/ *a.* exécrable.

abide /ə'baɪd/ *v.t.* supporter. **~ by,** respecter.

abiding /ə'baɪdɪŋ/ *a.* éternel.

ability /ə'bɪlətɪ/ *n.* aptitude *f.* (**to do,** à faire); (*talent*) talent *m.*

abject /'æbdʒekt/ *a.* abject.

ablaze /ə'bleɪz/ *a.* en feu. **~ with,** (*anger etc.: fig.*) enflammé de.

abl|**e** /'eɪbl/ *a.* (**-er, -est**) capable (**to, de**). **be ~e,** pouvoir; (*know how to*) savoir. **~y** *adv.* habilement.

ablutions /ə'blu:ʃnz/ *n. pl.* ablutions *f. pl.*

abnormal /æb'nɔ:ml/ *a.* anormal. **~ity** /-'mælətɪ/ *n.* anomalie *f.* **~ly** *adv.* (*unusually*) exceptionnellement.

aboard /ə'bɔ:d/ *adv.* à bord. —*prep.* à bord de.

abode /ə'bəʊd/ (*old use*) demeure *f.* **of no fixed ~,** sans domicile fixe.

aboli|**sh** /ə'bɒlɪʃ/ *v.t.* supprimer, abolir. **~tion** /æbə'lɪʃn/ *n.* suppression *f.*, abolition *f.*

abominable /ə'bɒmɪnəbl/ *a.* abominable.

abominat|e /ə'bɒmɪneɪt/ v.t. exécrer. **~ion** abomination f.

aboriginal /æbə'rɪdʒənl/ a. & n. aborigène (m.).

aborigines /æbə'rɪdʒəniːz/ n. pl. aborigènes m. pl.

abort /ə'bɔːt/ v.t. faire avorter. —v.i. avorter. **~ive** a. (attempt etc.) manqué.

abortion /ə'bɔːʃn/ n. avortement m. **have an ~**, se faire avorter.

abound /ə'baʊnd/ v.i. abonder (in, en).

about /ə'baʊt/ adv. (approximately) environ; (here and there) çà et là; (all round) partout, autour; (nearby) dans les parages; (of rumour) en circulation. —prep. au sujet de; (round) autour de; (somewhere in) dans. **~-face**, **~-turn** ns. (fig.) volteface f. invar. **~ here**, par ici. **be ~ to do**, être sur le point de faire. **how or what ~ leaving**, si on partait. **what's the film ~?**, quel est le sujet du film? **talk ~**, parler de.

above /ə'bʌv/ adv. au-dessus; (on page) ci-dessus. —prep. au-dessus de. **he is not ~ lying**, il n'est pas incapable de mentir. **~ all**, par-dessus tout. **~-board** a. honnête. **~-mentioned** a. mentionné ci-dessus.

abrasion /ə'breɪʒn/ n. frottement m.; (injury) écorchure f.

abrasive /ə'breɪsɪv/ a. abrasif; (manner) brusque. —n. abrasif m.

abreast /ə'brest/ a. de front. **keep ~ of**, se tenir au courant de.

abridge /ə'brɪdʒ/ v.t. abréger. **~ment** n. abrégement m., réduction f.; (abridged text) abrégé m.

abroad /ə'brɔːd/ adv. à l'étranger; (far and wide) de tous côtés.

abrupt /ə'brʌpt/ a. (sudden, curt) brusque; (steep) abrupt. **~ly** adv. (suddenly) brusquement; (curtly,

rudely) avec brusquerie. **~ness** n. brusquerie f.

abscess /'æbses/ n. abcès m.

abscond /əb'skɒnd/ v.i. s'enfuir.

abseil /'æbseɪl/ v.i. descendre en rappel.

absen|t[1] /'æbsənt/ a. absent; (look etc.) distrait. **~ce** n. absence f.; (lack) manque m. **in the ~ce of**, à défaut de. **~tly** adv. distraitement. **~t-minded** a. distrait. **~t-mindedness** n. distraction f.

absent[2] /əb'sent/ v. pr. **~ o.s.**, s'absenter.

absentee /æbsən'tiː/ n. absent(e) m. (f.). **~ism** n. absentéisme m.

absolute /'æbsəluːt/ a. absolu; (coward etc.: fam.) véritable. **~ly** adv. absolument.

absolution /æbsə'luːʃn/ n. absolution f.

absolve /əb'zɒlv/ v.t. (from sin) absoudre (from, de); (from vow etc.) délier (from, de).

absorb /əb'sɔːb/ v.t. absorber. **~ption** n. absorption f.

absorbent /əb'sɔːbənt/ a. absorbant. **~ cotton**, (Amer.) coton hydrophile m.

abst|ain /əb'steɪn/ v.i. s'abstenir (from, de). **~ention** n. /-enʃn/ n. abstention f.; (from drink) abstinence f.

abstemious /əb'stiːmɪəs/ a. sobre.

abstinen|ce /'æbstɪnəns/ n. abstinence f. **~t** a. sobre.

abstract[1] /'æbstrækt/ a. abstrait. —n. (quality) abstrait m.; (summary) résumé m.

abstract[2] /əb'strækt/ v.t. retirer, extraire. **~ion** /-kʃn/ n. extraction f.; (idea) abstraction f.

abstruse /əb'struːs/ a. obscur.

absurd /əb'sɜːd/ a. absurde. **~ity** n. absurdité f.

abundan|t /ə'bʌndənt/ a. abondant. **~ce** n. abondance f. **~tly** adv. (entirely) tout à fait.

abuse[1] /ə'bjuːz/ v.t. (misuse) abuser de; (ill-treat) maltraiter; (insult) injurier.

abuse[2] /ə'bjuːs/ n. (misuse) abus m. (of, de); (insults) injures f. pl. ~ive a. injurieux. get ~ive, devenir grossier.

abut /ə'bʌt/ v.i. (p.t. abutted) être contigu (on, à).

abysmal /ə'bɪzməl/ a. (great) profond; (bad: fam.) exécrable.

abyss /ə'bɪs/ n. abîme m.

academic /ækə'demɪk/ a. universitaire; (scholarly) intellectuel; (pej.) théorique. —n. universitaire m./f. ~ally /-lɪ/ adv. intellectuellement.

academy /ə'kædəmɪ/ n. (school) école f. A~y, (society) Académie f. ~ician /-'mɪʃn/ n. académicien(ne) m. (f.).

accede /ək'siːd/ v.i. ~ to, (request, post, throne) accéder à.

accelerat|e /ək'seləreɪt/ v.t. accélérer. —v.i. (speed up) s'accélérer; (auto.) accélérer. ~ion /-'reɪʃn/ n. accélération f.

accelerator /ək'seləreɪtə(r)/ n. (auto.) accélérateur m.

accent[1] /'æksənt/ n. accent m.

accent[2] /æk'sent/ v.t. accentuer.

accentuat|e /ək'sentʃʊeɪt/ v.t. accentuer. ~ion /-'eɪʃn/ n. accentuation f.

accept /ək'sept/ v.t. accepter. ~able a. acceptable. ~ance n. acceptation f.; (approval, favour) approbation f.

access /'ækses/ n. accès m. (to sth., à qch.; to s.o., auprès de qn.). ~ible /ək'sesəbl/ a. accessible. ~ road, route d'accès f.

accession /æk'seʃn/ n. accession f.; (thing added) nouvelle acquisition f.

accessory /ək'sesərɪ/ a. accessoire. —n. accessoire m.; (person: jurid.) complice m./f.

accident /'æksɪdənt/ n. accident m.; (chance) hasard m. ~al /-'dentl/ a. accidentel, fortuit. ~ally /-'dentəlɪ/ adv. involontairement. ~-prone, qui attire les accidents.

acclaim /ə'kleɪm/ v.t. acclamer. —n. acclamation(s) f. (pl.).

acclimat|e /'æklɪmeɪt/ v.t./i. (Amer.) (s')acclimater. ~ion /-'meɪʃn/ n. (Amer.) acclimatation f.

acclimatiz|e /ə'klaɪmətaɪz/ v.t./i. (s')acclimater. ~ation /-'zeɪʃn/ n. acclimatation f.

accommodat|e /ə'kɒmədeɪt/ v.t. loger, avoir de la place pour; (adapt) adapter; (supply) fournir; (oblige) obliger. ~ing a. obligeant. ~ion /-'deɪʃn/ n. (living premises) logement m.; (rented rooms) chambres f. pl.

accompan|y /ə'kʌmpənɪ/ v.t. accompagner. ~iment n. accompagnement m. ~ist n. accompagna|teur, -trice m., f.

accomplice /ə'kʌmplɪs/ n. complice m./f.

accomplish /ə'kʌmplɪʃ/ v.t. (perform) accomplir; (achieve) réaliser. ~ed a. accompli. ~ment n. accomplissement m. ~ments n. pl. (abilities) talents m. pl.

accord /ə'kɔːd/ v.i. concorder. —v.t. accorder. —n. accord m. of one's own ~, de sa propre initiative. ~ance n. in ~ance with, conformément à.

according /ə'kɔːdɪŋ/ adv. ~ to, selon, suivant; (person) d'après. ~ly adv. en conséquence.

accordion /ə'kɔːdɪən/ n. accordéon m.

accost /ə'kɒst/ v.t. aborder.

account /ə'kaʊnt/ n. (comm.) compte m.; (description) compte rendu m.; (importance) importance f. —v.t. considérer. ~ for, rendre compte de, expliquer. **on ~ of,** à cause de. **in no ~,** en aucun cas. **take into ~,** tenir compte de. **~able** *a.* responsable (**for,** de; **to,** envers). **~ability** /ə'bɪlətɪ/ *n.* responsabilité *f.*

accountan|t /ə'kaʊntənt/ *n.* comptable *m./f.,* expert-comptable *m.* **~cy** *n.* comptabilité *f.*

accredited /ə'kredɪtɪd/ *a.* accrédité.

accrue /ə'kruː/ *v.i.* s'accumuler. **~ to,** (*come to*) revenir à.

accumulat|e /ə'kjuːmjʊleɪt/ *v.t./i.* (s')accumuler. **~ion** /-'leɪʃn/ *n.* accumulation *f.*

accumulator /ə'kjuːmjʊleɪtə(r)/ *n.* (*battery*) accumulateur *m.*

accura|te /'ækjərət/ *a.* exact, précis. **~cy** *n.* exactitude *f.,* précision *f.* **~tely** *adv.* exactement, avec précision.

accus|e /ə'kjuːz/ *v.t.* accuser. **the ~ed,** l'accusé(e) *m.(f.).* **~ation** /ækjuː'zeɪʃn/ *n.* accusation *f.*

accustom /ə'kʌstəm/ *v.t.* accoutumer. **~ed** *a.* accoutumé. **become ~ed to,** s'accoutumer à.

ace /eɪs/ *n.* (*card, person*) as *m.*

ache /eɪk/ *n.* douleur *f.,* mal *m.* —*v.i.* faire mal. **my leg ~s,** ma jambe me fait mal, j'ai mal à la jambe.

achieve /ə'tʃiːv/ *v.t.* réaliser, accomplir; (*success*) obtenir. **~ment** *n.* réalisation *f.* (**of,** de); (*feat*) exploit *m.,* réussite *f.*

acid /'æsɪd/ *a. & n.* acide (*m.*). **~ity** /ə'sɪdətɪ/ *n.* acidité *f.* **~ rain,** pluies acides *f. pl.*

acknowledge /ək'nɒlɪdʒ/ *v.t.* reconnaître. **~** (*receipt of*), accuser réception de. **~ment** *n.* reconnaissance *f.;* accusé de réception *m.*

acme /'ækmɪ/ *n.* sommet *m.*

acne /'æknɪ/ *n.* acné *f.*

acorn /'eɪkɔːn/ *n.* (*bot.*) gland *m.*

acoustic /ə'kuːstɪk/ *a.* acoustique. **~s** *n. pl.* acoustique *f.*

acquaint /ə'kweɪnt/ *v.t.* **~ s.o. with sth.,** mettre qn. au courant de qch. **be ~ed with,** (*person*) connaître; (*fact*) savoir. **~ance** *n.* (*knowledge, person*) connaissance *f.*

acquiesce /ækwɪ'es/ *v.i.* consentir. **~nce** *n.* consentement *m.*

acqui|re /ə'kwaɪə(r)/ *v.t.* acquérir; (*habit*) prendre. **~sition** /ækwɪ'zɪʃn/ *n.* acquisition *f.* **~sitive** /ə'kwɪzətɪv/ *a.* avide, âpre au gain.

acquit /ə'kwɪt/ *v.t.* (*p.t.* **acquitted**) acquitter. **~ o.s. well,** bien s'en tirer. **~tal** *n.* acquittement *m.*

acre /'eɪkə(r)/ *n.* (*approx.*) demi-hectare *m.* **~age** *n.* superficie *f.*

acrid /'ækrɪd/ *a.* âcre.

acrimon|ious /ækrɪ'məʊnɪəs/ *a.* acerbe, acrimonieux. **~y** /'ækrɪmənɪ/ *n.* acrimonie *f.*

acrobat /'ækrəbæt/ *n.* acrobate *m./f.* **~ic** /-'bætɪk/ *a.* acrobatique. **~ics** /-'bætɪks/ *n. pl.* acrobatie *f.*

acronym /'ækrənɪm/ *n.* sigle *m.*

across /ə'krɒs/ *adv. & prep.* (*side to side*) d'un côté à l'autre (de); (*on other side*) de l'autre côté (**from,** de); (*crosswise*) en travers (de), à travers. **go** *or* **walk ~,** traverser.

acrylic /ə'krɪlɪk/ *a. & n.* acrylique (*m.*).

act /ækt/ *n.* (*deed, theatre*) acte *m.;* (*in variety show*) numéro *m.;* (*decree*) loi *f.* —*v.i.* agir; (*theatre*) jouer; (*function*) marcher; (*pretend*) jouer la comédie. —*v.t.* (*part, role*) jouer. **~ as,** servir de. **~ing** *a.* (*temporary*) intérimaire; *n.* (*theatre*) jeu *m.*

action /'ækʃn/ *n.* action *f.;* (*mil.*) combat *m.* **out of ~,** hors de service. **take ~,** agir.

activate /'æktɪveɪt/ *v.t.* activer. (*machine*) actionner; (*reaction*) activer.

active /'æktɪv/ *a.* actif; (*interest*) vif; (*volcano*) en activité. **~ism** *n.* activisme *m.* **~ist** *n.* activiste *m./f.* **~ity** /-'tɪvətɪ/ *n.* activité *f.*

ac|tor /'æktə(r)/ *n.* acteur *m.* **~tress** *n.* actrice *f.*

actual /'æktʃʊəl/ *a.* réel; (*example*) concret. **the ~ pen which,** le stylo même que. **in the ~ house,** (*the house itself*) dans la maison elle-même. **no ~ promise,** pas de promesse en tant que telle. **~ity** /-'ælətɪ/ *n.* réalité *f.* **~ly** *adv.* (*in fact*) en réalité, réellement.

actuary /'æktʃʊərɪ/ *n.* actuaire *m./f.*

acumen /'ækjʊmən, *Amer.* ə'kju:mən/ *n.* perspicacité *f.*

acupunctur|e /'ækjʊpʌŋktʃə(r)/ *n.* acupuncture *f.* **~ist** *n.* acupuncteur *m.*

acute /ə'kju:t/ *a.* aigu; (*mind*) pénétrant; (*emotion*) intense, vif; (*shortage*) grave. **~ly** *adv.* vivement. **~ness** *n.* intensité *f.*

ad /æd/ *n.* (*fam.*) annonce *f.*

AD *abbr.* après J.-C.

adamant /'ædəmənt/ *a.* inflexible.

Adam's apple /'ædəmz'æpl/ *n.* pomme d'Adam *f.*

adapt /ə'dæpt/ *v.t./i.* (s')adapter. **~ation** /-'teɪʃn/ *n.* adaptation *f.* **~or** *n.* (*electr.*) adaptateur *m.*; (*for two plugs*) prise multiple *f.*

adaptab|le /ə'dæptəbl/ *a.* souple; (*techn.*) adaptable. **~ility** /-'bɪlətɪ/ *n.* souplesse *f.*

add /æd/ *v.t./i.* ajouter. **~** (**up**), (*total*) additionner. **~ up to,** (*total*) s'élever à. **~ing machine,** machine à calculer *f.*

adder /'ædə(r)/ *n.* vipère *f.*

addict /'ædɪkt/ *n.* intoxiqué(e) *m. (f.)*; (*fig.*) fanatique *m./f.*

addict|ed /ə'dɪktɪd/ *a.* **~ed to,** (*drink*) adonné à. **be ~ed to,** (*fig.*) être fanatique de. **~ion** /-kʃn/ *n.* (*med.*) dépendance *f.*;

(*fig.*) manie *f.* **~ive** *a.* (*drug etc.*) qui crée une dépendance.

addition /ə'dɪʃn/ *n.* addition *f.* **in ~,** en outre. **~al** /-ʃənl/ *a.* supplémentaire.

additive /'ædɪtɪv/ *n.* additif *m.*

address /ə'dres/ *n.* adresse *f.*; (*speech*) allocution *f.* —*v.t.* adresser; (*speak to*) s'adresser à. **~ee** /ædre'si:/ *n.* destinataire *m./f.*

adenoids /'ædɪnɔɪdz/ *n. pl.* végétations (adénoïdes) *f. pl.*

adept /'ædept, *Amer.* ə'dept/ *a. & n.* expert (**at,** en) (*m.*).

adequa|te /'ædɪkwət/ *a.* suffisant; (*satisfactory*) satisfaisant. **~cy** *n.* quantité suffisante *f.*; (*of person*) compétence *f.* **~tely** *adv.* suffisamment.

adhere /əd'hɪə(r)/ *v.i.* adhérer (**to,** à). **~ to,** (*fig.*) respecter. **~nce** /-rəns/ *n.* adhésion *f.*

adhesion /əd'hi:ʒn/ *n.* (*grip*) adhérence *f.*; (*support: fig.*) adhésion *f.*

adhesive /əd'hi:sɪv/ *a. & n.* adhésif *m.*

ad infinitum /ædɪnfɪ'naɪtəm/ *adv.* à l'infini.

adjacent /ə'dʒeɪsnt/ *a.* contigu (**to,** à).

adjective /'ædʒɪktɪv/ *n.* adjectif *m.*

adjoin /ə'dʒɔɪn/ *v.t.* être contigu à.

adjourn /ə'dʒɜ:n/ *v.t.* ajourner. —*v.t./i.* **~** (**the meeting**), suspendre la séance. **~ to,** (*go*) se retirer à.

adjudicate /ə'dʒu:dɪkeɪt/ *v.t./i.* juger.

adjust /ə'dʒʌst/ *v.t.* (*machine*) régler; (*prices*) (r)ajuster; (*arrange*) rajuster, arranger. —*v.t./i.* (**o.s.**) **to,** s'adapter à. **~able** *a.* réglable. **~ment** *n.* (*techn.*) réglage *m.*; (*of person*) adaptation *f.*

ad lib /æd'lɪb/ *v.i.* (*p.t.* **ad libbed**) (*fam.*) improviser.

administer /əd'mɪnɪstə(r)/ *v.t.* administrer.

administration /ədmɪnɪ'streɪʃn/ *n.* administration *f.*

administrative /əd'mɪnɪstrətɪv/ *a.* administratif.

administrator /əd'mɪnɪstreɪtə(r)/ *n.* administra|teur, -trice *m., f.*

admirable /'ædmərəbl/ *a.* admirable.

admiral /'ædmərəl/ *n.* amiral *m.*

admir|e /əd'maɪə(r)/ *v.t.* admirer. **~ation** /ædmə'reɪʃn/ *n.* admiration *f.* **~er** *n.* admira|teur, -trice *m., f.*

admissible /əd'mɪsəbl/ *a.* admissible.

admission /əd'mɪʃn/ *n.* admission *f.*; (*to museum, theatre, etc.*) entrée *f.*; (*confession*) aveu *m.*

admit /əd'mɪt/ *v.t.* (*p.t.* **admitted**) laisser entrer; (*acknowledge*) reconnaître, admettre. **~ to,** avouer. **~tance** *n.* entrée *f.* **~tedly** *adv.* il est vrai (que).

admonish /əd'mɒnɪʃ/ *v.t.* réprimander.

ado /ə'du:/ *n.* **without more ~,** sans plus de cérémonies.

adolescen|ce /ædə'lesnt/ *n. & a.* adolescent(e) (*m.* (*f.*)). **~ce** *n.* adolescence *f.*

adopt /ə'dɒpt/ *v.t.* adopter. **~ed a.** (*child*) adoptif. **~ion** /-pʃn/ *n.* adoption *f.*

adoptive /ə'dɒptɪv/ *a.* adoptif.

ador|e /ə'dɔ:(r)/ *v.t.* adorer. **~able** *a.* adorable. **~ation** /ædə'reɪʃn/ *n.* adoration *f.*

adorn /ə'dɔ:n/ *v.t.* orner. **~ment** *n.* ornement *m.*

adrift /ə'drɪft/ *a. & adv.* à la dérive.

adroit /ə'drɔɪt/ *a.* adroit.

adulation /ædjʊ'leɪʃn/ *n.* adulation *f.*

adult /'ædʌlt/ *a. & n.* adulte (*m./f.*). **~hood** *n.* condition d'adulte *f.*

adulterate /ə'dʌltəreɪt/ *v.t.* falsifier, frelater, altérer.

adulter|y /ə'dʌltərɪ/ *n.* adultère *m.* **~er, ~ess** *ns.* épou|x, -se adultère *m., f.* **~ous** *a.* adultère.

advance /əd'vɑ:ns/ *v.t.* avancer. —*v.i.* (s')avancer; (*progress*) avancer. —*n.* avance *f.* —*a.* (*payment*) anticipé. **in ~,** à l'avance. **~d a.** avancé; (*studies*) supérieur. **~ment** *n.* avancement *m.*

advantage /əd'vɑ:ntɪdʒ/ *n.* avantage *m.* **take ~ of,** profiter de; (*person*) exploiter. **~ous** /ædvən'teɪdʒəs/ *a.* avantageux.

advent /'ædvənt/ *n.* arrivée *f.*

Advent /'ædvənt/ *n.* Avent *m.*

adventur|e /əd'ventʃə(r)/ *n.* aventure *f.* **~er** *n.* explora|teur, -trice *m., f.*; (*pej.*) aventur|ier, -ière *m., f.* **~ous** *a.* aventureux.

adverb /'ædvɜ:b/ *n.* adverbe *m.*

adversary /'ædvəsərɪ/ *n.* adversaire *m./f.*

advers|e /'ædvɜ:s/ *a.* défavorable. **~ity** /əd'vɜ:sətɪ/ *n.* adversité *f.*

advert /'ædvɜ:t/ *n.* (*fam.*) annonce *f.*; (*TV*) pub *f.*, publicité *f.* **~isement** /əd'vɜ:tɪsmənt/ *n.* publicité *f.*; (*in paper etc.*) annonce *f.*

advertis|e /'ædvətaɪz/ *v.t./i.* faire de la publicité (pour); (*sell*) mettre une annonce (pour vendre). **~ for,** (*seek*) chercher (par voie d'annonce). **~ing** *n.* publicité *f.* **~er** /-ə(r)/ *n.* annonceur *m.*

advice /əd'vaɪs/ *n.* conseil(s) *m.* (*pl.*); (*comm.*) avis *m.* **some ~, a piece of ~,** un conseil.

advis|e /əd'vaɪz/ *v.t.* conseiller; (*inform*) aviser. **~e against,** déconseiller. **~able** *a.* conseillé, prudent (**to,** de). **~er** *n.* conseil|ler, -ère *m., f.* **~ory** *a.* consultatif.

advocate¹ /'ædvəkət/ *n.* (*jurid.*) avocat *m.* **~s of,** les défenseurs de.

advocate² /'ædvəkeɪt/ v.t. recommander.

aegis /'iːdʒɪs/ n. **under the ~ of,** sous l'égide de f.

aeon /'iːən/ n. éternité f.

aerial /'eərɪəl/ a. aérien. —n. antenne f.

aerobatics /eərə'bætɪks/ n. pl. acrobatie aérienne f.

aerobics /eə'rəʊbɪks/ n. aérobic m.

aerodrome /'eərədrəʊm/ n. aérodrome m.

aerodynamic /eərəʊdaɪ'næmɪk/ a. aérodynamique.

aeroplane /'eərəpleɪn/ n. avion m.

aerosol /'eərəsɒl/ n. atomiseur m.

aesthetic /iːs'θetɪk, Amer. es-'θetɪk/ a. esthétique.

afar /ə'fɑː(r)/ adv. **from ~,** de loin.

affable /'æfəbl/ a. affable.

affair /ə'feə(r)/ n. (matter) affaire f.; (romance) liaison f.

affect /ə'fekt/ v.t. affecter. **~ation** /æfek'teɪʃn/ n. affectation f. **~ed** a. affecté.

affection /ə'fekʃn/ n. affection f.

affectionate /ə'fekʃənət/ a. affectueux.

affiliate /ə'fɪlɪeɪt/ v.t. affilier. **~ed company,** filiale f. **~ion** /-'eɪʃn/ n. affiliation f.

affinity /ə'fɪnətɪ/ n. affinité f.

affirm /ə'fɜːm/ v.t. affirmer. **~ation** /æfə'meɪʃn/ n. affirmation f.

affirmative /ə'fɜːmətɪv/ a. affirmatif. —n. affirmative f.

affix /ə'fɪks/ v.t. apposer.

afflict /ə'flɪkt/ v.t. affliger. **~ion** /-kʃn/ n. affliction f., détresse f.

affluen|t /'æfluənt/ a. riche. **~ce** n. richesse f.

afford /ə'fɔːd/ v.t. avoir les moyens d'acheter; (provide) fournir. **~ to do,** avoir les moyens de faire; (be able) se permettre de faire. **can you ~ the time?,** avez-vous le temps?

affray /ə'freɪ/ n. rixe f.

affront /ə'frʌnt/ n. affront m. —v.t. insulter.

afield /ə'fiːld/ adv. **far ~,** loin.

afloat /ə'fləʊt/ adv. à flot.

afoot /ə'fʊt/ adv. **sth. is ~,** il se trame or se prépare qch.

aforesaid /ə'fɔːsed/ a. susdit.

afraid /ə'freɪd/ a. **be ~,** avoir peur (of, to, de; that, que); (be sorry) regretter. **I am ~ that,** (regret to say) je regrette de dire que.

afresh /ə'freʃ/ adv. de nouveau.

Africa /'æfrɪkə/ n. Afrique f. **~n** a. & n. africain(e) (m. (f.)).

after /'ɑːftə(r)/ adv. & prep. après. —conj. après que. **~ doing,** après avoir fait. **~ all** après tout. **~-effect** n. suite f. **~-sales service,** service après-vente m. **~ the manner of,** d'après. **be ~,** (seek) chercher.

aftermath /'ɑːftəmæθ/ n. suites f. pl.

afternoon /ɑːftə'nuːn/ n. après-midi m./f. invar.

afters /'ɑːftəz/ n. pl. (fam.) dessert m.

aftershave /'ɑːftəʃeɪv/ n. lotion après-rasage f.

afterthought /'ɑːftəθɔːt/ n. réflexion après coup f. **as an ~,** en y repensant.

afterwards /'ɑːftəwədz/ adv. après, par la suite.

again /ə'gen/ adv. de nouveau, encore une fois; (besides) en outre. **do ~, see ~/etc.,** refaire, revoir/etc.

against /ə'genst/ prep. contre. **~ the law,** illégal.

age /eɪdʒ/ n. âge m. —v.t./i. (pres. p. **ageing**) vieillir. **~ group,** tranche d'âge f. **~ limit,** limite d'âge. **for ~s,** (fam.) une éternité. **of ~,** (jurid.) majeur. **ten years of ~,** âgé de dix ans. **~less** a. toujours jeune.

aged[1] /eɪdʒd/ *a.* ~ **six,** âgé de six ans.

aged[2] /eɪdʒd/ *a.* âgé, vieux.

agen|cy /eɪdʒənsɪ/ *n.* agence *f.*; (*means*) entremise *f.* ~**t** *n.* agent *m.*

agenda /əˈdʒendə/ *n.* ordre du jour *m.*

agglomeration /əɡlɒməˈreɪʃn/ *n.* agglomération *f.*

aggravat|e /ˈæɡrəveɪt/ *v.t.* (*make worse*) aggraver; (*annoy: fam.*) exaspérer. ~**ion** /-ˈveɪʃn/ *n.* aggravation *f.*; exaspération *f.*; (*trouble: fam.*) ennuis *m. pl.*

aggregate /ˈæɡrɪɡət/ *a. & n.* total (*m.*).

aggress|ive /əˈɡresɪv/ *a.* agressif. ~**ion** /-ʃn/ *n.* agression *f.* ~**iveness** *n.* agressivité *f.* ~**or** *n.* agresseur *m.*

aggrieved /əˈɡriːvd/ *a.* peiné.

aghast /əˈɡɑːst/ *a.* horrifié.

agile /ˈædʒaɪl, Amer. ˈædʒl/ *a.* agile. ~**ity** /əˈdʒɪlətɪ/ *n.* agilité *f.*

agitat|e /ˈædʒɪteɪt/ *v.t.* agiter. ~**ion** /-ˈteɪʃn/ *n.* agitation *f.* ~**or** *n.* agitateur, -trice *m., f.*

agnostic /æɡˈnɒstɪk/ *a. & n.* agnostique (*m./f.*).

ago /əˈɡəʊ/ *adv.* il y a. **a month** ~, il y a un mois. **long** ~, il y a longtemps. **how long** ~**?,** il y a combien de temps?

agog /əˈɡɒɡ/ *a.* impatient, en émoi.

agon|y /ˈæɡənɪ/ *n.* grande souffrance *f.*; (*mental*) angoisse *f.* ~**ize** *v.i.* souffrir. ~**ize over,** se torturer l'esprit pour. ~**ized** *a.* angoissé. ~**izing** *a.* angoissant.

agree /əˈɡriː/ *v.i.* être or se mettre d'accord (**on,** sur); (*of figures*) concorder. —*v.t.* (*date*) convenir de. ~ **that,** reconnaître que. ~ **to do,** accepter de faire. ~ **to sth.,** accepter qch. **onions don't** ~ **with me,** je ne digère pas les oignons. ~**d** *a.* (*time, place*) convenu. **be** ~**d,** être d'accord.

agreeable /əˈɡriːəbl/ *a.* agréable. **be** ~, (*willing*) être d'accord.

agreement /əˈɡriːmənt/ *n.* accord *m.* **in** ~, d'accord.

agricultur|e /ˈæɡrɪkʌltʃə(r)/ *n.* agriculture *f.* ~**al** /-ˈkʌltʃərəl/ *a.* agricole.

aground /əˈɡraʊnd/ *adv.* **run** ~, (*of ship*) (s')échouer.

ahead /əˈhed/ *adv.* (*in front*) en avant, devant; (*in advance*) à l'avance. ~ **of s.o.,** devant qn.; en avance sur qn. ~ **of time,** en avance. **straight** ~, tout droit.

aid /eɪd/ *v.t.* aider. —*n.* aide *f.* **in** ~ **of,** au profit de.

aide /eɪd/ *n.* aide *m./f.*

AIDS /eɪdz/ *n.* (*med.*) sida *m.*

ail /eɪl/ *v.t.* **what** ~**s you?,** qu'avez-vous? ~**ing** *a.* souffrant. ~**ment** *n.* maladie *f.*

aim /eɪm/ *v.t.* diriger; (*gun*) braquer (**at,** sur); (*remark*) destiner. —*v.i.* viser. ~ **but a.** ~ **at,** viser. ~ **to,** avoir l'intention de. **take** ~, viser. ~**less** *a.*, ~**lessly** *adv.* sans but.

air /eə(r)/ *n.* air *m.* —*v.t.* aérer; (*views*) exposer librement. —*a.* (*base etc.*) aérien. ~**bed** *n.* ~**conditioned** *a.* climatisé. ~**conditioning** *n.* climatisation *f.* ~ **force/hostess,** armée/ hôtesse de l'air *f.* ~ **letter,** aérogramme *m.* ~**mail,** poste aérienne *f.* **by** ~**mail,** par avion. ~ **raid,** attaque aérienne *f.* ~ **terminal,** aérogare *f.* ~ **traffic controller,** aiguilleur du ciel *m.* **by** ~, par avion. **in the** ~, (*rumour*) répandu; (*plan*) incertain. **on the** ~, sur l'antenne.

airborne /ˈeəbɔːn/ *a.* en (cours de) vol; (*troops*) aéroporté.

aircraft /ˈeəkrɑːft/ *n. invar.* avion *m.* ~**-carrier** *n.* porte-avions *m. invar.*

airfield /'eəfiːld/ n. terrain d'aviation m.

airgun /'eəgʌn/ n. carabine à air comprimé f.

airlift /'eəlɪft/ n. pont aérien m. —v.t. transporter par pont aérien.

airline /'eəlaɪn/ n. ligne aérienne f. ∼r /-ə(r)/ n. avion de ligne m.

airlock /'eəlɒk/ n. (in pipe) bulle d'air f.; (chamber: techn.) sas m.

airman /'eəmən/ n. (pl. -men) aviateur m.

airplane /'eəpleɪn/ n. (Amer.) avion m.

airport /'eəpɔːt/ n. aéroport m.

airsickness /'eəsɪknɪs/ n. mal de l'air m.

airtight /'eətaɪt/ a. hermétique.

airways /'eəweɪz/ n. pl. compagnie d'aviation f.

airworthy /'eəwɜːði/ a. en état de navigation.

airy /'eərɪ/ a. (-ier, -iest) bien aéré; (manner) désinvolte.

aisle /aɪl/ n. (of church) nef latérale f.; (gangway) couloir m.

ajar /ə'dʒɑː(r)/ adv. & a. entr'ouvert.

akin /ə'kɪn/ a. ∼ to, apparenté à.

alabaster /'æləbɑːstə(r)/ n. albâtre m.

à la carte /ɑːlɑː'kɑːt/ adv. & a. (culin.) à la carte.

alacrity /ə'lækrətɪ/ n. empressement m.

alarm /ə'lɑːm/ n. alarme f.; (clock) réveil m. —v.t. alarmer. ∼-clock n. réveil m., réveille-matin m. invar. ∼ist n. alarmiste m./f.

alas /ə'læs/ int. hélas.

albatross /'ælbətrɒs/ n. albatros m.

album /'ælbəm/ n. album m.

alcohol /'ælkəhɒl/ n. alcool m. ∼ic /-'hɒlɪk/ a. alcoolique; (drink) alcoolisé; n. alcoolique m./f. ∼ism n. alcoolisme m.

alcove /'ælkəʊv/ n. alcôve f.

ale /eɪl/ n. bière f.

alert /ə'lɜːt/ a. (lively) vif; (watchful) vigilant. —n. alerte f. —v.t. alerter. ∼ s.o. to, prévenir qn. de. **on the** ∼, sur le qui-vive. ∼ness n. vivacité f.; vigilance f.

A-level /'eɪlevl/ n. baccalauréat m.

algebra /'ældʒɪbrə/ n. algèbre f. ∼ic /-'breɪk/ a. algébrique.

Algeria /æl'dʒɪərɪə/ n. Algérie f. ∼n a. & n. algérien(ne) (m. (f.)).

algorithm /'ælgərɪðm/ n. algorithme m.

alias /'eɪlɪəs/ n. (pl. -ases) faux nom m. —adv. alias.

alibi /'ælɪbaɪ/ n. (pl. -is) alibi m.

alien /'eɪlɪən/ n. & a. étrang|er, -ère (m., f.) (to, à).

alienat|e /'eɪlɪəneɪt/ v.t. aliéner. ∼e one's friends/etc., s'aliéner ses amis/etc. ∼ion n. /-'neɪʃn/ n. aliénation f.

alight[1] /ə'laɪt/ v.i. (person) descendre; (bird) se poser.

alight[2] /ə'laɪt/ a. en feu, allumé.

align /ə'laɪn/ v.t. aligner. ∼ment n. alignement m.

alike /ə'laɪk/ a. semblable. —adv. de la même façon. **look or be** ∼, se ressembler.

alimony /'ælɪmənɪ/ Amer. -məʊnɪ/ n. pension alimentaire f.

alive /ə'laɪv/ a. vivant. ∼ to, sensible à, sensibilisé à. ∼ with, grouillant de.

alkali /'ælkəlaɪ/ n. (pl. -is) alcali m.

all /ɔːl/ a. tout, tous, toutes. —pron. tous, toutes; (everything) tout. —adv. tout. ∼ (the) men, tous les hommes. ∼ of it, (le) tout. ∼ of us, nous tous. ∼ but, presque. ∼ for sth., à fond pour qch. ∼ in, (exhausted) épuisé. ∼ in a. tout compris. ∼-in wrestling, catch m. ∼ out, à fond. ∼-out a. (effort) maximum. ∼ over, partout (sur or dans); (finished) fini. ∼ right, bien; (agreeing) bon! ∼ round, dans tous les domaines; (for all) pour

tous. ~-round *a.* général. ~
there, (*alert*) éveillé. ~ the
better, tant mieux. ~ the same,
tout de même. the best of ~, le
meilleur.

allay /ə'leɪ/ *v.t.* calmer.

allegation /ælɪ'geɪʃn/ *n.* allégation
f.

allege /ə'ledʒ/ *v.t.* prétendre. ~dly
/-ɪdlɪ/ *adv.* d'après ce qu'on dit.

allegiance /ə'liːdʒəns/ *n.* fidélité *f.*

allerg|y /'ælədʒɪ/ *n.* allergie *f.* ~ic
/ə'lɜːdʒɪk/ *a.* allergique (to, à).

alleviate /ə'liːvɪeɪt/ *v.t.* alléger.

alley /'ælɪ/ *n.* (*street*) ruelle *f.*

alliance /ə'laɪəns/ *n.* alliance *f.*

allied /'ælaɪd/ *a.* allié.

alligator /'ælɪgeɪtə(r)/ *n.* alligator
m.

allocat|e /'æləkeɪt/ *v.t.* (*assign*)
attribuer; (*share out*) distribuer.
~ion /-'keɪʃn/ *n.* allocation *f.*

allot /ə'lɒt/ *v.t.* (*p.t.* allotted)
attribuer. ~ment *n.* attribution
f.; (*share*) partage *m.*; (*land*)
parcelle de terre *f.* (*louée pour la
culture*).

allow /ə'laʊ/ *v.t.* permettre; (*grant*) accorder; (*reckon on*)
prévoir; (*agree*) reconnaître. ~
s.o. to, permettre à qn. de. ~ for,
tenir compte de.

allowance /ə'laʊəns/ *n.* allocation
f., indemnité *f.* make ~s for,
être indulgent envers; (*take into
account*) tenir compte de.

alloy /'ælɔɪ/ *n.* alliage *m.*

allude /ə'luːd/ *v.i.* ~ to, faire
allusion à.

allure /ə'lʊə(r)/ *v.t.* attirer.

allusion /ə'luːʒn/ *n.* allusion *f.*

ally¹ /'ælaɪ/ *n.* allié(e) *m.* (*f.*).

ally² /ə'laɪ/ *v.t.* allier. ~ o.s. with,
s'allier à ou avec.

almanac /'ɔːlmənæk/ *n.* almanach
m.

almighty /ɔːl'maɪtɪ/ *a.* tout-puis-
sant; (*very great: fam.*) sacré,
formidable.

almond /'ɑːmənd/ *n.* amande *f.*

almost /'ɔːlməʊst/ *adv.* presque.

alms /ɑːmz/ *n.* aumône *f.*

alone /ə'ləʊn/ *a. & adv.* seul.

along /ə'lɒŋ/ *prep.* le long de.
—*adv.* come ~, venir. go or
walk ~, passer. all ~, (*time*)
tout le temps, depuis le début. ~
with, avec.

alongside /əlɒŋ'saɪd/ *adv.* (*naut.*)
bord à bord. come ~, accoster.
—*prep.* le long de.

aloof /ə'luːf/ *adv.* à l'écart. —*a.*
distant. ~ness *n.* réserve *f.*

aloud /ə'laʊd/ *adv.* à haute voix.

alphabet /'ælfəbet/ *n.* alphabet *m.*
~ical /-'betɪkl/ *a.* alphabétique.

alpine /'ælpaɪn/ *a.* (*landscape*)
alpestre; (*climate*) alpin.

Alpine /'ælpaɪn/ *a.* des Alpes.

Alps /ælps/ *n. pl.* the ~, les Alpes
f. pl.

already /ɔːl'redɪ/ *adv.* déjà.

alright /ɔːl'raɪt/ *a. & adv.* = all
right.

Alsatian /æl'seɪʃn/ *n.* (*dog*) berger
allemand *m.*

also /'ɔːlsəʊ/ *adv.* aussi.

altar /'ɔːltə(r)/ *n.* autel *m.*

alter /'ɔːltə(r)/ *v.t./i.* changer.
~ation /-'reɪʃn/ *n.* changement
m.; (*to garment*) retouche *f.*

alternate¹ /ɔːl'tɜːnət/ *a.* alterné,
alternatif; (*Amer.*) = alternative. on ~ days/*etc.*, (*first one
then the other*) tous les deux
jours/*etc.* ~ly *adv.* tour à tour.

alternate² /'ɔːltəneɪt/ *v.i.* alterner.
—*v.t.* faire alterner.

alternative /ɔːl'tɜːnətɪv/ *a.* autre;
(*policy*) de rechange. —*n.* alternative *f.*, choix *m.* ~ly *adv.* comme
alternative. or ~ly, ou alors.

alternator /'ɔːltəneɪtə(r)/ *n.* alter-
nateur *m.*

although /ɔːl'ðəʊ/ *conj.* bien
que.

altitude /'æltɪtjuːd/ *n.* altitude *f.*

altogether /ɔːltə'geðə(r)/ *adv.*

(completely) tout à fait; *(on the whole)* à tout prendre.

aluminium /ælju'mɪnɪəm/ *(Amer.* **aluminum** /ə'lu:mɪnəm/) *n.* aluminium *m.*

always /'ɔːlweɪz/ *adv.* toujours.

am /æm/ *see* be.

a.m. /eɪ'em/ *am.* du matin.

amalgamate /ə'mælgəmeɪt/ *v.t./i.* (s')amalgamer; *(comm.)* fusionner.

amass /ə'mæs/ *v.t.* amasser.

amateur /'æmətə(r)/ *n.* amateur *m.* —*a.* *(musician etc.)* invar. **～ish** *a.* *(pej.)* d'amateur. **～ishly** *adv.* en amateur.

amaz|e /ə'meɪz/ *v.t.* étonner. **～ed** *a.* étonné. **～ement** *n.* étonnement *m.* **～ingly** *adv.* étonnamment.

ambassador /æm'bæsədə(r)/ *n.* ambassadeur *m.*

amber /'æmbə(r)/ *n.* ambre *m.*; *(auto.)* feu orange *m.*

ambigu|ous /æm'bɪgjʊəs/ *a.* ambigu. **～ity** /-'gjuːətɪ/ *n.* ambiguïté *f.*

ambiti|on /æm'bɪʃn/ *n.* ambition *f.* **～ous** *a.* ambitieux.

ambivalent /æm'bɪvələnt/ *a.* ambigu, ambivalent.

amble /'æmbl/ *v.i.* marcher sans se presser, s'avancer lentement.

ambulance /'æmbjʊləns/ *n.* ambulance *f.*

ambush /'æmbʊʃ/ *n.* embuscade *f.* —*v.t.* tendre une embuscade à.

amenable /ə'miːnəbl/ *a.* obligeant. **～ to,** *(responsive)* sensible à.

amend /ə'mend/ *v.t.* modifier, corriger. **～ment** *n.* *(to rule)* amendement *m.*

amends /ə'mendz/ *n. pl.* **make ～,** réparer son erreur.

amenities /ə'miːnətɪz/ *n. pl.* *(pleasant features)* attraits *m. pl.*; *(facilities)* aménagements *m. pl.*

America /ə'merɪkə/ *n.* Amérique *f.* **～n** *a. & n.* américain(e) *(m. (f.)).*

amiable /'eɪmɪəbl/ *a.* aimable.

amicable /'æmɪkəbl/ *a.* amical.

amid(st) /ə'mɪd(st)/ *prep.* au milieu de.

amiss /ə'mɪs/ *a. & adv.* mal. **sth. ～,** qch. qui ne va pas. **take sth. ～,** être offensé par qch.

ammonia /ə'məʊnɪə/ *n.* *(gas)* ammoniac *m.*; *(water)* ammoniaque *f.*

ammunition /æmjʊ'nɪʃn/ *n.* munitions *f. pl.*

amnesia /æm'niːzɪə/ *n.* amnésie *f.*

amnesty /'æmnəstɪ/ *n.* amnistie *f.*

amok /ə'mɒk/ *adv.* **run ～,** devenir fou furieux; *(crowd)* se déchaîner.

among(st) /ə'mʌŋ(st)/ *prep.* parmi, entre. **～ the crowd,** *(in the middle of)* parmi la foule. **～ the English/etc.,** *(race, group)* chez les Anglais/etc. **～ ourselves/etc.,** entre nous/etc.

amoral /eɪ'mɒrəl/ *a.* amoral.

amorous /'æmərəs/ *a.* amoureux.

amorphous /ə'mɔːfəs/ *a.* amorphe.

amount /ə'maʊnt/ *n.* quantité *f.*; *(total)* montant *m.*; *(sum of money)* somme *f.* —*v.i.* **～ to,** *(add up to)* s'élever à; *(be equivalent to)* revenir à.

amp /æmp/ *n.* *(fam.)* ampère *m.*

ampere /'æmpeə(r)/ *n.* ampère *m.*

amphibi|an /æm'fɪbɪən/ *n.* amphibie *m.* **～ous** *a.* amphibie.

ample /'æmpl/ *a.* (-er, -est) *(enough)* (bien) assez de; *(large, roomy)* ample. **～y** *adv.* amplement.

amplif|y /'æmplɪfaɪ/ *v.t.* amplifier. **～ier** *n.* amplificateur *m.*

amputat|e /'æmpjʊteɪt/ *v.t.* amputer. **～ion** /-'teɪʃn/ *n.* amputation *f.*

amuck /ə'mʌk/ *see* amok.

amuse /ə'mjuːz/ *v.t.* amuser. **～ment** *n.* amusement *m.*, divertissement *m.* **～ment arcade,** salle de jeux *f.*

an /æn, *unstressed* ən/ *see* a.

anachronism /ə'nækrɒnɪzəm/ *n.* anachronisme *m.*

anaem|ia /ə'niːmɪə/ *n.* anémie *f.* **~ic** *a.* anémique.

anaesthetic /ænɪs'θetɪk/ *n.* anesthésique *m.* **give an ~,** faire une anesthésie (**to,** à).

analogue, analog /'ænəlɒg/ *a.* analogique.

analogy /ə'nælədʒɪ/ *n.* analogie *f.*

analyse (*Amer.* **analyze**) /'ænəlaɪz/ *v.t.* analyser. **~t** /-ɪst/ *n.* analyste *m./f.*

analysis /ə'næləsɪs/ *n.* (*pl.* **-yses** /-əsiːz/) analyse *f.*

analytic(al) /ænə'lɪtɪk(l)/ *a.* analytique.

anarch|y /'ænəkɪ/ *n.* anarchie *f.* **~ist** *n.* anarchiste *m./f.*

anathema /ə'næθəmə/ *n.* **that is ~ to me,** j'ai cela en abomination.

anatom|y /ə'nætəmɪ/ *n.* anatomie *f.* **~ical** /ænə'tɒmɪkl/ *a.* anatomique.

ancest|or /'ænsestə(r)/ *n.* ancêtre *m.* **~ral** /-'sestrəl/ *a.* ancestral.

anchor /'æŋkə(r)/ *n.* ancre *f.* —*v.t.* mettre à l'ancre. —*v.i.* jeter l'ancre.

anchovy /'æntʃəvɪ/ *n.* anchois *m.*

ancient /'eɪnʃənt/ *a.* ancien.

ancillary /æn'sɪlərɪ/ *a.* auxiliaire.

and /ænd, *unstressed* ən(d)/ *conj.* et. **go ~ see him,** allez le voir. **richer ~ richer,** de plus en plus riche.

anecdote /'ænɪkdəʊt/ *n.* anecdote *f.*

anemia /ə'niːmɪə/ *n.* (*Amer.*) = **anaemia.**

anesthetic /ænɪs'θetɪk/ (*Amer.*) = **anaesthetic.**

anew /ə'njuː/ *adv.* de *or* à nouveau.

angel /'eɪndʒl/ *n.* ange *m.* **~ic** /æn'dʒelɪk/ *a.* angélique.

anger /'æŋgə(r)/ *n.* colère *f.* —*v.t.* mettre en colère, fâcher.

angle¹ /'æŋgl/ *n.* angle *m.*

angle² /'æŋgl/ *v.i.* pêcher (à la ligne). **~ for,** (*fig.*) quêter. **~r** /-ə(r)/ *n.* pêcheu|r, -se *m., f.*

Anglican /'æŋglɪkən/ *a.* & *n.* anglican(e) (*m.* (*f.*)).

Anglo- /'æŋgləʊ/ *pref.* anglo-.

Anglo-Saxon /'æŋgləʊ'sæksn/ *a.* & *n.* anglo-saxon(ne) (*m.* (*f.*)).

angr|y /'æŋgrɪ/ *a.* (**-ier, -iest**) fâché, en colère. **get ~y,** se fâcher, se mettre en colère (**with,** contre). **make s.o. ~y,** mettre qn. en colère. **~ily** *adv.* en colère.

anguish /'æŋgwɪʃ/ *n.* angoisse *f.*

angular /'æŋgjʊlə(r)/ *a.* (*features*) anguleux.

animal /'ænɪml/ *n.* & *a.* animal (*m.*).

animate¹ /'ænɪmət/ *a.* animé.

animate² /'ænɪmeɪt/ *v.t.* animer. **~ion** /-'meɪʃn/ *n.* animation *f.*

animosity /ænɪ'mɒsətɪ/ *n.* animosité *f.*

aniseed /'ænɪsiːd/ *n.* anis *m.*

ankle /'æŋkl/ *n.* cheville *f.* **~ sock,** socquette *f.*

annex /ə'neks/ *v.t.* annexer. **~ation** /ænek'seɪʃn/ *n.* annexion *f.*

annexe /'æneks/ *n.* annexe *f.*

annihilate /ə'naɪəleɪt/ *v.t.* anéantir.

anniversary /ænɪ'vɜːsərɪ/ *n.* anniversaire *m.*

announce /ə'naʊns/ *v.t.* annoncer. **~ment** *n.* annonce *f.* **~r** /-ə(r)/ *n.* (*radio, TV*) speaker(ine) *m.* (*f.*).

annoy /ə'nɔɪ/ *v.t.* agacer, ennuyer. **~ance** *n.* contrariété *f.* **~ed** *a.* fâché (**with,** contre). **get ~ed,** se fâcher. **~ing** *a.* ennuyeux.

annual /'ænjʊəl/ *a.* annuel. —*n.* publication annuelle *f.* **~ly** *adv.* annuellement.

annuity /ə'njuːətɪ/ *n.* rente (viagère) *f.*

annul /ə'nʌl/ *v.t.* (*p.t.* **annulled**) annuler. **~ment** *n.* annulation *f.*

anomaly /ə'nɒmǝli/ n. anomalie f.
~ous a. anormal.

anonymous /ə'nɒnimǝs/ a. anonyme. **~ity** /ænǝ'nimǝti/ n.
anonymat m.

anorak /'ænǝræk/ n. anorak m.

another /ə'nʌðǝ(r)/ a. & pron.
un(e) autre. **~ coffee,** (one more)
encore un café. **~ ten minutes,**
encore dix minutes, dix minutes
de plus.

answer /'ɑ:nsǝ(r)/ n. réponse f.;
(solution) solution f. —v.t.
répondre à; (prayer) exaucer.
—v.i. répondre. **~ the door,**
ouvrir la porte. **~ back,**
répondre. **~ for,** répondre de. **~
to,** (superior) dépendre de;
(description) répondre à. **~able** a.
responsable (for, de; to, devant).
~ing machine, répondeur m.

ant /ænt/ n. fourmi f.

antagonis|m /æn'tægǝnizǝm/ n.
antagonisme m. **~tic** /-'nistik/
a. antagoniste.

antagonize /æn'tægǝnaiz/ v.t.
provoquer l'hostilité de.

Antarctic /æn'tɑ:ktik/ a. & n.
antarctique (m.).

ante- /ænti/ pref. anti-, anté-.

antelope /'æntilǝup/ n. antilope f.

antenatal /'ænti'neitl/ a. prénatal.

antenna /æn'tenǝ/ n. (pl. **-ae** /-i:/)
(of insect) antenne f.; (pl. **-as;**
aerial: Amer.) antenne f.

anthem /'ænθǝm/ n. (relig.) motet
m.; (of country) hymne national
m.

anthology /æn'θɒlǝdʒi/ n. anthologie f.

anthropolog|y /ænθrǝ'pɒlǝdʒi/ n.
anthropologie f. **~ist** n. anthropologue m./f.

anti- /'ænti/ pref. anti-. **~-aircraft**
a. antiaérien.

antibiotic /æntibai'ɒtik/ n. antibiotique m.

antibody /'æntibɒdi/ n. anticorps
m.

antic /'æntik/ n. bouffonnerie f.

anticipat|e /æn'tisipeit/ v.t. (foresee, expect) prévoir, s'attendre à;
(forestall) devancer. **~ion**
/-'peiʃn/ n. attente f. **in ~ion of,**
en prévision or attente de.

anticlimax /ænti'klaimæks/ n.
(let-down) déception f. **it was an
~,** ça n'a pas répondu à l'attente.

anticlockwise /ænti'klɒkwaiz/
adv. & a. dans le sens inverse des
aiguilles d'une montre.

anticyclone /ænti'saiklǝun/ n. anticyclone m.

antidote /'æntidǝut/ n. antidote m.

antifreeze /'æntifri:z/ n. antigel m.

antihistamine /ænti'histǝmi:n/ n.
antihistaminique m.

antipathy /æn'tipǝθi/ n. antipathie f.

antiquated /'æntikweitid/ a. vieillot, suranné.

antique /æn'ti:k/ a. (old) ancien;
(from antiquity) antique. —n.
objet ancien m., antiquité f. **~
dealer,** antiquaire m./f. **~ shop,**
magasin d'antiquités m.

antiquity /æn'tikwǝti/ n. antiquité
f.

anti-Semitic /æntisi'mitik/ a. antisémite. **~sm** /-'semitizǝm/ n.
antisémitisme m.

antiseptic /ænti'septik/ a. & n.
antiseptique (m.).

antisocial /ænti'sǝuʃl/ a. asocial,
antisocial; (unsociable) insociable.

antithesis /æn'tiθǝsis/ n. (pl. **-eses**
/-ǝsi:z/) antithèse f.

antlers /'æntlǝz/ n. pl. bois m. pl.

anus /'einǝs/ n. anus m.

anvil /'ænvil/ n. enclume f.

anxiety /æŋ'zaiǝti/ n. (worry)
anxiété f.; (eagerness) impatience
f.

anxious /'æŋkʃǝs/ a. (troubled)
anxieux; (eager) impatient (to,
de). **~ly** adv. anxieusement;
impatiemment.

any /'enɪ/ a. (some) du, de l', de la, des; (after negative) de, d'; (every) tout; (no matter which) n'importe quel. **at ~ moment**, à tout moment. **have you ~ water?**, avez-vous de l'eau? —pron. (no matter which one) n'importe lequel; (someone) quelqu'un; (any amount of it or them) en. **I do not have ~**, je n'en ai pas. **did you see ~ of them?**, en avez-vous vu? —adv. (a little) un peu. **do you have ~ more?**, en avez-vous encore? **do you have ~ more tea?**, avez-vous encore du thé? **not ~**, nullement. **I don't do it ~ more**, je ne le fais plus.

anybody /'enɪbɒdɪ/ pron. n'importe qui; (somebody) quelqu'un; (after negative) personne. **he did not see ~**, il n'a vu personne.

anyhow /'enɪhaʊ/ adv. de toute façon; (badly) n'importe comment.

anyone /'enɪwʌn/ pron. = **anybody**.

anything /'enɪθɪŋ/ pron. n'importe quoi; (something) quelque chose; (after negative) rien. **he did not see ~**, il n'a rien vu. **~**, (cheap etc.) nullement. **~ you do**, tout ce que tu fais.

anyway /'enɪweɪ/ adv. de toute façon.

anywhere /'enɪweə(r)/ adv. n'importe où; (somewhere) quelque part; (after negative) nulle part. **he does not go ~**, il ne va nulle part. **~ you go**, partout où tu vas, où que tu ailles. **~ else**, partout ailleurs.

apart /ə'pɑːt/ adv. (on or to one side) à part; (separated) séparé; (into pieces) en pièces. **~ from**, à part, excepté. **ten metres ~**, (distant) à dix mètres l'un de l'autre. **come ~**, (break) tomber en morceaux; (machine) se démonter. **legs ~**, les jambes écartées. **keep ~**, séparer. **take ~**, démonter.

apartment /ə'pɑːtmənt/ n. (Amer.) appartement m. **~s**, logement m.

apathy /'æpəθɪ/ n. apathie f. **~etic** /-'θetɪk/ a. apathique.

ape /eɪp/ n. singe m. —v.t. singer.

aperitif /ə'perɪtɪf/ n. apéritif m.

aperture /'æpətʃə(r)/ n. ouverture f.

apex /'eɪpeks/ n. sommet m.

apiece /ə'piːs/ adv. chacun.

apologetic /əpɒlə'dʒetɪk/ a. (tone etc.) d'excuse. **be ~**, s'excuser. **~ally** /-lɪ/ adv. en s'excusant.

apologize /ə'pɒlədʒaɪz/ v.i. s'excuser (for, de; to, auprès de).

apology /ə'pɒlədʒɪ/ n. excuses f. pl.; (defence of belief) apologie f.

Apostle /ə'pɒsl/ n. apôtre m.

apostrophe /ə'pɒstrəfɪ/ n. apostrophe f.

appal /ə'pɔːl/ v.t. (p.t. appalled) épouvanter. **~ling** a. épouvantable.

apparatus /æpə'reɪtəs/ n. (machine & anat.) appareil m.

apparel /ə'pærəl/ n. habillement m.

apparent /ə'pærənt/ a. apparent. **~ly** adv. apparemment.

appeal /ə'piːl/ n. appel m.; (attractiveness) attrait m., charme m. —v.i. (jurid.) faire appel. **to s.o.**, (beg) faire appel à qn. **~ to s.o.**, (attract) plaire à qn. **~ to s.o. for sth.**, demander qch. à qn. **~ing** a. (attractive) attirant.

appear /ə'pɪə(r)/ v.i. apparaître; (arrive) se présenter; (seem, be published) sembler; (theatre) jouer. **~ on TV**, passer à la télé. **~ance** n. apparition f.; (aspect) apparence f.

appease /ə'piːz/ v.t. apaiser.

appendicitis /əpendɪ'saɪtɪs/ n. appendicite f.

appendix /ə'pendɪks/ n. (pl. -ices /-ɪsiːz/) appendice m.

appetite /'æpɪtaɪt/ n. appétit m.

appetizer /'æpɪtaɪzə(r)/ n. (snack) amuse-gueule m. invar.; (drink) apéritif m.

appetizing /'æpɪtaɪzɪŋ/ a. appétissant.

applau|d /ə'plɔːd/ v.t./i. applaudir; (decision) applaudir à. ~se n. applaudissements m. pl.

apple /'æpl/ n. pomme f. ~-tree n. pommier m.

appliance /ə'plaɪəns/ n. appareil m.

applicable /'æplɪkəbl/ a. applicable.

applicant /'æplɪkənt/ n. candidat(e) m. (f.) (for, à).

application /æplɪ'keɪʃn/ n. application f.; (request, form) demande f.; (for job) candidature f.

apply /ə'plaɪ/ v.t. appliquer. —v.i. ~ to, (refer) s'appliquer à; (ask) s'adresser à. ~ for, (job) postuler pour; (grant) demander. ~ o.s. to, s'appliquer à. **applied** a. appliqué.

appoint /ə'pɔɪnt/ v.t. (to post) nommer; (fix) désigner. well-~ed a. bien équipé. ~ment n. nomination f.; (meeting) rendezvous m. invar.; (job) poste m. **make an ~ment**, prendre rendez-vous (with, avec).

apportion /ə'pɔːʃn/ v.t. répartir.

apprais|e /ə'preɪz/ v.t. évaluer. ~al n. évaluation f.

appreciable /ə'priːʃəbl/ a. appréciable.

appreciat|e /ə'priːʃɪeɪt/ v.t. (like) apprécier; (understand) comprendre; (be grateful for) être reconnaissant de. —v.i. prendre de la valeur. ~ion /-'eɪʃn/ n. appréciation f.; (gratitude) reconnaissance f.; (rise) augmentation f. ~ive /ə'priːʃɪətɪv/ a. reconnaissant; (audience) enthousiaste.

apprehen|d /æprɪ'hend/ v.t. (arrest, fear) appréhender; (understand) comprendre. ~sion n. appréhension f.

apprehensive /æprɪ'hensɪv/ a. inquiet. **be ~ of**, craindre.

apprentice /ə'prentɪs/ n. apprenti m. —v.t. mettre en apprentissage. ~ship n. apprentissage m.

approach /ə'prəʊtʃ/ v.t. (s')approcher de; (accost) aborder; (with request) s'adresser à. —v.i. (s')approcher. —n. approche f. **an ~ to**, (problem) une façon d'aborder; (person) une démarche auprès de. ~able a. accessible; (person) abordable.

appropriate[1] /ə'prəʊprɪət/ a. approprié, propre. ~ly adv. à propos.

appropriate[2] /ə'prəʊprɪeɪt/ v.t. s'approprier.

approval /ə'pruːvl/ n. approbation f. **on ~**, à or sous condition.

approve /ə'pruːv/ v.t./i. approuver. ~ of, approuver. ~ingly adv. d'un air or d'un ton approbateur.

approximate[1] /ə'prɒksɪmət/ a. approximatif. ~ly adv. approximativement.

approximat|e[2] /ə'prɒksɪmeɪt/ v.i. ~e to, se rapprocher de. ~ion /-'meɪʃn/ n. approximation f.

apricot /'eɪprɪkɒt/ n. abricot m.

April /'eɪprəl/ n. avril m. **make an ~ fool of**, faire un poisson d'avril à.

apron /'eɪprən/ n. tablier m.

apse /æps/ n. (of church) abside f.

apt /æpt/ a. (suitable) approprié; (pupil) doué. **be ~ to**, avoir tendance à. ~ly adv. à propos.

aptitude /'æptɪtjuːd/ n. aptitude f.

aqualung /'ækwəlʌŋ/ n. scaphandre autonome m.

aquarium /ə'kweərɪəm/ n. (pl. -ums) aquarium m.

Aquarius /ə'kweərɪəs/ n. le Verseau.

aquatic /ə'kwætɪk/ a. aquatique; (*sport*) nautique.

aqueduct /'ækwɪdʌkt/ n. aqueduc m.

Arab /'ærəb/ n. & a. arabe (m./f.). ~ic a. & n. (*lang.*) arabe (m.). ~ic numerals, chiffres arabes m. pl.

Arabian /ə'reɪbɪən/ a. arabe.

arable /'ærəbl/ a. arable.

arbiter /'ɑːbɪtə(r)/ n. arbitre m.

arbitrary /'ɑːbɪtrərɪ/ a. arbitraire.

arbitrat|e /'ɑːbɪtreɪt/ v.i. arbitrer. ~ion /-'treɪʃn/ n. arbitrage m. ~or n. arbitre m.

arc /ɑːk/ n. arc m.

arcade /ɑː'keɪd/ n. (*shops*) galerie f.; (*arches*) arcades f. pl.

arch[1] /ɑːtʃ/ n. arche f.; (*in church etc.*) arc m.; (*of foot*) voûte plantaire f. —v.t./i. (s')arquer.

arch[2] /ɑːtʃ/ a. (*playful*) malicieux.

arch- /ɑːtʃ/ pref. (*hypocrite etc.*) grand, achevé.

archaeolog|y /ɑːkɪ'ɒlədʒɪ/ n. archéologie f. ~ical /-ə'lɒdʒɪkl/ a. archéologique. ~ist n. archéologue m./f.

archaic /ɑː'keɪɪk/ a. archaïque.

archbishop /ɑːtʃ'bɪʃəp/ n. archevêque m.

archeology /ɑːkɪ'ɒlədʒɪ/ n. (*Amer.*) = archaeology.

archer /'ɑːtʃə(r)/ n. archer m. ~y n. tir à l'arc m.

archetype /'ɑːkɪtaɪp/ n. archétype m., modèle m.

archipelago /ɑːkɪ'peləɡəʊ/ n. (pl. -os) archipel m.

architect /'ɑːkɪtekt/ n. architecte m.

architectur|e /'ɑːkɪtektʃə(r)/ n. architecture f. ~al /-'tektʃərəl/ a. architectural.

archiv|es /'ɑːkaɪvz/ n. pl. archives f. pl. ~ist /-ɪvɪst/ n. archiviste m./f.

archway /'ɑːtʃweɪ/ n. voûte f.

Arctic /'ɑːktɪk/ a. & n. arctique (m.). **arctic** a. glacial.

ardent /'ɑːdnt/ a. ardent. ~ly adv. ardemment.

ardour /'ɑːdə(r)/ n. ardeur f.

arduous /'ɑːdjʊəs/ a. ardu.

are /ɑː(r)/ see be.

area /'eərɪə/ n. (*surface*) superficie f.; (*region*) région f.; (*district*) quartier m.; (*fig.*) domaine m. **parking/picnic** ~, aire de parking/de pique-nique f.

arena /ə'riːnə/ n. arène f.

aren't /ɑːnt/ = are not.

Argentin|a /ɑːdʒən'tiːnə/ n. Argentine f. ~e /'ɑːdʒəntaɪn/, ~ian /-'tɪnɪən/ a. & n. argentin(e) (m. (f.)).

argue /'ɑːɡjuː/ v.i. (*quarrel*) se disputer; (*reason*) argumenter. —v.t. (*debate*) discuter. ~e that, alléguer que. ~able /-ʊəbl/ a. le cas selon certains. ~ably adv. selon certains.

argument /'ɑːɡjʊmənt/ n. dispute f.; (*reasoning*) argument m.; (*discussion*) débat m. ~ative /-'mentətɪv/ a. raisonneur, contrariant.

arid /'ærɪd/ a. aride.

Aries /'eəriːz/ n. le Bélier.

arise /ə'raɪz/ v.i. (p.t. **arose**, p.p. **arisen**) se présenter; (*old use*) se lever. ~ **from**, résulter de.

aristocracy /ærɪ'stɒkrəsɪ/ n. aristocratie f.

aristocrat /'ærɪstəkræt, *Amer.* ə'rɪstəkræt/ n. aristocrate m./f. ~ic /-'krætɪk/ a. aristocratique.

arithmetic /ə'rɪθmətɪk/ n. arithmétique f.

ark /ɑːk/ n. (*relig.*) arche f.

arm[1] /ɑːm/ n. bras m. ~ **in arm**, bras dessus bras dessous. ~**band** n. brassard m.

arm[2] /ɑːm/ v.t. armer. ~**ed robbery**, vol à main armée m.

armament /'ɑːməmənt/ n. armement m.

armchair /'ɑːmtʃeə(r)/ n. fauteuil m.

armistice /'ɑːmɪstɪs/ n. armistice m.

armour /'ɑːmə(r)/ n. armure f.; (on tanks etc.) blindage m. ~clad, ~ed adjs. blindé.

armoury /'ɑːmərɪ/ n. arsenal m.

armpit /'ɑːmpɪt/ n. aisselle f.

arms /ɑːmz/ n. pl. (weapons) armes f. pl. ~ dealer, trafiquant d'armes m.

army /'ɑːmɪ/ n. armée f.

aroma /ə'rəʊmə/ n. arôme m. ~tic /ˌærə'mætɪk/ a. aromatique.

arose /ə'rəʊz/ see **arise**.

around /ə'raʊnd/ adv. (tout) autour; (here and there) çà et là. —prep. autour de. ~ here, par ici.

arouse /ə'raʊz/ v.t. (awaken, cause) éveiller; (excite) exciter.

arrange /ə'reɪndʒ/ v.t. arranger; (time, date) fixer. ~ to, s'arranger pour. ~ment n. arrangement m. make ~ments, prendre des dispositions.

array /ə'reɪ/ v.t. (mil.) déployer; (dress) vêtir. —n. an ~ of, (display) un étalage impressionnant de.

arrears /ə'rɪəz/ n. pl. arriéré m. in ~, (rent) arriéré. he is in ~, il a des paiements en retard.

arrest /ə'rest/ v.t. arrêter; (attention) retenir. —n. arrestation f. under ~, en état d'arrestation.

arrival /ə'raɪvl/ n. arrivée f. new ~, nouveau venu m., nouvelle venue f.

arrive /ə'raɪv/ v.i. arriver.

arrogan|t /'ærəgənt/ a. arrogant. ~ce n. arrogance f. ~tly adv. avec arrogance.

arrow /'ærəʊ/ n. flèche f.

arse /ɑːs/ n. (sl.) cul m. (sl.).

arsenal /'ɑːsənl/ n. arsenal m.

arsenic /'ɑːsnɪk/ n. arsenic m.

arson /'ɑːsn/ n. incendie criminel m. ~ist n. incendiaire m./f.

art /ɑːt/ n. art m.; (fine arts) beaux-arts m. pl. ~s, (univ.) lettres f. pl. ~ gallery, (public) musée (d'art) m.; (private) galerie (d'art) ~ed f. ~ school, école des beaux-arts f.

artefact /'ɑːtɪfækt/ n. objet fabriqué m.

arter|y /'ɑːtərɪ/ n. artère f. ~ial /-'tɪərɪəl/ a. artériel. ~ial road, route principale f.

artful /'ɑːtfl/ a. astucieux, rusé. ~ness n. astuce f.

arthriti|s /ɑː'θraɪtɪs/ n. arthrite f. ~c /-ɪtɪk/ a. arthritique.

artichoke /'ɑːtɪtʃəʊk/ n. artichaut m.

article /'ɑːtɪkl/ n. article m. ~ of clothing, vêtement m. ~d a. (jurid.) en stage.

articulate¹ /ɑː'tɪkjʊlət/ a. (person) capable de s'exprimer clairement; (speech) distinct.

articulat|e² /ɑː'tɪkjʊleɪt/ v.t./i. articuler. ~ed lorry, semi-remorque m. ~ion /-'leɪʃn/ n. articulation f.

artifice /'ɑːtɪfɪs/ n. artifice m.

artificial /ɑːtɪ'fɪʃl/ a. artificiel. ~ity /-fɪ'ælətɪ/ n. manque de naturel m.

artillery /ɑː'tɪlərɪ/ n. artillerie f.

artisan /ɑːtɪ'zæn/ n. artisan m.

artist /'ɑːtɪst/ n. artiste m./f. ~ic /-'tɪstɪk/ a. artistique. ~ry n. art m.

artiste /ɑː'tiːst/ n. (entertainer) artiste m./f.

artless /'ɑːtlɪs/ a. ingénu, naïf.

artwork /'ɑːtwɜːk/ n. (of book) illustrations f. pl.

as /æz, unstressed əz/ adv. & conj. comme; (while) pendant que. as you get older, en vieillissant. as she came in, en entrant. as a mother, en tant que mère. **as a gift**, en cadeau. **as from Monday**, à partir de lundi. **as tall as**, aussi grand que. **as for**, **as to**, quant à. **as if**, comme si. **you look as if you're tired**, vous avez l'air (d'être) fatigué. **as much**, **as many**, autant (as, que). **as soon as**, aussitôt que. **as well**, aussi (as, bien que). **as wide as possible**, aussi large que possible.

asbestos /æz'bestɒs/ n. amiante f.

ascend /ə'send/ v.t. gravir; (throne) monter sur. —v.i. monter. **~ant** n. be in the **~ant**, monter.

ascent /ə'sent/ n. (climbing) ascension f.; (slope) côte f.

ascertain /æsə'teɪn/ v.t. s'assurer de. **~ that**, s'assurer que.

ascetic /ə'setɪk/ a. ascétique. —n. ascète m./f.

ascribe /ə'skraɪb/ v.t. attribuer.

ash[1] /æʃ/ n. **~(-tree)**, frêne m.

ash[2] /æʃ/ n. cendre f. **Ash Wednesday**, Mercredi des Cendres m. **~en** a. cendreux.

ashamed /ə'ʃeɪmd/ a. be **~**, avoir honte (of).

ashore /ə'ʃɔː(r)/ adv. à terre.

ashtray /'æʃtreɪ/ n. cendrier m.

Asia /'eɪʃə, Amer. 'eɪʒə/ n. Asie f. **~n** a. & n. asiatique (m./f.). the **~n community**, la communauté indo-pakistanaise. **~tic** /-ɪ'ætɪk/ a. asiatique.

aside /ə'saɪd/ adv. de côté. —n. aparté m. **~ from**, à part.

ask /ɑːsk/ v.t./i. demander; (a question) poser; (invite) inviter. **~ s.o. sth.**, demander qch. à qn. **~ s.o. to do**, demander à qn. de faire. **~ about**, (thing) se renseigner sur; (person) demander des nouvelles de. **~ for**, demander.

askance /ə'skæns/ adv. look **~ at**, regarder avec méfiance.

askew /ə'skjuː/ adv. & a. de travers.

asleep /ə'sliːp/ a. endormi; (numb) engourdi. —adv. fall **~**, s'endormir.

asparagus /ə'spærəgəs/ n. (plant) asperge f.; (culin.) asperges f. pl.

aspect /'æspekt/ n. aspect m.; (direction) orientation f.

aspersions /ə'spɜːʃnz/ n. pl. cast **~ on**, calomnier.

asphalt /'æsfælt, Amer. 'æsfɔːlt/ n. asphalte m. —v.t. asphalter.

asphyxiate /əs'fɪksieɪt/ v.t./i. (s')asphyxier. **~ion** /-'eɪʃn/ n. asphyxie f.

aspir|e /ə'spaɪə(r)/ v.i. **~e to**, aspirer à. **~ation** /æspə'reɪʃn/ n. aspiration f.

aspirin /'æsprɪn/ n. aspirine f.

ass /æs/ n. âne m.; (person: fam.) idiot(e) m. (f.).

assail /ə'seɪl/ v.t. assaillir. **~ant** n. agresseur m.

assassin /ə'sæsɪn/ n. assassin m.

assassinat|e /ə'sæsɪneɪt/ v.t. assassiner. **~ion** /-'neɪʃn/ n. assassinat m.

assault /ə'sɔːlt/ n. (mil.) assaut m.; (jurid.) agression f. —v.t. (person: jurid.) agresser.

assemble /ə'sembl/ v.t. (things) assembler; (people) rassembler. —v.i. s'assembler, se rassembler. **~age** n. assemblage m.

assembly /ə'semblɪ/ n. assemblée f. **~ line**, chaîne de montage f.

assent /ə'sent/ n. assentiment m. —v.i. consentir.

assert /ə'sɜːt/ v.t. affirmer; (one's rights) revendiquer. **~ion** /-ʃn/ n. affirmation f. **~ive** a. affirmatif, péremptoire.

assess /ə'ses/ v.t. évaluer; (payment) déterminer le montant de. **~ment** n. évaluation f. **~or** n. (valuer) expert m.

asset /'æset/ n. (advantage) atout m. **~s**, (comm.) actif m.

assiduous /ə'sɪdjuəs/ a. assidu.

assign /ə'saɪn/ v.t. (allot) assigner. ~ s.o. to, (appoint) affecter qn. à.

assignment /ə'saɪnmənt/ n. (task) mission f., tâche f.; (schol.) rapport m.

assimilat|e /ə'sɪməleɪt/ v.t./i. (s')assimiler. ~ion /-'leɪʃn/ n. assimilation f.

assist /ə'sɪst/ v.t./i. aider. ~ance n. aide f.

assistant /ə'sɪstənt/ n. aide m./f.; (in shop) vendeu|r, -se m., f. —a. (manager etc.) adjoint.

associat|e¹ /ə'səʊʃɪeɪt/ v.t. associer. —v.i. ~e with, fréquenter. ~ion /-'eɪʃn/ n. association f.

associate² /ə'səʊʃɪət/ n. & a. associé(e) (m. (f.)).

assort|ed /ə'sɔːtɪd/ a. divers; (foods) assortis. ~ment n. assortiment m. an ~ment of guests/etc., des invités/etc. divers.

assume /ə'sjuːm/ v.t. supposer, présumer; (power, attitude) prendre; (role, burden) assumer.

assumption /ə'sʌmpʃn/ n. (sth. supposed) supposition f.

assurance /ə'ʃʊərəns/ n. assurance f.

assure /ə'ʃʊə(r)/ v.t. assurer. ~d a. assuré. ~dly /-rɪdlɪ/ adv. assurément.

asterisk /'æstərɪsk/ n. astérisque m.

astern /ə'stɜːn/ adv. à l'arrière.

asthma /'æsmə/ n. asthme m. ~tic /-'mætɪk/ a. & n. asthmatique (m./f.).

astonish /ə'stɒnɪʃ/ v.t. étonner. ~ingly adv. étonnamment. ~ment n. étonnement m.

astound /ə'staʊnd/ v.t. stupéfier.

astray /ə'streɪ/ adv. & a. go ~, s'égarer. lead ~, égarer.

astride /ə'straɪd/ adv. & prep. à califourchon (sur).

astrolog|y /ə'strɒlədʒɪ/ n. astrologie f. ~er n. astrologue m.

astronaut /'æstrənɔːt/ n. astronaute m./f.

astronom|y /ə'strɒnəmɪ/ n. astronomie f. ~er n. astronome m. ~ical /æstrə'nɒmɪkl/ a. astronomique.

astute /ə'stjuːt/ a. astucieux. ~ness n. astuce f.

asylum /ə'saɪləm/ n. asile m.

at /ət, unstressed ət/ prep. à. at the doctor's/etc., chez le médecin/etc. surprised at, angry at. surprised at. not at all, pas du tout. no wind/etc. at all, (of any kind) pas le moindre vent/etc. at night, la nuit. at once, tout de suite; (simultaneously) à la fois. at sea, en mer. at times, parfois.

ate /et/ see eat.

atheis|t /'eɪθɪɪst/ n. athée m./f. ~m /-zəm/ n. athéisme m.

athlet|e /'æθliːt/ n. athlète m./f. ~ic /-'letɪk/ a. athlétique. ~ics /-'letɪks/ n. pl. athlétisme m.

Atlantic /ət'læntɪk/ a. atlantique. —n. ~ (Ocean), Atlantique m.

atlas /'ætləs/ n. atlas m.

atmospher|e /'ætməsfɪə(r)/ n. atmosphère f. ~ic /-'ferɪk/ a. atmosphérique.

atoll /'ætɒl/ n. atoll m.

atom /'ætəm/ n. atome m. ~ic /ə'tɒmɪk/ a. atomique. ~(ic) bomb, bombe atomique f.

atomize /'ætəmaɪz/ v.t. atomiser. ~r /-ə(r)/ n. atomiseur m.

atone /ə'təʊn/ v.i. ~ for, expier. ~ment n. expiation f.

atrocious /ə'trəʊʃəs/ a. atroce.

atrocity /ə'trɒsətɪ/ n. atrocité f.

atrophy /'ætrəfɪ/ n. atrophie f. —v.t./i. (s')atrophier.

attach /ə'tætʃ/ v.t./i. (s')attacher; (letter) joindre (to, à). ~ed a. be ~ed to, (like) être attaché à. the

~ed letter, la lettre ci-jointe. **~ment** n. (*accessory*) accessoire m.; (*affection*) attachement m.

attaché /ə'tæʃeɪ/ n. (*pol.*) attaché(e) m. (f.). **~ case,** mallette f.

attack /ə'tæk/ n. attaque f.; (*med.*) crise f. —*v.t.* attaquer. **~er** n. agresseur m., attaquant(e) m. (f.).

attain /ə'teɪn/ v.t. atteindre (à); (*gain*) acquérir. **~able** a. accessible. **~ment** n. acquisition f. (*of, de*). **~ments**, réussites f. pl.

attempt /ə'tempt/ v.t. tenter. —n. tentative f. **an ~ on s.o.'s life,** un attentat contre qn.

attend /ə'tend/ v.t. assister à; (*class*) suivre; (*school, church*) aller à; (*escort*) accompagner. —v.i. assister. **~ (to),** (*look after*) s'occuper de. **~ance** n. présence f.; (*people*) assistance f.

attendant /ə'tendənt/ n. employé(e) m. (f.); (*servant*) serviteur m. —a. concomitant.

attention /ə'tenʃn/ n. attention f.; **~!,** (*mil.*) garde-à-vous! **pay ~,** faire or prêter attention (to, à).

attentive /ə'tentɪv/ a. attentif; (*considerate*) attentionné. **~ly** adv. attentivement. **~ness** n. attention f.

attenuate /ə'tenjueɪt/ v.t. atténuer.

attest /ə'test/ v.t./i. **~ (to),** attester. **~ation** /æte'steɪʃn/ n. attestation f.

attic /'ætɪk/ n. grenier m.

attitude /'ætɪtjuːd/ n. attitude f.

attorney /ə'tɜːnɪ/ n. mandataire m.; (*Amer.*) avocat m.

attract /ə'trækt/ v.t. attirer. **~ion** /-kʃn/ n. attraction f.; (*charm*) attrait m.

attractive /ə'træktɪv/ a. attrayant, séduisant. **~ly** adv. agréablement. **~ness** n. attrait m., beauté f.

attribute[1] /ə'trɪbjuːt/ v.t. **~ to,** attribuer à.

attribute[2] /'ætrɪbjuːt/ n. attribut m.

attrition /ə'trɪʃn/ n. **war of ~,** guerre d'usure f.

aubergine /'əʊbəʒiːn/ n. aubergine f.

auburn /'ɔːbən/ a. châtain roux invar.

auction /'ɔːkʃn/ n. vente aux enchères f. —v.t. vendre aux enchères. **~eer** /-ə'nɪə(r)/ n. commissaire-priseur m.

audacious /ɔː'deɪʃəs/ a. audacieux. **~ty** /-æsəti/ n. audace f.

audible /'ɔːdəbl/ a. audible.

audience /'ɔːdɪəns/ n. auditoire m.; (*theatre, radio*) public m.; (*interview*) audience f.

audio typist /'ɔːdɪəʊ'taɪpɪst/ n. audiotypiste f.

audio-visual /ɔːdɪəʊ'vɪʒʊəl/ a. audio-visuel.

audit /'ɔːdɪt/ n. vérification des comptes f. —v.t. vérifier.

audition /ɔː'dɪʃn/ n. audition f. —v.t./i. auditionner.

auditor /'ɔːdɪtə(r)/ n. commissaire aux comptes m.

auditorium /ɔːdɪ'tɔːrɪəm/ n. (*of theatre etc.*) salle f.

augur /'ɔːgə(r)/ v.i. **~ well/ill,** être de bon/mauvais augure.

August /'ɔːgəst/ n. août m.

aunt /ɑːnt/ n. tante f.

au pair /əʊ'peə(r)/ n. jeune fille au pair f.

aura /'ɔːrə/ n. atmosphère f.

auspices /'ɔːspɪsɪz/ n. pl. auspices m. pl., égide f.

auspicious /ɔː'spɪʃəs/ a. favorable.

auster|e /ɔː'stɪə(r)/ a. austère. **~ity** /-erətɪ/ n. austérité f.

Australia /ɒ'streɪlɪə/ n. Australie f. **~n** a. & n. australien(ne) (m. (f.)).

Austria /'ɒstrɪə/ n. Autriche f. **~n** a. & n. autrichien(ne) (m. (f.)).

authentic /ɔː'θentɪk/ a. authentique. **~ity** /-ən'tɪsətɪ/ n. authenticité f.

authenticate /ɔː'θentɪkeɪt/ v.t. authentifier.

author /'ɔːθə(r)/ n. auteur m. **~ship** n. (origin) paternité f.

authoritarian /ɔːθɒrɪ'teərɪən/ a. autoritaire.

authority /ɔː'θɒrətɪ/ n. autorité f.; (permission) autorisation f., **~ative** /-ɪtətɪv/ a. (credible) qui fait autorité; (trusted) autorisé; (manner) autoritaire.

authorize /'ɔːθəraɪz/ v.t. autoriser. **~ation** /-'zeɪʃn/ n. autorisation f.

autistic /ɔː'tɪstɪk/ a. autistique.

autobiography /ɔːtəbaɪ'ɒgrəfɪ/ n. autobiographie f.

autocrat /'ɔːtəkræt/ n. autocrate m. **~ic** /-'krætɪk/ a. autocratique.

autograph /'ɔːtəgrɑːf/ n. autographe m. —v.t. signer, dédicacer.

auto-immune /ɔːtəʊɪ'mjuːn/ a. auto-immune.

automate /'ɔːtəmeɪt/ v.t. automatiser. **~ion** /-'meɪʃn/ n. automatisation f.

automatic /ɔːtə'mætɪk/ a. automatique. —n. (auto.) voiture automatique f. **~ally** /-klɪ/ adv. automatiquement.

automobile /'ɔːtəməbiːl/ n. (Amer.) auto(mobile) f.

autonomy /ɔː'tɒnəmɪ/ n. autonomie f. **~ous** a. autonome.

autopsy /'ɔːtɒpsɪ/ n. autopsie f.

autumn /'ɔːtəm/ n. automne m. **~al** /-'tʌmnəl/ a. automnal.

auxiliary /ɔːg'zɪlɪərɪ/ a. & n. auxiliaire (m./f.) **~** (verb), auxiliaire m.

avail /ə'veɪl/ v.t. **~ o.s. of,** profiter de. —n. **to no ~,** inutile. **to no ~,** sans résultat.

available /ə'veɪləbl/ a. disponible.

~ility /-'bɪlətɪ/ n. disponibilité f.

avalanche /'ævəlɑːnʃ/ n. avalanche f.

avant-garde /ævɑ̃'gɑːd/ a. d'avant-garde.

avarice /'ævərɪs/ n. avarice f. **~ious** /-'rɪʃəs/ a. avare.

avenge /ə'vendʒ/ v.t. venger. **~ o.s.,** se venger (on, de).

avenue /'ævənjuː/ n. avenue f.; (line of approach: fig.) voie f.

average /'ævərɪdʒ/ n. moyenne f. —a. moyen. —v.t./i. faire la moyenne de; (produce, do) faire en moyenne. **on ~,** en moyenne.

averse /ə'vɜːs/ a. **be ~e to,** répugner à. **~ion** /-ʃn/ n. aversion f.

avert /ə'vɜːt/ v.t. (turn away) détourner; (ward off) éviter.

aviary /'eɪvɪərɪ/ n. volière f.

aviation /eɪvɪ'eɪʃn/ n. aviation f.

avid /'ævɪd/ a. avide.

avocado /ævə'kɑːdəʊ/ n. (pl. -os) avocat m.

avoid /ə'vɔɪd/ v.t. éviter. **~able** a. évitable. **~ance** n. the **~ance of s.o./sth. is . . . ,** éviter qn./qch., c'est . . .

await /ə'weɪt/ v.t. attendre.

awake /ə'weɪk/ v.t./i. (p.t. **awoke,** p.p. **awoken**) (s')éveiller. —a. **be ~,** ne pas dormir, être (r)éveillé.

awaken /ə'weɪkən/ v.t./i. (s')éveiller.

award /ə'wɔːd/ v.t. attribuer. —n. récompense f., prix m.; (scholarship) bourse f. **pay ~,** augmentation (salariale) f.

aware /ə'weə(r)/ a. averti. **be ~ of,** (danger) être conscient de; (fact) savoir. **become ~ of,** prendre conscience de. **~ness** n. conscience f.

awash /ə'wɒʃ/ a. inondé (with, de).

away /ə'weɪ/ adv. (far) (au) loin;

(*absent*) absent, parti; (*persistently*) sans arrêt; (*entirely*) complètement. ~ **from**, loin de. **move** ~, s'écarter; (*to new home*) déménager. **six kilometres** ~, à six kilomètres (de distance). **take** ~, emporter. —*a. & n.* ~ (**match**), match à l'extérieur *m.*

awe /ɔː/ *n.* crainte (révérencielle) *f.* ~-**inspiring**, ~**some** *adjs.* terrifiant; (*sight*) imposant. ~**struck** *a.* terrifié.

awful /ˈɔːfl/ *a.* affreux. ~**ly** /-ˈɔːflɪ/ *adv.* (*badly*) affreusement; (*very. fam.*) rudement.

awhile /əˈwaɪl/ *adv.* quelque temps.

awkward /ˈɔːkwəd/ *a.* difficile; (*inconvenient*) inopportun; (*clumsy*) maladroit; (*embarrassing*) gênant; (*embarrassed*) gêné. ~**ly** *adv.* maladroitement; avec gêne. ~**ness** *n.* maladresse *f.*; (*discomfort*) gêne *f.*

awning /ˈɔːnɪŋ/ *n.* auvent *m.*; (*of shop*) store *m.*

awoke, awoken /əˈwəʊk, əˈwəʊkən/ *see* **awake**.

awry /əˈraɪ/ *adv.* **go** ~, mal tourner. **sth. is** ~, qch. ne va pas.

axe (*Amer.*) **ax** /æks/ *n.* hache *f.* —*v.t.* (*pres. p.* **axing**) réduire; (*eliminate*) supprimer; (*employee*) renvoyer.

axiom /ˈæksɪəm/ *n.* axiome *m.*

axis /ˈæksɪs/ *n.* (*pl.* **axes** /-siːz/) axe *m.*

axle /ˈæksl/ *n.* essieu *m.*

ay(e) /aɪ/ *adv. & n.* oui (*m. invar.*).

B

BA *abbr. see* **Bachelor of Arts.**

babble /ˈbæbl/ *v.i.* babiller; (*stream*) gazouiller. —*n.* babillage *m.*

baboon /bəˈbuːn/ *n.* babouin *m.*

baby /ˈbeɪbɪ/ *n.* bébé *m.* ~ **carriage**, (*Amer.*) voiture d'enfant *f.* ~**-sit** *v.i.* garder les enfants. ~**-sitter** *n.* baby-sitter *m./f.*

babyish /ˈbeɪbɪʃ/ *a.* enfantin.

bachelor /ˈbætʃələ(r)/ *n.* célibataire *m.* **B**~ **of Arts/Science**, licencié(e) ès lettres/sciences *m. (f.).*

back /bæk/ *n.* (*of person, hand, page, etc.*) dos *m.*; (*of house*) derrière *m.*; (*of vehicle*) arrière *m.*; (*of room*) fond *m.*; (*of chair*) dossier *m.*; (*football*) arrière *m.* —*a.* de derrière, arrière *invar.*; (*taxes*) arriéré. —*adv.* en arrière; (*returned*) de retour, rentré. —*v.t.* (*support*) appuyer; (*bet on*) miser sur; (*vehicle*) faire reculer. —*v.i.* (*of person, vehicle*) reculer. **at the** ~ **of beyond**, au diable. **at the** ~ **of the book**, à la fin du livre. **come** ~, revenir. **give** ~, rendre. **take** ~, reprendre. **I want it** ~, je veux le récupérer. **in** ~ **of**, (*Amer.*) derrière. ~-**bencher** *n.* (*pol.*) membre sans portefeuille *m.* ~ **down**, abandonner, se dégonfler. ~ **number**, vieux numéro *m.* ~ **out**, se dégager, se dégonfler; (*auto.*) sortir en reculant. ~-**pedal** *v.i.* pédaler en arrière; (*fig.*) faire machine arrière (**on**, à propos de). ~ **up**, (*support*) appuyer. ~-**up** *n.* appui *m.*; (*Amer., fam.*) embouteillage *m.*; (*comput.*) sauvegarde *f.*; *a.* de réserve; (*comput.*) de sauvegarde.

backache /ˈbækeɪk/ *n.* mal de reins *m.*, mal aux reins *m.*

backbiting /ˈbækbaɪtɪŋ/ *n.* médisance *f.*

backbone /ˈbækbəʊn/ *n.* colonne vertébrale *f.*

backdate /bækˈdeɪt/ *v.t.* antidater; (*arrangement*) rendre rétroactif.

backer /'bækə(r)/ n. partisan m.; (comm.) bailleur de fonds m.

backfire /bæk'faɪə(r)/ v.i. (auto.) pétarader; (fig.) mal tourner.

backgammon /bæk'gæmən/ n. trictrac m.

background /'bækgraʊnd/ n. fond m., arrière-plan m.; (context) contexte m.; (environment) milieu m.; (experience) formation f. —a. (music, noise) de fond.

backhand /'bækhænd/ n. revers m. ~ed a. équivoque. ~ed stroke, revers m. ~er n. revers m.; (bribe: sl.) pot de vin m.

backing /'bækɪŋ/ n. appui m.

backlash /'bæklæʃ/ n. choc en retour m., répercussions f. pl.

backlog /'bæklɒg/ n. accumulation (de travail) f.

backpack /'bækpæk/ n. sac à dos m.

backside /'bæksaɪd/ n. (buttocks: fam.) derrière m.

backstage /bæk'steɪdʒ/ a. & adv. dans les coulisses.

backstroke /'bækstrəʊk/ n. dos crawlé m.

backtrack /'bæktræk/ v.i. rebrousser chemin; (change one's opinion) faire marche arrière.

backward /'bækwəd/ a. (step etc.) en arrière; (retarded) arriéré.

backwards /'bækwədz/ adv. en arrière; (walk) à reculons; (read) à l'envers; (fall) à la renverse. **go ~ and forwards**, aller et venir.

backwater /'bækwɔːtə(r)/ n. (pej.) trou perdu m.

bacon /'beɪkən/ n. lard m.; (in rashers) bacon m.

bacteria /bæk'tɪərɪə/ n. pl. bactéries f. pl. ~l a. bactérien.

bad /bæd/ a. (worse, worst) mauvais; (wicked) méchant; (ill) malade; (accident) grave; (food) gâté. **feel ~**, se sentir mal. **go ~**, se gâter. **~ language**, gros mots

m. pl. **~-mannered** a. mal élevé. **~-tempered** a. grincheux. **~ly** adv. mal; (hurt) grièvement. **too ~!**, tant pis!; (I'm sorry) dommage! **want ~ly**, avoir grande envie de.

badge /bædʒ/ n. insigne m.; (of identity) plaque f.

badger /'bædʒə(r)/ n. blaireau m. —v.t. harceler.

badminton /'bædmɪntən/ n. badminton m.

baffle /'bæfl/ v.t. déconcerter.

bag /bæg/ n. sac m.; (luggage) bagages m.pl.; (under eyes) poches f. pl. —v.t. (p.t. bagged) mettre en sac; (take: fam.) s'adjuger. **~s of**, (fam.) beaucoup de.

baggage /'bægɪdʒ/ n. bagages m. pl. **~ reclaim**, livraison des bagages f.

baggy /'bægɪ/ a. trop grand.

bagpipes /'bægpaɪps/ n. pl. cornemuse f.

Bahamas /bə'hɑːməz/ n. pl. **the ~**, les Bahamas f. pl.

bail[1] /beɪl/ n. caution f. **on ~**, sous caution. —v.t. mettre en liberté (provisoire) sous caution. **~ out**, (fig.) sortir d'affaire.

bail[2] /beɪl/ n. (cricket) bâtonnet m.

bail[3] /beɪl/ v.t. (naut.) écoper.

bailiff /'beɪlɪf/ n. huissier m.

bait /beɪt/ n. appât m. —v.t. appâter; (fig.) tourmenter.

bak|e /beɪk/ v.t. (faire) cuire (au four). —v.i. cuire (au four); (person) faire du pain or des gâteaux. **~ed beans**, haricots blancs à la tomate m.pl. **~ed potato**, pomme de terre en robe des champs f. **~er** n. boulang|er, -ère m., f. **~ing** n. cuisson f. **~ing-powder** n. levure f.

bakery /'beɪkərɪ/ n. boulangerie f.

Balaclava /bælə'klɑːvə/ n. **~ (helmet)**, passe-montagne m.

balance /'bæləns/ *n.* équilibre *m.*; (*scales*) balance *f.*; (*outstanding sum: comm.*) solde *m.*; (*of payments, of trade*) balance *f.*; (*remainder*) reste *m.*; (*money in account*) position *f.* —*v.t.* tenir en équilibre; (*weigh up & comm.*) balancer; (*budget*) équilibrer; (*to compensate*) contrebalancer. —*v. i.* être en équilibre. **~d** *a.* équilibré.

balcony /'bælkənɪ/ *n.* balcon *m.*

bald /bɔːld/ *a.* (-**er, -est**) chauve; (*tyre*) lisse; (*fig.*) simple. **~ing** *a.* **be ~ing,** perdre ses cheveux. **~ness** *n.* calvitie *f.*

bale[1] /beɪl/ *n.* (*of cotton*) balle *f.*; (*of straw*) botte *f.*

bale[2] /beɪl/ *v.i.* **~ out,** sauter en parachute.

baleful /'beɪlfʊl/ *a.* sinistre.

balk /bɔːk/ *v.t.* contrecarrer. —*v.i.* **~ at,** reculer devant.

ball[1] /bɔːl/ *n.* (*golf, tennis, etc.*) balle *f.*; (*football*) ballon *m.*; (*croquet, billiards, etc.*) boule *f.*; (*of wool*) pelote *f.*; (*sphere*) boule *f.* **~-bearing** *n.* roulement à billes *m.* **~cock** *n.* robinet à flotteur *m.* **~-point** *n.* stylo à bille *m.*

ball[2] /bɔːl/ *n.* (*dance*) bal *m.*

ballad /'bæləd/ *n.* ballade *f.*

ballast /'bæləst/ *n.* lest *m.*

ballerina /bælə'riːnə/ *n.* ballerine *f.*

ballet /'bæleɪ/ *n.* ballet *m.*

ballistic /bə'lɪstɪk/ *a.* **~ missile,** engin balistique *m.*

balloon /bə'luːn/ *n.* ballon *m.*

ballot /'bælət/ *n.* scrutin *m.* **~ (paper)**, bulletin de vote *m.* **~ box** *n.* urne *f.* —*v.i.* (*p.t.* **balloted**) (*pol.*) voter. —*v.t.* (*members*) consulter par voie de scrutin.

ballroom /'bɔːlrʊm/ *n.* salle de bal *f.*

ballyhoo /bælɪ'huː/ *n.* (*publicity*) battage *m.*; (*uproar*) tapage *m.*

balm /bɑːm/ *n.* baume *m.* **~y** *a.* (*fragrant*) embaumé; (*mild*) doux; (*crazy: sl.*) dingue.

baloney /bə'ləʊnɪ/ *n.* (*sl.*) idioties *f. pl.*, calembredaines *f. pl.*

balustrade /bælə'streɪd/ *n.* balustrade *f.*

bamboo /bæm'buː/ *n.* bambou *m.*

ban /bæn/ *v.t.* (*p.t.* **banned**) interdire. **~ from,** exclure de. —*n.* interdiction *f.*

banal /bə'nɑːl, *Amer.* 'beɪnl/ *a.* banal. **~ity** /-ælətɪ/ *n.* banalité *f.*

banana /bə'nɑːnə/ *n.* banane *f.*

band /bænd/ *n.* (*strip, group of people*) bande *f.*; (*mus.*) orchestre *m.*; (*pop group*) groupe *m.* (*mil.*) fanfare *f.* —*v.i.* **~ together,** se liguer.

bandage /'bændɪdʒ/ *n.* pansement *m.* —*v.t.* bander, panser.

bandit /'bændɪt/ *n.* bandit *m.*

bandstand /'bændstænd/ *n.* kiosque à musique *m.*

bandwagon /'bændwægən/ *n.* **climb on the ~,** prendre le train en marche.

bandy[1] /'bændɪ/ *v.t.* **~ about,** (*rumours, ideas, etc.*) faire circuler.

bandy[2] /'bændɪ/ *a.* (-**ier, -iest**) qui a les jambes arquées.

bang /bæŋ/ *n.* (*blow, noise*) coup (violent) *m.*; (*explosion*) détonation *f.*; (*of door*) claquement *m.* —*v.t./i.* frapper; (*door*) claquer. —*int.* vlan. —*adv.* (*fam.*) exactement. **~ in the middle,** en plein milieu. **~ one's head,** se cogner la tête. **~s,** frange *f.*

banger /'bæŋə(r)/ *n.* (*firework*) pétard *m.*; (*culin., sl.*) saucisse *f.* (*old*) **~**, (*car: sl.*) guimbarde *f.*

bangle /'bæŋgl/ *n.* bracelet *m.*

banish /'bænɪʃ/ *v.t.* bannir.

banisters /'bænɪstəz/ *n. pl.* rampe (d'escalier) *f.*

banjo /'bændʒəʊ/ (pl. -os) banjo m.

bank¹ /bæŋk/ n. (of river) rive f.; (of earth) talus m.; (of sand) banc m. —v.t. (earth) amonceler; (fire) couvrir. —v.i. (aviat.) virer.

bank² /bæŋk/ n. banque f. —v.t. mettre en banque. —v.i. ~ with, avoir un compte à. ~ account, compte en banque m. ~ card, carte bancaire f. ~ holiday, jour férié m. ~ on, compter sur. ~ statement, relevé de compte m.

bank|ing /'bæŋkɪŋ/ n. opérations bancaires f. pl.; (as career) la banque. ~er n. banquier m.

banknote /'bæŋknəʊt/ n. billet de banque m.

bankrupt /'bæŋkrʌpt/ a. be ~, être en faillite. go ~, faire faillite. —n. failli(e) m. (f.). —v.t. mettre en faillite. ~cy n. faillite f.

banner /'bænə(r)/ n. bannière f.

banns /bænz/ n. pl. bans m. pl.

banquet /'bæŋkwɪt/ n. banquet m.

banter /'bæntə(r)/ n. plaisanterie f. —v.i. plaisanter.

bap /bæp/ n. petit pain m.

baptism /'bæptɪzəm/ n. baptême m.

Baptist /'bæptɪst/ n. baptiste m./f.

baptize /bæp'taɪz/ v.t. baptiser.

bar /bɑː(r)/ n. (of metal) barre f.; (on window & jurid.) barreau m.; (of chocolate) tablette f.; (pub) bar m.; (counter) comptoir m., bar m.; (division: mus.) mesure f.; (fig.) obstacle m. —v.t. (p.t. barred) (obstruct) barrer; (prohibit) interdire; (exclude) exclure. —prep. sauf. ~ code, code-barres m. invar. ~ of soap, savonnette f.

Barbados /bɑː'beɪdɒs/ n. Barbade f.

barbarian /bɑː'beəriən/ n. barbare m./f.

barbar|ic /bɑː'bærɪk/ a. barbare. ~ty /-ətɪ/ n. barbarie f.

barbarous /'bɑːbərəs/ a. barbare.

barbecue /'bɑːbɪkjuː/ n. barbecue m. —v.t. griller, rôtir (au barbecue).

barbed /bɑːbd/ a. ~ wire, fil de fer barbelé m.

barber /'bɑːbə(r)/ n. coiffeur m. (pour hommes).

barbiturate /bɑː'bɪtjʊrət/ n. barbiturique m.

bare /beə(r)/ a. (-er, -est) (not covered or adorned) nu; (cupboard) vide; (mere) simple. —v.t. mettre à nu.

barefaced /'beəfeɪst/ a. éhonté.

barefoot /'beəfʊt/ a. nu-pieds invar., pieds nus.

barely /'beəlɪ/ adv. à peine.

bargain /'bɑːgɪn/ n. (deal) marché m.; (cheap thing) occasion f. —v.i. négocier; (haggle) marchander. not ~ for, ne pas s'attendre à.

barge /bɑːdʒ/ n. chaland m. —v.i. ~ in, interrompre; (into room) faire irruption.

baritone /'bærɪtəʊn/ n. baryton m.

bark¹ /bɑːk/ n. (of tree) écorce f.

bark² /bɑːk/ n. (of dog) aboiement m. —v.i. aboyer.

barley /'bɑːlɪ/ n. orge f. ~ sugar, sucre d'orge m.

barmaid /'bɑːmeɪd/ n. serveuse f.

barman /'bɑːmən/ n. (pl. -men) barman m.

barmy /'bɑːmɪ/ a. (sl.) dingue.

barn /bɑːn/ n. grange f.

barometer /bə'rɒmɪtə(r)/ n. baromètre m.

baron /'bærən/ n. baron m. ~ess n. baronne f.

baroque /bə'rɒk, Amer. bə'rəʊk/ a. & n. baroque m.

barracks /'bærəks/ n. pl. caserne f.

barrage /'bærɑːʒ, Amer. bə'rɑːʒ/ n. (barrier) barrage m.; (mil.) tir de barrage m.; (of complaints) série f.

barrel /'bærəl/ n. tonneau m.; (of oil) baril m.; (of gun) canon m. ~ organ n. orgue de Barbarie m.

barren /'bærən/ a. stérile.

barricade /bærɪ'keɪd/ n. barricade f. —v.t. barricader.

barrier /'bærɪə(r)/ n. barrière f.

barring /'bɑːrɪŋ/ prep. sauf.

barrister /'bærɪstə(r)/ n. avocat m.

barrow /'bærəʊ/ n. charrette à bras f.; (wheelbarrow) brouette f.

bartender /'bɑːtendə(r)/ n. (Amer.) barman m.

barter /'bɑːtə(r)/ n. troc m., échange m. —v.t. troquer, échanger (for, contre).

base /beɪs/ n. base f. —v.t. baser (on, sur; in, à). —a. bas, ignoble. **~less** a. sans fondement.

baseball /'beɪsbɔːl/ n. base-ball m.

baseboard /'beɪsbɔːd/ n. (Amer.) plinthe f.

basement /'beɪsmənt/ n. sous-sol m.

bash /bæʃ/ v.t. cogner. —n. coup (violent) m. **have a ~ at**, (sl.) s'essayer à. **~ed in**, enfoncé.

bashful /'bæʃfl/ a. timide.

basic /'beɪsɪk/ a. fondamental, élémentaire. **the ~s**, les éléments de base m. pl. **~ally** /-klɪ/ adv. au fond.

basil /'bæzl, Amer. 'beɪzl/ n. basilic m.

basin /'beɪsn/ n. (for liquids) cuvette f.; (for food) bol m.; (for washing) lavabo m.; (of river) bassin m.

basis /'beɪsɪs/ n. (pl. bases /-siːz/) base f.

bask /bɑːsk/ v.i. se chauffer.

basket /'bɑːskɪt/ n. corbeille f.; (with handle) panier m.

basketball /'bɑːskɪtbɔːl/ n. basket(-ball) m.

Basque /bɑːsk/ a. & n. basque (m./f.).

bass¹ /beɪs/ a. (mus.) bas, grave. —n. (pl. basses) basse f.

bass² /bæs/ n. invar. (freshwater fish) perche f.; (sea) bar m.

bassoon /bə'suːn/ n. basson m.

bastard /'bɑːstəd/ n. bâtard(e) m. (f.); (sl.) salaud, -ope m., f.

baste¹ /beɪst/ v.t. (sew) bâtir.

baste² /beɪst/ v.t. (culin.) arroser.

bastion /'bæstɪən/ n. bastion m.

bat¹ /bæt/ n. (cricket etc.) batte f.; (table tennis) raquette f. —v.t. (p.t. batted) (ball) frapper. **not ~ an eyelid**, ne pas sourciller.

bat² /bæt/ n. (animal) chauve-souris f.

batch /bætʃ/ n. (of people) fournée f.; (of papers) paquet m.; (of goods) lot m.

bated /'beɪtɪd/ a. **with ~ breath**, en retenant son souffle.

bath /bɑːθ/ n. (pl. -s /bɑːðz/) bain m.; (tub) baignoire f. **(swimming) ~s**, piscine f. —v.t. donner un bain à —a. de bain. **have a ~**, prendre un bain. **~ mat**, tapis de bain f.

bathe /beɪð/ v.t. baigner. —v.i. se baigner; (Amer.) prendre un bain. —n. bain (de mer) m. **~r** /-ə(r)/ n. baigneur, -se m., f.

bathing /'beɪðɪŋ/ n. baignade f. **~-costume** n. maillot de bain m.

bathrobe /'bɑːθrəʊb/ n. (Amer.) robe de chambre f.

bathroom /'bɑːθrʊm/ n. salle de bains f.

baton /'bætən/ n. (mil.) bâton m.; (mus.) baguette f.

battalion /bə'tæljən/ n. bataillon m.

batter /'bætə(r)/ v.t. (strike) battre; (ill-treat) maltraiter. —n. (culin.) pâte (à frire) f. **~ed** a. (pan, car) cabossé; (face) meurtri. **~ing** n. **take a ~ing**, subir des coups.

battery /'bætərɪ/ n. (mil., auto.) batterie f.; (of torch, radio) pile f.

battle /'bætl/ n. bataille f.; (fig.) lutte f. —v.i. se battre.

battlefield /'bætlfiːld/ n. champ de bataille m.

battlements /'bætlmənts/ n. pl. (crenellations) créneaux m. pl.; (wall) remparts m. pl.

battleship /'bætlʃip/ n. cuirassé m.

baulk /bɔːk/ v.t./i. = **balk**.

bawd|y /'bɔːdɪ/ a. (-ier, -iest) paillard. —iness n. paillardise f.

bawl /bɔːl/ v.t./i. brailler.

bay[1] /beɪ/ n. (bot.) laurier m. ~-leaf n. feuille de laurier f.

bay[2] /beɪ/ n. (geog., archit.) baie f.; (area) aire f. ~ window, fenêtre en saillie f.

bay[3] /beɪ/ n. (bark) aboiement m. —v.i. aboyer. at ~, aux abois. keep or hold at ~, tenir à distance.

bayonet /'beɪənɪt/ n. baïonnette f.

bazaar /bə'zɑː(r)/ n. (shop, market) bazar m.; (sale) vente f.

BC abbr. (before Christ) avant J.-C.

be /biː/ v.i. (present tense am, are, is; p.t. was, were; p.p. been) être. be hot/right/etc., avoir chaud/ raison/etc. he is 30, (age) il a 30 ans. it is fine/cold/etc., (weather) il fait beau/froid/etc. I'm a painter—are you?, je suis peintre—ah oui?, how are you?, (health) comment allez-vous? he is to leave, (must) il doit partir; (will) il va partir, il est prévu qu'il parte. how much is it?, (cost) ça fait or c'est combien? be reading/walking/etc., (aux.) lire/ marcher/etc. the child was found, l'enfant a été retrouvé, on a retrouvé l'enfant. have been to, avoir été à, être allé à.

beach /biːtʃ/ n. plage f.

beacon /'biːkən/ n. (lighthouse) phare m.; (marker) balise f.

bead /biːd/ n. perle f.

beak /biːk/ n. bec m.

beaker /'biːkə(r)/ n. gobelet m.

beam /biːm/ n. (timber) poutre f.; (of light) rayon m.; (of torch)

faisceau m. —v.i. (radiate) rayonner. —v.t. (broadcast) diffuser. ~ing a. radieux.

bean /biːn/ n. haricot m.; (of coffee) grain m.

bear[1] /beə(r)/ n. ours m.

bear[2] /beə(r)/ v.t. (p.t. bore, p.p. borne) (carry, show, feel) porter; (endure, sustain) supporter; (child) mettre au monde. —v.i. ~ left/etc., (go) prendre à gauche/ etc. ~ in mind, tenir compte de. ~ on, se rapporter à. ~ out, corroborer. ~ up!, courage! ~able a. supportable. ~er n. porteu|r, -se m., f.

beard /bɪəd/ n. barbe f. ~ed a. barbu.

bearing /'beərɪŋ/ n. (behaviour) maintien m.; (relevance) rapport m. get one's ~s, s'orienter.

beast /biːst/ n. bête f.; (person) brute f.

beastly /'biːstlɪ/ a. (-ier, -iest) (fam.) détestable.

beat /biːt/ v.t./i. (p.t. beat, p.p. beaten) battre. —n. (of drum, heart) battement m.; (mus.) mesure f.; (of policeman) ronde f. ~ a retreat, battre en retraite. ~ it!, dégage! ~ s.o. down, faire baisser son prix à qn. ~ off the competition, éliminer la concurrence. ~ up, tabasser. it ~s me, (fam.) ça me dépasse. ~er n. batteur m. ~ing n. raclée f.

beautician /bjuː'tɪʃn/ n. esthéticien(ne) m. (f.).

beautiful /'bjuːtɪfl/ a. beau. ~ly /-flɪ/ adv. merveilleusement.

beautify /'bjuːtɪfaɪ/ v.t. embellir.

beauty /'bjuːtɪ/ n. beauté f. ~ parlour, institut de beauté m. ~ spot, grain de beauté m.; (fig.) site pittoresque m.

beaver /'biːvə(r)/ n. castor m.

became /bɪ'keɪm/ see **become**.

because /bɪ'kɒz/ conj. parce que. ~ of, à cause de.

beck /bek/ *n.* at the ~ and call of, aux ordres de.

beckon /'bekən/ *v.t./i.* ~ (to), faire signe à.

become /bɪ'kʌm/ *v.t./i.* (*p.t.* became, *p.p.* become) devenir; (*befit*) convenir à. what has ~ of her?, qu'est-elle devenue?

becoming /bɪ'kʌmɪŋ/ *a.* (*seemly*) bienséant; (*clothes*) seyant.

bed /bed/ *n.* lit *m.*; (*layer*) couche *f.*; (*of sea*) fond *m.*; (*of flowers*) parterre *m.* go to ~, (aller) se coucher. —*v.i.* (*p.t.* bedded) ~ down, se coucher. ~ding *n.* literie *f.*

bedbug /'bedbʌg/ *n.* punaise *f.*

bedclothes /'bedkləʊðz/ *n. pl.* couvertures *f. pl.* et draps *m. pl.*

bedevil /bɪ'devl/ *v.t.* (*p.t.* bedevilled) (*confuse*) embrouiller; (*plague*) tourmenter.

bedlam /'bedləm/ *n.* chahut *m.*

bedraggled /bɪ'drægld/ *a.* (*untidy*) débraillé.

bedridden /'bedrɪdn/ *a.* cloué au lit.

bedroom /'bedrʊm/ *n.* chambre (à coucher) *f.*

bedside /'bedsaɪd/ *n.* chevet *m.* ~ book, livre de chevet *m.*

bedsit /bed'sɪt/, **bedsitter** /'bedsɪt, -'sɪtə(r)/ *ns.* (*fam.*) *n.* chambre meublée *f.*, studio *m.*

bedspread /'bedspred/ *n.* dessus-de-lit *m. invar.*

bedtime /'bedtaɪm/ *n.* heure du coucher *f.*

bee /biː/ *n.* abeille *f.* make a ~-line for, aller tout droit vers.

beech /biːtʃ/ *n.* hêtre *m.*

beef /biːf/ *n.* bœuf *m.* —*v.i.* (*grumble. sl.*) rouspéter.

beefburger /'biːfbɜːgə(r)/ *n.* hamburger *m.*

beefeater /'biːfiːtə(r)/ *n.* hallebardier *m.*

beefy /'biːfɪ/ *a.* (-ier, -iest) musclé.

beehive /'biːhaɪv/ *n.* ruche *f.*

been /biːn/ *see* be.

beer /bɪə(r)/ *n.* bière *f.*

beet /biːt/ *n.* (*plant*) betterave *f.*

beetle /'biːtl/ *n.* scarabée *m.*

beetroot /'biːtruːt/ *n. invar.* (*culin.*) betterave *f.*

befall /bɪ'fɔːl/ *v.t.* (*p.t.* befell, *p.p.* befallen) arriver à.

befit /bɪ'fɪt/ *v.t.* (*p.t.* befitted) convenir à, seoir à.

before /bɪ'fɔː(r)/ *prep.* (*time*) avant; (*place*) devant. —*adv.* avant; (*already*) déjà. —*conj.* ~ leaving, avant de partir. ~ he leaves, avant qu'il (ne) parte. the day ~, la veille. two days ~, deux jours avant.

beforehand /bɪ'fɔːhænd/ *adv.* à l'avance, avant.

befriend /bɪ'frend/ *v.t.* offrir son amitié à, aider.

beg /beg/ *v.t.* (*p.t.* begged) (*entreat*) supplier (to do, de faire). ~ (for), (*money, food*) mendier; (*request*) solliciter, demander. —*v.i.* ~ (for alms), mendier. it is going ~ging, personne n'en veut.

began /bɪ'gæn/ *see* begin.

beggar /'begə(r)/ *n.* mendiant(e) *m.* (*f.*); (*sl.*) individu *m.*

begin /bɪ'gɪn/ *v.t./i.* (*p.t.* began, *p.p.* begun, *pres. p.* beginning) commencer (to do, à faire). ~ner *n.* débutant(e) *m.* (*f.*). ~ning *n.* commencement *m.*, début *m.*

begrudge /bɪ'grʌdʒ/ *v.t.* (*envy*) envier; (*give unwillingly*) donner à contrecœur. ~ doing, faire à contrecœur.

beguile /bɪ'gaɪl/ *v.t.* tromper.

begun /bɪ'gʌn/ *see* begin.

behalf /bɪ'hɑːf/ *n.* on ~ of, pour; (*as representative*) au nom de, pour (le compte de).

behave /bɪ'heɪv/ *v.i.* se conduire. ~ (o.s.), se conduire bien.

behaviour, (*Amer.*) **behavior**

/bɪ'hevjə(r)/ *n.* conduite *f.*, comportement *m.*

behead /bɪ'hed/ *v.t.* décapiter.

behind /bɪ'haɪnd/ *prep.* derrière; (*in time*) en retard sur. —*adv.* derrière; (*late*) en retard. —*n.* (*buttocks*) derrière *m.* leave ~, oublier.

behold /bɪ'həʊld/ *v.t.* (*p.t.* beheld) (*old use*) voir.

beige /beɪʒ/ *a.* & *n.* beige (*m.*).

being /'biːɪŋ/ *n.* (*person*) être *m.* **bring into** ~, créer. **come into** ~, prendre naissance.

belated /bɪ'leɪtɪd/ *a.* tardif.

belch /beltʃ/ *v.i.* faire un renvoi. —*v.t.* ~ **out**, (*smoke*) vomir. —*n.* renvoi *m.*

belfry /'belfrɪ/ *n.* beffroi *m.*

Belgium /'beldʒəm/ *n.* Belgique *f.* ~**an** *a.* & *n.* belge (*m./f.*).

belie /bɪ'laɪ/ *v.t.* démentir.

belief /bɪ'liːf/ *n.* croyance *f.*; (*trust*) confiance *f.*; (*faith: relig.*) foi *f.*

believe /bɪ'liːv/ *v.t./i.* croire. ~**e in**, croire à; (*deity*) croire en. ~**able** *a.* croyable. ~**er** *n.* croyant(e) *m.* (*f.*).

belittle /bɪ'lɪtl/ *v.t.* déprécier.

bell /bel/ *n.* cloche *f.*; (*small*) clochette *f.*; (*on door*) sonnette *f.*; (*of phone*) sonnerie *f.*

belligerent /bɪ'lɪdʒərənt/ *a.* & *n.* belligérant(e) (*m.* (*f.*)).

bellow /'beləʊ/ *v.t./i.* beugler.

bellows /'beləʊz/ *n. pl.* soufflet *m.*

belly /'belɪ/ *n.* ventre *m.* ~**ache** *n.* mal au ventre *m.*

bellyful /'belɪfʊl/ *n.* **have a** ~, en avoir plein le dos.

belong /bɪ'lɒŋ/ *v.i.* ~ **to**, appartenir à; (*club*) être membre de.

belongings /bɪ'lɒŋɪŋz/ *n. pl.* affaires *f. pl.*

beloved /bɪ'lʌvɪd/ *a.* & *n.* bien-aimé(e) (*m.* (*f.*)).

below /bɪ'ləʊ/ *prep.* au-dessous de; (*fig.*) indigne de. —*adv.* en dessous; (*on page*) ci-dessous.

belt /belt/ *n.* ceinture *f.*; (*techn.*) courroie *f.*; (*fig.*) région *f.* —*v.t.* (*hit: sl.*) rosser. —*v.i.* (*rush: sl.*) filer à toute allure.

beltway /'beltweɪ/ *n.* (*Amer.*) périphérique *m.*

bemused /bɪ'mjuːzd/ *a.* (*confused*) stupéfié; (*thoughtful*) pensif.

bench /bentʃ/ *n.* banc *m.*; (*working-table*) établi *m.* the ~, (*jurid.*) la magistrature (*assise*). ~**mark** *n.* repère *m.*

bend /bend/ *v.t./i.* (*p.t.* bent) (se) courber; (*arm, leg*) plier. —*n.* courbe *f.*; (*in road*) virage *m.*; (*of arm, knee*) pli *m.* ~ **down** or **over**, se pencher.

beneath /bɪ'niːθ/ *prep.* sous, au-dessous de; (*fig.*) indigne de. —*adv.* (au-)dessous.

benefactor /'benɪfæktə(r)/ *n.* bienfaiteur, -trice *m.*, *f.*

beneficial /benɪ'fɪʃl/ *a.* avantageux, favorable.

benefit /'benɪfɪt/ *n.* avantage *m.*; (*allowance*) allocation *f.* —*v.t.* (*p.t.* benefited, *pres. p.* benefiting) (*be useful to*) profiter à; (*do good to*) faire du bien à. ~ **from**, tirer profit de.

benevolent /bɪ'nevələnt/ *a.* bienveillant. ~**ce** *n.* bienveillance *f.*

benign /bɪ'naɪn/ *a.* (*kindly*) bienveillant; (*med.*) bénin.

bent /bent/ *see* **bend**. —*n.* (*talent*) aptitude *f.*; (*inclination*) penchant *m.* —*a.* tordu; (*sl.*) corrompu. ~ **on doing**, décidé à faire.

bequeath /bɪ'kwiːð/ *v.t.* léguer.

bequest /bɪ'kwest/ *n.* legs *m.*

bereaved /bɪ'riːvd/ *a.* the ~**d wife/***etc.*, la femme/*etc.* du disparu. ~**ment** *n.* deuil *m.*

beret /'bereɪ/ *n.* béret *m.*

Bermuda /bə'mjuːdə/ *n.* Bermudes *f. pl.*

berry /'berɪ/ *n.* baie *f.*

berserk /bə'sɜːk/ *a.* **go** ~, devenir fou furieux.

berth /bɜːθ/ n. (*in train, ship*) couchette f.; (*anchorage*) mouillage m. —v.i. mouiller. **give a wide ~ to**, éviter.

beseech /bɪ'siːtʃ/ v.t. (*p.t.* besought) implorer, supplier.

beset /bɪ'set/ v.t. (*p.t.* beset, *pres. p.* besetting) (*attack*) assaillir; (*surround*) entourer.

beside /bɪ'saɪd/ prep. à côté de. ~ o.s., hors de soi. ~ the point, sans rapport.

besides /bɪ'saɪdz/ prep. en plus de; (*except*) excepté. —adv. en plus.

besiege /bɪ'siːdʒ/ v.t. assiéger.

best /best/ a. meilleur. the ~ book/*etc.*, le meilleur livre/*etc.* —adv. (the) ~, (*sing etc.*) le mieux. —n. the ~ (one), le meilleur, la meilleure. ~ man, garçon d'honneur m. the ~ part of, la plus grande partie de. the ~ thing is to ..., le mieux est de ... do one's ~, faire de son mieux. make the ~ of, s'accommoder de.

bestow /bɪ'stəʊ/ v.t. accorder.

best-seller /best'selə(r)/ n. best-seller m., succès de librairie m.

bet /bet/ n. pari m. —v.t./i. (*p.t.* bet *or* betted, *pres. p.* betting) parier.

betray /bɪ'treɪ/ v.t. trahir. ~al n. trahison f.

better /'betə(r)/ a. meilleur. —adv. mieux.—v.t. (*improve*) améliorer; (*do better than*) surpasser.—n. one's ~s, ses supérieurs m. pl. be ~ off, (*financially*) avoir plus d'argent. he's ~ off at home, il est mieux chez lui. I had ~ go, je ferais mieux de partir. the ~ part of, la plus grande partie de. get ~, s'améliorer; (*recover*) se remettre. get the ~ of, l'emporter sur. so much the ~, tant mieux.

betting-shop /'betɪŋʃɒp/ n. bureau de P.M.U. m.

between /bɪ'twiːn/ prep. entre. —adv. in ~, au milieu.

beverage /'bevərɪdʒ/ n. boisson f.

bevy /'bevɪ/ n. essaim m.

beware /bɪ'weə(r)/ v.i. prendre garde (**of**, à).

bewilder /bɪ'wɪldə(r)/ v.t. désorienter, embarrasser. ~ment n. désorientation f.

bewitch /bɪ'wɪtʃ/ v.t. enchanter.

beyond /bɪ'jɒnd/ prep. au-delà de; (*doubt, reach*) hors de; (*besides*) excepté. —adv. au-delà. it is ~ me, ça me dépasse.

bias /'baɪəs/ n. (*inclination*) penchant m.; (*prejudice*) préjugé m. —v.t. (*p.t.* biased) influencer. ~ed a. partial.

bib /bɪb/ n. bavoir m.

Bible /'baɪbl/ n. Bible f.

biblical /'bɪblɪkl/ a. biblique.

bicarbonate /baɪ'kɑːbənət/ n. bicarbonate m.

biceps /'baɪseps/ n. biceps m.

bicker /'bɪkə(r)/ v.i. se chamailler.

bicycle /'baɪsɪkl/ n. bicyclette f. —v.i. faire de la bicyclette.

bid[1] /bɪd/ n. (*at auction*) offre f., enchère f.; (*attempt*) tentative f. —v.t./i. (*p.t.* bid, *pres. p.* bidding) (*offer*) faire une offre *or* une enchère (de). the highest ~der, le plus offrant.

bid[2] /bɪd/ v.t. (*p.t.* bade /bæd/, *p.p.* bidden *or* bid, *pres. p.* bidding) ordonner; (*say*) dire. ~ding n. ordre m.

bide /baɪd/ v.t. ~ one's time, attendre le bon moment.

biennial /baɪ'enɪəl/ a. biennal.

bifocals /baɪ'fəʊklz/ n. pl. lunettes bifocales f. pl.

big /bɪg/ a. (**bigger, biggest**) grand; (*in bulk*) gros; (*generous: sl.*) généreux. —adv. (*fam.*) en grand; (*earn: fam.*) gros. ~ business, les grandes affaires. ~-headed a. prétentieux. ~

shot, (sl.) huile f. **think ~**, (fam.) voir grand.

bigam|y /'bɪgəmɪ/ n. bigamie f. **~ist** n. bigame m./f. **~ous** a. bigame.

bigot /'bɪgət/ n. fanatique m./f. **~ed** a. fanatique. **~ry** n. fanatisme m.

bike /baɪk/ n. (fam.) vélo m.

bikini /bɪ'kiːnɪ/ n. (pl. **-is**) bikini m.

bilberry /'bɪlbərɪ/ n. myrtille f.

bile /baɪl/ n. bile f.

bilingual /baɪ'lɪŋgwəl/ a. bilingue.

bilious /'bɪlɪəs/ a. bilieux.

bill¹ /bɪl/ n. (invoice) facture f.; (in hotel, for sale, etc.) note f.; (in restaurant) addition f.; (of sale) acte m.; (pol.) projet de loi m.; (banknote: Amer.) billet de banque m. **~** (person: comm.) envoyer la facture à. (theatre) **on the ~**, à l'affiche.

bill² /bɪl/ n. (of bird) bec m.

billboard /'bɪlbɔːd/ n. panneau d'affichage m.

billet /'bɪlɪt/ n. cantonnement m. —v.t. (p.t. **billeted**) cantonner (on, chez).

billfold /'bɪlfəʊld/ n. (Amer.) portefeuille m.

billiards /'bɪljədz/ n. billard m.

billion /'bɪljən/ n. billion m.; (Amer.) milliard m.

billy-goat /'bɪlɪgəʊt/ n. bouc m.

bin /bɪn/ n. (for rubbish, litter) boîte (à ordures) f., poubelle f.; (for bread) huche f., coffre m.

binary /'baɪnərɪ/ a. binaire.

bind /baɪnd/ v.t. (p.t. **bound**) lier; (book) relier; (jurid.) obliger. —n. (bore: sl.) plaie f. be **~ing on**, être obligatoire pour.

binding /'baɪndɪŋ/ n. reliure f.

binge /bɪndʒ/ n. **go on a ~**, (spree: sl.) faire la bringue.

bingo /'bɪngəʊ/ n. loto m.

binoculars /bɪ'nɒkjʊləz/ n. pl. jumelles f. pl.

biochemistry /baɪəʊ'kemɪstrɪ/ n. biochimie f.

biodegradable /baɪəʊdɪ'greɪdəbl/ a. biodégradable.

biograph|y /baɪ'ɒgrəfɪ/ n. biographie f. **~er** n. biographe m./f.

biolog|y /baɪ'ɒlədʒɪ/ n. biologie f. **~ical** /-ə'lɒdʒɪkl/ a. biologique. **~ist** n. biologiste m./f.

biorhythm /'baɪəʊrɪðəm/ n. biorythme m.

birch /bɜːtʃ/ n. (tree) bouleau m.; (whip) verge f., fouet m.

bird /bɜːd/ n. oiseau m.; (fam.) individu m.; (girl: sl.) poule f.

Biro /'baɪərəʊ/ n. (pl. **-os**) (P.) stylo à bille m., Bic m. (P.).

birth /bɜːθ/ n. naissance f. **give ~**, accoucher. **~ certificate**, acte de naissance m. **~-control** n. contrôle des naissances m. **~-rate** n. natalité f.

birthday /'bɜːθdeɪ/ n. anniversaire m.

birthmark /'bɜːθmɑːk/ n. tache de vin f., envie f.

biscuit /'bɪskɪt/ n. biscuit m.; (Amer.) petit pain (au lait) m.

bisect /baɪ'sekt/ v.t. couper en deux.

bishop /'bɪʃəp/ n. évêque m.

bit¹ /bɪt/ n. morceau m.; (of horse) mors m.; (of tool) mèche f. **a ~**, (a little) un peu.

bit² /bɪt/ see **bite**.

bit³ /bɪt/ n. (comput.) bit m., élement binaire m.

bitch /bɪtʃ/ n. chienne f.; (woman: fam.) garce f. —v.i. (grumble: fam.) râler. **~y** a. (fam.) vache.

bite /baɪt/ v.t./i. (p.t. **bit**, p.p. **bitten**) mordre. —n. morsure f.; (by insect) piqûre f.; (mouthful) bouchée f. **~ one's nails**, se ronger les ongles. **have a ~**, manger un morceau.

biting /'baɪtɪŋ/ a. mordant.

bitter /'bɪtə(r)/ a. amer; (weather) glacial, âpre. —n. bière anglaise f.

~ly *adv.* amèrement. **it is ~ly cold**, il fait un temps glacial. **~ness** *n.* amertume *f.*

bitty /'bɪtɪ/ *a.* décousu.

bizarre /bɪ'zɑː(r)/ *a.* bizarre.

blab /blæb/ *v.i.* (*p.t.* **blabbed**) jaser.

black /blæk/ *a.* (**-er, -est**) noir. —*n.* (*colour*) noir *m.* **B~**, (*person*) Noir(e) *m. (f.).* —*v.t.* noircir; (*goods*) boycotter. **~ and blue**, couvert de bleus. **~ eye**, œil poché *m.* **~ ice**, verglas *m.* **~ list**, liste noire *f.* **~ market**, marché noir *m.* **~ sheep**, brebis galeuse *f.* **~ spot**, point noir *m.*

blackberry /'blækbərɪ/ *n.* mûre *f.*

blackbird /'blækbɜːd/ *n.* merle *m.*

blackboard /'blækbɔːd/ *n.* tableau noir *m.*

blackcurrant /'blæk'kʌrənt/ *n.* cassis *m.*

blacken /'blækən/ *v.t./i.* noircir.

blackhead /'blækhed/ *n.* point noir *m.*

blackleg /'blækleg/ *n.* jaune *m.*

blacklist /'blæklɪst/ *v.t.* mettre sur la liste noire *or* à l'index.

blackmail /'blækmeɪl/ *n.* chantage *m.* —*v.t.* faire chanter. **~er** *n.* maître-chanteur *m.*

blackout /'blækaʊt/ *n.* panne d'électricité *f.*; (*med.*) syncope *f.*

blacksmith /'blæksmɪθ/ *n.* forgeron *m.*

bladder /'blædə(r)/ *n.* vessie *f.*

blade /bleɪd/ *n.* (*of knife etc.*) lame *f.*; (*of propeller, oar*) pale *f.* **~ of grass**, brin d'herbe *m.*

blame /bleɪm/ *v.t.* accuser. —*n.* faute *f.* **s.o. for sth.**, reprocher qch. à qn. **he is to ~**, il est responsable (**for, de**). **~less** *a.* irréprochable.

bland /blænd/ *a.* (**-er, -est**) (*gentle*) doux; (*insipid*) fade.

blank /blæŋk/ *a.* blanc; (*look*) vide; (*cheque*) en blanc. —*n.* blanc *m.* **~ (cartridge)**, cartouche à blanc *f.*

blanket /'blæŋkɪt/ *n.* couverture *f.*; (*layer, fig.*) couche *f.* —*v.t.* (*p.t.* **blanketed**) recouvrir.

blare /bleə(r)/ *v.t./i.* beugler. —*n.* vacarme *m.*, beuglement *m.*

blarney /'blɑːnɪ/ *n.* boniment *m.*

blasé /'blɑːzeɪ/ *a.* blasé.

blasphem|y /'blæsfəmɪ/ *n.* blasphème *m.* **~ous** *a.* blasphématoire; (*person*) blasphémateur.

blast /blɑːst/ *n.* explosion *f.*; (*wave of air*) souffle *m.*; (*of wind*) rafale *f.*; (*noise from siren etc.*) coup *m.* —*v.t.* (*blow up*) faire sauter. **~ed** *a.* (*fam.*) maudit, fichu. **~ furnace** *n.* haut fourneau *m.* **~ off**, être mis à feu. **~-off** *n.* mise à feu *f.*

blatant /'bleɪtnt/ *a.* (*obvious*) flagrant; (*shameless*) éhonté.

blaze[1] /bleɪz/ *n.* flamme *f.*; (*conflagration*) incendie *m.*; (*fig.*) éclat *m.* —*v.i.* (*fire*) flamber; (*sky, eyes, etc.*) flamboyer.

blaze[2] /bleɪz/ *v.t.* **~ a trail**, montrer *or* marquer la voie.

blazer /'bleɪzə(r)/ *n.* blazer *m.*

bleach /bliːtʃ/ *n.* décolorant *m.*; (*for domestic use*) eau de Javel *f.* —*v.t./i.* blanchir; (*hair*) décolorer.

bleak /bliːk/ *a.* (**-er, -est**) morne.

bleary /'blɪərɪ/ *a.* (*eyes*) voilé.

bleat /bliːt/ *n.* bêlement *m.* —*v.i.* bêler.

bleed /bliːd/ *v.t./i.* (*p.t.* **bled**) saigner.

bleep /bliːp/ *n.* bip *m.* **~er** *n.* bip *m.*

blemish /'blemɪʃ/ *n.* tare *f.*, défaut *m.*; (*on reputation*) tache *f.* —*v.t.* entacher.

blend /blend/ *v.t./i.* (se) mélanger. —*n.* mélange *m.* **~er** *n.* mixer *n.*

bless /bles/ *v.t.* bénir. **be ~ed with**, avoir le bonheur de posséder. **~ing** *n.* bénédiction *f.*;

(*benefit*) avantage *m.*; (*stroke of luck*) chance *f.*

blessed /'blesɪd/ *a.* (*holy*) saint; (*damned*: *fam.*) sacré *f.*

blew /bluː/ *see* **blow**[1].

blight /blaɪt/ *n.* (*disease. bot.*) rouille *f.*; (*fig.*) fléau *m.*

blind /blaɪnd/ *a.* aveugle. —*v.t.* aveugler. —*n.* (*on window*) store *m.*; (*deception*) feinte *f.* **be ∼ to**, ne pas voir. **∼ alley**, impasse *f.* **∼ corner**, virage sans visibilité *m.* **∼ man**, aveugle *m.* **∼ spot**, (*auto.*) angle mort *m.* **∼ers** *n. pl.* (*Amer.*) œillères *f. pl.* **∼ly** *adv.* aveuglément. **∼ness** *n.* cécité *f.*

blindfold /'blaɪndfəʊld/ *a.* & *adv.* les yeux bandés. —*n.* bandeau *m.* —*v.t.* bander les yeux à.

blink /blɪŋk/ *v.i.* cligner des yeux; (*of light*) clignoter.

blinkers /'blɪŋkəz/ *n. pl.* œillères *f. pl.*

bliss /blɪs/ *n.* félicité *f.* **∼ful** *a.* bienheureux. **∼fully** *adv.* joyeusement, merveilleusement.

blister /'blɪstə(r)/ *n.* ampoule *f.* (*on paint*) cloque *f.* —*v.i.* se couvrir d'ampoules; cloquer.

blithe /blaɪð/ *a.* joyeux.

blitz /blɪts/ *n.* (*aviat.*) raid éclair *m.* —*v.t.* bombarder.

blizzard /'blɪzəd/ *n.* tempête de neige *f.*

bloated /'bləʊtɪd/ *a.* gonflé.

bloater /'bləʊtə(r)/ *n.* hareng saur *m.*

blob /blɒb/ *n.* (*drop*) (grosse) goutte *f.*; (*stain*) tache *f.*

bloc /blɒk/ *n.* bloc *m.*

block /blɒk/ *n.* bloc *m.*; (*buildings*) pâté de maisons *m.*; (*in pipe*) obstruction *f.* **∼ (of flats)**, immeuble *m.* —*v.t.* bloquer. **∼ letters**, majuscules *f. pl.* **∼age** *n.* obstruction *f.* **∼-buster** *n.* gros succès *m.*

blockade /blɒ'keɪd/ *n.* blocus *m.* —*v.t.* bloquer.

bloke /bləʊk/ *n.* (*fam.*) type *m.*

blond /blɒnd/ *a.* & *n.* blond (*m.*).

blonde /blɒnd/ *a.* & *n.* blonde (*f.*).

blood /blʌd/ *n.* sang *m.* —*a.* (*donor, bath, etc.*) de sang; (*bank, poisoning, etc.*) du sang; (*group, vessel*) sanguin. **∼-curdling** *a.* à tourner le sang. **∼less** *a.* (*fig.*) pacifique. **∼-pressure**, tension artérielle *f.* **∼-test**, prise de sang *f.*

bloodhound /'blʌdhaʊnd/ *n.* limier *m.*

bloodshed /'blʌdʃed/ *n.* effusion de sang *f.*

bloodshot /'blʌdʃɒt/ *a.* injecté de sang.

bloodstream /'blʌdstriːm/ *n.* sang *m.*

bloodthirsty /'blʌdθɜːstɪ/ *a.* sanguinaire.

bloody /'blʌdɪ/ *a.* (*-ier, -iest*) sanglant; (*sl.*) sacré. —*adv.* (*sl.*) vachement. **∼-minded** *a.* (*fam.*) hargneux, obstiné.

bloom /bluːm/ *n.* fleur *f.* —*v.i.* fleurir; (*fig.*) s'épanouir.

bloomer /'bluːmə(r)/ *n.* (*sl.*) gaffe *f.*

blossom /'blɒsəm/ *n.* fleur(s) *f.* (*pl.*). —*v.i.* fleurir; (*person*: *fig.*) s'épanouir.

blot /blɒt/ *n.* tache *f.* —*v.t.* (*p.t.* **blotted**) tacher; (*dry*) sécher. **∼ out**, effacer. **∼ter**, **∼ting-paper** *ns.* buvard *m.*

blotch /blɒtʃ/ *n.* tache *f.* **∼y** *a.* couvert de taches.

blouse /blaʊz/ *n.* chemisier *m.*

blow[1] /bləʊ/ *v.t./i.* (*p.t.* **blew**, *p.p.* **blown**) souffler; (*fuse*) (faire) sauter; (*squander*: *sl.*) claquer; (*opportunity*) rater. **∼ one's nose**, se moucher. **∼ a whistle**, siffler. **∼ away** *or* **off**, emporter. **∼-dry** *v.t.* sécher; *n.* brushing *m.* **∼ out**, (*candle*) souffler. **∼-out** *n.* (*of tyre*) éclatement *m.* **∼ over**, passer. **∼ up**, (faire) sauter; (*tyre*) gonfler; (*photo.*) aggrandir.

blow² /bləʊ/ n. coup m.

blowlamp /ˈbləʊlæmp/ n. chalumeau m.

blown /bləʊn/ see **blow¹**.

blowtorch /ˈbləʊtɔːtʃ/ n. (Amer.) chalumeau m.

blowy /ˈbləʊɪ/ a. it is ~, il y a du vent.

bludgeon /ˈblʌdʒən/ n. gourdin m. —v.t. matraquer.

blue /bluː/ a. (-er, -est) bleu; (film) porno. —n. bleu m. **come out of the ~**, être inattendu. **have the ~s**, avoir le cafard.

bluebell /ˈbluːbel/ n. jacinthe des bois f.

bluebottle /ˈbluːbɒtl/ n. mouche à viande f.

blueprint /ˈbluːprɪnt/ n. plan m.

bluff¹ /blʌf/ v.t./i. bluffer. —n. bluff m. **call s.o.'s ~**, dire chiche à qn.

bluff² /blʌf/ a. (person) brusque.

blunder /ˈblʌndə(r)/ v.i. faire une gaffe; (move) avancer à tâtons. —n. gaffe f.

blunt /blʌnt/ a. (knife) émoussé; (person) brusque. —v.t. émousser. **~ly** adv. carrément. **~ness** n. brusquerie f.

blur /blɜː(r)/ n. tache floue f. (p.t. **blurred**) rendre flou.

blurb /blɜːb/ n. résumé publicitaire m.

blurt /blɜːt/ v.t. ~ **out**, lâcher, dire.

blush /blʌʃ/ v.i. rougir. —n. rougeur f. **~er** n. blush m.

bluster /ˈblʌstə(r)/ v.i. (wind) faire rage; (swagger) fanfaronner. **~y** a. à bourrasques.

boar /bɔː(r)/ n. sanglier m.

board /bɔːd/ n. planche f.; (for notices) tableau m.; (food) pension f.; (committee) conseil m. —v.t./i. (bus, train) monter dans; (naut.) monter à bord (de). **~ of directors**, conseil d'administration m. **go by the ~**, passer à l'as.

full ~, pension complète f. **half ~**, demi-pension f. **on ~**, à bord. **~ up**, boucher. **~ with**, être en pension chez. **~er** n. pensionnaire m./f. **~ing-house** n. pension (de famille) f. **~ing-school** n. pensionnat m., pension f.

boast /bəʊst/ v.i. se vanter (**about**, de). —v.t. s'enorgueillir de. —n. vantardise f. **~er** n. vantard(e) m. (f.). **~ful** a. vantard. **~fully** adv. en se vantant.

boat /bəʊt/ n. bateau m.; (small) canot m. **in the same ~**, logé à la même enseigne. **~ing** n. canotage m.

boatswain /ˈbəʊsn/ n. maître d'équipage m.

bob¹ /bɒb/ v.i. (p.t. **bobbed**). **~ up and down**, monter et descendre.

bob² /bɒb/ n. invar. (sl.) shilling m.

bobby /ˈbɒbɪ/ n. (fam.) flic m.

bobsleigh /ˈbɒbsleɪ/ n. bob (sleigh) m.

bode /bəʊd/ v.i. ~ **well/ill**, être de bon/mauvais augure.

bodily /ˈbɒdɪlɪ/ a. physique, corporel. —adv. physiquement; (in person) en personne.

body /ˈbɒdɪ/ n. corps m.; (mass) masse f.; (organization) organisme m. **~(work)**, (auto.) carrosserie f. **the main ~ of**, le gros de. **~builder** n. culturiste m./f. **~building** n. culturisme m.

bodyguard /ˈbɒdɪɡɑːd/ n. garde du corps m.

bog /bɒɡ/ n. marécage m. —v.t. (p.t. **bogged**). **get ~ged down**, s'embourber.

boggle /ˈbɒɡl/ v.i. **the mind ~s**, on est stupéfait.

bogus /ˈbəʊɡəs/ a. faux.

bogy /ˈbəʊɡɪ/ n. (annoyance) embêtement m.; (man), croquemitaine m.

boil¹ /bɔɪl/ n. furoncle m.

boil² /bɔil/ v.t./i. (faire) bouillir. **bring to the ~**, porter à ébullition. **~ down to**, se ramener à. **~ over**, déborder. **~ing hot**, bouillant. **~ing point**, point d'ébullition m. **~ed** a. (egg) à la coque; (potatoes) à l'eau.

boiler /ˈbɔilə(r)/ n. chaudière f. **~ suit**, bleu (de travail) m.

boisterous /ˈbɔistərəs/ a. tapageur.

bold /bəuld/ a. (-er, -est) hardi; (cheeky) effronté; (type) gras. **~ness** n. hardiesse f.

Bolivia /bəˈliviə/ n. Bolivie f. **~n** a. & n. bolivien(ne) (m. (f.)).

bollard /ˈbɒləd/ n. (on road) borne f.

bolster /ˈbəulstə(r)/ n. traversin m. **—v.t.** soutenir.

bolt /bəult/ n. verrou m.; (for nut) boulon m.; (lightning) éclair m. **—v.t.** (door etc.) verrouiller; (food) engouffrer. **—v.i.** se sauver. **~ upright**, tout droit.

bomb /bɒm/ n. bombe f. **—v.t.** bombarder. **~ scare**, alerte à la bombe f. **~er** n. (aircraft) bombardier m.; (person) plastiqueur m.

bombard /bɒmˈbɑːd/ v.t. bombarder.

bombastic /bɒmˈbæstik/ a. grandiloquent.

bombshell /ˈbɒmʃel/ n. **be a ~**, tomber comme une bombe.

bona fide /bəunəˈfaidi/ a. de bonne foi.

bond /bɒnd/ n. (agreement) engagement m.; (link) lien m.; (comm.) obligation f., bon m. **in ~**, (entreposé) en douane.

bondage /ˈbɒndidʒ/ n. esclavage m.

bone /bəun/ n. os m.; (of fish) arête f. **—v.t.** désosser. **~-dry** a. tout à fait sec. **~ idle**, paresseux comme une couleuvre.

bonfire /ˈbɒnfaiə(r)/ n. feu m.; (for celebration) feu de joie m.

bonnet /ˈbɒnit/ n. (hat) bonnet m.; (of vehicle) capot m.

bonus /ˈbəunəs/ n. prime f.

bony /ˈbəuni/ a. (-ier, -iest) (thin) osseux; (meat) plein d'os; (fish) plein d'arêtes.

boo /buː/ int. hou. **—v.t./i.** huer. **—n.** huée f.

boob /buːb/ n. (blunder: sl.) gaffe f. **—v.i.** (sl.) gaffer.

booby-trap /ˈbuːbitræp/ n. engin piégé m. **—v.t.** (p.t. **-trapped**) piéger.

book /buk/ n. livre m.; (of tickets etc.) carnet m. **~s**, (comm.) comptes m. pl. **—v.t.** (reserve) réserver; (driver) faire un P.V. à; (player) prendre le nom de; (write down) inscrire. **—v.i.** retenir des places. **~able** a. qu'on peut retenir. **(fully) ~ed**, complet. **~ing office**, guichet m.

bookcase /ˈbukkeis/ n. bibliothèque f.

bookkeeping /ˈbukkiːpiŋ/ n. comptabilité f.

booklet /ˈbuklit/ n. brochure f.

bookmaker /ˈbukmeikə(r)/ n. bookmaker m.

bookseller /ˈbukselə(r)/n. libraire m./f.

bookshop /ˈbukʃɒp/ n. librairie f.

bookstall /ˈbukstɔːl/ n. kiosque (à journaux) m.

boom /buːm/ v.i. (gun, wind, etc.) gronder; (trade) prospérer. **—n.** grondement m.; (comm.) boom m., prospérité f.

boon /buːn/ n. (benefit) aubaine f.

boost /buːst/ v.t. stimuler; (morale) remonter; (price) augmenter; (publicize) faire de la réclame pour. **~**, **give a ~ to**, = **boost**.

boot /buːt/ n. (knee-length) botte f.; (ankle-length) chaussure (montante) f.; (for walking) chaussure de marche *f.*; (*sport*) chaussure de sport *f.*; (*of vehicle*) coffre *m.* —*v.t./i.* ~ **up**, (*comput.*) démarrer, lancer (le programme). **get the** ~, (*sl.*) être mis à la porte.

booth /buːð/ *n.* (*for telephone*) cabine *f.*; (*at fair*) baraque *f.*

booty /'buːtɪ/ *n.* butin *m.*

booze /buːz/ *v.i.* (*fam.*) boire (beaucoup). —*n.* (*fam.*) alcool *m.*; (*spree*) beuverie *f.*

border /'bɔːdə(r)/ *n.* (*edge*) bord *m.*; (*frontier*) frontière *f.*; (*in garden*) bordure *f.* —*v.i.* ~ **on**, (*be next to, come close to*) être voisin de, avoisiner.

borderline /'bɔːdəlaɪn/ *n.* ligne de démarcation *f.* ~ **case**, cas limite *m.*

bore[1] /bɔː(r)/ *see* **bear**[2].

bore[2] /bɔː(r)/ *v.t.* (*techn.*) forer.

bore[3] /bɔː(r)/ *v.t.* ennuyer. —*n.* raseu|r, -se *m.,f.*; (*thing*) ennui *m.* **be ~d**, s'ennuyer. ~**dom** *n.* ennui *m.* **boring** *a.* ennuyeux.

born /bɔːn/ *a.* né. **be ~**, naître.

borne /bɔːn/ *see* **bear**[2].

borough /'bʌrə/ *n.* municipalité *f.*

borrow /'bɒrəʊ/ *v.t.* emprunter (**from**, à). ~**ing** *n.* emprunt *m.*

bosom /'bʊzəm/ *n.* sein *m.* ~ **friend**, ami(e) intime *m.* (*f.*).

boss /bɒs/ *n.* (*fam.*) patron(ne) *m.* (*f.*) —*v.t.* ~ (**about**), (*fam.*) donner des ordres à, régenter.

bossy /'bɒsɪ/ *a.* autoritaire.

botan|y /'bɒtənɪ/ *n.* botanique *f.* ~**ical** /bə'tænɪkl/ *a.* botanique. ~**ist** *n.* botaniste *m./f.*

botch /bɒtʃ/ *v.t.* bâcler, saboter.

both /bəʊθ/ *a.* les deux. —*pron.* tous *or* toutes (les) deux, l'un(e) et l'autre. —*adv.* à la fois. ~ **the books**, les deux livres. **we ~ agree**, nous sommes tous les deux d'accord. **I bought ~** (**of them**), j'ai acheté les deux. **I saw ~ of you**, je vous ai vus tous les

deux. ~ **Paul and Anne**, (et) Paul et Anne.

bother /'bɒðə(r)/ *v.t.* (*annoy, worry*) ennuyer; (*disturb*) déranger. —*v.i.* se déranger. —*n.* ennui *m.*; (*effort*) peine *f.* **don't ~** (**calling**), ce n'est pas la peine (d'appeler). **don't ~ about us**, ne t'inquiète pas pour nous. **I can't be ~ed**, j'ai la flemme. **it's no ~**, ce n'est rien.

bottle /'bɒtl/ *n.* bouteille *f.*; (*for baby*) biberon *m.* —*v.t.* mettre en bouteille(s). ~ **bank**, collecteur (de verre usagé) *m.* ~**opener** *n.* ouvre-bouteille(s) *m.* ~ **up**, contenir.

bottleneck /'bɒtlnek/ *n.* (*traffic jam*) bouchon *m.*

bottom /'bɒtəm/ *n.* fond *m.*; (*of hill, page, etc.*) bas *m.*; (*buttocks*) derrière *m.* —*a.* inférieur; du bas. ~**less** *a.* insondable.

bough /baʊ/ *n.* rameau *m.*

bought /bɔːt/ *see* **buy**.

boulder /'bəʊldə(r)/ *n.* rocher *m.*

boulevard /'buːləvɑːd/ *n.* boulevard *m.*

bounce /baʊns/ *v.i.* rebondir; (*person*) faire des bonds, bondir; (*cheques*: *sl.*) être refusé. —*v.t.* faire rebondir. —*n.* rebond *m.*

bouncer /'baʊnsə(r)/ *n.* videur *m.*

bound[1] /baʊnd/ *v.i.* (*leap*) bondir. —*n.* bond *m.*

bound[2] /baʊnd/ *see* **bind**. —*a.* **be ~ for**, être en route pour, aller vers. ~ **to**, (*obliged*) obligé de; (*certain*) sûr de.

boundary /'baʊndrɪ/ *n.* limite *f.*

bound|s /baʊndz/ *n. pl.* limites *f. pl.* **out of ~s**, interdit. ~**ed by**, limité par. ~**less** *a.* sans bornes.

bouquet /bʊ'keɪ/ *n.* bouquet *m.*

bout /baʊt/ *n.* période *f.*; (*med.*) accès *m.*; (*boxing*) combat *m.*

boutique /buː'tiːk/ *n.* boutique (de mode) *f.*

bow[1] /bəʊ/ *n.* (*weapon*) arc *m.*;

(mus.) archet *m.*; *(knot)* nœud *m.*
~-legged *a.* aux jambes arquées.
~-tie *n.* nœud papillon *m.*

bow² /baʊ/ *n. (with head)* salut *m.*; *(with body)* révérence *f.* —*v.t./i.* (s')incliner.

bow³ /baʊ/ *n. (naut.)* proue *f.*

bowels /'baʊəlz/ *n. pl.* intestins *m. pl.*; *(fig.)* entrailles *f. pl.*

bowl¹ /baʊl/ *n.* cuvette *f.*; *(for food)* bol *m.*; *(for soup etc.)* assiette creuse *f.*

bowl² /baʊl/ *n. (ball)* boule *f.* —*v.t./i. (cricket)* lancer. **~ over**, bouleverser. **~ing** *n.* jeu de boules *m.* **~ing-alley** *n.* bowling *m.*

bowler¹ /'baʊlə(r)/ *n. (cricket)* lanceur *m.*

bowler² /'baʊlə(r)/ *n.* **~ (hat)**, (chapeau) melon *m.*

box¹ /bɒks/ *n.* boîte *f.*; *(cardboard)* carton *m.* *(theatre)* loge *f.* —*v.t.* mettre en boîte. **the ~**, *(fam.)* la télé. **~ in**, enfermer. **~-office** *n.* bureau de location *m.* **Boxing Day**, le lendemain de Noël.

box² /bɒks/ *v.t./i. (sport)* boxer. **~ s.o.'s ears**, gifler qn. **~ing** *n.* boxe *f.* **~ de boxe**.

boy /bɔɪ/ *n.* garçon *m.* **~-friend** *n.* (petit) ami *m.* **~hood** *n.* enfance *f.* **~ish** *a.* enfantin, de garçon.

boycott /'bɔɪkɒt/ *v.t.* boycotter. —*n.* boycottage *m.*

bra /brɑː/ *n.* soutien-gorge *m.*

brace /breɪs/ *n. (fastener)* attache *f.*; *(dental)* appareil *m.*; *(for bit)* vilbrequin *m.* **~s**, *(for trousers)* bretelles *f. pl.* —*v.t.* soutenir. **~ o.s.**, rassembler ses forces.

bracelet /'breɪslɪt/ *n.* bracelet *m.*

bracing /'breɪsɪŋ/ *a.* vivifiant.

bracken /'brækən/ *n.* fougère *f.*

bracket /'brækɪt/ *n. (for shelf etc.)* tasseau *m.*, support *m.*; *(group)* tranche *f.* **(round) ~**, *(printing sign)* parenthèse *f.* **(square) ~**, crochet *m.* —*v.t. (p.t.* **bracketed)**

mettre entre parenthèses *or* crochets.

brag /bræg/ *v.i. (p.t.* **bragged)** se vanter.

braid /breɪd/ *n. (trimming)* galon *m.*; *(of hair)* tresse *f.*

Braille /breɪl/ *n.* braille *m.*

brain /breɪn/ *n.* cerveau *m.* *(fig.)* intelligence *f.* —*v.t.* assommer. **~-child** *n.* invention personnelle *f.* **~-drain** *n.* exode des cerveaux *m.* **~less** *a.* stupide.

brainwash /'breɪnwɒʃ/ *v.t.* faire un lavage de cerveau à.

brainwave /'breɪnweɪv/ *n.* idée géniale *f.*, trouvaille *f.*

brainy /'breɪnɪ/ *a.* **(-ier, -iest)** intelligent.

braise /breɪz/ *v.t.* braiser.

brake /breɪk/ *n. (auto & fig.)* frein *m.* —*v.t./i.* freiner. **~ fluid**, liquide de frein *m.* **~ light**, feu de stop *m.* **~ lining**, garniture de frein *f.*

bramble /'bræmbl/ *n.* ronce *f.*

bran /bræn/ *n. (husks)* son *m.*

branch /brɑːntʃ/ *n.* branche *f.*; *(of road)* embranchement *m.*; *(comm.)* succursale *f.*; *(of bank)* agence *f.* —*v.i.* **~ (off)**, bifurquer.

brand /brænd/ *n.* marque *f.* —*v.t.* **~ s.o. as**, donner à qn. la réputation de. **~-new** *a.* tout neuf.

brandish /'brændɪʃ/ *v.t.* brandir.

brandy /'brændɪ/ *n.* cognac *m.*

brash /bræʃ/ *a.* effronté.

brass /brɑːs/ *n.* cuivre *m.* **get down to ~ tacks**, en venir aux choses sérieuses. **the ~**, *(mus.)* les cuivres *m. pl.* **top ~**, *(sl.)* gros bonnets *m. pl.*

brassière /'bræsɪə(r), *Amer.* brə'zɪər/ *n.* soutien-gorge *m.*

brat /bræt/ *n. (child: pej.)* môme *m./f.*; *(ill-behaved)* garnement *m.*

bravado /brə'vɑːdəʊ/ *n.* bravade *f.*

brave /breɪv/ *a.* **(-er, -est)**

courageux, brave. —*n.* (*American Indian*) brave *m.* —*v.t.* braver. ~**ry** /-ərɪ/ *n.* courage *m.*

bravo /'brɑːvəʊ/ *int.* bravo.

brawl /brɔːl/ *n.* bagarre *f.* —*v.i.* se bagarrer.

brawn /brɔːn/ *n.* muscles *m. pl.* ~**y** *a.* musclé.

bray /breɪ/ *n.* braiment *m.* —*v.i.* braire.

brazen /'breɪzn/ *a.* effronté.

brazier /'breɪzɪə(r)/ *n.* brasero *m.*

Brazil /brə'zɪl/ *n.* Brésil *m.* ~**ian** *a. & n.* brésilien(ne) (*m.* (*f.*)).

breach /briːtʃ/ *n.* violation *f.*; (*of contract*) rupture *f.*; (*gap*) brèche *f.* —*v.t.* ouvrir une brèche dans.

bread /bred/ *n.* pain *m.* ~ **and butter**, tartine *f.* ~**bin**, (*Amer.*) ~**box** *ns.* boîte à pain *f.* ~**winner** *n.* soutien de famille *m.*

breadcrumbs /'bredkrʌmz/ *n. pl.* (*culin.*) chapelure *f.*

breadline /'bredlaɪn/ *n.* **on the** ~, dans l'indigence.

breadth /bretθ/ *n.* largeur *f.*

break /breɪk/ *v.t.* (*p.t.* **broke**, *p.p.* **broken**) casser; (*smash into pieces*) briser; (*vow, silence, rank, etc.*) rompre; (*law*) violer; (*a record*) battre; (*news*) révéler; (*journey*) interrompre; (*heart, strike, ice*) briser. —*v.i.* (*se*) casser; se briser. —*n.* cassure *f.*, rupture *f.*; (*in relationship, continuity*) rupture *f.*; (*interval*) interruption *f.*; (*at school*) récréation *f.*, récré *f.*; (*for coffee*) pause *f.*; (*luck: fam.*) chance *f.* ~ **one's arm**, se casser le bras. ~ **away from**, quitter. ~ **down** *v.i.* (*collapse*) s'effondrer; (*fail*) échouer; (*machine*) tomber en panne; *v.t.* (*door*) enfoncer; (*analyse*) analyser. ~ **even**, rentrer dans ses frais. ~**in** *n.* cambriolage *m.* ~ **into**, cambrioler. ~ **off**, (se) détacher; (*suspend*) (*stop talking*)

s'interrompre. ~ **out**, (*fire, war, etc.*) éclater. ~ **up**, (*end*) (faire) cesser; (*couple*) rompre; (*marriage*) (se) briser; (*crowd*) (se) disperser; (*schools*) entrer en vacances. ~**able** *a.* cassable. ~**age** *n.* casse *f.*

breakdown /'breɪkdaʊn/ *n.* (*techn.*) panne *f.*; (*med.*) dépression *f.*; (*of figures*) analyse *f.* —*a.* (*auto.*) de dépannage.

breaker /'breɪkə(r)/ *n.* (*wave*) brisant *m.*

breakfast /'brekfəst/ *n.* petit déjeuner *m.*

breakthrough /'breɪkθruː/ *n.* percée *f.*

breakwater /'breɪkwɔːtə(r)/ *n.* brise-lames *m. invar.*

breast /brest/ *n.* sein *m.*; (*chest*) poitrine *f.* ~**feed** *v.t.* (*p.t.* **-fed**) allaiter. ~**stroke** *n.* brasse *f.*

breath /breθ/ *n.* souffle *m.*, haleine *f.* **out of** ~, essoufflé. **under one's** ~, tout bas. ~**less** *a.* essoufflé.

breathalyser /'breθəlaɪzə(r)/ *n.* alcootest *m.*

breath|e /briːð/ *v.t./i.* respirer. ~ **in**, inspirer. ~ **out**, expirer. ~**ing** *n.* respiration *f.*

breather /'briːðə(r)/ *n.* moment de repos *m.*

breathtaking /'breθteɪkɪŋ/ *a.* à vous couper le souffle.

bred /bred/ *see* **breed**.

breeches /'brɪtʃɪz/ *n. pl.* culotte *f.*

breed /briːd/ *v.t.* (*p.t.* **bred**) élever; (*give rise to*) engendrer. —*v.i.* se reproduire. —*n.* race *f.* ~**er** *n.* éleveur *m.* ~**ing** *n.* élevage *m.*; (*fig.*) éducation *f.*

breez|e /briːz/ *n.* brise *f.* ~**y** *a.* (*weather*) frais; (*cheerful*) jovial; (*casual*) désinvolte.

Breton /bretn/ *a. & n.* breton(ne) (*m.* (*f.*)).

brevity /'brevətɪ/ *n.* brièveté *f.*

brew /bruː/ *v.t.* (*beer*) brasser; (*tea*)

faire infuser. —*v.i.* fermenter; infuser; (*fig.*) se préparer. ~er /-/ *n.* décoction *f.* ~er *n.* brasseur *m.* ~ery *n.* brasserie *f.*

bribe /braɪb/ *n.* pot-de-vin *m.* —*v.t.* soudoyer, acheter. ~ry /-ərɪ/ *n.* corruption *f.*

brick /brɪk/ *n.* brique *f.*

bricklayer /'brɪkleɪə(r)/ *n.* maçon *m.*

bridal /'braɪdl/ *a.* nuptial.

bride /braɪd/ *n.* mariée *f.*

bridegroom /'braɪdgrʊm/ *n.* marié *m.*

bridesmaid /'braɪdzmeɪd/ *n.* demoiselle d'honneur *f.*

bridge[1] /brɪdʒ/ *n.* pont *m.*; (*naut.*) passerelle *f.*; (*of nose*) arête *f.* —*v.t.* ~ **a gap**, combler une lacune.

bridge[2] /brɪdʒ/ *n.* (*cards*) bridge *m.*

bridle /'braɪdl/ *n.* bride *f.* —*v.t.* brider. ~**path** *n.* allée cavalière *f.*

brief[1] /briːf/ *a.* (-er, -est) bref. ~**ly** *adv.* brièvement. ~**ness** *n.* brièveté *f.*

brief[2] /briːf/ *n.* instructions *f. pl.*; (*jurid.*) dossier *m.* —*v.t.* donner des instructions à. ~**ing** *n.* briefing *m.*

briefcase /'briːfkeɪs/ *n.* serviette *f.*

briefs /briːfs/ *n. pl.* slip *m.*

brigad|**e** /brɪ'geɪd/ *n.* brigade *f.* ~**ier** /-ə'dɪə(r)/ *n.* général de brigade *m.*

bright /braɪt/ *a.* (-er, -est) brillant, vif; (*day, room*) clair; (*cheerful*) gai; (*clever*) intelligent. ~**ly** *adv.* brillamment. ~**ness** *n.* éclat *m.*

brighten /'braɪtn/ *v.t.* égayer. —*v.i.* (*weather*) s'éclaircir; (*of face*) s'éclairer.

brillian|**t** /'brɪljənt/ *a.* brillant; (*light*) éclatant; (*very good: fam.*) super. ~**ce** *n.* éclat *m.*

brim /brɪm/ *n.* bord *m.* —*v.i.* (*p.t.* **brimmed**). ~ **over**, déborder.

brine /braɪn/ *n.* saumure *f.*

bring /brɪŋ/ *v.t.* (*p.t.* **brought**) (*thing*) apporter; (*person, vehicle*) amener. ~ **about**, provoquer. ~ **back**, rapporter; ramener. ~ **down**, faire tomber; (*shoot down, knock down*) abattre. ~ **for-ward**, avancer. ~ **off**, réussir. ~ **out**, (*take out*) sortir; (*show*) faire ressortir; (*book*) publier. ~ **round** *or* **to**, ranimer. ~ **to bear**, (*pressure etc.*) exercer. ~ **up**, élever; (*med.*) vomir; (*question*) soulever.

brink /brɪŋk/ *n.* bord *m.*

brisk /brɪsk/ *a.* (-er, -est) vif. ~**ness** *n.* vivacité *f.*

bristl|**e** /'brɪsl/ *n.* poil *m.* —*v.i.* se hérisser. ~**ing with**, hérissé de.

Britain /'brɪtn/ *n.* Grande-Bretagne *f.*

British /'brɪtɪʃ/ *a.* britannique. **the** ~, les Britanniques *m. pl.*

Briton /'brɪtn/ *n.* Britannique *m./f.*

Brittany /'brɪtənɪ/ *n.* Bretagne *f.*

brittle /'brɪtl/ *a.* fragile.

broach /brəʊtʃ/ *v.t.* entamer.

broad /brɔːd/ *a.* (-er, -est) large; (*daylight, outline*) grand. ~ **bean**, fève *f.* ~-**minded** *a.* d'esprit. ~**ly** *adv.* en gros.

broadcast /'brɔːdkɑːst/ *v.t./i.* (*p.t.* **broadcast**) diffuser; (*person*) parler à la télévision *or* à la radio. —*n.* émission *f.*

broaden /'brɔːdn/ *v.t./i.* (s')élar-gir.

broccoli /'brɒkəlɪ/ *n.* invar. brocoli *m.*

brochure /'brəʊʃə(r)/ *n.* brochure *f.*

broke /brəʊk/ *see* **break**. —*a.* (*penniless: sl.*) fauché.

broken /'brəʊkən/ *see* **break**. —*a.* ~ **English**, mauvais anglais *m.* ~-**hearted** *a.* au cœur brisé.

broker /'brəʊkə(r)/ *n.* courtier *m.*

brolly /'brolɪ/ n. (fam.) pépin m.

bronchitis /broŋ'kaɪtɪs/ n. bronchite f.

bronze /bronz/ n. bronze m. —v.t./i. (se) bronzer.

brooch /brəʊtʃ/ n. broche f.

brood /bru:d/ n. nichée f., couvée f. —v.i. couver; (fig.) méditer tristement. **~y** a. mélancolique.

brook[1] /brʊk/ n. ruisseau m.

brook[2] /brʊk/ v.t. souffrir.

broom /bru:m/ n. balai m.

broomstick /'bru:mstɪk/ n. manche à balai m.

broth /broθ/ n. bouillon m.

brothel /'broθl/ n. maison close f.

brother /'brʌðə(r)/ n. frère m. **~hood** n. fraternité f. **~-in-law** n. (pl. **~s-in-law**) beau-frère m. **~ly** a. fraternel.

brought /brɔːt/ see **bring**.

brow /braʊ/ n. front m.; (of hill) sommet m.

browbeat /'braʊbiːt/ v.t. (p.t. **-beat**, p.p. **-beaten**) intimider.

brown /braʊn/ a. (-er, -est) marron (invar.); (cheveux) brun. —n. marron m.; brun m. —v.t./i. brunir; (culin.) (faire) dorer. **be ~ed** (sl.) en avoir ras le bol. **~ bread**, pain bis m. **~ sugar**, cassonade f.

Brownie /'braʊnɪ/ n. jeannette f.

browse /braʊz/ v.i. feuilleter; (animal) brouter.

bruise /bruːz/ n. bleu m. —v.t. (hurt) faire un bleu à; (fruit) abîmer. **~d** a. couvert de bleus.

brunch /brʌntʃ/ n. petit déjeuner copieux m. (pris comme déjeuner).

brunette /bruː'net/ n. brunette f.

brunt /brʌnt/ n. the **~** of, le plus fort de.

brush /brʌʃ/ n. brosse f.; (skirmish) accrochage m.; (bushes) broussailles f. pl. —v.t. brosser. **~ against**, effleurer. **~ aside**, écarter. **give s.o. the ~-off**, (reject: fam.) envoyer promener qn. **~ up (on)**, se remettre à.

Brussels /'brʌslz/ n. Bruxelles m./f. **~ sprouts**, choux de Bruxelles m. pl.

brutal /'bruːtl/ a. brutal. **~ity** /-'tælɪtɪ/ n. brutalité f.

brute /bruːt/ n. brute f. **by ~ force**, de force.

B.Sc. abbr. see **Bachelor of Science**.

bubble /'bʌbl/ n. bulle f. —v.i. bouillonner. **~ bath**, bain moussant m. **~ over**, déborder.

buck[1] /bʌk/ n. mâle m. —v.i. ruer. **~ up**, (sl.) prendre courage; (hurry: sl.) se grouiller.

buck[2] /bʌk/ n. (Amer., sl.) dollar m.

buck[3] /bʌk/ n. **pass the ~**, rejeter la responsabilité (to, sur).

bucket /'bʌkɪt/ n. seau m. **~ shop**, agence de charters f.

buckle /'bʌkl/ n. boucle f. —v.t./i. (fasten) (se) boucler; (bend) voiler. **~ down to**, s'atteler à.

bud /bʌd/ n. bourgeon m. —v.i. (p.t. **budded**) bourgeonner.

Buddhist /'bʊdɪst/ a. & n. bouddhiste (m./f.). **~m** /-ɪzəm/ n. bouddhisme m.

budding /'bʌdɪŋ/ a. (talent etc.) naissant; (film star etc.) en herbe.

buddy /'bʌdɪ/ n. (fam.) copain m.

budge /bʌdʒ/ v.t./i. (faire) bouger.

budgerigar /'bʌdʒərɪgɑː(r)/ n. perruche f.

budget /'bʌdʒɪt/ n. budget m. —v.t. (p.t. **budgeted**) **~ for**, prévoir (dans son budget).

buff /bʌf/ n. (colour) chamois m.; (fam.) fanatique m./f.

buffalo /'bʌfələʊ/ n. (pl. **-oes** or **-o**) buffle m.; (Amer.) bison m.

buffer /'bʌfə(r)/ n. tampon m. **~ zone**, zone tampon f.

buffet[1] /'bʊfeɪ/ n. buffet m. **~ car**, buffet m.

buffet² /bʌfit/ n. (blow) soufflet m. —v.t. (p.t. **buffeted**) souffleter.

buffoon /bə'fu:n/ n. bouffon m.

bug /bʌg/ n. (insect) punaise f.; (any small insect) bestiole f.; (germ: sl.) microbe m.; (device: sl.) micro m.; (defect: sl.) défaut m. —v.t. (p.t. **bugged**) mettre des micros dans; (Amer., sl.) embêter.

buggy /bʌgi/ n. (child's) poussette f.

bugle /bju:gl/ n. clairon m.

build /bild/ v.t./i. (p.t. **built**) bâtir, construire. —n. carrure f. ~ **up**, (increase) augmenter, monter; (accumulate) (s')accumuler. ~-**up** n. accumulation f.; (fig.) publicité f. ~er n. entrepreneur m.; (workman) ouvrier m.

building /bildiŋ/ n. bâtiment m.; (dwelling) immeuble m. ~ **society**, caisse d'épargne-logement f.

built /bilt/ see **build**. ~-**in** a. encastré. ~-**up area**, agglomération f., zone urbanisée f.

bulb /bʌlb/ n. oignon m.; (electr.) ampoule f. ~**ous** a. bulbeux.

Bulgaria /bʌl'geəriə/ n. Bulgarie f. ~**n** a. & n. bulgare (m./f.).

bulge /bʌldʒ/ n. renflement m. —v.i. se renfler, être renflé. **be** ~**ing with**, être gonflé ou bourré de.

bulimia /bju:'limiə/ n. boulimie f.

bulk /bʌlk/ n. grosseur f. **in** ~, en gros; (loose) en vrac. **the** ~ **of**, la majeure partie de. ~**y** a. gros.

bull /bul/ n. taureau m. ~'s-**eye** n. centre de la cible) m.

bulldog /buldɒg/ n. bouledogue m.

bulldoze /buldəuz/ v.t. raser au bulldozer. ~r /-ə(r)/ n. bulldozer m.

bullet /bulit/ n. balle f. ~-**proof** a. pare-balles invar.; (vehicle) blindé.

bulletin /bulitin/ n. bulletin m.

bullfight /bulfait/ n. corrida f. ~er n. torero m.

bullion /buliən/ n. or or argent en lingots m.

bullring /buliŋ/ n. arène f.

bully /buli/ n. brute f.; tyran m. —v.t. (treat badly) brutaliser; (persecute) tyranniser; (coerce) forcer (into, à).

bum¹ /bʌm/ n. (sl.) derrière m.

bum² /bʌm/ n. (Amer., sl.) vagabond(e) m. (f.).

bumble-bee /bʌmblbi:/ n. bourdon m.

bump /bʌmp/ n. choc m.; (swelling) bosse f. —v.t./i. cogner, heurter. ~ **along**, cahoter. ~ **into**, (hit) rentrer dans; (meet) tomber sur. ~**y** a. cahoteux.

bumper /bʌmpə(r)/ n. pare-chocs m. invar. —a. exceptionnel.

bumptious /bʌmpʃəs/ a. prétentieux.

bun /bʌn/ n. (cake) petit pain au lait m.; (hair) chignon m.

bunch /bʌntʃ/ n. (of flowers) bouquet m.; (of keys) trousseau m.; (of people) groupe m.; (of bananas) régime m. ~ **of grapes**, grappe de raisin f.

bundle /bʌndl/ n. paquet m. —v.t. mettre en paquet; (push) pousser.

bung /bʌŋ/ n. bonde f. —v.t. boucher; (throw: sl.) flanquer.

bungalow /bʌŋgələu/ n. bungalow m.

bungle /bʌŋgl/ v.t. gâcher.

bunion /bʌnjən/ n. (med.) oignon m.

bunk¹ /bʌŋk/ n. couchette f. ~-**beds** n. pl. lits superposés m. pl.

bunk² /bʌŋk/ n. (nonsense: sl.) foutaise(s) f. (pl.).

bunker /bʌŋkə(r)/ n. (mil.) bunker m.

bunny /bʌni/ n. (children's use) (Jeannot) lapin m.

buoy /bɔi/ n. bouée f. —v.t. ~ **up**, (hearten) soutenir, encourager.

buoyan|t /'bɔɪənt/ a. (*cheerful*) gai. **∼cy** n. gaieté f.

burden /'bɜːdn/ n. fardeau m. —v.t. accabler. **∼some** a. lourd.

bureau /'bjʊərəʊ/ n. (pl. **-eaux** /-əʊz/) bureau m.

bureaucracy /bjʊə'rɒkrəsɪ/ n. bureaucratie f.

bureaucrat /'bjʊərəkræt/ n. bureaucrate m./f. **∼ic** /-'krætɪk/ a. bureaucratique.

burglar /'bɜːglə(r)/n. cambrioleur m. **∼ize** v.t. (Amer.) cambrioler. **∼ alarm**, alarme f. **∼y** n. cambriolage m.

burgle /'bɜːgl/ v.t. cambrioler.

Burgundy /'bɜːgəndɪ/ n. (*wine*) bourgogne f.

burial /'berɪəl/ n. enterrement m.

burlesque /bɜː'lesk/ n. (*imitation*) parodie f.

burly /'bɜːlɪ/ a. (**-ier, -iest**) costaud, solidement charpenté.

Burm|a /'bɜːmə/ n. Birmanie f. **∼ese** /-'miːz/ a. & n. birman(e) (m. (f.)).

burn /bɜːn/ v.t./i. (p.t. **burned** or **burnt**) brûler. —n. brûlure f. **∼ down** or **be ∼ed down**, être réduit en cendres. **∼er** n. brûleur m. **∼ing** a. (fig.) brûlant.

burnish /'bɜːnɪʃ/ v.t. polir.

burnt see **burn**.

burp /bɜːp/ n. (fam.) rot m. —v.i. (fam.) roter.

burrow /'bʌrəʊ/ n. terrier m. —v.t. creuser.

bursar /'bɜːsə(r)/ n. économe m./f.

bursary /'bɜːsərɪ/ n. bourse f.

burst /bɜːst/ v.t./i. (p.t. **burst**) crever, (faire) éclater. —n. explosion f.; (*of laughter*) éclat m.; (*surge*) élan m. **be ∼ing with**, déborder de. **∼ into**, faire irruption dans. **∼ into tears**, fondre en larmes. **∼ out laughing**, éclater de rire. **∼ pipe**, conduite qui a éclaté f.

bury /'berɪ/ v.t. (*person etc.*) enterrer; (*hide, cover*) enfouir; (*engross, thrust*) plonger.

bus /bʌs/ n. (pl. **buses**) (auto)bus m. —v.t. transporter en bus. —v.i. (p.t. **bussed**) prendre l'autobus. **∼-stop**, arrêt d'autobus m.

bush /bʊʃ/ n. buisson m.; (*land*) brousse f. **∼y** a. broussailleux.

business /'bɪznɪs/ n. (*task, concern*) affaire f.; (*commerce*) affaires f. pl.; (*line of work*) métier m.; (*shop*) commerce m. **he has no ∼ to**, il n'a pas le droit de. **mean ∼**, être sérieux. **that's none of your ∼!**, ça ne vous regarde pas! **∼man**, homme d'affaires m.

businesslike /'bɪznɪslaɪk/ a. sérieux.

busker /'bʌskə(r)/ n. musicien(ne) des rues m. (f.).

bust[1] /bʌst/ n. buste m.; (*bosom*) poitrine f.

bust[2] /bʌst/ v.t./i. (p.t. **busted** or **bust**) (burst: sl.) crever; (*break*: sl.) (se) casser. —a. (*broken, finished*: sl.) fichu. **∼-up** n. (sl.) engueulade f. **go ∼**, (sl.) faire faillite.

bustl|e /'bʌsl/ v.i. s'affairer. —n. affairement m., remue-ménage m. **∼ing** a. (*place*) bruyant, animé.

bus|y /'bɪzɪ/ a. (**-ier, -iest**) occupé; (*street*) animé; (*day*) chargé. —v.t. **∼y o.s. with**, s'occuper à. **∼ily** adv. activement.

busybody /'bɪzɪbɒdɪ/ n. **be a ∼**, faire la mouche du coche.

but /bʌt, unstressed bət/ conj. mais. —prep. sauf. —adv. (*only*) seulement. **∼ for**, sans. **nobody ∼**, personne d'autre que. **nothing ∼**, rien que.

butane /'bjuːteɪn/ n. butane m.

butcher /'bʊtʃə(r)/ n. boucher m. —v.t. massacrer. **∼y** n. boucherie f., massacre m.

butler /'bʌtlə(r)/ n. maître d'hôtel m.

butt /bʌt/ n. (of gun) crosse f.; (of cigarette) mégot m.; (target) cible f.; (barrel) tonneau; (Amer., fam.) derrière m. —v.i. ~ **in**, interrompre.

butter /'bʌtə(r)/ n. beurre m. —v.t. beurrer. ~**-bean** n. haricot blanc m. ~**-fingers** n. maladroit(e) m. (f.).

buttercup /'bʌtəkʌp/ n. bouton-d'or m.

butterfly /'bʌtəflaɪ/ n. papillon m.

buttock /'bʌtək/ n. fesse f.

button /'bʌtn/ n. bouton m. —v.t./i. ~ **(up)**, (se) boutonner.

buttonhole /'bʌtnhəʊl/ n. bouton-nière f. —v.t. accrocher.

buttress /'bʌtrɪs/ n. contrefort m. —v.t. soutenir.

buxom /'bʌksəm/ a. bien en chair.

buy /baɪ/ v.t. (p.t. **bought**) acheter (**from**, à); (believe: sl.) croire, avaler. —n. achat m. ~ **sth for s.o.** acheter qch. à qn., prendre qch. pour qn. ~**er** n. acheteu|r, -se m., f.

buzz /bʌz/ n. bourdonnement m. —v.i. bourdonner. ~ **off**, (sl.) ficher le camp. ~**er** n. sonnerie f.

by /baɪ/ prep. par, de; (near) à côté de; (before) avant; (means) en, à, par. **by bike**, à vélo. **by car**, en auto. **by day**, de jour. **by the kilo**, au kilo. **by running/etc.**, en courant/etc. **by sea**, par mer. ~ **that time**, à ce moment-là. **by the way**, à propos. —adv. (near) tout près. **by and large**, dans l'ensemble. **by-election** n. élection partielle f. **by-law** n. arrêté m.; (of club etc.) statut m. **by o.s.**, tout seul. **by-product** n. sous-produit m.; (fig.) conséquence. **by-road** n. chemin de traverse m.

bye(-bye) /baɪ('baɪ)/ int. (fam.) au revoir, salut.

bypass /'baɪpɑːs/ n. (auto.) route m. contourner f.; (med.) pontage m. —v.t. contourner.

bystander /'baɪstændə(r)/ n. specta|teur, -trice m., f.

byte /baɪt/ n. octet m.

byword /'baɪwɜːd/ n. **be a** ~ **for**, être connu pour.

C

cab /kæb/ n. taxi m.; (of lorry, train) cabine f.

cabaret /'kæbəreɪ/ n. spectacle (de cabaret) m.

cabbage /'kæbɪdʒ/ n. chou m.

cabin /'kæbɪn/ n. (hut) cabane f.; (in ship, aircraft) cabine f.

cabinet /'kæbɪnɪt/ n. (petite) armoire f., meuble de rangement m.; (for filing) classeur m. **C**~, (pol.) cabinet m. ~**-maker** n. ébéniste m.

cable /'keɪbl/ n. câble m. —v.t. câbler. ~**-car** n. téléphérique m. ~ **railway**, funiculaire m.

caboose /kə'buːs/ n. (rail., Amer.) fourgon m.

cache /kæʃ/ n. (place) cachette f. **a** ~ **of arms**, des armes cachées.

cackle /'kækl/ n. caquet m. —v.i. caqueter.

cactus /'kæktəs/ n. (pl. **-ti** /-taɪ/ or **-tuses**) cactus m.

caddie /'kædɪ/ n. (golf) caddie m.

caddy /'kædɪ/ n. boîte à thé f.

cadence /'keɪdns/ n. cadence f.

cadet /kə'det/ n. élève officier m.

cadge /kædʒ/ v.t. se faire payer, écornifler. —v.i. quémander. ~ **money from**, taper. ~**r** /-ə(r)/ n. écornifleu|r, -se m., f.

Caesarean /sɪ'zeərɪən/ a. ~ **(section)**, césarienne f.

café /'kæfeɪ/ n. café-restaurant m.

cafeteria /kæfɪ'tɪərɪə/ n. cafétéria f.

caffeine /'kæfi:n/ n. caféine f.

cage /keɪdʒ/ n. cage f. —v.t. mettre en cage.

cagey /'keɪdʒɪ/ a. (secretive: fam.) peu communicatif.

cagoule /kə'gu:l/ n. K-way n. (P.).

Cairo /'kaɪərəʊ/ n. le Caire m.

cajole /kə'dʒəʊl/ v.t. ~ s.o. into doing, faire l'enjoleur pour que qn. fasse.

cake /keɪk/ n. gâteau m. ~d a. durci. ~d with, raidi par.

calamit|y /kə'læmətɪ/ n. calamité f. ~ous a. désastreux.

calcium /'kælsɪəm/ n. calcium m.

calculat|e /'kælkjʊleɪt/ v.t./i. calculer; (Amer.) supposer. ~ed a. (action) délibéré. ~ing a. calculateur. ~ion /-'leɪʃn/ n. calcul m. ~or n. calculatrice f.

calculus /'kælkjʊləs/ n. (pl. -li /-laɪ/ or -luses) calcul m.

calendar /'kælɪndə(r)/ n. calendrier m.

calf[1] /kɑ:f/ n. (pl. calves) (young cow or bull) veau m.

calf[2] /kɑ:f/ n. (pl. calves) (of leg) mollet m.

calibre /'kælɪbə(r)/ n. calibre m.

calico /'kælɪkəʊ/ n. calicot m.

call /kɔ:l/ v.t./i. appeler. ~ (in or round), (visit) passer. —n. appel m.; (of bird) cri m.; visite f. be ~ed, (named) s'appeler. be on ~, être de garde. ~ back, rappeler; (visit) repasser. ~-box n. cabine téléphonique f. ~ for, (require) demander; (fetch) passer prendre. ~-girl n. call-girl f. ~ off, annuler. ~ out (to), appeler. ~ on, (visit) passer chez; (appeal to) faire appel à. ~ up, appeler (au téléphone); (mil.) mobiliser, appeler. ~er n. visiteu|r, -se m., f.; (on phone) personne qui appelle f. ~ing n. vocation f.

callous /'kæləs/ a., ~ly adv. sans pitié. ~ness n. manque de pitié m.

callow /'kæləʊ/ a. (-er, -est) inexpérimenté.

calm /kɑ:m/ a. (-er, -est) calme. —n. calme m. —v.t./i. ~ (down), (se) calmer. ~ness n. calme m.

calorie /'kælərɪ/ n. calorie f.

camber /'kæmbə(r)/ n. (of road) bombement m.

camcorder /'kæmkɔ:də(r)/ n. caméscope m.

came /keɪm/ see come.

camel /'kæml/ n. chameau m.

cameo /'kæmɪəʊ/ n. (pl. -os) camée m.

camera /'kæmərə/ n. appareil (-photo) m.; (for moving pictures) caméra f. in ~, à huis clos. ~man n. (pl. -men) caméraman m.

camouflage /'kæməflɑ:ʒ/ n. camouflage m. —v.t. camoufler.

camp[1] /kæmp/ n. camp m. —v.i. camper. ~-bed n. lit de camp m. ~er n. campeu|r, -se m., f. ~er (-van), camping-car m. ~ing n. camping m.

camp[2] /kæmp/ a. (mannered) affecté; (vulgar) de mauvais goût.

campaign /kæm'peɪn/ n. campagne f. —v.i. faire campagne.

campsite /'kæmpsaɪt/ n. (for holiday-makers) camping m.

campus /'kæmpəs/ n. (pl. -puses) campus m.

can[1] /kæn/ n. bidon m.; (sealed container for food) boîte f. —v.t. (p.t. canned) mettre en boîte. ~ it!, (Amer., sl.) ferme-la! ~ned music, musique de fond enregistrée f. ~-opener n. ouvre-boîte(s) m.

can[2] /kæn, unstressed kən/ v. aux. (be able to) pouvoir; (know how to) savoir.

Canad|a /'kænədə/ n. Canada m. ~ian /kə'neɪdɪən/ a. & n. canadien(ne) (m. (f.)).

canal /kə'næl/ *n.* canal *m.*

canary /kə'neərɪ/ *n.* canari *m.*

cancel /'kænsl/ *v.t./i.* (*p.t.* **cancelled**) (*call off, revoke*) annuler; (*cross out*) barrer; (*a stamp*) oblitérer. ~ **out**, (*fig.*) neutraliser. ~**lation** /-ə'leɪʃn/ *n.* annulation *f.*; oblitération *f.*

cancer /'kænsə(r)/ *n.* cancer *m.* ~**ous** *a.* cancéreux.

Cancer /'kænsə(r)/ *n.* le Cancer.

candid /'kændɪd/ *a.* franc. ~**ness** *n.* franchise *f.*

candida|te /'kændɪdeɪt/ *n.* candidat(e) *m.* (*f.*). ~**cy** /-əsɪ/ *n.* candidature *f.*

candle /'kændl/ *n.* bougie *f.*, chandelle *f.*; (*in church*) cierge *m.*

candlestick /'kændlstɪk/ *n.* bougeoir *m.*, chandelier *m.*

candour, (*Amer.*) **candor** /'kændə(r)/ *n.* franchise *f.*

candy /'kændɪ/ *n.* (*Amer.*) bonbon(s) *m.* (*pl.*). ~**-floss** *n.* barbe à papa *f.*

cane /keɪn/ *n.* canne *f.*; (*for baskets*) rotin *m.*; (*for punishment: schol.*) baguette *f.*, bâton *m.* —*v.t.* donner des coups de baguette or de bâton à, fustiger.

canine /'keɪnaɪn/ *a.* canin.

canister /'kænɪstə(r)/ *n.* boîte *f.*

cannabis /'kænəbɪs/ *n.* cannabis *m.*

cannibal /'kænɪbl/ *n.* cannibale *m./f.* ~**ism** *n.* cannibalisme *m.*

cannon /'kænən/ *n.* (*pl.* ~ *or* ~**s**) canon *m.* ~**-ball** *n.* boulet de canon *m.*

cannot /'kænət/ = **can not.**

canny /'kænɪ/ *a.* rusé, madré.

canoe /kə'nuː/ *n.* (*sport*) canoë *m.*, kayak *m.* —*v.i.* faire du canoë or du kayak. ~**ist** *n.* canoëiste *m./f.*

canon /'kænən/ *n.* (*clergyman*) chanoine *m.*; (*rule*) canon *m.*

canonize /'kænənaɪz/ *v.t.* canoniser.

canopy /'kænəpɪ/ *n.* dais *m.*; (*over doorway*) marquise *f.*

can't /kɑːnt/ = **can not.**

cantankerous /kæn'tæŋkərəs/ *a.* acariâtre, grincheux.

canteen /kæn'tiːn/ *n.* (*restaurant*) cantine *f.*; (*flask*) bidon *m.*

canter /'kæntə(r)/ *n.* petit galop *m.* —*v.i.* aller au petit galop.

canvas /'kænvəs/ *n.* toile *f.*

canvass /'kænvəs/ *v.t./i.* (*comm., pol.*) solliciter des commandes or des voix (de). ~**ing** *n.* (*comm.*) démarchage *m.*; (*pol.*) démarchage électoral *m.* ~ **opinion**, sonder l'opinion.

canyon /'kænjən/ *n.* cañon *m.*

cap /kæp/ *n.* (*hat*) casquette *f.*; (*of bottle, tube*) bouchon *m.*; (*of beer or milk bottle*) capsule *f.*; (*of pen*) capuchon *m.*; (*for toy gun*) amorce *f.* —*v.t.* (*p.t.* **capped**) (*bottle*) capsuler; (*outdo*) surpasser. ~**ped with,** coiffé de.

capab|le /'keɪpəbl/ *a.* (*person*) capable (**of, de**), compétent. **be** ~**le of,** (*of situation, text, etc.*) être susceptible de. ~**ility** /-'bɪlətɪ/ *n.* capacité *f.* ~**ly** *adv.* avec compétence.

capacity /kə'pæsətɪ/ *n.* capacité *f.* **in one's** ~ **as,** en sa qualité de.

cape[1] /keɪp/ *n.* (*cloak*) cape *f.*

cape[2] /keɪp/ *n.* (*geog.*) cap *m.*

caper[1] /'keɪpə(r)/ *v.i.* gambader. —*n.* (*prank*) farce *f.*; (*activity: sl.*) affaire *f.*

caper[2] /'keɪpə(r)/ *n.* (*culin.*) câpre *f.*

capital /'kæpɪtl/ *a.* capital. —*n.* (*town*) capitale *f.*; (*money*) capital *m.* ~ (**letter**), majuscule *f.*

capitalis|t /'kæpɪtəlɪst/ *a. & n.* capitaliste (*m./f.*). ~**m** /-zəm/ *n.* capitalisme *m.*

capitalize /'kæpɪtəlaɪz/ *v.i.* ~ **on,** tirer profit de.

capitulat|e /kə'pɪtʃuleɪt/ *v.i.* capituler. ~**ion** /-'leɪʃn/ *n.* capitulation *f.*

capricious /kəˈprɪʃəs/ a. capricieux.

Capricorn /ˈkæprɪkɔːn/ n. le Capricorne.

capsize /kæpˈsaɪz/ v.t./i. (faire) chavirer.

capsule /ˈkæpsjuːl/ n. capsule f.

captain /ˈkæptɪn/ n. capitaine m.

caption /ˈkæpʃn/ n. (for illustration) légende f.; (heading) soustitre m.

captivate /ˈkæptɪveɪt/ v.t. captiver.

captive /ˈkæptɪv/ a. & n. captif, -ve (m., f.). **~ity** /-ˈtɪvətɪ/ n. captivité f.

capture /ˈkæptʃə(r)/ v.t. (person, animal) prendre, capturer; (attention) retenir. —n. capture f.

car /kɑː(r)/ n. voiture f. **~ ferry**, ferry m. **~-park**, parking m. **~phone**, téléphone de voiture m. **~-wash** n. station de lavage f., lave-auto m.

carafe /kəˈræf/ n. carafe f.

caramel /ˈkærəmel/ n. caramel m.

carat /ˈkærət/ n. carat m.

caravan /ˈkærəvæn/ n. caravane f.

carbohydrate /kɑːbəʊˈhaɪdreɪt/ n. hydrate de carbone m.

carbon /ˈkɑːbən/ n. carbone m. **~ copy**, **~ paper**, carbone m.

carburettor, (Amer.) **carburetor** /kɑːbjʊˈretə(r)/ n. carburateur m.

carcass /ˈkɑːkəs/ n. carcasse f.

card /kɑːd/ n. carte f. **~-index** n. fichier m.

cardboard /ˈkɑːdbɔːd/ n. carton m.

cardiac /ˈkɑːdiæk/ a. cardiaque.

cardigan /ˈkɑːdɪgən/ n. cardigan m.

cardinal /ˈkɑːdɪnl/ a. cardinal. —n. (relig.) cardinal m.

care /keə(r)/ n. (attention) soin m., attention f.; (worry) souci m.; (protection) garde f. —v.i. **~ for**, s'intéresser à. **~ about**, s'occuper de; (invalid) soigner. **~ to** or **for**, aimer, vouloir. **I don't ~**, ça m'est égal. **take ~ of**, s'occuper de. **take ~ (of yourself)**, prends soin de toi. **take ~ to do sth.**, faire bien attention à faire qch.

career /kəˈrɪə(r)/ n. carrière f. —v.i. aller à toute vitesse.

carefree /ˈkeəfriː/ a. insouciant.

careful /ˈkeəfl/ a. soigneux; (cautious) prudent. **(be) ~!**, (fais) attention! **~ly** adv. avec soin.

careless /ˈkeəlɪs/ a. négligent; (work) peu soigné. **~ly** adv. négligemment. **~ness** n. négligence f.

caress /kəˈres/ n. caresse f. —v.t. caresser.

caretaker /ˈkeəteɪkə(r)/ n. gardien(ne) m. (f.). —a. (president) par intérim.

cargo /ˈkɑːgəʊ/ n. (pl. **-oes**) cargaison f. **~ boat**, cargo m.

Caribbean /kærɪˈbiːən/ a. caraïbe. —n. **the ~**, (sea) la mer des Caraïbes; (islands) les Antilles f. pl.

caricature /ˈkærɪkətjʊə(r)/ n. caricature f. —v.t. caricaturer.

caring /ˈkeərɪŋ/ a. (mother, son, etc.) aimant. —n. affection f.

carnage /ˈkɑːnɪdʒ/ n. carnage m.

carnal /ˈkɑːnl/ a. charnel.

carnation /kɑːˈneɪʃn/ n. œillet m.

carnival /ˈkɑːnɪvl/ n. carnaval m.

carol /ˈkærəl/ n. chant (de Noël) m.

carp[1] /kɑːp/ n. invar. carpe f.

carp[2] /kɑːp/ v.i. **~ (at)**, critiquer.

carpenter /ˈkɑːpɪntə(r)/ n. charpentier m.; (for light woodwork, furniture) menuisier m. **~ry** n. charpenterie f.; menuiserie f.

carpet /ˈkɑːpɪt/ n. tapis m. —v.t. (p.t. **carpeted**) recouvrir d'un tapis. **~-sweeper** n. balai mécanique m. **on the ~**, (fam.) sur la sellette.

carriage /'kærɪdʒ/ n. (rail & horse-drawn) voiture f.; (of goods) transport m.; (cost) port m.

carriageway /'kærɪdʒweɪ/ n. chaussée f.

carrier /'kærɪə(r)/ n. transporteur m.; (med.) porteu|r, -se m., f. ~ (**bag**), sac en plastique m.

carrot /'kærət/ n. carotte f.

carry /'kærɪ/ v.t./i. porter; (goods) transporter; (involve) comporter; (motion) voter. **be carried away**, s'emballer. ~**cot** n. porte-bébé m. ~ **off**, enlever; (prize) remporter. ~ **on**, continuer; (behave fam.) se conduire (mal). ~ **out**, (an order, plan) exécuter; (duty) accomplir; (task) effectuer.

cart /kɑːt/ n. charrette f. —v.t. transporter; (heavy object: sl.) trimballer.

cartilage /'kɑːtɪlɪdʒ/ n. cartilage m.

carton /'kɑːtn/ n. (box) carton m.; (of yoghurt, cream) pot m.; (of cigarettes) cartouche f.

cartoon /kɑː'tuːn/ n. dessin (humoristique) m.; (cinema) dessin animé m. ~**ist** n. dessina|teur, -trice m., f.

cartridge /'kɑːtrɪdʒ/ n. cartouche f.

carve /kɑːv/ v.t. tailler; (meat) découper.

cascade /kæs'keɪd/ n. cascade f. —v.i. tomber en cascade.

case¹ /keɪs/ n. cas m.; (jurid.) affaire f.; (phil.) arguments m. pl. **in ~ he comes**, au cas où il viendrait. **in ~ of fire**, en cas d'incendie. **in ~ of any problems**, au cas où il y aurait un problème. **in that ~**, à ce moment-là.

case² /keɪs/ n. (crate) caisse f.; (for camera, cigarettes, spectacles, etc.) étui m.; (suitcase) valise f.

cash /kæʃ/ n. argent m. —a. (price etc.) (au) comptant. —v.t. en-

caisser. ~ **a cheque**, (person) encaisser un chèque; (bank) payer un chèque. **pay ~**, payer comptant. **in ~**, en espèces. ~ **desk**, caisse f. ~ **dispenser**, distributeur de billets m. ~**flow** n. cash-flow m. ~ **in (on)**, profiter (de). ~ **register**, caisse enregistreuse f.

cashew /'kæʃuː/ n. noix de cajou f.

cashier /kæ'ʃɪə(r)/ n. caiss|ier, -ière m., f.

cashmere /'kæʃmɪə(r)/ n. cachemire m.

casino /kə'siːnəʊ/ n. (pl. -os) casino m.

cask /kɑːsk/ n. tonneau m.

casket /'kɑːskɪt/ n. (box) coffret m.; (coffin: Amer.) cercueil m.

casserole /'kæsərəʊl/ n. (utensil) cocotte f.; (stew) daube f.

cassette /kə'set/ n. cassette f.

cast /kɑːst/ v.t. (p.t. **cast**) (throw) jeter; (glance, look) jeter; (shadow) projeter; (vote) donner; (metal) couler. ~ (**off**), (shed) se dépouiller de. —n. (theatre) distribution f.; (of dice) coup m.; (mould) moule m.; (med.) plâtre m. ~ **iron**, fonte f. ~**-iron** a. de fonte; (fig.) solide. ~**-offs** n. pl. vieux vêtements m. pl.

castanets /kæstə'nets/ n. pl. castagnettes f. pl.

castaway /'kɑːstəweɪ/ n. naufragé(e) m. (f.).

caste /kɑːst/ n. caste f.

castle /'kɑːsl/ n. château m.; (chess) tour f.

castor /'kɑːstə(r)/ n. (wheel) roulette f. ~ **sugar**, sucre en poudre m.

castrat|e /kæ'streɪt/ v.t. châtrer. ~**ion** /-ʃn/ n. castration f.

casual /'kæʒʊəl/ a. (remark) fait au hasard; (meeting) fortuit; (attitude) désinvolte; (work) temporaire; (clothes) sport invar.

~ly adv. par hasard; (*carelessly*) avec désinvolture.

casualty /'kæʒʊəltɪ/ n. (*dead*) mort(e) m. (f.); (*injured*) blessé(e) m. (f.); (*accident victim*) accidenté(e) m. (f.).

cat /kæt/ n. chat m. **C~s-eyes** n. pl. (P.) catadioptres m. pl.

catalogue /'kætəlɒg/ n. catalogue m. —v.t. cataloguer.

catalyst /'kætəlɪst/ n. catalyseur m.

catapult /'kætəpʌlt/ n. lance-pierres m. invar. —v.t. catapulter.

cataract /'kætərækt/ n. (*waterfall & med.*) cataracte f.

catarrh /kə'tɑː(r)/ n. rhume m., catarrhe m.

catastroph|e /kə'tæstrəfɪ/ n. catastrophe f. **~ic** /kætə'strɒfɪk/ a. catastrophique.

catch /kætʃ/ v.t. (*p.t.* **caught**) attraper; (*grab*) prendre, saisir; (*catch unawares*) surprendre; (*jam, trap*) prendre; (*understand*) saisir. —v.i. prendre; (*get stuck*) se prendre (**in**, dans). —n. capture f., prise f.; (*on door*) loquet m.; (*fig.*) piège m. **~ fire**, prendre feu. **~ on**, (*fam.*) prendre, devenir populaire. **~ out**, prendre en faute. **~-phrase** n. slogan m. **~ sight of**, apercevoir. **~ s.o.'s eye**, attirer l'attention de qn. **~ up**, se rattraper. **~ up (with)**, rattraper.

catching /'kætʃɪŋ/ a. contagieux.

catchment /'kætʃmənt/ n. **~ area**, région desservie f.

catchy /'kætʃɪ/ a. facile à retenir.

categorical /kætɪ'gɒrɪkl/ a. catégorique.

category /'kætɪgərɪ/ n. catégorie f.

cater /'keɪtə(r)/ v.i. s'occuper de la nourriture. **~ for**, (*pander to*) satisfaire; (*of magazine etc.*) s'adresser à. **~er** n. traiteur m.

caterpillar /'kætəpɪlə(r)/ n. chenille f.

cathedral /kə'θiːdrəl/ n. cathédrale f.

catholic /'kæθəlɪk/ a. universel. **C~** a. & n. catholique (m./f.). **C~ism** /kə'θɒlɪsɪzəm/ n. catholicisme m.

cattle /'kætl/ n. pl. bétail m.

catty /'kætɪ/ a. méchant.

caucus /'kɔːkəs/ n. comité électoral m.

caught /kɔːt/ see **catch**.

cauliflower /'kɒlɪflaʊə(r)/ n. chou-fleur m.

cause /kɔːz/ n. cause f.; (*reason*) raison f., motif m. —v.t. causer. **~ sth. to grow/move/etc.**, faire pousser/bouger/etc. qch.

causeway /'kɔːzweɪ/ n. chaussée f.

caution /'kɔːʃn/ n. prudence f.; (*warning*) avertissement m. —v.t. avertir. **~ous** a. prudent. **~ously** adv. prudemment.

cavalier /kævə'lɪə(r)/ a. cavalier.

cavalry /'kævəlrɪ/ n. cavalerie f.

cave /keɪv/ n. caverne f., grotte f. —v.i. **~ in**, s'effondrer; (*agree*) céder.

caveman /'keɪvmæn/ n. (*pl.* **-men**) homme des cavernes m.

cavern /'kævən/ n. caverne f.

caviare, *Amer.* **caviar** /'kævɪɑː(r)/ n. caviar m.

caving /'keɪvɪŋ/ n. spéléologie f.

cavity /'kævətɪ/ n. cavité f.

cavort /kə'vɔːt/ v.i. gambader.

CD /siː'diː/ n. compact disc m.

cease /siːs/ v.t./i. cesser. **~-fire** n. cessez-le-feu m. invar. **~less** a. incessant.

cedar /'siːdə(r)/ n. cèdre m.

cede /siːd/ v.t. céder.

cedilla /sɪ'dɪlə/ n. cédille f.

ceiling /'siːlɪŋ/ n. plafond m.

celebrat|e /'selɪbreɪt/ v.t. (*perform, glorify*) célébrer; (*event*) fêter, célébrer. —v.i. **we shall ~e**, on va fêter ça. **~ion** /-'breɪʃn/ n. fête f.

celebrated /'selɪbreɪtɪd/ a. célèbre.

celebrity /sɪ'lebrətɪ/ n. célébrité f.

celery /'selərɪ/ n. céleri m.

cell /sel/ n. cellule f.; (electr.) élément m.

cellar /'selə(r)/ n. cave f.

cell|o /'tʃeləʊ/ n. (pl. -os) violoncelle m. **~ist** n. violoncelliste m./f.

Cellophane /'seləfeɪn/ n. (P.) cellophane f. (P.).

Celt /kelt/ n. Celte m./f. **~ic** a. celtique, celte.

cement /sɪ'ment/ n. ciment m. —v.t. cimenter. **~-mixer** n. bétonnière f.

cemetery /'semətrɪ/ n. cimetière m.

censor /'sensə(r)/ n. censeur m. —v.t. censurer. **the ~,** la censure. **~ship** n. censure f.

censure /'senʃə(r)/ n. blâme m. —v.t. blâmer.

census /'sensəs/ n. recensement m.

cent /sent/ n. (coin) cent m.

centenary /sen'tiːnərɪ, Amer. 'sentənərɪ/ n. centenaire m.

centigrade /'sentɪgreɪd/ a. centigrade.

centilitre, Amer. **centiliter** /'sentɪliːtə(r)/ n. centilitre m.

centimetre, Amer. **centimeter** /'sentɪmiːtə(r)/ n. centimètre m.

centipede /'sentɪpiːd/ n. millepattes m. invar.

central /'sentrəl/ a. central. **~ heating,** chauffage central m. **~ize** v.t. centraliser. **~ly** adv. (situated) au centre.

centre /'sentə(r)/ n. centre m. —v.t. (p.t. **centred**) centrer. —v.i. **~ on,** tourner autour de.

centrifugal /sen'trɪfjʊgl/ a. centrifuge.

century /'sentʃərɪ/ n. siècle m.

ceramic /sɪ'ræmɪk/ a. (art) céramique. (object) en céramique.

cereal /'sɪərɪəl/ n. céréale f.

cerebral /'serɪbrəl, Amer. sə'riːbrəl/ a. cérébral.

ceremonial /serɪ'məʊnɪəl/ a. de cérémonie. n. cérémonial m.

ceremon|y /'serɪmənɪ/ n. cérémonie f. **~ious** /-'məʊnɪəs/ a. solennel.

certain /'sɜːtn/ a. certain. **for ~,** avec certitude. **make ~ of,** s'assurer de. **~ly** adv. certainement. **~ty** n. certitude f.

certificate /sə'tɪfɪkət/ n. certificat m.

certify /'sɜːtɪfaɪ/ v.t. certifier.

cervical /sɜː'vaɪkl/ a. cervical.

cessation /se'seɪʃn/ n. cessation f.

cesspit, cesspool /'sespɪt, 'sespuːl/ ns. fosse d'aisances f.

chafe /tʃeɪf/ v.t. frotter (contre).

chaff /tʃɑːf/ v.t. taquiner.

chaffinch /'tʃæfɪntʃ/ n. pinson m.

chagrin /'ʃægrɪn/ n. vif dépit m.

chain /tʃeɪn/ n. chaîne f. —v.t. enchaîner. **~ reaction,** réaction en chaîne f. **~-smoke** v.i. fumer de manière ininterrompue. **~ store,** magasin à succursales multiples m.

chair /tʃeə(r)/ n. chaise f.; (armchair) fauteuil m.; (univ.) chaire f. —v.t. (preside over) présider.

chairman /'tʃeəmən/ n. (pl. -men) président(e) m. (f.).

chalet /'ʃæleɪ/ n. chalet m.

chalk /tʃɔːk/ n. craie f. **~y** a. crayeux.

challeng|e /'tʃælɪndʒ/ n. défi m.; (task) gageure f. —v.t. (summon) défier (to do, de faire); (question truth of) contester. **~er** n. (sport) challenger m. **~ing** a. stimulant.

chamber /'tʃeɪmbə(r)/ n. (old use) chambre f. **~ music,** musique de chambre f. **~-pot** n. pot de chambre m.

chambermaid /'tʃeɪmbəmeɪd/ n. femme de chambre f.

chamois /ˈʃæmɪ/ *n.* ~(-leather), peau de chamois *f.*

champagne /ʃæmˈpeɪn/ *n.* champagne *m.*

champion /ˈtʃæmpɪən/ *n.* champion(ne) *m. (f.).* —*v.t.* défendre. ~ship *n.* championnat *m.*

chance /tʃɑːns/ *n.* (*luck*) hasard *m.;* (*opportunity*) occasion *f.;* (*likelihood*) chances *f. pl.;* (*risk*) risque *m.* —*a.* fortuit. —*v.t.* ~ **doing,** prendre le risque de faire. ~ **it,** risquer le coup. **by** ~, par hasard. **by any** ~, par hasard. ~**s are that,** il est probable que.

chancellor /ˈtʃɑːnsələ(r)/ *n.* chancelier *m.* **C~ of the Exchequer,** Chancelier de l'Échiquier.

chancy /ˈtʃɑːnsɪ/ *a.* risqué.

chandelier /ʃændəˈlɪə(r)/ *n.* lustre *m.*

change /tʃeɪndʒ/ *v.t.* (*alter*) changer; (*exchange*) échanger (*for,* contre); (*money*) changer (*into,* en); (*exchange,* transpose) changer de; (*clothes*) changer. **~trains/one's dress/***etc.,* (*by substitution*) changer de train/de robe/*etc.* —*v.i.* changer; (*change clothes*) se changer. —*n.* changement *m.;* (*money*) monnaie *f.* **a ~ for the better,** une amélioration. **a ~ for the worse,** un changement en pire. ~ **into,** se transformer en; (*clothes*) mettre. **a ~ of clothes,** des vêtements de rechange. ~ **one's mind,** changer d'avis. ~ **over,** passer (**to,** à). **for a** ~, pour changer. ~**over** *n.* passage *m.* ~**able** *a.* changeant; (*weather*) variable. ~**ing** *a.* changeant. ~**ing room,** (*in shop*) cabine d'essayage; (*sport.*) vestiaire *m.*

channel /ˈtʃænl/ *n.* chenal *m.;* (*TV*) chaîne *f.;* (*medium, agency*) canal *m.;* (*groove*) rainure *f.* —*v.t.* (*p.t.* **channelled**) (*direct*) canaliser. **the (English) C~,** la Manche. **the C~ Islands,** les îles anglo-normandes *f. pl.*

chant /tʃɑːnt/ *n.* (*relig.*) psalmodie *f.;* (*of demonstrators*) chant (scandé) *m.* —*v.t./i.* psalmodier; (*demonstrators*) scander (des slogans).

chao|s /ˈkeɪɒs/ *n.* chaos *m.* ~**tic** /-ˈɒtɪk/ *a.* chaotique.

chap /tʃæp/ *n.* (*man: fam.*) type *m.*

chapel /ˈtʃæpl/ *n.* chapelle *f.;* (*Nonconformist*) église (nonconformiste) *f.*

chaperon /ˈʃæpərəʊn/ *n.* chaperon *m.* —*v.t.* chaperonner.

chaplain /ˈtʃæplɪn/ *n.* aumônier *m.*

chapped /tʃæpt/ *a.* gercé.

chapter /ˈtʃæptə(r)/ *n.* chapitre *m.*

char¹ /tʃɑː(r)/ *n.* (*fam.*) femme de ménage *f.*

char² /tʃɑː(r)/ *v.t.* (*p.t.* **charred**) carboniser.

character /ˈkærəktə(r)/ *n.* caractère *m.;* (*in novel, play*) personnage *m.* **of good** ~, de bonne réputation. ~**ize** *v.t.* caractériser.

characteristic /kærəktəˈrɪstɪk/ *a. & n.* caractéristique (*f.*). ~**ally** *adv.* typiquement.

charade /ʃəˈrɑːd/ *n.* charade *f.*

charcoal /ˈtʃɑːkəʊl/ *n.* charbon (de bois) *m.*

charge /tʃɑːdʒ/ *n.* prix *m.;* (*mil.*) charge *f.;* (*jurid.*) inculpation *f.,* accusation *f.;* (*task, custody*) charge *f.* ~**s,** frais *m. pl.* —*v.t.* faire payer; (*ask*) demander (**for,** pour); (*enemy, gun*) charger; (*jurid.*) inculper, accuser (**with,** de). —*v.i.* foncer, se précipiter. ~ **card,** carte d'achat *f.* ~ **it to my account,** mettez-le sur mon compte. **in** ~ **of,** responsable de. **take** ~ **of,** prendre en charge, se charger de. ~**able to,** (*comm.*) aux frais de.

charisma /kəˈrɪzmə/ *n.* magnétisme *m.* ~**tic** /kærɪzˈmætɪk/ *a.* charismatique.

charit|y /ˈtʃærətɪ/ *n.* charité *f.;*

(*society*) fondation charitable *f.* **~able** *a.* charitable.

charlatan /'ʃɑːlətən/ *n.* charlatan *m.*

charm /tʃɑːm/ *n.* charme *m.*; (*trinket*) amulette *f.* —*v.t.* charmer. **~ing** *a.* charmant.

chart /tʃɑːt/ *n.* (*naut.*) carte (*marine*) *f.*; (*table*) tableau *m.*, graphique *m.* —*v.t.* (*route*) porter sur la carte.

charter /'tʃɑːtə(r)/ *n.* charte *f.* ~ **(flight)**, charter *m.* —*v.t.* affréter. **~ed accountant,** expert-comptable *m.*

charwoman /'tʃɑːwʊmən/ *n.* (*pl.* **-women**) femme de ménage *f.*

chase /tʃeɪs/ *v.t.* poursuivre. —*v.i.* courir (*after,* après). —*n.* chasse *f.* ~ **away** *or* **off,** chasser.

chasm /'kæzəm/ *n.* abîme *m.*

chassis /'ʃæsɪ/ *n.* châssis *m.*

chaste /tʃeɪst/ *a.* chaste.

chastise /tʃæ'staɪz/ *v.t.* châtier.

chastity /'tʃæstətɪ/ *n.* chasteté *f.*

chat /tʃæt/ *n.* causette *f.* —*v.i.* (*p.t.* **chatted**) bavarder. **have a ~,** bavarder. **~ show,** talk-show *m.* ~ **up,** (*fam.*) draguer. **~ty** *a.* bavard.

chatter /'tʃætə(r)/ *n.* bavardage *m.* —*v.i.* bavarder. **his teeth are ~ing,** il claque des dents.

chatterbox /'tʃætəbɒks/ *n.* bavard(e) *m.* (*f.*).

chauffeur /'ʃəʊfə(r)/ *n.* chauffeur (de particulier) *m.*

chauvinis|t /'ʃəʊvɪnɪst/ *n.* chauvin(e) *m.* (*f.*). **male ~t,** (*pej.*) phallocrate *m.* **~m** /-zəm/ *n.* chauvinisme *m.*

cheap /tʃiːp/ *a.* (**-er, -est**) bon marché *invar.* (*fare, rate*) réduit; (*worthless*) sans valeur. **~er,** meilleur marché *invar.* **~(ly)** *adv.* à bon marché. **~ness** *n.* bas prix *m.*

cheapen /'tʃiːpən/ *v.t.* déprécier.

cheat /tʃiːt/ *v.i.* tricher; (*by fraud*) frauder. —*v.t.* (*defraud*) frauder; (*deceive*) tromper. —*n.* escroc *m.*

check[1] /tʃek/ *v.t./i.* vérifier; (*tickets*) contrôler; (*stop*) enrayer, arrêter; (*restrain*) contenir; (*rebuke*) réprimander; (*tick off:* *Amer.*) cocher. —*n.* vérification *f.*; contrôle *m.*; (*curb*) frein *m.*; (*chess*) échec *m.*; (*bill:* *Amer.*) addition *f.*; (*cheque:* *Amer.*) chèque *m.* ~ **in,** signer le registre; (*at airport*) passer à l'enregistrement. **~in** *n.* enregistrement *m.* **~-list** *n.* liste récapitulative *f.* ~ **out,** régler sa note. **~-out** *n.* caisse *f.* **~-point** *n.* contrôle *m.* ~ **up,** vérifier. ~ **up on,** (*detail*) vérifier; (*situation*) s'informer sur. **~-up** *n.* examen médical *m.*

check[2] /tʃek/ *n.* (*pattern*) carreaux *m. pl.* **~ed** *a.* à carreaux.

checking /'tʃekɪŋ/ *a.* ~ **account,** (*Amer.*) compte courant *m.*

checkmate /'tʃekmeɪt/ *n.* échec et mat *m.*

checkroom /'tʃekrʊm/ *n.* (*Amer.*) vestiaire *m.*

cheek /tʃiːk/ *n.* joue *f.*; (*impudence*) culot *m.* **~y** *a.* effronté.

cheer /tʃɪə(r)/ *n.* gaieté *f.* **~s,** acclamations *f. pl.*; (*when drinking*) à votre santé. —*v.t.* acclamer, applaudir. ~ **(up),** (*gladden*) remonter le moral à. ~ **up,** prendre courage. **~ful** *a.* gai. **~fulness** *n.* gaieté *f.*

cheerio /tʃɪərɪ'əʊ/ *int.* (*fam.*) salut.

cheese /tʃiːz/ *n.* fromage *m.*

cheetah /'tʃiːtə/ *n.* guépard *m.*

chef /ʃef/ *n.* (*cook*) chef *m.*

chemical /'kemɪkl/ *a.* chimique. —*n.* produit chimique *m.*

chemist /'kemɪst/ *n.* pharmacien(ne) *m.* (*f.*); (*scientist*) chimiste *m./f.* **~'s shop,** pharmacie *f.* **~ry** *n.* chimie *f.*

cheque /tʃek/ n. chèque m. ∼**book** n. chéquier m. ∼ **card**, carte bancaire f.

chequered /ˈtʃekəd/ a. (pattern) à carreaux; (fig.) mouvementé.

cherish /ˈtʃerɪʃ/ v.t. chérir; (hope) nourrir, caresser.

cherry /ˈtʃerɪ/ n. cerise f.

chess /tʃes/ n. échecs m. pl. ∼**board** n. échiquier m.

chest /tʃest/ n. (anat.) poitrine f.; (box) coffre m. ∼ **of drawers**, commode f.

chestnut /ˈtʃesnʌt/ n. châtaigne f.; (edible) marron m. châtaigne f.

chew /tʃuː/ v.t. mâcher. ∼**ing-gum** n. chewing-gum m.

chic /ʃiːk/ a. chic invar.

chick /tʃɪk/ n. poussin m.

chicken /ˈtʃɪkɪn/ n. poulet m. —a. (sl.) froussard. —v.i. ∼ **out**, (sl.) se dégonfler. ∼**pox** n. varicelle f.

chick-pea /ˈtʃɪkpiː/ n. pois chiche m.

chicory /ˈtʃɪkərɪ/ n. (for salad) endive f.; (in coffee) chicorée f.

chief /tʃiːf/ n. chef m. —a. principal. ∼**ly** adv. principalement.

chilblain /ˈtʃɪlbleɪn/ n. engelure f.

child /tʃaɪld/ n. (pl. **children** /ˈtʃɪldrən/) enfant m./f. ∼**hood** n. enfance f. ∼**ish** a. enfantin. ∼**less** a. sans enfants. ∼**like** a. innocent, candide. ∼**minder** n. nourrice f.

childbirth /ˈtʃaɪldbɜːθ/ n. accouchement m.

Chile /ˈtʃɪlɪ/ n. Chili m. ∼**an** a. & n. chilien(ne) (m. (f.)).

chill /tʃɪl/ n. froid m.; (med.) refroidissement m. —a. froid. —v.t. (person) donner froid à; (wine) rafraîchir; (food) mettre au frais. ∼**y** a. froid; (sensitive to cold) frileux. **be** or **feel** ∼**y**, avoir froid.

chilli /ˈtʃɪlɪ/ n. (pl. **-ies**) piment m.

chime /tʃaɪm/ n. carillon m. —v.t./i. carillonner.

chimney /ˈtʃɪmnɪ/ n. cheminée f. ∼**sweep** n. ramoneur m.

chimpanzee /tʃɪmpænˈziː/ n. chimpanzé m.

chin /tʃɪn/ n. menton m.

china /ˈtʃaɪnə/ n. porcelaine f.

Chin|**a** /ˈtʃaɪnə/ n. Chine f. ∼**ese** /-ˈniːz/ a. & n. chinois(e) (m. (f.)).

chink[1] /tʃɪŋk/ n. (slit) fente f.

chink[2] /tʃɪŋk/ n. tintement m. —v.t./i. (faire) tinter.

chip /tʃɪp/ n. (on plate etc.) ébréchure f.; (piece) éclat m.; (of wood) copeau m.; (culin.) frite f.; (microchip) microplaquette f., puce f. —v.t./i. (p.t. **chipped**) (s')ébrécher. ∼ **in**, (fam.) dire son mot; (with money: fam.) contribuer. (potato) ∼**s**, (Amer.) chips m. pl.

chipboard /ˈtʃɪpbɔːd/ n. aggloméré m.

chiropodist /kɪˈrɒpədɪst/ n. pédicure m./f.

chirp /tʃɜːp/ n. pépiement m. —v.i. pépier.

chirpy /ˈtʃɜːpɪ/ a. gai.

chisel /ˈtʃɪzl/ n. ciseau m. —v.t (p.t. **chiselled**) ciseler.

chit /tʃɪt/ n. note f., mot m.

chit-chat /ˈtʃɪttʃæt/ n. bavardage m.

chivalr|**y** /ˈʃɪvlrɪ/ n. galanterie f. ∼**ous** a. chevaleresque.

chives /tʃaɪvz/ n. pl. ciboulette f.

chlorine /ˈklɔːriːn/ n. chlore m.

choc-ice /ˈtʃɒkaɪs/ n. esquimau m.

chock /tʃɒk/ n. cale f. ∼**-a-block**, ∼**-full** adjs. archiplein.

chocolate /ˈtʃɒklət/ n. chocolat m.

choice /tʃɔɪs/ n. choix m. —a. de choix.

choir /ˈkwaɪə(r)/ n. chœur m.

choirboy /ˈkwaɪəbɔɪ/ n. jeune choriste m.

choke /tʃəʊk/ v.t./i. (s')étrangler. —n. starter m. ~ (up), boucher.

cholera /'kɒlərə/ n. choléra m.

cholesterol /kə'lestərɒl/ n. cholestérol m.

choose /tʃuːz/ v.t./i. (p.t. chose, p.p. chosen) choisir. ~ to do, décider de faire.

choosy /'tʃuːzɪ/ a. (fam.) exigeant.

chop /tʃɒp/ v.t./i. (p.t. chopped) (wood) couper (à la hache); (food) hacher. —n. (meat) côtelette f. ~ down, abattre. ~per n. hachoir m.; (sl.) hélicoptère m. ~ping-board n. planche à découper f.

choppy /'tʃɒpɪ/ a. (sea) agité.

chopstick /'tʃɒpstɪk/ n. baguette f.

choral /'kɔːrəl/ a. choral.

chord /kɔːd/ n. (mus.) accord m.

chore /tʃɔː(r)/ n. travail (routinier) m.; (unpleasant task) corvée f.

choreography /kɒrɪ'ɒgrəfɪ/ n. chorégraphie f.

chortle /'tʃɔːtl/ n. gloussement m. —v.i. glousser.

chorus /'kɔːrəs/ n. chœur m.; (of song) refrain m.

chose, chosen /tʃəʊz, 'tʃəʊzn/ see choose.

Christ /kraɪst/ n. le Christ m.

christen /'krɪsn/ v.t. baptiser. ~ing n. baptême m.

Christian /'krɪstʃən/ a. & n. chrétien(ne) (m. (f.)). ~ name, prénom m. ~ity /-stɪ'ænətɪ/ n. christianisme m.

Christmas /'krɪsməs/ n. Noël m. —a. (card, tree, etc.) de Noël. ~-box n. étrennes f. pl. ~ Day/Eve, le jour/la veille de Noël.

chrome /krəʊm/ n. chrome m.

chromium /'krəʊmɪəm/ n. chrome m.

chromosome /'krəʊməsəʊm/ n. chromosome m.

chronic /'krɒnɪk/ a. (situation, disease) chronique (bad: fam.) affreux.

chronicle /'krɒnɪkl/ n. chronique f.

chronology /krə'nɒlədʒɪ/ n. chronologie f. ~ical /krɒnə'lɒdʒɪkl/ a. chronologique.

chrysanthemum /krɪ'sænθəməm/ n. chrysanthème m.

chubby /'tʃʌbɪ/ a. (-ier, -iest) dodu, potelé.

chuck /tʃʌk/ v.t. (fam.) lancer. ~ away or out, (fam.) balancer.

chuckle /'tʃʌkl/ n. gloussement m. —v.i. glousser, rire.

chuffed /tʃʌft/ a. (sl.) bien content.

chum /tʃʌm/ n. cop|ain, -ine m., f. ~my a. amical. ~my with, copain avec.

chunk /tʃʌŋk/ n. (gros) morceau m.

chunky /'tʃʌŋkɪ/ a. trapu.

church /tʃɜːtʃ/ n. église f.

churchyard /'tʃɜːtʃjɑːd/ n. cimetière m.

churlish /'tʃɜːlɪʃ/ a. grossier.

churn /tʃɜːn/ n. baratte f.; (milk-can) bidon m. —v.t. baratter. ~ out, produire (en série).

chute /ʃuːt/ n. glissière f.; (for rubbish) vide-ordures m. invar.

chutney /'tʃʌtnɪ/ n. condiment (de fruits) m.

cider /'saɪdə(r)/ n. cidre m.

cigar /sɪ'gɑː(r)/ n. cigare m.

cigarette /sɪgə'ret/ n. cigarette f. ~ end, mégot m. ~-holder n. fume-cigarette m. invar.

cinder /'sɪndə(r)/ n. cendre f.

cine-camera /'sɪnɪkæmərə/ n. caméra f.

cinema /'sɪnəmə/ n. cinéma m.

cinnamon /'sɪnəmən/ n. cannelle f.

cipher /'saɪfə(r)/ n. (numeral, code) chiffre m.; (person) nullité f.

circle /'sɜːkl/ n. cercle m.; (theatre) balcon m. —v.t. (go round) faire le tour de; (word, error, etc.) entourer d'un cercle. —v.i. décrire des cercles.

circuit /'sɜ:kɪt/ *n.* circuit *m.* **~-breaker** *n.* disjoncteur *m.*

circuitous /sɜ:'kju:ɪtəs/ *a.* indirect.

circular /'sɜ:kjʊlə(r)/ *a. & n.* circulaire (*f.*).

circulat|e /'sɜ:kjʊleɪt/ *v.t./i.* (faire) circuler. **~ion** /-'leɪʃn/ *n.* circulation *f.*; (*of newspaper*) tirage *m.*

circumcis|e /'sɜ:kəmsaɪz/ *v.t.* circoncire. **~ion** /-'sɪʒn/ *n.* circoncision *f.*

circumference /sɜ:'kʌmfərəns/ *n.* circonférence *f.*

circumflex /'sɜ:kəmfleks/ *n.* circonflexe *m.*

circumspect /'sɜ:kəmspekt/ *a.* circonspect.

circumstance /'sɜ:kəmstəns/ *n.* circonstance *f.* **~s**, (*financial*) situation financière *f.*

circus /'sɜ:kəs/ *n.* cirque *m.*

cistern /'sɪstən/ *n.* réservoir *m.*

citadel /'sɪtədel/ *n.* citadelle *f.*

cit|e /saɪt/ *v.t.* citer. **~ation** /-'teɪʃn/ *n.* citation *f.*

citizen /'sɪtɪzn/ *n.* citoyen(ne) *m.* (*f.*); (*of town*) habitant(e) *m.* (*f.*). **~ship** *n.* citoyenneté *f.*

citrus /'sɪtrəs/ *a.* **~ fruit(s)**, agrumes *m. pl.*

city /'sɪtɪ/ *n.* (grande) ville *f.* **the C~**, la Cité de Londres.

civic /'sɪvɪk/ *a.* civique. **~ centre**, centre administratif *m.* **~s** *n. pl.* instruction civique *f.*

civil /'sɪvl/ *a.* civil; (*rights*) civique; (*defence*) passif. **~ engineer**, ingénieur civil *m.* **C~ Servant**, fonctionnaire *m./f.* **C~ Service**, fonction publique *f.* **~ war**, guerre civile *f.* **~ity** /sɪ'vɪlətɪ/ *n.* civilité *f.*

civilian /sɪ'vɪlɪən/ *a. & n.* civil(e) (*m.* (*f.*)).

civiliz|e /'sɪvɪlaɪz/ *v.t.* civiliser. **~ation** /-'zeɪʃn/ *n.* civilisation *f.*

civvies /'sɪvɪz/ *n. pl.* **in ~**, (*sl.*) en civil.

clad /klæd/ *a.* **~ in**, vêtu de.

claim /kleɪm/ *v.t.* revendiquer, réclamer; (*assert*) prétendre. —*n.* revendication *f.*, prétention *f.*; (*assertion*) affirmation *f.*; (*for insurance*) réclamation *f.*; (*right*) droit *m.*

claimant /'kleɪmənt/ *n.* (*of social benefits*) demandeur *m.*

clairvoyant /kleə'vɔɪənt/ *n.* voyant(e) *m.* (*f.*).

clam /klæm/ *n.* palourde *f.*

clamber /'klæmbə(r)/ *v.i.* grimper.

clammy /'klæmɪ/ *a.* (**-ier, -iest**) moite.

clamour /'klæmə(r)/ *n.* clameur *f.*, cris *m. pl.* —*v.i.* **~ for**, demander à grands cris.

clamp /klæmp/ *n.* agrafe *f.*; (*large*) crampon *m.*; (*for carpentry*) serre-joint(s) *m.*; (*for car*) sabot de Denver *m.* —*v.t.* serrer; (*car*) mettre un sabot de Denver à. **~ down on**, sévir contre.

clan /klæn/ *n.* clan *m.*

clandestine /klæn'destɪn/ *a.* clandestin.

clang /klæŋ/ *n.* son métallique *m.*

clanger /'klæŋə(r)/ *n.* (*sl.*) bévue *f.*

clap /klæp/ *v.t./i.* (*p.t.* **clapped**) applaudir; (*put forcibly*) mettre. —*n.* applaudissement *m.*; (*of thunder*) coup *m.* **~ one's hands**, battre des mains.

claptrap /'klæptræp/ *n.* baratin *m.*

claret /'klærət/ *n.* bordeaux rouge *m.*

clarif|y /'klærɪfaɪ/ *v.t./i.* (se) clarifier. **~ication** /-ɪ'keɪʃn/ *n.* clarification *f.*

clarinet /klærɪ'net/ *n.* clarinette *f.*

clarity /'klærətɪ/ *n.* clarté *f.*

clash /klæʃ/ *n.* choc *m.*; (*fig.*) conflit *m.* —*v.i.* (*metal objects*) s'entrechoquer; (*fig.*) se heurter.

clasp /klɑ:sp/ *n.* (*fastener*) fermoir *m.*, agrafe *f.* —*v.t.* serrer.

class /klɑːs/ *n.* classe *f.* –*v.t.* classer.

classic /'klæsɪk/ *a.* & *n.* classique (*m.*). ∼s, (*univ.*) les humanités *f. pl.* ∼al *a.* classique.

classif|y /'klæsɪfaɪ/ *v.t.* classifier. ∼**ication** -ɪ'keɪʃn/ *n.* classification *f.* ∼**ied** *a.* (*information etc.*) secret. ∼**ied advertisement**, petite annonce *f.*

classroom /'klɑːsrʊm/ *n.* salle de classe *f.*

classy /'klɑːsɪ/ *a.* (*sl.*) chic *invar.*

clatter /'klætə(r)/ *n.* cliquetis *m.* –*v.i.* cliqueter.

clause /klɔːz/ *n.* clause *f.*; (*gram.*) proposition *f.*

claustrophob|ia /klɔːstrə'fəʊbɪə/ *n.* claustrophobie *f.* ∼**ic** *a.* & *n.* claustrophobe (*m./f.*).

claw /klɔː/ *n.* (*of animal, small bird*) griffe *f.*; (*of bird of prey*) serre *f.*; (*of lobster*) pince *f.* –*v.t.* griffer.

clay /kleɪ/ *n.* argile *f.*

clean /kliːn/ *a.* (-**er**, -**est**) propre; (*shape, stroke, etc.*) net. –*adv.* complètement. –*v.t.* nettoyer. –*v.i.* ∼ **up**, faire le nettoyage. **one's teeth**, se brosser les dents. ∼**-shaven** *a.* glabre. ∼**er** *n.* (*at home*) femme de ménage *f.*; (*industrial*) agent de nettoyage *m./f.*; (*of clothes*) teintur|ier, -ière *m.*, *f.* ∼**ly** *adv.* proprement; (*sharply*) nettement.

cleanliness /'klenlɪnɪs/ *n.* propreté *f.*

cleans|e /klenz/ *v.t.* nettoyer; (*fig.*) purifier. ∼**ing cream**, crème démaquillante *f.*

clear /klɪə(r)/ *a.* (-**er**, -**est**) clair; (*glass*) transparent; (*profit*) net; (*road*) dégagé. –*adv.* complètement. –*v.t.* (*free*) dégager (**of**, **de**); (*table*) débarrasser; (*building*) évacuer; (*cheque*) encaisser; (*jump over*) franchir; (*debt*) liquider; (*jurid.*) disculper. ∼

(*away or* off), (*remove*) enlever. –*v.i.* (*fog*) se dissiper. ∼ **of**, (*away from*) à l'écart de. ∼ **off** *or* **out**, (*sl.*) décamper. ∼ **out**, (*clean*) nettoyer. ∼ **up**, (*tidy*) ranger; (*mystery*) éclaircir; (*of weather*) s'éclaircir. **make sth.** ∼, être très clair sur qch. ∼**-cut** *a.* net. ∼**ly** *adv.* clairement.

clearance /'klɪərəns/ *n.* (*permission*) autorisation *f.*; (*space*) dégagement *m.* ∼ **sale**, liquidation *f.*

clearing /'klɪərɪŋ/ *n.* clairière *f.*

clearway /'klɪəweɪ/ *n.* route à stationnement interdit *f.*

cleavage /'kliːvɪdʒ/ *n.* clivage *m.*; (*breasts*) décolleté *m.*

clef /klef/ *n.* (*mus.*) clé *f.*

cleft /kleft/ *n.* fissure *f.*

clemen|t /'klemənt/ *a.* clément. ∼**cy** *n.* clémence *f.*

clench /klentʃ/ *v.t.* serrer.

clergy /'klɜːdʒɪ/ *n.* clergé *m.* ∼**man** *n.* (*pl.* -**men**) ecclésiastique *m.*

cleric /'klerɪk/ *n.* clerc *m.* ∼**al** *a.* (*relig.*) clérical; (*of clerks*) de bureau, d'employé.

clerk /klɑːk, *Amer.* klɜːk/ *n.* employé(e) de bureau *m.* (*f.*); (*Amer.*) (*sales*) ∼, vendeu|r, -se *m.*, *f.*

clever /'klevə(r)/ *a.* (-**er**, -**est**) intelligent; (*skilful*) habile. ∼**ly** *adv.* intelligemment; habilement. ∼**ness** *n.* intelligence *f.*

cliché /'kliːʃeɪ/ *n.* cliché *m.*

click /klɪk/ *n.* déclic *m.* –*v.i.* faire un déclic; (*people: sl.*) s'entendre, se plaire. –*v.t.* (*heels, tongue*) faire claquer.

client /'klaɪənt/ *n.* client(e) *m.* (*f.*).

clientele /kliːɑːn'tel/ *n.* clientèle *f.*

cliff /klɪf/ *n.* falaise *f.*

climat|e /'klaɪmɪt/ *n.* climat *m.* ∼**ic** /-'mætɪk/ *a.* climatique.

climax /'klaɪmæks/ *n.* point culminant *m.*; (*sexual*) orgasme *m.*

climb /klaɪm/ v.t. (stairs) monter, grimper; (tree, ladder) monter or grimper à; (mountain) faire l'ascension de. —v.i. monter, grimper. —n. montée f. ~ **down**, (fig.) reculer. ~**down**, n. recul m. ~**er** n. (sport) alpiniste m./f.

clinch /klɪntʃ/ v.t. (a deal) conclure.

cling /klɪŋ/ v.i. (p.t. clung) se cramponner (to, à); (stick) coller. ~**film** n. (P.) film adhésif.

clinic /ˈklɪnɪk/ n. centre médical m.; (private) clinique f.

clinical /ˈklɪnɪkl/ a. clinique.

clink /klɪŋk/ n. tintement m. —v.t./i. (faire) tinter.

clinker /ˈklɪŋkə(r)/ n. mâchefer m.

clip¹ /klɪp/ n. (for paper) trombone m.; (for hair) barrette f.; (for tube) collier m. —v.t. (p.t. clipped) attacher (to, à).

clip² /klɪp/ v.t. (p.t. clipped) (cut) couper. —n. coupe f.; (of film) extrait m.; (blow: fam.) taloche f. ~**ping** n. coupure f.

clippers /ˈklɪpəz/ n. pl. tondeuse f.; (for nails) coupe-ongles m.

clique /kliːk/ n. clique f.

cloak /kləʊk/ n. (grande) cape f., manteau ample m.

cloakroom /ˈkləʊkrʊm/ n. vestiaire m.; (toilet) toilettes f. pl.

clobber /ˈklɒbə(r)/ n. (sl.) affaires f. pl. —v.t. (hit: sl.) rosser.

clock /klɒk/ n. pendule f.; (large) horloge f. —v.i. ~ **in** or **out**, pointer. ~ **up**, (miles etc.: fam.) faire. ~**tower** n. clocher m.

clockwise /ˈklɒkwaɪz/ a. & adv. dans le sens des aiguilles d'une montre.

clockwork /ˈklɒkwɜːk/ n. mécanisme m. —a. mécanique.

clog /klɒg/ n. sabot m. —v.t./i. (p.t. clogged) se boucher.

cloister /ˈklɔɪstə(r)/ n. cloître m.

close¹ /kləʊs/ a. (-er, -est) (near) proche (to, de); (link, collaboration) étroit; (examination) attentif; (friend) intime; (order, match) serré; (weather) lourd. ~ **together**, (crowded) serrés. ~ **by**, ~ **at hand**, tout près. ~**up** n. gros plan m. **have a** ~ **shave**, l'échapper belle. **keep a** ~ **watch on**, surveiller de près. ~**ly** adv. (follow) de près. ~**ness** n. proximité f.

close² /kləʊz/ v.t. fermer. —v.i. se fermer; (of shop etc.) fermer; (end) (se) terminer. —n. fin f. ~**d shop**, organisation qui exclut les travailleurs non syndiqués.

closet /ˈklɒzɪt/ n. (Amer.) placard m.

closure /ˈkləʊʒə(r)/ n. fermeture f.

clot /klɒt/ n. (of blood) caillot m.; (in sauce) grumeau m. —v.t./i. (p.t. clotted) (se) coaguler.

cloth /klɒθ/ n. tissu m.; (duster) linge m.; (table-cloth) nappe f.

clothe /kləʊð/ v.t. vêtir. ~**ing** n. vêtements m. pl.

clothes /kləʊðz/ n. pl. vêtements m. pl., habits m. pl. ~**brush** n. brosse à habits f. ~**hanger** n. cintre m. ~**line** n. corde à linge f. ~**peg**, (Amer.) ~**pin** ns. pince à linge f.

cloud /klaʊd/ n. nuage m. —v.i. se couvrir (de nuages); (become gloomy) s'assombrir. ~**y** a. (sky) couvert; (liquid) trouble.

cloudburst /ˈklaʊdbɜːst/ n. trombe d'eau f.

clout /klaʊt/ n. (blow) coup de poing m.; (power: fam.) pouvoir effectif m. —v.t. frapper.

clove /kləʊv/ n. clou de girofle m. ~ **of garlic**, gousse d'ail f.

clover /ˈkləʊvə(r)/ n. trèfle m.

clown /klaʊn/ n. clown m. —v.i. faire le clown.

cloy /klɔɪ/ v.t. écœurer.

club /klʌb/ n. (group) club m.; (weapon) massue f. ∼s, (cards) trèfle m. —v.t./i. (p.t. clubbed) matraquer. (golf) ∼, club (de golf) m. ∼ together, (share costs) se cotiser.

cluck /klʌk/ v.i. glousser.

clue /kluː/ n. indice m.; (in crossword) définition f. **I haven't a ∼**, (fam.) je n'en ai pas la moindre idée.

clump /klʌmp/ n. massif m.

clumsy /'klʌmzɪ/ a. (-ier, -iest) maladroit; (tool) peu commode. ∼iness n. maladresse f.

clung /klʌŋ/ see cling.

cluster /'klʌstə(r)/ n. (petit) groupe m. —v.i. se grouper.

clutch /klʌtʃ/ v.t. (hold) serrer fort; (grasp) saisir. —v.i. ∼ at, (try to grasp) essayer de saisir. —n. étreinte f.; (auto.) embrayage m.

clutter /'klʌtə(r)/ n. désordre m., fouillis m. —v.t. encombrer.

coach /kəʊtʃ/ n. autocar m.; (of train) wagon m.; (horse-drawn) carrosse m.; (sport) entraîneur, -se m., f. —v.t. donner des leçons (particulières) à; (sport) entraîner.

coagulate /kəʊ'ægjʊleɪt/ v.t./i. (se) coaguler.

coal /kəʊl/ n. charbon m. ∼-mine n. mine de charbon f.

coalfield /'kəʊlfiːld/ n. bassin houiller m.

coalition /kəʊə'lɪʃn/ n. coalition f.

coarse /kɔːs/ a. (-er, -est) grossier. ∼ness n. caractère grossier m.

coast /kəʊst/ n. côte f. —v.i. (car, bicycle) descendre en roue libre. ∼al a. côtier.

coaster /'kəʊstə(r)/ n. (ship) caboteur m.; (mat) dessous de verre m.

coastguard /'kəʊstɡɑːd/ n. garde-côte m.

coastline /'kəʊstlaɪm/ n. littoral m.

coat /kəʊt/ n. manteau m.; (of animal) pelage m.; (of paint) couche f. —v.t. enduire, couvrir; (with chocolate) enrober (with, de). ∼-hanger n. cintre m. ∼ of arms, armoiries f. pl. ∼ing n. couche f.

coax /kəʊks/ v.t. amadouer.

cob /kɒb/ n. (of corn) épi m.

cobble¹ /'kɒbl/ n. pavé m. ∼-stone n. pavé m.

cobble² /'kɒbl/ v.t. rapetasser.

cobbler /'kɒblə(r)/ n. (old use) cordonnier m.

cobweb /'kɒbweb/ n. toile d'araignée f.

cocaine /kəʊ'keɪn/ n. cocaïne f.

cock /kɒk/ n. (oiseau) mâle m.; (rooster) coq m. —v.t. (gun) armer; (ears) dresser. ∼-and-bull story, histoire à dormir debout f. ∼-eyed a. (askew: sl.) de travers. ∼-up n. (sl.) pagaille f.

cockerel /'kɒkərəl/ n. jeune coq m.

cockle /'kɒkl/ n. (culin.) coque f.

cockney /'kɒknɪ/ n. Cockney m./f.

cockpit /'kɒkpɪt/ n. poste de pilotage m.

cockroach /'kɒkrəʊtʃ/ n. cafard m.

cocksure /kɒk'ʃʊə(r)/ a. sûr de soi.

cocktail /'kɒkteɪl/ n. cocktail m. ∼ party, cocktail m. **fruit ∼**, macédoine (de fruits) f.

cocky /'kɒkɪ/ a. (-ier, -iest) trop sûr de soi, arrogant.

cocoa /'kəʊkəʊ/ n. cacao m.

coconut /'kəʊkənʌt/ n. noix de coco f.

cocoon /kə'kuːn/ n. cocon m.

COD abbr. (cash on delivery) paiement à la livraison m.

cod /kɒd/ n. invar. morue f. ∼-liver oil, huile de foie de morue f.

coddle /'kɒdl/ v.t. dorloter.

code /kəʊd/ n. code m. —v.t. coder.

codify /'kəʊdɪfaɪ/ v.t. codifier.

coeducational /kəʊedʒʊ'keɪʃənl/ a. (school, teaching) mixte.

coerc|e /kəʊ'ɜ:s/ v.t. contraindre. **~ion** /-ʃn/ n. contrainte f.

coexist /kəʊɪg'zɪst/ v.i. coexister. **~ence** n. coexistence f.

coffee /'kɒfɪ/ n. café m. **~ bar**, café m., cafétéria f. **~-pot** n. cafetière f. **~-table** n. table basse f.

coffer /'kɒfə(r)/ n. coffre m.

coffin /'kɒfɪn/ n. cercueil m.

cog /kɒg/ n. dent f.; (fig.) rouage m.

cogent /'kəʊdʒənt/ a. convaincant; (relevant) pertinent.

cognac /'kɒnjæk/ n. cognac m.

cohabit /kəʊ'hæbɪt/ v.i. vivre en concubinage.

coherent /kəʊ'hɪərənt/ a. cohérent.

coil /kɔɪl/ v.t./i. (s')enrouler. —n. rouleau m.; (one ring) spire f.; (contraceptive) stérilet m.

coin /kɔɪn/ n. pièce (de monnaie) f. —v.t. (word) inventer. **~age** n. monnaie f.; (fig.) invention f. **~-box** n. téléphone public m.

coincide /kəʊɪn'saɪd/ v.i. coïncider.

coinciden|ce /kəʊ'ɪnsɪdəns/ n. coïncidence f. **~tal** /-'dentl/ a. dû à une coïncidence.

coke /kəʊk/ n. coke m.

colander /'kʌləndə(r)/ n. passoire f.

cold /kəʊld/ a. (-er, -est) froid. be or feel **~**, avoir froid. it is **~**, il fait froid. —n. froid m.; (med.) rhume m. **~-blooded** a. sans pitié. **~ cream**, crème de beauté f. get **~ feet**, se dégonfler. **~-shoulder** v.t. snober. **~ sore**, bouton de fièvre m. **~ness** n. froideur f.

coleslaw /'kəʊlslɔ:/ n. salade de chou cru f.

colic /'kɒlɪk/ n. coliques f. pl.

collaborat|e /kə'læbəreɪt/ v.i. collaborer. **~ion** /-'reɪʃn/ n. collaboration f. **~or** n. collabora|teur, -trice m., f.

collage /'kɒlɑ:ʒ/ n. collage m.

collapse /kə'læps/ v.i. s'effondrer; (med.) avoir un malaise. —n. effondrement m.

collapsible /kə'læpsəbl/ a. pliant.

collar /'kɒlə(r)/ n. col m.; (of dog) collier m. —v.t. (take: sl.) piquer. **~-bone** n. clavicule f.

collateral /kə'lætərəl/ n. nantissement m.

colleague /'kɒli:g/ n. collègue m./f.

collect /kə'lekt/ v.t. rassembler; (pick up) ramasser; (call for) passer prendre; (money, rent) encaisser; (taxes) percevoir; (as hobby) collectionner. —v.i. se rassembler; (dust) s'amasser. —adv. call **~**, (Amer.) téléphoner en PCV. **~ion** /-kʃn/ n. collection f.; (in church) quête f.; (of mail) levée f. **~or** n. (as hobby) collectionneu|r, -se m., f.

collective /kə'lektɪv/ a. collectif.

college /'kɒlɪdʒ/ n. (for higher education) institut m., école f.; (within university) collège m. be at **~**, être en faculté.

collide /kə'laɪd/ v.i. entrer en collision (with, avec).

colliery /'kɒlɪərɪ/ n. houillère f.

collision /kə'lɪʒn/ n. collision f.

colloquial /kə'ləʊkwɪəl/ a. familier. **~ism** n. expression familière f.

collusion /kə'lu:ʒn/ n. collusion f.

colon /'kəʊlən/ n. (gram.) deux-points m. invar.; (anat.) côlon m.

colonel /'kɜ:nl/ n. colonel m.

colonize /'kɒlənaɪz/ v.t. coloniser.

colon|y /'kɒlənɪ/ n. colonie f. **~ial** /kə'ləʊnɪəl/ a. & n. colonial(e) (m. (f.)).

colossal /kə'lɒsl/ a. colossal.

colour /'kʌlə(r)/ n. couleur f. —a. (photo etc.) en couleur; (TV set) couleur invar. —v.t. colorer; (with crayon) colorier. **~-blind**

a. daltonien. **~-fast** *a.* grand teint. *invar.* **~ful** *a.* coloré; (*person*) haut en couleur. **~ing** *n.* (*of skin*) teint *m.*; (*in food*) colorant *m.*

coloured /'kʌləd/ *a.* (*person, pencil*) de couleur. —*n.* personne de couleur *f.*

colt /kəʊlt/ *n.* poulain *m.*

column /'kɒləm/ *n.* colonne *f.*

columnist /'kɒləmnɪst/ *n.* journaliste chroniqueur *m.*

coma /'kəʊmə/ *n.* coma *m.*

comb /kəʊm/ *n.* peigne *m.* —*v.t.* peigner; (*search*) ratisser. **~ one's hair**, se peigner.

combat /'kɒmbæt/ *n.* combat *m.* —*v.t.* (*p.t.* **combated**) combattre. **~ant** /-ətənt/ *n.* combattant(e) *m.* (*f.*).

combination /kɒmbɪ'neɪʃn/ *n.* combinaison *f.*

combine¹ /kəm'baɪn/ *v.t./i.* (se) combiner, (s')unir.

combine² /'kɒmbaɪn/ *n.* (*comm.*) trust *m.*, cartel *m.* **~ harvester**, moissonneuse-batteuse *f.*

combustion /kəm'bʌstʃən/ *n.* combustion *f.*

come /kʌm/ *v.i.* (*p.t.* **came**, *p.p.* **come**) venir; (*occur*) arriver; (*sexually*) jouir. **~ about**, arriver. **~ across**, rencontrer *or* trouver par hasard. **~ away** *or* **off**, se détacher, partir. **~ back**, revenir. **~-back** *n.* retour *f.*; (*retort*) réplique *f.* **~ by**, obtenir. **~ down**, descendre; (*price*) baisser. **~-down** *n.* humiliation *f.* **~ forward**, se présenter. **~ from**, être de. **~ in**, entrer. **~ in for**, recevoir. **~ into**, (*money*) hériter de. **~ off**, (*succeed*) réussir; (*fare*) s'en tirer. **~ on**, (*actor*) entrer en scène; (*light*) s'allumer; (*improve*) faire des progrès. **~ on!**, allez! **~ out**, sortir. **~ round** *or* **to**, revenir à soi. **~ through**, s'en tirer

(indemne de). **~ to**, (*amount*) revenir à; (*decision, conclusion*) arriver à. **~ up**, monter; (*fig.*) se présenter. **~ up against**, rencontrer. **get one's ~-uppance** *n.* (*fam.*) finir par recevoir ce qu'on mérite. **~ up with**, (*find*) trouver; (*produce*) produire.

comedian /kə'miːdɪən/ *n.* comique *m.*

comedy /'kɒmədɪ/ *n.* comédie *f.*

comely /'kʌmlɪ/ *a.* (**-ier, -iest**) (*old use*) avenant, beau.

comet /'kɒmɪt/ *n.* comète *f.*

comfort /'kʌmfət/ *n.* confort *m.*; (*consolation*) réconfort *m.* —*v.t.* consoler. **one's ~s**, ses aises. **~able** *a.* (*chair, car, etc.*) confortable; (*person*) à l'aise, bien; (*wealthy*) aisé.

comforter /'kʌmfətə(r)/ *n.* (*baby's dummy*) sucette *f.*; (*quilt: Amer.*) édredon *m.*

comfy /'kʌmfɪ/ *a.* (*fam.*) = **comfortable**.

comic /'kɒmɪk/ *a.* comique. —*n.* (*person*) comique *m.*; (*periodical*) comic *m.* **~ strip**, bande dessinée *f.* **~al** *a.* comique.

coming /'kʌmɪŋ/ *n.* arrivée *f.* —*a.* à venir. **~s and goings**, allées et venues *f. pl.*

comma /'kɒmə/ *n.* virgule *f.*

command /kə'mɑːnd/ *n.* (*authority*) commandement *m.*; (*order*) ordre *m.*; (*mastery*) maîtrise *f.* —*v.t.* commander (*s.o. to*, à qn. de); (*be able to use*) disposer de; (*require*) nécessiter; (*respect*) inspirer. **~er** *n.* commandant *m.* **~ing** *a.* imposant.

commandeer /kɒmən'dɪə(r)/ *v.t.* réquisitionner.

commandment /kə'mɑːndmənt/ *n.* commandement *n.*

commando /kə'mɑːndəʊ/ *n.* (*pl.* **-os**) commando *m.*

commemorat|e /kə'meməreɪt/ *v.t.* commémorer. **~ion** /-'reɪʃn/

commémoration f. **~ive** /-ətɪv/ a. commémoratif.

commence /kə'mens/ v.t./i. commencer. **~ment** n. commencement m.; (univ., Amer.) cérémonie de distribution des diplômes f.

commend /kə'mend/ v.t. (praise) louer; (entrust) confier. **~able** a. louable. **~ation** /komen'deɪʃn/ n. éloge m.

commensurate /kə'menʃərət/ a. proportionné.

comment /'koment/ n. commentaire m. —v.i. faire des commentaires. **~ on,** commenter.

commentary /'komntrɪ/ n. commentaire m.; (radio, TV) reportage m.

commentate /'komenteɪt/ v.i. faire un reportage. **~or** n. commentateur, -trice m., f.

commerce /'komɜːs/ n. commerce m.

commercial /kə'mɜːʃl/ a. commercial; (traveller) de commerce. —n. publicité f. **~ize** v.t. commercialiser.

commiserate /kə'mɪzəreɪt/ v.i. compatir (with, avec). **~ion** /-'reɪʃn/ n. commisération f.

commission /kə'mɪʃn/ n. commission f.; (order for work) commande f. —v.t. (order) commander; (mil.) nommer officier. **~ to do,** charger de faire. **out of ~,** hors service. **~er** n. préfet (de police) m.; (in E.C.) commissaire m.

commissionaire /kəmɪʃə'neə(r)/ n. commissionnaire m.

commit /kə'mɪt/ v.t. (p.t. committed) commettre; (entrust) confier. **~ o.s.,** s'engager. **~ perjury,** se parjurer. **~ suicide,** se suicider. **~ to memory,** apprendre par cœur. **~ment** n. engagement m.

committee /kə'mɪtɪ/ n. comité m.

commodity /kə'modətɪ/ n. produit m., article m.

common /'komən/ a. (-er, -est) (shared by all) commun; (usual) courant, commun; (vulgar) vulgaire, commun. —n. terrain communal m. **~ law,** droit coutumier m. **C~ Market,** Marché Commun m. **~-room** n. (schol.) salle commune f. **~ sense,** bon sens m. **House of C~s,** Chambre des Communes f. **in ~,** en commun. **~ly** adv. communément.

commoner /'komənə(r)/ n. roturier, -ière m., f.

commonplace /'komənpleɪs/ a. banal. —n. banalité f.

Commonwealth /'komənwelθ/ n. **the ~,** le Commonwealth m.

commotion /kə'məʊʃn/ n. agitation f., remue-ménage m. invar.

communal /'komjunl/ a. (shared) commun; (life) collectif.

commune /'komjuːn/ n. (group) communauté f.

communicate /kə'mjuːnɪkeɪt/ v.t./i. communiquer. **~ion** /-'keɪʃn/ n. communication f. **~ive** /-ətɪv/ a. communicatif.

communion /kə'mjuːnɪən/ n. communion f.

communiqué /kə'mjuːnɪkeɪ/ n. communiqué m.

Communis|t /'komjunɪst/ a. & n. communiste (m./f.) **~m** /-zəm/ n. communisme m.

community /kə'mjuːnətɪ/ n. communauté f.

commutation /komjuː'teɪʃn/ n. **~ ticket,** carte d'abonnement f.

commute /kə'mjuːt/ v.i. faire la navette. —v.t. (jurid.) commuer. **~r** /-ə(r)/ n. banlieusard(e) m. (f.).

compact¹ /kəm'pækt/ a. compact. **~** /'kompækt/ **disc,** (disque) compact m.

compact² /'kompækt/ n. (lady's case) poudrier m.

companion /kəm'pænjən/ n. compagnon, -agne m., f. **~ship** n. camaraderie f.

company /'kʌmpənɪ/ n. (*companionship, firm*) compagnie f.; (*guests*) invité(e)s m. (f.) pl.

comparable /'kɒmpərəbl/ a. comparable.

compar|e /kəm'peə(r)/ v.t. comparer (**with, to,** à). ∼**ed with** or **to,** en comparaison de. —v.i. être comparable. ∼**ative** /-'pærətɪv/ a. (*study, form*) comparatif; (*comfort etc.*) relatif. ∼**atively** /-'pærətɪvlɪ/ adv. relativement.

comparison /kəm'pærɪsn/ n. comparaison f.

compartment /kəm'pɑːtmənt/ n. compartiment m.

compass /'kʌmpəs/ n. (*for direction*) boussole f.; (*scope*) portée f. ∼**es,** (*for drawing*) compas m.

compassion /kəm'pæʃn/ n. compassion f. ∼**ate** a. compatissant.

compatib|le /kəm'pætəbl/ a. compatible. ∼**ility** /-'bɪlətɪ/ n. compatibilité f.

compatriot /kəm'pætrɪət/ n. compatriote m./f.

compel /kəm'pel/ v.t. (p.t. **compelled**) contraindre. ∼**ling** a. irrésistible.

compendium /kəm'pendɪəm/ n. abrégé m., résumé m.

compensat|e /'kɒmpənseɪt/ v.t./i. (*financially*) dédommager (**for,** de). ∼**e for sth.,** compenser qch. ∼**ion** /-'seɪʃn/ n. compensation f.; (*financial*) dédommagement m.

compete /kəm'piːt/ v.i. concourir. ∼ **with,** rivaliser avec.

competen|t /'kɒmpɪtənt/ a. compétent. ∼**ce** n. compétence f.

competition /kɒmpə'tɪʃn/ n. (*contest*) concours m.; (*sport*) compétition f.; (*comm.*) concurrence f.

competitive /kəm'petɪtɪv/ a. (*prices*) concurrentiel, compétitif. ∼ **examination,** concours m.

competitor /kəm'petɪtə(r)/ n. concurrent(e) m. (f.).

compile /kəm'paɪl/ v.t. (*list*) dresser; (*book*) rédiger. ∼**r** /-ə(r)/ n. rédac|teur, -trice m., f.

complacen|t /kəm'pleɪsnt/ a. content de soi. ∼**cy** contentement de soi m.

complain /kəm'pleɪn/ v.i. se plaindre (**about,** of, de).

complaint /kəm'pleɪnt/ n. plainte f.; (*in shop etc.*) réclamation f.; (*illness*) maladie f.

complement /'kɒmplɪmənt/ n. complément m. —v.t. compléter. ∼**ary** /-'mentrɪ/ a. complémentaire.

complet|e /kəm'pliːt/ a. complet; (*finished*) achevé; (*downright*) parfait. —v.t. achever; (*a form*) remplir. ∼**ely** adv. complètement. ∼**ion** /-ʃn/ n. achèvement m.

complex /'kɒmpleks/ a. complexe. —n. (*psych., archit.*) complexe m. ∼**ity** /kəm'pleksəti/ n. complexité f.

complexion /kəm'plekʃn/ n. (*of face*) teint m.; (*fig.*) caractère m.

compliance /kəm'plaɪəns/ n. (*agreement*) conformité f.

complicat|e /'kɒmplɪkeɪt/ v.t. compliquer. ∼**ed** a. compliqué. ∼**ion** /-'keɪʃn/ n. complication f.

complicity /kəm'plɪsətɪ/ n. complicité f.

compliment /'kɒmplɪmənt/ n. compliment m. —v.t. /'kɒmplɪment/ complimenter.

complimentary /kɒmplɪ'mentrɪ/ a. (*offert*) à titre gracieux; (*praising*) flatteur.

comply /kəm'plaɪ/ v.i. ∼ **with,** se conformer à, obéir à.

component /kəm'pəʊnənt/ n. (*of machine etc.*) pièce f.; (*chemical substance*) composant m.; (*element: fig.*) composante f. —a. constituant.

compose /kəm'pəʊz/ v.t. composer. ~ o.s., se calmer. ~d a. calme. ~r /-ə(r)/ n. (mus.) compositeur m.

composition /kɒmpə'zɪʃn/ n. composition f.

compost /'kɒmpɒst, Amer. 'kɒmpəʊst/ n. compost m.

composure /kəm'pəʊʒə(r)/ n. calme m.

compound[1] /'kɒmpaʊnd/ n. (substance, word) composé m.; (enclosure) enclos m. —a. composé.

compound[2] /kəm'paʊnd/ v.t. (problem etc.) aggraver.

comprehen|d /kɒmprɪ'hend/ v.t. comprendre. ~sion n. compréhension f.

comprehensive /kɒmprɪ'hensɪv/ a. étendu, complet; (insurance) tous-risques invar. ~ school, collège d'enseignement secondaire m.

compress /kəm'pres/ v.t. comprimer. ~ion /-ʃn/ n. compression f.

comprise /kəm'praɪz/ v.t. comprendre, inclure.

compromise /'kɒmprəmaɪz/ n. compromis m. —v.t. compromettre. —v.i. transiger, trouver un compromis. not ~ on, ne pas transiger sur.

compulsion /kəm'pʌlʃn/ n. contrainte f.

compulsive /kəm'pʌlsɪv/ a. (psych.) compulsif; (liar, smoker) invétéré.

compulsory /kəm'pʌlsərɪ/ a. obligatoire.

compunction /kəm'pʌŋkʃn/ n. scrupule m.

computer /kəm'pjuːtə(r)/ n. ordinateur m. ~ science, informatique f. ~ize v.t. informatiser.

comrade /'kɒmr(e)ɪd/ n. camarade m./f. ~ship n. camaraderie f.

con[1] /kɒn/ v.t. (p.t. conned) (sl.) rouler, escroquer (out of, de). —n. (sl.) escroquerie f. ~ s.o. into doing, arnaquer qn. en lui faisant faire. ~ man, (sl.) escroc m.

con[2] /kɒn/ see pro.

concave /'kɒnkeɪv/ a. concave.

conceal /kən'siːl/ v.t. dissimuler. ~ment n. dissimulation f.

concede /kən'siːd/ v.t. concéder. —v.i. céder.

conceit /kən'siːt/ n. suffisance f. ~ed a. suffisant.

conceivab|le /kən'siːvəbl/ a. concevable. ~ly adv. this may ~y be done, il est concevable que cela puisse se faire.

conceive /kən'siːv/ v.t./i. concevoir. ~ of, concevoir.

concentrat|e /'kɒnsntreɪt/ v.t./i. (se) concentrer. ~ion /-'treɪʃn/ n. concentration f.

concept /'kɒnsept/ n. concept m. ~ual /kən'septʃʊəl/ a. notionnel.

conception /kən'sepʃn/ n. conception f.

concern /kən'sɜːn/ n. (interest, business) affaire f.; (worry) inquiétude f.; (firm: comm.) entreprise f., affaire f. —v.t. concerner. ~ o.s. with, be ~ed with, s'occuper de. ~ing prep. en ce qui concerne.

concerned /kən'sɜːnd/ a. inquiet.

concert /'kɒnsət/ n. concert m. in ~, ensemble.

concerted /kən'sɜːtɪd/ a. concerté.

concertina /kɒnsə'tiːnə/ n. concertina m.

concerto /kən'tʃeətəʊ/ n. (pl. -os) concerto m.

concession /kən'seʃn/ n. concession f.

conciliation /kənsɪlɪ'eɪʃn/ n. conciliation f.

concise /kən'saɪs/ a. concis. ~ly adv. avec concision. ~ness n. concision f.

conclu|de /kən'kluːd/ v.t. conclure. —v.i. se terminer. **~ding** a. final. **~sion** n. conclusion f.

conclusive /kən'kluːsɪv/ a. concluant. **~ly** adv. de manière concluante.

concoct /kən'kɒkt/ v.t. confectionner; (invent: fig.) fabriquer. **~ion** /-kʃn/ n. mélange m.

concourse /'kɒŋkɔːs/ n. (rail.) hall m.

concrete /'kɒŋkriːt/ n. béton m. —a. concret. —v.t. bétonner. **~ mixer** n. bétonnière f.

concur /kən'kɜː(r)/ v.i. (p.t. **concurred**) être d'accord.

concurrently /kən'kʌrəntlɪ/ adv. simultanément.

concussion /kən'kʌʃn/ n. commotion (cérébrale) f.

condemn /kən'dem/ v.t. condamner. **~ation** /kɒndem'neɪʃn/ n. condamnation f.

condens|e /kən'dens/ v.t./i. (se) condenser. **~ation** /kɒnden-'seɪʃn/ n. condensation f.; (mist) buée f.

condescend /kɒndɪ'send/ v.i. condescendre.

condiment /'kɒndɪmənt/ n. condiment m.

condition /kən'dɪʃn/ n. condition f. —v.t. conditionner. **on ~ that**, à condition que. **~al** a. conditionnel. **be ~al upon**, dépendre de. **~er** n. après-shampooing m.

condolences /kən'dəʊlənsɪz/ n. pl. condoléances f. pl.

condom /'kɒndɒm/ n. préservatif m.

condominium /kɒndə'mɪnɪəm/ n. (Amer.) copropriété f.

condone /kən'dəʊn/ v.t. pardonner, fermer les yeux sur.

conducive /kən'djuːsɪv/ a. **~ to**, favorable à.

conduct[1] /kən'dʌkt/ v.t. conduire; (orchestra) diriger.

conduct[2] /'kɒndʌkt/ n. conduite f.

conduct|or /kən'dʌktə(r)/ n. chef d'orchestre m.; (of bus) receveur m.; (on train: Amer.) chef de train m.; (electr.) conducteur m. **~ress** n. receveuse f.

cone /kəʊn/ n. cône m.; (of ice-cream) cornet m.

confectioner /kən'fekʃənə(r)/ n. confiseu|r, -se m., f. **~y** n. confiserie f.

confederation /kənfedə'reɪʃn/ n. confédération f.

confer /kən'fɜː(r)/ v.t./i. (p.t. **conferred**) conférer.

conference /'kɒnfərəns/ n. conférence f.

confess /kən'fes/ v.t./i. avouer; (relig.) (se) confesser. **~ion** /-ʃn/ n. confession f.; (of crime) aveu m.

confessional /kən'feʃənl/ n. confessionnal m.

confetti /kən'fetɪ/ n. confettis m. pl.

confide /kən'faɪd/ v.t. confier. —v.i. **~ in**, se confier à.

confiden|t /'kɒnfɪdənt/ a. sûr. **~ce** n. (trust) confiance f.; (boldness) confiance en soi f.; (secret) confidence f. **~ce trick**, escroquerie f. **in ~ce**, en confidence.

confidential /kɒnfɪ'denʃl/ a. confidentiel.

configure /kən'fɪɡə(r)/ v.t. (comput.) configurer.

confine /kən'faɪn/ v.t. enfermer; (limit) limiter. **~d space**, espace réduit. **~d to**, limité à. **~ment** n. détention f.; (med.) couches f. pl.

confines /'kɒnfaɪnz/ n. pl. confins m. pl.

confirm /kən'fɜːm/ v.t. confirmer. **~ation** /kɒnfə'meɪʃn/ n. confirmation f. **~ed** a. (bachelor) endurci; (smoker) invétéré.

confiscat|e /'kɒnfɪskeɪt/ v.t. confisquer. **~ion** /-'keɪʃn/ n. confiscation f.

conflagration /ˌkɒnfləˈɡreɪʃn/ n. incendie m.

conflict[1] /ˈkɒnflɪkt/ n. conflit m.

conflict[2] /kənˈflɪkt/ v.i. (statements, views) être en contradiction (with, avec); (appointments) tomber en même temps (with, que). ~ing a. contradictoire.

conform /kənˈfɔːm/ v.t./i. (se) conformer. ~ist n. conformiste m./f.

confound /kənˈfaʊnd/ v.t. confondre. ~ed a. (fam.) sacré.

confront /kənˈfrʌnt/ v.t. affronter. ~ with, confronter avec. ~ation /kɒnfrʌnˈteɪʃn/ n. confrontation f.

confuse /kənˈfjuːz/ v.t. embrouiller; (mistake, confound) confondre. **become ~ed**, s'embrouiller. **I am ~ed**, je m'y perds. ~ing a. déroutant. ~ion /-ʒn/ n. confusion f.

congeal /kənˈdʒiːl/ v.t./i. (se) figer.

congenial /kənˈdʒiːnɪəl/ a. sympathique.

congenital /kənˈdʒenɪtl/ a. congénital.

congest|ed /kənˈdʒestɪd/ a. encombré; (med.) congestionné. ~ion /-stʃən/ n. (traffic) encombrement(s) m. (pl.); (med.) congestion f.

conglomerate /kənˈɡlɒmərət/ n. (comm.) conglomérat m.

congratulat|e /kənˈɡrætjʊleɪt/ v.t. féliciter (on, de). ~ions /-ˈleɪʃnz/ n. pl. félicitations f. pl.

congregat|e /ˈkɒŋɡrɪɡeɪt/ v.i. se rassembler. ~ion /-ˈɡeɪʃn/ n. assemblée f.

congress /ˈkɒŋɡres/ n. congrès m. **C~**, (Amer.) le Congrès.

conic(al) /ˈkɒnɪk(l)/ a. conique.

conifer /ˈkɒnɪfə(r)/ n. conifère m.

conjecture /kənˈdʒektʃə(r)/ n. conjecture f. —v.t./i. conjecturer.

conjugal /ˈkɒndʒʊɡl/ a. conjugal.

conjugat|e /ˈkɒndʒʊɡeɪt/ v.t. conjuguer. ~ion /-ˈɡeɪʃn/ n. conjugaison f.

conjunction /kənˈdʒʌŋkʃn/ n. conjonction f. **in ~ with**, conjointement avec.

conjunctivitis /kəndʒʌŋktɪˈvaɪtɪs/ n. conjonctivite f.

conjur|e /ˈkʌndʒə(r)/ v.i. faire des tours de passe-passe. —v.t. ~e up, faire apparaître. ~or n. prestidigita|teur, -trice m., f.

conk /kɒŋk/ v.i. ~ out, (sl.) tomber en panne.

conker /ˈkɒŋkə(r)/ n. (horse-chestnut fruit: fam.) marron m.

connect /kəˈnekt/ v.t./i. (se) relier; (in mind) faire le rapport entre; (install, wire up to mains) brancher. ~ with, (of train) assurer la correspondance avec. ~ed a. lié. **be ~ed with**, avoir rapport à; (deal with) avoir des rapports avec.

connection /kəˈnekʃn/ n. rapport m.; (rail.) correspondance f.; (phone call) communication f.; (electr.) contact m.; (joining piece) raccord m.; ~s, (comm.) relations f. pl.

conniv|e /kəˈnaɪv/ v.i. ~e at, se faire le complice de. ~ance n. connivence f.

connoisseur /kɒnəˈsɜː(r)/ n. connaisseur m.

connot|e /kəˈnəʊt/ v.t. connoter. ~ation /kɒnəˈteɪʃn/ n. connotation f.

conquer /ˈkɒŋkə(r)/ v.t. vaincre; (country) conquérir. ~or n. conquérant m.

conquest /ˈkɒŋkwest/ n. conquête f.

conscience /ˈkɒnʃəns/ n. conscience f.

conscientious /kɒnʃɪˈenʃəs/ a. consciencieux.

conscious /ˈkɒnʃəs/ a. conscient;

(*deliberate*) voulu. ∼ly *adv.* consciemment. ∼ness *n.* conscience *f.*; (*med.*) connaissance *f.*

conscript[1] /kən'skrɪpt/ *v.t.* recruter par conscription. ∼ion /-pʃn/ *n.* conscription *f.*

conscript[2] /'konskrɪpt/ *n.* conscrit *m.*

consecrate /'konsɪkreɪt/ *v.t.* consacrer.

consecutive /kən'sekjʊtɪv/ *a.* consécutif. ∼ly *adv.* consécutivement.

consensus /kən'sensəs/ *n.* consensus *m.*

consent /kən'sent/ *v.i.* consentir (**to**, à). —*n.* consentement *m.*

consequence /'konsɪkwəns/ *n.* conséquence *f.*

consequent /'konsɪkwənt/ *a.* résultant. ∼ly *adv.* par conséquent.

conservation /konsə'veɪʃn/ *n.* préservation *f.* ∼ **area**, zone classée *f.*

conservationist /konsə'veɪʃənɪst/ *n.* défenseur de l'environnement *m.*

conservative /kən'sɜ:vətɪv/ *a.* conservateur; (*estimate*) modeste. **C**∼ *a. & n.* conserva|teur, -trice (*m.* (*f.*)).

conservatory /kən'sɜ:vətrɪ/ *n.* (*greenhouse*) serre *f.*; (*room*) véranda *f.*

conserve /kən'sɜ:v/ *v.t.* conserver; (*energy*) économiser.

consider /kən'sɪdə(r)/ *v.t.* considérer; (*allow for*) tenir compte de; (*possibility*) envisager (**doing**, de faire). ∼**ation** /-'reɪʃn/ *n.* considération *f.*; (*respect*) égard(s) *m.* (*pl.*). ∼**ing** *prep.* compte tenu de.

considerabl|e /kən'sɪdərəbl/ *a.* considérable; (*much*) beaucoup de. ∼**y** *adv.* beaucoup, considérablement.

considerate /kən'sɪdərət/ *a.* prévenant, attentionné.

consign /kən'saɪn/ *v.t.* (*entrust*) confier; (*send*) expédier. ∼**ment** *n.* envoi *m.*

consist /kən'sɪst/ *v.i.* consister (**of**, en; **in doing**, à faire).

consisten|t /kən'sɪstənt/ *a.* cohérent. ∼**t with**, conforme à. ∼**cy** *n.* (*of liquids*) consistance *f.*; (*of argument*) cohérence *f.* ∼**tly** *adv.* régulièrement.

consol|e /kən'səʊl/ *v.t.* consoler. ∼**ation** /kɒnsə'leɪʃn/ *n.* consolation *f.*

consolidat|e /kən'sɒlɪdeɪt/ *v.t./i.* (se) consolider. ∼**ion** /-'deɪʃn/ *n.* consolidation *f.*

consonant /'konsənənt/ *n.* consonne *f.*

consort[1] /'konso:t/ *n.* époux *m.*, épouse *f.*

consort[2] /kən'so:t/ *v.i.* ∼ **with**, fréquenter.

consortium /kən'so:tɪəm/ *n.* (*pl.* -**tia**) consortium *m.*

conspicuous /kən'spɪkjʊəs/ *a.* (*easily seen*) en évidence; (*showy*) voyant; (*noteworthy*) remarquable.

conspiracy /kən'spɪrəsɪ/ *n.* conspiration *f.*

conspire /kən'spaɪə(r)/ *v.i.* (*person*) comploter (**to do**, de faire), conspirer; (*events*) conspirer (**to do**, à faire).

constable /'kʌnstəbl/ *n.* agent de police *m.*, gendarme *m.*

constant /'konstənt/ *a.* incessant; (*unchanging*) constant; (*friend*) fidèle. —*n.* constante *f.* ∼**ly** *adv.* constamment.

constellation /konstə'leɪʃn/ *n.* constellation *f.*

consternation /konstə'neɪʃn/ *n.* consternation *f.*

constipat|e /'konstɪpeɪt/ *v.t.* constiper. ∼**ion** /-'peɪʃn/ *n.* constipation *f.*

constituency /kən'stɪtjuənsɪ/ *n.* circonscription électorale *f.*

constituent /kən'stɪtjuənt/ *a.* constitutif. —*n.* élément constitutif *m.*; (*pol.*) élec|teur, -trice *m.*, *f.*

constitut|e /'kɒnstɪtjuːt/ *v.t.* constituer. **∼ion** /-'tjuːʃn/ *n.* constitution *f.* **∼ional** /-'tjuːʃənl/ *a.* constitutionnel; *n.* promenade *f.*

constrain /kən'streɪn/ *v.t.* contraindre.

constraint /kən'streɪnt/ *n.* contrainte *f.*

constrict /kən'strɪkt/ *v.t.* resserrer; (*movement*) gêner. **∼ion** /-kʃn/ *n.* resserrement *f.*

construct /kən'strʌkt/ *v.t.* construire. **∼ion** /-kʃn/ *n.* construction *f.* **∼ion worker,** ouvrier de bâtiment *m.*

constructive /kən'strʌktɪv/ *a.* constructif.

construe /kən'struː/ *v.t.* interpréter.

consul /'kɒnsl/ *n.* consul *m.* **∼ar** /-jʊlə(r)/ *a.* consulaire.

consulate /'kɒnsjʊlət/ *n.* consulat *m.*

consult /kən'sʌlt/ *v.t.* consulter. —*v.i.* **∼ with,** conférer avec. **∼ation** /kɒnsl'teɪʃn/ *n.* consultation *f.*

consultant /kən'sʌltənt/ *n.* conseil|ler, -ère *m.*, *f.*; (*med.*) spécialiste *m./f.*

consume /kən'sjuːm/ *v.t.* consommer; (*destroy*) consumer. **∼r** /-ə(r)/ *n.* consomma|teur, -trice *m.*, *f.* *a.* (*society*) de consommation.

consumerism /kən'sjuːmərɪzəm/ *n.* protection des consommateurs *f.*

consummate /'kɒnsəmeɪt/ *v.t.* consommer.

consumption /kən'sʌmpʃn/ *n.* consommation *f.*; (*med.*) phtisie *f.*

contact /'kɒntækt/ *n.* contact *m.*;

(*person*) relation *f.* —*v.t.* contacter. **∼ lenses,** lentilles (de contact) *f. pl.*

contagious /kən'teɪdʒəs/ *a.* contagieux.

contain /kən'teɪn/ *v.t.* contenir. **∼ o.s.,** se contenir. **∼er** *n.* récipient *m.*; (*for transport*) container *m.*

contaminate /kən'tæmɪneɪt/ *v.t.* contaminer. **∼ion** /-'neɪʃn/ *n.* contamination *f.*

contemplat|e /'kɒntempleɪt/ *v.t.* (*gaze at*) contempler; (*think about*) envisager. **∼ion** /-'pleɪʃn/ *n.* contemplation *f.*

contemporary /kən'temprərɪ/ *a.* & *n.* contemporain(e) (*m.* (*f.*)).

contempt /kən'tempt/ *n.* mépris *m.* **∼ible** *a.* méprisable. **∼uous** /-tʃʊəs/ *a.* méprisant.

contend /kən'tend/ *v.t.* soutenir. —*v.i.* **∼ with,** (*compete*) rivaliser avec; (*face*) faire face à. **∼er** *n.* adversaire *m./f.*

content[1] /kən'tent/ *a.* satisfait. —*v.t.* contenter. **∼ed** *a.* satisfait. **∼ment** *n.* contentement *m.*

content[2] /'kɒntent/ *n.* (*of letter*) contenu *m.*; (*amount*) teneur *f.* **∼s,** contenu *m.*

contention /kən'tenʃn/ *n.* dispute *f.*; (*claim*) affirmation *f.*

contest[1] /'kɒntest/ *n.* (*competition*) concours *m.*; (*fight*) combat *m.*

contest[2] /kən'test/ *v.t.* contester; (*compete for or in*) disputer. **∼ant** *n.* concurrent(e) *m.* (*f.*).

context /'kɒntekst/ *n.* contexte *m.*

continent /'kɒntɪnənt/ *n.* continent *m.* **the C∼,** l'Europe (continentale) *f.* **∼al** /-'nentl/ *a.* continental; européen. **∼al quilt,** couette *f.*

contingen|t /kən'tɪndʒənt/ *a.* **be ∼t upon,** dépendre de. —*n.* (*mil.*) contingent *m.* **∼cy** *n.* éventualité *f.* **∼cy plan,** plan d'urgence *m.*

continual /kən'tɪnjʊəl/ *a.* continuel. **∼ly** *adv.* continuellement.

continue /kən'tɪnjuː/ *v.t./i.* continuer; (*resume*) reprendre. **~ance** *n.* continuation *f.* **~ation** /-u'eɪʃn/ *n.* continuation *f.*; (*after interruption*) reprise *f.*; (*new episode*) suite *f.* **~ed** *a.* continu.

continuity /kɒntɪ'njuːətɪ/ *n.* continuité *f.*

continuous /kən'tɪnjʊəs/ *a.* continu. **~ stationery**, papier continu *m.* **~ly** *adv.* sans interruption, continûment.

contort /kən'tɔːt/ *v.t.* tordre. **~ o.s.**, se contorsionner. **~ion** /-ʃn/ *n.* torsion *f.*; contorsion *f.* **~ionist** /-ʃənɪst/ *n.* contorsionniste *m./f.*

contour /'kɒntʊə(r)/ *n.* contour *m.*

contraband /'kɒntrəbænd/ *n.* contrebande *f.*

contraception /kɒntrə'sepʃn/ *n.* contraception *f.*

contraceptive /kɒntrə'septɪv/ *a.* & *n.* contraceptif (*m.*).

contract[1] /'kɒntrækt/ *n.* contrat *m.*

contract[2] /kən'trækt/ *v.t./i.* (se) contracter. **~ion** /-kʃn/ *n.* contraction *f.*

contractor /kən'træktə(r)/ *n.* entrepreneur *m.*

contradict /kɒntrə'dɪkt/ *v.t.* contredire. **~ion** /-kʃn/ *n.* contradiction *f.* **~ory** *a.* contradictoire.

contralto /kən'træltəʊ/ *n.* (*pl.* -os) contralto *m.*

contraption /kən'træpʃn/ *n.* (*fam.*) engin *m.*, truc *m.*

contrary[1] /'kɒntrərɪ/ *a.* contraire (**to**, à). —*n.* contraire *m.* —*adv.* **~ to**, contrairement à. **on the ~**, au contraire.

contrary[2] /kən'treərɪ/ *a.* entêté.

contrast[1] /'kɒntrɑːst/ *n.* contraste *m.*

contrast[2] /kən'trɑːst/ *v.t./i.* contraster. **~ing** *a.* contrasté.

contravene /kɒntrə'viːn/ *v.t.* enfreindre. **~tion** /-'venʃn/ *n.* infraction *f.*

contribute /kən'trɪbjuːt/ *v.t.* donner. —*v.i.* **~ to**, contribuer à; (*take part*) participer à; (*newspaper*) collaborer à. **~ion** /kɒntrɪ'bjuːʃn/ *n.* contribution *f.* **~or** *n.* collaborateur, -trice *m.*, *f.*

contrivance /kən'traɪvəns/ *n.* (*device*) appareil *m.*, truc *m.*

contrive /kən'traɪv/ *v.t.* imaginer. **~ to do**, trouver moyen de faire. **~d** *a.* tortueux.

control /kən'trəʊl/ *v.t.* (*p.t.* **controlled**) (*a firm etc.*) diriger; (*check*) contrôler; (*restrain*) maîtriser. —*n.* contrôle *m.*; (*mastery*) maîtrise *f.* **~s**, commandes *f. pl.*; (*knobs*) boutons *m. pl.* **~ tower**, tour de contrôle *f.* **have under ~**, (*event*) avoir en main. **in ~ of**, maître de.

controversial /kɒntrə'vɜːʃl/ *a.* discutable, discuté.

controversy /'kɒntrəvɜːsɪ/ *n.* controverse *f.*

conurbation /kɒnɜː'beɪʃn/ *n.* agglomération *f.*, conurbation *f.*

convalesce /kɒnvə'les/ *v.i.* être en convalescence. **~nce** *n.* convalescence *f.* **~nt** *a.* & *n.* convalescent(e) (*m.* (*f.*)). **~nt home**, maison de convalescence *f.*

convector /kən'vektə(r)/ *n.* radiateur à convection *m.*

convene /kən'viːn/ *v.t.* convoquer. —*v.i.* se réunir.

convenience /kən'viːnɪəns/ *n.* commodité *f.* **~s**, toilettes *f. pl.* **all modern ~s**, tout le confort moderne. **at your ~**, quand cela vous conviendra, à votre convenance. **~ foods**, plats tout préparés *m. pl.*

convenient /kən'viːnɪənt/ *a.* commode, pratique; (*time*) bien choisi. **be ~ for**, convenir à. **~ly**

adv. (arrive) à propos. **~ly situated,** bien situé.

convent /'kɒnvənt/ *n.* couvent *m.*

convention /kən'venʃn/ *n. (assembly, agreement)* convention *f.*; *(custom)* usage *m.* **~al** *a.* conventionnel.

converge /kən'vɜːdʒ/ *v.i.* converger.

conversant /kən'vɜːsnt/ *a.* **be ~ with,** connaître; *(fact)* savoir; *(machinery)* s'y connaître en.

conversation /kɒnvə'seɪʃn/ *n.* conversation *f.* **~al** *a. (tone etc.)* de la conversation; *(French etc.)* de tous les jours. **~alist** *n.* causeu|r, -se *m.*, *f.*

converse[1] /kən'vɜːs/ *v.i.* s'entretenir, converser *(with,* avec).

converse[2] /'kɒnvɜːs/ *n. & a.* inverse (m.). **~ly** *adv.* inversement.

conver|t[1] /kən'vɜːt/ *v.t.* convertir; *(house)* aménager. —*v.i.* **~t into,** se transformer en. **~sion** /-ʃn/ *n.* conversion *f.* **~tible** *a.* convertible. —*n. (car)* décapotable *f.*

convert[2] /'kɒnvɜːt/ *n.* converti(e) *m. (f.).*

convex /'kɒnveks/ *a.* convexe.

convey /kən'veɪ/ *v.t. (wishes, order)* transmettre; *(goods, people)* transporter; *(idea, feeling)* communiquer. **~ance** *n.* transport *m.* **~or belt,** tapis roulant *m.*

convict[1] /kən'vɪkt/ *v.t.* déclarer coupable. **~ion** /-kʃn/ *n.* condamnation *f.*; *(opinion)* conviction *f.*

convict[2] /'kɒnvɪkt/ *n.* prisonn|ier, ère *m.*, *f.*

convinc|e /kən'vɪns/ *v.t.* convaincre. **~ing** *a.* convaincant.

convivial /kən'vɪvɪəl/ *a.* joyeux.

convoke /kən'vəʊk/ *v.t.* convoquer.

convoluted /'kɒnvəluːtɪd/ *a. (argument etc.)* compliqué.

convoy /'kɒnvɔɪ/ *n.* convoi *m.*

convuls|e /kən'vʌls/ *v.t.* convulser; *(fig.)* bouleverser. **be ~ed with laughter,** se tordre de rire. **~ion** /-ʃn/ *n.* convulsion *f.*

coo /kuː/ *v.i.* roucouler.

cook /kʊk/ *v.t./i.* (faire) cuire; *(of person)* faire la cuisine. —*n.* cuisin|ier, -ière *m.*, *f.* **~ up,** *(fam.)* fabriquer. **~ing** *n.* cuisine *f.*; *a.* de cuisine.

cooker /'kʊkə(r)/ *n. (stove)* cuisinière *f.*; *(apple)* pomme à cuire *f.*

cookery /'kʊkərɪ/ *n.* cuisine *f.* **~ book,** livre de cuisine *m.*

cookie /'kʊkɪ/ *n. (Amer.)* biscuit *m.*

cool /kuːl/ *a.* (-er, -est) frais; *(calm)* calme; *(unfriendly)* froid. —*n.* fraîcheur *f.*; *(calmness: sl.)* sang-froid *m.* —*v.t./i.* rafraîchir. **in the ~,** au frais. **~ box,** glacière *f.* **~er** *n. (for food)* glacière *f.*; **~ly** *adv.* calmement, froidement. **~ness** *n.* fraîcheur *f.*; froideur *f.*

coop /kuːp/ *n.* poulailler *m.* —*v.t.* **~ up,** enfermer.

co-operat|e /kəʊ'ɒpəreɪt/ *v.i.* coopérer. **~ion** /-'reɪʃn/ *n.* coopération *f.*

co-operative /kəʊ'ɒpərətɪv/ *a.* coopératif. —*n.* coopérative *f.*

co-opt /kəʊ'ɒpt/ *v.t.* coopter.

co-ordinat|e /kəʊ'ɔːdɪneɪt/ *v.t.* coordonner. **~ion** /-'neɪʃn/ *n.* coordination *f.*

cop /kɒp/ *v.t.* (*p.t.* copped) *(sl.)* piquer. —*n. (policeman: sl.)* flic *m.* **~ out,** *(sl.)* se dérober. **~-out** *n. (sl.)* dérobade *f.*

cope /kəʊp/ *v.i.* assurer. **~ with,** s'en sortir avec.

copious /'kəʊpɪəs/ *a.* copieux.

copper[1] /'kɒpə(r)/ *n.* cuivre *m.*; *(coin)* sou *m.* —*a.* de cuivre.

copper[2] /'kɒpə(r)/ *n. (sl.)* flic *m.*

coppice, copse /'kɒpɪs, kɒps/ *ns.* taillis *m.*

copulat|e /'kɒpjʊleɪt/ *v.i.* s'accoupler. **~ion** /-'leɪʃn/ *n.* copulation *f.*

copy /'kɒpɪ/ *n.* copie *f.*; (*of book, newspaper*) exemplaire *m.*; (*print photo.*) épreuve *f.* —*v.t./i.* copier. **~-writer** *n.* rédacteur-concepteur *m.*, rédactrice-conceptrice *f.*

copyright /'kɒpɪraɪt/ *n.* droit d'auteur *m.*, copyright *m.*

coral /'kɒrəl/ *a.* corail *m.*

cord /kɔːd/ *n.* (petite) corde *f.*; (*of curtain, pyjamas, etc.*) cordon *m.*; (*electr.*) cordon électrique *m.*; (*fabric*) velours côtelé *m.*

cordial /'kɔːdɪəl/ *a.* cordial. —*n.* (*fruit-flavoured drink*) sirop *m.*

cordon /'kɔːdn/ *n.* cordon *m.* —*v.t.* **~ off**, mettre un cordon autour de.

corduroy /'kɔːdərɔɪ/ *n.* velours côtelé *m.*, velours à côtes *m.*

core /kɔː(r)/ *n.* (*of apple*) trognon *m.*; (*of problem*) cœur *m.*; (*techn.*) noyau *m.* —*v.t.* vider.

cork /kɔːk/ *n.* liège *m.*; (*for bottle*) bouchon *m.* —*v.t.* boucher.

corkscrew /'kɔːkskruː/ *n.* tire-bouchon *m.*

corn[1] /kɔːn/ *n.* blé *m.*; (*maize: Amer.*) maïs *m.*; (*seed*) grain *m.* **~-cob** *n.* épi de maïs *m.*

corn[2] /kɔːn/ *n.* (*hard skin*) cor *m.*

cornea /'kɔːnɪə/ *n.* cornée *f.*

corned /kɔːnd/ *a.* **~ beef**, corned-beef *m.*

corner /'kɔːnə(r)/ *n.* coin *m.*; (*bend in road*) virage *m.*; (*football*) corner *m.* —*v.t.* coincer, acculer; (*market*) accaparer. —*v.i.* prendre un virage. **~-stone** *n.* pierre angulaire *f.*

cornet /'kɔːnɪt/ *n.* cornet *m.*

cornflakes /'kɔːnfleɪks/ *n. pl.* corn flakes *m. pl.*

cornflour /'kɔːnflaʊə(r)/ *n.* farine de maïs *f.*

cornice /'kɔːnɪs/ *n.* corniche *f.*

cornstarch /'kɔːnstɑːtʃ/ *n. Amer.* = **cornflour**.

cornucopia /kɔːnjʊ'kəʊpɪə/ *n.* corne d'abondance *f.*

Corn|wall /'kɔːnwəl/ *n.* Cornouailles *f.* **~ish** *a.* de Cornouailles *f.*

corny /'kɔːnɪ/ *a.* (**-ier, -iest**) (*trite: fam.*) rebattu; (*mawkish: fam.*) à l'eau de rose.

corollary /kə'rɒlərɪ/, *Amer.* 'kɒrələrɪ/ *n.* corollaire *m.*

coronary /'kɒrənərɪ/ *n.* infarctus *m.*

coronation /kɒrə'neɪʃn/ *n.* couronnement *m.*

coroner /'kɒrənə(r)/ *n.* coroner *m.*

corporal[1] /'kɔːpərəl/ *n.* caporal *m.*

corporal[2] /'kɔːpərəl/ *a.* **~ punishment**, châtiment corporel *m.*

corporate /'kɔːpərət/ *a.* en commun; (*body*) constitué.

corporation /kɔːpə'reɪʃn/ *n.* (*comm.*) société *f.*; (*of town*) municipalité *f.*

corps /kɔː(r)/ *n.* (*pl.* **corps** /kɔːz/) corps *m.*

corpse /kɔːps/ *n.* cadavre *m.*

corpulent /'kɔːpjʊlənt/ *a.* corpulent.

corpuscle /'kɔːpʌsl/ *n.* globule *m.*

corral /kə'rɑːl/ *n.* (*Amer.*) corral *m.*

correct /kə'rekt/ *a.* (*right*) exact, juste, correct; (*proper*) correct. **you are ~**, vous avez raison. —*v.t.* corriger. **~ion** /-kʃn/ *n.* correction *f.*

correlat|e /'kɒrəleɪt/ *v.t./i.* (faire) correspondre. **~ion** /-'leɪʃn/ *n.* corrélation *f.*

correspond /kɒrɪ'spɒnd/ *v.i.* correspondre. **~ence** *n.* correspondance *f.* **~ence course**, cours par correspondance *m.* **~ent** *n.* correspondant(e) *m.*(*f.*).

corridor /'kɒrɪdɔː(r)/ n. couloir m.

corroborate /kə'rɒbəreɪt/ v.t. corroborer.

corro|de /kə'rəʊd/ v.t./i. (se) corroder. **~sion** n. corrosion f.

corrosive /kə'rəʊsɪv/ a. corrosif.

corrugated /'kɒrəgeɪtɪd/ a. ondulé. **~ iron**, tôle ondulée f.

corrupt /kə'rʌpt/ a. corrompu. —v.t. corrompre. **~ion** /-pʃn/ n. corruption f.

corset /'kɔːsɪt/ n. (boned) corset m.; (elasticated) gaine f.

Corsica /'kɔːsɪkə/ n. Corse f.

cortisone /'kɔːtɪzəʊn/ n. cortisone f.

cos /kɒs/ n. laitue romaine f.

cosh /kɒʃ/ n. matraque f. —v.t. matraquer.

cosmetic /kɒz'metɪk/ n. produit de beauté m. —a. cosmétique; (fig., pej.) superficiel.

cosmic /'kɒzmɪk/ a. cosmique.

cosmonaut /'kɒzmənɔːt/ n. cosmonaute m./f.

cosmopolitan /kɒzmə'pɒlɪt(ə)n/ a. & n. cosmopolite (m./f.).

cosmos /'kɒzmɒs/ n. cosmos m.

Cossack /'kɒsæk/ n. cosaque m.

cosset /'kɒsɪt/ v.t. (p.t. cosseted) dorloter.

cost /kɒst/ v.t. (p.t. cost) coûter; (p.t. costed) établir le prix de. —n. coût m. **~s**, (jurid.) dépens m. pl. **at all ~s**, à tout prix. **to one's ~**, à ses dépens. **~-effective** a. rentable. **~-effectiveness** n. rentabilité f. **~ price**, prix de revient m. **~ of living**, coût de la vie.

co-star /'kəʊstɑː(r)/ n. partenaire m./f.

costly /'kɒstlɪ/ a. (-ier, -iest) coûteux; (valuable) précieux.

costume /'kɒstjuːm/ n. costume m.; (for swimming) maillot m. **~ jewellery**, bijoux de fantaisie m. pl.

cos|y /'kəʊzɪ/ a. (-ier, -iest) confortable, intime. —n. couvre-théière m. **~iness** n. confort m.

cot /kɒt/ n. lit d'enfant m.; (camp-bed: Amer.) lit de camp m.

cottage /'kɒtɪdʒ/ n. petite maison de campagne f.; (thatched) chaumière f. **~ cheese**, fromage blanc (maigre) m. **~ industry**, activité artisanale f. **~ pie**, hachis Parmentier m.

cotton /'kɒtn/ n. coton m.; (for sewing) fil (à coudre) m. —v.i. **~ on**, (sl.) piger. **~ candy**, (Amer.) barbe à papa f. **~ wool**, coton hydrophile m.

couch /kaʊtʃ/ n. divan m. —v.t. (express) formuler.

couchette /kuː'ʃet/ n. couchette f.

cough /kɒf/ v.i. tousser. —n. toux f. **~ up**, (sl.) cracher, payer.

could /kʊd, unstressed kəd/ p.t. of **can²**.

couldn't /'kʊdnt/ = **could not**.

council /'kaʊnsl/ n. conseil m. **~ house**, maison construite par la municipalité f., (approx.) H.L.M. m./f.

councillor /'kaʊnsələ(r)/ n. conseill|er, -ère municipal(e) m., f.

counsel /'kaʊnsl/ n. conseil m. —n. invar. (jurid.) avocat(e) m. (f.). **~lor** n. conseill|er, -ère m., f.

count¹ /kaʊnt/ v.t./i. compter. —n. compte m. **~ on**, compter sur.

count² /kaʊnt/ n. (nobleman) comte m.

countdown /'kaʊntdaʊn/ n. compte à rebours m.

countenance /'kaʊntɪnəns/ n. mine f. —v.t. admettre, approuver.

counter¹ /'kaʊntə(r)/ n. comptoir m.; (in bank etc.) guichet m.; (token) jeton m.

counter² /'kaʊntə(r)/ adv. **~ to**, à l'encontre de. —a. opposé. —v.t. opposer; (blow) parer. —v.i. riposter.

counter- /ˈkaʊntə(r)/ *pref.* contre-.

counteract /kaʊntərˈækt/ *v.t.* neutraliser.

counter-attack /ˈkaʊntərətæk/ *n.* contre-attaque *f.* —*v.t./i.* contre-attaquer.

counterbalance /ˈkaʊntəbæləns/ *n.* contrepoids *m.* —*v.t.* contrebalancer.

counter-clockwise /kaʊntə-ˈklɒkwaɪz/ *a. & adv.* (*Amer.*) dans le sens inverse des aiguilles d'une montre.

counterfeit /ˈkaʊntəfɪt/ *a. & n.* faux (*m.*). —*v.t.* contrefaire.

counterfoil /ˈkaʊntəfɔɪl/ *n.* souche *f.*

countermand /kaʊntəˈmɑːnd/ *v.t.* annuler.

counterpart /ˈkaʊntəpɑːt/ *n.* équivalent *m.*; (*person*) homologue *m./f.*

counter-productive /kaʊntə-prəˈdʌktɪv/ *a.* (*measure*) qui produit l'effet contraire.

countersign /ˈkaʊntəsaɪn/ *v.t.* contresigner.

counter-tenor /ˈkaʊntətenə(r)/ *n.* haute-contre *m.*

countess /ˈkaʊntɪs/ *n.* comtesse *f.*

countless /ˈkaʊntlɪs/ *a.* innombrable.

countrified /ˈkʌntrɪfaɪd/ *a.* rustique.

country /ˈkʌntrɪ/ *n.* (*land, region*) pays *m.*; (*homeland*) patrie *f.*; (*countryside*) campagne *f.* **~ dance,** danse folklorique *f.*

countryman /ˈkʌntrɪmən/ *n.* (*pl.* -men) campagnard *m.*; (*fellow citizen*) compatriote *m.*

countryside /ˈkʌntrɪsaɪd/ *n.* campagne *f.*

county /ˈkaʊntɪ/ *n.* comté *m.*

coup /kuː/ *n.* (*achievement*) joli coup *m.*; (*pol.*) coup d'état *m.*

coupé /ˈkuːpeɪ/ *n.* (*car*) coupé *m.*

couple /ˈkʌpl/ *n.* (*people, animals*) couple *m.* —*v.t./i.* (s')accoupler.

a **~ (of),** (*two or three*) deux ou trois.

coupon /ˈkuːpɒn/ *n.* coupon *m.*; (*for shopping*) bon *or* coupon de réduction *m.*

courage /ˈkʌrɪdʒ/ *n.* courage *m.* **~ous** /kəˈreɪdʒəs/ *a.* courageux.

courgette /kʊəˈʒet/ *n.* courgette *f.*

courier /ˈkʊrɪə(r)/ *n.* messager, -ère *m., f.*; (*for tourists*) guide *m.*

course /kɔːs/ *n.* cours *m.*; (*for training*) (*series*) série *f.*; (*culin.*) plat *m.*; (*for golf*) terrain *m.*; (*at sea*) itinéraire *m.* **change ~,** changer de cap. **~ (of action),** façon de faire *f.* **during the ~ of,** pendant. **in due ~,** en temps utile. **of ~,** bien sûr.

court /kɔːt/ *n.* cour *f.*; (*tennis*) court *m.* —*v.t.* faire la cour à; (*danger*) rechercher. **~ martial,** (*pl.* **courts martial**) conseil de guerre *m.* **~-martial** *v.t.* (*p.t.* -martialled) faire passer en conseil de guerre. **~-house** *n.* (*Amer.*) palais de justice *m.* **~ shoe,** escarpin *m.* **go to ~,** aller devant les tribunaux.

courteous /ˈkɜːtɪəs/ *a.* courtois.

courtesy /ˈkɜːtəsɪ/ *n.* courtoisie *f.* **by ~ of,** avec la permission de.

courtier /ˈkɔːtɪə(r)/ *n.* (*old use*) courtisan *m.*

courtroom /ˈkɔːtrʊm/ *n.* salle de tribunal *f.*

courtyard /ˈkɔːtjɑːd/ *n.* cour *f.*

cousin /ˈkʌzn/ *n.* cousin(e) *m.* (*f.*). **first ~,** cousin(e) germain(e) *m.* (*f.*).

cove /kəʊv/ *n.* anse *f.*, crique *f.*

covenant /ˈkʌvənənt/ *n.* convention *f.*

Coventry /ˈkɒvntrɪ/ *n.* **send to ~,** mettre en quarantaine.

cover /ˈkʌvə(r)/ *v.t.* couvrir. —*n.* (*for bed, book, etc.*) couverture *f.*; (*lid*) couvercle *m.*; (*for furniture*) housse *f.*; (*shelter*) abri *m.* **~ charge,** couvert *m.* **~ up,**

cacher; (*crime*) couvrir. **~ up for**, couvrir. **~up** *n.* tentative pour cacher la vérité *f.* **take ~**, se mettre à l'abri. **~ing** *n.* enveloppe *f.* **~ing letter**, lettre *f.* (*jointe à un document*).

coverage /'kʌvərɪdʒ/ *n.* reportage *m.*

coveralls /ˈkʌvərɔːlz/ (*Amer.*) bleu de travail *m.*

covert /'kʌvət, *Amer.* 'kəʊvɜːrt/ *a.* (*activity*) secret; (*threat*) voilé (*look*) dérobé.

covet /'kʌvɪt/ *v.t.* convoiter.

cow /kaʊ/ *n.* vache *f.*

coward /'kaʊəd/ *n.* lâche *m./f.* **~ly** *a.* lâche.

cowardice /'kaʊədɪs/ *n.* lâcheté *f.*

cowboy /'kaʊbɔɪ/ *n.* cow-boy *m.*

cower /'kaʊə(r)/ *v.i.* se recroqueviller (*sous l'effet de la peur*).

cowshed /'kaʊʃed/ *n.* étable *f.*

cox /kɒks/ *n.* barreur *m.* —*v.t.* barrer.

coxswain /'kɒksn/ *n.* barreur *m.*

coy /kɔɪ/ *a.* (**-er, -est**) (faussement) timide, qui fait le *or* la timide.

cozy /'kəʊzɪ/ *Amer.* = **cosy**.

crab /kræb/ *n.* crabe *m.* —*v.i.* (*p.t.* **crabbed**) rouspéter. **~apple** *n.* pomme sauvage *f.*

crack /kræk/ *n.* fente *f.*; (*in glass*) fêlure *f.*; (*noise*) craquement *m.*; (*joke: sl.*) plaisanterie *f.* —*a.* (*fam.*) d'élite, —*v.t./i.* (*break partially*) (se) fêler; (*split*) (se) fendre; (*nut*) casser; (*joke*) raconter; (*problem*) résoudre. **~ down on**, (*fam.*) sévir contre. **~ up**, (*fam.*) craquer. **get ~ing**, (*fam.*) s'y mettre.

cracked /krækt/ *a.* (*sl.*) cinglé.

cracker /'krækə(r)/ *n.* pétard *m.*; (*culin.*) biscuit (salé) *m.*

crackers /'krækəz/ *a.* (*sl.*) cinglé.

crackle /'krækl/ *v.i.* crépiter. —*n.* crépitement *m.*

crackpot /'krækpɒt/ *n.* (*sl.*) cinglé(e) *m.* (*f.*).

cradle /'kreɪdl/ *n.* berceau *m.* —*v.t.* bercer.

craft[1] /krɑːft/ *n.* métier artisanal *m.*; (*technique*) art *m.*; (*cunning*) ruse *f.*

craft[2] /krɑːft/ *n. invar.* (*boat*) bateau *m.*

craftsman /'krɑːftsmən/ *n.* (*pl.* **-men**) artisan *m.* **~ship** *n.* art *m.*

crafty /'krɑːftɪ/ *a.* (**-ier, -iest**) rusé.

crag /kræg/ *n.* rocher à pic *m.* **~gy** *a.* à pic; (*face*) rude.

cram /kræm/ *v.t./i.* (*p.t.* **crammed**). **~ (for an exam)**, bachoter. **~ into**, (*pack*) (s')entasser dans. **~ with**, (*fill*) bourrer de.

cramp /kræmp/ *n.* crampe *f.*

cramped /kræmpt/ *a.* à l'étroit.

cranberry /'krænbərɪ/ *n.* canneberge *f.*

crane /kreɪn/ *n.* grue *f.* —*v.t.* (*neck*) tendre.

crank[1] /kræŋk/ *n.* (*techn.*) manivelle *f.*

crank[2] /kræŋk/ *n.* excentrique *m./f.* **~y** *a.* excentrique; (*Amer.*) grincheux.

cranny /'krænɪ/ *n.* fissure *f.*

craps /kræps/ *n.* **shoot ~**, (*Amer.*) jouer aux dés.

crash /kræʃ/ *n.* accident *m.*; (*noise*) fracas *m.*; (*of thunder*) coup *m.*; (*of firm*) faillite *f.* —*v.t./i.* avoir un accident (avec); (*of plane*) s'écraser; (*two vehicles*) se percuter. —*a.* (*course*) intensif. **~ helmet** *n.* casque (anti-choc) *m.* **~ into**, rentrer dans. **~land** *v.i.* atterrir en catastrophe.

crass /kræs/ *a.* grossier.

crate /kreɪt/ *n.* cageot *m.*

crater /'kreɪtə(r)/ *n.* cratère *m.*

cravat /krə'væt/ *n.* foulard *m.*

crave /kreɪv/ *v.t./i.* **~e (for)**, désirer ardemment. **~ing** *n.* envie irrésistible *f.*

crawl /krɔːl/ v.i. ramper; (vehicle) se traîner. —n. (pace) pas m.; (swimming) crawl m. **be ~ing with,** grouiller de.

crayfish /ˈkreɪfɪʃ/ n. invar. écrevisse f.

crayon /ˈkreɪən/ n. crayon m.

craze /kreɪz/ n. engouement m.

crazed /kreɪzd/ a. affolé.

craz|y /ˈkreɪzɪ/ a. (-ier, -iest) fou. **~y about,** (person) fou de; (thing) fana or fou de. **~iness** n. folie f. **~y paving,** dallage irrégulier m.

creak /kriːk/ n. grincement m. —v.i. grincer. **~y** a. grinçant.

cream /kriːm/ n. crème f. —a. crème invar. —v.t. écrémer. **~ cheese,** fromage frais m. **~ off,** se servir en prenant. **~y** a. crémeux.

crease /kriːs/ n. pli m. —v.t./i. (se) froisser.

creat|e /kriːˈeɪt/ v.t. créer. **~ion** /-ʃn/ n. création f. **~ive** a. créateur. **~or** n. créa|teur, -trice m., f.

creature /ˈkriːtʃə(r)/ n. créature f.

crèche /kreʃ/ n. garderie f.

credence /ˈkriːdns/ n. **give ~ to,** ajouter foi à.

credentials /krɪˈdenʃlz/ n. pl. (identity) pièces d'identité f. pl.; (competence) références f. pl.

credib|le /ˈkredəbl/ a. (excuse etc.) croyable, plausible. **~ility** /-ˈbɪlətɪ/ n. crédibilité f.

credit /ˈkredɪt/ n. crédit m.; (honour) honneur m. **in ~,** créditeur. **~s,** (cinema) générique m. —a. (balance) créditeur. —v.t. (p.t. **credited**) croire; (comm.) créditer. **~ card,** carte de crédit f. **~ note,** avoir m. **~ s.o. with,** attribuer à qn. **~worthy** a. solvable. **~or** n. créan|cier, -ière m., f.

creditable /ˈkredɪtəbl/ a. méritoire, honorable.

credulous /ˈkredjʊləs/ a. crédule.

creed /kriːd/ n. credo m.

creek /kriːk/ n. crique f.; (Amer.) ruisseau m. **up the ~,** (sl.) dans le pétrin.

creep /kriːp/ v.i. (p.t. **crept**) ramper; (fig.) se glisser. —n. (person: sl.) pauvre type m. **give s.o. the ~s,** faire frissonner qn. **~er** n. liane f. **~y** a. qui fait frissonner.

cremat|e /krɪˈmeɪt/ v.t. incinérer. **~ion** /-ʃn/ n. incinération f.

crematorium /kremə'tɔːrɪəm/ n. (pl. **-ia**) crématorium m.

Creole /ˈkriːəʊl/ n. créole m./f.

crêpe /kreɪp/ n. crêpe m. **~ paper,** papier crêpon m.

crept /krept/ see creep.

crescendo /krɪˈʃendəʊ/ n. (pl. **-os**) crescendo m.

crescent /ˈkresnt/ n. croissant m.; (fig.) rue en demi-lune f.

cress /kres/ n. cresson m.

crest /krest/ n. crête f.; (coat of arms) armoiries f. pl.

Crete /kriːt/ n. Crète f.

cretin /ˈkretɪn, Amer. ˈkriːtn/ n. crétin(e) m. (f.). **~ous** a. crétin.

crevasse /krɪˈvæs/ n. crevasse f.

crevice /ˈkrevɪs/ n. fente f.

crew /kruː/ n. équipage m.; (gang) équipe f. **~ cut,** coupe en brosse f. **~ neck,** (col) ras du cou m.

crib[1] /krɪb/ n. lit d'enfant m.

crib[2] /krɪb/ n. v.t./i. (p.t. **cribbed**) copier. —n. (schol., fam.) traduction f., aide-mémoire m. invar.

crick /krɪk/ n. (in neck) torticolis m.

cricket[1] /ˈkrɪkɪt/ n. (sport) cricket m. **~er** n. joueur de cricket m.

cricket[2] /ˈkrɪkɪt/ n. (insect) grillon m.

crime /kraɪm/ n. crime m.; (minor) délit m.; (acts) criminalité f.

criminal /ˈkrɪmɪnl/ a. & n. criminel(le) (m. (f.)).

crimp /krɪmp/ v.t. (hair) friser.

crimson /ˈkrɪmzn/ a. & n. cramoisi (m.).

cringle /ˈkrɪndʒ/ v.i. reculer; (fig.) s'humilier. **~ing** a. servile.

crinkle /ˈkrɪŋkl/ v.t./i. (se) froisser. **~n.** pl.i m.

cripple /ˈkrɪpl/ n. infirme m./f. **—v.t.** estropier; (fig.) paralyser.

crisis /ˈkraɪsɪs/ n. (pl. **crises** /-siːz/) crise f.

crisp /krɪsp/ a. (-er, -est) (culin.) croquant; (air, reply) vif. **~s** n. pl. chips m. pl.

criss-cross /ˈkrɪskrɒs/ a. entre-croisé. **—v.t./i.** (s')entrecroiser.

criterion /kraɪˈtɪərɪən/ n. (pl. **-ia**) critère m.

critic /ˈkrɪtɪk/ n. critique m. **~al** a. critique. **~ally** adv. d'une manière critique; (ill) gravement.

criticism /ˈkrɪtɪsɪzəm/ n. critique f.

criticize /ˈkrɪtɪsaɪz/ v.t./i. critiquer.

croak /krəʊk/ n. (bird) croasse-ment; (frog) coassement m. **—v.i.** croasser; coasser.

crochet /ˈkrəʊʃeɪ/ n. crochet m. **—v.t.** faire au crochet.

crockery /ˈkrɒkərɪ/ n. vaisselle f.

crocodile /ˈkrɒkədaɪl/ n. crocodile m.

crocus /ˈkrəʊkəs/ n. (pl. **-uses**) crocus m.

crony /ˈkrəʊnɪ/ n. cop|ain, -ine m., f.

crook /krʊk/ n. (criminal: fam.) escroc m.; (stick) houlette f.

crooked /ˈkrʊkɪd/ a. tordu; (winding) tortueux; (askew) de travers; (dishonest: fig.) malhon-nête. **~ly** adv. de travers.

croon /kruːn/ v.t./i. chantonner.

crop /krɒp/ n. récolte f.; (fig.) quantité f. **—v.t.** (p.t. **cropped**) couper. **—v.i. ~ up**, se présenter.

croquet /ˈkrəʊkeɪ/ n. croquet m.

croquette /krəʊˈket/ n. croquette f.

cross /krɒs/ n. croix f.; (hybrid) hybride m. **—v.t./i.** traverser; (legs, animals) croiser; (cheque) barrer; (paths) se croiser. **—a.** en colère, fâché (with, contre). **~-check** v.t. vérifier (pour con-firmer). **~-country (running)**, cross m. **~ off or out**, rayer. **~ s.o.'s mind**, venir à l'esprit de qn. **~ talk at ~ purposes**, parler sans se comprendre. **~ly** adv. avec colère.

crossbar /ˈkrɒsbɑː(r)/ n. barre transversale f.

cross-examine /krɒsɪɡˈzæmɪn/ v.t. faire subir un examen contradic-toire à.

cross-eyed /ˈkrɒsaɪd/ a. **be ~**, loucher.

crossfire /ˈkrɒsfaɪə(r)/ n. feux croisés m. pl.

crossing /ˈkrɒsɪŋ/ n. (by boat) traversée f.; (on road) passage clouté m.

cross-reference /krɒsˈrefrəns/ n. renvoi m.

crossroads /ˈkrɒsrəʊdz/ n. carre-four m.

cross-section /krɒsˈsekʃn/ n. coupe transversale f.; (sample: fig.) échantillon m.

cross-wind /ˈkrɒswɪnd/ n. vent de travers m.

crosswise /ˈkrɒswaɪz/ adv. en travers.

crossword /ˈkrɒswɜːd/ n. mots croisés m. pl.

crotch /krɒtʃ/ n. (of garment) entre-jambes m. invar.

crotchet /ˈkrɒtʃɪt/ n. (mus.) noire f.

crotchety /ˈkrɒtʃɪtɪ/ a. grin-cheux.

crouch /kraʊtʃ/ v.i. s'accroupir.

crow /krəʊ/ n. corbeau m. **—v.i.** (of cock) (p.t. **crew**) chanter; (fig.) jubiler. **as the ~ flies**, à vol d'oiseau. **~'s feet**, pattes d'oie f. pl.

crowbar /'krəʊbɑ:(r)/ n. pied-de-biche m.

crowd /kraʊd/ n. foule f. —v.i. affluer. —v.t. remplir. ~ **into**, (s')entasser dans. ~ed a. plein.

crown /kraʊn/ n. couronne f.; (top part) sommet m. —v.t. couronner. C~ **Court**, Cour d'assises f. C~ **prince**, prince héritier m.

crucial /'kru:ʃl/ a. crucial.

crucifix /'kru:sifiks/ n. crucifix m.

crucif|y /'kru:sifaɪ/ v.t. crucifier. ~**ixion** /-'fikʃn/ n. crucifixion f.

crude /kru:d/ a. (-er, -est) (raw) brut; (rough, vulgar) grossier.

cruel /krʊəl/ a. (crueller, cruellest) cruel. ~**ty** n. cruauté f.

cruet /'kru:ɪt/ n. huilier m.

cruis|e /kru:z/ n. croisière f. —v.i. (ship) croiser; (tourists) faire une croisière; (vehicle) rouler. ~**er** n. croiseur m. ~**ing speed**, vitesse de croisière f.

crumb /krʌm/ n. miette f.

crumble /'krʌmbl/ v.t./i. (s')effriter; (bread) (s')émietter; (collapse) s'écrouler.

crummy /'krʌmɪ/ a. (-ier, -iest) (sl.) moche, minable.

crumpet /'krʌmpɪt/ n. (culin.) petite crêpe (grillée) f.

crumple /'krʌmpl/ v.t./i. (se) froisser.

crunch /krʌntʃ/ v.t. croquer. —n. (event) moment critique m. **when it comes to the** ~, quand ça devient sérieux.

crusade /kru:'seɪd/ n. croisade f. ~**r** /-ə(r)/ n. (knight) croisé m.; (fig.) militant(e) m. (f.).

crush /krʌʃ/ v.t. écraser; (clothes) froisser. —n. (crowd) presse f. **a** ~ **on**, (sl.) le béguin pour.

crust /krʌst/ n. croûte f. ~**y** a. croustillant.

crutch /krʌtʃ/ n. béquille f.; (crotch) entre-jambes m. invar.

crux /krʌks/ n. **the** ~ **of**, (problem etc.) le nœud de.

cry /kraɪ/ n. cri m. —v.i. (weep) pleurer; (call out) crier. ~-**baby** n. pleurnicheu|r, -se m., f. ~ **off**, abandonner.

crying /'kraɪɪŋ/ a. (evil etc.) flagrant. **a** ~ **shame**, une vraie honte.

crypt /krɪpt/ n. crypte f.

cryptic /'krɪptɪk/ a. énigmatique.

crystal /'krɪstl/ n. cristal m. ~-**clear** a. parfaitement clair. ~**lize** v.t./i. (se) cristalliser.

cub /kʌb/ n. petit m. **Cub** (Scout), louveteau m.

Cuba /'kju:bə/ n. Cuba m. ~**n** a. & n. cubain(e) m. (f.)).

cubby-hole /'kʌbɪhəʊl/ n. cagibi m.

cub|e /kju:b/ n. cube m. ~**ic** a. cubique; (metre etc.) cube.

cubicle /'kju:bɪkl/ n. (in room, hospital, etc.) box m.; (at swimming-pool) cabine f.

cuckoo /'kʊku:/ n. coucou m.

cucumber /'kju:kʌmbə(r)/ n. concombre m.

cuddl|e /'kʌdl/ v.t. câliner. —v.i. (kiss and) s'embrasser. —n. caresse f. ~**y** a. câlin, caressant.

cudgel /'kʌdʒl/ n. gourdin m.

cue¹ /kju:/ n. signal m.; (theatre) réplique f.

cue² /kju:/ n. (billiards) queue f.

cuff /kʌf/ n. manchette f.; (Amer.) revers m. —v.t. gifler. ~-**link** n. bouton de manchette m. **off the** ~, impromptu.

cul-de-sac /'kʌldəsæk/ n. (pl. **culs-de-sac**) impasse f.

culinary /'kʌlɪnərɪ/ a. culinaire.

cull /kʌl/ v.t. (select) choisir; (kill) abattre sélectivement.

culminat|e /'kʌlmɪneɪt/ v.i. ~**e in**, se terminer par. ~**ion** /-'neɪʃn/ n. point culminant m.

culprit /'kʌlprɪt/ n. coupable m./f.

cult /kʌlt/ n. culte m. ~ **movie**, film culte.

cultivat|e /'kʌltɪveɪt/ v.t. cultiver. ~**ion** /-'veɪʃn/ n. culture f.

cultural /'kʌltʃərəl/ a. culturel.

culture /'kʌltʃə(r)/ n. culture f. ~**d** a. cultivé.

cumbersome /'kʌmbəsəm/ a. encombrant.

cumulative /'kjuːmjʊlətɪv/ a. cumulatif.

cunning /'kʌnɪŋ/ a. rusé. —n. astuce f., ruse f.

cup /kʌp/ n. tasse f.; (prize) coupe f. **Cup final**, finale de la coupe f. ~ **size**, profondeur de bonnet f. ~**tie** n. match de coupe m.

cupboard /'kʌbəd/ n. placard m., armoire f.

cupful /'kʌpfʊl/ n. tasse f.

Cupid /'kjuːpɪd/ n. Cupidon m.

curable /'kjʊərəbl/ a. guérissable.

curate /'kjʊərət/ n. vicaire m.

curator /kjʊə'reɪtə(r)/ n. (of museum) conservateur m.

curb[1] /kɜːb/ n. (restraint) frein m. —v.t. (desires etc.) refréner; (price increase etc.) freiner.

curb[2], (Amer.) **kerb** /kɜːb/ n. bord du trottoir m.

curdle /'kɜːdl/ v.t./i. (se) cailler.

curds /kɜːdz/ n. pl. lait caillé m.

cure[1] /kjʊə(r)/ v.t. guérir; (fig.) éliminer. —n. (recovery) guérison f.; (remedy) remède m.

cure[2] /kjʊə(r)/ v.t. (culin.) fumer; (in brine) saler.

curfew /'kɜːfjuː/ n. couvre-feu m.

curio /'kjʊərɪəʊ/ n. (pl. -os) curiosité f., bibelot m.

curi|ous /'kjʊərɪəs/ a. curieux. ~**osity** /-'ɒsɪtɪ/ n. curiosité f.

curl /kɜːl/ v.t./i. (hair) boucler. —n. boucle f. ~ **up**, se pelotonner; (shrivel) se racornir.

curler /'kɜːlə(r)/ n. bigoudi m.

curly /'kɜːlɪ/ a. (-ier, -iest) bouclé.

currant /'kʌrənt/ n. raisin de Corinthe m.; (berry) groseille f.

currency /'kʌrənsɪ/ n. (money) monnaie f.; (acceptance) cours m. **foreign** ~, devises étrangères f. pl.

current /'kʌrənt/ a. (common) courant; (topical) actuel; (year etc.) en cours. —n. courant m. ~ **account**, compte courant m. ~ **events**, l'actualité f. ~**ly** adv. actuellement.

curriculum /kə'rɪkjʊləm/ n. (pl. -la) programme scolaire m. ~ **vitae**, curriculum vitae m.

curry[1] /'kʌrɪ/ n. curry m., cari m.

curry[2] /'kʌrɪ/ v.t. ~ **favour with**, chercher les bonnes grâces de.

curse /kɜːs/ n. malédiction f.; (oath) juron m. —v.t. maudire. —v.i. (swear) jurer.

cursor /'kɜːsə(r)/ n. curseur m.

cursory /'kɜːsərɪ/ a. (trop) rapide.

curt /kɜːt/ a. brusque.

curtail /kɜː'teɪl/ v.t. écourter, raccourcir; (expenses etc.) réduire.

curtain /'kɜːtn/ n. rideau m.

curtsy /'kɜːtsɪ/ n. révérence f. —v.i. faire une révérence.

curve /kɜːv/ n. courbe f. —v.t./i. (se) courber; (of road) tourner.

cushion /'kʊʃn/ n. coussin m. —v.t. (a blow) amortir; (fig.) protéger.

cushy /'kʊʃɪ/ a. (-ier, -iest) (job etc.: fam.) pépère.

custard /'kʌstəd/ n. crème anglaise f.; (set) crème renversée f.

custodian /kʌ'stəʊdɪən/ n. gardien(ne) m. (f.).

custody /'kʌstədɪ/ n. garde f.; (jurid.) détention préventive f.

custom /'kʌstəm/ n. coutume f.; (patronage: comm.) clientèle f. ~**built**, ~**made** adjs. fait etc. sur commande. ~**ary** a. d'usage.

customer /'kʌstəmə(r)/ n. client(e) m. (f.); (fam.) **an odd/a difficult** ~, un individu curieux/difficile.

customize /ˈkʌstəmaɪz/ v.t. personnaliser.

customs /ˈkʌstəmz/ n. pl. douane f. —a. douanier. ~ **officer,** douanier m.

cut /kʌt/ v.t./i. (p.t. cut, pres. p. cutting) couper; (hedge, jewel) tailler; (prices etc.) réduire. —n. coupure f.; (of clothes) coupe f.; (piece) morceau m.; réduction f. ~ **back** or **down (on),** réduire. ~**-back** n. réduction f. ~ **in,** (auto.) se rabattre. ~ **off,** couper; (fig.) isoler. ~ **out,** découper; (leave out) supprimer. ~**-price** a. à prix réduit. ~ **short,** (visit) écourter. ~ **up,** couper; (carve) découper. ~ **up about,** démoralisé par.

cute /kjuːt/ a. (-er, -est) (fam.) astucieux; (Amer.) mignon.

cuticle /ˈkjuːtɪkl/ n. petites peaux f. pl. (de l'ongle).

cutlery /ˈkʌtləri/ n. couverts m. pl.

cutlet /ˈkʌtlɪt/ n. côtelette f.

cutting /ˈkʌtɪŋ/ a. cinglant. —n. (from newspaper) coupure f.; (plant) bouture f. ~ **edge,** tranchant m.

CV abbr. see **curriculum vitae.**

cyanide /ˈsaɪənaɪd/ n. cyanure m.

cybernetics /saɪbəˈnetɪks/ n. cybernétique f.

cycl|e /ˈsaɪkl/ n. cycle m.; (bicycle) vélo m. —v.i. aller à vélo. ~**ing** n. cyclisme m. ~**ist** n. cycliste m./f.

cyclic(al) /ˈsaɪklɪk(l)/ a. cyclique.

cyclone /ˈsaɪkləʊn/ n. cyclone m.

cylind|er /ˈsɪlɪndə(r)/ n. cylindre m. ~**rical** /-ˈlɪndrɪkl/ a. cylindrique.

cymbal /ˈsɪmbl/ n. cymbale f.

cynic /ˈsɪnɪk/ n. cynique m./f. ~**al** a. cynique. ~**ism** /-sɪzəm/ n. cynisme m.

cypress /ˈsaɪprəs/ n. cyprès m.

Cypr|us /ˈsaɪprəs/ n. Chypre f. ~**iot** /ˈsɪprɪət/ a. & n. cypriote (m./f.).

cyst /sɪst/ n. kyste m. ~**ic fibrosis,** mucoviscidose f.

cystitis /sɪsˈtaɪtɪs/ n. cystite f.

czar /zɑː(r)/ n. tsar m.

Czech /tʃek/ a. & n. tchèque (m./f.).

Czechoslovak /tʃekəˈsləʊvæk/ a. & n. tchécoslovaque (m./f.). ~**ia** /-sləˈvækɪə/ n. Tchécoslovaquie f.

D

dab /dæb/ v.t. (p.t. dabbed) tamponner. —n. a ~ **of,** un petit coup de; (fam.) **be a ~ hand at,** avoir le coup de main pour. ~ **sth. on,** appliquer qch. à petits coups sur.

dabble /ˈdæbl/ v.i. ~ **in,** se mêler un peu de. ~**r** /-ə(r)/ n. amateur m.

dad /dæd/ n. (fam.) papa m. ~**dy** n. (children's use) papa m.

daffodil /ˈdæfədɪl/ n. jonquille f.

daft /dɑːft/ a. (-er, -est) idiot.

dagger /ˈdægə(r)/ n. poignard m.

dahlia /ˈdeɪlɪə/ n. dahlia m.

daily /ˈdeɪlɪ/ a. quotidien. —adv. tous les jours. —n. (newspaper) quotidien m.; (charwoman: fam.) femme de ménage f.

dainty /ˈdeɪntɪ/ a. (-ier, -iest) délicat.

dairy /ˈdeərɪ/ n. (on farm) laiterie f.; (shop) crémerie f. —a. laitier.

daisy /ˈdeɪzɪ/ n. pâquerette f. ~ **wheel,** marguerite f.

dale /deɪl/ n. vallée f.

dam /dæm/ n. barrage m. —v.t. (p.t. dammed) endiguer.

damag|e /ˈdæmɪdʒ/ n. dégâts m. pl., dommages m. pl.; (harm: fig.) préjudice m. ~**es,** (jurid.) dommages et intérêts m. pl. —v.t. abîmer; (fig.) nuire à. ~**ing** a. nuisible.

dame /deɪm/ n. (old use) dame f.; (Amer., sl.) fille f.

damn /dæm/ v.t. (swear at) maudire; (condemn, fig.) condamner. —int. zut, merde. —n. **not care a ~**, s'en foutre. —a. sacré. —adv. rudement. **~ation** /-ˈneɪʃn/ n. damnation f.

damp /dæmp/ n. humidité f. —a. (-er, -est) humide. —v.t. humecter; (fig.) refroidir. **~en** v.t. = damp. **~ness** n. humidité f.

dance /dɑːns/ v.t./i. danser. —n. danse f.; (gathering) bal m. **~ hall**, dancing m., salle de danse f. **~r** /-ə(r)/ n. danseu|r, -se m., f.

dandelion /ˈdændɪlaɪən/ n. pissenlit m.

dandruff /ˈdændrʌf/ n. pellicules f. pl.

dandy /ˈdændɪ/ n. dandy m.

Dane /deɪn/ n. Danois(e) m. (f.).

danger /ˈdeɪndʒə(r)/ n. danger m.; (risk) risque m. **be in ~ of**, risquer de. **~ous** a. dangereux.

dangle /ˈdæŋgl/ v.t./i. (se) balancer, (laisser) pendre. **~ sth. in front of s.o.**, (fig.) faire miroiter qch. à qn.

Danish /ˈdeɪnɪʃ/ a. danois. —n. (lang.) danois m.

dank /dæŋk/ a. (-er, -est) humide et froid.

dapper /ˈdæpə(r)/ a. élégant.

dare /deə(r)/ v.t. **~ (to) do**, oser faire. **~ s.o. to do**, défier qn. de faire. —n. défi m. **I ~ say**, je suppose (that, que).

daredevil /ˈdeədevl/ n. casse-cou m. invar.

daring /ˈdeərɪŋ/ a. audacieux.

dark /dɑːk/ a. (-er, -est) obscur, sombre, noir; (colour) foncé, sombre; (skin) brun, foncé; (gloomy) sombre. —n. noir m.; (nightfall) tombée de la nuit f. **~ horse**, individu aux talents inconnus m. **~-room** n. chambre noire f. **in the ~**, (fig.) dans

l'ignorance (about, de). **~ness** n. obscurité f.

darken /ˈdɑːkən/ v.t./i. (s')assombrir.

darling /ˈdɑːlɪŋ/ a. & n. chéri(e) (m. (f.)).

darn /dɑːn/ v.t. repriser.

dart /dɑːt/ n. fléchette f. **~s**, (game) fléchettes f. pl. —v.i. s'élancer.

dartboard /ˈdɑːtbɔːd/ n. cible f.

dash /dæʃ/ v.i. (hurry) se dépêcher; (forward etc.) se précipiter. —v.t. jeter (avec violence); (hopes) briser. —n. ruée f.; (stroke) tiret m. **a ~ of**, un peu de. **~ off**, (leave) partir en vitesse.

dashboard /ˈdæʃbɔːd/ n. tableau de bord m.

dashing /ˈdæʃɪŋ/ a. fringant.

data /ˈdeɪtə/ n. pl. données f. pl. **~ processing**, traitement des données m.

database /ˈdeɪtəbeɪs/ n. base de données f.

date¹ /deɪt/ n. date f.; (meeting: fam.) rendez-vous m. —v.t./i. dater; (go out with: fam.) sortir avec. **~ from**, dater de. **out of ~**, (old-fashioned) démodé; (passport) périmé. **to ~**, à ce jour. **up to ~**, (modern) moderne; (list) à jour. **~d** /-ɪd/ a. démodé.

date² /deɪt/ n. (fruit) datte f.

daub /dɔːb/ v.t. barbouiller.

daughter /ˈdɔːtə(r)/ n. fille f. **~-in-law** n. (pl. **~s-in-law**) belle-fille f.

daunt /dɔːnt/ v.t. décourager.

dauntless /ˈdɔːntlɪs/ a. intrépide.

dawdle /ˈdɔːdl/ v.i. lambiner. **~r** /-ə(r)/ n. lambin(e) m. (f.).

dawn /dɔːn/ n. aube f. —v.i. poindre; (fig.) naître. **it ~ed on me**, je m'en suis rendu compte.

day /deɪ/ n. jour m.; (whole day) journée f.; (period) époque f. **~-break** n. point du jour m. **~-dream** n. rêverie f.; v.i. rêvasser.

the ∼ **before,** la veille. the
following or **next** ∼, le lendemain.

daylight /'deɪlaɪt/ n. jour m.

daytime /'deɪtaɪm/ n. jour m.,
journée f.

daze /deɪz/ v.t. étourdir; (with
drugs) hébéter. —n. **in a** ∼,
étourdi; hébété.

dazzle /'dæzl/ v.t. éblouir.

deacon /'diːkən/ n. diacre m.

dead /ded/ a. mort; (numb) engourdi. —adv. complètement.
—n. **in the** ∼ **of,** au cœur de la
∼, les morts. ∼ **beat,** éreinté. ∼
end, impasse f. ∼**-end job,**
travail sans avenir m. **a** ∼ **loss,**
(thing) une perte de temps;
(person) une catastrophe. ∼**-pan**
a. impassible. **in** ∼ **centre,** au
beau milieu. **stop** ∼, s'arrêter
net. the race was a ∼ **heat,** ils
ont été classés ex aequo.

deaden /'dedn/ v.t. (sound, blow)
amortir; (pain) calmer.

deadline /'dedlaɪn/ n. date limite f.

deadlock /'dedlɒk/ n. impasse f.

deadly /'dedlɪ/ a. (-ier, -iest)
mortel; (weapon) meurtrier.

deaf /def/ a. (-er, -est) sourd. the
∼ **and dumb,** les sourds-muets.
∼**-aid** n. appareil acoustique m.
∼**ness** n. surdité f.

deafen /'defn/ v.t. assourdir.

deal /diːl/ v.t. (p.t. dealt) donner;
(a blow) porter. —v.i. (trade)
commercer. —n. affaire f.; (cards)
donne f. **a great** or **good** ∼,
beaucoup (of, de). ∼ **in,** faire le
commerce de. ∼ **with,** (handle,
manage) s'occuper de; (be about)
traiter de. ∼**er** n. marchand(e)
m. (f.); (agent) concessionnaire
m./f.

dealings /'diːlɪŋz/ n. pl. relations f.
pl.

dean /diːn/ n. doyen m.

dear /dɪə(r)/ a. (-er, -est) cher.
—n. (my) ∼, mon cher, ma chère;

(darling) (mon) chéri, (ma)
chérie. —adv. cher. —int. oh ∼!,
oh mon Dieu! ∼**ly** adv. tendrement; (pay) cher.

dearth /dɜːθ/ n. pénurie f.

death /deθ/ n. mort f. ∼ **certificate,** acte de décès m. ∼ **duty,**
droits de succession m. pl. ∼
penalty, peine de mort f. **it is a**
∼**-trap,** (place, vehicle) il y a un
danger de mort. ∼**ly** a. de mort,
mortel.

debar /dɪ'bɑː(r)/ v.t. (p.t. de-
barred) exclure.

debase /dɪ'beɪs/ v.t. avilir.

debate /dɪ'beɪt/ n. discussion f.,
débat m. —v.t. discuter. ∼**e**
whether, se demander si. ∼**able**
a. discutable.

debauch /dɪ'bɔːtʃ/ v.t. débaucher.
∼**ery** n. débauche f.

debilitate /dɪ'bɪlɪteɪt/ v.t. dé-
biliter.

debility /dɪ'bɪlɪtɪ/ n. débilité f.

debit /'debɪt/ n. débit m. **in** ∼,
débiteur. —a. (balance) débiteur.
—v.t. (p.t. **debited**) débiter.

debris /'deɪbriː/ n. débris m. pl.

debt /det/ n. dette f. **in** ∼, endetté.
∼**or** n. débit|teur, -trice m., f.

debunk /diː'bʌŋk/ v.t. (fam.)
démythifier.

decade /'dekeɪd/ n. décennie f.

decaden|t /'dekədənt/ a. décadent.
∼**ce** n. décadence f.

decaffeinated /diː'kæfɪneɪtɪd/ a.
décaféiné.

decanter /dɪ'kæntə(r)/ n. carafe f.

decathlon /dɪ'kæθlɒn/ n. décathlon m.

decay /dɪ'keɪ/ v.i. se gâter, pourrir;
(fig.) décliner. —n. pourriture f.;
(of tooth) carie f.; (fig.) déclin m.

deceased /dɪ'siːst/ a. décédé. —n.
défunt(e) m. (f.).

deceit /dɪ'siːt/ n. tromperie f. ∼**ful**
a. trompeur. ∼**fully** adv. d'une
manière trompeuse.

deceive /dɪ'siːv/ v.t. tromper.

December /dɪˈsembə(r)/ n. décembre m.

decen|t /ˈdiːsnt/ a. décent, convenable; (good: fam.) (assez) bon; (kind: fam.) gentil. **~cy** n. décence f. **~tly** adv. décemment.

decentralize /diːˈsentrəlaɪz/ v.t. décentraliser.

decept|ive /dɪˈseptɪv/ a. trompeur. **~ion** /-pʃn/ n. tromperie f.

decibel /ˈdesɪbel/ n. décibel m.

decide /dɪˈsaɪd/ v.t./i. décider; (question) régler. **~ on**, se décider pour. **~ to do**, décider de faire. **~d** /-ɪd/ a. (firm) résolu; (clear) net. **~dly** /-ɪdlɪ/ adv. résolument; nettement.

deciduous /dɪˈsɪdjʊəs/ a. à feuillage caduc.

decimal /ˈdesɪml/ a. décimal. —n. décimale f. **~ point**, virgule f.

decimate /ˈdesɪmeɪt/ v.t. décimer.

decipher /dɪˈsaɪfə(r)/ v.t. déchiffrer.

decision /dɪˈsɪʒn/ n. décision f.

decisive /dɪˈsaɪsɪv/ a. (conclusive) décisif; (firm) décidé. **~ly** adv. d'une façon décidée.

deck /dek/ n. pont m.; (of cards: Amer.) jeu m. **~chair** n. chaise longue f. **top ~**, (of bus) impériale f.

declar|e /dɪˈkleə(r)/ v.t. déclarer. **~ation** /deklǝˈreɪʃn/ n. déclaration f.

decline /dɪˈklaɪn/ v.t. refuser (poliment); (deteriorate) décliner; (fall) baisser. —n. déclin m.; baisse f.

decode /diːˈkəʊd/ v.t. décoder.

decompos|e /diːkəmˈpəʊz/ v.t./i. (se) décomposer. **~ition** /-ɒmpəˈzɪʃn/ n. décomposition f.

décor /ˈdeɪkɔː(r)/ n. décor m.

decorat|e /ˈdekəreɪt/ v.t. décorer; (room) peindre or tapisser. **~ion** /-ˈreɪʃn/ n. décoration f. **~ive** /-ətɪv/ a. décoratif.

decorator /ˈdekəreɪtə(r)/ n. peintre en bâtiment m. **(interior) ~**, décora|teur, -trice d'appartements m., f.

decorum /dɪˈkɔːrəm/ n. décorum m.

decoy¹ /ˈdiːkɔɪ/ n. (bird) appeau m.; (trap) piège m., leurre m.

decoy² /dɪˈkɔɪ/ v.t. attirer, appâter.

decrease /dɪˈkriːs/ v.t./i. diminuer. —n. /ˈdiːkriːs/ diminution f.

decree /dɪˈkriː/ n. (pol., relig.) décret m.; (jurid.) jugement m. —v.t. (p.t. decreed) décréter.

decrepit /dɪˈkrepɪt/ a. (building) délabré; (person) décrépit.

decry /dɪˈkraɪ/ v.t. dénigrer.

dedicat|e /ˈdedɪkeɪt/ v.t. dédier. **~e o.s. to**, se consacrer à. **~ed** a. dévoué. **~ion** /-ˈkeɪʃn/ n. dévouement m.; (in book) dédicace f.

deduce /dɪˈdjuːs/ v.t. déduire.

deduct /dɪˈdʌkt/ v.t. déduire; (from wages) retenir. **~ion** /-kʃn/ n. déduction f.; retenue f.

deed /diːd/ n. acte m.

deem /diːm/ v.t. juger.

deep /diːp/ a. (-er, -est) profond. —adv. profondément. **~ in thought**, absorbé dans ses pensées. **~ into the night**, tard dans la nuit. **~freeze** n. congélateur m.; v.t. congeler. **~fry**, frire. **~ly** adv. profondément.

deepen /ˈdiːpən/ v.t. approfondir. —v.i. devenir plus profond; (mystery, night) s'épaissir.

deer /dɪə(r)/ n. invar. cerf m.; (doe) biche f.

deface /dɪˈfeɪs/ v.t. dégrader.

defamation /defəˈmeɪʃn/ n. diffamation f.

default /dɪˈfɔːlt/ v.i. (jurid.) faire défaut. —n. **by ~**, (jurid.) par défaut. **win by ~**, gagner par forfait. —a. (comput.) par défaut.

defeat /dɪˈfiːt/ v.t. vaincre; (thwart) faire échouer. —n. défaite f.; (of plan etc.) échec m.

defect[1] /'di:fekt/ n. défaut m. **~ive** /dɪ'fektɪv/ a. défectueux.

defect[2] /dɪ'fekt/ v.i. faire défection. **~ to**, passer à. **~or** n. transfuge m./f.

defence /dɪ'fens/ n. défense f. **~less** a. sans défense.

defend /dɪ'fend/ v.t. défendre. **~ant** n. (jurid.) accusé(e) m. (f.). **~er**, défenseur n.

defense /dɪ'fens/ n. Amer. = **defence**.

defensive /dɪ'fensɪv/ a. défensif. **—n.** défensive f.

defer /dɪ'fɜː(r)/ v.t. (p.t. deferred) (postpone) différer, remettre.

deferen|ce /'defərəns/ n. déférence f. **~tial** /-'renʃl/ a. déférent.

defian|ce /dɪ'faɪəns/ n. défi m. **in ~ce of**, au mépris de. **~t** a. de défi. **~tly** adv. d'un air de défi.

deficien|t /dɪ'fɪʃnt/ a. insuffisant. **be ~t in**, manquer de. **~cy** n. insuffisance f.; (fault) défaut m.

deficit /'defɪsɪt/ n. déficit m.

defile /dɪ'faɪl/ v.t. souiller.

define /dɪ'faɪn/ v.t. définir.

definite /'defɪnɪt/ a. précis; (obvious) net; (firm) catégorique; (certain) certain. **~ly** adv. certainement; (clearly) nettement.

definition /defɪ'nɪʃn/ n. définition f.

definitive /dɪ'fɪnɪtɪv/ a. définitif.

deflat|e /dɪ'fleɪt/ v.t. dégonfler. **~ion** /-ʃn/ n. dégonflement m.; (comm.) déflation f.

deflect /dɪ'flekt/ v.t./i. (faire) dévier.

deforestation /di:fɒrɪ'steɪʃn/ n. déforestation f.

deform /dɪ'fɔːm/ v.t. déformer. **~ed** a. difforme. **~ity** n. difformité f.

defraud /dɪ'frɔːd/ v.t. (state, customs) frauder. **~ s.o. of sth.**, escroquer qch. à qn.

defray /dɪ'freɪ/ v.t. payer.

defrost /di:'frɒst/ v.t. dégivrer.

deft /deft/ a. (-er, -est) adroit. **~ness** n. adresse f.

defunct /dɪ'fʌŋkt/ a. défunt.

defuse /di:'fjuːz/ v.t. désamorcer.

defy /dɪ'faɪ/ v.t. défier; (attempts) résister à.

degenerate[1] /dɪ'dʒenəreɪt/ v.i. dégénérer (into, en).

degenerate[2] /dɪ'dʒenərət/ a. & n. dégénéré(e) (m. (f.)).

degrad|e /dɪ'greɪd/ v.t. dégrader. **~ation** /degrə'deɪʃn/ n. dégradation f.; (state) déchéance f.

degree /dɪ'griː/ n. degré m.; (univ.) diplôme universitaire m.; (Bachelor's degree) licence f.; **higher ~**, (univ.) maîtrise f. or doctorat m. **to such a ~ that**, à tel point que.

dehydrate /di:'haɪdreɪt/ v.t./i. (se) déshydrater.

de-ice /di:'aɪs/ v.t. dégivrer.

deign /deɪn/ v.t. **~ to do**, daigner faire.

deity /'di:ɪtɪ/ n. divinité f.

deject|ed /dɪ'dʒektɪd/ a. abattu. **~ion** /-kʃn/ n. abattement m.

delay /dɪ'leɪ/ v.t. retarder. **—v.i.** tarder. **—n.** (lateness, time overdue) retard m.; (waiting) délai m. **~ doing**, attendre pour faire.

delectable /dɪ'lektəbl/ a. délectable, très agréable.

delegate[1] /'delɪgət/ n. délégué(e) m. (f.).

delegat|e[2] /'delɪgeɪt/ v.t. déléguer. **~ion** /-'geɪʃn/ n. délégation f.

delete /dɪ'liːt/ v.t. effacer; (with line) barrer. **~ion** /-ʃn/ n. suppression f.; (with line) rature f.

deliberate[1] /dɪ'lɪbərət/ a. délibéré; (steps, manner) mesuré. **~ly** adv. exprès, délibérément.

deliberat|e[2] /dɪ'lɪbəreɪt/ v.i. délibérer. **—v.t.** considérer. **~ion** /-'reɪʃn/ n. délibération f.

delica|te /'delɪkət/ a. délicat. **~cy** n. délicatesse f.; (food) mets délicat or raffiné m.

delicatessen /delɪkə'tesn/ n. épicerie fine f., charcuterie f.

delicious /dɪ'lɪʃəs/ a. délicieux.

delight /dɪ'laɪt/ n. grand plaisir m., joie f., délice m. (f. in pl.); (thing) délice m. (f. in pl.). —v.t. réjouir. —v.i. ~ in, prendre plaisir à. **~ed** a. ravi. **~ful** a. charmant, très agréable.

delinquen|t /dɪ'lɪŋkwənt/ a. & n. délinquant(e) (m. (f.)) **~cy** n. délinquance f.

deliri|ous /dɪ'lɪrɪəs/ a. be **~ous**, délirer. **~um** n. délire m.

deliver /dɪ'lɪvə(r)/ v.t. (message) remettre; (goods) livrer; (letters) distribuer; (free) délivrer; (utter) prononcer; (med.) accoucher; (a blow) porter. **~ance** n. délivrance f. **~y** n. livraison f.; distribution f.; accouchement m.

delta /'deltə/ n. delta m.

delu|de /dɪ'luːd/ v.t. tromper. **~de o.s.**, se faire des illusions. **~sion** /-ʒn/ n. illusion f.

deluge /'deljuːdʒ/ n. déluge m. —v.t. inonder (with, de).

de luxe /də'lʌks/ a. de luxe.

delve /delv/ v.i. fouiller.

demagogue /'deməɡɒɡ/ n. démagogue m./f.

demand /dɪ'mɑːnd/ v.t. exiger; (in negotiations) réclamer. —n. exigence f.; (claim) revendication f.; (comm.) demande f. **in ~**, recherché. **on ~**, à la demande. **~ing** a. exigeant.

demarcation /diːmɑː'keɪʃn/ n. démarcation f.

demean /dɪ'miːn/ v.t. ~ **o.s.**, s'abaisser, s'avilir.

demeanour /dɪ'miːnə(r)/ n. (Amer.) **demeanor** n. comportement m.

demented /dɪ'mentɪd/ a. dément.

demerara /demə'reərə/ n. (brown sugar) cassonade f.

demise /dɪ'maɪz/ n. décès m.

demo /'deməʊ/ n. (pl. -os) (demonstration: fam.) manif f.

demobilize /diː'məʊbəlaɪz/ v.t. démobiliser.

democracy /dɪ'mɒkrəsɪ/ n. démocratie f.

democrat /'deməkræt/ n. démocrate m./f. **~ic** /-'krætɪk/ a. démocratique.

demoli|sh /dɪ'mɒlɪʃ/ v.t. démolir. **~tion** /demə'lɪʃn/ n. démolition f.

demon /'diːmən/ n. démon m.

demonstrat|e /'demənstreɪt/ v.t. démontrer. —v.i. (pol.) manifester. **~ion** /-'streɪʃn/ n. démonstration f.; (pol.) manifestation f. **~or** n. manifestant(e) m. (f.).

demonstrative /dɪ'mɒnstrətɪv/ a. démonstratif.

demoralize /dɪ'mɒrəlaɪz/ v.t. démoraliser.

demote /dɪ'məʊt/ v.t. rétrograder.

demure /dɪ'mjʊə(r)/ a. modeste.

den /den/ n. antre m.

denial /dɪ'naɪəl/ n. dénégation f.; (statement) démenti m.

denigrate /'denɪɡreɪt/ v.t. dénigrer.

denim /'denɪm/ n. toile de coton f. **~s**, (jeans) blue-jeans m. pl.

Denmark /'denmɑːk/ n. Danemark m.

denomination /dɪnɒmɪ'neɪʃn/ n. (relig.) confession f.; (money) valeur f.

denote /dɪ'nəʊt/ v.t. dénoter.

denounce /dɪ'naʊns/ v.t. dénoncer.

dens|e /dens/ a. (-er, -est) dense; (person) obtus. **~ely** adv. (packed etc.) très. **~ity** n. densité f.

dent /dent/ n. bosse f. —v.t. cabosser. **there is a ~ in the car door**, la portière est cabossée.

dental /'dentl/ a. dentaire. **~ floss**, fil dentaire m. **~ surgeon**, dentiste m./f.

dentist /'dentɪst/ n. dentiste m./f. ~ry n. art dentaire m.

dentures /'dentʃəz/ n. pl. dentier m.

denude /dɪ'njuːd/ v.t. dénuder.

denunciation /dɪnʌnsɪ'eɪʃn/ n. dénonciation f.

deny /dɪ'naɪ/ v.t. nier (that, que); (rumour) démentir; (disown) renier; (refuse) refuser.

deodorant /diː'əʊdərənt/ n. & a. déodorant (m.).

depart /dɪ'pɑːt/ v.i. partir. ~ from, (deviate) s'écarter de.

department /dɪ'pɑːtmənt/ n. département m.; (in shop) rayon m.; (in office) service m. D~ of Health, ministère de la santé m. ~ store, grand magasin m.

departure /dɪ'pɑːtʃə(r)/ n. départ m. a ~ from, (custom, diet, etc.) une entorse à.

depend /dɪ'pend/ v.i. dépendre (on, de). it (all) ~s, ça dépend. ~ on, (rely on) compter sur. ~ing on the weather, selon le temps qu'il fera. ~able a. sûr. ~ence n. dépendance f. ~ent a. dépendant. be ~ent on, dépendre de.

dependant /dɪ'pendənt/ n. personne à charge f.

depict /dɪ'pɪkt/ v.t. (describe) dépeindre; (in picture) représenter.

deplete /dɪ'pliːt/ v.t. (reduce) réduire; (use up) épuiser.

deplor|e /dɪ'plɔː(r)/ v.t. déplorer. ~able a. déplorable.

deploy /dɪ'plɔɪ/ v.t. déployer.

depopulate /diː'pɒpjʊleɪt/ v.t. dépeupler.

deport /dɪ'pɔːt/ v.t. expulser. ~ation /diːpɔː'teɪʃn/ n. expulsion f.

depose /dɪ'pəʊz/ v.t. déposer.

deposit /dɪ'pɒzɪt/ v.t. (p.t. deposited) déposer. —n. dépôt m.; (of payment) acompte m.; (to

reserve) arrhes f. pl.; (against damage) caution f.; (on bottle etc.) consigne f.; (of mineral) gisement m. ~ account, compte dépôt m. ~or n. (comm.) déposant(e) m. (f.), épargnant(e) m. (f.).

depot /'depəʊ, Amer. 'diːpəʊ/ n. dépôt m.; (Amer.) gare (routière) f.

deprav|e /dɪ'preɪv/ v.t. dépraver. ~ity /-'prævətɪ/ n. dépravation f.

deprecate /'deprəkeɪt/ v.t. désapprouver.

depreciat|e /dɪ'priːʃɪeɪt/ v.t./i. (se) déprécier. ~ion /-'eɪʃn/ n. dépréciation f.

depress /dɪ'pres/ v.t. (sadden) déprimer; (push down) appuyer sur. become ~ed, déprimer. ~ing a. déprimant. ~ion /-ʃn/ n. dépression f.

deprivation /deprɪ'veɪʃn/ n. privation f.

deprive /dɪ'praɪv/ v.t. ~ of, priver de. ~d a. (child etc.) déshérité.

depth /depθ/ n. profondeur f. be out of one's ~, perdre pied; (fig.) être perdu. in the ~s of, au plus profond de.

deputation /depjʊ'teɪʃn/ n. députation f.

deputize /'depjʊtaɪz/ v.i. assurer l'intérim (for, de). —v.t. (Amer.) déléguer, nommer.

deputy /'depjʊtɪ/ n. suppléant(e) m. (f.) —a. adjoint. ~ chairman, vice-président m.

derail /dɪ'reɪl/ v.t. faire dérailler. be ~ed, dérailler. ~ment n. déraillement m.

deranged /dɪ'reɪndʒd/ a. (mind) dérangé.

derelict /'derəlɪkt/ a. abandonné.

deri|de /dɪ'raɪd/ v.t. railler. ~sion /-'rɪʒn/ n. dérision f. ~sive a. (laughter, person) railleur.

derisory /dɪ'raɪsərɪ/ a. (scoffing) railleur; (offer etc.) dérisoire.

derivative /dɪˈrɪvətɪv/ a. & n. dérivé (m.).

deriv|e /dɪˈraɪv/ v.t. ~**e from**, tirer de. —v.i. ~**e from**, dériver de. ~**ation** /derɪˈveɪʃn/ n. dérivation f.

derogatory /dɪˈrɒgətrɪ/ a. (word) péjoratif; (remark) désobligeant.

derv /dɜːv/ n. gas-oil m., gazole m.

descend /dɪˈsend/ v.t./i. descendre. **be ~ed from**, descendre de. ~**ant** n. descendant(e) m. (f.).

descent /dɪˈsent/ n. descente f.; (lineage) origine f.

descri|be /dɪˈskraɪb/ v.t. décrire. ~**ption** /-ˈskrɪpʃn/ n. description f. ~**ptive** /-ˈskrɪptɪv/ a. descriptif.

desecrat|e /ˈdesɪkreɪt/ v.t. profaner. ~**ion** /-ˈkreɪʃn/ n. profanation f.

desert[1] /ˈdezət/ n. désert m. —a. désertique. ~ **island**, île déserte f.

desert[2] /dɪˈzɜːt/ v.t./i. déserter. ~**ed** a. désert. ~**er** n. déserteur m. ~**ion** /-ʃn/ n. désertion f.

deserts /dɪˈzɜːts/ n. pl. one's ~, ce qu'on mérite.

deserv|e /dɪˈzɜːv/ v.t. mériter (to, de). ~**edly** /-ɪdlɪ/ adv. à juste titre. ~**ing** a. (person) méritant; (action) méritoire.

design /dɪˈzaɪn/ n. (sketch) dessin m., plan m.; (construction) conception f.; (pattern) motif m.; (style of dress) modèle m.; (aim) dessein m. —v.t. (sketch) dessiner; (devise, intend) concevoir. ~**er** n. dessina|teur, -trice m., f.; (of fashion) styliste m./f.

designat|e /ˈdezɪgneɪt/ v.t. désigner. ~**ion** /-ˈneɪʃn/ n. désignation f.

desir|e /dɪˈzaɪə(r)/ n. désir m. —v.t. désirer. ~**able** a. désirable. ~**ability** /-əˈbɪlətɪ/ n. attrait m.

desk /desk/ n. bureau m.; (of pupil)

pupitre m.; (in hotel) réception f.; (in bank) caisse f.

desolat|e /ˈdesələt/ a. (place) désolé; (bleak: fig.) morne. ~**ion** /-ˈleɪʃn/ n. désolation f.

despair /dɪˈspeə(r)/ n. désespoir m. —v.i. désespérer (of, de).

despatch /dɪˈspætʃ/ v.t. = **dispatch**.

desperate /ˈdespərət/ a. désespéré; (criminal) prêt à tout. **be ~ for**, avoir une envie folle de. ~**ly** adv. désespérément; (worried) terriblement; (ill) gravement.

desperation /despəˈreɪʃn/ n. désespoir m. **in** or **out of ~**, en désespoir de cause.

despicable /dɪˈspɪkəbl/ a. méprisable, infâme.

despise /dɪˈspaɪz/ v.t. mépriser.

despite /dɪˈspaɪt/ prep. malgré.

desponden|t /dɪˈspɒndənt/ a. découragé. ~**cy** n. découragement m.

despot /ˈdespɒt/ n. despote m.

dessert /dɪˈzɜːt/ n. dessert m. ~**spoon** n. cuiller à dessert f. ~**spoonful** n. cuillerée à soupe f.

destination /destɪˈneɪʃn/ n. destination f.

destine /ˈdestɪn/ v.t. destiner.

destiny /ˈdestɪnɪ/ n. destin m.

destitute /ˈdestɪtjuːt/ a. indigent. ~ **of**, dénué de.

destr|oy /dɪˈstrɔɪ/ v.t. détruire; (animal) abattre. ~**uction** /-ʃn/ n. destruction f. ~**uctive** a. destructeur.

destroyer /dɪˈstrɔɪə(r)/ n. (warship) contre-torpilleur m.

detach /dɪˈtætʃ/ v.t. détacher. ~**able** a. détachable. ~**ed** a. détaché. ~**ed house**, maison individuelle f.

detachment /dɪˈtætʃmənt/ n. détachement m.

detail /ˈdiːteɪl/ n. détail m. —v.t. exposer en détail; (troops) détacher. **go into** ~, entrer dans le détail. ~**ed** *a.* détaillé.

detain /dɪ'teɪn/ *v.t.* retenir; (*in prison*) détenir. ~**ee** /di:teɪ'ni:/ *n.* détenu(e) *m.* (*f.*).

detect /dɪ'tekt/ *v.t.* découvrir; (*perceive*) distinguer; (*tumour*) dépister; (*mine*) détecter. ~**ion** /-kʃn/ *n.* découverte *f.*; dépistage *m.*; détection *f.* ~**or** *n.* détecteur *m.*

detective /dɪ'tektɪv/ *n.* policier *m.*; (*private*) détective *m.*

detention /dɪ'tenʃn/ *n.* détention *f.*; (*schol.*) retenue *f.*

deter /dɪ'tɜ:(r)/ *v.t.* (*p.t.* **deterred**) dissuader (**from**, de).

detergent /dɪ'tɜ:dʒənt/ *a.* & *n.* détergent (*m.*).

deteriorat|**e** /dɪ'tɪərɪəreɪt/ *v.i.* se détériorer. ~**ion** /-'reɪʃn/ *n.* détérioration *f.*

determin|**e** /dɪ'tɜ:mɪn/ *v.t.* déterminer. ~**e to do,** décider de faire. ~**ation** /-'neɪʃn/ *n.* détermination *f.* ~**ed** *a.* déterminé. ~**ed to do,** décidé à faire.

deterrent /dɪ'terənt, *Amer.* dɪ'tɜ:rənt/ *n.* force de dissuasion *f.*

detest /dɪ'test/ *v.t.* détester. ~**able** *a.* détestable.

detonat|**e** /'detəneɪt/ *v.t./i.* (faire) détoner. ~**ion** /-'neɪʃn/ *n.* détonation *f.* ~**or** *n.* détonateur *m.*

detour /'di:tʊə(r)/ *n.* détour *m.*

detract /dɪ'trækt/ *v.i.* ~ **from,** (*lessen*) diminuer.

detriment /'detrɪmənt/ *n.* détriment *m.* ~**al** /-'mentl/ *a.* préjudiciable (**to**, à).

devalu|**e** /di:'vælju:/ *v.t.* dévaluer. ~**ation** /-ju'eɪʃn/ *n.* dévaluation *f.*

devastat|**e** /'devəsteɪt/ *v.t.* dévaster; (*overwhelm*: *fig.*) accabler. ~**ing** *a.* accablant.

develop /dɪ'veləp/ *v.t./i.* (*p.t.* **developed**) (se) développer; (*contract*) contracter; (*build on, transform*) exploiter, aménager; (*change*) évoluer; (*appear*) se manifester. ~ **into,** devenir. ~**ing country,** pays en voie de développement *m.* ~**ment** *n.* développement *m.* (**housing**) ~, lotissement *m.* (**new**) ~**ment,** fait nouveau *m.*

deviant /'di:vɪənt/ *a.* anormal. —*n.* (*psych.*) déviant *m.*

deviat|**e** /'di:vɪeɪt/ *v.i.* dévier. ~**e from,** (*norm*) s'écarter de. ~**ion** /-'eɪʃn/ *n.* déviation *f.*

device /dɪ'vaɪs/ *n.* appareil *m.*; (*scheme*) procédé *m.*

devil /'devl/ *n.* diable *m.* ~**ish** *a.* diabolique.

devious /'di:vɪəs/ *a.* tortueux. **he is** ~, il a l'esprit tortueux.

devise /dɪ'vaɪz/ *v.t.* inventer; (*plan, means*) combiner, imaginer.

devoid /dɪ'vɔɪd/ *a.* ~ **of,** dénué de.

devolution /di:və'lu:ʃn/ *n.* décentralisation *f.*; (*of authority, power*) délégation *f.* (**to**, à).

devot|**e** /dɪ'vəʊt/ *v.t.* consacrer. ~**ed** *a.* dévoué. ~**edly** *adv.* avec dévouement. ~**ion** /-ʃn/ *n.* dévouement *m.*; (*relig.*) dévotion *f.* ~**ions,** (*relig.*) dévotions *f. pl.*

devotee /devə'ti:/ *n.* ~ **of,** passionné(e) de *m.* (*f.*).

devour /dɪ'vaʊə(r)/ *v.t.* dévorer.

devout /dɪ'vaʊt/ *a.* fervent.

dew /dju:/ *n.* rosée *f.*

dexterity /dek'sterətɪ/ *n.* dextérité *f.*

diabet|**es** /daɪə'bi:ti:z/ *n.* diabète *m.* ~**ic** /-'betɪk/ *a.* & *n.* diabétique (*m.*/*f.*).

diabolical /daɪə'bɒlɪkl/ *a.* diabolique; (*bad*: *fam.*) atroce.

diagnose /'daɪəgnəʊz/ *v.t.* diagnostiquer.

diagnosis /daɪəgˈnəʊsɪs/ n. (pl. -oses) /-siːz/) diagnostic m.

diagonal /daɪˈægənl/ a. diagonal. —n. diagonale f. **~ly** adv. en diagonale.

diagram /ˈdaɪəgræm/ n. schéma m.

dial /ˈdaɪəl/ n. cadran m. —v.t. (p.t. **dialled**) (number) faire; (person) appeler. **~ling code**, (Amer.) **~ code**, indicatif m. **~ling tone**, (Amer.) **~ tone**, tonalité f.

dialect /ˈdaɪəlekt/ n. dialecte m.

dialogue /ˈdaɪəlɒg/ n. dialogue m.

diameter /daɪˈæmɪtə(r)/ n. diamètre m.

diamond /ˈdaɪəmənd/ n. diamant m.; (shape) losange m.; (baseball) terrain m. **~s**, (cards) carreau m.

diaper /ˈdaɪəpə(r)/ n. (baby's nappy: Amer.) couche f.

diaphragm /ˈdaɪəfræm/ n. diaphragme m.

diarrhoea, (Amer.) **diarrhea** /daɪəˈrɪə/ n. diarrhée f.

diary /ˈdaɪərɪ/ n. (for appointments etc.) agenda m.; (appointments) emploi du temps m. (for private thoughts) journal intime m.

dice /daɪs/ n. invar. dé m. —v.t. (food) couper en dés.

dicey /ˈdaɪsɪ/ a. (fam.) risqué.

dictate /dɪkˈteɪt/ v.t./i. dicter. **~ion** /-ʃn/ n. dictée f.

dictates /ˈdɪkteɪts/ n. pl. préceptes m. pl.

dictator /dɪkˈteɪtə(r)/ n. dictateur m. **~ship** n. dictature f.

dictatorial /dɪktəˈtɔːrɪəl/ a. dictatorial.

diction /ˈdɪkʃn/ n. diction f.

dictionary /ˈdɪkʃənrɪ/ n. dictionnaire m.

did /dɪd/ see do.

diddle /ˈdɪdl/ v.t. (sl.) escroquer.

didn't /ˈdɪdnt/ = **did not**.

die[1] /daɪ/ v.i. (pres. p. **dying**) mourir. **~ down**, diminuer. **~ out**, disparaître. **be dying to**

do/for, mourir d'envie de faire/de.

die[2] /daɪ/ n. (metal mould) matrice f., étampe f.

die-hard /ˈdaɪhɑːd/ n. réactionnaire m./f.

diesel /ˈdiːzl/ n. diesel m. **~ engine**, moteur diesel m.

diet /ˈdaɪət/ n. (habitual food) alimentation f.; (restricted) régime m. —v.i. suivre un régime. **diet|etic** /daɪəˈtetɪk/ a. diététique. **~ician** n. diététicien(ne) m. (f.).

differ /ˈdɪfə(r)/ v.i. différer (**from**, de); (disagree) ne pas être d'accord.

differen|t /ˈdɪfrənt/ a. différent. **~ce** n. différence f.; (disagreement) différend m. **~tly** adv. différemment (**from**, de).

differential /dɪfəˈrenʃl/ a. & n. différentiel (m.).

differentiate /dɪfəˈrenʃɪeɪt/ v.t. différencier. —v.i. faire la différence (**between**, entre).

difficult /ˈdɪfɪkəlt/ a. difficile. **~y** n. difficulté f.

diffiden|t /ˈdɪfɪdənt/ a. qui manque d'assurance. **~ce** n. manque d'assurance f.

diffuse[1] /dɪˈfjuːs/ a. diffus.

diffuse[2] /dɪˈfjuːz/ v.t. diffuser. **~ion** /-ʒn/ n. diffusion f.

dig /dɪg/ v.t./i. (p.t. **dug**, pres. p. **digging**) creuser; (thrust) enfoncer. —n. (poke) coup de coude m.; (remark) coup de patte m.; (archael.) fouilles f. pl. **~s**, (lodgings: fam.) chambre meublée f. **~ (over)**, bêcher. **~ up**, déterrer.

digest[1] /dɪˈdʒest/ v.t./i. digérer. **~ible** a. digestible. **~ion** /-stʃən/ n. digestion f.

digest[2] /ˈdaɪdʒest/ n. sommaire m.

digestive /dɪˈdʒestɪv/ a. digestif.

digger /ˈdɪgə(r)/ n. (techn.) pelleteuse f., excavateur m.

digit /ˈdɪdʒɪt/ n. chiffre m.

digital /'dɪdʒɪtl/ a. (clock) numérique, à affichage numérique; (recording) numérique.

dignif|y /'dɪgnɪfaɪ/ v.t. donner de la dignité à. ~**ied** a. digne.

dignitary /'dɪgnɪtərɪ/ n. dignitaire m.

dignity /'dɪgnɪtɪ/ n. dignité f.

digress /daɪ'gres/ v.i. faire une digression. ~ **from**, s'écarter de. ~**ion** /-ʃn/ n. digression f.

dike /daɪk/ n. digue f.

dilapidated /dɪ'læpɪdeɪtɪd/ a. délabré.

dilat|e /daɪ'leɪt/ v.t./i. (se) dilater. ~**ion** /-ʃn/ n. dilatation f.

dilatory /'dɪlətərɪ/ a. dilatoire.

dilemma /dɪ'lemə/ n. dilemme m.

dilettante /dɪlɪ'tæntɪ/ n. dilettante m./f.

diligen|t /'dɪlɪdʒənt/ a. assidu. ~**ce** n. assiduité f.

dilly-dally /'dɪlɪdælɪ/ v.i. (fam.) lanterner.

dilute /daɪ'ljuːt/ v.t. diluer.

dim /dɪm/ a. (dimmer, dimmest) (weak) faible; (dark) sombre; (indistinct) vague; (fam.) stupide. —v.t./i. (p.t. dimmed) (light) (s')atténuer. ~**ly** adv. (shine) faiblement; (remember) vaguement. ~**mer** n. ~ (**switch**), variateur d'intensité m. ~**ness** n. faiblesse f.; (of room etc.) obscurité f.

dime /daɪm/ n. (in USA, Canada) pièce de dix cents f.

dimension /daɪ'menʃn/ n. dimension f.

diminish /dɪ'mɪnɪʃ/ v.t./i. diminuer.

diminutive /dɪ'mɪnjʊtɪv/ a. minuscule. —n. diminutif m.

dimple /'dɪmpl/ n. fossette f.

din /dɪn/ n. vacarme m.

dine /daɪn/ v.i. dîner. ~**r** /-ə(r)/ n. dîneur, -se m., f.; (rail.) wagon-restaurant m.; (Amer.) restaurant à service rapide m.

dinghy /'dɪŋgɪ/ n. canot m.; (inflatable) canot pneumatique m.

ding|y /'dɪndʒɪ/ a. (-ier, -iest) miteux, minable. ~**iness** n. aspect miteux or minable m.

dining-room /'daɪnɪŋrʊm/ n. salle à manger f.

dinner /'dɪnə(r)/ n. (evening meal) dîner m.; (lunch) déjeuner m. ~-**jacket** n. smoking m. ~ **party**, dîner m.

dinosaur /'daɪnəsɔː(r)/ n. dinosaure m.

dint /dɪnt/ n. **by** ~ **of**, à force de.

diocese /'daɪəsɪs/ n. diocèse m.

dip /dɪp/ v.t./i. (p.t. dipped) plonger. —n. (slope) déclivité f.; (in sea) bain rapide m. ~ **into**, (book) feuilleter; (savings) puiser dans. ~ **one's headlights**, se mettre en code.

diphtheria /dɪf'θɪərɪə/ n. diphtérie f.

diphthong /'dɪfθɒŋ/ n. diphtongue f.

diploma /dɪ'pləʊmə/ n. diplôme m.

diplomacy /dɪ'pləʊməsɪ/ n. diplomatie f.

diplomat /'dɪpləmæt/ n. diplomate m./f. ~**ic** /-'mætɪk/ a. (pol.) diplomatique; (tactful) diplomate.

dire /daɪə(r)/ a. (-er, -est) affreux; (need, poverty) extrême.

direct /dɪ'rekt/ a. direct. —adv. directement. —v.t. diriger; (letter, remark) adresser; (a play) mettre en scène. ~ **s.o. to**, indiquer à qn. le chemin de; (order) signifier à qn. de. ~**ness** n. franchise f.

direction /dɪ'rekʃn/ n. direction f.; (theatre) mise en scène f. ~**s**, indications f. pl. **ask** ~**s**, demander le chemin. ~**s for use**, mode d'emploi m.

directly /dɪ'rektlɪ/ adv. directement; (at once) tout de suite. —conj. dès que.

director /dɪˈrektə(r)/ n. direc|teur, -trice m., f.; (theatre) metteur en scène m.

directory /dɪˈrektərɪ/ n. (phone book) annuaire m.

dirt /dɜːt/ n. saleté f.; (earth) terre f. **~ cheap**, (sl.) très bon marché invar. **~-track** n. (sport) cendrée f.

dirty /ˈdɜːtɪ/ a. (-ier, -iest) sale; (word) grossier. **get ~**, se salir. **~v.t./i.** (se) salir.

disability /dɪsəˈbɪlətɪ/ n. handicap m.

disable /dɪsˈeɪbl/ v.t. rendre infirme. **~d** a. handicapé.

disadvantage /dɪsədˈvɑːntɪdʒ/ n. désavantage m. **~d** a. déshérité.

disagree /dɪsəˈɡriː/ v.i. ne pas être d'accord (**with**, avec). **~ with** s.o., (food, climate) ne pas convenir à qn. **~ment** n. désaccord m.; (quarrel) différend m.

disagreeable /dɪsəˈɡriːəbl/ a. désagréable.

disappear /dɪsəˈpɪə(r)/ v.i. disparaître. **~ance** n. disparition f.

disappoint /dɪsəˈpɔɪnt/ v.t. décevoir. **~ing** a. décevant. **~ed** a. déçu. **~ment** n. déception f.

disapprov|e /dɪsəˈpruːv/ v.i. **~e (of)**, désapprouver. **~al** n. désapprobation f.

disarm /dɪsˈɑːm/ v.t./i. désarmer. **~ament** n. désarmement m.

disarray /dɪsəˈreɪ/ n. désordre m.

disassociate /dɪsəˈsəʊʃɪeɪt/ v.t. = **dissociate**.

disast|er /dɪˈzɑːstə(r)/ n. désastre m. **~rous** a. désastreux.

disband /dɪsˈbænd/ v.t./i. (se) disperser.

disbelief /dɪsbɪˈliːf/ n. incrédulité f.

disc /dɪsk/ n. disque m.; (comput.) = **disk. ~ brake**, frein à disque m. **~ jockey**, disc-jockey m., animateur m.

discard /dɪsˈkɑːd/ v.t. se débarrasser de; (beliefs etc.) abandonner.

discern /dɪˈsɜːn/ v.t. discerner. **~ible** a. perceptible. **~ing** a. perspicace.

discharge¹ /dɪsˈtʃɑːdʒ/ v.t. (unload) décharger; (liquid) déverser; (duty) remplir; (dismiss) renvoyer; (prisoner) libérer. —v.i. (of pus) s'écouler.

discharge² /ˈdɪstʃɑːdʒ/ n. (med.) écoulement m.; (dismissal) renvoi m.; (electr.) décharge m.

disciple /dɪˈsaɪpl/ n. disciple m.

disciplin|e /ˈdɪsɪplɪn/ n. discipline f. —v.t. discipliner; (punish) punir. **~ary** a. disciplinaire.

disclaim /dɪsˈkleɪm/ v.t. désavouer. **~er** n. correctif m., précision f.

disclos|e /dɪsˈkləʊz/ v.t. révéler. **~ure** /-ʒə(r)/ n. révélation f.

disco /ˈdɪskəʊ/ n. (pl. -os) (club; fam.) discothèque f., disco m.

discolour /dɪsˈkʌlə(r)/ v.t./i. (se) décolorer. **~oration** /-ˈreɪʃn/ n. décoloration f.

discomfort /dɪsˈkʌmfət/ n. gêne f.

disconcert /dɪskənˈsɜːt/ v.t. déconcerter.

disconnect /dɪskəˈnekt/ v.t. détacher; (unplug) débrancher; (cut off) couper.

discontent /dɪskənˈtent/ n. mécontentement m. **~ed** a. mécontent.

discontinue /dɪskənˈtɪnjuː/ v.t. interrompre, cesser.

discord /ˈdɪskɔːd/ n. discorde f.; (mus.) dissonance f. **~ant** /-ˈskɔːdənt/ a. discordant.

discothèque /ˈdɪskətek/ n. discothèque f.

discount¹ /ˈdɪskaʊnt/ n. rabais m.

discount² /dɪsˈkaʊnt/ v.t. ne pas tenir compte de.

discourage /dɪsˈkʌrɪdʒ/ v.t. décourager.

discourse /'dɪskɔːs/ n. discours m.

discourteous /dɪs'kɜːtɪəs/ a. impoli, peu courtois.

discover /dɪ'skʌvə(r)/ v.t. découvrir. **~y** n. découverte f.

discredit /dɪs'kredɪt/ v.t. (p.t. **discredited**) discréditer. —n. discrédit m.

discreet /dɪ'skriːt/ a. discret. **~ly** adv. discrètement.

discrepancy /dɪ'skrepənsɪ/ n. contradiction f., incohérence f.

discretion /dɪ'skreʃn/ n. discrétion f.

discriminat|e /dɪ'skrɪmɪneɪt/ v.t./i. distinguer. **~e against**, faire de la discrimination contre. **~ing** a. (person) qui a du discernement. **~ion** /-'neɪʃn/ n. discernement m.; (bias) discrimination f.

discus /'dɪskəs/ n. disque m.

discuss /dɪ'skʌs/ v.t. (talk about) discuter de; (argue about, examine critically) discuter. **~ion** -ʃn/ n. discussion f.

disdain /dɪs'deɪn/ n. dédain m. **~ful** a. dédaigneux.

disease /dɪ'ziːz/ n. maladie f. **~d** a. malade.

disembark /dɪsɪm'bɑːk/ v.t./i. débarquer.

disembodied /dɪsɪm'bɒdɪd/ a. désincarné.

disenchant /dɪsɪn'tʃɑːnt/ v.t. désenchanter. **~ment** n. désenchantement m.

disengage /dɪsɪn'ɡeɪdʒ/ v.t. dégager; (mil.) retirer. —v.i. (mil.) retirer; (auto.) débrayer. **~ment** n. dégagement m.

disentangle /dɪsɪn'tæŋɡl/ v.t. démêler.

disfavour /dɪs'feɪvə(r)/ n. (Amer.) **disfavor** défaveur f.

disfigure /dɪs'fɪɡə(r)/ v.t. défigurer.

disgrace /dɪs'ɡreɪs/ n. (shame) honte f.; (disfavour) disgrâce f.

—v.t. déshonorer. **~d** a. (in disfavour) disgracié. **~ful** a. honteux.

disgruntled /dɪs'ɡrʌntld/ a. mécontent.

disguise /dɪs'ɡaɪz/ v.t. déguiser. —n. déguisement m. **in ~**, déguisé.

disgust /dɪs'ɡʌst/ n. dégoût m. —v.t. dégoûter. **~ing** a. dégoûtant.

dish /dɪʃ/ n. plat m. —v.t. **~ out**, (fam.) distribuer. **~ up**, servir. **the ~es**, (crockery) la vaisselle.

dishcloth /'dɪʃklɒθ/ n. lavette f.; (for drying) torchon m.

dishearten /dɪs'hɑːtn/ v.t. décourager.

dishevelled /dɪ'ʃevld/ a. échevelé.

dishonest /dɪs'ɒnɪst/ a. malhonnête. **~y** n. malhonnêteté f.

dishonour /dɪs'ɒnə(r)/ n. (Amer.) **dishonor** déshonneur m. —v.t. déshonorer. **~able** a. déshonorant. **~ably** adv. avec déshonneur.

dishwasher /'dɪʃwɒʃə(r)/ n. lave-vaisselle m. invar.

disillusion /dɪsɪ'luːʒn/ v.t. désillusionner. **~ment** n. désillusion f.

disincentive /dɪsɪn'sentɪv/ n. **be a ~ to**, décourager.

disinclined /dɪsɪn'klaɪnd/ a. **~ to**, peu disposé à.

disinfect /dɪsɪn'fekt/ v.t. désinfecter. **~ant** n. désinfectant m.

disinherit /dɪsɪn'herɪt/ v.t. déshériter.

disintegrate /dɪs'ɪntɪɡreɪt/ v.t./i. (se) désintégrer.

disinterested /dɪs'ɪntrəstɪd/ a. désintéressé.

disjointed /dɪs'dʒɔɪntɪd/ a. (talk) décousu.

disk /dɪsk/ n. (Amer.) = **disc**; (comput.) disque m. **~ drive**, drive m., lecteur de disquettes m.

diskette /dɪˈsket/ n. disquette f.

dislike /dɪsˈlaɪk/ n. aversion f. —v.t. ne pas aimer.

dislocat|e /ˈdɪsləkeɪt/ v.t. (limb) disloquer. **~ion** /-ˈkeɪʃn/ n. dislocation f.

dislodge /dɪsˈlɒdʒ/ v.t. (move) déplacer; (drive out) déloger.

disloyal /dɪsˈlɔɪəl/ a. déloyal. **~ty** n. déloyauté f.

dismal /ˈdɪzməl/ a. morne, triste.

dismantle /dɪsˈmæntl/ v.t. démonter, défaire.

dismay /dɪsˈmeɪ/ n. consternation f. —v.t. consterner.

dismiss /dɪsˈmɪs/ v.t. renvoyer; (appeal) rejeter; (from mind) écarter. **~al** n. renvoi m.

dismount /dɪsˈmaʊnt/ v.i. descendre, mettre pied à terre.

disobedien|t /dɪsəˈbiːdɪənt/ a. désobéissant. **~ce** n. désobéissance f.

disobey /dɪsəˈbeɪ/ v.t. désobéir à —v.i. désobéir.

disorder /dɪsˈɔːdə(r)/ n. désordre m.; (ailment) trouble(s) m. (pl.). **~ly** a. désordonné.

disorganize /dɪsˈɔːgənaɪz/ v.t. désorganiser.

disorientate /dɪsˈɔːrɪənteɪt/ v.t. désorienter.

disown /dɪsˈəʊn/ v.t. renier.

disparaging /dɪsˈpærɪdʒɪŋ/ a. désobligeant. **~ly** adv. de façon désobligeante.

disparity /dɪsˈpærətɪ/ n. disparité f., écart m.

dispassionate /dɪsˈpæʃənət/ a. impartial; (unemotional) calme.

dispatch /dɪsˈpætʃ/ v.t. (send, complete) expédier; (troops) envoyer. —n. expédition f.; (report) dépêche f. **~-rider** n. estafette f.

dispel /dɪsˈpel/ v.t. (p.t. dispelled) dissiper.

dispensary /dɪsˈpensərɪ/ n. pharmacie f., officine f.

dispense /dɪsˈpens/ v.t. distribuer; (medicine) préparer. —v.i. **~ with**, se passer de. **~r** /-ə(r)/ n. (container) distributeur m.

dispers|e /dɪsˈpɜːs/ v.t./i. (se) disperser. **~ion** n. dispersion f.

dispirited /dɪsˈpɪrɪtɪd/ a. découragé, abattu.

displace /dɪsˈpleɪs/ v.t. déplacer.

display /dɪsˈpleɪ/ v.t. montrer, exposer; (feelings) manifester. —n. exposition f.; manifestation f.; (comm.) étalage m.; (of computer) visuel m.

displeas|e /dɪsˈpliːz/ v.t. déplaire à. **~ed with**, mécontent de. **~ure** /-ˈpleʒə(r)/ n. mecontentement m.

disposable /dɪsˈpəʊzəbl/ a. à jeter.

dispos|e /dɪsˈpəʊz/ v.t. disposer. —v.i. **~ of**, se débarrasser de. well **~ed to**, bien disposé envers. **~al** n. (of waste) évacuation f. at s.o.'s **~al**, à la disposition de qn.

disposition /dɪspəˈzɪʃn/ n. disposition f.; (character) naturel m.

disproportionate /dɪsprəˈpɔːʃənət/ a. disproportionné.

disprove /dɪsˈpruːv/ v.t. réfuter.

dispute /dɪsˈpjuːt/ v.t. contester. —n. discussion f.; (pol.) conflit m. **in ~**, contesté.

disqualif|y /dɪsˈkwɒlɪfaɪ/ v.t. rendre inapte; (sport) disqualifier. **~y from driving**, retirer le permis à. **~ication** /-ɪˈkeɪʃn/ n. disqualification f.

disquiet /dɪsˈkwaɪət/ n. inquiétude f. **~ing** a. inquiétant.

disregard /dɪsrɪˈgɑːd/ v.t. ne pas tenir compte de. —n. indifférence f. (for, à).

disrepair /dɪsrɪˈpeə(r)/ n. mauvais état m., délabrement m.

disreputable /dɪsˈrepjʊtəbl/ a. peu recommendable.

disrepute /dɪsrɪˈpjuːt/ n. discrédit m.

disrespect /dɪsrɪ'spekt/ n. manque de respect m. ∼ful a. irrespectueux.

disrupt /dɪs'rʌpt/ v.t. (disturb, break up) perturber; (plans) déranger. ∼ion /-pʃn/ n. perturbation f. ∼ive a. perturbateur.

dissatisf|ied /dɪs'sætɪsfaɪd/ a. mécontent. ∼action /dɪsætɪs-'fækʃn/ n. mécontentement m.

dissect /dɪ'sekt/ v.t. disséquer. ∼ion /-kʃn/ n. dissection f.

disseminate /dɪ'semɪneɪt/ v.t. disséminer.

dissent /dɪ'sent/ v.i. différer (from, de). —n. dissentiment m.

dissertation /dɪsə'teɪʃn/ n. (univ.) mémoire m.

disservice /dɪs'sɜːvɪs/ n. mauvais service m.

dissident /'dɪsɪdənt/ a. & n. dissident(e) (m. (f.)).

dissimilar /dɪ'sɪmɪlə(r)/ a. dissemblable, différent.

dissipate /'dɪsɪpeɪt/ v.t./i. (se) dissiper; (efforts) gaspiller. ∼d /-ɪd/ a. (person) débauché.

dissociate /dɪ'səʊʃɪeɪt/ v.t. dissocier. ∼ o.s. from, se désolidariser de.

dissolute /'dɪsəljuːt/ a. dissolu.

dissolution /dɪsə'luːʃn/ n. dissolution f.

dissolve /dɪ'zɒlv/ v.t./i. (se) dissoudre.

dissuade /dɪ'sweɪd/ v.t. dissuader.

distance /'dɪstəns/ n. distance f. from a ∼, de loin. in the ∼, au loin.

distant /'dɪstənt/ a. éloigné, lointain; (relative) éloigné; (aloof) distant.

distaste /dɪs'teɪst/ n. dégoût m. ∼ful a. désagréable.

distemper /dɪs'tempə(r)/ n. (paint) badigeon m.; (animal disease) maladie f. —v.t. badigeonner.

distend /dɪs'tend/ v.t./i. (se) distendre.

distil /dɪ'stɪl/ v.t. (p.t. distilled) distiller. ∼lation /-'leɪʃn/ n. distillation f.

distillery /dɪ'stɪlərɪ/ n. distillerie f.

distinct /dɪ'stɪŋkt/ a. distinct; (marked) net. as ∼ from, par opposition à. ∼ion /-kʃn/ n. distinction f.; (in exam) mention très bien f. ∼ive a. distinctif. ∼ly adv. (see) distinctement; (forbid) expressément; (markedly) nettement.

distinguish /dɪ'stɪŋgwɪʃ/ v.t./i. distinguer. ∼ed a. distingué.

distort /dɪ'stɔːt/ v.t. déformer. ∼ion /-ʃn/ n. distorsion f.; (of facts) déformation f.

distract /dɪ'strækt/ v.t. distraire. ∼ed a. (distraught) éperdu. ∼ing a. gênant. ∼ion /-kʃn/ n. (lack of attention, entertainment) distraction f.

distraught /dɪ'strɔːt/ a. éperdu.

distress /dɪ'stres/ n. douleur f.; (poverty, danger) détresse f. —v.t. peiner. ∼ing a. pénible.

distribute /dɪ'strɪbjuːt/ v.t. distribuer. ∼ion /-'bjuːʃn/ n. distribution f. ∼or n. distributeur m.

district /'dɪstrɪkt/ n. région f.; (of town) quartier m.

distrust /dɪs'trʌst/ n. méfiance f. —v.t. se méfier de.

disturb /dɪs'tɜːb/ v.t. déranger; (alarm, worry) troubler. ∼ance n. dérangement m. (of, de); (noise) tapage m. ∼ances n. pl. (pol.) troubles m. pl. ∼ed a. troublé; (psychologically) perturbé. ∼ing a. troublant.

disused /dɪs'juːzd/ a. désaffecté.

ditch /dɪtʃ/ n. fossé m. —v.t. (sl.) abandonner.

dither /'dɪðə(r)/ v.i. hésiter.

ditto /'dɪtəʊ/ adv. idem m.

divan /dɪ'væn/ n. divan m.

div|e /daɪv/ v.i. plonger; (rush) se

préciper. —*n.* plongeon *m.*; (*of plane*) piqué *m.*; (*place: sl.*) bouge *m.* ∼**er** *n.* plongeu|r, ∼se *m.* ∼**ing-board** *n.* plongeoir *m.* ∼**ing-suit** *n.* tenue de plongée *f.*

diverge /daɪ'vɜːdʒ/ *v.i.* diverger.

divergent /daɪ'vɜːdʒənt/ *a.* divergent.

diverse /daɪ'vɜːs/ *a.* divers.

diversify /daɪ'vɜːsɪfaɪ/ *v.t.* diversifier.

diversity /daɪ'vɜːsətɪ/ *n.* diversité *f.*

diver|t /daɪ'vɜːt/ *v.t.* détourner; (*traffic*) dévier. ∼**sion** /-ʃn/ *n.* détournement *m.*; (*distraction*) diversion *f.*; (*of traffic*) déviation *f.*

divest /daɪ'vest/ *v.t.* ∼ **of**, (*strip of*) priver de, déposséder de.

divide /dɪ'vaɪd/ *v.t./i.* (se) diviser.

dividend /'dɪvɪdend/ *n.* dividende *m.*

divine /dɪ'vaɪn/ *a.* divin.

divinity /dɪ'vɪnɪtɪ/ *n.* divinité *f.*

division /dɪ'vɪʒn/ *n.* division *f.*

divorce /dɪ'vɔːs/ *n.* divorce *m.* (**from**, d'avec). —*v.t./i.* divorcer (d'avec). ∼**d** *a.* divorcé.

divorcee /dɪvɔː'siː, *Amer.* dɪvɔː'seɪ/ *n.* divorcé(e) *m.* (*f.*).

divulge /daɪ'vʌldʒ/ *v.t.* divulguer.

DIY *abbr. see* **do-it-yourself.**

dizz|y /'dɪzɪ/ *a.* (-**ier**, -**iest**) vertigineux. **be** *or* **feel** ∼**y**, avoir le vertige. ∼**iness** *n.* vertige *m.*

do /duː/ *v.t./i.* (*3 sing. present tense* **does**; *p.t.* **did**; *p.p.*, **done**) faire; (*progress, be suitable*) aller; (*be enough*) suffire; (*swindle: sl.*) avoir. **do well/badly**, se débrouiller bien/mal. **do the house**, peindre *ou* nettoyer *etc.* la maison. **well done!, bravo! well done**, (*culin.*) bien cuit. **done for**, (*fam.*) fichu. —*v. aux.* **do you see?**, voyez-vous? **do you live here?**—**I do**, est-ce que vous

habitez ici?—oui. **I do live here**, si, j'habite ici. **I do not smoke**, je ne fume pas. **don't you?**, **doesn't he?**, *etc.*, n'est-ce pas? —*n.* (*pl.* **dos** *or* **do's**) soirée *f.*, fête *f.* **dos and don'ts**, choses à faire et à ne pas faire. **do away with**, supprimer. **do in**, (*sl.*) tuer. **do-it-yourself** *n.* bricolage *m.*; *a.* (*shop, book*) de bricolage. **do out**, (*clean*) nettoyer. **do up**, (*fasten*) fermer; (*house*) refaire. **it's to do with the house**, c'est à propos de la maison. **it's nothing to do with me**, ça n'a rien à voir avec moi. **I could do with a holiday**, j'aurais bien besoin de vacances. **do without**, se passer de.

docile /'dəʊsaɪl/ *a.* docile.

dock[1] /dɒk/ *n.* dock *m.* —*v.t./i.* (se) mettre à quai. ∼**er** *n.* docker *m.*

dock[2] /dɒk/ *n.* (*jurid.*) banc des accusés *m.*

dock[3] /dɒk/ *v.t.* (*money*) retrancher.

dockyard /'dɒkjɑːd/ *n.* chantier naval *m.*

doctor /'dɒktə(r)/ *n.* médecin *m.*, docteur *m.*; (*univ.*) docteur *m.* —*v.t.* (*cat*) châtrer; (*fig.*) altérer.

doctorate /'dɒktərət/ *n.* doctorat *m.*

doctrine /'dɒktrɪn/ *n.* doctrine *f.*

document /'dɒkjʊmənt/ *n.* document *m.* ∼**ary** /-'mentrɪ/ *a.* & *n.* documentaire (*m.*). ∼**ation** /-'eɪʃn/ *n.* documentation *f.*

doddering /'dɒdərɪŋ/ *a.* gâteux.

dodge /dɒdʒ/ *v.t.* esquiver. —*v.i.* faire un saut de côté —*n.* (*fam.*) truc *m.*

dodgems /'dɒdʒəmz/ *n. pl.* autos tamponneuses *f. pl.*

dodgy /'dɒdʒɪ/ *a.* (-**ier**, -**iest**) (*fam.*: *difficult*) épineux, délicat; (*dangerous*) douteux.

doe /dəʊ/ *n.* (*deer*) biche *f.*

does /dʌz/ *see* **do.**

doesn't /'dʌznt/ = **does not.**

dog /dɒg/ n. chien m. —v.t. (p.t. **dogged**) poursuivre. **~-collar** n. (fam.) (faux) col d'ecclésiastique m. **~-eared** a. écorné.

dogged /'dɒgɪd/ a. obstiné.

dogma /'dɒgmə/ n. dogme m. **~tic** /-'mætɪk/ a. dogmatique.

dogsbody /'dɒgzbɒdɪ/ n. factotum m., bonne à tout faire f.

doily /'dɔɪlɪ/ n. napperon m.

doings /'duːɪŋz/ n. pl. (fam.) activités f. pl., occupations f. pl.

doldrums /'dɒldrəmz/ n. pl. **be in the ~,** (person) avoir le cafard.

dole /dəʊl/ v.t. **~ out,** distribuer. —n. (fam.) indemnité de chômage f. **on the ~,** (fam.) au chômage.

doleful /'dəʊlfl/ a. triste, morne.

doll /dɒl/ n. poupée f. —v.t. **~ up,** (fam.) bichonner.

dollar /'dɒlə(r)/ n. dollar m.

dollop /'dɒləp/ n. (of food etc.: fam.) gros morceau m.

dolphin /'dɒlfɪn/ n. dauphin m.

domain /də'meɪn/ n. domaine m.

dome /dəʊm/ n. dôme m.

domestic /də'mestɪk/ a. familial; (trade, flights, etc.) intérieur; (animal) domestique. **~ science,** arts ménagers m. pl. **~ated** a. (animal) domestiqué.

domesticity /dome'stɪsətɪ/ n. vie de famille f.

dominant /'dɒmɪnənt/ a. dominant.

dominate /'dɒmɪneɪt/ v.t./i. dominer. **~ion** /-'neɪʃn/ n. domination f.

domineering /dɒmɪ'nɪərɪŋ/ a. dominateur, autoritaire.

dominion /də'mɪnjən/ n. (British pol.) dominion m.

domino /'dɒmɪnəʊ/ n. (pl. -oes) domino m. **~es,** (game) dominos m. pl.

don¹ /dɒn/ v.t. (p.t. **donned**) revêtir, endosser.

don² /dɒn/ n. professeur d'université m.

donate /dəʊ'neɪt/ v.t. faire don de. **~ion** /-ʃn/ n. don m.

done /dʌn/ see **do.**

donkey /'dɒŋkɪ/ n. âne m. the **~-work** le sale boulot.

donor /'dəʊnə(r)/ n. dona|teur, -trice m., f.; (of blood) donneu|r, -se m., f.

don't /dəʊnt/ = **do not.**

doodle /'duːdl/ v.i. griffonner.

doom /duːm/ n. (ruin) ruine f.; (fate) destin m. —v.t. **be ~ed to,** être destiné or condamné à. **~ed (to failure)** voué à l'échec.

door /dɔː(r)/ n. porte f.; (of vehicle) portière f., porte f.

doorbell /'dɔːbel/ n. sonnette f.

doorman /'dɔːmən/ n. (pl. -men) portier m.

doormat /'dɔːmæt/ n. paillasson m.

doorstep /'dɔːstep/ n. pas de (la) porte m., seuil m.

doorway /'dɔːweɪ/ n. porte f.

dope /dəʊp/ n. (fam.) drogue f.; (idiot: sl.) imbécile m./f. —v.t. doper. **~y** a. (foolish: sl.) imbécile.

dormant /'dɔːmənt/ a. en sommeil.

dormitory /'dɔːmɪtrɪ/ Amer. /'dɔːmɪtɔːrɪ/ n. dortoir m.; (univ., Amer.) résidence f.

dormouse /'dɔːmaʊs/ n. (pl. -mice) loir m.

dose /dəʊs/ n. dose f. **~age** n. dose f.; (on label) posologie f.

doss /dɒs/ v.i. (sl.) roupiller. **~-house** n. asile de nuit m.

dossier /'dɒsɪə(r)/ n. dossier m.

dot /dɒt/ n. point m. **on the ~,** (fam.) à l'heure pile. **~-matrix** a. (printer) matriciel.

dote /dəʊt/ v.i. **~ on,** être gaga de.

dotted /'dɒtɪd/ a. (fabric) à pois. **~ line,** ligne en pointillés f. **~ with,** parsemé de.

dotty /'dɒtɪ/ a. (-ier, -iest) (fam.) cinglé, dingue.

double /'dʌbl/ a. double; (room, bed) pour deux personnes. —adv. deux fois. —n. double m.; (stuntman) doublure f. ~s, (tennis) double m. —v.t./i. doubler; (fold) plier en deux. at or on the ~, au pas de course. ~ the size, deux fois plus grand. pay ~, payer le double. ~-bass n. (mus.) contrebasse f. ~-breasted a. croisé. ~-check v.t. revérifier. ~ chin, double menton m. ~-cross v.t. tromper. ~-dealing n. double jeu m. ~-decker n. autobus à impériale m. ~ Dutch, de l'hébreu m.

doubly /'dʌblɪ/ adv. doublement.

doubt /daʊt/ n. doute m. —v.t. douter de. ~ if or that, douter que. ~ful a. incertain, douteux; (person) qui a des doutes. ~less adv. sans doute.

dough /dəʊ/ n. pâte f.; (money: sl.) fric m.

doughnut /'dəʊnʌt/ n. beignet m./f.

douse /daʊs/ v.t. arroser; (light, fire) éteindre.

dove /dʌv/ n. colombe f.

Dover /'dəʊvə(r)/ n. Douvres m./f.

dovetail /'dʌvteɪl/ v.t./i. (s')ajuster.

dowdy /'daʊdɪ/ a. (-ier, -iest) (clothes) sans chic, monotone.

down[1] /daʊn/ n. (fluff) duvet m.

down[2] /daʊn/ adv. en bas; (of sun) couché; (lower) plus bas. —prep. en bas de; (along) le long de. —v.t. (knock down, shoot down) abattre; (drink) vider. come or go ~, descendre. go ~ to the post office, aller à la poste. ~-and-out n. clochard(e) m. (f.). ~-hearted a. découragé. ~-market a. bas de gamme. ~-payment, acompte m. ~-to-earth a. terre-à-terre invar. ~

under, aux antipodes. ~ with, à bas.

downcast /'daʊnkɑːst/ a. démoralisé.

downfall /'daʊnfɔːl/ n. chute f.

downgrade /daʊn'greɪd/ v.t. déclasser.

downhill /daʊn'hɪl/ adv. go ~, descendre; (pej.) baisser.

downpour /'daʊnpɔː(r)/ n. grosse averse f.

downright /'daʊnraɪt/ a. (utter) véritable; (honest) franc. —adv. carrément.

downs /daʊnz/ n. pl. région de collines f.

downstairs /daʊn'steəz/ adv. en bas. —a. d'en bas.

downstream /'daʊnstriːm/ adv. en aval.

downtown /'daʊntaʊn/ a. (Amer.) du centre de la ville. ~ Boston/etc., le centre de Boston/etc.

downtrodden /'daʊntrɒdn/ a. opprimé.

downward /'daʊnwəd/ a. & adv., ~s adv. vers le bas.

dowry /'daʊərɪ/ n. dot f.

doze /dəʊz/ v.i. sommeiller. ~ off, s'assoupir. —n. somme m.

dozen /'dʌzn/ n. douzaine f. a ~ eggs, une douzaine d'œufs. ~s of, (fam.) des dizaines de.

Dr abbr. (Doctor) Docteur.

drab /dræb/ a. terne.

draft[1] /drɑːft/ n. (outline) brouillon m.; (comm.) traite f. —v.t. faire le brouillon de; (draw up) rédiger. the ~, (mil., Amer.) la conscription. a ~ treaty, un projet de traité.

draft[2] /drɑːft/ n. (Amer.) = **draught**.

drag /dræg/ v.t./i. (p.t. dragged) traîner; (river) draguer; (pull away) arracher. —n. (task: fam.) corvée f.; (person: fam.) raseu|r, -se m., f. in ~, en travesti. ~ on, s'éterniser.

dragon /'drægən/ n. dragon m.

dragon-fly /'drægənflaɪ/ n. libellule f.

drain /dreɪn/ v.t. (land) drainer; (vegetables) égoutter; (tank, glass) vider; (use up) épuiser. ~ (off), (liquid) faire écouler. —v.i. ~ (off), (of liquid) s'écouler. —n. (sewer) égout m. ~(-pipe), tuyau d'écoulement m. be a ~ on, pomper. ~ing-board n. égouttoir m.

drama /'drɑːmə/ n. art dramatique m., théâtre m.; (play, event) drame m. ~tic /drə'mætɪk/ a. (situation) dramatique; (increase) spectaculaire. ~tist /'dræmətɪst/ n. dramaturge m. ~tize /'dræmətaɪz/ v.t. adapter pour la scène; (fig.) dramatiser.

drank /dræŋk/ see **drink**.

drape /dreɪp/ v.t. draper. ~s n. pl. (Amer.) rideaux m. pl.

drastic /'dræstɪk/ a. sévère.

draught /drɑːft/ n. courant d'air m. ~s, (game) dames f. pl. ~ beer, bière à la pression f. ~y a. plein de courants d'air.

draughtsman /'drɑːftsmən/ n.(pl. -men) dessinateur, -trice industriel(le) m., f.

draw /drɔː/ v.t. (p.t. drew, p.p. drawn) (pull) tirer; (attract) attirer; (pass) passer; (picture) dessiner; (line) tracer. —v.i. dessiner; (sport) faire match nul; (come, move) venir. —n. (sport) match nul m.; (in lottery) tirage au sort m. ~ back, (recoil) reculer. ~ in, (days) diminuer. ~ near, (s')approcher (to, de). ~ out, (money) retirer. ~ up v.i. (stop) s'arrêter; v.t. (document) dresser; (chair) approcher.

drawback /'drɔːbæk/ n. inconvénient m.

drawbridge /'drɔːbrɪdʒ/ n. pontlevis m.

drawer /drɔː(r)/ n. tiroir m.

drawers /drɔːz/ n. pl. culotte f.

drawing /'drɔːɪŋ/ n. dessin m. ~board n. planche à dessin f. ~pin n. punaise f. ~-room n. salon m.

drawl /drɔːl/ n. voix traînante f.

drawn /drɔːn/ see **draw**. —a. (features) tiré; (match) nul.

dread /dred/ n. terreur f., crainte f. —v.t. redouter.

dreadful /'dredfl/ a. épouvantable, affreux. ~ly adv. terriblement.

dream /driːm/ n. rêve m. —v.t./i. (p.t. dreamed or dreamt) rêver. —a. (ideal) de ses rêves. ~ up, imaginer. ~er n. rêveu|r, -se m., f. ~y a. rêveur.

drear|y /'drɪərɪ/ a. (-ier, -iest) triste; (boring) monotone. ~iness n. tristesse f.; monotonie f.

dredge /dredʒ/ n. drague f. —v.t./i. draguer. ~r /-ə(r)/ n. dragueur m.

dregs /dregz/ n. pl. lie f.

drench /drentʃ/ v.t. tremper.

dress /dres/ n. robe f.; (clothing) tenue f. —v.t./i. (s')habiller; (food) assaisonner; (wound) panser. ~ circle, premier balcon m. ~ rehearsal, répétition générale f. ~ up as, se déguiser en. get ~ed, s'habiller.

dresser /'dresə(r)/ n. buffet m.; (actor's) habilleu|r, -se m., f.

dressing /'dresɪŋ/ n. (sauce) assaisonnement m.; (bandage) pansement m. ~-gown n. robe de chambre f. ~-room n. (sport) vestiaire m.; (theatre) loge f. ~table n. coiffeuse f.

dressmak|er /'dresmeɪkə(r)/ n. couturière f. ~ing n. couture f.

dressy /'dresɪ/ a. (-ier, -iest) chic invar.

drew /druː/ see **draw**.

dribble /'drɪbl/ v.i. couler goutte à

goutte; (*person*) baver; (*football*) dribbler.

dribs and drabs /drɪbz'dræbz/ *n. pl.* petites quantités *f. pl.*

dried /draɪd/ *a.* (*fruit etc.*) sec.

drier /'draɪə(r)/ *n.* séchoir *m.*

drift /drɪft/ *v.i.* aller à la dérive; (*pile up*) s'amonceler. —*n.* dérive *f.*; amoncellement *m.*; (*of events*) tournure *f.*; (*meaning*) sens *m.* **~ towards**, glisser vers. **(snow) ~**, congère *f.* **~er** *n.* personne sans but dans la vie *f.*

driftwood /'drɪftwʊd/ *n.* bois flotté *m.*

drill /drɪl/ *n.* (*tool*) perceuse *f.*; (*for teeth*) roulette *f.*; (*training*) exercice *m.*; (*procedure: fam.*) marche à suivre *f.* **(pneumatic) ~**, marteau piqueur *m.* —*v.t.* percer; (*train*) entraîner. —*v.i.* être à l'exercice.

drily /'draɪlɪ/ *adv.* sèchement.

drink /drɪŋk/ *v.t./i.* (*p.t.* **drank**, *p.p.* **drunk**) boire. —*n.* (*liquid*) boisson *f.*; (*glass of alcohol*) verre *m.* **a ~ of water**, un verre d'eau. **~able** *a.* (*not unhealthy*) potable; (*palatable*) buvable. **~er** *n.* buveu|r, -se *m.*, *f.* **~ing water**, eau potable *f.*

drip /drɪp/ *v.i.* (*p.t.* **dripped**) (dé)goutter; (*washing*) s'égoutter. —*n.* goutte *f.*; (*person: sl.*) lavette *f.* **~-dry** *v.t.* laisser égoutter; *a.* sans repassage.

dripping /'drɪpɪŋ/ *n.* (*Amer.* **~s**) graisse de rôti *f.*

drive /draɪv/ *v.t.* (*p.t.* **drove**, *p.p.* **driven**) chasser, pousser; (*vehicle*) conduire; (*machine*) actionner. —*v.i.* conduire. —*n.* promenade en voiture *f.*; (*private road*) allée *f.*; (*fig.*) énergie *f.*; (*psych.*) instinct *m.*; (*pol.*) campagne *f.*; (*auto.*) traction; (*golf, comput.*) drive *m.* **it's a two-hour ~**, c'est deux heures en voiture. **~ at**, en venir à. **~ away**, (*of

car*) partir. **~ in**, (*force in*) enfoncer. **~ mad**, rendre fou. **left-hand ~**, conduite à gauche *f.*

drivel /'drɪvl/ *n.* radotage *m.*

driver /'draɪvə(r)/ *n.* conduc|teur, -trice *m.*, *f.*, chauffeur *m.* **~'s license** (*Amer.*), permis de conduire *m.*

driving /'draɪvɪŋ/ *n.* conduite *f.* **~ licence**, permis de conduire *m.* **~ rain**, pluie battante *f.* **~ school**, auto-école *f.* **take one's ~ test**, passer son permis.

drizzle /'drɪzl/ *n.* bruine *f.* —*v.i.* bruiner.

dromedary /'dromədərɪ, (*Amer.*) 'drɒmədərɪ/ *n.* dromadaire *m.*

drone /drəʊn/ *n.* (*noise*) bourdonnement *m.*; (*bee*) faux bourdon *m.* —*v.i.* bourdonner; (*fig.*) parler d'une voix monotone.

drool /druːl/ *v.i.* baver (**over**, sur).

droop /druːp/ *v.i.* pencher, tomber.

drop /drɒp/ *n.* goutte *f.*; (*fall, lowering*) chute *f.* —*v.t./i.* (*p.t.* **dropped**) (laisser) tomber; (*decrease, lower*) baisser. **~ (off)**, (*person from car*) déposer. **~ a line**, écrire un mot (**to**, à). **~ in**, passer (**on**, chez). **~ off**, (*doze*) s'assoupir. **~ out**, se retirer (**of**, de); (*of student*) abandonner. **~-out** *n.* marginal(e) *m.* (*f.*), raté(e) *m.* (*f.*).

droppings /'drɒpɪŋz/ *n. pl.* crottes *f. pl.*

dross /drɒs/ *n.* déchets *m. pl.*

drought /draʊt/ *n.* sécheresse *f.*

drove /drəʊv/ *see* **drive**.

droves /drəʊvz/ *n. pl.* foule(s) *f. (pl.)*.

drown /draʊn/ *v.t./i.* (se) noyer.

drowsy /'draʊzɪ/ *a.* somnolent. **be or feel ~**, avoir envie de dormir.

drudge /drʌdʒ/ *n.* esclave du travail *m.* **~ry** /-ərɪ/ *n.* travail pénible et ingrat *m.*

drug /drʌg/ *n.* drogue *f.*; (*med.*)

médicament *m.* —*v.t.* (*p.t.* **drugged**) droguer. ∼ **addict**, drogué(e) *m.* (*f.*). ∼**gist** *n.* pharmacien(ne) *m.* (*f.*).

drugstore /'drʌgstɔː(r)/ *n.* (*Amer.*) drugstore *m.*

drum /drʌm/ *n.* tambour *m.*; (*for oil*) bidon *m.* ∼**s**, (*p.t.* **drummed**) tambouriner. —*v.t.* ∼ **into s.o.**, répéter sans cesse à qn. ∼ **up**, (*support*) susciter; (*business*) créer. ∼**mer** *n.* tambour *m.*; (*in pop group*) batteur *m.*

drumstick /'drʌmstɪk/ *n.* baguette de tambour *f.*; (*of chicken*) pilon *m.*

drunk /drʌŋk/ *see* **drink**. —*a.* ivre. **get** ∼, s'enivrer. —*n.*, ∼**ard** *n.* ivrogne(sse) *m.* (*f.*). ∼**en** *a.* ivre; (*habitually*) ivrogne. ∼**enness** *n.* ivresse *f.*

dry /draɪ/ *a.* (**drier**, **driest**) sec; (*day*) sans pluie. —*v.t./i.* (faire) sécher. **be** or **feel** ∼, avoir soif. ∼**-clean** *v.t.* nettoyer à sec. ∼**-cleaner** *n.* teinturier *m.* ∼ **run**, galop d'essai *m.* ∼ **up**, (*dry dishes*) essuyer la vaisselle; (*of supplies*) (se) tarir; (*be silent: fam.*) se taire. ∼**ness** *n.* sécheresse *f.*

dual /'djuːəl/ *a.* double. ∼ **carriageway**, route à quatre voies *f.* ∼**-purpose** *a.* qui fait double emploi.

dub /dʌb/ *v.t.* (*p.t.* **dubbed**) (*film*) doubler; (*nickname*) surnommer.

dubious /'djuːbɪəs/ *a.* (*pej.*) douteux. **be** ∼ **about sth.**, (*person*) avoir des doutes sur qch.

duchess /'dʌtʃɪs/ *n.* duchesse *f.*

duck /dʌk/ *n.* canard *m.* —*v.i.* se baisser subitement. —*v.t.* baisser; (*person*) plonger dans l'eau. ∼**ling** *n.* caneton *m.*

duct /dʌkt/ *n.* conduit *m.*

dud /dʌd/ *a.* (*tool etc.: sl.*) mal

fichu; (*coin: sl.*) faux; (*cheque: sl.*) sans provision. **be a** ∼, (*not work: sl.*) ne pas marcher.

dude /duːd/ *n.* (*Amer.*) dandy *m.*

due /djuː/ *a.* (*owing*) dû; (*expected*) attendu; (*proper*) qui convient. —*adv.* ∼ **east**/*etc.*, droit vers l'est/*etc.* —*n.* dû *m.* ∼**s**, droits *m. pl.*; (*of club*) cotisation *f.* ∼ **to**, à cause de; (*caused by*) dû à. **she's** ∼ **to leave now**, c'est prévu qu'elle parte maintenant. **in** ∼ **course**, (*eventually*) avec le temps; (*at the right time*) en temps et lieu.

duel /'djuːəl/ *n.* duel *m.*

duet /djuː'et/ *n.* duo *m.*

duffle /'dʌfl/ *a.* ∼ **bag**, sac de marin *m.* ∼ **coat**, duffel-coat *m.*

dug /dʌg/ *see* **dig**.

duke /djuːk/ *n.* duc *m.*

dull /dʌl/ *a.* (**-er**, **-est**) ennuyeux; (*colour*) terne; (*weather*) morne; (*sound*) sourd; (*stupid*) bête; (*blunt*) émoussé. —*v.t.* (*pain*) amortir; (*mind*) engourdir.

duly /'djuːlɪ/ *adv.* comme il convient; (*in due time*) en temps voulu.

dumb /dʌm/ *a.* (**-er**, **-est**) muet; (*stupid: fam.*) bête.

dumbfound /dʌm'faʊnd/ *v.t.* sidérer, ahurir.

dummy /'dʌmɪ/ *n.* (*comm.*) article factice *m.*; (*of tailor*) mannequin *m.*; (*of baby*) sucette *f.* —*a.* factice. ∼ **run**, galop d'essai *m.*

dump /dʌmp/ *v.t.* déposer; (*abandon: fam.*) se débarrasser de; (*comm.*) dumper. —*n.* tas d'ordures *m.*; (*refuse tip*) décharge *f.*; (*mil.*) dépôt *m.*; (*dull place: fam.*) trou *m.* **be in the** ∼**s**, (*fam.*) avoir le cafard.

dumpling /'dʌmplɪŋ/ *n.* boulette de pâte *f.*

dumpy /'dʌmpɪ/ *a.* (**-ier**, **-iest**) boulot, rondelet.

dunce /dʌns/ *n.* cancre *m.*, âne *m.*

dune /dju:n/ n. dune f.

dung /dʌŋ/ n. (excrement) bouse f., crotte f.; (manure) fumier m.

dungarees /dʌŋgə'ri:z/ n. pl. (overalls) salopette f.; (jeans: Amer.) jean m.

dungeon /'dʌndʒən/ n. cachot m.

dunk /dʌŋk/ v.t. tremper.

dupe /dju:p/ v.t. duper. —n. dupe f.

duplex /'dju:pleks/ n. duplex m.

duplicate¹ /'dju:plɪkət/ n. double m. —a. identique.

duplicat|e² /'dju:plɪkeɪt/ v.t. faire un double de; (on machine) polycopier. ∼or n. duplicateur m.

duplicity /dju:'plɪsɪtɪ/ n. duplicité f.

durable /'djʊərəbl/ a. (tough) résistant; (enduring) durable.

duration /dju'reɪʃn/ n. durée f.

duress /dju'res/ n. contrainte f.

during /'djʊərɪŋ/ prep. pendant.

dusk /dʌsk/ n. crépuscule m.

dusky /'dʌskɪ/ a. (-ier, -iest) foncé.

dust /dʌst/ n. poussière f. —v.t. épousseter; (sprinkle) saupoudrer (with, de). ∼-jacket n. jaquette f.

dustbin /'dʌstbɪn/ n. poubelle f.

duster /'dʌstə(r)/ n. chiffon m.

dustman /'dʌstmən/ n. (pl. -men) éboueur m.

dustpan /'dʌstpæn/ n. pelle à poussière f.

dusty /'dʌstɪ/ a. (-ier, -iest) poussiéreux.

Dutch /dʌtʃ/ a. hollandais. —n. (lang.) hollandais m. go ∼, partager les frais. ∼man n. Hollandais m. ∼woman n. Hollandaise f.

dutiful /'dju:tɪfl/ a. obéissant.

dut|y /'dju:tɪ/ n. devoir m.; (tax) droit m. ∼ies, (of official etc.) fonctions f. pl. ∼y-free a. horstaxe. on ∼y, de service.

duvet /'du:veɪ/ n. couette f.

dwarf /dwɔ:f/ n. (pl. -fs) nain(e) m. (f.). —v.t. rapetisser.

dwell /dwel/ v.i. (p.t. dwelt) demeurer. ∼ on, s'étendre sur. ∼er n. habitant(e) m. (f.). ∼ing n. habitation f.

dwindle /'dwɪndl/ v.i. diminuer.

dye /daɪ/ v.t. (pres. p. dyeing) teindre. —n. teinture f.

dying /'daɪɪŋ/ a. mourant; (art) qui se perd.

dynamic /daɪ'næmɪk/ a. dynamique.

dynamism /'daɪnəmɪzəm/ n. dynamisme m.

dynamite /'daɪnəmaɪt/ n. dynamite f. —v.t. dynamiter.

dynamo /'daɪnəməʊ/ n. (pl. -os) dynamo f.

dynasty /'dɪnəstɪ, Amer. 'daɪnəstɪ/ n. dynastie f.

dysentery /'dɪsntrɪ/ n. dysenterie f.

dyslex|ia /dɪs'leksɪə/ n. dyslexie f. ∼ic a. & n. dyslexique (m./f.)

E

each /i:tʃ/ a. chaque. —pron. chacun(e). ∼ one, chacun(e). ∼ other, l'un(e) l'autre, les un(e)s les autres. know ∼ other, se connaître. love ∼ other, s'aimer. a pound ∼, (get) une livre chacun; (cost) une livre chaque.

eager /'i:gə(r)/ a. impatient (to, de); (supporter, desire) ardent. be ∼ to, (want) avoir envie de. ∼ for, avide de. ∼ly adv. avec impatience or ardeur. ∼ness n. impatience f., désir m., ardeur f.

eagle /'i:gl/ n. aigle m.

ear¹ /ɪə(r)/ n. oreille f. ∼-drum n. tympan m. ∼-ring n. boucle d'oreille f.

ear[2] /ɪə(r)/ *n.* (*of corn*) épi *m.*

earache /ˈɪəreɪk/ *n.* mal à l'oreille *m.*, mal d'oreille *m.*

earl /ɜːl/ *n.* comte *m.*

earlier /ˈɜːlɪə(r)/ *a.* (*in series*) précédent; (*in history*) plus ancien, antérieur; (*in future*) plus avancé. —*adv.* précédemment; antérieurement; avant.

early /ˈɜːlɪ/ (-**ier**, -**iest**) *adv.* tôt, de bonne heure; (*ahead of time*) en avance. —*a.* premier; (*hour*) matinal; (*fruit*) précoce; (*retirement*) anticipé. **have an ～ dinner**, dîner tôt. **in ～ summer**, au début de l'été.

earmark /ˈɪəmɑːk/ *v.t.* destiner, réserver (**for**, à).

earn /ɜːn/ *v.t.* gagner; (*interest: comm.*) rapporter. **～ s.o. sth.**, (*bring*) valoir qch. à qn.

earnest /ˈɜːnɪst/ *a.* sérieux. **in ～**, sérieusement.

earnings /ˈɜːnɪŋz/ *n. pl.* salaire *m.*; (*profits*) bénéfices *m. pl.*

earphone /ˈɪəfəʊn/ *n.* écouteur *m.*

earshot /ˈɪəʃɒt/ *n.* **within ～**, à portée de voix.

earth /ɜːθ/ *n.* terre *f.* —*v.t.* (*electr.*) mettre à la terre. **why/how/where on ～ . . .?**, pourquoi/comment/où diable . . .? **～ly** *a.* terrestre.

earthenware /ˈɜːθnweə(r)/ *n.* faïence *f.*

earthquake /ˈɜːθkweɪk/ *n.* tremblement de terre *m.*

earthy /ˈɜːθɪ/ *a.* (*of earth*) terreux; (*coarse*) grossier.

earwig /ˈɪəwɪg/ *n.* perce-oreille *m.*

ease /iːz/ *n.* aisance *f.*, facilité *f.*; (*comfort*) bien-être *m.* —*v.t./i.* (se) calmer; (*relax*) (se) détendre; (*slow down*) ralentir; (*slide*) glisser. **at ～**, à l'aise; (*mil.*) au repos. **with ～**, aisément.

easel /ˈiːzl/ *n.* chevalet *m.*

east /iːst/ *n.* est *m.* —*a.* d'est. —*adv.* vers l'est. **the E～**, (*Orient*)

l'Orient *m.* **～erly** *a.* de l'est. **～ern** *a.* de l'est, oriental. **～ward** *a.* à l'est. **～wards** *adv.* vers l'est.

Easter /ˈiːstə(r)/ *n.* Pâques *f. pl.* (*or m. sing.*). **～ egg**, œuf de Pâques *m.*

easy /ˈiːzɪ/ *a.* (-**ier**, -**iest**) facile; (*relaxed*) aisé. **～ chair**, fauteuil *m.* **go ～ with**, (*fam.*) y aller doucement avec. **take it ～**, ne pas se fatiguer. **easily** *adv.* facilement.

easygoing /iːzɪˈgəʊɪŋ/ *a.* (*with people*) accommodant; (*relaxed*) décontracté.

eat /iːt/ *v.t./i.* (*p.t.* **ate**, *p.p.* **eaten**) manger; (*into*, ronger. **～able** *a.* mangeable. **～er** *n.* mangeu|r, -se *m., f.*

eau-de-Cologne /əʊdəkəˈləʊn/ *n.* eau de Cologne *f.*

eaves /iːvz/ *n. pl.* avant-toit *m.*

eavesdrop /ˈiːvzdrɒp/ *v.i.* (*p.t. -dropped*). **～ (on)**, écouter en cachette.

ebb /eb/ *n.* reflux *m.* —*v.i.* refluer; (*fig.*) décliner.

ebony /ˈebənɪ/ *n.* ébène *f.*

ebullient /ɪˈbʌlɪənt/ *a.* exubérant.

EC *abbr.* (*European Community*) CE.

eccentric /ɪkˈsentrɪk/ *a.* & *n.* excentrique (*m./f.*). **～ity** /eksenˈtrɪsətɪ/ *n.* excentricité *f.*

ecclesiastical /ɪkliːzɪˈæstɪkl/ *a.* ecclésiastique.

echo /ˈekəʊ/ *n.* (*pl.* -**oes**) écho *m.* —*v.t./i.* (*p.t.* **echoed**, *pres. p.* **echoing**) (se) répercuter; (*fig.*) répéter.

eclipse /ɪˈklɪps/ *n.* éclipse *f.* —*v.t.* éclipser.

ecology /iːˈkɒlədʒɪ/ *n.* écologie *f.* **～ical** /iːkəˈlɒdʒɪkl/ *a.* écologique.

economic /iːkəˈnɒmɪk/ *a.* économique; (*profitable*) rentable. **～al** *a.* économique; (*person*) économe. **～s** *n.* économie politique *f.*

economist /ɪˈkɒnəmɪst/ n. économiste m./f.

econom|y /ɪˈkɒnəmɪ/ n. économie f. ~ize v.i. ~ (on), économiser.

ecosystem /ˈiːkəʊsɪstəm/ n. écosystème m.

ecstasy /ˈekstəsɪ/ n. extase f.

ECU /ˈeɪkjuː/ n. ÉCU m.

eczema /ˈeksɪmə/ n. eczéma m.

eddy /ˈedɪ/ n. tourbillon m.

edge /edʒ/ n. bord m.; (of town) abords m. pl.; (of knife) tranchant m. —v.t. border. —v.i. (move) se glisser. **have the ~ on**, (fam.) l'emporter sur. on ~, énervé.

edgeways /ˈedʒweɪz/ adv. de côte. I **can't get a word in ~**, je ne peux pas placer un mot.

edging /ˈedʒɪŋ/ n. bordure f.

edgy /ˈedʒɪ/ a. énervé.

edible /ˈedɪbl/ a. mangeable; (not poisonous) comestible.

edict /ˈiːdɪkt/ n. décret m.

edifice /ˈedɪfɪs/ n. édifice m.

edify /ˈedɪfaɪ/ v.t. édifier.

edit /ˈedɪt/ v.t. (p.t. edited) (newspaper) diriger; (prepare text of) mettre au point, préparer; (write) rédiger; (cut) couper.

edition /ɪˈdɪʃn/ n. édition f.

editor /ˈedɪtə(r)/ n. (writer) rédac|teur, -trice m., f.; (annotator) édi|teur, -trice m., f. **the ~ (in chief)**, le rédacteur en chef. **~ial** /-ˈtɔːrɪəl/ a. de la rédaction; n. éditorial m.

educat|e /ˈedʒʊkeɪt/ v.t. instruire; (mind, public) éduquer. **~ed** a. instruit. **~ion** /-ˈkeɪʃn/ n. éducation f.; (schooling) enseignement m. **~ional** /-ˈkeɪʃənl/ a. pédagogique, éducatif.

EEC abbr. (European Economic Community) CEE f.

eel /iːl/ n. anguille f.

eerie /ˈɪərɪ/ a. (-ier, -iest) sinistre.

effect /ɪˈfekt/ n. effet m. —v.t. effectuer. **come into ~**, entrer en vigueur. **in ~**, effectivement. **take ~**, agir.

effective /ɪˈfektɪv/ a. efficace; (striking) frappant; (actual) effectif. **~ly** adv. efficacement; de manière frappante; effectivement. **~ness** n. efficacité f.

effeminate /ɪˈfemɪnət/ a. efféminé.

effervescent /efəˈvesnt/ a. effervescent.

efficien|t /ɪˈfɪʃnt/ a. efficace; (person) compétent. **~cy** n. efficacité f.; compétence f. **~tly** adv. efficacement.

effigy /ˈefɪdʒɪ/ n. effigie f.

effort /ˈefət/ n. effort m. **~less** a. facile.

effrontery /ɪˈfrʌntərɪ/ n. effronterie f.

effusive /ɪˈfjuːsɪv/ a. expansif.

e.g. /iːˈdʒiː/ abbr. par exemple.

egalitarian /ɪgælɪˈteərɪən/ a. égalitaire. —n. égalitariste m./f.

egg¹ /eg/ n. œuf m. **~-cup** n. coquetier m. **~-plant** n. aubergine f.

egg² /eg/ v.t. **~ on**, (fam.) inciter.

eggshell /ˈegʃel/ n. coquille d'œuf f.

ego /ˈiːgəʊ/ n. (pl. -os) moi m. **~(t)ism** n. égoïsme m. **~(t)ist** n. égoïste m./f.

Egypt /ˈiːdʒɪpt/ n. Égypte f. **~ian** /ɪˈdʒɪpʃn/ a. & n. égyptien(ne) (m. (f.)).

eh /eɪ/ int. (fam.) hein.

eiderdown /ˈaɪdədaʊn/ n. édredon m.

eight /eɪt/ a. & n. huit (m.). **eighth** /eɪtθ/ a. & n. huitième (m./f.).

eighteen /eɪˈtiːn/ a. & n. dix-huit (m.). **~th** a. & n. dix-huitième (m./f.).

eight|y /ˈeɪtɪ/ a. & n. quatre-vingts (m.). **~ieth** a. & n. quatre-vingtième (m./f.).

either /ˈaɪðə(r)/ a. & pron. l'un(e) ou l'autre; (with negative) ni l'un(e) ni l'autre; (each) chaque.

—*adv.* non plus.—*conj.* ~ ... or, ou (bien) ... ou (bien); (*with negative*) ni ... ni.

eject /ɪˈdʒekt/ *v.t.* éjecter. ~or **seat**, siège éjectable *m.*

eke /iːk/ *v.t.* ~ **out**, faire durer; (*living*) gagner difficilement.

elaborate[1] /ɪˈlæbərət/ *a.* compliqué, recherché.

elaborate[2] /ɪˈlæbəreɪt/ *v.t.* élaborer. —*v.i.* préciser. ~ **on**, s'étendre sur.

elapse /ɪˈlæps/ *v.i.* s'écouler.

elastic /ɪˈlæstɪk/ *a. & n.* élastique (*m.*). ~ **band**, élastique *m.* ~**ity** /elæˈstɪsɪtɪ/ *n.* élasticité *f.*

elated /ɪˈleɪtɪd/ *a.* fou de joie.

elbow /ˈelbəʊ/ *n.* coude *m.* ~ **room**, possibilité de manœuvre *f.*

elder[1] /ˈeldə(r)/ *a. & n.* aîné(e) (*m. (f.)*).

elder[2] /ˈeldə(r)/ *n.* (*tree*) sureau *m.*

elderly /ˈeldəlɪ/ *a.* (assez) âgé.

eldest /ˈeldɪst/ *a. & n.* aîné(e) (*m. (f.)*).

elect /ɪˈlekt/ *v.t.* élire. —*a.* (*president etc.*) futur. ~ **to do**, choisir de faire. ~**ion** /-kʃn/ *n.* élection *f.*

elector /ɪˈlektə(r)/ *n.* électeur, -trice *m.*, *f.* ~**al** *a.* électoral. ~**ate** *n.* électorat *m.*

electric /ɪˈlektrɪk/ *a.* électrique. ~ **blanket**, couverture chauffante *f.* ~**al** *a.* électrique.

electrician /ɪlekˈtrɪʃn/ *n.* électricien *m.*

electricity /ɪlekˈtrɪsətɪ/ *n.* électricité *f.*

electrify /ɪˈlektrɪfaɪ/ *v.t.* électrifier; (*excite*) électriser.

electrocute /ɪˈlektrəkjuːt/ *v.t.* électrocuter.

electron /ɪˈlektrɒn/ *n.* électron *m.*

electronic /ɪlekˈtrɒnɪk/ *a.* électronique. ~**s** *n.* électronique *f.*

elegan|**t** /ˈelɪɡənt/ *a.* élégant. ~**ce** *n.* élégance *f.* ~**tly** *adv.* élégamment.

element /ˈelɪmənt/ *n.* élément *m.*; (*of heater etc.*) résistance *f.* ~**ary** /-ˈmentrɪ/ *a.* élémentaire.

elephant /ˈelɪfənt/ *n.* éléphant *m.*

elevat|**e** /ˈelɪveɪt/ *v.t.* élever. ~**ion** /-ˈveɪʃn/ *n.* élévation *f.*

elevator /ˈelɪveɪtə(r)/ *n.* (*Amer.*) ascenseur *m.*

eleven /ɪˈlevn/ *a. & n.* onze (*m.*). ~**th** *a. & n.* onzième (*m./f.*).

elf /elf/ *n.* (*pl.* **elves**) lutin *m.*

elicit /ɪˈlɪsɪt/ *v.t.* obtenir (**from**, de).

eligible /ˈelɪdʒəbl/ *a.* admissible (**for**, à). be ~ **for**, (*entitled to*) avoir droit à.

eliminat|**e** /ɪˈlɪmɪneɪt/ *v.t.* éliminer. ~**ion** /-ˈneɪʃn/ *n.* élimination *f.*

élite /eɪˈliːt/ *n.* élite *f.* ~**ist** *a. & n.* élitiste (*m./f.*).

ellip|**se** /ɪˈlɪps/ *n.* ellipse *f.* ~**tical** *a.* elliptique.

elm /elm/ *n.* orme *m.*

elocution /eləˈkjuːʃn/ *n.* élocution *f.*

elongate /ˈiːlɒŋɡeɪt/ *v.t.* allonger.

elope /ɪˈləʊp/ *v.i.* s'enfuir. ~**ment** *n.* fugue (amoureuse) *f.*

eloquen|**t** /ˈeləkwənt/ *a.* éloquent. ~**ce** *n.* éloquence *f.* ~**tly** *adv.* avec éloquence.

else /els/ *adv. & adj.* d'autre. **everybody** ~, tous les autres. **nobody** ~, personne d'autre. **nothing** ~, rien d'autre. **or** ~, ou bien. **somewhere** ~, autre part. ~**where** *adv.* ailleurs.

elucidate /ɪˈluːsɪdeɪt/ *v.t.* élucider.

elude /ɪˈluːd/ *v.t.* échapper à; (*question*) éluder.

elusive /ɪˈluːsɪv/ *a.* insaisissable.

emaciated /ɪˈmeɪsɪeɪtɪd/ *a.* émacié.

emanate /ˈeməneɪt/ *v.i.* émaner.

emancipat|**e** /ɪˈmænsɪpeɪt/ *v.t.* émanciper. ~**ion** /-ˈpeɪʃn/ *n.* émancipation *f.*

embalm /ɪmˈbɑːm/ *v.t.* embaumer.

embankment /ɪmˈbæŋkmənt/ *n.* (*of river*) quai *m.*; (*of railway*) remblai *m.*, talus *m.*

embargo /ɪmˈbɑːgəʊ/ *n.* (*pl.* -oes) embargo *m.*

embark /ɪmˈbɑːk/ *v.t./i.* (s')embarquer. **∼ on,** (*business etc.*) se lancer dans; (*journey*) commencer. **∼ation** /embɑːˈkeɪʃn/ *n.* embarquement *m.*

embarrass /ɪmˈbærəs/ *v.t.* embarrasser, gêner. **∼ment** *n.* embarras *m.*, gêne *f.*

embassy /ˈembəsɪ/ *n.* ambassade *f.*

embed /ɪmˈbed/ *v.t.* (*p.t.* embedded) encastrer.

embellish /ɪmˈbelɪʃ/ *v.t.* embellir. **∼ment** *n.* enjolivement *m.*

embers /ˈembəz/ *n. pl.* braise *f.*

embezzle /ɪmˈbezl/ *v.t.* détourner. **∼ment** *n.* détournement de fonds *m.* **∼r** /-ə(r)/ *n.* escroc *m.*

embitter /ɪmˈbɪtə(r)/ *v.t.* (*person*) aigrir; (*situation*) envenimer.

emblem /ˈembləm/ *n.* emblème *m.*

embody /ɪmˈbɒdɪ/ *v.t.* incarner, exprimer; (*include*) contenir. **∼iment** *n.* incarnation *f.*

emboss /ɪmˈbɒs/ *v.t.* (*metal*) repousser; (*paper*) gaufrer.

embrace /ɪmˈbreɪs/ *v.t./i.* (s')embrasser. **∼***n.* étreinte *f.*

embroider /ɪmˈbrɔɪdə(r)/ *v.t.* broder. **∼y** *n.* broderie *f.*

embroil /ɪmˈbrɔɪl/ *v.t.* mêler (in, à).

embryo /ˈembrɪəʊ/ *n.* (*pl.* -os) embryon *m.* **∼nic** /-ˈɒnɪk/ *a.* embryonnaire.

emend /ɪˈmend/ *v.t.* corriger.

emerald /ˈemərəld/ *n.* émeraude *f.*

emerge /ɪˈmɜːdʒ/ *v.i.* apparaître. **∼nce** /-əns/ *n.* apparition *f.*

emergency /ɪˈmɜːdʒənsɪ/ *n.* (*crisis*) crise *f.*; (*urgent case:* med.) urgence *f.* d'urgence. **∼ exit,** sortie de secours *f.* **∼ landing,** atterrissage forcé. **in an ∼,** en cas d'urgence.

emery /ˈemərɪ/ *n.* émeri *m.*

emigrant /ˈemɪgrənt/ *n.* émigrant(e) *m.* (*f.*).

emigrat|e /ˈemɪgreɪt/ *v.i.* émigrer. **∼ion** /-ˈgreɪʃn/ *n.* émigration *f.*

eminen|t /ˈemɪnənt/ *a.* éminent. **∼ce** *n.* éminence *f.* **∼tly** *adv.* éminemment, parfaitement.

emissary /ˈemɪsərɪ/ *n.* émissaire *m.*

emi|t /ɪˈmɪt/ *v.t.* (*p.t.* **emitted**) émettre. **∼ssion** *n.* émission *f.*

emotion /ɪˈməʊʃn/ *n.* émotion *f.* **∼al** (*person, shock*) émotif; (*speech, scene*) émouvant.

emotive /ɪˈməʊtɪv/ *a.* émotif.

emperor /ˈempərə(r)/ *n.* empereur *m.*

emphasis /ˈemfəsɪs/ *n.* (on *word*) accent *m.* **lay ∼ on,** mettre l'accent sur.

emphasize /ˈemfəsaɪz/ *v.t.* souligner; (*syllable*) insister sur.

emphatic /ɪmˈfætɪk/ *a.* catégorique; (*manner*) énergique.

empire /ˈempaɪə(r)/ *n.* empire *m.*

employ /ɪmˈplɔɪ/ *v.t.* employer. **∼er** *n.* employeu|r, -se *m.*, *f.* **∼ment** *n.* emploi *m.* **∼ment agency,** agence de placement *f.*

employee /emplɔɪˈiː/ *n.* employé(e) *m.* (*f.*).

empower /ɪmˈpaʊə(r)/ *v.t.* autoriser (**to do, à** faire).

empress /ˈemprɪs/ *n.* impératrice *f.*

empt|y /ˈemptɪ/ *a.* (-ier, -est) vide; (*promise*) vain. —*v.t./i.* (se) vider. **∼y-handed** *a.* les mains vides. **on an ∼y stomach,** à jeun. **∼ies** *n. pl.* bouteilles vides *f. pl.* **∼iness** *n.* vide *m.*

emulat|e /ˈemjʊleɪt/ *v.t.* imiter. **∼ion** /-ˈleɪʃn/ *n.* (*comput.*) émulation *f.*

emulsion /ɪˈmʌlʃn/ *n.* émulsion *f.* **∼ (paint),** peinture-émulsion *f.*

enable /ɪˈneɪbl/ *v.t.* **∼ s.o. to,** permettre à qn. de.

enact /ɪ'nækt/ v.t. (*law*) promul-
guer; (*scene*) représenter.

enamel /ɪ'næml/ n. émail m. —v.t.
(*p.t.* **enamelled**) émailler.

enamoured /ɪ'næməd/ a. be ∼ of,
aimer beaucoup, être épris de.

encampment /ɪn'kæmpmənt/ n.
campement m.

encase /ɪn'keɪs/ v.t. (*cover*) recouvrir (**in**, de); (*enclose*) enfermer
(**in**, dans).

enchant /ɪn'tʃɑːnt/ v.t. enchanter.
∼**ing** a. enchanteur. ∼**ment** n.
enchantement m.

encircle /ɪn'sɜːkl/ v.t. encercler.

enclave /'enkleɪv/ n. enclave f.

enclose /ɪn'kləʊz/ v.t. (*land*)
clôturer; (*with letter*) joindre. ∼**d**
a. (*space*) clos; (*market*) couvert;
(*with letter*) ci-joint.

enclosure /ɪn'kləʊʒə(r)/ n. enceinte f.; (*comm.*) pièce jointe f.

encompass /ɪn'kʌmpəs/ v.t. (*include*) inclure.

encore /'ɒŋkɔː(r)/ int. & n. bis
(m.).

encounter /ɪn'kaʊntə(r)/ v.t. rencontrer. —n. rencontre f.

encourage /ɪn'kʌrɪdʒ/ v.t. encourager. ∼**ment** n. encouragement m.

encroach /ɪn'krəʊtʃ/ v.i. ∼ **upon**,
empiéter sur.

encumber /ɪn'kʌmbə(r)/ v.t. encombrer.

encyclical /ɪn'sɪklɪkl/ n. en-
cyclique f.

encyclopædia, encyclopedia
/ɪnsaɪklə'piːdɪə/ n. encyclopédie f.
∼**ic** a. encyclopédique.

end /end/ n. fin f.; (*farthest part*)
bout m. —v.t./i. (se) terminer. ∼
up doing, finir par faire. **come to
an** ∼, prendre fin. ∼**-product**,
produit fini m. **in the** ∼,
finalement. **no** ∼ **of**, (*fam.*)
énormément de. **on** ∼, (*upright*)
debout; (*in a row*) de suite. **put an**
∼ **to**, mettre fin à.

endanger /ɪn'deɪndʒə(r)/ v.t. mettre en danger.

endear|ing /ɪn'dɪərɪŋ/ a. atta-
chant. ∼**ment** n. parole tendre f.

endeavour, (*Amer.*) **endeavor**
/ɪn'devə(r)/ n. effort m. —v.i.
s'efforcer (**to**, de).

ending /'endɪŋ/ n. fin f.

endive /'endɪv/ n. chicorée f.

endless /'endlɪs/ a. interminable;
(*times*) innombrable; (*patience*)
infini.

endorse /ɪn'dɔːs/ v.t. (*document*)
endosser; (*action*) approuver.
∼**ment** n. (*auto.*) contravention
f.

endow /ɪn'daʊ/ v.t. doter. ∼**ed**
with, doté de. ∼**ment** n. dotation
f. (*of*, de).

endur|e /ɪn'djʊə(r)/ v.t. supporter.
—v.i. durer. ∼**able** a. suppor-
table. ∼**ance** n. endurance f.
∼**ing** a. durable.

enemy /'enəmɪ/ n. & a. ennemi(e)
(m. (f.)).

energetic /enə'dʒetɪk/ a. énergique.

energy /'enədʒɪ/ n. énergie f.

enforce /ɪn'fɔːs/ v.t. appliquer,
faire respecter; (*impose*) imposer
(**on**, à). ∼**d** a. forcé.

engage /ɪn'geɪdʒ/ v.t. engager.
—v.i. ∼ **in**, prendre part à. ∼**d** a.
fiancé; (*busy*) occupé. **get** ∼**d**, se
fiancer. ∼**ment** n. fiançailles f.
pl.; (*meeting*) rendez-vous m.;
(*undertaking*) engagement m.

engaging /ɪn'geɪdʒɪŋ/ a. engageant, séduisant.

engender /ɪn'dʒendə(r)/ v.t. engendrer.

engine /'endʒɪn/ n. moteur m.; (*of
train*) locomotive f.; (*of ship*)
machine f. ∼**-driver** n. mécanicien m.

engineer /endʒɪ'nɪə(r)/ n. ingénieur m.; (*appliance repair-
man*) dépanneur m. —v.t.
(*contrive*: *fam.*) machiner. ∼**ing**

n. (mechanical) mécanique *f.;*
(road-building etc.) génie *m.*

England /'ɪŋglənd/ *n.* Angleterre
f.

English /'ɪŋglɪʃ/ *a.* anglais. —*n.*
(lang.) anglais *m.* the ~, les Anglais
anglophone. **the ~,** les Anglais
m. pl. **~man** *n.* Anglais *m.*
~woman *n.* Anglaise *f.*

engrav|e /ɪn'greɪv/ *v.t.* graver.
~ing *n.* gravure *f.*

engrossed /ɪn'grəʊst/ *a.* absorbé
(in, par).

engulf /ɪn'gʌlf/ *v.t.* engouffrer.

enhance /ɪn'hɑːns/ *v.t.* rehausser;
(price, value) augmenter.

enigma /ɪ'nɪgmə/ *n.* énigme *f.*
~tic /enɪg'mætɪk/ *a.* énigmatique.

enjoy /ɪn'dʒɔɪ/ *v.t.* aimer *(doing,*
faire); *(benefit from)* jouir de. ~
o.s., s'amuser. ~ **your meal,**
bon appétit! **~able** *a.* agréable.
~ment *n.* plaisir *m.*

enlarge /ɪn'lɑːdʒ/ *v.t./i.* (s')agran-
dir. ~ **upon,** s'étendre sur.
~ment *n.* agrandissement *m.*

enlighten /ɪn'laɪtn/ *v.t.* éclairer.
~ment *n.* édification *f.;*
(information) éclaircissements
m. pl.

enlist /ɪn'lɪst/ *v.t. (person)*
recruter; *(fig.)* obtenir. —*v.i.*
s'engager.

enliven /ɪn'laɪvn/ *v.t.* animer.

enmity /'enmətɪ/ *n.* inimitié *f.*

enormity /ɪ'nɔːmətɪ/ *n.* énormité *f.*

enormous /ɪ'nɔːməs/ *a.* énorme.
~ly *adv.* énormément.

enough /ɪ'nʌf/ *adv. & n.* assez. —*a.*
assez de. ~ **glasses/time/**etc.,
assez de verres/de temps/*etc.*
have ~ of, en avoir assez de.

enquir|e /ɪn'kwaɪə(r)/ *v.t./i.* de-
mander. ~ **about,** se renseigner sur. **~y** *n.* demande de renseignements *f.*

enrage /ɪn'reɪdʒ/ *v.t.* mettre en
rage, rendre furieux.

enrich /ɪn'rɪtʃ/ *v.t.* enrichir.

enrol, *(Amer.)* **enroll** /ɪn'rəʊl/
v.t./i. (p.t. enrolled) (s')inscrire.
~ment *n.* inscription *f.*

ensconce /ɪn'skɒns/ *v.t.* ~ **o.s.,**
bien s'installer.

ensemble /ɒn'sɒmbl/ *n. (clothing*
& mus.) ensemble *m.*

ensign /'ensən, 'ensaɪn/ *n. (flag)*
pavillon *m.*

enslave /ɪn'sleɪv/ *v.t.* asservir.

ensue /ɪn'sjuː/ *v.i.* s'ensuivre.

ensure /ɪn'ʃʊə(r)/ *v.t.* assurer. ~
that, *(ascertain)* s'assurer que.

entail /ɪn'teɪl/ *v.t.* entraîner.

entangle /ɪn'tæŋgl/ *v.t.* emmêler.

enter /'entə(r)/ *v.t. (room, club,*
race, etc.) entrer dans; *(note down,*
register) inscrire; *(data)* entrer,
saisir. —*v.i.* entrer **(into,** dans).
~ **for,** s'inscrire à.

enterprise /'entəpraɪz/ *n.* entreprise *f.; (boldness)* initiative
f.

enterprising /'entəpraɪzɪŋ/ *a.*
entreprenant.

entertain /entə'teɪn/ *v.t.* amuser,
divertir; *(guests)* recevoir; *(ideas)*
considérer. **~er** *n.* artiste *m./f.*
~ing *a.* divertissant. **~ment** *n.*
amusement *m.,* divertissement
m.; (performance) spectacle *m.*

enthral, *(Amer.)* **enthrall**
/ɪn'θrɔːl/ *v.t. (p.t.* enthralled)
captiver.

enthuse /ɪn'θjuːz/ *v.i.* ~ **over,**
s'enthousiasmer pour.

enthusiasm /ɪn'θjuːzɪæzəm/ *n.* enthousiasme *m.*

enthusiast /ɪn'θjuːzɪæst/ *n.* fer-
vent(e) *m. (f.),* passionné(e) *m. (f.)*
(for, de). **~ic** /-'æstɪk/ *a.*
(supporter) enthousiaste. **be ~ic**
about, être enthousiasmé par.
~ically *adv.* /-'æstɪklɪ/ *adv.*
avec enthousiasme.

entice /ɪn'taɪs/ *v.t.* attirer. ~ **to**
do, entraîner à faire. **~ment** *n.*
(attraction) attrait *m.*

entire /ɪn'taɪə(r)/ a. entier. ~**ly** adv. entièrement.

entirety /ɪn'taɪərətɪ/ n. in its ~, en entier.

entitle /ɪn'taɪtl/ v.t. donner droit à (**to sth.**, à qch.; **to do**, de faire). ~**d** a. (book) intitulé. be ~**d to sth.**, avoir droit à qch. ~**ment** n. droit m.

entity /'entətɪ/ n. entité f.

entrails /'entreɪlz/ n. pl. entrailles f. pl.

entrance[1] /'entrəns/ n. (entering, way in) entrée f. (**to**, de); (right to enter) admission f. —a. (charge, exam) d'entrée.

entrance[2] /ɪn'trɑːns/ v.t. transporter.

entrant /'entrənt/ n. (sport) concurrent(e) m. (f.); (in exam) candidat(e) m. (f.).

entreat /ɪn'triːt/ v.t. supplier.

entrenched /ɪn'trentʃt/ a. ancré.

entrepreneur /ɒntrəprə'nɜː(r)/ n. entrepreneur m.

entrust /ɪn'trʌst/ v.t. confier.

entry /'entrɪ/ n. (entrance) entrée f.; (word on list) mot inscrit m. ~ **form**, feuille d'inscription f.

enumerate /ɪ'njuːməreɪt/ v.t. énumérer.

enunciate /ɪ'nʌnsɪeɪt/ v.t. (word) articuler; (ideas) énoncer.

envelop /ɪn'veləp/ v.t. (p.t. **enveloped**) envelopper.

envelope /'envələʊp/ n. enveloppe f.

enviable /'envɪəbl/ a. enviable.

envious /'envɪəs/ a. envieux (**of sth.**, de qch.). ~ **of s.o.**, jaloux de qn. ~**ly** adv. avec envie.

environment /ɪn'vaɪərənmənt/ n. milieu m.; (ecological) environnement m. ~**al** /-'mentl/ a. du milieu; de l'environnement. ~**alist** n. spécialiste de l'environnement m./f.

envisage /ɪn'vɪzɪdʒ/ v.t. envisager.

envoy /'envɔɪ/ n. envoyé(e) m. (f.).

envy /'envɪ/ n. envie f. —v.t. envier.

enzyme /'enzaɪm/ n. enzyme m.

ephemeral /ɪ'femərəl/ a. éphémère.

epic /'epɪk/ n. épopée f. —a. épique.

epidemic /epɪ'demɪk/ n. épidémie f.

epilep|sy /'epɪlepsɪ/ n. épilepsie f. ~**tic** /-'leptɪk/ a. & n. épileptique (m./f.).

episode /'epɪsəʊd/ n. épisode m.

epistle /ɪ'pɪsl/ n. épître f.

epitaph /'epɪtɑːf/ n. épitaphe f.

epithet /'epɪθet/ n. épithète f.

epitom|e /ɪ'pɪtəmɪ/ n. (embodiment) modèle m.; (summary) résumé m. ~**ize** v.t. incarner.

epoch /'iːpɒk/ n. époque f. ~**making** a. qui fait époque.

equal /'iːkwəl/ a. & n. égal(e) (m./f.).—v.t. (p.t. **equalled**) égaler. ~ **opportunities/rights**, égalité des chances/droits f. ~ **to**, (task) à la hauteur de. ~**ity** /ɪ'kwɒlətɪ/ n. égalité f. ~**ly** adv. également; (just as) tout aussi.

equalize /'iːkwəlaɪz/ v.t./i. égaliser. ~**r** /-ə(r)/ n. (goal) but égalisateur m.

equanimity /ekwə'nɪmətɪ/ n. égalité d'humeur f., calme m.

equate /ɪ'kweɪt/ v.t. assimiler, égaler (**with**, à).

equation /ɪ'kweɪʒn/ n. équation f.

equator /ɪ'kweɪtə(r)/ n. équateur m. ~**ial** /ekwə'tɔːrɪəl/ a. équatorial.

equilibrium /iːkwɪ'lɪbrɪəm/ n. équilibre m.

equinox /'iːkwɪnɒks/ n. équinoxe m.

equip /ɪ'kwɪp/ v.t. (p.t. **equipped**) équiper (**with**, de). ~**ment** n. équipement m.

equitable /'ekwɪtəbl/ a. équitable.

equity /'ekwətɪ/ n. équité f.

equivalen|t /ɪˈkwɪvələnt/ a. & n. équivalent (m.). **~ce** n. équivalence f.

equivocal /ɪˈkwɪvəkl/ a. équivoque.

era /ˈɪərə/ n. ère f., époque f.

eradicate /ɪˈrædɪkeɪt/ v.t. supprimer, éliminer.

erase /ɪˈreɪz/ v.t. effacer. **~r** /-ə(r)/ n. (rubber) gomme f.

erect /ɪˈrekt/ a. droit. —v.t. ériger. **~ion** /-kʃn/ n. érection f.

ermine /ˈɜːmɪn/ n. hermine f.

ero|de /ɪˈrəʊd/ v.t. ronger. **~sion** n. érosion f.

erotic /ɪˈrɒtɪk/ a. érotique. **~ism** /-sɪzəm/ n. érotisme m.

err /ɜː(r)/ v.i. (be mistaken) se tromper; (sin) pécher.

errand /ˈerənd/ n. course f.

erratic /ɪˈrætɪk/ a. (uneven) irrégulier; (person) capricieux.

erroneous /ɪˈrəʊnɪəs/ a. erroné.

error /ˈerə(r)/ n. erreur f.

erudit|e /ˈeruːdaɪt, Amer. ˈerjudaɪt/ a. érudit. **~ion** /-ˈdɪʃn/ n. érudition f.

erupt /ɪˈrʌpt/ v.i. (volcano) entrer en éruption; (fig.) éclater. **~ion** /-pʃn/ n. éruption f.

escalat|e /ˈeskəleɪt/ v.t./i. (s')intensifier; (of prices) monter en flèche. **~ion** /-ˈleɪʃn/ n. escalade f.

escalator /ˈeskəleɪtə(r)/ n. escalier mécanique m., escalator m.

escapade /eskəˈpeɪd/ n. fredaine f.

escape /ɪˈskeɪp/ v.i. s'échapper (from a place, d'un lieu); (prisoner) s'évader. —v.t. échapper à. —n. fuite f., évasion f.; (of gas etc.) fuite f. **~ from s.o.**, échapper à qn. **~ to**, s'enfuir dans. **have a lucky** or **narrow ~**, l'échapper belle.

escapism /ɪˈskeɪpɪzəm/ n. évasion (de la réalité) f.

escort¹ /ˈeskɔːt/ n. (guard) escorte f.; (of lady) cavalier m.

escort² /ɪˈskɔːt/ v.t. escorter.

Eskimo /ˈeskɪməʊ/ n. (pl. -os) Esquimau(de) m. (f.).

especial /ɪˈspeʃl/ a. particulier. **~ly** adv. particulièrement.

espionage /ˈespɪənɑːʒ/ n. espionnage m.

esplanade /ˈespləneɪd/ n. esplanade f.

espresso /eˈspresəʊ/ n. (pl. -os) (café) express m.

essay /ˈeseɪ/ n. essai m.; (schol.) rédacton f.; (univ.) dissertation f.

essence /ˈesns/ n. essence f.; (main point) essentiel m.

essential /ɪˈsenʃl/ a. essentiel. —n. pl. the **~s**, l'essentiel m. **~ly** adv. essentiellement.

establish /ɪˈstæblɪʃ/ v.t. établir; (business, state) fonder. **~ment** n. établissement m.; fondation f. **the E~ment**, les pouvoirs établis.

estate /ɪˈsteɪt/ n. (land) propriété f.; (possessions) biens m. pl.; (inheritance) succession f.; (district) cité f., complexe m. **~ agent**, agent immobilier m. **~ car**, break m.

esteem /ɪˈstiːm/ v.t. estimer. —n. estime f.

esthetic /esˈθetɪk/ a. (Amer.) = aesthetic.

estimate¹ /ˈestɪmət/ n. (calculation) estimation f.; (comm.) devis m.

estimat|e² /ˈestɪmeɪt/ v.t. estimer. **~ion** /-ˈmeɪʃn/ n. jugement m.; (high regard) estime f.

estuary /ˈestʃʊərɪ/ n. estuaire m.

etc. /et ˈsetərə/ adv. etc.

etching /ˈetʃɪŋ/ n. eau-forte f.

eternal /ɪˈtɜːnl/ a. éternel.

eternity /ɪˈtɜːnətɪ/ n. éternité f.

ether /ˈiːθə(r)/ n. éther m.

ethic /ˈeθɪk/ n. éthique f. **~s**, moralité f. **~al** a. éthique.

ethnic /ˈeθnɪk/ a. ethnique.

ethos /'iːθɒs/ *n.* génie *m.*

etiquette /'etɪket/ *n.* étiquette *f.*

etymology /etɪ'mɒlədʒɪ/ *n.* étymologie *f.*

eucalyptus /juːkə'lɪptəs/ *n.* (*pl.* -**tuses**) eucalyptus *m.*

eulogy /'juːlədʒɪ/ *n.* éloge *m.*

euphemism /'juːfəmɪzəm/ *n.* euphémisme *m.*

euphoria /juː'fɔːrɪə/ *n.* euphorie *f.*

eurocheque /'juərəʊtʃek/ *n.* eurochèque *m.*

Europe /'juərəp/ *n.* Europe *f.* ~**an** /-'pɪən/ *a. & n.* européen(ne) (*m. (f.)*). **E~an Community**, Communauté Européenne.

euthanasia /juːθə'neɪzɪə/ *n.* euthanasie *f.*

evacuat|**e** /ɪ'vækjʊeɪt/ *v.t.* évacuer. ~**ion** /-'eɪʃn/ *n.* évacuation *f.*

evade /ɪ'veɪd/ *v.t.* esquiver. ~ **tax**, frauder le fisc.

evaluate /ɪ'væljʊeɪt/ *v.t.* évaluer.

evangelical /iːvæn'dʒelɪkl/ *a.* évangélique.

evangelist /ɪ'vændʒəlɪst/ *n.* évangéliste *m.*

evaporat|**e** /ɪ'væpəreɪt/ *v.i.* s'évaporer. ~**ed milk**, lait concentré *m.* ~**ion** /-'reɪʃn/ *n.* évaporation *f.*

evasion /ɪ'veɪʒn/ *n.* fuite *f.* (of, devant); (*excuse*) subterfuge *m.* **tax** ~, fraude fiscale.

evasive /ɪ'veɪsɪv/ *a.* évasif.

eve /iːv/ *n.* veille *f.* (of, de).

even /'iːvn/ *a.* régulier; (*surface*) uni; (*equal, unvarying*) égal; (*number*) pair. —*v.t./i.* ~ (**out** *or* **up**), (s')égaliser. —*adv.* même. ~ **better**/*etc.*, (*still*) encore mieux/ *etc.* **get** ~ **with**, se venger de. ~**ly** *adv.* régulièrement; (*equally*) de manière égale.

evening /'iːvnɪŋ/ *n.* soir *m.*; (*whole evening, event*) soirée *f.*

event /ɪ'vent/ *n.* événement *m.*; (*sport*) épreuve *f.* **in the** ~ **of**, en cas de. ~**ful** *a.* mouvementé.

eventual /ɪ'ventʃʊəl/ *a.* final, définitif. ~**ity** /-'ælətɪ/ *n.* éventualité *f.* ~**ly** *adv.* en fin de compte; (*in future*) un jour ou l'autre.

ever /'evə(r)/ *adv.* jamais; (*at all times*) toujours. ~ **since** *prep. & adv.* depuis (ce moment-là); *conj.* depuis que. ~ **so**, (*fam.*) vraiment.

evergreen /'evəgriːn/ *n.* arbre à feuilles persistantes *m.*

everlasting /evə'lɑːstɪŋ/ *a.* éternel.

every /'evrɪ/ *a.* chaque. ~ **one**, chacun(e). ~ **other day**, un jour sur deux, tous les deux jours.

everybody /'evrɪbɒdɪ/ *pron.* tout le monde.

everyday /'evrɪdeɪ/ *a.* quotidien.

everyone /'evrɪwʌn/ *pron.* tout le monde.

everything /'evrɪθɪŋ/ *pron.* tout.

everywhere /'evrɪweə(r)/ *adv.* partout. ~ **he goes**, partout où il va.

evict /ɪ'vɪkt/ *v.t.* expulser. ~**ion** /-kʃn/ *n.* expulsion *f.*

evidence /'evɪdəns/ *n.* (*proof*) preuve(s) *f.* (*pl.*); (*certainty*) évidence *f.*; (*signs*) signes *m. pl.*; (*testimony*) témoignage *m.* **give** ~, témoigner. **in** ~, en vue.

evident /'evɪdənt/ *a.* évident. ~**ly** *adv.* de toute évidence.

evil /'iːvl/ *a.* mauvais. —*n.* mal *m.*

evo|**ke** /ɪ'vəʊk/ *v.t.* évoquer. ~**cative** /ɪ'vɒkətɪv/ *a.* évocateur.

evolution /iːvə'luːʃn/ *n.* évolution *f.*

evolve /ɪ'vɒlv/ *v.i.* se développer, évoluer. —*v.t.* développer.

ewe /juː/ *n.* brebis *f.*

ex- /eks/ *pref.* ex-, ancien.

exacerbate /ɪg'zæsəbeɪt/ *v.t.* exacerber.

exact /ɪg'zækt/ *a.* exact. ~**ly** *adv.* exactement. ~**ness** *n.* exactitude *f.*

exact² /ɪɡˈzækt/ v.t. exiger (from, de). **∼ing** a. exigeant.

exaggerat|e /ɪɡˈzædʒəreɪt/ v.t./i. exagérer. **∼ion** /-ˈreɪʃn/ n. exagération f.

exalted /ɪɡˈzɔːltɪd/ a. (in rank) de haut rang; (ideal) élevé.

exam /ɪɡˈzæm/ n. (fam.) examen m.

examination /ɪɡzæmɪˈneɪʃn/ n. examen m.

examine /ɪɡˈzæmɪn/ v.t. examiner; (witness etc.) interroger. **∼r** /-ə(r)/ n. examina|teur, -trice m., f.

example /ɪɡˈzɑːmpl/ n. exemple m. for **∼,** par exemple. make an **∼** of, punir pour l'exemple.

exasperat|e /ɪɡˈzæspəreɪt/ v.t. exaspérer. **∼ion** /-ˈreɪʃn/ n. exaspération f.

excavat|e /ˈekskəveɪt/ v.t. creuser; (uncover) déterrer. **∼ions** /-ˈveɪʃnz/ n. pl. (archaeol.) fouilles f. pl.

exceed /ɪkˈsiːd/ v.t. dépasser. **∼ingly** adv. extrêmement.

excel /ɪkˈsel/ v.i. (p.t. excelled) exceller. —v.t. surpasser.

excellen|t /ˈeksələnt/ a. excellent. **∼ce** n. excellence f. **∼tly** adv. admirablement, parfaitement.

except /ɪkˈsept/ prep. sauf, excepté. —v.t. excepter. **∼ for,** à part. **∼ing** prep. sauf, excepté.

exception /ɪkˈsepʃn/ n. exception f. take **∼ to,** s'offenser de.

exceptional /ɪkˈsepʃnl/ a. exceptionnel. **∼ly** adv. exceptionnellement.

excerpt /ˈeksɜːpt/ n. extrait m.

excess¹ /ɪkˈses/ n. excès m.

excess² /ˈekses/ a. excédentaire. **∼ fare,** supplément m. **∼ luggage,** excédent de bagages m.

excessive /ɪkˈsesɪv/ a. excessif. **∼ly** adv. excessivement.

exchange /ɪksˈtʃeɪndʒ/ v.t. échanger. —n. échange m.;

(between currencies) change m. **∼ rate,** taux d'échange m. (telephone) **∼,** central (téléphonique) m.

exchequer /ɪksˈtʃekə(r)/ n. (British pol.) Échiquier m.

excise /ˈeksaɪz/ n. impôt (indirect) m.

excit|e /ɪkˈsaɪt/ v.t. exciter; (enthuse) enthousiasmer. **∼able** a. excitable. **∼ed** a. excité. get **∼ed,** s'exciter. **∼ement** n. excitation f. **∼ing** a. passionnant.

exclaim /ɪkˈskleɪm/ v.t./i. exclamer, s'écrier.

exclamation /ekskləˈmeɪʃn/ n. exclamation f. **∼ mark** or **point** (Amer.), point d'exclamation m.

exclu|de /ɪkˈskluːd/ v.t. exclure. **∼sion** n. exclusion f.

exclusive /ɪkˈskluːsɪv/ a. (rights etc.) exclusif; (club etc.) sélect; (news item) en exclusivité. **∼ of** service/etc., service/etc. non compris. **∼ly** adv. exclusivement.

excrement /ˈekskrəmənt/ n. excrément(s) m (pl.).

excruciating /ɪkˈskruːʃɪeɪtɪŋ/ a. atroce, insupportable.

excursion /ɪkˈskɜːʃn/ n. excursion f.

excus|e¹ /ɪkˈskjuːz/ v.t. excuser. **∼e from,** (exempt) dispenser de. **∼e me!,** excusez-moi!, pardon! **∼able** a. excusable.

excuse² /ɪkˈskjuːs/ n. excuse f.

ex-directory /eksdɪˈrektərɪ/ a. qui n'est pas dans l'annuaire.

execute /ˈeksɪkjuːt/ v.t. exécuter.

execution /eksɪˈkjuːʃn/ n. exécution f. **∼er** n. bourreau m.

executive /ɪɡˈzekjʊtɪv/ n. (pouvoir) exécutif m.; (person) cadre m. —a. exécutif.

exemplary /ɪɡˈzemplərɪ/ a. exemplaire.

exemplify /ɪɡˈzemplɪfaɪ/ v.t. illustrer.

exempt /ɪɡ'zempt/ a. exempt (**from**, de). —v.t. exempter. ~**ion** /-pʃn/ n. exemption f.

exercise /'eksəsaɪz/ n. exercice m. —v.t. exercer; (*restraint, patience*) faire preuve de. —v.i. prendre de l'exercice. ~ **book**, cahier m.

exert /ɪɡ'zɜːt/ v.t. exercer. ~ **o.s.**, se dépenser, faire des efforts. ~**ion** /-ʃn/ n. effort m.

exhaust /ɪɡ'zɔːst/ v.t. épuiser. (*auto.*) (pot d')échappement m. ~**ed** a. épuisé. ~**ion** /-stʃən/ n. épuisement m.

exhaustive /ɪɡ'zɔːstɪv/ a. complet.

exhibit /ɪɡ'zɪbɪt/ v.t. exposer; (*fig.*) faire preuve de. —n. objet exposé m. ~**or** n. exposant(e) m. (f.).

exhibition /eksɪ'bɪʃn/ n. exposition f.; (*act of showing*) démonstration f. ~**ist** n. exhibitionniste m./f.

exhilarat|e /ɪɡ'zɪləreɪt/ v.t. transporter de joie; (*invigorate*) stimuler. ~**ing** a. euphorisant. ~**ion** /-'reɪʃn/ n. joie f.

exhort /ɪɡ'zɔːt/ v.t. exhorter (**to**, à).

exhume /eks'hjuːm/ v.t. exhumer.

exile /'eksaɪl/ n. exil m.; (*person*) exilé(e) m. (f.). —v.t. exiler.

exist /ɪɡ'zɪst/ v.i. exister. ~**ence** n. existence f. **be in** ~**ence**, exister. ~**ing** a. actuel.

exit /'eksɪt/ n. sortie f. —v.t./i. (*comput.*) sortir (de).

exodus /'eksədəs/ n. exode m.

exonerate /ɪɡ'zɒnəreɪt/ v.t. disculper, innocenter.

exorbitant /ɪɡ'zɔːbɪtənt/ a. exorbitant.

exorcize /'eksɔːsaɪz/ v.t. exorciser.

exotic /ɪɡ'zɒtɪk/ a. exotique.

expand /ɪk'spænd/ v.t./i. (*develop*) (se) développer; (*extend*) (s')étendre; (*metal, liquid*) (se) dilater. ~**sion** n. développement m.; dilatation f.; (*pol., comm.*) expansion f.

expanse /ɪk'spæns/ n. étendue f.

expatriate /eks'pætrɪət, *Amer.* eks'peɪtrɪət/ a. & n. expatrié(e) m. (f.).

expect /ɪk'spekt/ v.t. attendre, s'attendre à; (*suppose*) supposer; (*demand*) exiger; (*baby*) attendre. ~ **to do**, compter faire. ~**ation** /ekspek'teɪʃn/ n. attente f.

expectan|t /ɪk'spektənt/ a. ~**t look**, air d'attente m. ~**t mother**, future maman f. ~**cy** n. attente f.

expedient /ɪk'spiːdɪənt/ a. opportun. —n. expédient m.

expedite /'ekspɪdaɪt/ v.t. hâter.

expedition /ekspɪ'dɪʃn/ n. expédition f.

expel /ɪk'spel/ v.t. (*p.t.* **expelled**) expulser; (*from school*) renvoyer.

expend /ɪk'spend/ v.t. dépenser. ~**able** a. remplaçable.

expenditure /ɪk'spendɪtʃə(r)/ n. dépense(s) f. (pl.).

expense /ɪk'spens/ n. dépense f.; frais m. pl. **at s.o.'s** ~, aux dépens de qn. ~ **account**, note de frais f.

expensive /ɪk'spensɪv/ a. cher, coûteux; (*tastes, habits*) de luxe. ~**ly** adv. coûteusement.

experience /ɪk'spɪərɪəns/ n. expérience f.; (*adventure*) aventure f. —v.t. (*undergo*) connaître; (*feel*) éprouver. ~**d** a. expérimenté.

experiment /ɪk'sperɪmənt/ n. expérience f. —v.i. faire une expérience. ~**al** /-'mentl/ a. expérimental.

expert /'ekspɜːt/ n. expert(e) m. (f.). —a. expert. ~**ly** adv. habilement.

expertise /ekspɜː'tiːz/ n. compétence f. (**in**, en).

expir|e /ɪk'spaɪə(r)/ v.i. expirer. ~**ed** a. périmé. ~**y** n. expiration f.

expl|ain /ɪk'spleɪn/ v.t. expliquer.

∼anation /ɪksplə'neɪʃn/ n. explication f. **∼anatory** /-'ænətəri/ a. explicatif.

expletive /ɪk'spliːtɪv, Amer. 'eksplətɪv/ n. juron m.

explicit /ɪk'splɪsɪt/ a. explicite.

explo|de /ɪk'spləʊd/ v.t./i. (faire) exploser. **∼sion** n. explosion f. **∼sive** a. & n. explosif (m.).

exploit[1] /'eksplɔɪt/ n. exploit m.

exploit[2] /ɪk'splɔɪt/ v.t. exploiter. **∼ation** /eksplɔɪ'teɪʃn/ n. exploitation f.

exploratory /ɪk'splɒrətrɪ/ a. (talks: pol.) exploratoire.

explor|e /ɪk'splɔː(r)/ v.t. explorer; (fig.) examiner. **∼ation** /eksplə'reɪʃn/ n. exploration f. **∼er** n. explora|teur, -trice m., f.

exponent /ɪk'spəʊnənt/ n. interprète m. (of, de).

export[1] /ɪk'spɔːt/ v.t. exporter. **∼er** n. exportateur m.

export[2] /'ekspɔːt/ n. exportation f.

expos|e /ɪk'spəʊz/ v.t. exposer; (disclose) dévoiler. **∼ure** /-ʒə(r)/ n. exposition f.; (photo.) pose f. **die of ∼ure**, mourir de froid.

expound /ɪk'spaʊnd/ v.t. exposer.

express[1] /ɪk'spres/ a. formel, exprès; (letter) exprès invar. —adv. (by express post) (par) exprès. —n. (train) rapide m.; (less fast) express m. **∼ly** adv. expressément.

express[2] /ɪk'spres/ v.t. exprimer. **∼ion** /-ʃn/ n. expression f. **∼ive** a. expressif.

expressway /ɪk'spresweɪ/ n. voie express f.

expulsion /ɪk'spʌlʃn/ n. expulsion f.; (from school) renvoi m.

expurgate /'ekspɜːgeɪt/ v.t. expurger.

exquisite /'ekskwɪzɪt/ a. exquis. **∼ly** adv. d'une façon exquise.

ex-serviceman /eks'sɜːvɪsmən/ n. (pl. -men) ancien combattant m.

extant /ek'stænt/ a. existant.

extempore /ek'stempərɪ/ a. & adv. impromptu.

exten|d /ɪk'stend/ v.t. (increase) étendre, agrandir; (arm, leg) étendre; (prolong) prolonger; (house) agrandir; (grant) offrir. —v.i. (stretch) s'étendre; (in time) se prolonger. **∼sion** n. (of line, road) prolongement m.; (in time) prolongation f.; (building) annexe f.; (of phone) appareil supplémentaire m.; (phone number) poste m.; (cable, hose, etc.) rallonge f.

extensive /ɪk'stensɪv/ a. vaste; (study) profond; (damage etc.) important. **∼ly** adv. (much) beaucoup; (very) très.

extent /ɪk'stent/ n. (size, scope) étendue f.; (degree) mesure f. **to some ∼**, dans une certaine mesure. **to such an ∼ that**, à tel point que.

extenuating /ɪk'stenjʊeɪtɪŋ/ a. **∼ circumstances**, circonstances atténuantes.

exterior /ɪk'stɪərɪə(r)/ a. & n. extérieur (m.).

exterminat|e /ɪk'stɜːmɪneɪt/ v.t. exterminer. **∼ion** /-'neɪʃn/ n. extermination f.

external /ɪk'stɜːnl/ a. extérieur; (cause, medical use) externe. **∼ly** adv. extérieurement.

extinct /ɪk'stɪŋkt/ a. (species) disparu; (volcano, passion) éteint. **∼ion** /-kʃn/ n. extinction f.

extinguish /ɪk'stɪŋgwɪʃ/ v.t. éteindre. **∼er** n. extincteur m.

extol /ɪk'stəʊl/ v.t. (p.t. extolled) exalter, chanter les louanges de.

extort /ɪk'stɔːt/ v.t. extorquer (from, à). **∼ion** /-ʃn/ n. (jurid.) extorsion (de fonds) f.

extortionate /ɪk'stɔːʃənət/ a. exorbitant.

extra /'ekstrə/ a. de plus, supplémentaire. —adv. plus (que d'habitude). **~ strong,** extra-fort. —*n.* (*additional thing*) supplément *m.*; (*cinema*) figurant(e) *m.* (*f.*). **~ charge,** supplément *m.* **~ time,** (*football*) prolongation *f.*

extra- /'ekstrə/ *pref.* extra-.

extract¹ /ik'strækt/ *v.t.* extraire; (*promise, tooth*) arracher; (*fig.*) obtenir. **~ion** /-kʃn/ *n.* extraction *f.*

extract² /'ekstrækt/ *n.* extrait *m.*

extra-curricular /ekstrə-kə'rikjʊlə(r)/ *a.* parascolaire.

extradit|e /'ekstrədait/ *v.t.* extrader. **~ion** /-'diʃn/ *n.* extradition *f.*

extramarital /ekstrə'mærɪtl/ *a.* extra-conjugal.

extramural /ekstrə'mjʊərəl/ *a.* (*univ.*) hors faculté.

extraordinary /ik'strɔːdnri/ *a.* extraordinaire.

extravagan|t /ik'strævəgənt/ *a.* extravagant; (*wasteful*) prodigue. **~ce** *n.* extravagance *f.*; prodigalité *f.*

extrem|e /ik'striːm/ *a.* & *n.* extrême (*m.*). **~ely** *adv.* extrêmement. **~ist** *n.* extrémiste *m./f.*

extremity /ik'streməti/ *n.* extrémité *f.*

extricate /'ekstrikeit/ *v.t.* dégager.

extrovert /'ekstrəvɜːt/ *n.* extraverti(e) *m.* (*f.*).

exuberan|t /ig'zjuːbərənt/ *a.* exubérant. **~ce** *n.* exubérance *f.*

exude /ig'zjuːd/ *v.t.* (*charm etc.*) dégager.

exult /ig'zʌlt/ *v.i.* exulter.

eye /ai/ *n.* œil *m.* (*pl.* yeux). —*v.t.* (*p.t.* **eyed,** *pres. p.* **eyeing**) regarder. **keep an ~ on,** surveiller. **~-catching** *a.* qui attire l'attention. **~-opener** *n.* révélation *f.* **~-shadow** *n.* ombre à paupières *f.*

eyeball /'aibɔːl/ *n.* globe oculaire *m.*

eyebrow /'aibrau/ *n.* sourcil *m.*

eyeful /'aiful/ *n.* **get an ~,** (*fam.*) se rincer l'œil.

eyelash /'ailæʃ/ *n.* cil *m.*

eyelet /'ailɪt/ *n.* œillet *m.*

eyelid /'ailɪd/ *n.* paupière *f.*

eyesight /'aisait/ *n.* vue *f.*

eyesore /'aisɔː(r)/ *n.* horreur *f.*

eyewitness /'aiwitnis/ *n.* témoin oculaire *m.*

F

fable /'feibl/ *n.* fable *f.*

fabric /'fæbrik/ *n.* (*cloth*) tissu *m.*

fabrication /fæbri'keiʃn/ *n.* (*invention*) invention *f.*

fabulous /'fæbjuləs/ *a.* fabuleux; (*marvellous: fam.*) formidable.

façade /fə'sɑːd/ *n.* façade *f.*

face /feis/ *n.* visage *m.*, figure *f.*; (*aspect*) face *f.*; (*of clock*) cadran *m.* —*v.t.* être en face de; (*risk*) devoir affronter; (*confront*) faire face à, affronter. —*v.i.* se tourner; (*of house*) être exposé. **~-flannel** *n.* gant de toilette *m.* **~-lift** *n.* lifting *m.* **give a ~-lift to,** donner un coup de neuf à. **~ value,** (*comm.*) valeur nominale. **take sth. at ~ value,** prendre qch. au premier degré. **~ to face,** face à face. **~ up/down,** tourné vers le haut/bas. **~ up to,** faire face à. **in the ~ of,** **~d with,** face à. **make a (funny) ~,** faire une grimace.

faceless /'feislis/ *a.* anonyme.

facet /'fæsit/ *n.* facette *f.*

facetious /fə'siːʃəs/ *a.* facétieux.

facial /'feiʃl/ *a.* de la face, facial. —*n.* soin du visage *m.*

facile /'fæsail, *Amer.* 'fæsl/ *a.* facile, superficiel.

facilitate /fə'silɪteit/ *v.t.* faciliter.

facilit|y /fə'silɪti/ *n.* facilité *f.* **~ies,** (*equipment*) équipements *m. pl.*

facing /ˈfeɪsɪŋ/ *n.* parement *m.* —*prep.* en face de. —*a.* in face.

facsimile /fækˈsɪməlɪ/ *n.* facsimilé *m.* ~ **transmission**, télécopiage *m.*

fact /fækt/ *n.* fait *m.* **as a matter of** ~, **in** ~, en fait.

faction /ˈfækʃn/ *n.* faction *f.*

factor /ˈfæktə(r)/ *n.* facteur *m.*

factory /ˈfæktərɪ/ *n.* usine *f.*

factual /ˈfæktʃʊəl/ *a.* basé sur les faits.

faculty /ˈfækltɪ/ *n.* faculté *f.*

fad /fæd/ *n.* manie *f.*, folie *f.*

fade /feɪd/ *v.i.* (*sound*) s'affaiblir; (*memory*) s'évanouir; (*flower*) se faner; (*material*) déteindre; (*colour*) passer.

fag /fæg/ *n.* (*chore: fam.*) corvée *f.*; (*cigarette: sl.*) sèche *f.*; (*homosexual: Amer., sl.*) pédé *m.*

fagged /fægd/ *a.* (*tired*) éreinté.

fail /feɪl/ *v.i.* échouer; (*grow weak*) (s'a)faiblir; (*run short*) manquer; (*engine etc.*) tomber en panne. —*v.t.* (*exam*) échouer à; (*candidate*) refuser, recaler; (*disappoint*) décevoir. ~ **s.o.**, (*of words etc.*) manquer à qn. ~ **to do**, (*not do*) ne pas faire; (*not be able*) ne pas réussir à faire. **without** ~, à coup sûr.

failing /ˈfeɪlɪŋ/ *n.* défaut *m.* —*prep.* à défaut de.

failure /ˈfeɪljə(r)/ *n.* échec *m.*; (*person*) raté(e) *m.* (*f.*); (*breakdown*) panne *f.* ~ **to do**, (*inability*) incapacité de faire *f.*

faint /feɪnt/ *a.* (-**er**, -**est**) léger, faible. —*v.i.* s'évanouir. —*n.* évanouissement *m.* **feel** ~, (*ill*) se trouver mal. **I haven't the** ~**est idea**, je n'en ai pas la moindre idée. ~**-hearted** *a.* timide. ~**ly** *adv.* (*weakly*) faiblement; (*slightly*) légèrement. ~**ness** *n.* faiblesse *f.*

fair[1] /feə(r)/ *n.* foire *f.* ~**-ground** *n.* champ de foire *m.*

fair[2] /feə(r)/ *a.* (-**er**, -**est**) (*hair, person*) blond; (*skin etc.*) clair; (*just*) juste, équitable; (*weather*) beau; (*amount, quality*) raisonnable. —*adv.* (*play*) loyalement. ~ **play**, le fair-play. ~**ly** *adv.* (*justly*) équitablement; (*rather*) assez. ~**ness** *n.* justice *f.*

fairy /ˈfeərɪ/ *n.* fée *f.* ~ **story,** ~**tale** *n.* conte de fées *m.*

faith /feɪθ/ *n.* foi *f.* ~**-healer** *n.* guérisseur/-se *m.*, *f.*

faithful /ˈfeɪθfl/ *a.* fidèle. ~**ly** *adv.* fidèlement. ~**ness** *n.* fidélité *f.*

fake /feɪk/ *n.* (*forgery*) faux *m.*; (*person*) imposteur *m.* **it is a** ~, c'est faux. —*a.* faux. —*v.t.* (*copy*) faire un faux de; (*alter*) falsifier, truquer; (*illness*) simuler.

falcon /ˈfɔːlkən/ *n.* faucon *m.*

fall /fɔːl/ *v.i.* (*p.t.* **fell**, *p.p.* **fallen**) tomber. ~ *n.* chute *f.*; (*autumn: Amer.*) automne *m.* **Niagara F**~**s**, chutes du Niagara. ~ **back on**, se rabattre sur. ~ **behind**, prendre du retard. ~ **down** *or* **off**, tomber. ~ **for**, (*person: fam.*) tomber amoureux de; (*a trick: fam.*) se laisser prendre à. ~ **in**, (*mil.*) se mettre en rangs. ~ **off**, (*decrease*) diminuer. ~ **out**, se brouiller (**with**, avec). ~**-out** *n.* retombées *f. pl.* ~ **over**, tomber (par terre). ~ **short**, être insuffisant. ~ **through**, (*plans*) tomber à l'eau.

fallacy /ˈfæləsɪ/ *n.* erreur *f.*

fallible /ˈfæləbl/ *a.* faillible.

fallow /ˈfæləʊ/ *a.* en jachère.

false /fɔːls/ *a.* faux. ~**hood** *n.* mensonge *m.* ~**ly** *adv.* faussement. ~**ness** *n.* fausseté *f.*

falsetto /fɔːlˈsetəʊ/ *n.* (*pl.* -**os**) fausset *m.*

falsify /ˈfɔːlsɪfaɪ/ *v.t.* falsifier.

falter /ˈfɔːltə(r)/ *v.i.* vaciller; (*nerve*) faire défaut.

fame /feɪm/ *n.* renommée *f.*

famed /feɪmd/ a. renommé.

familiar /fə'mɪlɪə(r)/ a. familier. **be ~ with**, connaître. **~ity** /-'ærətɪ/ n. familiarité f. **~ize** v.t. familiariser.

family /'fæmɪlɪ/ n. famille f. —a. de famille, familial.

famine /'fæmɪn/ n. famine f.

famished /'fæmɪʃt/ a. affamé.

famous /'feɪməs/ a. célèbre. **~ly** adv. (very well: fam.) à merveille.

fan¹ /fæn/ n. ventilateur m.; (hand-held) éventail m. —v.t. (p.t. fanned) éventer; (fig.) attiser. —v.i. **~ out**, se déployer en éventail. **~ belt**, courroie de ventilateur f.

fan² /fæn/ n. (of person) fan m./f., admirateur, -trice m., f.; (enthusiast) fervent(e) m. (f.), passionné(e) m. (f.).

fanatic /fə'nætɪk/ n. fanatique m./f. **~al** a. fanatique. **~ism** /-sɪzəm/ n. fanatisme m.

fancier /'fænsɪə(r)/ n. (dog/etc.) **~**, amateur de chiens/etc.) m.

fanciful /'fænsɪfl/ a. fantaisiste.

fancy /'fænsɪ/ n. (whim, fantasy) fantaisie f.; (liking) goût m. —a. (buttons etc.) fantaisie invar.; (prices) extravagant; (impressive) impressionnant. —v.t. s'imaginer; (want: fam.) avoir envie de; (like: fam.) aimer. **take a ~ to s.o.**, se prendre d'affection pour qn. **it took my ~**, ça m'a plu. **~ dress**, déguisement m.

fanfare /'fænfeə(r)/ n. fanfare f.

fang /fæŋ/ n. (of dog etc.) croc m.; (of snake) crochet m.

fanlight /'fænlaɪt/ n. imposte f.

fantastic /fæn'tæstɪk/ a. fantastique.

fantas|y /'fæntəsɪ/ n. fantaisie f.; (day-dream) fantasme m. **~ize** v.i. faire des fantasmes.

far /fɑː(r)/ adv. loin; (much) beaucoup; (very) très. —a. lointain; (end, side) autre. **~ away**,

~ off, au loin. **as ~ as**, (up to) jusqu'à. **as ~ as I know**, autant que je sache. **~away** a. lointain. **by ~**, de loin. **~ from**, loin de. **the Far East**, l'Extrême-Orient m. **~fetched** a. bizarre. **~reaching** a. de grande portée.

farc|e /fɑːs/ n. farce f. **~ical** a. ridicule, grotesque.

fare /feə(r)/ n. (prix du) billet m.; (food) nourriture f. —v.i. (progress) aller; (manage) se débrouiller.

farewell /feə'wel/ int. & n. adieu (m.).

farm /fɑːm/ n. ferme f. —v.t. cultiver. —v.i. être fermier. **~ out**, céder en sous-traitance. **~ worker**, ouvrier, -ère agricole m., f. **~er** n. fermier m. **~ing** n. agriculture f.

farmhouse /'fɑːmhaʊs/ n. ferme f.

farmyard /'fɑːmjɑːd/ n. basse-cour f.

fart /fɑːt/ v.i. péter. —n. pet m.

farth|er /'fɑːðə(r)/ adv. plus loin. —a. plus éloigné. **~est** adv. le plus loin; a. le plus éloigné.

fascinat|e /'fæsɪneɪt/ v.t. fasciner. **~ion** /-'neɪʃn/ n. fascination f.

Fascis|t /'fæʃɪst/ n. fasciste m./f. **~m** /-zəm/ n. fascisme m.

fashion /'fæʃn/ n. (current style) mode f.; (manner) façon f. —v.t. façonner. **~ designer**, styliste m./f. **in ~**, à la mode. **out of ~**, démodé. **~able** a., **~ably** adv. à la mode.

fast¹ /fɑːst/ a. (-er, -est) rapide; (colour) grand teint invar.; fixe; (firm) fixe, solide. —adv. vite; (firmly) ferme. **be ~**, (clock etc.) avancer. **~ asleep**, profondément endormi. **~ food**, fast food m. restauration rapide f.

fast² /fɑːst/ v.i. (go without food) jeûner. —n. jeûne m.

fasten /'fɑːsn/ v.t./i. (s')attacher.

~er, ~ing ns. attache f., fermeture f.

fastidious /fə'stɪdɪəs/ a. difficile.

fat /fæt/ n. graisse f.; (on meat) gras m. —a. (fatter, fattest) gros, gras; (meat) gras; (sum, volume: fig.) gros. **a ~ lot,** (sl.) bien peu (of, de). **~-head** n. (fam.) imbécile m./f. **~ness** n. corpulence f.

fatal /'feɪtl/ a. mortel; (fateful, disastrous) fatal. **~ity** /fə'tælətɪ/ n. mort m. **~ly** adv. mortellement.

fatalist /'feɪtəlɪst/ n. fataliste m./f.

fate /feɪt/ n. (controlling power) destin m., sort m.; (one's lot) sort m. **~ful** a. fatidique.

fated /'feɪtɪd/ a. destiné (**to,** à).

father /'fɑːðə(r)/ n. père m. **~-in-law** n. (pl. **~s-in-law**) beau-père m. **~hood** n. paternité f. **~ly** a. paternel.

fathom /'fæðəm/ n. brasse f. (= 1,8 m.). —v.t. **~ (out),** comprendre.

fatigue /fə'tiːg/ n. fatigue f. —v.t. fatiguer.

fatten /'fætn/ v.t./i. engraisser. **~ing** a. qui fait grossir.

fatty /'fætɪ/ a. gras; (tissue) adipeux. —n. (person: fam.) gros(se) m. (f.).

fatuous /'fætjʊəs/ a. stupide.

faucet /'fɔːsɪt/ n. (Amer.) robinet m.

fault /fɔːlt/ n. (defect, failing) défaut m.; (blame) faute f.; (geol.) faille f. —v.t. **~ sth./s.o.,** trouver des défauts à qch./chez qn. **at ~,** fautif. **find ~ with,** critiquer. **~less** a. irréprochable. **~y** a. défectueux.

fauna /'fɔːnə/ n. faune f.

favour (Amer. **favor**) /'feɪvə(r)/ n. faveur f. —v.t. favoriser; (support) être en faveur de; (prefer) préférer. **do s.o. a ~,** rendre service à qn. **in ~ of,** pour. **~able** a. favorable. **~ably** adv. favorablement.

favourite /'feɪvərɪt/ a. & n. favori(te) (m. (f.)). **~ism** n. favoritisme m.

fawn[1] /fɔːn/ n. faon m. —a. fauve.

fawn[2] /fɔːn/ v.i. **~ on,** flatter bassement, flagorner.

fax /fæks/ n. fax m., télécopie f. —v.t. faxer, envoyer par télécopie. **~ machine,** télécopieur m.

FBI abbr. (Federal Bureau of Investigation) (Amer.) service d'enquêtes du Ministère de la Justice m.

fear /fɪə(r)/ n. crainte f., peur f.; (fig.) risque m. —v.t. craindre. **for ~ of/that,** de peur de/que. **~ful** a. (terrible) affreux; (timid) craintif. **~less** a. intrépide. **~lessness** n. intrépidité f.

fearsome /'fɪəsəm/ a. redoutable.

feasible /'fiːzəbl/ a. faisable; (likely) plausible. **~ility** /-'bɪlətɪ/ n. possibilité f.; plausibilité f.

feast /fiːst/ n. festin m.; (relig.) fête f. —v.i. festoyer. —v.t. régaler. **~ on,** se régaler de.

feat /fiːt/ n. exploit m.

feather /'feðə(r)/ n. plume f. —v.t. **~ one's nest,** s'enrichir. **~ duster,** plumeau m.

featherweight /'feðəweɪt/ n. poids plume m. invar.

feature /'fiːtʃə(r)/ n. caractéristique f.; (of person, face) trait m.; (film) long métrage m.; (article) article vedette m. —v.t. représenter; (give prominence to) mettre en vedette. —v.i. figurer (**in,** dans).

February /'februərɪ/ n. février m.

feckless /'feklɪs/ a. inepte.

fed /fed/ see **feed.** —a. **be ~ up,** (fam.) en avoir marre (**with,** de).

federal /'fedərəl/ a. fédéral. **~tion** /-'reɪʃn/ n. fédération f.

fee /fiː/ n. (for entrance) prix m.

~(s), (*of doctor etc.*) honoraires m. pl.; (*of actor, artist*) cachet m.; (*for tuition*) frais m. pl.; (*for enrolment*) droits m. pl.

feeble /fiːbl/ a. (**-er, -est**) faible. ~**-minded** a. faible d'esprit.

feed /fiːd/ v.t. (p.t. **fed**) nourrir, donner à manger à; (*suckle*) allaiter; (*supply*) alimenter. —v.i. se nourrir (**on**, de). —n. nourriture f.; (*of baby*) tétée f. ~ **in** information, rentrer des données. ~**er** n. alimentation f.

feedback /fiːdbæk/ n. réaction(s) f. (pl.); (*med., techn.*) feed-back m.

feel /fiːl/ v.t. (p.t. **felt**) (*touch*) tâter; (*be conscious of*) sentir; (*emotion*) ressentir; (*experience*) éprouver; (*think*) estimer. —v.i. (*tired, lonely, etc.*) se sentir. ~ **hot/thirsty/etc.**, avoir chaud/soif/etc. ~ **as if**, avoir l'impression que. ~ **awful**, (*ill*) se sentir malade. ~ **like**, (*want: fam.*) avoir envie de.

feeler /fiːlə(r)/ n. antenne f. put out a ~, lancer un ballon d'essai.

feeling /fiːlɪŋ/ n. sentiment m.; (*physical*) sensation f.

feet /fiːt/ see **foot**.

feign /feɪn/ v.t. feindre.

feint /feɪnt/ n. feinte f.

felicitous /fɪˈlɪsɪtəs/ a. heureux.

feline /fiːlaɪn/ a. félin.

fell¹ /fel/ v.t. (*cut down*) abattre.

fell² /fel/ see **fall**.

fellow /feləʊ/ n. compagnon m., camarade m.; (*of society*) membre m.; (*man: fam.*) type m. ~**countryman** n. compatriote m. ~**-passenger**, ~**-traveller** n. compagnon de voyage m. ~**ship** n. camaraderie f.; (*group*) association f.

felony /feləni/ n. crime m.

felt¹ /felt/ n. feutre m. ~**-tip** n. feutre m.

felt² /felt/ see **feel**.

female /fiːmeɪl/ a. (*animal etc.*) femelle; (*voice, sex, etc.*) féminin. —n. femme f.; (*animal*) femelle f.

feminin|e /femənɪn/ a. & n. féminin (m.). ~**ity** /-'nɪnətɪ/ n. féminité f.

feminist /femɪnɪst/ n. féministe m./f.

fenc|e /fens/ n. barrière f.; (*person: jurid.*) receleu|r, -se m., f. —v.t. ~**e** (**in**), clôturer. —v.i. (*sport*) faire de l'escrime. ~**er** n. escrimeu|r, -se m., f. ~**ing** n. escrime f.

fend /fend/ v.i. ~ **for o.s.**, se débrouiller tout seul. —v.t. ~ **off**, (*blow, attack*) parer.

fender /fendə(r)/ n. (*for fireplace*) garde-feu m. invar.; (*mudguard: Amer.*) garde-boue m. invar.

fennel /fenl/ n. (*culin.*) fenouil m.

ferment¹ /fəˈment/ v.t./i. (faire) fermenter. ~**ation** /fɜːmenˈteɪʃn/ n. fermentation f.

ferment² /fɜːment/ n. ferment m.; (*excitement: fig.*) agitation f.

fern /fɜːn/ n. fougère f.

feroc|ious /fəˈrəʊʃəs/ a. féroce. ~**ity** /-'rɒsətɪ/ n. férocité f.

ferret /ferɪt/ n. (*animal*) furet m. —v.i. (p.t. **ferreted**) fureter. —v.t. ~ **out**, dénicher.

ferry /ferɪ/ n. ferry m., bac m. —v.t. transporter.

fertil|e /fɜːtaɪl, Amer. 'fɜːtl/ a. fertile; (*person, animal*) fécond. ~**ity** /-'tɪlətɪ/ n. fertilité f.; fécondité f. ~**ize** /-əlaɪz/ v.t. fertiliser; féconder.

fertilizer /fɜːtəlaɪzə(r)/ n. engrais m.

fervent /fɜːvənt/ a. fervent.

fervour /fɜːvə(r)/ n. ferveur f.

fester /festə(r)/ v.i. (*wound*) suppurer; (*fig.*) rester sur le cœur.

festival /festɪvl/ n. festival m.; (*relig.*) fête f.

festiv|e /festɪv/ a. de fête, gai. ~**e**

season, période des fêtes *f.* ~ity
/fe'strvɪtɪ/ *n.* réjouissances *f. pl.*

festoon /fe'stuːn/ *v.i.* ~ with,
orner de.

fetch /fetʃ/ *v.t.* (go for) aller
chercher; (bring person) amener;
(bring thing) apporter; (be sold
for) rapporter.

fête /feɪt/ *n.* fête *f.* —*v.t.* fêter.

fetid /'fetɪd/ *a.* fétide.

fetish /'fetɪʃ/ *n.* (object) fétiche *m.*;
(psych.) obsession *f.*

fetter /'fetə(r)/ *v.t.* enchaîner. ~s
n. pl. chaînes *f. pl.*

feud /fjuːd/ *n.* querelle *f.*

feudal /'fjuːdl/ *a.* féodal.

fever /'fiːvə(r)/ *n.* fièvre *f.* ~ish *a.*
fiévreux.

few /fjuː/ *a. & n.* peu (de). ~
books, peu de livres. **they are**
~, ils sont peu nombreux. **a** ~ *a.*
quelques; *n.* quelques-un(e)s. **a**
good ~, **quite a** ~, (*fam.*) bon
nombre (de). ~**er** *a. & n.* moins
(de). **be** ~**er**, être moins
nombreux (**than**, que). ~**est** *a. &*
n. le moins (de).

fiancé /fɪ'ɒnseɪ/ *n.* fiancé *m.*

fiancée /fɪ'ɒnseɪ/ *n.* fiancée *f.*

fiasco /fɪ'æskəʊ/ *n.* (*pl.* -os) fiasco
m.

fib /fɪb/ *n.* mensonge *m.* ~**ber** *n.*
menteu|r, -se *m., f.*

fibre, *Amer.* **fiber** /'faɪbə(r)/ *n.*
fibre *f.* ~ **optics**, fibres optiques.

fibreglass, *Amer.* **fiberglass**
/'faɪbəglɑːs/ *n.* fibre de verre *f.*

fickle /'fɪkl/ *a.* inconstant.

fiction /'fɪkʃn/ *n.* fiction *f.* (**works**
of) ~, romans *m. pl.* ~**al** *a.* fictif.

fictitious /fɪk'tɪʃəs/ *a.* fictif.

fiddle /'fɪdl/ *n.* (*fam.*) violon *m.*;
(swindle: *sl.*) combine *f.* —*v.i.* (*sl.*)
frauder. —*v.t.* (*sl.*) falsifier. ~
with, (*fam.*) tripoter. ~**r** /-ə(r)/
n. (*fam.*) violoniste *m.*

fidelity /fɪ'delətɪ/ *n.* fidélité *f.*

fidget /'fɪdʒɪt/ *v.i.* (*p.t.* **fidgeted**)
remuer sans cesse. —*n.* **be a** ~,

être remuant. ~ **with**, tripoter.
~**y** *a.* remuant.

field /fiːld/ *n.* champ *m.*; (sport)
terrain *m.*; (fig.) domaine *m.*
—*v.t.* (ball: cricket) bloquer. ~
day *n.* grande occasion *f.* ~
glasses *n. pl.* jumelles *f. pl.* **F**~
Marshal, maréchal *m.*

fieldwork /'fiːldwɜːk/ *n.* travaux
pratiques *m. pl.*

fiend /fiːnd/ *n.* démon *m.* ~**ish** *a.*
diabolique.

fierce /fɪəs/ *a.* (-**er**, -**est**) féroce;
(storm, attack) violent. ~**ness** *n.*
férocité *f.*; violence *f.*

fiery /'faɪərɪ/ *a.* (-**ier**, -**iest**) (hot)
ardent; (spirited) fougueux.

fiesta /fɪ'estə/ *n.* fiesta *f.*

fifteen /fɪf'tiːn/ *a. & n.* quinze (*m.*).
~**th** *a. & n.* quinzième (*m./f.*).

fifth /fɪfθ/ *a. & n.* cinquième
(*m./f.*). ~ **column**, cinquième
colonne *f.*

fift|y /'fɪftɪ/ *a. & n.* cinquante (*m.*).
~**ieth** *a. & n.* cinquantième
(*m./f.*). **a** ~**y-fifty chance**,
(equal) une chance sur deux.

fig /fɪg/ *n.* figue *f.*

fight /faɪt/ *v.i.* (*p.t.* **fought**) se
battre; (struggle: fig.) lutter;
(quarrel) se disputer. —*v.t.* se
battre avec; (evil etc.: fig.) lutter
contre. —*n.* (struggle) lutte *f.*;
(quarrel) dispute *f.*; (brawl)
bagarre *f.*; (mil.) combat *m.* ~
back, se défendre. ~ **off**, surmonter. ~ **over sth.**, se disputer
qch. ~ **shy of**, fuir devant. ~**er**
n. (brawler, soldier) combattant
m.; (fig.) battant *m.*; (aircraft)
chasseur *m.* ~**ing** *n.* combats *m.*
pl.

figment /'fɪgmənt/ *n.* invention *f.*

figurative /'fɪɡjərətɪv/ *a.* figuré.

figure /'fɪɡə(r)/ *n.* (number) chiffre
m.; (diagram) figure *f.*; (shape)
forme *f.*; (body) ligne *f.* ~**s**,
arithmétique *f.* —*v.t.* s'imaginer.
—*v.i.* (appear) figurer. ~ **out**,

comprendre. **~-head** n. (person with no real power) prête-nom m.
~ of speech, façon de parler f.
that **~s**, (Amer., fam.) c'est logique.

filament /ˈfɪləmənt/ n. filament m.

filch /fɪltʃ/ v.t. voler, piquer.

file[1] /faɪl/ n. (tool) lime f. —v.t. limer. **~ings** n. pl. limaille f.

file[2] /faɪl/ n. dossier m., classeur m.; (comput.) fichier m.; (row) file f. —v.t. (papers) classer; (jurid.) déposer. —v.i. **~e in**, entrer en file. **~ past**, défiler devant. **~ing cabinet**, classeur m.

fill /fɪl/ v.t./i. (se) remplir. —n. **eat one's ~**, manger à sa faim. **have had one's ~**, en avoir assez. **~ in or up**, (form) remplir. **~ out**, (get fat) grossir. **~ up**, (auto.) faire le plein (d'essence).

fillet /ˈfɪlɪt, Amer. fɪˈleɪ/ n. filet m. —v.t. (p.t. **filleted**) découper en filets.

filling /ˈfɪlɪŋ/ n. (of tooth) plombage m.; (of sandwich) garniture f. **~ station**, station-service f.

filly /ˈfɪlɪ/ n. pouliche f.

film /fɪlm/ n. film m.; (photo.) pellicule f. —v.t. filmer. **~-goer** n. cinéphile m./f. **~ star**, vedette de cinéma f.

filter /ˈfɪltə(r)/ n. filtre m.; (traffic signal) flèche f. —v.t./i. filtrer; (of traffic) suivre la flèche. **~ coffee**, café-filtre m. **~-tip** n. bout filtre m.

filth, **~iness** n. /fɪlθ, fɪlθɪnəs/ n. saleté f. **~y** a. sale.

fin /fɪn/ n. (of fish, seal) nageoire f.; (of shark) aileron m.

final /ˈfaɪnl/ a. dernier; (conclusive) définitif. —n. (sport) finale f. **~ist** n. finaliste m./f. **~ly** adv. (lastly, at last) enfin, finalement; (once and for all) définitivement.

finale /fɪˈnɑːlɪ/ n. (mus.) finale m.

finalize /ˈfaɪnəlaɪz/ v.t. mettre au point, fixer.

financ|e /ˈfaɪnæns/ n. finance f. —a. financier. —v.t. financer. **~ier** /-ˈnænsɪə(r)/ n. financier m.

financial /faɪˈnænʃl/ a. financier. **~ly** adv. financièrement.

find /faɪnd/ v.t. (p.t. **found**) trouver; (sth. lost) retrouver. —n. trouvaille f. **~ out** v.t. découvrir; v.i. se renseigner (about, sur). **~ings** n. pl. conclusions f. pl.

fine[1] /faɪn/ n. amende f. —v.t. condamner à une amende.

fine[2] /faɪn/ a. (-er, -est) fin; (excellent) beau. —adv. (très) bien; (small) fin. **~ arts**, beaux-arts m. pl. **~ly** adv. (admirably) magnifiquement; (cut) fin.

finery /ˈfaɪnərɪ/ n. atours m. pl.

finesse /fɪˈnes/ n. finesse f.

finger /ˈfɪŋgə(r)/ n. doigt m. —v.t. palper. **~-nail** n. ongle m. **~-stall** n. doigtier m.

fingerprint /ˈfɪŋgəprɪnt/ n. empreinte digitale f.

fingertip /ˈfɪŋgətɪp/ n. bout du doigt m.

finicking, **finicky** /ˈfɪnɪkɪŋ, ˈfɪnɪkɪ/ adjs. méticuleux.

finish /ˈfɪnɪʃ/ v.t./i. finir. —n. fin f.; (of race) arrivée f.; (appearance) finition f. **~ doing**, finir de faire. **~ up doing**, finir par faire. **~ up in**, (land up in) se retrouver à.

finite /ˈfaɪnaɪt/ a. fini.

Fin|land /ˈfɪnlənd/ n. finlande f. **~n** n. finlandais(e) m. (f.). **~nish** a. finlandais; n. (lang.) finnois m.

fir /fɜː(r)/ n. sapin m.

fire /ˈfaɪə(r)/ n. feu m.; (conflagration) incendie m.; (heater) radiateur m. —v.t. (bullet etc.) tirer; (dismiss) renvoyer; (fig.) enflammer. —v.i. tirer (at, sur). **~ a gun**, tirer un coup de revolver or de fusil. **set ~ to**, mettre le feu à. ~ **alarm,** avertisseur d'incendie *m.* ~ **brigade,** pompiers *m. pl.* ~**engine** *n.* voiture de pompiers *f.* ~**-escape** *n.* escalier de secours *m.* ~ **extinguisher,** extincteur d'incendie *m.* ~ **station,** caserne de pompiers *f.*

firearm /'faɪərɑːm/ *n.* arme à feu *f.*

firecracker /'faɪəkrækə(r)/ *n.* (*Amer.*) pétard *m.*

firelight /'faɪəlaɪt/ *n.* lueur du feu *f.*

fireman /'faɪəmən/ *n.* (*pl.* -men) pompier *m.*

fireplace /'faɪəpleɪs/ *n.* cheminée *f.*

fireside /'faɪəsaɪd/ *n.* coin du feu *m.*

firewood /'faɪəwʊd/ *n.* bois de chauffage *m.*

firework /'faɪəwɜːk/ *n.* feu d'artifice *m.*

firing-squad /'faɪərɪŋskwɒd/ *n.* peloton d'exécution *m.*

firm[1] /fɜːm/ *n.* firme *f.*, société *f.*

firm[2] /fɜːm/ *a.* (-er, -est) ferme; (*belief*) solide. ~**ly** *adv.* fermement. ~**ness** *n.* fermeté *f.*

first /fɜːst/ *a.* premier. ~ *n.* premⅰer, -ière *m.*, *f.* —*adv.* d'abord, premièrement; (*arrive etc.*) le premier, la première. **at** ~, d'abord. **at** ~ **hand,** de première main. **at** ~ **sight,** à première vue. ~ **aid,** premiers soins *m. pl.* ~**class** *a.* de première classe. ~**floor,** (*Amer.*) rez-de-chaussée *m. invar.* ~ (**gear**), première (vitesse) *f.* **F**~ **Lady,** (*Amer.*) épouse du Président *f.* ~ **name,** prénom *m.* ~ **of all,** tout d'abord. ~**rate** *a.* de premier ordre. ~**ly** *adv.* premièrement.

fiscal /'fɪskl/ *a.* fiscal.

fish /fɪʃ/ *n.* (*usually invar.*) poisson *m.* —*v.i.* pêcher. ~ **for,** (*cod etc.*) pêcher. ~ **out,** (*from water*) repêcher; (*take out*: *fam.*) sortir. ~ **shop,** poissonnerie *f.* ~**ing** *n.* pêche *f.* **go** ~**ing,** aller à la pêche. ~**ing rod,** canne à pêche *f.* ~**y** *a.* de poisson; (*fig.*) louche.

fisherman /'fɪʃəmən/ *n.* (*pl.* -men) *n.* pêcheur *m.*

fishmonger /'fɪʃmʌŋgə(r)/ *n.* poissonnⅰier, -ière *m.*, *f.*

fission /'fɪʃn/ *n.* fission *f.*

fist /fɪst/ *n.* poing *m.*

fit[1] /fɪt/ *n.* (*bout*) accès *m.*, crise *f.*

fit[2] /fɪt/ *a.* (**fitter, fittest**) en bonne santé; (*proper*) convenable; (*good enough*) bon; (*able*) capable. —*v.t./i.* (*p.t.* **fitted**) (*clothes*) aller (à); (*match*) s'accorder (avec); (*put or go in or on*) (s')adapter (**to,** à); (*into space*) aller; (*install*) poser. —*n.* **be a good** ~, (*dress*) être à la bonne taille. **in no** ~ **state to do,** pas en état de faire. ~ **in,** *v.t.* caser; *v.i.* (*newcomer*) s'intégrer. ~ **out,** ~ **up,** équiper. ~**ness** *n.* santé *f.*; (*of remark*) justesse *f.*

fitful /'fɪtfl/ *a.* irrégulier.

fitment /'fɪtmənt/ *n.* meuble fixe *m.*

fitted /'fɪtɪd/ *a.* (*wardrobe*) encastré. ~ **carpet,** moquette *f.*

fitting /'fɪtɪŋ/ *a.* approprié. —*n.* essayage *m.* ~ **room,** cabine d'essayage *f.*

fittings /'fɪtɪŋz/ *n. pl.* (*in house*) installations *f. pl.*

five /faɪv/ *a. & n.* cinq (*m.*).

fiver /'faɪvə(r)/ *n.* (*fam.*) billet de cinq livres *m.*

fix /fɪks/ *v.t.* (*make firm, attach, decide*) fixer; (*mend*) réparer; (*deal with*) arranger. —*n.* **in a** ~, dans le pétrin. ~ **s.o. up with sth.,** trouver qch. à qn. ~**ed** *a.* fixe.

fixation /fɪk'seɪʃn/ *n.* fixation *f.*

fixture /'fɪkstʃə(r)/ *n.* (*sport*) match *m.* ~**s,** (*in house*) installations *f. pl.*

fizz /fɪz/ v.i. pétiller. —n. pétillement m. ~**y** a. gazeux.

fizzle /ˈfɪzl/ v.i. pétiller. ~ **out**, (plan etc.) finir en queue de poisson.

flab /flæb/ n. (fam.) corpulence f. ~**by** /ˈflæbɪ/ a. flasque.

flabbergast /ˈflæbəgɑːst/ v.t. sidérer, ahurir.

flag[1] /flæg/ n. drapeau m.; (naut.) pavillon m. —v.t. (p.t. **flagged**). ~ **(down)**, faire signe de s'arrêter à. ~**pole** n. mât m.

flag[2] /flæg/ v.i. (p.t. **flagged**) (weaken) faiblir; (sick person) s'affaiblir; (droop) dépérir.

flagon /ˈflægən/ n. bouteille f.

flagrant /ˈfleɪɡrənt/ a. flagrant.

flagstone /ˈflægstəʊn/ n. dalle f.

flair /fleə(r)/ n. flair m.

flak /flæk/ n. (fam.) critiques f.pl.

flake /fleɪk/ n. flocon m.; (of paint, metal) écaille f. —v.i. s'écailler. ~**y** a. (paint) écailleux.

flamboyant /flæmˈbɔɪənt/ a. (colour) éclatant; (manner) extravagant.

flame /fleɪm/ n. flamme f. —v.i. flamber. **burst into** ~**s**, exploser. **go up in** ~**s**, brûler.

flamingo /fləˈmɪŋɡəʊ/ n. (pl. -os) flamant (rose) m.

flammable /ˈflæməbl/ a. inflammable.

flan /flæn/ n. tarte f.; (custard tart) flan m.

flank /flæŋk/ n. flanc m. —v.t. flanquer.

flannel /ˈflænl/ n. flannelle f.; (for face) gant de toilette m.

flannelette /flænəˈlet/ n. pilou m.

flap /flæp/ v.i. (p.t. **flapped**) battre. —v.t. ~ **its wings**, battre des ailes. —n. (of pocket) rabat m.; (of table) abattant m. **get into a** ~, (fam.) s'affoler.

flare /fleə(r)/ v.i. ~ **up**, s'enflammer, flamber; (fighting) éclater; (person) s'emporter. —n.

flamboiement m.; (mil.) fusée éclairante f.; (in skirt) évasement m. ~**d** a. (skirt) évasé.

flash /flæʃ/ v.i. briller; (on and off) clignoter. —v.t. faire briller; (aim torch) diriger (**at**, sur); (flaunt) étaler. —n. éclair m., éclat m.; (of news, camera) flash m. **in a** ~, en un éclair. ~ **one's headlights**, faire un appel de phares. ~ **past**, passer à toute vitesse.

flashback /ˈflæʃbæk/ n. retour en arrière m.

flashlight /ˈflæʃlaɪt/ n. (torch) lampe électrique f.

flashy /ˈflæʃɪ/ a. voyant.

flask /flɑːsk/ n. flacon m.; (vacuum flask) thermos m./f. invar. (P.).

flat /flæt/ a. (**flatter**, **flattest**) plat; (tyre) à plat; (refusal) catégorique; (fare, rate) fixe. —adv. (say) carrément. —n. (rooms) appartement m.; (tyre: fam.) crevaison f.; (mus.) bémol m. ~ **out**, (drive) à toute vitesse; (work) d'arrache-pied. ~**pack** a. en kit. ~**ly** adv. catégoriquement. ~**ness** n. égalité f.

flatten /ˈflætn/ v.t./i. (s')aplatir.

flatter /ˈflætə(r)/ v.t. flatter. ~**er** n. flatteu|r, -se m., f. ~**ing** a. flatteur. ~**y** n. flatterie f.

flatulence /ˈflætjʊləns/ n. flatulence f.

flaunt /flɔːnt/ v.t. étaler, afficher.

flautist /ˈflɔːtɪst/ n. flûtiste m./f.

flavour /ˈfleɪvə(r)/ (Amer.) **flavor** n. goût m.; (of ice-cream etc.) parfum m. —v.t. parfumer, assaisonner. ~**ing** n. arôme synthétique m.

flaw /flɔː/ n. défaut m. ~**ed** a. imparfait. ~**less** a. parfait.

flax /flæks/ n. lin m. ~**en** a. de lin.

flea /fliː/ n. puce f. ~ **market**, marché aux puces m.

fleck /flek/ n. petite tache f.

fled /fled/ see **flee**.

fledged /fledʒd/ a. **fully-**~,

(*doctor etc.*) diplômé; (*member, citizen*) à part entière.

flee /fliː/ *v.i.* (*p.t.* **fled**) s'enfuir. —*v.t.* s'enfuir de; (*danger*) fuir.

fleece /fliːs/ *n.* toison *f.* —*v.t.* voler.

fleet /fliːt/ *n.* (*naut., aviat.*) flotte *f.* **a ~ of vehicles**, un parc automobile.

fleeting /ˈfliːtɪŋ/ *a.* très bref.

Flemish /ˈflemɪʃ/ *a.* flamand. —*n.* (*lang.*) flamand *m.*

flesh /fleʃ/ *n.* chair *f.* **one's (own) ~ and blood**, les siens *m. pl.* **~y** *a.* charnu.

flew /fluː/ *see* **fly**[2].

flex[1] /fleks/ *v.t.* (*knee etc.*) fléchir; (*muscle*) faire jouer.

flex[2] /fleks/ *n.* (*electr.*) fil souple *m.*

flexib|le /ˈfleksəbl/ *a.* flexible. **~ility** /-ˈbɪlətɪ/ *n.* flexibilité *f.*

flexitime /ˈfleksɪtaɪm/ *n.* horaire variable *m.*

flick /flɪk/ *n.* petit coup *m.* —*v.t.* donner un petit coup à. **~-knife** *n.* couteau à cran d'arrêt *m.* **~ through**, feuilleter.

flicker /ˈflɪkə(r)/ *v.i.* vaciller. —*n.* vacillement *m.*; (*light*) lueur *f.*

flier /ˈflaɪə(r)/ *n.* = **flyer**.

flies /flaɪz/ *n. pl.* (*on trousers: fam.*) braguette *f.*

flight[1] /flaɪt/ *n.* (*of bird, plane, etc.*) vol *m.* **~-deck** *n.* poste de pilotage *m.* **~ of stairs**, escalier *m.*

flight[2] /flaɪt/ *n.* (*fleeing*) fuite *f.* **put to ~**, mettre en fuite. **take ~**, prendre la fuite.

flimsy /ˈflɪmzɪ/ *a.* (**-ier, -iest**) (*pej.*) mince, peu solide.

flinch /flɪntʃ/ *v.i.* (*wince*) broncher; (*draw back*) reculer.

fling /flɪŋ/ *v.t.* (*p.t.* **flung**) jeter. —*n.* **have a ~**, faire la fête.

flint /flɪnt/ *n.* silex *m.*; (*for lighter*) pierre *f.*

flip /flɪp/ *v.t.* (*p.t.* **flipped**) donner un petit coup à. —*n.* chiquenaude *f.* **~ through**, feuilleter. **~flops** *n. pl.* tongs *f. pl.*

flippant /ˈflɪpənt/ *a.* désinvolte.

flipper /ˈflɪpə(r)/ *n.* (*of seal etc.*) nageoire *f.*; (*of swimmer*) palme *f.*

flirt /flɜːt/ *v.i.* flirter. —*n.* flirteu|r, -se *m., f.* **~ation** /-ˈteɪʃn/ *n.* flirt *m.*

flit /flɪt/ *v.i.* (*p.t.* **flitted**) voltiger.

float /fləʊt/ *v.t./i.* (faire) flotter. —*n.* flotteur *m.*; (*cart*) char *m.*

flock /flɒk/ *n.* (*of sheep etc.*) troupeau *m.*; (*of people*) foule *f.* —*v.i.* venir en foule.

flog /flɒɡ/ *v.t.* (*p.t.* **flogged**) (*beat*) fouetter; (*sell: sl.*) vendre.

flood /flʌd/ *n.* inondation *f.*; (*fig.*) flot *m.* —*v.t.* inonder. —*v.i.* (*building etc.*) être inondé; (*river*) déborder; (*people: fig.*) affluer.

floodlight /ˈflʌdlaɪt/ *n.* projecteur *m.* —*v.t.* (*p.t.* **floodlit**) illuminer.

floor /flɔː(r)/ *n.* sol *m.*, plancher *m.*; (*for dancing*) piste *f.*; (*storey*) étage *m.* —*v.t.* (*knock down*) terrasser; (*baffle*) stupéfier. **~board** *n.* planche *f.*

flop /flɒp/ *v.i.* (*p.t.* **flopped**) s'agiter faiblement; (*drop*) s'affaler; (*fail: sl.*) échouer. —*n.* (*sl.*) échec *m.*, fiasco *m.* **~py** *a.* lâche, flasque. **~py (disk)**, disquette *f.*

flora /ˈflɔːrə/ *n.* flore *f.*

floral /ˈflɔːrəl/ *a.* floral.

florid /ˈflɒrɪd/ *a.* fleuri.

florist /ˈflɒrɪst/ *n.* fleuriste *m./f.*

flounce /flaʊns/ *n.* volant *m.*

flounder[1] /ˈflaʊndə(r)/ *v.i.* patauger (avec difficulté).

flounder[2] /ˈflaʊndə(r)/ *n.* (*fish: Amer.*) flet *m.*, plie *f.*

flour /ˈflaʊə(r)/ *n.* farine *f.* **~y** *a.* farineux.

flourish /ˈflʌrɪʃ/ *v.i.* prospérer. —*v.t.* brandir. —*n.* geste élégant *m.*; (*curve*) fioriture *f.*

flout /flaʊt/ *v.t.* faire fi de.

flow /fləʊ/ *v.i.* couler; (*circulate*) circuler; (*traffic*) s'écouler; (*hang loosely*) flotter. —*n.* (*of liquid,* *traffic*) écoulement *m.*; (*of tide*) flux *m.*; (*of orders, words: fig.*) flot *m.* ~ **chart**, organigramme *m.* ~ **in**, affluer. ~ **into**, (*of river*) se jeter dans.

flower /'flauə(r)/ *n.* fleur *f.* —*v.i.* fleurir. ~**-bed** *n.* plate-bande *f.* ~**ed** *a.* à fleurs. ~**y** *a.* fleuri.

flown /fləun/ *see* **fly**².

flu /flu:/ *n.* (*fam.*) grippe *f.*

fluctuat|e /'flʌktʃueɪt/ *v.i.* varier. ~**ion** /-'eɪʃn/ *n.* variation *f.*

flue /flu:/ *n.* (*duct*) tuyau *m.*

fluen|t /'flu:ənt/ *a.* (*style*) aisé. **be** ~**t** (**in a language**), parler (une langue) couramment. ~**cy** *n.* facilité *f.* ~**tly** *adv.* avec facilité; (*lang.*) couramment.

fluff /flʌf/ *n.* peluche(s) *f.* (*pl.*); (*down*) duvet *m.* ~**y** *a.* pelucheux.

fluid /'flu:ɪd/ *a. & n.* fluide (*m.*).

fluke /flu:k/ *n.* coup de chance *m.*

flung /flʌŋ/ *see* **fling**.

flunk /flʌŋk/ *v.t./i.* (*Amer., fam.*) être collé (à).

fluorescent /fluə'resnt/ *a.* fluorescent.

fluoride /'fluəraɪd/ *n.* (*in toothpaste, water*) fluor *m.*

flurry /'flʌrɪ/ *n.* (*squall*) rafale *f.*; (*fig.*) agitation *f.*

flush¹ /flʌʃ/ *v.i.* rougir. —*v.t.* nettoyer à grande eau. —*n.* (*blush*) rougeur *f.*; (*fig.*) excitation *f.* —*a.* ~ **with**, (*level with*) au ras de. ~ **the toilet**, tirer la chasse d'eau.

flush² /flʌʃ/ *v.t.* ~ **out**, chasser.

fluster /'flʌstə(r)/ *v.t.* énerver.

flute /flu:t/ *n.* flûte *f.*

flutter /'flʌtə(r)/ *v.i.* voleter; (*of wings*) battre. —*n.* (*of wings*) battement *m.*; (*fig.*) agitation *f.*; (*bet: fam.*) pari *m.*

flux /flʌks/ *n.* changement continuel *m.*

fly¹ /flaɪ/ *n.* mouche *f.*

fly² /flaɪ/ *v.i.* (*p.t.* **flew**, *p.p.* **flown**) voler; (*of passengers*) voyager en

avion; (*of flag*) flotter; (*rush*) filer. —*v.t.* (*aircraft*) piloter; (*passengers, goods*) transporter par avion; (*flag*) arborer. —*n.* (*of trousers*) braguette *f.* ~ **off**, s'envoler.

flyer /'flaɪə(r)/ *n.* aviateur *m.*; (*circular: Amer.*) prospectus *m.*

flying /'flaɪŋ/ *a.* (*saucer etc.*) volant. —*n.* (*activity*) aviation *f.* ~ **buttress**, arc-boutant *m.* **with** ~ **colours**, haut la main. ~ **start**, excellent départ *m.* ~ **visit**, visite éclair *f.* (*a. invar.*).

flyover /'flaɪəuvə(r)/ *n.* (*road*) toboggan *m.*, saut-de-mouton *m.*

flyweight /'flaɪweɪt/ *n.* poids mouche *m.*

foal /fəul/ *n.* poulain *m.*

foam /fəum/ *n.* écume *f.*, mousse *f.* —*v.i.* écumer, mousser. ~ (**rubber**) *n.* caoutchouc mousse *m.*

fob /fɒb/ *v.t.* (*p.t.* **fobbed**) ~ **off on** (**to**) **s.o.**, (*palm off*) refiler à qn. ~ **s.o. off with**, forcer qn. à se contenter de.

focal /'fəukl/ *a.* focal.

focus /'fəukəs/ *n.* (*pl.* **-cuses** *or* **-ci** /-saɪ/) foyer *m.*; (*fig.*) centre *m.* —*v.t./i.* (*p.t.* **focused**) (*faire*) converger; (*instrument*) mettre au point; (*with camera*) faire la mise au point (**on**, sur); (*fig.*) (se) concentrer. **be in/out of** ~, être/ne pas être au point.

fodder /'fɒdə(r)/ *n.* fourrage *m.*

foe /fəu/ *n.* ennemi(e) *m.*(*f.*).

foetus /'fi:təs/ *n.* (*pl.* **-tuses**) fœtus *m.*

fog /fɒg/ *n.* brouillard *m.* —*v.t./i.* (*p.t.* **fogged**) (*window etc.*) (s')embuer. ~**-horn** *n.* (*naut.*) corne de brume *f.* ~**gy** *a.* brumeux. **it is** ~**gy**, il fait du brouillard.

fog(e)y /'fəugɪ/ *n.* (**old**) ~, vieille baderne *f.*

foible /'fɔɪbl/ *n.* faiblesse *f.*

foil¹ /fɔɪl/ *n.* (*tin foil*) papier

d'aluminium *m.*; (*fig.*) repoussoir *m.*

foil² /fɔɪl/ *v.t.* thwart) déjouer.

foist /fɔɪst/ *v.t.* imposer (**on**, à).

fold¹ /fəʊld/ *v.t./i.* (se) plier; (*arms*) croiser; (*fail*) s'effondrer. —*n.* pli *m.* **~er** *n.* (*file*) chemise *f.*; (*leaflet*) dépliant *m.* **~ing** *a.* pliant.

fold² /fəʊld/ *n.* (*for sheep*) parc à moutons *m.*; (*relig.*) bercail *m.*

foliage /ˈfəʊlɪdʒ/ *n.* feuillage *m.*

folk /fəʊk/ *n.* gens *m. pl.* **~s**, parents *m. pl.* —*a.* folklorique.

folklore /ˈfəʊklɔː(r)/ *n.* folklore *m.*

follow /ˈfɒləʊ/ *v.t./i.* suivre. **it ~s that**, il s'ensuit que. **~ suit**, en faire autant. **~ up**, (*letter etc.*) donner suite à. **~er** *n.* partisan *m.* **~ing** *n.* partisans *m. pl.*; *a.* suivant; *prep.* à la suite de.

folly /ˈfɒlɪ/ *n.* sottise *f.*

foment /fəʊˈment/ *v.t.* fomenter.

fond /fɒnd/ *a.* (**-er, -est**) (*loving*) affectueux; (*hope*) cher. **be ~ of**, aimer. **~ness** *n.* affection *f.*; (*for things*) attachement *m.*

fondle /ˈfɒndl/ *v.t.* caresser.

food /fuːd/ *n.* nourriture *f.* —*a.* alimentaire. **French ~**, la cuisine française. **~ processor**, robot (ménager) *m.*

fool /fuːl/ *n.* idiot(e) *m. (f.).* —*v.t.* duper. —*v.i.* **~ around**, faire l'idiot.

foolhardy /ˈfuːlhɑːdɪ/ *a.* téméraire.

foolish /ˈfuːlɪʃ/ *a.* idiot. **~ly** *adv.* sottement. **~ness** *n.* sottise *f.*

foolproof /ˈfuːlpruːf/ *a.* infaillible.

foot /fʊt/ *n.* (*pl.* **feet**) pied *m.*; (*measure*) pied *m.* (= 30.48 *cm.*); (*of stairs, page*) bas *m.* —*v.t.* (*bill*) payer. **~-bridge** *n.* passerelle *f.* **on ~**, à pied. **on or to one's feet**, debout. **under s.o.'s feet**, dans les jambes de qn.

footage /ˈfʊtɪdʒ/ *n.* (*of film*) métrage *m.*

football /ˈfʊtbɔːl/ *n.* (*ball*) ballon *m.*; (*game*) football *m.* **~ pools**, paris sur les matchs de football *m. pl.* **~er** *n.* footballeur *m.*

foothills /ˈfʊthɪlz/ *n. pl.* contreforts *m. pl.*

foothold /ˈfʊthəʊld/ *n.* prise *f.*

footing /ˈfʊtɪŋ/ *n.* prise (de pied) *f.*, équilibre *m.*; (*fig.*) situation *f.* **on an equal ~**, sur un pied d'égalité.

footlights /ˈfʊtlaɪts/ *n. pl.* rampe *f.*

footman /ˈfʊtmən/ *n.* (*pl.* **-men**) valet de pied *m.*

footnote /ˈfʊtnəʊt/ *n.* note (en bas de la page) *f.*

footpath /ˈfʊtpɑːθ/ *n.* sentier *m.*; (*at the side of the road*) chemin *m.*

footprint /ˈfʊtprɪnt/ *n.* empreinte (de pied) *f.*

footsore /ˈfʊtsɔː(r)/ *a.* **be ~**, avoir les pieds douloureux.

footstep /ˈfʊtstep/ *n.* pas *m.*

footwear /ˈfʊtweə(r)/ *n.* chaussures *f. pl.*

for /fɔː(r), *unstressed* fə(r)/ *prep.* pour; (*during*) pendant; (*before*) avant. —*conj.* car. **a liking ~**, le goût de. **look ~**, chercher. **pay ~**, payer. **he has been away ~**, il est absent depuis. **he stopped ~ ten minutes**, il s'est arrêté (pendant) dix minutes. **it continues ~ ten kilometres**, ça continue pendant dix kilomètres. **~ ever**, pour toujours. **~ good**, pour de bon. **~ all my work**, malgré mon travail.

forage /ˈfɒrɪdʒ/ *v.i.* fourrager. —*n.* fourrage *m.*

foray /ˈfɒreɪ/ *n.* incursion *f.*

forbade /fəˈbæd/ *see* **forbid**.

forbear /fɔːˈbeə(r)/ *v.t./i.* (*p.t.* **forbore**, *p.p.* **forborne**) s'abstenir. **~ance** *n.* patience *f.*

forbid /fəˈbɪd/ *v.t.* (*p.t.* **forbade**, *p.p.* **forbidden**) interdire, défendre (**s.o. to do**, à qn. de faire). **~ s.o. sth.**, interdire *or* défendre qch. à qn. **you are ～den to leave**, il vous est interdit de partir.

forbidding /fə'bɪdɪŋ/ a. menaçant.

force /fɔːs/ n. force f. —v.t. forcer. **～ into**, faire entrer de force. **～ on**, imposer à. **come into ～**, entrer en vigueur. **the ～s**, les forces armées. f. pl. **～d** a. forcé. **～ful** a. énergique.

force-feed /'fɔːsfiːd/ v.t. (p.t. **-fed**) nourrir de force.

forceps /'fɔːseps/ n. invar. forceps m.

forcibl|e /'fɔːsəbl/ a., **～y** adv. de force.

ford /fɔːd/ n. gué m. —v.t. passer à gué.

fore /fɔː(r)/ a. antérieur. —n. **to the ～**, en évidence.

forearm /'fɔːrɑːm/ n. avant-bras m. invar.

foreboding /fɔː'bəʊdɪŋ/ n. pressentiment m.

forecast /'fɔːkɑːst/ v.t. (p.t. **forecast**) prévoir. —n. prévision f.

forecourt /'fɔːkɔːt/ n. (of garage) devant m.; (of station) cour f.

forefathers /'fɔːfɑːðəz/ n. pl. aïeux m. pl.

forefinger /'fɔːfɪŋɡə(r)/ n. index m.

forefront /'fɔːfrʌnt/ n. premier rang m.

foregone /'fɔːɡɒn/ a. **～ conclusion**, résultat à prévoir m.

foreground /'fɔːɡraʊnd/ n. premier plan m.

forehead /'fɒrɪd/ n. front m.

foreign /'fɒrən/ a. étranger; (trade) extérieur; (travel) à l'étranger. **～er** n. étrang|er, -ère m., f.

foreman /'fɔːmən/ n. (pl. **-men**) contremaître m.

foremost /'fɔːməʊst/ a. le plus éminent. —adv. **first and ～**, tout d'abord.

forename /'fɔːneɪm/ n. prénom n.

forensic /fə'rensɪk/ a. médicolégal. **～ medicine**, médecine légale f.

foreplay /'fɔːpleɪ/ n. préliminaires m. pl.

forerunner /'fɔːrʌnə(r)/ n. précurseur m.

foresee /fɔː'siː/ v.t. (p.t. **-saw**, p.p. **-seen**) prévoir. **～able** a. prévisible.

foreshadow /fɔː'ʃædəʊ/ v.t. présager, laisser prévoir.

foresight /'fɔːsaɪt/ n. prévoyance f.

forest /'fɒrɪst/ n. forêt f.

forestall /fɔː'stɔːl/ v.t. devancer.

forestry /'fɒrɪstrɪ/ n. sylviculture f.

foretaste /'fɔːteɪst/ n. avant-goût m.

foretell /fɔː'tel/ v.t. (p.t. **foretold**) prédire.

forever /fə'revə(r)/ adv. toujours.

forewarn /fɔː'wɔːn/ v.t. avertir.

foreword /'fɔːwɜːd/ n. avant-propos m. invar.

forfeit /'fɔːfɪt/ n. (penalty) peine f.; (in game) gage m. —v.t. perdre.

forgave /fə'ɡeɪv/ see **forgive**.

forge[1] /fɔːdʒ/ v.i. **～ ahead**, aller de l'avant, avancer.

forge[2] /fɔːdʒ/ n. forge f. —v.t. (metal, friendship) forger; (copy) contrefaire, falsifier. **～r** /-ə(r)/ n. faussaire m. **～ry** /-ərɪ/ n. faux m., contrefaçon f.

forget /fə'ɡet/ v.t./i. (p.t. **forgot**, p.p. **forgotten**) oublier. **～-me-not** n. myosotis m. **～ o.s.**, s'oublier. **～ful** a. distrait. **～ful of**, oublieux de.

forgive /fə'ɡɪv/ v.t. (p.t. **forgave**, p.p. **forgiven**) pardonner (**s.o. for sth.**, qch. à qn.). **～ness** n. pardon m.

forgo /fɔː'ɡəʊ/ v.t. (p.t. **forwent**, p.p. **forgone**) renoncer à.

fork /fɔːk/ n. fourchette f.; (for digging etc.) fourche f.; (in road)

bifurcation f. —v.i. (road) bifurquer. **~-lift truck**, chariot élévateur m. **~ out**, (sl.) payer. **~ed** a. fourchu.

forlorn /fə'lɔːn/ a. triste, abandonné. **~ hope**, mince espoir m.

form /fɔːm/ n. forme f.; (document) formulaire m.; (schol.) classe f. —v.t./i. (se) former. **on ~**, en forme.

formal /'fɔːml/ a. officiel, en bonne et due forme; (person) compassé, cérémonieux; (dress) de cérémonie; (denial, grammar) formel; (language) soutenu. **~ity** /-'mælətɪ/ n. cérémonial m.; (requirement) formalité f. **~ly** adv. officiellement.

format /'fɔːmæt/ n. format m. —v.t. (p.t. **formatted**) (disk) initialiser, formater.

formation /fɔː'meɪʃn/ n. formation f.

formative /'fɔːmətɪv/ a. formateur.

former /'fɔːmə(r)/ a. ancien; (first of two) premier. **the ~**, celui-là, celle-là. **~ly** adv. autrefois.

formidable /'fɔːmɪdəbl/ a. redoutable, terrible.

formula /'fɔːmjʊlə/ n. (pl. **-ae** /-iː/ or **-as**) formule f.

formulate /'fɔːmjʊleɪt/ v.t. formuler.

forsake /fə'seɪk/ v.t. (p.t. **forsook**, p.p. **forsaken**) abandonner.

fort /fɔːt/ n. (mil.) fort m.

forte /'fɔːteɪ/ n. (talent) fort m.

forth /fɔːθ/ adv. en avant. **and so ~**, et ainsi de suite. **go back and ~**, aller et venir.

forthcoming /fɔːθ'kʌmɪŋ/ a. à venir, prochain; (sociable: fam.) communicatif.

forthright /'fɔːθraɪt/ a. direct.

forthwith /fɔːθ'wɪθ/ adv. sur-le-champ.

fortif|y /'fɔːtɪfaɪ/ v.t. fortifier.

~ication /-ɪ'keɪʃn/ n. fortification f.

fortitude /'fɔːtɪtjuːd/ n. courage m.

fortnight /'fɔːtnaɪt/ n. quinze jours m. pl., quinzaine f. **~ly** a. bimensuel; adv. tous les quinze jours.

fortress /'fɔːtrɪs/ n. forteresse f.

fortuitous /fɔː'tjuːɪtəs/ a. fortuit.

fortunate /'fɔːtʃənət/ a. heureux. **be ~**, avoir de la chance. **~ly** adv. heureusement.

fortune /'fɔːtʃuːn/ n. fortune f. **~-teller** n. diseuse de bonne aventure f. **have the good ~ to**, avoir la chance de.

fort|y /'fɔːtɪ/ a. & n. quarante (m.). **~y winks**, un petit somme. **~ieth** a. & n. quarantième (m./f.).

forum /'fɔːrəm/ n. forum m.

forward /'fɔːwəd/ a. en avant; (advanced) précoce; (pert) effronté. —n. (sport) avant m. —adv. en avant. —v.t. (letter) faire suivre; (goods) expédier; (fig.) favoriser. **come ~**, se présenter. **go ~**, avancer. **~ness** n. précocité f.

forwards /'fɔːwədz/ adv. en avant.

fossil /'fɒsl/ n. & a. fossile (m.).

foster /'fɒstə(r)/ v.t. (promote) encourager; (child) élever. **~-child** n. enfant adoptif m. **~-mother** n. mère adoptive f.

fought /fɔːt/ see **fight**.

foul /faʊl/ a. (**-er, -est**) (smell, weather, etc.) infect; (place, action) immonde; (language) ordurier. —n. (football) faute f. —v.t. souiller, encrasser. **~-mouthed** a. au langage ordurier. **~ play**, jeu irrégulier m.; (crime) acte criminel m. **~ up**, (sl.) gâcher.

found[1] /faʊnd/ see **find**.

found[2] /faʊnd/ v.t. fonder. **~ation** /-'deɪʃn/ n. fondation f.; (basis) fondement m.; (make-up)

fond de teint *m.* ～**er**[1] *n.*
fonda|teur, -trice *m., f.*

founder[2] /ˈfaʊndə(r)/ *v.i.* sombrer.

foundry /ˈfaʊndrɪ/ *n.* fonderie *f.*

fountain /ˈfaʊntɪn/ *n.* fontaine *f.*
～**-pen** *n.* stylo à encre *m.*

four /fɔː(r)/ *a. & n.* quatre (*m.*).
～**fold** *a.* quadruple (*a.*) au
quadruple. ～**th** *a. & n.* quatrième
(*m./f.*). ～**-wheel drive,** quatre
roues motrices; (*car*) quatre-
quatre *f.*

foursome /ˈfɔːsəm/ *n.* partie à
quatre *f.*

fourteen /fɔːˈtiːn/ *a. & n.* quatorze
(*m.*). ～**th** *a. & n.* quatorzième
(*m./f.*).

fowl /faʊl/ *n.* volaille *f.*

fox /fɒks/ *n.* renard *m.* —*v.t.*
(*baffle*) mystifier; (*deceive*) tromper.

foyer /ˈfɔɪeɪ/ *n.* (*hall*) foyer *m.*

fraction /ˈfrækʃn/ *n.* fraction *f.*

fracture /ˈfræktʃə(r)/ *n.* fracture *f.*
—*v.t./i.* (se) fracturer.

fragile /ˈfrædʒaɪl, *Amer.* ˈfrædʒəl/
a. fragile.

fragment /ˈfrægmənt/ *n.* fragment
m. ～**ary** *a.* fragmentaire.

fragran|t /ˈfreɪɡrənt/ *a.* parfumé.
～**ce** *n.* parfum *m.*

frail /freɪl/ *a.* (-**er**, -**est**) frêle.

frame /freɪm/ *n.* charpente *f.*; (*of
picture*) cadre *m.*; (*of window*)
châssis *m.*; (*of spectacles*) monture
f. —*v.t.* encadrer; (*fig.*) formuler;
(*jurid., sl.*) monter un coup
contre. ～ **of mind,** humeur *f.*

framework /ˈfreɪmwɜːk/ *n.* structure *f.*; (*context*) cadre *m.*

franc /fræŋk/ *n.* franc *m.*

France /frɑːns/ *n.* France *f.*

franchise /ˈfræntʃaɪz/ *n.* (*pol.*)
droit de vote *m.*; (*comm.*) franchise *f.*

Franco- /ˈfræŋkəʊ/ *pref.* franco-.

frank[1] /fræŋk/ *a.* franc. ～**ly** *adv.*
franchement. ～**ness** *n.* franchise
f.

frank[2] /fræŋk/ *v.t.* affranchir.

frantic /ˈfræntɪk/ *a.* frénétique. ～
with, fou de.

fratern|al /frəˈtɜːnl/ *a.* fraternel. ～
ity *n.* (*bond*) fraternité *f.*;
(*group, club*) confrérie *f.*

fraternize /ˈfrætənaɪz/ *v.i.* frater-
niser (**with,** avec).

fraud /frɔːd/ *n.* (*deception*) fraude
f.; (*person*) imposteur *m.* ～**ulent**
a. frauduleux.

fraught /frɔːt/ *a.* (*tense*) tendu. ～
with, chargé de.

fray[1] /freɪ/ *n.* rixe *f.*

fray[2] /freɪ/ *v.t./i.* (s')effilocher.

freak /friːk/ *n.* phénomène *m.* —*a.*
anormal. ～**ish** *a.* anormal.

freckle /ˈfrekl/ *n.* tache de rousseur *f.* ～**d** *a.* couvert de taches de
rousseur.

free /friː/ *a.* (**freer** /ˈfriːə(r)/, **freest**
/ˈfriːɪst/) libre; (*gratis*) gratuit;
(*lavish*) généreux. —*v.t.* (*p.t.*
freed) libérer; (*clear*) dégager. ～
enterprise, la libre entreprise. *a.*
～ **hand,** carte blanche *f.* ～
kick, coup franc *m.* ～**lance** *a. &
n.* free-lance (*m./f.*), indépen-
dant(e) *m., f.* ～ (**of charge**),
gratuit(ement). ～**-range** *a.*
(*eggs*) de ferme. ～**wheel** *v.i.*
descendre en roue libre. ～
wheeling *a.* sans contraintes. ～
ly *adv.* librement.

freedom /ˈfriːdəm/ *n.* liberté *f.*

Freemason /ˈfriːmeɪsn/ *n.* franc-
maçon *m.* ～**ry** *n.* franc-
maçonnerie *f.*

freeway /ˈfriːweɪ/ *n.* (*Amer.*)
autoroute *f.*

freeze /friːz/ *v.t./i.* (*p.t.* **froze,** *p.p.*
frozen) geler; (*culin.*) (se) con-
geler; (*wages etc.*) bloquer. —*n.*
gel *m.*; blocage *m.* ～**-dried** *a.*
lyophilisé. ～**er** *n.* congélateur *m.*
～**ing** *a.* glacial. **below** ～**ing,** au-
dessous de zéro.

freight /freɪt/ *n.* fret *m.* ～**er** *n.*
(*ship*) cargo *m.*

French /frentʃ/ a. français. —n. (lang.) français m. ~ **bean,** haricot vert m. ~ **fries,** frites f. pl. ~**-speaking** a. francophone. ~ **window** n. porte-fenêtre f. **the** ~, les Français m. pl. ~**man** n. Français m. ~**woman** n. Française f.

frenz|y /ˈfrenzi/ n. frénésie f. ~**ied** a. frénétique.

frequen|t¹ /ˈfriːkwənt/ a. fréquent. ~**cy** n. fréquence f. ~**tly** adv. fréquemment.

frequent² /frɪˈkwent/ v.t. fréquenter.

fresco /ˈfreskəʊ/ n. (pl. -os) fresque f.

fresh /freʃ/ a. (-er, -est) frais; (different, additional) nouveau; (cheeky: fam.) culotté. ~**ly** adv. nouvellement. ~**ness** n. fraîcheur f.

freshen /ˈfreʃn/ v.i. (weather) fraîchir. ~ **up,** (person) se rafraîchir.

fresher /ˈfreʃə(r)/ n., **freshman** /ˈfreʃmən/ n. (pl. -men) bizuth m./f.

freshwater /ˈfreʃwɔːtə(r)/ a. d'eau douce.

fret /fret/ v.i. (p.t. **fretted**) se tracasser. ~**ful** a. ronchon, insatisfait.

friar /ˈfraɪə(r)/ n. moine m., frère m.

friction /ˈfrɪkʃn/ n. friction f.

Friday /ˈfraɪdɪ/ n. vendredi m.

fridge /frɪdʒ/ n. frigo m.

fried /fraɪd/ see **fry.** —a. frit. ~ **eggs,** œufs sur le plat m. pl.

friend /frend/ n. ami(e) m. (f.). ~**ship** n. amitié f.

friend|ly /ˈfrendlɪ/ a. (-ier, -iest) amical, gentil. **F~y Society,** mutuelle f., société de prévoyance f. ~**iness** n. gentillesse f.

frieze /friːz/ n. frise f.

frigate /ˈfrɪgət/ n. frégate f.

fright /fraɪt/ n. peur f.; (person,

thing) horreur f. ~**ful** a. affreux. ~**fully** adv. affreusement.

frighten /ˈfraɪtn/ v.t. effrayer. ~ **off,** faire fuir. ~**ed** a. effrayé. **be** ~**ed,** avoir peur (**of,** de). ~**ing** a. effrayant.

frigid /ˈfrɪdʒɪd/ a. froid, glacial; (psych.) frigide. ~**ity** /-ˈdʒɪdətɪ/ n. frigidité f.

frill /frɪl/ n. (trimming) fanfreluche f. **with no** ~**s,** très simple.

fringe /frɪndʒ/ n. (edging, hair) frange f.; (of area) bordure f.; (of society) marge f. ~ **benefits,** avantages sociaux m. pl.

frisk /frɪsk/ v.t. (search) fouiller.

frisky /ˈfrɪskɪ/ a. (-ier, -iest) fringant, frétillant.

fritter¹ /ˈfrɪtə(r)/ n. beignet m.

fritter² /ˈfrɪtə(r)/ v.t. ~ **away,** gaspiller.

frivol|ous /ˈfrɪvələs/ a. frivole. ~**ity** /-ˈvɒlətɪ/ n. frivolité f.

frizzy /ˈfrɪzɪ/ a. crépu, crêpelé.

fro /frəʊ/ see **to and fro.**

frock /frɒk/ n. robe f.

frog /frɒg/ n. grenouille f. **a** ~ **in one's throat,** un chat dans la gorge.

frogman /ˈfrɒgmən/ n. (pl. -men) homme-grenouille m.

frolic /ˈfrɒlɪk/ v.i. (p.t. **frolicked**) s'ébattre. —n. ébats m. pl.

from /frɒm, unstressed frəm/ prep. de; (with time, prices, etc.) à partir de, de; (habit, conviction, etc.) par; (according to) d'après. **take** ~ **s.o.,** prendre à qn. **take** ~ **one's pocket,** prendre dans sa poche.

front /frʌnt/ n. (of car, train, etc.) avant m.; (of garment, building) devant m.; (mil., pol.) front m.; (of book, pamphlet, etc.) début m.; (appearance: fig.) façade f. —a. de devant, avant invar.; (first) premier. **in** ~ **door,** porte d'entrée f. ~**-wheel drive,** traction avant

f. in ~ (of), devant. ~age f. façade f. ~al a. frontal; (attack) de front.

frontier /ˈfrʌntɪə(r)/ n. frontière f.

frost /frɒst/ n. gel m., gelée f.; (on glass etc.) givre m. —v.t./i. (se) givrer. ~bite n. gelure (f.) bitten a. gelé. ~ed a. (glass) dépoli. ~ing n. (icing: Amer.) glace f. ~y a. (weather, welcome) glacial; (window) givré.

froth /frɒθ/ n. mousse f., écume f. —v.i. mousser, écumer. ~y a. mousseux.

frown /fraʊn/ v.i. froncer les sourcils. —n. froncement de sourcils m. ~ on, désapprouver.

froze /frəʊz/ see freeze.

frozen /ˈfrəʊzn/ see freeze. —a. congelé.

frugal /ˈfruːgl/ a. (person) économe; (meal, life) frugal. ~ly adv. (live) simplement.

fruit /fruːt/ n. fruit m.; (collectively) fruits m. pl. ~ machine, machine à sous f. ~ salad, salade de fruits f. ~erer n. fruitler, -ière m., f. ~y a. (taste) fruité.

fruit|ful /ˈfruːtfl/ a. (discussions) fructueux. ~less a. stérile.

fruition /fruːˈɪʃn/ n. come to ~, se réaliser.

frustrat|e /frʌˈstreɪt/ v.t. (plan) faire échouer; (person: psych.) frustrer; (upset: fam.) exaspérer. ~ion /-ʃn/ n. (psych.) frustration f.; (disappointment) déception f.

fry[1] /fraɪ/ v.t./i. (p.t. fried) (faire) frire. ~ing-pan n. poêle (à frire) f.

fry[2] /fraɪ/ n. the small ~, le menu fretin.

fuddy-duddy /ˈfʌdɪdʌdɪ/ n. be a ~, (sl.) être vieux jeu invar.

fudge /fʌdʒ/ n. (sorte de) caramel mou m. —v.t. se dérober à.

fuel /ˈfjuːəl/ n. combustible m.; (for car engine) carburant m. —v.t.

(p.t. fuelled) alimenter en combustible.

fugitive /ˈfjuːdʒɪtɪv/ n. & a. fugitif, -ve (m., f.).

fugue /fjuːg/ n. (mus.) fugue f.

fulfil /fʊlˈfɪl/ v.t. (p.t. fulfilled) accomplir, réaliser; (condition) remplir. ~ o.s., s'épanouir. ~ling a. satisfaisant. ~ment n. réalisation f.; épanouissement m.

full /fʊl/ a. (-er, -est) plein (of, de); (bus, hotel) complet; (programme) chargé; (name) complet; (skirt) ample. —n. in ~, intégral(ement). to the ~, complètement. be ~ (up), n'avoir plus faim. ~ back, (sport) arrière m. ~ moon, pleine lune f. ~-scale a. (drawing etc.) grandeur nature invar.; (fig.) de grande envergure. at ~ speed, à toute vitesse. ~ stop, point m. ~-time a. & adv. à plein temps. ~y adv. complètement.

fulsome /ˈfʊlsəm/ a. excessif.

fumble /ˈfʌmbl/ v.i. tâtonner, fouiller. ~ with, tripoter.

fume /fjuːm/ v.i. rager. ~s n. pl. exhalaisons f. pl., vapeurs f. pl.

fumigate /ˈfjuːmɪgeɪt/ v.t. désinfecter.

fun /fʌn/ n. amusement m. be ~, être chouette. for ~, pour rire. ~-fair n. fête foraine f. make ~ of, se moquer de.

function /ˈfʌŋkʃn/ n. (purpose, duty) fonction f.; (event) réception f. —v.i. fonctionner. ~al a. fonctionnel.

fund /fʌnd/ n. fonds m. —v.t. fournir les fonds pour.

fundamental /fʌndəˈmentl/ a. fondamental. ~ist n. intégriste m./f. ~ism n. intégrisme m.

funeral /ˈfjuːnərəl/ n. enterrement m., funérailles f. pl. —a. funèbre.

fungus /ˈfʌŋgəs/ n. (pl. -gi /-gaɪ/) (plant) champignon m.; (mould) moisissure f.

funicular /fjuːˈnɪkjʊlə(r)/ n. funiculaire m.

funk /fʌŋk/ m. **be in a ~**, *(afraid: sl.)* avoir la frousse; *(depressed: Amer., sl.)* être déprimé.

funnel /ˈfʌnl/ n. *(for pouring)* entonnoir m.; *(of ship)* cheminée f.

funn|y /ˈfʌnɪ/ a. *(-ier, -iest)* drôle; *(odd)* bizarre. **~y business**, quelque chose de louche. **~ily** adv. drôlement; bizarrement.

fur /fɜː(r)/ n. fourrure f.; *(in kettle)* tartre m.

furious /ˈfjʊərɪəs/ a. furieux. **~ly** adv. furieusement.

furnace /ˈfɜːnɪs/ n. fourneau m.

furnish /ˈfɜːnɪʃ/ v.t. *(with furniture)* meubler; *(supply)* fournir. **~ings** n. pl. ameublement m.

furniture /ˈfɜːnɪtʃə(r)/ n. meubles m. pl., mobilier m.

furrow /ˈfʌrəʊ/ n. sillon m.

furry /ˈfɜːrɪ/ a. *(animal)* à fourrure; *(toy)* en peluche.

further /ˈfɜːðə(r)/ a. plus éloigné; *(additional)* supplémentaire. —adv. plus loin; *(more)* davantage. —v.t. avancer. **~er education**, formation continue f. **~est** a. le plus éloigné; adv. le plus loin.

furthermore /ˈfɜːðəmɔː(r)/ adv. en outre, de plus.

furtive /ˈfɜːtɪv/ a. furtif.

fury /ˈfjʊərɪ/ n. fureur f.

fuse¹ /fjuːz/ v.t./i. *(melt)* fondre; *(unite: fig.)* fusionner. —n. fusible m., plomb m. **~ the lights etc.**, faire sauter les plombs.

fuse² /fjuːz/ n. *(of bomb)* amorce f.

fuselage /ˈfjuːzəlɑːʒ/ n. fuselage m.

fusion /ˈfjuːʒn/ n. fusion f.

fuss /fʌs/ n. *(when upset)* histoire(s) f. (pl.); *(when excited)* agitation f. —v.i. s'agiter. **make a ~**, faire des histoires; s'agiter; *(about food)* faire des chichis. **make a ~ of**, faire grand cas de.

~y a. *(finicky)* tatillon; *(hard to please)* difficile.

futile /ˈfjuːtaɪl/ a. futile, vain.

future /ˈfjuːtʃə(r)/ a. futur. —n. avenir m.; *(gram.)* futur m. **in ~**, à l'avenir.

fuzz /fʌz/ n. *(fluff, growth)* duvet m.; *(police: sl.)* flics m. pl.

fuzzy /ˈfʌzɪ/ a. *(hair)* crépu; *(photograph)* flou; *(person: fam.)* à l'esprit confus.

G

gabardine /ˈɡæbədiːn/ n. gabardine f.

gabble /ˈɡæbl/ v.t./i. bredouiller. —n. baragouin m.

gable /ˈɡeɪbl/ n. pignon m.

gad /ɡæd/ v.i. *(p.t. gadded)*. **~ about**, se promener, aller çà et là.

gadget /ˈɡædʒɪt/ n. gadget m.

Gaelic /ˈɡeɪlɪk/ n. gaélique m.

gaffe /ɡæf/ n. *(blunder)* gaffe f.

gag /ɡæg/ n. bâillon m.; *(joke)* gag m. —v.t. *(p.t. gagged)* bâillonner.

gaiety /ˈɡeɪətɪ/ n. gaieté f.

gaily /ˈɡeɪlɪ/ adv. gaiement.

gain /ɡeɪn/ v.t. gagner; *(speed, weight)* prendre. —v.i. *(of clock)* avancer. —n. acquisition f.; *(profit)* gain m. **~ful** a. profitable.

gait /ɡeɪt/ n. démarche f.

gala /ˈɡɑːlə/ n. *(festive occasion)* gala m.; *(sport)* concours m.

galaxy /ˈɡæləksɪ/ n. galaxie f.

gale /ɡeɪl/ n. tempête f.

gall /ɡɔːl/ n. bile f.; *(fig.)* fiel m.; *(impudence: sl.)* culot m. **~-bladder** n. vésicule biliaire f.

gallant /ˈɡælənt/ a. *(brave)* courageux; *(chivalrous)* galant. **~ry** n. courage m.

galleon /ˈɡælɪən/ n. galion m.

gallery /ˈɡælərɪ/ n. galerie f. **(art) ~**, *(public)* musée m.

galley /'gælɪ/ n. (ship) galère f.; (kitchen) cambuse f.

Gallic /'gælɪk/ a. français. **~ism** /-sɪzəm/ n. gallicisme m.

gallivant /gælɪ'vænt/ v.i. (fam.) se promener, aller çà et là.

gallon /'gælən/ n. gallon m. (imperial = 4.546 litres; Amer. = 3.785 litres).

gallop /'gæləp/ n. galop m. —v.i. (p.t. galloped) galoper.

gallows /'gæləʊz/ n. potence f.

galore /gə'lɔ:(r)/ adv. en abondance, à gogo.

galosh /gə'lɒʃ/ n. (overshoe) caoutchouc m.

galvanize /'gælvənaɪz/ v.t. galvaniser.

gambit /'gæmbɪt/ n. (opening) ~, (move) première démarche f.; (ploy) stratagème m.

gambl|e /'gæmbl/ v.t./i. jouer. —n. (venture) entreprise risquée f.; (bet) pari m.; (risk) risque m. ~e on, miser sur. ~er n. joueur|r, -se m., f. ~ing n. le jeu.

game¹ /geɪm/ n. jeu m.; (football) match m.; (tennis) partie f.; (animals, birds) gibier m. —a. (brave) brave. ~ for, prêt à.

game² /geɪm/ a. (lame) estropié.

gamekeeper /'geɪmki:pə(r)/ n. garde-chasse m.

gammon /'gæmən/ n. jambon fumé m.

gamut /'gæmət/ n. gamme f.

gamy /'geɪmɪ/ a. faisandé.

gang /gæŋ/ n. bande f. —v.i. ~ up, se liguer (on, against, contre).

gangling /'gæŋglɪŋ/ a. dégingandé, grand et maigre.

gangrene /'gæŋgri:n/ n. gangrène f.

gangster /'gæŋstə(r)/ n. gangster m.

gangway /'gæŋweɪ/ n. passage m.; (aisle) allée f.; (of ship) passerelle f.

gaol /dʒeɪl/ n. & v.t. = **jail**.

gap /gæp/ n. trou m., vide m.; (in time) intervalle m.; (in education) lacune f.; (difference) écart m.

gap|e /geɪp/ v.i. rester bouche bée. **~ing** a. béant.

garage /'gæra:ʒ, Amer. gə'ra:ʒ/ n. garage m. —v.t. mettre au garage.

garb /ga:b/ n. costume m.

garbage /'ga:bɪdʒ/ n. ordures f. pl.

garble /'ga:bl/ v.t. déformer.

garden /'ga:dn/ n. jardin m. —v.i. jardiner. ~er n. jardin|ier, -ière m., f. ~ing n. jardinage m.

gargle /'ga:gl/ v.i. se gargariser. —n. gargarisme m.

gargoyle /'ga:gɔɪl/ n. gargouille f.

garish /'geərɪʃ/ a. voyant, criard.

garland /'ga:lənd/ n. guirlande f.

garlic /'ga:lɪk/ n. ail m.

garment /'ga:mənt/ n. vêtement m.

garnish /'ga:nɪʃ/ v.t. garnir (with, de). —n. garniture f.

garret /'gærət/ n. mansarde f.

garrison /'gærɪsn/ n. garnison f.

garrulous /'gærələs/ a. loquace.

garter /'ga:tə(r)/ n. jarretière f. ~ belt n. porte-jarretelles n.m. invar.

gas /gæs/ n. (pl. gases) gaz m.; (med.) anesthésique m.; (petrol: Amer., fam.) essence f. —a. (mask, pipe) à gaz. —v.t. asphyxier; (mil.) gazer. —v.i. (fam.) bavarder.

gash /gæʃ/ n. entaille f. —v.t. entailler.

gasket /'gæskɪt/ n. (auto.) joint de culasse m.; (for pressure cooker) rondelle f.

gasoline /'gæsəli:n/ n. (petrol: Amer.) essence f.

gasp /ga:sp/ v.i. haleter; (in surprise, fig.) avoir le souffle coupé. —n. halètement m.

gassy /'gæsɪ/ a. gazeux.

gastric /'gæstrɪk/ a. gastrique.

gastronomy /gæ'strɒnəmɪ/ *n.* gastronomie *f.*

gate /geɪt/ *n.* porte *f.*; (*of metal*) grille *f.*; (*barrier*) barrière *f.*

gatecrash /'geɪtkræʃ/ *v.t./i.* venir sans invitation (à). **~er** *n.* intrus(e) *m.(f.).*

gateway /'geɪtweɪ/ *n.* porte *f.*

gather /'gæðə(r)/ *v.t.* (*people, objects*) rassembler; (*pick up*) ramasser; (*flowers*) cueillir; (*fig.*) comprendre; (*sewing*) froncer. —*v.i.* (*people*) se rassembler; (*crowd*) se former; (*pile up*) s'accumuler. **~ speed,** prendre de la vitesse. **~ing** *n.* rassemblement *m.*

gaudy /'gɔːdɪ/ *a.* (-ier, -iest) voyant, criard.

gauge /geɪdʒ/ *n.* jauge *f.*, indicateur *m.* —*v.t.* jauger, évaluer.

gaunt /gɔːnt/ *a.* (*lean*) émacié; (*grim*) lugubre.

gauntlet /'gɔːntlɪt/ *n.* **run the ~ of,** subir (l'assaut de).

gauze /gɔːz/ *n.* gaze *f.*

gave /geɪv/ *see* **give.**

gawky /'gɔːkɪ/ *a.* (-ier, -iest) gauche, maladroit.

gawp (*or* **gawk**) /gɔːp, gɔːk/ *v.i.* **~ (at),** regarder bouche bée.

gay /geɪ/ *a.* (-er, -est) (*joyful*) gai; (*fam.*) gay *invar.* —*n.* gay *m./f.*

gaze /geɪz/ *v.i.* **~ (at),** regarder (fixement). —*n.* regard (fixe) *m.*

gazelle /gə'zel/ *n.* gazelle *f.*

gazette /gə'zet/ *n.* journal (officiel) *m.*

GB *abbr. see* **Great Britain.**

gear /gɪə(r)/ *n.* équipement *m.*; (*techn.*) engrenage *m.*; (*auto.*) vitesse *f.* —*v.t.* adapter. **~-lever,** (*Amer.*) **~-shift** *ns.* levier de vitesse *m.* **in ~,** en prise. **out of ~,** au point mort.

gearbox /'gɪəbɒks/ *n.* (*auto.*) boîte de vitesses *f.*

geese /giːs/ *see* **goose.**

gel /dʒel/ *n.* gelée *f.*; (*for hair*) gel *m.*

gelatine /'dʒelətiːn/ *n.* gélatine *f.*

gelignite /'dʒelɪgnaɪt/ *n.* nitroglycérine *f.*

gem /dʒem/ *n.* pierre précieuse *f.*

Gemini /'dʒemɪnaɪ/ *n.* les Gémeaux *m. pl.*

gender /'dʒendə(r)/ *n.* genre *m.*

gene /dʒiːn/ *n.* gène *m.*

genealogy /dʒiːnɪ'ælədʒɪ/ *n.* généalogie *f.*

general /'dʒenrəl/ *a.* général. —*n.* général *m.* **~ election,** élections législatives *f. pl.* **~ practitioner,** (*med.*) généraliste *m.* **in ~,** en général. **~ly** *adv.* généralement.

generaliz|e /'dʒenrəlaɪz/ *v.t./i.* généraliser. **~ation** /-'zeɪʃn/ *n.* généralisation *f.*

generate /'dʒenəreɪt/ *v.t.* produire.

generation /dʒenə'reɪʃn/ *n.* génération *f.*

generator /'dʒenəreɪtə(r)/ *n.* (*electr.*) groupe électrogène *m.*

gener|ous /'dʒenərəs/ *a.* généreux; (*plentiful*) copieux. **~osity** /-'rɒsətɪ/ *n.* générosité *f.*

genetic /dʒɪ'netɪk/ *a.* génétique. **~s** *n.* génétique *f.*

Geneva /dʒɪ'niːvə/ *n.* Genève *m./f.*

genial /'dʒiːnɪəl/ *a.* affable, sympathique; (*climate*) doux.

genital /'dʒenɪtl/ *a.* génital. **~s** *n. pl.* organes génitaux *m. pl.*

genius /'dʒiːnɪəs/ *n.* (*pl.* -uses) génie *m.*

genocide /'dʒenəsaɪd/ *n.* génocide *m.*

gent /dʒent/ *n.* (*sl.*) monsieur *m.*

genteel /dʒen'tiːl/ *a.* distingué.

gentl|e /'dʒentl/ *a.* (-er, -est) (*mild, kind*) doux; (*slight*) léger; (*hint*) discret. **~eness** *n.* douceur *f.* **~y** *adv.* doucement.

gentleman /'dʒentlmən/ *n.* (*pl.* -men) (*man*) monsieur *m.*; (*wellbred*) gentleman *m.*

genuine /'dʒenjʊɪn/ *a.* (*true*) véritable; (*person, belief*) sincère.

geograph|y /dʒɪ'ɒɡrəfɪ/ *n.* géographie *f.* ∼**er** *n.* géographe *m./f.* ∼**ical** /dʒɪə'ɡræfɪkl/ *a.* géographique.

geolog|y /dʒɪ'ɒlədʒɪ/ *n.* géologie *f.* ∼**ical** /dʒɪə'lɒdʒɪkl/ *a.* géologique. ∼**ist** *n.* géologue *m./f.*

geometr|y /dʒɪ'ɒmɪtrɪ/ *n.* géométrie *f.* ∼**ic(al)** /dʒɪə'metrɪk(l)/ *a.* géométrique.

geranium /dʒɪ'reɪnɪəm/ *n.* géranium *m.*

geriatric /dʒerɪ'ætrɪk/ *a.* gériatrique.

germ /dʒɜːm/ *n.* (*rudiment, seed*) germe *m.*; (*med.*) microbe *m.*

German /'dʒɜːmən/ *a. & n.* allemand(e) (*m.* (*f.*)); (*lang.*) allemand *m.* ∼ **measles**, rubéole *f.* ∼**shepherd**, (*dog: Amer.*) berger allemand *m.* ∼**ic** /dʒə'mænɪk/ *a.* germanique. ∼**y** *n.* Allemagne *f.*

germinate /'dʒɜːmɪneɪt/ *v.t./i.* (faire) germer.

gestation /dʒe'steɪʃn/ *n.* gestation *f.*

gesticulate /dʒe'stɪkjʊleɪt/ *v.i.* gesticuler.

gesture /'dʒestʃə(r)/ *n.* geste *m.*

get /ɡet/ *v.t.* (*p.t. & p.p.* **got**, *p.p. Amer.* **gotten**, *pres. p.* **getting**) avoir, obtenir, recevoir; (*catch*) prendre; (*buy*) acheter, prendre; (*find*) trouver; (*fetch*) aller chercher; (*understand: sl.*) comprendre. ∼ **s.o. to do sth.**, faire faire qch. à qn. ∼ **sth. done**, faire faire qch. **did you** ∼ **that number?**, tu as relevé le numéro? —*v.i.* aller, arriver (**to**, à); (*become*) devenir; (*start*) se mettre (**to**, à); (*manage*) parvenir (**to**, à). ∼ **married/ready/etc.**, se marier/se préparer/*etc.* ∼ **promoted/hurt/etc.**, être promu/blessé/*etc.* ∼ **arrested/**

robbed/*etc.*, se faire arrêter/voler/*etc.* **you** ∼ **to use the computer**, vous utilisez l'ordinateur. **it's** ∼**ting to be annoying**, ça commence à être agaçant. ∼ **about**, (*person*) se déplacer. ∼ **across**, (*cross*) traverser. ∼ **along** *or* **by**, (*manage*) se débrouiller. ∼ **along** *or* **on**, (*progress*) avancer. ∼ **along** *or* **on with**, s'entendre avec. ∼ **at**, (*reach*) parvenir à. **what are you** ∼**ting at?**, où veux-tu en venir? ∼ **away**, partir; (*escape*) s'échapper. ∼ **back** *v.i.* revenir; *v.t.* (*recover*) récupérer. ∼ **by** *or* **through**, (*pass*) passer. ∼ **down** *v.t./i.* descendre; (*depress*) déprimer. ∼ **in**, entrer, arriver. ∼ **into**, (*car*) monter dans; (*dress*) mettre. ∼ **into trouble**, avoir des ennuis. ∼ **off** *v.i.* (*from bus etc.*) descendre; (*leave*) partir; (*jurid.*) être acquitté; *v.t.* (*remove*) enlever. ∼ **on**, (*on train etc.*) monter; (*succeed*) réussir. ∼ **on with**, (*job*) récupérer. ∼ **on**, (*person*) s'entendre avec. ∼ **out**, sortir. ∼ **out of**, (*fig.*) se soustraire à. ∼ **over**, (*illness*) se remettre de. ∼ **round**, (*rule*) contourner; (*person*) entortiller. ∼ **through**, (*finish*) finir. ∼ **up** *v.i.* se lever; *v.t.* (*climb, bring*) monter. ∼**-up** *n.* (*clothes: fam.*) mise *f.*

getaway /'ɡetəweɪ/ *n.* fuite *f.*

geyser /'ɡiːzə(r)/ *n.* chauffe-eau *m. invar.*; (*geol.*) geyser *m.*

Ghana /'ɡɑːnə/ *n.* Ghana *m.*

ghastly /'ɡɑːstlɪ/ *a.* (**-ier, -iest**) affreux; (*pale*) blême.

gherkin /'ɡɜːkɪn/ *n.* cornichon *m.*

ghetto /'ɡetəʊ/ *n.* (*pl.* **-os**) ghetto *m.*

ghost /ɡəʊst/ *n.* fantôme *m.* ∼**ly** *a.* spectral.

giant /'dʒaɪənt/ *n. & a.* géant (*m.*).

gibberish /'dʒɪbərɪʃ/ *n.* baragouin *m.*, charabia *m.*

gibe /dʒaɪb/ n. raillerie f. —v.i. ∼ (at), railler.

giblets /ˈdʒɪblɪts/ n. pl. abattis m. pl.

gidd|y /ˈgɪdɪ/ a. (-ier, -iest) vertigineux. **be** or **feel** ∼**y**, avoir le vertige. ∼**iness** n. vertige m.

gift /gɪft/ n. cadeau m.; (ability) don m. ∼**-wrap** v.t. (p.t. **-wrapped**) faire un paquet-cadeau de.

gifted /ˈgɪftɪd/ a. doué.

gig /gɪg/ n. (fam.) concert m.

gigantic /dʒaɪˈgæntɪk/ a. gigantesque.

giggle /ˈgɪgl/ v.i. ricaner (sottement), glousser. —n. ricanement m. **the** ∼**s**, le fou rire.

gild /gɪld/ v.t. dorer.

gill /dʒɪl/ n. (approx.) décilitre (imperial = 0.15 litre; Amer. = 0.12 litre).

gills /gɪlz/ n. pl. ouïes f. pl.

gilt /gɪlt/ a. doré. —n. dorure f. ∼**-edged** a. (comm.) de tout repos.

gimmick /ˈgɪmɪk/ n. truc m.

gin /dʒɪn/ n. gin m.

ginger /ˈdʒɪndʒə(r)/ n. gingembre m. —a. roux. ∼ **ale**, ∼ **beer**, boisson gazeuse au gingembre f.

gingerbread /ˈdʒɪndʒəbred/ n. pain d'épice m.

gingerly /ˈdʒɪndʒəlɪ/ adv. avec précaution.

gipsy /ˈdʒɪpsɪ/ n. = gypsy.

giraffe /dʒɪˈrɑːf/ n. girafe f.

girder /ˈgɜːdə(r)/ n. poutre f.

girdle /ˈgɜːdl/ n. (belt) ceinture f.; (corset) gaine f.

girl /gɜːl/ n. (child) fille f.; (young woman) (jeune) fille f. ∼**-friend** n. amie f.; (of boy) petite amie f. ∼**hood** n. enfance f., jeunesse f. ∼**ish** a. de (jeune) fille.

giro /ˈdʒaɪərəʊ/ n. (pl. -os) virement bancaire m.; (cheque: fam.) mandat m.

girth /gɜːθ/ n. circonférence f.

gist /dʒɪst/ n. essentiel m.

give /gɪv/ v.t. (p.t. **gave**, p.p. **given**) donner; (gesture) faire; (laugh, sigh, etc.) pousser. ∼ **s.o. sth.**, donner qch. à qn. —v.i. donner; (yield) céder; (stretch) se détendre. —n. élasticité f. ∼ **away**, donner; (secret) trahir. ∼ **back**, rendre. ∼ **in**, (yield) se rendre. ∼ **off**, dégager. ∼ **out** v.t. distribuer; (become used up) s'épuiser. ∼ **over**, (devote) consacrer; (stop: fam.) cesser. ∼ **up** v.t./i. (renounce) renoncer (à); (yield) céder. ∼ **o.s. up**, se rendre. ∼ **way**, céder; (collapse) s'effondrer.

given /ˈgɪvn/ see give. —a. donné. ∼ **name**, prénom m.

glacier /ˈglæsɪə(r)/, Amer. /ˈgleɪʃər/ n. glacier m.

glad /glæd/ a. content. ∼**ly** adv. avec plaisir.

gladden /ˈglædn/ v.t. réjouir.

gladiolus /glædɪˈəʊləs/ n. (pl. -li /-laɪ/) glaïeul m.

glam|our /ˈglæmə(r)/ n. enchantement m., séduction f. ∼**orize** v.t. rendre séduisant. ∼**orous** a. séduisant, ensorcelant.

glance /glɑːns/ n. coup d'œil m. —v.i. ∼ **at**, jeter un coup d'œil à.

gland /glænd/ n. glande f.

glar|e /gleə(r)/ v.i. briller très fort. —n. éclat (aveuglant) m.; (stare: fig.) regard furieux m. ∼**e at**, regarder d'un air furieux. ∼**ing** a. éblouissant; (obvious) flagrant.

glass /glɑːs/ n. verre m.; (mirror) miroir m. ∼**es**, (spectacles) lunettes f. pl. ∼**y** a. vitreux.

glaze /gleɪz/ v.t. (door etc.) vitrer; (pottery) vernisser. —n. vernis m.

gleam /gliːm/ n. lueur f. —v.i. luire.

glean /gliːn/ v.t. glaner.

glee /gliː/ n. joie f. ∼ **club**, chorale f. ∼**ful** a. joyeux.

glen /glen/ n. vallon m.

glib /glɪb/ a. (person: pej.) qui a la

parole facile *or* du bagou; (*reply*, *excuse*) désinvolte, spécieux. ~**ly** *adv*. avec désinvolture.

glide /glaɪd/ *v.i.* glisser; (*of plane*) planer. ~**r** /-ə(r)/ *n.* planeur *m.*

glimmer /ˈglɪmə(r)/ *n.* lueur *f.* —*v.i.* luire.

glimpse /glɪmps/ *n.* aperçu *m.* **catch a** ~ **of**, entrevoir.

glint /glɪnt/ *n.* éclair *m.* —*v.i.* étinceler.

glisten /ˈglɪsn/ *v.i.* briller, luire.

glitter /ˈglɪtə(r)/ *v.i.* scintiller. —*n.* scintillement *m.*

gloat /gləʊt/ *v.i.* jubiler (**over**, à l'idée de).

global /ˈgləʊbl/ *a.* (*world-wide*) mondial; (*all-embracing*) global.

globe /gləʊb/ *n.* globe *m.*

gloom /gluːm/ *n.* obscurité *f.*; (*sadness*: *fig.*) tristesse *f.* ~**y** *a.* triste; (*pessimistic*) pessimiste.

glorif|y /ˈglɔːrɪfaɪ/ *v.t.* glorifier. **a** ~**ied waitress**/*etc.*, à peine plus qu'une serveuse/*etc.*

glorious /ˈglɔːrɪəs/ *a.* splendide; (*deed, hero, etc.*) glorieux.

glory /ˈglɔːrɪ/ *n.* gloire *f.*; (*beauty*) splendeur *f.* —*v.i.* ~ **in**, s'enorgueillir de.

gloss /glɒs/ *n.* lustre *m.*, brillant *m.* —*a.* brillant. ~ **over**, (*make light of*) glisser sur; (*cover up*) dissimuler. ~**y** *a.* brillant.

glossary /ˈglɒsərɪ/ *n.* glossaire *m.*

glove /glʌv/ *n.* gant *m.* ~ **compartment**, (*auto.*) vide-poches *m. invar.* ~**d** *a.* ganté.

glow /gləʊ/ *v.i.* rougeoyer; (*person, eyes*) rayonner. —*n.* rougeoiement *m.*, éclat *m.* ~**ing** *a.* (*account etc.*) enthousiaste.

glucose /ˈgluːkəʊs/ *n.* glucose *m.*

glue /gluː/ *n.* colle *f.* —*v.t.* (*pres. p.* **gluing**) coller.

glum /glʌm/ *a.* (**glummer, glummest**) triste, morne.

glut /glʌt/ *n.* surabondance *f.*

glutton /ˈglʌtn/ *n.* glouton(ne) *m.*

(*f.*). ~**ous** *a.* glouton. ~**y** *n.* gloutonnerie *f.*

glycerine /ˈglɪsəriːn/ *n.* glycérine *f.*

gnarled /nɑːld/ *a.* noueux.

gnash /næʃ/ *v.t.* ~ **one's teeth**, grincer des dents.

gnat /næt/ *n.* (*fly*) cousin *m.*

gnaw /nɔː/ *v.t./i.* ronger.

gnome /nəʊm/ *n.* gnome *m.*

go /gəʊ/ *v.i.* (*p.t.* **went**, *p.p.* **gone**) aller; (*leave*) partir; (*work*) marcher; (*become*) devenir; (*be sold*) se vendre; (*vanish*) disparaître. **my coat's gone**, mon manteau n'est plus là. ~ **via Paris**, passer par Paris. ~ **by car/on foot**, aller en voiture/à pied. ~ **for a walk/ride**, aller se promener/ faire un tour en voiture. **go red/dry**/*etc.*, rougir/tarir/*etc.* **don't** ~ **telling him**, ne va pas lui dire. ~ **riding/shopping**/ *etc.*, faire du cheval/les courses/ *etc.* —*n.* (*pl.* **goes**) (*try*) coup *m.*; (*success*) réussite *f.*; (*turn*) tour *m.*; (*energy*) dynamisme *m.* **have a** ~, essayer. **be** ~**ing to do**, aller faire. ~ **across**, traverser. ~ **ahead!**, allez-y! ~**-ahead** *n.* feu vert *m.*; *a.* dynamique. ~ **away**, s'en aller. ~ **back**, retourner. (*go home*) rentrer. ~ **back on**, (*promise etc.*) revenir sur. ~ **bad** *or* **off**, se gâter. ~ **between** *n.* intermédiaire *m./f.* ~ **by**, (*pass*) passer. ~ **down**, descendre; (*sun*) se coucher. ~ **for**, aller chercher; (*like*) aimer; (*attack*: *sl.*) attaquer. ~ **in**, (r)entrer. ~ **in for** (*exam*) se présenter à. ~ **into**, entrer dans; (*subject*) examiner. ~**-kart** *n.* kart *m.* ~ **off**, partir; (*explode*) sauter; (*ring*) sonner; (*take place*) se dérouler; (*dislike*) revenir de. ~ **on**, continuer; (*happen*) se passer. ~ **out**, sortir; (*light, fire*) s'éteindre. ~ **over**, (*cross*)

traverser; (*pass*) passer. ~ **over**
or **through**, (*check*) vérifier; (*search*) fouiller. ~ **round**, (*be enough*) suffire. ~**-slow** grève perlée *f.* ~ **through**, (*suffer*) subir. ~ **under**, (*sink*) couler; (*fail*) échouer. ~ **up**, monter. ~ **without**, se passer de. **on the** ~, actif.

goad /gəʊd/ *v.t.* aiguillonner.

goal /gəʊl/ *n.* but *m.* ~**-post** *n.* poteau de but *m.*

goalkeeper /ˈgəʊlkiːpə(r)/ *n.* gardien de but *m.*

goat /gəʊt/ *n.* chèvre *f.*

goatee /gəʊˈtiː/ *n.* barbiche *f.*

gobble /ˈgɒbl/ *v.t.* engouffrer.

goblet /ˈgɒblɪt/ *n.* verre à pied *m.*

goblin /ˈgɒblɪn/ *n.* lutin *m.*

God /gɒd/ *n.* Dieu *m.* ~**-forsaken** *a.* perdu.

god /gɒd/ *n.* dieu *m.* ~**dess** *n.* déesse *f.* ~**ly** *a.* dévot.

god|child /ˈgɒdtʃaɪld/ *n.* (*pl.* **-children**) filleul(e) *m. (f.).* ~**daughter** *n.* filleule *f.* ~**father** *n.* parrain *m.* ~**mother** *n.* marraine *f.* ~**son** *n.* filleul *m.*

godsend /ˈgɒdsend/ *n.* aubaine *f.*

goggle /ˈgɒgl/ *v.i.* ~ (**at**), regarder avec de gros yeux.

goggles /ˈgɒglz/ *n. pl.* lunettes (protectrices) *f. pl.*

going /ˈgəʊɪŋ/ *n.* **it is slow/hard** ~, c'est lent/difficile. —*a.* (*price, rate*) actuel. ~**s-on** *n. pl.* activités (bizarres) *f. pl.*

gold /gəʊld/ *n.* or *m.* —*a.* en or, d'or. ~**-mine** *n.* mine d'or *f.*

golden /ˈgəʊldən/ *a.* d'or; (*in colour*) doré; (*opportunity*) unique. ~ **wedding**, noces d'or *f. pl.*

goldfish /ˈgəʊldfɪʃ/ *n. invar.* poisson rouge *m.*

gold-plated /ˈgəʊldˈpleɪtɪd/ *a.* plaqué or.

goldsmith /ˈgəʊldsmɪθ/ *n.* orfèvre *m.*

golf /gɒlf/ *n.* golf *m.* ~ **ball**, balle

de golf *f.*; (*on typewriter*) boule *f.* ~**-course** *n.* terrain de golf *m.* ~**er** *n.* joueu|r, -se de golf *m., f.*

gondol|a /ˈgɒndələ/ *n.* gondole *f.* ~**ier** /-ˈlɪə(r)/ *n.* gondolier *m.*

gone /gɒn/ *see* **go**. —*a.* parti. ~ **six o'clock**, six heures passées. **the butter's all** ~, il n'y a plus de beurre.

gong /gɒŋ/ *n.* gong *m.*

good /gʊd/ *a.* (**better**, **best**) bon; (*weather*) beau; (*well-behaved*) sage. —*n.* bien *m.* **as** ~ **as**, (*almost*) pratiquement. **that's** ~ **of you**, c'est gentil (de ta part). **be** ~ **with**, savoir s'y prendre avec. **do** ~, faire du bien. **feel** ~, se sentir bien. ~**-for-nothing** *a.* & *n.* propre à rien (*m./f.*). **G-Friday**, Vendredi saint *m.* **G-afternoon**, ~**-morning** *ints.* bonjour. ~**-evening** *int.* bonsoir. ~**-looking** *a.* beau. ~**-natured** *a.* gentil. ~ **name**, réputation *f.* ~**-night** *int.* bonsoir, bonne nuit. **it is** ~ **for you**, ça vous fait du bien. **is it any** ~?, est-ce que c'est bien? **it's no** ~, ça ne vaut rien. **it is no** ~ **shouting**/*etc.*, ça ne sert à rien de crier/*etc.* **for** ~, pour toujours. ~**ness** *n.* bonté *f.* **my** ~**ness!**, mon Dieu!

goodbye /gʊdˈbaɪ/ *int.* & *n.* au revoir (*m.*).

goods /gʊdz/ *n. pl.* marchandises *f. pl.*

goodwill /gʊdˈwɪl/ *n.* bonne volonté *f.*

goody /ˈgʊdɪ/ *n.* (*fam.*) bonne chose *f.* ~**-goody** *n.* petit(e) saint(e) *m. (f.).*

gooey /ˈguːɪ/ *a.* (*sl.*) poisseux.

goof /guːf/ *v.i.* (*Amer.*) gaffer.

goose /guːs/ *n.* (*pl.* **geese**) oie *f.* ~**-flesh**, ~**-pimples** *ns.* chair de poule *f.*

gooseberry /ˈgʊzbərɪ/ *n.* groseille à maquereau *f.*

gore[1] /gɔː(r)/ *n.* (*blood*) sang *m.*

gore[2] /gɔː(r)/ v.t. encorner.

gorge /gɔːdʒ/ n. (geog.) gorge f. —v.t. ~ o.s., se gorger.

gorgeous /ˈgɔːdʒəs/ a. magnifique, splendide, formidable.

gorilla /gəˈrɪlə/ n. gorille m.

gormless /ˈgɔːmlɪs/ a. (sl.) stupide.

gorse /gɔːs/ n. invar. ajonc(s) m. (pl.).

gory /ˈgɔːrɪ/ a. (-ier, -iest) sanglant; (horrific: fig.) horrible.

gosh /gɒʃ/ int. mince (alors).

gospel /ˈgɒspl/ n. évangile m. the G~, l'Évangile m.

gossip /ˈgɒsɪp/ n. bavardage(s) m. (pl.), commérage(s) m. (pl.); (person) bavard(e) m. (f.). —v.i. (p.t. gossiped) bavarder. ~y a. bavard.

got /gɒt/ see **get**. —have ~, avoir. have ~ to do, devoir faire.

Gothic /ˈgɒθɪk/ a. gothique.

gouge /gaʊdʒ/ v.t. ~ out, arracher.

gourmet /ˈguəmeɪ/ n. gourmet m.

gout /gaʊt/ n. (med.) goutte f.

govern /ˈgʌvn/ v.t./i. gouverner. ~ess /-ənɪs/ n. gouvernante f. ~or /-ənə(r)/ n. gouverneur m.

government /ˈgʌvənmənt/ n. gouvernement m. ~al /-ˈmentl/ a. gouvernemental.

gown /gaʊn/ n. robe f.; (of judge, teacher) toge f.

GP abbr. see **general practitioner**.

grab /græb/ v.t. (p.t. grabbed) saisir.

grace /greɪs/ n. grâce f. —v.t. (honour) honorer; (adorn) orner. ~ful a. gracieux.

gracious /ˈgreɪʃəs/ a. (kind) bienveillant; (elegant) élégant.

gradation /grəˈdeɪʃn/ n. gradation f.

grade /greɪd/ n. catégorie f.; (of goods) qualité f.; (on scale) grade m.; (school mark) note f.; (class: Amer.) classe f. —v.t. classer;

(school work) noter. ~ crossing, (Amer.) passage à niveau m. ~ school, (Amer.) école primaire f.

gradient /ˈgreɪdɪənt/ n. (slope) inclinaison f.

gradual /ˈgrædʒʊəl/ a. progressif, graduel. ~ly adv. progressivement, peu à peu.

graduate[1] /ˈgrædʒʊət/ n. (univ.) diplômé(e) m. (f.).

graduat|e[2] /ˈgrædʒʊeɪt/ v.i. obtenir son diplôme. —v.t. graduer. ~ion /-ˈeɪʃn/ n. remise de diplômes f.

graffiti /grəˈfiːtiː/ n. pl. graffiti m. pl.

graft[1] /grɑːft/ n. (med., bot.) greffe f. (work) boulot. —v.t. greffer; (work) trimer.

graft[2] /grɑːft/ n. (bribery: fam.) corruption f.

grain /greɪn/ n. (seed, quantity, texture) grain m.; (in wood) fibre f.

gram /græm/ n. gramme m.

gramm|ar /ˈgræmə(r)/ n. grammaire f. ~atical /grəˈmætɪkl/ a. grammatical.

grand /grænd/ a. (-er, -est) magnifique; (duke, chorus) grand. ~ piano, piano à queue m.

grandad /ˈgrændæd/ n. (fam.) papy m.

grand|child /ˈgræn(d)tʃaɪld/ n. (pl. -children) petit(e)-enfant m. (f.). ~daughter n. petite-fille f. ~father n. grand-père m. ~mother n. grand-mère f. ~parents n. pl. grands-parents m. pl. ~son n. petit-fils m.

grandeur /ˈgrændʒə(r)/ n. grandeur f.

grandiose /ˈgrændɪəʊs/ a. grandiose.

grandma /ˈgrændmɑː/ n. = granny.

grandstand /ˈgræn(d)stænd/ n. tribune f.

granite /ˈgrænɪt/ n. granit m.

granny /'grænɪ/ n. (fam.) grand-maman f., mémé f., mamie f.

grant /grɑːnt/ v.t. (give) accorder; (request) accéder à; (admit) admettre (that, que). —n. subvention f.; (univ.) bourse f. **take sth. for** ~ed, considérer qch. comme une chose acquise.

granulated /'grænjʊleɪtɪd/ a. ~ **sugar**, sucre semoule m.

granule /'grænjuːl/ n. granule m.

grape /greɪp/ n. grain de raisin m. ~s, raisin(s) m. (pl.).

grapefruit /'greɪpfruːt/ n. invar. pamplemousse m.

graph /grɑːf/ n. graphique m.

graphic /'græfɪk/ a. (arts etc.) graphique; (fig.) vivant, explicite. ~s n. pl. (comput.) graphiques m. pl.

grapple /'græpl/ v.i. ~ **with**, affronter, être aux prises avec.

grasp /grɑːsp/ v.t. saisir. —n. (hold) prise f.; (strength of hand) poigne f.; (reach) portée f.; (fig.) compréhension f.

grasping /'grɑːspɪŋ/ a. rapace.

grass /grɑːs/ n. herbe f. ~ **roots**, peuple m.; (pol.) base f. ~-**roots** a. populaire. ~**y** a. herbeux.

grasshopper /'grɑːshɒpə(r)/ n. sauterelle f.

grassland /'grɑːslænd/ n. prairie f.

grate[1] /greɪt/ n. (fireplace) foyer m.; (frame) grille f.

grate[2] /greɪt/ v.t. râper. —v.i. grincer. ~**r** /-ə(r)/ n. râpe f.

grateful /'greɪtfl/ a. reconnaissant. ~**ly** adv. avec reconnaissance.

gratify /'grætɪfaɪ/ v.t. satisfaire; (please) faire plaisir à. ~**ied** a. très heureux. ~**ying** a. agréable.

grating /'greɪtɪŋ/ n. grille f.

gratis /'greɪtɪs, 'grætɪs/ a. & adv. gratis (a. invar.).

gratitude /'grætɪtjuːd/ n. gratitude f.

gratuitous /grə'tjuːɪtəs/ a. gratuit.

gratuity /grə'tjuːətɪ/ n. (tip) pourboire m.; (bounty: mil.) prime f.

grave[1] /greɪv/ n. tombe f. ~-**digger** n. fossoyeur m.

grave[2] /greɪv/ a. (-er, -est) (serious) grave. ~**ly** adv. gravement.

grave[3] /grɑːv/ a. ~ **accent**, accent grave m.

gravel /'grævl/ n. gravier m.

gravestone /'greɪvstəʊn/ n. pierre tombale f.

graveyard /'greɪvjɑːd/ n. cimetière m.

gravitate /'grævɪteɪt/ v.i. graviter. ~**ion** /-'teɪʃn/ n. gravitation f.

gravity /'grævətɪ/ n. (seriousness) gravité f.; (force) pesanteur f.

gravy /'greɪvɪ/ n. jus (de viande) m.

gray /greɪ/ a. & n. = **grey**.

graze[1] /greɪz/ v.t./i. (eat) paître.

graze[2] /greɪz/ v.t. (touch) frôler; (scrape) écorcher. —n. écorchure f.

greas|**e** /griːs/ n. graisse f. —v.t. graisser. ~**e-proof paper**, papier sulfurisé m. ~**y** a. graisseux.

great /greɪt/ a. (-er, -est) grand; (very good: fam.) magnifique. ~ **Britain**, Grande-Bretagne f. ~**grandfather** n. arrière-grand-père m. ~**grandmother** n. arrière-grand-mère f. ~**ly** adv. (very) très; (much) beaucoup. ~**ness** n. grandeur f.

Greece /griːs/ n. Grèce f.

greed /griːd/ n. avidité f.; (for food) gourmandise f. ~**y** a. avide; gourmand.

Greek /griːk/ a. & n. grec(que) (m. (f.)); (lang.) grec m.

green /griːn/ a. (-er, -est) vert; (fig.) naïf. —n. vert m.; (grass) pelouse f.; (golf) green m. ~**s**, légumes verts m. pl. ~ **belt**, ceinture verte f. ~ **light**, feu vert m. ~**ery** n. verdure f.

greengage /'gri:ngeɪdʒ/ n. (plum) reine-claude f.

greengrocer /'gri:ngrəʊsə(r)/ n. marchand(e) de fruits et légumes m. (f.).

greenhouse /'gri:nhaʊs/ n. serre f.

greet /gri:t/ v.t. (receive) accueillir; (address politely) saluer. ∼ing n. accueil m. ∼ings n. pl. compliments m. pl.; (wishes) vœux m. pl. ∼ings card, carte de vœux f.

gregarious /grɪ'geərɪəs/ a. (instinct) grégaire; (person) sociable.

grenade /grɪ'neɪd/ n. grenade f.

grew /gru:/ see grow.

grey /greɪ/ a. (-er, -est) gris; (fig.) triste. —n. gris m. go ∼, (hair, person) grisonner.

greyhound /'greɪhaʊnd/ n. lévrier m.

grid /grɪd/ n. grille f.; (network: electr.) réseau m.; (culin.) gril m.

grief /gri:f/ n. chagrin m. come to ∼, (person) avoir un malheur; (fail) tourner mal.

grievance /'gri:vns/ n. grief m.

grieve /gri:v/ v.t./i. (s')affliger. ∼ for, pleurer.

grill /grɪl/ n. (cooking device) gril m.; (food) grillade f.; (auto.) calandre f. —v.t./i. griller; (interrogate) cuisiner.

grille /grɪl/ n. grille f.

grim /grɪm/ a. (grimmer, grimmest) sinistre.

grimace /grɪ'meɪs/ n. grimace f. —v.i. grimacer.

grim|e /graɪm/ n. crasse f. ∼y a. crasseux.

grin /grɪn/ v.i. (p.t. grinned) sourire. —n. (large) sourire m.

grind /graɪnd/ v.t. (p.t. ground) écraser; (coffee) moudre; (sharpen) aiguiser. —n. corvée f. ∼ one's teeth, grincer des dents. ∼ to a halt, devenir paralysé.

grip /grɪp/ v.t. (p.t. gripped) saisir; (interest) passionner. —n. prise f.; (strength of hand) poigne

f.; (bag) sac de voyage m. come to ∼s, en venir aux prises.

gripe /graɪp/ n. ∼s, (med.) coliques f. pl. —v.i. (grumble: sl.) râler.

grisly /'grɪzlɪ/ a. (-ier, -iest) macabre, horrible.

gristle /'grɪsl/ n. cartilage m.

grit /grɪt/ n. gravillon m., sable m.; (fig.) courage m. —v.t. (p.t. gritted) (road) sabler; (teeth) serrer.

grizzle /'grɪzl/ v.i. (cry) pleurnicher.

groan /grəʊn/ v.i. gémir. —n. gémissement m.

grocer /'grəʊsə(r)/ n. épic|ier, -ière m., f. ∼ies n. pl. (goods) épicerie f. ∼y n. (shop) épicerie f.

grog /grɒg/ n. grog m.

groggy /'grɒgɪ/ a. (weak) faible; (unsteady) chancelant; (ill) mal fichu.

groin /grɔɪn/ n. aine f.

groom /gru:m/ n. marié m.; (for horses) valet d'écurie m. —v.t. (horse) panser; (fig.) préparer.

groove /gru:v/ n. (for door etc.) rainure f.; (in record) sillon m.

grope /grəʊp/ v.i. tâtonner. ∼ for, chercher à tâtons.

gross /grəʊs/ a. (-er, -est) (coarse) grossier; (comm.) brut. —n. invar. grosse f. ∼ly adv. grossièrement; (very) extrêmement.

grotesque /grəʊ'tesk/ a. grotesque, horrible.

grotto /'grɒtəʊ/ n. (pl. -oes) grotte f.

grotty /'grɒtɪ/ a. (sl.) moche.

grouch /graʊtʃ/ v.i. (grumble: fam.) rouspéter, râler.

ground¹ /graʊnd/ n. terre f., sol m.; (area) terrain m.; (reason) raison f.; (electr., Amer.) masse f. ∼s, terres f. pl., parc m.; (of coffee) marc m. —v.t./i. (naut.) échouer; (aircraft) retenir au sol. on the ∼, par terre. lose ∼, perdre du terrain. ～ **floor**, rez-de-chaussée *m. invar.* ～ **rule**, règle de base *f.* ～**less** *a.* sans fondement. ～ **swell**, lame de fond *f.*

ground² /graʊnd/ *see* grind. —*a.* ～ **beef**, (*Amer.*) bifteck haché *m.*

grounding /ˈgraʊndɪŋ/ *n.* connaissances (de base) *f. pl.*

groundsheet /ˈgraʊndʃiːt/ *n.* tapis de sol *m.*

groundwork /ˈgraʊndwɜːk/ *n.* travail préparatoire *m.*

group /gruːp/ *n.* groupe *m.* —*v.t./i.* (se) grouper.

grouse¹ /graʊs/ *n. invar.* (*bird*) coq de bruyère *m.*, grouse *f.*

grouse² /graʊs/ *v.i.* (*grumble: fam.*) rouspéter, râler.

grove /grəʊv/ *n.* bocage *m.*

grovel /ˈgrɒvl/ *v.i.* (*p.t.* grovelled) ramper. ～**ling** *a.* rampant.

grow /grəʊ/ *v.i.* (*p.t* grew, *p.p.* grown) grandir; (*of plant*) pousser; (*become*) devenir. —*v.t.* cultiver. ～ **up**, devenir adulte, grandir. ～**er** *n.* cultiva|teur, -trice *m., f.* ～**ing** *a.* grandissant.

growl /graʊl/ *v.i.* grogner. —*n.* grognement *m.*

grown /grəʊn/ *see* grow. —*a.* adulte. ～**up** *a.* & *n.* adulte (*m./f.*).

growth /grəʊθ/ *n.* croissance *f.*; (*in numbers*) accroissement *m.*; (*of hair, tooth*) pousse *f.*; (*med.*) tumeur *f.*

grub /grʌb/ *n.* (*larva*) larve *f.*; (*food: sl.*) bouffe *f.*

grubby /ˈgrʌbɪ/ *a.* (-ier, -iest) sale.

grudge /grʌdʒ/ *v.t.* ～ **doing**, faire à contrecœur. ～ **s.o. sth.**, (*success, wealth*) en vouloir à qn. de qch. —*n.* rancune *f.* **have a** ～ **against**, en vouloir à. **grudgingly** *adv.* à contrecœur.

gruelling /ˈgruːəlɪŋ/ *a.* exténuant.

gruesome /ˈgruːsəm/ *a.* macabre.

gruff /grʌf/ *a.* (-er, -est) bourru.

grumble /ˈgrʌmbl/ *v.i.* ronchonner, grogner (**at**, après).

grumpy /ˈgrʌmpɪ/ *a.* (-ier, -iest) grincheux, grognon.

grunt /grʌnt/ *v.i.* grogner. —*n.* grognement *m.*

guarantee /gærənˈtiː/ *n.* garantie *f.* —*v.t.* garantir. ～**or** *n.* garant(e) *m.* (*f.*).

guard /gɑːd/ *v.t.* protéger; (*watch*) surveiller. —*v.i.* ～ **against**, se protéger contre. —*n.* (*vigilance, mil., group*) garde *f.*; (*person*) garde *m.*; (*on train*) chef de train *m.* ～**ian** *n.* gardien(ne) *m.* (*f.*); (*of orphan*) tu|teur, -trice *m., f.*

guarded /ˈgɑːdɪd/ *a.* prudent.

guerrilla /gəˈrɪlə/ *n.* guérillero *m.* ～ **warfare**, guérilla *f.*

guess /ges/ *v.t./i.* deviner; (*suppose*) penser. —*n.* conjecture *f.*

guesswork /ˈgeswɜːk/ *n.* conjectures *f. pl.*

guest /gest/ *n.* invité(e) *m.* (*f.*); (*in hotel*) client(e) *m.* (*f.*). ～**-house** *n.* pension *f.* ～**-room** *n.* chambre d'ami *f.*

guffaw /gəˈfɔː/ *n.* gros rire *m.* —*v.i.* s'esclaffer, rire bruyamment.

guidance /ˈgaɪdns/ *n.* (*advice*) conseils *m. pl.*; (*information*) information *f.*

guide /gaɪd/ *n.* (*person, book*) guide *m.* —*v.t.* guider. ～**d** /-ɪd/ *a.* ～**d missile**, missile téléguidé *m.* ～**-dog** *n.* chien d'aveugle *m.* ～**-lines** *n. pl.* grandes lignes *f. pl.*

Guide /gaɪd/ *n.* (*girl*) guide *f.*

guidebook /ˈgaɪdbʊk/ *n.* guide *m.*

guild /gɪld/ *n.* corporation *f.*

guile /gaɪl/ *n.* ruse *f.*

guillotine /ˈgɪlətiːn/ *n.* guillotine *f.*; (*for paper*) massicot *m.*

guilt /gɪlt/ *n.* culpabilité *f.* ～**y** *a.* coupable.

guinea-pig /ˈgɪnɪpɪg/ *n.* cobaye *m.*

guinea-fowl /ˈgɪnɪfaʊl/ *n.* pintade *f.*

guise /gaɪz/ n. apparence f.

guitar /gɪ'tɑː(r)/ n. guitare f. **~ist** n. guitariste m./f.

gulf /gʌlf/ n. (part of sea) golfe m.; (hollow) gouffre m.

gull /gʌl/ n. mouette f., goéland m.

gullet /'gʌlɪt/ n. gosier m.

gullible /'gʌləbl/ a. crédule.

gully /'gʌlɪ/ n. (ravine) ravine f.; (drain) rigole f.

gulp /gʌlp/ v.t. ~ (down), avaler en vitesse. —v.i. (from fear etc.) avoir un serrement de gorge. —n. gorgée f.

gum¹ /gʌm/ n. (anat.) gencive f.

gum² /gʌm/ n. (from tree) gomme f.; (glue) colle f.; (for chewing) chewing-gum m. —v.t. (p.t. gummed) gommer.

gumboil /'gʌmbɔɪl/ n. abcès dentaire m.

gumboot /'gʌmbuːt/ n. botte de caoutchouc f.

gumption /'gʌmpʃn/ n. (fam.) initiative f., courage m., audace f.

gun /gʌn/ n. (pistol) revolver m.; (rifle) fusil m.; (large) canon m. —v.t. (p.t. gunned). ~ down, abattre. ~ner n. artilleur m.

gunfire /'gʌnfaɪə(r)/ n. fusillade f.

gunge /gʌndʒ/ n. (sl.) crasse f.

gunman /'gʌnmən/ n. (pl. -men) bandit armé m.

gunpowder /'gʌnpaʊdə(r)/ n. poudre à canon f.

gunshot /'gʌnʃɒt/ n. coup de feu m.

gurgle /'gɜːgl/ n. glouglou m. —v.i. glouglouter.

guru /'guruː/ n. (pl. -us) gourou m.

gush /gʌʃ/ v.i. ~ (out), jaillir. —n. jaillissement m.

gust /gʌst/ n. rafale f.; (of smoke) bouffée f. ~y a. venteux.

gusto /'gʌstəʊ/ n. enthousiasme m.

gut /gʌt/ n. boyau m. ~s, boyaux m. pl., ventre m.; (courage: fam.) cran m. —v.t. (p.t. gutted) (fish) vider; (of fire) dévaster.

gutter /'gʌtə(r)/ n. (on roof) gouttière f.; (in street) caniveau m.

guttural /'gʌtərəl/ a. guttural.

guy /gaɪ/ n. (man: fam.) type m.

guzzle /'gʌzl/ v.t./i. (eat) bâfrer; (drink: Amer.) boire d'un trait.

gym /dʒɪm/ n. (fam.) gymnase m.; (fam.) gym (nastique) f. **~slip** n. tunique f. **~nasium** n. gymnase m.

gymnast /'dʒɪmnæst/ n. gymnaste m./f. **~ics** /-'næstɪks/ n. pl. gymnastique f.

gynaecology /gaɪnɪ'kɒlədʒɪ/ n. gynécologie f. **~ist** n. gynécologue m./f.

gypsy /'dʒɪpsɪ/ n. bohémien(ne) m. (f.).

gyrate /dʒaɪ'reɪt/ v.i. tournoyer.

H

haberdashery /hæbə'dæʃərɪ/ n. mercerie f.

habit /'hæbɪt/ n. habitude f.; (costume: relig.) habit m. **be in/get into the ~ of,** avoir/prendre l'habitude de.

habit|able /'hæbɪtəbl/ a. habitable. **~ation** /-'teɪʃn/ n. habitation f.

habitat /'hæbɪtæt/ n. habitat m.

habitual /hə'bɪtʃʊəl/ a. (usual) habituel; (smoker, liar) invétéré. **~ly** adv. habituellement.

hack¹ /hæk/ n. (old horse) haridelle f.; (writer) nègre m., écrivailleur, se, m.f.

hack² /hæk/ v.t. hacher, tailler.

hackneyed /'hæknɪd/ a. rebattu.

had /hæd/ see have.

haddock /'hædək/ n. invar. églefin m. smoked **~,** haddock m.

haemorrhage /'hemərɪdʒ/ n. hémorragie f.

haemorrhoids /'heməroidz/ *n. pl.* hémorroïdes *f. pl.*

hag /hæg/ *n.* (vieille) sorcière *f.*

haggard /'hægəd/ *a.* (*person*) qui a le visage défait; (*face, look*) défait, hagard.

haggle /'hægl/ *v.i.* marchander. ~ **over,** (*object*) marchander; (*price*) discuter.

Hague (The) /(ðə)'heɪg/ *n.* La Haye.

hail[1] /heɪl/ *v.t.* (greet) saluer; (*taxi*) héler. —*v.i.* ~ **from,** venir de.

hail[2] /heɪl/ *n.* grêle *f.* —*v.i.* grêler.

hailstone /'heɪlstəʊn/ *n.* grêlon *m.*

hair /heə(r)/ *n.* (on head) cheveux *m. pl.*; (on body, of animal) poils *m. pl.*; (single strand on head) cheveu *m.*; (on body) poil *m.* ~**do** *n.* (*fam.*) coiffure *f.* ~**-drier** *n.* séchoir (à cheveux) *m.* ~**grip** *n.* pince à cheveux *f.* ~**-raising** *a.* horrifique. ~ **remover,** dépilatoire *m.* ~**-style** *n.* coiffure *f.*

hairbrush /'heəbrʌʃ/ *n.* brosse à cheveux *f.*

haircut /'heəkʌt/ *n.* coupe de cheveux *f.* **have a** ~, se faire couper les cheveux.

hairdresser /'heədresə(r)/ *n.* coiffeu|r, -se *m., f.*

hairpin /'heəpɪn/ *n.* épingle à cheveux *f.*

hairy /'heərɪ/ *a.* (**-ier, -iest**) poilu; (*terrifying: sl.*) horrifique.

hake /heɪk/ *n. invar.* colin *m.*

hale /heɪl/ *a.* vigoureux.

half /hɑːf/ *n.* (*pl.* **halves**) moitié *f.*, demi(e) *m.* (*f.*). —*a.* demi. ~ *n.* moitié. ~ **a dozen,** une demi-douzaine. ~ **an hour,** une demi-heure. **four and a** ~, quatre et demi(e). ~ **and half,** moitié moitié. **in** ~, en deux. ~**-back** *n.* (*sport*) demi *m.* ~**-caste** *n.* métis(se) *m.* (*f.*). ~**-hearted** *a.* tiède. **at** ~**-mast** *adv.* en berne. ~ **measure,** demi-mesure *f.* ~

price, moitié prix. ~**-term** *n.* congé de (de)mi-trimestre *m.* ~**time** *n.* mi-temps *f.* ~**-way** *adv.* à mi-chemin. ~**-wit** *n.* imbécile *m./f.*

halibut /'hælɪbət/ *n. invar.* (*fish*) flétan *m.*

hall /hɔːl/ *n.* (room) salle *f.*; (*entrance*) vestibule *m.*; (*mansion*) manoir *m.*; (*corridor*) couloir *m.* ~ **of residence,** foyer d'étudiants *m.*

hallelujah /hælɪ'luːjə/ *int. & n. =* **alleluia.**

hallmark /'hɔːlmɑːk/ *n.* (on gold etc.) poinçon *m.*; (*fig.*) sceau *m.*

hallo /hə'ləʊ/ *int. & n.* bonjour (*m.*). ~**!,** (on telephone) allô!; (in surprise) tiens!

hallow /'hæləʊ/ *v.t.* sanctifier.

Hallowe'en /hæləʊ'iːn/ *n.* la veille de la Toussaint.

hallucination /həluːsɪ'neɪʃn/ *n.* hallucination *f.*

halo /'heɪləʊ/ *n.* (*pl.* **-oes**) auréole *f.*

halt /hɔːlt/ *n.* halte *f.* —*v.t./i.* (s')arrêter.

halve /hɑːv/ *v.t.* diviser en deux; (*time etc.*) réduire de moitié.

ham /hæm/ *n.* jambon *m.*; (*theatre sl.*) cabotin(e) *m.* (*f.*). ~**-fisted** *a.* maladroit.

hamburger /'hæmbɜːgə(r)/ *n.* hamburger *m.*

hamlet /'hæmlɪt/ *n.* hameau *m.*

hammer /'hæmə(r)/ *n.* marteau *m.* —*v.t./i.* marteler, frapper; (*defeat*) battre à plate couture. ~ **out,** (*differences*) arranger; (*agreement*) arriver à.

hammock /'hæmək/ *n.* hamac *m.*

hamper[1] /'hæmpə(r)/ *n.* panier *m.*

hamper[2] /'hæmpə(r)/ *v.t.* gêner.

hamster /'hæmstə(r)/ *n.* hamster *m.*

hand /hænd/ *n.* main *f.*; (of clock) aiguille *f.*; (writing) écriture *f.*; (worker) ouvr|ier, -ière *m., f.*;

(cards) jeu m. —v.t. donner. **at** ~, proche. ~-**baggage** n. bagages à main m. pl. **give s.o. a** ~, donner un coup de main à qn. ~ **in** or **over**, remettre. ~ **out**, distribuer. ~-**out** n. prospectus m.; (money) aumône f. **on** ~, disponible. **on one's** ~s, (fig.) sur les bras. **on the one** ~ ... **on the other** ~, d'une part ... d'autre part. **to** ~, à portée de la main.

handbag /ˈhændbæg/ n. sac à main m.

handbook /ˈhændbʊk/ n. manuel m.

handbrake /ˈhændbreɪk/ n. frein à main m.

handcuffs /ˈhændkʌfs/ n. pl. menottes f. pl.

handful /ˈhændfʊl/ n. poignée f.; **he's a** ~!, c'est du boulot!

handicap /ˈhændɪkæp/ n. handicap m. —v.t. (p.t. handicapped) handicaper.

handicraft /ˈhændɪkrɑːft/ n. travaux manuels m. pl., artisanat m.

handiwork /ˈhændɪwɜːk/ n. ouvrage m.

handkerchief /ˈhæŋkətʃɪf/ n. (pl. -fs) mouchoir m.

handle /ˈhændl/ n. (of door etc.) poignée f.; (of implement) manche m.; (of cup etc.) anse f.; (of pan etc.) queue f.; (for turning) manivelle f. —v.t. manier; (deal with) s'occuper de; (touch) toucher à.

handlebar /ˈhændlbɑː(r)/ n. guidon m.

handshake /ˈhændʃeɪk/ n. poignée de main f.

handsome /ˈhænsəm/ a. (good-looking) beau; (generous) généreux; (large) considérable.

handwriting /ˈhændraɪtɪŋ/ n. écriture f.

handy /ˈhændɪ/ a. (-ier, -iest) (useful) commode, utile; (person) adroit; (near) accessible.

handyman /ˈhændɪmæn/ n. (pl. -men) bricoleur m.; (servant) homme à tout faire m.

hang /hæŋ/ v.t. (p.t. hung) suspendre, accrocher; (p.t. hanged) (criminal) pendre. —v.i. pendre. —n. **get the** ~ **of doing**, trouver le truc pour faire. ~ **about**, traîner. ~-**gliding** n. vol libre m. ~ **on**, (hold out) tenir bon; (wait: sl.) attendre. ~ **out** v.i. pendre; (live: sl.) crécher; (spend time: sl.) passer son temps; v.t. (washing) étendre. ~ **up**, (telephone) raccrocher. ~-**up** n. (sl.) complexe m.

hangar /ˈhæŋə(r)/ n. hangar m.

hanger /ˈhæŋə(r)/ n. (for clothes) cintre m. ~-**on** n. parasite m.

hangover /ˈhæŋəʊvə(r)/ n. (after drinking) gueule de bois f.

hanker /ˈhæŋkə(r)/ v.i. ~ **after**, avoir envie de. ~**ing** n. envie f.

hanky-panky /ˈhæŋkɪpæŋkɪ/ n. (trickery: sl.) manigances f. pl.

haphazard /hæpˈhæzəd/ a., ~**ly** adv. au petit bonheur, au hasard.

hapless /ˈhæplɪs/ a. infortuné.

happen /ˈhæpən/ v.i. arriver, se passer. **it so** ~s that, il se trouve que. **he** ~s **to know** that, il se trouve qu'il sait que. ~**ing** n. événement m.

happ|y /ˈhæpɪ/ a. (-ier, -iest) heureux. **I'm not** ~ **about the idea**, je n'aime pas trop l'idée. ~ **with sth.**, satisfait de qch. ~**y medium** or **mean**, juste milieu m. ~**ily** adv. joyeusement; (fortunately) heureusement. ~**iness** n. bonheur m. ~**y-go-lucky** a. insouciant.

harass /ˈhærəs/ v.t. harceler. ~**ment** n. harcèlement m.

harbour, (Amer.) **harbor** /ˈhɑːbə(r)/ n. port m. —v.t. (shelter) héberger.

hard /hɑːd/ a. (-er, -est) dur;

(*difficult*) difficile, dur. —*adv.*
dur; (*think*) sérieusement; (*pull*)
fort. **~ and fast**, concret. **~-
boiled egg**, œuf dur *m.* **~ by**,
tout près. **~ disk**, disque dur *m.*
~ done by, mal traité. **~-
headed** *a.* réaliste. **~ of hearing**, dur d'oreille. **the ~ of
hearing**, les malentendants *m.
pl.* **~-line** *a.* pur et dur. **~-
shoulder**, accotement stabilisé
m. **~ up**, (*fam.*) fauché. **~-
wearing** *a.* solide. **~-working**
a. travailleur. **~ness** *n.* dureté *f.*

hardboard /'hɑːdbɔːd/ *n.* Isorel *m.*
(P.).

harden /'hɑːdn/ *v.t./i.* durcir.

hardly /'hɑːdlɪ/ *adv.* à peine. **~
ever**, presque jamais.

hardship /'hɑːdʃɪp/ *n.* **~(s)**,
épreuves *f. pl.*, souffrance *f.*

hardware /'hɑːdweə(r)/ *n.* (*metal
goods*) quincaillerie *f.*; (*machinery, of computer*) matériel *m.*

hardy /'hɑːdɪ/ *a.* (**-ier, iest**)
résistant.

hare /heə(r)/ *n.* lièvre *m.* **~
around**, courir partout. **~-
brained** *a.* écervelé.

hark /hɑːk/ *v.i.* écouter. **~ back
to**, revenir sur.

harm /hɑːm/ *n.* (*hurt*) mal *m.*;
(*wrong*) tort *m.* —*v.t.* (*hurt*) faire
du mal à; (*wrong*) faire du tort à;
(*object*) endommager. **there is no
~ in**, il n'y a pas de mal à. **~ful** *a.*
nuisible. **~less** *a.* inoffensif.

harmonica /hɑː'mɒnɪkə/ *n.* harmonica *m.*

harmon|y /'hɑːmənɪ/ *n.* harmonie
f. **~ious** /-'məʊnɪəs/ *a.* har-
monieux. **~ize** *v.t./i.* (s')harmo-
niser.

harness /'hɑːnɪs/ *n.* harnais *m.*
—*v.t.* (*horse*) harnacher; (*control*)
maîtriser; (*use*) exploiter.

harp /hɑːp/ *n.* harpe *f.* —*v.i.* **~ on
(about)**, rabâcher. **~ist** *n.* har-
piste *m./f.*

harpoon /hɑː'puːn/ *n.* harpon *m.*

harpsichord /'hɑːpsɪkɔːd/ *n.*
clavecin *m.*

harrowing /'hærəʊɪŋ/ *a.* dé-
chirant, qui déchire le cœur.

harsh /hɑːʃ/ *a.* (**-er, -est**) dur,
rude; (*taste*) âpre; (*sound*) rude,
âpre. **~ly** *adv.* durement. **~ness**
n. dureté *f.*

harvest /'hɑːvɪst/ *n.* moisson *f.*,
récolte *f.* **the wine ~**, les
vendanges *f. pl.* —*v.t.* moison-
ner, récolter. **~er** *n.* moisson-
neuse *f.*

has /hæz/ *see* have.

hash /hæʃ/ *n.* (*culin.*) hachis *m.*;
(*fig.*) gâchis *m.* **make a ~ of**,
(*bungle: sl.*) saboter.

hashish /'hæʃiʃ/ *n.* ha(s)chisch *m.*

hassle /'hæsl/ *n.* (*fam.*) dif-
ficulté(s) *f* (*pl.*); (*bother, effort:
fam.*) mal *m.*, peine *f.*; (*quarrel:
fam.*) chamaillerie *f.* —*v.t.*
(*harass: fam.*) harceler.

haste /heɪst/ *n.* hâte *f.* **in ~**, à la
hâte. **make ~**, se hâter.

hasten /'heɪsn/ *v.t./i.* (se) hâter.

hast|y /'heɪstɪ/ *a.* (**-ier, -iest**)
précipité. **~ily** *adv.* à la hâte.

hat /hæt/ *n.* chapeau *m.* **a ~ trick**,
trois succès consécutifs.

hatch¹ /hætʃ/ *n.* (*for food*) passe-
plat *m.*; (*naut.*) écoutille *f.*

hatch² /hætʃ/ *v.t./i.* (faire) éclore.

hatchback /'hætʃbæk/ *n.* voiture
avec hayon arrière *f.*

hatchet /'hætʃɪt/ *n.* hachette *f.*

hate /heɪt/ *n.* haine *f.* —*v.t.* haïr.
~ful *a.* haïssable.

hatred /'heɪtrɪd/ *n.* haine *f.*

haughty /'hɔːtɪ/ *a.* (**-ier, -iest**)
hautain.

haul /hɔːl/ *v.t.* traîner, tirer. —*n.*
(*of thieves*) butin *m.*; (*catch*) prise
f.; (*journey*) voyage *m.* **~age** *n.*
camionnage *m.* **~ier** *n.* camionneur *m.*

haunch /hɔːntʃ/ *n.* **on one's ~es**,
accroupi.

haunt /hɔ:nt/ v.t. hanter. —n. endroit favori m.

have /hæv/ v.t. (3 sing. present tense **has**; p.t. **had**) avoir; (meal, bath, etc.) prendre; (walk, dream, etc.) faire. —v. aux. avoir; (with aller, partir, etc. & pronominal verbs) être. ~ **it out with**, s'expliquer avec. ~ **just done**, venir de faire. ~**sth. done**, faire faire qch. ~ **to do**, devoir faire. **the ~s and have-nots**, les riches et les pauvres m. pl.

haven /ˈheɪvn/ n. havre m., abri m.

haversack /ˈhævəsæk/ n. musette f.

havoc /ˈhævək/ n. ravages m. pl.

haw /hɔ:/ see **hum**.

hawk[1] /hɔ:k/ n. faucon m.

hawk[2] /hɔ:k/ v.t. colporter. ~**er** n. colporteu|r, ~se m., f.

hawthorn /ˈhɔ:θɔ:n/ n. aubépine f.

hay /heɪ/ n. foin m. ~ **fever**, rhume des foins m.

haystack /ˈheɪstæk/ n. meule de foin f.

haywire /ˈheɪwaɪə(r)/ a. **go** ~, (plans) se désorganiser; (machine) se détraquer.

hazard /ˈhæzəd/ n. risque m. —v.t. risquer, hasarder. ~ **warning lights**, feux de détresse m. pl. ~**ous** a. hasardeux, risqué.

haze /heɪz/ n. brume f.

hazel /ˈheɪzl/ n. (bush) noisetier m. ~**nut** n. noisette f.

hazy /ˈheɪzɪ/ a. (-ier, -iest) (misty) brumeux; (fig.) flou, vague.

he /hi:/ pron. il; (emphatic) lui. —n. mâle m.

head /hed/ n. tête f.; (leader) chef m.; (of beer) mousse f. —a. principal. —v.t. être à la tête de. —v.i. ~ **for**, se diriger vers. ~**dress** n. coiffure f.; (lady's) coiffe f. ~**-on** a. & adv. de plein fouet. ~ **first**, la tête la première. ~**s or tails?**, pile ou face? ~ **office**, siège m. ~ **rest**, appui-tête m. ~

the ball, faire une tête. ~ **waiter**, maître d'hôtel m. ~**er** n. (football) tête f.

headache /ˈhedeɪk/ n. mal de tête m.

heading /ˈhedɪŋ/ n. titre m.; (subject category) rubrique f.

headlamp /ˈhedlæmp/ n. phare m.

headland /ˈhedlənd/ n. cap m.

headlight /ˈhedlaɪt/ n. phare m.

headline /ˈhedlaɪn/ n. titre m.

headlong /ˈhedlɒŋ/ adv. (in a rush) à toute allure.

head|**master** /hedˈmɑ:stə(r)/ (of school) directeur m. ~**mistress** n. directrice f.

headphone /ˈhedfəʊn/ n. écouteur m. ~**s**, casque (à écouteurs) m.

headquarters /hedˈkwɔ:təz/ n. pl. siège m., bureau central m.; (mil.) quartier général m.

headstrong /ˈhedstrɒŋ/ a. têtu.

headway /ˈhedweɪ/ n. progrès m. (pl.) **make** ~, faire des progrès.

heady /ˈhedɪ/ a. (-ier, -iest) (wine) capiteux; (exciting) grisant.

heal /hi:l/ v.t./i. guérir.

health /helθ/ n. santé f. ~ **centre**, dispensaire m. ~ **foods**, aliments diététiques m. pl. ~ **insurance**, assurance médicale f. ~**y** a. sain; (person) en bonne santé.

heap /hi:p/ n. tas m. —v.t. entasser. ~**s of**, (fam.) des tas de.

hear /hɪə(r)/ v.t./i. (p.t. **heard** /hɜ:d/) entendre. **hear, hear!**, bravo! ~ **from**, recevoir des nouvelles de. ~ **of** or **about**, entendre parler de. **not** ~ **of**, (refuse to allow) ne pas entendre parler de. ~**ing** n. ouïe f.; (of witness) audition f.; (of case) audience f. ~**ing-aid** n. appareil acoustique m.

hearsay /ˈhɪəseɪ/ n. ouï-dire m. invar. **from** ~, par ouï-dire.

hearse /hɜ:s/ n. corbillard m.

heart /hɑ:t/ n. cœur m. ~**s**, (cards)

cœur *m*. **at** ◣, **au foud. by** ◣, **par cœur**. ◣ **attack**, crise cardiaque *f*. ◣**-break** *n*. chagrin *m*. ◣**-breaking** *a*. navrant. **be** ◣**-broken**, avoir le cœur brisé. ◣**-to-heart** *a*. à cœur ouvert. **lose** ◣, perdre courage.

heartache /'hɑːteɪk/ *n*. chagrin *m*.

heartburn /'hɑːtbɜːn/ *n*. brûlures d'estomac *f. pl*.

hearten /'hɑːtn/ *v.t.* encourager.

heartfelt /'hɑːtfelt/ *a*. sincère.

hearth /hɑːθ/ *n*. foyer *m*.

heartless /'hɑːtlɪs/ *a*. cruel.

heart|y /'hɑːtɪ/ *a*. (**-ier, -iest**) (*sincere*) chaleureux; (*meal*) gros. ◣**ily** *adv*. (*eat*) avec appétit.

heat /hiːt/ *n*. chaleur *f*.; (*excitement: fig.*) feu *m*.; (*contest*) éliminatoire *f*. —*v.t./i.* chauffer. ◣ **stroke**, insolation *f*. ◣ **up**, (*food*) réchauffer. ◣ **wave**, vague de chaleur *f*. ◣**er** *n*. radiateur *m*. ◣**ing** *n*. chauffage *m*.

heated /'hiːtɪd/ *a*. (*fig.*) passionné.

heath /hiːθ/ *n*. (*area*) lande *f*.

heathen /'hiːðn/ *n*. païen(ne) *m*. (*f.*).

heather /'heðə(r)/ *n*. bruyère *f*.

heave /hiːv/ *v.t./i.* (*lift*) (se) soulever; (*a sigh*) pousser; (*throw: fam.*) lancer; (*retch*) avoir des nausées.

heaven /hevn/ *n*. ciel *m*. ◣**ly** *a*. céleste; (*pleasing: fam.*) divin.

heav|y /'hevɪ/ *a*. (**-ier, -iest**) lourd; (*cold, work, etc.*) gros; (*traffic*) dense. ◣**y goods vehicle**, poids lourd *m*. ◣**y-handed** *a*. maladroit. ◣**ily** *adv*. lourdement; (*smoke, drink*) beaucoup.

heavyweight /'hevɪweɪt/ *n*. poids lourd *m*.

Hebrew /'hiːbruː/ *a*. hébreu (*m. only*), hébraïque. —*n*. (*lang.*) hébreu *m*.

heckle /'hekl/ *v.t.* (*speaker*) interrompre, interpeller.

hectic /'hektɪk/ *a*. très bousculé, trépidant, agité.

hedge /hedʒ/ *n*. haie *f*. —*v.t.* entourer. —*v.i.* (*in answering*) répondre évasivement. ◣ **one's bets**, protéger ses arrières.

hedgehog /'hedʒhɒg/ *n*. hérisson *m*.

heed /hiːd/ *v.t.* faire attention à. —*n*. **pay** ◣ **to**, faire attention à. ◣**less** *a*. ◣**less of**, inattentif à.

heel /hiːl/ *n*. talon *m*.; (*man: sl.*) salaud *m*. **down at** ◣, (*Amer.*) **down at the** ◣**s**, miteux.

hefty /'heftɪ/ *a*. (**-ier, -iest**) gros, lourd.

heifer /'hefə(r)/ *n*. génisse *f*.

height /haɪt/ *n*. hauteur *f*.; (*of person*) taille *f*.; (*of plane, mountain*) altitude *f*.; (*of fame, glory*) apogée *m*.; (*of joy, folly, pain*) comble *m*.

heighten /'haɪtn/ *v.t.* (*raise*) rehausser; (*fig.*) augmenter.

heinous /'heɪnəs/ *a*. atroce.

heir /eə(r)/ *n*. héritier *m*. ◣**ess** *n*. héritière *f*.

heirloom /'eəluːm/ *n*. bijou (meuble, tableau, *etc.*) de famille *m*.

held /held/ *see* **hold**[1].

helicopter /'helɪkɒptə(r)/ *n*. hélicoptère *m*.

heliport /'helɪpɔːt/ *n*. héliport *m*.

hell /hel/ *n*. enfer *m*. ◣**-bent** *a*. acharné (**on, à**). ◣**ish** *a*. infernal.

hello /hə'ləʊ/ *int.* & *n.* = **hallo**.

helm /helm/ *n*. (*of ship*) barre *f*.

helmet /'helmɪt/ *n*. casque *m*.

help /help/ *v.t./i.* aider. —*n*. aide *f*.; (*employees*) personnel *m*.; (*charwoman*) femme de ménage *f*. ◣ **o.s. to**, se servir de. **he cannot** ◣ **laughing**, il ne peut pas s'empêcher de rire. ◣**er** *n*. aide *m./f.* ◣**ful** *a*. utile; (*person*) serviable. ◣**less** *a*. impuissant.

helping /'helpɪŋ/ *n*. portion *f*.

helter-skelter /heltə'skeltə(r)/ *n.* toboggan *m.* —*adv.* pêle-mêle.

hem /hem/ *n.* ourlet *m.* —*v.t.* (*p.t.* **hemmed**) ourler. **~ in**, enfermer.

hemisphere /'hemɪsfɪə(r)/ *n.* hémisphère *m.*

hemorrhage /'hemərɪdʒ/ *n.* (*Amer.*) = **haemorrhage**.

hemorrhoids /'hemərɔɪdz/ *n. pl.* (*Amer.*) = **haemorrhoids**.

hen /hen/ *n.* poule *f.*

hence /hens/ *adv.* (*for this reason*) d'où; (*from now*) d'ici. **~forth** *adv.* désormais.

henchman /'hentʃmən/ *n.* (*pl.* -men) acolyte *m.*, homme de main *m.*

henpecked /'henpekt/ *a.* dominé or harcelé par sa femme.

hepatitis /hepə'taɪtɪs/ *n.* hépatite *f.*

her /hɜː(r)/ *pron.* la, l'*; (*after prep.*) elle. (**to**) **~**, lui. **I know ~**, je la connais. —*a.* son, sa, *pl.* ses.

herald /'herəld/ *v.t.* annoncer.

herb /hɜːb, *Amer.* ɜːb/ *n.* herbe *f.* **~s**, (*culin.*) fines herbes *f. pl.*

herd /hɜːd/ *n.* troupeau *m.* —*v.t./i.* **~ together**, (s')entasser.

here /hɪə(r)/ *adv.* ici. **~!**, (*take this*) tenez! **is ~**, **~ are**, voici. **I'm ~**, je suis là. **~abouts** *adv.* par ici.

hereafter /hɪər'ɑːftə(r)/ *adv.* après; (*in book*) ci-après.

hereby /hɪə'baɪ/ *adv.* par le présent acte; (*in letter*) par la présente.

hereditary /hə'redɪtərɪ/ *a.* héréditaire.

heredity /hə'redətɪ/ *n.* hérédité *f.*

here|sy /'herəsɪ/ *n.* hérésie *f.* **~tic** *n.* hérétique *m./f.*

herewith /hɪə'wɪð/ *adv.* (*comm.*) avec ceci, ci-joint.

heritage /'herɪtɪdʒ/ *n.* patrimoine *m.*, héritage *m.*

hermit /'hɜːmɪt/ *n.* ermite *m.*

hernia /'hɜːnɪə/ *n.* hernie *f.*

hero /'hɪərəʊ/ *n.* (*pl.* -oes) héros *m.* **~ine** /'herəʊɪn/ *n.* héroïne *f.* **~ism** /'herəʊɪzəm/ *n.* héroïsme *m.*

heroic /hɪ'rəʊɪk/ *a.* héroïque.

heroin /'herəʊɪn/ *n.* héroïne *f.*

heron /'herən/ *n.* héron *m.*

herpes /'hɜːpiːz/ *n.* herpès *m.*

herring /'herɪŋ/ *n.* hareng *m.*

hers /hɜːz/ *poss. pron.* le sien, la sienne, les sien(ne)s. **it is ~**, c'est à elle or le sien.

herself /hɜː'self/ *pron.* elle-même; (*reflexive*) se; (*after prep.*) elle.

hesitant /'hezɪtənt/ *a.* hésitant.

hesitat|e /'hezɪteɪt/ *v.i.* hésiter. **~ion** /-'teɪʃn/ *n.* hésitation *f.*

het /het/ *a.* **~ up**, (*sl.*) énervé.

heterosexual /hetərəʊ'seksjʊəl/ *a. & n.* hétérosexuel(le) (*m.* (*f.*)).

hexagon /'heksəgən/ *n.* hexagone *m.* **~al** /-'ægənl/ *a.* hexagonal.

hey /heɪ/ *int.* dites donc.

heyday /'heɪdeɪ/ *n.* apogée *m.*

HGV *abbr.* **see heavy goods vehicle.**

hi /haɪ/ *int.* (*greeting*: *Amer.*) salut.

hibernat|e /'haɪbəneɪt/ *v.i.* hiberner. **~ion** /-'neɪʃn/ *n.* hibernation *f.*

hiccup /'hɪkʌp/ *n.* hoquet *m.* —*v.i.* hoqueter. (**the**) **~s**, le hoquet.

hide[1] /haɪd/ *v.t.* (*p.t.* **hid**, *p.p.* **hidden**) cacher (**from**, à). —*v.i.* se cacher (**from**, de). **go into hiding**, se cacher. **~out** *n.* (*fam.*) cachette *f.*

hide[2] /haɪd/ *n.* (*skin*) peau *f.*

hideous /'hɪdɪəs/ *a.* (*dreadful*) atroce; (*ugly*) hideux.

hiding /'haɪdɪŋ/ *n.* (*thrashing*: *fam.*) correction *f.*

hierarchy /'haɪərɑːkɪ/ *n.* hiérarchie *f.*

hi-fi /haɪ'faɪ/ *a. & n.* hi-fi *a. & f. invar.*; (*machine*) chaîne hi-fi *f.*

high /haɪ/ *a.* (**-er, -est**) haut; (*price, number*) élevé; (*priest, speed*) grand; (*voice*) aigu. —*n.* a

(new) ∼, (recorded level) un record. —adv. haut. ∼ **chair**, chaise haute f. ∼**-handed** a. autoritaire. ∼**-jump**, saut en hauteur m. ∼**-level** a. de haut niveau. ∼**-rise** building, tour f. ∼ **road**, grand-route f. ∼ **school**, lycée m. **in the** ∼ **season**, en pleine saison. ∼ **speed** a. ultra-rapide. ∼ **spot**, (fam.) point culminant m. ∼ **street**, grand-rue f. ∼**-strung** a. (Amer.) nerveux. ∼ **tea**, goûter-dîner m. ∼**er education**, enseignement supérieur m.

highbrow /'haɪbraʊ/ a. & n. intellectuel(le) (m. (f.)).

highlight /'haɪlaɪt/ n. (vivid moment) moment fort m. ∼**s**, (in hair) balayage m. recorded ∼**s**, extraits enregistrés m. pl. —v.t. (emphasize) souligner.

highly /'haɪlɪ/ adv. extrêmement; (paid) très bien. ∼**-strung** a. nerveux. **speak/think** ∼ **of**, dire/penser du bien de.

Highness /'haɪnɪs/ n. Altesse f.

highway /'haɪweɪ/ n. route nationale f. ∼ **code**, code de la route m.

hijack /'haɪdʒæk/ v.t. détourner. —n. détournement m. ∼**er** m. pirate (de l'air) m.

hike /haɪk/ n. randonnée f. —v.i. faire de la randonnée. **price** ∼, hausse de prix f. ∼**r** /-ə(r)/ n. randonneu|r, -se m.f.

hilarious /hɪ'leərɪəs/ a. (funny) désopilant.

hill /hɪl/ n. colline f.; (slope) côte f. ∼**y** a. accidenté.

hillside /'hɪlsaɪd/ n. coteau m.

hilt /hɪlt/ n. (of sword) garde f. **to the** ∼, tout à fait, au maximum.

him /hɪm/ pron. le, l'*; (after prep.) lui. **(to)** ∼, lui. **I know** ∼, je le connais.

himself /hɪm'self/ pron. lui-même; (reflexive) se; (after prep.) lui.

hind /haɪnd/ a. de derrière.

hind|er /'hɪndə(r)/ v.t. (hamper) gêner; (prevent) empêcher. ∼**rance** n. obstacle m., gêne f.

hindsight /'haɪndsaɪt/ n. **with** ∼, rétrospectivement.

Hindu /hɪn'duː/ a. & n. hindou(e) (m. (f.)). ∼**ism** /'hɪnduːɪzəm/ n. hindouisme m.

hinge /hɪndʒ/ n. charnière f. —v.i. ∼ **on**, (depend on) dépendre de.

hint /hɪnt/ n. allusion f.; (advice) conseil m. —v.t. laisser entendre. —v.i. ∼ **at**, faire allusion à.

hip /hɪp/ n. hanche f.

hippie /'hɪpɪ/ n. hippie m./f.

hippopotamus /hɪpə'pɒtəməs/ n. (pl. **-muses**) hippopotame m.

hire /'haɪə(r)/ v.t. (thing) louer; (person) engager. —n. location f. ∼**-car** n. voiture de location f. ∼**-purchase** n. achat à crédit m., vente à crédit f.

his /hɪz/ a. son, sa, pl. ses. —poss. pron. le sien, la sienne, les sien(ne)s. **it is** ∼, c'est à lui or le sien.

hiss /hɪs/ n. sifflement m. —v.t./i. siffler.

historian /hɪ'stɔːrɪən/ n. historien(ne) m. (f.).

history /'hɪstərɪ/ n. histoire f. **make** ∼**y**, entrer dans l'histoire. ∼**ic(al)** /hɪ'stɒrɪk(l)/ a. historique.

hit /hɪt/ v.t. (p.t. **hit**, pres. p. **hitting**) frapper; (knock against, collide with) heurter; (find) trouver; (affect, reach) toucher. —v.i. ∼ **on**, (find) tomber sur. —n. (blow) coup m.; (fig.) succès m.; (song) tube m. ∼ **it off**, s'entendre bien (with, avec). ∼**-or-miss** a. fait au petit bonheur.

hitch /hɪtʃ/ v.t. (fasten) accrocher. —n. (snag) anicroche f. ∼ **a lift**, ∼**-hike** v.i. faire de l'auto-stop. ∼**-hiker** n. auto-stoppeu|r, -se m., f. ∼ **up**, (pull up) remonter.

hi-tech /haɪˈtek/ a. & n. high-tech (m.) invar.

hitherto /hɪðəˈtuː/ adv. jusqu'ici.

HIV abbr. HIV. ~-**positive** a. séropositif.

hive /haɪv/ n. ruche f. —v.t. ~ **off**, séparer; (industry) vendre.

hoard /hɔːd/ v.t. amasser. —n. réserve(s) f. (pl.); (of money) magot m., trésor m.

hoarding /ˈhɔːdɪŋ/ n. panneau d'affichage m.

hoar-frost /ˈhɔːfrɒst/ n. givre m.

hoarse /hɔːs/ a. (-er, -est) enroué. ~**ness** n. enrouement m.

hoax /həʊks/ n. canular m. —v.t. faire un canular à.

hob /hɒb/ n. plaque chauffante f.

hobble /ˈhɒbl/ v.i. clopiner.

hobby /ˈhɒbɪ/ n. passe-temps m. invar. ~-**horse** n. (fig.) dada m.

hob-nob /ˈhɒbnɒb/ v.i. (p.t. hob-nobbed) ~ **with**, frayer avec.

hock¹ /hɒk/ n. vin du Rhin m.

hock² /hɒk/ n. (pawn: sl.) mettre au clou.

hockey /ˈhɒkɪ/ n. hockey m.

hoe /həʊ/ n. binette f. —v.t. (pres. p. **hoeing**) biner.

hog /hɒg/ n. cochon m. —v.t. (p.t. **hogged**) (fam.) accaparer.

hoist /hɔɪst/ v.t. hisser. —n. palan m.

hold¹ /həʊld/ v.t. (p.t. **held**) tenir; (contain) contenir; (interest, breath, etc.) retenir; (possess) avoir; (believe) maintenir. —v.i. (of rope, weather, etc.) tenir. —n. prise f. **get** ~ **of**, saisir; (fig.) trouver. **on** ~, en suspens. **~ back**, (contain) retenir; (hide) cacher. **~ down**, (job) garder; (in struggle) retenir. **~ on**, (stand firm) tenir bon; (wait) attendre. **~ on to**, (keep) garder; (cling to) se cramponner à. **~ one's tongue**, se taire. **~ out** v.t. (offer) offrir; v.i. (resist) tenir le coup. **~ (the line), please**, ne quittez pas.

~ up, (support) soutenir; (delay) retarder; (rob) attaquer. **~-up** n. retard m.; (of traffic) bouchon m.; (robbery) hold-up m. invar. **not ~ with**, désapprouver. **~er** n. déten|teur, -trice m., f.; (of post) titulaire m./f.; (for object) support m.

hold² /həʊld/ n. (of ship) cale f.

holdall /ˈhəʊldɔːl/ n. (bag) fourre-tout m. invar.

holding /ˈhəʊldɪŋ/ n. (possession, land) possession f. ~ **company**, holding m.

hole /həʊl/ n. trou m. —v.t. trouer.

holiday /ˈhɒlədeɪ/ n. vacances f. pl.; (public) jour férié m.; (day off) congé m. —v.i. passer ses vacances. —a. de vacances. ~-**maker** n. vacanc|ier, -ière m., f.

holiness /ˈhəʊlɪnɪs/ n. sainteté f.

holistic /həʊˈlɪstɪk/ a. holistique.

Holland /ˈhɒlənd/ n. Hollande f.

hollow /ˈhɒləʊ/ a. creux; (fig.) faux. —n. creux m. —v.t. creuser.

holly /ˈhɒlɪ/ n. houx m.

holster /ˈhəʊlstə(r)/ n. étui de revolver m.

holy /ˈhəʊlɪ/ a. (-ier, -iest) saint, sacré; (water) bénit. **H~ Ghost**, **H~ Spirit**, Saint-Esprit m.

homage /ˈhɒmɪdʒ/ n. hommage m.

home /həʊm/ n. maison f., foyer m.; (institution) maison f.; (for soldiers, workers) foyer m.; (country) pays natal m. —a. de la maison, du foyer; (of family) de famille; (pol.) national, intérieur; (match, visit) à domicile. —adv. (at) ~, à la maison, chez soi. **come** or **go** ~, rentrer; (from abroad) rentrer dans son pays. **feel at** ~ **with**, être à l'aise avec. **H~ Counties**, région autour de Londres f. ~-**made** a. (food) fait maison; (clothes) fait à la maison. **H~ Office**, ministère de l'Intérieur m. **H~ Secretary**, ministre de l'Intérieur m.

town, ville natale *f.* ~ **truth**, vérité bien sentie *f.* ~**less** *a.* sans abri.

homeland /'həʊmlænd/ *n.* patrie *f.*

homely /'həʊmlɪ/ *a.* (**-ier**, **-iest**) simple; (*person: Amer.*) assez laid.

homesick /'həʊmsɪk/ *a.* **be ~**, avoir le mal du pays.

homeward /'həʊmwəd/ *a.* (*journey*) de retour.

homework /'həʊmwɜːk/ *n.* devoirs *m. pl.*

homicide /'hɒmɪsaɪd/ *n.* homicide *m.*

homœopath|y /həʊmɪ'ɒpəθɪ/ *n.* homéopathie *f.* ~**ic** *a.* homéopathique.

homogeneous /hɒmə'dʒiːnɪəs/ *a.* homogène.

homosexual /hɒmə'sekʃʊəl/ *a.* & *n.* homosexuel(le) (*m.* (*f.*)).

honest /'ɒnɪst/ *a.* honnête; (*frank*) franc. ~**ly** *adv.* honnêtement; franchement. ~**y** *n.* honnêteté *f.*

honey /'hʌnɪ/ *n.* miel *m.*; (*person: fam.*) chéri(e) *m.* (*f.*).

honeycomb /'hʌnɪkəʊm/ *n.* rayon de miel *m.*

honeymoon /'hʌnɪmuːn/ *n.* lune de miel *f.*

honk /hɒŋk/ *v.i.* klaxonner.

honorary /'ɒnərərɪ/ *a.* (*person*) honoraire; (*duties*) honorifique.

honour, (*Amer.*) **honor** /'ɒnə(r)/ *n.* honneur *m.* —*v.t.* honorer. ~**able** *a.* honorable.

hood /hʊd/ *n.* capuchon *m.*; (*car roof*) capote *f.*; (*car engine cover: Amer.*) capot *m.*

hoodlum /'huːdləm/ *n.* voyou *m.*

hoodwink /'hʊdwɪŋk/ *v.t.* tromper.

hoof /huːf/ *n.* (*pl.* **-fs**) sabot *m.*

hook /hʊk/ *n.* crochet *m.*; (*on garment*) agrafe *f.*; (*for fishing*) hameçon *m.* —*v.t./i.* (s')accrocher; (*garment*) (s')agrafer. **off the ~**, tiré d'affaire; (*phone*) décroché.

hooked /hʊkt/ *a.* crochu. ~ **on**, (*sl.*) adonné à.

hooker /'hʊkə(r)/ *n.* (*rugby*) talonneur *m.*; (*Amer., sl.*) prostituée *f.*

hookey /'hʊkɪ/ *n.* **play ~**, (*Amer., sl.*) faire l'école buissonnière.

hooligan /'huːlɪgən/ *n.* houligan *m.*

hoop /huːp/ *n.* (*toy etc.*) cerceau *m.*

hooray /hʊ'reɪ/ *int.* & *n.* = **hurrah**.

hoot /huːt/ *n.* (h)ululement *m.*; coup de klaxon *m.*; huée *f.* —*v.i.* (*owl*) (h)ululer; (*of car*) klaxonner; (*jeer*) huer. ~**er** *n.* klaxon *m.* (P.); (*of factory*) sirène *f.*

Hoover /'huːvə(r)/ *n.* (P.) aspirateur *m.* —*v.t.* passer à l'aspirateur.

hop[1] /hɒp/ *v.i.* (*p.t.* **hopped**) sauter (à cloche-pied). —*n.* saut *m.*; (*flight*) étape *f.* ~ **in**, (*fam.*) monter. ~ **it**, (*sl.*) décamper. ~ **out**, (*fam.*) descendre.

hop[2] /hɒp/ *n.* ~(**s**), houblon *m.*

hope /həʊp/ *n.* espoir *m.* —*v.t./i.* espérer. ~ **for**, espérer (avoir). **I ~ so**, je l'espère. ~**ful** *a.* encourageant. **be ~ful (that)**, avoir bon espoir (que). ~**fully** *adv.* avec espoir; (*it is hoped*) on l'espère. ~**less** *a.* sans espoir; (*useless: fig.*) nul. ~**lessly** *adv.* sans espoir *m.*

hopscotch /'hɒpskɒtʃ/ *n.* marelle *f.*

horde /hɔːd/ *n.* horde *f.*, foule *f.*

horizon /hə'raɪzn/ *n.* horizon *m.*

horizontal /hɒrɪ'zɒntl/ *a.* horizontal.

hormone /'hɔːməʊn/ *n.* hormone *f.*

horn /hɔːn/ *n.* corne *f.*; (*of car*) klaxon *m.* (P.); (*mus.*) cor *m.* —*v.i.* ~ **in**, (*sl.*) interrompre. ~**y** *a.* (*hands*) calleux.

hornet /'hɔːnɪt/ *n.* frelon *m.*

horoscope /'hɒrəskəʊp/ *n.* horoscope *m.*

horrible /'hɒrəbl/ a. horrible.

horrid /'hɒrɪd/ a. horrible.

horrific /hə'rɪfɪk/ a. horrifiant.

horr|or /'hɒrə(r)/ n. horreur f. —a. (film etc.) d'épouvante. **~ify** v.t. horrifier.

hors-d'œuvre /ɔ:'dɜ:vrə/ n. hors d'œuvre m. invar.

horse /hɔ:s/ n. cheval m. **~chestnut** n. marron (d'Inde) m. **~race** n. course de chevaux f. **~radish** n. raifort m. **~sense**, (fam.) bon sens m.

horseback /'hɔ:sbæk/ n. on **~**, à cheval.

horseman /'hɔ:smən/ n. (pl. -men) cavalier m.

horsepower /'hɔ:spauə(r)/ n. (unit) cheval (vapeur) m.

horseshoe /'hɔ:sʃu:/ n. fer à cheval m.

horsy /'hɔ:sɪ/ a. (face etc.) chevalin.

horticultur|e /'hɔ:tɪkʌltʃə(r)/ n. horticulture f. **~al** /-'kʌltʃərəl/ a. horticole.

hose /həʊz/ n. (tube) tuyau m. —v.t. arroser. **~-pipe** n. tuyau m.

hosiery /'həʊzɪərɪ/ n. bonneterie f.

hospice /'hɒspɪs/ n. hospice m.

hospit|able /hɒ'spɪtəbl/ a. hospitalier. **~ably** adv. avec hospitalité. **~ality** /-'tælətɪ/ n. hospitalité f.

hospital /'hɒspɪtl/ n. hôpital m.

host¹ /həʊst/ n. (to guests) hôte m.; (on TV) animateur m. **~ess** n. hôtesse f.

host² /həʊst/ n. **a ~ of**, une foule de.

host³ /həʊst/ n. (relig.) hostie f.

hostage /'hɒstɪdʒ/ n. otage m.

hostel /'hɒstl/ n. foyer m. **(youth) ~**, auberge (de jeunesse) f.

hostil|e /'hɒstaɪl/ a. hostile. **~ity** /hɒ'stɪlətɪ/ n. hostilité f.

hot /hɒt/ a. (**hotter**, **hottest**) chaud; (culin.) épicé; (news)

récent. **be** or **feel ~**, avoir chaud. **it is ~**, il fait chaud. —v.t./i. (p.t. **hotted**) **~ up**, (fam.) chauffer. **~ dog**, hot-dog m. **~ line**, téléphone rouge m. **~ shot**, (Amer., sl.) crack m. **~water bottle**, bouillotte f. **in ~ water**, (fam.) dans le pétrin. **~ly** adv. vivement.

hotbed /'hɒtbed/ n. foyer m.

hotchpotch /'hɒtʃpɒtʃ/ n. fatras m.

hotel /həʊ'tel/ n. hôtel m. **~ier** /-ɪeɪ/ n. hôtel|ier, -ière m., f.

hothead /'hɒthed/ n. tête brûlée f. **~ed** a. impétueux.

hotplate /'hɒtpleɪt/ n. plaque chauffante f.

hound /haʊnd/ n. chien courant m. —v.t. poursuivre.

hour /'aʊə(r)/ n. heure f. **~ly** a. & adv. toutes les heures. **~ly rate**, tarif horaire m. **paid ~ly**, payé à l'heure.

house¹ /haʊs/ n. (pl. -s /'haʊzɪz/) n. maison f.; (theatre) salle f.; (pol.) chambre f. **~-proud** a. méticuleux. **~-warming** n. pendaison de la crémaillère f.

house² /haʊz/ v.t. loger; (of building) abriter; (keep) garder.

housebreaking /'haʊsbreɪkɪŋ/ n. cambriolage m.

housecoat /'haʊskəʊt/ n. blouse f., tablier m.

household /'haʊshəʊld/ n. (house, family) ménage m. —a. ménager. **~er** n. occupant(e) m. (f.); (owner) propriétaire m./f.

housekeep|er /'haʊski:pə(r)/ n. gouvernante f. **~ing** n. ménage m.

housewife /'haʊswaɪf/ n. (pl. -wives) ménagère f.

housework /'haʊswɜ:k/ n. ménage m. travaux de ménage m. pl.

housing /'haʊzɪŋ/ n. logement m. **~ association**, service de logement m. **~ development**, cité f.

hovel /'hɒvl/ n. taudis m.

hover /'hɒvə(r)/ v.i. (bird, threat, etc.) planer; (loiter) rôder.

hovercraft /'hɒvəkrɑːft/ n. aéroglisseur m.

how /haʊ/ adv. comment. ~ long/tall is ...?, quelle est la longueur/hauteur de ...? ~ pretty!, comme or que c'est joli! ~ about a walk?, si on faisait une promenade? ~ are you?, comment allez-vous? ~ do you do?, (introduction) enchanté. ~ many?, ~ much?, combien?

however /haʊ'evə(r)/ adv. de quelque manière que; (nevertheless) cependant. ~ small/delicate/etc. it may be, quelque petit/délicat/etc. que ce soit.

howl /haʊl/ n. hurlement m. —v.i. hurler.

howler /'haʊlə(r)/ n. (fam.) bévue f.

HP abbr. see **hire-purchase**.

hp abbr. see **horsepower**.

HQ abbr. see **headquarters**.

hub /hʌb/ n. moyeu m.; (fig.) centre m. ~cap n. enjoliveur m.

hubbub /'hʌbʌb/ n. vacarme m.

huddle /'hʌdl/ v.i. se blottir.

hue[1] /hjuː/ n. (colour) teinte f.

hue[2] /hjuː/ n. ~ and cry, clameur f.

huff /hʌf/ n. in a ~, fâché, vexé.

hug /hʌɡ/ v.t. (p.t. hugged) serrer dans ses bras; (keep close to) serrer. —n. étreinte f.

huge /hjuːdʒ/ a. énorme. ~ly adv. énormément.

hulk /hʌlk/ n. (of ship) épave f.; (person) mastodonte m.

hull /hʌl/ n. (of ship) coque f.

hullo /hə'ləʊ/ int. & n. = **hallo**.

hum /hʌm/ v.t./i. (p.t. hummed) (person) fredonner; (insect) bourdonner; (engine) vrombir. —n. bourdonnement m.; vrombissement m. ~ and haw, hésiter.

human /'hjuːmən/ a. humain. —n. être humain m. ~itarian /-mənɪ'teərɪən/ a. humanitaire.

humane /hjuː'meɪn/ a. humain, plein d'humanité.

humanity /hjuː'mænətɪ/ n. humanité f.

humble /'hʌmbl/ a. (-er, -est) humble. —v.t. humilier. ~y adv. humblement.

humbug /'hʌmbʌɡ/ n. (false talk) hypocrisie f.

humdrum /'hʌmdrʌm/ a. monotone.

humid /'hjuːmɪd/ a. humide. ~ity /-'ɪmdətɪ/ n. humidité f.

humiliate /hjuː'mɪlɪeɪt/ v.t. humilier. ~ion /-'eɪʃn/ n. humiliation f.

humility /hjuː'mɪlətɪ/ n. humilité f.

humorist /'hjuːmərɪst/ n. humoriste m./f.

humour, (Amer.) **humor** /'hjuːmə(r)/ n. humour m.; (mood) humeur f. —v.t. ménager. ~ous a. humoristique; (person) plein d'humour. ~ously adv. avec humour.

hump /hʌmp/ n. bosse f. —v.t. voûter. the ~, (sl.) le cafard.

hunch[1] /hʌntʃ/ v.t. voûter.

hunch[2] /hʌntʃ/ n. petite idée f.

hunchback /'hʌntʃbæk/ n. bossu(e) m. (f.).

hundred /'hʌndrəd/ a. & n. cent (m.). ~s of, des centaines de. ~fold a. centuple; adv. au centuple. ~th a. & n. centième (m./f.).

hundredweight /'hʌndrədweɪt/ n. 50.8 kg.; (Amer.) 45.36 kg.

hung /hʌŋ/ see **hang**.

Hungar|y /'hʌŋɡərɪ/ n. Hongrie f. ~ian /-'ɡeərɪən/ a. & n. hongrois(e) (m. (f.)).

hunger /'hʌŋɡə(r)/ n. faim f. —v.i. ~ for, avoir faim de. ~-strike n. grève de la faim f.

hungr|y /'hʌŋgrɪ/ a. (-ier, -iest) affamé. **be ~y**, avoir faim. **~ily** adv. avidement.

hunk /hʌŋk/ n. gros morceau m.

hunt /hʌnt/ v.t./i. chasser. —n. chasse f. **~ for**, chercher. **~er** n. chasseur m. **~ing** n. chasse f.

hurdle /'hɜːdl/ n. (sport) haie f.; (fig.) obstacle m.

hurl /hɜːl/ v.t. lancer.

hurrah, hurray /hʊ'rɑː, hʊ'reɪ/ int. & n. hourra (m.).

hurricane /'hʌrɪkən, Amer. 'hʌrɪkeɪn/ n. ouragan m.

hurried /'hʌrɪd/ a. précipité. **~ly** adv. précipitamment.

hurry /'hʌrɪ/ v.i. se dépêcher, se presser. —v.t. presser, activer. —n. hâte f. **in a ~**, pressé.

hurt /hɜːt/ v.t./i. (p.t. hurt) faire mal (à); (injure, offend) blesser. —a. blessé. —n. mal m. **~ful** a. blessant.

hurtle /'hɜːtl/ v.t. lancer. —v.i. **~ along**, avancer à toute vitesse.

husband /'hʌzbənd/ n. mari m.

hush /hʌʃ/ v.t. faire taire. —n. silence m. **~-hush** a. (fam.) ultra-secret. **~ up**, (news etc.) étouffer.

husk /hʌsk/ n. (of grain) enveloppe f.

husky /'hʌskɪ/ a. (-ier, -iest) (hoarse) rauque; (burly) costaud. —n. chien de traîneau m.

hustle /'hʌsl/ v.t. (push, rush) bousculer. —v.i. (work busily; Amer.) se démener. —n. bousculade f. **~ and bustle**, agitation f.

hut /hʌt/ n. cabane f.

hutch /hʌtʃ/ n. clapier m.

hyacinth /'haɪəsɪnθ/ n. jacinthe f.

hybrid /'haɪbrɪd/ a. & n. hybride (m.).

hydrangea /haɪ'dreɪndʒə/ n. hortensia m.

hydrant /'haɪdrənt/ n. **(fire) ~**, bouche d'incendie f.

hydraulic /haɪ'drɔːlɪk/ a. hydraulique.

hydroelectric /haɪdrəʊɪ'lektrɪk/ a. hydro-électrique.

hydrofoil /'haɪdrəʊfɔɪl/ n. hydroptère m.

hydrogen /'haɪdrədʒən/ n. hydrogène m. **~ bomb**, bombe à hydrogène f.

hyena /haɪ'iːnə/ n. hyène f.

hygiene /'haɪdʒiːn/ n. hygiène f.

hygienic /haɪ'dʒiːnɪk/ a. hygiénique.

hymn /hɪm/ n. cantique m., hymne m.

hype /haɪp/ n. tapage publicitaire m. —v.t. faire du tapage autour de.

hyper- /haɪpə(r)/ pref. hyper-.

hypermarket /'haɪpəmɑːkɪt/ n. hypermarché m.

hyphen /'haɪfn/ n. trait d'union m. **~ate** v.t. mettre un trait d'union à.

hypno|sis /hɪp'nəʊsɪs/ n. hypnose f. **~tic** /-'nɒtɪk/ a. hypnotique.

hypnot|ize /'hɪpnətaɪz/ v.t. hypnotiser. **~ism** n. hypnotisme m.

hypochondriac /haɪpə'kɒndriæk/ n. malade imaginaire m./f.

hypocrisy /hɪ'pɒkrəsɪ/ n. hypocrisie f.

hypocrit|e /'hɪpəkrɪt/ n. hypocrite m./f. **~ical** /-'krɪtɪkl/ a. hypocrite.

hypodermic /haɪpə'dɜːmɪk/ a. hypodermique. —n. seringue hypodermique f.

hypothermia /haɪpə'θɜːmɪə/ n. hypothermie f.

hypothe|sis /haɪ'pɒθəsɪs/ n. (pl. -theses /-siːz/) hypothèse f. **~tical** /-ə'θetɪkl/ a. hypothétique.

hyster|ia /hɪ'stɪərɪə/ n. hystérie f. **~ical** /-erɪkl/ a. hystérique; (person) surexcité.

hysterics /hɪ'sterɪks/ n. pl. crise de nerfs or de rire f.

I

I /aɪ/ *pron.* je, j'*; (*stressed*) moi.

ice /aɪs/ *n.* glace *f.; (on road)* verglas *m.* —*v.t.* (*cake*) glacer. —*v.i.* ~ (**up**), (*window*) se givrer; (*river*) geler. ~-**cream** *n.* glace *f.* ~-**cube** *n.* glaçon *m.* ~ **hockey**, hockey sur glace *m.* ~ **lolly**, glace (*sur bâtonnet*) *f.* ~ **rink**, patinoire *f.* ~ **skate**, patin à glace *m.*

iceberg /ˈaɪsbɜːɡ/ *n.* iceberg *m.*

icebox /ˈaɪsbɒks/ *n.* (*Amer.*) réfrigérateur *m.*

Iceland /ˈaɪslənd/ *n.* Islande *f.* ~**er** *n.* Islandais(e) *m.* (*f.*). ~**ic** /-ˈlændɪk/ *a.* islandais; *n.* (*lang.*) islandais *m.*

icicle /ˈaɪsɪkl/ *n.* glaçon *m.*

icing /ˈaɪsɪŋ/ *n.* (*sugar*) glace *f.*

icon /ˈaɪkɒn/ *n.* icône *f.*

icy /ˈaɪsɪ/ *a.* (-**ier**, -**iest**) (*hands, wind*) glacé; (*road*) verglacé; (*manner, welcome*) glacial.

idea /aɪˈdɪə/ *n.* idée *f.*

ideal /aɪˈdɪəl/ *a.* idéal. —*n.* idéal *m.* ~**ize** *v.t.* idéaliser. ~**ly** *adv.* idéalement.

idealis|t /aɪˈdɪəlɪst/ *n.* idéaliste *m./f.* ~**m** /-zəm/ *n.* idéalisme *m.* ~**tic** /-ˈlɪstɪk/ *a.* idéaliste.

identical /aɪˈdentɪkl/ *a.* identique.

identif|y /aɪˈdentɪfaɪ/ *v.t.* identifier. —*v.i.* ~**y with**, s'identifier à. ~**ication** /-ɪˈkeɪʃn/ *n.* identification *f.; (*papers*) une pièce d'identité.

identikit /aɪˈdentɪkɪt/ *n.* ~ **picture**, portrait-robot *m.*

identity /aɪˈdentətɪ/ *n.* identité *f.*

ideolog|y /aɪdɪˈɒlədʒɪ/ *n.* idéologie *f.* ~**ical** /-əˈlɒdʒɪkl/ *a.* idéologique.

idiocy /ˈɪdɪəsɪ/ *n.* idiotie *f.*

idiom /ˈɪdɪəm/ *n.* expression idiomatique *f.; (*language*) idiome *m.* ~**atic** /-ˈmætɪk/ *a.* idiomatique.

idiosyncrasy /ɪdɪəˈsɪŋkrəsɪ/ *n.* particularité *f.*

idiot /ˈɪdɪət/ *n.* idiot(e) *m.* (*f.*). ~**ic** /-ˈɒtɪk/ *a.* idiot.

idle /ˈaɪdl/ *a.* (-**er**, -**est**) désœuvré, oisif; (*lazy*) paresseux; (*unemployed*) sans travail; (*machine*) au repos; (*fig.*) vain. —*v.i.* (*engine*) tourner au ralenti. —*v.t.* ~ **away**, gaspiller. ~**ness** *n.* oisiveté *f.* ~**r** /-ə(r)/ *n.* oisif, -ve *m., f.*

idol /ˈaɪdl/ *n.* idole *f.* ~**ize** *v.t.* idolâtrer.

idyllic /ɪˈdɪlɪk, *Amer.* aɪˈdɪlɪk/ *a.* idyllique.

i.e. *abbr.* c'est-à-dire.

if /ɪf/ *conj.* si.

igloo /ˈɪɡluː/ *n.* igloo *m.*

ignite /ɪɡˈnaɪt/ *v.t./i.* (s')enflammer.

ignition /ɪɡˈnɪʃn/ *n.* (*auto.*) allumage *m.* ~ **key**, clé de contact. ~ (**switch**), contact *m.*

ignorant /ˈɪɡnərənt/ *a.* ignorant (*of*, de). ~**ce** *n.* ignorance *f.* ~**tly** *adv.* par ignorance.

ignore /ɪɡˈnɔː(r)/ *v.t.* ne faire *or* prêter aucune attention à; (*person in street etc.*) faire semblant de ne pas voir; (*facts*) ne pas tenir compte de.

ilk /ɪlk/ *n.* (*kind: fam.*) acabit *m.*

ill /ɪl/ *a.* malade; (*bad*) mauvais. —*adv.* mal. ~ **n.** mal *m.* ~-**advised** *a.* peu judicieux. ~ **at ease**, mal à l'aise. ~-**bred** *a.* mal élevé. ~-**fated** *a.* malheureux. ~ **feeling**, ressentiment *m.* ~-**gotten** *a.* mal acquis. ~-**natured** *a.* désagréable. ~-**treat** *v.t.* maltraiter. ~ **will**, malveillance *f.*

illegal /ɪˈliːɡl/ *a.* illégal.

illegible /ɪˈledʒəbl/ *a.* illisible.

illegitima|te /ɪlɪˈdʒɪtɪmət/ a. illégitime. ~cy n. illégitimité f.

illitera|te /ɪˈlɪtərət/ a. & n. illettré(e) (m. (f.)), analphabète m./f. ~cy n. analphabétisme m.

illness /ˈɪlnɪs/ n. maladie f.

illogical /ɪˈlɒdʒɪkl/ a. illogique.

illuminat|e /ɪˈluːmɪneɪt/ v.t. éclairer; (decorate with lights) illuminer. ~ion /-ˈneɪʃn/ n. éclairage f.; illumination f.

illusion /ɪˈluːʒn/ n. illusion f.

illusory /ɪˈluːsərɪ/ a. illusoire.

illustrat|e /ˈɪləstreɪt/ v.t. illustrer. ~ion /-ˈstreɪʃn/ n. illustration f. ~ive /-ətɪv/ a. qui illustre.

illustrious /ɪˈlʌstrɪəs/ a. illustre.

image /ˈɪmɪdʒ/ n. image f. (public) ~, (of firm, person) image de marque f. ~ry /-ərɪ/ n. images f. pl.

imaginary /ɪˈmædʒɪnərɪ/ a. imaginaire.

imaginat|ion /ɪmædʒɪˈneɪʃn/ n. imagination f. ~ive /ɪˈmædʒɪnətɪv/ a. plein d'imagination.

imagin|e /ɪˈmædʒɪn/ v.t. (picture to o.s.) (s')imaginer; (suppose) imaginer. ~able a. imaginable.

imbalance /ɪmˈbæləns/ n. déséquilibre m.

imbecile /ˈɪmbəsiːl/ n. & a. imbécile (m./f.).

imbue /ɪmˈbjuː/ v.t. imprégner.

imitat|e /ˈɪmɪteɪt/ v.t. imiter. ~ion /-ˈteɪʃn/ n. imitation f. ~or n. imita|teur, -trice m., f.

immaculate /ɪˈmækjʊlət/ a. (room, dress, etc.) impeccable.

immaterial /ɪməˈtɪərɪəl/ a. sans importance (to, pour; that, que).

immature /ɪməˈtjʊə(r)/ a. pas mûr; (person) immature.

immediate /ɪˈmiːdɪət/ a. immédiat. ~ly adv. immédiatement; conj. dès que.

immens|e /ɪˈmens/ a. immense. ~ely adv. extrêmement, immensément. ~ity n. immensité f.

immers|e /ɪˈmɜːs/ v.t. plonger, immerger. ~ion /-ˈɜːʃn/ n. immersion f. ~ion heater, chauffe-eau (électrique) m. invar.

immigr|ate /ˈɪmɪɡreɪt/ v.t. immigrer. ~ant n. & a. immigré(e) (m. (f.)); (newly-arrived) immigrant(e) (m. (f.)). ~ation /-ˈɡreɪʃn/ n. immigration f. go through ~ation, passer le contrôle des passeports.

imminen|t /ˈɪmɪnənt/ a. imminent. ~ce n. imminence f.

immobil|e /ɪˈməʊbaɪl, Amer. ɪˈməʊbl/ a. immobile. ~ize /-əlaɪz/ v.t. immobiliser.

immoderate /ɪˈmɒdərət/ a. immodéré.

immoral /ɪˈmɒrəl/ a. immoral. ~ity /ɪməˈrælɪtɪ/ n. immoralité f.

immortal /ɪˈmɔːtl/ a. immortel. ~ity /-ˈtælɪtɪ/ n. immortalité f. ~ize v.t. immortaliser.

immun|e /ɪˈmjuːn/ a. immunisé (from, to, contre). ~ity n. immunité f.

immuniz|e /ˈɪmjʊnaɪz/ v.t. immuniser. ~ation /-ˈzeɪʃn/ n. immunisation f.

imp /ɪmp/ n. lutin m.

impact /ˈɪmpækt/ n. impact m.

impair /ɪmˈpeə(r)/ v.t. détériorer.

impart /ɪmˈpɑːt/ v.t. communiquer, transmettre.

impartial /ɪmˈpɑːʃl/ a. impartial. ~ity /-ʃɪˈælətɪ/ n. impartialité f.

impassable /ɪmˈpɑːsəbl/ a. (barrier etc.) infranchissable; (road) impraticable.

impasse /ˈæmpɑːs, Amer. ˈɪmpæs/ n. impasse f.

impassioned /ɪmˈpæʃnd/ n. passionné.

impassive /ɪmˈpæsɪv/ a. impassible.

impatien|t /ɪmˈpeɪʃnt/ a. impatient. get ~t, s'impatienter. ~ce n. impatience f. ~tly adv. impatiemment.

impeccable /ɪm'pekəbl/ a. impeccable.

impede /ɪm'piːd/ v.t. gêner.

impediment /ɪm'pedɪmənt/ n. obstacle m. **(speech)** ~, défaut d'élocution m.

impel /ɪm'pel/ v.t. (p.t. **impelled**) pousser, forcer **(to do**, à faire).

impending /ɪm'pendɪŋ/ a. imminent.

impenetrable /ɪm'penɪtrəbl/ a. impénétrable.

imperative /ɪm'perətɪv/ a. nécessaire; (need etc.) impérieux. —n. (gram.) impératif m.

imperceptible /ɪmpə'septəbl/ a. imperceptible.

imperfect /ɪm'pɜːfɪkt/ a. imparfait; (faulty) défectueux. ~**ion** /-ə'fekʃn/ n. imperfection f.

imperial /ɪm'pɪərɪəl/ a. impérial; (measure) légal (au Royaume-Uni). ~**ism** n. impérialisme m.

imperil /ɪm'perəl/ v.t. (p.t. **imperilled**) mettre en péril.

imperious /ɪm'pɪərɪəs/ a. impérieux.

impersonal /ɪm'pɜːsənl/ a. impersonnel.

impersonat|e /ɪm'pɜːsəneɪt/ v.t. se faire passer pour; (mimic) imiter. ~**ion** /-'neɪʃn/ n. imitation f. ~**or** n. imita|teur, -trice m., f.

impertinen|t /ɪm'pɜːtɪnənt/ a. impertinent. ~**ce** n. impertinence f. ~**tly** adv. avec impertinence.

impervious /ɪm'pɜːvɪəs/ a. ~ **to**, imperméable à.

impetuous /ɪm'petʃʊəs/ a. impétueux.

impetus /'ɪmpɪtəs/ n. impulsion f.

impinge /ɪm'pɪndʒ/ v.i. ~ **on**, affecter; (encroach) empiéter sur.

impish /'ɪmpɪʃ/ a. espiègle.

implacable /ɪm'plækəbl/ a. implacable.

implant /ɪm'plɑːnt/ v.t. implanter. —n. implant m.

implement¹ /'ɪmplɪmənt/ n. (tool) outil m.; (utensil) ustensile m.

implement² /'ɪmplɪment/ v.t. exécuter, mettre en pratique.

implicat|e /'ɪmplɪkeɪt/ v.t. impliquer. ~**ion** /-'keɪʃn/ n. implication f.

implicit /ɪm'plɪsɪt/ a. (implied) implicite; (unquestioning) absolu.

implore /ɪm'plɔː(r)/ v.t. implorer.

impl|y /ɪm'plaɪ/ v.t. (assume, mean) impliquer; (insinuate) laisser entendre. ~**ied** a. implicite.

impolite /ɪmpə'laɪt/ a. impoli.

imponderable /ɪm'pondərəbl/ a. & n. impondérable (m.).

import¹ /ɪm'pɔːt/ v.t. importer. ~**ation** /-'teɪʃn/ n. importation f. ~**er** n. importa|teur, -trice m., f.

import² /'ɪmpɔːt/ n. (article) importation f.; (meaning) sens m.

important /ɪm'pɔːtnt/ a. important. ~**ce** n. importance f.

impos|e /ɪm'pəʊz/ v.t. imposer. —v.i. ~ **on**, abuser de l'amabilité de. ~**ition** /-ə'zɪʃn/ n. imposition f.; (fig.) dérangement m.

imposing /ɪm'pəʊzɪŋ/ a. imposant.

impossibl|e /ɪm'posəbl/ a. impossible. ~**ility** /-'bɪlətɪ/ n. impossibilité f.

impostor /ɪm'postə(r)/ n. imposteur m.

impoten|t /'ɪmpətənt/ a. impuissant. ~**ce** n. impuissance f.

impound /ɪm'paʊnd/ v.t. confisquer, saisir.

impoverish /ɪm'povərɪʃ/ v.t. appauvrir.

impracticable /ɪm'præktɪkəbl/ a. impraticable.

impractical /ɪm'præktɪkl/ a. peu pratique.

imprecise /ɪmprɪ'saɪs/ a. imprécis.

impregnable /ɪm'pregnəbl/ a. imprenable; (fig.) inattaquable.

impregnate /ˈɪmpregneɪt/ *v.t.* im- prégner **(with,** de).

impresario /ɪmprɪˈsɑːrɪəʊ/ *n.* (*pl.* **-os)** imprésario *m.*

impress /ɪmˈpres/ *v.t.* impression- ner; (*imprint*) imprimer. **~ on s.o.,** faire comprendre à qn.

impression /ɪmˈpreʃn/ *n.* impres- sion *f.* **~able** *a.* impression- nable.

impressive /ɪmˈpresɪv/ *a.* impres- sionnant.

imprint[1] /ˈɪmprɪnt/ *n.* empreinte *f.*

imprint[2] /ɪmˈprɪnt/ *v.t.* imprimer.

imprison /ɪmˈprɪzn/ *v.t.* empri- sonner. **~ment** *n.* emprisonnement *m.,* prison *f.*

improbab|le /ɪmˈprɒbəbl/ *a.* (*not likely*) improbable; (*incredible*) invraisemblable. **~ility** /-ˈbɪlətɪ/ *n.* improbabilité *f.*

impromptu /ɪmˈprɒmptjuː/ *a.* & *adv.* impromptu.

improp|er /ɪmˈprɒpə(r)/ *a.* incon- venant, indécent; (*wrong*) incor- rect. **~riety** /-əˈpraɪətɪ/ *n.* inconvenance *f.*

improve /ɪmˈpruːv/ *v.t./i.* (s')amé- liorer. **~ment** *n.* amélioration *f.*

improvis|e /ˈɪmprəvaɪz/ *v.t./i.* im- proviser. **~ation** /-ˈzeɪʃn/ *n.* improvisation *f.*

imprudent /ɪmˈpruːdnt/ *a.* impru- dent.

impuden|t /ˈɪmpjʊdnt/ *a.* impu- dent. **~ce** *n.* impudence *f.*

impulse /ˈɪmpʌls/ *n.* impulsion *f.* **on ~,** sur un coup de tête.

impulsive /ɪmˈpʌlsɪv/ *a.* impulsif. **~ly** *adv.* par impulsion.

impunity /ɪmˈpjuːnətɪ/ *n.* im- punité *f.* **with ~,** impunément.

impur|e /ɪmˈpjʊə(r)/ *a.* impur. **~ity** *n.* impureté *f.*

impute /ɪmˈpjuːt/ *v.t.* imputer.

in /ɪn/ *prep.* dans, à, en. *—adv.* (*inside*) dedans; (*at home*) là, à la maison; (*in fashion*) à la mode. **in**

the box/garden, dans la boîte/le jardin. **in Paris/school,** à Paris/l'école. **in town,** en ville. **in the country,** à la campagne. **in winter/English,** en hiver/ anglais. **in India,** en Inde. **in Japan,** au Japon. **in a firm manner/voice,** d'une manière/ voix ferme. **in blue,** en bleu. **in ink,** à l'encre. **in uniform,** en uniforme. **in a skirt,** en jupe. **in a whisper,** en chuchotant. **in a loud voice,** d'une voix forte. **in winter,** en hiver. **in spring,** au printemps. **in an hour,** (*at end of*) au bout d'une heure. **in an hour('s time),** dans une heure. **in (the space of) an hour,** en une heure. **in doing,** en faisant. **in the evening,** le soir. **one in** ten, un sur dix. **in between,** entre les deux; (*time*) entretemps. **the best in,** le meilleur de. **we are in for,** on va avoir. **in-laws** *n. pl.* (*fam.*) beaux-parents *m. pl.* **in-patient** *n.* malade hospita- lisé(e) *m.(f.).* **the ins and outs of,** les tenants et aboutissants de. **in so far as,** dans la mesure où.

inability /ɪnəˈbɪlətɪ/ *n.* incapacité *f.* (**to do,** de faire).

inaccessible /ɪnækˈsesəbl/ *a.* inac- cessible.

inaccurate /ɪnˈækjərət/ *a.* inexact.

inaction /ɪnˈækʃn/ *n.* inaction *f.*

inactive /ɪnˈæktɪv/ *a.* inactif. **~ity** /-ˈtɪvətɪ/ *n.* inaction *f.*

inadequa|te /ɪnˈædɪkwət/ *a.* insuf- fisant. **~cy** *n.* insuffisance *f.*

inadmissible /ɪnədˈmɪsəbl/ *a.* inadmissible.

inadvertently /ɪnədˈvɜːtntlɪ/ *adv.* par mégarde.

inadvisable /ɪnədˈvaɪzəbl/ *a.* déconseillé, pas recommandé.

inane /ɪˈneɪn/ *a.* inepte.

inanimate /ɪnˈænɪmət/ *a.* inanimé.

inappropriate /ɪnəˈprəʊprɪət/ *a.* inopportun; (*term*) inapproprié.

inarticulate /ɪnɑːˈtɪkjʊlət/ a. qui a du mal à s'exprimer.

inasmuch as /ɪnəzˈmʌtʃəz/ adv. en ce sens que; (because) vu que.

inattentive /ɪnəˈtentɪv/ a. inattentif.

inaudible /ɪnˈɔːdɪbl/ a. inaudible.

inaugural /ɪˈnɔːɡjʊrəl/ a. inaugural.

inaugurat|e /ɪˈnɔːɡjʊreɪt/ v.t. (open, begin) inaugurer; (person) investir. **∼ion** /-ˈreɪʃn/ n. inauguration f.; investiture f.

inauspicious /ɪnɔːˈspɪʃəs/ a. peu propice.

inborn /ɪnˈbɔːn/ a. inné.

inbred /ɪnˈbred/ a. (inborn) inné.

inc. abbr. (incorporated) S.A.

incalculable /ɪnˈkælkjʊləbl/ a. incalculable.

incapable /ɪnˈkeɪpəbl/ a. incapable.

incapacit|y /ɪnkəˈpæsətɪ/ n. incapacité f. **∼ate** v.t. rendre incapable (de travailler etc.).

incarcerate /ɪnˈkɑːsəreɪt/ v.t. incarcérer.

incarnat|e /ɪnˈkɑːneɪt/ a. incarné. **∼ion** /-ˈneɪʃn/ n. incarnation f.

incendiary /ɪnˈsendɪərɪ/ a. incendiaire. —n. (bomb) bombe incendiaire f.

incense¹ /ˈɪnsens/ n. encens m.

incense² /ɪnˈsens/ v.t. mettre en fureur.

incentive /ɪnˈsentɪv/ n. motivation f.; (payment) prime (d'encouragement) f.

inception /ɪnˈsepʃn/ n. début m.

incessant /ɪnˈsesnt/ a. incessant. **∼ly** adv. sans cesse.

incest /ˈɪnsest/ n. inceste m. **∼uous** /ɪnˈsestjʊəs/ a. incestueux.

inch /ɪntʃ/ n. pouce m. (= 2.54 cm.). —v.i. avancer doucement.

incidence /ˈɪnsɪdəns/ n. fréquence f.

incident /ˈɪnsɪdənt/ n. incident m.; (in play, film, etc.) épisode m.

incidental /ɪnsɪˈdentl/ a. accessoire. **∼ly** adv. accessoirement; (by the way) à propos.

incinerat|e /ɪnˈsɪnəreɪt/ v.t. incinérer. **∼or** n. incinérateur m.

incipient /ɪnˈsɪpɪənt/ a. naissant.

incision /ɪnˈsɪʒn/ n. incision f.

incisive /ɪnˈsaɪsɪv/ a. incisif.

incite /ɪnˈsaɪt/ v.t. inciter, pousser. **∼ment** n. incitation f.

inclement /ɪnˈklemənt/ a. inclément, rigoureux.

inclination /ɪnklɪˈneɪʃn/ n. (propensity, bowing) inclination f.

incline¹ /ɪnˈklaɪn/ v.t./i. incliner. **be ∼d to**, avoir tendance à.

incline² /ˈɪnklaɪn/ n. pente f.

inclu|de /ɪnˈkluːd/ v.t. comprendre, inclure. **∼ding** prep. (y) compris. **∼sion** n. inclusion f.

inclusive /ɪnˈkluːsɪv/ a. & adv. inclus, compris. **be ∼ of**, comprendre, inclure.

incognito /ɪnkɒɡˈniːtəʊ/ adv. incognito.

incoherent /ɪnkəʊˈhɪərənt/ a. incohérent.

income /ˈɪnkʌm/ n. revenu m. **∼ tax**, impôt sur le revenu m.

incoming /ˈɪnkʌmɪŋ/ a. (tide) montant; (tenant etc.) nouveau.

incomparable /ɪnˈkɒmprəbl/ a. incomparable.

incompatible /ɪnkəmˈpætəbl/ a. incompatible.

incompeten|t /ɪnˈkɒmpɪtənt/ a. incompétent. **∼ce** n. incompétence f.

incomplete /ɪnkəmˈpliːt/ a. incomplet.

incomprehensible /ɪnkɒmprɪˈhensəbl/ a. incompréhensible.

inconceivable /ɪnkənˈsiːvəbl/ a. inconcevable.

inconclusive /ɪnkənˈkluːsɪv/ a. peu concluant.

incongruous /ɪnˈkɒŋgrʊəs/ a. déplacé, incongru.

inconsequential /ɪnkɒnsɪˈkwenʃl/ a. sans importance.

inconsiderate /ɪnkənˈsɪdərət/ a. (person) qui ne se soucie pas des autres; (act) irréfléchi.

inconsisten|t /ɪnkənˈsɪstənt/ a. (treatment) sans cohérence, inconséquent; (argument) contradictoire; (performance) irrégulier. ~t with, incompatible avec. ~cy n. inconséquence f. contradiction f.; irrégularité f.

inconspicuous /ɪnkənˈspɪkjʊəs/ a. peu en évidence.

incontinen|t /ɪnˈkɒntɪnənt/ a. incontinent. ~ce n. incontinence f.

inconvenien|t /ɪnkənˈviːnɪənt/ a. incommode, peu pratique; (time) mal choisi. be ~t for, ne pas convenir à. ~ce n. dérangement m.; (drawback) inconvénient m.; v.t. déranger.

incorporate /ɪnˈkɔːpəreɪt/ v.t. incorporer; (include) contenir.

incorrect /ɪnkəˈrekt/ a. inexact.

incorrigible /ɪnˈkɒrɪdʒəbl/ a. incorrigible.

incorruptible /ɪnkəˈrʌptəbl/ a. incorruptible.

increas|e[1] /ɪnˈkriːs/ v.t./i. augmenter. ~ing a. croissant. ~ingly adv. de plus en plus.

increase[2] /ˈɪnkriːs/ n. augmentation f. (in, of, de). be on the ~, augmenter.

incredible /ɪnˈkredəbl/ a. incroyable.

incredulous /ɪnˈkredjʊləs/ a. incrédule.

increment /ˈɪnkrəmənt/ n. augmentation f.

incriminat|e /ɪnˈkrɪmɪneɪt/ v.t. incriminer. ~ing a. compromettant.

incubat|e /ˈɪnkjʊbeɪt/ v.t. (eggs) couver. ~ion /-ˈbeɪʃn/ n. incubation f. ~or n. couveuse f.

inculcate /ˈɪnkʌlkeɪt/ v.t. inculquer.

incumbent /ɪnˈkʌmbənt/ n. (pol., relig.) titulaire m./f.

incur /ɪnˈkɜː(r)/ v.t. (p.t. incurred) encourir; (debts) contracter; (anger) s'exposer à.

incurable /ɪnˈkjʊərəbl/ a. incurable.

incursion /ɪnˈkɜːʃn/ n. incursion f.

indebted /ɪnˈdetɪd/ a. ~ to s.o., redevable à qn. (for, de).

indecen|t /ɪnˈdiːsnt/ a. indécent. ~cy n. indécence f.

indecision /ɪndɪˈsɪʒn/ n. indécision f.

indecisive /ɪndɪˈsaɪsɪv/ a. indécis; (ending) peu concluant.

indeed /ɪnˈdiːd/ adv. en effet, vraiment.

indefensible /ɪndɪˈfensɪbl/ a. indéfendable.

indefinable /ɪndɪˈfaɪnəbl/ a. indéfinissable.

indefinite /ɪnˈdefɪnɪt/ a. indéfini; (time) indéterminé. ~ly adv. indéfiniment.

indelible /ɪnˈdeləbl/ a. indélébile.

indemni|fy /ɪnˈdemnɪfaɪ/ v.t. (compensate) indemniser (for, de); (safeguard) garantir. ~ty /-nətɪ/ n. indemnité f.; garantie f.

indent /ɪnˈdent/ v.t. (text) renfoncer. ~ation /-ˈteɪʃn/ n. (outline) découpure f.

independen|t /ɪndɪˈpendənt/ a. indépendant. ~ce n. indépendance f. ~tly adv. de façon indépendante. ~tly of, indépendamment de.

indescribable /ɪndɪˈskraɪbəbl/ a. indescriptible.

indestructible /ɪndɪˈstrʌktəbl/ a. indestructible.

indeterminate /ɪndɪˈtɜːmɪnət/ a. indéterminé.

index /ˈɪndeks/ n. (pl. indexes)

(figure) indice *m.*; *(in book)* index *m.*; *(in library)* catalogue *m.* —*v.t.* classer. ~**card,** fiche *f.* ~**finger** index *m.* ~**-linked** *a.* indexé.

India /'ɪndɪə/ *n.* Inde *f.* ~**n** *a. & n.* indien(ne) *(m. (f.))*. ~**n summer,** été de la Saint-Martin *m.*

indicat|e /'ɪndɪkeɪt/ *v.t.* indiquer. ~**ion** /-'keɪʃn/ *n.* indication *f.* ~**or** *n.* *(device)* indicateur *m.*; *(on vehicle)* clignotant *m.*; *(board)* tableau *m.*

indicative /ɪn'dɪkətɪv/ *a.* indicatif. —*n.* *(gram.)* indicatif *m.*

indict /ɪn'daɪt/ *v.t.* accuser. ~**ment** *n.* accusation *f.*

indifferen|t /ɪn'dɪfrənt/ *a.* indifférent; *(not good)* médiocre. ~**ce** *n.* indifférence *f.*

indigenous /ɪn'dɪdʒɪnəs/ *a.* indigène.

indigest|ion /ɪndɪ'dʒestʃən/ *n.* indigestion *f.* ~**ible** /-təbl/ *a.* indigeste.

indign|ant /ɪn'dɪgnənt/ *a.* indigné. ~**ation** /-'neɪʃn/ *n.* indignation *f.*

indigo /'ɪndɪgəʊ/ *n.* indigo *m.*

indirect /ɪndɪ'rekt/ *a.* indirect. ~**ly** *adv.* indirectement.

indiscr|eet /ɪndɪ'skriːt/ *a.* indiscret; *(not wary)* imprudent. ~**etion** /-eʃn/ *n.* indiscrétion *f.*

indiscriminate /ɪndɪ'skrɪmɪnət/ *a.* qui manque de discernement; *(random)* fait au hasard. ~**ly** *adv.* sans discernement; au hasard.

indispensable /ɪndɪ'spensəbl/ *a.* indispensable.

indispos|ed /ɪndɪ'spəʊzd/ *a.* indisposé, souffrant. ~**ition** /-ə'zɪʃn/ *n.* indisposition *f.*

indisputable /ɪndɪ'spjuːtəbl/ *a.* incontestable.

indistinct /ɪndɪ'stɪŋkt/ *a.* indistinct.

indistinguishable /ɪndɪ'stɪŋgwɪʃəbl/ *a.* indifférenciable.

individual /ɪndɪ'vɪdʒʊəl/ *a.* individuel. —*n.* individu *m.* ~**ist** *n.* *m./f.* ~**ity** /-'ælətɪ/ *n.* individualité *f.* ~**ly** *adv.* individuellement.

indivisible /ɪndɪ'vɪzəbl/ *a.* indivisible.

indoctrinat|e /ɪn'dɒktrɪneɪt/ *v.t.* endoctriner. ~**ion** /-'neɪʃn/ *n.* endoctrinement *m.*

indolen|t /'ɪndələnt/ *a.* indolent. ~**ce** *n.* indolence *f.*

indomitable /ɪn'dɒmɪtəbl/ *a.* indomptable.

Indonesia /ɪndəʊ'niːzɪə/ *n.* Indonésie *f.* ~**n** *a. & n.* indonésien(ne) *(m. (f.))*.

indoor /'ɪndɔː(r)/ *a.* *(clothes etc.)* d'intérieur; *(under cover)* couvert. ~**s** /ɪn'dɔːz/ *adv.* à l'intérieur.

induce /ɪn'djuːs/ *v.t.* *(influence)* persuader; *(cause)* provoquer. ~**ment** *n.* encouragement *m.*

induct /ɪn'dʌkt/ *v.t.* investir, installer; *(mil., Amer.)* incorporer.

indulge /ɪn'dʌldʒ/ *v.t.* *(desires)* satisfaire; *(person)* se montrer indulgent pour, gâter. —*v.i.* ~**in,** se livrer à, s'offrir.

indulgen|t /ɪn'dʌldʒənt/ *a.* indulgent. ~**ce** *n.* indulgence *f.*; *(treat)* gâterie *f.*

industrial /ɪn'dʌstrɪəl/ *a.* industriel; *(unrest etc.)* ouvrier; *(action)* revendicatif; *(accident)* du travail. ~**ist** *n.* industriel(le) *m.(f.)*. ~**ized** *a.* industrialisé.

industrious /ɪn'dʌstrɪəs/ *a.* travailleur, appliqué.

industry /'ɪndəstrɪ/ *n.* industrie *f.*; *(zeal)* application *f.*

inebriated /ɪ'niːbrɪeɪtɪd/ *a.* ivre.

inedible /ɪn'edɪbl/ *a.* *(food)* immangeable.

ineffective /ɪnɪ'fektɪv/ *a.* inefficace; *(person)* incapable.

ineffectual /ɪnɪ'fektʃʊəl/ *a.* inefficace; *(person)* incapable.

inefficien|t /ɪnɪˈfɪʃnt/ *a.* inefficace; (*person*) incompétent. **~cy** *n.* inefficacité *f.*; incompétence *f.*

ineligible /ɪnˈelɪdʒəbl/ *a.* inéligible. **be ~ for**, ne pas avoir droit à.

inept /ɪˈnept/ *a.* (*absurd*) inepte; (*out of place*) mal à propos.

inequality /ɪnɪˈkwɒlətɪ/ *n.* inégalité *f.*

inert /ɪˈnɜːt/ *a.* inerte.

inertia /ɪˈnɜːʃə/ *n.* inertie *f.*

inescapable /ɪnɪˈskeɪpəbl/ *a.* inéluctable.

inevitab|le /ɪnˈevɪtəbl/ *a.* inévitable. **~y** *adv.* inévitablement.

inexact /ɪnɪɡˈzækt/ *a.* inexact.

inexcusable /ɪnɪkˈskjuːzəbl/ *a.* inexcusable.

inexhaustible /ɪnɪɡˈzɔːstəbl/ *a.* inépuisable.

inexorable /ɪnˈeksərəbl/ *a.* inexorable.

inexpensive /ɪnɪkˈspensɪv/ *a.* bon marché *invar.*, pas cher.

inexperience /ɪnɪkˈspɪərɪəns/ *n.* inexpérience *f.* **~d** *a.* inexpérimenté.

inexplicable /ɪnɪkˈsplɪkəbl/ *a.* inexplicable.

inextricable /ɪnɪkˈstrɪkəbl/ *a.* inextricable.

infallib|le /ɪnˈfæləbl/ *a.* infaillible. **~ility** /-ˈbɪlətɪ/ *n.* infaillibilité *f.*

infam|ous /ˈɪnfəməs/ *a.* infâme. **~y** *n.* infamie *f.*

infan|t /ˈɪnfənt/ *n.* (*baby*) nourrisson *m.*; (*at school*) petit(e) enfant *m.(f.).* **~cy** *n.* petite enfance *f.*; (*fig.*) enfance *f.*

infantile /ˈɪnfəntaɪl/ *a.* infantile.

infantry /ˈɪnfəntrɪ/ *n.* infanterie *f.*

infatuat|ed /ɪnˈfætʃʊeɪtɪd/ *a.* **~ed with**, engoué de. **~ion** /-ˈeɪʃn/ *n.* engouement *m.*, béguin *m.*

infect /ɪnˈfekt/ *v.t.* infecter. **~ s.o. with**, communiquer à qn. **~ion** /-kʃn/ *n.* infection *f.*

infectious /ɪnˈfekʃəs/ *a.* (*med.*) infectieux; (*fig.*) contagieux.

infer /ɪnˈfɜː(r)/ *v.t.* (*p.t.* **inferred**) déduire. **~ence** /ˈɪnfərəns/ *n.* déduction *f.*

inferior /ɪnˈfɪərɪə(r)/ *a.* inférieur (**to**, à); (*work, product*) de qualité inférieure. **—n.** inférieur(e) *m. (f.).* **~ity** /-ˈɒrətɪ/ *n.* infériorité *f.*

infernal /ɪnˈfɜːnl/ *a.* infernal. **~ly** *adv.* (*fam.*) atrocement.

inferno /ɪnˈfɜːnəʊ/ *n.* (*pl.* **-os**) (*hell*) enfer *m.*; (*blaze*) incendie *m.*

infertil|e /ɪnˈfɜːtaɪl, *Amer.* ɪnˈfɜːtl/ *a.* infertile. **~ity** /-əˈtɪlətɪ/ *n.* infertilité *f.*

infest /ɪnˈfest/ *v.t.* infester.

infidelity /ɪnfɪˈdelətɪ/ *n.* infidélité *f.*

infighting /ˈɪnfaɪtɪŋ/ *n.* querelles internes *f. pl.*

infiltrat|e /ˈɪnfɪltreɪt/ *v.t./i.* s'infiltrer (dans). **~ion** /-ˈtreɪʃn/ *n.* infiltration *f.*

infinite /ˈɪnfɪnɪt/ *a.* infini. **~ly** *adv.* infiniment.

infinitesimal /ɪnfɪnɪˈtesɪml/ *a.* infinitésimal.

infinitive /ɪnˈfɪnətɪv/ *n.* infinitif *m.*

infinity /ɪnˈfɪnətɪ/ *n.* infinité *f.*

infirm /ɪnˈfɜːm/ *a.* infirme. **~ity** *n.* infirmité *f.*

infirmary /ɪnˈfɜːmərɪ/ *n.* hôpital *m.*; (*sick-bay*) infirmerie *f.*

inflame /ɪnˈfleɪm/ *v.t.* enflammer. **~mable** /-æməbl/ *a.* inflammable. **~mation** /-əˈmeɪʃn/ *n.* inflammation *f.*

inflammatory /ɪnˈflæmətrɪ/ *a.* incendiaire.

inflat|e /ɪnˈfleɪt/ *v.t.* (*balloon, prices, etc.*) gonfler. **~able** *a.* gonflable.

inflation /ɪnˈfleɪʃn/ *n.* inflation *f.* **~ary** *a.* inflationniste.

inflection /ɪnˈflekʃn/ *n.* inflexion *f.*; (*suffix: gram.*) désinence *f.*

inflexible /ɪnˈfleksəbl/ *a.* inflexible.

inflict /ɪnˈflɪkt/ *v.t.* infliger (**on**, à).

influence /'ɪnfluəns/ n. influence f. —v.t. influencer. **under the ~,** (drunk. fam.) en état d'ivresse.

influential /ɪnflu'enʃl/ a. influent.

influenza /ɪnflu'enzə/ n. grippe f.

influx /'ɪnflʌks/ n. afflux m.

inform /ɪn'fɔːm/ v.t. informer (of, de). **keep ~ed,** tenir au courant. **~ant** n. informa|teur, -trice m., f. **~er** n. indica|teur, -trice m., f.

informal /ɪn'fɔːml/ a. (simple) simple, sans cérémonie; (unofficial) officieux; (colloquial) familier. **~ity** /-'mælətɪ/ n. simplicité f. **~ly** adv. sans cérémonie.

information /ɪnfə'meɪʃn/ n. renseignement(s) m. (pl.), information(s) f. (pl.). **some ~,** un renseignement. **~ technology,** informatique f.

informative /ɪn'fɔːmətɪv/ a. instructif.

infra-red /ɪnfrə'red/ a. infrarouge.

infrastructure /'ɪnfrəstrʌktʃə(r)/ n. infrastructure f.

infrequent /ɪn'friːkwənt/ a. peu fréquent. **~ly** adv. rarement.

infringe /ɪn'frɪndʒ/ v.t. contrevenir à. **~ on,** empiéter sur. **~ment** n. infraction f.

infuriate /ɪn'fjʊərɪeɪt/ v.t. exaspérer, rendre furieux.

infus|e /ɪn'fjuːz/ v.t. infuser. **~ion** /-ʒn/ n. infusion f.

ingen|ious /ɪn'dʒiːnɪəs/ a. ingénieux. **~uity** /-ɪ'njuːətɪ/ n. ingéniosité f.

ingenuous /ɪn'dʒenjʊəs/ a. ingénu.

ingot /'ɪŋgət/ n. lingot m.

ingrained /ɪn'greɪnd/ a. enraciné.

ingratiate /ɪn'greɪʃɪeɪt/ v.t. **~ o.s. with,** gagner les bonnes grâces de.

ingratitude /ɪn'grætɪtjuːd/ n. ingratitude f.

ingredient /ɪn'griːdɪənt/ n. ingrédient m.

inhabit /ɪn'hæbɪt/ v.t. habiter. **~able** a. habitable. **~ant** n. habitant(e) m. (f.).

inhale /ɪn'heɪl/ v.t. inhaler; (tobacco smoke) avaler. **~r** n. spray m.

inherent /ɪn'hɪərənt/ a. inhérent. **~ly** adv. en soi, intrinsèquement.

inherit /ɪn'herɪt/ v.t. hériter (de). **~ance** n. héritage m.

inhibit /ɪn'hɪbɪt/ v.t. (hinder) gêner; (prevent) empêcher. **be ~ed,** avoir des inhibitions. **~ion** /-'bɪʃn/ n. inhibition f.

inhospitable /ɪnhɒ'spɪtəbl/ a. inhospitalier.

inhuman /ɪn'hjuːmən/ a. (brutal, not human) inhumain. **~ity** /-'mænətɪ/ n. inhumanité f.

inhumane /ɪnhjuː'meɪn/ a. (unkind) inhumain.

inimitable /ɪ'nɪmɪtəbl/ a. inimitable.

iniquit|ous /ɪ'nɪkwɪtəs/ a. inique. **~y** /-ɒtɪ/ n. iniquité f.

initial /ɪ'nɪʃl/ n. initiale f. —v.t. (p.t. initialled) parapher. —a. initial. **~ly** adv. initialement.

initiat|e /ɪ'nɪʃɪeɪt/ v.t. (begin) amorcer; (scheme) lancer; (person) initier (into, à). **~ion** /-'eɪʃn/ n. initiation f.; (start) amorce f.

initiative /ɪ'nɪʃətɪv/ n. initiative f.

inject /ɪn'dʒekt/ v.t. injecter; (new element: fig.) insuffler. **~ion** /-kʃn/ n. injection f., piqûre f.

injunction /ɪn'dʒʌŋkʃn/ n. (court order) ordonnance f.

injure /'ɪndʒə(r)/ v.t. blesser; (do wrong to) nuire à.

injury /'ɪndʒərɪ/ n. (physical) blessure f.; (wrong) préjudice m.

injustice /ɪn'dʒʌstɪs/ n. injustice f.

ink /ɪŋk/ n. encre f. **~-well** n. encrier m. **~y** a. taché d'encre.

inkling /'ɪŋklɪŋ/ n. petite idée f.

inland /'ɪnlənd/ a. intérieur.

—*adv.* /ɪn'lænd/ à l'intérieur. **I~ Revenue,** fisc *m.*

in-laws /'ɪnlɔ:z/ *n. pl.* (*parents*) beaux-parents; (*family*) belle-famille *f.*

inlay[1] /ɪn'leɪ/ *v.t.* (*p.t.* **inlaid**) incruster.

inlay[2] /'ɪnleɪ/ *n.* incrustation *f.*

inlet /'ɪnlet/ *n.* bras de mer *m.*; (*techn.*) arrivée *f.*

inmate /'ɪnmeɪt/ *n.* (*of asylum*) interné(e) *m.* (*f.*); (*of prison*) détenu(e) *m.* (*f.*).

inn /ɪn/ *n.* auberge *f.*

innards /'ɪnədz/ *n. pl.* (*fam.*) entrailles *f. pl.*

innate /ɪ'neɪt/ *a.* inné.

inner /'ɪnə(r)/ *a.* intérieur, interne; (*fig.*) profond, intime. **~city,** quartiers défavorisés *m. pl.* **~most** *a.* le plus profond. **~tube,** chambre à air *f.*

innings /'ɪnɪŋz/ *n. invar.* tour de batte *m.*; (*fig.*) tour *m.*

innkeeper /'ɪnkiːpə(r)/ *n.* aubergiste *m./f.*

innocen|t /'ɪnəsnt/ *a. & n.* innocent(e) (*m.* (*f.*)). **~ce** *n.* innocence *f.*

innocuous /ɪ'nɒkjʊəs/ *a.* inoffensif.

innovat|e /'ɪnəveɪt/ *v.i.* innover. **~ion** /-'veɪʃn/ *n.* innovation *f.* **~or** *n.* innova|teur, -trice *m., f.*

innuendo /ɪnju:'endəʊ/ *n.* (*pl. -oes*) insinuation *f.*

innumerable /ɪ'nju:mərəbl/ *a.* innombrable.

inoculat|e /ɪ'nɒkjuleɪt/ *v.t.* inoculer. **~ion** /-'leɪʃn/ *n.* inoculation *f.*

inoffensive /ɪnə'fensɪv/ *a.* inoffensif.

inoperative /ɪn'ɒpərətɪv/ *a.* inopérant.

inopportune /ɪn'ɒpətjuːn/ *a.* inopportun.

inordinate /ɪ'nɔːdɪnət/ *a.* excessif. **~ly** *adv.* excessivement.

input /'ɪnpʊt/ *n.* (*data*) données *f. pl.*; (*computer process*) entrée *f.*; (*power: electr.*) énergie *f.*

inquest /'ɪnkwest/ *n.* enquête *f.*

inquire /ɪn'kwaɪə(r)/ *v.t./i.* = **enquire.**

inquiry /ɪn'kwaɪərɪ/ *n.* enquête *f.*

inquisition /ɪnkwɪ'zɪʃn/ *n.* inquisition *f.*

inquisitive /ɪn'kwɪzətɪv/ *a.* curieux; (*prying*) indiscret.

inroad /'ɪnrəʊd/ *n.* incursion *f.*

insan|e /ɪn'seɪn/ *a.* fou. **~ity** /ɪn'sænətɪ/ *n.* folie *f.*, démence *f.*

insanitary /ɪn'sænɪtrɪ/ *a.* insalubre, malsain.

insatiable /ɪn'seɪʃəbl/ *a.* insatiable.

inscri|be /ɪn'skraɪb/ *v.t.* inscrire; (*book*) dédicacer. **~ption** /-ɪpʃn/ *n.* inscription *f.*; dédicace *f.*

inscrutable /ɪn'skruːtəbl/ *a.* impénétrable.

insect /'ɪnsekt/ *n.* insecte *m.*

insecticide /ɪn'sektɪsaɪd/ *n.* insecticide *m.*

insecur|e /ɪnsɪ'kjʊə(r)/ *a.* (*not firm*) peu solide; (*unsafe*) peu sûr; (*worried*) anxieux. **~ity** *n.* insécurité *f.*

insemination /ɪnsemɪ'neɪʃn/ *n.* insémination *f.*

insensible /ɪn'sensəbl/ *a.* insensible; (*unconscious*) inconscient.

insensitive /ɪn'sensətɪv/ *a.* insensible.

inseparable /ɪn'seprəbl/ *a.* inséparable.

insert[1] /ɪn'sɜːt/ *v.t.* insérer. **~ion** /-ʃn/ *n.* insertion *f.*

insert[2] /'ɪnsɜːt/ *n.* insertion *f.*; (*advertising*) encart *m.*

in-service /ɪn'sɜːvɪs/ *a.* (*training*) continu.

inshore /ɪn'ʃɔː(r)/ *a.* côtier.

inside /ɪn'saɪd/ *n.* intérieur *m.* **~(s),** (*fam.*) entrailles *f. pl.* —*a.* intérieur. —*adv.* à l'intérieur, dedans. —*prep.* à l'intérieur de; (*of time*) en moins de. ~ **out**, à l'envers; (*thoroughly*) à fond.

insidious /ɪnˈsɪdɪəs/ *a.* insidieux.

insight /ˈɪnsaɪt/ *n.* (*perception*) perspicacité *f.*; (*idea*) aperçu *m.*

insignia /ɪnˈsɪgnɪə/ *n. pl.* insignes *m. pl.*

insignificant /ɪnsɪgˈnɪfɪkənt/ *a.* insignifiant.

insincer|e /ɪnsɪnˈsɪə(r)/ *a.* peu sincère. ~**ity** /-ˈserətɪ/ *n.* manque de sincérité *m.*

insinuat|e /ɪnˈsɪnjʊeɪt/ *v.t.* insinuer. ~**ion** /-ˈeɪʃn/ *n.* insinuation *f.*

insipid /ɪnˈsɪpɪd/ *a.* insipide.

insist /ɪnˈsɪst/ *v.t./i.* insister. ~ **on**, affirmer; (*demand*) exiger. ~ **on doing**, insister pour faire.

insisten|t /ɪnˈsɪstənt/ *a.* insistant. ~**ce** *n.* insistance *f.* ~**tly** *adv.* avec insistance.

insole /ˈɪnsəʊl/ *n.* (*separate*) semelle *f.*

insolen|t /ˈɪnsələnt/ *a.* insolent. ~**ce** *n.* insolence *f.*

insoluble /ɪnˈsɒljʊbl/ *a.* insoluble.

insolvent /ɪnˈsɒlvənt/ *a.* insolvable.

insomnia /ɪnˈsɒmnɪə/ *n.* insomnie *f.* ~**c** /-ɪæk/ *n.* insomniaque *m./f.*

inspect /ɪnˈspekt/ *v.t.* inspecter; (*tickets*) contrôler. ~**ion** /-kʃn/ *n.* inspection *f.*; contrôle *m.* ~**or** *n.* inspec|teur, -trice *m.*, *f.*; (*on train, bus*) contrôleur, -se *m.*, *f.*

inspir|e /ɪnˈspaɪə(r)/ *v.t.* inspirer. ~**ation** /-əˈreɪʃn/ *n.* inspiration *f.*

instability /ɪnstəˈbɪlətɪ/ *n.* instabilité *f.*

install /ɪnˈstɔːl/ *v.t.* installer. ~**ation** /-əˈleɪʃn/ *n.* installation *f.*

instalment /ɪnˈstɔːlmənt/ *n.* (*payment*) acompte *m.*; versement *m.*; (*of serial*) épisode *m.*

instance /ˈɪnstəns/ *n.* exemple *m.*; (*case*) cas *m.* **for** ~, par exemple. **in the first** ~, en premier lieu.

instant /ˈɪnstənt/ *a.* immédiat; (*food*) instantané. —*n.* instant *m.* ~**ly** *adv.* immédiatement.

instantaneous /ɪnstənˈteɪnɪəs/ *a.* instantané.

instead /ɪnˈsted/ *adv.* plutôt. ~ **of doing**, au lieu de faire. ~ **of s.o.**, à la place de qn.

instep /ˈɪnstep/ *n.* cou-de-pied *m.*

instigat|e /ˈɪnstɪgeɪt/ *v.t.* provoquer. ~**ion** /-ˈgeɪʃn/ *n.* instigation *f.* ~**or** *n.* instiga|teur, -trice *m.*, *f.*

instil /ɪnˈstɪl/ *v.t.* (*p.t.* instilled) inculquer; (*inspire*) insuffler.

instinct /ˈɪnstɪŋkt/ *n.* instinct *m.* ~**ive** /-ˈstɪŋktɪv/ *a.* instinctif.

institut|e /ˈɪnstɪtjuːt/ *n.* institut *m.* —*v.t.* instituer; (*inquiry etc.*) entamer. ~**ion** /-ˈtjuːʃn/ *n.* institution *f.*; (*school, hospital*) établissement *m.*

instruct /ɪnˈstrʌkt/ *v.t.* instruire; (*order*) ordonner. ~ **s.o. in sth.**, enseigner qch. à qn. ~ **s.o. to do**, ordonner à qn. de faire. ~**ion** /-kʃn/ *n.* instruction *f.* ~**ions** /-kʃnz/ *n. pl.* (*for use*) mode d'emploi *m.* ~**ive** *a.* instructif. ~**or** *n.* professeur *m.*; (*skiing, driving*) moni|teur, -trice *m.*, *f.*

instrument /ˈɪnstrʊmənt/ *n.* instrument *m.* ~ **panel**, tableau de bord *m.*

instrumental /ɪnstrʊˈmentl/ *a.* instrumental. **be** ~ **in**, contribuer à. ~**ist** *n.* instrumentaliste *m./f.*

insubordinat|e /ɪnsəˈbɔːdɪnət/ *a.* insubordonné. ~**ion** /-ˈneɪʃn/ *n.* insubordination *f.*

insufferable /ɪnˈsʌfrəbl/ *a.* intolérable, insupportable.

insufficient /ɪnsəˈfɪʃnt/ *a.* insuffisant. ~**ly** *adv.* insuffisamment.

insular /'ɪnsjʊlə(r)/ a. insulaire; (mind, person: fig.) borné.

insulat|e /'ɪnsjʊleɪt/ v.t. (room, wire, etc.) isoler. **~ing tape,** chatterton m. **~ion** /-'leɪʃn/ n. isolation f.

insulin /'ɪnsjʊlɪn/ n. insuline f.

insult[1] /ɪn'sʌlt/ v.t. insulter.

insult[2] /'ɪnsʌlt/ n. insulte f.

insuperable /ɪn'sjuːprəbl/ a. insurmontable.

insur|e /ɪn'ʃʊə(r)/ v.t. assurer. **~ that,** (ensure: Amer.) s'assurer que. **~ance** n. assurance f.

insurmountable /ɪnsə'maʊntəbl/ a. insurmontable.

insurrection /ɪnsə'rekʃn/ n. insurrection f.

intact /ɪn'tækt/ a. intact.

intake /'ɪnteɪk/ n. admission(s) f. (pl.); (techn.) prise f.

intangible /ɪn'tændʒəbl/ a. intangible.

integral /'ɪntɪɡrəl/ a. intégral. **be an ~ part of,** faire partie intégrante de.

integrat|e /'ɪntɪɡreɪt/ v.t./i. (s')intégrer. **~ion** /-'ɡreɪʃn/ n. intégration f.; (racial) déségrégation f.

integrity /ɪn'teɡrɪtɪ/ n. intégrité f.

intellect /'ɪntəlekt/ n. intelligence f. **~ual** /-'lektʃʊəl/ a. & n. intellectuel(le) (m. (f.)).

intelligen|t /ɪn'telɪdʒənt/ a. intelligent. **~ce** n. intelligence f.; (mil.) renseignements m. pl. **~tly** adv. intelligemment.

intelligentsia /ɪntelɪ'dʒentsɪə/ n. intelligentsia f.

intelligible /ɪn'telɪdʒəbl/ a. intelligible.

intemperance /ɪn'tempərəns/ n. (drunkenness) ivrognerie f.

intend /ɪn'tend/ v.t. destiner. **~ to do,** avoir l'intention de faire. **~ed** a. (deliberate) intentionnel; (planned) prévu; n. (future spouse: fam.) promis(e) m. (f.).

intens|e /ɪn'tens/ a. intense; (person) passionné. **~ely** adv. (to live etc.) intensément; (very) extrêmement. **~ity** n. intensité f.

intensif|y /ɪn'tensɪfaɪ/ v.t. intensifier. **~ication** /-ɪ'keɪʃn/ n. intensification f.

intensive /ɪn'tensɪv/ a. intensif. **in ~ care,** en réanimation.

intent /ɪn'tent/ n. intention f. —a. attentif. **~ on,** absorbé par. **~ on doing,** résolu à faire. **~ly** adv. attentivement.

intention /ɪn'tenʃn/ n. intention f. **~al** a. intentionnel.

inter /ɪn'tɜː(r)/ v.t. (p.t. **interred**) enterrer.

inter- /'ɪntə(r)/ pref. inter-.

interact /ɪntə'rækt/ v.i. avoir une action réciproque. **~ion** /-kʃn/ n. interaction f.

intercede /ɪntə'siːd/ v.i. intercéder.

intercept /ɪntə'sept/ v.t. intercepter. **~ion** /-pʃn/ n. interception f.

interchange /'ɪntətʃeɪndʒ/ n. (road junction) échangeur m.

interchangeable /ɪntə'tʃeɪndʒəbl/ a. interchangeable.

intercom /'ɪntəkɒm/ n. interphone m.

interconnected /ɪntəkə'nektɪd/ a. (facts, events, etc.) lié.

intercourse /'ɪntəkɔːs/ n. (sexual, social) rapports m. pl.

interest /'ɪntrəst/ n. intérêt m.; (stake) intérêts m. pl. —v.t. intéresser. **~ rates,** taux d'intérêt m. pl. **~ed** a. intéressé. **be ~ed in,** s'intéresser à. **~ing** a. intéressant.

interface /'ɪntəfeɪs/ n. (comput.) interface f.; (fig.) zone de rencontre f.

interfer|e /ɪntə'fɪə(r)/ v.i. se mêler des affaires des autres. **~e in,** s'ingérer dans. **~e with,** (plans) créer un contretemps avec; (work) s'immiscer dans; (radio) faire des interférences avec; (lock) toucher à. **~ence** n. ingérence f.; (radio) parasites m. pl.

interim /ˈɪntərɪm/ n. intérim m. —a. intérimaire.

interior /ɪnˈtɪərɪə(r)/ n. intérieur m. —a. intérieur.

interjection /ɪntəˈdʒekʃn/ n. interjection f.

interlinked /ɪntəˈlɪŋkt/ a. lié.

interlock /ɪntəˈlɒk/ v.t./i. (techn.) (s')emboîter, (s')enclencher.

interloper /ˈɪntələʊpə(r)/ n. intrus(e) m. (f.).

interlude /ˈɪntəluːd/ n. intervalle m.; (theatre, mus.) interlude m.

intermarr|iage /ɪntəˈmærɪdʒ/ n. mariage entre membres de races différentes m. **~y** v.i. se marier (entre eux).

intermediary /ɪntəˈmiːdɪərɪ/ a. & n. intermédiaire (m./f.).

intermediate /ɪntəˈmiːdɪət/ a. intermédiaire; (exam etc.) moyen.

interminable /ɪnˈtɜːmɪnəbl/ a. interminable.

intermission /ɪntəˈmɪʃn/ n. pause f.; (theatre etc.) entracte m.

intermittent /ɪntəˈmɪtnt/ a. intermittent. **~ly** adv. par intermittence.

intern¹ /ɪnˈtɜːn/ v.t. interner. **~ee** /-ˈniː/ n. interné(e) m. (f.). **~ment** n. internement m.

intern² /ˈɪntɜːn/ n. (doctor: Amer.) interne m./f.

internal /ɪnˈtɜːnl/ a. interne; (domestic: pol.) intérieur. I~ Revenue, (Amer.) fisc m. **~ly** adv. intérieurement.

international /ɪntəˈnæʃnəl/ a. & n. international (m.).

interplay /ˈɪntəpleɪ/ n. jeu m., interaction f.

interpolate /ɪnˈtɜːpəleɪt/ v.t. interpoler.

interpret /ɪnˈtɜːprɪt/ v.t. interpréter. —v.i. faire l'interprète. **~ation** /-ˈteɪʃn/ n. interprétation f. **~er** n. interprète m./f.

interrelated /ɪntərɪˈleɪtɪd/ a. en corrélation, lié.

interrogat|e /ɪnˈterəgeɪt/ v.t. interroger. **~ion** /-ˈgeɪʃn/ n. interrogation f. (of, de); (session of questions) interrogatoire m.

interrogative /ɪntəˈrɒgətɪv/ a. & n. interrogatif (m.).

interrupt /ɪntəˈrʌpt/ v.t. interrompre. **~ion** /-pʃn/ n. interruption f.

intersect /ɪntəˈsekt/ v.t./i. (lines, roads) (se) couper. **~ion** /-kʃn/ n. intersection f.; (crossroads) croisement m.

interspersed /ɪntəˈspɜːst/ a. (scattered) dispersé. **~ with**, parsemé de.

intertwine /ɪntəˈtwaɪn/ v.t./i. (s')entrelacer.

interval /ˈɪntəvl/ n. intervalle m.; (theatre) entracte m. **at ~s**, par intervalles.

interven|e /ɪntəˈviːn/ v.i. intervenir; (of time) s'écouler (between, entre); (happen) survenir. **~tion** /-ˈvenʃn/ n. intervention f.

interview /ˈɪntəvjuː/ n. (with reporter) interview f.; (for job etc.) entrevue f. —v.t. interviewer. **~er** n. interviewer m.

intestine /ɪnˈtestɪn/ n. intestin m. **~al** a. intestinal.

intima|te¹ /ˈɪntɪmət/ a. intime; (detailed) profond. **~cy** n. intimité f. **~tely** adv. intimement.

intimate² /ˈɪntɪmeɪt/ v.t. (state) annoncer; (imply) suggérer.

intimidat|e /ɪnˈtɪmɪdeɪt/ v.t. intimider. **~ion** /-ˈdeɪʃn/ n. intimidation f.

into /ˈɪntuː, unstressed ˈɪntə/ prep. (put, go, fall, etc.) dans; (divide, translate, etc.) en.

intolerable /ɪnˈtɒlərəbl/ *a.* intolérable.

intoleran|t /ɪnˈtɒlərənt/ *a.* intolérant. **～ce** *n.* intolérance *f.*

intonation /ɪntəˈneɪʃn/ *n.* intonation *f.*

intoxicat|e /ɪnˈtɒksɪkeɪt/ *v.t.* enivrer. **～ed** *a.* ivre. **～ion** /-ˈkeɪʃn/ *n.* ivresse *f.*

intra- /ˈɪntrə/ *pref.* intra-.

intractable /ɪnˈtræktəbl/ *a.* très difficile.

intransigent /ɪnˈtrænsɪdʒənt/ *a.* intransigeant.

intransitive /ɪnˈtrænsətɪv/ *a.* (*verb*) intransitif.

intravenous /ɪntrəˈviːnəs/ *a.* (*med.*) intraveineux.

intrepid /ɪnˈtrepɪd/ *a.* intrépide.

intrica|te /ˈɪntrɪkət/ *a.* complexe. **～cy** *n.* complexité *f.*

intrigue /ɪnˈtriːɡ/ *v.t./i.* intriguer. —*n.* intrigue *f.* **～ing** *a.* très intéressant; (*curious*) curieux.

intrinsic /ɪnˈtrɪnsɪk/ *a.* intrinsèque. **～ally** /-klɪ/ *adv.* intrinsèquement.

introduce /ɪntrəˈdjuːs/ *v.t.* (*bring in, insert*) introduire; (*programme, question*) présenter. **～ s.o. to,** (*person*) présenter à; (*subject*) faire connaître à qn.

introduct|ion /ɪntrəˈdʌkʃn/ *n.* introduction *f.*; (*to person*) présentation *f.* **～ory** /-tərɪ/ *a.* (*letter, words*) d'introduction.

introspective /ɪntrəˈspektɪv/ *a.* introspectif.

introvert /ˈɪntrəvɜːt/ *n.* introverti(e) *m.* (*f.*).

intru|de /ɪnˈtruːd/ *v.i.* (*person*) s'imposer (**on s.o.,** à qn.), déranger. **～der** *n.* intrus(e) *m.* (*f.*). **～sion** *n.* intrusion *f.*

intuit|ion /ɪntjuːˈɪʃn/ *n.* intuition *f.* **～ive** /ɪnˈtjuːɪtɪv/ *a.* intuitif.

inundat|e /ˈɪnʌndeɪt/ *v.t.* inonder (**with,** de). **～ion** /-ˈdeɪʃn/ *n.* inondation *f.*

invade /ɪnˈveɪd/ *v.t.* envahir. **～r** /-ə(r)/ *n.* envahisseu|r, -se *m., f.*

invalid¹ /ˈɪnvəlɪd/ *n.* malade *m./f.*; (*disabled*) infirme *m./f.*

invalid² /ɪnˈvælɪd/ *a.* non valable. **～ate** *v.t.* invalider.

invaluable /ɪnˈvæljʊəbl/ *a.* inestimable.

invariab|le /ɪnˈveərɪəbl/ *a.* invariable. **～ly** *adv.* invariablement.

invasion /ɪnˈveɪʒn/ *n.* invasion *f.*

invective /ɪnˈvektɪv/ *n.* invective *f.*

inveigh /ɪnˈveɪ/ *v.i.* invectiver.

inveigle /ɪnˈveɪɡl/ *v.t.* persuader.

invent /ɪnˈvent/ *v.t.* inventer. **～ion** /-enʃn/ *n.* invention *f.* **～ive** *a.* inventif. **～or** *n.* inven|teur, -trice *m., f.*

inventory /ˈɪnvəntrɪ/ *n.* inventaire *m.*

inverse /ɪnˈvɜːs/ *a. & n.* inverse (*m.*). **～ly** *adv.* inversement.

inver|t /ɪnˈvɜːt/ *v.t.* intervertir. **～ted commas,** guillemets *m. pl.* **～sion** *n.* inversion *f.*

invest /ɪnˈvest/ *v.t.* investir (*time, effort*: *fig.*) consacrer. —*v.i.* faire un investissement. **～ in,** (*buy*: *fam.*) se payer. **～ment** *n.* investissement *m.* **～or** *n.* actionnaire *m./f.*; (*saver*) épargnant(e) *m.* (*f.*).

investigat|e /ɪnˈvestɪɡeɪt/ *v.t.* étudier; (*crime etc.*) enquêter sur. **～ion** /-ˈɡeɪʃn/ *n.* investigation *f.* **under ～ion,** à l'étude. **～or** *n.* (*police*) enquêteu|r, -se *m., f.*

inveterate /ɪnˈvetərət/ *a.* invétéré.

invidious /ɪnˈvɪdɪəs/ *a.* (*hateful*) odieux; (*unfair*) injuste.

invigilat|e /ɪnˈvɪdʒɪleɪt/ *v.i.* (*schol.*) être de surveillance. **～or** *n.* surveillant(e) *m.* (*f.*).

invigorate /ɪnˈvɪɡəreɪt/ *v.t.* vivifier; (*encourage*) stimuler.

invincible /ɪnˈvɪnsəbl/ *a.* invincible.

invisible /ɪnˈvɪzəbl/ *a.* invisible.

invit|e /ɪnˈvaɪt/ *v.t.* inviter; (*ask*

for) demander. **~ation** /ın-vı'teıʃn/ *n.* invitation *f.* **~ing** *a.* (*meal, smile, etc.*) engageant.

invoice /'ınvɔıs/ *n.* facture *f.* —*v.t.* facturer.

invoke /ın'vəʊk/ *v.t.* invoquer.

involuntary /ın'vɒlǝntrı/ *a.* involontaire.

involve /ın'vɒlv/ *v.t.* entraîner; (*people*) faire participer. **~d** *a.* (*complex*) compliqué; (*at stake*) en jeu. **be ~d in**, (*work*) participer à; (*crime*) être mêlé à. **~ment** *n.* participation *f.* (**in**, à).

invulnerable /ın'vʌlnǝrǝbl/ *a.* invulnérable.

inward /'ınwǝd/ *a.* & *adv.* vers l'intérieur; (*feeling etc.*) intérieur. **~ly** *adv.* intérieurement. **~s** *adv.* vers l'intérieur.

iodine /'aıǝdi:n/ *n.* iode *m.*; (*antiseptic*) teinture d'iode *f.*

iota /aı'ǝʊtǝ/ *n.* (*amount*) brin *m.*

IOU /aıǝʊ'ju:/ *abbr.* (*I owe you*) reconnaissance de dette *f.*

IQ /aı'kju:/ *abbr.* (*intelligence quotient*) QI *m.*

Iran /ı'rɑ:n/ *n.* Iran *m.* **~ian** /ı'reımıǝn/ *a.* & *n.* iranien(ne) (*m.* (*f.*)).

Iraq /ı'rɑ:k/ *n.* Irak *m.* **~i** *a.* & *n.* irakien(ne) (*m.* (*f.*)).

irascible /ı'ræsǝbl/ *a.* irascible.

irate /aı'reıt/ *a.* en colère, furieux.

ire /'aıǝ(r)/ *n.* courroux *m.*

Ireland /'aıǝlǝnd/ *n.* Irlande *f.*

iris /'aıǝrıs/ *n.* (*anat., bot.*) iris *m.*

Irish /'aıǝrıʃ/ *a.* irlandais. —*n.* (*lang.*) irlandais *m.* **~man** *n.* Irlandais *m.* **~woman** *n.* Irlandaise *f.*

irk /ɜ:k/ *v.t.* ennuyer. **~some** *a.* ennuyeux.

iron /'aıǝn/ *n.* fer *m.*; (*appliance*) fer (à repasser) *m.* —*a.* de fer. —*v.t.* repasser. **I~ Curtain**, rideau de fer *m.* **~ out**, faire disparaître. **~ing-board** *n.* planche à repasser *f.*

ironic(al) /aı'rɒnık(l)/ *a.* ironique.

ironmonger /'aıǝnmʌŋgǝ(r)/ *n.* quincaillier *m.* **~y** *n.* quincaillerie *f.*

ironwork /'aıǝnwɜ:k/ *n.* ferronnerie *f.*

irony /'aıǝrǝnı/ *n.* ironie *f.*

irrational /ı'ræʃǝnl/ *a.* irrationnel; (*person*) pas rationnel.

irreconcilable /ırekǝn'saılǝbl/ *a.* irréconciliable; (*incompatible*) inconciliable.

irrefutable /ı'refjutǝbl/ *a.* irréfutable.

irregular /ı'regjʊlǝ(r)/ *a.* irrégulier. **~ity** /-'lærǝtı/ *n.* irrégularité *f.*

irrelevan|t /ı'relǝvǝnt/ *a.* sans rapport (**to**, avec). **~ce** *n.* manque de rapport *m.*

irreparable /ı'repǝrǝbl/ *a.* irréparable, irrémédiable.

irreplaceable /ırı'pleısǝbl/ *a.* irremplaçable.

irrepressible /ırı'presǝbl/ *a.* irrépressible.

irresistible /ırı'zıstǝbl/ *a.* irrésistible.

irresolute /ı'rezǝlu:t/ *a.* irrésolu.

irrespective /ırı'spektıv/ *a.* **~ of**, sans tenir compte de.

irresponsible /ırı'spɒnsǝbl/ *a.* irresponsable.

irretrievable /ırı'tri:vǝbl/ *a.* irréparable.

irreverent /ı'revǝrǝnt/ *a.* irrévérencieux.

irreversible /ırı'vɜ:sǝbl/ *a.* irréversible; (*decision*) irrévocable.

irrevocable /ı'revǝkǝbl/ *a.* irrévocable.

irrigat|e /'ırıgeıt/ *v.t.* irriguer. **~ion** /-'geıʃn/ *n.* irrigation *f.*

irritable /'ırıtǝbl/ *a.* irritable.

irritat|e /'ırıteıt/ *v.t.* irriter. **be ~ed by**, être énervé par. **~ing** *a.* énervant. **~ion** /-'teıʃn/ *n.* irritation *f.*

is /ɪz/ *see* be.
Islam /'ɪzlɑːm/ *n.* Islam *m.* **~ic**
/ɪz'læmɪk/ *a.* islamique.
island /'aɪlənd/ *n.* île *f.* **traffic ~**,
refuge *m.* **~er** *n.* insulaire *m./f.*
isle /aɪl/ *n.* île *f.*
isolat|e /'aɪsəleɪt/ *v.t.* isoler. **~ion**
/-'leɪʃn/ *n.* isolement *m.*
isotope /'aɪsətəʊp/ *n.* isotope *m.*
Israel /'ɪzreɪl/ *n.* Israël *m.* **~i**
/ɪz'reɪlɪ/ *a. & n.* israélien(ne) (*m.*
(*f.*)).
issue /'ɪʃuː/ *n.* question *f.*;
(*outcome*) résultat *m.*; (*of
magazine etc.*) numéro *m.*; (*of
stamps etc.*) émission *f.*; (*offspring*) descendance *f.* —*v.t.*
distribuer, donner; (*stamps etc.*)
émettre; (*book*) publier; (*order*)
donner. —*v.i.* **~ from**, sortir de.
at ~, en cause. **take ~**, engager
une controverse.
isthmus /'ɪsməs/ *n.* isthme *m.*
it /ɪt/ *pron.* (*subject*) il, elle; (*object*)
le, la, l'*; (*impersonal subject*) il;
(*non-specific*) ce, c*, cela, ça. **it
is**, (*quiet, my book, etc.*) c'est. **it
is/cold/warm/late/etc.**, il fait
froid/chaud/tard/etc. **that's it**,
c'est ça. **who is it?**, qui est-ce? **of
it, from it**, en. **in it, at it, to
it**, y.
IT *abbr. see* **information technology.**
italic /ɪ'tælɪk/ *a.* italique. **~s** *n. pl.*
italique *m.*
Ital|y /'ɪtəlɪ/ *n.* Italie *f.* **~ian**
/ɪ'tæljən/ *a. & n.* italien(ne) (*m.*
(*f.*)); (*lang.*) italien *m.*
itch /ɪtʃ/ *n.* démangeaison *f.* —*v.i.*
démanger. **my arm ~es**, mon
bras me démange. **I am ~ing to**,
ça me démange de. **~y** *a.* qui
démange.
item /'aɪtəm/ *n.* article *m.*, chose *f.*;
(*on agenda*) question *f.* **news ~**,
nouvelle *f.* **~ize** *v.t.* détailler.
itinerant /aɪ'tɪnərənt/ *a.* itinérant *m.*;
(*musician, actor*) ambulant.

itinerary /aɪ'tɪnərərɪ/ *n.* itinéraire
m.
its /ɪts/ *a.* son, sa, *pl.* ses.
it's /ɪts/ = **it is, it has.**
itself /ɪt'self/ *pron.* lui-même, elle-
même; (*reflexive*) se.
IUD *abbr.* (*intrauterine device*)
stérilet *m.*
ivory /'aɪvərɪ/ *n.* ivoire *m.* **~
tower**, tour d'ivoire *f.*
ivy /'aɪvɪ/ *n.* lierre *m.*

J

jab /dʒæb/ *v.t.* (*p.t.* **jabbed**)
(*thrust*) enfoncer; (*prick*) piquer.
—*n.* coup *m.*; (*injection*) piqûre *f.*
jabber /'dʒæbə(r)/ *v.i.* jacasser,
bavarder; (*indistinctly*) bredouiller. —*n.* bavardage *m.*
jack /dʒæk/ *n.* (*techn.*) cric *m.*;
(*cards*) valet *m.*; (*plug*) fiche *f.*
—*v.t.* **~ up**, soulever (avec un
cric).
jackal /'dʒækɔːl/ *n.* chacal *m.*
jackass /'dʒækæs/ *n.* âne *m.*
jackdaw /'dʒækdɔː/ *n.* choucas *m.*
jacket /'dʒækɪt/ *n.* veste *f.*, veston
m.; (*of book*) jaquette *f.*
jack-knife /'dʒæknaɪf/ *n.* couteau
pliant *m.* —*v.i.* (*lorry*) faire un
tête-à-queue.
jackpot /'dʒækpɒt/ *n.* gros lot *m.*
hit the ~, gagner le gros lot.
Jacuzzi /dʒə'kuːzɪ/ *n.* (P.) bain à
remous *m.*
jade /dʒeɪd/ *n.* (*stone*) jade *m.*
jaded /'dʒeɪdɪd/ *a.* las; (*appetite*)
blasé.
jagged /'dʒægɪd/ *a.* dentelé.
jail /dʒeɪl/ *n.* prison *f.* —*v.t.* mettre
en prison. **~er** *n.* geôlier *m.*
jalopy /dʒə'lɒpɪ/ *n.* vieux tacot *m.*
jam[1] /dʒæm/ *n.* confiture *f.*
jam[2] /dʒæm/ *v.t./i.* (*p.t.* **jammed**)
(*wedge, become wedged*) (se) coin-
cer; (*cram*) (s')entasser; (*street*

etc.) encombrer; *(thrust)* enfoncer; *(radio)* brouiller. —*n.* foule *f.;* *(of traffic)* embouteillage *m.;* *(situation: fam.)* pétrin *m.* ~**packed** *a.* (*fam.*) bourré.

Jamaica /dʒəˈmeɪkə/ *n.* Jamaïque *f.*

jangle /ˈdʒæŋgl/ *n.* cliquetis *m.* —*v.t/i.* (faire) cliqueter.

janitor /ˈdʒænɪtə(r)/ *n.* concierge *m.*

January /ˈdʒænjʊərɪ/ *n.* janvier *m.*

Japan /dʒəˈpæn/ *n.* Japon *m.* ~**ese** /dʒæpəˈniːz/ *a. & n.* japonais(e) *(m. (f.));* *(lang.)* japonais *m.*

jar[1] /dʒɑː(r)/ *n.* pot *m.,* bocal *m.*

jar[2] /dʒɑː(r)/ *v.i.* *(p.t.* **jarred**) grincer; *(of colours etc.)* détonner. —*v.t.* ébranler. —*n.* son discordant *m.* ~**ring** *a.* discordant.

jargon /ˈdʒɑːgən/ *n.* jargon *m.*

jasmine /ˈdʒæsmɪn/ *n.* jasmin *m.*

jaundice /ˈdʒɔːndɪs/ *n.* jaunisse *f.*

jaundiced /ˈdʒɔːndɪst/ *a. (envious)* envieux; *(bitter)* aigri.

jaunt /dʒɔːnt/ *n. (trip)* balade *f.*

jaunty /ˈdʒɔːntɪ/ *a.* (**-ier, -iest**) *(cheerful, sprightly)* allègre.

javelin /ˈdʒævlɪn/ *n.* javelot *m.*

jaw /dʒɔː/ *n.* mâchoire *f.* —*v.i.* *(talk: sl.)* jacasser.

jay /dʒeɪ/ *n.* geai *m.* ~**-walk** *v.i.* traverser la chaussée imprudemment.

jazz /dʒæz/ *n.* jazz *m.* —*v.t.* ~ **up,** animer. ~**y** *a.* tape-à-l'œil *invar.*

jealous /ˈdʒeləs/ *a.* jaloux. ~**y** *n.* jalousie *f.*

jeans /dʒiːnz/ *n. pl.* (blue-)jean *m.*

jeep /dʒiːp/ *n.* jeep *f.*

jeer /dʒɪə(r)/ *v.t/i.* ~ **(at),** railler; *(boo)* huer. —*n.* raillerie *f.;* huée *f.*

jell /dʒel/ *v.i. (set: fam.)* prendre. ~**ied** *a.* en gelée.

jelly /ˈdʒelɪ/ *n.* gelée *f.*

jellyfish /ˈdʒelɪfɪʃ/ *n.* méduse *f.*

jeopard|**y** /ˈdʒepədɪ/ *n.* péril *m.* ~**ize** *v.t.* mettre en péril.

jerk /dʒɜːk/ *n.* secousse *f.;* *(fool: sl.)* idiot *m.;* *(creep: sl.)* salaud *m.* —*v.t.* donner une secousse à. ~**ily** *adv.* par saccades. ~**y** *a.* saccadé.

jersey /ˈdʒɜːzɪ/ *n. (garment)* chandail *m.,* tricot *m.;* *(fabric)* jersey *m.*

jest /dʒest/ *n.* plaisanterie *f.* —*v.i.* plaisanter. ~**er** *n.* bouffon *m.*

Jesus /ˈdʒiːzəs/ *n.* Jésus *m.*

jet[1] /dʒet/ *n. (mineral)* jais *m.* ~**black** *a.* de jais.

jet[2] /dʒet/ *n. (stream)* jet *m.;* *(plane)* avion à réaction *m.,* jet *m.* ~ **lag,** fatigue due au décalage horaire *f.* ~**-propelled** *a.* à réaction.

jettison /ˈdʒetɪsn/ *v.t.* jeter à la mer; *(aviat.)* larguer; *(fig.)* abandonner.

jetty /ˈdʒetɪ/ *n. (breakwater)* jetée *f.*

Jew /dʒuː/ *n.* Juif *m.* ~**ess** *n.* Juive *f.*

jewel /ˈdʒuːəl/ *n.* bijou *m.* ~**led** *a.* orné de bijoux. ~**ler** *n.* bijoutier, -ière *m., f.* ~**lery** *n.* bijoux *m. pl.*

Jewish /ˈdʒuːɪʃ/ *a.* juif.

Jewry /ˈdʒʊərɪ/ *n.* les Juifs *m. pl.*

jib /dʒɪb/ *v.i.* *(p.t.* **jibbed**) regimber *(at,* devant). —*n. (sail)* foc *m.*

jibe /dʒaɪb/ *n.* = **gibe.**

jiffy /ˈdʒɪfɪ/ *n. (fam.)* instant *m.*

jig /dʒɪg/ *n. (dance)* gigue *f.*

jiggle /ˈdʒɪgl/ *v.t.* secouer légèrement.

jigsaw /ˈdʒɪgsɔː/ *n.* puzzle *m.*

jilt /dʒɪlt/ *v.t.* laisser tomber.

jingle /ˈdʒɪŋgl/ *v.t/i.* (faire) tinter. —*n.* tintement *m.;* *(advertising)* jingle *m.,* sonal *m.*

jinx /dʒɪŋks/ *n. (person: fam.)* porte-malheur *m. invar.;* *(spell: fig.)* mauvais sort *m.*

jitter|**s** /ˈdʒɪtəz/ *n. pl.* **the** ~**s,** *(fam.)* la frousse *f.* ~**y** /-ərɪ/ *a.* **be** ~**y,** *(fam.)* avoir la frousse.

job /dʒɒb/ *n.* travail *m.;* *(post)*

poste *m.* **have a ~ doing**, avoir du mal à faire. **it is a good ~ that**, heureusement que. **~less** *a.* sans travail, au chômage.

jobcentre /'dʒɒbsentə(r)/ *n.* agence (nationale) pour l'emploi *f.*

jockey /'dʒɒkɪ/ *n.* jockey *m.* —*v.t.* (*manœuvre*) manœuvrer.

jocular /'dʒɒkjʊlə(r)/ *a.* jovial.

jog /dʒɒg/ *v.t.* (*p.t.* **jogged**) pousser; (*memory*) rafraîchir. —*v.i.* faire du jogging. **~ging** *n.* jogging *m.*

join /dʒɔɪn/ *v.t.* joindre, unir; (*club*) devenir membre de; (*political group*) adhérer à; (*army*) s'engager dans. **~ s.o.**, (*in activity*) se joindre à qn.; (*meet*) rejoindre qn. —*v.i.* (*roads etc.*) se rejoindre. —*n.* joint *m.* **~ in**, participer (à). **~ up**, (*mil.*) s'engager.

joiner /'dʒɔɪnə(r)/ *n.* menuisier *m.*

joint /dʒɔɪnt/ *a.* (*account, venture*) commun. *n.* (*join*) joint *m.*; (*anat.*) articulation *f.*; (*culin.*) rôti *m.*; (*place: sl.*) boîte *f.* **~ author**, coauteur *m.* **out of ~**, déboîté. **~ly** *adv.* conjointement.

joist /dʒɔɪst/ *n.* solive *f.*

joke /dʒəʊk/ *n.* plaisanterie *f.*; (*trick*) farce *f.* —*v.i.* plaisanter. **it's no ~e**, ce n'est pas drôle. **~er** *n.* blagueu|r, -se *m.f.*; (*pej.*) petit malin *m.*; (*cards*) joker *m.* **~ingly** *adv.* pour rire.

jolly /'dʒɒlɪ/ *a.* (**-ier, -iest**) gai. —*adv.* (*fam.*) rudement. **~ification** /-fɪ'keɪʃn/, **~ity** *ns.* réjouissances *f. pl.*

jolt /dʒəʊlt/ *v.t./i.* (*vehicle, passenger*) cahoter; (*shake*) secouer. —*n.* cahot *m.*; secousse *f.*

Jordan /'dʒɔːdn/ *n.* Jordanie *f.*

jostle /'dʒɒsl/ *v.t./i.* (*push*) bousculer; (*push each other*) se bousculer.

jot /dʒɒt/ *n.* brin *m.* —*v.t.* (*p.t.* **jotted**) **~ down**, noter. **~ter** *n.* (*pad*) bloc-notes *m.*

journal /'dʒɜːnl/ *n.* journal *m.* **~ism** *n.* journalisme *m.* **~ist** *n.* journaliste *m./f.* **~ese** /-'liːz/ *n.* jargon des journalistes *m.*

journey /'dʒɜːnɪ/ *n.* voyage *m.*; (*distance*) trajet *m.* —*v.i.* voyager.

jovial /'dʒəʊvɪəl/ *a.* jovial.

joy /dʒɔɪ/ *n.* joie *f.* **~-riding** *n.* courses en voitures volées *f. pl.* **~ful, ~ous** *adjs.* joyeux.

joystick /'dʒɔɪstɪk/ *n.* (*comput.*) manette *f.*

jubil|ant /'dʒuːbɪlənt/ *a.* débordant de joie. **be ~ant**, jubiler. **~ation** /-'leɪʃn/ *n.* jubilation *f.*

jubilee /'dʒuːbɪliː/ *n.* jubilé *m.*

Judaism /'dʒuːdeɪɪzm/ *n.* judaïsme *m.*

judder /'dʒʌdə(r)/ *v.i.* vibrer. —*n.* vibration *f.*

judge /dʒʌdʒ/ *n.* juge *m.* —*v.t.* juger. **judging by**, à juger de. **~ment** *n.* jugement *m.*

judic|iary /dʒuː'dɪʃərɪ/ *n.* magistrature *f.* **~ial** *a.* judiciaire.

judicious /dʒuː'dɪʃəs/ *a.* judicieux.

judo /'dʒuːdəʊ/ *n.* judo *m.*

jug /dʒʌg/ *n.* cruche *f.*, pichet *m.*

juggernaut /'dʒʌgənɔːt/ *n.* (*lorry*) poids lourd *m.*, mastodonte *m.*

juggle /'dʒʌgl/ *v.t./i.* jongler (avec). **~r** /-ə(r)/ *n.* jongleu|r, -se *m.*, *f.*

juic|e /dʒuːs/ *n.* jus *m.* **~y** *a.* juteux; (*details etc.: fam.*) croustillant.

juke-box /'dʒuːkbɒks/ *n.* juke-box *m.*

July /dʒuː'laɪ/ *n.* juillet *m.*

jumble /'dʒʌmbl/ *v.t.* mélanger. —*n.* (*muddle*) fouillis *m.* **~ sale**, vente (de charité) *f.*

jumbo /'dʒʌmbəʊ/ *a.* **~ jet**, avion géant *m.*, jumbo-jet *m.*

jump /dʒʌmp/ *v.t./i.* sauter; (*start*) sursauter; (*of price etc.*) faire un

bond. —n. saut m.; sursaut m.;
(*increase*) hausse f. ~ **at**, sauter
sur. ~**-leads** n. pl. câbles de
démarrage m. pl. ~ **the gun**, agir
prématurément. ~ **the queue**,
resquiller.

jumper /'dʒʌmpə(r)/ n. pull-(over)
m.; (*dress: Amer.*) robe chasuble f.

jumpy /'dʒʌmpɪ/ a. nerveux.

junction /'dʒʌŋkʃn/ n. jonction f.;
(*of roads etc.*) embranchement m.

juncture /'dʒʌŋktʃə(r)/ n. moment
m.; (*state of affairs*) conjoncture f.

June /dʒuːn/ n. juin m.

jungle /'dʒʌŋgl/ n. jungle f.

junior /'dʒuːnɪə(r)/ a. (*in age*) plus
jeune (**to**, que); (*in rank*) subalterne; (*school*) élémentaire;
(*executive, doctor*) jeune. —n.
cadet(te) m. (f.); (*schol.*) petit(e)
élève m. (f.); (*sport*) junior m./f.

junk /dʒʌŋk/ n. bric-à-brac m.
invar.; (*poor material*) camelote f.
—v.t. (*Amer., sl.*) balancer. ~
food, saloperies f. pl. ~**-shop** n.
boutique de brocanteur f.

junkie /'dʒʌŋkɪ/ n. (*sl.*) drogué(e)
m. (f.).

junta /'dʒʌntə/ n. junte f.

jurisdiction /dʒʊərɪs'dɪkʃn/ n.
juridiction f.

jurisprudence /dʒʊərɪs'pruːdəns/
n. jurisprudence f.

juror /'dʒʊərə(r)/ n. juré m.

jury /'dʒʊərɪ/ n. jury m.

just /dʒʌst/ a. (*fair*) juste. —adv.
juste, exactement; (*only, slightly*)
juste; (*simply*) tout simplement.
he has/had ~ **left**/*etc.*, il
vient/venait de partir/*etc.* **have**
~ **missed**, avoir manqué de peu.
it's ~ **a cold**, ce n'est qu'un
rhume. ~ **as tall**/*etc.*, tout aussi
grand/*etc.* (**as**, que). ~ **as well**,
heureusement (que). ~ **listen!**,
écoutez donc! ~**ly** adv. avec
justice.

justice /'dʒʌstɪs/ n. justice f. **J**~
of the Peace, juge de paix m.

justifiabl|e /dʒʌstɪ'faɪəbl/ a. jus-
tifiable. ~**y** adv. avec raison.

justif|y /'dʒʌstɪfaɪ/ v.t. justifier.
~**ication** /-ɪ'keɪʃn/ n. justification f.

jut /dʒʌt/ v.i. (p.t. jutted). ~ **out**,
faire saillie, dépasser.

juvenile /'dʒuːvənaɪl/ a. (*youthful*)
juvénile; (*childish*) puéril; (*de-
linquent*) jeune; (*court*) pour
enfants. —n. jeune m./f.

juxtapose /dʒʌkstə'pəʊz/ v.t. juxtaposer.

K

kaleidoscope /kə'laɪdəskəʊp/ n.
kaléidoscope.

kangaroo /kæŋgə'ruː/ n. kangourou m.

karate /kə'rɑːtɪ/ n. karaté m.

kebab /kə'bæb/ n. brochette f.

keel /kiːl/ n. (*of ship*) quille f. —v.i.
~ **over**, chavirer.

keen /kiːn/ a. (-er, -est) (*interest,
wind, feeling, etc.*) vif; (*mind,
analysis*) pénétrant; (*edge, appetite*) aiguisé; (*eager*) enthousiaste. **be** ~ **on**, (*person,
thing: fam.*) aimer beaucoup. **be**
~ **to do** or **on doing**, tenir
beaucoup à faire. ~**ly** adv.
vivement; avec enthousiasme.
~**ness** n. vivacité f.; enthousiasme m.

keep /kiːp/ v.t. (p.t. kept) garder;
(*promise, shop, diary, etc.*) tenir;
(*family*) entretenir; (*animals*)
élever; (*rule etc.*) respecter;
(*celebrate*) célébrer; (*delay*) retenir; (*prevent*) empêcher; (*conceal*) cacher. —v.i. (*food*) se
garder; (*remain*) rester. ~ (**on**),
continuer (**doing**, à faire). —n.
subsistance f.; (*of castle*) donjon
m. **for** ~**s**, (*fam.*) pour toujours.
~ **back** v.t. retenir; v.i. ne pas

s'approcher. **~ s.o. from doing,** empêcher qn. de faire. **~ in/out,** empêcher d'entrer/de sortir. **~ up, (se)** maintenir. **~ up (with),** suivre. **~er** n. gardien(ne) m. (f.). **~fit** n. exercices physiques m. pl.

keeping /'ki:pɪŋ/ n. garde f. **in ~ with,** en accord avec.

keepsake /'ki:pseɪk/ n. (thing) souvenir m.

keg /keg/ n. tonnelet m.

kennel /'kenl/ n. niche f.

Kenya /'kenjə/ n. Kenya m.

kept /kept/ see keep.

kerb /kɜ:b/ n. bord du trottoir m.

kerfuffle /kə'fʌfl/ n. (fuss. fam.) histoire(s) f. (pl.).

kernel /'kɜ:nl/ n. amande f.

kerosene /'kerəsi:n/ n. (aviation fuel) kérosène m.; (paraffin) pétrole (lampant) m.

ketchup /'ketʃəp/ n. ketchup m.

kettle /'ketl/ n. bouilloire f.

key /ki:/ n. clef f.; (of piano etc.) touche f. —a. clef (f. invar.). **~ring** n. porte-clefs m. invar. —v.t. **~ in,** (comput.) saisir. **~ up,** surexciter.

keyboard /'ki:bɔ:d/ n. clavier m.

keyhole /'ki:həʊl/ n. trou de la serrure m.

keynote /'ki:nəʊt/ n. (of speech etc.) note dominante f.

keystone /'ki:stəʊn/ n. (archit., fig.) clef de voûte f.

khaki /'kɑ:ki/ a. kaki invar.

kibbutz /kɪ'bʊts/ n. (pl. -im /-i:m/) kibboutz m.

kick /kɪk/ v.t./i. donner un coup de pied (à); (of horse) ruer. —n. coup de pied m.; (thrill: fam.) plaisir m.; (of gun) recul m. **~off** n. coup d'envoi m. **~ out,** (fam.) flanquer dehors. **~ up,** (fuss, racket: fam.) faire.

kid /kɪd/ n. (goat, leather) chevreau m.; (child: sl.) gosse m./f. —v.t./i. (p.t. kidded) blaguer.

kidnap /'kɪdnæp/ v.t. (p.t. kidnapped) enlever, kidnapper. **~ping** n. enlèvement m.

kidney /'kɪdnɪ/ n. rein m.; (culin.) rognon m.

kill /kɪl/ v.t. tuer; (fig.) mettre fin à. —n. mise à mort f. **~er** n. tueu|r, -se m., f. **~ing** n. massacre m., meurtre m.; a. (funny: fam.) tordant; (tiring: fam.) tuant.

killjoy /'kɪldʒɔɪ/ n. rabat-joie m. invar., trouble-fête m./f. invar.

kiln /kɪln/ n. four m.

kilo /'ki:ləʊ/ n. (pl. -os) kilo m.

kilobyte /'kɪləbaɪt/ n. kilo-octet m.

kilogram /'kɪləgræm/ n. kilogramme m.

kilohertz /'kɪləhɜːts/ n. kilohertz m.

kilometre /'kɪləmiːtə(r)/ n. kilomètre m.

kilowatt /'kɪləwɒt/ n. kilowatt m.

kilt /kɪlt/ n. kilt m.

kin /kɪn/ n. parents m. pl.

kind[1] /kaɪnd/ n. genre m., sorte f., espèce f. **in ~,** en nature f. **~ of,** (somewhat: fam.) un peu. **be two of a ~,** se rassembler.

kind[2] /kaɪnd/ a. (-er, -est) gentil, bon. **~-hearted** a. bon. **~ness** n. bonté f.

kindergarten /'kɪndəgɑːtn/ n. jardin d'enfants m.

kindle /'kɪndl/ v.t./i. (s')allumer.

kindly /'kaɪndlɪ/ a. (-ier, -iest) bienveillant. —adv. avec bonté. **~ wait/etc.,** voulez-vous avoir la bonté d'attendre/etc.

kindred /'kɪndrɪd/ a. apparenté. **~ spirit,** personne qui a les mêmes goûts f., âme sœur f.

kinetic /kɪ'netɪk/ a. cinétique.

king /kɪŋ/ n. roi m. **~-size(d)** a. géant.

kingdom /'kɪŋdəm/ n. royaume m.; (bot.) règne m.

kingfisher /'kɪŋfɪʃə(r)/ n. martin-pêcheur m.

kink /kɪŋk/ n. (in rope) entortille-
ment m.; déformation f.; (fig.)
perversion f. ~y a. (fam.)
perverti.

kiosk /'kiːɒsk/ n. kiosque m.
telephone ~, cabine téléphonique f.

kip /kɪp/ n. roupillon m. —v.i.
(p.t. **kipped**) (sl.) roupiller.

kipper /'kɪpə(r)/ n. hareng fumé m.

kirby-grip /'kɜːbɪɡrɪp/ n. pince à
cheveux f.

kiss /kɪs/ n. baiser m. —v.t./i.
(s')embrasser.

kit /kɪt/ n. équipement m.;
(clothing) affaires f. pl.; (set of
tools etc.) trousse f.; (for assembly) kit m. —v.t. (p.t. **kitted**)
~ **out**, équiper.

kitbag /'kɪtbæɡ/ n. sac m. (de
marin etc.).

kitchen /'kɪtʃɪn/ n. cuisine f. ~
garden, jardin potager m.

kitchenette /kɪtʃɪ'net/ n. kitchenette f.

kite /kaɪt/ n. (toy) cerf-volant m.

kith /kɪθ/ n. ~ **and kin**, parents et
amis m. pl.

kitten /'kɪtn/ n. chaton m.

kitty /'kɪtɪ/ n. (fund) cagnotte f.

knack /næk/ n. truc m., chic m.

knapsack /'næpsæk/ n. sac à dos
m.

knave /neɪv/ n. (cards) valet m.

knead /niːd/ v.t. pétrir.

knee /niː/ n. genou m.

kneecap /'niːkæp/ n. rotule f.

kneel /niːl/ v.i. (p.t. **knelt**). ~
(**down**), s'agenouiller.

knell /nel/ n. glas m.

knew /njuː/ see **know**.

knickers /'nɪkəz/ n. pl. (woman's
undergarment) culotte f., slip m.

knife /naɪf/ n. (pl. **knives**) couteau
m. —v.t. poignarder.

knight /naɪt/ n. chevalier m.;
(chess) cavalier m. —v.t. faire ou
armer chevalier. ~**hood** n. titre
de chevalier m.

knit /nɪt/ v.t./i. (p.t. **knitted** or
knit) tricoter; (bones etc.) (se)
souder. ~ **one's brow**, froncer
les sourcils. ~**ting** n. tricot
m.

knitwear /'nɪtweə(r)/ n. tricots m.
pl.

knob /nɒb/ n. bouton m.

knock /nɒk/ v.t./i. frapper, cogner;
(criticize: sl.) critiquer. —n. coup
m. ~ **about** v.t. malmener; v.i.
vadrouiller. ~ **down**, (chair,
pedestrian) renverser; (demolish)
abattre; (reduce) baisser. ~-
down a. (price) très bas. ~
kneed a. cagneux. ~ **off** v.t. faire
tomber; (fam.) expédier; v.i.
(fam.) s'arrêter de travailler. ~
out, (by blow) assommer; (tire)
épuiser. ~-**out** n. (boxing) knock-
out m. ~ **over**, renverser. ~ **up**,
(meal etc.) préparer en vitesse.
~**er** n. heurtoir m.

knot /nɒt/ n. nœud m. —v.t. (p.t.
knotted) nouer. ~**ty** /'nɒtɪ/ a.
noueux; (problem) épineux.

know /nəʊ/ v.t./i. (p.t. **knew**, p.p.
known) savoir (that, que);
(person, place) connaître. ~ **how**
to do, savoir comment faire. —n.
in the ~, (fam.) dans le secret, au
courant. ~ **about**, (cars etc.) s'y
connaître en. ~-**all**, (Amer.) ~-
it-all n. je-sais-tout m./f. ~-**how**
n. technique f. ~ **of**, connaître,
avoir entendu parler de. ~**ingly**
adv. (consciously) sciemment.

knowledge /'nɒlɪdʒ/ n. connaissance f.; (learning) connaissances
f. pl. ~**able** a. bien informé.

known /nəʊn/ see **know**. —a.
connu; (recognized) reconnu.

knuckle /'nʌkl/ n. articulation du
doigt f. —v.i. ~ **under**, se
soumettre.

Koran /kə'rɑːn/ n. Coran m.

Korea /kə'rɪə/ n. Corée f.

kosher /'kəʊʃə(r)/ a. kascher
invar.

kowtow /kaʊˈtaʊ/ v.i. se prosterner (**to**, devant).

kudos /ˈkjuːdɒs/ n. (fam.) gloire f.

Kurd /kɜːd/ a. & n. kurde m./f.

L

lab /læb/ n. (fam.) labo m.

label /ˈleɪbl/ n. étiquette f. —v.t. (p.t. labelled) étiqueter.

laboratory /ləˈbɒrətrɪ. Amer. ˈlæbrətɔːrɪ/ n. laboratoire m.

laborious /ləˈbɔːrɪəs/ a. laborieux.

labour /ˈleɪbə(r)/ n. travail m.; (workers) main-d'œuvre f. —v.i. peiner. —v.t. trop insister sur. in ~, en train d'accoucher, en couches. ~ed a. laborieux.

Labour /ˈleɪbə(r)/ n. le parti travailliste m. —a. travailliste.

labourer /ˈleɪbərə(r)/ n. manœuvre m.; (on farm) ouvrier agricole m.

labyrinth /ˈlæbərɪnθ/ n. labyrinthe m.

lace /leɪs/ n. dentelle f.; (of shoe) lacet m. —v.t. (fasten) lacer; (drink) arroser. ~-ups n. pl. chaussures à lacets f. pl.

lacerate /ˈlæsəreɪt/ v.t. lacérer.

lack /læk/ n. manque m. —v.t. manquer de. be ~ing, manquer (in, de). for ~ of, faute de.

lackadaisical /lækəˈdeɪzɪkl/ a. indolent, apathique.

lackey /ˈlækɪ/ n. laquais m.

laconic /ləˈkɒnɪk/ a. laconique.

lacquer /ˈlækə(r)/ n. laque f.

lad /læd/ n. garçon m., gars m.

ladder /ˈlædə(r)/ n. échelle f.; (in stocking) maille filée f. —v.t./i. (stocking) filer.

laden /ˈleɪdn/ a. chargé (with, de).

ladle /ˈleɪdl/ n. louche f.

lady /ˈleɪdɪ/ n. dame f. ~-friend, amie f. ~-in-waiting n. dame d'honneur f. young ~, jeune

femme or fille f. ~like a. distingué.

lady|bird /ˈleɪdɪbɜːd/ n. coccinelle f. ~bug n. (Amer.) coccinelle f.

lag[1] /læg/ v.i. (p.t. lagged) traîner. —n. (interval) décalage m.

lag[2] /læg/ v.t. (p.t. lagged) (pipes) calorifuger.

lager /ˈlɑːgə(r)/ n. bière blonde f.

lagoon /ləˈguːn/ n. lagune f.

laid /leɪd/ see **lay**[2]. ~-back a. (fam.) cool.

lain /leɪn/ see **lie**[2].

lair /leə(r)/ n. tanière f.

laity /ˈleɪətɪ/ n. laïques m. pl.

lake /leɪk/ n. lac m.

lamb /læm/ n. agneau m.

lambswool /ˈlæmzwʊl/ n. laine d'agneau f.

lame /leɪm/ a. (-er, -est) boiteux; (excuse) faible. ~ly adv. (argue) sans conviction. ~ duck, canard boiteux m.

lament /ləˈment/ n. lamentation f. —v.t./i. se lamenter (sur). ~able a. lamentable.

laminated /ˈlæmɪneɪtɪd/ a. laminé.

lamp /læmp/ n. lampe f.

lamppost /ˈlæmppəʊst/ n. réverbère m.

lampshade /ˈlæmpʃeɪd/ n. abat-jour m. invar.

lance /lɑːns/ n. lance f. —v.t. (med.) inciser.

lancet /ˈlɑːnsɪt/ n. bistouri m.

land /lænd/ n. terre f.; (plot) terrain m.; (country) pays m. —a. terrestre; (policy, reform) agraire. —v.t./i. débarquer; (aircraft) (se) poser, (faire) atterrir; (fall) tomber; (obtain) décrocher; (put) mettre; (a blow) porter. ~locked a. sans accès à la mer. ~up, se retrouver.

landed /ˈlændɪd/ a. foncier.

landing /ˈlændɪŋ/ n. débarquement m.; (aviat.) atterrissage m.; (top of stairs) palier m. ~-stage *n.* débarcadère *m.* **~-strip** *n.* piste d'atterrissage *f.*

land|lady /ˈlændleɪd/ *n.* propriétaire *f.*; (*of inn*) patronne *f.* **~lord** *n.* propriétaire *m.*; patron *m.*

landmark /ˈlændmɑːk/ *n.* (point de) repère *m.*

landscape /ˈlæn(d)skeɪp/ *n.* paysage *m.* —*v.t.* aménager.

landslide /ˈlændslaɪd/ *n.* glissement de terrain *m.*; (*pol.*) razde-marée (électoral) *m. invar.*

lane /leɪn/ *n.* (*path*, *road*) chemin *m.*; (*strip of road*) voie *f.*; (*of traffic*) file *f.*; (*aviat.*) couloir *m.*

language /ˈlæŋgwɪdʒ/ *n.* langue *f.*; (*speech*, *style*) langage *m.* **~ laboratory**, laboratoire de langue *m.*

languid /ˈlæŋgwɪd/ *a.* languissant.

languish /ˈlæŋgwɪʃ/ *v.i.* languir.

lank /læŋk/ *a.* grand et maigre.

lanky /ˈlæŋkɪ/ *a.* (-**ier**, -**iest**) dégingandé, grand et maigre.

lanolin /ˈlænəlɪn/ *n.* lanoline *f.*

lantern /ˈlæntən/ *n.* lanterne *f.*

lap[1] /læp/ *n.* genoux *m. pl.*; (*sport*) tour (de piste) *m.* —*v.t./i.* (*p.t.* **lapped**) **~ over**, (se) chevaucher.

lap[2] /læp/ *v.t.* (*p.t.* **lapped**). **~ up**, laper. —*v.i.* (*waves*) clapoter.

lapel /ləˈpel/ *n.* revers *m.*

lapse /læps/ *v.i.* (*decline*) se dégrader; (*expire*) se périmer. —*n.* défaillance *f.*, erreur *f.*; (*of time*) intervalle *m.* **~ into**, retomber dans.

larceny /ˈlɑːsənɪ/ *n.* vol simple *m.*

lard /lɑːd/ *n.* saindoux *m.*

larder /ˈlɑːdə(r)/ *n.* garde-manger *m. invar.*

large /lɑːdʒ/ *a.* (-**er**, -**est**) grand, gros. **at ~**, en liberté. **by and ~**, en général. **~ly** *adv.* en grande mesure. **~ness** *n.* grandeur *f.*

lark[1] /lɑːk/ *n.* (*bird*) alouette *f.*

lark[2] /lɑːk/ *n.* (*bit of fun*: *fam.*) rigolade *f.* —*v.i.* (*fam.*) rigoler.

larva /ˈlɑːvə/ *n.* (*pl.* -**vae** /-viː/) larve *f.*

laryngitis /lærɪnˈdʒaɪtɪs/ *n.* laryngite *f.*

larynx /ˈlærɪŋks/ *n.* larynx *m.*

lasagne /ləˈzænjə/ *n.* lasagne *f.*

laser /ˈleɪzə(r)/ *n.* laser *m.* **~ printer**, imprimante laser *f.*

lash /læʃ/ *v.t.* fouetter. —*n.* coup de fouet *m.*; (*eyelash*) cil *m.* **~ out**, (*spend*) dépenser follement. **~ out against**, attaquer.

lashings /ˈlæʃɪŋz/ *n. pl.* **~ of**, (*cream etc.*: *sl.*) des masses de.

lass /læs/ *n.* jeune fille *f.*

lasso /læˈsuː/ *n.* (*pl.* -**os**) lasso *m.*

last[1] /lɑːst/ *a.* dernier. —*adv.* en dernier; (*most recently*) la dernière fois. —*n.* dern|ier, -ière *m.*, *f.*; (*remainder*) reste *m.* **at (long) ~**, enfin. **~-ditch** *a.* ultime. **~-minute** *a.* de dernière minute. **~ night**, hier soir. **the ~ straw**, le comble. **the ~ word**, le mot de la fin. **on its ~ legs**, sur le point de rendre l'âme. **~ly** *adv.* en dernier lieu.

last[2] /lɑːst/ *v.i.* durer. **~ing** *a.* durable.

latch /lætʃ/ *n.* loquet *m.*

late /leɪt/ *a.* (-**er**, -**est**) (*not on time*) en retard; (*recent*) récent; (*former*) ancien; (*hour*, *fruit*, *etc.*) tardif; (*deceased*) défunt. **the late Mrs X**, feu Mme X. **~st** /-st/, (*last*) dernier. —*adv.* (*not early*) tard; (*not on time*) en retard. **in ~ July**, fin juillet. **of ~**, dernièrement. **~ness** *n.* retard *m.*; (*of event*) heure tardive *f.*

latecomer /ˈleɪtkʌmə(r)/ *n.* retardataire *m./f.*

lately /ˈleɪtlɪ/ *adv.* dernièrement.

latent /ˈleɪtnt/ *a.* latent.

lateral /ˈlætərəl/ *a.* latéral.

lathe /leɪð/ *n.* tour *m.*

lather /ˈlɑːðə(r)/ *n.* mousse *f.* —*v.t.* savonner. —*v.i.* mousser.

Latin /'lætɪn/ *n.* (*lang.*) latin *m.*
　　—*a.* latin. **～ America**, Amérique latine *f.*

latitude /'lætɪtjuːd/ *n.* latitude *f.*

latrine /lə'triːn/ *n.* latrines *f. pl.*

latter /'lætə(r)/ *a.* dernier. **the ～**, celui-ci, celle-ci. **～-day** *a.* moderne. **～ly** *adv.* dernièrement.

lattice /'lætɪs/ *n.* treillage *m.*

laudable /'lɔːdəbl/ *a.* louable.

laugh /lɑːf/ *v.i.* rire (**at**, de). —*n.* rire *m.* **～able** *a.* ridicule. **～ing-stock** *n.* objet de risée *m.*

laughter /'lɑːftə(r)/ *n.* (*act*) rire *m.*; (*sound of laughs*) rires *m. pl.*

launch¹ /lɔːntʃ/ *v.t.* lancer. —*n.* lancement *m.* **～ (out) into**, se lancer dans. **～ing pad**, aire de lancement *f.*

launch² /lɔːntʃ/ *n.* (*boat*) vedette *f.*

launder /'lɔːndə(r)/ *v.t.* blanchir.

launderette /lɔːn'dret/ *n.* laverie automatique *f.*

laundry /'lɔːndrɪ/ *n.* (*place*) blanchisserie *f.*; (*clothes*) linge *m.*

laurel /'lɒrəl/ *n.* laurier *m.*

lava /'lɑːvə/ *n.* lave *f.*

lavatory /'lævətrɪ/ *n.* cabinets *m. pl.*

lavender /'lævəndə(r)/ *n.* lavande *f.*

lavish /'lævɪʃ/ *a.* (*person*) prodigue; (*plentiful*) copieux; (*lush*) somptueux. —*v.t.* prodiguer (**on**, à). **～ly** *adv.* copieusement.

law /lɔː/ *n.* loi *f.*; (*profession, subject of study*) droit *m.* **～-abiding** *a.* respectueux des lois. **～ and order**, l'ordre public. **～ful** *a.* légal. **～fully** *adv.* légalement. **～less** *a.* sans loi.

lawcourt /'lɔːkɔːt/ *n.* tribunal *m.*

lawn /lɔːn/ *n.* pelouse *f.*, gazon *m.* **～-mower** *n.* tondeuse à gazon *f.* **～ tennis**, tennis (sur gazon) *m.*

lawsuit /'lɔːsuːt/ *n.* procès *m.*

lawyer /'lɔːjə(r)/ *n.* avocat *m.*

lax /læks/ *a.* négligent; (*morals*

etc.) relâché. **～ity** *n.* négligence *f.*

laxative /'læksətɪv/ *n.* laxatif *m.*

lay¹ /leɪ/ *a.* (*non-clerical*) laïque; (*opinion etc.*) d'un profane.

lay² /leɪ/ *v.t.* (*p.t.* **laid**) poser, mettre; (*trap*) tendre; (*table*) mettre; (*plan*) former; (*eggs*) pondre. —*v.i.* pondre. **～ aside**, mettre de côté. **～ down**, (dé)poser; (*condition*) (im)poser. **～ hold of**, saisir. **～ off** *v.t.* (*worker*) licencier; *v.i.* (*fam.*) arrêter. **～-off** *n.* licenciement *m.* **～ on**, (*provide*) fournir. **～ out**, (*design*) dessiner; (*display*) disposer; (*money*) dépenser. **～ up**, (*store*) amasser. **～ waste**, ravager.

lay³ /leɪ/ *see* **lie**².

layabout /'leɪəbaʊt/ *n.* fainéant(e) *m.* (*f.*).

lay-by /'leɪbaɪ/ *n.* (*pl.* **-bys**) petite aire de stationnement *f.*

layer /'leɪə(r)/ *n.* couche *f.*

layman /'leɪmən/ *n.* (*pl.* **-men**) profane *m.*

layout /'leɪaʊt/ *n.* disposition *f.*

laze /leɪz/ *v.i.* paresser.

laz|y /'leɪzɪ/ *a.* (**-ier**, **-iest**) paresseux. **～iness** *n.* paresse *f.* **～y-bones** *n.* flemmard(e) *m.* (*f.*).

lead¹ /liːd/ *v.t./i.* (*p.t.* **led**) mener; (*team etc.*) diriger; (*life*) mener; (*induce*) amener. **～ to**, conduire à, mener à. —*n.* avance *f.*; (*clue*) indice *m.*; (*leash*) laisse *f.*; (*theatre*) premier rôle *m.*; (*wire*) fil *m.*; (*example*) exemple *m.* **in the ～**, en tête. **～ away**, emmener. **～ up to**, (*precede*) venir à; (*precede*) précéder.

lead² /led/ *n.* plomb *m.*; (*of pencil*) mine *f.* **～en** *a.* (*sky*) de plomb (*humour*) lourd.

leader /'liːdə(r)/ *n.* chef *m.*; (*of country, club, etc.*) dirigeant(e) *m.* (*f.*); (*leading article*) éditorial *m.* **～ship** *n.* direction *f.*

leading /'li:dɪŋ/ a. principal. **~ article,** éditorial m.

leaf /li:f/ n. (pl. **leaves**) feuille f.; (of table) rallonge f. —v.i. **~ through,** feuilleter. **~y** a. feuillu.

leaflet /'li:flɪt/ n. prospectus m.

league /li:g/ n. ligue f.; (sport) championnat m. **in ~ with,** de mèche avec.

leak /li:k/ n. fuite f. —v.i. fuir; (news: fig.) s'ébruiter. —v.t. répandre; (fig.) divulguer. **~age** n. fuite f. **~y** a. qui a une fuite.

lean[1] /li:n/ a. (-**er**, -**est**) maigre. —n. (of meat) maigre m. **~ness** n. maigreur f.

lean[2] /li:n/ v.t./i. (p.t. **leaned** or **leant** /lent/) (rest) (s')appuyer; (slope) pencher. **~ out,** se pencher à l'extérieur. **~ over,** (of person) se pencher. **~to** n. appentis m.

leaning /'li:nɪŋ/ a. penché —n. tendance f.

leap /li:p/ v.i. (p.t. **leaped** or **leapt** /lept/) bondir. —n. bond m. **~-frog** n. saute-mouton m. invar.; v.i. (p.t. **-frogged**) sauter (over, par-dessus). **~ year,** année bissextile f.

learn /lɜ:n/ v.t./i. (p.t. **learned** or **learnt**) apprendre (**to do,** à faire). **~er** n. débutant(e) m. (f.).

learn|ed /'lɜ:nɪd/ a. érudit. **~ing** n. érudition f., connaissances f. pl.

lease /li:s/ n. bail m. —v.t. louer à bail.

leaseback /'li:sbæk/ n. cession-bail f.

leash /li:ʃ/ n. laisse f.

least /li:st/ a. **the ~,** (smallest amount of) le moins de; (slightest) le or la moindre. —n. le moins. —adv. le moins; (with adjective) le or la moins. **at ~,** au moins.

leather /'leðə(r)/ n. cuir m.

leave /li:v/ v.t. (p.t. **left**) laisser; (depart from) quitter. —n. (holiday) congé m.; (consent) permission f. **be left (over),** rester. **~ alone,** (thing) ne pas toucher à; (person) laisser tranquille. **~ behind,** laisser. **~ out,** omettre. **on ~,** (mil.) en permission. **take one's ~,** prendre congé (**of,** de).

leavings /'li:vɪŋz/ n. pl. restes m. pl.

Leban|on /'lebənən/ n. Liban m. **~ese** /-'ni:z/ a. & n. libanais(e) (m. (f.)).

lecher /'letʃə(r)/ n. débauché m. **~ous** a. lubrique. **~y** n. lubricité f.

lectern /'lektən/ n. lutrin m.

lecture /'lektʃə(r)/ n. cours m., conférence f.; (rebuke) réprimande f. —v.t./i. faire un cours or une conférence (à); (rebuke) réprimander. **~r** /-ə(r)/ n. conférenci|er, -ière m., f., (univ.) enseignant(e) m. (f.).

led /led/ see **lead**[1].

ledge /ledʒ/ n. (window) rebord m.; (rock) saillie f.

ledger /'ledʒə(r)/ n. grand livre m.

lee /li:/ n. côté sous le vent m.

leek /li:k/ n. poireau m.

leech /li:tʃ/ n. sangsue f.

leer /lɪə(r)/ v.i. **~ (at),** lorgner. —n. regard sournois m.

leeway /'li:weɪ/ n. (naut.) dérive f.; (fig.) liberté d'action f. **make up ~,** rattraper le retard.

left[1] /left/ see **leave**. **~ luggage (office),** consigne f. **~-overs** n. restes m. pl.

left[2] /left/ a. gauche. —adv. à gauche. —n. gauche f. **~-hand** a. à or de gauche. **~-handed** a. gaucher. **~-wing** a. (pol.) de gauche.

leftist /'leftɪst/ n. gauchiste m./f.

leg /leg/ n. jambe f.; (of animal) patte f.; (of table) pied m.; (of chicken) cuisse f.; (of lamb) gigot m.; (*of journey*) étape f. **~-room** n. place pour les jambes f. **~-warmers** n. pl. jambières f. pl.

legacy /'legəsɪ/ n. legs m.

legal /'liːgl/ a. légal; (*affairs etc.*) juridique. **~ity** /liːˈgælɪtɪ/ n. légalité f. **~ly** adv. légalement.

legalize /'liːgəlaɪz/ v.t. légaliser.

legend /'ledʒənd/ n. légende f. **~ary** a. légendaire.

leggings /'legɪnz/ n. pl. collant sans pieds m.

legib|le /'ledʒəbl/ a. lisible. **~ility** /-'bɪlɪtɪ/ n. lisibilité f. **~ly** adv. lisiblement.

legion /'liːdʒən/ n. légion f. **~naire** n. légionnaire m. **~naire's disease**, maladie du légionnaire f.

legislat|e /'ledʒɪsleɪt/ v.i. légiférer. **~ion** /-'leɪʃn/ n. (*body of laws*) législation f.; (*law*) loi f.

legislat|ive /'ledʒɪslətɪv/ a. législatif. **~ure** /-eɪtʃə(r)/ n. corps législatif m.

legitima|te /lɪˈdʒɪtɪmət/ a. légitime. **~cy** n. légitimité f.

leisure /'leʒə(r)/ n. loisir(s) m. (pl.). **at one's ~**, à tête reposée. **~ centre**, centre de loisirs m. **~ly** a. lent; adv. sans se presser.

lemon /'lemən/ n. citron m.

lemonade /lemə'neɪd/ n. (*fizzy*) limonade f.; (*still*) citronnade f.

lend /lend/ v.t. (*p.t.* lent) prêter; (*contribute*) donner. **~ itself to**, se prêter à. **~er** n. prêteu|r, -se m., f. **~ing** n. prêt m.

length /leŋθ/ n. longueur f.; (*in time*) durée f.; (*section*) morceau m. **at ~**, (*at last*) enfin & (*at great*) **~**, longuement. **~y** a. long.

lengthen /'leŋθən/ v.t./i. (s')allonger.

lengthways /'leŋθweɪz/ adv. dans le sens de la longueur.

lenien|t /'liːnɪənt/ a. indulgent. **~cy** n. indulgence f. **~tly** adv. avec indulgence.

lens /lenz/ n. lentille f.; (*of spectacles*) verre m.; (*photo.*) objectif m.

lent /lent/ see lend.

Lent /lent/ n. Carême m.

lentil /'lentl/ n. (*bean*) lentille f.

Leo /'liːəʊ/ n. le Lion.

leopard /'lepəd/ n. léopard m.

leotard /'liːətɑːd/ n. body m.

leper /'lepə(r)/ n. lépreu|x, -se m., f.

leprosy /'leprəsɪ/ n. lèpre f.

lesbian /'lezbɪən/ n. lesbienne f. **~a.** lesbien.

lesion /'liːʒn/ n. lésion f.

less /les/ a. (*in quantity etc.*) moins de (**than**, que). **—adv., n. & prep.** moins. **~ than**, (*with numbers*) moins de. **work/etc. ~ than**, travailler/*etc.* moins que. **ten pounds/etc. ~**, dix livres/*etc.* de moins. **~ and less**, de moins en moins. **~er a.** moindre.

lessen /'lesn/ v.t./i. diminuer.

lesson /'lesn/ n. leçon f.

lest /lest/ conj. de peur que or de.

let /let/ v.t. (*p.t.* let, *pres. p.* letting) laisser; (*lease*) louer. **—v. aux. ~ us do, ~'s do**, faisons. **~ him do**, qu'il fasse. **~ me know the results**, informe-moi des résultats. **—n.** location f. **~ alone**, (*thing*) ne pas toucher à; (*person*) laisser tranquille; (*never mind*) encore moins. **~ down**, baisser; (*deflate*) dégonfler; (*fig.*) décevoir. **~-down** n. déception f. **~ go** v.t./i. lâcher prise. **~ sb. in/out**, laisser or faire entrer/sortir qn. **~ a dress out**, élargir une robe. **~ o.s. in for**, (*task*) s'engager à; (*trouble*) s'attirer. **~ off**, (*explode*, *fire*) faire éclater or partir; (*excuse*) dispenser; (*not punish*) ne pas punir. **~ up**, (*fam.*) s'arrêter. **~-up** n. répit m.

lethal /'liːθl/ a. mortel; (*weapon*) meurtrier.

letharg|y /'leθədʒɪ/ n. léthargie f. **~ic** /lɪ'θɑːdʒɪk/ a. léthargique.

letter /'letə(r)/ n. lettre f. **~-bomb** n. lettre piégée f. **~-box** n. boîte à or aux lettres f. **~ing** n. (letters) caractères m. pl.

lettuce /'letɪs/ n. laitue f., salade f.

leukaemia /luːˈkiːmɪə/ n. leucémie f.

level /'levl/ a. plat, uni; (on surface) horizontal; (in height) au même niveau (**with**, que); (in score) à égalité. —n. niveau m. (**spirit**) **~**, niveau à bulle m. —v.t. (p.t. levelled) niveler; (aim) diriger. **be on the ~**, (fam.) être franc. **~ crossing**, passage à niveau m. **~-headed** a. équilibré.

lever /'liːvə(r)/ n. levier m. —v.t. soulever au moyen d'un levier.

leverage /'liːvərɪdʒ/ n. influence f.

levity /'levətɪ/ n. légèreté f.

levy /'levɪ/ v.t. (tax) (pré)lever. —n. impôt m.

lewd /ljuːd/ a. (-er, -est) obscène.

liab|le /'laɪəbl/ a. **be ~ to do**, avoir tendance à faire, pouvoir faire. **~ to**, (illness etc.) sujet à; (fine) passible de. **~ for**, responsable de.

liabilit|y /laɪəˈbɪlətɪ/ n. responsabilité f.; (fam.) handicap m. **~ies**, (debts) dettes f. pl.

liais|e /lɪˈeɪz/ v.i. (fam.) faire la liaison. **~on** /-on/ n. liaison f.

liar /'laɪə(r)/ n. menteu|r, -se m., f.

libel /'laɪbl/ n. diffamation f. —v.t. (p.t. libelled) diffamer.

liberal /'lɪbərəl/ a. libéral; (generous) généreux, libéral. **~ly** adv. libéralement.

Liberal /'lɪbərəl/ a. & n. (pol.) libéral(e) (m. (f.)).

liberat|e /'lɪbəreɪt/ v.t. libérer. **~ion** /-ˈreɪʃn/ n. libération f.

liberty /'lɪbətɪ/ n. liberté f. **at ~ to**, libre de v.t. **take ~ies**, prendre des libertés.

libido /lɪˈbiːdəʊ/ n. libido f.

Libra /'liːbrə/ n. la Balance.

librar|y /'laɪbrərɪ/ n. bibliothèque f. **~ian** /-ˈbreərɪən/ n. bibliothécaire m./f.

libretto /lɪˈbretəʊ/ n. (pl. -os) (mus.) livret m.

Libya /'lɪbɪə/ n. Libye f. **~n a.** & n. libyen(ne) (m. (f.)).

lice /laɪs/ see **louse**.

licence, Amer. **license**[1] /'laɪsns/ n. permis m.; (for television) redevance f.; (comm.) licence f.; (liberty; fig.) licence f. **~ plate**, plaque minéralogique f.

license[2] /'laɪsns/ v.t. accorder un permis à, autoriser.

licentious /laɪˈsenʃəs/ a. licencieux.

lichen /'laɪkən/ n. lichen m.

lick /lɪk/ v.t. lécher; (defeat: sl.) rosser. —n. coup de langue m. **~ one's chops**, se lécher les babines.

licorice /'lɪkərɪs/ n. (Amer.) réglisse f.

lid /lɪd/ n. couvercle m.

lido /'liːdəʊ/ n. (pl. -os) piscine en plein air f.

lie[1] /laɪ/ n. mensonge m. —v.i. (p.t. lied, pres. p. lying) (tell lies) mentir. **give the ~ to**, démentir.

lie[2] /laɪ/ v.i. (p.t. lay, p.p. lain, pres. p. lying) s'allonger; (remain) rester; (be) se trouver être; (in grave) reposer. **be lying**, être allongé. **~ down**, s'allonger. **~ in, have a ~-in**, faire la grasse matinée. **~ low**, se cacher.

lieu /ljuː/ n. **in ~ of**, au lieu de.

lieutenant /lefˈtenənt, Amer. luːˈtenənt/ n. lieutenant m.

life /laɪf/ n. (pl. lives) vie f. **~ cycle**, cycle de vie m. **~-guard** n. sauveteur m. **~ insurance**, assurance-vie f. **~-jacket**, **~ preserver**, n. gilet de sauvetage m. **~-size(d)** a. grandeur nature invar. **~-style** n. style de vie m.

lifebelt /ˈlaɪfbelt/ n. bouée de sauvetage f.

lifeboat /ˈlaɪfbəʊt/ n. canot de sauvetage m.

lifebuoy /ˈlaɪfbɔɪ/ n. bouée de sauvetage f.

lifeless /ˈlaɪflɪs/ a. sans vie.

lifelike /ˈlaɪflaɪk/ a. très ressemblant.

lifelong /ˈlaɪflɒŋ/ a. de toute la vie.

lifetime /ˈlaɪftaɪm/ n. vie f. in one's ~, de son vivant.

lift /lɪft/ v.t. lever; (steal: fam.) voler. —v.i. (of fog) se lever. —n. (in building) ascenseur m. give a ~ to, emmener (en voiture). ~-off n. (aviat.) décollage m.

ligament /ˈlɪɡəmənt/ n. ligament m.

light[1] /laɪt/ n. lumière f.; (lamp) lampe f.; (for fire, on vehicle, etc.) feu m.; (headlight) phare m. —a. (not dark) clair. —v.t. (p.t. lit or lighted) allumer; (room etc.) éclairer; (match) frotter. bring to ~, révéler. come to ~, être révélé. have you got a ~?, vous avez du feu? ~ bulb, ampoule f. ~ pen, crayon optique m. ~ up v.i. s'allumer; v.t. (room) éclairer. ~-year n. année lumière f.

light[2] /laɪt/ a. (-er, -est) (not heavy) léger. ~-fingered a. chapardeur. ~-headed a. (dizzy) qui a un vertige; (frivolous) étourdi. ~-hearted a. gai. ~ly adv. légèrement. ~ness n. légèreté f.

lighten[1] /ˈlaɪtn/ v.t. (give light to) éclairer; (make brighter) éclaircir.

lighten[2] /ˈlaɪtn/ v.t. (make less heavy) alléger.

lighter /ˈlaɪtə(r)/ n. briquet m.; (for stove) allume-gaz m. invar.

lighthouse /ˈlaɪthaʊs/ n. phare m.

lighting /ˈlaɪtɪŋ/ n. éclairage m. ~ technician, éclairagiste m./f.

lightning /ˈlaɪtnɪŋ/ n. éclair(s) m. (pl.), foudre f. —a. éclair invar.

lightweight /ˈlaɪtweɪt/ a. léger. —n. (boxing) poids léger m.

like[1] /laɪk/ a. semblable, pareil. —prep. comme. —conj. (fam.) comme. —n. pareil m. be ~-minded, avoir les mêmes sentiments. the ~s of you, des gens comme vous.

like[2] /laɪk/ v.t. aimer (bien). ~s n. pl. goûts m. pl. I should ~, je voudrais, j'aimerais. would you ~?, voulez-vous? ~able a. sympathique.

likely /ˈlaɪklɪ/ a. (-ier, -iest) probable. —adv. probablement. he is ~y to do, il fera probablement. not ~y!, (fam.) pas question! ~ihood n. probabilité f.

liken /ˈlaɪkən/ v.t. comparer.

likeness /ˈlaɪknɪs/ n. ressemblance f.

likewise /ˈlaɪkwaɪz/ adv. de même.

liking /ˈlaɪkɪŋ/ n. (for thing) penchant m.; (for person) affection f.

lilac /ˈlaɪlək/ n. lilas m. —a. lilas invar.

lily /ˈlɪlɪ/ n. lis m., lys m. ~ of the valley, muguet m.

limb /lɪm/ n. membre m. out on a ~, isolé (et vulnérable).

limber /ˈlɪmbə(r)/ v.i. ~ up, faire des exercices d'assouplissement.

limbo /ˈlɪmbəʊ/ n. be in ~, (forgotten) être tombé dans l'oubli.

lime[1] /laɪm/ n. chaux f.

lime[2] /laɪm/ n. (fruit) citron vert m.

lime[3] /laɪm/ n. (~-tree) tilleul m.

limelight /ˈlaɪmlaɪt/ n. in the ~, en vedette.

limerick /ˈlɪmərɪk/ n. poème humoristique m. (de cinq vers).

limit /ˈlɪmɪt/ n. limite f. —v.t. limiter. ~ed company, société

anonyme *f.* ~**ation** /-'teɪʃn/ *n.*

limitation *f.* ~**less** *a.* sans limites.

limousine /'lɪməziːn/ *n.* (car) limousine *f.*

limp[1] /lɪmp/ *v.i.* boiter. —*n.* have a ~, boiter.

limp[2] /lɪmp/ *a.* (**-er, -est**) mou.

limpid /'lɪmpɪd/ *a.* limpide.

linctus /'lɪŋktəs/ *n.* sirop *m.*

line[1] /laɪn/ *n.* ligne *f.*; (track) voie *f.*; (wrinkle) ride *f.*; (row) rangée *f.*, file *f.*; (of poem) vers *m.*; (rope) corde *f.*; (of goods) gamme *f.*; (queue: Amer.) queue *f.* —*v.t.* (paper) régler; (streets etc.) border. **be in ~ for,** avoir de bonnes chances d'avoir. **in ~ with,** en accord avec. **stand in ~,** faire la queue. **~ up,** (s')aligner; (in queue) faire la queue. **~ sth. up,** prévoir qch.

line[2] /laɪn/ *v.t.* (garment) doubler; (fill) remplir, garnir.

lineage /'lɪnɪdʒ/ *n.* lignée *f.*

linear /'lɪnɪə(r)/ *a.* linéaire.

linen /'lɪnɪn/ *n.* (sheets etc.) linge *m.*; (material) lin *m.*, toile de lin *f.*

liner /'laɪnə(r)/ *n.* paquebot *m.*

linesman /'laɪnzmən/ *n.* (football) juge de touche *m.*

linger /'lɪŋɡə(r)/ *v.i.* s'attarder; (smells etc.) persister.

lingerie /'lænʒərɪ/ *n.* lingerie *f.*

lingo /'lɪŋɡəʊ/ *n.* (*pl.* **-os**) (hum., fam.) jargon *m.*

linguist /'lɪŋɡwɪst/ *n.* linguiste *m./f.*

linguistic /lɪŋ'ɡwɪstɪk/ *a.* linguistique. ~**s** *n.* linguistique *f.*

lining /'laɪnɪŋ/ *n.* doublure *f.*

link /lɪŋk/ *n.* lien *m.*; (of chain) maillon *m.* —*v.t.* relier; (relate) (re)lier. ~ **up,** (of roads) se rejoindre. ~**age** *n.* lien *m.* ~**up** *n.* liaison *f.*

links /lɪŋks/ *n. invar.* terrain de golf *m.*

lino /'laɪnəʊ/ *n.* (*pl.* **-os**) lino *m.*

linoleum /lɪ'nəʊlɪəm/ *n.* linoléum *m.*

lint /lɪnt/ *n.* (med.) tissu ouaté *m.*; (fluff) peluche(s) *f.* (*pl.*).

lion /'laɪən/ *n.* lion *m.* **take the ~'s share,** se tailler la part du lion. ~**ess** *n.* lionne *f.*

lip /lɪp/ *n.* lèvre *f.*; (edge) rebord *m.* ~**-read** *v.t./i.* lire sur les lèvres. **pay ~-service to,** n'approuver que pour la forme.

lipsalve /'lɪpsælv/ *n.* baume pour les lèvres *m.*

lipstick /'lɪpstɪk/ *n.* rouge (à lèvres) *m.*

liquefy /'lɪkwɪfaɪ/ *v.t./i.* (se) liquéfier.

liqueur /lɪ'kjʊə(r)/ *n.* liqueur *f.*

liquid /'lɪkwɪd/ *n. & a.* liquide (*m.*). ~**ize** *v.t.* passer au mixeur. ~**izer** *n.* mixeur *m.*

liquidat|e /'lɪkwɪdeɪt/ *v.t.* liquider. ~**ion** /-'deɪʃn/ *n.* liquidation *f.* **go into ~ion,** déposer son bilan.

liquor /'lɪkə(r)/ *n.* alcool *m.*

liquorice /'lɪkərɪs/ *n.* réglisse *f.*

lira /'lɪərə/ *n.* (*pl.* **lire** /'lɪəreɪ/ or **liras**) lire *f.*

lisp /lɪsp/ *n.* zézaiement *m.* —*v.i.* zézayer. **with a ~,** en zézayant.

list[1] /lɪst/ *n.* liste *f.* —*v.t.* dresser la liste de.

list[2] /lɪst/ *v.i.* (ship) giter.

listen /'lɪsn/ *v.i.* écouter. ~ **to,** ~ **in (to),** écouter. ~**er** *n.* audi|teur, -trice *m./f.*

listless /'lɪstlɪs/ *a.* apathique.

lit /lɪt/ *see* **light**[1].

litany /'lɪtənɪ/ *n.* litanie *f.*

liter /'liːtə(r)/ *see* **litre**.

literal /'lɪtərəl/ *a.* littéral; (person) prosaïque. ~**ly** *adv.* littéralement.

literary /'lɪtərərɪ/ *a.* littéraire.

litera|te /'lɪtərət/ *a.* qui sait lire et écrire. ~**cy** *n.* capacité de lire et écrire *f.*

literature /'lɪtrətʃə(r)/ *n.* littérature *f.*; (fig.) documentation *f.*

lithe /laɪð/ a. souple, agile.

litigation /lɪtɪˈgeɪʃn/ n. litige m.

litre, (Amer.) liter /ˈliːtə(r)/ n. litre m.

litter /ˈlɪtə(r)/ n. détritus m. pl.; papiers m. pl.; (animals) portée f. —v.t. éparpiller; (make untidy) laisser des détritus dans. ~bin n. poubelle f. ~ed with, jonché de.

little /ˈlɪtl/ a. petit; (not much) peu de. —n. peu m. —adv. peu. a ~, un peu (de).

liturgy /ˈlɪtədʒɪ/ n. liturgie f.

live¹ /laɪv/ a. vivant; (wire) sous tension; (broadcast) en direct. be a ~ wire, être très dynamique.

live² /lɪv/ v.t./i. vivre; (reside) habiter, vivre. ~ down, faire oublier. ~ it up, mener la belle vie. ~ on, (feed o.s. on) vivre de; (continue) survivre. ~ up to, se montrer à la hauteur de.

livelihood /ˈlaɪvlɪhʊd/ n. moyens d'existence m. pl.

lively /ˈlaɪvlɪ/ a. (-ier, -iest) vif, vivant. ~iness n. vivacité f.

liven /ˈlaɪvn/ v.t./i. ~ up, (s')animer; (cheer up) (s')égayer.

liver /ˈlɪvə(r)/ n. foie m.

livery /ˈlɪvərɪ/ n. livrée f.

livestock /ˈlaɪvstɒk/ n. bétail m.

livid /ˈlɪvɪd/ a. livide; (angry: fam.) furieux.

living /ˈlɪvɪŋ/ a. vivant. —n. vie f. make a ~, gagner sa vie. ~ conditions, conditions de vie f. pl. ~-room n. salle de séjour f.

lizard /ˈlɪzəd/ n. lézard m.

llama /ˈlɑːmə/ n. lama m.

load /ləʊd/ n. charge f.; (loaded goods) chargement m., charge f.; (weight, strain) poids m. ~s of, (fam.) des masses de. —v.t. charger. ~ed a. (dice) pipé; (wealthy: sl.) riche.

loaf¹ /ləʊf/ n. (pl. loaves) pain m.

loaf² /ləʊf/ v.i. ~ (about),

fainéanter. ~er n. fainéant(e) m.

loam /ləʊm/ n. terreau m.

loan /ləʊn/ n. prêt m.; (money borrowed) emprunt m. —v.t. (lend: fam.) prêter.

loath /ləʊθ/ a. peu disposé (to, à).

loathe /ləʊð/ v.t. détester. ~ing n. dégoût m. ~some a. dégoûtant.

lobby /ˈlɒbɪ/ n. entrée f., vestibule m.; (pol.) lobby m., groupe de pression m. —v.t. faire pression sur.

lobe /ləʊb/ n. lobe m.

lobster /ˈlɒbstə(r)/ n. homard m.

local /ˈləʊkl/ a. local; (shops etc.) du quartier. —n. personne du coin f.; (pub: fam.) pub du coin m. ~ government, administration locale f. ~ly adv. localement; (nearby) dans les environs.

locale /ləʊˈkɑːl/ n. lieu m.

locality /ləʊˈkælətɪ/ n. (district) région f.; (position) lieu m.

localized /ˈləʊkəlaɪzd/ a. localisé.

locate /ləʊˈkeɪt/ v.t. (situate) situer; (find) repérer. ~ion /-ʃn/ n. emplacement m. on ~ion, (cinema) en extérieur.

lock¹ /lɒk/ n. mèche de cheveux f.

lock² /lɒk/ n. (of door etc.) serrure f.; (on canal) écluse f. —v.t./i. fermer à clef; (wheels: auto.) (se) bloquer. ~ in or up, (person) enfermer. ~ out, (by mistake) enfermer dehors. ~-out m. lock-out m. invar. ~-up n. (shop) boutique f.; (garage) box m.

locker /ˈlɒkə(r)/ n. casier m.

locket /ˈlɒkɪt/ n. médaillon m.

locksmith /ˈlɒksmɪθ/ n. serrurier m.

locomotion /ˌləʊkəˈməʊʃn/ n. locomotion f.

locomotive /ˈləʊkəməʊtɪv/ n. locomotive f.

locum /ˈləʊkəm/ n. (doctor etc.) remplaçant(e) m. (f.).

locust /ˈləʊkəst/ n. criquet m., sauterelle f.

lodge /lɒdʒ/ n. (house) pavillon de gardien or de chasse) m.; (of porter) loge f. —v.t. loger; (money, complaint) déposer. —v.i. être logé (with, chez); (become fixed) se loger. —**~r** /-ə(r)/ n. locataire m./f., pensionnaire m./f.

lodgings /ˈlɒdʒɪŋz/ n. chambre (meublée) f.; (flat) logement m.

loft /lɒft/ n. grenier m.

lofty /ˈlɒftɪ/ a. (-ier, -iest) (tall, noble) élevé; (haughty) hautain.

log /lɒg/ n. (of wood) bûche f. **~(-book)**, (naut.) journal de bord m.; (auto.) (équivalent de la) carte grise f. —v.t. (p.t. logged) noter; (distance) parcourir. **~ on**, entrer. **~ off**, sortir.

logarithm /ˈlɒgərɪðəm/ n. logarithme m.

loggerheads /ˈlɒgəhedz/ n. pl. **at ~**, en désaccord.

logic /ˈlɒdʒɪk/ a. logique. **~al** a. logique. **~ally** adv. logiquement.

logistics /ləˈdʒɪstɪks/ n. logistique f.

logo /ˈləʊgəʊ/ n. (pl. -os) (fam.) emblème m.

loin /lɔɪn/ n. (culin.) filet m. **~s**, reins m. pl.

loiter /ˈlɔɪtə(r)/ v.i. traîner.

loll /lɒl/ v.i. se prélasser.

lollipop /ˈlɒlɪpɒp/ n. sucette f. **~y** n. (fam.) sucette f.; (sl.) fric m.

London /ˈlʌndən/ n. Londres m./f. **~er** n. Londonien(ne) m. (f.).

lone /ləʊn/ a. solitaire. **~r** /-ə(r)/ n. solitaire m./f. **~some** a. solitaire.

lonely /ˈləʊnlɪ/ a. (-ier, -iest) solitaire; (person) seul, solitaire.

long¹ /lɒŋ/ a. (-er, -est) long. —adv. longtemps. how **~ is?**, quelle est la longueur de? how **~ is?**, (in time) quelle est la durée de? how **~?**, combien de temps? he will

not be **~**, il n'en a pas pour longtemps. a **~ time**, longtemps. as or so **~ as**, pourvu que. before **~**, avant peu. I no **~er** do, je ne fais plus. **~-distance** a. (flight) sur long parcours; (phone call) interurbain. **~ face**, grimace f. (fam.). **~-johns**, (fam.) caleçon long m. **~ jump**, saut en longueur m. **~-playing record**, microsillon m. **~-range** a. à longue portée; (forecast) à long terme. **~-sighted** a. presbyte. **~-standing** a. de longue date. **~-suffering** a. très patient. **~-term** a. à long terme. **~ wave**, grandes ondes f. pl. **~-winded** a. (speaker etc.) verbeux.

long² /lɒŋ/ v.i. avoir bien or très envie (for, to, de). **~ for s.o.** (pine for) languir après qn. **~ing** n. envie f.; (nostalgia) nostalgie f.

longevity /lɒnˈdʒevətɪ/ n. longévité f.

longhand /ˈlɒŋhænd/ n. écriture courante f.

longitude /ˈlɒndʒɪtjuːd/ n. longitude f.

loo /luː/ n. (fam.) toilettes f. pl.

look /lʊk/ v.t./i. regarder; (seem) avoir l'air. —n. regard m.; (appearance) air m., aspect m. (good) **~s**, beauté f. **~ after**, s'occuper de, soigner. **~ at**, regarder. **~ back on**, repenser à. **~ down on**, mépriser. **~ for**, chercher. **~ forward to**, attendre avec impatience. **~ in on**, passer voir. **~ into**, examiner. **~ like**, ressembler à, avoir l'air de. **~ out**, faire attention. **~ out for**, chercher; (watch) guetter. **~-out** n. (mil.) poste de guet m.; (person) guetteur m. **be on the ~-out for**, rechercher. **~ round**, se retourner. **~ up**, (word) chercher; (visit) passer voir. **~ up to**, respecter. **~-alike** n. sosie m. **~ing-glass** n. glace f.

loom¹ /lu:m/ n. métier à tisser m.

loom² /lu:m/ v.i. surgir; (event etc.: fig.) paraître imminent.

loony /'lu:nɪ/ n. & a. (sl.) fou, folle (m., f.).

loop /lu:p/ n. boucle f. —v.t. boucler.

loophole /'lu:phəʊl/ n. (in rule) échappatoire f.

loose /lu:s/ a. (-er, -est) (knot etc.) desserré; (page etc.) détaché; (clothes) ample, lâche; (tooth) qui bouge; (lax) relâché; (not packed) en vrac; (inexact) vague; (pej.) immoral. at a ~ end, (Amer.) at ~ ends, désœuvré. come ~, bouger. ~ly adv. sans serrer; (roughly) vaguement.

loosen /'lu:sn/ v.t. (slacken) desserrer; (untie) défaire.

loot /lu:t/ n. butin m. —v.t. piller. ~er n. pillard(e) m. (f.). ~ing n. pillage m.

lop /lɒp/ v.t. (p.t. lopped). ~ off, couper.

lop-sided /lɒp'saɪdɪd/ a. de travers.

lord /lɔ:d/ n. seigneur m.; (British title) lord m.; the L~, le Seigneur. (good) L~!, mon Dieu! ~ly a. noble; (haughty) hautain.

lore /lɔ:(r)/ n. traditions f. pl.

lorry /'lɒrɪ/ n. camion m.

lose /lu:z/ v.t./i. (p.t. lost) perdre. get lost, se perdre. ~r /-ə(r)/ n. perdant(e) m. (f.).

loss /lɒs/ n. perte f. be at a ~, être perplexe. be at a ~ to, être incapable de. heat ~, déperdition de chaleur f.

lost /lɒst/ see lose. —a. perdu. ~ property, (Amer.) ~ and found, objets trouvés m. pl.

lot¹ /lɒt/ n. (fate) sort m.; (at auction) lot m.; (land) lotissement m.

lot² /lɒt/ n. the ~, (le) tout m.; (people) tous m. pl., toutes f. pl. a

~ (of), ~s (of), (fam.) beaucoup (de). quite a ~ (of), (fam.) pas mal (de).

lotion /'ləʊʃn/ n. lotion f.

lottery /'lɒtərɪ/ n. loterie f.

loud /laʊd/ a. (-er, -est) bruyant, fort. —adv. fort. ~ hailer, portevoix m. invar. out ~, tout haut. ~ly adv. fort.

loudspeaker /laʊd'spi:kə(r)/ n. haut-parleur m.

lounge /laʊndʒ/ v.i. paresser. —n. salon m. ~ suit, costume m.

louse /laʊs/ n. (pl. lice) pou m.

lousy /'laʊzɪ/ a. (-ier, -iest) pouilleux; (bad: sl.) infect.

lout /laʊt/ n. rustre m.

lovable /'lʌvəbl/ a. adorable.

love /lʌv/ n. amour m.; (tennis) zéro m. —v.t. aimer; (like greatly) aimer (beaucoup) (to do, faire). in ~, amoureux (with, de). ~ affair, liaison amoureuse f. ~ life, vie amoureuse f. make ~, faire l'amour.

lovely /'lʌvlɪ/ a. (-ier, -iest) joli; (delightful: fam.) très agréable.

lover /'lʌvə(r)/ n. amant m.; (devotee) amateur m. (of, de).

lovesick /'lʌvsɪk/ a. amoureux.

loving /'lʌvɪŋ/ a. affectueux.

low¹ /ləʊ/ v.i. meugler.

low² /ləʊ/ a. & adv. (-er, -est) bas. —n. (low pressure) dépression f. reach a (new) ~, atteindre son niveau le plus bas. ~ in sth., à faible teneur en qch. ~-calorie a. basses-calories. ~-cut a. décolleté. ~-down a. méprisable; n. (fam.) renseignements m. pl. ~-fat a. maigre. ~-key a. modéré; (discreet) discret. ~-lying a. à faible altitude.

lowbrow /'ləʊbraʊ/ a. peu intellectuel.

lower /'ləʊə(r)/ a. & adv. see low². —v.t. baisser. ~ o.s., s'abaisser.

lowlands /'ləʊləndz/ n. pl. plaine(s) f. (pl.).

lowly /ˈləʊlɪ/ a. (-ier, -iest) humble.

loyal /ˈlɔɪəl/ a. loyal. ~ly adv. loyalement. ~ty n. loyauté f.

lozenge /ˈlɒzɪndʒ/ n. (shape) losange m.; (tablet) pastille f.

LP abbr. see **long-playing record**.

Ltd. abbr. (Limited) SA.

lubric|ate /ˈluːbrɪkeɪt/ v.t. graisser, lubrifier. ~ant n. lubrifiant m. ~ation /-ˈkeɪʃn/ n. graissage m.

lucid /ˈluːsɪd/ a. lucide. ~ity /luːˈsɪdətɪ/ n. lucidité f.

luck /lʌk/ n. chance f. **bad** ~, malchance f. **good** ~!, bonne chance!

luck|y /ˈlʌkɪ/ a. (-ier, -iest) qui a de la chance, heureux; (event) heureux; (number) qui porte bonheur. **it's** ~**y that**, c'est une chance que. ~**ily** adv. heureusement.

lucrative /ˈluːkrətɪv/ a. lucratif.

ludicrous /ˈluːdɪkrəs/ a. ridicule.

lug /lʌɡ/ v.t. (p.t. **lugged**) traîner.

luggage /ˈlʌɡɪdʒ/ n. bagages m. pl. ~-**rack** n. porte-bagages m. invar.

lukewarm /ˈluːkwɔːm/ a. tiède.

lull /lʌl/ v.t. (soothe, send to sleep) endormir. —n. accalmie f.

lullaby /ˈlʌləbaɪ/ n. berceuse f.

lumbago /lʌmˈbeɪɡəʊ/ n. lumbago m.

lumber /ˈlʌmbə(r)/ n. bric-à-brac m. invar.; (wood) bois de charpente m. —v.t. ~ **s.o. with**, (chore etc.) coller à qn.

lumberjack /ˈlʌmbədʒæk/ n. (Amer.) bûcheron m.

luminous /ˈluːmɪnəs/ a. lumineux.

lump /lʌmp/ n. morceau m.; (swelling on body) grosseur f.; (in liquid) grumeau m. —v.t. ~ **together**, réunir. ~ **sum**, somme globale f. ~**y** a. (sauce) grumeleux; (bumpy) bosselé.

lunacy /ˈluːnəsɪ/ n. folie f.

lunar /ˈluːnə(r)/ a. lunaire.

lunatic /ˈluːnətɪk/ n. fou, folle m., f.

lunch /lʌntʃ/ n. déjeuner m. —v.i. déjeuner. ~ **box**, cantine f.

luncheon /ˈlʌntʃən/ n. déjeuner m. ~ **meat**, (approx.) saucisson m. ~ **voucher**, chèque-repas m.

lung /lʌŋ/ n. poumon m.

lunge /lʌndʒ/ n. mouvement brusque en avant m. —v.i. s'élancer (**at**, sur).

lurch[1] /lɜːtʃ/ n. **leave in the** ~, planter là, laisser en plan.

lurch[2] /lɜːtʃ/ v.i. (person) tituber.

lure /lʊə(r)/ v.t. appâter, attirer. —n. (attraction) attrait m., appât m.

lurid /ˈlʊərɪd/ a. choquant, affreux; (gaudy) voyant.

lurk /lɜːk/ v.i. se cacher; (in ambush) s'embusquer; (prowl) rôder. **a** ~**ing suspicion**, **a** petit soupçon.

luscious /ˈlʌʃəs/ a. appétissant.

lush /lʌʃ/ a. luxuriant. —n. (Amer., fam.) ivrogne(sse) m. (f.).

lust /lʌst/ n. luxure f.; (fig.) convoitise f. —v.i. ~ **after**, convoiter.

lustre /ˈlʌstə(r)/ n. lustre m.

lusty /ˈlʌstɪ/ a. (-ier, -iest) robuste.

lute /luːt/ n. (mus.) luth m.

Luxemburg /ˈlʌksəmbɜːɡ/ n. Luxembourg m.

luxuriant /lʌɡˈʒʊərɪənt/ a. luxuriant.

luxurious /lʌɡˈʒʊərɪəs/ a. luxueux.

luxury /ˈlʌkʃərɪ/ n. luxe m. —a. de luxe.

lying /ˈlaɪɪŋ/ see **lie**[1], **lie**[2]. —n. le mensonge m.

lynch /lɪntʃ/ v.t. lyncher.

lynx /lɪŋks/ n. lynx m.

lyric /ˈlɪrɪk/ a. lyrique. ~**s** n. pl. paroles f. pl. ~**al** a. lyrique. ~**ism** /-sɪzəm/ n. lyrisme f.

M

MA *abbr. see* Master of Arts.
mac /mæk/ *n. (fam.)* imper *m.*
macaroni /mækə'rəʊnɪ/ *n.* macaronis *m. pl.*
macaroon /mækə'ru:n/ *n.* macaron *m.*
mace /meɪs/ *n. (staff)* masse *f.*
Mach /mɑːk/ *n.* **~ (number)**, (nombre de) Mach *m.*
machiavellian /mækɪə'velɪən/ *a.* machiavélique.
machinations /mækɪ'neɪʃnz/ *n. pl.* machinations *f. pl.*
machine /mə'ʃiːn/ *n.* machine *f.* —*v.t. (sew)* coudre à la machine; *(techn.)* usiner. **~ code,** code machine *m.* **~-gun** *n.* mitrailleuse *f.*; *v.t. (p.t.* **-gunned)** mitrailler. **~-readable** *a.* en langage machine. **~ tool,** machine-outil *f.*
machinery /mə'ʃiːnərɪ/ *n.* machinerie *f.*; *(working parts & fig.)* mécanisme(s) *m. (pl.).*
machinist /mə'ʃiːnɪst/ *n. (operator)* opéra|teur, -trice sur machine *m.*, *f.*; *(on sewing-machine)* piqueu|r, -se *m.*, *f.*
macho /'mætʃəʊ/ *n. (pl.* **-os)** macho *m.* —*a.* macho *invar.*
mackerel /'mækrəl/ *n. invar. (fish)* maquereau *m.*
mackintosh /'mækɪntɒʃ/ *n.* imperméable *m.*
macrobiotic /mækrəʊbaɪ'ɒtɪk/ *a.* macrobiotique.
mad /mæd/ *a.* **(madder, maddest)** fou; *(foolish)* insensé; *(dog etc.)* enragé; *(angry. fam.)* furieux. **be ~ about,** se passionner pour; *(person)* être fou de. **drive s.o. ~,** exaspérer qn. **like ~,** comme un fou. **~ly** *adv. (interested, in love, etc.)* follement; *(frantically)* comme un fou. **~ness** *n.* folie *f.*

Madagascar /mædə'gæskə(r)/ *n.* Madagascar *f.*
madam /'mædəm/ *n.* madame *f.*; *(unmarried)* mademoiselle *f.*
madden /'mædn/ *v.t.* exaspérer.
made /meɪd/ *see* **make. ~ to measure,** fait sur mesure.
Madeira /mə'dɪərə/ *n. (wine)* madère *m.*
madhouse /'mædhaʊs/ *n. (fam.)* maison de fous *f.*
madman /'mædmən/ *n. (pl.* **-men)** fou *m.*
madrigal /'mædrɪgl/ *n.* madrigal *m.*
magazine /mægə'ziːn/ *n.* revue *f.*, magazine *m.*; *(of gun)* magasin *m.*
magenta /mə'dʒentə/ *a.* magenta *(invar.).*
maggot /'mægət/ *n.* ver *m.*, asticot *m.* **~y** *a.* véreux.
magic /'mædʒɪk/ *n.* magie *f.* —*a.* magique. **~al** *a.* magique.
magician /mə'dʒɪʃn/ *n.* magicien(ne) *m. (f.).*
magistrate /'mædʒɪstreɪt/ *n.* magistrat *m.*
magnanim|ous /mæg'nænɪməs/ *a.* magnanime. **~ity** /-ə'nɪmətɪ/ *n.* magnanimité *f.*
magnate /'mægneɪt/ *n.* magnat *m.*
magnesia /mæg'niːʃə/ *n.* magnésie *f.*
magnet /'mægnɪt/ *n.* aimant *m.* **~ic** /-'netɪk/ *a.* magnétique. **~ism** *n.* magnétisme *m.* **~ize** *v.t.* magnétiser.
magneto /mæg'niːtəʊ/ *n. (pl.* **os)** magnéto *m.*
magnificen|t /mæg'nɪfɪsnt/ *a.* magnifique. **~ce** *n.* magnificence *f.*
magnif|y /'mægnɪfaɪ/ *v.t.* grossir; *(sound)* amplifier; *(fig.)* exagérer. **~ication** /-ɪ'keɪʃn/ *n.* grossissement *m.*; amplification *f.* **~ier** *n.* **~ying glass,** loupe *f.*

magnitude /'mægnɪtjuːd/ n. (*importance*) ampleur f.; (*size*) grandeur f.

magnolia /mæg'nəʊlɪə/ n. magnolia m.

magnum /'mægnəm/ n. magnum m.

magpie /'mægpaɪ/ n. pie f.

mahogany /mə'hɒgənɪ/ n. acajou m.

maid /meɪd/ n. (*servant*) bonne f.; (*girl: old use*) jeune fille f.

maiden /'meɪdn/ n. (*old use*) jeune fille f. —a. (*aunt*) célibataire; (*voyage*) premier. ~ **name**, nom de jeune fille f. ~**hood** n. virginité f. ~**ly** a. virginal.

mail[1] /meɪl/ n. poste f.; (*letters*) courrier m. —a. (*bag, van*) postal. —v.t. envoyer par la poste. ~ **box**, boîte à lettres f. ~**ing list**, liste d'adresses f. ~ **order**, vente par correspondance f. ~ **shot**, publipostage m.

mail[2] /meɪl/ n. (*armour*) cotte de mailles f.

mailman /'meɪlmæn/ n. (*pl.* -men) (*Amer.*) facteur m.

maim /meɪm/ v.t. mutiler.

main[1] /meɪn/ a. principal. —n. in the ~, en général. —n. in the ~, en général, grande ligne f. a ~ road, une grande route. ~**ly** adv. principalement, surtout.

main[2] /meɪn/ n. (*water/gas*) ~, conduite d'eau/de gaz f. the ~**s** (*electr.*) le secteur.

mainframe n. unité centrale f.

mainland /'meɪnlənd/ n. continent m.

mainspring /'meɪnsprɪŋ/ n. ressort principal m.; (*motive: fig.*) mobile principal m.

mainstay /'meɪnsteɪ/ n. soutien m.

mainstream /'meɪnstriːm/ n. tendance principale f., ligne f.

maintain /meɪn'teɪn/ v.t. (*continue, keep, assert*) maintenir; (*house, machine, family*) entretenir; (*rights*) soutenir.

maintenance /'meɪntənəns/ n. (*care*) entretien m.; (*continuation*) maintien m.; (*allowance*) pension alimentaire f.

maisonette /meɪzə'net/ n. duplex m.

maize /meɪz/ n. maïs m.

majestic /mə'dʒestɪk/ a. majestueux.

majesty /'mædʒəstɪ/ n. majesté f.

major /'meɪdʒə(r)/ a. majeur. —n. commandant m. —v.i. ~ **in**, (*univ., Amer.*) se spécialiser en. ~ **road**, route à priorité f.

Majorca /mə'dʒɔːkə/ n. Majorque f.

majority /mə'dʒɒrətɪ/ n. majorité f. —a. majoritaire. **the ~ of people**, la plupart des gens.

make /meɪk/ v.t./i. (*p.t.* made) faire; (*manufacture*) fabriquer; (*friends*) se faire; (*money*) gagner, se faire; (*decision*) prendre; (*destination*) arriver à; (*cause to be*) rendre. ~ **s.o. do sth.**, faire faire qch. à qn.; (*force*) obliger qn. à faire qch. —n. fabrication f.; (*brand*) marque f. **be made of**, être fait de. ~ **o.s. at home**, se mettre à l'aise. ~ **s.o. happy**, rendre qn. heureux. ~ **it**, arriver; (*succeed*) réussir. I ~ **it two o'clock**, j'ai deux heures. I ~ **it 150**, d'après moi, ça fait 150. I **cannot ~ anything of it**, je n'y comprends rien. **can you ~ Friday?**, vendredi, c'est possible? ~ **as if to**, faire mine de. ~**believe**, faire semblant. ~**believe**, a. feint, illusoire; n. fantaisie f. ~ **do**, (*manage*) se débrouiller (**with**, avec). ~ **do with**, (*content o.s.*) se contenter de. ~ **for**, se diriger vers; (*cause*) tendre à créer. ~ **good** v.i. réussir; v.t. compenser; (*repair*) réparer. ~ **off**, filer (**with**, avec). ~ **out** v.t. distinguer; (*understand*) comprendre; (*draw up*)

faire; (*assert*) prétendre; *v.i.*
(*fam.*) se débrouiller. ~ **over**,
céder (**to**, à); (*convert*) transformer. ~ **up** *v.t.* faire, former;
(*story*) inventer; (*deficit*) combler;
v.i. se réconcilier. ~ **up** (**one's**
face), se maquiller. ~-**up** *n.*
maquillage *m.*; (*of object*) constitution *f.*; (*psych.*) caractère *m.*
~ **up for**, compenser; (*time*)
rattraper. ~ **up one's mind**, se
décider. ~ **up to**, concilier les
bonnes grâces de.
maker /'meɪkə(r)/ *n.* fabricant *m.*
makeshift /'meɪkʃɪft/ *n.* expédient
m. —*a.* provisoire.
making /'meɪkɪŋ/ *n.* **be the ~ of**,
faire le succès de. **he has the ~s**
of, il a l'étoffe de.
maladjusted /mælə'dʒʌstɪd/ *a.* inadapté.
maladministration /mælədmɪn-
ɪ'streɪʃn/ *n.* mauvaise gestion *f.*
malaise /mæ'leɪz/ *n.* malaise *m.*
malaria /mə'leərɪə/ *n.* malaria *f.*
Malay /mə'leɪ/ *a.* & *n.* malais(e) (*m.*
(*f.*)). ~**sia** *n.* Malaysia *f.*
Malaya /mə'leɪə/ *n.* Malaisie *f.*
male /meɪl/ *a.* (*voice, sex*) masculin; (*bot., techn.*) mâle. —*n.*
mâle *m.*
malevolen|t /mə'levələnt/ *a.* mal-
veillant. ~**ce** *n.* malveillance *f.*
malform|ation /mælfɔː'meɪʃn/ *n.*
malformation *f.* ~**ed** *a.* difforme.
malfunction /mæl'fʌŋkʃn/ *n.*
mauvais fonctionnement *m.* —*v.i.*
mal fonctionner.
malice /'mælɪs/ *n.* méchanceté *f.*
malicious /mə'lɪʃəs/ *a.* méchant.
~**ly** *adv.* méchamment.
malign /mə'laɪn/ *a.* pernicieux.
—*v.t.* calomnier.
malignan|t /mə'lɪgnənt/ *a.* mal-
veillant; (*tumour*) malin. ~**cy** *n.*
malveillance *f.*; malignité *f.*
malinger /mə'lɪŋgə(r)/ *v.i.* feindre
la maladie. ~**er** *n.* simulateur,
-trice *m.*, *f.*

mall /mɔːl/ *n.* (**shopping**) ~,
centre commercial *m.*
malleable /'mælɪəbl/ *a.* malléable.
mallet /'mælɪt/ *n.* maillet *m.*
malnutrition /mælnjuː'trɪʃn/ *n.*
sous-alimentation *f.*
malpractice /mæl'præktɪs/ *n.*
faute professionnelle *f.*
malt /mɔːlt/ *n.* malt *m.* ~ **whisky**,
whisky pur malt *m.*
Malt|a /'mɔːltə/ *n.* Malte *f.* ~**ese**
/-'tiːz/ *a.* & *n.* maltais(e) (*m.*
(*f.*)).
maltreat /mæl'triːt/ *v.t.* maltraiter. ~**ment** *n.* mauvais traitement *m.*
mammal /'mæml/ *n.* mammifère
m.
mammoth /'mæməθ/ *n.* mammouth *m.* —*a.* monstre.
man /mæn/ *n.* (*pl.* **men**) homme
m.; (*in sports team*) joueur *m.*;
(*chess*) pièce *f.* —*v.t.* (*p.t.*
manned) pourvoir en hommes;
(*ship*) armer; (*guns*) servir; (*be on*
duty at) être de service à ~-**hour**
n. heure de main-d'œuvre *f.* ~ **in**
the street, homme de la rue *m.*
~-**made** *a.* artificiel. ~-**sized** *a.*
grand. ~ **to man**, d'homme à
homme. ~**ned space flight**, vol
spatial habité *m.*
manage /'mænɪdʒ/ *v.t.* diriger;
(*shop, affairs*) gérer; (*handle*)
manier. **I could ~ another**
drink, (*fam.*) je prendrais bien
encore un verre. **can you ~**
Friday?, vendredi, c'est possible? —*v.i.* se débrouiller. ~ **to**
do, réussir à faire. ~**able** *a.* (*tool,*
size, person, etc.) maniable; (*job*)
faisable. ~**ment** *n.* direction *f.*;
(*of shop*) gestion *f.* **managing**
director, directeur général *m.*
manager /'mænɪdʒə(r)/ *n.* direc|-
teur, -trice *m.*, *f.*; (*of shop*)
gérant(e) *m.*(*f.*); (*of actor*) impresario *m.* ~**ess** /-'res/ *n.*
directrice *f.*; gérante *f.* ~**ial**

/-'dʒɔːrɪəl/ a. directorial. **~ial staff**, cadres m. pl.

mandarin /'mændərɪn/ n. mandarin m.; (orange) mandarine f.

mandate /'mændeɪt/ n. mandat m.

mandatory /'mændətrɪ/ a. obligatoire.

mane /meɪn/ n. crinière f.

manful /'mænfl/ a. courageux.

manganese /'mæŋgə'niːz/ n. manganèse m.

mangetout /mɑ̃ŋ'tuː/ n. mangetout m. invar.

mangle[1] /'mæŋgl/ n. (for wringing) essoreuse f.; (for smoothing) calandre f.

mangle[2] /'mæŋgl/ v.t. mutiler.

mango /'mæŋgəʊ/ n. (pl. -oes) mangue f.

manhandle /'mænhændl/ v.t. maltraiter, malmener.

manhole /'mænhəʊl/ n. trou d'homme m., regard m.

manhood /'mænhʊd/ n. âge d'homme m.; (quality) virilité f.

mania /'meɪnɪə/ n. manie f. **~c** /-ɪæk/ n. maniaque m./f., fou m., folle f.

manic-depressive /'mænɪkdɪ'presɪv/ a. & n. maniaco-dépressif(-ive) (m. f.).

manicure /'mænɪkjʊə(r)/ n. soin des mains m. —v.t. soigner, manucurer. **~ist** n. manucure m./f.

manifest /'mænɪfest/ a. manifeste. —v.t. manifester. **~ation** /-'steɪʃn/ n. manifestation f.

manifesto /mænɪ'festəʊ/ n. (pl. -os) manifeste m.

manifold /'mænɪfəʊld/ a. multiple. —n. (auto.) collecteur m.

manipulat|e /mə'nɪpjʊleɪt/ v.t. (tool, person) manipuler. **~ion** /-'leɪʃn/ n. manipulation f.

mankind /mæn'kaɪnd/ n. genre humain m.

manly /'mænlɪ/ a. viril.

manner /'mænə(r)/ n. manière f.; (attitude) attitude f.; (kind) sorte f. **~s**, (social behaviour) manières f. pl. **~ed** a. maniéré.

mannerism /'mænərɪzəm/ n. trait particulier m.

manœuvre /mə'nuːvə(r)/ n. manœuvre f. —v.t./i. manœuvrer.

manor /'mænə(r)/ n. manoir m.

manpower /'mænpaʊə(r)/ n. main-d'œuvre f.

manservant /'mænsɜːvənt/ n. (pl. **menservants**) domestique m.

mansion /'mænʃn/ n. château m.

manslaughter /'mænslɔːtə(r)/ n. homicide involontaire m.

mantelpiece /'mæntlpiːs/ n. (shelf) cheminée f.

manual /'mænjʊəl/ a. manuel m. (handbook) manuel m.

manufacture /mænjʊ'fæktʃə(r)/ v.t. fabriquer. —n. fabrication f. **~r** /-ə(r)/ n. fabricant m.

manure /mə'njʊə(r)/ n. fumier m.; (artificial) engrais m.

manuscript /'mænjʊskrɪpt/ n. manuscrit m.

many /'menɪ/ a. & n. beaucoup (de). **a great or good ~**, un grand nombre (de). **~ a**, bien des.

Maori /'maʊrɪ/ a. maori. —n. Maori(e m. (f.).

map /mæp/ n. carte f.; (of streets etc.) plan m. —v.t. (p.t. **mapped**) faire la carte de. **~ out**, (route) tracer; (arrange) organiser.

maple /'meɪpl/ n. érable m.

mar /mɑː(r)/ v.t. (p.t. **marred**) gâter; (spoil beauty of) déparer.

marathon /'mærəθən/ n. marathon m.

marble /'mɑːbl/ n. marbre m.; (for game) bille f.

March /mɑːtʃ/ n. mars m.

march /mɑːtʃ/ v.i. (mil.) marcher (au pas). **~ off/etc.**, partir/etc. allégrement. —v.t. **~ off**, (lead away) emmener. —n. marche f. **~-past** n. défilé m.

mare /meə(r)/ *n.* jument *f.*

margarine /maːdʒəˈriːn/ *n.* margarine *f.*

margin /ˈmaːdʒɪn/ *n.* marge *f.* ~**al** *a.* marginal; (*increase etc.*) léger, faible. ~**al seat,** (*pol.*) siège chaudement disputé *m.* ~**alize** *v.t.* marginaliser. ~**ally** *adv.* très légèrement.

marigold /ˈmærɪɡəʊld/ *n.* souci *m.*

marijuana /mærɪˈwaːnə/ *n.* marijuana *f.*

marina /məˈriːnə/ *n.* marina *f.*

marinate /ˈmærɪneɪt/ *v.t.* mariner.

marine /məˈriːn/ *a.* marin. —*n.* (*shipping*) marine *f.*; (*sailor*) fusilier marin *m.*

marionette /mærɪəˈnet/ *n.* marionnette *f.*

marital /ˈmærɪtl/ *a.* conjugal. ~ **status,** situation de famille *f.*

maritime /ˈmærɪtaɪm/ *a.* maritime.

marjoram /ˈmaːdʒərəm/ *n.* marjolaine *f.*

mark¹ /maːk/ *n.* (*currency*) mark *m.*

mark² /maːk/ *n.* marque *f.*; (*trace*) trace *f.*, marque *f.*; (*schol.*) note *f.*; (*target*) but *m.* —*v.t.* marquer; (*exam*) corriger. ~ **out,** délimiter; (*person*) désigner. ~ **time,** marquer le pas. ~**er** *n.* marque *f.* ~**ing** *n.* (*marks*) marques *f.pl.*

marked /maːkt/ *a.* marqué. ~**ly** /-ɪdlɪ/ *adv.* visiblement.

market /ˈmaːkɪt/ *n.* marché *m.* —*v.t.* (*sell*) vendre; (*launch*) commercialiser. ~ **garden,** jardin maraîcher *m.* ~**-place** *n.* marché *m.* ~ **research,** étude de marché *f.* ~ **value,** valeur marchande *f.* **on the** ~, en vente. ~**ing** *n.* marketing *m.*

marksman /ˈmaːksmən/ *n.* (*pl.* -**men**) tireur d'élite *m.*

marmalade /ˈmaːməleɪd/ *n.* confiture d'oranges *f.*

maroon /məˈruːn/ *n.* bordeaux *m. invar.* —*a.* bordeaux *invar.*

marooned /məˈruːnd/ *a.* abandonné; (*snow-bound etc.*) bloqué.

marquee /maːˈkiː/ *n.* grande tente *f.*; (*awning: Amer.*) marquise *f.*

marquis /ˈmaːkwɪs/ *n.* marquis *m.*

marriage /ˈmærɪdʒ/ *n.* mariage *m.* ~**able** *a.* nubile, mariable.

marrow /ˈmærəʊ/ *n.* (*of bone*) moelle *f.*; (*vegetable*) courge *f.*

marr|y /ˈmærɪ/ *v.t.* épouser; (*give or unite in marriage*) marier. —*v.i.* se marier. ~**ied** *a.* marié; (*life*) conjugal. **get** ~**ied,** se marier (**to,** avec).

Mars /maːz/ *n.* (*planet*) Mars *f.*

marsh /maːʃ/ *n.* marais *m.* ~**y** *a.* marécageux.

marshal /ˈmaːʃl/ *n.* maréchal *m.*; (*at event*) membre du service d'ordre *m.* —*v.t.* (*p.t.* **marshalled**) rassembler.

marshmallow /maːʃˈmæləʊ/ *n.* guimauve *f.*

martial /ˈmaːʃl/ *a.* martial. ~ **law,** loi martiale *f.*

martyr /ˈmaːtə(r)/ *n.* martyr(e) *m.* (*f.*). —*v.t.* martyriser. ~**dom** *n.* martyre *m.*

marvel /ˈmaːvl/ *n.* merveille *f.* —*v.i.* (*p.t.* **marvelled**) s'émerveiller (**at,** de).

marvellous /ˈmaːvələs/ *a.* merveilleux.

Marxis|t /ˈmaːksɪst/ *a.* & *n.* marxiste (*m./f.*). ~**m** /-zəm/ *n.* marxisme *m.*

marzipan /ˈmaːzɪpæn/ *n.* pâte d'amandes *f.*

mascara /mæˈskaːrə/ *n.* mascara *m.*

mascot /ˈmæskət/ *n.* mascotte *f.*

masculin|e /ˈmæskjʊlɪn/ *a.* & *n.* masculin (*m.*). ~**ity** /-ˈlɪnətɪ/ *n.* masculinité *f.*

mash /mæʃ/ *n.* pâtée *f.*; (*potatoes: fam.*) purée *f.* —*v.t.* écraser. ~**ed**

potatoes, purée (de pommes de terre) f.

mask /mɑːsk/ n. masque m. —v.t. masquer.

masochis|t /ˈmæsəkɪst/ n. masochiste m./f. ~m /-zəm/ n. masochisme m.

mason /ˈmeɪsn/ n. (builder) maçon m. ~ry n. maçonnerie f.

Mason /ˈmeɪsn/ n. maçon m. ~ic /məˈsɒnɪk/ a. maçonnique.

masquerade /mɑːskəˈreɪd/ n. mascarade f. —v.i. ~ as, se faire passer pour.

mass¹ /mæs/ n. (relig.) messe f.

mass² /mæs/ n. masse f. —v.t./i. (se) masser. ~-produce v.t. fabriquer en série. the ~es, les masses f.pl. the ~ media, les media m.pl.

massacre /ˈmæsəkə(r)/ n. massacre m. —v.t. massacrer.

massage /ˈmæsɑːʒ, Amer. məˈsɑːʒ/ n. massage m. —v.t. masser.

masseu|r /mæˈsɜː(r)/ n. masseur m. ~se /-ɜːz/ n. masseuse f.

massive /ˈmæsɪv/ a. (large) énorme; (heavy) massif.

mast /mɑːst/ n. mât m.; (for radio, TV) pylône m.

master /ˈmɑːstə(r)/ n. maître m.; (in secondary school) professeur m. —v.t. maîtriser. ~-key n. passe-partout m. invar. ~-mind n. (of scheme etc.) cerveau m.; diriger. M~ of Arts/etc., titulaire d'une maîtrise ès lettres/etc. m./f. ~-stroke n. coup de maître m. ~y n. maîtrise f.

masterly /ˈmɑːstəlɪ/ a. magistral.

masterpiece /ˈmɑːstəpiːs/ n. chef-d'œuvre m.

mastiff /ˈmæstɪf/ n. dogue m.

masturbat|e /ˈmæstəbeɪt/ v.t./i. se masturber. ~ion /-ˈbeɪʃn/ n. masturbation f.

mat /mæt/ n. (petit) tapis m., natte f.; (at door) paillasson m.

match¹ /mætʃ/ n. allumette f.

match² /mætʃ/ n. (sport) match m.; (equal) égal(e) m. (f.); (marriage) mariage m.; (s.o. to marry) parti m. —v.t. opposer; (go with) aller avec; (cups etc.) assortir; (equal) égaler. be a ~ for, pouvoir tenir tête à. —v.i. (be alike) être assorti. ~ing a. assorti.

matchbox /ˈmætʃbɒks/ n. boîte à allumettes f.

mate¹ /meɪt/ n. camarade m./f.; (of animal) compagnon m., compagne f.; (assistant) aide m./f. —v.t./i. (s')accoupler (with, avec).

mate² /meɪt/ n. (chess) mat m.

material /məˈtɪərɪəl/ n. matière f.; (fabric) tissu m.; (documents, for building) matériau(x) m. (pl.). ~s, (equipment) matériel m. —a. matériel; (fig.) important. ~istic /-ˈlɪstɪk/ a. matérialiste.

materialize /məˈtɪərɪəlaɪz/ v.i. se matérialiser, se réaliser.

maternal /məˈtɜːnl/ a. maternel.

maternity /məˈtɜːnətɪ/ n. maternité f. —a. (clothes) de grossesse. ~ hospital, maternité f. ~ leave, congé maternité m.

mathematic|s /mæθəˈmætɪks/ n. & n. pl. mathématiques f. pl. ~ian /-əˈtɪʃn/ n. mathématicien(ne) m. (f.). ~al a. mathématique.

maths /mæθs/ (Amer. math /mæθ/) n. & n. pl. (fam.) maths f. pl.

matinée /ˈmætɪneɪ/ n. matinée f.

mating /ˈmeɪtɪŋ/ n. accouplement m. ~ season, saison des amours f.

matriculat|e /məˈtrɪkjʊleɪt/ v.t./i. (s')inscrire. ~ion /-ˈleɪʃn/ n. inscription f.

matrimon|y /ˈmætrɪmənɪ/ n. mariage m. ~ial /-ˈməʊnɪəl/ a. matrimonial.

matrix /'meɪtrɪks/ n. (pl. matrices /-ɪsiːz/) matrice f.

matron /'meɪtrən/ n. (married, elderly) dame âgée f.; (in hospital: former use) infirmière-major f. **~ly** a. d'âge mûr; (manner) très digne.

matt /mæt/ a. mat.

matted /'mætɪd/ a. (hair) emmêlé.

matter /'mætə(r)/ n. (substance) matière f.; (affair) affaire f.; (pus) pus m. —v.i. importer. **as a ~ of fact,** en fait. **it does not ~,** ça ne fait rien. **~-of-fact** a. terre à terre invar. **no ~ what happens,** quoi qu'il arrive. **what is the ~?,** qu'est-ce qu'il y a?

mattress /'mætrɪs/ n. matelas m.

matur|e /mə'tjʊə(r)/ a. mûr. —v.t./i. (se) mûrir. **~ity** n. maturité f.

maul /mɔːl/ v.t. déchiqueter.

Mauritius /mə'rɪʃəs/ n. île Maurice f.

mausoleum /mɔːsə'lɪəm/ n. mausolée m.

mauve /məʊv/ a. & n. mauve (m.).

maverick /'mævərɪk/ n. non-conformiste.

maxim /'mæksɪm/ n. maxime f.

maxim|um /'mæksɪməm/ a. & n. (pl. -ima) maximum (m.). **~ize** v.t. porter au maximum.

may /meɪ/ v. aux. (p.t. might) pouvoir. **he ~/might come,** il peut/pourrait venir. **you might have,** vous auriez pu. **you ~ leave,** vous pouvez partir. **~ I smoke?,** puis-je fumer? **~ he be happy,** qu'il soit heureux. **I ~ or might as well stay,** je ferais aussi bien de rester.

May /meɪ/ n. mai m. **~ Day,** le Premier Mai.

maybe /'meɪbiː/ adv. peut-être.

mayhem /'meɪhem/ n. (havoc) ravages m. pl.

mayonnaise /meɪə'neɪz/ n. mayonnaise f.

mayor /meə(r)/ n. maire m. **~ess** n. (wife) femme du maire f.

maze /meɪz/ n. labyrinthe m.

MBA (abbr.) (Master of Business Administration) magistère en gestion commercial.

me /miː/ pron. me, m'*; (after prep.) moi. **(to) ~,** me, m'*. **he knows ~,** il me connaît.

meadow /'medəʊ/ n. pré m.

meagre /'miːgə(r)/ a. maigre.

meal¹ /miːl/ n. repas m.

meal² /miːl/ n. (grain) farine f.

mealy-mouthed /miːlɪ'maʊðd/ a. mielleux.

mean¹ /miːn/ a. (-er, -est) (poor) misérable; (miserly) avare; (unkind) méchant. **~ness** n. avarice f.; méchanceté f.

mean² /miːn/ a. moyen. —n. milieu m.; (average) moyenne f. **in the ~ time,** en attendant.

mean³ /miːn/ v.t. (p.t. meant /ment/) vouloir dire, signifier; (involve) entraîner. **I ~ that!,** je suis sérieux. **be meant for,** être destiné à. **~ to do,** avoir l'intention de faire.

meander /mɪ'ændə(r)/ v.i. faire des méandres.

meaning /'miːnɪŋ/ n. sens m., signification f. **~ful** a. significatif. **~less** a. denué de sens.

means /miːnz/ n. moyen(s) m. (pl.). **by ~ of sth.,** au moyen de qch. —n. pl. (wealth) moyens financiers m. pl. **by all ~,** certainement. **by no ~,** nullement.

meant /ment/ see **mean²**.

mean|time /'miːntaɪm/, **~while** advs. en attendant.

measles /'miːzlz/ n. rougeole f.

measly /'miːzlɪ/ a. (sl.) minable.

measurable /'meʒərəbl/ a. mesurable.

measure /'meʒə(r)/ n. mesure f.; (ruler) règle f. —v.t./i. mesurer. **~ up to,** être à la hauteur de. **~d** a. mesuré. **~ment** n. mesure f.

meat /miːt/ *n.* viande *f.* ~y *a.* de viande; (*fig.*) substantiel.

mechanic /mɪˈkænɪk/ *n.* mécanicien(ne) *m.* (*f.*).

mechanic|al /mɪˈkænɪkl/ *a.* mécanique. ~s *n.* (*science*) mécanique *f.*; *n. pl.* mécanisme *m.*

mechan|ism /ˈmekənɪzəm/ *n.* mécanisme *m.* ~ize *v.t.* mécaniser.

medal /ˈmedl/ *n.* médaille *f.* ~list *n.* médaillé(e) *m.* (*f.*). **be a gold** ~**list,** être médaille d'or.

medallion /mɪˈdælɪən/ *n.* (*medal, portrait, etc.*) médaillon *m.*

meddle /ˈmedl/ *v.i.* (*interfere*) se mêler (**in, de**); (*tinker*) toucher (**with,** à). ~**some** *a.* importun.

media /ˈmiːdɪə/ *see* **medium.** —*n. pl.* the ~, les media *m. pl.* **talk to the** ~, parler à la presse.

median /ˈmiːdɪən/ *a.* médian. —*n.* médiane *f.*

mediat|e /ˈmiːdɪeɪt/ *v.i.* servir d'intermédiaire. ~**ion** /-ˈeɪʃn/ *n.* médiation *f.* ~**or** *n.* média|teur, -trice *m., f.*

medical /ˈmedɪkl/ *a.* médical; (*student*) en médecine. —*n.* (*fam.*) visite médicale *f.*

medicat|ed /ˈmedɪkeɪtɪd/ *a.* médical. ~**ion** /-ˈkeɪʃn/ *n.* médicaments *m. pl.*

medicin|e /ˈmedsn/ *n.* (*science*) médecine *f.*; (*substance*) médicament *m.* ~**al** /mɪˈdɪsɪnl/ *a.* médicinal.

medieval /medɪˈiːvl/ *a.* médiéval.

mediocr|e /miːdɪˈəʊkə(r)/ *a.* médiocre. ~**ity** /-ˈɒkrəti/ *n.* médiocrité *f.*

meditat|e /ˈmedɪteɪt/ *v.t./i.* méditer. ~**ion** /-ˈteɪʃn/ *n.* méditation *f.*

Mediterranean /medɪtəˈreɪnɪən/ *a.* méditerranéen. —*n.* the ~, la Méditerranée *f.*

medium /ˈmiːdɪəm/ *n.* (*pl.* **media**) milieu *m.*; (*for transmitting data*

etc.) support *m.*; (*pl.* **mediums**) (*person*) médium *m.* —*a.* moyen.

medley /ˈmedlɪ/ *n.* mélange *m.*; (*mus.*) pot-pourri *m.*

meek /miːk/ *a.* (**-er, -est**) doux.

meet /miːt/ *v.t.* (*p.t.* **met**) rencontrer; (*see again*) retrouver; (*fetch*) (aller) chercher; (*be introduced to*) faire la connaissance de; (*face*) faire face à; (*requirement*) satisfaire. —*v.i.* se rencontrer; (*see each other again*) se retrouver; (*in session*) se réunir.

meeting /ˈmiːtɪŋ/ *n.* réunion *f.*; (*between two people*) rencontre *f.*

megalomania /megələʊˈmeɪnɪə/ *n.* mégalomanie *f.* ~**c** /-ˈæk/ *n.* mégalomane *m./f.*

megaphone /ˈmegəfəʊn/ *n.* porte-voix *m. invar.*

melamine /ˈmeləmiːn/ *n.* mélamine *f.*

melanchol|y /ˈmelənkəlɪ/ *n.* mélancolie *f.* —*a.* mélancolique. ~**ic** /-ˈkɒlɪk/ *a.* mélancolique.

mellow /ˈmeləʊ/ *a.* (**-er, -est**) (*fruit*) mûr; (*sound, colour*) moelleux, doux; (*person*) mûri. —*v.t./i.* (*mature*) mûrir; (*soften*) (s')adoucir.

melodious /mɪˈləʊdɪəs/ *a.* mélodieux.

melodrama /ˈmelədrɑːmə/ *n.* mélodrame *m.* ~**tic** /-əˈmætɪk/ *a.* mélodramatique.

melod|y /ˈmelədɪ/ *n.* mélodie *f.* ~**ic** /mɪˈlɒdɪk/ *a.* mélodique.

melon /ˈmelən/ *n.* melon *m.*

melt /melt/ *v.t./i.* (faire) fondre. ~**ing-pot** *n.* creuset *m.*

member /ˈmembə(r)/ *n.* membre *m.* **M~ of Parliament,** député *m.* ~**ship** *n.* adhésion *f.*; (*members*) membres *m. pl.*; (*fee*) cotisation *f.*

membrane /ˈmembreɪn/ *n.* membrane *f.*

memento /mɪˈmentəʊ/ *n.* (*pl.* **-oes**) (*object*) souvenir *m.*

memo /'meməʊ/ n. (pl. -os) (fam.) note f.

memoir /'memwɑ:(r)/ n. (record, essay) mémoire m.

memorable /'memərəbl/ a. mémorable.

memorandum /memə'rændəm/ n. (pl. -ums) note f.

memorial /mɪ'mɔ:rɪəl/ n. monument m. —a. commémoratif.

memorize /'meməraɪz/ v.t. apprendre par cœur.

memory /'meməri/ n. (mind, in computer) mémoire f.; (thing remembered) souvenir m. from ～, de mémoire. in ～ of, à la mémoire de.

men /men/ see **man**.

menac|e /'menəs/ n. menace f.; (nuisance) peste f. —v.t. menacer. ～ing a. menaçant.

menagerie /mɪ'nædʒərɪ/ n. ménagerie f.

mend /mend/ v.t. réparer; (darn) raccommoder. —n. raccommodage m. ～ one's ways, s'amender. on the ～, en voie de guérison.

menial /'mi:nɪəl/ a. servile.

meningitis /menɪn'dʒaɪtɪs/ n. méningite f.

menopause /'menəpɔ:z/ n. ménopause f.

menstruation /menstru'eɪʃn/ n. menstruation f.

mental /'mentl/ a. mental; (hospital) psychiatrique. ～ block, blocage m.

mentality /men'tælətɪ/ n. mentalité f.

menthol /'menθɒl/ n. menthol m. —a. mentholé.

mention /'menʃn/ v.t. mentionner. —n. mention f. don't ～ it!, il n'y a pas de quoi!, je vous en prie!

mentor /'mentɔ:(r)/ n. mentor m.

menu /'menju:/ n. (food, on computer) menu m.; (list) carte f.

MEP (abbr.) (member of the European Parliament) député européen m.

mercenary /'mɜ:sɪnərɪ/ a. & n. mercenaire (m.).

merchandise /'mɜ:tʃəndaɪz/ n. marchandises f. pl.

merchant /'mɜ:tʃənt/ n. marchand m. —a. (ship, navy) marchand. ～ bank, banque de commerce f.

merciful /'mɜ:sɪfl/ a. miséricordieux. ～ly adv. (fortunately: fam.) Dieu merci.

merciless /'mɜ:sɪlɪs/ a. impitoyable, implacable.

mercury /'mɜ:kjʊrɪ/ n. mercure m.

mercy /'mɜ:sɪ/ n. pitié f. at the ～ of, à la merci de.

mere /mɪə(r)/ a. simple. ～ly adv. simplement.

merest /'mɪərɪst/ a. moindre.

merg|e /mɜ:dʒ/ v.t./i. (se) mêler (with, à); (companies: comm.) fusionner. ～r /-ə(r)/ n. fusion f.

meridian /mə'rɪdɪən/ n. méridien m.

meringue /mə'ræŋ/ n. meringue f.

merit /'merɪt/ n. mérite m. —v.t. (p.t. merited) mériter.

mermaid /'mɜ:meɪd/ n. sirène f.

merriment /'merɪmənt/ n. gaieté f.

merry /'merɪ/ a. (-ier, -iest) gai. make ～, faire la fête. ～-go-round n. manège m. ～-making n. réjouissances f. pl. **merrily** adv. gaiement.

mesh /meʃ/ n. maille f.; (fabric) tissu à mailles m.; (network) réseau m.

mesmerize /'mezməraɪz/ v.t. hypnotiser.

mess /mes/ n. désordre m., gâchis m.; (dirt) saleté f.; (mil.) mess m. —v.t. ～ up, gâcher. —v.i. ～ about, s'amuser; (dawdle) traîner. ～ with, (tinker with) tripoter. make a ～ of, gâcher.

message /'mesɪdʒ/ n. message m.

messenger /'mesɪndʒə(r)/ n. messager m.

Messrs /'mesəz/ n. pl. ~ **Smith**, Messieurs or MM. Smith.

messy /'mesɪ/ a. (**-ier, -iest**) en désordre; (*dirty*) sale.

met /met/ *see* meet.

metabolic /metə'bɒlɪk/ *adj.* métabolique.

metabolism /mɪ'tæbəlɪzəm/ n. métabolisme m.

metal /'metl/ n. métal m. —a. de métal. ~**lic** /mɪ'tælɪk/ a. métallique; (*paint, colour*) métallisé.

metallurgy /mɪ'tælədʒɪ, *Amer.* 'metəlɜːdʒɪ/ n. métallurgie f.

metamorphosis /metə'mɔːfəsɪs/ n. (pl. **-phoses** /-siːz/) métamorphose f.

metaphor /'metəfə(r)/ n. métaphore f. ~**ical** /-'fɒrɪkl/ a. métaphorique.

mete /miːt/ v.t. ~ **out**, donner, distribuer; (*justice*) rendre.

meteor /'miːtɪə(r)/ n. météore m.

meteorite /'miːtɪəraɪt/ n. météorite m.

meteorolog|y /miːtɪə'rɒlədʒɪ/ n. météorologie f. ~**ical** /-ə'lɒdʒɪkl/ a. météorologique.

meter[1] /'miːtə(r)/ n. compteur m.

meter[2] /'miːtə(r)/ n. (*Amer.*) = metre.

method /'meθəd/ n. méthode f.

methodical /mɪ'θɒdɪkl/ a. méthodique.

Methodist /'meθədɪst/ n. & a. méthodiste (m./f.).

methodology /meθə'dɒlədʒɪ/ n. méthodologie f.

methylated /'meθɪleɪtɪd/ a. ~ **spirit**, alcool à brûler m.

meticulous /mɪ'tɪkjʊləs/ a. méticuleux.

metre /'miːtə(r)/ n. mètre m.

metric /'metrɪk/ a. métrique. ~**ation** /-'keɪʃn/ n. adoption du système métrique f.

metropol|is /mə'trɒpəlɪs/ n. (*city*)

métropole f. ~**itan** /metrə'pɒlɪtən/ a. métropolitain.

mettle /'metl/ n. courage m.

mew /mjuː/ n. miaulement m. —v.i. miauler.

mews /mjuːz/ n. pl. (*dwellings*) appartements chic aménagés dans des anciennes écuries m. pl.

Mexic|o /'meksɪkəʊ/ n. Mexique m. ~**an** a. & n. mexicain(e) (m. (f.)).

miaow /miːˈaʊ/ n. & v.i. = mew.

mice /maɪs/ *see* mouse.

mickey /'mɪkɪ/ n. **take the ~ out of**, (*sl.*) se moquer de.

micro- /'maɪkrəʊ/ *pref.* micro-.

microbe /'maɪkrəʊb/ n. microbe m.

microchip /'maɪkrəʊtʃɪp/ n. microplaquette f., puce f.

microclimate /'maɪkrəʊklaɪmət/ n. microclimat m.

microcomputer /maɪkrəʊkəm'pjuːtə(r)/ n. micro(-ordinateur) m.

microcosm /'maɪkrəʊkɒzm/ n. microcosme m.

microfilm /'maɪkrəʊfɪlm/ n. microfilm m.

microlight /'maɪkrəʊlaɪt/ n. U.L.M. m.

microphone /'maɪkrəfəʊn/ n. microphone m.

microprocessor /maɪkrəʊ'prəʊsesə(r)/ n. microprocesseur m.

microscop|e /'maɪkrəskəʊp/ n. microscope m. ~**ic** /-'skɒpɪk/ a. microscopique.

microwave /'maɪkrəweɪv/ n. micro-onde f. ~ **oven**, four à micro-ondes m.

mid /mɪd/ a. **in ~ air**/*etc.*, en plein ciel/*etc.* **in ~ March**/*etc.*, à la mi-mars/*etc.* **in ~ ocean**/*etc.*, au milieu de l'océan/*etc.*

midday /mɪd'deɪ/ n. midi m.

middle /'mɪdl/ a. du milieu; (*quality*) moyen. —n. milieu m. **in the ~ of**, au milieu de. ~**-aged** a. d'un certain âge. **M~ Ages**,

moyen âge m. **~ class,** classe
moyenne f. **~-class** a. bourgeois.
M~ East, Proche-Orient m.
middleman /ˈmɪdlmæn/ n. (pl.
-men) intermédiaire m.
middling /ˈmɪdlɪŋ/ a. moyen.
midge /mɪdʒ/ n. moucheron m.
midget /ˈmɪdʒɪt/ n. nain(e) m. (f.).
—a. minuscule.
Midlands /ˈmɪdləndz/ n. pl. région
du centre de l'Angleterre f.
midnight /ˈmɪdnaɪt/ n. minuit f.
midriff /ˈmɪdrɪf/ n. ventre m.
midst /mɪdst/ n. **in the ~ of,** au
milieu de. **in our ~,** parmi nous.
midsummer /mɪdˈsʌmə(r)/ n.
milieu de l'été m.; (solstice)
solstice d'été m.
midway /mɪdˈweɪ/ adv. à
mi-chemin.
midwife /ˈmɪdwaɪf/ n. (pl. **-wives**)
sage-femme f.
might[1] /maɪt/ n. puissance f. **~y**
a. puissant; (very great: fam.) très
grand; adv. (fam.) rudement.
might[2] /maɪt/ see **may.**
migraine /ˈmiːɡreɪn, Amer. ˈmaɪ-
ɡreɪn/ n. migraine f.
migrant /ˈmaɪɡrənt/ a. & n. (bird)
migrateur (m.); (worker) émi-
grant(e) (m. (f.)).
migrat|e /maɪˈɡreɪt/ v.i. émigrer.
~ion /-ʃn/ n. migration f.
mike /maɪk/ n. (fam.) micro m.
mild /maɪld/ a. (**-er, -est**) doux;
(illness) bénin. **~ly** adv. doucement. **to put it ~ly,** pour ne rien
exagérer. **~ness** n. douceur f.
mildew /ˈmɪldjuː/ n. moisissure f.
mile /maɪl/ n. mille m. (= 1.6 km.).
~s too big/etc., (fam.) beaucoup
trop grand/etc. **~age** n. (loosely)
kilométrage m.
milestone /ˈmaɪlstəʊn/ n. borne f.
(event, stage; fig.) jalon m.
militant /ˈmɪlɪtənt/ a. & n.
militant(e) (m. (f.)).
military /ˈmɪlɪtrɪ/ a. militaire.
militate /ˈmɪlɪteɪt/ v.i. militer.

militia /mɪˈlɪʃə/ n. milice f.
milk /mɪlk/ n. lait m. —a. (product)
laitier. —v.t. (cow etc.) traire;
(fig.) exploiter. **~ shake,** milk-
shake m. **~y** a. (diet) lacté;
(colour) laiteux; (tea etc.) au lait.
M~y Way, Voie lactée f.
milkman /ˈmɪlkmən, Amer.
ˈmɪlkmæn/ n. (pl. **-men**) laitier m.
mill /mɪl/ n. moulin m.; (factory)
usine f. —v.t. moudre. —v.i. **~
around,** tourner en rond;
(crowd) grouiller. **~er** n.
meunier m.
millennium /mɪˈlenɪəm/ n. (pl.
-ums) millénaire m.
millet /ˈmɪlɪt/ n. millet m.
milli- /ˈmɪlɪ/ pref. milli-.
millimetre /ˈmɪlɪmiːtə(r)/ n. millimètre m.
milliner /ˈmɪlɪnə(r)/ n. modiste f.
million /ˈmɪljən/ n. million m. **a ~
pounds,** un million de livres.
~aire /-ˈneə(r)/ n. millionnaire
m.
millstone /ˈmɪlstəʊn/ n. meule f.;
(burden: fig.) boulet m.
milometer /maɪˈlɒmɪtə(r)/ n.
compteur kilométrique m.
mime /maɪm/ n. (actor) mime
m./f.; (art) (art du) mime m.
—v.t./i. mimer.
mimic /ˈmɪmɪk/ v.t. (p.t.
mimicked) imiter. —n. imita-
teur, -trice m., f. **~ry** n. imitation
f.
mince /mɪns/ v.t. hacher. —n.
viande hachée f. **~ pie,** tarte aux
fruits confits f. **not to ~
matters,** ne pas mâcher ses mots.
~r /-ə(r)/ n. (machine) hachoir m.
mincemeat /ˈmɪnsmiːt/ n. hachis
de fruits confits m. **make ~ of,**
anéantir, pulvériser.
mind /maɪnd/ n. esprit m.; (sanity)
raison f.; (opinion) avis m. —v.t.
(have charge of) s'occuper de;
(heed) faire attention à. **be on
s.o.'s ~,** préoccuper qn. **bear**

that in ∼, ne l'oubliez pas.
change one's ∼, changer d'avis.
make up one's ∼, se décider (**to**,
à). **I do not** ∼ **the noise**/*etc*., le
bruit/*etc*. ne me dérange pas. **I do
not** ∼, ça m'est égal. **would you**
∼ **checking?**, je peux vous
demander de vérifier? ∼**ful** *a*.
attentif (**of**, à). ∼**less** *a*. irréfléchi.

minder /'maɪndə(r)/ *n*. (*for child*)
gardien(ne) *m*. (*f*.); (*for protection*) ange gardien *m*.

mine[1] /maɪn/*poss. pron.* le mien, la
mienne, les mien(ne)s. **it is** ∼,
c'est à moi or le mien.

min|e[2] /maɪn/ *n*. mine *f*. —*v.t.*
extraire; (*mil*.) miner. ∼**er** *n*.
mineur *m*. ∼**ing** *n*. exploitation
minière *f*.; *a*. minier.

minefield /'maɪnfiːld/ *n*. champ de
mines *m*.

mineral /'mɪnərəl/ *n*. & *a*. minéral
(*m*.). ∼ (**water**), (*fizzy soft drink*)
boisson gazeuse *f*. ∼ **water**,
(*natural*) eau minérale *f*.

minesweeper /'maɪnswiːpə(r)/ *n*.
(*ship*) dragueur de mines *m*.

mingle /'mɪŋgl/ *v.t./i.* (se) mêler
(**with**, à).

mingy /'mɪndʒɪ/ *a*. (*fam*.) radin.

mini- /'mɪnɪ/ *pref.* mini-.

miniatur|e /'mɪnɪtʃə(r)/ *a*. & *n*.
miniature (*f*.). ∼**ize** *v.t.* mini-
aturiser.

minibus /'mɪnɪbʌs/ *n*. minibus *m*.

minicab /'mɪnɪkæb/ *n*. taxi *m*.

minim /'mɪnɪm/ *n*. blanche *f*.

minim|um /'mɪnɪməm/ *a*. & *n*. (*pl.
-ima*) minimum (*m*.). ∼**al** *a*.
minimal. ∼**ize** *v.t.* minimiser.

minist|er /'mɪnɪstə(r)/ *n*. ministre
m. ∼**erial** /-'stɪərɪəl/ *a*. ministériel. ∼**ry** *n*. ministère *m*.

mink /mɪŋk/ *n*. vison *m*.

minor /'maɪnə(r)/ *a*. petit, mineur.
—*n*. (*jurid*.) mineur(e) *m*. (*f*.).

minority /maɪ'nɒrətɪ/ *n*. minorité
f. —*a*. minoritaire.

mint[1] /mɪnt/ *n*., **the M**∼, l'Hôtel de
la Monnaie *m*. **a** ∼, une fortune.
—*v.t.* frapper. **in** ∼ **condition**, à
l'état neuf.

mint[2] /mɪnt/ *n*. (*plant*) menthe *f*.;
(*sweet*) pastille de menthe *f*.

minus /'maɪnəs/ *prep.* moins;
(*without: fam*.) sans. —*n*. (*sign*)
moins *m*. ∼ **sign**, moins
m.

minute[1] /'mɪnɪt/ *n*. minute *f*. ∼**s**,
(*of meeting*) procès-verbal *m*.

minute[2] /maɪ'njuːt/ *a*. (*tiny*)
minuscule; (*detailed*) minutieux.

miracle /'mɪrəkl/ *n*. miracle *m*.
∼**ulous** /mɪ'rækjʊləs/ *a*. mira-
culeux.

mirage /'mɪrɑːʒ/ *n*. mirage *m*.

mire /maɪə(r)/ *n*. fange *f*.

mirror /'mɪrə(r)/ *n*. miroir *m*.,
glace *f*. —*v.t.* refléter.

mirth /mɜːθ/ *n*. gaieté *f*.

misadventure /mɪsəd'ventʃə(r)/
n. mésaventure *f*.

misanthropist /mɪs'ænθrəpɪst/ *n*.
misanthrope *m*.

misapprehension /mɪsæprɪ-
'henʃn/ *n*. malentendu *m*.

misbehav|e /mɪsbɪ'heɪv/ *v.i.* se
conduire mal. ∼**iour** *n*. mauvaise conduite *f*.

miscalculat|e /mɪs'kælkjʊleɪt/ *v.t.*
mal calculer. —*v.i.* se tromper.
∼**ion** /-'leɪʃn/ *n*. erreur de calcul
f.

miscarr|y /mɪs'kærɪ/ *v.i.* faire une
fausse couche. ∼**iage** /-ɪdʒ/ *n*.
fausse couche *f*. ∼**iage of justice**, erreur judiciaire *f*.

miscellaneous /mɪsə'leɪnɪəs/ *a*.
divers.

mischief /'mɪstʃɪf/ *n*. (*foolish
conduct*) espièglerie *f*.; (*harm*)
mal *m*. **get into** ∼, faire des
sottises.

mischievous /'mɪstʃɪvəs/ *a*.
espiègle; (*malicious*) méchant.

misconception /mɪskən'sepʃn/ *n*.
idée fausse *f*.

misconduct /mɪs'kɒndʌkt/ n. mauvaise conduite f.

misconstrue /mɪskən'struː/ v.t. mal interpréter.

misdeed /mɪs'diːd/ n. méfait m.

misdemeanour /mɪsdɪ'miːnə(r)/ n. (jurid.) délit m.

misdirect /mɪsdɪ'rekt/ v.t. (person) mal renseigner.

miser /'maɪzə(r)/ n. avare m./f. ~ly a. avare.

miserable /'mɪzrəbl/ a. (sad) malheureux; (wretched) misérable; (unpleasant) affreux.

misery /'mɪzərɪ/ n. (unhappiness) malheur m.; (pain) souffrances f. pl.; (poverty) misère f.; (person: fam.) grincheu|x, -se m., f.

misfire /mɪs'faɪə(r)/ v.i. (plan etc.) rater; (engine) avoir des ratés.

misfit /'mɪsfɪt/ n. inadapté(e) m. (f.).

misfortune /mɪs'fɔːtʃuːn/ n. malheur m.

misgiving /mɪs'gɪvɪŋ/ n. (doubt) doute m.; (apprehension) crainte f.

misguided /mɪs'gaɪdɪd/ a. (foolish) imprudent; (mistaken) erroné. be ~, (person) se tromper.

mishap /'mɪshæp/ n. mésaventure f., contretemps m.

misinform /mɪsɪn'fɔːm/ v.t. mal renseigner.

misinterpret /mɪsɪn'tɜːprɪt/ v.t. mal interpréter.

misjudge /mɪs'dʒʌdʒ/ v.t. mal juger.

mislay /mɪs'leɪ/ v.t. (p.t. mislaid) égarer.

mislead /mɪs'liːd/ v.t. (p.t. misled) tromper. ~ing a. trompeur.

mismanage /mɪs'mænɪdʒ/ v.t. mal gérer. ~ment n. mauvaise gestion f.

misnomer /mɪs'nəʊmə(r)/ n. terme impropre m.

misplace /mɪs'pleɪs/ v.t. mal placer; (lose) égarer.

misprint /'mɪsprɪnt/ n. faute d'impression f., coquille f.

misread /mɪs'riːd/ v.t. (p.t. misread /mɪs'red/) mal lire; (intentions) mal comprendre.

misrepresent /mɪsreprɪ'zent/ v.t. présenter sous un faux jour.

miss¹ /mɪs/ v.t./i. manquer; (deceased person etc.) regretter. he ~es her/Paris/etc., elle/Paris/etc. lui manque. I ~ you, tu me manques. you're ~ing the point, vous n'avez rien compris. —n. coup manqué m. it was a near ~, on l'a échappé belle or de peu. ~ out, omettre. ~ out on sth, rater qch.

miss² /mɪs/ n. (pl. misses) mademoiselle f. (pl. mesdemoiselles). M~ Smith, Mademoiselle or Mlle Smith.

misshapen /mɪs'ʃeɪpən/ a. difforme.

missile /'mɪsaɪl/ n. (mil.) missile m.; (object thrown) projectile m.

missing /'mɪsɪŋ/ a. (person) disparu; (thing) qui manque. something's ~, il manque quelque chose.

mission /'mɪʃn/ n. mission f.

missionary /'mɪʃənrɪ/ n. missionnaire m./f.

missive /'mɪsɪv/ n. missive f.

misspell /mɪs'spel/ v.t. (p.t. misspelt or misspelled) mal écrire.

mist /mɪst/ n. brume f.; (on window) buée f. —v.t./i. (s')embuer.

mistake /mɪ'steɪk/ n. erreur f. —v.t. (p.t. mistook, p.p. mistaken) mal comprendre; (choose wrongly) se tromper de. by ~, par erreur. make a ~, faire une erreur. ~ for, prendre pour. ~n /-ən/ a. erroné. be ~n, se tromper. ~nly /-ənlɪ/ adv. par erreur.

mistletoe /'mɪsltəʊ/ *n.* gui *m.*

mistreat /mɪs'triːt/ *v.t.* maltraiter.

mistress /'mɪstrɪs/ *n.* maîtresse *f.*

mistrust /mɪs'trʌst/ *v.t.* se méfier de. —*n.* méfiance *f.*

misty /'mɪstɪ/ *a.* (**-ier, -iest**) brumeux; (*window*) embué.

misunderstand /mɪsʌndə'stænd/ *v.t.* (*p.t.* **-stood**) mal comprendre. ∼**ing** *n.* malentendu *m.*

misuse[1] /mɪs'juːz/ *v.t.* mal employer; (*power etc.*) abuser de.

misuse[2] /mɪs'juːs/ *n.* mauvais emploi *m.*; (*unfair use*) abus *m.*

mitigat|e /'mɪtɪgeɪt/ *v.t.* atténuer. ∼**ing circumstances**, circonstances atténuantes *f.pl.*

mitten /'mɪtn/ *n.* moufle *f.*

mix /mɪks/ *v.t./i.* (se) mélanger. —*n.* mélange *m.* ∼ **up**, mélanger; (*bewilder*) embrouiller; (*mistake, confuse*) confondre (**with**, avec). ∼-**up** *n.* confusion *f.* ∼ **with**, (*people*) fréquenter. ∼**er** *n.* (*culin.*) mélangeur *m.* **be a good** ∼**er**, être sociable. ∼**er tap**, mélangeur *m.*

mixed /mɪkst/ *a.* (*school etc.*) mixte; (*assorted*) assorti. **be** ∼-**up**, (*fam.*) avoir des problèmes.

mixture /'mɪkstʃə(r)/ *n.* mélange *m.*; (*for cough*) sirop *m.*

moan /məʊn/ *n.* gémissement *m.* —*v.i.* gémir; (*complain*) grogner. ∼**er** *n.* (*grumbler*) grognon *m.*

moat /məʊt/ *n.* douve(s) *f.* (*pl.*).

mob /mɒb/ *n.* (*crowd*) cohue *f.*; (*gang: sl.*) bande *f.* —*v.t.* (*p.t.* **mobbed**) assiéger.

mobile /'məʊbaɪl/ *a.* mobile. ∼**e home**, caravane *f.* ∼ **mobile** *m.* ∼**ity** /-'bɪlətɪ/ *n.* mobilité *f.*

mobiliz|e /'məʊbɪlaɪz/ *v.t./i.* mobiliser. ∼**ation** /-'zeɪʃn/ *n.* mobilisation *f.*

moccasin /'mɒkəsɪn/ *n.* mocassin *m.*

mock /mɒk/ *v.t./i.* se moquer (de). —*a.* faux. ∼-**up** *n.* maquette *f.*

mockery /'mɒkərɪ/ *n.* moquerie *f.* **a** ∼ **of**, une parodie de.

mode /məʊd/ *n.* (*way, method*) mode *m.*; (*fashion*) mode *f.*

model /'mɒdl/ *n.* modèle *m.*; (*of toy*) modèle réduit *m.*; (*artist's*) modèle *m.*; (*for fashion*) mannequin *m.* —*a.* modèle; (*car etc.*) modèle réduit *invar.* —*v.t.* (*p.t.* **modelled**) (*clothes*) présenter. —*v.i.* être mannequin; (*pose*) poser. ∼**ling** *n.* métier de mannequin *m.*

modem /'məʊdem/ *n.* modem *m.*

moderate[1] /'mɒdərət/ *a. & n.* modéré(e) (*m. (f.)*). ∼**ly** *adv.* (*in moderation*) modérément; (*fairly*) moyennement.

moderat|e[2] /'mɒdəreɪt/ *v.t./i.* (se) modérer. ∼**ion** /-'reɪʃn/ *n.* modération *f.* **in** ∼**ion**, avec modération.

modern /'mɒdn/ *a.* moderne. ∼ **languages**, langues vivantes *f. pl.* ∼**ize** *v.t.* moderniser.

modest /'mɒdɪst/ *a.* modeste. ∼**y** *n.* modestie *f.*

modicum /'mɒdɪkəm/ *n.* **a** ∼ **of**, un peu de.

modif|y /'mɒdɪfaɪ/ *v.t.* modifier. ∼**ication** /-ɪ'keɪʃn/ *n.* modification *f.*

modular /'mɒdjʊlə(r)/ *a.* modulaire

modulat|e /'mɒdjʊleɪt/ *v.t./i.* moduler. ∼**ion** /-'leɪʃn/ *n.* modulation *f.*

module /'mɒdjuːl/ *n.* module *m.*

mohair /'məʊheə(r)/ *n.* mohair *m.*

moist /mɔɪst/ *a.* (**-er, -est**) humide, moite. ∼**ure** /'mɔɪstʃə(r)/ *n.* humidité *f.* ∼**urizer** /mɔɪs-tʃəraɪz(r)/ *n.* produit hydratant.

moisten /'mɔɪsn/ *v.t.* humecter.

molar /'məʊlə(r)/ *n.* molaire *f.*

molasses /mə'læsɪz/ *n.* mélasse *f.*

mold /məʊld/ (*Amer.*) = **mould**.

mole[1] /məʊl/ *n.* grain de beauté *m.*

mole² /məʊl/ *n.* (*animal*) taupe *f.*

molecule /'mɒlɪkjuːl/ *n.* molécule *f.*

molest /mə'lest/ *v.t.* (*pester*) importuner; (*ill-treat*) molester.

mollusc /'mɒləsk/ *n.* mollusque *m.*

mollycoddle /'mɒlɪkɒdl/ *v.t.* dorloter, chouchouter.

molten /'məʊltən/ *a.* en fusion.

mom /mɒm/ *n.* (*Amer.*) maman *f.*

moment /'məʊmənt/ *n.* moment *m.*

momentar|y /'məʊməntrɪ, Amer. -terɪ/ *a.* momentané. ~**ily** (*Amer.* /-'terəlɪ/) *adv.* momentanément; (*soon: Amer.*) très bientôt.

momentous /mə'mentəs/ *a.* important.

momentum /mə'mentəm/ *n.* élan *m.*

Monaco /'mɒnəkəʊ/ *n.* Monaco *f.*

monarch /'mɒnək/ *n.* monarque *m.* ~**y** *n.* monarchie *f.*

monaster|y /'mɒnəstrɪ/ *n.* monastère *m.* ~**ic** /mə'næstɪk/ *a.* monastique.

Monday /'mʌndɪ/ *n.* lundi *m.*

monetarist /'mʌnɪtərɪst/ *n.* monétariste *m./f.*

monetary /'mʌnɪtrɪ/ *a.* monétaire.

money /'mʌnɪ/ *n.* argent *m.* ~**s**, sommes d'argent *f. pl.* ~**-box** *n.* tirelire *f.* ~**-lender** *n.* prêteu|r, -se *m., f.* ~**order**, mandat *m.* ~**-spinner** *n.* mine d'or *f.*

mongrel /'mʌŋgrəl/ *n.* (chien) bâtard *m.*

monitor /'mɒnɪtə(r)/ *n.* (*pupil*) chef de classe *m.*; (*techn.*) moniteur *m.* —*v.t.* contrôler; (*broadcast*) écouter.

monk /mʌŋk/ *n.* moine *m.*

monkey /'mʌŋkɪ/ *n.* singe *m.* ~**nut** *n.* cacahuète *f.* ~**-wrench** *n.* clef à molette *f.*

mono /'mɒnəʊ/ *n.* (*pl.* -os) mono *f.* —*a.* mono invar.

monochrome /'mɒnəkrəʊm/ *a. & n.* (en) noir et blanc (*m.*).

monogram /'mɒnəgræm/ *n.* monogramme *m.*

monologue /'mɒnəlɒg/ *n.* monologue *m.*

monopol|y /mə'nɒpəlɪ/ *n.* monopole *m.* ~**ize** *v.t.* monopoliser.

monotone /'mɒnətəʊn/ *n.* ton uniforme *m.*

monoton|ous /mə'nɒtənəs/ *a.* monotone. ~**y** *n.* monotonie *f.*

monsoon /mɒn'suːn/ *n.* mousson *f.*

monst|er /'mɒnstə(r)/ *n.* monstre *m.* ~**rous** *a.* monstrueux.

monstrosity /mɒn'strɒsətɪ/ *n.* monstruosité *f.*

month /mʌnθ/ *n.* mois *m.*

monthly /'mʌnθlɪ/ *a.* mensuel. —*adv.* mensuellement. —*n.* (*periodical*) mensuel *m.*

monument /'mɒnjʊmənt/ *n.* monument *m.* ~**al** /-'mentl/ *a.* monumental.

moo /muː/ *n.* meuglement *m.* —*v.i.* meugler.

mooch /muːtʃ/ *v.i.* (*sl.*) flâner. —*v.t.* (*Amer., sl.*) se procurer.

mood /muːd/ *n.* humeur *f.* **in a good/bad** ~, de bonne/mauvaise humeur. ~**y** *a.* d'humeur changeante; (*sullen*) maussade.

moon /muːn/ *n.* lune *f.*

moon|light /'muːnlaɪt/ *n.* clair de lune *m.* ~**lit** *a.* éclairé par la lune.

moonlighting /'muːnlaɪtɪŋ/ *n.* (*fam.*) travail au noir *m.*

moor¹ /mʊə(r)/ *n.* lande *f.*

moor² /mʊə(r)/ *v.t.* amarrer. ~**ings** *n. pl.* (*chains etc.*) amarres *f. pl.*; (*place*) mouillage *m.*

moose /muːs/ *n. invar.* élan *m.*

moot /muːt/ *a.* discutable. —*v.t.* (*question*) soulever.

mop /mɒp/ *n.* balai à franges *m.* —*v.t.* (*p.t.* **mopped**). ~ (**up**), éponger. ~ **of hair**, tignasse *f.*

moped /'məʊped/ *n.* cyclomoteur *m.*

moral /'mɒrəl/ a. moral. —.
morale f. ～s, moralité f. ～ize
v.i. moraliser. ～ly adv. moralement.

morale /mə'rɑːl/ n. moral m.

morality /mə'rælətɪ/ n. moralité f.

morass /mə'ræs/ n. marais m.

morbid /'mɔːbɪd/ a. morbide.

more /mɔː(r)/ a. (a greater amount
of) plus de (than, que). — n. &
adv. plus (than, que). (some) ～
tea/pens/etc., (additional) encore du thé/des stylos/etc. no ～
bread/etc., plus de pain/etc. I
want no ～, I do not want any
～, je n'en veux plus. ～ or less,
plus ou moins.

moreover /mɔː'rəʊvə(r)/ adv. de
plus, en outre.

morgue /mɔːg/ n. morgue f.

moribund /'mɒrɪbʌnd/ a. moribond.

morning /'mɔːnɪŋ/ n. matin m.;
(whole morning) matinée f.

Morocc|o /mə'rɒkəʊ/ n. Maroc m.
～an a. & n. marocain(e) (m.
(f.)).

moron /'mɔːrɒn/ n. crétin(e) m.
(f.).

morose /mə'rəʊs/ a. morose.

morphine /'mɔːfiːn/ n. morphine f.

Morse /mɔːs/ n. ～ (code), morse
m.

morsel /'mɔːsl/ n. petit morceau
m.; (of food) bouchée f.

mortal /'mɔːtl/ a. & n. mortel(le)
(m.(f.)). ～ity /mɔː'tælətɪ/ n.
mortalité f.

mortar /'mɔːtə(r)/ n. mortier m.

mortgage /'mɔːgɪdʒ/ n. crédit immobilier m. —v.t. hypothéquer.

mortify /'mɔːtɪfaɪ/ v.t. mortifier.

mortise /'mɔːtɪs/ n. ～ lock
serrure encastrée f.

mortuary /'mɔːtʃərɪ/ n. morgue f.

mosaic /məʊ'zeɪk/ n. mosaïque
f.

Moscow /'mɒskəʊ/ n. Moscou
m./f.

Moses /'məʊzɪz/ a. ～ basket,
moïse m.

mosque /mɒsk/ n. mosquée f.

mosquito /mə'skiːtəʊ/ n. (pl. -oes)
moustique m.

moss /mɒs/ n. mousse f. ～y a.
moussu.

most /məʊst/ a. (the greatest
amount of) le plus de; (the
majority of) la plupart de. — n. le
plus. —adv. (le) plus; (very) fort.
～ of, la plus grande partie de;
(majority) la plupart de. at ～,
tout au plus. for the ～ part,
pour la plupart. make the ～ of,
profiter de. ～ly adv. surtout.

motel /məʊ'tel/ n. motel m.

moth /mɒθ/ n. papillon de nuit m.;
(in cloth) mite f. ～-ball n. boule
de naphtaline f.; v.t. mettre en
réserve. ～-eaten a. mité.

mother /'mʌðə(r)/ n. mère f. —v.t.
entourer de soins maternels,
materner. ～hood n. maternité f.
～-in-law n. (pl. ～s-in-law)
belle-mère f. ～-of-pearl n. nacre
f. M～'s Day, la fête des mères.
～-to-be n. future maman f.
～ tongue, langue maternelle
f.

motherly /'mʌðəlɪ/ a. maternel.

motif /məʊ'tiːf/ n. motif m.

motion /'məʊʃn/ n. mouvement
m.; (proposal) motion f. —v.t./i.
～ (to) s.o. to, faire signe à qn. de.
～less a. immobile. ～ picture,
(Amer.) film m.

motivat|e /'məʊtɪveɪt/ v.t. mo-
tiver. ～ion /-'veɪʃn/ n. motivation f.

motive /'məʊtɪv/ n. motif m.

motley /'mɒtlɪ/ a. bigarré.

motor /'məʊtə(r)/ n. moteur m.;
(car) auto f. —a. (anat.) moteur;
(boat) à moteur. ～ in auto. ～ go in
auto. ～ bike, (fam.) moto f. ～
car, auto f. ～ cycle, moto-
cyclette f. ～-cyclist n. moto-
cycliste m./f. ～ home, (Amer.)

camping-car *m.* ~**ing** *n.* (*sport*) l'automobile *f.* ~**ized** *a.* motorisé ~ **vehicle**, véhicule automobile *m.*

motorist /'məʊtərɪst/ *n.* automobiliste *m./f.*

motorway /'məʊtəweɪ/ *n.* autoroute *f.*

mottled /'mɒtld/ *a.* tacheté.

motto /'mɒtəʊ/ *n.* (*pl.* -**oes**) devise *f.*

mould[1] /məʊld/ *n.* moule *m.* —*v.t.* mouler; (*influence*) former. ~**ing** *n.* (*on wall etc.*) moulure *f.*

mould[2] /məʊld/ *n.* (*fungus, rot*) moisissure *f.* ~**y** *a.* moisi.

moult /məʊlt/ *v.i.* muer.

mound /maʊnd/ *n.* monticule *m.*, tertre *m.*; (*pile: fig.*) tas *m.*

mount[1] /maʊnt/ *n.* (*hill*) mont *m.*

mount[2] /maʊnt/ *v.t./i.* monter. —*n.* monture *f.* ~ **up**, s'accumuler; (*add up*) chiffrer (**to**, à).

mountain /'maʊntɪn/ *n.* montagne *f.* ~ **bike**, (vélo) tout terrain *m.*, vtt *m.* ~**ous** *a.* montagneux.

mountaineer /maʊntɪ'nɪə(r)/ *n.* alpiniste *m./f.* ~**ing** *n.* alpinisme *m.*

mourn /mɔ:n/ *v.t./i.* ~ (**for**), pleurer. ~**er** *n.* personne qui suit le cortège funèbre *f.* ~**ing** *n.* deuil *m.*

mournful /'mɔ:nfl/ *a.* triste.

mouse /maʊs/ *n.* (*pl.* **mice**) souris *f.*

mousetrap /'maʊstræp/ *n.* souricière *f.*

mousse /mu:s/ *n.* mousse *f.*

moustache /mə'stɑ:ʃ, *Amer.* 'mʌstæʃ/ *n.* moustache *f.*

mousy /'maʊsɪ/ *a.* (*hair*) d'un brun terne; (*fig.*) timide.

mouth /maʊθ/ *n.* bouche *f.*; (*of dog, cat, etc.*) gueule *f.* ~**-organ** *n.* harmonica *m.*

mouthful /'maʊθfʊl/ *n.* bouchée *f.*

mouthpiece /'maʊθpi:s/ *n.* (*mus.*) embouchure *f.*; (*person: fig.*) porte-parole *m. invar.*

mouthwash /'maʊθwɒʃ/ *n.* eau dentifrice *f.*

mouthwatering /'maʊθwɔ:trɪŋ/ *a.* qui fait venir l'eau à la bouche.

movable /'mu:vəbl/ *a.* mobile.

move /mu:v/ *v.t./i.* remuer, (se) déplacer, bouger; (*incite*) pousser; (*emotionally*) émouvoir; (*propose*) proposer; (*depart*) partir; (*act*) agir. ~ (**out**), déménager. —*n.* mouvement *m.*; (*in game*) coup *m.*; (*player's turn*) tour *m.*; (*procedure: fig.*) démarche *f.*; (*house change*) déménagement *m.* ~ **back**, (faire) reculer. ~ **forward** *or* **on**, (faire) avancer. ~ **in**, emménager. ~ **over**, se pousser. **on the** ~, en marche.

movement /'mu:vmənt/ *n.* mouvement *m.*

movie /'mu:vɪ/ *n.* (*Amer.*) film *m.* **the** ~**s**, le cinéma. ~ **camera**, (*Amer.*) caméra *f.*

moving /'mu:vɪŋ/ *a.* en mouvement; (*touching*) émouvant.

mow /məʊ/ *v.t.* (*p.p.* **mowed** *or* **mown**) (*corn etc.*) faucher; (*lawn*) tondre. ~ **down**, faucher. ~**er** *n.* (*for lawn*) tondeuse *f.*

MP *abbr. see* **Member of Parliament.**

Mr /'mɪstə(r)/ *n.* (*pl.* **Messrs**) ~ **Smith**, Monsieur *or* M. Smith.

Mrs /'mɪsɪz/ *n.* (*pl.* **Mrs**) ~ **Smith**, Madame *or* Mme Smith. **the** ~ **Smith**, Mesdames *or* Mmes Smith.

Ms /mɪz/ *n.* (*title of married or unmarried woman*). ~ **Smith**, Madame *or* Mme Smith.

much /mʌtʃ/ *a.* beaucoup de. —*adv. & n.* beaucoup.

muck /mʌk/ *n.* fumier *m.*; (*dirt: fam.*) saleté *f.* —*v.i.* ~ **about**, (*sl.*) s'amuser. ~ **about with,**

(*sl.*) tripoter. **~ in**, (*sl.*) participer. —*v.t.* **~ up**, (*sl.*) gâcher. **~y** *a.* sale.

mucus /'mjuːkəs/ *n.* mucus *m.*

mud /mʌd/ *n.* boue *f.* **~dy** *a.* couvert de boue.

muddle /'mʌdl/ *v.t.* embrouiller. —*v.i.* **~ through**, se débrouiller. —*n.* désordre *m.*, confusion *f.*; (*mix-up*) confusion *f.*

mudguard /'mʌdgaːd/ *n.* garde-boue *m. invar.*

muff /mʌf/ *n.* manchon *m.*

muffin /'mʌfɪn/ *n.* muffin *m.* (*petit pain rond et plat*).

muffle /'mʌfl/ *v.t.* emmitoufler; (*sound*) assourdir. **~r** /-ə(r)/ *n.* (*scarf*) cache-nez *m. invar.*; (*Amer.: auto.*) silencieux *m.*

mug /mʌg/ *n.* tasse *f.*; (*in plastic, metal*) gobelet *m.*; (*for beer*) chope *f.*; (*face: sl.*) gueule *f.*; (*fool: sl.*) idiot *n.* (*m.f.*) —*v.t.* (*p.t.* **mugged**) agresser. **~ger** *n.* agresseur *m.* **~ging** *n.* agression *f.*

muggy /'mʌgɪ/ *a.* lourd.

mule /mjuːl/ *n.* (*male*) mulet *m.*; (*female*) mule *f.*

mull[1] /mʌl/ *v.t.* (*wine*) chauffer.

mull[2] /mʌl/ *v.t.* **~ over**, ruminer.

multi- /'mʌltɪ/ *pref.* multi-.

multicoloured /'mʌltɪkʌləd/ *a.* multicolore.

multifarious /mʌltɪ'feərɪəs/ *a.* divers.

multinational /mʌltɪ'næʃnəl/ *a. & n.* multinational(e) (*f.*).

multiple /'mʌltɪpl/ *a. & n.* multiple (*m.*). **~ sclerosis**, sclérose en plaques *f.*

multipl|y /'mʌltɪplaɪ/ *v.t./i.* (se) multiplier. **~ication** /-ɪ'keɪʃn/ *n.* multiplication *f.*

multistorey /mʌltɪ'stɔːrɪ/ *a.* (*car park*) à étages.

multitude /'mʌltɪtjuːd/ *n.* multitude *f.*

mum[1] /mʌm/ *a.* **keep ~**, (*fam.*) garder le silence.

mum[2] /mʌm/ *n.* (*fam.*) maman *f.*

mumble /'mʌmbl/ *v.t./i.* marmotter, marmonner.

mummy[1] /'mʌmɪ/ *n.* (*embalmed body*) momie *f.*

mummy[2] /'mʌmɪ/ *n.* (*mother: fam.*) maman *f.*

mumps /mʌmps/ *n.* oreillons *m. pl.*

munch /mʌntʃ/ *v.t./i.* mastiquer.

mundane /mʌn'deɪn/ *a.* banal.

municipal /mjuː'nɪsɪpl/ *a.* municipal. **~ity** /-'pælətɪ/ *n.* municipalité *f.*

munitions /mjuː'nɪʃnz/ *n. pl.* munitions *f. pl.*

mural /'mjʊərəl/ *a.* mural. —*n.* peinture murale *f.*

murder /'mɜːdə(r)/ *n.* meurtre *m.* —*v.t.* assassiner; (*ruin: fam.*) massacrer. **~er** *n.* meurtrier *m.*, assassin *m.* **~ous** *a.* meurtrier.

murky /'mɜːkɪ/ *a.* (**-ier**, **-iest**) (*night, plans, etc.*) sombre, ténébreux; (*liquid*) épais, sale.

murmur /'mɜːmə(r)/ *n.* murmure *m.* —*v.t./i.* murmurer.

muscle /'mʌsl/ *n.* muscle *m.* —*v.i.* **~ in**, (*sl.*) s'introduire de force (**on**, dans).

muscular /'mʌskjʊlə(r)/ *a.* musculaire; (*brawny*) musclé.

muse /mjuːz/ *v.i.* méditer.

museum /mjuː'zɪəm/ *n.* musée *m.*

mush /mʌʃ/ *n.* (*pulp, soft food*) bouillie *f.* **~y** *a.* mou.

mushroom /'mʌʃrʊm/ *n.* champignon *m.* —*v.i.* pousser comme des champignons.

music /'mjuːzɪk/ *n.* musique *f.* **~al** *a.* musical; (*instrument*) de musique; (*talented*) doué pour la musique; *n.* comédie musicale *f.*

musician /mjuː'zɪʃn/ *n.* musicien(ne) *m.* (*f.*).

musk /mʌsk/ *n.* musc *m.*

Muslim /'mʊzlɪm/ *a. & n.* musulman(e) (*m.* (*f.*)).

muslin /'mʌzlɪn/ *n.* mousseline *f.*

mussel /'mʌsl/ *n.* moule *f.*

must /mʌst/ *v. aux.* devoir. **you ~ go**, vous devez partir, il faut que vous partiez. **he ~ be old**, il doit être vieux. **I ~ have done it**, j'ai dû le faire. —*n.* **be a ~**, *(fam.)* être un must.

mustard /'mʌstəd/ *n.* moutarde *f.*

muster /'mʌstə(r)/ *v.t./i.* (se) rassembler.

musty /'mʌstɪ/ *a.* (**-ier, -iest**) *(room, etc.)* qui sent le moisi; *(smell, taste)* de moisi.

mutant /'mju:tənt/ *a. & n.* mutant *(m.)*.

mutation /mju:'teɪʃn/ *n.* mutation *f.*

mute /mju:t/ *a. & n.* muet(te) *(m. (f.))*. **~d** /-ɪd/ *a.* *(colour, sound)* sourd, atténué; *(criticism)* voilé.

mutilat|e /'mju:tɪleɪt/ *v.t.* mutiler. **~ion** /-'leɪʃn/ *n.* mutilation *f.*

mutin|y /'mju:tɪnɪ/ *n.* mutinerie *f.* —*v.i.* se mutiner. **~ous** *a.* *(sailor etc.)* mutiné; *(fig.)* rebelle.

mutter /'mʌtə(r)/ *v.t./i.* marmonner, murmurer.

mutton /'mʌtn/ *n.* mouton *m.*

mutual /'mju:tʃʊəl/ *a.* mutuel; *(common to two or more: fam.)* commun. **~ly** *adv.* mutuellement.

muzzle /'mʌzl/ *n.* *(snout)* museau *m.*; *(device)* muselière *f.*; *(of gun)* gueule *f.* —*v.t.* museler.

my /maɪ/ *a.* mon, ma, *pl.* mes.

myopic /maɪ'ɒpɪk/ *a.* myope.

myself /maɪ'self/ *pron.* moi-même; *(reflexive)* me, m'*; *(after prep.)* moi.

mysterious /mɪ'stɪərɪəs/ *a.* mystérieux.

mystery /'mɪstərɪ/ *n.* mystère *m.*

mystic /'mɪstɪk/ *a. & n.* mystique *(m./f.)* **~al** *a.* mystique. **~ism** /-sɪzəm/ *n.* mysticisme *m.*

mystify /'mɪstɪfaɪ/ *v.t.* laisser perplexe.

mystique /mɪ'sti:k/ *n.* mystique *f.*

myth /mɪθ/ *n.* mythe *m.* **~ical** *a.* mythique.

mythology /mɪ'θɒlədʒɪ/ *n.* mythologie *f.*

N

nab /næb/ *v.t.* *(p.t.* **nabbed**) *(arrest: sl.)* épingler, attraper.

nag /næg/ *v.t./i.* *(p.t.* **nagged**) critiquer; *(pester)* harceler.

nagging /'nægɪŋ/ *a.* persistant.

nail /neɪl/ *n.* clou *m.*; *(of finger, toe)* ongle *m.* —*v.t.* clouer. **~-brush** *n.* brosse à ongles *f.* **~-file** *n.* lime à ongles *f.* **~ polish**, vernis à ongles *m.* **on the ~**, *(pay)* sans tarder, tout de suite.

naïve /naɪ'i:v/ *a.* naïf.

naked /'neɪkɪd/ *a.* nu. **to the ~ eye**, à l'œil nu. **~ly** *adv.* à nu. **~ness** *n.* nudité *f.*

name /neɪm/ *n.* nom *m.*; *(fig.)* réputation *f.* —*v.t.* nommer; *(fix)* fixer. **be ~d after**, porter le nom de. **~less** *a.* sans nom, anonyme.

namely /'neɪmlɪ/ *adv.* à savoir.

namesake /'neɪmseɪk/ *n.* *(person)* homonyme *m.*

nanny /'nænɪ/ *n.* nounou *f.* **~-goat** *n.* chèvre *f.*

nap /næp/ *n.* somme *m.* —*v.i.* *(p.t.* **napped**) faire un somme. **catch ~ping**, prendre au dépourvu.

nape /neɪp/ *n.* nuque *f.*

napkin /'næpkɪn/ *n.* *(at meals)* serviette *f.*; *(for baby)* couche *f.*

nappy /'næpɪ/ *n.* couche *f.*

narcotic /nɑ:'kɒtɪk/ *a. & n.* narcotique *(m.)*.

narrat|e /nə'reɪt/ *v.t.* raconter. **~ion** /-ʃn/ *n.* narration *f.* **~or** *n.* narra|teur, -trice *m., f.*

narrative /'nærətɪv/ *n.* récit *m.*

narrow /'nærəʊ/ *a.* (**-er, -est**) étroit. —*v.t./i.* (se) rétrécir; *(limit)* (se) limiter. **~ down the**

choices, limiter les choix. **~ly** *adv.* étroitement; *(just)* de justesse. **~-minded** *a.* à l'esprit étroit; *(ideas etc.)* étroit. **~ness** *n.* étroitesse *f.*

nasal /'neɪzl/ *a.* nasal.

nast|y /'nɑːstɪ/ *a.* (-ier, -iest) mauvais, désagréable; *(malicious)* méchant. **~ily** *adv.* désagréablement; méchamment. **~iness** *n.* (*malice*) méchanceté *f.*

nation /'neɪʃn/ *n.* nation *f.* **~-wide** *a.* dans l'ensemble du pays.

national /'næʃnəl/ *a.* national. —*n.* ressortissant(e) *m. (f.).* **~ anthem,** hymne national *m.* **~ism** *n.* nationalisme *m.* **~ize** *v.t.* nationaliser. **~ly** *adv.* à l'échelle nationale.

nationality /næʃə'nælətɪ/ *n.* nationalité *f.*

native /'neɪtɪv/ *n.* (*local inhabitant*) autochtone *m./f.*; *(non-European)* indigène *m./f.* —*a.* indigène; *(country)* natal; *(inborn)* inné. **be a ~ of,** être originaire de. **~ language,** langue maternelle *f.* **~ speaker of French,** personne de langue maternelle française *f.*

Nativity /nə'tɪvətɪ/ *n.* **the ~,** la Nativité *f.*

natter /'nætə(r)/ *v.i.* bavarder.

natural /'nætʃrəl/ *a.* naturel. **~ history,** histoire naturelle *f.* **~ist** *n.* naturaliste *m./f.* **~ly** *adv.* (*normally, of course*) naturellement; *(by nature)* de nature.

naturaliz|e /'nætʃrəlaɪz/ *v.t.* naturaliser. **~ation** /-'zeɪʃn/ *n.* naturalisation *f.*

nature /'neɪtʃə(r)/ *n.* nature *f.*

naught /nɔːt/ *n.* (*old use*) rien *m.*

naught|y /'nɔːtɪ/ *a.* (-ier, -iest) vilain, méchant; *(indecent)* grivois. **~ily** *adv.* mal.

nause|a /'nɔːsɪə/ *n.* nausée *f.* **~ous** *a.* nauséabond.

nauseate /'nɔːsɪeɪt/ *v.t.* écœurer.

nautical /'nɔːtɪkl/ *a.* nautique.

naval /'neɪvl/ *a.* (*battle etc.*) naval; *(officer)* de marine.

nave /neɪv/ *n.* (*of church*) nef *f.*

navel /'neɪvl/ *n.* nombril *m.*

navigable /'nævɪgəbl/ *a.* navigable.

navigat|e /'nævɪgeɪt/ *v.t.* (*sea etc.*) naviguer sur; *(ship)* piloter. —*v.i.* naviguer. **~ion** /-'geɪʃn/ *n.* navigation *f.* **~or** *n.* navigateur *m.*

navvy /'nævɪ/ *n.* terrassier *m.*

navy /'neɪvɪ/ *n.* marine *f.* **~ (blue),** bleu marine *invar.*

near /nɪə(r)/ *adv.* près. —*prep.* près de. —*a.* proche. —*v.t.* approcher de. **draw ~,** (s')approcher (to, de). **~ by** *adv.* tout près. **N~ East,** Proche-Orient *m.* **~ to,** près de. **~ness** *n.* proximité *f.* **~-sighted** *a.* myope.

nearby /nɪə'baɪ/ *a.* proche.

nearly /'nɪəlɪ/ *adv.* presque. **I ~ forgot,** j'ai failli oublier. **not ~ as pretty/etc. as,** loin d'être aussi joli/*etc.* que.

nearside /'nɪəsaɪd/ *a.* (*auto.*) du côté du passager.

neat /niːt/ *a.* (-er, -est) soigné, net; *(room etc.)* bien rangé; *(clever)* habile; *(whisky, brandy, etc.)* sec. **~ly** *adv.* avec soin; habilement. **~ness** *n.* netteté *f.*

nebulous /'nebjʊləs/ *a.* nébuleux.

necessar|y /'nesəsərɪ/ *a.* nécessaire. **~ies** *n. pl.* nécessaire *m.* **~ily** *adv.* nécessairement.

necessitate /nɪ'sesɪteɪt/ *v.t.* nécessiter.

necessity /nɪ'sesətɪ/ *n.* nécessité *f.*; *(thing)* chose indispensable *f.*

neck /nek/ *n.* cou *m.*; *(of dress)* encolure *f.* **~ and neck,** à égalité.

necklace /'neklɪs/ *n.* collier *m.*

neckline /'neklaɪn/ *n.* encolure *f.*

necktie /'nektaɪ/ *n.* cravate *f.*

nectarine /'nektərɪn/ n. brugnon m., nectarine f.

need /niːd/ n. besoin m. —v.t. avoir besoin de; (demand) demander. **you ∼ not come**, vous n'êtes pas obligé de venir. **∼less** a. inutile. **∼lessly** adv. inutilement.

needle /'niːdl/ n. aiguille f. —v.t. (annoy. fam.) asticoter, agacer.

needlework /'niːdlwɜːk/ n. couture f.; (object) ouvrage (à l'aiguille) m.

needy /'niːdɪ/ a. (-ier, -iest) nécessiteux, indigent.

negation /nɪ'geɪʃn/ n. négation f.

negative /'negətɪv/ a. négatif. —n. (of photograph) négatif m.; (word: gram.) négation f. **in the ∼**, (answer) par la négative. (gram.) à la forme négative. **∼ly** adv. négativement.

neglect /nɪ'glekt/ v.t. négliger, laisser à l'abandon. —n. manque de soins m. **(state of) ∼**, abandon m. **∼ to do**, négliger de faire. **∼ful** a. négligent.

négligé /'neglɪʒeɪ/ n. négligé m.

negligen|t /'neglɪdʒənt/ a. négligent. **∼ce** n. négligence f.

negligible /'neglɪdʒəbl/ a. négligeable.

negotiable /nɪ'gəʊʃəbl/ a. négociable.

negotiat|e /nɪ'gəʊʃɪeɪt/ v.t./i. négocier. **∼ion** /-'eɪʃn/ n. négociation f. **∼or** n. négocia|teur, -trice m., f.

Negr|o /'niːgrəʊ/ n. (pl. -oes) Noir m. —a. noir; (art, music) nègre. **∼ess** n. Noire f.

neigh /neɪ/ n. hennissement m. —v.i. hennir.

neighbour, Amer. **neighbor** /'neɪbə(r)/ n. voisin(e) m. (f.). **∼hood** n. voisinage m.; quartier m. **in the ∼hood of**, aux alentours de. **∼ing** a. voisin.

neighbourly /'neɪbəlɪ/ a. amical.

neither /'naɪðə(r)/ a. & pron. aucun(e) des deux; ni l'un(e) ni l'autre. —adv. ni. —conj. (ne) non plus. **∼ big nor small**, ni grand ni petit. **∼ am I coming**, je ne viendrai pas non plus.

neon /'niːɒn/ n. néon m. —a. (lamp etc.) au néon.

nephew /'nevjuː, Amer. 'nefjuː/ n. neveu m.

nerve /nɜːv/ n. nerf m.; (courage) courage m.; (calm) sang-froid m.; (impudence: fam.) culot m. **∼s**, (before exams etc.) le trac m. **∼-racking** a. éprouvant.

nervous /'nɜːvəs/ a. nerveux. **be or feel ∼**, (afraid) avoir peur. **∼ breakdown**, dépression nerveuse f. **∼ly** adv. (tensely) nerveusement; (timidly) craintivement. **∼ness** n. nervosité f.; (fear) crainte f.

nervy /'nɜːvɪ/ a. = **nervous**; (Amer., fam.) effronté.

nest /nest/ n. nid m. —v.i. nicher. **∼-egg** n. pécule m.

nestle /'nesl/ v.i. se blottir.

net¹ /net/ n. filet m. —v.t. (p.t. netted) prendre au filet. **∼ting** n. (nets) filets m. pl.; (wire) treillis m.; (fabric) voile m.

net² /net/ a. (weight etc.) net.

netball /'netbɔːl/ n. netball m.

Netherlands /'neðələndz/ n. pl. **the ∼**, les Pays-Bas m. pl.

nettle /'netl/ n. ortie f.

network /'netwɜːk/ n. réseau m.

neuralgia /njʊə'rældʒə/ n. névralgie f.

neuro|sis /njʊə'rəʊsɪs/ n. (pl. -oses /-siːz/) névrose f. **∼tic** /-'rɒtɪk/ a. & n. névrosé(e) (m. (f.)).

neuter /'njuːtə(r)/ a. & n. neutre (m.). —v.t. (castrate) castrer.

neutral /'njuːtrəl/ a. neutre. **∼ (gear)**, (auto.) point mort m. **∼ity** /-'trælətɪ/ n. neutralité f.

neutron /'njuːtrɒn/ n. neutron m. **∼ bomb**, bombe à neutrons f.

never /'nevə(r)/ *adv.* (ne) jamais; (*not: fam.*) (ne) pas. **he ∼ refuses,** il ne refuse jamais. **I ∼ saw him,** (*fam.*) je ne l'ai pas vu. **∼ again,** plus jamais. **∼ mind,** (*don't worry*) ne vous en faites pas; (*it doesn't matter*) peu importe. **∼-ending** *a.* interminable.

nevertheless /nevəðə'les/ *adv.* néanmoins, toutefois.

new /nju:/ *a.* (**-er, -est**) nouveau; (*brand-new*) neuf. **∼-born** *a.* nouveau-né. **∼-laid egg,** œuf frais *m.* **∼ moon,** nouvelle lune *f.* **∼ year,** nouvel an. **New Year's Day,** le jour de l'an. **New Year's Eve,** la Saint-Sylvestre. **New Zealand,** Nouvelle-Zélande *f.* **New Zealander,** Néo-Zélandais(e) *m.* (*f.*). **∼ness** *n.* nouveauté *f.*

newcomer /'nju:kʌmə(r)/ *n.* nouveau venu *m.*, nouvelle venue *f.*

newfangled /nju:'fæŋgld/ *a.* (*pej.*) moderne, neuf.

newly /'nju:lı/ *adv.* nouvellement. **∼-weds** *n. pl.* nouveaux mariés *m. pl.*

news /nju:z/ *n.* nouvelle(s) *f.* (*pl.*). (*radio, press*) informations *f. pl.*, (*TV*) actualités *f. pl.* **∼ agency,** agence de presse *f.* **∼caster, ∼-reader** *ns.* présenta|teur, trice *m., f.*

newsagent /'nju:zeıdʒənt/ *n.* marchand(e) de journaux *m.*(*f.*).

newsletter /'nju:zletə(r)/ *n.* bulletin *m.*

newspaper /'nju:speıpə(r)/ *n.* journal *m.*

newsreel /'nju:zri:l/ *n.* actualités *f. pl.*

newt /nju:t/ *n.* triton *m.*

next /nekst/ *a.* prochain; (*adjoining*) voisin; (*following*) suivant. —*adv.* la prochaine fois; (*afterwards*) ensuite. —*n.* suivant(e) *m.*(*f.*). **∼ door,** à côté

(to, de). **∼-door.** *a.* d'à côté. **∼ of kin,** parent le plus proche *m.* **∼ to,** à côté de.

nib /nıb/ *n.* bec *m.*, plume *f.*

nibble /'nıbl/ *v.t./i.* grignoter.

nice /naıs/ *a.* (**-er, -est**) agréable, bon; (*kind*) gentil; (*pretty*) joli; (*respectable*) bien *invar.*; (*subtle*) délicat. **∼ly** *adv.* agréablement; gentiment; (*well*) bien.

nicety /'naısətı/ *n.* subtilité *f.*

niche /nıtʃ, ni:ʃ/ *n.* (*recess*) niche *f.*; (*fig.*) place *f.*, situation *f.*

nick /nık/ *n.* petite entaille *f.* —*v.t.* (*steal, arrest: sl.*) piquer. **in the ∼ of time,** juste à temps.

nickel /'nıkl/ *n.* nickel *m.*; (*Amer.*) pièce de cinq cents *f.*

nickname /'nıkneım/ *n.* surnom *m.*; (*short form*) diminutif *m.* —*v.t.* surnommer.

nicotine /'nıkəti:n/ *n.* nicotine *f.*

niece /ni:s/ *n.* nièce *f.*

nifty /'nıftı/ *a.* (*sl.*) chic *invar.*

Nigeria /naı'dʒıərıə/ *n.* Nigéria *m./f.* **∼n** *a. & n.* nigérian(e) (*m.* (*f.*)).

niggardly /'nıgədlı/ *a.* chiche.

niggling /'nıglıŋ/ *a.* (*person*) tatillon; (*detail*) insignifiant.

night /naıt/ *n.* nuit *f.*; (*evening*) soir *m.* —*a.* de nuit. **∼-cap** *n.* boisson *f.* (*avant d'aller se coucher*). **∼-club** *n.* boîte de nuit *f.* **∼-dress, ∼-gown, ∼ie** *ns.* chemise de nuit *f.* **∼-life** *n.* vie nocturne *f.* **∼-school** *n.* cours du soir *m.* **∼-time** *n.* nuit *f.* **∼-watchman** *n.* veilleur de nuit *m.*

nightfall /'naıtfɔ:l/ *n.* tombée de la nuit *f.*

nightingale /'naıtıŋgeıl/ *n.* rossignol *m.*

nightly /'naıtlı/ *a. & adv.* (de) chaque nuit *or* soir.

nightmare /'naıtmeə(r)/ *n.* cauchemar *m.*

nil /nıl/ *n.* rien *m.*; (*sport*) zéro *m.* —*a.* (*chances, risk, etc.*) nul.

nimble /'nɪmbl/ a. (-er, -est) agile.

nin|e /naɪn/ a. & n. neuf (m.). **~th** a. & n. neuvième (m./f.).

nineteen /naɪn'tiːn/ a. & n. dix-neuf (m.). **~th** a. & n. dix-neuvième (m./f.).

ninet|y /'naɪntɪ/ a. & n. quatre-vingt-dix (m.). **~ieth** a. & n. quatre-vingt-dixième (m./f.).

nip /nɪp/ v.t./i. (p.t. nipped) (pinch) pincer; (rush: sl.) courir. **~out/back/**etc., sortir/rentrer/ etc. rapidement. —n. pincement m.; (cold) fraîcheur f.

nipper /'nɪpə(r)/ n. (sl.) gosse m./f.

nipple /'nɪpl/ n. bout de sein m.; (of baby's bottle) tétine f.

nippy /'nɪpɪ/ a. (-ier, -iest) (fam.) alerte; (chilly: fam.) frais.

nitrogen /'naɪtrədʒən/ n. azote m.

nitwit /'nɪtwɪt/ n. (fam.) imbécile m./f.

no /nəʊ/ a. aucun(e); pas de. —adv. non. —n. (pl. noes) non m. invar. **no man/**etc., aucun homme/etc. **no money/time/**etc., pas d'argent/de temps/etc. **no man's land,** no man's land m. **no one** = **nobody. no smoking/entry,** défense de fumer/d'entrer. **no way!,** (fam.) pas question!

nob|le /'nəʊbl/ a. (-er, -est) noble. **~ility** /-'bɪlɪtɪ/ n. noblesse f.

nobleman /'nəʊblmən/ n. (pl. -men) noble m.

nobody /'nəʊbədɪ/ pron. (ne) personne. —n. nullité f. **he knows ~,** il ne connaît personne. **~ is there,** personne n'est là.

nocturnal /nɒk'tɜːnl/ a. nocturne.

nod /nɒd/ v.t./i. (p.t. nodded) **~ (one's head),** faire un signe de tête. **~ off,** s'endormir. —n. signe de tête m.

noise /nɔɪz/ n. bruit m. **~less** a. silencieux.

nois|y /'nɔɪzɪ/ a. (-ier, -iest) bruyant. **~ily** adv. bruyamment.

nomad /'nəʊmæd/ n. nomade m./f. **~ic** /-'mædɪk/ a. nomade.

nominal /'nɒmɪnl/ a. symbolique, nominal; (value) nominal. **~ly** adv. nominalement.

nominat|e /'nɒmɪneɪt/ v.t. nommer; (put forward) proposer. **~ion** /-'neɪʃn/ n. nomination f.

non- /nɒn/ pref. non-. **~-iron** a. qui ne se repasse pas. **~-skid** a. antidérapant. **~-stick** a. à revêtement antiadhésif.

non-commissioned /nɒnkə'mɪʃnd/ a. **~ officer,** sous-officier m.

non-committal /nɒnkə'mɪtl/ a. évasif.

nondescript /'nɒndɪskrɪpt/ a. indéfinissable.

none /nʌn/ pron. aucun(e). **~ of us,** aucun de nous. **I have ~,** je n'en ai pas. **~ of the money was used,** l'argent n'a pas du tout été utilisé. —adv. **~ too,** pas tellement. **he is ~ the happier,** il n'en est pas plus heureux.

nonentity /nɒ'nentətɪ/ n. nullité f.

non-existent /nɒnɪg'zɪstənt/ a. inexistant.

nonplussed /nɒn'plʌst/ a. perplexe, déconcerté.

nonsens|e /'nɒnsəns/ n. absurdités f. pl. **~ical** /-'sensɪkl/ a. absurde.

non-smoker /nɒn'sməʊkə(r)/ n. non-fumeur m.

non-stop /nɒn'stɒp/ a. (train, flight) direct. —adv. sans arrêt.

noodles /'nuːdlz/ n. pl. nouilles f. pl.

nook /nʊk/ n. (re)coin m.

noon /nuːn/ n. midi m.

noose /nuːs/ n. nœud coulant m.

nor /nɔː(r)/ adv. ni. —conj. (ne) non plus. **~ shall I come,** je ne viendrai pas non plus.

norm /nɔːm/ n. norme f.

normal /'nɔːml/ a. normal. **~ity** /nɔː'mælətɪ/ n. normalité f. **~ly** adv. normalement.

Norman /'nɔːmən/ a. & n. normand(e) (m.(f.)). **~dy** n. Normandie f.

north /nɔːθ/ n. nord m. —a. nord invar., du nord. —adv. vers le nord. **N~ America,** Amérique du Nord f. **N~ American** a. & n. nord-américain(e) (m. (f.)). **~east** n. nord-est m. **~erly** /'nɔːðəlɪ/ a. du nord. **~ward** a. au nord. **~wards** adv. vers le nord. **~west** n. nord-ouest m.

northern /'nɔːðən/ a. du nord. **~er** n. habitant(e) du nord m. (f.).

Norw|ay /'nɔːweɪ/ n. Norvège f. **~egian** /nɔː'wiːdʒən/ a. & n. norvégien(ne) (m. (f.)).

nose /nəʊz/ n. nez m. —v.i. **~ about,** fouiner.

nosebleed /'nəʊzbliːd/ n. saignement de nez m.

nosedive /'nəʊzdaɪv/ n. piqué m. —v.i. descendre en piqué.

nostalg|ia /nɒ'stældʒə/ n. nostalgie f. **~ic** a. nostalgique.

nostril /'nɒstrəl/ n. narine f.; (of horse) naseau m.

nosy /'nəʊzɪ/ a. (-ier, -iest) (fam.) curieux, indiscret.

not /nɒt/ adv. (ne) pas. **I do ~ know,** je ne sais pas. **~ at all,** pas du tout. **~ yet,** pas encore. **I suppose ~,** je suppose que non.

notable /'nəʊtəbl/ a. notable. —n. (person) notable m.

notably /'nəʊtəblɪ/ adv. notamment.

notary /'nəʊtərɪ/ n. notaire m.

notation /nəʊ'teɪʃn/ n. notation f.

notch /nɒtʃ/ n. entaille f. —v.t. **~ up,** (score etc.) marquer.

note /nəʊt/ n. note f.; (banknote) billet m.; (short letter) mot m. —v.t. noter; (notice) remarquer.

notebook /'nəʊtbʊk/ n. carnet m.

noted /'nəʊtɪd/ a. connu (for, pour).

notepaper /'nəʊtpeɪpə(r)/ n. papier à lettres m.

noteworthy /'nəʊtwɜːðɪ/ a. remarquable.

nothing /'nʌθɪŋ/ pron. (ne) rien. —n. rien m.; (person) nullité f. —adv. nullement. **he eats ~,** il ne mange rien. **~ big/etc.,** rien de grand/etc. **~ else,** rien d'autre. **~ much,** pas grand-chose. **for ~,** pour rien, gratis.

notice /'nəʊtɪs/ n. avis m., annonce f.; (poster) affiche f. **(advance) ~,** préavis m. **at short ~,** dans des délais très brefs. **give in one's ~,** donner sa démission. —v.t. remarquer, observer. **~board** n. tableau d'affichage m. **take ~,** faire attention (of, à).

noticeab|le /'nəʊtɪsəbl/ a. visible. **~y** adv. visiblement.

notif|y /'nəʊtɪfaɪ/ v.t. (inform) aviser; (make known) notifier. **~ication** /-ɪ'keɪʃn/ n. avis m.

notion /'nəʊʃn/ n. idée, notion f. **~s,** (sewing goods etc.: Amer.) mercerie f.

notor|ious /nəʊ'tɔːrɪəs/ a. (tristement) célèbre. **~iety** /-ə'raɪətɪ/ n. notoriété f. **~iously** adv. notoirement.

notwithstanding /nɒtwɪθ'stændɪŋ/ prep. malgré. —adv. néanmoins.

nougat /'nuːɡɑː/ n. nougat m.

nought /nɔːt/ n. zéro m.

noun /naʊn/ n. nom m.

nourish /'nʌrɪʃ/ v.t. nourrir. **~ing** a. nourrissant. **~ment** n. nourriture f.

novel /'nɒvl/ n. roman m. —a. nouveau. **~ist** n. roman|cier, -ière m., f. **~ty** n. nouveauté f.

November /nəʊ'vembə(r)/ n. novembre m.

novice /'nɒvɪs/ n. novice m./f.

now /naʊ/ adv. maintenant. —conj. maintenant que. **just ~,** en ce moment; (a moment ago) tout à l'heure; **(a moment ago) ~ and again, ~ and then,** de temps à autre.

nowadays /'nauədeiz/ *adv.* de nos jours.

nowhere /'nəuweə(r)/ *adv.* nulle part.

nozzle /'nɒzl/ *n.* (*tip*) embout *m.*; (*of hose*) lance *f.*

nuance /'nju:ɑːns/ *n.* nuance *f.*

nuclear /'nju:klɪə(r)/ *a.* nucléaire.

nucleus /'nju:klɪəs/ *n.* (*pl.* -lei /-lɪaɪ/) noyau *m.*

nud|e /nju:d/ *a.* nu. —*n.* nu *m.* **in the ~,** tout nu. **~ity** *n.* nudité *f.*

nudge /nʌdʒ/ *v.t.* pousser du coude. —*n.* coup de coude *m.*

nudis|t /'nju:dist/ *n.* nudiste *m./f.* **~m** /-zəm/ *n.* nudisme *m.*

nuisance /'nju:sns/ *n.* (*thing, event*) ennui *m.*; (*person*) peste *f.* **be a ~,** être embêtant.

null /nʌl/ *a.* nul. **~ify** *v.t.* infirmer.

numb /nʌm/ *a.* engourdi. —*v.t.* engourdir.

number /'nʌmbə(r)/ *n.* nombre *m.*; (*of ticket, house, page, etc.*) numéro *m.* —*v.t.* numéroter; (*count, include*) compter. **a ~ of people,** plusieurs personnes. **~-plate** *n.* plaque d'immatriculation *f.*

numeral /'nju:mərəl/ *n.* chiffre *m.*

numerate /'nju:mərət/ *a.* qui sait calculer.

numerical /nju:'merɪkl/ *a.* numérique.

numerous /'nju:mərəs/ *a.* nombreux.

nun /nʌn/ *n.* religieuse *f.*

nurs|e /nɜːs/ *n.* infirmière *f.*, infirmier *m.*; (*nanny*) nurse *f.* —*v.t.* soigner; (*hope etc.*) nourrir. **~ing home,** clinique *f.*

nursemaid /'nɜːsmeɪd/ *n.* bonne d'enfants *f.*

nursery /'nɜːsərɪ/ *n.* chambre d'enfants *f.*; (*for plants*) pépinière *f.* **(day) ~,** crèche *f.* **~ rhyme,** chanson enfantine *f.*, comptine *f.*

~ school, (école) maternelle *f.* **~ slope,** piste facile *f.*

nurture /'nɜːtʃə(r)/ *v.t.* élever.

nut /nʌt/ *n.* (*walnut, Brazil nut, etc.*) noix *f.*; (*hazelnut*) noisette *f.*; (*peanut*) cacahuète *f.*; (*techn.*) écrou *m.*; (*sl.*) idiot(e) *m.* (*f.*).

nutcrackers /'nʌtkrækəz/ *n. pl.* casse-noix *m. invar.*

nutmeg /'nʌtmeg/ *n.* muscade *f.*

nutrient /'nju:trɪənt/ *n.* substance nutritive *f.*

nutrit|ion /nju:'trɪʃn/ *n.* nutrition *f.* **~ious** *a.* nutritif.

nuts /nʌts/ *a.* (*crazy: sl.*) cinglé.

nutshell /'nʌtʃel/ *n.* coquille de noix *f.* **in a ~,** en un mot.

nuzzle /'nʌzl/ *v.i.* **~ up to,** coller son museau à.

nylon /'naɪlɒn/ *n.* nylon *m.* **~s,** bas nylon *m. pl.*

O

oaf /əuf/ *n.* (*pl.* **oafs**) lourdaud(e) *m.* (*f.*).

oak /əuk/ *n.* chêne *m.*

OAP *abbr.* (*old-age pensioner*) retraité(e) *m.* (*f.*), personne âgée *f.*

oar /ɔː(r)/ *n.* aviron *m.*, rame *f.*

oasis /əu'eisis/ *n.* (*pl.* **oases** /-siːz/) oasis *f.*

oath /əuθ/ *n.* (*promise*) serment *m.*; (*swear-word*) juron *m.*

oatmeal /'əutmiːl/ *n.* farine d'avoine *f.*, flocons d'avoine *m. pl.*

oats /əuts/ *n. pl.* avoine *f.*

obedien|t /ə'biːdɪənt/ *a.* obéissant. **~ce** *n.* obéissance *f.* **~tly** *adv.* docilement, avec soumission.

obes|e /əu'biːs/ *a.* obèse. **~ity** *n.* obésité *f.*

obey /ə'beɪ/ *v.t./i.* obéir (à).

obituary /ə'bɪtʃuəri/ *n.* nécrologie *f.*

object¹ /'ɒbdʒɪkt/ *n.* (*thing*) objet *m.*; (*aim*) but *m.*, objet *m.*; (*gram.*)

complément (d'objet) m. **money/** etc. **is no ~,** l'argent/etc. ne pose pas de problèmes.

object² /əb'dʒekt/ v.i. protester. —v.t. **that,** objecter que. **~ to,** (behaviour) désapprouver; (plan) protester contre. **~ion** /-kʃn/ n. objection f.; (drawback) inconvénient m.

objectionable /əb'dʒekʃnəbl/ a. désagréable.

objectiv|e /əb'dʒektɪv/ a. objectif. —n. objectif m. **~ity** /ɒbdʒek-'tɪvətɪ/ n. objectivité f.

obligat|e /'ɒblɪgeɪt/ v.t. obliger. **~ion** /-'geɪʃn/ n. obligation f. **under an ~ion to s.o.,** redevable à qn. (for, de).

obligatory /ə'blɪɡətrɪ/ a. obligatoire.

oblig|e /ə'blaɪdʒ/ v.t. obliger. **~ to do,** obliger à faire. **~ed** a. obligé (to, de). **~ed to s.o.,** redevable à qn. **~ing** a. obligeant. **~ingly** adv. obligeamment.

oblique /ə'bliːk/ a. oblique; (reference etc.; fig.) indirect.

obliterat|e /ə'blɪtəreɪt/ v.t. effacer. **~ion** /-'reɪʃn/ n. effacement m.

oblivion /ə'blɪvɪən/ n. oubli m.

oblivious /ə'blɪvɪəs/ a. (unaware) inconscient (to, of, de).

oblong /'ɒblɒŋ/ a. oblong. —n. rectangle m.

obnoxious /əb'nɒkʃəs/ a. odieux.

oboe /'əʊbəʊ/ n. hautbois m.

obscen|e /əb'siːn/ a. obscène. **~ity** /-enətɪ/ n. obscénité f.

obscur|e /əb'skjʊə(r)/ a. obscur. —v.t. obscurcir; (conceal) cacher. **~ely** adv. obscurément. **~ity** n. obscurité f.

obsequious /əb'siːkwɪəs/ a. obséquieux.

observan|t /əb'zɜːvənt/ a. observateur. **~ce** n. observance f.

observatory /əb'zɜːvətrɪ/ n. observatoire m.

observ|e /əb'zɜːv/ v.t. observer; (remark) remarquer. **~ation** /ɒbzə'veɪʃn/ n. observation f. **~er** n. observa|teur, -trice m., f.

obsess /əb'ses/ v.t. obséder. **~ion** /-ʃn/ n. obsession f. **~ive** a. obsédant; (psych.) obsessionnel.

obsolete /'ɒbsəliːt/ a. dépassé.

obstacle /'ɒbstəkl/ n. obstacle m.

obstetric|s /əb'stetrɪks/ n. obstétrique f. **~ian** /ɒbstɪ'trɪʃn/ n. médecin accoucheur m.

obstina|te /'ɒbstɪnət/ a. obstiné. **~cy** n. obstination f. **~tely** adv. obstinément.

obstruct /əb'strʌkt/ v.t. (block) boucher; (congest) encombrer; (hinder) entraver. **~ion** /-kʃn/ n. (act) obstruction f.; (thing) obstacle m.; (traffic jam) encombrement m.

obtain /əb'teɪn/ v.t. obtenir. —v.i. avoir cours. **~able** a. disponible.

obtrusive /əb'truːsɪv/ a. importun; (thing) trop en évidence.

obtuse /əb'tjuːs/ a. obtus.

obviate /'ɒbvɪeɪt/ v.t. éviter.

obvious /'ɒbvɪəs/ a. évident, manifeste. **~ly** adv. manifestement.

occasion /ə'keɪʒn/ n. occasion f.; (big event) événement m. —v.t. occasionner. **on ~,** à l'occasion.

occasional /ə'keɪʒənl/ a. fait, pris, etc. de temps en temps; (visitor etc.) qui vient de temps en temps. **~ly** adv. de temps en temps. **very ~ly,** rarement.

occult /ɒ'kʌlt/ a. occulte.

occupation /ɒkjʊ'peɪʃn/ n. (activity, occupying) occupation f.; (job) métier m., profession f. **~al** a. professionnel, du métier. **~al therapy** ergothérapie f.

occup|y /'ɒkjʊpaɪ/ v.t. occuper. **~ant, ~ier** ns. occupant(e) m. (f.).

occur /ə'kɜː(r)/ v.i. (p.t. **occurred**)

se produire; (*arise*) se présenter. ∼ **to s.o.**, venir à l'esprit de qn.

occurrence /ə'kʌrəns/ *n.* événement *m.* **a frequent** ∼, une chose qui arrive souvent.

ocean /'əʊʃn/ *n.* océan *m.*

o'clock /ə'klɒk/ *adv.* **it is six** ∼/*etc.*, il est six heures/*etc.*

octagon /'ɒktəgən/ *n.* octogone *m.*

octane /'ɒkteɪn/ *n.* octane *m.*

octave /'ɒktɪv/ *n.* octave *f.*

October /ɒk'təʊbə(r)/ *n.* octobre *m.*

octopus /'ɒktəpəs/ *n.* (*pl.* -**puses**) pieuvre *f.*

odd /ɒd/ *a.* (-**er**, -**est**) bizarre; (*number*) impair; (*left over*) qui reste; (*not of set*) dépareillé; (*occasional*) fait, *pars, etc.* de temps en temps. ∼ **jobs**, menus travaux *m. pl.* **twenty** ∼, vingt et quelques. ∼**ity** *n.* bizarrerie *f.* ∼**ly** *adv.* bizarrement.

oddment /'ɒdmənt/ *n.* fin de série *f.*

odds /ɒdz/ *n. pl.* chances *f. pl.*; (*in betting*) cote *f.* (**on, at**). **at** ∼, en désaccord. **it makes no** ∼, ça ne fait rien. ∼ **and ends**, des petites choses.

ode /əʊd/ *n.* ode *f.*

odious /'əʊdɪəs/ *a.* odieux.

odour, *Amer.* **odor** /'əʊdə(r)/ *n.* odeur *f.* ∼**less** *a.* inodore.

of /ɒv, *unstressed* əv/ *prep.* de. **of the, du, de la, pl. des. of it, of them,** en. **a friend of mine,** un de mes amis. **six of them,** six d'entre eux. **the fifth of June**/*etc.*, le cinq juin /*etc.* **a litre of water,** un litre d'eau; **made of steel,** en acier.

off /ɒf/ *adv.* parti, absent; (*switched off*) éteint; (*tap*) fermé; (*taken off*) enlevé, détaché; (*cancelled*) annulé. —*prep.* de; (*distant from*) éloigné de. **go** ∼,

(*leave*) partir; (*milk*) tourner; (*food*) s'abîmer. **be better** ∼, (*in a better position, richer*) être mieux. **a day** ∼, un jour de congé. **20%** ∼, une réduction de 20%. **take sth.** ∼, (*a surface*) prendre qch. sur. ∼-**beat** *a.* original. **on the** ∼ **chance (that)**, au cas où. ∼ **colour**, (*ill*) patraque. ∼ **color**, (*improper: Amer.*) scabreux. ∼**licence** *n.* débit de vins *m.* ∼-**line** *a.* autonome; (*switched off*) déconnecté. ∼**load** *v.t.* décharger. ∼-**peak** *a.* (*hours*) creux; (*rate*) des heures creuses. ∼-**putting** *a.* (*fam.*) rebutant. ∼-**stage** *a. & adv.* dans les coulisses. ∼-**white** *a.* blanc cassé *invar.*

offal /'ɒfl/ *n.* abats *m. pl.*

offence /ə'fens/ *n.* délit *m.* **give** ∼ **to,** offenser. **take** ∼, s'offenser (**at, de**).

offend /ə'fend/ *v.t.* offenser; (*fig.*) choquer. **be** ∼**ed,** s'offenser (**at, de**). ∼**er** *n.* délinquant(e) *m.* (*f.*).

offensive /ə'fensɪv/ *a.* offensant; (*disgusting*) dégoûtant; (*weapon*) offensif. —*n.* offensive *f.*

offer /'ɒfə(r)/ *v.t.* (*p.t.* **offered**) offrir. —*n.* offre *f.* **on** ∼, en promotion. ∼**ing** *n.* offrande *f.*

offhand /ɒf'hænd/ *a.* désinvolte. —*adv.* à l'improviste.

office /'ɒfɪs/ *n.* bureau *m.*; (*duty*) fonction *f.*; (*surgery: Amer.*) cabinet *m.* —*a.* de bureau. **good** ∼**s,** bons offices *m. pl.* **in** ∼, au pouvoir. ∼ **building,** immeuble de bureaux *m.*

officer /'ɒfɪsə(r)/ *n.* (*army etc.*) officier *m.*; (*policeman*) agent *m.*

official /ə'fɪʃl/ *a.* officiel. —*n.* officiel *m.*; (*civil servant*) fonctionnaire *m.*/*f.* ∼**ly** *adv.* officiellement.

officiate /ə'fɪʃɪeɪt/ *v.i.* (*priest*) officier; (*president*) présider.

officious /ə'fɪʃəs/ *a.* trop zélé.

offing /'ɒfɪŋ/ n. in the ~, en perspective.

offset /'ɒfset/ v.t. (p.t. -set, pres. p. -setting) compenser.

offshoot /'ɒfʃuːt/ n. (bot.) rejeton m.; (fig.) ramification f.

offshore /ɒfˈʃɔː(r)/ a. (waters) côtier; (exploration) en mer; (banking) dans les paladis fiscaux.

offside /ɒfˈsaɪd/ a. (sport) hors jeu invar.; (auto.) du côté du conducteur.

offspring /'ɒfsprɪŋ/ n. invar. progéniture f.

often /'ɒfn/ adv. souvent. how ~?, combien de fois? every so ~, de temps en temps.

ogle /'əʊgl/ v.t. lorgner.

ogre /'əʊgə(r)/ n. ogre m.

oh /əʊ/ int. oh, ah.

oil /ɔɪl/ n. huile f.; (petroleum) pétrole m.; (for heating) mazout m. —v.t. graisser. ~-painting n. peinture à l'huile f. ~-tanker n. pétrolier m. ~y a. graisseux.

oilfield /'ɔɪlfiːld/ n. gisement pétrolifère m.

oilskins /'ɔɪlskɪnz/ n. pl. ciré m.

ointment /'ɔɪntmənt/ n. pommade f., onguent m.

OK /əʊˈkeɪ/ a. & adv. (fam.) bien.

old /əʊld/ a. (-er, -est) vieux; (person) âgé; (former) ancien. how ~ is he?, quel âge a-t-il? he is eight years ~, il a huit ans. of ~, jadis. ~ age, vieillesse f. old-age pensioner, retraité(e) m. (f.) ~ boy, ancien élève m.; (fellow: fam.) vieux m. ~er, ~est, (son etc.) aîné. ~-fashioned a. démodé; (person) vieux jeu invar. ~ maid, vieille fille f. ~ man, vieillard m., vieux m. ~-time a. ancien, vieux, vieille f.

olive /'ɒlɪv/ n. olive f. —a. olive invar. ~ oil, huile d'olive f.

Olympic /əˈlɪmpɪk/ a. olympique.

~s n. pl., ~ Games, Jeux olympiques m. pl.

omelette /'ɒmlɪt/ n. omelette f.

omen /'əʊmen/ n. augure m.

ominous /'ɒmɪnəs/ a. de mauvais augure; (fig.) menaçant.

omi|t /ə'mɪt/ v.t. (p.t. omitted) omettre. ~ssion n. omission f.

on /ɒn/ prep. sur. —adv. en avant; (switched on) allumé; (tap) ouvert; (machine) en marche; (put on) mis. on foot/time/etc., à pied/l'heure/etc. on arriving, en arrivant. on Tuesday, mardi. on Tuesdays, le mardi. walk/etc. on, continuer à marcher/etc. be on, (of film) passer. the meeting/deal is still on, la réunion/le marché est maintenu(e). be on at, (fam.) être après. on and off, de temps en temps.

once /wʌns/ adv. une fois; (formerly) autrefois. —conj. une fois que. all at ~, tout à coup. ~-over n. (fam.) coup d'œil rapide m.

oncoming /'ɒnkʌmɪŋ/ a. (vehicle etc.) qui approche.

one /wʌn/ a. & n. un(e) (m. (f.)). —pron. un(e) m. (f.); (impersonal) on. ~ (and only), seul (et unique). a big/red/etc.. ~, un(e) grand(e)/rouge/etc. this/that ~, celui-ci/-là, celle-ci/-là. ~ another, l'un(e)/l'autre. ~-eyed, borgne. ~-off a. (fam.), ~ of a kind, (Amer.) unique, exceptionnel. ~-sided a. (biased) partial; (unequal) inégal. ~-way a. (street) à sens unique; (ticket) simple.

oneself /wʌn'self/ pron. soi-même; (reflexive) se.

ongoing /'ɒngəʊɪŋ/ a. qui continue à évoluer.

onion /'ʌnjən/ n. oignon m.

onlooker /'ɒnlʊkə(r)/ n. spectateur, -trice m., f.

only /ˈəʊnlɪ/ a. seul. **an ~ son**/etc., un fils/etc. unique. —adv. & conj. seulement. **he ~ has six,** il n'en a que six, il en a six seulement. **~ too,** extrêmement.

onset /ˈɒnset/ n. début m.

onslaught /ˈɒnslɔːt/ n. attaque f.

onus /ˈəʊnəs/ n. **the ~ is on me**/etc., c'est ma/etc. responsabilité **(to,** de).

onward(s) /ˈɒnwəd(z)/ adv. en avant.

onyx /ˈɒnɪks/ n. onyx m.

ooze /uːz/ v.i. suinter.

opal /ˈəʊpl/ n. opale f.

opaque /əʊˈpeɪk/ a. opaque.

open /ˈəʊpən/ a. ouvert; **(view)** dégagé; **(free to all)** public; **(undisguised)** manifeste; **(question)** en attente. —v.t./i. **(s')**ouvrir; **(of shop, play)** ouvrir. **in the ~ air,** en plein air. **~-ended** a. sans limite **(de durée etc.); (system)** qui peut évoluer. **~-heart** a. **(surgery)** à cœur ouvert. **keep ~ house,** tenir table ouverte. **~ out** or **up, (s')**ouvrir. **~-minded** a. à l'esprit ouvert. **~-plan** a. sans cloisons. **~ secret,** secret de Polichinelle m.

opener /ˈəʊpənə(r)/ n. ouvre-boîte(s) m., ouvre-bouteille(s) m.

opening /ˈəʊpənɪŋ/ n. ouverture f.; **(job)** débouché m., poste vacant m.

openly /ˈəʊpənlɪ/ adv. ouvertement.

opera /ˈɒpərə/ n. opéra m. **~ glasses** n. pl. jumelles f. pl. **~tic** /ɒpəˈrætɪk/ a. d'opéra.

operate /ˈɒpəreɪt/ v.t./i. opérer; **(techn.)** (faire) fonctionner. **~e on, (med.)** opérer. **~ing theatre,** salle d'opération f. **~ion** /-ˈreɪʃn/ n. opération f. **have an ~ion,** se faire opérer. **in ~ion,** en vigueur; **(techn.)** en service. **~or** n. opérat|eur, -trice m., f.; **(telephonist)** standardiste m./f.

operational /ɒpəˈreɪʃənl/ a. opérationnel.

operative /ˈɒpərətɪv/ a. **(med.)** opératoire; **(law etc.)** en vigueur.

operetta /ɒpəˈretə/ n. opérette f.

opinion /əˈpɪnjən/ n. opinion f., avis m. **~ated** a. dogmatique.

opium /ˈəʊpɪəm/ n. opium m.

opponent /əˈpəʊnənt/ n. adversaire m./f.

opportune /ˈɒpətjuːn/ a. opportun.

opportunist /ɒpəˈtjuːnɪst/ n. opportuniste m./f.

opportunity /ɒpəˈtjuːnətɪ/ n. occasion f. **(to do,** de faire).

oppos|e /əˈpəʊz/ v.t. s'opposer à. **~ed to,** opposé à. **~ing** a. opposé.

opposite /ˈɒpəzɪt/ a. opposé. —n. contraire m., opposé m. —adv. en face. —prep. **~ (to),** en face de. **one's ~ number,** son homologue m./f.

opposition /ɒpəˈzɪʃn/ n. opposition f.; **(mil.)** résistance f.

oppress /əˈpres/ v.t. opprimer. **~ion** /-ʃn/ n. oppression f. **~ive** a. **(cruel)** oppressif; **(heat)** oppressant. **~or** n. oppresseur m.

opt /ɒpt/ v.i. **~ for,** opter pour. **~ out,** refuser de participer **(of,** à). **~ to do,** choisir de faire.

optical /ˈɒptɪkl/ a. optique. **~ illusion,** illusion d'optique f.

optician /ɒpˈtɪʃn/ n. opticien(ne) m. (f.).

optimis|t /ˈɒptɪmɪst/ n. optimiste m./f. **~m** /-zəm/ n. optimisme m. **~tic** /-ˈmɪstɪk/ a. optimiste. **~tically** /-ˈmɪstɪklɪ/ adv. avec optimisme.

optimum /ˈɒptɪməm/ a. & n. **(pl. -ima)** optimum **(m.).**

option /ˈɒpʃn/ n. choix m., option f.

optional /ˈɒpʃənl/ a. facultatif. **~ extras,** accessoires en option m. pl.

opulen|t /'ɔpjulənt/ *a.* opulent. **~ce** *n.* opulence *f.*

or /ɔː(r)/ *conj.* ou; (*with negative*) ni.

oracle /'ɔrəkl/ *n.* oracle *m.*

oral /'ɔːrəl/ *a.* oral. —*n.* (*examination: fam.*) oral *m.*

orange /'ɔrindʒ/ *n.* (*fruit*) orange *f.* —*a.* (*colour*) orange *invar.*

orangeade /ɔrindʒ'eid/ *n.* orangeade *f.*

orator /'ɔrətə(r)/ *n.* orateur, -trice *m., f.* **~y** /-tri/ *n.* rhétorique *f.*

oratorio /ɔrə'tɔːriəʊ/ *n.* (*pl.* -os) oratorio *m.*

orbit /'ɔːbit/ *n.* orbite *f.* —*v.t.* graviter autour de, orbiter.

orchard /'ɔːtʃəd/ *n.* verger *m.*

orchestra /'ɔːkistrə/ *n.* orchestre *m.* **~ stalls** (*Amer.*), fauteuils d'orchestre *m. pl.* /-l'kestrəl/ *a.* orchestral.

orchestrate /'ɔːkistreit/ *v.t.* orchestrer.

orchid /'ɔːkid/ *n.* orchidée *f.*

ordain /ɔː'dein/ *v.t.* décréter (**that**, que); (*relig.*) ordonner.

ordeal /ɔː'diːl/ *n.* épreuve *f.*

order /'ɔːdə(r)/ *n.* ordre *m.*; (*comm.*) commande *f.* —*v.t.* ordonner; (*goods etc.*) commander. **in ~**, (*tidy*) en ordre; (*document*) en règle; (*fitting*) de règle. **in ~ that**, pour que. **in ~ to**, pour. **~ s.o. to**, ordonner à qn. de.

orderly /'ɔːdəli/ *a.* (*tidy*) ordonné; (*not unruly*) discipliné. —*n.* (*mil.*) planton *m.*; (*med.*) garçon de salle *m.*

ordinary /'ɔːdinri/ *a.* (*usual*) ordinaire; (*average*) moyen.

ordination /ɔːdi'neiʃn/ *n.* (*relig.*) ordination *f.*

ore /ɔː(r)/ *n.* mineral *m.*

organ /'ɔːgən/ *n.* organe *m.*; (*mus.*) orgue *m.* **~ist** *n.* organiste *m./f.*

organic /ɔː'gænik/ *a.* organique.

organism /'ɔːgənizəm/ *n.* organisme *m.*

organiz|e /'ɔːgənaiz/ *v.t.* organiser. **~ation** /-'zeiʃn/ *n.* organisation *f.* **~er** *n.* organisa|teur, -trice *m., f.*

orgasm /'ɔːgæzəm/ *n.* orgasme *m.*

orgy /'ɔːdʒi/ *n.* orgie *f.*

Orient /'ɔːriənt/ *n.* **the ~**, l'Orient *m.* **~al** /-'entl/ *n.* Oriental(e) *m.* (*f.*).

oriental /ɔːri'entl/ *a.* oriental.

orient(at)e /'ɔːriənt(eit)/ *v.t.* orienter. **~ion** /-'teiʃn/ *n.* orientation *f.*

orifice /'ɔrifis/ *n.* orifice *m.*

origin /'ɔridʒin/ *n.* origine *f.*

original /ə'ridʒənl/ *a.* (*first*) originel; (*not copied*) original. **~ity** /-'næləti/ *n.* originalité *f.* **~ly** *adv.* (*at the outset*) à l'origine; (*write etc.*) originalement.

originat|e /ə'ridʒineit/ *v.i.* (*plan*) prendre naissance. —*v.t.* être l'auteur de. **~e from**, provenir de; (*person*) venir de. **~or** *n.* auteur *m.*

ornament /'ɔːnəmənt/ *n.* (*decoration*) ornement *m.*; (*object*) objet décoratif *m.* **~al** /-'mentl/ *a.* ornemental. **~ation** /-en'teiʃn/ *n.* ornementation *f.*

ornate /ɔː'neit/ *a.* richement orné.

ornithology /ɔːni'θɔlədʒi/ *n.* ornithologie *f.*

orphan /'ɔːfn/ *n.* orphelin(e) *m.* (*f.*). —*v.t.* rendre orphelin. **~age** *n.* orphelinat *m.*

orthodox /'ɔːθədɔks/ *a.* orthodoxe. **~y** *n.* orthodoxie *f.*

orthopaedic /ɔːθə'piːdik/ *a.* orthopédique.

oscillate /'ɔsileit/ *v.i.* osciller.

ostensibl|e /ɔ'tensəbl/ *a.* apparent, prétendu. **~y** *adv.* apparemment, prétendument.

ostentati|on /ɔsten'teiʃn/ *n.* ostentation *f.* **~ous** *a.* prétentieux.

osteopath /'ɔstiəpæθ/ *n.* ostéopathe *m./f.*

ostracize /ˈɒstrəsaɪz/ *v.t.* frapper d'ostracisme.

ostrich /ˈɒstrɪtʃ/ *n.* autruche *f.*

other /ˈʌðə(r)/ *a.* autre. —*n.* & *pron.* autre *m./f.* —*adv.* ∼ **than**, autrement que; (*except*) à part. **(some)** ∼**s**, d'autres. **the** ∼ **one**, l'autre *m./f.*

otherwise /ˈʌðəwaɪz/ *adv.* autrement.

otter /ˈɒtə(r)/ *n.* loutre *f.*

ouch /aʊtʃ/ *int.* aïe!

ought /ɔːt/ *v. aux.* devoir. **you** ∼ **to stay**, vous devriez rester. **he** ∼ **to succeed**, il devrait réussir. **I** ∼ **to have done it**, j'aurais dû le faire.

ounce /aʊns/ *n.* once *f.* (*= 28.35 g.*).

our /ˈaʊə(r)/ *a.* notre, *pl.* nos.

ours /ˈaʊəz/ *poss.* le *or* la nôtre, les nôtres.

ourselves /aʊəˈselvz/ *pron.* nous-mêmes; (*reflexive & after prep.*) nous.

oust /aʊst/ *v.t.* évincer.

out /aʊt/ *adv.* dehors; (*sun*) levé. **be** ∼, (*person, book*) être sorti; (*light*) être éteint; (*flower*) être épanoui; (*tide*) être bas; (*secret*) se savoir; (*wrong*) se tromper. **be** ∼ **to do**, être résolu à faire. **run/etc.** ∼, sortir en courant/*etc.* ∼**-and-out** *a.* absolu. ∼ **of**, hors de; (*without*) sans, à court de. ∼ **of pity/etc.**, par pitié/*etc.* **made** ∼ **of**, fait en *or* de. **take** ∼ **of**, prendre dans. **5** ∼ **of 6**, 5 sur 6. ∼ **of date**, démodé; (*not valid*) périmé. ∼ **of doors**, dehors. ∼ **of hand**, (*situation*) dont on n'est plus maître. ∼ **of line**, (*impertinent: Amer.*) incorrect. ∼ **of one's mind**, fou. ∼ **of order**, (*broken*) en panne. ∼ **of place**, (*object, remark*) déplacé. ∼ **of the way**, écarté. **get** ∼ **of the way!** écarte-toi! ∼ **of work**, sans travail. ∼**-patient** *n.* malade en consultation externe *m./f.*

outbid /aʊtˈbɪd/ *v.t.* (*p.t.* -**bid**, *pres. p.* -**bidding**) enchérir sur.

outboard /ˈaʊtbɔːd/ *a.* (*motor*) hors-bord *invar.*

outbreak /ˈaʊtbreɪk/ *n.* (*of war etc.*) début *m.*; (*of violence, boils*) éruption *f.*

outburst /ˈaʊtbɜːst/ *n.* explosion *f.*

outcast /ˈaʊtkɑːst/ *n.* paria *m.*

outclass /aʊtˈklɑːs/ *v.t.* surclasser.

outcome /ˈaʊtkʌm/ *n.* résultat *m.*

outcrop /ˈaʊtkrɒp/ *n.* affleurement.

outcry /ˈaʊtkraɪ/ *n.* tollé *m.*

outdated /aʊtˈdeɪtɪd/ *a.* démodé.

outdo /aʊtˈduː/ *v.t.* (*p.t.* -**did**, *p.p.* -**done**) surpasser.

outdoor /ˈaʊtdɔː(r)/ *a.* de *or* en plein air. ∼**s** /-ˈdɔːz/ *adv.* dehors.

outer /ˈaʊtə(r)/ *a.* extérieur. ∼ **space**, espace (cosmique) *m.*

outfit /ˈaʊtfɪt/ *n.* (*articles*) équipement *m.*; (*clothes*) tenue *f.*; (*group: fam.*) équipe *f.* ∼**ter** *n.* spécialiste de confection *m./f.*

outgoing /ˈaʊtɡəʊɪŋ/ *a.* (*minister, tenant*) sortant; (*sociable*) ouvert. ∼**s** *n. pl.* dépenses *f. pl.*

outgrow /aʊtˈɡrəʊ/ *v.t.* (*p.t.* -**grew**, *p.p.* -**grown**) (*clothes*) devenir trop grand pour; (*habit*) dépasser.

outhouse /ˈaʊthaʊs/ *n.* appentis *m.*; (*of mansion*) dépendance *f.*; (*Amer.*) cabinets extérieurs *m. pl.*

outing /ˈaʊtɪŋ/ *n.* sortie *f.*

outlandish /aʊtˈlændɪʃ/ *a.* bizarre, étrange.

outlaw /ˈaʊtlɔː/ *n.* hors-la-loi *m. invar.* —*v.t.* proscrire.

outlay /ˈaʊtleɪ/ *n.* dépenses *f. pl.*

outlet /ˈaʊtlet/ *n.* (*for water, gases*) sortie *f.*; (*for goods*) débouché *m.*; (*for feelings*) exutoire *m.*

outline /ˈaʊtlaɪn/ *n.* contour *m.*; (*summary*) esquisse *f.* **(main)** ∼**s**, grandes lignes *f. pl.* —*v.t.* tracer le contour de; (*summarize*) exposer sommairement.

outlive /aʊt'lɪv/ v.t. survivre à.

outlook /'aʊtlʊk/ n. perspective f.

outlying /aʊt'laɪɪŋ/ a. écarté.

outmoded /aʊt'məʊdɪd/ a. démodé.

outnumber /aʊt'nʌmbə(r)/ v.t. surpasser en nombre.

outpost /'aʊtpəʊst/ n. avant-poste m.

output /'aʊtpʊt/ n. rendement m.; (comput.) sortie f. —v.t/i. (comput.) sortir.

outrage /'aʊtreɪdʒ/ n. atrocité f.; (scandal) scandale m. —v.t. (morals) outrager; (person) scandaliser.

outrageous /aʊt'reɪdʒəs/ a. scandaleux, atroce.

outright /aʊt'raɪt/ adv. complètement; (at once) sur le coup; (frankly) carrément. —a. /'aʊtraɪt/ complet; (refusal) net.

outset /'aʊtset/ n. début m.

outside[1] /aʊt'saɪd/ n. extérieur m. —adv. (au) dehors. —prep. en dehors de; (in front of) devant.

outside[2] /'aʊtsaɪd/ a. extérieur.

outsider /aʊt'saɪdə(r)/ n. étranger, -ère m., f.; (sport) outsider m.

outsize /'aʊtsaɪz/ a. grande taille invar.

outskirts /'aʊtskɜːts/ n. pl. banlieue f.

outspoken /aʊt'spəʊkən/ a. franc.

outstanding /aʊt'stændɪŋ/ a. exceptionnel; (not settled) en suspens.

outstretched /aʊt'stretʃt/ a. (arm) tendu.

outstrip /aʊt'strɪp/ v.t. (p.t. -stripped) devancer, surpasser.

outward /aʊt'wəd/ a. & adv. vers l'extérieur; (sign etc.) extérieur; (journey) d'aller. —ly adv. extérieurement. —s adv. vers l'extérieur.

outweigh /aʊt'weɪ/ v.t. (exceed in importance) l'emporter sur.

outwit /aʊt'wɪt/ v.t. (p.t. -witted) duper, être plus malin que.

oval /'əʊvl/ n. & a. ovale (m.).

ovary /'əʊvərɪ/ n. ovaire m.

ovation /ə'veɪʃn/ n. ovation f.

oven /'ʌvn/ n. four m.

over /'əʊvə(r)/ prep. sur, au-dessus de; (across) de l'autre côté de; (during) pendant; (more than) plus de. —adv. (par-)dessus; (ended) fini; (past) passé; (too) trop; (more) plus. **jump/etc.** ~, sauter/etc. par-dessus. ~ **the radio,** à la radio. **ask** ~, inviter chez soi. **he has some** ~, il lui en reste. **all** ~ **(the table),** partout (sur la table). ~ **and above,** en plus de. ~ **and over,** à maintes reprises. ~ **here,** par ici. ~ **there,** là-bas.

over- /'əʊvə(r)/ pref. sur-, trop.

overall[1] /'əʊvərɔːl/ n. blouse f. ~**s,** bleu(s) de travail m. (pl.).

overall[2] /əʊvər'ɔːl/ a. global, d'ensemble; (length, width) total. —adv. globalement.

overawe /əʊvər'ɔː/ v.t. intimider.

overbalance /əʊvə'bæləns/ v.t./i. (faire) basculer.

overbearing /əʊvə'beərɪŋ/ a. autoritaire.

overboard /'əʊvəbɔːd/ adv. pardessus bord.

overbook /əʊvə'bʊk/ v.t. accepter trop de réservations pour.

overcast /'əʊvəkɑːst/ a. couvert.

overcharge /əʊvə'tʃɑːdʒ/ v.t. ~ s.o. (for), faire payer trop cher à qn.

overcoat /'əʊvəkəʊt/ n. pardessus m.

overcome /əʊvə'kʌm/ v.t. (p.t. -came, p.p. -come) triompher de; (difficulty) surmonter, triompher de. ~ **by,** accablé de.

overcrowded /əʊvə'kraʊdɪd/ a. bondé; (country) surpeuplé.

overdo /əʊvə'duː/ v.t. (p.t. -did, p.p. -done) exagérer; (culin.) trop cuire. ~ **it**, (*overwork*) se surmener.

overdose /ˈəʊvədəʊs/ n. overdose f., surdose f.

overdraft /ˈəʊvədrɑːft/ n. découvert m.

overdraw /əʊvəˈdrɔː/ v.t. (p.t. **-drew**, p.p. **-drawn**) (*one's account*) mettre à découvert.

overdrive /əʊvəˈdraɪv/ n. surmultipliée f.

overdue /əʊvəˈdjuː/ a. en retard; (*belated*) tardif; (*bill*) impayé.

overestimate /əʊvərˈestɪmeɪt/ v.t. surestimer.

overexposed /əʊvərɪkˈspəʊzd/ a. surexposé.

overflow[1] /əʊvəˈfləʊ/ v.i. déborder.

overflow[2] /ˈəʊvəfləʊ/ n. (*outlet*) trop-plein m.

overgrown /əʊvəˈgrəʊn/ a. (*garden etc.*) envahi par la végétation.

overhang /əʊvəˈhæŋ/ v.t. (p.t. **-hung**) surplomber. —v.i. faire saillie.

overhaul[1] /əʊvəˈhɔːl/ v.t. réviser.

overhaul[2] /ˈəʊvəhɔːl/ n. révision f.

overhead[1] /əʊvəˈhed/ adv. au-dessus; (*in sky*) dans le ciel.

overhead[2] /ˈəʊvəhed/ a. aérien. ~s n. pl. frais généraux m. pl. ~ **projector**, rétroprojecteur m.

overhear /əʊvəˈhɪə(r)/ v.t. (p.t. **-heard**) surprendre, entendre.

overjoyed /əʊvəˈdʒɔɪd/ a. ravi.

overland /ˈəʊvəlænd/, /əʊvəˈlænd/ par voie de terre.

overlap /əʊvəˈlæp/ v.t./i. (p.t. **-lapped**) (se) chevaucher.

overleaf /əʊvəˈliːf/ adv. au verso.

overload /əʊvəˈləʊd/ v.t. surcharger.

overlook /əʊvəˈlʊk/ v.t. oublier, négliger; (*of window, house*) donner sur; (*of tower*) dominer.

overly /ˈəʊvəlɪ/ adv. excessivement.

overnight /əʊvəˈnaɪt/ adv. (pendant) la nuit; (*instantly: fig.*) du jour au lendemain. —a. /ˈəʊvənaɪt/ (*train etc.*) de nuit; (*stay etc.*) d'une nuit; (*fig.*) soudain.

overpay /əʊvəˈpeɪ/ v.t. (p.t. **-paid**) (*person*) surpayer.

overpower /əʊvəˈpaʊə(r)/ v.t. subjuguer; (*opponent*) maîtriser; (*fig.*) accabler. ~**ing** a. irrésistible; (*heat, smell*) accablant.

overpriced /əʊvəˈpraɪst/ a. trop cher.

overrate /əʊvəˈreɪt/ v.t. surestimer. ~**d** /-ɪd/ a. surfait.

overreach /əʊvəˈriːtʃ/ v. pr. ~ **o.s.**, trop entreprendre.

overreact /əʊvərɪˈækt/ v.i. réagir excessivement.

override /əʊvəˈraɪd/ v.t. (p.t. **-rode**, p.p. **-ridden**) passer outre à. ~**ing** a. prépondérant; (*importance*) majeur.

overripe /ˈəʊvəraɪp/ a. trop mûr.

overrule /əʊvəˈruːl/ v.t. rejeter.

overrun /əʊvəˈrʌn/ v.t. (p.t. **-ran**, p.p. **-run**, pres. p. **-running**) envahir; (*a limit*) aller au-delà de. —v.i. (*meeting*) durer plus longtemps que prévu.

overseas /əʊvəˈsiːz/ a. d'outre-mer, étranger. —adv. outre-mer, à l'étranger.

oversee /əʊvəˈsiː/ v.t. (p.t. **-saw**, p.p. **-seen**) surveiller. ~**r** /ˈəʊvəsɪə(r)/ n. contremaître m.

overshadow /əʊvəˈʃædəʊ/ v.t. (*darken*) assombrir; (*fig.*) éclipser.

overshoot /əʊvəˈʃuːt/ v.t. (p.t. **-shot**) dépasser.

oversight /ˈəʊvəsaɪt/ n. omission f.

oversleep /əʊvəˈsliːp/ v.i. (p.t. **-slept**) se réveiller trop tard.

overt /ˈəʊvɜːt/ a. manifeste.

overtake /əʊvəˈteɪk/ v.t./i. (p.t. **-took**, p.p. **-taken**) dépasser; (*vehicle*) doubler, dépasser; (*surprise*) surprendre.

overtax /əʊvəˈtæks/ v.t. (*strain*) fatiguer; (*taxpayer*) surimposer.

overthrow /əʊvəˈθrəʊ/ v.t. (*p.t. -threw, p.p. -thrown*) renverser.

overtime /ˈəʊvətaɪm/ n. heures supplémentaires f. pl.

overtone /ˈəʊvətəʊn/ n. nuance f.

overture /ˈəʊvətjʊə(r)/ n. ouverture f.

overturn /əʊvəˈtɜːn/ v.t./i. (se) renverser.

overweight /əʊvəˈweɪt/ a. be ~, peser trop.

overwhelm /əʊvəˈwelm/ v.t. accabler; (*defeat*) écraser; (*amaze*) bouleverser. ~ing a. accablant; (*victory*) écrasant; (*urge*) irrésistible.

overwork /əʊvəˈwɜːk/ v.t./i. (se) surmener. —n. surmenage m.

overwrought /əʊvəˈrɔːt/ a. à bout.

ow|e /əʊ/ v.t. devoir. ~ing a. dû. ~ing to, à cause de.

owl /aʊl/ n. hibou m.

own¹ /əʊn/ a. propre. **a house**/*etc.* **of one's** ~, sa propre maison/*etc.*, une maison/*etc.* à soi. **get one's** ~ **back**, (*fam.*) prendre sa revanche. **on one's** ~, bien se défendre. **on one's** ~, tout seul.

own² /əʊn/ v.t. posséder. ~ **up (to)**, (*fam.*) avouer. ~**er** n. propriétaire m./f. ~**ership** n. possession f. (**of**, de); (*right*) propriété f.

ox /ɒks/ n. (pl. **oxen**) bœuf m.

oxygen /ˈɒksɪdʒən/ n. oxygène m.

oyster /ˈɔɪstə(r)/ n. huître f.

ozone /ˈəʊzəʊn/ n. ozone m. ~ **layer**, couche d'ozone f.

P

pace /peɪs/ n. pas m.; (*speed*) allure f.; —v.t. (*room etc.*) arpenter.

—v.i. ~ (**up and down**), faire les cent pas. **keep** ~ **with**, suivre.

pacemaker /ˈpeɪsmeɪkə(r)/ n. (*med.*) stimulateur cardiaque m.

Pacific /pəˈsɪfɪk/ a. pacifique. n. ~ (**Ocean**), Pacifique m.

pacifist /ˈpæsɪfɪst/ n. pacifiste m./f.

pacif|y /ˈpæsɪfaɪ/ v.t. (*country*) pacifier; (*person*) apaiser. ~**ier** n. (*Amer.*) sucette f.

pack /pæk/ n. paquet m.; (*mil.*) sac m.; (*of hounds*) meute f.; (*of thieves*) bande f.; (*of lies*) tissu m. —v.t. emballer; (*suitcase*) faire; (*box, room*) remplir; (*press down*) tasser. —v.i. ~ (**one's bags**), faire ses valises. ~ **into**, (*cram*) (s')entasser dans. ~ **off**, expédier. **send** ~**ing**, envoyer promener. ~**ed** a. (*crowded*) bondé. ~**ed lunch**, repas froid m. ~**ing** n. (*action, material*) emballage m. ~**ing case**, caisse f.

package /ˈpækɪdʒ/ n. paquet m. —v.t. empaqueter. ~ **deal**, forfait m. ~ **tour**, voyage organisé m.

packet /ˈpækɪt/ n. paquet m.

pact /pækt/ n. pacte m.

pad¹ /pæd/ n. bloc(-notes) m.; (*for ink*) tampon m. (**launching**) ~, rampe (de lancement) f. —v.t. (*p.t.* **padded**) rembourrer; (*text: fig.*) délayer. ~**ding** n. rembourrage m.; délayage m.

pad² /pæd/ v.i. (*p.t.* **padded**) (*walk*) marcher à pas feutrés.

paddle¹ /ˈpædl/ n. pagaie f. —v.t. ~ **a canoe**, pagayer. ~**-steamer** n. bateau à roues m.

paddl|e² /ˈpædl/ v.i. barboter, se mouiller les pieds. ~**ing pool**, pataugeoire f.

paddock /ˈpædək/ n. paddock m.

paddy(-field) /ˈpædɪ(fiːld)/ n. rizière f.

padlock /ˈpædlɒk/ n. cadenas m. —v.t. cadenasser.

paediatrician /piːdɪəˈtrɪʃn/ n. pédiatre m./f.

pagan /'peɪgən/ a. & n. païen(ne) (m. (f.)).

page¹ /peɪdʒ/ n. (of book etc.) page f.

page² /peɪdʒ/ n. (in hotel) chasseur m. (at wedding) page m. —v.t. (faire) appeler.

pageant /'pædʒənt/ n. spectacle (historique) m. ∼ry n. pompe f.

pagoda /pə'gəʊdə/ n. pagode f.

paid /peɪd/ see **pay**. —a. put ∼ to, (fam.) mettre fin à.

pail /peɪl/ n. seau m.

pain /peɪn/ n. douleur f. ∼s, efforts m. pl. —v.t. (grieve) peiner. be in ∼, souffrir. take ∼s to, se donner du mal pour. ∼-killer n. analgésique m. ∼less a. indolore.

painful /'peɪnfl/ a. douloureux; (laborious) pénible.

painstaking /'peɪnzteɪkɪŋ/ a. assidu, appliqué.

paint /peɪnt/ n. peinture f. ∼s, (in tube, box) couleurs f. pl. —v.t./i. peindre. ∼er n. peintre m. ∼ing n. peinture f.

paintbrush /'peɪntbrʌʃ/ n. pinceau m.

paintwork /'peɪntwɜːk/ n. peintures f. pl.

pair /peə(r)/ n. paire f.; (of people) couple m. a ∼ of trousers, un pantalon. —v.i. ∼ off, (at dance etc.) former un couple.

pajamas /pə'dʒɑːməz/ n.pl. (Amer.) pyjama m.

Pakistan /pɑːkɪ'stɑːn/ n. Pakistan. m. ∼i a. & n. pakistanais(e) (m. (f.)).

pal /pæl/ n. (fam.) cop|ain, -ine m., f.

palace /'pælɪs/ n. palais m.

palat|e /'pælət/ n. (of mouth) palais m. ∼able a. agréable au goût.

palatial /pə'leɪʃl/ a. somptueux.

palaver /pə'lɑːvə(r)/ n. (fuss: fam.) histoire(s) f. (pl.).

pale /peɪl/ a. (-er, -est) pâle. —v.i. pâlir. ∼ness n. pâleur f.

Palestin|e /'pælɪstaɪn/ n. Palestine f. ∼ian /-'stɪnɪən/ a. & n. palestinien(ne) (m. (f.)).

pall /pɔːl/ n. voile m.

pallet /'pælɪt/ n. palette f.

pallid /'pælɪd/ a. pâle.

palm /pɑːm/ n. (of hand) paume f.; (tree) palmier m.; (symbol) palme f. —v.t. ∼ off, (thing) refiler, coller (on, à); (person) coller. P∼ Sunday, dimanche des Rameaux m.

palmist /'pɑːmɪst/ n. chiromancien(ne) m. (f.).

palpable /'pælpəbl/ a. manifeste.

palpitat|e /'pælpɪteɪt/ v.i. palpiter. ∼ion /-'teɪʃn/ n. palpitation f.

paltry /'pɔːltrɪ/ a. (-ier, -iest) dérisoire, piètre.

pamper /'pæmpə(r)/ v.t. dorloter.

pamphlet /'pæmflɪt/ n. brochure f.

pan /pæn/ n. casserole f.; (for frying) poêle f.; (of lavatory) cuvette f. —v.t. (p.t. panned) (fam.) critiquer.

panacea /pænə'sɪə/ n. panacée f.

panache /pə'næʃ/ n. panache m.

pancake /'pænkeɪk/ n. crêpe f.

pancreas /'pæŋkrɪəs/ n. pancréas m.

panda /'pændə/ n. panda m. ∼ car, voiture pie (de la police) f.

pandemonium /pændɪ'məʊnɪəm/ n. tumulte m., chaos m.

pander /'pændə(r)/ v.i. ∼ to, (person, taste) flatter bassement.

pane /peɪn/ n. carreau m., vitre f.

panel /'pænl/ n. (of door etc.) panneau m.; (jury) jury m.; (speakers: TV) invités m. pl. (instrument) ∼, tableau de bord m. ∼ of experts, groupe d'experts m. ∼led a. lambrissé. ∼ling n. lambrissage m. ∼list n. (TV) invité(e) (de tribune) m. (f.).

pang /pæŋ/ n. pincement au cœur m. ∼s, (of hunger, death) affres f.

pl. ~s of conscience, remords *m. pl.*

panic /ˈpænɪk/ *n.* panique *f.* —*v.t./i.* (*p.t.* panicked) (s')affoler, paniquer. ~-stricken *a.* pris de panique, affolé.

panorama /pænəˈrɑːmə/ *n.* panorama *m.*

pansy /ˈpænzɪ/ *n.* (*bot.*) pensée *f.*

pant /pænt/ *v.i.* haleter.

panther /ˈpænθə(r)/ *n.* panthère *f.*

panties /ˈpæntɪz/ *n. pl.* (*fam.*) slip *m.*, culotte *f.* (*de femme*).

pantihose /ˈpæntɪhəʊz/ *n.* (*Amer.*) collant *m.*

pantomime /ˈpæntəmaɪm/ *n.* (*show*) spectacle de Noël *m.*; (*mime*) pantomime *f.*

pantry /ˈpæntrɪ/ *n.* office *m.*

pants /pænts/ *n. pl.* (*underwear: fam.*) slip *m.*; (*trousers: fam. & Amer.*) pantalon *m.*

papacy /ˈpeɪpəsɪ/ *n.* papauté *f.*

papal /ˈpeɪpl/ *a.* papal.

paper /ˈpeɪpə(r)/ *n.* papier *m.*; (*newspaper*) journal *m.*; (*exam*) épreuve *f.*; (*essay*) exposé *m.*; (*wallpaper*) papier peint *m.*; (*identity*) ~s papiers (d'identité) *m. pl.* —*v.t.* (*room*) tapisser. on ~, par écrit. ~-clip *n.* trombone *m.*

paperback /ˈpeɪpəbæk/ *a. & n.* ~ (book), livre broché *m.*

paperweight /ˈpeɪpəweɪt/ *n.* presse-papiers *m. invar.*

paperwork /ˈpeɪpəwɜːk/ *n.* paperasserie *f.*

paprika /ˈpæprɪkə/ *n.* paprika *m.*

par /pɑː(r)/ *n.* be below ~, ne pas être en forme. on a ~ with, à égalité avec.

parable /ˈpærəbl/ *n.* parabole *f.*

parachute /ˈpærəʃuːt/ *n.* parachute *m.* —*v.i.* descendre en parachute. ~ist *n.* parachutiste *m./f.*

parade /pəˈreɪd/ *n.* (*procession*) défilé *m.*; (*ceremony, display*) parade *f.*; (*street*) avenue *f.* —*v.i.* défiler. —*v.t.* faire parade de.

paradise /ˈpærədaɪs/ *n.* paradis *m.*

paradox /ˈpærədɒks/ *n.* paradoxe *m.* ~ical /-ˈdɒksɪkl/ *a.* paradoxal.

paraffin /ˈpærəfɪn/ *n.* pétrole (lampant) *m.*; (*wax*) paraffine *f.*

paragon /ˈpærəgən/ *n.* modèle *m.*

paragraph /ˈpærəgrɑːf/ *n.* paragraphe *m.*

parallel /ˈpærəlel/ *a.* parallèle. —*n.* (*line*) parallèle *f.*; (*comparison & geog.*) parallèle *m.* —*v.t.* (*p.t.* paralleled) être semblable à; (*match*) égaler.

paralyse /ˈpærəlaɪz/ *v.t.* paralyser.

paraly|sis /pəˈræləsɪs/ *n.* paralysie *f.* ~tic /-ˈlɪtɪk/ *a. & n.* paralytique (*m./f.*).

paramedic /ˌpærəˈmedɪk/ *n.* auxiliaire médical(e) *m.* (*f.*).

parameter /pəˈræmɪtə(r)/ *n.* paramètre *m.*

paramount /ˈpærəmaʊnt/ *a.* primordial, fondamental.

paranoi|a /ˌpærəˈnɔɪə/ *n.* paranoïa *f.* ~d *a.* paranoïaque; (*fam.*) parano *invar.*

parapet /ˈpærəpɪt/ *n.* parapet *m.*

paraphernalia /ˌpærəfəˈneɪlɪə/ *n.* attirail *m.*, équipement *m.*

paraphrase /ˈpærəfreɪz/ *n.* paraphrase *f.* —*v.t.* paraphraser.

parasite /ˈpærəsaɪt/ *n.* parasite *m.*

parasol /ˈpærəsɒl/ *n.* ombrelle *f.*; (*on table, at beach*) parasol *m.*

paratrooper /ˈpærətruːpə(r)/ *n.* (*mil.*) parachutiste *m.*

parcel /ˈpɑːsl/ *n.* colis *m.*, paquet *m.* —*v.t.* (*p.t.* parcelled). ~ out, diviser en parcelles.

parch /pɑːtʃ/ *v.t.* dessécher. be ~ed, (*person*) avoir très soif.

parchment /ˈpɑːtʃmənt/ *n.* parchemin *m.*

pardon /ˈpɑːdn/ *n.* pardon *m.*; (*jurid.*) grâce *m.* —*v.t.* (*p.t.*

pardoned) pardonner (s.o. for sth., qch. à qn.); gracier. **I beg your ~**, pardon.

pare /peə(r)/ v.t. (clip) rogner; (peel) éplucher.

parent /'peərənt/ n. père m., mère f. **~s**, parents m. pl. **~al** /pə'rentl/ a. des parents. **~hood** n. l'état de parent m.

parenthesis /pə'renθəsɪs/ n. (pl. -theses /-siːz/) parenthèse f.

Paris /'pærɪs/ n. Paris m./f. **~ian** /pə'rɪzɪən, Amer. pə'riːʒn/ a. & n. parisien(ne) (m. (f.)).

parish /'pærɪʃ/ n. (relig.) paroisse f.; (municipal) commune f. **~ioner** /pə'rɪʃənə(r)/ n. paroissien(ne) m. (f.).

parity /'pærətɪ/ n. parité f.

park /paːk/ n. parc m. —v.t./i. (se) garer; (remain parked) stationner. **~ing-lot** n. (Amer.) parking m. **~ing-meter** n. parcmètre m. **~ing ticket**, procès-verbal m.

parka /'paːkə/ n. parka m./f.

parlance /'paːləns/ n. langage m.

parliament /'paːləmənt/ n. parlement m. **~ary** /-'mentrɪ/ a. parlementaire.

parlour, (Amer.) **parlor** /'paːlə(r)/ n. salon m.

parochial /pə'rəʊkɪəl/ a. (relig.) paroissial; (fig.) borné, provincial.

parody /'pærədɪ/ n. parodie f. —v.t. parodier.

parole /pə'rəʊl/ n. **on ~**, en liberté conditionnelle.

parquet /'paːkeɪ/ n. parquet m.

parrot /'pærət/ n. perroquet m.

parry /'pærɪ/ v.t. (sport) parer; (question etc.) esquiver. —n. parade f.

parsimonious /paːsɪ'məʊnɪəs/ a. parcimonieux.

parsley /'paːslɪ/ n. persil m.

parsnip /'paːsnɪp/ n. panais m.

parson /'paːsn/ n. pasteur m.

part /paːt/ n. partie f.; (of serial) épisode m.; (of machine) pièce f.; (theatre) rôle m.; (side in dispute) parti m. —a. partiel. —adv. en partie. —v.t./i. (separate) séparer. **in ~**, en partie. **on the ~ of**, de la part de. **~-exchange** n. reprise f. **~ of speech**, catégorie grammaticale f. **~-time** a. & adv. à temps partiel. **~ with**, se séparer de. **take ~ in**, participer à. **in these ~s**, dans la région, dans le coin.

partake /paː'teɪk/ v.i. (p.t. **took**, p.p. **-taken**) participer (in, à).

partial /'paːʃl/ a. partiel; (biased) partial. **be ~ to**, avoir une prédilection pour. **~ity** /-ʃɪ'ælətɪ/ n. (bias) partialité f.; (fondness) prédilection f. **~ly** adv. partiellement.

participate /paː'tɪsɪpeɪt/ v.i. participer (in, à). **~ant** n. participant(e) m. (f.). **~ation** /-'peɪʃn/ n. participation f.

participle /'paːtɪsɪpl/ n. participe m.

particle /'paːtɪkl/ n. particule f.

particular /pə'tɪkjʊlə(r)/ a. particulier; (fussy) difficile; (careful) méticuleux. **that ~ man**, cet homme-là en particulier. **~s** n. pl. détails m. pl. **in ~**, en particulier. **~ly** adv. particulièrement.

parting /'paːtɪŋ/ n. séparation f.; (in hair) raie f. —a. d'adieu.

partisan /paːtɪ'zæn, Amer. 'paːtɪzn/ n. partisan(e) m. (f.).

partition /paː'tɪʃn/ n. (of room) cloison f.; (pol.) partage m., partition f. —v.t. (room) cloisonner; (country) partager.

partly /'paːtlɪ/ adv. en partie.

partner /'paːtnə(r)/ n. associé(e) m. (f.); (sport) partenaire m./f. **~ship** n. association f.

partridge /'paːtrɪdʒ/ n. perdrix f.

party /'paːtɪ/ n. fête f.; (formal)

réception f.; (for young people) boum f.; (group) groupe m.; équipe f.; (pol.) parti m.; (jurid.) partie f. **~ line,** (telephone) ligne commune f.

pass /pɑːs/ v.t./i. (p.t. **passed**) passer; (overtake) dépasser; (in exam) être reçu (à); (approve) accepter, autoriser; (remark) faire; (judgement) prononcer; (law, bill) voter. **~ (by),** (building) passer devant; (person) croiser. —n. (permit) laissez-passer m. invar.; (ticket) carte (d'abonnement) f.; (geog.) col m.; (sport) passe f. **~ (mark),** (in exam) moyenne f. **make a ~ at,** (fam.) faire des avances à. **~ away,** mourir. **~ out or round,** distribuer. **~ out,** (faint. fam.) s'évanouir. **~ over,** (overlook) passer sur. **~ up,** (forego. fam.) laisser passer.

passable /ˈpɑːsəbl/ a. (adequate) passable; (road) praticable.

passage /ˈpæsɪdʒ/ n. (way through, text, etc.) passage m.; (voyage) traversée f.; (corridor) couloir m.

passenger /ˈpæsɪndʒə(r)/ n. passage|r, -ère m., f.; (in train) voyageu|r, -se m., f.

passer-by /pɑːsəˈbaɪ/ n. (pl. **passers-by**) passant(e) m. (f.).

passing /ˈpɑːsɪŋ/ a. (fleeting) fugitif, passager.

passion /ˈpæʃn/ n. passion f. **~ate** a. passionné. **~ately** adv. passionnément.

passive /ˈpæsɪv/ a. passif. **~ness** n. passivité f.

Passover /ˈpɑːsəʊvə(r)/ n. Pâque f.

passport /ˈpɑːspɔːt/ n. passeport m.

password /ˈpɑːswɜːd/ n. mot de passe m.

past /pɑːst/ a. passé; (former) ancien. —n. passé m. —prep. au-delà de; (in front of) devant. —adv. devant. **the ~ months,**

ces derniers mois. **~ midnight,** minuit passé. **10 ~ 6,** six heures dix.

pasta /ˈpæstə/ n. pâtes f. pl.

paste /peɪst/ n. (glue) colle f.; (dough) pâte f.; (of fish, meat) pâté m.; (jewellery) strass m. —v.t. coller.

pastel /ˈpæstl/ n. pastel m. —a. pastel invar.

pasteurize /ˈpæstʃəraɪz/ v.t. pasteuriser.

pastiche /pæˈstiːʃ/ n. pastiche m.

pastille /ˈpæstɪl/ n. pastille f.

pastime /ˈpɑːstaɪm/ n. passetemps m. invar.

pastoral /ˈpɑːstərəl/ a. pastoral.

pastry /ˈpeɪstrɪ/ n. (dough) pâte f.; (tart) pâtisserie f.

pasture /ˈpɑːstʃə(r)/ n. pâturage m.

pasty[1] /ˈpæstɪ/ n. petit pâté m.

pasty[2] /ˈpeɪstɪ/ a. pâteux.

pat /pæt/ v.t. (p.t. **patted**) tapoter. —n. petite tape f. —adv. & a. à propos; (ready) tout prêt.

patch /pætʃ/ n. pièce f.; (over eye) bandeau m.; (spot) tache f.; (of vegetables) carré m. —v.t. **~ up,** rapiécer; (fig.) régler. **bad ~,** période difficile f. **not be a ~ on,** ne pas arriver à la cheville de. **~y** a. inégal.

patchwork /ˈpætʃwɜːk/ n. patchwork m.

pâté /ˈpæteɪ/ n. pâté m.

patent /ˈpeɪtnt/ a. patent. —n. brevet (d'invention) m. —v.t. breveter. **~ leather,** cuir verni m. **~ly** adv. manifestement.

paternal /pəˈtɜːnl/ a. paternel.

paternity /pəˈtɜːnətɪ/ n. paternité f.

path /pɑːθ/ n. (pl. **-s** /pɑːðz/) sentier m., chemin m.; (in park) allée f.; (of rocket) trajectoire f.

pathetic /pəˈθetɪk/ a. pitoyable; (bad: fam.) minable.

pathology /pəˈθɒlədʒɪ/ n. pathologie f.

pathos /'peɪθɒs/ n. pathétique m.

patience /'peɪʃns/ n. patience f.

patient /'peɪʃnt/ a. patient. —n. malade m./f., patient(e) m. (f.). ~ly adv. patiemment.

patio /'pætɪəʊ/ n. (pl. -os) patio m.

patriot /'pætrɪət, 'peɪtrɪət/ n. patriote m./f. ~ic /-'ɒtɪk/ a. patriotique; (person) patriote. ~ism n. patriotisme m.

patrol /pə'trəʊl/ n. patrouille f. —v.t./i. patrouiller (dans). ~ car, voiture de police f.

patrolman /pə'trəʊlmən/ n. (pl. -men /-men/) (Amer.) agent de police m.

patron /'peɪtrən/ n. (of the arts) mécène m. (customer) client(e) m. (f.). ~ saint, saint(e) patron(ne) m. (f.).

patron|age /'pætrənɪdʒ/ n. clientèle f.; (support) patronage m. ~ize v.t. être client de; (fig.) traiter avec condescendance.

patter¹ /'pætə(r)/ n. (of steps) bruit m.; (of rain) crépitement m.

patter² /'pætə(r)/ n. (speech) baratin m.

pattern /'pætn/ n. motif m., dessin m.; (for sewing) patron m.; (procedure, type) schéma m.; (example) exemple m.

paunch /pɔːntʃ/ n. panse f.

pauper /'pɔːpə(r)/ n. indigent(e) m. (f.), pauvre m., pauvresse f.

pause /pɔːz/ n. pause f. —v.i. faire une pause; (hesitate) hésiter.

pav|e /peɪv/ v.t. paver. ~e the way, ouvrir la voie (for, à). ~ing-stone n. pavé m.

pavement /'peɪvmənt/ n. trottoir m.; (Amer.) chaussée f.

pavilion /pə'vɪljən/ n. pavillon m.

paw /pɔː/ n. patte f. —v.t. (of animal) donner des coups de patte à; (touch: fam.) tripoter.

pawn¹ /pɔːn/ n. (chess & fig.) pion m.

pawn² /pɔːn/ v.t. mettre en gage. —n. in ~, en gage. ~-shop n. mont-de-piété m.

pawnbroker /'pɔːnbrəʊkə(r)/ n. prêteur sur gages m.

pay /peɪ/ v.t./i. (p.t. paid) payer; (yield: comm.) rapporter; (compliment, visit) faire. —n. salaire m., paie f. in the ~ of, à la solde de. ~ attention, faire attention (to, à). ~ back, rembourser. ~ for, payer. ~ homage, rendre hommage (to, à). ~ in, verser (to, à). ~ off, (finir de payer); (succeed: fam.) être payant. ~ out, payer, verser.

payable /'peɪəbl/ a. payable.

payment /'peɪmənt/ n. paiement m.; (regular) versement m. (reward) récompense f.

payroll /'peɪrəʊl/ n. registre du personnel m. be on the ~ of, être membre du personnel de.

pea /piː/ n. (petit) pois m. ~-shooter n. sarbacane f.

peace /piːs/ n. paix f. ~ of mind, tranquillité d'esprit f. ~able a. pacifique.

peaceful /'piːsfl/ a. paisible; (intention, measure) pacifique.

peacemaker /'piːsmeɪkə(r)/ n. conciliateur, -trice m., f.

peach /piːtʃ/ n. pêche f.

peacock /'piːkɒk/ n. paon m.

peak /piːk/ n. sommet m.; (of mountain) pic m.; (maximum) maximum m. ~ hours, heures de pointe f. pl. ~ed cap, casquette f.

peaky /'piːki/ a. (pale) pâlot; (puny) chétif; (ill) patraque.

peal /piːl/ n. (of bells) carillon m.; (of laughter) éclat m.

peanut /'piːnʌt/ n. cacahuète f. ~s, (money: sl.) une bagatelle.

pear /peə(r)/ n. poire f.

pearl /pɜːl/ n. perle f. ~y a. nacré.

peasant /'peznt/ n. paysan(ne) m. (f.).

peat /piːt/ n. tourbe f.

pebble /'pebl/ n. caillou m.; (on beach) galet m.

peck /pek/ v.t./i. (food etc.) picorer; (attack) donner des coups de bec (à). —n. coup de bec m. **a ~ on the cheek**, une bise.

peckish /'pekɪʃ/ a. be ~, (fam.) avoir faim.

peculiar /pɪ'kjuːlɪə(r)/ a. (odd) bizarre; (special) particulier (to, à). **~ity** /-'ærətɪ/ n. bizarrerie f.

pedal /'pedl/ n. pédale f. —v.i. pédaler.

pedantic /pɪ'dæntɪk/ a. pédant.

peddle /'pedl/ v.t. colporter; (drugs) revendre.

pedestal /'pedɪstl/ n. piédestal m.

pedestrian /pɪ'destrɪən/ n. piéton m. —a. (precinct, street) piétonnier; (fig.) prosaïque. **~ crossing**, passage piétons m.

pedigree /'pedɪgriː/ n. (of person) ascendance f.; (of animal) pedigree m. —a. (cattle etc.) de race.

pedlar /'pedlə(r)/ n. camelot m.; (door-to-door) colporteu|r, -se m., f.

pee /piː/ v.i. (fam.) faire pipi.

peek /piːk/ v.i. & n. = **peep**[1].

peel /piːl/ n. épluchure(s) f (pl.); (of orange) écorce f. —v.t. (fruit, vegetables) éplucher. —v.i. (of skin) peler; (of paint) s'écailler. **~ings** n. pl. épluchures f pl.

peep[1] /piːp/ v.i. jeter un coup d'œil (furtif) (at, à). —n. coup d'œil (furtif) m. **~-hole** n. judas m. **P~ing Tom**, voyeur m.

peep[2] /piːp/ v.i. (chirp) pépier.

peer[1] /pɪə(r)/ v.i. **~ (at)**, regarder attentivement, scruter.

peer[2] /pɪə(r)/ n. (equal, noble) pair m. **~age** n. pairie f.

peeved /piːvd/ a. (sl.) irrité.

peevish /'piːvɪʃ/ a. grincheux.

peg /peg/ n. cheville f.; (for clothes) pince à linge f.; (to hang coats etc.)

patère f.; (for tent) piquet m. —v.t. (p.t. pegged) (prices) stabiliser. **buy off the ~**, acheter en prêt-à-porter.

pejorative /pɪ'dʒɒrətɪv/ a. péjoratif.

pelican /'pelɪkən/ n. pélican m. **~ crossing**, passage clouté avec feux de signalisation m.

pellet /'pelɪt/ n. (round mass) boulette f.; (for gun) plomb m.

pelt[1] /pelt/ n. (skin) peau f.

pelt[2] /pelt/ v.t. bombarder (with, de). —v.i. pleuvoir à torrents.

pelvis /'pelvɪs/ n. (anat.) bassin m.

pen[1] /pen/ n. (for sheep etc.) enclos m.; (for baby, cattle) parc m.

pen[2] /pen/ n. stylo m.; (to be dipped in ink) plume f. —v.t. (p.t. penned) écrire. **~friend** n. correspondant(e) m. (f.). **~name** n. pseudonyme m.

penal /'piːnl/ a. pénal. **~ize** v.t. pénaliser; (fig.) handicaper.

penalty /'penltɪ/ n. peine f.; (fine) amende f.; (sport) pénalité f.

penance /'penəns/ n. pénitence f.

pence /pens/ see **penny**.

pencil /'pensl/ n. crayon m. —v.t. (p.t. pencilled) crayonner. **~ in**, noter provisoirement. **~-sharpener** n. taille-crayon(s) m.

pendant /'pendənt/ n. pendentif m.

pending /'pendɪŋ/ a. en suspens. —prep. (until) en attendant.

pendulum /'pendjʊləm/ n. pendule m.; (of clock) balancier m.

penetrat|e /'penɪtreɪt/ v.t. (enter) pénétrer dans; (understand, permeate) pénétrer. —v.i. pénétrer. **~ing a.** pénétrant. **~ion** /-'treɪʃn/ n. pénétration f.

penguin /'peŋgwɪn/ n. manchot m., pingouin m.

penicillin /penɪ'sɪlɪn/ n. pénicilline f.

peninsula /pə'nɪnsjʊlə/ n. péninsule f.

penis /'piːnɪs/ n. pénis m.

peniten|t /'penɪtənt/ a. & n. pénitent(e) (m. (f.)). **~ce** n. pénitence f.

penitentiary /penɪ'tenʃərɪ/ n. (Amer.) prison f., pénitencier m.

penknife /'pennaɪf/ n. (pl. -knives) canif m.

pennant /'penənt/ n. flamme f.

penniless /'penɪlɪs/ a. sans le sou.

penny /'penɪ/ n. (pl. pennies or pence) penny m.; (fig.) sou m.

pension /'penʃn/ n. pension f.; (for retirement) retraite f. —v.t. **~ off**, mettre à la retraite. **~ scheme**, caisse de retraite f. **~able** a. qui a droit à une retraite. **~er** n. (old-age) **~er**, retraité(e) m. (f.), personne âgée f.

pensive /'pensɪv/ a. pensif.

Pentecost /'pentɪkɒst/ n. Pentecôte f. **~al** a. pentecôtiste.

penthouse /'penthaʊs/ n. appartement de luxe m. (sur le toit d'un immeuble).

pent-up /pent'ʌp/ a. refoulé.

penultimate /pen'ʌltɪmət/ a. avant-dernier.

people /'piːpl/ n. pl. gens m. pl., personnes f. pl. —n. peuple m. —v.t. peupler. **English/etc. ~**, les Anglais/etc. m. pl. **~ say**, on dit.

pep /pep/ n. entrain m. —v.t. **~ up**, donner de l'entrain à. **~ talk**, discours d'encouragement m.

pepper /'pepə(r)/ n. poivre m.; (vegetable) poivron m. —v.t. (culin.) poivrer. **~y** a. poivré.

peppermint /'pepəmɪnt/ n. (plant) menthe poivrée f.; (sweet) bonbon à la menthe m.

per /pɜː(r)/ prep. par. **~ annum**, par an. **~ cent**, pour cent. **~ kilo/etc.**, le kilo/etc. **~ ten km.** hour, dix km à l'heure.

perceive /pə'siːv/ v.t. percevoir; (notice) s'apercevoir de. **~ that**, s'apercevoir que.

percentage /pə'sentɪdʒ/ n. pourcentage m.

perceptible /pə'septəbl/ a. perceptible.

percept|ion /pə'sepʃn/ n. perception f. **~ive** /-tɪv/ a. pénétrant.

perch /pɜːtʃ/ n. (of bird) perchoir m. —v.i. (se) percher.

percolat|e /'pɜːkəleɪt/ v.t. passer. —v.i. filtrer. **~or** n. cafetière f.

percussion /pə'kʌʃn/ n. percussion f.

peremptory /pə'remptərɪ/ a. péremptoire.

perennial /pə'renɪəl/ a. perpétuel; (plant) vivace.

perfect[1] /'pɜːfɪkt/ a. parfait. **~ly** adv. parfaitement.

perfect[2] /pə'fekt/ v.t. parfaire, mettre au point. **~ion** /-kʃn/ n. perfection f. **to ~ion**, à la perfection. **~ionist** /-kʃənɪst/ n. perfectionniste m./f.

perforat|e /'pɜːfəreɪt/ v.t. perforer. **~ion** /-'reɪʃn/ n. perforation f.; (line of holes) pointillé m.

perform /pə'fɔːm/ v.t. exécuter, faire; (a function) remplir; (mus., theatre) interpréter, jouer. —v.i. jouer; (behave, function) se comporter. **~ance** n. exécution f.; interprétation f.; (of car, team) performance f.; (show) représentation f.; séance f.; (fuss) histoire f. **~er** n. artiste m./f.

perfume /'pɜːfjuːm/ n. parfum m.

perfunctory /pə'fʌŋktərɪ/ a. négligent, superficiel.

perhaps /pə'hæps/ adv. peut-être.

peril /'perəl/ n. péril m. **~ous** a. périlleux.

perimeter /pə'rɪmɪtə(r)/ n. périmètre m.

period /'pɪərɪəd/ n. période f., époque f.; (era) époque f.; (lesson) cours m.; (gram.) point m.; (med.) règles f. pl. —a. d'époque. **~ic** /-'ɒdɪk/ a. périodique. **~ically** /-'ɒdɪklɪ/ adv. périodiquement.

periodical /pɪərɪ'ɒdɪkl/ n. périodique m.

peripher|y /pə'rɪfərɪ/ n. périphérie f. ~al a. périphérique; (of lesser importance: fig.) accessoire; n. (comput.) périphérique m.

periscope /'perɪskəʊp/ n. périscope m.

perish /'perɪʃ/ v.i. périr; (rot) se détériorer. ~able a. périssable.

perjur|e /'pɜːdʒə(r)/ v.pr. ~e o.s., se parjurer. ~y n. parjure m.

perk[1] /pɜːk/ v.t./i. ~ up, (fam.) (se) remonter. ~y a. (fam.) gai.

perk[2] /pɜːk/ n. (fam.) avantage m.

perm /pɜːm/ n. permanente f. —v.t. **have one's hair ~ed**, se faire faire une permanente.

permanen|t /'pɜːmənənt/ a. permanent. ~ce n. permanence f. ~tly adv. à titre permanent.

permeable /'pɜːmɪəbl/ a. perméable.

permeate /'pɜːmɪeɪt/ v.t. imprégner, se répandre dans.

permissible /pə'mɪsəbl/ a. permis.

permission /pə'mɪʃn/ n. permission f.

permissive /pə'mɪsɪv/ a. tolérant, laxiste. ~ness n. laxisme m.

permit[1] /pə'mɪt/ v.t. (p.t. **permitted**) permettre (s.o. to, à qn. de), autoriser (s.o. to, qn. à).

permit[2] /'pɜːmɪt/ n. permis m.; (pass) laissez-passer m. invar.

permutation /pɜːmjuː'teɪʃn/ n. permutation f.

pernicious /pə'nɪʃəs/ a. nocif, pernicieux; (med.) pernicieux.

peroxide /pə'rɒksaɪd/ n. eau oxygénée f.

perpendicular /pɜːpən'dɪkjʊlə(r)/ a. & n. perpendiculaire (f.).

perpetrat|e /'pɜːpɪtreɪt/ v.t. perpétrer. ~or n. auteur m.

perpetual /pə'petʃʊəl/ a. perpétuel.

perpetuate /pə'petʃʊeɪt/ v.t. perpétuer.

perplex /pə'pleks/ v.t. rendre perplexe. ~ed a. perplexe. ~ing a. déroutant. ~ity n. perplexité f.

persecut|e /'pɜːsɪkjuːt/ v.t. persécuter. ~ion /-'kjuːʃn/ n. persécution f.

persever|e /pɜːsɪ'vɪə(r)/ v.i. persévérer. ~ance n. persévérance f.

Persian /'pɜːʃn/ a. & n. (lang.) persan (m.). ~ **Gulf**, golfe persique m.

persist /pə'sɪst/ v.i. persister (**in doing**, à faire). ~ence n. persistance f. ~ent a. (cough, snow, etc.) persistant; (obstinate) obstiné; (continual) continuel. ~ently adv. avec persistance.

person /'pɜːsn/ n. personne f. **in ~**, en personne. ~able a. beau.

personal /'pɜːsənl/ a. personnel; (hygiene, habits) intime; (secretary) particulier. ~ly adv. personnellement. ~ **stereo**, baladeur m.

personality /pɜːsə'nælətɪ/ n. personnalité f.; (on TV) vedette f.

personify /pə'sɒnɪfaɪ/ v.t. personnifier.

personnel /pɜːsə'nel/ n. personnel m.

perspective /pə'spektɪv/ n. perspective f.

Perspex /'pɜːspeks/ n. (P.) plexiglas m. (P.).

perspir|e /pə'spaɪə(r)/ v.i. transpirer. ~ation /-'reɪʃn/ n. transpiration f.

persua|de /pə'sweɪd/ v.t. persuader (to, de). ~sion /-eɪʒn/ n. persuasion f.

persuasive /pə'sweɪsɪv/ a. (person, speech, etc.) persuasif. ~ly adv. d'une manière persuasive.

pert /pɜːt/ a. (saucy) impertinent; (lively) plein d'entrain. ~ly adv. avec impertinence.

pertain /pə'teɪn/ v.i. ~ **to**, se rapporter à.

pertinent /'pɜ:tɪmənt/ a. pertinent. ~**ly** adv. pertinemment.

perturb /pə'tɜ:b/ v.t. troubler.

Peru /pə'ru:/ n. Pérou m. ~**vian** a. & n. péruvien(ne) (m. (f.)).

peruse /pə'ru:z/ v.t. lire (attentivement). ~**al** n. lecture f.

pervade /pə'veɪd/ v.t. imprégner, envahir. ~**sive** a. (mood, dust) envahissant.

perverse /pə'vɜ:s/ a. (stubborn) entêté; (wicked) pervers. ~**ity** n. perversité f.

pervert[1] /pə'vɜ:t/ v.t. pervertir. ~**sion** n. perversion f.

pervert[2] /'pɜ:vɜ:t/ n. perverti(e) m. (f.), dépravé(e) m. (f.).

peseta /pə'seɪtə/ n. peseta f.

pessimis|t /'pesɪmɪst/ n. pessimiste m./f. ~**m** /-zəm/ n. pessimisme m. ~**tic** /-'mɪstɪk/ a. pessimiste. ~**tically** /-'mɪstɪklɪ/ adv. avec pessimisme.

pest /pest/ n. insecte or animal nuisible m.; (person: fam.) enquiquineu|r, -se m., f.

pester /'pestə(r)/ v.t. harceler.

pesticide /'pestɪsaɪd/ n. pesticide m., insecticide m.

pet /pet/ n. animal (domestique) m.; (favourite) chouchou(te) m. (f.). —a. (tame) apprivoisé. —v.t. (p.t. petted) caresser; (sexually) peloter. ~ **hate**, bête noire f. ~ **name**, diminutif m.

petal /'petl/ n. pétale m.

peter /'pi:tə(r)/ v.i. ~ **out**, (supplies) s'épuiser; (road) finir.

petite /pə'ti:t/ a. (woman) menue.

petition /pɪ'tɪʃn/ n. pétition f. —v.t. adresser une pétition à.

petrify /'petrɪfaɪ/ v.t. pétrifier; (scare: fig.) pétrifier de peur.

petrol /'petrəl/ n. essence f. ~ **bomb**, cocktail molotov m. ~ **station**, station-service f. ~ **tank**, réservoir d'essence.

petroleum /pɪ'trəʊlɪəm/ n. pétrole m.

petticoat /'petɪkəʊt/ n. jupon m.

petty /'petɪ/ a. (-ier, -iest) (minor) petit; (mean) mesquin. ~ **cash**, petite caisse f.

petulan|t /'petjʊlənt/ a. irritable. ~**ce** n. irritabilité f.

pew /pju:/ n. banc (d'église) m.

pewter /'pju:tə(r)/ n. étain m.

phallic /'fælɪk/ a. phallique.

phantom /'fæntəm/ n. fantôme m.

pharmaceutical /fɑ:mə'sju:tɪkl/ a. pharmaceutique.

pharmac|y /'fɑ:məsɪ/ n. pharmacie f. ~**ist** n. pharmacien(ne) m. (f.).

pharyngitis /færɪn'dʒaɪtɪs/ n. pharyngite f.

phase /feɪz/ n. phase f. —v.t. ~ **in/out**, introduire/retirer progressivement.

pheasant /'feznt/ n. faisan m.

phenomen|on /fɪ'nɒmɪnən/ n. (pl. -ena) phénomène m. ~**al** a. phénoménal.

phew /fju:/ int. ouf.

phial /'faɪəl/ n. fiole f.

philanderer /fɪ'lændərə(r)/ n. coureur (de femmes) m.

philanthrop|ist /fɪ'lænθrəpɪst/ n. philanthrope m./f. ~**ic** /-ən'θrɒpɪk/ a. philanthropique.

philately /fɪ'lætəlɪ/ n. philatélie f. ~**ist** n. philatéliste m./f.

philharmonic /fɪlɑ:'mɒnɪk/ a. philharmonique.

Philippines /'fɪlɪpi:nz/ n. pl. the ~, les Philippines f. pl.

philistine /'fɪlɪstaɪn, Amer. 'fɪlɪsti:n/ n. philistin m.

philosoph|y /fɪ'lɒsəfɪ/ n. philosophie f. ~**er** n. philosophe m./f. ~**ical** /-ə'sɒfɪkl/ a. philosophique; (resigned) philosophe.

phlegm /flem/ n. (med.) mucosité f.

phlegmatic /fleg'mætɪk/ a. flegmatique.

phobia /'fəʊbɪə/ n. phobie f.

phone /fəʊn/ n. téléphone m. —v.t. (person) téléphoner à; (message) téléphoner. —v.i. téléphoner. ∼ back, rappeler. on the ∼, au téléphone. ∼ book, annuaire m. ∼ box, ∼ booth, cabine téléphonique f. ∼ call, coup de fil m. ∼-in n. émission à ligne ouverte f.

phonecard /ˈfəʊnkɑːd/ n. télé-carte f.

phonetic /fəˈnetɪk/ a. phonétique.

phoney /ˈfəʊnɪ/ a. (-ier, -iest) (sl.) faux. —n. (person: sl.) charlatan m. it's a ∼, (sl.) c'est faux.

phosphate /ˈfɒsfeɪt/ n. phosphate m.

phosphorus /ˈfɒsfərəs/ n. phosphore m.

photo /ˈfəʊtəʊ/ n. (pl. -os) (fam.) photo f.

photocop|y /ˈfəʊtəʊkɒpɪ/ n. photocopie f. —v.t. photocopier. ∼ier n. photocopieuse f.

photogenic /fəʊtəʊˈdʒenɪk/ a. photogénique.

photograph /ˈfəʊtəgrɑːf/ n. photographie f. —v.t. photographier. ∼er /fəˈtɒgrəfə(r)/ n. photographe m./f. ∼ic /-ˈgræfɪk/ a. photographique. ∼y /fəˈtɒgrəfɪ/ n. (activity) photographie f.

phrase /freɪz/ n. expression f.; (idiom & gram.) locution f. —v.t. exprimer, formuler. ∼-book n. guide de conversation m.

physical /ˈfɪzɪkl/ a. physique. ∼ly adv. physiquement.

physician /fɪˈzɪʃn/ n. médecin m.

physicist /ˈfɪzɪsɪst/ n. physicien(ne) m. (f.).

physics /ˈfɪzɪks/ n. physique f.

physiology /fɪzɪˈɒlədʒɪ/ n. physiologie f.

physiotherap|y /fɪzɪəʊˈθerəpɪ/ n. kinésithérapie f. ∼ist n. kinésithérapeute m./f.

physique /fɪˈziːk/ n. constitution f.; (appearance) physique m.

pian|o /pɪˈænəʊ/ n. (pl. -os) piano m. ∼ist /ˈpɪənɪst/ n. pianiste m./f.

piazza /pɪˈætsə/ n. (square) place f.

pick[1] /pɪk/ (tool) n. pioche f.

pick[2] /pɪk/ v.t. choisir; (flower etc.) cueillir; (lock) crocheter; (nose) se curer; (pockets) faire. ∼ (off), enlever. —n. choix m.; (best) meilleur(e) m. (f.). ∼ a quarrel with, chercher querelle à. ∼ holes in, relever les défauts de. the ∼ of, ce qu'il y a de mieux dans. ∼ off, (mil.) abattre un à un. ∼ on, harceler. ∼ out, choisir; (identify) distinguer. ∼ up v.t. ramasser; (sth. fallen) relever; (weight) soulever; (habit, passenger, speed, etc.) prendre; (learn) apprendre; v.i. s'améliorer. ∼-me-up n. remontant m. ∼-up n. partenaire de rencontre m./f.; (truck, stylus-holder) pick-up m.

pickaxe /ˈpɪkæks/ n. pioche f.

picket /ˈpɪkɪt/ n. (single striker) gréviste m./f.; (stake) piquet m. ∼ (line), piquet de grève m. —v.t. (p.t. picketed) mettre un piquet de grève devant.

pickings /ˈpɪkɪŋz/ n. pl. restes m. pl.

pickle /ˈpɪkl/ n. vinaigre m.; (brine) saumure f. ∼s, pickles m. pl.; (Amer.) concombres m.pl. —v.t. conserver dans du vinaigre or de la saumure. in a ∼, (fam.) dans le pétrin.

pickpocket /ˈpɪkpɒkɪt/ n. (thief) pickpocket m.

picnic /ˈpɪknɪk/ n. pique-nique m. —v.i. (p.t. picnicked) pique-niquer.

pictorial /pɪkˈtɔːrɪəl/ a. illustré.

picture /ˈpɪktʃə(r)/ n. image f.; (painting) tableau m.; (photograph) photo f.; (drawing) dessin m.; (film) film m.; (fig.) description f.; tableau m. —v.t. s'imaginer; (describe) dépeindre.

the **~s**, *(cinema)* le cinéma. **~ book**, livre d'images *m*.

picturesque /ˌpɪktʃəˈresk/ *a.* pittoresque.

piddling /ˈpɪdlɪŋ/ *a. (fam.)* dérisoire.

pidgin /ˈpɪdʒɪn/ *a.* **~ English**, pidgin *m*.

pie /paɪ/ *n.* tarte *f.*; *(of meat)* pâté en croûte *m.* **~ chart**, camembert *m*.

piebald /ˈpaɪbɔːld/ *a.* pie *invar*.

piece /piːs/ *n.* morceau *m.*; *(of currency, machine, etc.)* pièce *f.* **—v.t.** **~ (together)**, (r)assembler. **a ~ of advice/furniture/ etc.**, un conseil/meuble/*etc.* **~ work** *n.* travail à la pièce *m.* **go to ~s**, *(fam.)* s'effondrer. **take to ~s**, démonter.

piecemeal /ˈpiːsmiːl/ *a.* par bribes.

pier /pɪə(r)/ *n. (promenade)* jetée *f*.

pierc|e /pɪəs/ *v.t.* percer. **~ing** *a.* perçant; *(cold)* glacial.

piety /ˈpaɪətɪ/ *n.* piété *f*.

piffl|e /ˈpɪfl/ *n. (sl.)* fadaises *f. pl.* **~ing** *a. (sl.)* insignifiant.

pig /pɪg/ *n.* cochon *m.* **~-headed** *a.* entêté.

pigeon /ˈpɪdʒən/ *n.* pigeon *m.* **~ hole** *n.* casier *m.*; *v.t.* classer.

piggy /ˈpɪgɪ/ *a.* porcin; *(greedy: fam.)* goinfre. **~-back** *adv.* sur le dos. **~ bank**, tirelire *f*.

pigment /ˈpɪgmənt/ *n.* pigment *m.* **~ation** /-enˈteɪʃn/ *n.* pigmentation *f*.

pigsty /ˈpɪgstaɪ/ *n.* porcherie *f*.

pigtail /ˈpɪgteɪl/ *n.* natte *f*.

pike /paɪk/ *n. invar. (fish)* brochet *m*.

pilchard /ˈpɪltʃəd/ *n.* pilchard *m*.

pile /paɪl/ *n.* pile *f.*, tas *m.*; *(of carpet)* poils *m.pl.* **—v.t.** **~ (up)**, *(stack)* empiler. **—v.i.** **~ into**, s'empiler dans. **~ up**, *(accumulate)* (s')accumuler. **a ~ of**, *(fam.)* un tas de. **~-up** *n. (auto.)* carambolage *m*.

piles /paɪlz/ *n. pl. (fam.)* hémorroïdes *f. pl*.

pilfer /ˈpɪlfə(r)/ *v.t.* chaparder. **~age** *n.* chapardage *m*.

pilgrim /ˈpɪlgrɪm/ *n.* pèlerin *m.* **~age** *n.* pèlerinage *m*.

pill /pɪl/ *n.* pilule *f*.

pillage /ˈpɪlɪdʒ/ *n.* pillage *m.* **—v.t.** piller. **—v.i.** se livrer au pillage.

pillar /ˈpɪlə(r)/ *n.* pilier *m.* **~-box** *n.* boîte à *or* aux lettres *f*.

pillion /ˈpɪljən/ *n.* siège arrière *m.* **ride ~**, monter derrière.

pillory /ˈpɪlərɪ/ *n.* pilori *m*.

pillow /ˈpɪləʊ/ *n.* oreiller *m*.

pillowcase /ˈpɪləʊkeɪs/ *n.* taie d'oreiller *f*.

pilot /ˈpaɪlət/ *n.* pilote *m.* **—a.** pilote. **—v.t.** *(p.t.* **piloted)** piloter. **~-light** *n.* veilleuse *f*.

pimento /pɪˈmentəʊ/ *n. (pl. -os)* piment *m*.

pimp /pɪmp/ *n.* souteneur *m*.

pimpl|e /ˈpɪmpl/ *n.* bouton *m.* **~y** *a.* boutonneux.

pin /pɪn/ *n.* épingle *f.*; *(techn.)* goupille *f.* **—v.t.** *(p.t.* **pinned)** épingler, attacher; *(hold down)* clouer. **have ~s and needles**, avoir des fourmis. **~ s.o. down**, *(fig.)* forcer qn. à se décider. **~ point** *v.t.* repérer, définir. **~ up**, afficher. **~-up** *n. (fam.)* pin-up *f. invar*.

pinafore /ˈpɪnəfɔː(r)/ *n.* tablier *m*.

pincers /ˈpɪnsəz/ *n. pl.* tenailles *f. pl*.

pinch /pɪntʃ/ *v.t.* pincer; *(steal: sl.)* piquer. **—v.i.** *(be too tight)* serrer. **—n.** *(mark)* pinçon *m.*; *(of salt)* pincée *f.* **at a ~**, au besoin.

pincushion /ˈpɪnkʊʃn/ *n.* pelote à épingles *f*.

pine[1] /paɪn/ *n. (tree)* pin *m.* **~ cone** *n.* pomme de pin *f*.

pine[2] /paɪn/ *v.i.* **~ away**, dépérir. **~ for**, languir après.

pineapple /ˈpaɪnæpl/ *n.* ananas *m*.

ping /pɪŋ/ *n.* bruit métallique *m*.

ping-pong /ˈpɪŋpɒŋ/ *n.* ping-pong *m.*

pink /pɪŋk/ *a.* & *n.* rose (*m.*).

pinnacle /ˈpɪnəkl/ *n.* pinacle *m.*

pint /paɪnt/ *n.* pinte *f.* (*imperial* = 0.57 *litre*; *Amer.* = 0.47 *litre*).

pioneer /paɪəˈnɪə(r)/ *n.* pionnier *m.* —*v.t.* être le premier à faire, utiliser, étudier, *etc.*

pious /ˈpaɪəs/ *a.* pieux.

pip[1] /pɪp/ *n.* (*seed*) pépin *m.*

pip[2] /pɪp/ *n.* (*sound*) top *m.*

pipe /paɪp/ *n.* tuyau *m.*; (*of smoker*) pipe *f.*; (*mus.*) pipeau *m.* —*v.t.* transporter par tuyau. **~-cleaner** *n.* cure-pipe *m.* **~ down**, se taire. **~-dream** *n.* chimère *f.*

pipeline /ˈpaɪplaɪn/ *n.* pipeline *m.* **in the ~**, en route.

piping /ˈpaɪpɪŋ/ *n.* tuyau(x) *m.* (*pl.*). **~ hot**, très chaud.

piquant /ˈpiːkənt/ *a.* piquant.

pique /piːk/ *n.* dépit *m.*

pira|te /ˈpaɪərət/ *n.* pirate *m.* —*v.t.* pirater. **~cy** *n.* piraterie *f.*

Pisces /ˈpaɪsiːz/ *n.* les Poissons *m. pl.*

pistachio /pɪˈstæʃɪəʊ/ *n.* (*pl.* -os) pistache *f.*

pistol /ˈpɪstl/ *n.* pistolet *m.*

piston /ˈpɪstən/ *n.* piston *m.*

pit /pɪt/ *n.* fosse *f.*, trou *m.*; (*mine*) puits *m.*; (*quarry*) carrière *f.*; (*for orchestra*) fosse *f.*; (*of stomach*) creux *m.*; (*of cherry etc.: Amer.*) noyau *m.* —*v.t.* (*p.t.* pitted) trouer; (*fig.*) opposer. **~ o.s. against**, se mesurer à.

pitch[1] /pɪtʃ/ *n.* (*tar*) poix *f.* **~-black** *a.* d'un noir d'ébène.

pitch[2] /pɪtʃ/ *v.t.* lancer; (*tent*) dresser. —*v.i.* (*of ship*) tanguer. —*n.* degré *m.*; (*of voice*) hauteur *f.*; (*mus.*) ton *m.*; (*sport*) terrain *m.* **~ed battle**, bataille rangée *f.* **a high-~ed voice**, une voix aiguë. **~ in**, (*fam.*) contribuer. **~ into**, (*fam.*) s'attaquer à.

pitcher /ˈpɪtʃə(r)/ *n.* cruche *f.*

pitchfork /ˈpɪtʃfɔːk/ *n.* fourche à foin *f.*

pitfall /ˈpɪtfɔːl/ *n.* piège *m.*

pith /pɪθ/ *n.* (*of orange*) peau blanche *f.*; (*essence: fig.*) moelle *f.*

pithy /ˈpɪθɪ/ *a.* (-ier, -iest) (*terse*) concis; (*forceful*) vigoureux.

piti|ful /ˈpɪtɪfl/ *a.* pitoyable. **~less** *a.* impitoyable.

pittance /ˈpɪtns/ *n.* revenu *or* salaire dérisoire *m.*

pity /ˈpɪtɪ/ *n.* pitié *f.*; (*regrettable fact*) dommage *m.* —*v.t.* plaindre. **take ~ on**, avoir pitié de. **what a ~**, quel dommage. **it's a ~**, c'est dommage.

pivot /ˈpɪvət/ *n.* pivot *m.* —*v.i.* (*p.t.* pivoted) pivoter.

pixie /ˈpɪksɪ/ *n.* lutin *m.*

pizza /ˈpiːtsə/ *n.* pizza *f.*

placard /ˈplækɑːd/ *n.* affiche *f.*

placate /pləˈkeɪt, Amer.* ˈpleɪkeɪt/ *v.t.* calmer.

place /pleɪs/ *n.* endroit *m.*, lieu *m.*; (*house*) maison *f.*; (*seat, rank, etc.*) place *f.* —*v.t.* placer; (*an order*) passer; (*remember*) situer. **at or to my ~**, chez moi. **be ~d**, (*in race*) se placer. **change ~s**, changer de place. **in the first ~**, d'abord. **out of ~**, déplacé. **take ~**, avoir lieu. **~-mat** *n.* set *m.*

placenta /pləˈsentə/ *n.* placenta *m.*

placid /ˈplæsɪd/ *a.* placide.

plagiar|ize /ˈpleɪdʒəraɪz/ *v.t.* plagier. **~ism** *n.* plagiat *m.*

plague /pleɪg/ *n.* peste *f.*; (*nuisance: fam.*) fléau *m.* —*v.t.* harceler.

plaice /pleɪs/ *n. invar.* carrelet *m.*

plaid /plæd/ *n.* tissu écossais *m.*

plain /pleɪn/ *a.* (-er, -est) clair; (*candid*) franc; (*simple*) simple; (*not pretty*) sans beauté; (*not patterned*) uni. —*adv.* franchement. —*n.* plaine *f.* **~ chocolate**, chocolat noir. **in ~ clothes**, en

civil. **~ly** *adv.* clairement; franchement; simplement.
~ness *n.* simplicité *f.*

plaintiff /'pleɪntɪf/ *n.* plaignant(e)
m. (*f.*).

plaintive /'pleɪntɪv/ *a.* plaintif.

plait /plæt/ *v.t.* tresser, natter. —*n.*
tresse *f.*, natte *f.*

plan /plæn/ *n.* projet *m.*, plan *m.*;
(*diagram*) plan *m.* —*v.t.* (*p.t.*
planned) prévoir; projeter;
(*arrange*) organiser; (*design*) concevoir; (*economy, work*) planifier.
—*v.i.* faire des projets. **~ to do**,
avoir l'intention de faire.

plane[1] /pleɪn/ *n.* (*tree*) platane *m.*

plane[2] /pleɪn/ *n.* (*level*) plan *m.*;
(*aeroplane*) avion *m.* —*a.* plan.

plane[3] /pleɪn/ *n.* (*tool*) rabot *m.*
—*v.t.* raboter.

planet /'plænɪt/ *n.* planète *f.* **~ary**
a. planétaire.

plank /plæŋk/ *n.* planche *f.*

plankton /'plæŋktn/ *n.* plancton *m.*

planning /'plænɪŋ/ *n.* (*pol., comm.*)
planification *f.* **family ~**, planning familial *m.* **~ permission**,
permis de construire *m.*

plant /plɑːnt/ *n.* plante *f.*; (*techn.*)
matériel *m.*; (*factory*) usine *f.*
—*v.t.* planter; (*bomb*) (dé)poser.
~ation /-'teɪʃn/ *n.* plantation *f.*

plaque /plɑːk/ *n.* plaque *f.*

plasma /'plæzmə/ *n.* plasma *m.*

plaster /'plɑːstə(r)/ *n.* plâtre *m.*;
(*adhesive*) sparadrap *m.* —*v.t.*
plâtrer; (*cover*) tapisser (**with**,
de). **in ~**, dans le plâtre. **~ of
Paris**, plâtre à mouler *m.* **~er** *n.*
plâtrier *m.*

plastic /'plæstɪk/ *a.* en plastique;
(*art, substance*) plastique. —*n.*
plastique *m.* **~ surgery**,
chirurgie esthétique *f.*

Plasticine /'plæstɪsiːn/ *n.* (P.) pâte
à modeler *f.*

plate /pleɪt/ *n.* assiette *f.*; (*of metal*)
plaque *f.*; (*gold or silver dishes*)
vaisselle plate *f.*; (*in book*)

gravure *f.* —*v.t.* (*metal*) plaquer.
~ful *n.* (*pl.* **-fuls**) assiettée *f.*

plateau /'plætəʊ/ *n.* (*pl.* **-eaux**
/-əʊz/) plateau *m.*

platform /'plætfɔːm/ *n.* (*in classroom, hall, etc.*) estrade *f.*; (*for
speaking*) tribune *f.*; (*rail.*) quai
m.; (*of bus & pol.*) plate-forme *f.*

platinum /'plætɪnəm/ *n.* platine *m.*

platitude /'plætɪtjuːd/ *n.* platitude
f.

platonic /plə'tɒnɪk/ *a.* platonique.

platoon /plə'tuːn/ *n.* (*mil.*) section
f.

platter /'plætə(r)/ *n.* plat *m.*

plausible /'plɔːzəbl/ *a.* plausible.

play /pleɪ/ *v.t./i.* jouer; (*instrument*) jouer de; (*record*) passer;
(*game*) jouer à; (*opponent*) jouer
contre; (*match*) disputer. —*n.* jeu
m.; (*theatre*) pièce *f.* **~act** *v.i.*
jouer la comédie. **~ down**,
minimiser. **~group**, **~school**
ns. garderie *f.* **~off** *n.* (*sport*)
belle *f.* **~ on**, (*take advantage of*)
jouer sur. **~ on words**, jeu de
mots *m.* **~ed out**, épuisé. **~pen**
n. parc *m.* **~ safe**, ne pas prendre
de risques. **~ up**, (*fam.*) créer des
problèmes (à). **~ up to**, flatter.
~er *n.* joueu|r, -se *m.*, *f.*

playboy /'pleɪbɔɪ/ *n.* play-boy *m.*

playful /'pleɪfl/ *a.* enjoué; (*child*)
joueur. **~ly** *adv.* avec espièglerie.

playground /'pleɪgraʊnd/ *n.* cour
de récréation *f.*

playing /'pleɪɪŋ/ *n.* jeu *m.* **~card**
n. carte à jouer *f.* **~field** *n.*
terrain de sport *m.*

playmate /'pleɪmeɪt/ *n.* camarade
m./f., cop|ain, -ine *m.*, *f.*

plaything /'pleɪθɪŋ/ *n.* jouet *m.*

playwright /'pleɪraɪt/ *n.* dramaturge *m./f.*

plc *abbr.* (**public limited company**)
SA.

plea /pliː/ *n.* (*entreaty*) supplica-
tion *f.*; (*reason*) excuse *f.*; (*jurid.*)
défense *f.*

plead /pliːd/ *v.t./i.* (*jurid.*) plaider; (*as excuse*) alléguer. ~ **for**, (*beg for*) implorer. ~ **with**, (*beg*) implorer.

pleasant /'pleznt/ *a.* agréable. ~**ly** *adv.* agréablement.

please /pliːz/ *v.t./i.* plaire (à), faire plaisir (à). —*adv.* s'il vous or te plaît. ~ **o.s.**, **do as one** ~**s**, faire ce qu'on veut. ~**d** *a.* content (**with**, de). **pleasing** *a.* agréable.

pleasur|e /'pleʒə(r)/ *n.* plaisir *m.* ~**able** *a.* très agréable.

pleat /pliːt/ *n.* pli *m.* —*v.t.* plisser.

plebiscite /'plebɪsɪt/ *n.* plébiscite *m.*

pledge /pledʒ/ *n.* (*token*) gage *m.*; (*fig.*) promesse *f.* —*v.t.* promettre; (*pawn*) engager.

plentiful /'plentɪfl/ *a.* abondant.

plenty /'plentɪ/ *n.* abondance *f.* ~ (**of**), (*a great deal*) beaucoup (de); (*enough*) assez (de).

pleurisy /'plʊərəsɪ/ *n.* pleurésie *f.*

pliable /'plaɪəbl/ *a.* souple.

pliers /'plaɪəz/ *n. pl.* pince(s) *f. (pl.)*.

plight /plaɪt/ *n.* triste situation *f.*

plimsoll /'plɪms(ə)l/ *n.* chaussure de gym *f.*

plinth /plɪnθ/ *n.* socle *m.*

plod /plɒd/ *v.i.* (*p.t.* **plodded**) avancer péniblement *or* d'un pas lent; (*work*) bûcher. ~**der** *n.* bûcheu|r, -se *m., f.* ~**ding** *a.* lent.

plonk /plɒŋk/ *n.* (*sl.*) pinard *m.* —*v.t.* ~ **down**, poser lourdement.

plot /plɒt/ *n.* complot *m.*; (*of novel etc.*) intrigue *f.* ~ (**of land**), terrain *m.* —*v.t./i.* (*p.t.* **plotted**) comploter; (*mark out*) tracer.

plough /plaʊ/ *n.* charrue *f.* —*v.t./i.* labourer. ~ **back**, réinvestir. ~ **into**, rentrer dans. ~ **through**, avancer péniblement dans.

plow /plaʊ/ *n. & v.t./i.* (*Amer.*) = **plough**.

ploy /plɔɪ/ *n.* (*fam.*) stratagème *m.*

pluck /plʌk/ *v.t.* cueillir; (*bird*) plumer; (*eyebrows*) épiler; (*strings: mus.*) pincer. —*n.* courage *m.* ~ **up courage**, prendre son courage à deux mains. ~**y** *a.* courageux.

plug /plʌg/ *n.* (*of cloth, paper, etc.*) tampon *m.*; (*for sink etc.*) bonde *f.*; (*electr.*) fiche *f.*, prise *f.* —*v.t.* (*p.t.* **plugged**) (*hole*) boucher; (*publicize: fam.*) faire du battage autour de. —*v.i.* ~ **away**, (*work: fam.*) bosser. ~ **in**, brancher. ~**hole** *n.* vidange *f.*

plum /plʌm/ *n.* prune *f.* ~ **job**, travail en *or* *m.* ~ **pudding**, (plum-)pudding *m.*

plumb /plʌm/ *adv.* tout à fait. —*v.t.* (*probe*) sonder. ~**line** *n.* fil à plomb *m.*

plumb|er /'plʌmə(r)/ *n.* plombier *m.* ~**ing** *n.* plomberie *f.*

plum|e /pluːm/ *n.* plume(s) *f. (pl.)*. ~**age** *n.* plumage *m.*

plummet /'plʌmɪt/ *v.i.* (*p.t.* **plummeted**) tomber, plonger.

plump /plʌmp/ *a.* (-**er**, -**est**) potelé, dodu. —*v.i.* ~ **for**, choisir. ~**ness** *n.* rondeur *f.*

plunder /'plʌndə(r)/ *v.t.* piller. —*n.* (*act*) pillage *m.*; (*goods*) butin *m.*

plunge /plʌndʒ/ *v.t.* (*dive, thrust*) plonger; (*fall*) tomber. —*n.* plongeon *m.*; (*fall*) chute *f.* **take the** ~, se jeter à l'eau.

plunger /'plʌndʒə(r)/ *n.* (*for sink etc.*) ventouse *f.*, débouchoir *m.*

plural /'plʊərəl/ *a.* pluriel; (*noun*) au pluriel. —*n.* pluriel *m.*

plus /plʌs/ *prep.* plus. —*a.* (*electr. & fig.*) positif. —*n.* signe plus *m.*; (*fig.*) atout *m.* **ten** ~, plus de dix.

plush(y) /plʌʃ(ɪ)/ *a.* somptueux.

ply /plaɪ/ *v.t.* (*tool*) manier; (*trade*) exercer. —*v.i.* faire la navette. ~ **s.o. with drink**, offrir continuellement à boire à qn.

plywood /'plaɪwʊd/ n. contreplaqué m.

p.m. /pi:'em/ adv. de l'après-midi or du soir.

pneumatic /nju:'mætɪk/ a. pneumatique. **~ drill**, marteau-piqueur m.

pneumonia /nju:'məʊnɪə/ n. pneumonie f.

PO abbr. see Post Office.

poach /pəʊtʃ/ v.t./i. (game) braconner; (staff) débaucher; (culin.) pocher. **~er** n. braconnier m.

pocket /'pɒkɪt/ n. poche f. —a. de poche. —v.t. empocher. **be out of ~**, avoir perdu de l'argent. **~-book** n. (notebook) carnet m.; (wallet: Amer.) portefeuille m.; (handbag: Amer.) sac à main m. **~-money** n. argent de poche m.

pock-marked /'pɒkmɑːkt/ a. (face etc.) grêlé.

pod /pɒd/ n. (peas etc.) cosse f.; (vanilla) gousse f.

podgy /'pɒdʒɪ/ a. (**-ier**, **-iest**) dodu.

poem /'pəʊɪm/ n. poème m.

poet /'pəʊɪt/ n. poète m. **~ic** /-'etɪk/ a. poétique.

poetry /'pəʊɪtrɪ/ n. poésie f.

poignant /'pɔɪnjənt/ a. poignant.

point /pɔɪnt/ n. point m.; (tip) pointe f.; (decimal point) virgule f.; (meaning) sens m., intérêt m.; (remark) remarque f. **~s**, (rail.) aiguillage m. —v.t. indiquer du doigt (at or to s.o., qn.). **~ out that**, **make the ~ that**, faire remarquer que. **good ~s**, qualités f. pl. **make a ~ of doing**, ne pas manquer de faire. **on the ~ of**, sur le point de. **~-blank** a. & adv. à bout portant. **~ in time**, moment m. **~ of view**, point de vue m. **~ out**, signaler. **to the ~**, pertinent. **what is the ~?**, à quoi bon?

pointed /'pɔɪntɪd/ a. pointu; (remark) lourd de sens.

pointer /'pɔɪntə(r)/ n. (indicator) index m.; (dog) chien d'arrêt m.; (advice: fam.) tuyau m.

pointless /'pɔɪntlɪs/ a. inutile.

poise /pɔɪz/ n. équilibre m.; (carriage) maintien m.; (fig.) assurance f. **~d** a. en équilibre; (confident) assuré. **~d for**, prêt à.

poison /'pɔɪzn/ n. poison m. —v.t. empoisonner. **~ous** a. (substance etc.) toxique; (plant) vénéneux; (snake) venimeux.

poke /pəʊk/ v.t./i. (push) pousser; (fire) tisonner; (thrust) fourrer. —n. (petit) coup m. **~ about**, fureter. **~ fun at**, se moquer de. **~ out**, (head) sortir.

poker[1] /'pəʊkə(r)/ n. tisonnier m.

poker[2] /'pəʊkə(r)/ n. (cards) poker m.

poky /'pəʊkɪ/ a. (**-ier**, **-iest**) (small) exigu; (slow: Amer.) lent.

Poland /'pəʊlənd/ n. Pologne f.

polar /'pəʊlə(r)/ a. polaire. **~ bear**, ours blanc m.

polarize /'pəʊləraɪz/ v.t. polariser.

Polaroid /'pəʊlərɔɪd/ n. (P.) polaroïd (P.) m.

pole[1] /pəʊl/ n. (fixed) poteau m.; (rod) perche f.; (for flag) mât m. **~-vault** n. saut à la perche m.

pole[2] /pəʊl/ n. (geog.) pôle m.

Pole /pəʊl/ n. Polonais(e) m. (f.).

polemic /pə'lemɪk/ n. polémique f.

police /pə'liːs/ n. police f. —v.t. faire la police dans. **~ state**, état policier m. **~ station**, commissariat de police m.

police|man /pə'liːsmən/ n. (pl. **-men**) agent de police m. **~woman** (pl. **-women**) femme-agent f.

policy[1] /'pɒlɪsɪ/ n. politique f.

policy[2] /'pɒlɪsɪ/ n. (insurance) police (d'assurance) f.

polio(myelitis) /'pəʊlɪəʊ(maɪə-'laɪtɪs)/ n. polio(myélite) f.

polish /'pɒlɪʃ/ v.t. polir; (*shoes, floor*) cirer. —n. (*for shoes*) cirage m.; (*for floor*) encaustique f.; (*for nails*) vernis m.; (*shine*) poli m.; (*fig.*) raffinement m. ~ **off**, finir en vitesse. ~ **up**, (*language*) perfectionner. ~**ed** a. raffiné.

Polish /'pəʊlɪʃ/ a. polonais. —n. (*lang.*) polonais m.

polite /pə'laɪt/ a. poli. ~**ly** adv. poliment. ~**ness** n. politesse f.

political /pə'lɪtɪkl/ a. politique.

politician /pɒlɪ'tɪʃn/ n. homme politique m., femme politique f.

politics /'pɒlətɪks/ n. politique f.

polka /'pɒlkə, *Amer.* 'pəʊlkə/ n. polka f. ~ **dots**, pois m. pl.

poll /pəʊl/ n. scrutin m.; (*survey*) sondage m. —v.t. (*votes*) obtenir. **go to the ~s**, aller aux urnes. ~**ing-booth** n. isoloir m. ~**ing station**, bureau de vote m.

pollen /'pɒlən/ n. pollen m.

pollut|e /pə'luːt/ v.t. polluer. ~**ion** /-ʃn/ n. pollution f.

polo /'pəʊləʊ/ n. polo m. ~ **neck**, col roulé m. ~ **shirt**, polo m.

polyester /pɒlɪ'estə(r)/ n. polyester m.

polygamy /pə'lɪgəmɪ/ n. polygamie f.

polytechnic /pɒlɪ'teknɪk/ n. institut universitaire de technologie m.

polythene /'pɒlɪθiːn/ n. polythène m., polyéthylène m.

pomegranate /'pɒmɪgrænɪt/ n. (*fruit*) grenade f.

pomp /pɒmp/ n. pompe f.

pompon /'pɒmpɒn/ n. pompon m.

pomp|ous /'pɒmpəs/ a. pompeux. ~**osity** /-'pɒsətɪ/ n. solennité f.

pond /pɒnd/ n. étang m.; (*artificial*) bassin m.; (*stagnant*) mare f.

ponder /'pɒndə(r)/ v.t./i. réfléchir (à), méditer (sur).

ponderous /'pɒndərəs/ a. pesant.

pong /pɒŋ/ n. (*stink: sl.*) puanteur f. —v.i. (*sl.*) puer.

pony /'pəʊnɪ/ n. poney m. ~**-tail** n. queue de cheval f.

poodle /'puːdl/ n. caniche m.

pool[1] /puːl/ n. (*puddle*) flaque f.; (*pond*) étang m.; (*of blood*) mare f.; (*of swimming*) piscine f.

pool[2] /puːl/ n. (*fund*) fonds commun m., (*of ideas*) réservoir m.; (*of typists*) pool m.; (*snooker*) billard américain m. ~**s**, pari mutuel sur le football m. —v.t. mettre en commun.

poor /pɔː(r)/ a. (-er, -est) pauvre; (*not good*) médiocre, mauvais. ~**ly** adv. mal; a. malade.

pop[1] /pɒp/ n. (*noise*) bruit sec m. —v.t./i. (*p.t.* **popped**) (*burst*) crever; (*put*) mettre. ~ **in/out/off**, entrer/sortir/partir. ~ **over**, faire un saut (**to see s.o.**, chez qn.). ~ **up**, surgir.

pop[2] /pɒp/ n. (*mus.*) musique pop f. —a. pop invar.

popcorn /'pɒpkɔːn/ n. pop-corn m.

pope /pəʊp/ n. pape m.

poplar /'pɒplə(r)/ n. peuplier m.

poppy /'pɒpɪ/ n. pavot m.; (*wild*) coquelicot m.

popsicle /'pɒpsɪkl/ n. (P.) (*Amer.*) glace à l'eau f.

popular /'pɒpjʊlə(r)/ a. populaire; (*in fashion*) en vogue. **be ~ with**, plaire à. ~**ity** /-'lærətɪ/ n. popularité f. ~**ize** v.t. populariser. ~**ly** adv. communément.

populat|e /'pɒpjʊleɪt/ v.t. peupler. ~**ion** /-'leɪʃn/ n. population f.

populous /'pɒpjʊləs/ a. populeux.

porcelain /'pɔːsəlɪn/ n. porcelaine f.

porch /pɔːtʃ/ n. porche m.

porcupine /'pɔːkjʊpaɪn/ n. (*rodent*) porc-épic m.

pore[1] /pɔː(r)/ n. pore m.

pore[2] /pɔː(r)/ v.i. ~ **over**, étudier minutieusement.

pork /pɔːk/ n. (food) porc m.

pornograph|y /pɔːˈnɒgrəfɪ/ n. pornographie f. **~ic** /-əˈgræfɪk/ a. pornographique.

porous /ˈpɔːrəs/ a. poreux.

porpoise /ˈpɔːpəs/ n. marsouin m.

porridge /ˈpɒrɪdʒ/ n. porridge m.

port[1] /pɔːt/ n. (harbour) port m. **~ of call**, escale f.

port[2] /pɔːt/ n. (left: naut.) bâbord m.

port[3] /pɔːt/ n. (wine) porto m.

portable /ˈpɔːtəbl/ a. portatif.

portal /ˈpɔːtl/ n. portail m.

porter[1] /ˈpɔːtə(r)/ n. (carrier) porteur m.

porter[2] /ˈpɔːtə(r)/ n. (door-keeper) portier m.

portfolio /pɔːtˈfəʊliəʊ/ n. (pl. -os) (pol., comm.) portefeuille m.

porthole /ˈpɔːthəʊl/ n. hublot m.

portico /ˈpɔːtɪkəʊ/ n. (pl. -oes) portique m.

portion /ˈpɔːʃn/ n. (share, helping) portion f.; (part) partie f.

portly /ˈpɔːtlɪ/ a. (-ier, -iest) corpulent (et digne).

portrait /ˈpɔːtrɪt/ n. portrait m.

portray /pɔːˈtreɪ/ v.t. représenter. **~al** n. portrait m., peinture f.

Portug|al /ˈpɔːtjʊgl/ n. Portugal m. **~uese** /-ˈgiːz/ a. & n. invar. portugais(e) (m. & f.)).

pose /pəʊz/ v.t./i. poser. —n. pose f. **~ as**, (expert etc.) se poser en.

poser /ˈpəʊzə(r)/ n. colle f.

posh /pɒʃ/ a. (sl.) chic invar.

position /pəˈzɪʃn/ n. position f.; (job, state) situation f. —v.t. placer.

positive /ˈpɒzətɪv/ a. (test, help, etc.) positif; (sure) sûr, certain; (real) véritable, vrai. **~ly** adv. positivement; (absolutely) complètement.

possess /pəˈzes/ v.t. posséder. **~ion** /-ʃn/ n. possession f. **take ~ion of**, prendre possession de. **~or** n. possesseur m.

possessive /pəˈzesɪv/ a. possessif.

possib|le /ˈpɒsəbl/ a. possible. **~ility** /-ˈbɪlətɪ/ n. possibilité f.

possibly /ˈpɒsəblɪ/ adv. peut-être. **if I ~ can**, si cela m'est possible. **I cannot ~ leave**, il m'est impossible de partir.

post[1] /pəʊst/ n. (pole) poteau m. —v.t. (up), (a notice) afficher.

post[2] /pəʊst/ n. (station, job) poste m. —v.t. (appoint) affecter.

post[3] /pəʊst/ n. (mail service) poste f.; (letters) courrier m. —a. postal. —v.t. (put in box) poster; (send) envoyer (par la poste). **catch the last ~**, attraper la dernière levée. **keep ~ed**, tenir au courant. **~box** n. boîte à or aux lettres f. **~code** n. code postal m. **P~ Office**, postes f.pl.; (in France) Postes et Télécommunications f. pl. **~ office**, bureau de poste m., poste f.

post- /pəʊst/ pref. post-.

postage /ˈpəʊstɪdʒ/ n. tarif postal m., frais de port m.pl.

postal /ˈpəʊstl/ a. postal. **~ order**, mandat m. **~ worker**, employé(e) des postes m. (f.).

postcard /ˈpəʊstkɑːd/ n. carte postale f.

poster /ˈpəʊstə(r)/ n. affiche f.; (for decoration) poster m.

posterior /pɒˈstɪərɪə(r)/ n. postérieur m.

posterity /pɒˈsterətɪ/ n. postérité f.

postgraduate /pəʊstˈgrædʒʊət/ n. étudiant(e) de troisième cycle m. (f.).

posthumous /ˈpɒstjʊməs/ a. posthume. **~ly** adv. à titre posthume.

postman /ˈpəʊstmən/ n. (pl. -men) facteur m.

postmark /ˈpəʊstmɑːk/ n. cachet de la poste m.

postmaster /ˈpəʊstmɑːstə(r)/ n. receveur des postes m.

post-mortem /ˌpəʊstˈmɔːtəm/ *n.* autopsie *f.*

postpone /pəˈspəʊn/ *v.t.* remettre. **~ment** *n.* ajournement *m.*

postscript /ˈpəʊskrɪpt/ *n.* (*to letter*) post-scriptum *m. invar.*

postulate /ˈpɒstjʊleɪt/ *v.t.* postuler.

posture /ˈpɒstʃə(r)/ *n.* posture *f.* —*v.i.* (*affectedly*) prendre des poses.

post-war /ˈpəʊstwɔː(r)/ *a.* d'après-guerre.

pot /pɒt/ *n.* pot *m.*; (*for cooking*) marmite *f.*; (*drug: sl.*) marie-jeanne *f.* —*v.t.* (*plants*) mettre en pot. **go to ~,** (*sl.*) aller à la ruine. **~-belly** *n.* gros ventre *m.* **take ~ luck,** tenter sa chance. **take a ~-shot at,** faire un carton sur.

potato /pəˈteɪtəʊ/ *n.* (*pl.* -oes) pomme de terre *f.*

poten|t /ˈpəʊtnt/ *a.* puissant; (*drink*) fort. **~cy** *n.* puissance *f.*

potential /pəˈtenʃl/ *a.* & *n.* potentiel (*m.*). **~ly** *adv.* potentiellement.

pot-hol|e /ˈpɒthəʊl/ *n.* (*in rock*) caverne *f.*; (*in road*) nid de poule *m.* **~ing** *n.* spéléologie *f.*

potion /ˈpəʊʃn/ *n.* potion *f.*

potted /ˈpɒtɪd/ *a.* (*plant etc.*) en pot; (*preserved*) en conserve; (*abridged*) condensé.

potter[1] /ˈpɒtə(r)/ *n.* potier *m.* **~y** *n.* (*art*) poterie *f.*; (*objects*) poteries *f.pl.*

potter[2] /ˈpɒtə(r)/ *v.i.* bricoler.

potty /ˈpɒtɪ/ *a.* (-ier, -iest) (*crazy: sl.*) toqué. —*n.* pot *m.*

pouch /paʊtʃ/ *n.* poche *f.*; (*for tobacco*) blague *f.*

pouffe /puːf/ *n.* pouf *m.*

poultice /ˈpəʊltɪs/ *n.* cataplasme *m.*

poult|ry /ˈpəʊltrɪ/ *n.* volaille *f.* **~erer** *n.* marchand de volailles *m.*

pounce /paʊns/ *v.i.* bondir (**on,** sur). —*n.* bond *m.*

pound[1] /paʊnd/ *n.* (*weight*) livre *f.* (= 454 *g.*); (*money*) livre *f.*

pound[2] /paʊnd/ *n.* (*for dogs, cars*) fourrière *f.*

pound[3] /paʊnd/ *v.t.* (*crush*) piler; (*bombard*) pilonner. —*v.i.* frapper fort; (*of heart*) battre fort; (*walk*) marcher à pas lourds.

pour /pɔː(r)/ *v.t.* verser. —*v.i.* couler, ruisseler (**from,** de); (*rain*) pleuvoir à torrents. **~ in/out,** (*people*) arriver/sortir en masse. **~ off** *or* **out,** vider. **~ing rain,** pluie torrentielle *f.*

pout /paʊt/ *v.t./i.* **~ (one's lips),** faire la moue. —*n.* moue *f.*

poverty /ˈpɒvətɪ/ *n.* misère *f.*, pauvreté *f.*

powder /ˈpaʊdə(r)/ *n.* poudre *f.* —*v.t.* poudrer. **~ed** *a.* en poudre. **~y** *a.* poudreux. **~-room** *n.* toilettes pour dames *f. pl.*

power /ˈpaʊə(r)/ *n.* puissance *f.*; (*ability, authority*) pouvoir *m.*; (*energy*) énergie *f.*; (*electr.*) courant *m.* **~ cut,** coupure de courant *f.* **~ed by,** fonctionnant à; (*jet etc.*) propulsé par. **~less** *a.* impuissant. **~ point,** prise de courant *f.* **~-station** *n.* centrale électrique *f.*

powerful /ˈpaʊəfl/ *a.* puissant. **~ly** *adv.* puissamment.

practicable /ˈpræktɪkəbl/ *a.* praticable.

practical /ˈpræktɪkl/ *a.* pratique. **~ity** /-ˈkælətɪ/ *n.* sens *or* aspect pratique *m.* **~ joke,** farce *f.*

practically /ˈpræktɪklɪ/ *adv.* pratiquement.

practice /ˈpræktɪs/ *n.* pratique *f.*; (*of profession*) exercice *m.*; (*sport*) entraînement *m.*; (*clients*) clientèle *f.* **be in ~,** (*doctor, lawyer*) exercer. **in ~,** (*in fact*) en pratique; (*well-trained*) en forme.

out of ~, rouillé. **put into** ~,
mettre en pratique.

practis|e /'præktɪs/ *v.t./i.* (*musician, typist, etc.*) s'exercer (à);
(*sport*) s'entraîner (à); (*put into practice*) pratiquer; (*profession*)
exercer. **~ed** *a.* expérimenté.
~ing *a.* (*Catholic etc.*) pratiquant.

practitioner /præk'tɪʃənə(r)/ *n.*
praticien(ne) *m.* (*f.*).

pragmatic /præg'mætɪk/ *a.* pragmatique.

prairie /'preərɪ/ *n.* (*in North America*) prairie *f.*

praise /preɪz/ *v.t.* louer. —*n.*
éloge(s) *m.* (*pl.*), louange(s) *f.* (*pl.*).

praiseworthy /'preɪzwɜːðɪ/ *a.*
digne d'éloges.

pram /præm/ *n.* voiture d'enfant *f.*,
landau *m.*

prance /prɑːns/ *v.i.* caracoler.

prank /præŋk/ *n.* farce *f.*

prattle /'prætl/ *v.i.* jaser.

prawn /prɔːn/ *n.* crevette rose *f.*

pray /preɪ/ *v.i.* prier.

prayer /preə(r)/ *n.* prière *f.*

pre- /priː/ *pref.* pré-.

preach /priːtʃ/ *v.t./i.* prêcher. **~ at**
or **to**, prêcher. **~er** *n.*
prédicateur *m.*

preamble /priː'æmbl/ *n.* préambule *m.*

pre-arrange /priːə'reɪndʒ/ *v.t.*
fixer à l'avance.

precarious /prɪ'keərɪəs/ *a.* précaire.

precaution /prɪ'kɔːʃn/ *n.* précaution *f.* **~ary** *a.* de précaution.

preced|e /prɪ'siːd/ *v.t.* précéder.
~ing *a.* précédent.

precedence /'presɪdəns/ *n.* priorité *f.*; (*in rank*) préséance *f.*

precedent /'presɪdənt/ *n.* précédent *m.*

precept /'priːsept/ *n.* précepte *m.*

precinct /'priːsɪŋkt/ *n.* enceinte *f.*;
(*pedestrian area*) zone *f.*; (*district: Amer.*) circonscription *f.*

precious /'preʃəs/ *a.* précieux.
—*adv.* (*very: fam.*) très.

precipice /'presɪpɪs/ *n.* (*geog.*) à-pic *m. invar.*; (*fig.*) précipice *m.*

precipitat|e /prɪ'sɪpɪteɪt/ *v.t.* (*person, event, chemical*) précipiter.
—*a.* /-ɪtət/ précipité. **~ion**
/-'teɪʃn/ *n.* précipitation *f.*

précis /'preɪsiː/ *n. invar.* précis *m.*

precis|e /prɪ'saɪs/ *a.* précis;
(*careful*) méticuleux. **~ely** *adv.*
précisément. **~ion** /-'sɪʒn/ *n.*
précision *f.*

preclude /prɪ'kluːd/ *v.t.* (*prevent*)
empêcher; (*rule out*) exclure.

precocious /prɪ'kəʊʃəs/ *a.* précoce.

preconc|eived /priːkən'siːvd/ *a.*
préconçu. **~eption** *n.* préconception *f.*

pre-condition /priːkən'dɪʃn/ *n.*
condition requise *f.*

predator /'predətə(r)/ *n.* prédateur *m.* **~y** *a.* rapace.

predecessor /'priːdɪsesə(r)/ *n.*
prédécesseur *m.*

predicament /prɪ'dɪkəmənt/ *n.*
mauvaise situation *or* passe *f.*

predict /prɪ'dɪkt/ *v.t.* prédire.
~able *a.* prévisible. **~ion** /-kʃn/
n. prédiction *f.*

predispose /priːdɪ'spəʊz/ *v.t.*
prédisposer (**to do,** à faire).

predominant /prɪ'dɒmɪnənt/ *a.*
prédominant. **~ly** *adv.* pour la
plupart.

predominate /prɪ'dɒmɪneɪt/ *v.i.*
prédominer.

pre-eminent /priː'emɪnənt/ *a.*
prééminent.

pre-empt /priː'empt/ *v.t.* (*buy*)
acquérir d'avance; (*stop*) prévenir. **~ive** *a.* preventif.

preen /priːn/ *v.t.* (*bird*) lisser. **~ o.s.,** (*person*) se bichonner.

prefab /'priːfæb/ *n.* (*fam.*) bâtiment préfabriqué *m.* **~ricated**
/-'fæbrɪkeɪtɪd/ *a.* préfabriqué.

preface /'prefɪs/ n. préface f.

prefect /'priːfekt/ n. (pupil) élève chargé(e) de la discipline m.(f.); (official) préfet m.

prefer /prɪ'fɜː(r)/ v.t. (p.t. preferred) préférer (**to do**, faire). **~able** /'prefrəbl/ a. préférable. **~ably** adv. de préférence.

preferen|ce /'prefrəns/ n. préférence f. **~tial** /-ə'renʃl/ a. préférentiel.

prefix /'priːfɪks/ n. préfixe m.

pregnan|t /'pregnənt/ a. (woman) enceinte; (animal) pleine. **~cy** n. (of woman) grossesse f.

prehistoric /priːhɪ'stɒrɪk/ a. préhistorique.

prejudge /priː'dʒʌdʒ/ v.t. préjuger de; (person) juger d'avance.

prejudice /'predʒʊdɪs/ n. préjugé(s) m. (pl.); (harm) préjudice m. —v.t. (claim) porter préjudice à; (person) prévenir. **~d** a. partial; (person) qui a des préjugés.

preliminar|y /prɪ'lɪmɪnərɪ/ a. préliminaire. **~ies** n. pl. préliminaires m. pl.

prelude /'preljuːd/ n. prélude m.

pre-marital /priː'mærɪtl/ a. avant le mariage.

premature /'premətjʊə(r)/ a. prématuré.

premeditated /priː'medɪteɪtɪd/ a. prémédité.

premier /'premɪə(r)/ a. premier. —n. premier ministre m.

première /'premɪeə(r)/ n. première f.

premises /'premɪsɪz/ n. pl. locaux m. pl. **on the ~**, sur les lieux.

premiss /'premɪs/ n. prémisse f.

premium /'priːmɪəm/ n. prime f. **be at a ~**, faire prime.

premonition /priːmə'nɪʃn/ n. prémonition f., pressentiment m.

preoccupation /priːɒkjʊ'peɪʃn/ n. préoccupation f. **~ied** /-'ɒkjʊpaɪd/ a. préoccupé.

prep /prep/ n. (work) devoirs m.pl. **~ school** = **preparatory school.**

preparation /prepə'reɪʃn/ n. préparation f. **~s**, préparatifs m. pl.

preparatory /prɪ'pærətrɪ/ a. préparatoire. **~ school**, école primaire privée f.; (Amer.) école secondaire privée f.

prepare /prɪ'peə(r)/ v.t./i. (se) préparer (**for**, à). **be ~d for** (expect) s'attendre à. **~d to**, prêt à.

prepay /priː'peɪ/ v.t. (p.t. **-paid**) payer d'avance.

preponderance /prɪ'pɒndərəns/ n. prédominance f.

preposition /prepə'zɪʃn/ n. préposition f.

preposterous /prɪ'pɒstərəs/ a. absurde, ridicule.

prerequisite /priː'rekwɪzɪt/ n. condition préalable f.

prerogative /prɪ'rɒgətɪv/ n. prérogative f.

Presbyterian /prezbɪ'tɪərɪən/ a. & n. presbytérien(ne) (m. (f.)).

prescri|be /prɪ'skraɪb/ v.t. prescrire. **~ption** /-ɪpʃn/n. prescription f.; (med.) ordonnance f.

presence /'prezns/ n. présence f. **~ of mind**, présence d'esprit f.

present[1] /'preznt/ a. présent. —n. présent m. **at ~**, à présent. **for the ~**, pour le moment. **~-day** a. actuel.

present[2] /'preznt/ n. (gift) cadeau m.

present[3] /prɪ'zent/ v.t. présenter; (film, concert, etc.) donner. **~ s.o. with**, offrir à qn. **~able** a. présentable. **~ation** /prezn'teɪʃn/ n. présentation f. **~er** n. présenta|teur, -trice m., f.

presently /'prezntlɪ/ adv. bientôt; (now: Amer.) en ce moment.

preservative /prɪ'zɜːvətɪv/ n. (culin.) agent de conservation m.

preserv|e /prɪ'zɜːv/ v.t. préserver; (*maintain & culin.*) conserver. —n. réserve f.; (*fig.*) domaine m.; (*jam*) confiture f. **~ation** /preza'veɪʃn/ n. conservation f.

preside /prɪ'zaɪd/ v.i. présider. **~ over**, présider.

presiden|t /'prezɪdənt/ n. président(e) m. (f.). **~cy** n. présidence f. **~tial** /-'denʃl/ a. présidentiel.

press /pres/ v.t./i. (*button etc.*) appuyer (sur); (*squeeze*) presser; (*iron*) repasser; (*pursue*) poursuivre. —n. (*newspapers, machine*) presse f.; (*for wine*) pressoir m. **be ~ed for**, (*time etc.*) manquer de. **~ for sth.**, faire pression pour avoir qch. **~s.o. to do sth.**, pousser qn. à faire qch. **~ conference/cutting**, conférence/coupure de presse f. **~ on**, continuer (**with sth.**, qch.). **~ release**, communiqué de presse m. **~-stud** n. bouton-pression m. **~-up** n. traction f.

pressing /'presɪŋ/ a. pressant.

pressure /'preʃə(r)/ n. pression f. —v.t. faire pression sur. **~cooker** n. cocotte-minute f. **~ group**, groupe de pression m.

pressurize /'preʃəraɪz/ v.t. (*cabin etc.*) pressuriser; (*person*) faire pression sur.

prestige /pre'stiːʒ/ n. prestige m.

prestigious /pre'stɪdʒəs/ a. prestigieux.

presumably /prɪ'zjuːməblɪ/ adv. vraisemblablement.

presum|e /prɪ'zjuːm/ v.t. (*suppose*) présumer. **~e to**, (*venture*) se permettre de. **~ption** /-'zʌmpʃn/ n. présomption f.

presumptuous /prɪ'zʌmptʃʊəs/ a. présomptueux.

pretence, (*Amer.*) **pretense** /prɪ'tens/ n. feinte f., simulation f.; (*claim*) prétention f.; (*pretext*) prétexte m.

pretend /prɪ'tend/ v.t./i. faire semblant (**to do**, de faire). **~ to**, (*lay claim to*) prétendre à.

pretentious /prɪ'tenʃəs/ a. prétentieux.

pretext /'priːtekst/ n. prétexte m.

pretty /'prɪtɪ/ a. (-**ier**, -**iest**) joli. —adv. assez. **~ much**, presque.

prevail /prɪ'veɪl/ v.t. prédominer; (*win*) prévaloir. **~ on**, persuader (**to do**, de faire). **~ing** a. actuel; (*wind*) dominant.

prevalen|t /'prevələnt/ a. répandu. **~ce** n. fréquence f.

prevent /prɪ'vent/ v.t. empêcher (**from doing**, de faire). **~able** a. évitable. **~ion** /-enʃn/ n. prévention f. **~ive** a. préventif.

preview /'priːvjuː/ n. avant-première f.; (*fig.*) aperçu m.

previous /'priːvɪəs/ a. précédent, antérieur. **~ to**, avant. **~ly** adv. précédemment, auparavant.

pre-war /'priːwɔː(r)/ a. d'avant-guerre.

prey /preɪ/ n. proie f. —v.i. **~ on**, faire sa proie de; (*worry*) préoccuper. **bird of ~**, rapace m.

price /praɪs/ n. prix m. —v.t. fixer le prix de. **~less** a. inestimable; (*amusing*: sl.) impayable.

pricey /'praɪsɪ/ a. (*fam.*) coûteux.

prick /prɪk/ v.t. (*with pin etc.*) piquer. —n. piqûre f. **~ up one's ears**, dresser l'oreille.

prickl|e /'prɪkl/ n. piquant m.; (*sensation*) picotement m. **~y** a. piquant; (*person*) irritable.

pride /praɪd/ n. orgueil m.; (*satisfaction*) fierté f. —v. pr. **~ o.s. on**, s'enorgueillir de. **~ of place**, place d'honneur f.

priest /priːst/ n. prêtre m. **~hood** n. sacerdoce m. **~ly** a. sacerdotal.

prig /prɪg/ n. petit saint m., pharisien(ne) m. (f.). **~gish** a. hypocrite.

prim /prɪm/ a. (**primmer**, **primmest**) guindé, méticuleux.

primar|y /'praɪmərɪ/ a. (school, elections, etc.) primaire; (chief, basic) premier, fondamental. —n. (pol.: Amer.) primaire m. ~ily Amer. /-'merɪlɪ/ adv. essentiellement.

prime[1] /praɪm/ a. principal, premier; (first-rate) excellent. **P~ Minister**, Premier Ministre m. the ~ **of life**, la force de l'âge.

prime[2] /praɪm/ v.t. (pump, gun) amorcer; (surface) apprêter. ~r[1] /-ə(r)/ n. (paint etc.) apprêt m.

primer[2] /'praɪmə(r)/ n. (schoolbook) premier livre m.

primeval /praɪ'miːvl/ a. primitif.

primitive /'prɪmɪtɪv/ a. primitif.

primrose /'prɪmrəʊz/ n. primevère (jaune) f.

prince /prɪns/ n. prince m. ~ly a. princier.

princess /prɪn'ses/ n. princesse f.

principal /'prɪnsəpl/ a. principal. —n. (of school etc.) direc|teur, -trice m., f. ~ly adv. principalement.

principle /'prɪnsəpl/ n. principe m. **in/on ~**, en/par principe.

print /prɪnt/ v.t. imprimer; (write in capitals) écrire en majuscules. —n. (of foot etc.) empreinte f.; (letters) caractères m. pl.; (photograph) épreuve f.; (engraving) gravure f. **in ~**, disponible. **out of ~**, épuisé. ~**out** n. listage m. ~**ed matter**, imprimés m. pl.

print|er /'prɪntə(r)/ n. (person) imprimeur m.; (comput.) imprimante f. ~**ing** n. impression f.

prior[1] /'praɪə(r)/ a. précédent. ~ **to**, prep. avant (de).

prior[2] /'praɪə(r)/ n. (relig.) prieur m. ~y n. prieuré m.

priority /praɪ'ɒrətɪ/ n. priorité f. **take ~**, avoir la priorité (over, sur).

prise /praɪz/ v.t. forcer. ~ **open**, ouvrir en forçant.

prism /'prɪzəm/ n. prisme m.

prison /'prɪzn/ n. prison f. ~**er** n. prisonn|ier, -ière m., f. ~ **officer**, gardien(ne) de prison m. (f.).

pristine /'prɪstiːn/ a. primitif; (condition) parfait.

privacy /'prɪvəsɪ/ n. intimité f., solitude f.

private /'praɪvɪt/ a. privé; (confidential) personnel; (lessons, house, etc.) particulier; (ceremony) intime. —n. (soldier) simple soldat m. **in ~**, en privé; (of ceremony) dans l'intimité. ~**ly** adv. en privé; dans l'intimité; (inwardly) intérieurement.

privation /praɪ'veɪʃn/ n. privation f.

privet /'prɪvɪt/ n. (bot.) troène m.

privilege /'prɪvɪlɪdʒ/ n. privilège m. ~**d** a. privilégié. **be ~d to**, avoir le privilège de.

privy /'prɪvɪ/ a. ~ **to**, au fait de.

prize /praɪz/ n. prix m. —a. (entry etc.) primé; (fool etc.) parfait. —v.t. (value) priser. ~**fighter** n. boxeur professionnel m. ~**win-ner** n. lauréat(e) m. (f.); (in lottery etc.) gagnant(e) m. (f.).

pro /prəʊ/ n. **the ~s and cons**, le pour et le contre.

pro- /prəʊ/ pref. pro-.

probab|le /'prɒbəbl/ a. probable. ~**ility** /-'bɪlətɪ/ n. probabilité f. ~**ly** adv. probablement.

probation /prə'beɪʃn/ n. (testing) essai m.; (jurid.) liberté surveillée f. ~**ary** a. d'essai.

probe /prəʊb/ n. (device) sonde f.; (fig.) enquête f. —v.t. sonder. —v.i. ~ **into**, sonder.

problem /'prɒbləm/ n. problème m. —a. difficile. ~**atic** /-'mætɪk/ a. problématique.

procedure /prə'siːdʒə(r)/ n. procédure f.; (way of doing sth.) démarche à suivre f.

proceed /prə'siːd/ v.i. (go) aller,

avancer; (*pass*) passer (**to**, à); (*act*) procéder. **~ (with)**, (*continue*) continuer. **~ to do**, se mettre à faire. **~ing** *n.* procédé *m.*

proceedings /prə'siːdɪŋz/ *n. pl.* (*discussions*) débats *m. pl.*; (*meeting*) réunion *f.*; (*report*) actes *m. pl.*; (*jurid.*) poursuites *f. pl.*

proceeds /'prəʊsiːdz/ *n. pl.* (*profits*) produit *m.*, bénéfices *m. pl.*

process /'prəʊses/ *n.* processus *m.*; (*method*) procédé *m.* —*v.t.* (*material, data*) traiter. **in ~**, en cours. **in the ~ of doing**, en train de faire.

procession /prə'seʃn/ *n.* défilé *m.*

proclaim /prə'kleɪm/ *v.t.* proclamer. **~amation** /prɒklə'meɪʃn/ *n.* proclamation *f.*

procrastinate /prə'kræstɪneɪt/ *v.i.* différer, tergiverser.

procreation /prəʊkrɪ'eɪʃn/ *n.* procréation *f.*

procure /prə'kjʊə(r)/ *v.t.* obtenir.

prod /prɒd/ *v.t./i.* (*p.t.* **prodded**) pousser. —*n.* poussée *f.*, coup *m.*

prodigal /'prɒdɪɡl/ *a.* prodigue.

prodigious /prə'dɪdʒəs/ *a.* prodigieux.

prodigy /'prɒdɪdʒɪ/ *n.* prodige *m.*

produce[1] /prə'djuːs/ *v.t./i.* produire; (*bring out*) sortir; (*show*) présenter; (*cause*) provoquer; (*theatre, TV*) mettre en scène; (*radio*) réaliser; (*cinema*) produire. **~er** *n.* metteur en scène *m.*; réalisateur *m.*; producteur *m.* **~tion** /-'dʌkʃn/ *n.* production *f.*; mise en scène *f.*; réalisation *f.*

produce[2] /'prɒdjuːs/ *n.* (*food etc.*) produits *m. pl.*

product /'prɒdʌkt/ *n.* produit *m.*

productive /prə'dʌktɪv/ *a.* productif. **~ity** /prɒdʌk'tɪvətɪ/ *n.* productivité *f.*

profane /prə'feɪn/ *a.* sacrilège; (*secular*) profane. **~ity** /-'fænətɪ/ *n.* (*oath*) juron *m.*

profess /prə'fes/ *v.t.* professer. **~ to do**, prétendre faire.

profession /prə'feʃn/ *n.* profession *f.* **~al** *a.* professionnel; (*of high quality*) de professionnel; (*person*) qui exerce une profession libérale; *n.* professionnel(le) *m. (f.).*

professor /prə'fesə(r)/ *n.* professeur (titulaire d'une chaire) *m.*

proficient /prə'fɪʃnt/ *a.* compétent. **~cy** *n.* compétence *f.*

profile /'prəʊfaɪl/ *n.* profil *m.*

profit /'prɒfɪt/ *n.* profit *m.*, bénéfice *m.* —*v.i.* (*p.t.* **profited**). **~ by**, tirer profit de. **~able** *a.* rentable.

profound /prə'faʊnd/ *a.* profond. **~ly** *adv.* profondément.

profuse /prə'fjuːs/ *a.* abondant. **~ in**, (*lavish in*) prodigue de. **~ely** *adv.* en abondance; (*apologize*) avec effusion. **~ion** /-ʒn/ *n.* profusion *f.*

progeny /'prɒdʒənɪ/ *n.* progéniture *f.*

program /'prəʊɡræm/ *n.* (*Amer.*) = **programme. (computer) ~**, programme *m.* —*v.t.* (*p.t.* **programmed**) programmer. **~mer** *n.* programmeur,-se *m.,f.* **~ming** *n.* (*on computer*) programmation *f.*

programme /'prəʊɡræm/ *n.* programme *m.*; (*broadcast*) émission *f.*

progress[1] /'prəʊɡres/ *n.* progrès *m.* (*pl.*). **in ~**, en cours. **make ~**, faire des progrès. **~ report**, compte-rendu *m.*

progress[2] /prə'ɡres/ *v.i.* (*advance, improve*) progresser. **~ion** /-ʃn/ *n.* progression *f.*

progressive /prə'ɡresɪv/ *a.* progressif; (*reforming*) progressiste. **~ly** *adv.* progressivement.

prohibit /prə'hɪbɪt/ v.t. interdire (**s.o. from doing**, à qn. de faire).

prohibitive /prə'hɪbɪtɪv/ a. (*price etc.*) prohibitif.

project[1] /prə'dʒekt/ v.t. projeter. —v.i. (*jut out*) être en saillie. ~**ion** /-kʃn/ n. projection f.; saillie f.

project[2] /'prɒdʒekt/ n. (*plan*) projet m.; (*undertaking*) entreprise f.; (*schol.*) dossier m.

projectile /prə'dʒektaɪl/ n. projectile m.

projector /prə'dʒektə(r)/ n. (*cinema etc.*) projecteur m.

proletari|**at** /prəʊlɪ'teərɪət/ n. prolétariat m. ~**an** a. prolétarien; n. prolétaire m./f.

proliferat|**e** /prə'lɪfəreɪt/ v.i. proliférer. ~**ion** /-'reɪʃn/ n. prolifération f.

prolific /prə'lɪfɪk/ a. prolifique.

prologue /'prəʊlɒg/ n. prologue m.

prolong /prə'lɒŋ/ v.t. prolonger.

promenade /prɒmə'nɑːd/ n. promenade f. —v.t./i. (se) promener.

prominen|**t** /'prɒmɪnənt/ a. (*projecting*) proéminent; (*conspicuous*) bien en vue; (*fig.*) important. ~**ce** n. proéminence f.; importance f. ~**tly** adv. bien en vue.

promiscu|**ous** /prə'mɪskjʊəs/ a. qui a plusieurs partenaires, (*pej.*) de mœurs faciles. ~**ity** /prɒmɪ-'skjuːəti/ n. les partenaires multiples; (*pej.*) liberté de mœurs f.

promis|**e** /'prɒmɪs/ n. promesse f. —v.t./i. promettre. ~**ing** a. prometteur; (*person*) qui promet.

promot|**e** /prə'məʊt/ v.t. promouvoir; (*advertise*) faire la promotion de. ~**ion** /-'məʊʃn/ n. (*of person, sales, etc.*) promotion f.

prompt /prɒmpt/ a. rapide; (*punctual*) à l'heure, ponctuel. —adv. (*on the dot*) pile. —v.t. inciter; (*cause*) provoquer; (*theatre*) souffler (son rôle) à. ~**er** n. souffleu|r, -se m., f. ~**ly** adv.

rapidement; ponctuellement. ~**ness** n. rapidité f.

prone /prəʊn/ a. couché sur le ventre. ~ **to**, prédisposé à.

prong /prɒŋ/ n. (*of fork*) dent f.

pronoun /'prəʊnaʊn/ n. pronom m.

pron|**ounce** /prə'naʊns/ v.t. prononcer. ~**ouncement** n. déclaration f. ~**unciation** /-ʌnsɪ'eɪʃn/ n. prononciation f.

pronounced /prə'naʊnst/ a. (*noticeable*) prononcé.

proof /pruːf/ n. (*evidence*) preuve f.; (*test, trial copy*) épreuve f.; (*of liquor*) teneur en alcool f. —a. ~ **against**, à l'épreuve de.

prop[1] /prɒp/ n. support m. —v.t. (*p.t. propped*). ~ **(up)**, (*support*) étayer; (*lean*) appuyer.

prop[2] /prɒp/ n. (*theatre, fam.*) accessoire m.

propaganda /prɒpə'gændə/ n. propagande f.

propagat|**e** /'prɒpəgeɪt/ v.t./i. (se) propager. ~**ion** /-'geɪʃn/ n. propagation f.

propane /'prəʊpeɪn/ n. propane m.

propel /prə'pel/ v.t. (*p.t. propelled*) propulser. ~**ling pencil**, porte-mine m. invar.

propeller /prə'pelə(r)/ n. hélice f.

proper /'prɒpə(r)/ a. correct, bon; (*seemly*) convenable; (*real*) vrai; (*thorough: fam.*) parfait. ~ **noun**, nom propre m. ~**ly** adv. correctement, comme il faut; (*rightly*) avec raison.

property /'prɒpəti/ n. propriété f.; (*things owned*) biens m. pl., propriété f. —a. immobilier, foncier.

prophecy /'prɒfəsi/ n. prophétie f.

prophesy /'prɒfəsaɪ/ v.t./i. prophétiser. ~ **that**, prédire que.

prophet /'prɒfɪt/ n. prophète m. ~**ic** /prə'fetɪk/ a. prophétique.

proportion /prə'pɔːʃn/ n. (*ratio,*

dimension) proportion f.; (amount) partie f. ~al, ~ate adjs. proportionnel.

proposal /prə'pəʊzl/ n. proposition f.; (of marriage) demande en mariage f.

propos|e /prə'pəʊz/ v.t. proposer. —v.i. ~e to, faire une demande en mariage à. ~e to do, se proposer de faire. ~ition /prɒpə'zɪʃn/ n. proposition f.; (matter: fam.) affaire f.; v.t. (fam.) faire des propositions malhonnêtes à.

propound /prə'paʊnd/ v.t. (theory etc.) proposer.

proprietor /prə'praɪətə(r)/ n. propriétaire m./f.

propriety /prə'praɪətɪ/ n. (correct behaviour) bienséance f.

propulsion /prə'pʌlʃn/ n. propulsion f.

prosaic /prə'zeɪɪk/ a. prosaïque.

proscribe /prə'skraɪb/ v.t. proscrire.

prose /prəʊz/ n. prose f.; (translation) thème m.

prosecut|e /'prɒsɪkjuːt/ v.t. poursuivre. ~ion /-'kjuːʃn/ n. poursuites f. pl. ~or n. procureur m.

prospect¹ /'prɒspekt/ n. perspective f.; (chance) espoir m. a job with ~s, un travail avec des perspectives d'avenir.

prospect² /prə'spekt/ v.t./i. prospecter. ~or n. prospecteur m.

prospective /prə'spektɪv/ a. (future) futur; (possible) éventuel.

prospectus /prə'spektəs/ n. prospectus m.; (univ.) guide m.

prosper /'prɒspə(r)/ v.i. prospérer.

prosper|ous /'prɒspərəs/ a. prospère. ~ity /-'sperətɪ/ n. prospérité f.

prostate /'prɒsteɪt/ n. prostate f.

prostitut|e /'prɒstɪtjuːt/ n. prostituée f. ~ion /-'tjuːʃn/ n. prostitution f.

prostrate /'prɒstreɪt/ a. (prone) à plat ventre; (submissive) prosterné; (exhausted) prostré

protagonist /prə'tægənɪst/ n. protagoniste m.

protect /prə'tekt/ v.t. protéger. ~ion /-kʃn/ n. protection f. ~or n. protecteur, -trice m., f.

protective /prə'tektɪv/ a. protecteur; (clothes) de protection.

protégé /'prɒtɪʒeɪ/ n. protégé m. ~e n. protégée f.

protein /'prəʊtiːn/ n. protéine f.

protest¹ /'prəʊtest/ n. protestation f. under ~, en protestant.

protest² /prə'test/ v.t./i. protester. ~er n. (pol.) manifestant(e) m. (f.).

Protestant /'prɒtɪstənt/ a. & n. protestant(e) (m. (f.)).

protocol /'prəʊtəkɒl/ n. protocole m.

prototype /'prəʊtətaɪp/ n. prototype m.

protract /prə'trækt/ v.t. prolonger, faire traîner. ~ed a. prolongé.

protractor /prə'træktə(r)/ n. (for measuring) rapporteur m.

protrude /prə'truːd/ v.i. dépasser.

proud /praʊd/ a. (-er, -est) fier, orgueilleux. ~ly adv. fièrement.

prove /pruːv/ v.t. prouver. ~ (to be) easy/etc., se révéler facile/etc. ~ o.s., faire ses preuves. ~n a. prouvé.

proverb /'prɒvɜːb/ n. proverbe m. ~ial /prə'vɜːbɪəl/ a. proverbial.

provide /prə'vaɪd/ v.t. fournir (s.o. with sth., qch. à qn.). —v.i. ~ for, (allow for) prévoir; (guard against) parer à; (person) pourvoir aux besoins de.

provided /prə'vaɪdɪd/ conj. ~ that, à condition que.

providence /'prɒvɪdəns/ n. providence f.

providing /prə'vaɪdɪŋ/ conj. = provided.

provinc|e /'prɒvɪns/ n. province f.;

(fig.) compétence *f.* ∼ial /prə'vɪnʃl/ *a. & n.* provincial(e) (*m.* (*f.*)).

provision /prə'vɪʒn/ *n.* (*stock*) provision *f.*; (*supplying*) fourniture *f.*; (*stipulation*) disposition *f.* ∼s, (*food*) provisions *f. pl.*

provisional /prə'vɪʒnl/ *a.* provisoire. ∼ly *adv.* provisoirement.

proviso /prə'vaɪzəʊ/ *n.* (*pl.* -os) condition *f.*, stipulation *f.*

provo|ke /prə'vəʊk/ *v.t.* provoquer. ∼cation /prɒvə'keɪʃn/ *n.* provocation *f.* ∼cative /-'vɒkətɪv/ *a.* provocant(e).

prow /praʊ/ *n.* proue *f.*

prowess /'praʊɪs/ *n.* prouesse *f.*

prowl /praʊl/ *v.i.* rôder. — *n.* be on the ∼, rôder. ∼er *n.* rôdeu|r, -se *m.*, *f.*

proximity /prɒk'sɪmətɪ/ *n.* proximité *f.*

proxy /'prɒksɪ/ *n.* by ∼, par procuration.

prud|e /pruːd/ *n.* prude *f.* ∼ish *a.* prude.

pruden|t /'pruːdnt/ *a.* prudent. ∼ce *n.* prudence *f.* ∼tly *adv.* prudemment.

prune¹ /pruːn/ *n.* pruneau *m.*

prune² /pruːn/ *v.t.* (*cut*) tailler.

pry¹ /praɪ/ *v.i.* être indiscret. ∼ into, fourrer son nez dans.

pry² /praɪ/ *v.t.* (*Amer.*) = **prise**.

psalm /sɑːm/ *n.* psaume *m.*

pseudo- /'sjuːdəʊ/ *pref.* pseudo-.

pseudonym /'sjuːdənɪm/ *n.* pseudonyme *m.*

psoriasis /sə'raɪəsɪs/ *n.* psoriasis *m.*

psyche /'saɪkɪ/ *n.* psyché *f.*

psychiatr|y /saɪ'kaɪətrɪ/ *n.* psychiatrie *f.* ∼ic /-ɪ'ætrɪk/ *a.* psychiatrique. ∼ist *n.* psychiatre *m.*/*f.*

psychic /'saɪkɪk/ *a.* (*phenomenon etc.*) métapsychique; (*person*) doué de télépathie.

psychoanalys|e /saɪkəʊ'ænəlaɪz/ *v.t.* psychanalyser. ∼t /-ɪst/ *n.* psychanalyste *m.*/*f.*

psychoanalysis /saɪkəʊə'næləsɪs/ *n.* psychanalyse *f.*

psycholog|y /saɪ'kɒlədʒɪ/ *n.* psychologie *f.* ∼ical /-ə'lɒdʒɪkl/ *a.* psychologique. ∼ist *n.* psychologue *m.*/*f.*

psychopath /'saɪkəʊpæθ/ *n.* psychopathe *m.*/*f.*

psychosomatic /saɪkəʊsə'mætɪk/ *a.* psychosomatique.

psychotherap|y /saɪkəʊ'θerəpɪ/ *n.* psychothérapie *f.* ∼ist *n.* psychothérapeute *m.*/*f.*

pub /pʌb/ *n.* pub *m.*

puberty /'pjuːbətɪ/ *n.* puberté *f.*

public /'pʌblɪk/ *a.* public; (*library etc.*) municipal. **in ∼**, en public. ∼ **address system**, sonorisation *f.* (*dans un lieu public*). ∼ **house**, pub *m.* ∼ **relations**, relations publiques *f. pl.* ∼ **school**, école privée *f.*; (*Amer.*) école publique *f.* ∼ **servant**, fonctionnaire *m.*/*f.* ∼-**spirited** *a.* dévoué au bien public. ∼ **transport**, transports en commun *m. pl.* ∼ly *adv.* publiquement.

publican /'pʌblɪkən/ *n.* patron(ne) de pub *m.* (*f.*).

publication /pʌblɪ'keɪʃn/ *n.* publication *f.*

publicity /pʌb'lɪsɪtɪ/ *n.* publicité *f.*

publicize /'pʌblɪsaɪz/ *v.t.* faire connaître au public.

publish /'pʌblɪʃ/ *v.t.* publier. ∼er *n.* éditeur *m.* ∼ing *n.* édition *f.*

puck /pʌk/ *n.* (*ice hockey*) palet *m.*

pucker /'pʌkə(r)/ *v.t.*/*i.* (se) plisser.

pudding /'pʊdɪŋ/ *n.* dessert *m.*; (*steamed*) pudding *m.* **black ∼**, boudin *m.* **rice ∼**, riz au lait *m.*

puddle /'pʌdl/ *n.* flaque d'eau *f.*

pudgy /'pʌdʒɪ/ *a.* (-ier, -iest) dodu.

puerile /'pjʊəraɪl/ *a.* puéril.

puff /pʌf/ n. bouffée f. —v.t./i. souffler. ~ **at,** (cigar) tirer sur. ~ **out,** (swell) (se) gonfler.

puffy /'pʌfɪ/ a. gonflé.

pugnacious /pʌg'neɪʃəs/ a. batailleur, combatif.

pug-nosed /'pʌgnəʊzd/ a. camus.

pull /pʊl/ v.t./i. tirer; (muscle) se froisser. —n. traction f.; (fig.) attraction f.; (influence) influence f. **give a** ~, tirer. ~ **a face,** faire une grimace. ~ **one's weight,** faire sa part du travail. ~ **s.o.'s leg,** faire marcher qn. ~ **apart,** mettre en morceaux. ~ **away,** (auto.) démarrer. ~ **back** or **out,** (withdraw) (se) retirer. ~ **down,** baisser; (building) démolir. ~ **in,** (enter) (stop) s'arrêter. ~ **off,** enlever; (fig.) réussir. ~ **out,** (from bag etc.) sortir; (extract) arracher; (auto.) déboîter. ~ **over,** (auto.) se ranger. ~ **round** or **through,** s'en tirer. ~ **o.s. together,** se ressaisir. ~ **up,** remonter; (uproot) déraciner; (auto.) (s')arrêter.

pulley /'pʊlɪ/ n. poulie f.

pullover /'pʊləʊvə(r)/ n. pull (-over) m.

pulp /pʌlp/ n. (of fruit) pulpe f.; (for paper) pâte à papier f.

pulpit /'pʊlpɪt/ n. chaire f.

pulsate /pʌl'seɪt/ v.i. battre.

pulse /pʌls/ n. (med.) pouls m.

pulverize /'pʌlvəraɪz/ v.t. (grind, defeat) pulvériser.

pummel /'pʌml/ v.t. (p.t. pummelled) bourrer de coups.

pump[1] /pʌmp/ n. pompe f. —v.t./i. pomper; (person) soutirer des renseignements à. ~ **up,** gonfler.

pump[2] /pʌmp/ n. (plimsoll) tennis m.; (for dancing) escarpin m.

pumpkin /'pʌmpkɪn/ n. potiron m.

pun /pʌn/ n. jeu de mots m.

punch[1] /pʌntʃ/ v.t. donner un coup de poing à; (perforate) poinçonner; (a hole) faire. —n. coup de

poing m.; (vigour: sl.) punch m.; (device) poinçonneuse f. ~ **drunk** a. sonné. ~**-line,** chute f. ~**-up** n. (fam.) bagarre f.

punch[2] /pʌntʃ/ n. (drink) punch m.

punctual /'pʌŋktʃʊəl/ a. à l'heure; (habitually) ponctuel. ~**ity** /-'ælətɪ/ n. ponctualité f. ~**ly** adv. à l'heure; ponctuellement.

punctuat|e /'pʌŋktʃʊeɪt/ v.t. ponctuer. ~**ion** /-'eɪʃn/ n. ponctuation f.

puncture /'pʌŋktʃə(r)/ n. (in tyre) crevaison f. —v.t./i. crever.

pundit /'pʌndɪt/ n. expert m.

pungent /'pʌndʒənt/ a. âcre.

punish /'pʌnɪʃ/ v.t. punir (for sth., de qch.). ~**able** a. punissable (by, de). ~**ment** n. punition f.

punitive /'pjuːnɪtɪv/ a. punitif.

punk /pʌŋk/ n. (music, fan) punk m.; (person: Amer., fam.) salaud m.

punt[1] /pʌnt/ n. (boat) bachot m.

punt[2] /pʌnt/ v.i. (bet) parier.

puny /'pjuːnɪ/ a. (-ier, -iest) chétif.

pup(py) /'pʌp(ɪ)/ n. chiot m.

pupil /'pjuːpl/ n. (person) élève m./f.; (of eye) pupille f.

puppet /'pʌpɪt/ n. marionnette f.

purchase /'pɜːtʃəs/ v.t. acheter (**from s.o.,** à qn.). —n. achat m. ~**r** /-ə(r)/ n. acheteu|r, -se m., f.

pur|e /pjʊə(r)/ a. (-er, -est) pur. ~**ely** adv. purement. ~**ity** n. pureté f.

purgatory /'pɜːgətrɪ/ n. purgatoire m.

purge /pɜːdʒ/ v.t. purger (**of,** de). —n. purge f.

purif|y /'pjʊərɪfaɪ/ v.t. purifier. ~**ication** /-ɪ'keɪʃn/ n. purification f.

purist /'pjʊərɪst/ n. puriste m./f.

puritan /'pjʊərɪtən/ n. puritain(e) m. (f.). ~**ical** /-'tænɪkl/ a. puritain.

purple /'pɜːpl/ a. & n. violet (m.).

purport /pə'pɔːt/ v.t. ~ to be, (claim) prétendre être.

purpose /'pɜːpəs/ n. but m.; (fig.) résolution f. on ~, exprès. ~-built a. construit spécialement. to no ~, sans résultat.

purr /pɜː(r)/ n. ronronnement m. —v.i. ronronner.

purse /pɜːs/ n. porte-monnaie a. invar.; (handbag: Amer.) sac à main m. —v.t. (lips) pincer.

pursue /pə'sjuː/ v.t. poursuivre. ~r /-ə(r)/ n. poursuivant(e) m. (f.).

pursuit /pə'sjuːt/ n. poursuite f.; (fig.) activité f., occupation f.

purveyor /pə'veɪə(r)/ n. fournisseur m.

pus /pʌs/ n. pus m.

push /pʊʃ/ v.t./i. pousser; (button) appuyer sur; (thrust) enfoncer; (recommend: fam.) proposer avec insistance. —n. poussée f.; (effort) gros effort m.; (drive) dynamisme m. be ~ed for, (time etc.) manquer de. be ~ing thirty/ etc., (fam.) friser la trentaine/etc. give the ~ to, (sl.) flanquer à la porte. ~ around, bousculer qn. ~ back, repousser. ~-chair n. poussette f. ~er n. revendeu|r, -se (de drogue) m., f. ~ off, (sl.) filer. ~ on, continuer. ~-over n. jeu d'enfant m. ~ up, (lift) relever; (prices) faire monter. ~-up n. (Amer.) traction f. ~y a. (fam.) autoritaire.

pushing /'pʊʃɪŋ/ a. arriviste.

puss /pʊs/ n. (cat) minet(te) m. (f.).

put /pʊt/ v.t./i. (p.t. put, pres. p. putting) mettre, placer, poser; (question) poser. ~ the damage at a million, estimer les dégâts à un million; I'd put it at a thousand, je dirais un millier. ~ sth. tactfully, dire qch. avec tact. ~ across, communiquer. ~ away, ranger; (fig.) enfermer.

~ back, remettre; (delay) retarder. ~ by, mettre de côté. ~ down, (dé)poser; (write) inscrire; (pay) verser; (suppress) réprimer. ~ forward, (plan) soumettre. ~ in, (insert) introduire; (fix) installer; (submit) soumettre. ~ in for, faire une demande de. ~ off, (postpone) renvoyer à plus tard; (disconcert) déconcerter; (displease) rebuter. ~ s.o. off sth., dégoûter qn. de qch. ~ on, (clothes, radio) mettre; (light) allumer; (speed, accent, weight) prendre. ~ out, sortir; (stretch) (é)tendre; (extinguish) éteindre; (disconcert) déconcerter; (inconvenience) déranger. ~ up, lever, remonter; (building) construire; (notice) mettre; (price) augmenter; (guest) héberger; (offer) offrir. ~-up job, coup monté m. ~ up with, supporter.

putt /pʌt/ n. (golf) putt m.

putter /'pʌtə(r)/ v.i. (Amer.) bricoler.

putty /'pʌtɪ/ n. mastic m.

puzzle /'pʌzl/ n. énigme f.; (game) casse-tête m. invar.; (jigsaw) puzzle m. —v.t. rendre perplexe. —v.i. se creuser la tête.

pygmy /'pɪɡmɪ/ n. pygmée m.

pyjamas /pə'dʒɑːməz/ n. pl. pyjama m.

pylon /'paɪlɒn/ n. pylône m.

pyramid /'pɪrəmɪd/ n. pyramide f.

Pyrenees /pɪrə'niːz/ n. pl. the ~, les Pyrénées f.

python /'paɪθn/ n. python m.

Q

quack[1] /kwæk/ n. (of duck) coin-coin m. invar.

quack[2] /kwæk/ n. charlatan m.

quad /kwɒd/ (fam.) = quadrangle, quadruplet.

quadrangle /'kwɒdræŋgl/ (of college) n. cour f.

quadruped /'kwɒdruped/ n. quadrupède m.

quadruple /kwɒ'druːpl/ a. & n. quadruple (m.). —v.t./i. quadrupler. **~ts** /-plts/ n. pl. quadruplé(e)s m. (f.) pl.

quagmire /'kwægmaɪə(r)/ n. (bog) bourbier m.

quail /kweɪl/ n. (bird) caille f.

quaint /kweɪnt/ a. (-er, -est) pittoresque; (old) vieillot; (odd) bizarre. **~ness** n. pittoresque m.

quake /kweɪk/ v.i. trembler. —n. (fam.) tremblement de terre m.

Quaker /'kweɪkə(r)/ n. quaker(esse) m. (f.).

qualification /kwɒlɪfɪ'keɪʃn/ n. diplôme m.; (ability) compétence f.; (fig.) réserve f., restriction f.

qualif|y /'kwɒlɪfaɪ/ v.t. qualifier; (modify: fig.) mettre des réserves à; (statement) nuancer. —v.i. obtenir son diplôme (as, de); (sport) se qualifier; (fig.) remplir les conditions requises. **~ied** a. diplômé; (able) qualifié (to do, pour faire); (fig.) conditionnel; (success) modéré. **~ying** a. (round) éliminatoire; (candidates) qualifiés.

qualit|y /'kwɒlətɪ/ n. qualité f. **~ative** /-tətɪv/ a. qualitatif.

qualm /kwɑːm/ n. scrupule m.

quandary /'kwɒndərɪ/ n. embarras m., dilemme m.

quantit|y /'kwɒntətɪ/ n. quantité f. **~ative** /-tətɪv/ a. quantitatif.

quarantine /'kwɒrəntiːn/ n. (isolation) quarantaine f.

quarrel /'kwɒrəl/ n. dispute f., querelle f. —v.i. (p.t. quarrelled) se disputer. **~some** a. querelleur.

quarry[1] /'kwɒrɪ/ n. (prey) proie f.

quarry[2] /'kwɒrɪ/ n. (excavation) carrière f. —v.t. extraire.

quart /kwɔːt/ n. (approx.) litre m.

quarter /'kwɔːtə(r)/ n. quart m.; (of year) trimestre m.; (25 cents: Amer.) quart de dollar m.; (district) quartier m. **~s**, logement(s) m. (pl.) —v.t. diviser en quatre; (mil.) cantonner. **from all ~s**, de toutes parts. **~-final** n. quart de finale m. **~ly** a. trimestriel; adv. trimestriellement.

quartermaster /'kwɔːtəmɑːstə(r)/ n. (mil.) intendant m.

quartet /kwɔː'tet/ n. quatuor m.

quartz /kwɔːts/ n. quartz m. —a. (watch etc.) à quartz.

quash /kwɒʃ/ v.t. (suppress) étouffer; (jurid.) annuler.

quasi- /'kweɪsaɪ/ pref. quasi-.

quaver /'kweɪvə(r)/ v.i. trembler, chevroter. —n. (mus.) croche f.

quay /kiː/ n. (naut.) quai m. **~side** n. (edge of quay) quai m.

queasy /'kwiːzɪ/ a. (stomach) délicat. **feel ~**, avoir mal au cœur.

queen /kwiːn/ n. reine f.; (cards) dame f. **~ mother**, reine mère f.

queer /kwɪə(r)/ a. (-er, -est) étrange; (dubious) louche; (ill) patraque. —n. (sl.) homosexuel m.

quell /kwel/ v.t. réprimer.

quench /kwentʃ/ v.t. éteindre; (thirst) étancher; (desire) étouffer.

query /'kwɪərɪ/ n. question f. —v.t. mettre en question.

quest /kwest/ n. recherche f.

question /'kwestʃən/ n. question f. —v.t. interroger; (doubt) mettre en question, douter de. **a ~ of money**, une question d'argent. **in ~**, en question. **no ~ of**, pas question de. **out of the ~**, hors de question. **~ mark**, point d'interrogation m.

questionable /'kwestʃənəbl/ a. discutable.

questionnaire /ˌkwestʃəˈneə(r)/ n. questionnaire m.

queue /kju:/ n. queue f. —v.i. (pres. p. queuing) faire la queue.

quibble /ˈkwɪbl/ v.i. ergoter.

quick /kwɪk/ a. (-er, -est) rapide. —adv. vite. —n. a ~ one, (fam.) un petit verre. cut to the ~, piquer au vif. be ~, (hurry) se dépêcher. have a ~ temper, s'emporter facilement. ~ly adv. rapidement, vite. ~-witted a. vif.

quicken /ˈkwɪkən/ v.t./i. (s)accélérer.

quicksand /ˈkwɪksænd/ n. ~(s), sables mouvants m. pl.

quid /kwɪd/ n. invar. (sl.) livre f.

quiet /ˈkwaɪət/ a. (-er, -est) (calm, still) tranquille; (silent) silencieux; (gentle) doux; (discreet) discret. —n. tranquillité f. keep ~, se taire. on the ~, en cachette. ~ly adv. tranquillement; silencieusement; doucement; discrètement. ~ness n. tranquillité f.

quieten /ˈkwaɪətn/ v.t./i. (se) calmer.

quill /kwɪl/ n. plume (d'oie) f.

quilt /kwɪlt/ n. édredon m. (continental) ~, couette f. —v.t. matelasser.

quinine /ˈkwɪniːn. Amer. ˈkwaɪnaɪn/ n. quinine f.

quintet /kwɪnˈtet/ n. quintette m.

quintuplets /ˈkwɪntjuːplɪts/ n. pl. quintuplé(e)s m. (f.) pl.

quip /kwɪp/ n. mot piquant m.

quirk /kwɜːk/ n. bizarrerie f.

quit /kwɪt/ v.t. (p.t. quitted) quitter. —v.i. abandonner; (resign) démissionner. ~ doing, (cease: Amer.) cesser de faire.

quite /kwaɪt/ adv. tout à fait, vraiment; (rather) assez. ~ (so)!, parfaitement! ~ a few, un assez grand nombre (de).

quits /kwɪts/ a. quitte (with, envers). call it ~, en rester là.

quiver /ˈkwɪvə(r)/ v.i. trembler.

quiz /kwɪz/ n. (pl. quizzes) test m.; (game) jeu-concours m. —v.t. (p.t. quizzed) questionner.

quizzical /ˈkwɪzɪkl/ a. moqueur.

quorum /ˈkwɔːrəm/ n. quorum m.

quota /ˈkwəʊtə/ n. quota m.

quotation /kwəʊˈteɪʃn/ n. citation f.; (price) devis m.; (stock exchange) cotation f. ~ marks, guillemets m. pl.

quote /kwəʊt/ v.t. citer; (reference: comm.) rappeler; (price) indiquer; (share price) coter. —v.i. ~ for, faire un devis pour. ~ from, citer. —n. (estimate) devis; (fam.) = quotation. in ~s, (fam.) entre guillemets.

quotient /ˈkwəʊʃnt/ n. quotient m.

R

rabbi /ˈræbaɪ/ n. rabbin m.

rabbit /ˈræbɪt/ n. lapin m.

rabble /ˈræbl/ n. (crowd) cohue f. the ~, (pej.) la populace.

rabid /ˈræbɪd/ a. enragé.

rabies /ˈreɪbiːz/ n. (disease) rage f.

race[1] /reɪs/ n. course f. —v.t. (horse) faire courir; (engine) emballer. ~ (against), faire la course à. —v.i. courir; (rush) foncer. ~-track n. piste f.; (for horses) champ de courses m.

race[2] /reɪs/ n. (group) race f. —a. racial; (relations) entre les races.

racecourse /ˈreɪskɔːs/ n. champ de courses m.

racehorse /ˈreɪshɔːs/ n. cheval de course m.

racial /ˈreɪʃl/ a. racial.

racing /ˈreɪsɪŋ/ n. courses f. pl. ~ car, voiture de course f.

racis|**t** /ˈreɪsɪst/ a. & n. raciste (m./f.). ~**m** /-zəm/ n. racisme m.

rack[1] /ræk/ *n.* (*shelf*) étagère *f.*; (*pigeon-holes*) casier *m.*; (*for luggage*) porte-bagages *m. invar.*; (*for dishes*) égouttoir *m.*; (*on car roof*) galerie *f.* —*v.t.* ~ **one's brains,** se creuser la cervelle.

rack[2] /ræk/ *n.* **go to** ~ **and ruin,** aller à la ruine; (*building*) tomber en ruine.

racket[1] /'rækɪt/ *n.* raquette *f.*

racket[2] /'rækɪt/ *n.* (*din*) tapage *m.*; (*dealings*) combine *f.*; (*crime*) racket *m.* ~**eer** /-ə'tɪə(r)/ *n.* racketteur *m.*

racy /'reɪsɪ/ *a.* (**-ier, -iest**) fougueux, piquant; (*Amer.*) risqué.

radar /'reɪda:(r)/ *n.* radar *m.* —*a.* (*system etc.*) radar *invar.*

radial /'reɪdɪəl/ *a.* (*tyre*) à carcasse radiale.

radian|t /'reɪdɪənt/ *a.* rayonnant. ~**ce** *n.* éclat *m.* ~**tly** *adv.* avec éclat.

radiat|e /'reɪdɪeɪt/ *v.t.* dégager. —*v.i.* rayonner (**from,** de). ~**ion** /-'eɪʃn/ *n.* rayonnement *m.*; (*radioactivity*) radiation *f.*

radiator /'reɪdɪeɪtə(r)/ *n.* radiateur *m.*

radical /'rædɪkl/ *a.* radical. —*n.* (*person: pol.*) radical(e) *m.* (*f.*).

radio /'reɪdɪəʊ/ *n.* (*pl.* **-os**) radio *f.* —*v.t.* (*message*) envoyer par radio; (*person*) appeler par radio.

radioactiv|e /reɪdɪəʊ'æktɪv/ *a.* radioactif. ~**ity** /-'tɪvətɪ/ *n.* radioactivité *f.*

radiographer /reɪdɪ'ɒɡrəfə(r)/ *n.* radiologue *m./f.*

radish /'rædɪʃ/ *n.* radis *m.*

radius /'reɪdɪəs/ *n.* (*pl.* **-dii** /-dɪaɪ/) rayon *m.*

raffle /'ræfl/ *n.* tombola *f.*

raft /rɑ:ft/ *n.* radeau *m.*

rafter /'rɑ:ftə(r)/ *n.* chevron *m.*

rag[1] /ræɡ/ *n.* lambeau *m.*, loque *f.*; (*for wiping*) chiffon *m.*; (*newspaper*) torchon *m.* **in** ~**s,** (*person*) en haillons; (*clothes*) en lambeaux. ~ **doll,** poupée de chiffon *f.*

rag[2] /ræɡ/ *v.t.* (*p.t.* **ragged**) (*tease: sl.*) taquiner. —*n.* (*univ., sl.*) carnaval *m.* (*pour une œuvre de charité*).

ragamuffin /'ræɡəmʌfɪn/ *n.* va-nu-pieds *m. invar.*

rage /reɪdʒ/ *n.* rage *f.*, fureur *f.* —*v.i.* rager; (*storm, battle*) faire rage. **be all the** ~, faire fureur.

ragged /'ræɡɪd/ *a.* (*clothes, person*) loqueteux; (*edge*) déchiqueté.

raging /'reɪdʒɪŋ/ *a.* (*storm, fever, etc.*) violent.

raid /reɪd/ *n.* (*mil.*) raid *m.*; (*by police*) rafle *f.*; (*by criminals*) hold-up *m. invar.* —*v.t.* faire un raid or une rafle *or* un hold-up dans. ~**er** *n.* (*person*) bandit *m.*, pillard *m.* ~**ers** *n. pl.* (*mil.*) commando *m.*

rail /reɪl/ *n.* (*on balcony*) balustrade *f.*; (*stairs*) main courante *f.*, rampe *f.*; (*for train*) rail *m.*; (*for curtain*) tringle *f.* **by** ~, par chemin de fer.

railing /'reɪlɪŋ/ *n.* ~**s,** grille *f.*

railroad /'reɪlrəʊd/ *n.* (*Amer.*) = **railway.**

railway /'reɪlweɪ/ *n.* chemin de fer *m.* ~ **line,** voie ferrée *f.* ~**man** *n.* (*pl.* **-men**) cheminot *m.* ~ **station,** gare *f.*

rain /reɪn/ *n.* pluie *f.* —*v.i.* pleuvoir. ~ **forest,** forêt (humide) tropicale *f.* ~**storm** *n.* trombe d'eau *f.* ~**water** *n.* eau de pluie *f.*

rainbow /'reɪnbəʊ/ *n.* arc-en-ciel *m.*

raincoat /'reɪnkəʊt/ *n.* imperméable *m.*

rainfall /'reɪnfɔ:l/ *n.* précipitation *f.*

rainy /'reɪnɪ/ *a.* (**-ier, -iest**) pluvieux; (*season*) des pluies.

raise /reɪz/ *v.t.* lever; (*breed, build*)

élever; (*question etc.*) soulever; (*price etc.*) relever; (*money etc.*) obtenir; (*voice*) élever. —*n.* (*Amer.*) augmentation *f.*

raisin /ˈreɪzn/ *n.* raisin sec *m.*

rake[1] /reɪk/ *n.* râteau *m.* —*v.t.* (*garden*) ratisser; (*search*) fouiller dans. ~ **in**, (*money*) amasser. ~**-off** *n.* (*fam.*) profit *m.* ~ **up**, (*memories, past*) remuer.

rake[2] /reɪk/ *n.* (*man*) débauché *m.*

rally /ˈrælɪ/ *v.t./i.* (se) rallier; (*strength*) reprendre; (*after illness*) aller mieux. —*n.* rassemblement *m.*; (*auto.*) rallye *m.*; (*tennis*) échange *m.* ~ **round**, venir en aide.

ram /ræm/ *n.* bélier *m.* —*v.t.* (*p.t.* **rammed**) (*thrust*) enfoncer; (*crash into*) emboutir, percuter.

RAM /ræm/ *abbr.* (*random access memory*) mémoire vive *f.*

rambl|e /ˈræmbl/ *n.* randonnée *f.* —*v.i.* faire une randonnée. ~**e on**, parler (sans cesse), divaguer. ~**er** *n.* randonneu|r, -se, *m.*, *f.* ~**ing** *a.* (*speech*) décousu.

ramification /ræmɪfɪˈkeɪʃn/ *n.* ramification *f.*

ramp /ræmp/ *n.* (*slope*) rampe *f.*; (*in garage*) pont de graissage *m.*

rampage[1] /ræmˈpeɪdʒ/ *v.i.* se livrer à des actes de violence, se déchaîner.

rampage[2] /ˈræmpeɪdʒ/ *n.* **go on the** ~ = **rampage**[1].

rampant /ˈræmpənt/ *a.* **be** ~, (*disease etc.*) sévir, être répandu.

rampart /ˈræmpɑːt/ *n.* rempart *m.*

ramshackle /ˈræmʃækl/ *a.* délabré.

ran /ræn/ *see* **run**.

rancid /ˈrænsɪd/ *a.* rance.

rancour /ˈræŋkə(r)/ *n.* rancœur *f.*

random /ˈrændəm/ *a.* fait, pris, *etc.* au hasard, aléatoire (*techn.*). —*n.* **at** ~, au hasard.

randy /ˈrændɪ/ *a.* (**-ier**, **-iest**) (*fam.*) excité, en chaleur.

rang /ræŋ/ *see* **ring**[2].

range /reɪndʒ/ *n.* (*distance*) portée *f.*; (*of aircraft etc.*) rayon d'action *m.*; (*series*) gamme *f.*; (*scale*) échelle *f.*; (*choice*) choix *m.*; (*domain*) champ *m.*; (*of mountains*) chaîne *f.*; (*stove*) cuisinière *f.* —*v.i.* s'étendre; (*vary*) varier.

ranger /ˈreɪndʒə(r)/ *n.* garde forestier *m.*

rank[1] /ræŋk/ *n.* rang *m.*; (*grade: mil.*) grade *m.*, rang *m.* —*v.t./i.* ~ **among**, compter parmi. **the** ~ **and file**, les gens ordinaires.

rank[2] /ræŋk/ *a.* (**-er, -est**) (*plants: pej.*) luxuriant; (*smell*) fétide; (*complete*) absolu.

rankle /ˈræŋkl/ *v.i.* ~ **with s.o.**, rester sur le cœur à qn.

ransack /ˈrænsæk/ *v.t.* (*search*) fouiller; (*pillage*) saccager.

ransom /ˈrænsəm/ *n.* rançon *f.* —*v.t.* rançonner; (*redeem*) racheter. **hold to** ~, rançonner.

rant /rænt/ *v.i.* tempêter.

rap /ræp/ *n.* petit coup sec *m.* —*v.t./i.* (*p.t.* **rapped**) frapper.

rape /reɪp/ *v.t.* violer. —*n.* viol *m.*

rapid /ˈræpɪd/ *a.* rapide. ~**ity** /rəˈpɪdətɪ/ *n.* rapidité *f.* ~**s** *n. pl.* (*of river*) rapides *m. pl.*

rapist /ˈreɪpɪst/ *n.* violeur *m.*

rapport /ræˈpɔː(r)/ *n.* rapport *m.*

rapt /ræpt/ *a.* (*attention*) profond. ~ **in**, plongé dans.

raptur|e /ˈræptʃə(r)/ *n.* extase *f.* ~**ous** *a.* (*person*) en extase; (*welcome etc.*) frénétique.

rare[1] /reə(r)/ *a.* (**-er, -est**) rare. ~**ely** *adv.* rarement. ~**ity** *n.* rareté *f.*

rare[2] /reə(r)/ *a.* (**-er, -est**) (*culin.*) saignant.

rarefied /ˈreərɪfaɪd/ *a.* raréfié.

raring /ˈreərɪŋ/ *a.* ~ **to**, (*fam.*) impatient de.

rascal /ˈrɑːskl/ *n.* coquin(e) *m.* (*f.*).

rash[1] /ræʃ/ *n.* (*med.*) éruption *f.*, rougeurs *f. pl.*

rash² /ræʃ/ a. (-er, -est) imprudent. **~ly** adv. imprudemment. **~ness** n. imprudence f.

rasher /'ræʃə(r)/ n. tranche (de lard) f.

raspberry /'rɑːzbrɪ/ n. framboise f.

rasping /'rɑːspɪŋ/ a. grinçant.

rat /ræt/ n. rat m. —v.i. (p.t. ratted). **~ on**, (desert) lâcher; (inform on) dénoncer. **~ race**, foire d'empoigne f.

rate /reɪt/ n. (ratio, level) taux m.; (speed) allure f.; (price) tarif m. **~s**, (taxes) impôts locaux m. pl. —v.t. évaluer; (consider) considérer; (deserve: Amer.) mériter. —v.i. **~ as**, être considéré comme. **at any ~**, en tout cas. **at the ~ of**, (on the basis of) à raison de.

ratepayer /'reɪtpeɪə(r)/ n. contribuable m./f.

rather /'rɑːðə(r)/ adv. (by preference) plutôt; (fairly) assez, plutôt; (a little) un peu. **I would ~ go**, j'aimerais mieux partir. **~ than go**, plutôt que de partir.

ratif|**y** /'rætɪfaɪ/ v.t. ratifier. **~ication** /-ɪ'keɪʃn/ n. ratification f.

rating /'reɪtɪŋ/ n. classement m.; (sailor) matelot m.; (number) indice m. **the ~s**, (TV) l'audimat (P.).

ratio /'reɪʃɪəʊ/ n. (pl. -os) proportion f.

ration /'ræʃn/ n. ration f. —v.t. rationner.

rational /'ræʃənl/ a. rationnel; (person) raisonnable.

rationalize /'ræʃənəlaɪz/ v.t. tenter de justifier; (organize) rationaliser.

rattle /'rætl/ v.i. faire du bruit; (of bottles) cliqueter; (v.t.) secouer; (sl.) agacer. —n. bruit (de ferraille) m.; cliquetis m.; (toy)

hochet m. **~ off**, débiter en vitesse.

rattlesnake /'rætlsneɪk/ n. serpent à sonnette m., crotale m.

raucous /'rɔːkəs/ a. rauque.

raunchy /'rɔːntʃɪ/ a. (-ier, -iest) (Amer., sl.) cochon.

ravage /'rævɪdʒ/ v.t. ravager. **~s** /-ɪz/ n. pl. ravages m. pl.

rav|**e** /reɪv/ v.i. divaguer; (in anger) tempêter. **~e about**, s'extasier sur. **~ings** n. pl. divagations f. pl.

raven /'reɪvn/ n. corbeau m.

ravenous /'rævənəs/ a. vorace. **I am ~**, je meurs de faim.

ravine /rə'viːn/ n. ravin m.

raving /'reɪvɪŋ/ a. **~ lunatic**, fou furieux m., folle furieuse f.

ravioli /rævɪ'əʊlɪ/ n. ravioli m. pl.

ravish /'rævɪʃ/ v.t. (rape) ravir. **~ing** a. (enchanting) ravissant.

raw /rɔː/ a. (-er, -est) cru; (not processed) brut; (wound) à vif; (immature) inexpérimenté. **get a ~ deal**, être mal traité. **~ materials**, matières premières f. pl.

ray /reɪ/ n. (of light etc.) rayon m. **~ of hope**, lueur d'espoir f.

raze /reɪz/ v.t. (destroy) raser.

razor /'reɪzə(r)/ n. rasoir m. **~-blade** n. lame de rasoir f.

re /riː/ prep. concernant.

re- /riː/ pref. re-, ré-, r-.

reach /riːtʃ/ v.t./i. atteindre, arriver à; (contact) joindre; (hand over) passer. —v.i. s'étendre. —n. portée f. **~ for**, tendre la main pour prendre. **within ~ of**, à portée de; (close to) à proximité de.

react /rɪ'ækt/ v.i. réagir.

reaction /rɪ'ækʃn/ n. réaction f. **~ary** a. & n. réactionnaire (m./f.).

reactor /rɪ'æktə(r)/ n. réacteur m.

read /riːd/ v.t./i. (p.t. read /red/)

lire; *(fig.)* comprendre; *(study)* étudier; *(of instrument)* indiquer. —*n. (fam.)* lecture *f.* ∼ **about** s.o., lire un article sur qn. ∼**out**, lire à haute voix. ∼**able** *a.* agréable *or* facile à lire. ∼**ing** *n.* lecture *f.*; indication *f.* ∼**ing-glasses** *pl. n.* lunettes pour lire *f. pl.* ∼**ing-lamp** *n.* lampe de bureau *f.* ∼**out** *n.* affichage *m.*

reader /'riːdə(r)/ *n.* lec|teur, -trice *m., f.* ∼**ship** *n.* lecteurs *m. pl.*

readily /'redɪlɪ/ *adv. (willingly)* volontiers; *(easily)* facilement.

readiness /'redɪnɪs/ *n.* empressement *m.* in ∼, prêt (for, à).

readjust /riːə'dʒʌst/ *v.t.* rajuster. —*v.i.* se réadapter (to, à).

ready /'redɪ/ *a.* (-ier, -iest) prêt; *(quick)* prompt. —*n.* at the ∼, tout prêt. ∼**-made** *a.* tout fait. ∼ **money**, (argent) liquide *m.* ∼**-reckoner**, barème *m.* ∼**-to-wear** *a.* prêt-à-porter.

real /rɪəl/ *a.* vrai, véritable, réel. —*adv. (Amer., fam.)* vraiment. ∼ **estate**, biens fonciers *m. pl.*

realis|t /'rɪəlɪst/ *n.* réaliste *m./f.* ∼**m** /-zəm/ *n.* réalisme *m.* ∼**tic** /-'lɪstɪk/ *a.* réaliste. ∼**tically** /-'lɪstɪklɪ/ *adv.* avec réalisme.

reality /rɪ'ælətɪ/ *n.* réalité *f.*

realize /'rɪəlaɪz/ *v.t.* se rendre compte de, comprendre; *(fulfil, turn into cash)* réaliser; *(price)* atteindre. ∼**ation** /-'zeɪʃn/ *n.* prise de conscience *f.*; réalisation *f.*

really /'rɪəlɪ/ *adv.* vraiment.

realtor /'rɪəltə(r)/ *n. (Amer.)* agent immobilier *m.*

realm /relm/ *n.* royaume *m.*

reap /riːp/ *v.t. (crop, field)* moissonner; *(fig.)* récolter.

reappear /riːə'pɪə(r)/ *v.i.* réapparaître, reparaître.

reappraisal /riːə'preɪzl/ *n.* réévaluation *f.*

rear¹ /rɪə(r)/ *n.* arrière *m.; derrière m.* —*a.* arrière *invar.*, de derrière. ∼**-view mirror**, rétroviseur *m.*

rear² /rɪə(r)/ *v.t. (bring up, breed)* élever. —*v.i. (horse)* se cabrer. ∼ **one's head**, dresser la tête.

rearguard /'rɪəgɑːd/ *n. (mil.)* arrière-garde *f.*

rearm /riː'ɑːm/ *v.t./i.* réarmer.

rearrange /riːə'reɪndʒ/ *v.t.* réarranger.

reason /'riːzn/ *n.* raison *f.* —*v.i.* raisonner. **it stands to** ∼ **that**, de toute évidence. **we have** ∼ **to believe that**, on a tout lieu de croire que. **there is no** ∼ **to panic**, il n'y a pas de raison de paniquer. ∼ **with**, raisonner. **everything within** ∼, tout dans les limites normales. ∼**ing** *n.* raisonnement *m.*

reasonable /'riːznəbl/ *a.* raisonnable.

reassur|e /riːə'ʃʊə(r)/ *v.t.* rassurer. ∼**ance** *n.* réconfort *m.*

rebate /'riːbeɪt/ *n.* remboursement (partiel) *m.*; *(discount)* rabais *m.*

rebel¹ /rebl/ *n. & a.* rebelle *(m./f.).*

rebel² /rɪ'bel/ *v.i. (p.t.* rebelled) se rebeller. ∼**lion** *n.* rébellion *f.* ∼**lious** *a.* rebelle.

rebound¹ /rɪ'baʊnd/ *v.i.* rebondir. ∼ **on**, *(backfire)* se retourner contre—. ∼² /'riːbaʊnd/ *n.* rebond *m.*

rebuff /rɪ'bʌf/ *v.t.* repousser. —*n.* rebuffade *f.*

rebuild /riː'bɪld/ *v.t.* reconstruire.

rebuke /rɪ'bjuːk/ *v.t.* réprimander. —*n.* réprimande *f.*, reproche *m.*

rebuttal /rɪ'bʌtl/ *n.* réfutation *f.*

recall /rɪ'kɔːl/ *v.t. (to s.o., call back)* rappeler; *(remember)* se rappeler. —*n.* rappel *m.*

recant /rɪ'kænt/ *v.i.* se rétracter.

recap /'riːkæp/ *v.t./i. (p.t.* recapped) *(fam.)* récapituler. —*n. (fam.)* récapitulation *f.*

recapitulat|e /riːkəˈpɪtʃuleɪt/ *v.t./i.* récapituler. **∼ion** /-ˈleɪʃn/ *n.* récapitulation *f.*

recapture /riːˈkæptʃə(r)/ *v.t.* reprendre; (*recall*) recréer.

reced|e /rɪˈsiːd/ *v.i.* s'éloigner. **his hair is ∼ing**, son front se dégarnit. **∼ing** *a.* (*forehead*) fuyant.

receipt /rɪˈsiːt/ *n.* (*written*) reçu *m.*; (*of letter*) réception *f.* **∼s,** (*money: comm.*) recettes *f. pl.*

receive /rɪˈsiːv/ *v.t.* recevoir. **∼r** /-ə(r)/ *n.* (*of stolen goods*) receleu|r, -se *m.*, *f.*; (*telephone*) combiné *m.*

recent /ˈriːsnt/ *a.* récent. **∼ly** *adv.* récemment.

receptacle /rɪˈseptəkl/ *n.* récipient *m.*

reception /rɪˈsepʃn/ *n.* réception *f.* **give s.o. a warm ∼,** donner un accueil chaleureux à qn. **∼ist** *n.* réceptionniste *m./f.*

receptive /rɪˈseptɪv/ *a.* réceptif.

recess /rɪˈses/ *n.* (*alcove*) renfoncement *m.*; (*nook*) recoin *m.*; (*holiday*) vacances *f. pl.*; (*schol., Amer.*) récréation *f.*

recession /rɪˈseʃn/ *n.* récession *f.*

recharge /riːˈtʃɑːdʒ/ *v.t.* recharger.

recipe /ˈresəpɪ/ *n.* recette *f.*

recipient /rɪˈsɪpɪənt/ *n.* (*of honour*) récipiendaire *m.*; (*of letter*) destinataire *m./f.*

reciprocal /rɪˈsɪprəkl/ *a.* réciproque.

reciprocate /rɪˈsɪprəkeɪt/ *v.t.* offrir en retour. —*v.i.* en faire autant.

recital /rɪˈsaɪtl/ *n.* récital *m.*

recite /rɪˈsaɪt/ *v.t.* (*poem, lesson, etc.*) réciter; (*list*) énumérer.

reckless /ˈreklɪs/ *a.* imprudent. **∼ly** *adv.* imprudemment.

reckon /ˈrekən/ *v.t./i.* calculer; (*judge*) considérer; (*think*) penser. **∼ on/with,** compter sur/ avec. **∼ing** *n.* calcul(s) *m.* (*pl.*).

reclaim /rɪˈkleɪm/ *v.t.* (*seek return of*) réclamer; (*land*) défricher; (*flooded land*) assécher.

reclin|e /rɪˈklaɪn/ *v.i.* être étendu. **∼ing** *a.* (*person*) étendu; (*seat*) à dossier réglable.

recluse /rɪˈkluːs/ *n.* reclus(e) *m.* (*f.*), ermite *m.*

recognition /rekəgˈnɪʃn/ *n.* reconnaissance *f.* **beyond ∼,** méconnaissable. **gain ∼,** être reconnu.

recognize /ˈrekəgnaɪz/ *v.t.* reconnaître.

recoil /rɪˈkɔɪl/ *v.i.* reculer (**from,** devant).

recollect /rekəˈlekt/ *v.t.* se souvenir de, se rappeler. **∼ion** /-kʃn/ *n.* souvenir *m.*

recommend /rekəˈmend/ *v.t.* recommander. **∼ation** /-ˈdeɪʃn/ *n.* recommandation *f.*

recompense /ˈrekəmpens/ *v.t.* (ré)compenser. —*n.* récompense *f.*

reconcil|e /ˈrekənsaɪl/ *v.t.* (*people*) réconcilier; (*facts*) concilier. **∼e o.s. to,** se résigner à. **∼iation** /-sɪlɪˈeɪʃn/ *n.* réconciliation *f.*

recondition /riːkənˈdɪʃn/ *v.t.* remettre à neuf, réviser.

reconnoitre /rekəˈnɔɪtə(r)/ *v.t.* (*pres. p.* **-tring**) (*mil.*) reconnaître. **∼aissance** /rɪˈkɒnɪsns/ *n.* reconnaissance *f.*

reconsider /riːkənˈsɪdə(r)/ *v.t.* reconsidérer. —*v.i.* se déjuger.

reconstruct /riːkənˈstrʌkt/ *v.t.* reconstruire; (*crime*) reconstituer.

record¹ /rɪˈkɔːd/ *v.t./i.* (*in register, on tape, etc.*) enregistrer; (*in diary*) noter. **∼ that,** rapporter que. **∼ing** *n.* enregistrement *m.*

record² /ˈrekɔːd/ *n.* (*report*) rapport *m.*; (*register*) registre *m.*; (*mention*) mention *f.*; (*file*) dossier *m.*; (*fig.*) résultats *m. pl.*; (*mus.*) disque *m.*; (*sport*) record *m.* (**criminal**) **∼,** casier

judiciaire m. —a. record invar.
off the ∼, officieusement. ∼-
holder n. déten|teur, -trice du
record m., f. ∼-player n.
électrophone m.
recorder /rɪ'kɔːdə(r)/ n. (mus.)
flûte à bec f.
recount /rɪ'kaʊnt/ v.t. raconter.
re-count /riː'kaʊnt/ v.t. recomp-
ter.
recoup /rɪ'kuːp/ v.t. récupérer.
recourse /rɪ'kɔːs/ n. recours m.
have ∼ to, avoir recours à.
recover /rɪ'kʌvə(r)/ v.t. récupérer.
—v.i. se remettre; (med.) se
rétablir; (economy) se redresser.
∼y n. récupération f.; (med.)
rétablissement m.
recreation /rekrɪ'eɪʃn/ n. récréation f. ∼al a. de récréation.
recrimination /rɪkrɪmɪ'neɪʃn/ n.
contre-accusation f.
recruit /rɪ'kruːt/ n. recrue f. —v.t.
recruter. ∼ment n. recrutement
m.
rectang|le /'rektæŋgl/ n. rectangle
m. ∼ular /-'tæŋgjʊlə(r)/ a.
rectangulaire.
rectif|y /'rektɪfaɪ/ v.t. rectifier.
∼ication /-ɪ'keɪʃn/ n. rectifica-
tion f.
recuperate /rɪ'kjuːpəreɪt/ v.t.
récupérer. —v.i. (med.) se
rétablir.
recur /rɪ'kɜː(r)/ v.i. (p.t. recurred)
revenir, se répéter.
recurren|t /rɪ'kʌrənt/ a. fréquent.
∼ce n. répétition f., retour m.
recycle /riː'saɪkl/ v.t. recycler.
red /red/ a. (redder, reddest)
rouge; (hair) roux. —n. rouge m.
in the ∼, en déficit. roll out the
∼ carpet for, recevoir en grande
pompe. Red Cross, Croix-
Rouge f. ∼-handed a. en flagrant
délit. ∼ herring, fausse piste f.
∼-hot a. brûlant. the ∼ light, le
feu rouge m. ∼ tape, paperasserie f., bureaucratie f.

redcurrant /red'kʌrənt/ n.
groseille f.
redden /'redn/ v.t./i. rougir.
reddish /'redɪʃ/ a. rougeâtre.
redecorate /riː'dekəreɪt/ v.t. (re-
paint etc.) repeindre, refaire.
redeem /rɪ'diːm/ v.t. racheter.
∼ing quality, qualité qui
rachète les défauts f. redemption n. /rɪ'dempʃn/ rachat m.
redeploy /riːdɪ'plɔɪ/ v.t. réorganiser; (troops) répartir.
redirect /riːdaɪə'rekt/ v.t. (letter)
faire suivre.
redness /'rednɪs/ n. rougeur f.
redo /riː'duː/ v.t. (p.t. -did, p.p.
-done) refaire.
redolent /'redələnt/ a. ∼ of, qui
évoque.
redouble /rɪ'dʌbl/ v.t. redoubler.
redress /rɪ'dres/ v.t. (wrong etc.)
redresser. —n. réparation f.
reduc|e /rɪ'djuːs/ v.t. réduire;
(temperature etc.) faire baisser.
∼tion /rɪ'dʌkʃn/ n. réduction f.
redundan|t /rɪ'dʌndənt/ a. super-
flu; (worker) licencié. make ∼,
licencier. ∼cy n. licenciement
m.; (word, phrase) pléonasme m.
reed /riːd/ n. (plant) roseau m.;
(mus.) anche f.
reef /riːf/ n. récif m., écueil m.
reek /riːk/ n. puanteur f. —v.i. ∼
(of), puer.
reel /riːl/ n. (of thread) bobine f.;
(of film) bande f.; (winding device)
dévidoir m. —v.i. chanceler. —v.t.
∼ off, réciter.
refectory /rɪ'fektərɪ/ n. réfectoire
m.
refer /rɪ'fɜː(r)/ v.t./i. (p.t. re-
ferred). ∼ to, (allude to) faire
allusion à; (concern) s'appliquer
à; (consult) consulter; (submit)
soumettre à; (direct) renvoyer
à.
referee /refə'riː/ n. arbitre m.; (for
job) répondant(e) m. (f.). —v.t.
(p.t. refereed) arbitrer.

reference /'refrəns/ n. référence f.; (mention) allusion f.; (person) répondant(e) m. (f.). **in** or **with ~ to**, en ce qui concerne; (comm.) suite à. **~ book**, ouvrage de référence m.

referendum /refə'rendəm/ n. (pl. **-ums**) référendum m.

refill[1] /ri:'fɪl/ v.t. remplir (à nouveau); (pen etc.) recharger.

refill[2] /'ri:fɪl/ n. (of pen, lighter, lipstick) recharge f.

refine /rɪ'faɪn/ v.t. raffiner. **~d** a. raffiné. **~ment** n. raffinement m.; (techn.) raffinage m. **~ry** /-ərɪ/ n. raffinerie f.

reflate /ri:'fleɪt/ v.t. relancer.

reflect /rɪ'flekt/ v.t. refléter; (of mirror) réfléchir, refléter. —v.i. réfléchir (**on**, à). **~ on s.o.**, (glory etc.) (faire) rejaillir sur qn.; (pej.) donner une mauvaise impression de qn. **~ion** /-kʃn/ n. réflexion f.; (image) reflet m. **on ~ion**, réflexion faite. **~or** n. réflecteur m.

reflective /rɪ'flektɪv/ a. réfléchissant.

reflex /'ri:fleks/ a. & n. réflexe (m.).

reflexive /rɪ'fleksɪv/ a. (gram.) réfléchi.

reform /rɪ'fɔ:m/ v.t. réformer. —v.i. (person) s'amender. —n. réforme f. **~er** n. réforma|teur, -trice m., f.

refract /rɪ'frækt/ v.t. réfracter.

refrain[1] /rɪ'freɪn/ n. refrain m.

refrain[2] /rɪ'freɪn/ v.i. s'abstenir (**from**, de).

refresh /rɪ'freʃ/ v.t. rafraîchir; (of rest etc.) ragaillardir, délasser. **~ing** a. (drink) rafraîchissant; (sleep) réparateur. **~ments** n. pl. rafraîchissements m. pl.

refresher /rɪ'freʃə(r)/ a. (course) de perfectionnement.

refrigerat|e /rɪ'frɪdʒəreɪt/ v.t. réfrigérer. **~or** n. réfrigérateur m.

refuel /ri:'fjʊəl/ v.t./i. (p.t. **refuelled**) (se) ravitailler.

refuge /'refju:dʒ/ n. refuge m. **take ~**, se réfugier.

refugee /refjʊ'dʒi:/ n. réfugié(e) m.

refund /rɪ'fʌnd/ v.t. rembourser. —n. /'ri:fʌnd/ remboursement m.

refurbish /ri:'fɜ:bɪʃ/ v.t. remettre à neuf.

refus|e[1] /rɪ'fju:z/ v.t./i. refuser. **~al** n. refus m.

refuse[2] /'refju:s/ n. ordures f. pl.

refute /rɪ'fju:t/ v.t. réfuter.

regain /rɪ'geɪn/ v.t. retrouver; (lost ground) regagner.

regal /'ri:gl/ a. royal, majestueux.

regalia /rɪ'geɪlɪə/ n. pl. (insignia) insignes (royaux) m. pl.

regard /rɪ'gɑ:d/ v.t. considérer. —n. considération f., estime f. **~s**, amitiés f. pl. **in this ~**, à cet égard. **as ~s**, **~ing** prep. en ce qui concerne.

regardless /rɪ'gɑ:dlɪs/ adv. quand même. **~ of**, sans tenir compte de.

regatta /rɪ'gætə/ n. régates f. pl.

regenerat|e /rɪ'dʒenəreɪt/ v.t. régénérer. **~ion** /-'reɪʃn/ n. régénération f.

regen|t /'ri:dʒənt/ n. régent(e) m. (f.). **~cy** n. régence f.

regime /reɪ'ʒi:m/ n. régime m.

regiment /'redʒɪmənt/ n. régiment m. **~al** /-'mentl/ a. d'un régiment. **~ation** /-en'teɪʃn/ n. discipline excessive f.

region /'ri:dʒən/ n. région f. **in the ~ of**, environ. **~al** a. régional.

register /'redʒɪstə(r)/ n. registre m. —v.t. enregistrer; (vehicle) immatriculer; (birth) déclarer; (letter) recommander; (indicate) indiquer; (express) exprimer. —v.i. (enrol) s'inscrire; (fig.) être compris. **~er office**, bureau d'état civil m. **~ration** /-'streɪʃn/ n. enregistrement m.; inscription *f.*; (*vehicle document*) carte grise *f.* **~ration (number)**, (*auto.*) numéro d'immatriculation *m.*

registrar /redʒɪˈstrɑː(r)/ *n.* officier de l'état civil *m.*; (*univ.*) secrétaire général *m.*

regret /rɪˈgret/ *n.* regret *m.* —*v.t.* (*p.t.* **regretted**) regretter (**to do**, de faire). **~fully** *adv.* à regret. **~table** *a.* regrettable, fâcheux. **~tably** *adv.* malheureusement; (*small, poor, etc.*) fâcheusement.

regroup /riːˈgruːp/ *v.t./i.* (se) regrouper.

regular /ˈregjʊlə(r)/ *a.* régulier; (*usual*) habituel; (*thorough: fam.*) vrai. —*n.* (*fam.*) habitué(e) *m.* (*f.*). **~ity** /-ˈlærəti/ *n.* régularité *f.* **~ly** *adv.* régulièrement.

regulat|e /ˈregjʊleɪt/ *v.t.* régler. **~ion** /-ˈleɪʃn/ *n.* réglage *m.*; (*rule*) règlement *m.*

rehabilitat|e /riːəˈbɪlɪteɪt/ *v.t.* réadapter; (*in public esteem*) réhabiliter. **~ion** /-ˈteɪʃn/ *n.* réadaptation *f.*; réhabilitation *f.*

rehash¹ /riːˈhæʃ/ *v.t.* remanier.

rehash² /ˈriːhæʃ/ *n.* réchauffé *m.*

rehears|e /rɪˈhɜːs/ *v.t./i.* (*theatre*) répéter. **~al** *n.* répétition *f.*

re-heat /riːˈhiːt/ *v.t.* réchauffer.

reign /reɪn/ *n.* règne *m.* —*v.i.* régner (**over**, sur).

reimburse /riːɪmˈbɜːs/ *v.t.* rembourser.

rein /reɪn/ *n.* rêne *f.*

reindeer /ˈreɪndɪə(r)/ *n. invar.* renne *m.*

reinforce /riːɪnˈfɔːs/ *v.t.* renforcer. **~ment** *n.* renforcement *m.* **~ments** *n. pl.* renforts *m. pl.* **~d concrete**, béton armé *m.*

reinstate /riːɪnˈsteɪt/ *v.t.* réintégrer, rétablir.

reiterate /riːˈɪtəreɪt/ *v.t.* réitérer.

reject¹ /rɪˈdʒekt/ *v.t.* (*offer, plea, etc.*) rejeter; (*book, goods, etc.*) refuser. **~ion** /-kʃn/ *n.* rejet *m.*; refus *m.*

reject² /ˈriːdʒekt/ *n.* (article de) rebut *m.*

rejoic|e /rɪˈdʒɔɪs/ *v.i.* se réjouir. **~ing** *n.* réjouissance *f.*

rejuvenate /rɪˈdʒuːvəneɪt/ *v.t.* rajeunir.

relapse /rɪˈlæps/ *n.* rechute *f.* —*v.i.* rechuter. **~ into**, retomber dans.

relate /rɪˈleɪt/ *v.t.* raconter; (*associate*) rapprocher. —*v.i.* **~ to**, se rapporter à; (*get on with*) s'entendre avec. **~d** /-ɪd/ *a.* (*ideas etc.*) lié. **~d to s.o.**, parent(e) de qn.

relation /rɪˈleɪʃn/ *n.* rapport *m.*; (*person*) parent(e) *m.* (*f.*). **~ship** *n.* lien de parenté *m.*; (*link*) rapport *m.*; (*affair*) liaison *f.*

relative /ˈrelətɪv/ *n.* parent(e) *m.* (*f.*). —*a.* relatif; (*respective*) respectif. **~ly** *adv.* relativement.

relax /rɪˈlæks/ *v.t./i.* (*less tense*) (se) relâcher; (*for pleasure*) se détendre. **~ation** /riːlækˈseɪʃn/ *n.* relâchement *m.*; détente *f.* **~ing** *a.* délassant.

relay¹ /ˈriːleɪ/ *n.* relais *m.* **~ race**, course de relais *f.*

relay² /rɪˈleɪ/ *v.t.* relayer.

release /rɪˈliːs/ *v.t.* libérer; (*bomb*) lâcher; (*film*) sortir; (*news*) publier; (*smoke*) dégager; (*spring*) déclencher. —*n.* libération *f.*; sortie *f.*; (*record*) nouveau disque *m.* (*of pollution*) émission *f.*

relegate /ˈrelɪgeɪt/ *v.t.* reléguer.

relent /rɪˈlent/ *v.i.* se laisser fléchir. **~less** *a.* impitoyable.

relevan|t /ˈreləvənt/ *a.* pertinent. **be ~t to**, avoir rapport à. **~ce** *n.* pertinence *f.*, rapport *m.*

reliab|le /rɪˈlaɪəbl/ *a.* sérieux, sûr; (*machine*) fiable. **~ility** /-ˈbɪləti/ *n.* sérieux *m.*; fiabilité *f.*

reliance /rɪˈlaɪəns/ *n.* dépendance *f.*; (*trust*) confiance *f.*

relic /ˈrelɪk/ *n.* relique *f.* **~s**, (*of past*) vestiges *m. pl.*

relief /rɪˈliːf/ *n.* soulagement *m.*

(from, à); (assistance) secours m.; (outline, design) relief m. **~ road**, route de délestage f.

relieve /rɪˈliːv/ v.t. soulager; (help) secourir; (take over from) relayer.

religion /rɪˈlɪdʒən/ n. religion f.

religious /rɪˈlɪdʒəs/ a. religieux.

relinquish /rɪˈlɪŋkwɪʃ/ v.t. abandonner; (relax hold of) lâcher.

relish /ˈrelɪʃ/ n. plaisir m., goût m.; (culin.) assaisonnement m. —v.t. savourer; (idea etc.) aimer.

relocate /riːləʊˈkeɪt/ v.t. (company) déplacer; (employee) muter. —v.i. se déplacer, déménager.

reluctan|**t** /rɪˈlʌktənt/ a. fait, donné, etc. à contrecœur. **~t to**, peu disposé à. **~ce** n. répugnance f. **~tly** adv. à contrecœur.

rely /rɪˈlaɪ/ v.i. **~ on**, compter sur; (financially) dépendre de.

remain /rɪˈmeɪn/ v.i. rester. **~s** n. pl. restes m. pl.

remainder /rɪˈmeɪndə(r)/ n. reste m.; (book) invendu soldé m.

remand /rɪˈmɑːnd/ v.t. mettre en détention préventive. —n. **on ~**, en détention préventive.

remark /rɪˈmɑːk/ n. remarque f. —v.t. remarquer. —v.i. **~ on**, faire des commentaires sur. **~able** a. remarquable.

remarry /riːˈmærɪ/ v.i. se remarier.

remed|**y** /ˈremədɪ/ n. remède m. —v.t. remédier à. **~ial** /rɪˈmiːdɪəl/ a. (class etc.) de rattrapage; (treatment med.) curatif.

rememb|**er** /rɪˈmembə(r)/ v.t. se souvenir de, se rappeler. **~er to do**, ne pas oublier de faire. **~rance** n. souvenir m.

remind /rɪˈmaɪnd/ v.t. rappeler (**s.o. of sth.**, qch. à qn.). **~s.o. to do**, rappeler à qn. qu'il doit faire. **~er** n. (letter, signal) rappel m.

reminisce /remɪˈnɪs/ v.i. évoquer ses souvenirs. **~nces** n. pl. réminiscences f. pl.

reminiscent /remɪˈnɪsnt/ a. **~ of**, qui rappelle, qui évoque.

remiss /rɪˈmɪs/ a. négligent.

remission /rɪˈmɪʃn/ n. rémission f.; (jurid.) remise (de peine) f.

remit /rɪˈmɪt/ v.t. (p.t. remitted) (money) envoyer; (debt) remettre. **~tance** n. paiement m.

remnant /ˈremnənt/ n. reste m., débris m.; (trace) vestige m.; (of cloth) coupon m.

remodel /riːˈmɒdl/ v.t. (p.t. remodelled) remodeler.

remorse /rɪˈmɔːs/ n. remords m. (pl.). **~ful** a. plein de remords. **~less** a. implacable.

remote /rɪˈməʊt/ a. (place, time) lointain; (person) distant; (slight) vague. **~ control**, télécommande f. **~ly** adv. au loin; vaguement. **~ness** n. éloignement m.

removable /rɪˈmuːvəbl/ a. (detachable) amovible.

remov|**e** /rɪˈmuːv/ v.t. enlever; (lead away) emmener; (dismiss) renvoyer; (do away with) supprimer. **~al** n. enlèvement m.; renvoi m.; suppression f.; (from house) déménagement m. **~al men**, déménageurs m. pl. **~er** n. (for paint) décapant m.

remunerat|**e** /rɪˈmjuːnəreɪt/ v.t. rémunérer. **~ion** /-ˈreɪʃn/ n. rémunération f.

rename /riːˈneɪm/ v.t. rebaptiser.

render /ˈrendə(r)/ v.t. (give, make) rendre; (mus.) interpréter. **~ing** n. interprétation f.

rendezvous /ˈrɒndɪvuː/ n. (pl. **-vous** /-vuːz/) rendez-vous m. invar.

renegade /ˈrenɪgeɪd/ n. renégat(e) m. (f.).

renew /rɪˈnjuː/ v.t. renouveler; (resume) reprendre. **~able** a. renouvelable. **~al** n. renouvellement m.; reprise f.

renounce /rɪˈnaʊns/ v.t. renoncer à; (disown) renier.

renovat|e /ʹrenəveɪt/ v.t. rénover. ∼ion /-ʹveɪʃn/ n. rénovation f.

renown /rɪʹnaʊn/ n. renommée f. ∼ed a. renommé.

rent /rent/ n. loyer m. —v.t. louer. for ∼, à louer. ∼al n. prix de location m.

renunciation /rɪnʌnsɪʹeɪʃn/ n. renonciation f.

reopen /riːʹəʊpən/ v.t./i. rouvrir. ∼ing n. réouverture f.

reorganize /riːʹɔːɡənaɪz/ v.t. réorganiser.

rep /rep/ n. (comm., fam.) représentant(e) m. (f.).

repair /rɪʹpeə(r)/ v.t. réparer. —n. réparation f. in good/bad ∼, en bon/mauvais état. ∼er n. réparateur m.

repartee /repɑːʹtiː/ n. repartie f.

repatriat|e /riːʹpætrɪeɪt/ v.t. rapatrier. ∼ion /-ʹeɪʃn/ n. rapatriement m.

repay /riːʹpeɪ/ v.t. (p.t. repaid) rembourser; (reward) récompenser. ∼ment n. remboursement m.; récompense f. monthly ∼ments, mensualités f. pl.

repeal /rɪʹpiːl/ v.t. abroger, annuler. —n. abrogation f.

repeat /rɪʹpiːt/ v.t./i. répéter; (renew) renouveler. —n. répétition f.; (broadcast) reprise f. ∼ itself, ∼ o.s., se répéter.

repeatedly /rɪʹpiːtɪdlɪ/ adv. à maintes reprises.

repel /rɪʹpel/ v.t. (p.t. repelled) repousser. ∼lent a. repoussant.

repent /rɪʹpent/ v.i. se repentir (of, de). ∼ance n. repentir m. ∼ant a. repentant.

repercussion /riːpəʹkʌʃn/ n. répercussion f.

repertoire /ʹrepətwɑː(r)/ n. répertoire m.

repertory /ʹrepətrɪ/ n. répertoire m. ∼ (theatre), théâtre de répertoire m.

repetit|ion /repɪʹtɪʃn/ n. répétition f. ∼ious /-ʹtɪʃəs/, ∼ive /rɪʹpetɪtɪv/ adjs. plein de répétitions.

replace /rɪʹpleɪs/ v.t. remettre; (take the place of) remplacer. ∼ment n. remplacement m. (of, de); (person) remplaçant(e) m. (f.); (new part) pièce de rechange f.

replay /ʹriːpleɪ/ n. (sport) match rejoué m.; (recording) répétition immédiate f.

replenish /rɪʹplenɪʃ/ v.t. (refill) remplir; (renew) renouveler.

replica /ʹreplɪkə/ n. copie exacte f.

reply /rɪʹplaɪ/ v.t./i. répondre. —n. réponse f.

report /rɪʹpɔːt/ v.t. rapporter, annoncer (that, que); (notify) signaler; (denounce) dénoncer. —v.i. faire un rapport (on), (news item) faire un reportage sur. ∼ to, (go) se présenter chez. —n. rapport m.; (in press) reportage m.; (schol.) bulletin m.; (sound) détonation f. ∼edly adv. selon ce qu'on dit.

reporter /rɪʹpɔːtə(r)/ n. reporter m.

repose /rɪʹpəʊz/ n. repos m.

repossess /riːpəʹzes/ v.t. reprendre.

represent /reprɪʹzent/ v.t. représenter. ∼ation /-ʹteɪʃn/ n. représentation f. make ∼ations to, protester auprès de.

representative /reprɪʹzentətɪv/ a. représentatif, typique (of, de). —n. représentant(e) m. (f.).

repress /rɪʹpres/ v.t. réprimer. ∼ion /-ʃn/ n. répression f. ∼ive a. répressif.

reprieve /rɪʹpriːv/ n. (delay) sursis m.; (pardon) grâce f. —v.t. accorder un sursis à; gracier.

reprimand /ʹreprɪmɑːnd/ v.t. réprimander. —n. réprimande f.

reprint /ʹriːprɪnt/ n. réimpression f.; (offprint) tiré à part m.

reprisals /rɪ'praɪzlz/ n. pl. représailles f. pl.

reproach /rɪ'prəʊtʃ/ v.t. reprocher (s.o. for sth., qch. à qn.). —n. reproche m. ~ful a. de reproche, réprobateur. ~fully adv. avec reproche.

reproduce /riːprə'djuːs/ v.t./i. (se) reproduire. ~tion /-'dʌkʃn/ n. reproduction f. ~tive /-'dʌktɪv/ a. reproducteur.

reptile /'reptaɪl/ n. reptile m.

republic /rɪ'pʌblɪk/ n. république f. ~an a. & n. républicain(e) (m. (f.)).

repudiate /rɪ'pjuːdɪeɪt/ v.t. répudier; (treaty) refuser d'honorer.

repugnan|t /rɪ'pʌgnənt/ a. répugnant. ~ce n. répugnance f.

repuls|e /rɪ'pʌls/ v.t. repousser. ~ion /-ʃn/ n. répulsion f. ~ive a. repoussant.

reputable /'repjʊtəbl/ a. honorable, de bonne réputation.

reputation /repjʊ'teɪʃn/ n. réputation f.

repute /rɪ'pjuːt/ n. réputation f. ~d /-ɪd/ a. réputé. ~dly /-ɪdlɪ/ adv. d'après ce qu'on dit.

request /rɪ'kwest/ n. demande f. —v.t. demander (of, from, à). ~ stop, arrêt facultatif m.

requiem /'rekwɪem/ n. requiem m.

require rɪ'kwaɪə(r) v.t. (of thing) demander; (of person) avoir besoin de; (demand, order) exiger. ~d a. requis. ~ment n. exigence f.; (condition) condition (requise) f.

requisite /'rekwɪzɪt/ a. nécessaire. —n. chose nécessaire f. ~s, (for travel etc.) articles m. pl.

requisition /rekwɪ'zɪʃn/ n. réquisition f. —v.t. réquisitionner.

re-route /riː'ruːt/ v.t. dérouter.

resale /'riːseɪl/ n. revente f.

rescind /rɪ'sɪnd/ v.t. annuler.

rescue /'reskjuː/ v.t. sauver. —n.

sauvetage m. (of, de); (help) secours m. ~r /-ə(r)/ n. sauveteur m.

research /rɪ'sɜːtʃ/ n. recherche(s) f.(pl.). —v.t./i. faire de recherches (sur). ~er n. chercheu|r, -se m., f.

resembl|e /rɪ'zembl/ v.t. ressembler à ~ance n. ressemblance f.

resent /rɪ'zent/ v.t. être indigné de, s'offenser de. ~ful a. plein de ressentiment, indigné. ~ment n. ressentiment m.

reservation /rezə'veɪʃn/ n. réserve f.; (booking) réservation f.; (Amer.) réserve (indienne) f. make a ~, réserver.

reserve /rɪ'zɜːv/ v.t. réserver. —n. (reticence, stock, land) réserve f.; (sport) remplaçant(e) m. (f.). in ~, en réserve. the ~s, (mil.) les réserves f. pl. ~d a. (person, room) réservé.

reservist /rɪ'zɜːvɪst/ n. (mil.) réserviste m.

reservoir /'rezəvwɑː(r)/ n. (lake, supply, etc.) réservoir m.

reshape /riː'ʃeɪp/ v.t. remodeler.

reshuffle /riː'ʃʌfl/ v.t. (pol.) remanier. —n. (pol.) remaniement (ministériel) m.

reside /rɪ'zaɪd/ v.i. résider.

residen|t /'rezɪdənt/ a. résidant. be ~t, résider. —n. habitant(e) m. (f.); (foreigner) résident(e) m. (f.); (in hotel) pensionnaire m./f. ~ce n. résidence f.; (of students) foyer m. in ~ce, (doctor) résidant; (students) au foyer.

residential /rezɪ'denʃl/ a. résidentiel.

residue /'rezɪdjuː/ n. résidu m.

resign /rɪ'zaɪn/ v.t. abandonner; (job) démissionner de. —v.i. démissionner. ~ o.s. to, se résigner à. ~ation /rezɪg'neɪʃn/ n. résignation f.; (from job) démission f. ~ed a. résigné.

resilien|t /rɪ'zɪlɪənt/ a. élastique; (*person*) qui a du ressort. **~ce** n. élasticité f.; ressort m.

resin /'rezɪn/ n. résine f.

resist /rɪ'zɪst/ v.t./i. résister (à). **~ance** n. résistance f. **~ant** a. (*med.*) rebelle; (*metal*) résistant.

resolute /'rezəluːt/ a. résolu. **~ion** /-'luːʃn/ n. résolution f.

resolve /rɪ'zɒlv/ v.t. résoudre (**to** do, de faire). —n. résolution f. **~d** a. résolu (**to do**, à faire).

resonan|t /'rezənənt/ a. résonnant. **~ce** n. résonance f.

resort /rɪ'zɔːt/ v.i. **~ to**, avoir recours à. —n. (*recourse*) recours m.; (*place*) station f. **in the last ~**, en dernier ressort.

resound /rɪ'zaʊnd/ v.i. retentir (**with**, de). **~ing** a. retentissant.

resource /rɪ'sɔːs/ n. (*expedient*) ressource f. **~s**, (*wealth etc.*) ressources f. pl. **~ful** a. ingénieux. **~fulness** n. ingéniosité f.

respect /rɪ'spekt/ n. respect m.; (*aspect*) égard m. —v.t. respecter. **with ~ to**, à l'égard de, relativement à. **~ful** a. respectueux.

respectab|le /rɪ'spektəbl/ a. respectable. **~ility** /-'bɪlətɪ/ n. respectabilité f. **~ly** adv. convenablement.

respective /rɪ'spektɪv/ a. respectif. **~ly** adv. respectivement.

respiration /respə'reɪʃn/ n. respiration f.

respite /'resp(a)ɪt/ n. répit m.

resplendent /rɪ'splendənt/ a. resplendissant.

respond /rɪ'spɒnd/ v.i. répondre (**to**, à) **~ to**, (*react to*) réagir à.

response /rɪ'spɒns/ n. réponse f.

responsib|le /rɪ'spɒnsəbl/ a. responsable; (*job*) qui comporte des responsabilités. **~ility** /-'bɪlətɪ/ n. responsabilité f. **~ly** adv. de façon responsable.

responsive /rɪ'spɒnsɪv/ a. qui réagit bien. **~ to**, sensible à.

rest[1] /rest/ v.t./i. (se) reposer; (*lean*) (s')appuyer (**on**, sur); (*be buried, lie*) reposer. —n. (*repose*) repos m.; (*support*) support m. **have a ~**, se reposer; (*at work*) prendre une pause. **~-room** n. (*Amer.*) toilettes f. pl.

rest[2] /rest/ v.i. (*remain*) demeurer. —n. (*remainder*) reste m. (**of**, de). **the ~ (of the)**, (*others, other*) les autres. **it ~s with him to**, il lui appartient de.

restaurant /'restərɒnt/ n. restaurant m.

restful /'restfl/ a. reposant.

restitution /restɪ'tjuːʃn/ n. (*for injury*) compensation f.

restive /'restɪv/ a. rétif.

restless /'restlɪs/ a. agité. **~ly** adv. avec agitation, fébrilement.

restor|e /rɪ'stɔː(r)/ v.t. rétablir; (*building*) restaurer. **~e sth. to** s.o., restituer qch. à qn. **~ation** /restə'reɪʃn/ n. rétablissement m.; restauration f. **~er** n. (*art*) restaura|teur, -trice m.,f.

restrain /rɪ'streɪn/ v.t. contenir. **~ s.o. from**, retenir qn. de. **~ed** a. (*moderate*) mesuré; (*in control of self*) maître de soi. **~t** n. contrainte f.; (*moderation*) retenue f.

restrict /rɪ'strɪkt/ v.t. restreindre. **~ion** /-kʃn/ n. restriction f. **~ive** a. restrictif.

restructure /riː'strʌktʃə(r)/ v.t. restructurer.

result /rɪ'zʌlt/ n. résultat m. —v.i. résulter. **~ in**, aboutir à.

resum|e /rɪ'zjuːm/ v.t./i. reprendre. **~ption** /rɪ'zʌmpʃn/ n. reprise f.

résumé /'rezjuːmeɪ/ n. résumé m.; (*of career: Amer.*) CV m., curriculum vitae m.

resurgence /rɪ'sɜːdʒəns/ n. réapparition f.

resurrect /rezə'rekt/ v.t. ressusciter. **~ion** -k∫n/ n. résurrection f.

resuscitate /rɪ'sʌsɪteɪt/ v.t. réanimer.

retail /'ri:teɪl/ n. détail m. —a. & adv. au détail. —v.t./i. (se) vendre (au détail). **~er**n. détaillant(e)m. (f.).

retain /rɪ'teɪn/ v.t. (hold back, remember) retenir; (keep) conserver.

retaliat|e /rɪ'tælɪeɪt/ v.i. riposter. **~ion** -/'eɪ∫n/ n. représailles f. pl.

retarded /rɪ'tɑːdɪd/ a. arriéré.

retch /retʃ/ v.i. avoir un haut-le-cœur.

retentive /rɪ'tentɪv/ a. (memory) fidèle. **~ of**, qui retient.

rethink /ri:'θɪŋk/ v.t. (p.t. rethought) repenser.

reticen|t /'retɪsnt/a. réticent. **~ce** n. réticence f.

retina /'retɪnə/ n. rétine f.

retinue /'retɪnju:/ n. suite f.

retire /rɪ'taɪə(r)/ v.i. (from work) prendre sa retraite; (withdraw) se retirer; (go to bed) se coucher. —v.t. mettre à la retraite. **~d** a. retraité. **~ment** n. retraite f.

retiring /rɪ'taɪərɪŋ/ a. réservé.

retort /rɪ'tɔːt/ v.t./i. répliquer. —n. réplique f.

retrace /ri:'treɪs/ v.t. **~ one's steps**, revenir sur ses pas.

retract /rɪ'trækt/ v.t./i. (se) rétracter.

retrain /ri:'treɪn/ v.t./i. (se) recycler.

retread /ri:'tred/ n. pneu rechapé m.

retreat /rɪ'tri:t/ v.i. (mil.) battre en retraite. —n. retraite f.

retrial /ri:'traɪəl/ n. nouveau procès m.

retribution /retrɪ'bju:∫n/ n. châtiment m.; (vengeance) vengeance f.

retriev|e /rɪ'tri:v/ v.t. (recover)

récupérer; (restore) rétablir; (put right) réparer. **~al** n. récupération f.; (of information) recherche documentaire f. **~er** n. (dog) chien d'arrêt m.

retrograde /'retrəgreɪd/ a. rétrograde —v.i. rétrograder.

retrospect /'retrəspekt/ n. **in ~**, rétrospectivement.

return /rɪ'tɜːn/ v.i. (come back) revenir; (go back) retourner; (go home) rentrer. —v.t. (give back) rendre; (bring back) rapporter; (send back) renvoyer; (put back) remettre. —n. retour m.; (yield) rapport m. **~s**, (comm.) bénéfices m. pl. **in ~ for**, en échange de. **~ journey**, voyage de retour m. **~ match**, match retour m. **~ ticket**, aller-retour m.

reunion /ri:'ju:nɪən/ n. réunion f.

reunite /ri:ju:'naɪt/ v.t. réunir.

rev /rev/ n. (auto., fam.) tour m. —v.t./i. (p.t. revved). **~ (up)**, (engine: fam.) (s')emballer.

revamp /ri:'væmp/ v.t. rénover.

reveal /rɪ'vi:l/ v.t. révéler; (allow to appear) laisser voir. **~ing** a. révélateur.

revel /'revl/ v.i. (p.t. revelled) faire bombance. **~ in**, se délecter de. **~ry** n. festivités f. pl.

revelation /revə'leɪ∫n/ n. révélation f.

revenge /rɪ'vendʒ/ n. vengeance f.; (sport) revanche f. —v.t. venger.

revenue /'revənju:/ n. revenu m.

reverberate /rɪ'vɜːbəreɪt/ v.i. (sound, light) se répercuter.

revere /rɪ'vɪə(r)/ v.t. révérer. **~nce** /'revərəns/ n. vénération f.

reverend /'revərənd/ a. révérend.

reverent /'revərənt/ a. respectueux.

reverie /'revərɪ/ n. rêverie f.

revers|e /rɪ'vɜːs/ a. contraire, inverse. —n. contraire m.; (back) revers m.; envers m.; (gear) marche arrière f. —v.t. (situation, bracket, *etc.*) renverser; (*order*) inverser; (*decision*) annuler. —*v.i.* (*auto.*) faire marche arrière. ∼**al** *n.* renversement *m.*; (*of view*) revirement *m.*

revert /rɪ'vɜːt/ *v.i.* ∼ **to**, revenir à.

review /rɪ'vjuː/ *n.* (*inspection, magazine*) revue *f.*; (*of book etc.*) critique *f.* —*v.t.* passer en revue; (*situation*) réexaminer; faire la critique de. ∼**er** *n.* critique *m.*

revis|e /rɪ'vaɪz/ *v.t.* réviser; (*text*) revoir. ∼**ion** /-ʒn/ *n.* révision *f.*

revitalize /riː'vaɪtəlaɪz/ *v.t.* revitaliser, revivifier.

reviv|e /rɪ'vaɪv/ *v.t.* (*person, hopes*) ranimer; (*play*) reprendre; (*custom*) rétablir. —*v.i.* se ranimer. ∼**al** *n.* (*resumption*) reprise *f.*; (*of faith*) renouveau *m.*

revoke /rɪ'vəʊk/ *v.t.* révoquer.

revolt /rɪ'vəʊlt/ *v.t./i.* (se) révolter. —*n.* révolte *f.*

revolting /rɪ'vəʊltɪŋ/ *a.* dégoûtant.

revolution /revə'luːʃn/ *n.* révolution *f.* ∼**ary** *a.* & *n.* révolutionnaire (*m./f.*). ∼**ize** *v.t.* révolutionner.

revolv|e /rɪ'vɒlv/ *v.i.* tourner. ∼**ing door**, tambour *m.*

revolver /rɪ'vɒlvə(r)/ *n.* revolver *m.*

revulsion /rɪ'vʌlʃn/ *n.* dégoût *m.*

reward /rɪ'wɔːd/ *n.* récompense *f.* —*v.t.* récompenser (**for**, de). ∼**ing** *a.* rémunérateur; (*worthwhile*) qui (en) vaut la peine.

rewind /riː'waɪnd/ *v.t.* (*p.t.* **rewound**) (*tape, film*) rembobiner.

rewire /riː'waɪə(r)/ *v.t.* refaire l'installation électrique de.

reword /riː'wɜːd/ *v.t.* reformuler.

rewrite /riː'raɪt/ *v.t.* récrire.

rhapsody /'ræpsədɪ/ *n.* rhapsodie *f.*

rhetoric /'retərɪk/ *n.* rhétorique *f.* ∼**al** /rɪ'tɒrɪkl/ *a.* (de) rhétorique; (*question*) de pure forme.

rheumati|c /ruː'mætɪk/ *a.* (*pain*) rhumatismal; (*person*) rhumatisant. ∼**sm** /'ruːmətɪzəm/ *n.* rhumatisme *m.*

rhinoceros /raɪ'nɒsərəs/ *n.* (*pl.* -**oses**) rhinocéros *m.*

rhubarb /'ruːbɑːb/ *n.* rhubarbe *f.*

rhyme /raɪm/ *n.* rime *f.*; (*poem*) vers *m. pl.* —*v.t./i.* (faire) rimer.

rhythm /'rɪðəm/ *n.* rythme *m.* ∼**ic(al)** /'rɪðmɪk(l)/ *a.* rythmique.

rib /rɪb/ *n.* côte *f.*

ribald /'rɪbld/ *a.* grivois.

ribbon /'rɪbən/ *n.* ruban *m.* **in** ∼**s**, (*torn pieces*) en lambeaux.

rice /raɪs/ *n.* riz *m.*

rich /rɪtʃ/ *a.* (-**er**, -**est**) riche. ∼**es** *n. pl.* richesses *f. pl.* ∼**ly** *adv.* richement; (*fully*) pleinement. ∼**ness** *n.* richesse *f.*

rickety /'rɪkətɪ/ *a.* branlant.

ricochet /'rɪkəʃeɪ/ *n.* ricochet *m.* —*v.i.* (*p.t.* **ricocheted** /-ʃeɪd/) ricocher.

rid /rɪd/ *v.t.* (*p.t.* **rid**, *pres. p.* **ridding**) débarrasser (**of**, de). **get** ∼ **of**, se débarrasser de.

riddance /'rɪdns/ *n.* **good** ∼!, bon débarras!

ridden /'rɪdn/ *see* **ride**.

riddle[1] /'rɪdl/ *n.* énigme *f.*

riddle[2] /'rɪdl/ *v.t.* ∼ **with**, (*bullets*) cribler de; (*mistakes*) bourrer de.

ride /raɪd/ *v.i.* (*p.t.* **rode**, *p.p.* **ridden**) aller (à bicyclette, à cheval, *etc.*); (*in car*) rouler. ∼ **(a horse)**, (*go riding as sport*) monter (à cheval). —*v.t.* (*a particular horse*) monter; (*distance*) parcourir. —*n.* promenade *f.*, tour *m.*; (*distance*) trajet *m.* **give s.o. a** ∼, (*Amer.*) prendre qn. en voiture. **go for a** ∼, aller faire un tour (à bicyclette, à cheval, *etc.*). ∼**r** /-ə(r)/ *n.* cavali|er, -ière *m., f.*; (*in horse race*) jockey *m.*; (*cyclist*) cycliste *m./f.*; (*motorcyclist*) motocycliste *m./f.*; (*in document*) annexe *f.*

ridge /rɪdʒ/ n. arête f., crête f.

ridicule /'rɪdɪkjuːl/ n. ridicule m. —v.t. ridiculiser.

ridiculous /rɪ'dɪkjʊləs/ a. ridicule.

riding /'raɪdɪŋ/ n. équitation f.

rife /raɪf/ a. **be ~**, être répandu, sévir. **~ with**, abondant en.

riff-raff /'rɪfræf/ n. canaille f.

rifle /'raɪfl/ n. fusil m. —v.t. (rob) dévaliser.

rift /rɪft/ n. (crack) fissure f.; (between people) désaccord m.

rig¹ /rɪg/ v.t. (p.t. **rigged**) (equip) équiper. —n. (for oil) derrick m. **~ out**, habiller. **~out** n. (fam.) tenue f. **~ up**, (arrange) arranger.

rig² /rɪg/ v.t. (p.t. **rigged**) (election, match, etc.) truquer.

right /raɪt/ a. (morally) bon; (fair) juste; (best) bon, qu'il faut; (not left) droit. **be ~**, (person) avoir raison (**to**, de); (calculation, watch) être exact. —n. (entitlement) droit m.; (not left) droite f.; (not evil) le bien. —v.t. (a wrong, sth. fallen, etc.) redresser. —adv. (not left) à droite; (directly) tout droit; (exactly) bien, juste; (completely) tout à fait. **be in the ~**, avoir raison. **by ~**, normalement. **on the ~**, à droite. **put ~**, arranger, rectifier. **~ angle**, angle droit m. **~ away**, tout de suite. **~-hand** a. à or de droite. **~ hand man**, bras droit m. **~-handed** a. droitier. **~ now**, (at once) tout de suite; (at present) en ce moment. **~ of way**, (auto.) priorité f. **~-wing** a. (pol.) de droite.

righteous /'raɪtʃəs/ a. (person) vertueux; (cause, anger) juste.

rightful /'raɪtfl/ a. légitime. **~ly** adv. à juste titre.

rightly /'raɪtlɪ/ adv. correctement; (with reason) à juste titre.

rigid /'rɪdʒɪd/ a. rigide. **~ity** /rɪ'dʒɪdətɪ/ n. rigidité f.

rigmarole /'rɪgmərəʊl/ n. charabia m.; (procedure) comédie f.

rigour /'rɪgə(r)/ n. rigueur f. **~orous** a. rigoureux.

rile /raɪl/ v.t. (fam.) agacer.

rim /rɪm/ n. bord m.; (of wheel) jante f. **~med** a. bordé.

rind /raɪnd/ n. (on cheese) croûte f.; (on bacon) couenne f.; (on fruit) écorce f.

ring¹ /rɪŋ/ n. anneau m.; (with stone) bague f.; (circle) cercle m.; (boxing) ring m.; (arena) piste f. —v.t. entourer; (word in text etc.) entourer d'un cercle. **(wedding) ~**, alliance f. **~ road**, périphérique m.

ring² /rɪŋ/ v.t./i. (p.t. **rang**, p.p. **rung**) (of words etc.) retentir. —n. sonnerie f. **give s.o. a ~**, donner un coup de fil à qn. **~ the bell**, sonner. **~ back**, rappeler. **~ off**, raccrocher. **~ up**, téléphoner (à). **~ing** n. (of bell) sonnerie f. **~ing tone**, tonalité f.

ringleader /'rɪŋliːdə(r)/ n. chef m.

rink /rɪŋk/ n. patinoire f.

rinse /rɪns/ v.t. rincer. **~ out**, rincer. —n. rinçage m.

riot /'raɪət/ n. émeute f.; (of colours) orgie f. —v.i. faire une émeute. **run ~**, se déchaîner. **~er** n. émeutier, -ière m., f.

riotous /'raɪətəs/ a. turbulent.

rip /rɪp/ v.t./i. (p.t. **ripped**) (se) déchirer. —n. déchirure f. **let ~**, (not check) laisser courir. **~ off**, (sl.) rouler. **~-off** n. (sl.) vol m.

ripe /raɪp/ a. (-er, -est) mûr. **~ness** n. maturité f.

ripen /'raɪpən/ v.t./i. mûrir.

ripple /'rɪpl/ n. ride f., ondulation f.; (sound) murmure m. —v.t./i. (water) (se) rider.

rise /raɪz/ v.i. (p.t. **rose**, p.p. **risen**) (go upwards, increase) monter, s'élever; (stand up, get up from *bed*) se lever; (*rebel*) se soulever (*sun, curtain*) se lever; (*water*) monter. —*n*. (*slope*) pente *f*.; (*of curtain*) lever *m*.; (*increase*) hausse *f*.; (*in pay*) augmentation *f*.; (*progress, boom*) essor *m*. **give ~ to**, donner lieu à. **~ up**, se soulever. **~ r** /-ǝ(r)/ *n*. **be an early ~r**, se lever tôt.

rising /'raɪzɪŋ/ *n*. (*revolt*) soulèvement *m*. —*a*. (*increasing*) croissant; (*price*) qui monte; (*tide*) montant; (*sun*) levant. **~ generation**, nouvelle génération *f*.

risk /rɪsk/ *n*. risque *m*. —*v.t*. risquer. **at ~**, menacé. **~ doing**, (*venture*) se risquer à faire. **~y** *a*. risqué.

rissole /'rɪsǝʊl/ *n*. croquette *f*.

rite /raɪt/ *n*. rite *m*. **last ~s**, derniers sacrements *m. pl*.

ritual /'rɪtʃʊǝl/ *a. & n*. rituel (*m*.).

rival /'raɪvl/ *n*. rival(e) *m*. (*f*.). —*a*. rival; (*claim*) opposé. —*v.t*. (*p.t*. **rivalled**) rivaliser avec. **~ry** *n*. rivalité *f*.

river /'rɪvǝ(r)/ *n*. rivière *f*.; (*flowing into sea & fig*.) fleuve *m*. —*a*. (*fishing, traffic, etc*.) fluvial.

rivet /'rɪvɪt/ *n*. (*bolt*) rivet *m*. —*v.t*. (*p.t*. **riveted**) river, riveter. **~ing** *a*. fascinant.

Riviera /rɪvɪ'eǝrǝ/ *n*. **the (French) ~**, la Côte d'Azur.

road /rǝʊd/ *n*. route *f*.; (*in town*) rue *f*.; (*small*) chemin *m*. —*a*. (*sign, safety*) routier. **the ~ to**, (*glory, etc.: fig*.) le chemin de. **~block** *n*. barrage routier *m*. **~hog** *n*. chauffard *m*. **~-map** *n*. carte routière *f*. **~works** *n. pl*. travaux *m. pl*.

roadside /'rǝʊdsaɪd/ *n*. bord de la route *m*.

roadway /'rǝʊdweɪ/ *n*. chaussée *f*.

roadworthy /'rǝʊdwɜ:ðɪ/ *a*. en état de marche.

roam /rǝʊm/ *v.i*. errer. —*v.t*. (*streets, seas, etc*.) parcourir.

roar /rɔ:(r)/ *n*. hurlement *m*.; rugissement *m*.; grondement *m*. —*v.t./i*. hurler; (*of lion, wind*) rugir; (*of lorry, thunder*) gronder. **~ with laughter**, rire aux éclats.

roaring /'rɔ:rɪŋ/ *a*. (*trade, success*) très gros. **~ fire**, belle flambée *f*.

roast /rǝʊst/ *v.t./i*. rôtir. —*n*. (*roast or roasting meat*) rôti *m*. —*a*. rôti. **~ beef**, rôti de bœuf *m*.

rob /rɒb/ *v.t*. (*p.t*. **robbed**) voler (s.o. of sth., qch. à qn.); (*bank, house*) dévaliser; (*deprive*) priver (of, de). **~ber** *n*. voleu|r;-se *m., f*. **~bery** *n*. vol *m*.

robe /rǝʊb/ *n*. (*of judge etc*.) robe *f*.; (*dressing-gown*) peignoir *m*.

robin /'rɒbɪn/ *n*. rouge-gorge *m*.

robot /'rǝʊbɒt/ *n*. robot *m*.

robust /rǝʊ'bʌst/ *a*. robuste.

rock[1] /rɒk/ *n*. roche *f*.; (*rock face, boulder*) rocher *m*.; (*hurled stone*) pierre *f*.; (*sweet*) sucre d'orge *m*. **on the ~s**, (*drink*) avec des glaçons; (*marriage*) en crise. **~bottom** *a*. (*fam*.) très bas. **~climbing** *n*. varappe *f*.

rock[2] /rɒk/ *v.t./i*. (se) balancer; (*shake*) (faire) trembler; (*child*) bercer. —*n*. (*mus*.) rock *m*. **~ing-chair** *n*. fauteuil à bascule *m*.

rockery /'rɒkǝrɪ/ *n*. rocaille *f*.

rocket /'rɒkɪt/ *n*. fusée *f*.

rocky /'rɒkɪ/ *a*. (-ier, -iest) (*ground*) rocailleux; (*hill*) rocheux; (*shaky: fig*.) branlant.

rod /rɒd/ *n*. (*metal*) tige *f*.; (*for curtain*) tringle *f*.; (*wooden*) baguette *f*.; (*for fishing*) canne à pêche *f*.

rode /rǝʊd/ *see* ride.

rodent /'rǝʊdnt/ *n*. rongeur *m*.

rodeo /rǝʊ'deɪǝʊ, *Amer*. 'rǝʊdɪǝʊ/ *n*. (*pl*. **-os**) rodéo *m*.

roe[1] /rǝʊ/ *n*. œufs de poisson *m. pl*.

roe[2] /rǝʊ/ *n*. (*pl*. roe *or* roes) (*deer*) chevreuil *m*.

rogue /rəʊg/ *n.* (*dishonest*) bandit, voleu|r, -se *m.*, *f.*; (*mischievous*) coquin(e) *m.* (*f.*). **~ish** *a.* coquin.

role /rəʊl/ *n.* rôle *m.*. **~-playing** *n.* jeu de rôle *m.*.

roll /rəʊl/ *v.t./i.* rouler. **~ (about),** (*child, dog*) se rouler. —*n.* rouleau *m.*; (*list*) liste *f.*; (*bread*) petit pain *m.*; (*of drum, thunder*) roulement *m.*; (*of ship*) roulis *m.* be **~ing (in money),** (*fam.*) rouler sur l'or. **~-bar** *n.* arceau de sécurité *m.*. **~-call** *n.* appel *m.*. **~ing-pin** *n.* rouleau à pâtisserie *m.*. **~ out,** étendre. **~ over,** (*turn over*) se retourner. **~ up** *v.t.* (*sleeves*) retrousser; *v.i.* (*fam.*) s'amener.

roller /'rəʊlə(r)/ *n.* rouleau *m.*. **~-blind** *n.* store *m.*. **~-coaster** *n.* montagnes russes *f. pl.*. **~-skate** *n.* patin à roulettes *m.*.

rollicking /'rɒlɪkɪŋ/ *a.* exubérant.

rolling /'rəʊlɪŋ/ *a.* onduleux.

ROM (*abbr.*) (*read-only memory*) mémoire morte *f.*.

Roman /'rəʊmən/ *a.* & *n.* romain(e) (*m.* (*f.*)). **~ Catholic** *a.* & *n.* catholique *a.* (*m./f.*). **~ numerals,** chiffres romains *m. pl.*.

romance /rə'mæns/ *n.* roman d'amour *m.*; (*love*) amour *m.*; (*affair*) idylle *f.*; (*fig.*) poésie *f.*.

Romania /rəʊ'meɪnɪə/ *n.* Roumanie *f.*. **~n** *a.* & *n.* roumain(e) (*m.* (*f.*)).

romantic /rə'mæntɪk/ *a.* (*of love etc.*) romantique; (*of the imagination*) romanesque. **~ally** *adv.* (*behave*) en romantique.

romp /rɒmp/ *v.i.* s'ébattre; (*fig.*) réussir. —*n.* have **a ~,** s'ébattre.

roof /ruːf/ *n.* (*pl.* roofs) toit *m.*; (*of tunnel*) plafond *m.*; (*of mouth*) palais *m.*. —*v.t.* recouvrir. **~ing** *n.* toiture *f.*. **~-rack** *n.* galerie *f.*. **~-top** *n.* toit *m.*.

rook¹ /rʊk/ *n.* (*bird*) corneille *f.*.

rook² /rʊk/ *n.* (*chess*) tour *f.*.

room /ruːm/ *n.* pièce *f.*; (*bedroom*) chambre *f.*; (*large hall*) salle *f.*; (*space*) place *f.*. **~-mate** *n.* camarade de chambre *m./f.*. **~y** *a.* spacieux; (*clothes*) ample.

roost /ruːst/ *n.* perchoir *m.*. —*v.i.* percher. **~er** /'ruːstə(r)/ *n.* coq *m.*.

root¹ /ruːt/ *n.* racine *f.*; (*source*) origine *f.*. —*v.t./i.* (s')enraciner. **~ out,** extirper. **take ~,** prendre racine. **~less** *a.* sans racines.

root² /ruːt/ *v.i.* **~ about,** fouiller. **~ for,** (*Amer., fam.*) encourager.

rope /rəʊp/ *n.* corde *f.*. —*v.t.* attacher. **know the ~s,** être au courant. **~ in,** (*person*) enrôler.

rosary /'rəʊzərɪ/ *n.* chapelet *m.*.

rose¹ /rəʊz/ *n.* (*flower*) rose *f.*; (*colour*) rose *m.*; (*nozzle*) pomme *f.*.

rose² /rəʊz/ *see* rise.

rosé /'rəʊzeɪ/ *n.* rosé *m.*.

rosette /rəʊ'zet/ *n.* (*sport*) cocarde *f.*; (*officer's*) rosette *f.*.

roster /'rɒstə(r)/ *n.* liste (de service) *f.*, tableau (de service) *m.*.

rostrum /'rɒstrəm/ *n.* (*pl.* **-tra**) tribune *f.*; (*sport*) podium *m.*.

rosy /'rəʊzɪ/ *a.* (**-ier, -iest**) rose; (*hopeful*) plein d'espoir.

rot /rɒt/ *v.t./i.* (*p.t.* rotted) pourrir. —*n.* pourriture *f.*; (*nonsense: sl.*) bêtises *f. pl.*, âneries *f. pl.*.

rota /'rəʊtə/ *n.* liste (de service) *f.*.

rotary /'rəʊtərɪ/ *a.* rotatif.

rotat|e /rəʊ'teɪt/ *v.t./i.* (faire) tourner; (*change round*) alterner. **~ing** *a.* tournant. **~ion** /-ʃn/ *n.* rotation *f.*.

rote /rəʊt/ *n.* **by ~,** machinalement.

rotten /'rɒtn/ *a.* pourri; (*tooth*) gâté; (*bad: fam.*) mauvais, sale.

rotund /rəʊ'tʌnd/ *a.* rond.

rouge /ruːʒ/ *n.* rouge (à joues) *m.*.

rough /rʌf/ *a.* (**-er, -est**) (*manners*) rude; (*to touch*) rugueux;

(*ground*) accidenté; (*violent*) brutal; (*bad*) mauvais; (*estimate etc.*) approximatif; (*diamond*) brut. —*adv.* (*live*) à la dure; (*play*) brutalement. —*v.t.* **~ it,** vivre à la dure. **~-and-ready** *a.* (*solution etc.*) grossier (mais efficace). **~-and-tumble** *n.* mêlée *f.* **~ out,** ébaucher. **~ paper,** papier brouillon *m.* **~ly** *adv.* rudement; (*approximately*) à peu près. **~ness** *n.* rudesse *f.*; brutalité *f.*

roughage /ˈrʌfɪdʒ/ *n.* fibres (alimentaires) *f. pl.*

roulette /ruːˈlet/ *n.* roulette *f.*

round /raʊnd/ *a.* (*-er, -est*) rond. —*n.* (*circle*) rond *m.*; (*slice*) tranche *f.*; (*of visits, drinks*) tournée *f.*; (*mil.*) ronde *f.*; (*competition*) partie *f.*, manche *f.*; (*boxing*) round *m.*; (*of talks*) série *f.* —*prep.* autour de. —*adv.* autour. —*v.t.* (*object*) arrondir; (*corner*) tourner. **go** *or* **come ~ to,** (*a friend etc.*) passer chez. **I'm going ~ the corner,** je vais juste à côté. **enough to go ~,** assez pour tout le monde. **go the ~s,** circuler. **she lives ~ here** elle habite par ici; (*fig.*) à peu près. **~ about,** (*near by*) par ici; (*fig.*) à peu près. **~ of applause,** applaudissements *m. pl.* **~ off,** terminer. **~ the clock,** vingt-quatre heures sur vingt-quatre. **~ trip,** voyage aller-retour *m.* **~ up,** rassembler. **~ up** *n.* rassemblement *m.*; (*of suspects*) rafle *f.*

roundabout /ˈraʊndəbaʊt/ *n.* manège *m.*; (*for traffic*) rond-point (à sens giratoire) *m.* —*a.* indirect.

rounders /ˈraʊndəz/ *n.* sorte de base-ball *m.*

roundly /ˈraʊndlɪ/ *adv.* (*bluntly*) franchement.

rous|e /raʊz/ *v.t.* éveiller; (*wake up*) réveiller. **be ~ed,** (*angry*)

être en colère. **~ing** *a.* (*speech, music*) excitant; (*cheers*) frénétique.

rout /raʊt/ *n.* (*defeat*) déroute *f.* —*v.t.* mettre en déroute.

route /ruːt/ *n.* itinéraire *m.*, parcours *m.*; (*naut., aviat.*) route *f.*

routine /ruːˈtiːn/ *n.* routine *f.* —*a.* de routine. **daily ~,** travail quotidien *m.*

rov|e /rəʊv/ *v.t./i.* errer (dans). **~ing** *a.* (*life*) vagabond.

row[1] /rəʊ/ *n.* rangée *f.*, rang *m.* in a **~,** (*consecutive*) consécutif.

row[2] /rəʊ/ *v.i.* ramer; (*sport*) faire de l'aviron. —*v.t.* faire aller à la rame. **~ing** *n.* aviron *m.* **~(ing)-boat** *n.* bateau à rames *m.*

row[3] /raʊ/ *n.* (*noise: fam.*) tapage *m.*; (*quarrel, fam.*) engueulade *f.* —*v.i.* (*fam.*) s'engueuler.

rowdy /ˈraʊdɪ/ *a.* (*-ier, -iest*) tapageur. —*n.* voyou *m.*

royal /ˈrɔɪəl/ *a.* royal. **~ly** *adv.* (*treat, live, etc.*) royalement.

royal|ty /ˈrɔɪəltɪ/ *n.* famille royale *f.* **~ies,** droits d'auteur *m. pl.*

rub /rʌb/ *v.t./i.* (*p.t.* **rubbed**) frotter. —*n.* friction *f.* **~ it in,** insister là-dessus. **~ off on,** déteindre sur. **~ out,** (s')effacer.

rubber /ˈrʌbə(r)/ *n.* caoutchouc *m.*; (*eraser*) gomme *f.* **~ band,** élastique *m.* **~ stamp,** tampon *m.* **~-stamp** *v.t.* approuver. **~y** *a.* caoutchouteux.

rubbish /ˈrʌbɪʃ/ *n.* (*refuse*) ordures *f. pl.*; (*junk*) saletés *f. pl.*; (*fig.*) bêtises *f. pl.* **~y** *a.* sans valeur.

rubble /ˈrʌbl/ *n.* décombres *m. pl.*

ruby /ˈruːbɪ/ *n.* rubis *m.*

rucksack /ˈrʌksæk/ *n.* sac à dos *m.*

rudder /ˈrʌdə(r)/ *n.* gouvernail *m.*

ruddy /ˈrʌdɪ/ *a.* (*-ier, -iest*) coloré, rougeâtre; (*damned: sl.*) fichu.

rude /ruːd/ *a.* (*-er, -est*) impoli, grossier; (*improper*) indécent; (*shock, blow*) brutal. **~ly** *adv.*

impoliment. **~ness** n. impolitesse f.; indécence f.; brutalité f.

rudiment /'ru:dɪmənt/ n. rudiment m. **~ary** /-'mentrɪ/ a. rudimentaire.

rueful /'ru:fl/ a. triste.

ruffian /'rʌfɪən/ n. voyou m.

ruffle /'rʌfl/ v.t. (hair) ébouriffer; (clothes) froisser; (person) contrarier. —n. (frill) ruche f.

rug /rʌg/ n. petit tapis m.

Rugby /'rʌgbɪ/ n. **~** (football), rugby m.

rugged /'rʌgɪd/ a. (surface) rude, rugueux; (ground) accidenté; (character, features) rude.

ruin /'ru:ɪn/ n. ruine f. —v.t. (destroy) ruiner; (damage) abîmer; (spoil) gâter. **~ous** a. ruineux.

rule /ru:l/ n. règle f.; (regulation) règlement m.; (pol.) gouvernement m. —v.t. gouverner; (master) dominer; (decide) décider. —v.i. régner. **as a ~,** en règle générale. **~ out,** exclure. **~d paper,** papier réglé m. **~r** /-ə(r)/ n. dirigeant(e) m. (f.), gouvernant m.; (measure) règle f.

ruling /'ru:lɪŋ/ a. (class) dirigeant; (party) au pouvoir. —n. décision f.

rum /rʌm/ n. rhum m.

rumble /'rʌmbl/ v.i. gronder; (stomach) gargouiller. —n. grondement m.; gargouillement m.

rummage /'rʌmɪdʒ/ v.i. fouiller.

rumour, (Amer. **rumor**) /'ru:mə(r)/ n. bruit m., rumeur f. **there's a ~ that,** le bruit court que.

rump /rʌmp/ n. (of horse etc.) croupe f.; (of fowl) croupion m.; (steak) romsteck m.

rumpus /'rʌmpəs/ n. (uproar, fam.) chahut m.

run /rʌn/ v.i. (p.t. **ran,** p.p. **run,** pres. p. **running**) courir; (flow) couler; (pass) passer; (function) marcher; (melt) fondre; (extend) s'étendre; (of bus etc.) circuler; (of play) se jouer; (last) durer; (of colour in washing) déteindre; (in election) être candidat. —v.t. (manage) diriger; (event) organiser; (risk, race) courir; (house) tenir; (blockade) forcer; (temperature, errand) faire; (comput.) exécuter. —n. course f.; (journey) parcours m.; (outing) promenade f.; (rush) ruée f.; (series) série f.; (in cricket) point m. **have the ~ of,** avoir à sa disposition. **in the long ~,** avec le temps. **on the ~,** en fuite. **~ across,** rencontrer par hasard. **~ away,** s'enfuir. **~ down,** descendre en courant; (of vehicle) renverser; (production) réduire progressivement; (belittle) dénigrer. **be ~ down,** (weak etc.) être sans forces or mal fichu. **~ in,** (vehicle) roder. **~ into,** (hit) heurter. **~ off,** (copies) tirer. **~-of-the-mill** a. ordinaire. **~ out,** (be used up) s'épuiser; (of lease) expirer. **~ out of,** manquer de. **~ over,** (of vehicle) écraser; (details) revoir. **~ through sth.,** regarder qch. rapidement. **~ sth. through,** passer qch. à travers qch. **~ up,** (bill) accumuler. **the ~-up to,** la période qui précède.

runaway /'rʌnəweɪ/ n. fugitif/-ve m., f. —a. fugitif; (horse, vehicle) fou; (inflation) galopant.

rung[1] /rʌŋ/ n. (of ladder) barreau m.

rung[2] /rʌŋ/ see **ring**[2].

runner /'rʌnə(r)/ n. coureu|r, -se m., f. **~ bean,** haricot (grimpant) m. **~-up** n. second(e) m., f.

running /'rʌnɪŋ/ n. course f.; (of business) gestion f.; (of machine) marche f. —a. (commentary) suivi; (*water*) courant. **be in the ~ for**, être sur les rangs pour. **four days/etc.**, quatre jours/etc. de suite.

runny /'rʌnɪ/ a. (*nose*) qui coule.

runt /rʌnt/ n. avorton m.

runway /'rʌnweɪ/ n. piste f.

rupture /'rʌptʃə(r)/ n. (*breaking*, *breach*) rupture f.; (*med.*) hernie f. —v.t./i. (se) rompre. **~ o.s.**, se donner une hernie.

rural /'rʊərəl/ a. rural.

ruse /ruːz/ n. (*trick*) ruse f.

rush¹ /rʌʃ/ n. (*plant*) jonc m.

rush² /rʌʃ/ v.i. (*move*) se précipiter; (*be in a hurry*) se dépêcher. —v.t. faire, envoyer, etc. en vitesse; (*person*) bousculer; (*mil.*) prendre d'assaut. —n. ruée f.; (*haste*) bousculade f. **in a ~**, pressé. **~-hour** n. heure de pointe f.

rusk /rʌsk/ n. biscotte f.

russet /'rʌsɪt/ a. roussâtre, roux.

Russia /'rʌʃə/ n. Russie f. **~n** a. & n. russe (m./f.); (*lang.*) russe m.

rust /rʌst/ n. rouille f. —v.t./i. rouiller. **~-proof** a. inoxydable. **~y** a. (*tool, person, etc.*) rouillé.

rustic /'rʌstɪk/ a. rustique.

rustle /'rʌsl/ v.t./i. (*leaves*) (faire) bruire; (*steal: Amer.*) voler. **~ up**, (*food etc.: fam.*) préparer.

rut /rʌt/ n. ornière f. **be in a ~**, rester dans l'ornière.

ruthless /'ruːθlɪs/ a. impitoyable. **~ness** n. cruauté f.

rye /raɪ/ n. seigle m.; (*whisky*) whisky m. (*à base de seigle*).

S

sabbath /'sæbəθ/ n. (*Jewish*) sabbat m.; (*Christian*) dimanche m.

sabbatical /sə'bætɪkl/ a. (*univ.*) sabbatique.

sabot|age /'sæbətɑːʒ/ n. sabotage m. —v.t. saboter. **~eur** /-'tɜː(r)/ n. saboteu|r, -se m., f.

saccharin /'sækərɪn/ n. saccharine f.

sachet /'sæʃeɪ/ n. sachet m.

sack¹ /sæk/ n. (*bag*) sac m. (*fam.*) renvoyer. **get the ~**, (*fam.*) être renvoyé. **~ing** n. toile à sac f.; (*dismissal: fam.*) renvoi m.

sack² /sæk/ v.t. (*plunder*) saccager.

sacrament /'sækrəmənt/ n. sacrement m.

sacred /'seɪkrɪd/ a. sacré.

sacrifice /'sækrɪfaɪs/ n. sacrifice m. —v.t. sacrifier.

sacrileg|e /'sækrɪlɪdʒ/ n. sacrilège m. **~ious** /-'lɪdʒəs/ a. sacrilège.

sad /sæd/ a. (**sadder**, **saddest**) triste. **~ly** adv. tristement; (*unfortunately*) malheureusement. **~ness** n. tristesse f.

sadden /'sædn/ v.t. attrister.

saddle /'sædl/ n. selle f. —v.t. (*horse*) seller. **~ s.o. with**, (*task, person*) coller à qn. **in the ~**, bien en selle. **~-bag** n. sacoche f.

sadis|t /'seɪdɪst/ n. sadique m./f. **~m** /-zəm/ n. sadisme m. **~tic** /sə'dɪstɪk/ a. sadique.

safari /sə'fɑːrɪ/ n. safari m.

safe /seɪf/ a. (**-er**, **-est**) (*not dangerous*) sans danger; (*reliable*) sûr; (*out of danger*) en sécurité; (*after accident*) sain et sauf; (*wise: fig.*) prudent. —n. coffre-fort m. **to be on the ~ side**, pour être sûr. **in ~ keeping**, en sécurité. **~ conduct**, sauf-conduit m. **~ from**, à l'abri de. **~ly** adv. sans danger; (*in safe place*) en sûreté.

safeguard /'seɪfɡɑːd/ n. sauvegarde f. —v.t. sauvegarder.

safety /'seɪftɪ/ n. sécurité f. **~-belt** n. ceinture de sécurité f. **~-pin** n. épingle de sûreté f. **~-valve** n. soupape de sûreté f.

saffron /'sæfrən/ n. safran m.
sag /sæg/ v.i. (p.t. **sagged**) s'affaisser, fléchir. **~ging** a. affaissé.
saga /'sɑːgə/ n. saga f.
sage[1] /seɪdʒ/ n. (herb) sauge f.
sage[2] /seɪdʒ/ a. & n. sage (m.).
Sagittarius /sædʒɪ'teərɪəs/ n. le Sagittaire.
said /sed/ see **say**.
sail /seɪl/ n. voile f.; (journey) tour en bateau m. —v.i. naviguer; (leave) partir; (sport) faire de la voile; (glide) glisser. —v.t. (boat) piloter. **~ing-boat**, **~ing-ship** ns. bateau à voiles m.
sailor /'seɪlə(r)/ n. marin m.
saint /seɪnt/ n. saint m. (f.). **~ly** a. (person, act, etc.) saint.
sake /seɪk/ n. for the **~** of, pour, pour l'amour de.
salad /'sæləd/ n. salade f. **~-dressing** n. vinaigrette f.
salami /sə'lɑːmɪ/ n. salami m.
salar|y /'sælərɪ/ n. traitement m., salaire m. **~ied** a. salarié.
sale /seɪl/ n. vente f. **~s**, (at reduced prices) soldes m. pl. **~s assistant**, (Amer.) **~s clerk**, vendeu|r, -se m., f., à vendre. on **~**, en vente; (at a reduced price; Amer.) en solde. **~-room** n. salle des ventes f.
saleable /'seɪləbl/ a. vendable.
sales|man /'seɪlzmən/ n. (pl. **-men**) (in shop) vendeur m.; (traveller) représentant m. **~woman** n. (pl. **-women**) vendeuse f.; représentante f.
salient /'seɪlɪənt/ a. saillant.
saline /'seɪlaɪn/ a. salin. —n. sérum physiologique m.
saliva /sə'laɪvə/ n. salive f.
sallow /'sæləʊ/ a. (-er, -est) (complexion) jaunâtre.
salmon /'sæmən/ n. invar. saumon m.
salon /'sælɒn/ n. salon m.
saloon /sə'luːn/ n. (on ship) salon

m.; (bar: Amer.) bar m., saloon m. **~ (car)**, berline f.
salt /sɔːlt/ n. sel m. —a. (culin.) salé; (water) de mer. —v.t. saler. **~-cellar** n. salière f. **~y** a. salé.
salutary /'sæljʊtrɪ/ a. salutaire.
salute /sə'luːt/ n. (mil.) salut m. —v.t. saluer. —v.i. faire un salut.
salvage /'sælvɪdʒ/ n. sauvetage m.; (of waste) récupération f.; (goods) objets sauvés m. pl. —v.t. sauver; (for re-use) récupérer.
salvation /sæl'veɪʃn/ n. salut m.
salvo /'sælvəʊ/ n. (pl. **-oes**) salve f.
same /seɪm/ a. même (as, que). —pron. the **~**, le or la même, les mêmes. at the **~** time, en même temps. the **~** (thing), la même chose.
sample /'sɑːmpl/ n. échantillon m.; (of blood) prélèvement m. —v.t. essayer; (food) goûter.
sanatorium /sænə'tɔːrɪəm/ n. (pl. **-iums**) sanatorium m.
sanctify /'sæŋktɪfaɪ/ v.t. sanctifier.
sanctimonious /sæŋktɪ'məʊnɪəs/ a. (person) bigot; (air, tone) de petit saint.
sanction /'sæŋkʃn/ n. sanction f. —v.t. sanctionner.
sanctity /'sæŋktətɪ/ n. sainteté f.
sanctuary /'sæŋktʃʊərɪ/ n. (relig.) sanctuaire m.; (for animals) réserve f.; (refuge) asile m.
sand /sænd/ n. sable m. **~s**, (beach) plage f. —v.t. sabler. **~-castle** n. château de sable m. **~-pit**, (Amer.) **~-box** n. bac à sable m.
sandal /'sændl/ n. sandale f.
sandpaper /'sændpeɪpə(r)/ n. papier de verre m. —v.t. poncer.
sandstone /'sændstəʊn/ n. grès m.
sandwich /'sændwɪdʒ/ n. sandwich m. —v.t. **~ed between**, pris en sandwich entre. **~ course**, stage de formation continue à mi-temps m.

sandy /'sændɪ/ a. sablonneux, de sable; (*hair*) blond roux *invar.*

sane /seɪn/ a. (**-er, -est**) (*view etc.*) sain; (*person*) sain d'esprit. **~ly** adv. sainement.

sang /sæŋ/ *see* sing.

sanitary /'sænɪtrɪ/ a. (*clean*) hygiénique; (*system etc.*) sanitaire. **~ towel**, (*Amer.*) **~ napkin**, serviette hygiénique f.

sanitation /sænɪ'teɪʃn/ n. hygiène (publique) f.; (*drainage etc.*) système sanitaire m.

sanity /'sænətɪ/ n. santé mentale f.; (*good sense: fig.*) bon sens m.

sank /sæŋk/ *see* sink.

Santa Claus /'sæntəklɔːz/ n. le père Noël m.

sap /sæp/ n. (*of plants*) sève f. —v.t. (*p.t.* sapped) (*undermine*) saper.

sapphire /'sæfaɪə(r)/ n. saphir m.

sarcas|m /'sɑːkæzəm/ n. sarcasme m. **~tic** /sɑː'kæstɪk/ a. sarcastique.

sardine /sɑː'diːn/ n. sardine f.

Sardinia /sɑː'dɪnɪə/ n. Sardaigne f.

sardonic /sɑː'dɒnɪk/ a. sardonique.

sash /sæʃ/ n. (*on uniform*) écharpe f.; (*on dress*) ceinture f. **~-window**, fenêtre à guillotine f.

sat /sæt/ *see* sit.

satanic /sə'tænɪk/ a. satanique.

satchel /'sætʃl/ n. cartable m.

satellite /'sætəlaɪt/ n. & a. satellite (m.). **~ dish**, antenne parabolique f.

satin /'sætɪn/ n. satin m.

satir|e /'sætaɪə(r)/ n. satire f. **~ical** /sə'tɪrɪkl/ a. satirique.

satisfactor|y /sætɪs'fæktərɪ/ a. satisfaisant. **~ily** adv. d'une manière satisfaisante.

satisf|y /'sætɪsfaɪ/ v.t. satisfaire; (*convince*) convaincre. **~action** /-'fækʃn/ n. satisfaction f. **~ying** a. satisfaisant.

satsuma /sæt'suːmə/ n. mandarine f.

saturat|e /'sætʃəreɪt/ v.t. saturer. **~ed** a. (*wet*) trempé. **~ion** /-'reɪʃn/ n. saturation f.

Saturday /'sætədɪ/ n. samedi m.

sauce /sɔːs/ n. sauce f.; (*impudence: sl.*) toupet m.

saucepan /'sɔːspən/ n. casserole f.

saucer /'sɔːsə(r)/ n. soucoupe f.

saucy /'sɔːsɪ/ a. (**-ier, -iest**) impertinent; (*boldly smart*) coquin.

Saudi Arabia /saʊdɪə'reɪbɪə/ n. Arabie Séoudite f.

sauna /'sɔːnə/ n. sauna m.

saunter /'sɔːntə(r)/ v.i. flâner.

sausage /'sɒsɪdʒ/ n. saucisse f.; (*pre-cooked*) saucisson m.

savage /'sævɪdʒ/ a. (*fierce*) féroce; (*wild*) sauvage. —n. sauvage m./f. —v.t. attaquer férocement. **~ry** n. sauvagerie f.

sav|e /seɪv/ v.t. sauver; (*money*) économiser; (*time*) (faire) gagner; (*keep*) garder; (*prevent*) éviter (**from**, de). —n. (*football*) arrêt m. —prep. sauf. **~er** n. épargnant(e) m. (f.). **~ing** n. (*of time, money*) économie f. **~ings** n. pl. économies f. pl.

saviour, (*Amer.*) **savior** /'seɪvjə(r)/ n. sauveur m.

savour, (*Amer.*) **savor** /'seɪvə(r)/ n. saveur f. —v.t. savourer. **~y** a. (*tasty*) savoureux; (*culin.*) salé.

saw[1] /sɔː/ *see* see[1].

saw[2] /sɔː/ n. scie f. —v.t. (*p.t.* sawed, *p.p.* sawn /sɔːn/ *or* sawed) scier.

sawdust /'sɔːdʌst/ n. sciure f.

saxophone /'sæksəfəʊn/ n. saxophone m.

say /seɪ/ v.t./i. (*p.t.* said /sed/) dire; (*prayer*) faire. —n. **have a ~**, dire son mot; (*in decision*) avoir voix au chapitre. I **~!**, dites donc!

saying /'seɪɪŋ/ n. proverbe m.

scab /skæb/ n. (*on sore*) croûte f.; (*blackleg: fam.*) jaune m.

scaffold /'skæfəʊld/ *n.* (*gallows*) échafaud *m.* **∼ing** /-əldɪŋ/ *n.* (*for workmen*) échafaudage *m.*

scald /skɔːld/ *v.t.* (*injure, cleanse*) ébouillanter. —*n.* brûlure *f.*

scale[1] /skeɪl/ *n.* (*of fish*) écaille *f.*

scale[2] /skeɪl/ *n.* (*for measuring, size, etc.*) échelle *f.*; (*mus.*) gamme *f.*; (*of salaries, charges*) barème *m.* **on a small/etc. ∼**, sur une petite *etc.* échelle. **∼ model**, maquette *f.* —*v.t.* (*climb*) escalader. **∼ down**, réduire (proportionnellement).

scales /skeɪlz/ *n. pl.* (*for weighing*) balance *f.*

scallop /'skɒləp/ *n.* coquille Saint-Jacques *f.*

scalp /skælp/ *n.* cuir chevelu *m.* —*v.t.* (*mutilate*) scalper.

scalpel /'skælp(ə)l/ *n.* scalpel *m.*

scamper /'skæmpə(r)/ *v.i.* courir, trotter. **∼ away**, détaler.

scampi /'skæmpɪ/ *n. pl.* grosses crevettes *f. pl.*, gambas *f. pl.*

scan /skæn/ *v.t.* (*p.t.* **scanned**) scruter; (*quickly*) parcourir; (*poetry*) scander; (*of radar*) balayer. —*n.* (*ultrasound*) échographie *f.*

scandal /'skændl/ *n.* (*disgrace, outrage*) scandale *m.*; (*gossip*) cancans *m. pl.* **∼ous** *a.* scandaleux.

scandalize /'skændəlaɪz/ *v.t.* scandaliser.

Scandinavia /skændɪ'neɪvɪə/ *n.* Scandinavie *f.* **∼n** *a. & n.* scandinave (*m./f.*).

scant /skænt/ *a.* insuffisant.

scant|ly /'skæntɪ/ *a.* (**-ier, -iest**) insuffisant; (*clothing*) sommaire. **∼ily** *adv.* insuffisamment. **∼ily dressed**, à peine vêtu.

scapegoat /'skeɪpɡəʊt/ *n.* bouc émissaire *m.*

scar /skɑː(r)/ *n.* cicatrice *f.* —*v.t.* (*p.t.* **scarred**) marquer d'une cicatrice; (*fig.*) marquer.

scarc|e /skeəs/ *a.* (**-er, -est**) rare. **make o.s. ∼e**, (*fam.*) se sauver. **∼ity** *n.* rareté *f.*, pénurie *f.*

scarcely /'skeəslɪ/ *adv.* à peine.

scare /skeə(r)/ *v.t.* faire peur à. —*n.* peur *f.* **be ∼d**, avoir peur. **bomb ∼**, alerte à la bombe *f.*

scarecrow /'skeəkrəʊ/ *n.* épouvantail *m.*

scarf /skɑːf/ *n.* (*pl.* **scarves**) écharpe *f.*; (*over head*) foulard *m.*

scarlet /'skɑːlət/ *a.* écarlate. **∼ fever**, scarlatine *f.*

scary /'skeərɪ/ *a.* (**-ier, -iest**) (*fam.*) qui fait peur, effrayant.

scathing /'skeɪðɪŋ/ *a.* cinglant.

scatter /'skætə(r)/ *v.t.* (*throw*) éparpiller, répandre; (*disperse*) disperser. —*v.i.* se disperser. **∼brain** *n.* écervelé(e) *m.* (*f.*).

scavenge /'skævɪndʒ/ *v.i.* fouiller (dans les ordures). **∼r** /-ə(r)/ *n.* (*vagrant*) personne qui fouille dans les ordures *f.*

scenario /sɪ'nɑːrɪəʊ/ *n.* (*pl.* **-os**) scénario *m.*

scene /siːn/ *n.* (*of accident, crime*) lieu(x) *m.* (*pl.*); (*sight*) spectacle *m.*; (*incident*) incident *m.* **behind the ∼s**, en coulisse. **to make a ∼**, faire un esclandre.

scenery /'siːnərɪ/ *n.* paysage *m.*; (*theatre*) décor(s) *m.* (*pl.*).

scenic /'siːnɪk/ *a.* pittoresque.

scent /sent/ *n.* (*perfume*) parfum *m.*; (*trail*) piste *f.* —*v.t.* flairer; (*make fragrant*) parfumer.

sceptic /'skeptɪk/ *n.* sceptique *m./f.* **∼al** *a.* sceptique. **∼ism** /-sɪzəm/ *n.* scepticisme *m.*

schedule /'ʃedjuːl/, *Amer.* /'skedʒʊl/ *n.* horaire *m.*; (*for job*) planning *m.* —*v.t.* prévoir. **behind ∼**, en retard. **on ∼**, (*train*) à l'heure; (*work*) dans les temps. **∼d flight**, vol régulier *m.*

scheme /skiːm/ *n.* plan *m.*; (*dishonest*) combine *f.*; (*fig.*)

arrangement *m.* —*v.i.* intriguer.
pension ~, caisse de retraite *f.*
~**r** /-ǝ(r)/ *n.* intrigant(e) *m.* (*f.*).
schism /'sɪzǝm/ *n.* schisme *m.*
schizophrenic /skɪtsǝʊ'frenɪk/ *a.*
& *n.* schizophrène (*m./f.*).
scholar /'skɒlǝ(r)/ *n.* érudit(e) *m.*
(*f.*). ~**ly** *a.* érudit. ~**ship** *n.*
érudition *f.*; (*grant*) bourse *f.*
school /sku:l/ *n.* école *f.*;
(*secondary*) lycée *m.*; (*of university*) faculté *f.* —*a.* (*age, year,
holidays*) scolaire. —*v.t.* (*person*)
éduquer; (*animal*) dresser. ~**ing**
n. (*education*) instruction *f.*;
(*attendance*) scolarité *f.*
school|boy /'sku:lbɔɪ/ *n.* écolier *m.*
~**girl** *n.* écolière *f.*
school|master /'sku:lmɑ:stǝ(r)/
~**mistress**, ~**teacher** *ns.*
(*primary*) institu|teur, -trice *m.*,
f.; (*secondary*) professeur *m.*
schooner /'sku:nǝ(r)/ *n.* goélette
f.
sciatica /saɪ'ætɪkǝ/ *n.* sciatique *f.*
scien|ce /'saɪǝns/ *n.* science *f.* ~**ce
fiction**, science-fiction *f.* ~**tific**
/-'tɪfɪk/ *a.* scientifique.
scientist /'saɪǝntɪst/ *n.* scientifique
m./f.
scintillate /'sɪntɪleɪt/ *v.i.* scintiller;
(*person: fig.*) briller.
scissors /'sɪzǝz/ *n. pl.* ciseaux *m.
pl.*
scoff[1] /skɒf/ *v.i.* ~ **at**, se moquer
de.
scoff[2] /skɒf/ *v.t.* (*eat: sl.*) bouffer.
scold /skǝʊld/ *v.t.* réprimander.
~**ing** *n.* réprimande *f.*
scone /skɒn/ *n.* petit pain au lait
m., galette *f.*
scoop /sku:p/ *n.* (*for grain, sugar*)
pelle (à main) *f.*; (*for food*) cuiller
f.; (*ice cream*) boule *f.*; (*news*)
exclusivité *f.* —*v.t.* (*pick up*)
ramasser. ~ **out**, creuser. ~ **up**,
ramasser.
scoot /sku:t/ *v.i.* (*fam.*) filer.
scooter /'sku:tǝ(r)/ *n.* (*child's*)

trottinette *f.*; (*motor cycle*) scooter
m.
scope /skǝʊp/ *n.* étendue *f.*;
(*competence*) compétence *f.*;
(*opportunity*) possibilité(s) *f.*
(*pl.*).
scorch /skɔ:tʃ/ *v.t.* brûler, roussir.
~**ing** *a.* brûlant, très chaud.
score /skɔ:(r)/ *n.* score *m.*; (*mus.*)
partition *f.* —*v.t.* marquer;
(*success*) remporter. —*v.i.* marquer un point; (*football*) marquer
un but; (*keep score*) compter les
points. **a** ~ **(of)**, (*twenty*) vingt.
on that ~, à cet égard. ~ **out**,
rayer. ~**board** *n.* tableau *m.* ~**r**
/-ǝ(r)/ *n.* (*sport*) marqueur *m.*
scorn /skɔ:n/ *n.* mépris *m.* —*v.t.*
mépriser. ~**ful** *a.* méprisant.
~**fully** *adv.* avec mépris.
Scorpio /'skɔ:pɪǝʊ/ *n.* le Scorpion.
scorpion /'skɔ:pɪǝn/ *n.* scorpion
m.
Scot /skɒt/ *n.* Écossais(e) *m.* (*f.*).
~**tish** *a.* écossais.
Scotch /skɒtʃ/ *a.* écossais. —*n.*
whisky *m.*, scotch *m.*
scotch /skɒtʃ/ *v.t.* mettre fin à.
scot-free /skɒt'fri:/ *a.* & *adv.* sans
être puni; (*gratis*) sans payer.
Scotland /'skɒtlǝnd/ *n.* Écosse *f.*
Scots /skɒts/ *a.* écossais. ~**man** *n.*
Écossais *m.* ~**woman** *n.* Écos-
saise *f.*
scoundrel /'skaʊndrǝl/ *n.* vaurien
m., bandit *m.*, gredin(e) *m.* (*f.*).
scour[1] /'skaʊǝ(r)/ *v.t.* (*pan*)
récurer. ~**er** *n.* tampon à récurer
m.
scour[2] /'skaʊǝ(r)/ *v.t.* (*search*)
parcourir.
scourge /skɜ:dʒ/ *n.* fléau *m.*
scout /skaʊt/ *n.* (*mil.*) éclaireur *m.*
—*v.i.* ~ **around (for)**, chercher.
Scout /skaʊt/ *n.* (*boy*) scout *m.*,
éclaireur *m.* ~**ing** *n.* scoutisme
m.
scowl /skaʊl/ *n.* air renfrogné *m.*
—*v.i.* faire la tête (**at**, à).

scraggy /'skrægɪ/ a. (-ier, -iest) décharné, efflanqué.

scram /skræm/ v.i. (sl.) se tirer.

scramble /'skræmbl/ v.i. (clamber) grimper. —v.t. (eggs) brouiller. —n. bousculade f., ruée f. ~ **for**, se bousculer pour avoir.

scrap[1] /skræp/ n. petit morceau m. ~**s,** (of metal, fabric, etc.) déchets m. pl.; (of food) restes m. pl. —v.t. (p.t. **scrapped**) mettre au rebut; (plan etc.) abandonner. ~**-book** n. album m. **on the ~-heap,** mis au rebut. ~**-iron** n. ferraille f. ~**-paper** n. brouillon m. ~**py** a. fragmentaire.

scrap[2] /skræp/ n. (fight: fam.) bagarre f., dispute f.

scrape /skreɪp/ v.t. racler, gratter; (graze) érafler. —v.i. (rub) frotter. —n. raclement m.; éraflure f. **in a ~,** dans une mauvaise passe. ~ **through,** réussir de justesse. ~ **together,** réunir. ~**r** /-ə(r)/ n. racloir m.

scratch /skrætʃ/ v.t./i. (se) gratter; (with claw, nail) griffer; (graze) érafler; (mark) rayer. —n. éraflure f. **start from ~,** partir de zéro. **up to ~,** au niveau voulu.

scrawl /skrɔːl/ n. gribouillage m. —v.t./i. gribouiller.

scrawny /'skrɔːnɪ/ a. (-ier, -iest) décharné, émacié.

scream /skriːm/ v.t./i. crier, hurler. —n. cri (perçant) m.

scree /skriː/ n. éboulis m.

screech /skriːtʃ/ v.i. (scream) hurler; (of brakes) grincer. —n. hurlement m.; grincement m.

screen /skriːn/ n. écran m.; (folding) paravent m. —v.t. (conceal) masquer; (protect) protéger; (film) projeter; (candidates) filtrer; (med.) faire subir un test de dépistage. ~**ing** n. projection f.

screenplay /'skriːnpleɪ/ n. scénario m.

screw /skruː/ n. vis f. —v.t. visser.

~ **up,** (eyes) plisser; (ruin: sl.) bousiller.

screwdriver /'skruːdraɪvə(r)/ n. tournevis m.

screwy /'skruːɪ/ a. (-ier, -iest) (crazy: sl.) cinglé.

scribble /'skrɪbl/ v.t./i. griffonner. —n. griffonnage m.

scribe /skraɪb/ n. scribe m.

script /skrɪpt/ n. écriture f.; (of film) scénario m.; (of play) texte m. ~**-writer** n. scénariste m./f.

Scriptures /'skrɪptʃəz/ n. pl. **the** ~, l'Écriture (sainte) f.

scroll /skrəʊl/ n. rouleau m. —v.t./i. (comput.) (faire) défiler.

scrounge /skraʊndʒ/ v.t. (meal) faire payer; (steal) chiper. —v.i. (beg) quémander. ~ **money from,** taper. ~**r** /-ə(r)/ n. parasite m.; (of money) tapeu|r, -se m., f.

scrub[1] /skrʌb/ n. (land) broussailles f. pl.

scrub[2] /skrʌb/ v.t./i. (p.t. **scrubbed**) nettoyer (à la brosse), frotter. —n. nettoyage m.

scruff /skrʌf/ n. **by the ~ of the neck,** par la peau du cou.

scruffy /'skrʌfɪ/ a. (-ier, -iest) (fam.) miteux, sale.

scrum /skrʌm/ n. (Rugby) mêlée f.

scruple /'skruːpl/ n. scrupule m.

scrupulous /'skruːpjʊləs/ a. scrupuleux. ~**ly** adv. scrupuleusement. ~**ly clean,** impeccable.

scrutin|y /'skruːtɪnɪ/ n. examen minutieux m. ~**ize** v.t. scruter.

scuba-diving /'skuːbədaɪvɪŋ/ n. plongée soumarine f.

scuff /skʌf/ v.t. (scratch) érafler.

scuffle /'skʌfl/ n. bagarre f.

sculpt /skʌlpt/ v.t./i. sculpter. ~**or** n. sculpteur m. ~**ure** /-tʃə(r)/ n. sculpture f.; v.t./i. sculpter.

scum /skʌm/ n. (on liquid) écume f.; (people: pej.) racaille f.

scurf /skɜːf/ n. pellicules f. pl.

scurrilous /ˈskʌrɪləs/ a. grossier, injurieux, venimeux.

scurry /ˈskʌrɪ/ v.i. courir (for, pour chercher). ~ off, filer.

scuttle[1] /ˈskʌtl/ v.t. (ship) saborder.

scuttle[2] /ˈskʌtl/ v.i. ~ away, se sauver, filer.

scythe /saɪð/ n. faux f.

sea /siː/ n. mer f. —a. de (la) mer, marin. **at** ~, en mer. **by** ~, par mer. ~**-green** a. vert glauque invar. ~**-level** n. niveau de la mer m. ~**shell**, coquillage m. ~**shore** n. rivage m.

seaboard /ˈsiːbɔːd/ n. littoral m.

seafarer /ˈsiːfeərə(r)/ n. marin m.

seafood /ˈsiːfuːd/ n. fruits de mer m. pl.

seagull /ˈsiːɡʌl/ n. mouette f.

seal[1] /siːl/ n. (animal) phoque m.

seal[2] /siːl/ n. sceau m. (with wax) cachet m. —v.t. sceller; cacheter; (stick down) coller. ~**ing-wax** n. cire à cacheter f. ~ **off**, (area) boucler.

seam /siːm/ n. (in cloth etc.) couture f.; (of coal) veine f.

seaman /ˈsiːmən/ n. (pl. -men) marin m.

seamy /ˈsiːmɪ/ a. ~ **side**, côté sordide m.

seance /ˈseɪɑːns/ n. séance de spiritisme f.

seaplane /ˈsiːpleɪn/ n. hydravion m.

seaport /ˈsiːpɔːt/ n. port de mer m.

search /sɜːtʃ/ v.t./i. fouiller; (study) examiner. —n. fouille f.; (quest) recherche(s) f. (pl.). **in** ~ **of**, à la recherche de. ~ **for**, chercher. ~**party** n. équipe de secours f. ~**warrant** n. mandat de perquisition f. ~**ing** a. (piercing) pénétrant.

searchlight /ˈsɜːtʃlaɪt/ n. projecteur m.

seasick /ˈsiːsɪk/ a. **be** ~, avoir le mal de mer.

seaside /ˈsiːsaɪd/ n. bord de la mer m.

season /ˈsiːzn/ n. saison f. —v.t. assaisonner. **in** ~, de saison. ~**able** a. qui convient à la saison. ~**al** a. saisonnier. ~**ing** n. assaisonnement m. ~**-ticket** n. carte d'abonnement f.

seasoned /ˈsiːznd/ a. expérimenté.

seat /siːt/ n. siège m.; (place) place f.; (of trousers) fond m. —v.t. (put) placer; (have seats for) avoir des places assises pour. **be** ~**ed**, **take a** ~, s'asseoir. ~**-belt** n. ceinture de sécurité f.

seaweed /ˈsiːwiːd/ n. algues f. pl.

seaworthy /ˈsiːwɜːðɪ/ a. en état de naviguer.

secateurs /sekəˈtɜːz/ n. pl. sécateur m.

seced|**e** /sɪˈsiːd/ v.i. faire sécession. ~**ssion** /-ʃn/ n. sécession f.

seclu|**de** /sɪˈkluːd/ v.t. isoler. ~**ded** a. isolé. ~**sion** /-ʒn/ n. solitude f.

second[1] /ˈsekənd/ a. deuxième, second. —n. deuxième m./f.; second(e) m. (f.); (unit of time) seconde f. ~**s**, (goods) articles de second choix m. —adv. (in race etc.) en seconde place. —v.t. (proposal) appuyer. ~**-best** a. de second choix, numéro deux invar. ~**-class** a. de deuxième classe m. ~ **hand**, de seconde main. ~**-hand** a. & adv. d'occasion; (n. on clock) trotteuse f. ~**-rate** a. médiocre. **have** ~ **thoughts**, avoir des doutes, changer d'avis. **on** ~ **thoughts**, (Amer.) on ~ **thought**, à la réflexion. ~**ly** adv. deuxièmement.

second[2] /sɪˈkɒnd/ v.t. (transfer) détacher (to, à). ~**ment** n. détachement m.

secondary /ˈsekəndrɪ/ a. secondaire. ~ **school**, lycée m., collège m.

secrecy /ˈsiːkrəsɪ/ n. secret m.

secret /ˈsiːkrɪt/ a. secret. —n. secret m. **in ~**, en secret. **~ly** adv. en secret, secrètement.

secretariat /sekrəˈteərɪət/ n. secrétariat m.

secretar|y /ˈsekrətrɪ/ n. secrétaire m./f. **S~y of State**, m. et (Amer.) ministre des Affaires étrangères m.; **~ial** /-ˈteərɪəl/ a. (work etc.) de secrétaire.

secret|e /sɪˈkriːt/ v.t. (med.) sécréter. **~ion** /-ʃn/ n. sécrétion f.

secretive /ˈsiːkrətɪv/ a. cachottier.

sect /sekt/ n. secte f. **~arian** /-ˈteərɪən/ a. sectaire.

section /ˈsekʃn/ n. section f.; (of country, town) partie f.; (in store) rayon m.; (newspaper column) rubrique f.

sector /ˈsektə(r)/ n. secteur m.

secular /ˈsekjʊlə(r)/ a. (school etc.) laïque; (art, music, etc.) profane.

secure /sɪˈkjʊə(r)/ a. (safe) en sûreté; (in mind) tranquille; (psychologically) sécurisé; (firm) solide; (against attack) sûr; (window etc.) bien fermé. —v.t. attacher; (obtain) s'assurer; (ensure) assurer. **~ly** adv. solidement; (safely) en sûreté.

security /sɪˈkjʊərətɪ/ n. (safety) sécurité f.; (for loan) caution f. **~ guard**, vigile m.

sedan /sɪˈdæn/ n. (Amer.) berline f.

sedate[1] /sɪˈdeɪt/ a. calme.

sedat|e[2] /sɪˈdeɪt/ v.t. donner un sédatif à. **~ion** /-ʃn/ n. sédation f.

sedative /ˈsedətɪv/ n. sédatif m.

sedentary /ˈsedntrɪ/ a. sédentaire.

sediment /ˈsedɪmənt/ n. sédiment m.

sedition /sɪˈdɪʃn/ n. sédition f.

seduce /sɪˈdjuːs/ v.t. séduire. **~r** /-ə(r)/ n. séduc|teur, -trice m., f.

seduct|ion /sɪˈdʌkʃn/ n. séduction f. **~ive** /-tɪv/ a. séduisant.

see[1] /siː/ v.t./i. (p.t. saw, p.p. seen)

voir; (escort) (r)accompagner. **~ about or to**, s'occuper de. **~ through**, (task) mener à bonne fin; (person) deviner (le jeu de). **~ (to it) that**, veiller à ce que. **~ you (soon)!**, à bientôt! **~ing that**, vu que.

see[2] /siː/ n. (of bishop) évêché m.

seed /siːd/ n. graine f.; (collectively) graines f. pl.; (origin: fig.) germe m.; (tennis) tête de série f. **go to ~**, (plant) monter en graine; (person) se laisser aller. **~ling** n. plant m.

seedy /ˈsiːdɪ/ a. (-ier, -iest) miteux.

seek /siːk/ v.t. (p.t. sought) chercher. **~ out**, aller chercher.

seem /siːm/ v.i. sembler. **~ingly** adv. apparemment.

seemly /ˈsiːmlɪ/ adv. convenable.

seen /siːn/ see **see[1]**.

seep /siːp/ v.i. (ooze) suinter. **~ into**, s'infiltrer dans. **~age** n. suintement m.; infiltration f.

see-saw /ˈsiːsɔː/ n. balançoire f., tape-cul m. —v.t. osciller.

seethe /siːð/ v.i. **~ with**, (anger) bouillir de; (people) grouiller de.

segment /ˈsegmənt/ n. segment m.; (of orange) quartier m.

segregat|e /ˈsegrɪgeɪt/ v.t. séparer. **~ion** /-ˈgeɪʃn/ n. ségrégation f.

seize /siːz/ v.t. saisir; (take possession of) s'emparer de. —v.i. **~ on**, (chance etc.) saisir. **~ up**, (engine etc.) se gripper.

seizure /ˈsiːʒə(r)/ n. (med.) crise f.

seldom /ˈseldəm/ adv. rarement.

select /sɪˈlekt/ v.t. choisir, sélectionner. —a. choisi; (exclusive) sélect. **~ion** /-kʃn/ n. sélection f.

selective /sɪˈlektɪv/ a. sélectif.

self /self/ n. (pl. selves) (on cheque) moi-même. **the ~**, le moi m. invar. **your good ~**, vous-même.

self- /self/ pref. **~assurance** n.

assurance *f*. **~-assured** *a*. sûr de soi. **~-catering** *a*. où l'on fait la cuisine soi-même. **~-centred**, (*Amer*.) **~-centered** *a*. égocentrique, (*Amer*.) **~-coloured**, (*Amer*.) **~-colored** *a*. uni. **~-confidence** *n*. confiance en soi *f*. **~-confident** *a*. sûr de soi. **~-conscious** *a*. gêné, timide. **~-contained** *a*. (*flat*) indépendant. **~-control** *n*. maîtrise de soi *f*. **~-defence** *n*. autodéfense *f*.; (*jurid*.) légitime défense *f*. **~-denial** *n*. abnégation *f*. **~-employed** *a*. qui travaille à son compte. **~-esteem** *n*. amour-propre *m*. **~-evident** *a*. évident. **~-government** *n*. autonomie *f*. **~-indulgent** *a*. qui se permet tout. **~-interest** *n*. intérêt personnel *m*. **~-portrait** *n*. autoportrait *m*. **~-possessed** *a*. assuré. **~-reliant** *a*. indépendant. **~-respect** *n*. respect de soi *m*., dignité *f*. **~-righteous** *a*. satisfait de soi. **~-sacrifice** *n*. abnégation *f*. **~-satisfied** *a*. content de soi. **~-seeking** *a*. égoïste. **~-service** *a*. & *n*. libre-service (*m*.). **~-styled** *a*. soi-disant. **~-sufficient** *a*. indépendant. **~-willed** *a*. entêté.

selfish /'selfɪʃ/ *a*. égoïste; (*motive*) intéressé. **~ness** *n*. égoïsme *m*.

selfless /'selflɪs/ *a*. désintéressé.

sell /sel/ *v.t./i.* (*p.t.* **sold**) (se) vendre. **~-by date**, date limite de vente *f*. be sold out of, n'avoir plus de. **~ off**, liquider. **~ out**, *n*. trahison *f*. it was a **~-out**, on a vendu tous les billets. **~ up**, vendre son fonds, sa maison, *etc*. **~er** *n*. vendeu|r, -se *m*., *f*.

Sellotape /'seləʊteɪp/ *n*. (P.) scotch *m*. (P.).

semantic /sɪ'mæntɪk/ *a*. sémantique. **~s** *n*. sémantique *f*.

semaphore /'seməfɔː(r)/ *n*. signaux à bras *m. pl.*; (*device*: rail.) sémaphore *m*.

semblance /'sembləns/ *n*. semblant *m*.

semen /'siːmən/ *n*. sperme *m*.

semester /sɪ'mestə(r)/ *n*. (*univ*., *Amer*.) semestre *m*.

semi- /'semɪ/ *pref*. semi-, demi-.

semibreve /'semɪbriːv/ *n*. (*mus*.) ronde *f*.

semicirc|le /'semɪsɜːkl/ *n*. demi-cercle *m*. **~ular** /-'sɜːkjʊlə(r)/ *a*. en demi-cercle.

semicolon /semɪ'kəʊlən/ *n*. point-virgule *m*.

semiconductor /semɪkən'dʌktə(r)/ *n*. semi-conducteur *n*.

semi-detached /semɪ'dɪtætʃt/ *a*. **~ house**, maison jumelle *f*.

semifinal /semɪ'faɪnl/ *n*. demi-finale *f*.

seminar /'semɪnɑː(r)/ *n*. séminaire *m*.

seminary /'semɪnərɪ/ *n*. séminaire *m*.

semiquaver /'semɪkweɪvə(r)/ *n*. (*mus*.) double croche *f*.

Semit|e /'siːmaɪt, *Amer*. 'semaɪt/ *n*. Sémite *m./f.* **~ic** /sɪ'mɪtɪk/ *a*. sémite; (*lang*.) sémitique.

semolina /semə'liːnə/ *n*. semoule *f*.

senat|e /'senɪt/ *n*. sénat *m*. **~or** /-ətə(r)/ *n*. sénateur *m*.

send /send/ *v.t./i.* (*p.t.* **sent**) envoyer. **~** *away*, (*dismiss*) renvoyer. **~** (*away or off*) **for**, commander (par la poste). **~ back**, renvoyer. **~ for**, (*person*, *help*) envoyer chercher. **~ a player off**, renvoyer un joueur. **~off** *n*. adieux chaleureux *m. pl.* **~ up**, (*fam*.) parodier. **~er** *n*. expédi|teur, -trice *m*., *f*.

senile /'siːnaɪl/ *a*. sénile. **~ity** /sɪ'nɪlətɪ/ *n*. sénilité *f*.

senior /'siːnɪə(r)/ *a*. plus âgé (to, que); (*in rank*) supérieur; (*teacher, partner*) principal. — *n*. aîné(e) *m*. (*f*.); (*schol*.) grand(e) *m*. (*f*.). **~ citizen**, personne âgée *f*.

~ity /-'ɒrətɪ/ n. priorité d'âge f.; supériorité f.; (in service) ancienneté f.

sensation /sen'seɪʃn/ n. sensation f. ~al a. (event) qui fait sensation; (wonderful) sensationnel.

sense /sens/ n. sens m.; (sensation) sensation f.; (mental impression) sentiment m.; (common sense) bon sens m. ~s, (mind) raison f. —v.t. (pres)sentir. **make** ~, avoir du sens. **make** ~ **of**, comprendre. ~less a. stupide; (med.) sans connaissance.

sensibilit|y /sensə'bɪlətɪ/ n. sensibilité f. ~ies, susceptibilité f.

sensible /'sensəbl/ a. raisonnable, sensé; (clothing) fonctionnel.

sensitiv|e /'sensətɪv/ a. sensible (to, à); (touchy) susceptible. ~ity /-'tɪvətɪ/ n. sensibilité f.

sensory /'sensərɪ/ a. sensoriel.

sensual /'senʃʊəl/ a. sensuel. ~ity /-'ælətɪ/ n. sensualité f.

sensuous /'senʃʊəs/ a. sensuel.

sent /sent/ see send.

sentence /'sentəns/ n. phrase f.; (decision, jurid.) jugement m., condamnation f.; (punishment) peine f. —v.t. ~ **to**, condamner à.

sentiment /'sentɪmənt/ n. sentiment m.

sentimental /sentɪ'mentl/ a. sentimental. ~ity /-'tælətɪ/ n. sentimentalité f.

sentry /'sentrɪ/ n. sentinelle f.

separable /'sepərəbl/ a. séparable.

separate¹ /'seprət/ a. séparé, différent; (independent) indépendant. ~s n. pl. coordonnés m. pl. ~ly adv. séparément.

separat|e² /'sepəreɪt/ v.t./i. (se) séparer. ~ion /-'reɪʃn/ n. séparation f.

September /sep'tembə(r)/ n. septembre m.

septic /'septɪk/ a. (wound) infecté. ~ **tank**, fosse septique f.

sequel /'siːkwəl/ n. suite f.

sequence /'siːkwəns/ n. (order) ordre m.; (series) suite f.; (of film) séquence f.

sequin /'siːkwɪn/ n. paillette f.

serenade /serə'neɪd/ n. sérénade f. —v.t. donner une sérénade à.

seren|e /sɪ'riːn/ a. serein. ~ity /-enətɪ/ n. sérénité f.

sergeant /'sɑːdʒənt/ n. (mil.) sergent m.; (policeman) brigadier m.

serial /'sɪərɪəl/ n. (story) feuilleton m. —a. (number) de série.

series /'sɪərɪz/ n. invar. série f.

serious /'sɪərɪəs/ a. sérieux; (very bad, critical) grave, sérieux. ~ly adv. sérieusement, gravement. **take** ~ly, prendre au sérieux. ~ness n. sérieux m.

sermon /'sɜːmən/ n. sermon m.

serpent /'sɜːpənt/ n. serpent m.

serrated /sɪ'reɪtɪd/ a. (edge) en dents de scie.

serum /'sɪərəm/ n. (pl. -a) sérum m.

servant /'sɜːvənt/ n. domestique m./f.; (of God etc.) serviteur m.

serve /sɜːv/ v.t./i. servir; (undergo, carry out) faire; (of transport) desservir. —n. (tennis) service m. ~ **as/to**, servir de/à. ~ **its purpose**, remplir sa fonction.

service /'sɜːvɪs/ n. service m.; (maintenance) révision f.; (relig.) office m. ~s, (mil.) forces armées f. pl. —v.t. (car etc.) réviser. **of** ~ **to**, utile à. ~ **area**, (auto.) aire de services f. ~ **charge**, service m. ~ **station**, station- service f.

serviceable /'sɜːvɪsəbl/ a. (usable) utilisable; (useful) commode; (durable) solide.

serviceman /'sɜːvɪsmən/ n. (pl. -men) militaire m.

serviette /sɜːvɪ'et/ n. serviette f.

servile /'sɜːvaɪl/ a. servile.

session /'seʃn/ n. séance f.; (univ.) année (universitaire) f.; (univ., Amer.) semestre m.

set /set/ v.t. (p.t. **set**, pres. p. **setting**) mettre; (put down) poser, mettre; (limit etc.) fixer; (watch, clock) régler; (example, task) donner; (for printing) composer; (in plaster) plâtrer. —v.i. (of sun) se coucher; (of jelly) prendre. —n. (of chairs, stamps, etc.) série f.; (of knives, keys, etc.) jeu m.; (of people) groupe m.; (TV, radio) poste m.; (style of hair) mise en plis f.; (theatre) décor m.; (tennis) set m.; (mathematics) ensemble m. —a. fixe; (in habits) régulier; (meal) à prix fixe; (book) au programme. **~ against** sth., opposé à. be **~ on** doing, être résolu à faire. **~ about** or **to**, se mettre à. **~ back**, (delay) retarder; (cost: sl.) coûter. **~-back** n. revers m. **~ fire to**, mettre le feu à. **~ free**, libérer. **~ in**, (take hold) s'installer, commencer. **~ off** or **out**, partir. **~ off**, (mechanism, activity) déclencher; (bomb) faire éclater. **~ out**, (state) exposer; (arrange) disposer. **~ out to do** sth., entreprendre de faire qch. **~ sail**, partir. **~ square**, équerre f. **~ to**, (about to) sur le point de. **~-to** n. querelle f. **~ to music**, mettre en musique. **~ up**, (establish) fonder, établir; (launch) lancer. **~-up** n. (fam.) affaire f.

settee /se'ti:/ n. canapé m.

setting /'setɪŋ/ n. cadre m.

settle /'setl/ v.t. (arrange, pay) régler; (date) fixer; (nerves) calmer. —v.i. (come to rest) se poser; (live) s'installer. **~ down**, se calmer; (become orderly) se ranger. **~ for**, accepter. **~ in**, s'installer. **~ up (with)**, régler. **~r** /-ə(r)/ n. colon m.

settlement /'setlmənt/ n. règlement m. (of, de); (agreement) accord m.; (place) colonie f.

seven /'sevn/ a. & n. sept (m.). **~th** a. & n. septième (m./f.).

seventeen /sevn'ti:n/ a. & n. dix-sept (m.). **~th** a. & n. dix-septième (m./f.).

seventy /'sevntɪ/ a. & n. soixante-dix (m.). **~ieth** a. & n. soixante-dixième (m./f.).

sever /'sevə(r)/ v.t. (cut) couper; (relations) rompre. **~ance** n. (breaking off) rupture f. **~ance pay**, indemnité de licenciement f.

several /'sevrəl/ a. & pron. plusieurs.

severe /sɪ'vɪə(r)/ a. (-er, -est) sévère; (violent) violent; (serious) grave. **~ely** adv. sévèrement; gravement. **~ity** /sɪ'verətɪ/ n. sévérité f.; violence f.; gravité f.

sew /səʊ/ v.t./i. (p.t. **sewed**, p.p. **sewn** or **sewed**) coudre. **~ing** n. couture f. **~ing-machine** n. machine à coudre f.

sewage /'su:ɪdʒ/ n. eaux d'égout f. pl., vidanges f. pl.

sewer /'su:ə(r)/ n. égout m.

sewn /səʊn/ see **sew**.

sex /seks/ n. sexe m. —a. (life) sexuel. **have ~**, avoir des rapports (sexuels). **~ maniac**, obsédé(e) sexuel(le) m. (f.). **~y** a. sexy invar.

sexist /'seksɪst/ a. & n. sexiste (m./f.).

sextet /seks'tet/ n. sextuor m.

sexual /'sekʃʊəl/ a. sexuel. **~ intercourse**, rapports sexuels m. pl. **~ity** /-'ælətɪ/ n. sexualité f.

shabby /'ʃæbɪ/ a. (-ier, -iest) (place, object) minable, miteux; (person) pauvrement vêtu; (mean) mesquin. **~ily** adv. (dress) pauvrement; (act) mesquinement.

shack /ʃæk/ n. cabane f.

shackles /'ʃæklz/ n. pl. chaînes f. pl.

shade /ʃeɪd/ n. ombre f.; (of colour,

opinion) nuance f.; (for lamp) abat-jour m.; (blind: Amer.) store m. **a ~ bigger**/etc., légèrement plus grand/etc. —v.t. (of person etc.) abriter; (of tree) ombrager.

shadow /ˈʃædəʊ/ n. ombre f. —v.t. (follow) filer. **S~ Cabinet**, cabinet fantôme m. **~y** a. ombragé; (dubious: fig.) vague.

shady /ˈʃeɪdɪ/ a. (-ier, -iest) ombragé; (dubious: fig.) louche.

shaft /ʃɑːft/ n. (of arrow) hampe f.; (axle) arbre m.; (of mine) puits m.; (of light) rayon m.

shaggy /ˈʃægɪ/ a. (-ier, -iest) (beard) hirsute; (hair) broussailleux; (animal) à longs poils.

shake /ʃeɪk/ v.t. (p.t. **shook**, p.p. **shaken**) secouer; (bottle) agiter; (house, belief, etc.) ébranler. —v.i. trembler. —n. secousse f. **~ hands with**, serrer la main à. **~ off**, (get rid of) se débarrasser de. **~ one's head**, (in refusal) dire non de la tête. **~ up**, (disturb, rouse, mix contents of) secouer. **~-up** n. (upheaval) remaniement m.

shaky /ˈʃeɪkɪ/ a. (-ier, -iest) (hand, voice) tremblant; (table etc.) branlant; (weak: fig.) faible.

shall /ʃæl, unstressed ʃ(ə)l/ v. aux. **I ~ do**, je ferai. **we ~ do**, nous ferons.

shallot /ʃəˈlɒt/ n. échalote f.

shallow /ˈʃæləʊ/ a. (-er, -est) peu profond; (fig.) superficiel.

sham /ʃæm/ n. comédie f.; (person) imposteur m.; (jewel) imitation f. —a. faux; (affected) feint. —v.t. (p.t. **shammed**) feindre.

shambles /ˈʃæmblz/ n. pl. (mess: fam.) désordre m., pagaille f.

shame /ʃeɪm/ n. honte f. —v.t. faire honte à. **it's a ~**, c'est dommage. **~ful** a. honteux. **~fully** adv. honteusement. **~less** a. éhonté.

shamefaced /ʃeɪmˈfeɪst/ a. honteux.

shampoo /ʃæmˈpuː/ n. shampooing m. —v.t. faire un shampooing à, shampooiner.

shandy /ˈʃændɪ/ n. panaché m.

shan't /ʃɑːnt/ = **shall not**.

shanty /ˈʃæntɪ/ n. (shack) baraque f. **~ town**, bidonville m.

shape /ʃeɪp/ n. forme f. —v.t. (fashion, mould) façonner; (future etc.: fig.) déterminer. —v.i. **~ up**, (plan etc.) prendre tournure or forme; (person etc.) faire des progrès. **~less** a. informe.

shapely /ˈʃeɪplɪ/ a. (-ier, -iest) (leg, person) bien tourné.

share /ʃeə(r)/ n. part f.; (comm.) action f. —v.t./i. partager; (feature) avoir en commun. **~ out** n. partage m.

shareholder /ˈʃeəhəʊldə(r)/ n. actionnaire m./f.

shark /ʃɑːk/ n. requin m.

sharp /ʃɑːp/ a. (-er, -est) (knife etc.) tranchant; (pin etc.) pointu; (point) aigu; (acute) vif; (sudden) brusque; (dishonest) peu scrupuleux. —adv. (stop) net. **six o'clock**/etc. **~**, six heures/etc. pile. —n. (mus.) dièse m. **~ly** adv. (harshly) vivement; (suddenly) brusquement.

sharpen /ˈʃɑːpən/ v.t. aiguiser; (pencil) tailler. **~er** n. (for pencil) taille-crayon/s f.

shatter /ˈʃætə(r)/ v.t./i. (glass etc.) (faire) voler en éclats, (se) briser; (upset, ruin) anéantir.

shave /ʃeɪv/ v.t./i. (se) raser. —n. **have a ~e**, se raser. **~en** a. rasé. **~er** n. rasoir électrique m. **~ing-brush** n. blaireau m. **~ing-cream** n. crème à raser f.

shaving /ˈʃeɪvɪŋ/ n. copeau m.

shawl /ʃɔːl/ n. châle m.

she /ʃiː/ pron. elle. —n. femelle f.

sheaf /ʃiːf/ n. (pl. **sheaves**) gerbe f.

shear /ʃɪə(r)/ v.t. (p.p. **shorn** or **sheared**) (sheep etc.) tondre. **~ off**, se détacher.

shears /ʃɪəz/ n. pl. cisaille(s) f. (pl.).

sheath /ʃiːθ/ n. (pl. -s /ʃiːðz/) gaine f., fourreau m.; (*contraceptive*) préservatif m.

sheathe /ʃiːð/ v.t. rengainer.

shed[1] /ʃed/ n. remise f.

shed[2] /ʃed/ v.t. (p.t. **shed**, pres. p. **shedding**) perdre; (*light, tears*) répandre.

sheen /ʃiːn/ n. lustre m.

sheep /ʃiːp/ n. invar. mouton m. **~-dog** n. chien de berger m.

sheepish /ʃiːpɪʃ/ a. penaud. **~ly** adv. d'un air penaud.

sheepskin /ʃiːpskɪn/ n. peau de mouton f.

sheer /ʃɪə(r)/ a. pur (et simple); (*steep*) à pic; (*fabric*) très fin. —adv. à pic, verticalement.

sheet /ʃiːt/ n. drap m.; (*of paper*) feuille f.; (*of glass, ice*) plaque f.

sheikh /ʃeɪk/ n. cheik m.

shelf /ʃelf/ n. (pl. **shelves**) rayon m. étagère f. **on the ~**, (*person*) laissé pour compte.

shell /ʃel/ n. coquille f.; (*on beach*) coquillage m.; (*of building*) carcasse f.; (*explosive*) obus m. —v.t. (*nut etc.*) décortiquer; (*peas*) écosser; (*mil.*) bombarder.

shellfish /ʃelfɪʃ/ n. invar. (*lobster etc.*) crustacé(s)m. (pl.); (*mollusc*) coquillage(s) m. (pl.).

shelter /ʃeltə(r)/ n. abri m. —v.t./i. (s')abriter; (*give shelter to*) donner asile à. **~ed** a. (*life etc.*) protégé.

shelve /ʃelv/ v.t. (*plan etc.*) laisser en suspens, remettre à plus tard.

shelving /ʃelvɪŋ/ n. (*shelves*) rayonnage(s) m. (pl.).

shepherd /ʃepəd/ n. berger m. —v.t. (*people*) guider. **~'s pie**, hachis Parmentier m.

sherbet /ʃɜːbət/ n. jus de fruits m.; (*powder*) poudre acidulée f.; (*water-ice: Amer.*) sorbet m.

sheriff /ʃerɪf/ n. shérif m.

sherry /ʃerɪ/ n. xérès m.

shield /ʃiːld/ n. bouclier m.; (*screen*) écran m. —v.t. protéger.

shift /ʃɪft/ v.t./i. (se) déplacer, bouger; (*exchange, alter*) changer de. —n. changement m.; (*workers*) équipe f.; (*work*) poste m.; (*auto.: Amer.*) levier de vitesse m. **make ~**, se débrouiller. **~ work**, travail par roulement.

shiftless /ʃɪftlɪs/ a. paresseux.

shifty /ʃɪftɪ/ a. (-ier, -iest) louche.

shilling /ʃɪlɪŋ/ n. shilling m.

shilly-shally /ʃɪlɪʃælɪ/ v.i. hésiter, balancer.

shimmer /ʃɪmə(r)/ v.i. chatoyer. —n. chatoiement m.

shin /ʃɪn/ n. tibia m.

shine /ʃaɪn/ v.t./i. (p.t. **shone** /ʃɒn/) (faire) briller. —n. éclat m., brillant m. **~ one's torch** or **the light (on)**, éclairer.

shingle /ʃɪŋgl/ n. (*pebbles*) galets m. pl.; (*on roof*) bardeau m.

shingles /ʃɪŋglz/ n. pl. (*med.*) zona m.

shiny /ʃaɪnɪ/ a. (-ier, -iest) brillant.

ship /ʃɪp/ n. bateau m., navire m. —v.t. (p.t. **shipped**) transporter; (*send*) expédier; (*load*) embarquer. **~ment** n. cargaison f., envoi m. **~per** n. expéditeur m. **~ping** n. (*ships*) navigation f., navires m. pl.

shipbuilding /ʃɪpbɪldɪŋ/ n. construction navale f.

shipshape /ʃɪpʃeɪp/ adv. & a. parfaitement en ordre.

shipwreck /ʃɪprek/ n. naufrage m. **~ed** a. naufragé. **be ~ed**, faire naufrage.

shipyard /ʃɪpjɑːd/ n. chantier naval m.

shirk /ʃɜːk/ v.t. esquiver. **~er** n. tire-au-flanc m. invar.

shirt /ʃɜːt/ n. chemise f.; (*of woman*) chemisier m. **in ~-sleeves**, en bras de chemise.

shiver /'ʃɪvə(r)/ *v.i.* frissonner.
—*n.* frisson *m.*

shoal /ʃəʊl/ *n.* (*of fish*) banc *m.*

shock /ʃɒk/ *n.* choc *m.*, secousse *f.*;
(*electr.*) décharge *f.*; (*med.*) choc
m. —*a.* (*result*) choc *invar.*;
(*tactics*) de choc. —*v.t.* choquer.
∼ **absorber**, amortisseur *m.* **be
a** ∼**er**, (*fam.*) être affreux. ∼**ing**
a. choquant; (*bad:* *fam.*) affreux.
∼**ingly** *adv.* (*fam.*) affreusement.

shodd|y /'ʃɒdɪ/ *a.* (-**ier**, -**iest**) mal
fait, mauvais. ∼**ily** *adv.* mal.

shoe /ʃuː/ *n.* chaussure *f.*, soulier
m.; (*of horse*) fer (à cheval) *m.*; (*in
vehicle*) sabot (de frein) *m.* —*v.t.*
(*p.t.* **shod** /ʃɒd/, *pres. p.* **shoeing**)
(*horse*) ferrer. ∼ **repairer**, cordonnier *m.* **on a** ∼**string**, avec
très peu d'argent.

shoehorn /'ʃuːhɔːn/ *n.* chausse-
pied *m.*

shoelace /'ʃuːleɪs/ *n.* lacet *m.*

shoemaker /'ʃuːmeɪkə(r)/ *n.* cordonnier *m.*

shone /ʃɒn/ *see* **shine.**

shoo /ʃuː/ *v.t.* chasser.

shook /ʃʊk/ *see* **shake.**

shoot /ʃuːt/ *v.t.* (*p.t.* **shot**) (*gun*)
tirer un coup de; (*missile, glance*)
lancer; (*kill, wound*) tuer, blesser
(d'un coup de fusil, de pistolet,
etc.); (*execute*) fusiller; (*hunt*)
chasser; (*film*) tourner. —*v.i.*
tirer (**at**, sur). —*n.* (*bot.*) pousse *f.*
∼ **down**, abattre. ∼ **out**, (*rush*)
sortir en vitesse. ∼ **up**, (*spurt*)
jaillir; (*grow*) pousser vite. **hear**
∼**ing**, entendre des coups de feu.
∼**ing-range** *n.* stand de tir *m.*
∼**ing star**, étoile filante *f.*

shop /ʃɒp/ *n.* magasin *m.*, boutique
f.; (*workshop*) atelier *m.* —*v.i.*
(*p.t.* **shopped**) faire ses courses.
∼ **around**, comparer les prix. ∼
assistant, vendeu|r, -se *m., f.* ∼
floor *n.* (*workers*) ouvriers *m. pl.*
∼**per** *n.* acheteu|r, -se *m., f.* ∼

soiled, (*Amer.*) ∼**-worn** *adjs.*
abîmé. ∼ **steward**, délégué(e)
syndical(e) *m.* (*f.*). ∼ **window**,
vitrine *f.*

shopkeeper /'ʃɒpkiːpə(r)/ *n.* com-
merçant(e) *m. (f.).*

shoplift|er /'ʃɒplɪftə(r)/ *n.* voleu|r,
-se à l'étalage *m., f.* ∼**ing** *n.* vol à
l'étalage *m.*

shopping /'ʃɒpɪŋ/ *n.* (*goods*)
achats *m. pl.* **go** ∼, faire ses
courses. ∼ **bag**, sac à provisions
m. ∼ **centre**, centre commercial
m.

shore /ʃɔː(r)/ *n.* rivage *m.*

shorn /ʃɔːn/ *see* **shear.** —*a.* ∼ **of**,
dépouillé de.

short /ʃɔːt/ *a.* (-**er**, -**est**) court;
(*person*) petit; (*brief*) court, bref;
(*curt*) brusque. **be** ∼ **(of)**, (*lack*)
manquer (de). —*adv.* (*stop*) net.
—*n.* (*electr.*) court-circuit *m.*;
(*film*) court-metrage *m.* ∼**s**,
(*trousers*) short *m.* ∼ **of money**,
à court d'argent. **I'm two** ∼, il
m'en manque deux. ∼ **of doing**
sth., à moins de faire qch.
everything ∼ **of**, tout sauf.
nothing ∼ **of**, rien de moins que.
cut ∼, écourter. **cut s.o.** ∼,
couper court à qn. **fall** ∼ **of**, ne
pas arriver à. **he is called Tom**
for ∼, son diminutif est Tom. **in**
∼, en bref. ∼**-change** *v.t.* (*cheat*)
rouler. ∼ **circuit**, court-circuit
m. ∼**-circuit** *v.t.* court-circuiter.
∼ **cut**, raccourci *m.* ∼**-handed**
a. à court de personnel. ∼ **list**,
liste des candidats choisis *f.* ∼**-
lived** *a.* éphémère. ∼**-sighted** *a.*
myope. ∼**-staffed** *a.* à court de
personnel. ∼ **story**, nouvelle *f.*
∼**-term** *a.* à court terme. ∼
wave, ondes courtes *f. pl.*

shortage /'ʃɔːtɪdʒ/ *n.* manque *m.*

shortbread /'ʃɔːtbred/ *n.* sablé
m.

shortcoming /'ʃɔːtkʌmɪŋ/ *n.*
défaut *m.*

shorten /'ʃɔːtn/ v.t. raccourcir.

shortfall /'ʃɔːtfɔːl/ n. déficit m.

shorthand /'ʃɔːthænd/ n. sténo (-graphie) f. ~ **typist**, sténo-dactylo f.

shortly /'ʃɔːtlɪ/ adv. bientôt.

shot /ʃɒt/ see **shoot**. —n. (firing, attempt, etc.) coup de feu m.; (person) tireur m.; (bullet) balle f.; (photograph) photo f.; (injection) piqûre f. **like a ~**, comme une flèche. ~-**gun** n. fusil de chasse m.

should /ʃʊd, unstressed ʃəd/ v.aux. devoir. **you ~ help me**, vous devriez m'aider. **I ~ have stayed**, j'aurais dû rester. **I ~ like to**, j'aimerais bien. **if he ~ come**, s'il vient.

shoulder /'ʃəʊldə(r)/ n. épaule f. —v.t. (responsibility) endosser; (burden) se charger de. ~-**bag** n. sac à bandoulière m. ~-**blade** n. omoplate f. ~-**pad** n. épaulette f.

shout /ʃaʊt/ n. cri m. —v.t./i. crier. ~ **at**, enguueler. ~ **down**, huer.

shove /ʃʌv/ n. poussée f. —v.t./i. pousser; (put: fam.) ficher. ~ **off**, (depart: fam.) se tirer.

shovel /'ʃʌvl/ n. pelle f. —v.t. (p.t. **shovelled**) pelleter.

show /ʃəʊ/ v.t. (p.t. **showed**, p.p. **shown**) montrer; (of dial, needle) indiquer; (put on display) exposer; (film) donner; (conduct) conduire. —v.i. (be visible) se voir. —n. démonstration f.; (ostentation) parade f.; (exhibition) exposition f., salon m.; (theatre) spectacle m.; (cinema) séance f. **for ~**, pour l'effet. **on ~**, exposé. ~-**down** n. épreuve de force f. ~-**jumping** n. concours hippique m. ~ **off** v.t étaler; v.i. poser, crâner. ~-**off** n. poseu|r, -se m., f. ~-**piece** n. modèle du genre m. ~ **s.o. in/out**, faire entrer/sortir qn. ~ **up**, (faire) ressortir; (appear: fam.) se

montrer. ~-**ing** n. performance f.; (cinema) séance f.

shower /'ʃaʊə(r)/ n. (of rain) averse f.; (of blows etc.) grêle f.; (for washing) douche f. —v.t. ~ **with**, couvrir de. —v.i. se doucher. ~**y** a. pluvieux.

showerproof /'ʃaʊəpruːf/ a. imperméable.

showmanship /'ʃəʊmənʃɪp/ n. art de la mise en scène m.

shown /ʃəʊn/ see **show**.

showroom /'ʃəʊrʊm/ n. salle d'exposition f.

showy /'ʃəʊɪ/ a. (-ier, -iest) voyant; (manner) prétentieux.

shrank /ʃræŋk/ see **shrink**.

shrapnel /'ʃræpn(ə)l/ n. éclats d'obus m. pl.

shred /ʃred/ n. lambeau m.; (least amount: fig.) parcelle f. —v.t. (p.t. **shredded**) déchiqueter; (culin.) râper. ~**der** n. destructeur de documents m.

shrew /ʃruː/ n. (woman) mégère f.

shrewd /ʃruːd/ a. (-er, -est) astucieux. ~**ness** n. astuce f.

shriek /ʃriːk/ n. hurlement m. —v.t./i. hurler.

shrift /ʃrɪft/ n. **give s.o. short ~**, traiter qn. sans ménagement.

shrill /ʃrɪl/ a. strident, aigu.

shrimp /ʃrɪmp/ n. crevette f.

shrine /ʃraɪn/ n. (place) lieu saint m.; (tomb) châsse f.

shrink /ʃrɪŋk/ v.t./i. (p.t. **shrank**, p.p. **shrunk**) rétrécir; (lessen) diminuer. ~ **from**, reculer devant. ~**age** n. rétrécissement m.

shrivel /'ʃrɪvl/ v.t./i. (p.t. **shrivelled**) (se) ratatiner.

shroud /ʃraʊd/ n. linceul m. —v.t. (veil) envelopper.

Shrove /ʃrəʊv/ n. ~ **Tuesday**, Mardi gras m.

shrub /ʃrʌb/ n. arbuste m. ~**bery** n. arbustes m. pl.

shrug /ʃrʌg/ v.t. (p.t. **shrugged**)

~ **one's shoulders,** hausser les épaules. —n. haussement d'épaules m. ~ **sth. off,** réagir avec indifférence à qch.

shrunk /ʃrʌŋk/ *see* **shrink.** ~**en** a. rétréci; (*person*) ratatiné.

shudder /'ʃʌdə(r)/ v.i. frémir. —n. frémissement m.

shuffle /'ʃʌfl/ v.t. (*feet*) traîner; (*cards*) battre. —v.i. traîner les pieds. —n. démarche traînante f.

shun /ʃʌn/ v.t. (*p.t.* **shunned**) éviter, fuir.

shunt /ʃʌnt/ v.t. (*train*) aiguiller.

shush /ʃuʃ/ int. (*fam.*) chut.

shut /ʃʌt/ v.t. (*p.t.* **shut,** *pres. p.* **shutting**) fermer. —v.i. se fermer; (*of shop, bank, etc.*) fermer. ~**down** n. *ou* up, fermer. ~**in** *or* up, enfermer. ~**up** v.i. (*fam.*) se taire; v.t. (*fam.*) faire taire.

shutter /'ʃʌtə(r)/ n. volet m.; (*photo.*) obturateur m.

shuttle /'ʃʌtl/ n. (*bus etc.*) navette f. —v.i. faire la navette. —v.t. transporter. ~ **service,** navette f.

shuttlecock /'ʃʌtlkɒk/ n. (*badminton*) volant m.

shy /ʃaɪ/ a. (-**er**, -**est**) timide. —v.i. reculer. ~**ness** n. timidité f.

Siamese /saɪə'miːz/ a. siamois.

sibling /'sɪblɪŋ/ n. frère m., sœur f.

Sicily /'sɪsɪlɪ/ n. Sicile f.

sick /sɪk/ a. malade; (*humour*) macabre. **be** ~, (*vomit*) vomir. **be** ~ **of,** en avoir assez *or* marre de. **feel** ~, avoir mal au cœur. ~**bay** n. infirmerie f. ~**leave** n. congé maladie m. ~**pay** n. assurance-maladie f. ~**room** n. chambre de malade f.

sicken /'sɪkən/ v.t. écœurer. —v.i. **be** ~**ing for,** (*illness*) couver.

sickle /'sɪkl/ n. faucille f.

sickly /'sɪklɪ/ a. (-**ier**, -**iest**) (*person*) maladif; (*taste, smell, etc.*) écœurant.

sickness /'sɪknɪs/ n. maladie f.

side /saɪd/ n. côté m.; (*of road, river*) bord m.; (*of hill*) flanc m.; (*sport*) équipe f. —a. latéral. —v.i. ~ **with,** se ranger du côté de. **on the** ~, (*extra*) en plus; (*secretly*) en catimini. ~ **by side,** côte à côte. ~**car** n. side-car m. ~**effect** n. effet secondaire m. ~**saddle** adv. en amazone. ~**show** n. petite attraction f. ~**step** v.t. (*p.t.* -**stepped**) éviter. ~**street** n. rue latérale f. ~**track** v.t. faire dévier de son sujet.

sideboard /'saɪdbɔːd/ n. buffet m. ~**s,** (*whiskers: sl.*) pattes f. pl.

sideburns /'saɪdbɜːnz/ n. pl. pattes f. pl., rouflaquettes f. pl.

sidelight /'saɪdlaɪt/ n. (*auto.*) veilleuse f., lanterne f.

sideline /'saɪdlaɪn/ n. activité secondaire f.

sidewalk /'saɪdwɔːk/ n. (*Amer.*) trottoir m.

side|ways /'saɪdweɪz/, ~**long** adv. & a. de côté.

siding /'saɪdɪŋ/ n. voie de garage f.

sidle /'saɪdl/ v.i. avancer furtivement (**up to,** vers).

siege /siːdʒ/ n. siège m.

siesta /sɪ'estə/ n. sieste f.

sieve /sɪv/ n. tamis m.; (*for liquids*) passoire f. —v.t. tamiser.

sift /sɪft/ v.t. tamiser. —v.i. ~ **through,** examiner.

sigh /saɪ/ n. soupir m. —v.t./i. soupirer.

sight /saɪt/ n. vue f.; (*scene*) spectacle m.; (*on gun*) mire f. —v.t. apercevoir. **at** *or* **on** ~, à vue. **catch** ~ **of,** apercevoir. **in** ~, visible. **lose** ~ **of,** perdre de vue.

sightsee|ing /'saɪtsiːɪŋ/ n. tourisme m. ~**r** /-ə(r)/ n. touriste m./f.

sign /saɪn/ n. signe m.; (*notice*)

panneau *m.* —*v.t./i.* signer. ~ **language,** (*for deaf*) langage des sourds-muets *m.* ~ **on,** (*when unemployed*) s'inscrire au chômage. ~ **up,** (s')enrôler.

signal /ˈsɪɡnəl/ *n.* signal *m.* —*v.t.* (*p.t.* **signalled**) communiquer (par signaux); (*person*) faire signe à. ~**box** *n.* poste d'aiguillage *m.*

signalman /ˈsɪɡnəlmən/ *n.* (*pl.* **-men**) (*rail.*) aiguilleur *m.*

signatory /ˈsɪɡnətrɪ/ *n.* signataire *m./f.*

signature /ˈsɪɡnətʃə(r)/ *n.* signature *f.* ~ **tune,** indicatif musical *m.*

signet-ring /ˈsɪɡnɪtrɪŋ/ *n.* chevalière *f.*

significan|t /sɪɡˈnɪfɪkənt/ *a.* important; (*meaningful*) significatif. ~**ce** *n.* importance *f.*; (*meaning*) signification *f.* ~**tly** *adv.* (*much*) sensiblement.

signify /ˈsɪɡnɪfaɪ/ *v.t.* signifier.

signpost /ˈsaɪnpəʊst/ *n.* poteau indicateur *m.*

silence /ˈsaɪləns/ *n.* silence *m.* —*v.t.* faire taire. ~**r** /-ə(r)/ *n.* (*on gun, car*) silencieux *m.*

silent /ˈsaɪlənt/ *a.* silencieux; (*film*) muet. ~**ly** *adv.* silencieusement.

silhouette /sɪluːˈet/ *n.* silhouette *f.* —*v.t.* **be** ~**d against,** se profiler contre.

silicon /ˈsɪlɪkən/ *n.* silicium *m.* ~ **chip,** microplaquette *f.*

silk /sɪlk/ *n.* soie *f.* ~**en,** ~**y** *adjs.* soyeux.

sill /sɪl/ *n.* rebord *m.*

silly /ˈsɪlɪ/ *a.* (**-ier, -iest**) bête, idiot.

silo /ˈsaɪləʊ/ *n.* (*pl.* **-os**) silo *m.*

silt /sɪlt/ *n.* vase *f.*

silver /ˈsɪlvə(r)/ *n.* argent *m.*; (*silverware*) argenterie *f.* —*a.* en argent, d'argent. ~ **wedding,** noces d'argent *f. pl.* ~**y** *a.* argenté; (*sound*) argentin.

silversmith /ˈsɪlvəsmɪθ/ *n.* orfèvre *m.*

silverware /ˈsɪlvəweə(r)/ *n.* argenterie *f.*

similar /ˈsɪmɪlə(r)/ *a.* semblable (**to, à**). ~**ity** /-ˈlærətɪ/ *n.* ressemblance *f.* ~**ly** *adv.* de même.

simile /ˈsɪmɪlɪ/ *n.* comparaison *f.*

simmer /ˈsɪmə(r)/ *v.t./i.* (*soup etc.*) mijoter; (*water*) (laisser) frémir; (*smoulder: fig.*) couver. ~ **down,** se calmer.

simper /ˈsɪmpə(r)/ *v.i.* minauder. ~**ing** *a.* minaudier.

simple /ˈsɪmpl/ *a.* (**-er, -est**) simple. ~**-minded** *a.* simple d'esprit. ~**icity** /-ˈplɪsətɪ/ *n.* simplicité *f.* ~**y** *adv.* simplement; (*absolutely*) absolument.

simplify /ˈsɪmplɪfaɪ/ *v.t.* simplifier. ~**ication** /-ɪˈkeɪʃn/ *n.* simplification *f.*

simplistic /sɪmˈplɪstɪk/ *a.* simpliste.

simulat|e /ˈsɪmjʊleɪt/ *v.t.* simuler. ~**ion** /-ˈleɪʃn/ *n.* simulation *f.*

simultaneous /ˌsɪmlˈteɪnɪəs, *Amer.* saɪmlˈteɪnɪəs/ *a.* simultané. ~**ly** *adv.* simultanément.

sin /sɪn/ *n.* péché *m.* —*v.i.* (*p.t.* **sinned**) pécher.

since /sɪns/ *prep. & adv.* depuis. —*conj.* depuis que; (*because*) puisque. ~ **then,** depuis.

sincer|e /sɪnˈsɪə(r)/ *a.* sincère. ~**ely** *adv.* sincèrement. ~**ity** /-ˈserətɪ/ *n.* sincérité *f.*

sinew /ˈsɪnjuː/ *n.* tendon *m.* ~**s,** muscles *m. pl.*

sinful /ˈsɪnfl/ *a.* (*act*) coupable, qui constitue un péché; (*shocking*) scandaleux.

sing /sɪŋ/ *v.t./i.* (*p.t.* **sang,** *p.p.* **sung**) chanter. ~**er** *n.* chanteu|r, -se *m., f.*

singe /sɪndʒ/ *v.t.* (*pres. p.* **singeing**) brûler légèrement, roussir.

single /'sɪŋgl/ a. seul; (*not double*) simple; (*unmarried*) célibataire; (*room, bed*) pour une personne; (*ticket*) simple. —n. (*ticket*) aller simple m.; (*record*) 45 tours m. invar. **~s**, (*tennis*) simple m. **~s bar**, bar pour les célibataires m. —v.t. **~ out**, choisir. in **~ file**, en file indienne. **~-handed** a. sans aide. **~-minded** a. tenace. **~ parent**, parent seul m.

singly adv. un à un.

singlet /'sɪŋglɪt/ n. maillot de corps m.

singsong /'sɪŋsɒŋ/ n. have a **~**, chanter en chœur. —a. (*voice*) monotone.

singular /'sɪŋgjʊlə(r)/ n. singulier m. —a. (*uncommon & gram.*) singulier; (*noun*) au singulier. **~ly** adv. singulièrement.

sinister /'sɪnɪstə(r)/ a. sinistre.

sink /sɪŋk/ v.t./i. (*p.t.* sank, *p.p.* sunk) (faire) couler; (*of ground, person*) s'affaisser; (*well*) creuser; (*money*) investir. —n. (*in kitchen*) évier m.; (*wash-basin*) lavabo m. **~ in**, (*fig.*) être compris. **~ into** v.t. (*thrust*) enfoncer dans; v.i. (*go deep*) s'enfoncer dans. **~ unit**, bloc-evier m.

sinner /'sɪnə(r)/ n. péch|eur, -eresse m., f.

sinuous /'sɪnjʊəs/ a. sinueux.

sinus /'saɪnəs/ n. (*pl.* -uses) (*anat.*) sinus m.

sip /sɪp/ n. petite gorgée f. —v.t. (*p.t.* sipped) boire à petites gorgées.

siphon /'saɪfn/ n. siphon m. —v.t. **~ off**, siphonner.

sir /sɜː(r)/ n. monsieur m. Sir, (*title*) Sir m.

siren /'saɪərən/ n. sirène f.

sirloin /'sɜːlɔɪn/ n. faux-filet m., aloyau m.; (*Amer.*) romsteck m.

sissy /'sɪsɪ/ n. personne efféminée f.; (*coward*) dégonflé(e) m. (f.).

sister /'sɪstə(r)/ n. sœur f.; (*nurse*) infirmière en chef f. **~-in-law** (*pl.* **~s-in-law**) belle-sœur f. **~ly** a. fraternel.

sit /sɪt/ v.t./i. (*p.t.* sat, *pres. p.* sitting) (s')asseoir; (*of committee etc.*) siéger. **~ (for)**, (*exam*) se présenter à. be **~ting**, être assis. **~ around**, ne rien faire. **~ down**, s'asseoir. **~ in on a meeting**, assister à une réunion pour écouter. **~-in** n. sit-in m. invar. **~ting** n. séance f.; (*in restaurant*) service m. **~ting-room** n. salon m.

site /saɪt/ n. emplacement m. (**building**) **~**, chantier m. —v.t. placer, construire, situer.

situat|e /'sɪtjʊeɪt/ v.t. situer. be **~ed**, être situé. **~ion** /-'eɪʃn/ n. situation f.

six /sɪks/ a. & n. six (m.). **~th** a. & n. sixième (m./f.).

sixteen /sɪk'stiːn/ a. & n. seize (m.). **~th** a. & n. seizième (m./f.).

sixt|y /'sɪkstɪ/ a. & n. soixante (m.). **~ieth** a. & n. soixantième (m./f.).

size /saɪz/ n. dimension f.; (*of person, garment, etc.*) taille f.; (*of shoes*) pointure f.; (*of sum, salary*) montant m.; (*extent*) ampleur f. —v.t. **~ up**, (*fam.*) jauger, juger. **~able** a. assez grand.

sizzle /'sɪzl/ v.i. grésiller.

skate[1] /skeɪt/ n. invar. (*fish*) raie f.

skat|e[2] /skeɪt/ n. patin m. —v.i. patiner. **~er** n. patineu|r, -se m., f. **~ing** n. patinage m. **~ing-rink** n. patinoire f.

skateboard /'skeɪtbɔːd/ n. skateboard m., planche à roulettes f.

skeleton /'skelɪtən/ n. squelette m. **~on crew or staff**, effectifs minimums m. pl. **~al** a. squelettique.

sketch /sketʃ/ n. esquisse f., croquis m.; (*theatre*) sketch m. —v.t. faire un croquis de, esquisser. —v.i. faire des esquisses. **~ out,** esquisser. **~ pad,** bloc à dessins.

sketchy /ˈsketʃɪ/ a. (-ier, -iest) sommaire, incomplet.

skew /skjuː/ n. on the **~,** de travers. **~-whiff** a. (fam.) de travers.

skewer /ˈskjʊə(r)/ n. brochette f.

ski /skiː/ n. (pl. -is) ski m. —a. de ski. —v.i. (p.t. **ski'd** or **skied,** pres. p. **skiing**) skier; (go skiing) faire du ski. **~ jump,** saut à skis m. **~ lift,** remonte-pente m. **~er** n. skieu|r, -se m./f. **~ing** n. ski m.

skid /skɪd/ v.i. (p.t. **skidded**) déraper. —n. dérapage m.

skilful /ˈskɪlfl/ a. habile.

skill /skɪl/ n. habileté f.; (craft) métier m. **~s,** aptitudes f. pl. **~ed** a. habile; (worker) qualifié.

skim /skɪm/ v.t. (p.t. **skimmed**) écumer; (milk) écrémer; (pass or glide over) effleurer. —v.i. **~ through,** parcourir.

skimp /skɪmp/ v.t./i. **~ (on),** lésiner (sur).

skimpy /ˈskɪmpɪ/ a. (-ier, -iest) (clothes) étriqué; (meal) chiche.

skin /skɪn/ n. peau f. —v.t. (p.t. **skinned**) (animal) écorcher; (fruit) éplucher. **~-diving** n. plongée sous-marine f. **~-tight** a. collant.

skinflint /ˈskɪnflɪnt/ n. avare m./f.

skinny /ˈskɪnɪ/ a. (-ier, -iest) maigre, maigrichon.

skint /skɪnt/ a. (sl.) fauché.

skip¹ /skɪp/ v.i. (p.t. **skipped**) sautiller; (with rope) sauter à la corde. —v.t. (page, class, etc.) sauter. —n. petit saut m. **~ping-rope** n. corde à sauter f.

skip² /skɪp/ n. (container) benne f.

skipper /ˈskɪpə(r)/ n. capitaine m.

skirmish /ˈskɜːmɪʃ/ n. escarmouche f., accrochage m.

skirt /skɜːt/ n. jupe f. —v.t. contourner. **~ing-board** n. plinthe f.

skit /skɪt/ n. sketch satirique m.

skittle /ˈskɪtl/ n. quille f.

skive /skaɪv/ v.i. (sl.) tirer au flanc.

skivvy /ˈskɪvɪ/ n. (fam.) boniche f.

skulk /skʌlk/ v.i. (move) rôder furtivement; (hide) se cacher.

skull /skʌl/ n. crâne m. **~-cap** n. calotte f.

skunk /skʌŋk/ n. (animal) mouffette f.; (person: sl.) salaud m.

sky /skaɪ/ n. ciel m. **~-blue** a. & n. bleu ciel a. & m. invar.

skylight /ˈskaɪlaɪt/ n. lucarne f.

skyscraper /ˈskaɪskreɪpə(r)/ n. gratte-ciel m. invar.

slab /slæb/ n. plaque f., bloc m.; (of paving-stone) dalle f.

slack /slæk/ a. (-er, -est) (rope) lâche; (person) négligent; (business) stagnant; (period) creux. —n. the **~,** (in rope) du mou —v.t./i. (se) relâcher.

slacken /ˈslækən/ v.t./i. (se) relâcher; (slow) (se) ralentir.

slacks /slæks/ n. pl. pantalon m.

slag /slæg/ n. scories f. pl. **~-heap** n. crassier m.

slain /sleɪn/ see slay.

slake /sleɪk/ v.t. étancher.

slalom /ˈslɑːləm/ n. slalom m.

slam /slæm/ v.t./i. (p.t. **slammed**) (door etc.) claquer; (throw) flanquer; (criticize: sl.) critiquer. —n. (noise) claquement m.

slander /ˈslɑːndə(r)/ n. diffamation f., calomnie f. —v.t. diffamer, calomnier. **~ous** a. diffamatoire.

slang /slæŋ/ n. argot m. **~y** a. argotique.

slant /slɑːnt/ v.t./i. (faire) pencher; (news) présenter sous un certain jour. —n. inclinaison f.; (bias) angle m. **~ed** a. partial. be **~ing,** être penché.

slap /slæp/ v.t. (p.t. **slapped**) (strike) donner une claque à; (face) gifler; (put) flanquer. —n. claque f.; gifle f. —adv. tout droit.

~-happy a. (carefree: fam.) insouciant; (dazed: fam.) abruti. **~-up meal**, (sl.) gueuleton m.

slapdash /'slæpdæʃ/ a. fait, qui travaille etc. n'importe comment.

slapstick /'slæpstɪk/ n. grosse farce f.

slash /slæʃ/ v.t. (cut) taillader; (sever) trancher; (fig.) réduire (radicalement). —n. taillade f.

slat /slæt/ n. (in blind) lamelle f.; (on bed) latte f.

slate /sleɪt/ n. ardoise f. —v.t. (fam.) critiquer, éreinter.

slaughter /'slɔːtə(r)/ v.t. massacrer; (animals) abattre. —n. massacre m.; abattage m.

slaughterhouse /'slɔːtəhaʊs/ n. abattoir m.

Slav /slɑːv/ a. & n. slave (m./f.). **~onic** /slə'vɒnɪk/a. (lang.) slave.

slave /sleɪv/ n. esclave m./f. —v.i. trimer. **~-driver** n. négr|ier, -ière m., f. **~ry** /-ərɪ/ n. esclavage m.

slavish /'sleɪvɪʃ/ a. servile.

slay /sleɪ/ v.t. (p.t. slew, p.p. slain) tuer.

sleazy /'sliːzɪ/ a. (-ier, -iest) (fam.) sordide, miteux.

sledge /sledʒ/ n. luge f.; (horse-drawn) traîneau m. **~-hammer** n. marteau de forgeron m.

sleek /sliːk/ a. (-er, -est) lisse, brillant; (manner) onctueux.

sleep /sliːp/ n. sommeil m. —v.i. (p.t. slept) dormir; (spend the night) coucher. —v.t. loger. **go to ~**, s'endormir. **~ in**, faire la grasse matinée. **~er** n. dormeu|r, -se m., f.; (beam: rail) traverse f.; (berth) couchette f. **~ing-bag** n. sac de couchage m. **~ing pill** n. somnifère m. **~less** a. sans sommeil. **~-walker** n. somnambule m./f.

sleepy /'sliːpɪ/ a. (-ier, -iest) somnolent. **be ~y**, avoir sommeil. **~ily** adv. à moitié endormi.

sleet /sliːt/ n. neige fondue f.; (coat of ice: Amer.) verglas m. —v.i. tomber de la neige fondue.

sleeve /sliːv/ n. manche f.; (of record) pochette f. **up one's ~**, en réserve. **~less** a. sans manches.

sleigh /sleɪ/ n. traîneau m.

sleight /slaɪt/ n. **~ of hand**, prestidigitation f.

slender /'slendə(r)/ a. mince, svelte; (scanty: fig.) faible.

slept /slept/ see sleep.

sleuth /sluːθ/ n. limier m.

slew¹ /sluː/ v.i. (turn) virer.

slew² /sluː/ see slay.

slice /slaɪs/ n. tranche f. —v.t. couper (en tranches).

slick /slɪk/ a. (unctuous) mielleux; (cunning) astucieux. —n. (oil) **~**, nappe de pétrole f., marée noire f.

slide /slaɪd/ v.t./i. (p.t. slid) glisser. —n. glissade f.; (fall: fig.) baisse f.; (in playground) tobboggan m.; (for hair) barrette f. (photo.) diapositive f. **~ into**, (go silently) se glisser dans. **~-rule** n. règle à calcul f. **sliding** a. (door, panel) à glissière, à coulisse. **sliding scale**, échelle mobile f.

slight /slaɪt/ a. (-er, -est) petit, léger; (slender) mince; (frail) frêle. —v.t. (insult) offenser. —n. affront m. **~est** a. moindre. **~ly** adv. légèrement, un peu.

slim /slɪm/ a. (slimmer, slimmest) mince. —v.i. (p.t. slimmed) maigrir. **~ness** n. minceur f.

slim|e /slaɪm/ n. boue (visqueuse) f.; (on river-bed) vase f. **~y** a. boueux; vaseux; (sticky, servile) visqueux.

sling /slɪŋ/ n. (weapon, toy) fronde f.; (bandage) écharpe f. —v.t. (p.t. slung) jeter, lancer.

slip /slɪp/ v.t./i. (p.t. slipped) glisser. —n. faux pas m.; (mistake) erreur f.; (petticoat) combinaison f.; (paper) fiche f. **give the ~ to**, fausser compagnie à. ~ away, s'esquiver. ~-cover n. (Amer.) housse f. ~ into, (go) se glisser dans; (clothes) mettre. ~ of the tongue, lapsus m. ~ped disc, hernie discale f. ~-road n. bretelle f. ~ s.o.'s mind, échapper à qn. ~-stream n. sillage m. ~ up, (fam.) gaffer. ~-up n. (fam.) gaffe f.

slipper /'slɪpə(r)/ n. pantoufle f.

slippery /'slɪpərɪ/ a. glissant.

slipshod /'slɪpʃɒd/ a. (person) négligent; (work) négligé.

slit /slɪt/ n. fente f. —v.t. (p.t. slit, pres. p. slitting) couper, fendre.

slither /'slɪðə(r)/ v.i. glisser.

sliver /'slɪvə(r)/ n. (of cheese etc.) lamelle f.; (splinter) éclat m.

slob /slɒb/ n. (fam.) rustre m.

slobber /'slɒbə(r)/ v.i. baver.

slog /slɒg/ v.t. (p.t. slogged) (hit) frapper dur. —v.i. (work) trimer. —n. (work) travail dur m.; (effort) gros effort m.

slogan /'sləʊgən/ n. slogan m.

slop /slɒp/ v.t./i. (p.t. slopped) (se) répandre. ~s n. pl. eaux sales f. pl.

slop|e /sləʊp/ v.i. être en pente; (of handwriting) pencher. ~e n. pente f.; (of mountain) flanc m. ~ing a. en pente.

sloppy /'slɒpɪ/ a. (-ier, -iest) (ground) détrempé; (food) liquide; (work) négligé; (person) négligent; (fig.) sentimental.

slosh /slɒʃ/ v.t. (fam.) répandre; (hit: sl.) frapper. —v.i. patauger.

slot /slɒt/ n. fente f. —v.t./i. (p.t. slotted) (s')insérer. ~-machine n. distributeur automatique m.; (for gambling) machine à sous f.

sloth /sləʊθ/ n. paresse f.

slouch /slaʊtʃ/ v.i. avoir le dos voûté; (move) marcher le dos voûté.

sloven|ly /'slʌvnlɪ/ a. débraillé. ~iness n. débraillé m.

slow /sləʊ/ a. (-er, -est) lent.

—adv. lentement. —v.t./i. ralentir. be ~, (clock etc.) retarder. in ~ motion, au ralenti. ~ly adv. lentement. ~ness n. lenteur f.

slow|coach /'sləʊkəʊtʃ/, (Amer.) ~poke ns. lambin(e) m. (f.).

sludge /slʌdʒ/ n. gadoue f., boue f.

slug /slʌg/ n. (mollusc) limace f.; (bullet) balle f.; (blow) coup m.

sluggish /'slʌgɪʃ/ a. lent, mou.

sluice /slu:s/ n. (gate) vanne f.

slum /slʌm/ n. taudis m.

slumber /'slʌmbə(r)/ n. sommeil. m. —v.i. dormir.

slump /slʌmp/ n. effondrement m.; baisse f.; (in business) marasme m. —v.i. (collapse, fall limply) s'effondrer; (decrease) baisser.

slung /slʌŋ/ see sling.

slur /slɜ:(r)/ v.t./i. (p.t. slurred) (spoken words) mal articuler. —n. bredouillement m.; (discredit) atteinte f. (on, à).

slush /slʌʃ/ n. (snow) neige fondue f. ~ fund, fonds servant à des pots-de-vin m. ~y a. (road) couvert de neige fondue.

slut /slʌt/ n. (dirty) souillon f.; (immoral) dévergondée f.

sly /slaɪ/ a. (slyer, slyest) (crafty) rusé; (secretive) sournois. —n. on the ~, en cachette. ~ly adv. sournoisement.

smack[1] /smæk/ n. tape f.; (on face) gifle f. —v.t. donner une tape à; gifler. —adv. (fam.) tout droit.

smack[2] /smæk/ v.i. ~ of sth., (have flavour) sentir qch.

small /smɔ:l/ a. (-er, -est) petit. —n. ~ of the back, creux des reins m. —adv. (cut etc.) menu. ~ness n. petitesse f. ~ ads, petites annonces f. pl. ~ business, les petites entreprises. ~ change, petite monnaie f. ~ talk, menus propos m. pl. ~ time a. petit, peu important.

smallholding /'smɔ:lhəʊldɪŋ/ n. petite ferme f.

smallpox /'smɔːlpɒks/ n. variole f.

smarmy /'smɑːmɪ/ a. (-ier, -iest) (fam.) obséquieux, patelin.

smart /smɑːt/ a. (-er, -est) élégant; (clever) astucieux, intelligent; (brisk) rapide. —v.i. (of wound etc.) brûler. ∼ly adv. élégamment. ∼ness n. élégance f.

smarten /'smɑːtn/ v.t./i. ∼ (up), embellir. ∼ (o.s.) up, se faire beau; (tidy) s'arranger.

smash /smæʃ/ v.t./i. (se) briser, (se) fracasser; (opponent, record) pulvériser. —n. (noise) fracas m.; (blow) coup m.; (fig.) collision f.

smashing /'smæʃɪŋ/ a. (fam.) formidable, épatant.

smattering /'smætərɪŋ/ n. a ∼ of, des notions de.

smear /smɪə(r)/ v.t. (stain) tacher; (coat) enduire; (discredit: fig.) entacher. —n. tache f. ∼ test, frottis m.

smell /smel/ n. odeur f.; (sense) odorat m. —v.t./i. (p.t. smelt or smelled) sentir. ∼ of, sentir. ∼y a. malodorant, qui pue.

smelt[1] /smelt/ see smell.

smelt[2] /smelt/ v.t. (ore) fondre.

smile /smaɪl/ n. sourire m. —v.i. sourire. ∼ing a. souriant.

smirk /smɜːk/ n. sourire affecté m.

smith /smɪθ/ n. forgeron m.

smithereens /smɪðə'riːnz/ n. pl. to or in ∼, en mille morceaux.

smitten /'smɪtn/ a. (in love) épris (with, de).

smock /smɒk/ n. blouse f.

smog /smɒg/ n. brouillard mélangé de fumée m., smog m.

smoke /sməʊk/ n. fumée f. —v.t./i. fumer. **have a** ∼, fumer. ∼d a. fumé. ∼less a. (fuel) non polluant. ∼r /-ə(r)/ n. fumeu/r, -se m., f. ∼-screen n. écran de fumée m.; (fig.) manœuvre de diversion f. smoky a. (air) enfumé.

smooth /smuːð/ a. (-er, -est) lisse,

(movement) régulier; (manners, cream) onctueux; (flight) sans turbulence; (changes) sans heurt. —v.t. lisser. ∼ out, (fig.) faire disparaître. ∼ly adv. facilement, doucement.

smother /'smʌðə(r)/ v.t. (stifle) étouffer; (cover) couvrir.

smoulder /'sməʊldə(r)/ v.i. (fire, discontent, etc.) couver.

smudge /smʌdʒ/ n. tache f. —v.t./i. (se) salir, (se) tacher.

smug /smʌg/ a. (smugger, smuggest) suffisant. ∼ly adv. avec suffisance. ∼ness n. suffisance f.

smuggl|e /'smʌgl/ v.t. passer (en contrebande). ∼er n. contreband|ier, -ière m., f. ∼ing n. contrebande f.

smut /smʌt/ n. saleté f. ∼ty a. indécent.

snack /snæk/ n. casse-croûte m. invar. ∼-bar n. snack(-bar) m.

snag /snæg/ n. difficulté f., inconvénient m.; (in cloth) accroc m.

snail /sneɪl/ n. escargot m. at a ∼'s pace, à un pas de tortue.

snake /sneɪk/ n. serpent m.

snap /snæp/ v.t./i. (p.t. snapped) (whip, fingers, etc.) (faire) claquer; (break) (se) casser net; (say) dire sèchement. —n. claquement m.; (photograph) instantané m.; (press-stud: Amer.) bouton-pression m. —a. soudain. ∼ at, (bite) happer; (angrily) être cassant avec. ∼ up, (buy) sauter sur.

snappy /'snæpɪ/ a. (-ier, -iest) (brisk: fam.) prompt, rapide. **make it** ∼, (fam.) se dépêcher.

snapshot /'snæpʃɒt/ n. instantané m., photo f.

snare /sneə(r)/ n. piège m.

snarl /snɑːl/ v.i. gronder (en montrant les dents). —n. grondement m. ∼-up n. embouteillage m.

snatch /snætʃ/ v.t. (grab) saisir; (steal) voler. ∼ from s.o., arracher à qn. —*n.* (*theft*) vol *m.*; (*short part*) fragment *m.*

sneak /sniːk/ *v.i.* aller furtivement. —*n.* (*schol.*, *sl.*) rapporteu|r, -se *m.*, *f.* ~y *a.* sournois.

sneakers /ˈsniːkəz/ *n. pl.* (*shoes*) tennis *m. pl.*

sneaking /ˈsniːkɪŋ/ *a.* caché.

sneer /snɪə(r)/ *n.* ricanement *m.* —*v.i.* ricaner.

sneeze /sniːz/ *n.* éternuement *m.* —*v.i.* éternuer.

snide /snaɪd/ *a.* (*fam.*) narquois.

sniff /snɪf/ *v.t./i.* renifler. —*n.* reniflement *m.*

snigger /ˈsnɪgə(r)/ *n.* ricanement *m.* —*v.i.* ricaner.

snip /snɪp/ *v.t.* (*p.t.* **snipped**) couper. —*n.* morceau coupé *m.*; (*bargain*: *sl.*) bonne affaire *f.*

snipe /snaɪp/ *v.i.* canarder. ~r /-ə(r)/ *n.* tireur embusqué *m.*

snippet /ˈsnɪpɪt/ *n.* bribe *f.*

snivel /ˈsnɪvl/ *v.i.* (*p.t.* **snivelled**) pleurnicher.

snob /snɒb/ *n.* snob *m.*/*f.* ~bery *n.* snobisme *m.* ~bish *a.* snob *invar.*

snooker /ˈsnuːkə(r)/ *n.* (*sorte de*) jeu de billard *m.*

snoop /snuːp/ *v.i.* (*fam.*) fourrer son nez partout. ~ **on**, espionner.

snooty /ˈsnuːtɪ/ *a.* (*-ier*, *-iest*) (*fam.*) snob *invar.*, hautain.

snooze /snuːz/ *n.* petit somme *m.* —*v.i.* faire un petit somme.

snore /snɔː(r)/ *n.* ronflement *m.* —*v.i.* ronfler.

snorkel /ˈsnɔːkl/ *n.* tuba *m.*

snort /snɔːt/ *n.* grognement *m.* —*v.i.* (*person*) grogner; (*horse*) s'ébrouer.

snotty /ˈsnɒtɪ/ *a.* morveux.

snout /snaʊt/ *n.* museau *m.*

snow /snəʊ/ *n.* neige *f.* —*v.i.* neiger. **be** ~**ed under with**, être submergé de. ~**bound** *a.* bloqué par la neige. ~**drift** *n.* congère *f.* ~**plough** *n.* chasse-neige *m.*

invar. ~**shoe** *n.* raquette *f.* ~y *a.* neigeux.

snowball /ˈsnəʊbɔːl/ *n.* boule de neige *f.* —*v.i.* faire boule de neige.

snowdrop /ˈsnəʊdrɒp/ *n.* perce-neige *m./f.* *invar.*

snowfall /ˈsnəʊfɔːl/ *n.* chute de neige *f.*

snowflake /ˈsnəʊfleɪk/ *n.* flocon de neige *m.*

snowman /ˈsnəʊmæn/ *n.* (*pl.* **-men**) bonhomme de neige *m.*

snowstorm /ˈsnəʊstɔːm/ *n.* tempête de neige *f.*

snub /snʌb/ *v.t.* (*p.t.* **snubbed**) (*person*) snober; (*offer*) repousser. —*n.* rebuffade *f.*

snub-nosed /snʌbˈnəʊzd/ *a.* au nez retroussé.

snuff[1] /snʌf/ *n.* tabac à priser *m.*

snuff[2] /snʌf/ *v.t.* (*candle*) moucher.

snuffle /ˈsnʌfl/ *v.i.* renifler.

snug /snʌg/ *a.* (**snugger**, **snuggest**) (*cosy*) comfortable; (*tight*) bien ajusté; (*safe*) sûr.

snuggle /ˈsnʌgl/ *v.i.* se pelotonner.

so /səʊ/ *adv.* si, tellement; (*thus*) ainsi. —*conj.* donc, alors. **so am I**, moi aussi. **so good**/*etc.* **as**, aussi bon/*etc.* que. **so does he**, lui aussi. **that is so**, c'est ça. **I think so**, je pense que oui. **five or so**, environ cinq. **so-and-so** *n.* un(e) tel(le) *m.* (*f.*). **so as to**, de manière à. **so-called** *a.* soi-disant *invar.* **so far**, jusqu'ici. **so long!**, (*fam.*) à bientôt! **so many**, **so much**, tant (de). **so-so** *a.* & *adv.* comme ci comme ça. **so that**, pour que.

soak /səʊk/ *v.t./i.* (faire) tremper (**in**, dans). ~ **in** or **up**, absorber. ~**ing** *a.* trempé.

soap /səʊp/ *n.* savon *m.* —*v.t.* savonner. ~ **opera**, feuilleton *m.* ~ **powder**, lessive *f.* ~y *a.* savonneux.

soar /sɔː(r)/ *v.i.* monter (en flèche).

sob /sɒb/ *n.* sanglot *m.* —*v.i.* (*p.t.* **sobbed**) sangloter.

sober /'səʊbə(r)/ a. qui n'est pas ivre; (*serious*) sérieux; (*colour*) sobre. —v.t./i. ~ up, dessoûler.

soccer /'sɒkə(r)/ n. (*fam.*) football m.

sociable /'səʊʃəbl/ a. sociable.

social /'səʊʃl/ a. social; (*gathering, life*) mondain. —n. réunion (amicale) f., fête f. ~ly adv. socialement; (*meet*) en société. ~ **security**, aide sociale f.; (*for old age: Amer.*) pension (de retraite) f. ~ **worker**, assistant(e) social(e) m. (f.).

socialis|t /'səʊʃəlɪst/ n. socialiste m./f. ~m /-zəm/ n. socialisme m.

socialize /'səʊʃəlaɪz/ v.i. se mêler aux autres. ~ **with**, fréquenter.

society /sə'saɪətɪ/ n. société f.

sociolog|y /səʊsɪ'ɒlədʒɪ/ n. sociologie f. ~**ical** /-ə'lɒdʒɪkl/ a. sociologique. ~**ist** n. sociologue m./f.

sock[1] /sɒk/ n. chaussette f.

sock[2] /sɒk/ v.t. (*hit: sl.*) flanquer un coup (de poing) à.

socket /'sɒkɪt/ n. cavité f.; (*for lamp*) douille f.; (*electr.*) prise (de courant) f.; (*of tooth*) alvéole f.

soda /'səʊdə/ n. soude f. ~ **(-pop)**, (*Amer.*) soda m. ~ **(-water)**, soda m., eau de Seltz f.

sodden /'sɒdn/ a. détrempé.

sodium /'səʊdɪəm/ n. sodium m.

sofa /'səʊfə/ n. canapé m., sofa m.

soft /sɒft/ a. (-er, -est) (*gentle, lenient*) doux; (*not hard*) doux, mou; (*heart, wood*) tendre; (*silly*) ramolli; (*easy: sl.*) facile. ~ **drink**, boisson non alcoolisée f. ~**ly** adv. doucement. ~**ness** n. douceur f. ~ **spot**, faible m.

soften /'sɒfn/ v.t./i. (se) ramollir; (*tone down, lessen*) (s')adoucir.

software /'sɒftweə(r)/ n. (*for computer*) logiciel m.

softwood /'sɒftwʊd/ n. bois tendre m.

soggy /'sɒgɪ/ a. (-ier, -iest) détrempé; (*bread etc.*) ramolli.

soil[1] /sɔɪl/ n. sol m., terre f.

soil[2] /sɔɪl/ v.t./i. (se) salir.

solar /'səʊlə(r)/ a. solaire.

sold /səʊld/ see **sell**. —a. ~ **out**, épuisé.

solder /'sɒldə(r)/ Amer. 'sɒdər/ n. soudure f. —v.t. souder. ~**ing iron**, fer à souder m.

soldier /'səʊldʒə(r)/ n. soldat m. —v.i. ~ **on**, (*fam.*) persévérer.

sole[1] /səʊl/ n. (*of foot*) plante f.; (*of shoe*) semelle f.

sole[2] /səʊl/ n. (*fish*) sole f.

sole[3] /səʊl/ a. unique, seul. ~**ly** adv. uniquement.

solemn /'sɒləm/ a. (*formal*) solennel; (*not cheerful*) grave. ~**ity** /sə'lemnətɪ/ n. solennité f. ~**ly** adv. solennellement; gravement.

solicit /sə'lɪsɪt/ v.t. (*seek*) solliciter. —v.i. (*of prostitute*) racoler.

solicitor /sə'lɪsɪtə(r)/ n. avoué m.

solid /'sɒlɪd/ a. solide; (*not hollow*) plein; (*gold*) massif; (*mass*) compact; (*meal*) substantiel. —n. solide m. ~**s**, (*food*) aliments solides m. pl. ~**-state** a. à circuits intégrés. ~**ity** /sə'lɪdətɪ/ n. solidité f. ~**ly** adv. solidement.

solidarity /sɒlɪ'dærətɪ/ n. solidarité f.

solidify /sə'lɪdɪfaɪ/ v.t./i. (se) solidifier.

soliloquy /sə'lɪləkwɪ/ n. monologue m., soliloque m.

solitary /'sɒlɪtrɪ/ a. (*alone, lonely*) solitaire; (*only, single*) seul.

solitude /'sɒlɪtjuːd/ n. solitude f.

solo /'səʊləʊ/ n. (pl. **-os**) solo m. —a. (*mus.*) solo invar.; (*flight*) en solitaire. ~**ist** n. soliste m./f.

solstice /'sɒlstɪs/ n. solstice m.

soluble /'sɒljʊbl/ a. soluble.

solution /sə'luːʃn/ n. solution f.

solv|e /sɒlv/ v.t. résoudre. ~**able** a. soluble.

solvent /'sɒlvənt/ a. (*comm.*) solvable. —n. (dis)solvant *m.*

sombre /'sɒmbə(r)/ a. sombre.

some /sʌm/ a. (*quantity, number*) du, de l'*, de la, des; (*unspecified, some or other*) un(e), quelque; (*a little*) un peu de; (*a certain*) un(e) certain(e), quelque; (*contrasted with others*) quelques, certain(e)s. —pron. quelques-un(e)s; (*certain quantity of it or them*) en; (*a little*) un peu. —adv. (*approximately*) quelque. **pour ~ milk**, versez du lait. **buy ~ flowers**, achetez des fleurs. **~ people like them**, il y a des gens qui les aiment. **~ of my friends**, quelques amis à moi. **he wants ~**, il en veut. **~ book (or other)**, un livre (quelconque), quelque livre. **~ time ago**, il y a un certain temps.

somebody /'sʌmbədɪ/ pron. quelqu'un. —n. be a **~**, être quelqu'un.

somehow /'sʌmhaʊ/ adv. d'une manière ou d'une autre; (*for some reason*) je ne sais pas pourquoi.

someone /'sʌmwʌn/ pron. & n. = **somebody**.

someplace /'sʌmpleɪs/ adv. (*Amer.*) = **somewhere**.

somersault /'sʌməsɔːlt/ n. culbute *f.* —v.i. faire la culbute.

something /'sʌmθɪŋ/ pron. & n. quelque chose (*m.*). **~ good/etc.** quelque chose de bon/*etc.* **~ like**, un peu comme.

sometime /'sʌmtaɪm/ adv. un jour. —a. (*former*) ancien. **~ in June**, en juin.

sometimes /'sʌmtaɪmz/ adv. quelquefois, parfois.

somewhat /'sʌmwɒt/ adv. quelque peu, un peu.

somewhere /'sʌmweə(r)/ adv. quelque part.

son /sʌn/ n. fils *m.* **~-in-law** n. (*pl.* **~s-in-law**) beau-fils *m.*, gendre *m.*

sonar /'səʊnɑː(r)/ n. sonar *m.*

sonata /sə'nɑːtə/ n. sonate *f.*

song /sɒŋ/ n. chanson *f.* **going for a ~**, à vendre pour une bouchée de pain.

sonic /'sɒnɪk/ a. **~ boom**, bang supersonique *m.*

sonnet /'sɒnɪt/ n. sonnet *m.*

sonny /'sʌnɪ/ n. (*fam.*) fiston *m.*

soon /suːn/ adv. (-er, -est) bientôt; (*early*) tôt. **I would ~er stay**, j'aimerais mieux rester. **~ after**, peu après. **~er or later**, tôt ou tard.

soot /sʊt/ n. suie *f.* **~y** a. couvert de suie.

sooth|e /suːð/ v.t. calmer. **~ing** a. (*remedy, words, etc.*) calmant.

sophisticated /sə'fɪstɪkeɪtɪd/ a. raffiné; (*machine etc.*) sophistiqué.

sophomore /'sɒfəmɔː(r)/ n. (*Amer.*) étudiant(e) de seconde année *m.* (*f.*).

soporific /sɒpə'rɪfɪk/ a. soporifique.

sopping /'sɒpɪŋ/ a. trempé.

soppy /'sɒpɪ/ a. (-ier, -iest) (*fam.*) sentimental; (*silly: fam.*) bête.

soprano /sə'prɑːnəʊ/ n. (*pl.* -os) (*voice*) soprano *m.*; (*singer*) soprano *m./f.*

sorcerer /'sɔːsərə(r)/ n. sorcier *m.*

sordid /'sɔːdɪd/ a. sordide.

sore /sɔː(r)/ a. (-er, -est) douloureux; (*vexed*) en rogne (at, with, contre). —n. plaie *f.*

sorely /'sɔːlɪ/ adv. fortement.

sorrow /'sɒrəʊ/ n. chagrin *m.* **~ful** a. triste.

sorry /'sɒrɪ/ a. (-ier, -iest) (*regretful*) désolé (to, de; that, que); (*wretched*) triste. **feel ~ for**, plaindre. **~!**, pardon!

sort /sɔːt/ n. genre *m.*, sorte *f.*, espèce *f.*; (*person: fam.*) type *m.* —v.t. **~ (out)**, (*classify*) trier. **what ~ of?**, quel genre de? **be out of ~s**, ne pas être dans son assiette. **~ out**, (tidy) ranger; (arrange) arranger; (problem) régler.

SOS /esəʊ'es/ n. SOS m.

soufflé /'suːfleɪ/ n. soufflé m.

sought /sɔːt/ see **seek**.

soul /səʊl/ n. âme f. **~-destroying** a. démoralisant.

soulful /'səʊlfl/ a. plein de sentiment, très expressif.

sound¹ /saʊnd/ n. son m., bruit m. —v.t./i. sonner; (seem) sembler (as if, que). **~ a horn**, klaxonner. **~ barrier**, mur du son m. **~like**, sembler être. **~-proof** a. insonorisé; v.t. insonoriser. **~-track** n. bande sonore f.

sound² /saʊnd/ a. (-er, -est) solide; (healthy) sain; (sensible) sensé. **~ asleep**, profondément endormi. **~ly** adv. solidement; (sleep) profondément.

sound³ /saʊnd/ v.t. (test) sonder. **~ out**, sonder.

soup /suːp/ n. soupe f., potage m. **in the ~**, (sl.) dans le pétrin.

sour /'saʊə(r)/ a. (-er, -est) aigre. —v.t./i. (s')aigrir.

source /sɔːs/ n. source f.

south /saʊθ/ n. sud m. —a. sud invar., du sud. —adv. vers le sud. **S~ Africa/America**, Afrique/Amérique du Sud f. **S~ African** a. & n. sud-africain(e) (m. (f.)). **S~ American** a. & n. sud-américain(e) (m. (f.)). **~-east** n. sud-est m. **~erly** /'sʌðəlɪ/ a. du sud. **~ward** a. au sud. **~wards** adv. vers le sud. **~-west** n. sud-ouest m.

southern /'sʌðən/ a. du sud. **~er** n. habitant(e) du sud m. (f.).

souvenir /suːvə'nɪə(r)/ n. (thing) souvenir m.

sovereign /'sɒvrɪn/ n. & a. souverain(e) (m. (f.)). **~ty** n. souveraineté f.

Soviet /'səʊvɪət/ a. soviétique. **the ~ Union**, l'Union soviétique f.

sow¹ /səʊ/ v.t. (p.t. sowed, p.p. sowed or sown) (seed etc.) semer; (land) ensemencer.

sow² /saʊ/ n. (pig) truie f.

soya, soy /'sɔɪə, sɔɪ/ n. **~ bean**, graine de soja f. **~ sauce**, sauce soja f.

spa /spaː/ n. station thermale f.

space /speɪs/ n. espace m.; (room) place f.; (period) période f. —a. (research etc.) spatial. —v.t. (out), espacer.

space|craft /'speɪskrɑːft/ n. invar., **~ship** n. engin spatial m.

spacesuit /'speɪssuːt/ n. scaphandre m.

spacious /'speɪʃəs/ a. spacieux.

spade¹ /speɪd/ n. (large, for garden) bêche f.; (child's) pelle f.

spade² /speɪd/ n. (cards) pique m.

spadework /'speɪdwɜːk/ n. (fig.) travail préparatoire m.

spaghetti /spə'getɪ/ n. spaghetti m. pl.

Spa|in /speɪn/ n. Espagne f. **~niard** /'spænɪəd/ n. Espagnol(e) m. (f.). **~nish** /'spænɪʃ/ a. espagnol; n. (lang.) espagnol m.

span¹ /spæn/ n. (of arch) portée f.; (of wings) envergure f.; (of time) durée f. —v.t. (p.t. spanned) enjamber; (in time) embrasser.

span² /spæn/ see **spick**.

spaniel /'spænɪəl/ n. épagneul m.

spank /spæŋk/ v.t. donner une fessée à. **~ing** n. fessée f.

spanner /'spænə(r)/ n. (tool) clé (plate) f.; (adjustable) clé à molette f.

spar /spaː(r)/ v.i. (p.t. sparred) s'entraîner (à la boxe).

spare /speə(r)/ v.t. épargner; (do without) se passer de; (afford to give) donner, accorder; (use with restraint) ménager. —a. en réserve; (surplus) de trop; (tyre, shoes, etc.) de rechange; (room, bed) d'ami. —n. **~ (part)**, pièce de rechange *f.* ∼ **time**, loisirs *m. pl.* **are there any** ∼ **tickets?** y a-t-il encore des places?

sparing /'speəriŋ/ *a.* frugal. ∼ **of**, avare de. ∼**ly** *adv.* en petite quantité.

spark /spɑːk/ *n.* étincelle *f.* —*v.t.* ∼ **off**, (*initiate*) provoquer. ∼**(ing)-plug** *n.* bougie *f.*

sparkle /'spɑːkl/ *v.i.* étinceler. —*n.* étincellement *m.*

sparkling /'spɑːklɪŋ/ *a.* (*wine*) mousseux, pétillant; (*eyes*) pétillant.

sparrow /'spærəʊ/ *n.* moineau *m.*

sparse /spɑːs/ *a.* clairsemé. ∼**ly** *adv.* (*furnished* etc.) peu.

spartan /'spɑːtn/ *a.* spartiate.

spasm /'spæzəm/ *n.* (*of muscle*) spasme *m.*; (*of coughing, anger, etc.*) accès *m.*

spasmodic /spæz'mɒdɪk/ *a.* intermittent.

spastic /'spæstɪk/ *n.* handicapé(e) moteur *m.* (*f.*).

spat /spæt/ *see* spit¹.

spate /speɪt/ *n.* **a** ∼ **of**, (*letters* etc.) une avalanche de.

spatter /'spætə(r)/ *v.t.* éclabousser (**with**, de).

spatula /'spætjʊlə/ *n.* spatule *f.*

spawn /spɔːn/ *n.* frai *m.*, œufs *m. pl.* —*v.t.* pondre. —*v.i.* frayer.

speak /spiːk/ *v.i.* (*p.t.* **spoke**, *p.p.* **spoken**) parler. —*v.t.* (*say*) dire; (*language*) parler. ∼ **up**, parler plus fort.

speaker /'spiːkə(r)/ *n.* (*in public*) orateur *m.*; (*pol.*) président; (*loudspeaker*) baffle *m.* **be a French/a good/**etc. ∼, parler français/bien/ etc.

spear /spɪə(r)/ *n.* lance *f.*

spearhead /'spɪəhed/ *n.* fer de lance *m.* —*v.t.* (*lead*) mener.

spearmint /'spɪəmɪnt/ *n.* menthe verte *f.*—*a.* à la menthe.

spec /spek/ *n.* **on** ∼, (*as speculation: fam.*) à tout hasard.

special /'speʃl/ *a.* spécial; (*exceptional*) exceptionnel. ∼**ity** /-'ælətɪ/, (*Amer.*) ∼**ty** *n.* spécialité *f.* ∼**ly** *adv.* spécialement.

specialist /'speʃəlɪst/ *n.* spécialiste *m./f.*

specialize /'speʃəlaɪz/ *v.i.* se spécialiser (**in**, en). ∼**d** *a.* spécialisé.

species /'spiːʃiːz/ *n. invar.* espèce *f.*

specific /spə'sɪfɪk/ *a.* précis, explicite. ∼**ally** *adv.* explicitement; (*exactly*) précisément.

specify /'spesɪfaɪ/ *v.t.* spécifier. ∼**ication** /-ɪ'keɪʃn/ *n.* spécification *f.*; (*details*) prescriptions *f. pl.*

specimen /'spesɪmɪn/ *n.* spécimen *m.*, échantillon *m.*

speck /spek/ *n.* (*stain*) (petite) tache *f.*; (*particle*) grain *m.*

speckled /'spekld/ *a.* tacheté.

specs /speks/ *n. pl.* (*fam.*) lunettes *f. pl.*

spectacle /'spektəkl/ *n.* spectacle *m.* ∼**s**, lunettes *f. pl.*

spectacular /spek'tækjʊlə(r)/ *a.* spectaculaire.

spectator /spek'teɪtə(r)/ *n.* spectateur, -trice *m., f.*

spectre /'spektə(r)/ *n.* spectre *m.*

spectrum /'spektrəm/ *n.* (*pl.* **-tra**) spectre *m.*; (*of ideas* etc.) gamme *f.*

speculat|e /'spekjʊleɪt/ *v.i.* s'interroger (**about**, sur); (*comm.*) spéculer. ∼**ion** /-'leɪʃn/ *n.* conjectures *f. pl.*; (*comm.*) spéculation *f.* ∼**or** *n.* spéculateur, -trice *m., f.*

speech /spiːtʃ/ *n.* (*faculty*) parole *f.*; (*diction*) élocution *f.*; (*dialect*) langage *m.*; (*address*) discours *m.* ∼**less** *a.* muet (**with**, de).

speed /spiːd/ *n.* (*of movement*) vitesse *f.*; (*swiftness*) rapidité *f.* —*v.i.* (*p.t.* **sped** /sped/) aller vite; (*p.t.* **speeded**) (*drive too fast*) aller trop vite. ∼ **limit**, limitation de vitesse *f.* ∼ **up**, accélérer; (*of pace*) s'accélérer. ∼**ing** *n.* excès de vitesse *m.*

speedboat /'spi:dbəut/ n. vedette f.

speedometer /spi'dɒmɪtə(r)/ n. compteur (de vitesse) m.

speedway /'spi:dweɪ/ n. piste pour motos f.; (Amer.) autodrome m.

speed|y /'spi:dɪ/ a. (-ier, -iest) rapide. **~ily** adv. rapidement.

spell[1] /spel/ n. (magic) charme m., sortilège m.; (curse) sort m.

spell[2] /spel/ v.t./i. (p.t. spelled or spelt) (mean) signifier. **~ out**, épeler; (explain) expliquer. **~ing** n. orthographe f. **~ing mistake,** faute d'orthographe f.

spell[3] /spel/ n. (courte) période f.

spend /spend/ v.t. (p.t. spent) (money) dépenser (on, pour); (time, holiday) passer; (energy) consacrer (on, à). —v.i. dépenser.

spendthrift /'spendθrɪft/ n. dépens|ier, -ière m., f.

spent /spent/ see spend. —a. (used) utilisé; (person) épuisé.

sperm /spɜ:m/ n. (pl. sperms or sperm) (semen) sperme m.; (cell) spermatozoïde m. **~icide** n. spermicide m.

spew /spju:/ v.t./i. vomir.

sphere /sfɪə(r)/ n. sphère f.

spherical /'sferɪkl/ a. sphérique.

spic|e /spaɪs/ n. épice f.; (fig.) piquant m. **~y** a. épicé; piquant.

spick /spɪk/ a. **~ and span,** impeccable, d'une propreté parfaite.

spider /'spaɪdə(r)/ n. araignée f.

spiel /ʃpi:l/ (Amer.) spi:l/ n. baratin m.

spik|e /spaɪk/ n. (of metal etc.) pointe f. **~y** a. garni de pointes.

spill /spɪl/ v.t. (p.t. spilled or spilt) renverser, répandre. —v.i. se répandre. **~ over,** déborder.

spin /spɪn/ v.t./i. (p.t. spun, pres. p. spinning) (wool, web, of spinner) filer; (turn) (faire) tourner; (story) débiter. —n. (movement, excursion) tour m. **~ out,** faire durer.

~drier n. essoreuse f. **~ning-wheel** n. rouet m. **~off** n. avantage accessoire m.; (by-product) dérivé m.

spinach /'spɪnɪdʒ/ n. (plant) épinard m.; (as food) épinards m. pl.

spinal /'spaɪnl/ a. vertébral. **~ cord,** moelle épinière f.

spindl|e /'spɪndl/ n. fuseau m. **~y** a. filiforme, grêle.

spine /spaɪn/ n. colonne vertébrale f.; (prickle) piquant m.

spineless /'spaɪnlɪs/ a. (fig.) sans caractère, mou, lâche.

spinster /'spɪnstə(r)/ n. célibataire f.; (pej.) vieille fille f.

spiral /'spaɪərəl/ a. en spirale; (staircase) en colimaçon. —n. spirale f. —v.i. (p.t. spiralled) (prices) monter en flèche.

spire /'spaɪə(r)/ n. flèche f.

spirit /'spɪrɪt/ n. esprit m.; (boldness) courage m. **~s,** (morale) moral m.; (drink) spiritueux m. pl. —v.t. **~ away,** faire disparaître. **~-level** n. niveau à bulle m.

spirited /'spɪrɪtɪd/ a. fougueux.

spiritual /'spɪrɪtʃʊəl/ a. spirituel. —n. (song) (negro-)spiritual m.

spit[1] /spɪt/ v.t./i. (p.t. spat or spit, pres. p. spitting) cracher; (of rain) crachiner. —n. crachat(s) m. (pl.) **~ out,** cracher. **the ~ting image of,** le portrait craché or vivant de.

spit[2] /spɪt/ n. (for meat) broche f.

spite /spaɪt/ n. rancune f. —v.t. contrarier. **in ~ of,** malgré. **~ful** a. méchant, rancunier. **~fully** adv. méchamment.

spittle /'spɪtl/ n. crachat(s) m. (pl.).

splash /splæʃ/ v.t. éclabousser. —v.i. faire des éclaboussures. **~ (about),** patauger. —n. (act, mark) éclaboussure f.; (sound) plouf m.; (of colour) tache f.

spleen /spli:n/ n. (anat.) rate f.

splendid /'splendɪd/ a. magnifique, splendide.

splendour /'splendə(r)/ n. splendeur f., éclat m.

splint /splɪnt/ n. (med.) attelle f.

splinter /'splɪntə(r)/ n. éclat m.; (in finger) écharde f. ~ **group**, groupe dissident m.

split /splɪt/ v.t./i. (p.t. **split**, pres.p. **splitting**) (se) fendre; (tear) (se) déchirer; (divide) (se) diviser; (share) partager. —n. fente f.; déchirure f.; (share: fam.) part f., partage m.; (quarrel) rupture f.; (pol.) scission f. ~ **up**, (couple) rompre. **a** ~ **second**, un rien de temps. ~ **one's sides**, se tordre (de rire).

splurge /splɜːdʒ/ v.i. (fam.) faire de folles dépenses.

splutter /'splʌtə(r)/ v.i. crachoter; (stammer) bafouiller; (engine) tousser; (fat) crépiter.

spoil /spɔɪl/ v.t. (p.t. **spoilt** or **spoiled**) (pamper) gâter; (ruin) abîmer; (mar) gâcher, gâter. —n. ~**(s)**, (plunder) butin m. ~**sport** n. trouble-fête m./f. invar.

spoke[1] /spəʊk/ n. rayon m.

spoke[2], **spoken** /spəʊk, 'spəʊkən/ see **speak**.

spokesman /'spəʊksmən/ n. (pl. -men) porte-parole m.

sponge /spʌndʒ/ n. éponge f. —v.t. éponger. —v.i. ~ **on**, vivre aux crochets de. ~**bag** n. trousse de toilette f. ~**cake** n. génoise f. ~**r** /-ə(r)/ n. parasite m. **spongy** a. spongieux.

sponsor /'spɒnsə(r)/ n. (of concert) parrain m., sponsor m.; (surety) garant m.; (for membership) parrain m., marraine f. —v.t. parrainer, sponsoriser; (member) parrainer. ~**ship** n. patronage m.; parrainage m.

spontane|ous /spɒn'teɪnɪəs/ a. spontané. ~**ity** /-tə'niːətɪ/ n.

spontanéité f. ~**ously** adv. spontanément.

spoof /spuːf/ n. (fam.) parodie f.

spool /spuːl/ n. bobine f.

spoon /spuːn/ n. cuiller f. ~**feed** v.t. (p.t. -fed) nourrir à la cuiller; (help: fig.) mâcher la besogne à. ~**ful** n. (pl. -fuls) cuillerée f.

sporadic /spə'rædɪk/ a. sporadique.

sport /spɔːt/ n. sport m. **(good)** ~, (person: sl.) chic type m. —v.t. (display) exhiber, arborer. ~**s car/coat**, voiture/veste de sport f. ~**y** a. (fam.) sportif.

sporting /'spɔːtɪŋ/ a. sportif. **a** ~ **chance**, une assez bonne chance.

sports|man /'spɔːtsmən/ n. (pl. -men) sportif m. ~**manship** n. sportivité f. ~**woman** n. (pl. -women) sportive f.

spot /spɒt/ n. (mark, stain) tache f.; (dot) point m.; (in pattern) pois m.; (drop) goutte f.; (place) endroit m.; (pimple) bouton m. —v.t. (p.t. **spotted**) (fam.) apercevoir. **a** ~ **of**, (fam.) un peu de. **be in a** ~, (fam.) avoir un problème. **on the** ~, sur place; (without delay) sur le coup. ~ **check**, contrôle à l'improviste m. ~**ted** a. tacheté; (fabric) à pois. ~**ty** a. (skin) boutonneux.

spotless /'spɒtlɪs/ a. impeccable.

spotlight /'spɒtlaɪt/ n. (lamp) projecteur m., spot m.

spouse /spaʊs/ n. époux m., épouse f.

spout /spaʊt/ n. (of vessel) bec m.; (of liquid) jet m. —v.i. jaillir. **up the** ~, (ruined: sl.) fichu.

sprain /spreɪn/ n. entorse f., foulure f. —v.t. ~ **one's wrist/ etc.**, se fouler le poignet/etc.

sprang /spræŋ/ see **spring**.

sprawl /sprɔːl/ v.i. (town, person, etc.) s'étaler. —n. étalement m.

spray[1] /spreɪ/ n. (of flowers) gerbe f.

spray[2] /spreɪ/ n. (water) gerbe d'eau f.; (from sea) embruns m.

pl.; (*device*) bombe *f.*, atomiseur *m.* —v.t. (*surface, insecticide*) vaporiser; (*plant etc.*) arroser; (*crops*) traiter.

spread /spred/ v.t./i. (p.t. **spread**) (*stretch, extend*) (s')étendre; (*news, fear, etc.*) (se) répandre; (*illness*) se propager; (*butter etc.*) (s')étaler. —n. propagation *f.*; (*of population*) distribution *f.*; (*paste*) pâte à tartiner *f.*; (*food*) belle table *f.* **~-eagled** a. bras et jambes écartés.

spreadsheet /'spredʃiːt/ n. tableur *m.*

spree /spriː/ n. go on a **~**, (*have fun: fam.*) faire la noce.

sprig /sprɪg/ n. (*shoot*) brin *m.*; (*twig*) brindille *f.*

sprightly /'spraɪtlɪ/ a. (**-ier, -iest**) alerte, vif.

spring /sprɪŋ/ v.i. (p.t. **sprang**, p.p. **sprung**) bondir. —v.t. faire, annoncer, *etc.* à l'improviste (**on**, à). —n. bond *m.*; (*device*) ressort *m.*; (*season*) printemps *m.*; (*of water*) source *f.* **~-clean** v.t. nettoyer de fond en comble. **~ from**, provenir de. **~ onion**, oignon blanc *m.* **~ up**, surgir.

springboard /'sprɪŋbɔːd/ n. tremplin *m.*

springtime /'sprɪŋtaɪm/ n. printemps *m.*

springy /'sprɪŋɪ/ a. (**-ier, -iest**) élastique.

sprinkle /'sprɪŋkl/ v.t. (*with liquid*) arroser (**with**, de); (*with salt, flour*) saupoudrer (**with**, de). **~ sand/etc.**, répandre du sable/*etc.* **~r** /-ər/ n. (*in garden*) arroseur *m.*; (*for fires*) extincteur (à déclenchement) automatique *m.*

sprinkling /'sprɪŋklɪŋ/ n. (*amount*) petite quantité *f.*

sprint /sprɪnt/ v.i. (*sport*) sprinter. —n. sprint *m.* **~er** n. sprinteur|r, -se *m.*, *f.*

sprout /spraʊt/ v.t./i. pousser.

—n. (*on plant etc.*) pousse *f.* (**Brussels**) **~s**, choux de Bruxelles *m. pl.*

spruce[1] /spruːs/ a. pimpant. —v.t. **~ o.s. up**, se faire beau.

spruce[2] /spruːs/ n. (*tree*) épicéa *m.*

sprung /sprʌŋ/ see **spring**. —a. (*mattress etc.*) à ressorts.

spry /spraɪ/ a. (**spryer, spryest**) alerte, vif.

spud /spʌd/ n. (*sl.*) patate *f.*

spun /spʌn/ see **spin**.

spur /spɜː(r)/ n. (*of rider, cock, etc.*) éperon *m.*; (*stimulus*) aiguillon *m.* —v.t. (p.t. **spurred**) éperonner. **on the ~ of the moment**, sous l'impulsion du moment.

spurious /'spjʊərɪəs/ a. faux.

spurn /spɜːn/ v.t. repousser.

spurt /spɜːt/ v.i. jaillir; (*fig.*) accélérer. —n. jet *m.*; (*at work*) coup de collier *m.*

spy /spaɪ/ n. espion(ne) *m.* (*f.*). —v.i. espionner. —v.t. apercevoir. **~ on**, espionner. **~ out**, reconnaître.

squabble /'skwɒbl/ v.i. se chamailler. —n. chamaillerie *f.*

squad /skwɒd/ n. (*of soldiers etc.*) escouade *f.*; (*sport*) équipe *f.*

squadron /'skwɒdrən/ n. (*mil.*) escadron *m.*; (*aviat.*) escadrille *f.*; (*naut.*) escadre *f.*

squal|id /'skwɒlɪd/ a. sordide. **~or** n. conditions sordides *f. pl.*

squall /skwɔːl/ n. rafale *f.*

squander /'skwɒndə(r)/ v.t. (*money, time, etc.*) gaspiller.

square /skweə(r)/ n. carré *m.*; (*open space in town*) place *f.*; (*instrument*) équerre *f.* —a. carré; (*honest*) honnête; (*meal*) solide; (*fam.*) ringard. (**all**) **~**, (*quits*) quitte. —v.t. (*settle*) régler. —v.i. (*agree*) cadrer (**with**, avec). **~ up to**, faire face à. **~ metre**, mètre carré *m.* **~ly** adv. carrément.

squash /skwɒʃ/ v.t. écraser; (*crowd*) serrer. —n. (*game*)

squash *m.*; (*marrow: Amer.*) courge *f.* lemon ~, citronnade *f.* orange ~, orangeade *f.* ~y a. mou.

squat /skwɒt/ *v.i.* (*p.t.* squatted) s'accroupir. —*a.* (*dumpy*) trapu. ~ **in a house**, squatteriser une maison. ~**ter** *n.* squatter *m.*

squawk /skwɔːk/ *n.* cri rauque *m.* —*v.i.* pousser un cri rauque.

squeak /skwiːk/ *n.* petit cri *m.*; (*of door etc.*) grincement *m.* —*v.i.* crier; grincer. ~**y** *a.* grinçant.

squeal /skwiːl/ *n.* cri aigu *m.* —*v.i.* pousser un cri aigu. ~ **on**, (*inform on: sl.*) dénoncer.

squeamish /ˈskwiːmɪʃ/ *a.* (*too*) délicat, facilement dégoûté.

squeeze /skwiːz/ *v.t.* presser; (*hand, arm*) serrer; (*extract*) exprimer (from, de); (*extort*) soutirer (from, à). —*v.i.* (*force one's way*) se glisser. —*n.* pression *f.*; (*comm.*) restrictions de crédit *f. pl.*

squelch /skweltʃ/ *v.i.* faire flic flac. —*v.t.* (*suppress*) supprimer.

squid /skwɪd/ *n.* calmar *m.*

squiggle /ˈskwɪgl/ *n.* ligne onduleuse *f.*

squint /skwɪnt/ *v.i.* loucher; (*with half-shut eyes*) plisser les yeux. —*n.* (*med.*) strabisme *m.*

squire /ˈskwaɪə(r)/ *n.* propriétaire terrien *m.*

squirm /skwɜːm/ *v.i.* se tortiller.

squirrel /ˈskwɪrəl, *Amer.* ˈskwɜːrəl/ *n.* écureuil *m.*

squirt /skwɜːt/ *v.t./i.* (faire) jaillir. —*n.* jet *m.*

stab /stæb/ *v.t.* (*p.t.* stabbed) (*with knife etc.*) poignarder. —*n.* coup (de couteau) *m.* **have a ~ at sth.**, essayer de faire qch.

stabilize /ˈsteɪbəlaɪz/ *v.t.* stabiliser.

stab|le[1] /ˈsteɪbl/ *a.* (-er, -est) stable. ~**ility** /stəˈbɪlətɪ/ *n.* stabilité *f.*

stable[2] /ˈsteɪbl/ *n.* écurie *f.* ~**-boy** *n.* lad *m.*

stack /stæk/ *n.* tas *m.* —*v.t.* (up), entasser, empiler.

stadium /ˈsteɪdɪəm/ *n.* stade *m.*

staff /stɑːf/ *n.* personnel *m.*; (*in school*) professeurs *m. pl.*; (*mil.*) état-major *m.*; (*stick*) bâton *m.* —*v.t.* pourvoir en personnel.

stag /stæg/ *n.* cerf *m.* **have a ~ party**, enterrer sa vie de garçon.

stage /steɪdʒ/ *n.* (*theatre*) scène *f.*; (*phase*) stade *m.*, étape *f.*; (*platform in hall*) estrade *f.* —*v.t.* mettre en scène; (*fig.*) organiser. **go on the ~**, faire du théâtre. ~**-coach** *n.* (*old use*) diligence *f.* ~**door**, entrée des artistes *f.* ~**fright**, trac *m.* ~**-manage** *v.t.* monter, organiser. ~**-manager** *n.* régisseur *m.*

stagger /ˈstægə(r)/ *v.i.* chanceler. —*v.t.* (*shock*) stupéfier; (*holidays etc.*) étaler. ~**ing** *a.* stupéfiant.

stagnant /ˈstægnənt/ *a.* stagnant.

stagna|te /stægˈneɪt/ *v.i.* stagner. ~**tion** /-ʃn/ *n.* stagnation *f.*

staid /steɪd/ *a.* sérieux.

stain /steɪn/ *v.t.* tacher; (*wood etc.*) colorer. —*n.* tache *f.*; (*colouring*) colorant *m.* ~**ed glass window**, vitrail *m.* ~**less steel**, acier inoxydable *m.* ~ **remover**, détachant *m.*

stair /steə(r)/ *n.* marche *f.* **the ~s**, l'escalier *m.*

stair|case /ˈsteəkeɪs/, ~**way** *ns.* escalier *m.*

stake /steɪk/ *n.* (*post*) pieu *m.*; (*wager*) enjeu *m.* —*v.t.* (*area*) jalonner; (*wager*) jouer. **at ~**, en jeu. ~ **a claim to**, revendiquer.

stale /steɪl/ *a.* (-er, -est) pas frais; (*bread*) rassis; (*smell*) de renfermé; (*news*) vieux. ~**ness** *n.* manque de fraîcheur *m.*

stalemate /ˈsteɪlmeɪt/ *n.* (*chess*) pat *m.*; (*fig.*) impasse *f.*

stalk¹ /stɔːk/ n. (of plant) tige f.

stalk² /stɔːk/ v.i. marcher de façon guindée. —v.t. (prey) traquer.

stall /stɔːl/ n. (in stable) stalle f.; (in market) éventaire m. ~s, (theatre) orchestre m. —v.t./i. (auto.) caler. ~ (for time), temporiser.

stallion /'stæljən/ n. étalon m.

stalwart /'stɔːlwət/ n. (supporter) partisan(e) fidèle m. (f.).

stamina /'stæminə/ n. résistance f.

stammer /'stæmə(r)/ v.t./i. bégayer. —n. bégaiement m.

stamp /stæmp/ v.t./i. ~ (one's foot), taper du pied. —v.t. (letter etc.) timbrer. n. (for postage, marking) timbre m.; (mark: fig.) sceau m. ~-collecting n. philatélie f. ~ out, supprimer.

stampede /stæm'piːd/ n. fuite désordonnée f.; (rush: fig.) ruée f. —v.i. s'enfuir en désordre; se ruer.

stance /stæns/ n. position f.

stand /stænd/ v.i. (p.t. stood) être or se tenir (debout); (rise) se lever; (be situated) se trouver; (rest) reposer; (pol.) être candidat (for, à). —v.t. mettre (debout); (tolerate) supporter. —n. position f.; (mil.) résistance f.; (for lamp etc.) support m.; (at fair) stand m.; (in street) kiosque m.; (for spectators) tribune f.; (jurid., Amer.) barre f. **make a ~**, prendre position. **~ a chance**, avoir une chance. **~ back**, reculer. **~ by or around**, ne rien faire. **~ by**, (be ready) se tenir prêt; (promise, person) rester fidèle à. **~-by** a. de réserve; n. **be a ~-by**, être de réserve. **~ down**, se désister. **for**, représenter; (fam.) supporter. **~ in for**, remplacer. **~ in** n. remplaçant(e) m. (f.). **~ in line**, (Amer.) faire la queue. **~ offish** a. (fam.) distant. **~ out**,

(be conspicuous) ressortir. **~ to reason**, être logique. **~ up**, se lever. **~ up for**, défendre. **~ up to**, résister à.

standard /'stændəd/ n. norme f.; (level) niveau (voulu) m.; (flag) étendard m. ~s, (morals) principes m. pl. —a. ordinaire. **~ lamp**, lampadaire m. **~ of living**, niveau de vie m.

standardize /'stændədaɪz/ v.t. standardiser.

standing /'stændɪŋ/ a. debout invar.; (army, offer) permanent. —n. position f., réputation f.; (duration) durée f. **~ order**, prélèvement bancaire m. **~ room**, places debout f. pl.

standpoint /'stændpɔɪnt/ n. point de vue m.

standstill /'stændstɪl/ n. **at a ~**, immobile. **bring/come to a ~**, (s')immobiliser.

stank /stæŋk/ see stink.

stanza /'stænzə/ n. strophe f.

staple¹ /'steɪpl/ n. agrafe f. —v.t. agrafer. **~r** /-ə(r)/ n. agrafeuse f.

staple² /'steɪpl/ a. principal, de base.

star /stɑː(r)/ n. étoile f.; (famous person) vedette f. —v.t. (p.t. **starred**) (of film) avoir pour vedette. —v.i. **~ in**, être la vedette de. **~dom** n. célébrité f.

starboard /'stɑːbəd/ n. tribord m.

starch /stɑːtʃ/ n. amidon m.; (in food) fécule f. —v.t. amidonner. **~y** a. féculent; (stiff) guindé.

stare /steə(r)/ v.i. **~ at**, regarder fixement. —n. regard fixe m.

starfish /'stɑːfɪʃ/ n. étoile de mer f.

stark /stɑːk/ a. (-er, -est) (desolate) désolé; (severe) austère; (utter) complet; (fact etc.) brutal. —adv. complètement.

starling /'stɑːlɪŋ/ n. étourneau m.

starlit /'stɑːlɪt/ a. étoilé.

starry /'stɑːrɪ/ a. étoilé. **~-eyed** a. naïf, (trop) optimiste.

start /stɑːt/ v.t./i. commencer; (machine) (se) mettre en marche; (fashion etc.) lancer; (cause) provoquer; (jump) sursauter; (of vehicle) démarrer. —n. commencement m., début m.; (of race) départ m.; (lead) avance f.; (jump) sursaut m. ~ **to do,** commencer or se mettre à faire. ~ **off doing,** commencer par faire. ~ **out,** partir. ~ **up a business,** lancer une affaire. ~**er** n. (auto.) démarreur m.; (runner) partant m.; (culin.) entrée f. ~**ing point,** point de départ m. ~**ing tomorrow,** à partir de demain.

startle /'stɑːtl/ v.t. (make jump) faire tressaillir; (shock) alarmer.

starv|**e** /stɑːv/ v.t./i. mourir de faim. —v.t. affamer; (deprive) priver. ~**ation** /-'veɪʃn/ n. faim f.

stash /stæʃ/ v.t. (hide: sl.) cacher.

state /steɪt/ n. état m.; (pomp) apparat m. **S**~, (pol.) État m. —a. d'État, de l'État; (school) public. —v.t. affirmer (that, que); (views) exprimer; (fix) fixer. **the S**~**s,** les États-Unis. **get into a** ~, s'affoler.

stateless /'steɪtlɪs/ a. apatride.

stately /'steɪtlɪ/ a. (-ier, -iest) majestueux. ~ **home,** château m.

statement /'steɪtmənt/ n. déclaration f.; (of account) relevé m.

statesman /'steɪtsmən/ n. (pl. -men) homme d'État m.

static /'stætɪk/ a. statique. —n. (radio, TV) parasites m. pl.

station /'steɪʃn/ n. station f.; (rail.) gare f.; (mil.) poste m.; (rank) condition f. —v.t. poster, placer. ~**ed at** or **in,** (mil.) en garnison à. ~ **wagon,** (Amer.) break m.

stationary /'steɪʃənrɪ/ a. immobile, stationnaire; (vehicle) à l'arrêt.

stationer /'steɪʃənə(r)/ n. papet|ier, -ière m., f. ~**'s shop,** papeterie f. ~**y** n. papeterie f.

statistic /stə'tɪstɪk/ n. statistique f. ~**s,** (science) statistique f. ~**al** a. statistique.

statue /'stætʃuː/ n. statue f.

stature /'stætʃə(r)/ n. stature f.

status /'steɪtəs/ n. (pl. -uses) situation f., statut m.; (prestige) standing m. ~ **quo,** statu quo m.

statut|**e** /'stætʃuːt/ n. loi f. ~**es,** (rules) statuts m. pl. ~**ory** /-ʊtrɪ/ a. statutaire; (holiday) légal.

staunch /stɔːntʃ/ a. (-er, -est) (friend etc.) loyal, fidèle.

stave /steɪv/ n. (mus.) portée f. —v.t. ~ **off,** éviter, conjurer.

stay /steɪ/ v.i. rester; (spend time) séjourner; (reside) loger. —v.t. (hunger) tromper. —n. séjour m. ~ **away from,** (school etc.) ne pas aller à. ~ **behind/on/late/etc.,** rester. ~ **in/out,** rester à la maison/dehors. ~ **up (late),** veiller, se coucher tard.

stead /sted/ n. **stand s.o. in good** ~, être bien utile à qn.

steadfast /'stedfɑːst/ a. ferme.

stead|**y** /'stedɪ/ a. (-ier, -iest) stable; (hand, voice) ferme; (regular) régulier; (staid) sérieux. —v.t. maintenir, assurer; (calm) calmer. ~**ily** adv. fermement; régulièrement.

steak /steɪk/ n. steak m., bifteck m.; (of fish) darne f.

steal /stiːl/ v.t./i. (p.t. **stole,** p.p. **stolen**) voler (**from s.o.,** à qn.).

stealth /stelθ/ n. **by** ~, furtivement. ~**y** a. furtif.

steam /stiːm/ n. vapeur f.; (on glass) buée f. —v.t. (cook) cuire à la vapeur; (window) embuer. —v.i. fumer. ~**-engine** n. machine à vapeur f. ~ **iron,** fer à vapeur m. ~**y** a. humide.

steamer /'stiːmə(r)/ n. (culin.) cuit-vapeur m.; (also ~**ship**) (bateau à) vapeur m.

steamroller /'stiːmrəʊlə(r)/ n. rouleau compresseur m.

steel /stiːl/ n. acier m. —v. pr. ~ o.s., s'endurcir, se cuirasser. ~ **industry,** sidérurgie f.

steep[1] /stiːp/ v.t. (soak) tremper. ~**ed in,** (fig.) imprégné de.

steep[2] /stiːp/ a. (-er, -est) raide, rapide; (price: fam.) excessif. ~**ly** adv. **rise** ~**ly,** (slope, price) monter rapidement.

steeple /ˈstiːpl/ n. clocher m.

steeplechase /ˈstiːpltʃeɪs/ n. (race) steeple(-chase) m.

steer[1] /stɪə(r)/ n. (ox) bouvillon m.

steer[2] /stɪə(r)/ v.t. diriger; (ship) gouverner; (fig.) guider. —v.i. (in ship) gouverner. ~ **clear of,** éviter. ~**ing** n. (auto.) direction f. ~**ing-wheel** n. volant m.

stem[1] /stem/ n. tige f.; (of glass) pied m. —v.i. (p.t. stemmed) ~ **from,** provenir de.

stem[2] /stem/ v.t. (p.t. stemmed) (check, stop) endiguer, contenir.

stench /stentʃ/ n. puanteur f.

stencil /ˈstensl/ n. pochoir m.; (for typing) stencil m. —v.t. (p.t. stencilled) (document) polycopier.

stenographer /steˈnɒɡrəfə(r)/ n. (Amer.) sténodactylo f.

step /step/ v.i. (p.t. stepped) marcher, aller. —v.t. ~ **up,** augmenter. —n. pas m.; (stair) marche f.; (of train) marchepied m.; (action) mesure f. ~**s,** (ladder) escabeau m. **in** ~, au pas; (fig.) conforme (with, à). ~ **down,** (resign) démissionner; (from ladder) descendre. ~ **forward,** (faire un) pas en avant. ~ **up,** (pressure) augmenter. ~ **in,** (intervene) intervenir. ~**ladder** n. escabeau m. ~**ping-stone** n. (fig.) tremplin m.

step|**brother** /ˈstepbrʌðə(r)/ n. demi-frère m. ~**daughter** n. belle-fille f. ~**father** n. beau-père m. ~**mother** n. belle-mère f.

~**sister** n. demi-sœur f. ~**son** n. beau-fils m.

stereo /ˈsteriəʊ/ n. (pl. -os) stéréo f.; (record-player) chaîne stéréo f. —a. stéréo invar. ~**phonic** /-əˈfɒnɪk/ a. stéréophonique.

stereotype /ˈsteriətaip/ n. stéréotype m. ~**d** a. stéréotypé.

steril|**e** /ˈsteraɪl, Amer. ˈsterəl/ a. stérile. ~**ity** /stəˈrɪlətɪ/ n. stérilité f.

steriliz|**e** /ˈsterɪlaiz/ v.t. stériliser. ~**ation** /-ˈzeɪʃn/ n. stérilisation f.

sterling /ˈstɜːlɪŋ/ n. livre(s) sterling f. (pl.). —a. sterling invar.; (silver) fin; (fig.) excellent.

stern[1] /stɜːn/ a. (-er, -est) sévère.

stern[2] /stɜːn/ n. (of ship) arrière m.

steroid /ˈstɪərɔɪd/ n. stéroïde m.

stethoscope /ˈsteθəskəʊp/ n. stéthoscope m.

stew /stjuː/ v.t./i. cuire à la casserole. —n. ragoût m. ~**ed fruit,** compote f. ~**ed tea,** thé trop infusé m. ~**pan** n. cocotte f.

steward /stjʊəd/ n. (of club etc.) intendant m.; (on ship etc.) steward m. ~**ess** /-ˈdes/ n. hôtesse f.

stick[1] /stɪk/ n. bâton m.; (for walking) canne f.

stick[2] /stɪk/ v.t. (p.t. stuck) (glue) coller; (thrust) enfoncer; (put: fam.) mettre; (endure: sl.) supporter. —v.i. (adhere) coller, adhérer; (to pan) attacher; (remain: fam.) rester; (be jammed) être coincé. **be stuck with s.o.,** (fam.) se farcir qn. **be stuck in-the-mud** n. encroûté(e)m.(f.). ~ **at,** persévérer dans. ~ **out,** (head etc.) sortir; (tongue) tirer; v.i. (protrude) dépasser. ~ **to,** (promise etc.) rester fidèle à. ~ **up for,** (fam.) défendre. ~**ing-plaster** n. sparadrap m.

sticker /ˈstɪkə(r)/ n. autocollant m.

stickler /ˈstɪklə(r)/ n. **be a** ~ **for,** insister sur.

sticky /'stɪkɪ/ a. (-ier, -iest) poisseux; (*label, tape*) adhésif.

stiff /stɪf/ a. (-er, -est) raide; (*limb, joint*) ankylosé; (*tough*) dur; (*drink*) fort; (*price*) élevé; (*manner*) guindé. ~ **neck**, torticolis m. ~**ness** n. raideur f.

stiffen /'stɪfn/ v.t./i. (se) raidir.

stifle /'staɪfl/ v.t./i. étouffer.

stigma /'stɪgmə/ n. (pl. -as) stigmate m. ~**tize** v.t. stigmatiser.

stile /staɪl/ n. échalier m.

stiletto /stɪ'letəʊ/ a. & n. (pl. -os) ~**s**, ~ **heels** talons aiguille.

still[1] /stɪl/ a. immobile; (*quiet*) calme, tranquille. ~ **water**, eau dormante. —*adv*. encore, toujours; (*even*) encore; (*nevertheless*) tout de même. **keep** ~!, arrête de bouger! ~ **life**, nature morte f.

still[2] /stɪl/ n. (*apparatus*) alambic m.

stillborn /'stɪlbɔːn/ a. mort-né.

stilted /'stɪltɪd/ a. guindé.

stilts /stɪlts/ n. pl. échasses f. pl.

stimul|ate /'stɪmjʊleɪt/ v.t. stimuler. ~**ant** n. stimulant m. ~**ation** /-'leɪʃn/ n. stimulation f.

stimulus /'stɪmjʊləs/ n. (pl. -li /-laɪ/) (*spur*) stimulant m.

sting /stɪŋ/ n. piqûre f.; (*organ*) dard m. —v.t./i. (p.t. **stung**) piquer. ~**ing** a. (*fig.*) cinglant.

stingy /'stɪndʒɪ/ a. (-ier, -iest) avare (**with**, de).

stink /stɪŋk/ n. puanteur f. —v.i. (p.t. **stank** or **stunk**, p.p. **stunk**). ~ (**of**), puer. —v.t. ~ **out**, (*room etc.*) empester.

stinker /'stɪŋkə(r)/ n. (*thing: sl.*) vacherie f.; (*person: sl.*) vache f.

stint /stɪnt/ v.i. ~ **on**, lésiner sur. —n. (*work*) tour m.

stipulat|e /'stɪpjʊleɪt/ v.t. stipuler. ~**ion** /-'leɪʃn/ n. stipulation f.

stir /stɜː(r)/ v.t./i. (p.t. **stirred**) (*move*) remuer; (*excite*) exciter. —n. agitation f. ~ **up**, (*trouble etc.*) provoquer.

stirrup /'stɪrəp/ n. étrier m.

stitch /stɪtʃ/ n. point m.; (*in knitting*) maille f.; (*med.*) point de suture m.; (*muscle pain*) point de côté m. —v.t. coudre. **be in** ~**es**, (*fam.*) avoir le fou rire.

stoat /stəʊt/ n. hermine f.

stock /stɒk/ n. réserve f.; (*comm.*) stock m.; (*financial*) valeurs f. pl.; (*family*) souche f.; (*soup*) bouillon m. —a. (*goods*) courant. —v.t. (*shop etc.*) approvisionner; (*sell*) vendre. —v.i. ~ **up**, s'approvisionner (**with**, de). ~**car** n. stock-car n. ~ **cube**, bouillon-cube m. **S~ Exchange**, ~ **market**, Bourse f. ~ **phrase**, cliché m. ~**taking** n. (*comm.*) inventaire m. **in** ~, en stock. **we're out of** ~, il n'y en a plus. **take** ~, (*fig.*) faire le point.

stockbroker /'stɒkbrəʊkə(r)/ n. agent de change m.

stocking /'stɒkɪŋ/ n. bas m.

stockist /'stɒkɪst/ n. stockiste m.

stockpile /'stɒkpaɪl/ n. stock m. —v.t. stocker; (*arms*) amasser.

stocky /'stɒkɪ/ a. (-ier, -iest) trapu.

stodge /stɒdʒ/ n. (*fam.*) aliment(s) lourd(s) m. (pl.). ~**y** a. lourd.

stoic /'stəʊɪk/ n. stoïque m./f. ~**al** a. stoïque. ~**ism** /-sɪzəm/ n. stoïcisme m.

stoke /stəʊk/ v.t. (*boiler, fire*) garnir, alimenter.

stole[1] /stəʊl/ n. (*garment*) étole f.

stole[2], **stolen** /stəʊl, 'stəʊlən/ see **steal**.

stolid /'stɒlɪd/ a. flegmatique.

stomach /'stʌmək/ n. estomac m.; (*abdomen*) ventre m. —v.t. (*put up with*) supporter. ~**ache** n. mal à l'estomac or au ventre m.

ston|e /stəʊn/ n. pierre f.; (*pebble*) caillou m.; (*in fruit*) noyau m.; (*weight*) 6.350 kg. — m. —v.t. lapider; (*fruit*) dénoyauter. ~**e-cold/-deaf**, complètement froid/sourd. **~y** a. pierreux. **~y-broke** a. (sl.) fauché.

stonemason /ˈstəʊnmeɪsn/ n. maçon m., tailleur de pierre m.

stood /stʊd/ see stand.

stooge /stuːdʒ/ n. (actor) comparse m./f.; (fig.) fantoche m., laquais m.

stool /stuːl/ n. tabouret m.

stoop /stuːp/ v.i. (bend) se baisser; (condescend) s'abaisser. —n. have a **~**, être voûté.

stop /stɒp/ v.t./i. (p.t. stopped) arrêter (doing, de faire); (moving, talking) s'arrêter; (prevent) empêcher (from, de); (hole, leak, etc.) boucher; (of pain, noise, etc.) cesser; (stay: fam.) rester. —n. arrêt m.; (full stop) point m. **~ off**, s'arrêter. **~ up**, boucher. **~(-over)**, halte f.; (port of call) escale f. **~-light** n. (on vehicle) stop m. **~-watch** n. chronomètre m.

stopgap /ˈstɒpgæp/ n. bouche-trou m. —a. intérimaire.

stoppage /ˈstɒpɪdʒ/ n. arrêt m.; (of work) arrêt de travail m.; (of pay) retenue f.

stopper /ˈstɒpə(r)/ n. bouchon m.

storage /ˈstɔːrɪdʒ/ n. (of goods, food, etc.) emmagasinage m. **~ heater**, radiateur électrique à accumulation m. **~ space**, espace de rangement m.

store /stɔː(r)/ n. réserve f.; (warehouse) entrepôt m.; (shop) grand magasin m.; (Amer.) magasin m. —v.t. (for future) mettre en réserve; (in warehouse, mind) emmagasiner. have in **~ for**, réserver à. set **~ by**, attacher du prix à. **~-room** n. réserve f.

storey /ˈstɔːrɪ/ n. étage m.

stork /stɔːk/ n. cigogne f.

storm /stɔːm/ n. tempête f., orage m. —v.t. prendre d'assaut. —v.i. (rage) tempêter. **~y** a. orageux.

story /ˈstɔːrɪ/ n. histoire f. (in press) article m.; (storey: Amer.) étage m. **~ book**, livre d'histoires m. **~-teller** n. conteu|r, -se m., f.; (liar: fam.) menteu|r, -se m., f.

stout /staʊt/ a. (-er, -est) corpulent; (strong) solide. —n. bière brune f. **~ness** n. corpulence f.

stove /stəʊv/ n. (for cooking) cuisinière f.; (heater) poêle m.

stow /stəʊ/ v.t. **~ away**, (put away) ranger; (hide) cacher. —v.i. voyager clandestinement.

stowaway /ˈstəʊəweɪ/ n. passag|er, -ère clandestin(e) m., f.

straddle /ˈstrædl/ v.t. être à cheval sur, enjamber.

straggle /ˈstrægl/ v.i. (lag behind) traîner en désordre. **~r** /-ə(r)/ n. traînard(e) m. (f.).

straight /streɪt/ a. (-er, -est) droit; (tidy) en ordre; (frank) franc. —adv. (in straight line) droit; (direct) tout droit. —n. ligne droite f. **~ ahead** or **on**, tout droit. **~ away**, tout de suite. **~ face**, visage sérieux m. get sth. **~**, mettre qch. au clair. **~ off**, (fam.) sans hésiter.

straighten /ˈstreɪtn/ v.t. (nail, situation, etc.) redresser; (tidy) arranger.

straightforward /streɪtˈfɔːwəd/ a. honnête; (easy) simple.

strain[1] /streɪn/ n. (breed) race f.; (streak) tendance f.

strain[2] /streɪn/ v.t. (rope, ears) tendre; (limb) fouler; (eyes) fatiguer; (muscle) froisser; (filter) passer; (vegetables) égoutter; (fig.) mettre à l'épreuve. —v.i. fournir des efforts. —n. tension f.; (fig.) effort m. **~s**, (tune: mus.) accents m. pl. **~ed** a. forcé; (relations) tendu. **~er** n. passoire f.

strait /streɪt/ n. détroit m. **~s**,

détroit *m.*; (*fig.*) embarras *m.* **~-jacket** *n.* camisole de force *f.* **~-laced** *a.* collet monté invar.

strand /strænd/ *n.* (*thread*) fil *m.*, brin *m.*; (*lock of hair*) mèche *f.*

stranded /'strændɪd/ *a.* (*person*) en rade; (*ship*) échoué.

strange /streɪndʒ/ *a.* (**-er, -est**) étrange; (*unknown*) inconnu. **~ly** *adv.* étrangement. **~ness** *n.* étrangeté *f.*

stranger /'streɪndʒə(r)/ *n.* inconnu(e) *m.* (*f.*).

strangle /'stræŋgl/ *v.t.* étrangler.

stranglehold /'stræŋglhəʊld/ *n.* **have a ~ on**, tenir à la gorge.

strap /stræp/ *n.* (*of leather etc.*) courroie *f.*; (*of dress*) bretelle *f.*; (*of watch*) bracelet *m.* —*v.t.* (*p.t.* **strapped**) attacher.

strapping /'stræpɪŋ/ *a.* costaud.

stratagem /'strætədʒəm/ *n.* stratagème *m.*

strategic /strə'tiːdʒɪk/ *a.* stratégique.

strategy /'strætədʒɪ/ *n.* stratégie *f.*

stratum /'strɑːtəm/ *n.* (*pl.* **strata**) couche *f.*

straw /strɔː/ *n.* paille *f.* **the last ~**, le comble.

strawberry /'strɔːbrɪ/ *n.* fraise *f.*

stray /streɪ/ *v.i.* s'égarer; (*deviate*) s'écarter. —*a.* perdu; (*isolated*) isolé. —*n.* animal perdu *m.*

streak /striːk/ *n.* raie *f.*, bande *f.*; (*trace*) trace *f.*; (*period*) période *f.*; (*tendency*) tendance *f.* —*v.t.* (*mark*) strier. —*v.i.* filer à toute allure. **~y** *a.* strié.

stream /striːm/ *n.* ruisseau *m.*; (*current*) courant *m.*; (*flow*) flot *m.*; (*in schools*) classe (de niveau) *f.* —*v.i.* ruisseler (**with**, de); (*eyes, nose*) couler.

streamer /'striːmə(r)/ *n.* (*of paper*) serpentin *m.*; (*flag*) banderole *f.*

streamline /'striːmlaɪn/ *v.t.* rationaliser. **~d** *a.* (*shape*) aérodynamique.

street /striːt/ *n.* rue *f.* **~ lamp**, réverbère *m.* **~ map**, plan des rues *m.*

streetcar /'striːtkɑː(r)/ *n.* (*Amer.*) tramway *m.*

strength /streŋθ/ *n.* force *f.*; (*of wall, fabric, etc.*) solidité *f.* **on the ~ of**, en vertu de.

strengthen /'streŋθn/ *v.t.* renforcer, fortifier.

strenuous /'strenjʊəs/ *a.* énergique; (*arduous*) ardu; (*tiring*) fatigant. **~ly** *adv.* énergiquement.

stress /stres/ *n.* accent *m.*; (*pressure*) pression *f.*; (*med.*) stress *m.* —*v.t.* souligner, insister sur.

stretch /stretʃ/ *v.t.* (*pull taut*) tendre; (*arm, leg*) étendre; (*neck*) tendre; (*clothes*) étirer; (*truth etc.*) forcer. —*v.i.* s'étendre; (*of person, clothes*) s'étirer. —*n.* étendue *f.*; (*period*) période *f.*; (*of road*) tronçon *m.* —*a.* (*fabric*) extensible. **~ one's legs**, se dégourdir les jambes. **at a ~**, d'affilée.

stretcher /'stretʃə(r)/ *n.* brancard *m.*

strew /struː/ *v.t.* (*p.t.* **strewed**, *p.p.* **strewed** *or* **strewn**) (*scatter*) répandre; (*cover*) joncher.

stricken /'strɪkən/ *a.* **~ with**, frappé *or* atteint de.

strict /strɪkt/ *a.* (**-er, -est**) strict. **~ly** *adv.* strictement. **~ness** *n.* sévérité *f.*

stride /straɪd/ *v.i.* (*p.t.* **strode**, *p.p.* **stridden**) faire de grands pas. —*n.* grand pas *m.*

strident /'straɪdnt/ *a.* strident.

strife /straɪf/ *n.* conflit(s) *m.* (*pl.*).

strike /straɪk/ *v.t.* (*p.t.* **struck**) frapper; (*blow*) donner; (*match*) frotter; (*gold etc.*) trouver. —*v.i.* faire grève; (*attack*) attaquer; (*clock*) sonner. —*n.* (*of workers*) grève *f.*; (*mil.*) attaque *f.*; (*find*) découvrante f. **on ~**, en grève. **~ off** or **out**, rayer. **~ up a friendship**, lier amitié. **(with, avec).**

striker /ˈstraɪkə(r)/ n. gréviste m./f.; (football) buteur m.

striking /ˈstraɪkɪŋ/ a. frappant.

string /strɪŋ/ n. ficelle f.; (of violin, racket, etc.) corde f.; (of pearls) collier m.; (of lies etc.) chapelet m. —v.t. (p.t. **strung**) (thread) enfiler. **the ~s**, (mus.) les cordes. **~ bean**, haricot vert m. **pull ~s**, faire jouer ses relations, faire marcher le piston. **~ out**, (s')échelonner. **~ed** a. (instrument) à cordes. **~y** a. filandreux.

stringent /ˈstrɪndʒənt/ a. rigoureux, strict.

strip¹ /strɪp/ v.t./i. (p.t. **stripped**) (undress) (se) déshabiller; (machine) démonter; (deprive) dépouiller. **~per** n. strip-teaseuse f.; (solvent) décapant m. **~-tease** n. strip-tease m.

strip² /strɪp/ n. bande f. **comic ~**, bande dessinée f. **~ light**, néon m.

stripe /straɪp/ n. rayure f., raie f. **~d** a. rayé.

strive /straɪv/ v.i. (p.t. **strove**, p.p. **striven**) s'efforcer (**to**, de).

strode /strəʊd/ see **stride**.

stroke¹ /strəʊk/ n. coup m.; (of pen) trait m.; (swimming) nage f.; (med.) attaque f., congestion f. **at a ~**, d'un seul coup.

stroke² /strəʊk/ v.t. (with hand) caresser. —n. caresse f.

stroll /strəʊl/ v.i. flâner. —n. petit tour m. **~ in/**etc., entrer/etc. tranquillement. **~er** n. (Amer.) poussette f.

strong /strɒŋ/ a. (-er, -est) fort; (shoes, fabric, etc.) solide. **be fifty/**etc. **~**, être au nombre de cinquante/etc. **~-box** n. coffrefort m. **~-minded** a. résolu. **~-**

room n. chambre forte f. **~ly** adv. (greatly) fortement; (with energy) avec force; (deeply) profondément.

stronghold /ˈstrɒŋhəʊld/ n. bastion m.

strove /strəʊv/ see **strive**.

struck /strʌk/ see **strike**. —a. **~ on**, (sl.) impressionné par.

structur|e /ˈstrʌktʃə(r)/ n. (of cell, poem, etc.) structure f.; (building) construction f. **~al** a. structural, de (la) construction.

struggle /ˈstrʌgl/ v.i. lutter, se battre. —n. lutte f.; (effort) effort m. **have a ~ to**, avoir du mal à.

strum /strʌm/ v.t. (p.t. **strummed**) (banjo etc.) gratter de.

strung /strʌŋ/ see **string**. —a. **~ up**, (tense) nerveux.

strut /strʌt/ n. (support) étai m. —v.i. (p.t. **strutted**) se pavaner.

stub /stʌb/ n. bout m.; (of tree) souche f.; (counterfoil) talon m. —v.t. (p.t. **stubbed**). **~ one's toe**, se cogner le doigt de pied. **~ out**, écraser.

stubble /ˈstʌbl/ n. (on chin) barbe de plusieurs jours f.; (remains of wheat) chaume m.

stubborn /ˈstʌbən/ a. opiniâtre, obstiné. **~ly** adv. obstinément. **~ness** n. opiniâtreté f.

stubby /ˈstʌbɪ/ a. (-ier, -iest) (finger) épais; (person) trapu.

stuck /stʌk/ see **stick**². —a. (jammed) coincé. **I'm ~**, (for answer) je sèche. **~-up** a. (sl.) prétentieux.

stud¹ /stʌd/ n. clou m.; (for collar) bouton m. —v.t. (p.t. **studded**) clouter. **~ded with**, parsemé de.

stud² /stʌd/ n. (horses) écurie f. **~(-farm)** n. haras m.

student /ˈstjuːdnt/ n. (univ.) étudiant(e) m. (f.); (schol.) élève m./f. —a. (restaurant, life, residence) universitaire.

studied /'stʌdɪd/ a. étudié.

studio /'stjuːdɪəʊ/ n. (pl. **-os**) studio m. —v. **flat**, studio m.

studious /'stjuːdɪəs/ a. (person) studieux; (deliberate) étudié. **~ly** adv. (carefully) avec soin.

study /'stʌdɪ/ n. étude f.; (office) bureau m. —v.t./i. étudier.

stuff /stʌf/ n. substance f.; (sl.) chose(s) f. (pl.). —v.t. rembourrer; (animal) empailler; (cram) bourrer; (culin.) farcir; (block up) boucher; (put) fourrer. **~ing** n. bourre f.; (culin.) farce f.

stuffy /'stʌfɪ/ a. (-ier, -iest) mal aéré; (dull: fam.) vieux jeu invar.

stumble /'stʌmbl/ v.i. trébucher. **~e across** or **on**, tomber sur. **~ing-block** n. pierre d'achoppement f.

stump /stʌmp/ n. (of tree) souche f.; (of limb) moignon m.; (of pencil) bout m.

stumped /stʌmpt/ a. (baffled: fam.) embarrassé.

stun /stʌn/ v.t. (p.t. **stunned**) étourdir; (bewilder) stupéfier.

stung /stʌŋ/ see **sting**.

stunk /stʌŋk/ see **stink**.

stunning /'stʌnɪŋ/ a. (delightful: fam.) sensationnel.

stunt[1] /stʌnt/ v.t. (growth) retarder. **~ed** a. (person) rabougri.

stunt[2] /stʌnt/ n. (feat: fam.) tour de force m.; (trick: fam.) truc m.; (dangerous) cascade f. **~ man** n. cascadeur m.

stupefy /'stjuːpɪfaɪ/ v.t. abrutir; (amaze) stupéfier.

stupendous /stjuː'pendəs/ a. prodigieux, formidable.

stupid /'stjuːpɪd/ a. stupide, bête. **~ity** /-'pɪdətɪ/ n. stupidité f. **~ly** adv. stupidement, bêtement.

stupor /'stjuːpə(r)/ n. stupeur f.

sturdy /'stɜːdɪ/ a. (-ier, -iest) robuste. **~iness** n. robustesse f.

stutter /'stʌtə(r)/ v.i. bégayer. —n. bégaiement m.

sty[1] /staɪ/ n. (pigsty) porcherie f.

sty[2] /staɪ/ n. (on eye) orgelet m.

style /staɪl/ n. style m.; (fashion) mode f.; (sort) genre m.; (pattern) modèle m. —v.t. (design) créer. **do sth. in ~e**, faire qch. avec classe. **~e s.o.'s hair**, coiffer qn. **~ist** n. (of hair) coiffeur, -se m., f.

stylish /'staɪlɪʃ/ a. élégant.

stylized /'staɪlaɪzd/ a. stylisé.

stylus /'staɪləs/ n. (pl. **-uses**) (of record-player) saphir m.

suave /swɑːv/ a. (urbane) courtois; (smooth: pej.) doucereux.

sub- /sʌb/ pref. sous-, sub-.

subconscious /sʌb'kɒnʃəs/ a. & n. inconscient (m.), subconscient (m.). **~ly** adv. inconsciemment.

subcontract /sʌbkən'trækt/ v.t. sous-traiter.

subdivide /sʌbdɪ'vaɪd/ v.t. subdiviser.

subdue /səb'djuː/ v.t. (feeling) maîtriser; (country) subjuguer. **~d** a. (weak) faible; (light) tamisé; (person, criticism) retenu.

subject[1] /'sʌbdʒɪkt/ a. (state etc.) soumis. —n. sujet m.; (school., univ.) matière f.; (citizen) ressortissant(e) m. (f.), sujet(te) m. (f.). **~matter** n. contenu m. **~ to**, soumis à; (liable to, dependent on) sujet à.

subject[2] /səb'dʒekt/ v.t. soumettre. **~ion** /-kʃn/ n. soumission f.

subjective /səb'dʒektɪv/ a. subjectif.

subjunctive /səb'dʒʌŋktɪv/ a. & n. subjonctif (m.).

sublet /sʌb'let/ v.t. sous-louer.

sublime /sə'blaɪm/ a. sublime.

submarine /sʌbmə'riːn/ n. sous-marin m.

submerge /səb'mɜːdʒ/ v.t. submerger. —v.i. plonger.

submissive /səb'mɪsɪv/ a. soumis.

submit /səb'mɪt/ v.t./i. (p.t. **submitted**) (se) soumettre (**to**, à). **~ssion** n. soumission f.

subordinate¹ /sə'bɔːdɪnət/ a. subalterne; (gram.) subordonné. —n. subordonné(e) m. (f.).

subordinate² /sə'bɔːdɪneɪt/ v.t. subordonner (to, à).

subpoena /səb'piːnə/ n. (pl. -as) (jurid.) citation f., assignation f.

subroutine /'sʌbruːtiːn/ n. sous-programme m.

subscribe /səb'skraɪb/ v.t./i. verser (de l'argent) (to, à). ~ to, (loan, theory) souscrire à; (newspaper) s'abonner à, être abonné à. ~r /-ə(r)/ n. abonné(e) m. (f.).

subscription /səb'skrɪpʃn/ n. souscription f.; abonnement m.; (membership dues) cotisation f.

subsequent /'sʌbsɪkwənt/ a. (later) ultérieur; (next) suivant. ~ly adv. par la suite.

subside /səb'saɪd/ v.i. (land etc.) s'affaisser; (flood, wind) baisser. ~nce /-əns/ n. affaissement m.

subsidiary /səb'sɪdɪərɪ/ a. accessoire. —n. (comm.) filiale f.

subsid|y /'sʌbsədɪ/ n. subvention f. ~ize /-ɪdaɪz/ v.t. subventionner.

subsist /səb'sɪst/ v.i. subsister. ~ence n. subsistance f.

substance /'sʌbstəns/ n. substance f.

substandard /sʌb'stændəd/ a. de qualité inférieure.

substantial /səb'stænʃl/ a. considérable; (meal) substantiel. ~ly adv. considérablement.

substantiate /səb'stænʃɪeɪt/ v.t. justifier, prouver.

substitut|e /'sʌbstɪtjuːt/ n. succédané m.; (person) remplaçant(e) m. (f.). —v.t. substituer (for, à). ~ion /-'tjuːʃn/ n. substitution f.

subterfuge /'sʌbtəfjuːdʒ/ n. subterfuge m.

subterranean /sʌbtə'reɪnɪən/ a. souterrain.

subtitle /'sʌbtaɪtl/ n. sous-titre m.

subtle /'sʌtl/ a. (-er, -est) subtil. ~ty n. subtilité f.

subtotal /sʌb'təʊtl/ n. total partiel m.

subtract /səb'trækt/ v.t. soustraire. ~ion /-kʃn/ n. soustraction f.

suburb /'sʌbɜːb/ n. faubourg m., banlieue f. ~s, banlieue f. ~an /sə'bɜːbən/ a. de banlieue.

suburbia /sə'bɜːbɪə/ n. la banlieue.

subversive /səb'vɜːsɪv/ a. subversif.

subver|t /səb'vɜːt/ v.t. renverser. ~sion /-ʃn/ n. subversion f.

subway /'sʌbweɪ/ n. passage souterrain m.; (Amer.) métro m.

succeed /sək'siːd/ v.i. réussir (in doing, à faire). —v.t. (follow) succéder à. ~ing a. suivant.

success /sək'ses/ n. succès m., réussite f.

successful /sək'sesfl/ a. réussi, couronné de succès; (favourable) heureux; (in exam) reçu. be ~ in doing, réussir à faire. ~ly adv. avec succès.

succession /sək'seʃn/ n. succession f. in ~, de suite.

successive /sək'sesɪv/ a. successif. **six** ~ **days,** six jours consécutifs.

successor /sək'sesə(r)/ n. successeur m.

succinct /sək'sɪŋkt/ a. succinct.

succulent /'sʌkjʊlənt/ a. succulent.

succumb /sə'kʌm/ v.i. succomber.

such /sʌtʃ/ a. & pron. tel(le), tel(le)s; (so much) tant (de). —adv. si. ~ **a book**/etc., un tel livre/etc. ~ **books**/etc., de tels livres/etc. ~ **courage**/etc., tant de courage/etc. ~ **a big house,** une si grande maison. ~ **as,** comme, tel que. **as** ~, en tant que tel. **there's no** ~ **thing,** ça n'existe pas. ~**-and-such** a. tel ou tel.

suck /sʌk/ v.t. sucer. ~ **in** or **up**, aspirer. ~**er** n. (rubber pad) ventouse f.; (person: sl.) dupe f.

suction /'sʌkʃn/ n. succion f.

sudden /'sʌdn/ a. soudain, subit. **all of a** ~, tout à coup. ~**ly** adv. subitement, brusquement. ~**ness** n. soudaineté f.

suds /sʌdz/ n. pl. (froth) mousse de savon f.

sue /suː/ v.t. (pres. p. **suing**) poursuivre (en justice).

suede /sweɪd/ n. daim m.

suet /'suːɪt/ n. graisse de rognon f.

suffer /'sʌfə(r)/ v.t./i. souffrir, (loss, attack, etc.) subir. ~**er** n. victime f., malade m./f. ~**ing** n. souffrance(s) f. (pl.).

suffice /sə'faɪs/ v.i. suffire.

sufficient /sə'fɪʃnt/ a. (enough) suffisamment de; (big enough) suffisant. ~**ly** adv. suffisamment.

suffix /'sʌfɪks/ n. suffixe m.

suffocat|**e** /'sʌfəkeɪt/ v.t./i. suffoquer. ~**ion** /-'keɪʃn/ n. suffocation f.; (med.) asphyxie f.

suffused /sə'fjuːzd/ a. ~ **with**, (light, tears) baigné de.

sugar /'ʃʊɡə(r)/ n. sucre m. —v.t. sucrer. ~**y** a. sucré.

suggest /sə'dʒest/ v.t. suggérer. ~**ion** /-tʃn/ n. suggestion f.

suggestive /sə'dʒestɪv/ a. suggestif. **be** ~ **of**, suggérer.

suicid|**e** /'suːɪsaɪd/ n. suicide m. **commit** ~**e**, se suicider. ~**al** /-'saɪdl/ a. suicidaire.

suit /suːt/ n. costume m.; (woman's) tailleur m.; (cards) couleur f. —v.t. convenir à; (of garment, style, etc.) aller à; (adapt) adapter. ~**ability** n. (of action etc.) à-propos m.; (of candidate) aptitude(s) f. (pl.). ~**able** a. qui convient (for, à), convenable. ~**ably** adv. convenablement. ~**ed** a. (well) ~**ed**, (matched) bien assorti. ~**ed to**, fait pour, apte à.

suitcase /'suːtkeɪs/ n. valise f.

suite /swiːt/ n. (rooms, retinue) suite f.; (furniture) mobilier m.

suitor /'suːtə(r)/ n. soupirant m.

sulfur /'sʌlfər/ n. (Amer.) = **sulphur**.

sulk /sʌlk/ v.i. bouder. ~**y** a. boudeur, maussade.

sullen /'sʌlən/ a. maussade. ~**ly** adv. d'un air maussade.

sulphur /'sʌlfə(r)/ n. soufre m. ~**ic** /-'fjʊərɪk/ a. ~**ic acid**, acide sulfurique m.

sultan /'sʌltən/ n. sultan m.

sultana /sʌl'tɑːnə/ n. raisin de Smyrne m., raisin sec m.

sultry /'sʌltrɪ/ a. (-ier, -iest) étouffant, lourd; (fig.) sensuel.

sum /sʌm/ n. somme f.; (in arithmetic) calcul m. —v.t./i. (p.t. **summed**) récapituler; (assess) évaluer.

summar|**y** /'sʌmərɪ/ n. résumé m. —a. sommaire. ~**ize** v.t. résumer.

summer /'sʌmə(r)/ n. été m. —a. d'été. ~**time** n. (season) été m. ~**y** a. estival.

summit /'sʌmɪt/ n. sommet m. ~ (conference), (pol.) (conférence f. au) sommet m.

summon /'sʌmən/ v.t. appeler; (meeting, s.o. to meeting) convoquer. ~ **up**, (strength, courage, etc.) rassembler.

summons /'sʌmənz/ n. (jurid.) assignation f. —v.t. assigner.

sump /sʌmp/ n. (auto.) carter m.

sumptuous /'sʌmptʃʊəs/ a. somptueux, luxueux.

sun /sʌn/ n. soleil m. —v.t. (p.t. **sunned**) ~ **o.s.**, se chauffer au soleil. ~**glasses** n. pl. lunettes de soleil f. pl. ~**roof** n. toit ouvrant m. ~**tan** n. bronzage m. ~**tanned** a. bronzé.

sunbathe /'sʌnbeɪð/ v.i. prendre un bain de soleil.

sunburn /'sʌnbɜ:n/ n. coup de soleil m. **~t** a. brûlé par le soleil.

Sunday /'sʌndɪ/ n. dimanche m. **~ school**, catéchisme m.

sundial /'sʌndaɪəl/ n. cadran solaire m.

sundown /'sʌndaʊn/ n. = sunset.

sundry /'sʌndrɪ/ a. divers. **~ies** n. pl. articles divers m. pl. **all and ~y**, tout le monde.

sunflower /'sʌnflaʊə(r)/ n. tournesol m.

sung /sʌŋ/ see sing.

sunk /sʌŋk/ see sink.

sunken /'sʌŋkən/ a. (ship etc.) submergé; (eyes) creux.

sunlight /'sʌnlaɪt/ n. soleil m.

sunny /'sʌnɪ/ a. (-ier, -iest) (room, day, etc.) ensoleillé.

sunrise /'sʌnraɪz/ n. lever du soleil m.

sunset /'sʌnset/ n. coucher du soleil m.

sunshade /'sʌnʃeɪd/ n. (lady's) ombrelle f.; (awning) parasol m.

sunshine /'sʌnʃaɪn/ n. soleil m.

sunstroke /'sʌnstrəʊk/ n. insolation f.

super /'su:pə(r)/ a. (sl.) formidable.

superb /su:'pɜ:b/ a. superbe.

supercilious /su:pə'sɪlɪəs/ a. hautain, dédaigneux.

superficial /su:pə'fɪʃl/ a. superficiel. **~ity** /-ɪ'ælətɪ/ n. caractère superficiel m. **~ly** adv. superficiellement.

superfluous /su:'pɜ:fluəs/ a. superflu.

superhuman /su:pə'hju:mən/ a. surhumain.

superimpose /su:pərɪm'pəʊz/ v.t. superposer (on, à).

superintendent /su:pərɪn'tendənt/ n. direc|teur, -trice m., f.; (of police) commissaire m.

superior /su:'pɪərɪə(r)/ a. & n. supérieur(e) (m. (f.)). **~ity** /-'ɒrətɪ/ n. supériorité f.

superlative /su:'pɜ:lətɪv/ a. suprême. —n. (gram.) superlatif m.

superman /'su:pəmæn/ n. (pl. -men) surhomme m.

supermarket /'su:pəmɑ:kɪt/ n. supermarché m.

supernatural /su:pə'nætʃrəl/ a. surnaturel.

superpower /'su:pəpaʊə(r)/ n. superpuissance f.

supersede /su:pə'si:d/ v.t. remplacer, supplanter.

supersonic /su:pə'sɒnɪk/ a. supersonique.

superstiti|on /su:pə'stɪʃn/ n. superstition f. **~ous** a. superstitieux.

superstore /'su:pəstɔ:(r)/ n. hypermarché m.

supertanker /'su:pətæŋkə(r)/ n. pétrolier géant m.

supervis|e /'su:pəvaɪz/ v.t. surveiller, diriger. **~ion** /-'vɪʒn/ n. surveillance f. **~or** n. surveillant(e) m. (f.); (shop) chef de rayon m.; (firm) chef de service m. **~ory** /-'vaɪzərɪ/ a. de surveillance.

supper /'sʌpə(r)/ n. dîner m.; (late at night) souper m.

supple /'sʌpl/ a. souple.

supplement[1] /'sʌplɪmənt/ n. supplément m. **~ary** /-'mentrɪ/ a. supplémentaire.

supplement[2] /'sʌplɪment/ v.t. compléter.

supplier /sə'plaɪə(r)/ n. fournisseur m.

suppl|y /sə'plaɪ/ v.t. fournir; (equip) pourvoir; (feed) alimenter (with, en). —n. provision f.; (of gas etc.) alimentation f. **~ies**, (food) vivres m. pl.; (material) fournitures f. pl. **~y teacher**, (professeur) suppléant(e) m. (f.).

support /sə'pɔ:t/ v.t. soutenir; (family) assurer la subsistance de; (endure) supporter. —n.

soutien *m.*, appui *m.*; (*techn.*) support *m.* ~**er** *n.* partisan(e) *m.* (*f.*); (*sport*) supporter *m.* ~**ive** *a.* qui soutient et encourage.

suppos|e /sə'pəʊz/ *v.t./i.* supposer. **be ~ed to do**, être censé faire, devoir faire. ~**ing he comes**, supposons qu'il vienne. ~**ition** /sʌpə'zɪʃn/ *n.* supposition *f.*

supposedly /sə'pəʊzɪdlɪ/ *adv.* soi-disant, prétendument.

suppress /sə'pres/ *v.t.* (*put an end to*) supprimer; (*restrain*) réprimer; (*stifle*) étouffer. ~**ion** /-ʃn/ *n.* suppression *f.*; répression *f.*

supreme /suː'priːm/ *a.* suprême. ~**acy** /-eməsɪ/ *n.* suprématie *f.*

surcharge /'sɜːtʃɑːdʒ/ *n.* prix supplémentaire *m.*; (*tax*) surtaxe *f.*; (*on stamp*) surcharge *f.*

sure /ʃɔː(r)/ *a.* (-**er**, -**est**) sûr. —*adv.* (*Amer., fam.*) pour sûr. **make ~ of**, s'assurer de. **make ~ that**, vérifier que. ~**ly** *adv.* sûrement.

surety /'ʃɔːrətɪ/ *n.* caution *f.*

surf /sɜːf/ *n.* (*waves*) ressac *m.* ~**ing** *n.* surf *m.*

surface /'sɜːfɪs/ *n.* surface *f.* —*a.* superficiel. —*v.t.* revêtir. —*v.i.* faire surface; (*fig.*) réapparaître. ~ **mail**, courrier maritime *m.*

surfboard /'sɜːfbɔːd/ *n.* planche de surf *f.*

surfeit /'sɜːfɪt/ *n.* excès *m.* (**of**, de).

surge /sɜːdʒ/ *v.i.* (*of crowd*) déferler; (*of waves*) s'enfler; (*increase*) monter. —*n.* (*wave*) vague *f.*; (*rise*) montée *f.*

surgeon /'sɜːdʒən/ *n.* chirurgien *m.*

surg|ery /'sɜːdʒərɪ/ *n.* chirurgie *f.*; (*office*) cabinet *m.*; (*session*) consultation *f.* **need ~ery**, devoir être opéré. ~**ical** *a.* chirurgical. ~**ical spirit**, alcool à 90 degrés *m.*

surly /'sɜːlɪ/ *a.* (-**ier**, -**iest**) bourru.

surmise /sə'maɪz/ *v.t.* conjecturer. —*n.* conjecture *f.*

surmount /sə'maʊnt/ *v.t.* (*overcome, cap*) surmonter.

surname /'sɜːneɪm/ *n.* nom de famille *m.*

surpass /sə'pɑːs/ *v.t.* surpasser.

surplus /'sɜːpləs/ *n.* surplus *m.* —*a.* en surplus.

surpris|e /sə'praɪz/ *n.* surprise *f.* —*v.t.* surprendre. ~**ed** *a.* surpris (**at**, de). ~**ing** *a.* surprenant. ~**ingly** *adv.* étonnamment.

surrender /sə'rendə(r)/ *v.i.* se rendre. —*v.t.* (*hand over*) remettre; (*mil.*) rendre. —*n.* (*mil.*) reddition *f.*; (*of passport etc.*) remise *f.*

surreptitious /sʌrəp'tɪʃəs/ *a.* subreptice, furtif.

surround /sə'raʊnd/ *v.t.* entourer; (*mil.*) encercler. ~**ing** *a.* environnant. ~**ings** *n. pl.* environs *m. pl.*; (*setting*) cadre *m.*

surveillance /sɜː'veɪləns/ *n.* surveillance *f.*

survey[1] /sə'veɪ/ *v.t.* (*review*) passer en revue; (*inquire into*) enquêter sur; (*building*) inspecter. ~**or** *n.* expert (géomètre) *m.*

survey[2] /'sɜːveɪ/ *n.* (*inquiry*) enquête *f.*; inspection *f.*; (*general view*) vue d'ensemble *f.*

survival /sə'vaɪvl/ *n.* survie *f.*; (*relic*) vestige *m.*

surviv|e /sə'vaɪv/ *v.t./i.* survivre (**à**). ~**or** *n.* survivant(e) *m.* (*f.*).

susceptib|le /sə'septəbl/ *a.* sensible (**to**, à). ~**le to**, (*prone to*) prédisposé à. ~**ility** /-'bɪlətɪ/ *n.* sensibilité *f.*; prédisposition *f.*

suspect[1] /sə'spekt/ *v.t.* soupçonner; (*doubt*) douter de.

suspect[2] /'sʌspekt/ *n. & a.* suspect(e) (*m.* (*f.*)).

suspen|d /sə'spend/ *v.t.* (*hang, stop*) suspendre; (*licence*) retirer provisoirement. ~**ded sentence**, condamnation avec sursis *f.* ~**sion** *n.* suspension *f.*; retrait provisoire *m.* ~**sion bridge**, pont suspendu *m.*

suspender /sə'spendə(r)/ *n.* jarretelle *f.* ~**s** (*braces: Amer.*) bretelles *f. pl.* ~ **belt**, porte-jarretelles *m.*

suspense /sə'spens/ *n.* attente *f.*; (*in book etc.*) suspense *m.*

suspicion /sə'spɪʃn/ *n.* soupçon *m.*; (*distrust*) méfiance *f.*

suspicious /səs'pɪʃəs/ *a.* soupçonneux; (*causing suspicion*) suspect. **be** ~ **of**, (*distrust*) se méfier de. ~**ly** *adv.* de façon suspecte.

sustain /sə'steɪn/ *v.t.* supporter; (*effort etc.*) soutenir; (*suffer*) subir.

sustenance /'sʌstɪnəns/ *n.* (*food*) nourriture *f.*; (*quality*) valeur nutritive *f.*

swab /swɒb/ *n.* (*pad*) tampon *m.*

swagger /'swægə(r)/ *v.i.* (*walk*) se pavaner, parader.

swallow[1] /'swɒləʊ/ *v.t./i.* avaler. ~ **up**, (*absorb, engulf*) engloutir.

swallow[2] /'swɒləʊ/ *n.* hirondelle *f.*

swam /swæm/ *see* swim.

swamp /swɒmp/ *n.* marais *m.* —*v.t.* (*flood, overwhelm*) submerger. ~**y** *a.* marécageux.

swan /swɒn/ *n.* cygne *m.* ~**-song** *n.* (*fig.*) chant du cygne *m.*

swank /swæŋk/ *n.* (*behaviour: fam.*) épate *f.*, esbroufe *f.*; (*person: fam.*) crâneur, -se *m.*, *f.* —*v.i.* (*show off: fam.*) crâner.

swap /swɒp/ *v.t./i.* (*p.t.* swapped) (*fam.*) échanger. —*n.* (*fam.*) échange *m.*

swarm /swɔːm/ *n.* (*of insects, people*) essaim *m.* —*v.i.* fourmiller. ~ **into** *or* **round**, (*crowd*) envahir.

swarthy /'swɔːðɪ/ *a.* (**-ier, -iest**) noiraud; (*complexion*) basané.

swastika /'swɒstɪkə/ *n.* (*Nazi*) croix gammée *f.*

swat /swɒt/ *v.t.* (*p.t.* swatted) (*fly etc.*) écraser.

sway /sweɪ/ *v.t./i.* (se) balancer; (*influence*) influencer. —*n.* balancement *m.*; (*rule*) empire *m.*

swear /sweə(r)/ *v.t./i.* (*p.t.* swore, *p.p.* sworn) jurer (**to sth.**, de qch.). ~ **at**, injurier. ~ **by sth.**, (*fam.*) ne jurer que par qch. ~**word** *n.* juron *m.*

sweat /swet/ *n.* sueur *f.* —*v.i.* suer. ~**-shirt** *n.* sweat-shirt *m.* ~**y** *a.* en sueur.

sweater /'swetə(r)/ *n.* pull-over *m.*

swede /swiːd/ *n.* rutabaga *m.*

Swede /swiːd/ *n.* Suédois(e) *m.* (*f.*). ~**en** *n.* Suède *f.* ~**ish** *a.* suédois; *n.* (*lang.*) suédois *m.*

sweep /swiːp/ *v.t./i.* (*p.t.* swept) balayer; (*carry away*) emporter, entraîner; (*chimney*) ramoner. —*n.* coup de balai *m.*; (*curve*) courbe *f.*; (*movement*) geste *m.*, mouvement *m.*; (*for chimneys*) ramoneur *m.* ~ **by**, passer rapidement *or* majestueusement. ~ **out**, balayer. ~**er** *n.* (*for carpet*) balai mécanique *m.*; (*football*) arrière volant *m.* ~**ing** *a.* (*gesture*) large; (*action*) qui va loin; (*statement*) trop général.

sweet /swiːt/ *a.* (**-er, -est**) (*not sour, pleasant*) doux; (*not savoury*) sucré; (*charming: fam.*) gentil. —*n.* bonbon *m.*; (*dish*) dessert *m.*; (*person*) chéri(e) *m.* (*f.*). **have a** ~ **tooth**, aimer les sucreries. ~ **corn**, maïs *m.* ~ **pea**, pois de senteur *m.* ~ **shop**, confiserie *f.* ~**ly** *adv.* gentiment. ~**ness** *n.* douceur *f.*; goût sucré *m.*

sweeten /'swiːtn/ *v.t.* sucrer; (*fig.*) adoucir. ~**er** *n.* édulcorant *m.*

sweetheart /'swiːthɑːt/ *n.* petit(e) ami(e) *m.* (*f.*); (*term of endearment*) chéri(e) *m.* (*f.*).

swell /swel/ *v.t./i.* (*p.t.* swelled, *p.p.* swollen *or* swelled), (*increase*) grossir; (*expand*) (se) gonfler; (*of hand, face*) enfler. —*n.* (*of sea*) houle *f.* —*a.* (*fam.*) formidable. **~ing** *n.* (*med.*) enflure *f.*

swelter /'swelta(r)/ *v.i.* étouffer. **~ing** *a.* étouffant.

swept /swept/ *see* **sweep.**

swerve /swɜːv/ *v.i.* faire un écart.

swift /swift/ *a.* (-er, -est) rapide. —*n.* (*bird*) martinet *m.* **~ly** *adv.* rapidement. **~ness** *n.* rapidité *f.*

swig /swig/ *v.t.* (*p.t.* **swigged**) (*drink: fam.*) lamper. —*n.* (*fam.*) lampée *f.*, coup *m.*

swill /swil/ *v.t.* rincer; (*drink*) lamper. —*n.* (*pig-food*) pâtée *f.*

swim /swim/ *v.i.* (*p.t.* **swam**, *p.p.* **swum**, *pres. p.* **swimming**) nager; (*be dizzy*) tourner. —*v.t.* traverser à la nage; (*distance*) nager. —*n.* baignade *f.* **go for a ~**, aller se baigner. **~mer** *n.* nageu|r, -se *m.*, *f.* **~ming** *n.* natation *f.* **~ming-bath**, **~ming-pool** *ns.* piscine *f.* **~suit** *n.* maillot de bain *m.*

swindle /'swindl/ *v.t.* escroquer. —*n.* escroquerie *f.* **~r** /-ə(r)/ *n.* escroc *m.*

swine /swain/ *n. pl.* (*pigs*) pourceaux *m. pl.* —*n. invar.* (*person: fam.*) salaud *m.*

swing /swiŋ/ *v.t./i.* (*p.t.* **swung**) (se) balancer; (*turn round*) tourner; (*of pendulum*) osciller. —*n.* balancement *m.*; (*seat*) balançoire *f.*; (*of opinion*) revirement *m.* (**towards**, en faveur de); (*mus.*) rythme *m.* **be in full ~**, battre son plein. **~ round**, (*of person*) se retourner.

swingeing /'swindʒɪŋ/ *a.* écrasant.

swipe /swaip/ *v.t.* (*hit: fam.*) frapper; (*steal: fam.*) piquer. —*n.* (*hit: fam.*) grand coup *m.*

swirl /swɜːl/ *v.i.* tourbillonner. —*n.* tourbillon *m.*

swish /swif/ *v.i.* (*hiss*) siffler,

cingler l'air. —*a.* (*fam.*) chic *invar.*

Swiss /swis/ *a.* suisse. —*n. invar.* Suisse(sse) *m.* (*f.*).

switch /switf/ *n.* bouton (électrique) *m.*, interrupteur *m.*; (*shift*) changement *m.*, revirement *m.* —*v.t.* (*transfer*) transférer; (*exchange*) échanger (**for**, contre); (*reverse positions of*) changer de place. **~ trains/etc.**, (*change*) changer de train/etc. —*v.i.* (*go over*) passer. **~ off**, éteindre. **~ on**, mettre, allumer.

switchback /'switfbæk/ *n.* montagnes russes *f. pl.*

switchboard /'switfbɔːd/ *n.* (*telephone*) standard *m.*

Switzerland /'switsələnd/ *n.* Suisse *f.*

swivel /'swivl/ *v.t./i.* (*p.t.* **swivelled**) (faire) pivoter.

swollen /'swəulən/ *see* **swell.**

swoon /swuːn/ *v.i.* se pâmer.

swoop /swuːp/ *v.i.* (*bird*) fondre; (*police*) faire une descente, foncer. —*n.* (*police raid*) descente *f.*

sword /sɔːd/ *n.* épée *f.*

swore /swɔː(r)/ *see* **swear.**

sworn /swɔːn/ *see* **swear.** —*a.* (*enemy*) juré; (*ally*) dévoué.

swot /swot/ *v.t./i.* (*p.t.* **swotted**) (*study: sl.*) bûcher. —*n.* (*sl.*) bûcheu|r, -se *m.*, *f.*

swum /swʌm/ *see* **swim.**

swung /swʌŋ/ *see* **swing.**

sycamore /'sikəmɔː(r)/ *n.* (*maple*) sycomore *m.*; (*Amer.*) platane *m.*

syllable /'siləbl/ *n.* syllabe *f.*

syllabus /'siləbəs/ *n.* (*pl.* -uses) (*schol., univ.*) programme *m.*

symbol /'simbl/ *n.* symbole *m.* **~ic(al)** /-'bolik(l)/ *a.* symbolique. **~ism** *n.* symbolisme *m.*

symbolize /'simbəlaiz/ *v.t.* symboliser.

symmetr|y /'simətri/ *n.* symétrie *f.* **~ical** /si'metrikl/ *a.* symétrique.

sympathize /'sɪmpəθaɪz/ v.i. ~
with, (pity) plaindre; (fig.) comprendre les sentiments de. ~r
/ə(r)/ n. sympathisant(e) m. (f.).

sympath|y /'sɪmpəθɪ/ n. (pity)
compassion f.; (fig.) compréhension f.; (solidarity) solidarité f.;
(condolences) condoléances f. pl.
be in ~y with, comprendre, être
en accord avec. ~etic /-'θetɪk/ a.
compatissant; (fig.) compréhensif. ~etically /-'θetɪklɪ/ adv.
avec compassion; (fig.) avec compréhension.

symphon|y /'sɪmfənɪ/ n. symphonie f. ~a. symphonique. ~ic
/-'fɒnɪk/ a. symphonique.

symposium /sɪm'pəʊzɪəm/ n. (pl.
-ia) symposium m.

symptom /'sɪmptəm/ n. symptôme m. ~atic /-'mætɪk/ a.
symptomatique (of, de).

synagogue /'sɪnəgɒg/ n. synagogue f.

synchronize /'sɪŋkrənaɪz/ v.t.
synchroniser.

syndicate /'sɪndɪkət/ n. syndicat
m.

syndrome /'sɪndrəʊm/ n. syndrome m.

synonym /'sɪnənɪm/ n. synonyme
m. ~ous /sɪ'nɒnɪməs/ a. synonyme.

synopsis /sɪ'nɒpsɪs/ n. (pl. -opses
/-siːz/) résumé m.

syntax /'sɪntæks/ n. syntaxe f.

synthesis /'sɪnθəsɪs/ n. (pl. -theses
/-siːz/) synthèse f.

synthetic /sɪn'θetɪk/ a. synthétique.

syphilis /'sɪfɪlɪs/ n. syphilis f.

Syria /'sɪrɪə/ n. Syrie f. ~n a. & n.
syrien(ne) (m. (f.)).

syringe /sɪ'rɪndʒ/ n. seringue f.

syrup /'sɪrəp/ n. (liquid) sirop m.;
(treacle) mélasse raffinée f. ~y a.
sirupeux.

system /'sɪstəm/ n. système m.;
(body) organisme m.; (order)

méthode f. ~s analyst, analyste-
programmeur|r,-se m.,f. ~s disk,
disque système m.

systematic /sɪstə'mætɪk/ a. systématique.

T

tab /tæb/ n. (flap) languette f.,
patte f.; (loop) attache f.; (label)
étiquette f.; (Amer., fam.) addition f. keep ~s on, (fam.)
surveiller.

table /'teɪbl/ n. table f. —v.t.
présenter; (postpone) ajourner.
—a. (lamp, wine) de table. at ~, à
table. lay or set the ~, mettre la
table. ~-cloth n. nappe f. ~-mat
n. dessous-de-plat m. invar.;
(cloth) set m. ~ of contents,
table des matières f. ~ tennis,
ping-pong m.

tablespoon /'teɪblspuːn/ n. cuiller
à soupe f. ~ful n. (pl. ~fuls)
cuillerée à soupe f.

tablet /'tæblɪt/ n. (of stone) plaque
f.; (drug) comprimé m.

tabloid /'tæblɔɪd/ n. tabloïd m.
the ~ press, la presse populaire f.

taboo /tə'buː/ n. & a. tabou (m.).

tabulator /'tæbjʊleɪtə(r)/ n. (on
typewriter) tabulateur m.

tacit /'tæsɪt/ a. tacite.

taciturn /'tæsɪtɜːn/ a. taciturne.

tack /tæk/ n. (nail) broquette f.;
(stitch) point de bâti m.; (course of
action) voie f. —v.t. (nail) clouer;
(stitch) bâtir; (add) ajouter. —v.i.
(naut.) louvoyer.

tackle /'tækl/ n. équipement m.,
matériel m.; (football) plaquage
m. —v.t. (problem etc.) s'attaquer
à; (football player) plaquer.

tacky /'tækɪ/ a. (-ier, -iest) poisseux, pas sec; (shabby, mean:
Amer.) moche.

tact /tækt/ *n.* tact *m.* ~**ful** *a.* plein de tact. ~**fully** *adv.* avec tact. ~**less** *a.* qui manque de tact. ~**lessly** *adv.* sans tact.

tactic /'tæktɪk/ *n.* tactique *f.* ~**s** *n. & n. pl.* tactique *f.* ~**al** *a.* tactique.

tactile /'tæktaɪl/ *a.* tactile.

tadpole /'tædpəʊl/ *n.* têtard *m.*

tag /tæg/ *n.* (*label*) étiquette *f.*; (*end piece*) bout *m.*; (*phrase*) cliché *m.* —*v.t.* (*p.t.* **tagged**) étiqueter; (*join*) ajouter. —*v.i.* ~ **along**, (*fam.*) suivre.

tail /teɪl/ *n.* queue *f.*; (*of shirt*) pan *m.* ~**s**, (*coat*) habit *m.* ~**s!**, (*tossing coin*) pile! —*v.t.* (*follow*) filer. —*v.i.* ~ **away** *or* **off**, diminuer. ~**back** *n.* (*traffic*) bouchon *m.* ~**end** *n.* fin *f.*, bout *m.* ~**gate** *n.* hayon arrière *m.*

tailcoat /'teɪlkəʊt/ *n.* habit *m.*

tailor /'teɪlə(r)/ *n.* tailleur *m.* —*v.t.* (*garment*) façonner; (*fig.*) adapter. ~**-made** *a.* fait sur mesure. ~**-made for**, (*fig.*) fait pour.

tainted /'teɪntɪd/ *a.* (*infected*) infecté; (*decayed*) gâté; (*fig.*) souillé.

take /teɪk/ *v.t./i.* (*p.t.* **took**, *p.p.* **taken**) prendre; (*carry*) (ap)porter (**to**, à); (*escort*) accompagner, amener; (*contain*) contenir; (*tolerate*) supporter; (*prize*) remporter; (*exam*) passer; (*choice*) faire; (*precedence*) avoir. ~ **sth. from s.o.**, prendre qch. à qn. ~ **sth. from a place**, prendre qch. d'un endroit. ~ **s.o. home**, ramener qn. chez lui. **be** ~**n by** *or* **with**, être impressionné par. **be** ~**n ill**, tomber malade. **it** ~**s time/courage/** *etc.* **to**, il faut du temps/du courage/ *etc.* pour. ~ **after**, ressembler à. ~ **apart**, démonter. ~ **away**, (*object*) emporter; (*person*) emmener; (*remove*) enlever (**from**, à). ~**away** *n.* (*meal*) plat à emporter

m.; (*shop*) restaurant qui fait de plats à emporter *m.* ~ **back**, reprendre; (*return*) rendre; (*accompany*) raccompagner; (*statement*) retirer. ~ **down**, (*object*) descendre; (*notes*) prendre. ~ **in**, (*object*) rentrer; (*include*) inclure; (*cheat*) tromper; (*grasp*) saisir. ~ **it that**, supposer que. ~ **off** *v.t.* enlever; (*mimic*) imiter; *v.i.* (*aviat.*) décoller. ~**off** *n.* imitation *f.*; (*aviat.*) décollage *m.* ~ **on**, (*task*, *staff*, *passenger*, *etc.*) prendre; (*challenger*) relever le défi de. ~ **out**, sortir; (*stain etc.*) enlever. ~ **over** *v.t.* (*factory*, *country*, *etc.*) prendre la direction de; (*firm: comm.*) racheter; *v.i.* (*of dictator*) prendre le pouvoir. ~ **over from**, (*relieve*) prendre la relève de; (*succeed*) prendre la succession de. ~**over** *n.* (*pol.*) prise de pouvoir *f.*; (*comm.*) rachat *m.* ~ **part**, participer (**in**, à). ~ **place**, avoir lieu. ~ **sides**, prendre parti (**with**, pour). ~ **to**, se prendre d'amitié pour; (*activity*) prendre goût à. ~ **to doing**, se mettre à faire. ~ **up**, (*object*) monter; (*hobby*) se mettre à; (*occupy*) prendre; (*resume*) reprendre. ~ **up with**, se lier avec.

takings /'teɪkɪŋz/ *n. pl.* recette *f.*

talcum /'tælkəm/ *n.* talc *m.* ~ **powder**, talc *m.*

tale /teɪl/ *n.* conte *m.*; (*report*) récit *m.*; (*lie*) histoire *f.*

talent /'tælənt/ *n.* talent *m.* ~**ed** *a.* doué, qui a du talent.

talk /tɔːk/ *v.t./i.* parler; (*say*) dire; (*chat*) bavarder. —*n.* conversation *f.*, entretien *m.*; (*words*) propos *m. pl.*; (*lecture*) exposé *m.* ~ **into doing**, persuader de faire. ~ **over**, discuter (de). ~-**show** *n.* talk-show *m.* ~**er** *n.* causeu|r, -se *m.*, *f.* ~**ing-to** *n.* (*fam.*) réprimande *f.*

talkative /'tɔːkətɪv/ a. bavard.

tall /tɔːl/ a. (-er, -est) (high) haut; (person) grand. ~ **story**, (fam.) histoire invraisemblable f.

tallboy /'tɔːlbɔɪ/ n. commode f.

tally /'tælɪ/ v.i. correspondre (**with**, à), s'accorder (**with**, avec).

tambourine /tæmbə'riːn/ n. tambourin m.

tame /teɪm/ a. (-er, -est) apprivoisé; (dull) insipide. —v.t. apprivoiser; (lion) dompter. ~**r** /-ə(r)/ n. dompteu|r, -se m., f.

tamper /'tæmpə(r)/ v.i. ~ **with**, toucher à, tripoter; (text) altérer.

tampon /'tæmpɒn/ n. (med.) tampon hygiénique m.

tan /tæn/ v.t./i. (p.t. tanned) bronzer; (hide) tanner. —n. bronzage m. —a. marron clair invar.

tandem /'tændəm/ n. (bicycle) tandem m. **in** ~, en tandem.

tang /tæŋ/ n. (taste) saveur forte f.; (smell) odeur forte f.

tangent /'tændʒənt/ n. tangente f.

tangerine /tændʒə'riːn/ n. mandarine f.

tangible /'tændʒəbl/ a. tangible.

tangle /'tæŋgl/ v.t. enchevêtrer. —n. enchevêtrement m. **become** ~**d**, s'enchevêtrer.

tango /'tæŋgəʊ/ n. (pl. -os) tango m.

tank /tæŋk/ n. réservoir m.; (vat) cuve f.; (for fish) aquarium m.; (mil.) char m., tank m.

tankard /'tæŋkəd/ n. chope f.

tanker /'tæŋkə(r)/ n. camion-citerne m.; (ship) pétrolier m.

tantaliz|e /'tæntəlaɪz/ v.t. tourmenter. ~**ing** a. tentant.

tantamount /'tæntəmaʊnt/ a. **be** ~ **to**, équivaloir à.

tantrum /'tæntrəm/ n. crise de colère or de rage f.

tap¹ /tæp/ n. (for water etc.) robinet m. —v.t. (p.t. tapped) (resources) exploiter; (telephone) mettre sur table d'écoute. **on** ~, (fam.) disponible.

tap² /tæp/ v.t./i. (p.t. tapped) frapper (doucement). —n. petit coup m. ~**-dance** n. claquettes f. pl.

tape /teɪp/ n. ruban m.; (sticky) ruban adhésif m. (magnetic) ~, bande (magnétique) f. —v.t. (tie) attacher; (record) coller; (record) enregistrer. ~-**measure** n. mètre (à) ruban m. ~-**recorder**, magnétophone m.

taper /'teɪpə(r)/ n. (for lighting) bougie f. —v.t./i. (s')effiler. ~ **off**, (diminish) diminuer. ~**ed**, ~**ing** adjs. (fingers etc.) effilé, fuselé; (trousers) étroit du bas.

tapestry /'tæpɪstrɪ/ n. tapisserie f.

tapioca /tæpɪ'əʊkə/ n. tapioca m.

tar /tɑː(r)/ n. goudron m. —v.t. (p.t. tarred) goudronner.

tardy /'tɑːdɪ/ a. (-ier, -iest) (slow) lent; (belated) tardif.

target /'tɑːgɪt/ n. cible f.; (objective) objectif m. —v.t. prendre pour cible.

tariff /'tærɪf/ n. (charges) tarif m.; (on imports) tarif douanier m.

Tarmac /'tɑːmæk/ n. (P.) macadam (goudronné) m.; (runway) piste f.

tarnish /'tɑːnɪʃ/ v.t./i. (se) ternir.

tarpaulin /tɑː'pɔːlɪn/ n. bâche goudronnée f.

tarragon /'tærəgən/ n. estragon m.

tart¹ /tɑːt/ a. (-er, -est) acide.

tart² /tɑːt/ n. tarte f.; (prostitute, sl.) poule f. —v.t. ~ **up**, (pej., sl.) embellir (sans le moindre goût).

tartan /'tɑːtn/ n. tartan m. —a. écossais.

tartar /'tɑːtə(r)/ n. tartre m. ~ **sauce**, sauce tartare f.

task /tɑːsk/ n. tâche f., travail m. **take to** ~, réprimander. ~ **force**, détachement spécial m.

tassel /'tæsl/ n. gland m., pompon m.

taste /teɪst/ n. goût m. —v.t. (eat,

enjoy) goûter; (_try_) goûter à; (_perceive taste of_) sentir le goût de. —_v.i._ ~ of or like, avoir un goût de. **have a** ~ **of**, (_experience_) goûter de. ~**less** _a._ sans goût; (_fig._) de mauvais goût.

tasteful /'teɪstfl/ _a._ de bon goût. ~**ly** _adv._ avec goût.

tasty /'teɪstɪ/ _a._ (**-ier**, **-iest**) délicieux, savoureux.

tat /tæt/ _see_ **tit²**.

tatter|s /'tætəz/ _n. pl._ lambeaux _m. pl._ ~**ed** /'tætəd/ _a._ en lambeaux.

tattoo¹ /tə'tuː/ _n._ (_mil._) spectacle militaire _m._

tattoo² /tə'tuː/ _v.t._ tatouer. —_n._ tatouage _m._

tatty /'tætɪ/ _a._ (**-ier**, **-iest**) (_shabby. fam._) miteux, minable.

taught /tɔːt/ _see_ **teach**.

taunt /tɔːnt/ _v.t._ railler. —_n._ raillerie _f._ ~**ing** _a._ railleur.

Taurus /'tɔːrəs/ _n._ le Taureau.

taut /tɔːt/ _a._ tendu.

tavern /'tævən/ _n._ taverne _f._

tawdry /'tɔːdrɪ/ _a._ (**-ier**, **-iest**) (_showy_) tape-à-l'œil _invar._

tax /tæks/ _n._ taxe _f._, impôt _m._; (_on income_) impôts _m. pl._ —_v.t._ imposer; (_put to test: fig._) mettre à l'épreuve. ~**able** _a._ imposable. ~**ation** /-'seɪʃn/ _n._ imposition _f._; (_taxes_) impôts _m. pl._ ~**-collector** _n._ percepteur _m._ ~**-deductible** _a._ déductible d'impôts. ~ **disc**, vignette _f._ ~**-free** _a._ exempt d'impôts. ~**ing** _a._ (_fig._) éprouvant. ~**-haven** paradis fiscal _m._ ~ **inspector**, inspecteur des impôts _m._ ~ **relief**, dégrèvement fiscal _m._ ~ **return**, déclaration d'impôts _f._

taxi /'tæksɪ/ _n._ (_pl._ **-is**) taxi _m._ —_v.i._ (_p.t._ **taxied**, _pres. p_ **taxiing**) (_aviat._) rouler au sol. ~**-cab** _n._ taxi _m._ ~ **rank**, ~ **stand**, station de taxi _f._

taxpayer /'tækspeɪə(r)/ _n._ contribuable _m./f._

tea /tiː/ _n._ thé _m._; (_snack_) goûter _m._ ~**-bag** _n._ sachet de thé _m._ ~**break** _n._ pause-thé _f._ ~**-leaf** _n._ feuille de thé _f._ ~**-set** _n._ service à thé _m._ ~**-shop** _n._ salon de thé _m._ ~**-towel** _n._ torchon _m._

teach /tiːtʃ/ _v.t._ (_p.t._ **taught**) apprendre (**s.o. sth.**, qch. à qn.); (_in school_) enseigner (**s.o. sth.**, qch. à qn.). —_v.i._ enseigner. ~**er** _n._ professeur _m._; (_primary_) instituteur, -trice _m., f._; (_member of teaching profession_) enseignant(e) _m. (f.)._ ~**ing** _n._ enseignement _m._; _a._ pédagogique; (_staff_) enseignant.

teacup /'tiːkʌp/ _n._ tasse à thé _f._

teak /tiːk/ _n._ (_wood_) teck _m._

team /tiːm/ _n._ équipe _f._; (_of animals_) attelage _m._ —_v.i._ ~ **up**, faire équipe (**with**, avec). ~**work** _n._ travail d'équipe _m._

teapot /'tiːpɒt/ _n._ théière _f._

tear¹ /teə(r)/ _v.t./i._ (_p.t._ **tore**, _p.p._ **torn**) (se) déchirer; (_snatch_) arracher (**from**, à); (_rush_) aller à toute vitesse. —_n._ déchirure _f._

tear² /tɪə(r)/ _n._ larme _f._ **in** ~**s**, en larmes. ~**-gas** _n._ gaz lacrymogène _m._

tearful /'tɪəfl/ _a._ (_voice_) larmoyant; (_person_) en larmes. ~**ly** _adv._ en pleurant, les larmes aux yeux.

tease /tiːz/ _v.t._ taquiner. —_n._ (_person: fam._) taquin(e) _m. (f.)._

teaspoon /'tiːspuːn/ _n._ petite cuiller _f._ ~**ful** _n._ (_pl._ **-fuls**) cuillerée à café _f._

teat /tiːt/ _n._ (_of bottle, animal_) tétine _f._

technical /'teknɪkl/ _a._ technique. ~**ity** /-'kælətɪ/ _n._ détail technique _m._ ~**ly** _adv._ techniquement.

technician /tek'nɪʃn/ _n._ technicien(ne) _m. (f.)._

technique /tek'niːk/ _n._ technique _f._

technolog|y /tek'nɒlədʒɪ/ n. technologie f. **~ical** /-ə'lɒdʒɪk/ a. technologique.

teddy /'tedɪ/ a. **~ bear**, ours en peluche m.

tedious /'tiːdɪəs/ a. fastidieux.

tedium /'tiːdɪəm/ n. ennui m.

tee /tiː/ n. (golf) tee m.

teem[1] /tiːm/ v.i. (swarm) grouiller (with, de).

teem[2] /tiːm/ v.i. **~ (with rain)**, pleuvoir à torrents.

teenage /'tiːneɪdʒ/ a. (d')adolescent. **~d** a. adolescent. **~r** /-ə(r)/ n. adolescent(e) m. (f.).

teens /tiːnz/ n. pl. **in one's ~**, adolescent.

teeny /'tiːnɪ/ a. (-ier, -iest) (tiny: fam.) minuscule.

teeter /'tiːtə(r)/ v.i. chanceler.

teeth /tiːθ/ see **tooth**.

teeth|e /tiːð/ v.i. faire ses dents. **~ing troubles**, (fig.) difficultés initiales f. pl.

teetotaller /tiː'təʊtlə(r)/ n. personne qui ne boit pas d'alcool f.

telecommunications /telɪkəmjuːnɪ'keɪʃnz/ n. pl. télécommunications f. pl.

telegram /'telɪɡræm/ n. télégramme m.

telegraph /'telɪɡrɑːf/ n. télégraphe m. —a. télégraphique. **~ic** /-'ɡræfɪk/ a. télégraphique.

telepath|y /tɪ'lepəθɪ/ n. télépathie f. **~ic** /telɪ'pæθɪk/ a. télépathique.

telephone /'telɪfəʊn/ n. téléphone m. —v.t. (person) téléphoner à; (message) téléphoner. —v.i. téléphoner. **~ book**, annuaire m. **~ box** n., **~ booth**, cabine téléphonique f. **~ call**, coup de téléphone m. **~ number**, numéro de téléphone m.

telephonist /tɪ'lefənɪst/ n. (in exchange) téléphoniste m./f.

telephoto /telɪ'fəʊtəʊ/ a. **~ lens**, téléobjectif m.

telescop|e /'telɪskəʊp/ n. télescope m. —v.t./i. (se) télescoper. **~ic** /-'skɒpɪk/ a. télescopique.

teletext /'telɪtekst/ n. télétexte m.

televise /'telɪvaɪz/ v.t. téléviser.

television /'telɪvɪʒn/ n. télévision f. **~ set**, poste de télévision m.

telex /'teleks/ n. télex m. —v.t. envoyer par télex.

tell /tel/ v.t. (p.t. **told**) dire (s.o. sth., qch. à qn.); (story) raconter; (distinguish) distinguer. —v.i. avoir un effet; (know) savoir. **~ of**, parler de. **~ off**, (fam.) gronder. **~tale** n. rapporteu|r, -se m. f.; a. révélateur. **~ tales**, rapporter.

teller /'telə(r)/ n. (in bank) caiss|ier, -ière m., f.

telling /'telɪŋ/ a. révélateur.

telly /'telɪ/ n. (fam.) télé f.

temerity /tɪ'merətɪ/ n. témérité f.

temp /temp/ n. (temporary employee: fam.) intérimaire m./f. —v.i. faire de l'intérim.

temper /'tempə(r)/ n. humeur f.; (anger) colère f. —v.t. (metal) tremper; (fig.) tempérer. **lose one's ~**, se mettre en colère.

temperament /'tempramənt/ n. tempérament m. **~al** /-'mentl/ a. capricieux; (innate) inné.

temperance /'tempərəns/ n. (in drinking) tempérance f.

temperate /'tempərət/ a. tempéré.

temperature /'temprətʃə(r)/ n. température f. **have a ~**, avoir (de) la fièvre or de la température.

tempest /'tempɪst/ n. tempête f.

tempestuous /tem'pestʃʊəs/ a. (meeting etc.) orageux.

template /'templ(e)ɪt/ n. patron m.

temple[1] /'templ/ n. temple m.

temple[2] /'templ/ n. (of head) tempe f.

tempo /'tempəʊ/ n. (pl. -os) tempo m.

temporal /'tempərəl/ a. temporel.

temporar|y /'tempǝrɪ/ a. temporaire, provisoire. **~ily** adv. temporairement, provisoirement.

tempt /tempt/ v.t. tenter. **~ s.o. to do**, donner envie à qn. de faire. **~ation** /-'teɪʃn/ n. tentation f. **~ing** a. tentant.

ten /ten/ a. & n. dix (m.).

tenable /'tenǝbl/ a. défendable.

tenac|ious /tɪ'neɪʃǝs/ a. tenace. **~ity** /-'æsɪtɪ/ n. ténacité f.

tenancy /'tenǝnsɪ/ n. location f.

tenant /'tenǝnt/ n. locataire m./f.

tend[1] /tend/ v.t. s'occuper de.

tend[2] /tend/ v.i. **~ to**, (be apt to) avoir tendance à.

tendency /'tendǝnsɪ/ n. tendance f.

tender[1] /'tendǝ(r)/ a. tendre; (sore, painful) sensible. **~ly** adv. tendrement. **~ness** n. tendresse f.

tender[2] /'tendǝ(r)/ v.t. offrir, donner. —v.i. faire une soumission. —n. (comm.) soumission f. **be legal ~**, (money) avoir cours. **put sth. out to ~**, faire un appel d'offres pour qch.

tendon /'tendǝn/ n. tendon m.

tenement /'tenǝmǝnt/ n. maison de rapport f., H.L.M. m./f.; (slum: Amer.) taudis m.

tenet /'tenɪt/ n. principe m.

tenner /'tenǝ(r)/ n. (fam.) billet de dix livres m.

tennis /'tenɪs/ n. tennis m. —a. de tennis. **~ shoes**, tennis m. pl.

tenor /'tenǝ(r)/ n. (meaning) sens général m.; (mus.) ténor m.

tense[1] /tens/ n. (gram.) temps m.

tense[2] /tens/ a. (-er, -est) tendu. —v.t. (muscles) tendre, raidir. —v.i. (of face) se crisper. **~ness** n. tension f.

tension /'tenʃn/ n. tension f.

tent /tent/ n. tente f.

tentacle /'tentǝkl/ n. tentacule m.

tentative /'tentǝtɪv/ a. provisoire; (hesitant) timide. **~ly** adv. provisoirement; timidement.

tenterhooks /'tentǝhʊks/ n. pl. **on ~**, sur des charbons ardents.

tenth /tenθ/ a. & n. dixième (m./f.).

tenuous /'tenjʊǝs/ a. ténu.

tenure /'tenjʊǝ(r)/ n. (in job, office) (période de) jouissance f. **have ~**, être titulaire.

tepid /'tepɪd/ a. tiède.

term /tɜːm/ n. (word, limit) terme m.; (of imprisonment) temps; (in school etc.) trimestre m.; (Amer.) semestre m. **~s**, conditions f. pl. —v.t. appeler, **on good/bad ~s**, en bons/mauvais termes. **in the short/long ~**, à court/long terme **come to ~s**, arriver à un accord. **come to ~s with sth.**, accepter qch. **~ of office**, (pol.) mandat m.

terminal /'tɜːmɪnl/ a. terminal, final; (med.) en phase terminale. —n. (oil, computer) terminal m.; (rail.) terminus m.; (electr.) borne f. (air) **~**, aérogare f.

terminat|e /'tɜːmɪneɪt/ v.t. mettre fin à. —v.i. prendre fin. **~ion** /-'neɪʃn/ n. fin f.

terminology /tɜːmɪ'nɒlǝdʒɪ/ n. terminologie f.

terminus /'tɜːmɪnǝs/ n. (pl. -ni /-naɪ/) (station) terminus m.

terrace /'terǝs/ n. terrasse f.; (houses) rangée de maisons contiguës f. **the ~s**, (sport) les gradins m. pl.

terracotta /terǝ'kɒtǝ/ n. terre cuite f.

terrain /te'reɪn/ n. terrain m.

terrib|le /'terǝbl/ a. affreux, atroce. **~y** adv. affreusement; (very) terriblement.

terrier /'terɪǝ(r)/ n. (dog) terrier m.

terrific /tǝ'rɪfɪk/ a. (fam.) terrible. **~ally** /-klɪ/ adv. (very: fam.) terriblement; (very well: fam.) terriblement bien.

terrify /'terɪfaɪ/ v.t. terrifier. **be ~ied of**, avoir très peur de.

territorial /terɪˈtɔːrɪəl/ *a.* territorial.

territory /ˈterɪtərɪ/ *n.* territoire *m.*

terror /ˈterə(r)/ *n.* terreur *f.*

terroris|t /ˈterərɪst/ *n.* terroriste *m./f.* **~m** /-zəm/ *n.* terrorisme *m.*

terrorize /ˈterəraɪz/ *v.t.* terroriser.

terse /tɜːs/ *a.* concis, laconique.

test /test/ *n.* examen *m.*, analyse *f.*; (*of goods*) contrôle *m.*; (*of machine etc.*) essai *m.*; (*in school*) interrogation *f.*; (*of strength etc.*: *fig.*) épreuve *f.* —*v.t.* examiner, analyser; (*check*) contrôler; (*try*) essayer; (*pupil*) donner une interrogation à; (*fig.*) éprouver. **driving ~**, (épreuve *f.* du) permis de conduire *m.* **~ match**, match international *m.* **~ pilot**, pilote d'essai *m.* **~-tube** *n.* éprouvette *f.*

testament /ˈtestəmənt/ *n.* testament *m.* **Old/New T~**, Ancien/Nouveau Testament *m.*

testicle /ˈtestɪkl/ *n.* testicule *m.*

testify /ˈtestɪfaɪ/ *v.t./i.* témoigner (**to**, de). **~ that**, témoigner que.

testimony /ˈtestɪmənɪ/ *n.* témoignage *m.*

testy /ˈtestɪ/ *a.* grincheux.

tetanus /ˈtetənəs/ *n.* tétanos *m.*

tetchy /ˈtetʃɪ/ *a.* grincheux.

tether /ˈteðə(r)/ *v.t.* attacher. —*n.* **at the end of one's ~**, à bout.

text /tekst/ *n.* texte *m.*

textbook /ˈtekstbʊk/ *n.* manuel *m.*

textile /ˈtekstaɪl/ *n. & a.* textile (*m.*).

texture /ˈtekstʃə(r)/ *n.* (*of paper etc.*) grain *m.*; (*of fabric*) texture *f.*

Thai /taɪ/ *a. & n.* thaïlandais(e) (*m.* (*f.*)). **~land** *n.* Thaïlande *f.*

Thames /temz/ *n.* Tamise *f.*

than /ðæn, *unstressed* ðən/ *conj.* que, qu'*. (*with numbers*) de. **more/less ~ ten**, plus/moins de dix.

thank /θæŋk/ *v.t.* remercier. **~s** *n.*

pl. remerciements *m. pl.* **~ you!**, merci! **~s!**, (*fam.*) merci! **~s to**, grâce à. **T~sgiving (Day)**, (*Amer.*) jour d'action de grâces *m.* (*fête nationale*).

thankful /ˈθæŋkfl/ *a.* reconnaissant (**for**, de). **~ly** *adv.* (*happily*) heureusement.

thankless /ˈθæŋklɪs/ *a.* ingrat.

that /ðæt, *unstressed* ðət/ *a. pl.* **those** ce *or* cet*, cette. those, ces. —*pron.* ce *or* c'*, cela, ça. **~ (one)**, celui-là, celle-là. **those (ones)**, ceux-là, celles-là. —*adv.* si, aussi. —*rel. pron.* (*subject*) qui; (*object*) que, qu'*. —*conj.* que, qu'*. **~ boy**, ce garçon *m.* **~ boy** (*with emphasis*) ce garçon-là. **~ is, c'est. ~ is (to say)**, c'est-à-dire. **after ~**, après ça *or* cela. **the day ~**, le jour où. **the man ~ married her**, l'homme qui l'a épousée. **the man ~ she married**, l'homme qu'elle a épousé. **the car ~ I came in**, la voiture dans laquelle je suis venu. **~ big**, grand comme ça. **~ many, ~ much**, tant que ça.

thatch /θætʃ/ *n.* chaume *m.* **~ed** *a.* en chaume. **~ed cottage**, chaumière *f.*

thaw /θɔː/ *v.t./i.* (faire) dégeler; (*snow*) (faire) fondre. —*n.* dégel *m.*

the /*before vowel* ðɪ, *before consonant* ðə, *stressed* ðiː/ *a.* le *or* l'*, la *or* l'*, *pl.* les *or* les. **~ day**, le *or* l'*, de la, *pl.* des. **to ~**, au, à l'*, à la, *pl.* aux. **~ third of June**, le trois juin.

theatre /ˈθɪətə(r)/ *n.* théâtre *m.*

theatrical /θɪˈætrɪkl/ *a.* théâtral.

theft /θeft/ *n.* vol *m.*

their /ðeə(r)/ *a.* leur, *pl.* leurs.

theirs /ðeəz/ *poss. pron.* le *or* la leur, *pl.* les leurs.

them /ðem, *unstressed* ðəm/ *pron.* les; (*after prep.*) eux, elles. (**to**) **~**, leur. **I know ~**, je les connais.

theme /θiːm/ n. thème m. ∼ **song**, (in film etc.) chanson principale f.

themselves /ðəm'selvz/ pron. eux-mêmes, elles-mêmes; (reflexive) se; (after prep.) eux, elles.

then /ðen/ adv. alors; (next) ensuite, puis; (therefore) alors, donc. —a. d'alors. **from ∼ on**, dès lors.

theology /θɪ'ɒlədʒɪ/ n. théologie f. ∼**ian** /θɪə'ləʊdʒən/ n. théologien(ne) m. (f.).

theorem /'θɪərəm/ n. théorème m.

theory /'θɪərɪ/ n. théorie f. ∼**etical** /-'retɪk/ a. théorique.

therapeutic /θerə'pjuːtɪk/ a. thérapeutique.

therapy /'θerəpɪ/ n. thérapie f.

there /ðeə(r)/ adv. là; (with verb) y; (over there) là-bas. —int. allez. he **goes** ∼, il y va. on va ∼, là-dessus. ∼ **is**, ∼ **are**, il y a; (pointing) voilà. ∼, ∼!, allons, allons! ∼**abouts** adv. par là. ∼**after** adv. par la suite. ∼**by** adv. de cette manière.

therefore /'ðeəfɔː(r)/ adv. donc.

thermal /'θɜːml/ a. thermique.

thermometer /θə'mɒmɪtə(r)/ n. thermomètre m.

thermonuclear /θɜːməʊ'njuːklɪə(r)/ a. thermonucléaire.

Thermos /'θɜːməs/ n. (P.) thermos m./f. invar. (P.)

thermostat /'θɜːməstæt/ n. thermostat m.

thesaurus /θɪ'sɔːrəs/ n. (pl. -ri /-raɪ/) dictionnaire de synonymes m.

these /ðiːz/ see **this**.

thesis /'θiːsɪs/ n. (pl. theses /-siːz/) thèse f.

they /ðeɪ/ pron. ils, elles; (emphatic) eux, elles; (people in general) on.

thick /θɪk/ a. (-er, -est) épais; (stupid) bête; (friends: fam.) très lié. —adv. = **thickly**. —n. in the ∼ **of**, au plus gros de. ∼**ly** adv.

(grow) dru; (spread) en couche épaisse. ∼**ness** n. épaisseur f. ∼-**skinned** a. peu sensible.

thicken /'θɪkən/ v.t./i. (s')épaissir.

thicket /'θɪkɪt/ n. trapu.

thief /θiːf/ n. (pl. thieves) voleu|r, -se m., f.

thigh /θaɪ/ n. cuisse f.

thimble /'θɪmbl/ n. dé (à coudre) m.

thin /θɪn/ a. (thinner, thinnest) mince; (person) maigre, mince; (sparse) clairsemé; (fine) fin. —adv. = **thinly**. —v.t./i. (p.t. thinned) (liquid) (s')éclaircir. ∼ **out**, (in quantity) (s')éclaircir. ∼**ly** adv. (slightly) légèrement. ∼**ner** n. diluant m. ∼**ness** n. minceur f.; maigreur f.

thing /θɪŋ/ n. chose f. ∼**s**, (belongings) affaires f. pl. **the best** ∼ **is to**, le mieux est de. **the (right)** ∼, ce qu'il faut (for s.o., à qn.).

think /θɪŋk/ v.t./i. (p.t. thought) penser (about, of, à); (carefully) réfléchir (about, of, à); (believe) croire. I ∼ **so**, je crois que oui. ∼ **better of it**, se raviser. ∼ **nothing of**, trouver naturel de. ∼ **of**, (hold opinion of) penser de. I'm ∼**ing of going**, je pense que j'irai peut-être. ∼ **over**, bien réfléchir à. ∼-**tank** n. comité d'experts m. ∼ **up**, inventer. ∼**er** n. penseu|r, -se m., f.

third /θɜːd/ a. troisième. —n. troisième m./f.; (fraction) tiers m. ∼**ly** adv. troisièmement. ∼-**rate** a. très inférieur. **T∼ World**, Tiers-Monde m.

thirst /θɜːst/ n. soif f. ∼**y** a. **be** ∼**y**, avoir soif. **make** ∼**y**, donner soif à.

thirteen /θɜː'tiːn/ a. & n. treize (m.). ∼**th** a. & n. treizième (m./f.).

thirt|y /'θɜːtɪ/ a. & n. trente (m.). ∼**ieth** a. & n. trentième (m./f.).

this /ðɪs/ a. (pl. these) ce or cet*,

cette. **these**, ces. —*pron.* ce or c'*, ceci. **~ (one)**, celui-ci, celle-ci. **these (ones)**, ceux-ci, celles-ci. **~ boy**, ce garçon; (*with emphasis*) ce garçon-ci. **~ is a mistake**, c'est une erreur. **~ is the book**, voici le livre. **~ is my son**, je vous présente mon fils. **~ is Anne speaking**, c'est Anne à l'appareil. **~**, après ceci.

thistle /'θɪsl/ *n.* chardon *m.*

thorn /θɔːn/ *n.* épine *f.* **~y** *a.* épineux.

thorough /'θʌrə/ *a.* consciencieux; (*deep*) profond; (*cleaning, washing*) à fond. **~ly** *adv.* (*clean, study, etc.*) à fond; (*very*) tout à fait.

thoroughbred /'θʌrəbred/ *n.* (*horse etc.*) pur-sang *m. invar.*

thoroughfare /'θʌrəfeə(r)/ *n.* grande artère *f.*

those /ðəʊz/ *see* **that**.

though /ðəʊ/ *conj.* bien que. —*adv.* (*fam.*) cependant.

thought /θɔːt/ *see* **think**. —*n.* pensée *f.*; (*idea*) idée *f.*

thoughtful /'θɔːtfl/ *a.* pensif; (*considerate*) attentionné. **~ly** *adv.* pensivement; avec considération.

thoughtless /'θɔːtlɪs/ *a.* étourdi. **~ly** *adv.* étourdiment.

thousand /'θaʊznd/ *a. & n.* mille (*m. invar.*). **~s of**, des milliers de.

thrash /θræʃ/ *v.t.* rosser; (*defeat*) écraser. **~ about**, se débattre. **~ out**, discuter à fond.

thread /θred/ *n.* (*yarn & fig.*) fil *m.*; (*of screw*) pas *m.* —*v.t.* enfiler. **~ one's way**, se faufiler.

threadbare /'θredbeə(r)/ *a.* râpé.

threat /θret/ *n.* menace *f.*

threaten /'θretn/ *v.t./i.* menacer (**with**, de). **~ingly** *adv.* d'un air menaçant.

three /θriː/ *a. & n.* trois (*m.*). **~-dimensional** *a.* en trois dimensions.

thresh /θreʃ/ *v.t.* (*corn etc.*) battre.

threshold /'θreʃəʊld/ *n.* seuil *m.*

threw /θruː/ *see* **throw**.

thrift /θrɪft/ *n.* économie *f.* **~y** *a.* économe.

thrill /θrɪl/ *n.* émotion *f.*, frisson *m.* —*v.t.* transporter (de joie). —*v.i.* frissonner (de joie). **be ~ed**, être ravi. **~ing** *a.* excitant.

thriller /'θrɪlə(r)/ *n.* livre or film à suspense *m.*

thriv|**e** /θraɪv/ *v.i.* (*p.t.* **thrived** or **throve**, *p.p.* **thrived** or **thriven**) prospérer. **he ~es on it**, cela lui réussit. **~ing** *a.* prospère.

throat /θrəʊt/ *n.* gorge *f.* **have a sore ~**, avoir mal à la gorge.

throb /θrɒb/ *v.i.* (*p.t.* **throbbed**) (*wound*) causer des élancements; (*heart*) palpiter; (*fig.*) vibrer. —*n.* (*pain*) élancement *m.*; palpitation *f.* **~bing** *a.* (*pain*) lancinant.

throes /θrəʊz/ *n. pl.* **in the ~ of**, au milieu de, aux prises avec.

thrombosis /θrɒm'bəʊsɪs/ *n.* thrombose *f.*

throne /θrəʊn/ *n.* trône *m.*

throng /θrɒŋ/ *n.* foule *f.* —*v.t.* (*streets etc.*) se presser dans. —*v.i.* (*arrive*) affluer.

throttle /'θrɒtl/ *n.* (*auto.*) accélérateur *m.* —*v.t.* étrangler.

through /θruː/ *prep.* à travers; (*during*) pendant; (*by means or way of, out of*) par; (*by reason of*) grâce à, à cause de. —*adv.* à travers; (*entirely*) jusqu'au bout. —*a.* (*train etc.*) direct. **be ~**, (*finished*) avoir fini. **come or go ~**, (*cross, pierce*) traverser. **I'm putting you ~**, je vous passe votre correspondant.

throughout /θruː'aʊt/ *prep.* **~ the country**/*etc.*, dans tout le pays/*etc.* **~ the day**/*etc.*, pendant toute la journée/*etc.* —*adv.* (*place*) partout; (*time*) tout le temps.

throw /θrəʊ/ v.t. (p.t. threw, p.p. thrown) jeter, lancer; (baffle: fam.) déconcerter. — n. jet m.; (of dice) coup m. ~ **a party,** (fam.) faire une fête. ~ **away,** jeter. ~ **away** a. à jeter. ~ **off,** (get rid of) se débarrasser de. ~ **out,** jeter; (person) expulser; (reject) rejeter. ~ **over,** (desert) plaquer. ~ **up,** (one's arms) lever; (resign from) abandonner; (vomit: fam.) vomir.

thru /θruː/ prep., adv. & a. (Amer.) = **through.**

thrush /θrʌʃ/ n. (bird) grive f.

thrust /θrʌst/ v.t. (p.t. thrust) pousser. — n. poussée f. ~ **into,** (put) enforcer dans, mettre dans. ~ **upon,** (force on) imposer à.

thud /θʌd/ n. bruit sourd m.

thug /θʌg/ n. voyou m., bandit m.

thumb /θʌm/ n. pouce m. — v.t. (book) feuilleter. ~ **a lift,** faire de l'auto-stop. ~**-index,** répertoire à onglets m.

thumbtack /ˈθʌmtæk/ n. (Amer.) punaise f.

thump /θʌmp/ v.t./i. cogner (sur); (of heart) battre fort. — n. grand coup m. ~**ing** a. (fam.) énorme.

thunder /ˈθʌndə(r)/ n. tonnerre m. — v.i. (weather, person, etc.) tonner. ~ **past,** passer dans un bruit de tonnerre. ~**y** a. orageux.

thunderbolt /ˈθʌndəbəʊlt/ n. coup de foudre m.; (event: fig.) coup de tonnerre m.

thunderstorm /ˈθʌndəstɔːm/ n. orage m.

Thursday /ˈθɜːzdɪ/ n. jeudi m.

thus /ðʌs/ adv. ainsi.

thwart /θwɔːt/ v.t. contrecarrer.

thyme /taɪm/ n. thym m.

thyroid /ˈθaɪrɔɪd/ n. thyroïde f.

tiara /tɪˈɑːrə/ n. diadème m.

tic /tɪk/ n. tic (nerveux) m.

tick[1] /tɪk/ n. (sound) tic-tac m.; (mark) coche f.; (moment: fam.) instant m. — v.i. faire tic-tac.

— v.t. ~ **(off),** cocher. ~ **off,** (fam.) réprimander. ~ **over,** (engine, factory) tourner au ralenti.

tick[2] /tɪk/ n. (insect) tique f.

ticket /ˈtɪkɪt/ n. billet m.; (for bus, cloakroom, etc.) ticket m.; (label) étiquette f. ~**-collector** n. contrôleu|r, -se m., f. ~**-office** n. guichet m.

tickle /ˈtɪkl/ v.t. chatouiller; (amuse: fig.) amuser. — n. chatouillement m.

ticklish /ˈtɪklɪʃ/ a. chatouilleux.

tidal /ˈtaɪdl/ a. qui a des marées. ~ **wave,** raz-de-marée m. invar.

tiddly-winks /ˈtɪdlɪwɪŋks/ n. (game) jeu de puce m.

tide /taɪd/ n. marée f.; (of events) cours m. — v.t. ~ **over,** dépanner.

tidings /ˈtaɪdɪŋz/ n. pl. nouvelles f. pl.

tid|y /ˈtaɪdɪ/ a. (-ier, -iest) (room) bien rangé; (appearance, work) soigné; (methodical) ordonné; (amount: fam.) joli. — v.t./i. ranger. ~**y o.s.,** s'arranger. ~**ily** adv. avec soin. ~**iness** n. ordre m.

tie /taɪ/ v.t. (pres. p. **tying**) attacher, nouer; (a knot) faire; (link) lier.—v.i. (darts etc.) finir à égalité de points; (football) faire match nul; (in race) être ex aequo. — n. attache f.; (necktie) cravate f.; (link) lien m.; égalité (de points) f.; match nul m. ~ **down,** attacher; (job) bloquer. ~ **s.o. down to,** (date) forcer qn. à respecter. ~ **in with,** être lié à. ~ **up,** attacher; (money) immobiliser; (occupy) occuper. ~ **up in** (link) lien m.; (auto., Amer.) bouchon m.

tier /tɪə(r)/ n. étage m., niveau m.; (in stadium etc.) gradin m.

tiff /tɪf/ n. petite querelle f.

tiger /ˈtaɪgə(r)/ n. tigre m.

tight /taɪt/ a. (-er, -est) (clothes) étroit, juste; (rope) tendu; (lid) solidement fixé; (control) strict; (knot, collar, schedule) serré; (drunk: fam.) ivre. —adv. (hold, sleep, etc.) bien; (squeeze) fort. **~ corner,** situation difficile f. **~-fisted** a. avare. **~ly** adv. bien; (squeeze) fort.

tighten /'taɪtn/ v.t./i. (se) tendre; (bolt etc.) (se) resserrer; (control etc.) renforcer. **~ up on,** se montrer plus strict à l'égard de.

tightrope /'taɪtrəʊp/ n. corde raide f. **~ walker,** funambule m./f.

tights /taɪts/ n. pl. collant m.

tile /taɪl/ n. (on wall, floor) carreau m.; (on roof) tuile f. —v.t. carreler; couvrir de tuiles.

till¹ /tɪl/ v.t. (land) cultiver.

till² /tɪl/ prep. & conj. = **until**.

till³ /tɪl/ n. caisse (enregistreuse) f.

tilt /tɪlt/ v.t./i. pencher. —n. (slope) inclinaison f. **(at) full ~,** à toute vitesse.

timber /'tɪmbə(r)/ n. bois (de construction) m.; (trees) arbres m. pl.

time /taɪm/ n. temps m.; (moment) moment m.; (epoch) époque f.; (by clock) heure f.; (occasion) fois f.; (rhythm) mesure f. **~s,** (multiplying) fois f. pl. —v.t. choisir le moment de; (measure) minuter; (sport) chronométrer. **any ~,** n'importe quand. **behind the ~s,** en retard sur son temps. **for the ~ being,** pour le moment. **from ~ to time,** de temps en temps. **have a good ~,** s'amuser. **in no ~,** à temps; (eventually) avec le temps. **a long ~,** longtemps. **on ~,** à l'heure. **what's the ~?,** quelle heure est-il? **~ bomb,** bombe à retardement f. **~-honoured** a. consacré (par l'usage). **~-lag** n. décalage m. **~-limit** n. délai m. **~-scale** n. délais fixés m. pl. **~ off,** du temps libre. **~ zone,** fuseau horaire m.

timeless /'taɪmlɪs/ a. éternel.

timely /'taɪmlɪ/ a. à propos.

timer /'taɪmə(r)/ n. (for cooker etc.) minuteur m.; (on video) programmateur; (culin.) compte-minutes m. invar.; (with sand) sablier m.

timetable /'taɪmteɪbl/ n. horaire m.

timid /'tɪmɪd/ a. timide; (fearful) peureux. **~ly** adv. timidement.

timing /'taɪmɪŋ/ n. (measuring) minutage m.; (moment) moment m.; (of artist) rythme m.

tin /tɪn/ n. étain m.; (container) boîte f. **~(plate),** fer-blanc m. —v.t. (p.t. **tinned**) mettre en boîte. **~ foil,** papier d'aluminium m. **~ny** a. métallique. **~-opener** n. ouvre-boîte(s) m.

tinge /tɪndʒ/ v.t. teinter (**with,** de). —n. teinte f.

tingle /'tɪŋgl/ v.i. (prickle) picoter. —n. picotement m.

tinker /'tɪŋkə(r)/ n. rétameur m. —v.i. **~ (with),** bricoler.

tinkle /'tɪŋkl/ n. tintement m.; (fam.) coup de téléphone m.

tinsel /'tɪnsl/ n. cheveux d'ange m. pl., guirlandes de Noël f. pl.

tint /tɪnt/ n. teinte f.; (for hair) shampooing colorant m. —v.t. (glass, paper) teinter.

tiny /'taɪnɪ/ a. (-ier, -iest) minuscule, tout petit.

tip¹ /tɪp/ n. bout m.; (cover) embout m. **~ped cigarette,** cigarette (à bout) filtre f.

tip² /tɪp/ v.t./i. (p.t. **tipped**) (tilt) pencher; (overturn) (faire) basculer; (pour) verser; (empty) déverser; (give money) donner un pourboire à. —n. (money) pourboire m.; (advice) tuyau m.; (for rubbish) décharge f. **~ off,**

prévenir. **~-off** n. tuyau m. (pour prévenir).

tipsy /'tɪpsɪ/ a. un peu ivre, gris.

tiptoe /'tɪptəʊ/ n. **on ~,** sur la pointe des pieds.

tiptop /'tɪptɒp/ a. (fam.) excellent. **~e of,** se lasser de. **~eless** a. infatigable. **~ing** a. fatigant.

tire¹ /'taɪə(r)/ v.t./i. (se) fatiguer.

tire² /'taɪə(r)/ n. (Amer.) pneu m.

tired /'taɪəd/ a. fatigué. **be ~ of,** en avoir assez de.

tiresome /'taɪəsəm/ a. ennuyeux.

tissue /'tɪʃuː/ n. tissu m.; (handkerchief) mouchoir en papier m. **~-paper** n. papier de soie m.

tit¹ /tɪt/ n. (bird) mésange f.

tit² /tɪt/ n. **give ~ for tat,** rendre coup pour coup.

titbit /'tɪtbɪt/ n. friandise f.

titillate /'tɪtɪleɪt/ v.t. exciter.

title /'taɪtl/ n. titre m. **~-deed** n. titre de propriété m. **~-role** n. rôle principal m.

titter /'tɪtə(r)/ v.i. rigoler.

titular /'tɪtjʊlə(r)/ a. (ruler etc.) nominal.

to /tuː, unstressed tə/ prep. à; (towards) vers; (of attitude) envers. —adv. **push** or **pull to,** (close) fermer. **to France**/etc., en France/etc. **to town,** en ville. **to Canada**/etc., au Canada/etc. **to the baker's**/etc., chez le boulanger/etc. **the road/door/** etc. **to,** la route/porte/etc. de. **to me/her**/etc., me/lui/etc. **to do/** **sit**/etc., faire/s'asseoir/etc. **I wrote to tell her,** j'ai écrit pour lui dire. **I tried to help you,** j'ai essayé de t'aider. **ten to six,** (by clock) six heures moins dix. **go to and fro,** aller et venir. **husband**/etc. **-to-be** n. futur mari/ etc. m.

toad /təʊd/ n. crapaud m.

toadstool /'təʊdstuːl/ n. champignon (vénéneux) m.

toast /təʊst/ n. pain grillé m., toast m.; (drink) toast m. —v.t. (bread) faire griller; (drink to) porter un toast à; (event) arroser. **~er** n. grille-pain m. invar.

tobacco /tə'bækəʊ/ n. tabac m.

tobacconist /tə'bækənɪst/ n. marchand(e) de tabac m. (f.). **~'s shop,** tabac m.

toboggan /tə'bɒgən/ n. toboggan m., luge f.

today /tə'deɪ/ n. & adv. aujourd'hui m.

toddler /'tɒdlə(r)/ n. tout(e) petit(e) enfant m./f.

toddy /'tɒdɪ/ n. (drink) grog m.

toe /təʊ/ n. orteil m.; (of shoe) bout m. —v.t. **~ the line,** se conformer. **on one's ~s,** vigilant. **~hold** n. prise (précaire) f.

toffee /'tɒfɪ/ n. caramel m. **~ apple** n. pomme caramélisée f.

together /tə'geðə(r)/ adv. ensemble; (at same time) en même temps. **~ with,** avec. **~ness** n. camaraderie f.

toil /tɔɪl/ v.i. peiner. —n. labeur m.

toilet /'tɔɪlɪt/ n. toilettes f. pl.; (grooming) toilette f. **~-paper** n. papier hygiénique m. **~-roll** n. rouleau de papier hygiénique m. **~ water,** eau de toilette f.

toiletries /'tɔɪlɪtrɪz/ n. pl. articles de toilette m. pl.

token /'təʊkən/ n. témoignage m., marque f.; (voucher) bon m.; (coin) jeton m. —a. symbolique.

told /təʊld/ see **tell.** —a. **all ~,** (all in all) en tout.

tolerab|le /'tɒlərəbl/ a. tolérable; (not bad) passable. **~y** adv. (work, play, etc.) passablement.

toleran|t /'tɒlərənt/ a. tolérant (of, à l'égard de). **~ce** n. tolérance f. **~tly** adv. avec tolérance.

tolerate /'tɒləreɪt/ v.t. tolérer.

toll¹ /təʊl/ n. péage m. **death ~,** nombre de morts m. **take its ~,** (of age) faire sentir son poids.

toll² /təʊl/ v.i. (of bell) sonner.

tom /tɒm/, ~**-cat** *ns.* matou *m.*

tomato /təˈmɑːtəʊ, *Amer.* təˈmeɪtəʊ/ *n.* (*pl.* -oes) tomate *f.*

tomb /tuːm/ *n.* tombeau *m.*

tombola /tɒmˈbəʊlə/ *n.* tombola *f.*

tomboy /ˈtɒmbɔɪ/ *n.* garçon manqué *m.*

tombstone /ˈtuːmstəʊn/ *n.* pierre tombale *f.*

tomfoolery /tɒmˈfuːlərɪ/ *n.* âneries *f. pl.*, bêtises *f. pl.*

tomorrow /təˈmɒrəʊ/ *n. & adv.* demain (*m.*). ~ **morning/night,** demain matin/soir. **the day after** ~, après-demain.

ton /tʌn/ *n.* tonne *f.* (= 1016 kg). (**metric**) ~, tonne *f.* (= 1000 kg.). ~**s of,** (*fam.*) des masses de.

tone /təʊn/ *n.* ton *m.*; (*of radio, telephone, etc.*) tonalité *f.* —*v.t.* ~ **down,** atténuer. —*v.i.* ~ **in,** s'harmoniser (**with,** avec). ~-**deaf** *a.* qui n'a pas d'oreille. ~ **up,** (*muscles*) tonifier.

tongs /tɒŋz/ *n. pl.* pinces *f. pl.*; (*for sugar*) pince *f.*; (*for hair*) fer *m.*

tongue /tʌŋ/ *n.* langue *f.* ~-**tied** *a.* muet. ~-**twister** *n.* phrase difficile à prononcer *f.* **with one's** ~ **in one's cheek,** ironiquement.

tonic /ˈtɒnɪk/ *n.* (*med.*) tonique *m.* —*a.* (*effect, accent*) tonique. ~ (**water**), tonic *m.*

tonight /təˈnaɪt/ *n. & adv.* cette nuit (*f.*); (*evening*) ce soir (*m.*).

tonne /tʌn/ *n.* (*metric*) tonne *f.*

tonsil /ˈtɒnsl/ *n.* amygdale *f.*

tonsillitis /tɒnsɪˈlaɪtɪs/ *n.* amygdalite *f.*

too /tuː/ *adv.* trop; (*also*) aussi. ~ **many** *a.* trop de; *n.* trop. ~ **much** *a.* trop de; *adv. & n.* trop.

took /tʊk/ *see* take.

tool /tuːl/ *n.* outil *m.* ~-**bag** *n.* trousse à outils *f.*

toot /tuːt/ *n.* coup de klaxon *m.* —*v.t./i.* ~ (**the horn**), klaxonner.

tooth /tuːθ/ *n.* (*pl.* teeth) dent *f.* ~**less** *a.* édenté.

toothache /ˈtuːθeɪk/ *n.* mal de dents *m.*

toothbrush /ˈtuːθbrʌʃ/ *n.* brosse à dents *f.*

toothcomb /ˈtuːθkəʊm/ *n.* peigne fin *m.*

toothpaste /ˈtuːθpeɪst/ *n.* dentifrice *m.*, pâte dentifrice *f.*

toothpick /ˈtuːθpɪk/ *n.* cure-dent *m.*

top[1] /tɒp/ *n.* (*highest point*) sommet *m.*; (*upper part*) haut *m.*; (*upper surface*) dessus *m.*; (*lid*) couvercle *m.*; (*of bottle, tube*) bouchon *m.*; (*of beer bottle*) capsule *f.*; (*of list*) tête *f.* —*a.* (*shelf etc.*) du haut; (*floor*) dernier; (*in rank*) premier; (*best*) meilleur; (*distinguished*) éminent; (*maximum*) maximum. —*v.t.* (*p.t.* topped) (*exceed*) dépasser; (*list*) venir en tête de. **from** ~ **to bottom,** de fond en comble. **on** ~ **of,** sur; (*fig.*) en plus de. ~ **hat,** haut-de-forme *m.* ~-**heavy** *a.* trop lourd du haut. ~-**level** *a.* du plus haut niveau. ~-**notch** *a.* excellent. ~-**quality** *a.* de la plus haute qualité. ~ **secret,** ultra-secret. ~ **up,** remplir. ~**ped with,** surmonté de; (*cream etc.*: *culin.*) nappé de.

top[2] /tɒp/ *n.* (*toy*) toupie *f.*

topic /ˈtɒpɪk/ *n.* sujet *m.*

topical /ˈtɒpɪkl/ *a.* d'actualité.

topless /ˈtɒplɪs/ *a.* aux seins nus.

topple /ˈtɒpl/ *v.t./i.* (faire) tomber, (faire) basculer.

topsy-turvy /tɒpsɪˈtɜːvɪ/ *adv. & a.* sens dessus dessous.

torch /tɔːtʃ/ *n.* (*electric*) lampe de poche *f.*; (*flaming*) torche *f.*

tore /tɔː(r)/ *see* tear[1].

torment[1] /ˈtɔːment/ *n.* tourment *m.*

torment[2] /tɔːˈment/ *v.t.* tourmenter; (*annoy*) agacer.

torn /tɔːn/ *see* **tear**[1].

tornado /tɔːˈneɪdəʊ/ *n.* (*pl.* **-oes**) tornade *f.*

torpedo /tɔːˈpiːdəʊ/ *n.* (*pl.* **-oes**) torpille *f.* —*v.t.* torpiller.

torrent /ˈtɒrənt/ *n.* torrent *m.* ~**ial** /təˈrenʃl/ *a.* torrentiel.

torrid /ˈtɒrɪd/ *a.* (*climate etc.*) torride; (*fig.*) passionné.

torso /ˈtɔːsəʊ/ *n.* (*pl.* **-os**) torse *m.*

tortoise /ˈtɔːtəs/ *n.* tortue *f.*

tortoiseshell /ˈtɔːtəsʃel/ *n.* (*for ornaments etc.*) écaille *f.*

tortuous /ˈtɔːtʃʊəs/ *a.* tortueux.

torture /ˈtɔːtʃə(r)/ *n.* torture *f.*, supplice *m.* —*v.t.* torturer. ~**r** /-ə(r)/ *n.* tortionnaire *m.*

Tory /ˈtɔːrɪ/ *n.* tory *m.* —*a.* tory (*f. invar.*).

toss /tɒs/ *v.t.* jeter, lancer; (*shake*) agiter. —*v.i.* s'agiter. ~ **up**, tirer à pile ou face (*for*, pour).

tot[1] /tɒt/ *n.* petit(e) enfant *m.(f.)*; (*glass: fam.*) petit verre *m.*

tot[2] /tɒt/ *v.t.* (*p.t.* **totted**) ~ **up**, (*fam.*) additionner.

total /ˈtəʊtl/ *a.* total. —*n.* total *m.* —*v.t.* (*p.t.* **totalled**) (*find total of*) totaliser; (*amount to*) s'élever à. ~**ity** /-ˈtælətɪ/ *n.* totalité *f.* ~**ly** *adv.* totalement.

totalitarian /ˌtəʊtælɪˈteərɪən/ *a.* totalitaire.

totter /ˈtɒtə(r)/ *v.i.* chanceler.

touch /tʌtʃ/ *v.t./i.* toucher; (*of ends, gardens, etc.*) se toucher; (*tamper with*) toucher à. —*n.* (*sense*) toucher *m.*; (*contact*) contact *m.*; (*of colour*) touche *f.*; (*football*) touche *f.* **a** ~ **of**, (*small amount*) un peu de. **get in** ~ **with**, contacter. **lose** ~, perdre contact. **be out of** ~, n'être plus dans le coup. ~ **down**, (*aviat.*) atterrir. ~**line** *n.* (ligne de) touche *f.* ~ **off**, (*explode*) faire partir; (*cause*) déclencher. ~ **on**,

(*mention*) aborder. ~ **up**, retoucher.

touchdown /ˈtʌtʃdaʊn/ *n.* atterrissage *m.*; (*sport, Amer.*) but *m.*

touching /ˈtʌtʃɪŋ/ *a.* touchant.

touchstone /ˈtʌtʃstəʊn/ *n.* pierre de touche *f.*

touchy /ˈtʌtʃɪ/ *a.* susceptible.

tough /tʌf/ *a.* (**-er**, **-est**) (*hard, difficult*) dur; (*strong*) solide; (*relentless*) acharné. —*n.* ~ (*guy*), dur *m.* ~ **luck!**, (*fam.*) tant pis! ~**ness** *n.* dureté *f.*; solidité *f.*

toughen /ˈtʌfn/ *v.t.* (*strengthen*) renforcer; (*person*) endurcir.

toupee /ˈtuːpeɪ/ *n.* postiche *m.*

tour /tʊə(r)/ *n.* voyage *m.*; (*visit*) visite *f.*; (*by team etc.*) tournée *f.* —*v.t.* visiter. **on** ~, en tournée. ~ **operator**, voyagiste *m.*

tourism /ˈtʊərɪzəm/ *n.* tourisme *m.*

tourist /ˈtʊərɪst/ *n.* touriste *m./f.* —*a.* touristique. ~ **office**, syndicat d'initiative *m.*

tournament /ˈtɔːnəmənt/ *n.* (*sport & medieval*) tournoi *m.*

tousle /ˈtaʊzl/ *v.t.* ébouriffer.

tout /taʊt/ *v.i.* ~ (**for**), racoler. —*v.t.* (*sell*) revendre. —*n.* racoleu|r, -se *m.*, *f.*; revendeu|r, -se *m.*, *f.*

tow /təʊ/ *v.t.* remorquer. —*n.* remorque *f.* **on** ~, en remorque. ~ **away**, (*vehicle*) (faire) enlever. ~**path** *n.* chemin de halage *m.* ~ **truck**, dépanneuse *f.*

toward(s) /təˈwɔːd(z), *Amer.* tɔːd(z)/ *prep.* vers; (*of attitude*) envers.

towel /ˈtaʊəl/ *n.* serviette *f.*; (*teatowel*) torchon *m.* ~**ling** *n.* tissu-éponge *m.*

tower /ˈtaʊə(r)/ *n.* tour *f.* —*v.i.* ~ **above**, dominer. ~ **block**, tour *f.*, immeuble *m.* ~**ing** *a.* très haut.

town /taʊn/ *n.* ville *f.* **go to** ~, (*fam.*) mettre le paquet. ~

council, conseil municipal *m.* ~
hall, hôtel de ville *m.*
toxic /'tɒksɪk/ *a.* toxique.
toxin /'tɒksɪn/ *n.* toxine *f.*
toy /tɔɪ/ *n.* jouet *m.* —*v.i.* ~ **with**,
(*object*) jouer avec; (*idea*)
caresser.
toyshop /'tɔɪʃɒp/ *n.* magasin de
jouets *m.*

trace /treɪs/ *n.* trace *f.* —*v.t.* suivre
or retrouver la trace de; (*draw*)
tracer; (*with tracing-paper*) décalquer; (*relate*) retracer.
tracing /'treɪsɪŋ/ *n.* calque *m.* ~
paper *n.* papier-calque *m. invar.*
track /træk/ *n.* (*of person etc.*) trace
f., piste *f.*; (*path, race-track & of
tape*) piste *f.*; (*on disc*) plage *f.*; (*of
rocket etc.*) trajectoire *f.*; (*rail.*)
voie *f.* —*v.t.* suivre la trace *or* la
trajectoire de. **keep** ~ **of**, suivre.
~ **down**, (*find*) retrouver; (*hunt*)
traquer. ~ **suit**, survêtement *m.*;
(*with sweatshirt*) jogging *m.*
tract[1] /trækt/ *n.* (*land*) étendue *f.*;
(*anat.*) appareil *m.*
tract[2] /trækt/ *n.* (*pamphlet*) tract
m.
tractor /'træktə(r)/ *n.* tracteur *m.*
trade /treɪd/ *n.* commerce *m.*; (*job*)
métier *m.*; (*swap*) échange *m.*
—*v.i.* faire du commerce. —*v.t.*
échanger. ~ **deficit**, déficit commercial *m.* ~ **in**, (*used article*)
faire reprendre. ~**-in** *n.* reprise *f.*
~ **mark**, marque de fabrique *f.*
(*name*) marque déposée *f.* ~**-off**
n. (*fam.*) compromis *m.* ~ **on**,
(*exploit*) abuser de. ~ **union**,
syndicat *m.* ~**-unionist** *n.* syn-
dicaliste *m./f.* ~**r** /-ə(r)/ *n.*
négociant(e) *m.* (*f.*), commer-
çant(e) *m.* (*f.*).
tradesman /'treɪdzmən/ *n.* (*pl.*
-men) commerçant *m.*
trading /'treɪdɪŋ/ *n.* commerce *m.*
~ **estate**, zone industrielle *f.*
tradition /trə'dɪʃn/ *n.* tradition *f.*
~**al** *a.* traditionnel.

traffic /'træfɪk/ *n.* trafic *m.*; (*on
road*) circulation *f.* —*v.i.* (*p.t.*
trafficked) trafiquer (**in**, de). ~
circle, (*Amer.*) rond-point *m.* ~
cone, cône de délimitation de
voie *m.* ~ **jam**, embouteillage *m.*
~**-lights** *n. pl.* feux (de circulation) *m. pl.* ~ **warden**, contrac-
tuel(le) *m.* (*f.*).
tragedy /'trædʒədɪ/ *n.* tragédie *f.*
tragic /'trædʒɪk/ *a.* tragique.
trail /treɪl/ *v.t./i.* traîner; (*of plant*)
ramper; (*track*) suivre. —*n.* (*of
powder etc.*) traînée *f.*; (*track*)
piste *f.*; (*beaten path*) sentier *m.*
~ **behind**, traîner.
trailer /'treɪlə(r)/ *n.* remorque *f.*;
(*caravan: Amer.*) caravane *f.*;
(*film*) bande-annonce *f.*
train /treɪn/ *n.* (*rail.*) train *m.*;
(*underground*) rame *f.*; (*procession*) file *f.*; (*of dress*) traîne *f.*
—*v.t.* (*instruct, develop*) former;
(*sportsman*) entraîner; (*animal*)
dresser; (*ear*) exercer; (*aim*)
braquer. —*v.i.* recevoir une formation; s'entraîner. ~**ed** *a.*
(*skilled*) qualifié; (*doctor etc.*)
diplômé. ~**er** *n.* (*sport*) entraîneur *m.*, -se *m.*, *f.* ~**ers**, (*shoes*)
chaussures de sport *f. pl.* ~**ing** *n.*
formation *f.*; entraînement *m.*;
dressage *m.*
trainee /treɪ'niː/ *n.* stagiaire *m./
f.*
traipse /treɪps/ *v.i.* (*fam.*) traîner.
trait /treɪ(t)/ *n.* trait *m.*
traitor /'treɪtə(r)/ *n.* traître *m.*
tram /træm/ *n.* tram(way) *m.*
tramp /træmp/ *v.i.* marcher (d'un
pas lourd). —*v.t.* parcourir. —*n.*
pas lourds *m. pl.*; (*vagrant*)
clochard(e) *m.* (*f.*); (*Amer., sl.*)
dévergondée *f.*; (*hike*) randonnée
f.
trample /'træmpl/ *v.t./i.* ~ (**on**),
piétiner; (*fig.*) fouler aux pieds.
trampoline /'træmpəliːn/ *n.* (*canvas sheet*) trampoline *m.*

trance /trɑːns/ n. transe f.

tranquil /'træŋkwɪl/ a. tranquille. **~lity** /-'kwɪlətɪ/ n. tranquillité f.

tranquillizer /'træŋkwɪlaɪzə(r)/ n. (drug) tranquillisant m.

transact /træn'zækt/ v.t. traiter. **~ion** /-kʃn/ n. transaction f.

transatlantic /trænzət'læntɪk/ a. transatlantique.

transcend /træn'send/ v.t. transcender. **~ent** a. transcendant.

transcript /'trænskrɪpt/ n. (written copy) transcription f.

transfer[1] /træns'fɜː(r)/ v.t. (p.t. **transferred**) transférer; (power) faire passer. —v.i. être transféré. **~ the charges**, (telephone) téléphoner en PCV.

transfer[2] /'trænsfɜː(r)/ n. transfert m.; (of power) passation f.; (image) décalcomanie f.; (sticker) autocollant m.

transform /træns'fɔːm/ v.t. transformer. **~ation** /-ə'meɪʃn/ n. transformation f. **~er** n. (electr.) transformateur m.

transfusion /træns'fjuːʒn/ n. (of blood) transfusion f.

transient /'trænzɪənt/ a. transitoire, éphémère.

transistor /træn'zɪstə(r)/ n. (device, radio set) transistor m.

transit /'trænsɪt/ n. transit m.

transition /træn'zɪʃn/ n. transition f. **~al** a. transitoire.

transitive /'trænsɪtɪv/ a. transitif.

transitory /'trænsɪtərɪ/ a. transitoire.

translat|**e** /trænz'leɪt/ v.t. traduire. **~ion** /-ʃn/ n. traduction f. **~or** n. traducteur, -trice m., f.

translucent /trænz'luːsnt/ a. translucide.

transmi|**t** /trænz'mɪt/ v.t. (p.t. **transmitted**) (pass on etc.) transmettre; (broadcast) émettre. **~ssion** n. transmission f.; émission f. **~tter** n. émetteur m.

transparen|**t** /træns'pærənt/ a. transparent. **~cy** n. transparence f.; (photo.) diapositive f.

transpire /træn'spaɪə(r)/ v.i. s'avérer; (happen: fam.) arriver.

transplant[1] /træns'plɑːnt/ v.t. transplanter; (med.) greffer.

transplant[2] /'trænsplɑːnt/ n. transplantation f.; greffe f.

transport[1] /træn'spɔːt/ v.t. (carry, delight) transporter. **~ation** /-'teɪʃn/ n. transport m.

transport[2] /'trænspɔːt/ n. (of goods, delight, etc.) transport m.

transpose /træn'spəʊz/ v.t. transposer.

transverse /'trænzvɜːs/ a. transversal.

transvestite /trænz'vestaɪt/ n. travesti(e) m. (f.).

trap /træp/ n. piège m. —v.t. (p.t. **trapped**) (jam, pin down) coincer; (cut off) bloquer; (snare) prendre au piège. **~per** n. trappeur m.

trapdoor /træp'dɔː(r)/ n. trappe f.

trapeze /trə'piːz/ n. trapèze m.

trappings /'træpɪŋz/ n. pl. (fig.) signes extérieurs m. pl., apparat m.

trash /træʃ/ n. (junk) saleté(s) f. (pl.); (refuse) ordures f. pl.; (nonsense) idioties f. pl. **~can** n. (Amer.) poubelle f. **~y** a. qui ne vaut rien, de mauvaise qualité.

trauma /'trɔːmə/ n. traumatisme m. **~tic** /-'mætɪk/ a. traumatisant.

travel /'trævl/ v.i. (p.t. **travelled**, Amer. **traveled**) voyager; (of vehicle, bullet, etc.) aller. —v.t. parcourir. —n. voyage(s) m. (pl.). **~ agent**, agent de voyage m. **~ler** n. voyageur, -se m., f. **~ler's cheque**, chèque de voyage m. **~ling** n. voyage(s) m. (pl.). **~ sickness**, mal des transports m.

travesty /'trævəstɪ/ n. parodie f., simulacre m. —v.t. travestir.

trawler /'trɔːlə(r)/ n. chalutier m.

tray /treɪ/ n. plateau m.; (on office desk) corbeille f.

treacherous /'tretʃərəs/ a. traître. ~ly adv. traîtreusement.

treachery /'tretʃərɪ/ n. traîtrise f.

treacle /'triːkl/ n. mélasse f.

tread /tred/ v.i. (p.t. trod, p.p. trodden) marcher (on, sur). —v.t. parcourir (à pied); (soil; fig.) fouler. —n. démarche f.; (sound) bruit m. de) pas m. pl.; (of tyre) chape f. ~ sth. into, (carpet) étaler qch. sur (avec les pieds).

treason /'triːzn/ n. trahison f.

treasure /'treʒə(r)/ n. trésor m. —v.t. attacher une grande valeur à; (store) conserver. ~r /-ə(r)/ n. trésor|ier, -ière m., f.

treasury /'treʒərɪ/ n. trésorerie f. the T~, le ministère des Finances.

treat /triːt/ v.t. traiter (consider) considérer. —n. (pleasure) plaisir m., régal m.; (present) gâterie f.; (food) régal m. ~ s.o. to sth., offrir qch. à qn.

treatise /'triːtɪz/ n. traité m.

treatment /'triːtmənt/ n. traitement m.

treaty /'triːtɪ/ n. (pact) traité m.

treble /'trebl/ a. triple. —v.t./i. tripler. —n. (voice; mus.) soprano m. ~e clef, clé de sol f. ~y adv. triplement.

tree /triː/ n. arbre m. ~-top n. cime (d'un arbre) f.

trek /trek/ n. voyage pénible m.; (sport) randonnée f. —v.i. (p.t. trekked) voyager (péniblement); (sport) faire de la randonnée.

trellis /'trelɪs/ n. treillage m.

tremble /'trembl/ v.i. trembler.

tremendous /trɪ'mendəs/ a. énorme; (excellent; fam.) fantastique. ~ly adv. fantastiquement.

tremor /'tremə(r)/ n. tremblement

m. (earth) ~, secousse (sismique) f.

trench /trentʃ/ n. tranchée f.

trend /trend/ n. tendance f.; (fashion) mode f. ~-setter n. lanceu|r, -se de mode m., f. ~y a. (fam.) dans le vent.

trepidation /trepɪ'deɪʃn/ n. (fear) inquiétude f.

trespass /'trespəs/ v.i. s'introduire sans autorisation (on, dans). ~er n. intrus(e) m. (f.).

tresses /'tresɪz/ n. pl. chevelure f.

trestle /'tresl/ n. tréteau m. ~-table n. table à tréteaux f.

tri- /traɪ/ pref. tri-.

trial /'traɪəl/ n. (jurid.) procès m.; (test) essai m.; (ordeal) épreuve f. go on ~, passer en jugement. ~ and error, tâtonnements m. pl. ~ run, galop d'essai m.

triangle /'traɪæŋgl/ n. triangle m. ~ular /-'æŋgjʊlə(r)/ a. triangulaire.

trible /traɪb/ n. tribu f. ~al a. tribal.

tribulation /trɪbjʊ'leɪʃn/ n. tribulation f.

tribunal /traɪ'bjuːnl/ n. tribunal m.; (mil.) commission f.

tributary /'trɪbjʊtərɪ/ n. affluent m.

tribute /'trɪbjuːt/ n. tribut m. pay ~ to, rendre hommage à.

trick /trɪk/ n. astuce f., ruse f.; (joke, feat of skill) tour m.; (habit) manie f. —v.t. tromper. do the ~, (fam.) faire l'affaire.

trickery /'trɪkərɪ/ n. ruse f.

trickle /'trɪkl/ v.i. dégouliner. ~ in/out, arriver or partir en petit nombre. —n. filet m.; (fig.) petit nombre m.

tricky /'trɪkɪ/ a. (crafty) rusé; (problem) délicat, difficile.

tricycle /'traɪsɪkl/ n. tricycle m.

trifle /'traɪfl/ n. bagatelle f.; (cake) diplomate m. —v.i. ~ with, jouer avec. a ~, (small amount) un peu.

trifling /'traɪflɪŋ/ a. insignifiant.

trigger /'trɪɡə(r)/ n. (of gun) gâchette f., détente f. —v.t. ~ (off), (initiate) déclencher.

trilby /'trɪlbɪ/ n. (hat) feutre m.

trim /trɪm/ a. (trimmer, trimmest) net, soigné; (figure) svelte. —v.t. (p.t. trimmed) (cut) couper légèrement; (hair) rafraîchir; (budget) réduire. —n. (cut) coupe légère f.; (decoration) garniture f. in ~, en bon ordre; (fit) en forme. ~ with, (decorate) orner de. ~ming(s) n. (pl.) garniture(s) f. (pl.).

Trinity /'trɪnətɪ/ n. Trinité f.

trinket /'trɪŋkɪt/ n. colifichet m.

trio /'triːəʊ/ n. (pl. -os) trio m.

trip /trɪp/ v.t./i. (p.t. tripped) (faire) trébucher; (go lightly) marcher d'un pas léger. —n. (journey) voyage m.; (outing) excursion f.; (stumble) faux pas m.

tripe /traɪp/ n. (food) tripes f. pl.; (nonsense: sl.) bêtises f. pl.

triple /'trɪpl/ a. triple. —v.t./i. tripler. ~ts /-plɪts/ n. pl. triplé(e)s m. (f.) pl.

tripod /'traɪpɒd/ n. trépied m.

trite /traɪt/ a. banal.

triumph /'traɪəmf/ n. triomphe m. —v.i. triompher (over, de). ~al /-'ʌmfl/ a. triomphal. ~ant /-'ʌmfənt/ a. triomphant, triomphal. ~antly /-'ʌmfəntlɪ/ adv. en triomphe.

trivial /'trɪvɪəl/ a. insignifiant. ~ize v.t. considérer comme insignifiant.

trod, trodden /trɒd, 'trɒdn/ see **tread**.

trolley /'trɒlɪ/ n. chariot m. (tea-)~, table roulante f. ~-bus n. trolleybus m.

trombone /trɒm'bəʊn/ n. (mus.) trombone m.

troop /truːp/ n. bande f. ~s, (mil.)

troupes f. pl. —v.i. ~ in/out, entrer/sortir en bande. ~er n. soldat de cavalerie m. ~ing the colour, le salut au drapeau.

trophy /'trəʊfɪ/ n. trophée m.

tropic /'trɒpɪk/ n. tropique m. ~s, tropiques m. pl. ~al a. tropical.

trot /trɒt/ n. trot m. —v.i. (p.t. trotted) trotter. on the ~, (fam.) de suite. ~ out, (produce: fam.) sortir; (state: fam.) formuler.

trouble /'trʌbl/ n. ennui(s) m. (pl.), difficulté(s) f. (pl.); (pains, effort) mal m., peine f. ~(s), ennuis m. pl.; (unrest) conflits m. pl. —v.t./i. (bother) (se) déranger; (worry) ennuyer. be in ~, avoir des ennuis. go to a lot of ~, se donner du mal. what's the ~?, quel est le problème? ~d a. inquiet; (period) agité. ~maker n. provoca|teur, -trice m., f. ~shooter n. personne appelée pour désamorcer une crise.

troublesome /'trʌblsəm/ a. ennuyeux, pénible.

trough /trɒf/ n. (drinking) abreuvoir m.; (feeding) auge f. ~ (of low pressure), dépression f.

trounce /traʊns/ v.t. (defeat) écraser; (thrash) rosser.

troupe /truːp/ n. (theatre) troupe f.

trousers /'traʊzəz/ n. pl. pantalon m. short ~, culotte courte f.

trousseau /'truːsəʊ/ n. (pl. -s /-əʊz/) (of bride) trousseau m.

trout /traʊt/ n. invar. truite f.

trowel /'traʊəl/ n. (garden) déplantoir m.; (for mortar) truelle f.

truant /'truːənt/ n. absentéiste m./f.; (schol.) élève absent(e) sans permission m.(f.). play ~t, sécher les cours. ~cy n. absentéisme m.

truce /truːs/ n. trêve f.

truck /trʌk/ n. (lorry) camion m.; (cart) chariot m.; (rail.) wagon m., plateforme f. ~-driver n. camionneur m.

truculent /'trʌkjʊlənt/ a. agressif.

trudge /trʌdʒ/ v.i. marcher péniblement, se traîner.

true /truː/ a. (-er, -est) vrai; (accurate) exact; (faithful) fidèle.

truffle /'trʌfl/ n. truffe f.

truly /'truːlɪ/ adv. vraiment; (faithfully) fidèlement; (truthfully) sincèrement.

trump /trʌmp/ n. atout m. —v.t. ~ up, inventer. ~ card, atout m.

trumpet /'trʌmpɪt/ n. trompette f.

truncate /trʌŋ'keɪt/ v.t. tronquer.

trundle /'trʌndl/ v.t./i. rouler bruyamment.

trunk /trʌŋk/ n. (of tree, body) tronc m.; (of elephant) trompe f.; (box) malle f.; (auto., Amer.) coffre m. ~s, (for swimming) slip de bain m. ~-call n. communication interurbaine f. ~-road n. route nationale f.

truss /trʌs/ n. (med.) bandage herniaire m. —v.t. (fowl) trousser.

trust /trʌst/ n. confiance f.; (association) trust m. —v.t. avoir confiance en. —v.i. ~ in or to, s'en remettre à. in ~, en dépôt. on ~, de confiance. ● s.o. with, confier à qn. ~ed a. (friend etc.) éprouvé, sûr. ~ful, ~ing adjs. confiant. ~y a. fidèle.

trustee /trʌs'tiː/ n. administra|teur, -trice m., f.

trustworthy /'trʌstwɜːðɪ/ a. digne de confiance.

truth /truːθ/ n. (pl. -s /truːðz/) vérité f. ~ful a. (account etc.) véridique; (person) qui dit la vérité. ~fully adv. sincèrement.

try /traɪ/ v.t./i. (p.t. tried) essayer; (be a strain on) éprouver; (jurid.) juger. —n. (attempt) essai m.; (Rugby) essai m. ~ on or out, essayer. ~ to do, essayer de faire. ~ing a. éprouvant.

tsar /zɑː(r)/ n. tsar m.

T-shirt /'tiːʃɜːt/ n. tee-shirt m.

tub /tʌb/ n. baquet m., cuve f.; (bath: fam.) baignoire f.

tuba /'tjuːbə/ n. tuba m.

tubby /'tʌbɪ/ a. (-ier, -iest) dodu.

tub|e /tjuːb/ n. tube m.; (railway: fam.) métro m.; (in tyre) chambre à air f. ~ing n. tubes m. pl.

tuberculosis /tjuːbɜːkjʊ'ləʊsɪs/ n. tuberculose f.

tubular /'tjuːbjʊlə(r)/ a. tubulaire.

tuck /tʌk/ n. (fold) rempli m., (re)pli m. —v.t. (put away, place) ranger; (hide) cacher. —v.i. ~ in or into, (eat: sl.) attaquer. ~ in, (shirt) rentrer; (blanket, person) border. ~-shop n. (schol.) boutique à provisions f.

Tuesday /'tjuːzdɪ/ n. mardi m.

tuft /tʌft/ n. (of hair etc.) touffe f.

tug /tʌg/ v.t. (p.t. tugged) tirer fort (sur). —v.i. tirer fort. —n. (boat) remorqueur m. ~ of war, jeu de la corde tirée m.

tuition /tjuː'ɪʃn/ n. cours m. pl.; (fee) frais de scolarité m. pl.

tulip /'tjuːlɪp/ n. tulipe f.

tumble /'tʌmbl/ v.i. (fall) dégringoler. —n. chute f. ~-drier n. séchoir à linge (à air chaud) m. ~ to, (realize: fam.) piger.

tumbledown /'tʌmbldaʊn/ a. délabré, en ruine.

tumbler /'tʌmblə(r)/ n. gobelet m.

tummy /'tʌmɪ/ n. (fam.) ventre m.

tumour /'tjuːmə(r)/ n. tumeur f.

tumult /'tjuːmʌlt/ n. tumulte m. ~uous /-'mʌltʃʊəs/ a. tumultueux.

tuna /'tjuːnə/ n. invar. thon m.

tune /tjuːn/ n. air m. —v.t. (engine) régler; (mus.) accorder. —v.i. ~ in (to), (radio, TV) écouter. be in ~/out of ~, (instrument) être accordé/désaccordé; (singer) chanter juste/faux. ~ful a. mélodieux. tuning-fork n. diapason m. ~ up, (orchestra) accorder leurs instruments.

tunic /'tjuːnɪk/ n. tunique f.

Tunisia /tjuːˈnɪzɪə/ n. Tunisie f. ~n a. & n. tunisien(ne) (m. (f.)).

tunnel /'tʌnl/ n. tunnel m.; (in mine) galerie f. —v.i. (p.t. tunnelled) creuser un tunnel (into, dans).

turban /'tɜːbən/ n. turban m.

turbine /'tɜːbaɪn/ n. turbine f.

turbo /'tɜːbəʊ/ n. turbo m.

turbulen|t /'tɜːbjʊlənt/ a. turbulent. ~ce n. turbulence f.

tureen /tjʊˈriːn/ n. soupière f.

turf /tɜːf/ n. (pl. turf or turves) gazon m. —v.t. ~ out, (sl.) jeter dehors. the ~, (racing) le turf.

turgid /'tɜːdʒɪd/ a. (speech, style) boursouflé, ampoulé.

Turk /tɜːk/ n. Turc m., Turque f. ~ey n. Turquie f. ~ish a. turc; n. (lang.) turc m.

turkey /'tɜːkɪ/ n. dindon m., dinde f.; (as food) dinde f.

turmoil /'tɜːmɔɪl/ n. trouble m., chaos m. in ~, en ébullition.

turn /tɜːn/ v.t./i. tourner; (of person) se tourner; (to other side) retourner; (change) (se) transformer (into, en); (become) devenir; (deflect) détourner; (milk) tourner. —n. tour m.; (in road) tournant m.; (of mind, events) tournure f.; (illness: fam.) crise f. do a good ~, rendre service. in ~, à tour de rôle. speak out of ~, commettre une indiscrétion. take ~s, se relayer. ~ against, se retourner contre. ~ away v.i. se détourner (from, de); v.t. (avert) détourner; (refuse) refuser; (send back) renvoyer. ~ back v.i. (return) retourner; (vehicle) faire demi-tour; v.t. (fold) rabattre. ~ down, refuser; (fold) rabattre; (reduce) baisser. ~ in, (go to bed: fam.) se coucher. ~ off, (light etc.) éteindre; (engine) arrêter; (tap) fermer; (of driver) tourner. ~off n. (auto.)

embranchement m. ~ on, (light etc.) allumer; (engine) allumer; (tap) ouvrir. ~ out v.t. (light) éteindre; (empty) vider; (produce) produire; v.i. (transpire) s'avérer; (come: fam.) venir. ~out n. assistance f. ~ over, (se) retourner. ~ round n. (se) retourner. ~-round n. revirement m. ~ up v.i. arriver; (be found) se retrouver; v.t. (find) déterrer; (collar) remonter. ~ up n. (of trousers) revers m.

turning /'tɜːnɪŋ/ n. rue (latérale) f.; (bend) tournant m. ~-point n. tournant m.

turnip /'tɜːnɪp/ n. navet m.

turnover /'tɜːnəʊvə(r)/ n. (pie, tart) chausson m.; (money) chiffre d'affaires m.

turnpike /'tɜːnpaɪk/ n. (Amer.) autoroute à péage f.

turnstile /'tɜːnstaɪl/ n. (gate) tourniquet m.

turntable /'tɜːnteɪbl/ n. (for record) platine f.; plateau m.

turpentine /'tɜːpəntaɪn/ n. térébenthine f.

turquoise /'tɜːkwɔɪz/ a. turquoise invar.

turret /'tʌrɪt/ n. tourelle f.

turtle /'tɜːtl/ n. tortue (de mer) f. ~-neck a. à col montant, roulé.

tusk /tʌsk/ n. (tooth) défense f.

tussle /'tʌsl/ n. bagarre f., lutte f.

tutor /'tjuːtə(r)/ n. précep|teur, -trice m., f.; (univ.) direc|teur, -trice d'études m., f.

tutorial /tjuːˈtɔːrɪəl/ n. (univ.) séance d'études or de travaux pratiques f.

tuxedo /tʌkˈsiːdəʊ/ n. (pl. -os) (Amer.) smoking m.

TV /tiːˈviː/ n. télé f.

twaddle /'twɒdl/ n. fadaises f. pl.

twang /twæŋ/ n. (son: mus.) pincement m.; (in voice) nasillement m. —v.t./i. (faire) vibrer.

tweed /twiːd/ n. tweed m.

tweezers /'twi:zəz/ *n. pl.* pince (à épiler) *f.*

twel|ve /twelv/ *a. & n.* douze (*m.*). ~**fth** *a. & n.* douzième (*m./f.*). ~**ve (o'clock)**, midi *m.* or minuit *m.*

twent|y /'twentɪ/ *a. & n.* vingt (*m.*). ~**ieth** *a. & n.* vingtième (*m./f.*).

twice /twaɪs/ *adv.* deux fois.

twiddle /'twɪdl/ *v.t./i.* ~ **(with)**, (*fiddle with*) tripoter. ~ **one's thumbs**, se tourner les pouces.

twig[1] /twɪg/ *n.* brindille *f.*

twig[2] /twɪg/ *v.t./i.* (*p.t.* **twigged**) (*understand: fam.*) piger.

twilight /'twaɪlaɪt/ *n.* crépuscule *m.* —*a.* crépusculaire.

twin /twɪn/ *n. & a.* jumeau, -elle (*m.*, *f.*). —*v.t.* (*p.t.* **twinned**) jumeler. ~**ning** *n.* jumelage *m.*

twine /twaɪn/ *n.* ficelle *f.* —*v.t./i.* (*wind*) (s')enlacer.

twinge /twɪndʒ/ *n.* élancement *m.*; (*remorse*) remords *m.*

twinkle /'twɪŋkl/ *v.i.* (*star etc.*) scintiller; (*eye*) pétiller. —*n.* scintillement *m.*; pétillement *m.*

twirl /twɜːl/ *v.t./i.* (faire) tournoyer.

twist /twɪst/ *v.t.* tordre; (*weave together*) entortiller; (*roll*) enrouler; (*distort*) déformer. —*v.i.* (*rope etc.*) s'entortiller; (*road*) zigzaguer. —*n.* torsion *f.*; (*in rope*) tortillon *m.*; (*in road*) tournant *m.*; (*of events*) tournure *f.*, tour *m.*

twit /twɪt/ *n.* (*fam.*) idiot(e) *m.* (*f.*).

twitch /twɪtʃ/ *v.t./i.* (se) contracter nerveusement. —*n.* (*tic*) tic *m.*; (*jerk*) secousse *f.*

two /tu:/ *a. & n.* deux (*m.*). in or of ~ **minds**, indécis. put ~ **and two together**, faire le rapport. ~**-faced** *a.* hypocrite. ~**fold** *a.* double; *adv.* au double. ~**-piece** *n.* (*garment*) deux-pièces *m. invar.*

twosome /'tu:səm/ *n.* couple *m.*

tycoon /taɪ'ku:n/ *n.* magnat *m.*

tying /'taɪɪŋ/ *see* tie.

type /taɪp/ *n.* (*example*) type *m.*; (*kind*) genre *m.*, sorte *f.*; (*person: fam.*) type *m.*; (*print*) caractères *m. pl.* —*v.t./i.* (*write*) taper (à la machine). ~**-cast** *a.* catégorisé (as, comme).

typescript /'taɪpskrɪpt/ *n.* manuscrit dactylographié *m.*

typewrit|er /'taɪpraɪtə(r)/ *n.* machine à écrire *f.* ~**ten** /-ɪtn/ *a.* dactylographié.

typhoid /'taɪfɔɪd/ *n.* ~ **(fever)**, typhoïde *f.*

typhoon /taɪ'fu:n/ *n.* typhon *m.*

typical /'tɪpɪkl/ *a.* typique. ~**ly** *adv.* typiquement.

typify /'tɪpɪfaɪ/ *v.t.* être typique de.

typing /'taɪpɪŋ/ *n.* dactylo(graphie) *f.*

typist /'taɪpɪst/ *n.* dactylo *f.*

tyrann|y /'tɪrənɪ/ *n.* tyrannie *f.* ~**ical** /tɪ'rænɪkl/ *a.* tyrannique.

tyrant /'taɪərənt/ *n.* tyran *m.*

tyre /'taɪə(r)/ *n.* pneu *m.*

U

ubiquitous /juː'bɪkwɪtəs/ *a.* omniprésent, qu'on trouve partout.

udder /'ʌdə(r)/ *n.* pis *m.*, mamelle *f.*

UFO /'juːfəʊ/ *n.* (*pl.* **-Os**) OVNI *m.*

Uganda /juː'gændə/ *n.* Ouganda *m.*

ugl|y /'ʌglɪ/ *a.* (**-ier, -iest**) laid. ~**iness** *n.* laideur *f.*

UK *abbr. see* United Kingdom.

ulcer /'ʌlsə(r)/ *n.* ulcère *m.*

ulterior /ʌl'tɪərɪə(r)/ *a.* ultérieur. ~ **motive**, arrière-pensée *f.*

ultimate /'ʌltɪmət/ *a.* dernier, ultime; (*definitive*) définitif; (*basic*) fondamental. ~**ly** *adv.* à la fin; (*in the last analysis*) en fin de compte.

ultimatum /ʌltɪ'meɪtəm/ *n.* (*pl.* **-ums**) ultimatum *m.*

ultra- /'ʌltrə/ *pref.* ultra-.

ultrasound /'ʌltrəsaund/ n. ultra-son m.

ultraviolet /ʌltrə'vaɪələt/ a. ultra-violet.

umbilical /ʌm'bɪlɪkl/ a. ~ **cord**, cordon ombilical m.

umbrella /ʌm'brelə/ n. parapluie m.

umpire /'ʌmpaɪə(r)/ n. (sport) arbitre m. —v.t. arbitrer.

umpteen /'ʌmptiːn/ a. (many: sl.) un tas de. ~**th** a. (fam.) énième.

UN abbr. (United Nations) ONU f.

un- /ʌn/ pref. in-, dé(s)-, non, peu, mal, sans.

unabated /ʌnə'beɪtɪd/ a. non diminué, aussi fort qu'avant.

unable /ʌn'eɪbl/ a. incapable. (through circumstances) dans l'impossibilité (to do, de faire).

unacceptable /ʌnək'septəbl/ a. inacceptable, inadmissible.

unaccountab|le /ʌnə'kaʊntəbl/ a. (strange) inexplicable. ~**ly** adv. inexplicablement.

unaccustomed /ʌnə'kʌstəmd/ a. inaccoutumé. ~ **to**, peu habitué à.

unadulterated /ʌnə'dʌltəreɪtɪd/ a. (pure, sheer) pur.

unaided /ʌn'eɪdɪd/ a. sans aide.

unanim|ous /juː'nænɪməs/ a. una-nime. ~**ity** /-ə'nɪmətɪ/ n. una-nimité f. ~**ously** adv. à l'unanimité.

unarmed /ʌn'ɑːmd/ a. non armé.

unashamed /ʌnə'ʃeɪmd/ a. éhonté. ~**ly** /-ɪdlɪ/ adv. sans vergogne.

unassuming /ʌnə'sjuːmɪŋ/ a. modeste, sans prétention.

unattached /ʌnə'tætʃt/ a. libre.

unattainable /ʌnə'teɪnəbl/ a. inac-cessible.

unattended /ʌnə'tendɪd/ a. (laissé) sans surveillance.

unattractive /ʌnə'træktɪv/ a. peu séduisant, laid; (offer) peu inté-ressant.

unauthorized /ʌn'ɔːθəraɪzd/ a. non autorisé.

unavailable /ʌnə'veɪləbl/ a. pas disponible.

unavoidab|le /ʌnə'vɔɪdəbl/ a. iné-vitable. ~**y** adv. inévitable-ment.

unaware /ʌnə'weə(r)/ a. be ~ of, ignorer. ~**s** /-eəz/ adv. au dépourvu.

unbalanced /ʌn'bælənst/ a. (mind, person) déséquilibré.

unbearable /ʌn'beərəbl/ a. insup-portable.

unbeat|able /ʌn'biːtəbl/ a. imbat-table. ~**en** a. non battu.

unbeknown(st) /ʌnbɪ'nəʊn(st)/ a. ~ **(st) to**, (fam.) à l'insu de.

unbelievable /ʌnbɪ'liːvəbl/ a. in-croyable.

unbend /ʌn'bend/ v.i. (p.t. unbent) (relax) se détendre.

unbiased /ʌn'baɪəst/ a. impartial.

unblock /ʌn'blɒk/ v.t. déboucher.

unborn /ʌn'bɔːn/ a. futur, à venir.

unbounded /ʌn'baʊndɪd/ a. il-limité.

unbreakable /ʌn'breɪkəbl/ a. in-cassable.

unbridled /ʌn'braɪdld/ a. débridé.

unbroken /ʌn'brəʊkən/ a. (intact) intact; (continuous) continu.

unburden /ʌn'bɜːdn/ v.pr. ~ **o.s.**, (open one's heart) s'épancher.

unbutton /ʌn'bʌtn/ v.t. débouton-ner.

uncalled-for /ʌn'kɔːldfɔː(r)/ a. in-justifié, superflu.

uncanny /ʌn'kænɪ/ a. (-ier, -iest) étrange, mystérieux.

unceasing /ʌn'siːsɪŋ/ a. incessant.

unceremonious /ʌnserɪ'məʊnɪəs/ a. sans façon, brusque.

uncertain /ʌn'sɜːtn/ a. incertain. be ~ **whether**, ne pas savoir exactement si (to do, on doit faire). ~**ty** n. incertitude f.

unchang|ed /ʌn'tʃeɪndʒd/ a. in-changé. ~**ing** a. immuable.

uncivilized /ʌnˈsɪvɪlaɪzd/ a. barbare.

uncle /ˈʌŋkl/ n. oncle m.

uncomfortable /ʌnˈkʌmftəbl/ a. (thing) peu confortable; (unpleasant) désagréable. **feel** or **be ~,** (person) être mal à l'aise.

uncommon /ʌnˈkɒmən/ a. rare. **~ly** adv. remarquablement.

uncompromising /ʌnˈkɒmprəmaɪzɪŋ/ a. intransigeant.

unconcerned /ʌnkənˈsɜːnd/ a. (indifferent) indifférent (by, à).

unconditional /ʌnkənˈdɪʃənl/ a. inconditionnel.

unconscious /ʌnˈkɒnʃəs/ a. sans connaissance, inanimé; (not aware) inconscient (of, de) —n. inconscient m. **~ly** adv. inconsciemment.

unconventional /ʌnkənˈvenʃənl/ a. peu conventionnel.

uncooperative /ʌnkəʊˈɒpərətɪv/ a. peu coopératif.

uncork /ʌnˈkɔːk/ v.t. déboucher.

uncouth /ʌnˈkuːθ/ a. grossier.

uncover /ʌnˈkʌvə(r)/ v.t. découvrir.

undecided /ʌndɪˈsaɪdɪd/ a. indécis.

undefinable /ʌndɪˈfaɪnəbl/ a. indéfinissable.

undeniable /ʌndɪˈnaɪəbl/ a. indéniable, incontestable.

under /ˈʌndə(r)/ prep. sous; (less than) moins de; (according to) selon. —adv. au-dessous. **~ age**, mineur. **~ it/there**, là-dessous. **~-side** n. dessous m. **~ way**, (in progress) en cours; (on the way) en route.

under- /ˈʌndə(r)/ pref. sous-.

undercarriage /ˈʌndəkærɪdʒ/ n. (aviat.) train d'atterrissage m.

underclothes /ˈʌndəkləʊðz/ n. pl. sous-vêtements m. pl.

undercoat /ˈʌndəkəʊt/ n. (of paint) couche de fond f.

undercover /ʌndəˈkʌvə(r)/ (agent, operation) a. secret.

undercurrent /ˈʌndəkʌrənt/ n. courant (profond) m.

undercut /ʌndəˈkʌt/ v.t. (p.t. undercut, pres. p. undercutting) (comm.) vendre moins cher que.

underdeveloped /ʌndədɪˈveləpt/ a. sous-développé.

underdog /ˈʌndədɒg/ n. (pol.) opprimé(e) m. (f.); (socially) déshérité(e) m. (f.).

underdone /ʌndəˈdʌn/ a. pas assez cuit; (steak) saignant.

underestimate /ʌndərˈestɪmeɪt/ v.t. sous-estimer.

underfed /ʌndəˈfed/ a. sous-alimenté.

underfoot /ʌndəˈfʊt/ adv. sous les pieds.

undergo /ʌndəˈgəʊ/ v.t. (p.t. -went, pp. -gone) subir.

undergraduate /ʌndəˈgrædʒuət/ n. étudiant(e) (qui prépare la licence) m. (f.).

underground[1] /ʌndəˈgraʊnd/ adv. sous terre.

underground[2] /ˈʌndəgraʊnd/ a. souterrain; (secret) clandestin. —n. (rail.) métro m.

undergrowth /ˈʌndəgrəʊθ/ n. sous-bois m. invar.

underhand /ˈʌndəhænd/ a. (deceitful) sournois.

under‖line /ʌndəˈlaɪ/ v.t. (p.t. -lay, p.p. -lain, pres. p. -lying) sous-tendre. **~lying** a. fondamental.

underline /ʌndəˈlaɪn/ v.t. souligner.

undermine /ʌndəˈmaɪn/ v.t. (cliff, society, etc.) miner, saper.

underneath /ʌndəˈniːθ/ prep. sous. —adv. (en) dessous.

underpaid /ʌndəˈpeɪd/ a. sous-payé.

underpants /ˈʌndəpænts/ n. pl. (man's) slip m.

underpass /ˈʌndəpɑːs/ n. (for cars, people) passage souterrain m.

underprivileged /ʌndə'prɪvɪlɪdʒd/ a. défavorisé.

underrate /ʌndə'reɪt/ v.t. sous-estimer.

undershirt /'ʌndəʃɜːt/ n. (*Amer.*) maillot (de corps) m.

undershorts /'ʌndəʃɔːts/ n. pl. (*Amer.*) caleçon m.

underskirt /'ʌndəskɜːt/ n. jupon m.

understand /ʌndə'stænd/ v.t./i. (p.t. **-stood**) comprendre. **~able** a. compréhensible. **~ing** a. compréhensif; n. compréhension f.; (*agreement*) entente f.

understatement /'ʌndəsteɪtmənt/ n. litote f. **that's an ~**, c'est en deçà de la vérité.

understudy /'ʌndəstʌdɪ/ n. (*theatre*) doublure f.

undertak|e /ʌndə'teɪk/ v.t. (p.t. **-took**, p.p. **-taken**) entreprendre; (*responsibility*) assumer. **~e to**, s'engager à. **~ing** n. (*task*) entreprise f.; (*promise*) promesse f.

undertaker /'ʌndəteɪkə(r)/ n. entrepreneur de pompes funèbres m.

undertone /'ʌndətəʊn/ n. **in an ~**, à mi-voix.

undervalue /ʌndə'væljuː/ v.t. sous-évaluer.

underwater /ʌndə'wɔːtə(r)/ a. sous-marin. —adv. sous l'eau.

underwear /'ʌndəweə(r)/ n. sous-vêtements m. pl.

underwent /ʌndə'went/ see **undergo**.

underworld /'ʌndəwɜːld/ n. (*of crime*) milieu m., pègre f.

undeserved /ʌndɪ'zɜːvd/ a. immérité.

undesirable /ʌndɪ'zaɪərəbl/ a. peu souhaitable; (*person*) indésirable.

undies /'ʌndɪz/ n. pl. (*female underwear*; fam.) dessous m. pl.

undignified /ʌn'dɪgnɪfaɪd/ a. qui manque de dignité, sans dignité.

undisputed /ʌndɪ'spjuːtɪd/ a. incontesté.

undistinguished /ʌndɪ'stɪŋgwɪʃt/ a. médiocre.

undo /ʌn'duː/ v.t. (p.t. **-did**, p.p. **-done** /-dʌn/) défaire, détacher; (a wrong) réparer. **leave ~ne**, ne pas faire.

undoubted /ʌn'daʊtɪd/ a. indubitable. **~ly** adv. indubitablement.

undreamt /ʌn'dremt/ a. **~ of**, insoupçonné, inimaginable.

undress /ʌn'dres/ v.t./i. (se) déshabiller. **get ~ed**, se déshabiller.

undu|e /ʌn'djuː/ a. excessif. **~ly** adv. excessivement.

undulate /'ʌndjʊleɪt/ v.i. onduler.

undying /ʌn'daɪŋ/ a. éternel.

unearth /ʌn'ɜːθ/ v.t. déterrer.

unearthly /ʌn'ɜːθlɪ/ a. mystérieux. **~ hour**, (fam.) heure indue f.

uneasy /ʌn'iːzɪ/ a. (ill at ease) mal à l'aise; (worried) inquiet; (situation) difficile.

uneducated /ʌn'edʒʊkeɪtɪd/ a. (person) inculte; (speech) populaire.

unemploy|ed /ʌnɪm'plɔɪd/ a. en chômage. **~ment** n. chômage m. **~ment benefit**, allocations de chômage f. pl.

unending /ʌn'endɪŋ/ a. interminable, sans fin.

unequal /ʌn'iːkwəl/ a. inégal. **~led** a. inégalé.

unerring /ʌn'ɜːrɪŋ/ a. infaillible.

uneven /ʌn'iːvn/ a. inégal.

uneventful /ʌnɪ'ventfl/ a. sans incident.

unexpected /ʌnɪk'spektɪd/ a. inattendu, imprévu. **~ly** adv. subitement; (arrive) à l'improviste.

unfailing /ʌn'feɪlɪŋ/ a. constant, continuel; (loyal) fidèle.

unfair /ʌn'feə(r)/ a. injuste. **~ness** n. injustice f.

unfaithful /ʌnˈfeɪθfl/ a. infidèle.

unfamiliar /ʌnfəˈmɪlɪə(r)/ a. inconnu, peu familier. **be ~ with**, ne pas connaître.

unfashionable /ʌnˈfæʃənəbl/ a. (clothes) démodé. **it's ~ to**, ce n'est pas à la mode de.

unfasten /ʌnˈfɑːsn/ v.t. défaire.

unfavourable /ʌnˈfeɪvərəbl/ a. défavorable.

unfeeling /ʌnˈfiːlɪŋ/ a. insensible.

unfinished /ʌnˈfɪnɪʃt/ a. inachevé.

unfit /ʌnˈfɪt/ a. (med.) pas en forme; (unsuitable) impropre (for, à). **~ to**, (unable) pas en état de.

unflinching /ʌnˈflɪntʃɪŋ/ a. (fearless) intrépide.

unfold /ʌnˈfəʊld/ v.t. déplier; (expose) exposer. —v.i. se dérouler.

unforeseen /ʌnfɔːˈsiːn/ a. imprévu.

unforgettable /ʌnfəˈɡetəbl/ a. inoubliable.

unforgivable /ʌnfəˈɡɪvəbl/ a. impardonnable, inexcusable.

unfortunate /ʌnˈfɔːtʃənət/ a. malheureux; (event) fâcheux. **~ly** adv. malheureusement.

unfounded /ʌnˈfaʊndɪd/ a. (rumour etc.) sans fondement.

unfriendly /ʌnˈfrendlɪ/ a. peu amical, froid.

ungainly /ʌnˈɡeɪnlɪ/ a. gauche.

ungodly /ʌnˈɡɒdlɪ/ a. impie. **~ hour**, (fam.) heure indue f.

ungrateful /ʌnˈɡreɪtfl/ a. ingrat.

unhapp|y /ʌnˈhæpɪ/ a. (-ier, -iest) malheureux, triste; (not pleased) mécontent (with, de). **~ily** adv. malheureusement. **~iness** n. tristesse f.

unharmed /ʌnˈhɑːmd/ a. indemne, sain et sauf.

unhealthy /ʌnˈhelθɪ/ a. (-ier, -iest) (climate etc.) malsain; (person) en mauvaise santé.

unheard-of /ʌnˈhɜːdɒv/ a. inouï.

unhinge /ʌnˈhɪndʒ/ v.t. (person, mind) déséquilibrer.

unholy /ʌnˈhəʊlɪ/ a. (-ier, -iest) (person, act, etc.) impie; (great: fam.) invraisemblable.

unhook /ʌnˈhʊk/ v.t. décrocher; (dress) dégrafer.

unhoped /ʌnˈhəʊpt/ a. **~ for**, inespéré.

unhurt /ʌnˈhɜːt/ a. indemne.

unicorn /ˈjuːnɪkɔːn/ n. licorne f.

uniform /ˈjuːnɪfɔːm/ n. uniforme m. —a. uniforme. **~ity** /-ˈfɔːmətɪ/ n. uniformité f. **~ly** adv. uniformément.

unif|y /ˈjuːnɪfaɪ/ v.t. unifier. **~ication** /-ɪˈkeɪʃn/ n. unification f.

unilateral /juːnɪˈlætrəl/ a. unilatéral.

unimaginable /ʌnɪˈmædʒɪnəbl/ a. inimaginable.

unimportant /ʌnɪmˈpɔːtnt/ a. peu important.

uninhabited /ʌnɪnˈhæbɪtɪd/ a. inhabité.

unintentional /ʌnɪnˈtenʃənl/ a. involontaire.

uninterest|ed /ʌnˈɪntrəstɪd/ a. indifférent (in, à). **~ing** a. peu intéressant.

union /ˈjuːnɪən/ n. union f.; (trade union) syndicat m. **~ist** n. syndiqué·e m. (f.). **U~ Jack**, drapeau britannique m.

unique /juːˈniːk/ a. unique. **~ly** adv. exceptionnellement.

unisex /ˈjuːnɪseks/ a. unisexe.

unison /ˈjuːnɪsn/ n. **in ~**, à l'unisson.

unit /ˈjuːnɪt/ n. unité f.; (of furniture etc.) élément m., bloc m. **~ trust**, (équivalent d'une) SICAV f.

unite /juːˈnaɪt/ v.t./i. (s')unir. **U~d Kingdom**, Royaume-Uni m. **U~d Nations**, Nations Unies f.

pl. U∼d States (of America), États-Unis (d'Amérique) *m. pl.*

unity /'juːnətɪ/ *n.* unité *f.*; *(harmony: fig.)* harmonie *f.*

universal /juːnɪ'vɜːsl/ *a.* universel.

universe /'juːnɪvɜːs/ *n.* univers *m.*

university /juːnɪ'vɜːsɪtɪ/ *n.* université *f.* —*a.* universitaire; *(student, teacher)* d'université.

unjust /ʌn'dʒʌst/ *a.* injuste.

unkempt /ʌn'kempt/ *a.* négligé.

unkind /ʌn'kaɪnd/ *a.* pas gentil, méchant. ∼**ly** *adv.* méchamment.

unknowingly /ʌn'nəʊɪŋlɪ/ *adv.* sans le savoir, inconsciemment.

unknown /ʌn'nəʊn/ *a.* inconnu. —*n.* the ∼, l'inconnu *m.*

unleash /ʌn'liːʃ/ *v.t.* déchaîner.

unless /ən'les/ *conj.* à moins que.

unlike /ʌn'laɪk/ *a. (brothers etc.)* différents. —*prep.* à la différence de; *(different from)* très différent de.

unlikely /ʌn'laɪklɪ/ *a.* improbable. ∼**ihood** *n.* improbabilité *f.*

unlimited /ʌn'lɪmɪtɪd/ *a.* illimité.

unlisted /ʌn'lɪstɪd/ *a. (comm.)* non inscrit à la cote; *(Amer.)* qui n'est pas dans l'annuaire.

unload /ʌn'ləʊd/ *v.t.* décharger.

unlock /ʌn'lɒk/ *v.t.* ouvrir.

unlucky /ʌn'lʌkɪ/ *a.* (-ier, -iest) malheureux; *(number)* qui porte malheur. ∼**ily** *adv.* malheureusement.

unmarried /ʌn'mærɪd/ *a.* célibataire, qui n'est pas marié.

unmask /ʌn'mɑːsk/ *v.t.* démasquer.

unmistakable /ʌnmɪ'steɪkəbl/ *a. (voice etc.)* facilement reconnaissable; *(clear)* très net.

unmitigated /ʌn'mɪtɪgeɪtɪd/ *a. (absolute)* absolu.

unmoved /ʌn'muːvd/ *a.* indifférent (by, à), insensible (by, à).

unnatural /ʌn'nætʃrəl/ *a.* pas naturel, anormal.

unnecessary /ʌn'nesəsərɪ/ *a.* inutile; *(superfluous)* superflu.

unnerve /ʌn'nɜːv/ *v.t.* troubler.

unnoticed /ʌn'nəʊtɪst/ *a.* inaperçu.

unobtainable /ʌnəb'teɪnəbl/ *n.* impossible à obtenir.

unobtrusive /ʌnəb'truːsɪv/ *a. (person, object)* discret.

unofficial /ʌnə'fɪʃl/ *a.* officieux.

unorthodox /ʌn'ɔːθədɒks/ *a.* peu orthodoxe.

unpack /ʌn'pæk/ *v.t. (suitcase etc.)* défaire; *(contents)* déballer. —*v.i.* défaire sa valise.

unpalatable /ʌn'pælətəbl/ *a. (food, fact, etc.)* désagréable.

unparalleled /ʌn'pærəleld/ *a.* incomparable.

unpleasant /ʌn'pleznt/ *a.* désagréable (to, avec).

unplug /ʌn'plʌg/ *v.t. (electr.)* débrancher; *(unblock)* déboucher.

unpopular /ʌn'pɒpjʊlə(r)/ *a.* impopulaire. ∼ with, mal vu de.

unprecedented /ʌn'presɪdentɪd/ *a.* sans précédent.

unpredictable /ʌnprɪ'dɪktəbl/ *a.* imprévisible.

unprepared /ʌnprɪ'peəd/ *a.* non préparé; *(person)* qui n'a rien préparé. be ∼ for, *(not expect)* ne pas s'attendre à.

unpretentious /ʌnprɪ'tenʃəs/ *a.* sans prétention(s).

unprincipled /ʌn'prɪnsəpld/ *a.* sans scrupules.

unprofessional /ʌnprə'feʃənl/ *a. (work)* d'amateur; *(conduct)* contraire au code professionnel.

unpublished /ʌn'pʌblɪʃt/ *a.* inédit.

unqualified /ʌn'kwɒlɪfaɪd/ *a.* non diplômé; *(success etc.)* total. be ∼ to, ne pas être qualifié pour.

unquestionable /ʌn'kwestʃənəbl/ *a.* incontestable. ∼**y** *adv.* incontestablement.

unravel /ʌnˈrævl/ v.t. (p.t. **unravelled**) démêler, débrouiller.

unreal /ʌnˈrɪəl/ a. irréel.

unreasonable /ʌnˈriːznəbl/ a. déraisonnable, peu raisonnable.

unrecognizable /ʌnˈrekəgˈnaɪzəbl/ a. méconnaissable.

unrelated /ʌnrɪˈleɪtɪd/ a. (facts) sans rapport (to, avec).

unreliable /ʌnrɪˈlaɪəbl/ a. peu sérieux; (machine) peu fiable.

unremitting /ʌnrɪˈmɪtɪŋ/ a. (effort) acharné; (emotion) inaltérable.

unreservedly /ʌnrɪˈzɜːvɪdlɪ/ adv. sans réserve.

unrest /ʌnˈrest/ n. troubles m. pl.

unrivalled /ʌnˈraɪvld/ a. sans égal, incomparable.

unroll /ʌnˈrəʊl/ v.t. dérouler.

unruffled /ʌnˈrʌfld/ a. (person) qui n'a pas perdu son calme.

unruly /ʌnˈruːlɪ/ a. indiscipliné.

unsafe /ʌnˈseɪf/ a. (dangerous) dangereux; (person) en danger.

unsaid /ʌnˈsed/ a. **leave ∼,** passer sous silence.

unsatisfactory /ʌnsætɪsˈfæktərɪ/ a. peu satisfaisant.

unsavoury /ʌnˈseɪvərɪ/ a. désagréable, répugnant.

unscathed /ʌnˈskeɪðd/ a. indemne.

unscheduled /ʌnˈʃedjuːld, Amer. ʌnˈskedjuːld/ a. pas prévu.

unscrew /ʌnˈskruː/ v.t. dévisser.

unscrupulous /ʌnˈskruːpjʊləs/ a. sans scrupules, malhonnête.

unseemly /ʌnˈsiːmlɪ/ a. inconvenant, incorrect, incongru.

unseen /ʌnˈsiːn/ a. inaperçu. —n. (translation) version f.

unsettle /ʌnˈsetl/ v.t. troubler. **∼d** a. (weather) instable.

unshakeable /ʌnˈʃeɪkəbl/ a. (person, belief, etc.) inébranlable.

unshaven /ʌnˈʃeɪvn/ a. pas rasé.

unsightly /ʌnˈsaɪtlɪ/ a. laid.

unskilled /ʌnˈskɪld/ a. inexpert; (worker) non qualifié.

unsociable /ʌnˈsəʊʃəbl/ a. insociable, farouche.

unsophisticated /ʌnsəˈfɪstɪkeɪtɪd/ a. peu sophistiqué, simple.

unsound /ʌnˈsaʊnd/ a. peu solide. **of ∼ mind,** fou.

unspeakable /ʌnˈspiːkəbl/ a. indescriptible; (bad) innommable.

unspecified /ʌnˈspesɪfaɪd/ a. indéterminé.

unstable /ʌnˈsteɪbl/ a. instable.

unsteady /ʌnˈstedɪ/ a. (step) chancelant; (ladder) instable; (hand) mal assuré.

unstuck /ʌnˈstʌk/ a. décollé. **come ∼,** (fail: fam.) échouer.

unsuccessful /ʌnsəkˈsesfl/ a. (result, candidate) malheureux; (attempt) infructueux. **be ∼,** ne pas réussir (**in doing,** à faire).

unsuit|able /ʌnˈsuːtəbl/ a. qui ne convient pas (for, à), peu approprié. **∼ed** a. inapte (to, à).

unsure /ʌnˈʃɔː(r)/ a. incertain.

unsuspecting /ʌnsəˈspektɪŋ/ a. qui ne se doute de rien.

unsympathetic /ʌnsɪmpəˈθetɪk/ a. (unhelpful) peu compréhensif; (unpleasant) antipathique.

untangle /ʌnˈtæŋgl/ v.t. démêler.

untenable /ʌnˈtenəbl/ a. intenable.

unthinkable /ʌnˈθɪŋkəbl/ a. impensable, inconcevable.

untid|y /ʌnˈtaɪdɪ/ a. (-ier, -iest) (person) désordonné; (clothes, hair, room) en désordre; (work) mal soigné. **∼ily** adv. sans soin.

untie /ʌnˈtaɪ/ v.t. (knot, parcel) défaire; (person) détacher.

until /ʌnˈtɪl/ prep. jusqu'à. **not ∼,** pas avant. —conj. jusqu'à ce que; (before) avant que.

untimely /ʌnˈtaɪmlɪ/ a. inopportun; (death) prématuré.

untold /ʌnˈtəʊld/ a. incalculable.

untoward /ʌntəˈwɔːd/ a. fâcheux.

untrue /ʌnˈtruː/ a. faux.

unused[1] /ʌnˈjuːzd/ a. (*new*) neuf; (*not in use*) inutilisé.

unused[2] /ʌnˈjuːst/ a. ~ **to**, peu habitué à.

unusual /ʌnˈjuːʒʊəl/ a. exceptionnel; (*strange*) insolite, étrange. ~**ly** adv. exceptionnellement.

unveil /ʌnˈveɪl/ v.t. dévoiler.

unwanted /ʌnˈwɒntɪd/ a. (*useless*) superflu; (*child*) non désiré.

unwelcome /ʌnˈwelkəm/ a. fâcheux; (*guest*) importun.

unwell /ʌnˈwel/ a. indisposé.

unwieldy /ʌnˈwiːldɪ/ a. difficile à manier.

unwilling /ʌnˈwɪlɪŋ/ a. peu disposé (**to**, à); (*victim*) récalcitrant. ~**ly** adv. à contrecœur.

unwind /ʌnˈwaɪnd/ v.t./i. (*p.t.* **unwound** /ʌnˈwaʊnd/) (se) dérouler; (*relax: fam.*) se détendre.

unwise /ʌnˈwaɪz/ a. imprudent.

unwittingly /ʌnˈwɪtɪŋlɪ/ adv. involontairement.

unworkable /ʌnˈwɜːkəbl/ a. (*plan etc.*) irréalisable.

unworthy /ʌnˈwɜːðɪ/ a. indigne.

unwrap /ʌnˈræp/ v.t. (*p.t.* **unwrapped**) ouvrir, défaire.

unwritten /ʌnˈrɪtn/ a. (*agreement*) verbal, tacite.

up /ʌp/ adv. en haut, en l'air; (*sun, curtain*) levé; (*out of bed*) levé, debout; (*finished*) fini. **be up**, (*level, price*) avoir monté. —prep. (*a hill*) en haut de; (*a tree*) dans; (*a ladder*) sur. —v.t. (*p.t.* **upped**) augmenter. **come or go up**, monter. **up in the bedroom**, là-haut dans la chambre. **up there**, là-haut. **up to**, jusqu'à; (*task*) à la hauteur de. **it is up to you**, ça dépend de vous (**to**, de). **be up to sth.**, (*able*) être capable de qch.; (*do*) faire qch.; (*plot*) préparer qch. **be up to**, (*in book*) en être à. **be up against**, faire face à. **be up in**, (*fam.*) s'y connaître en. **feel up to doing**, (*able*) être de taille à

faire. **have ups and downs**, connaître des hauts et des bas. **up-and-coming** a. prometteur. **up-market** a. haut-de-gamme. **up to date**, moderne; (*news*) récent.

upbringing /ˈʌpbrɪŋɪŋ/ n. éducation f.

update /ʌpˈdeɪt/ v.t. mettre à jour.

upgrade /ʌpˈgreɪd/ v.t. (*person*) promouvoir; (*job*) revaloriser.

upheaval /ʌpˈhiːvl/ n. bouleversement m.

uphill /ʌpˈhɪl/ a. qui monte; (*fig.*) difficile. —adv. **go** ~, monter.

uphold /ʌpˈhəʊld/ v.t. (*p.t.* **upheld**) maintenir.

upholster /ʌpˈhəʊlstə(r)/ v.t. (*pad*) rembourrer; (*cover*) recouvrir. ~**y** n. (*in vehicle*) garniture f.

upkeep /ˈʌpkiːp/ n. entretien m.

upon /əˈpɒn/ prep. sur.

upper /ˈʌpə(r)/ a. supérieur. —n. (*of shoe*) empeigne f. **have the** ~ **hand**, avoir le dessus. ~ **class**, aristocratie f. ~**most** a. (*highest*) le plus haut.

upright /ˈʌpraɪt/ a. droit. —n. (*post*) montant m.

uprising /ʌpˈraɪzɪŋ/ n. soulèvement m., insurrection f.

uproar /ˈʌprɔː(r)/ n. tumulte m.

uproot /ʌpˈruːt/ v.t. déraciner.

upset[1] /ʌpˈset/ v.t. (*p.t.* **upset**, *pres. p.* **upsetting**) (*overturn*) renverser; (*plan, stomach*) déranger; (*person*) contrarier, affliger. —a. peiné.

upset[2] /ˈʌpset/ n. dérangement m.; (*distress*) chagrin m.

upshot /ˈʌpʃɒt/ n. résultat m.

upside-down /ʌpsaɪdˈdaʊn/ adv. (*in position, in disorder*) à l'envers, sens dessus dessous.

upstairs /ʌpˈsteəz/ adv. en haut. —a. (*flat etc.*) d'en haut.

upstart /ˈʌpstɑːt/ n. (*pej.*) parvenu(e) m. (f.).

upstream /ʌpˈstriːm/ adv. en amont.

upsurge /'ʌpsɜːdʒ/ n. recrudescence f.; (of anger) accès m.

uptake /'ʌpteɪk/ n. **be quick on the ∼,** comprendre vite.

uptight /ʌp'taɪt/ a. (tense. fam.) crispé; (angry. fam.) en colère.

upturn /'ʌptɜːn/ n. amélioration f.

upward /'ʌpwəd/ a. & adv., **∼s** adv. vers le haut.

uranium /jʊ'reɪnɪəm/ n. uranium m.

urban /'ɜːbən/ a. urbain.

urbane /ɜː'beɪn/ a. courtois.

urchin /'ɜːtʃɪn/ n. garnement m.

urge /ɜːdʒ/ v.t. conseiller vivement (**to do,** de faire). — n. forte envie f. **∼ on,** (impel) encourager.

urgent /'ɜːdʒənt/ a. urgent; (request) pressant. **∼cy** n. urgence f.; (of request, tone) insistance f. **∼tly** adv. d'urgence.

urinal /jʊə'raɪnl/ n. urinoir m.

urin|e /'jʊərɪn/ n. urine f. **∼ate** v.i. uriner.

urn /ɜːn/ n. urne f. (for tea, coffee) fontaine f.

us /ʌs, unstressed əs/ pron. nous. (to us,) nous.

US abbr. see **United States.**

USA abbr. see **United States of America.**

usable /'juːzəbl/ a. utilisable.

usage /'juːsɪdʒ/ n. usage m.

use¹ /juːz/ v.t. se servir de, utiliser; (consume) consommer. **∼ up,** épuiser. **∼r** /-ə(r)/ n. usager m. **∼r-friendly** a. facile d'emploi.

use² /juːs/ n. usage m., emploi m. **in ∼,** en usage. **it is no ∼ shouting/**etc., ça ne sert à rien de crier/etc. **make ∼ of,** se servir de. **of ∼,** utile.

used¹ /juːzd/ a. (second-hand) d'occasion.

used² /juːst/ p.t. **he ∼ to do,** il faisait (autrefois), il avait l'habitude de faire. **—a. ∼ to,** habitué à.

use|ful /'juːsfl/ a. utile. **∼fully** adv.

utilement. **∼less** a. inutile; (person) incompétent.

usher /'ʌʃə(r)/ n. (in theatre, hall) placeur m. **—v.t. ∼ in,** faire entrer. **∼ette** n. ouvreuse f.

USSR abbr. (Union of Soviet Socialist Republics) URSS f.

usual /'juːʒʊəl/ a. habituel, normal. **as ∼,** comme d'habitude. **∼ly** adv. d'habitude.

usurp /juː'zɜːp/ v.t. usurper.

utensil /juː'tensl/ n. ustensile m.

uterus /'juːtərəs/ n. utérus m.

utilitarian /juːtɪlɪ'teərɪən/ a. utilitaire.

utility /juː'tɪlətɪ/ n. utilité f. (public) **∼,** service public m.

utilize /'juːtɪlaɪz/ v.t. utiliser.

utmost /'ʌtməʊst/ a. (furthest, most intense) extrême. **the ∼ care/**etc., (greatest) le plus grand soin/etc. **—n. do one's ∼,** faire tout son possible.

Utopia /juː'təʊpɪə/ n. utopie f. **∼n** a. utopique.

utter¹ /'ʌtə(r)/ a. complet, absolu. **∼ly** adv. complètement.

utter² /'ʌtə(r)/ v.t. proférer; (sigh, shout) pousser. **∼ance** n. déclaration f. **give ∼ance to,** exprimer.

U-turn /'juːtɜːn/ n. demi-tour m.

V

vacan|t /'veɪkənt/ a. (post) vacant; (seat etc.) libre; (look) vague. **∼cy** n. (post) poste vacant m.; (room) chambre disponible f.

vacate /və'keɪt, Amer. 'veɪkeɪt/ v.t. quitter.

vacation /veɪ'keɪʃn/ n. (Amer.) vacances f. pl.

vaccinat|e /'væksɪneɪt/ v.t. vacciner. **∼ion** /-'neɪʃn/ n. vaccination f.

vaccine /'væksiːn/ n. vaccin m.

vacuum /'vækjʊəm/ n. (pl. **-cuums** or **-cua**) vide m. ~ **cleaner**, aspirateur m. ~ **flask**, bouteille thermos f. (P.). ~ **packed** a. emballé sous vide.

vagabond /'vægəbɒnd/ n. vagabond(e) m. (f.).

vagina /və'dʒaɪnə/ n. vagin m.

vagrant /'veɪɡrənt/ n. vagabond(e) m. (f.), clochard(e) m. (f.).

vague /veɪɡ/ a. (-er, -est) vague; (outline) flou. be ~, ne pas préciser. ~**ly** adv. vaguement.

vain /veɪn/ a. (-er, -est) (conceited) vaniteux; (useless) vain. in ~, en vain. ~**ly** adv. en vain.

valentine /'væləntaɪn/ n. (card) carte de la Saint-Valentin f.

valet /'vælɪt, 'væleɪ/ n. (man-servant) valet de chambre m.

valiant /'væliənt/ a. courageux.

valid /'vælɪd/ a. valable. ~**ity** /və'lɪdətɪ/ n. validité f.

validate /'vælɪdeɪt/ v.t. valider.

valley /'vælɪ/ n. vallée f.

valour, (Amer.) **valor** /'vælə(r)/ n. courage m.

valuable /'væljʊəbl/ a. (object) de valeur; (help etc.) précieux. ~**s** n. pl. objets de valeur m. pl.

valuation /væljʊ'eɪʃn/ n. expertise f.; (of house) évaluation f.

value /'væljuː/ n. valeur f. —v.t. (appraise) évaluer; (cherish) attacher de la valeur à. ~ **added tax**, taxe à la valeur ajoutée f., TVA f. ~**d** a. estimé. ~**r** /-ə(r)/ n. expert m.

valve /vælv/ n. (techn.) soupape f.; (of tyre) valve f.; (radio) lampe f.

vampire /'væmpaɪə(r)/ n. vampire m.

van /væn/ n. (vehicle) camionnette f.; (rail.) fourgon m.

vandal /'vændl/ n. vandale m./f. ~**ism** /-əlɪzəm/ n. vandalisme m.

vandalize /'vændəlaɪz/ v.t. abîmer, détruire, saccager.

vanguard /'vænɡɑːd/ n. (of army, progress, etc.) avant-garde f.

vanilla /və'nɪlə/ n. vanille f.

vanish /'vænɪʃ/ v.i. disparaître.

vanity /'vænətɪ/ n. vanité f. ~ **case**, mallette de toilette f.

vantage-point /'vɑːntɪdʒpɔɪnt/ n. (place) excellent point de vue m.

vapour /'veɪpə(r)/ n. vapeur f.

vari|**able** /'veərɪəbl/ a. variable. ~**ation** /-'eɪʃn/ n. variation f. ~**ed** /-ɪd/ a. varié.

variance /'veərɪəns/ n. **at ~**, en désaccord (with, avec).

variant /'veərɪənt/ a. différent. —n. variante f.

varicose /'værɪkəʊs/ a. ~ **veins**, varices f. pl.

variety /və'raɪətɪ/ n. variété f.; (entertainment) variétés f. pl.

various /'veərɪəs/ a. divers. ~**ly** adv. diversement.

varnish /'vɑːnɪʃ/ n. vernis m. —v.t. vernir.

vary /'veərɪ/ v.t./i. varier.

vase /vɑːz, Amer. veɪs/ n. vase m.

vast /vɑːst/ a. vaste, immense. ~**ly** adv. infiniment, extrêmement. ~**ness** n. immensité f.

vat /væt/ n. cuve f.

VAT /viːeɪ'tiː, væt/ abbr. (value added tax) TVA f.

vault[1] /vɔːlt/ n. (roof) voûte f.; (in bank) chambre forte f.; (tomb) caveau m.; (cellar) cave f.

vault[2] /vɔːlt/ v.t./i. sauter. —n. saut m.

vaunt /vɔːnt/ v.t. vanter.

VCR abbr. see **video cassette recorder**.

VDU abbr. see **visual display unit**.

veal /viːl/ n. (meat) veau m.

veer /vɪə(r)/ v.i. tourner, virer.

vegan /'viːɡən/ a. & n. végétalien (-ne) (m. (f.)).

vegetable /'vedʒtəbl/ n. légume m. —a. végétal. ~ **garden**, (jardin) potager m.

vegetarian /vedʒɪ'teərɪən/ a. & n. végétarien(ne) (m. (f.)).

vegetate /'vedʒɪteɪt/ v.i. végéter.

vegetation /vedʒɪ'teɪʃn/ n. végétation f.

vehement /'viːəmənt/ a. véhément. **~ly** adv. avec véhémence.

vehicle /'viːɪkl/ n. véhicule m.

veil /veɪl/ n. voile m. —v.t. voiler.

vein /veɪn/ n. (in body, rock) veine f.; (on leaf) nervure f. (mood) esprit m.

velocity /vɪ'lɒsətɪ/ n. vélocité f.

velvet /'velvɪt/ n. velours m.

vending-machine /'vendɪŋməʃiːn/ n. distributeur automatique m.

vendor /'vendə(r)/ n. vendeu|r, -se m., f.

veneer /və'nɪə(r)/ n. placage m.; (appearance: fig.) vernis m.

venerable /'venərəbl/ a. vénérable.

venereal /və'nɪərɪəl/ a. vénérien.

venetian /və'niːʃn/ a. **~ blind**, jalousie f.

vengeance /'vendʒəns/ n. vengeance f. **with a ~**, furieusement.

venison /'venɪzn/ n. venaison f.

venom /'venəm/ n. venin m. **~ous** /'venəməs/ a. venimeux.

vent¹ /vent/ n. (in coat) fente f.

vent² /vent/ n. (hole) orifice m.; (for air) bouche d'aération f. —v.t. (anger) décharger (on, sur). **give ~ to**, donner libre cours à.

ventilat|e /'ventɪleɪt/ v.t. ventiler. **~ion** /-'leɪʃn/ n. ventilation f. **~or** n. ventilateur m.

ventriloquist /ven'trɪləkwɪst/ n. ventriloque m./f.

venture /'ventʃə(r)/ n. entreprise f. —v.t./i. (se) risquer.

venue /'venjuː/ n. lieu de rencontre or de rendez-vous m.

veranda /və'rændə/ n. véranda f.

verb /vɜːb/ n. verbe m.

verbal /'vɜːbl/ a. verbal.

verbatim /vɜː'beɪtɪm/ adv. textuellement, mot pour mot.

verdict /'vɜːdɪkt/ n. verdict m.

verge /vɜːdʒ/ n. bord m. —v.i. **~ on**, friser, frôler. **on the ~ of doing**, sur le point de faire.

verif|y /'verɪfaɪ/ v.t. vérifier. **~ication** /-ɪ'keɪʃn/ n. vérification f.

vermicelli /vɜːmɪ'selɪ/ n. vermicelle(s) m. (pl.).

vermin /'vɜːmɪn/ n. vermine f.

vermouth /'vɜːməθ/ n. vermouth m.

vernacular /və'nækjʊlə(r)/ n. langue f.; (regional) dialecte m.

versatile /'vɜːsətaɪl, Amer. 'vɜːsətl/ a. (person) aux talents variés; (mind) souple. **~ity** /-'tɪlətɪ/ n. souplesse f. **her ~ity**, la variété de ses talents.

verse /vɜːs/ n. strophe f.; (of Bible) verset m.; (poetry) vers m. pl.

versed /vɜːst/ a. **~ in**, versé dans.

version /'vɜːʃn/ n. version f.

versus /'vɜːsəs/ prep. contre.

vertebra /'vɜːtɪbrə/ n. (pl. -brae /-briː/) vertèbre f.

vertical /'vɜːtɪkl/ a. vertical. **~ly** adv. verticalement.

vertigo /'vɜːtɪgəʊ/ n. vertige m.

verve /vɜːv/ n. fougue f.

very /'verɪ/ adv. très. —a. (actual) même. **the ~ day/etc.**, le jour/etc. même. **at the ~ end**, tout à la fin. **the ~ first**, le tout premier. **~ much**, beaucoup.

vessel /'vesl/ n. (duct, ship) vaisseau m.

vest /vest/ n. maillot de corps m.; (waistcoat: Amer.) gilet m.

vested /'vestɪd/ a. **~ interests**, droits acquis m. pl., intérêts m. pl.

vestige /'vestɪdʒ/ n. vestige m.

vestry /'vestrɪ/ n. sacristie f.

vet /vet/ n. (fam.) vétérinaire m./f. —v.t. (p.t. vetted) (candidate etc.) examiner (de près).

veteran /'vetərən/ n. vétéran m. **(war)** ~, ancien combattant m.

veterinary /'vetərɪnərɪ/ a. vétérinaire. ~ **surgeon**, vétérinaire m./f.

veto /'viːtəʊ/ n. (pl. -oes) veto m.; (right) droit de veto m. —v.t. mettre son veto à.

vex /veks/ v.t. contrarier, irriter. ~**ed question**, question controversée f.

via /'vaɪə/ prep. via, par.

viable /'vaɪəbl/ a. (baby, plan, firm) viable.

viaduct /'vaɪədʌkt/ n. viaduc m.

vibrant /'vaɪbrənt/ a. vibrant.

vibrat|e /vaɪ'breɪt/ v.t./i. (faire) vibrer. ~**ion** /-ʃn/ n. vibration f.

vicar /'vɪkə(r)/ n. pasteur m. ~**age** n. presbytère m.

vicarious /vɪ'keərɪəs/ a. (emotion) ressenti indirectement.

vice¹ /vaɪs/ n. (depravity) vice m.

vice² /vaɪs/ n. (techn.) étau m.

vice- /vaɪs/ pref. vice-.

vice versa /'vaɪsɪ'vɜːsə/ adv. vice versa.

vicinity /vɪ'sɪnətɪ/ n. environs m. pl. **in the** ~ **of**, aux environs de.

vicious /'vɪʃəs/ a. (spiteful) méchant; (violent) brutal. ~ **circle**, cercle vicieux m. ~**ly** adv. méchamment; brutalement.

victim /'vɪktɪm/ n. victime f.

victimiz|e /'vɪktɪmaɪz/ v.t. persécuter, martyriser. ~**ation** /-'zeɪʃn/ n. persécution f.

victor /'vɪktə(r)/ n. vainqueur m.

Victorian /vɪk'tɔːrɪən/ a. & n. victorien(ne) (m. (f.)).

victor|y /'vɪktərɪ/ n. victoire f. ~**ious** /-'tɔːrɪəs/ a. victorieux.

video /'vɪdɪəʊ/ a. (game, camera) vidéo invar. —n. (recorder) magnétoscope m.; (film) vidéo f. ~ **cassette**, vidéocassette f. ~ **(cassette) recorder**, magnétoscope m. —v.t. (programme) enregistrer.

videotape /'vɪdɪəʊteɪp/ n. bande vidéo f. —v.t. (programme) enregistrer; (wedding) filmer avec une caméra vidéo.

vie /vaɪ/ v.i. (pres. p. vying) rivaliser (with, avec).

view /vjuː/ n. vue f. —v.t. (watch) regarder; (consider) considérer (as, comme); (house) visiter. in my ~, à mon avis. in ~ of, compte tenu de. on ~, exposé. with a ~ to, dans le but de. ~**er** n. (TV) téléspecta|teur, -trice m., f.; (for slides) visionneuse f.

viewfinder /'vjuːfaɪndə(r)/ n. viseur m.

viewpoint /'vjuːpɔɪnt/ n. point de vue m.

vigil /'vɪdʒɪl/ n. veille f.; (over sick person, corpse) veillée f.

vigilan|t /'vɪdʒɪlənt/ a. vigilant. ~**ce** n. vigilance f.

vig|our (Amer.) **vigor** /'vɪgə(r)/ n. vigueur f. ~**orous** a. vigoureux.

vile /vaɪl/ a. (base) infâme, vil; (bad) abominable, exécrable.

vilify /'vɪlɪfaɪ/ v.t. diffamer.

villa /'vɪlə/ n. villa f., pavillon m.

village /'vɪlɪdʒ/ n. village m. ~**r** /-ə(r)/ n. villageois(e) m. (f.).

villain /'vɪlən/ n. scélérat m., bandit m.; (in story etc.) méchant m. ~**y** n. infamie f.

vindicat|e /'vɪndɪkeɪt/ v.t. justifier. ~**ion** /-'keɪʃn/ n. justification f.

vindictive /vɪn'dɪktɪv/ a. vindicatif.

vine /vaɪn/ n. vigne f.

vinegar /'vɪnɪgə(r)/ n. vinaigre m.

vineyard /'vɪnjəd/ n. vignoble m.

vintage /'vɪntɪdʒ/ n. (year) année f., millésime m. —a. (wine) de grand cru; (car) d'époque.

vinyl /'vaɪnɪl/ n. vinyle m.

viola /vɪ'əʊlə/ n. (mus.) alto m.

violat|e /'vaɪəleɪt/ v.t. violer. ~**ion** /-'leɪʃn/ n. violation f.

violen|t /'vaɪələt/ *a.* violent. **~ce** *n.* violence *f.* **~tly** *adv.* violemment, avec violence.

violet /'vaɪələt/ *n.* (*bot.*) violette *f.*; (*colour*) violet *m.* —*a.* violet.

violin /vaɪə'lɪn/ *n.* violon *m.* **~ist** *n.* violoniste *m./f.*

VIP /viːaɪ'piː/ *abbr.* (*very important person*) personnage de marque *m.*

viper /'vaɪpə(r)/ *n.* vipère *f.*

virgin /'vɜːdʒɪn/ *n.* (*woman*) vierge *f.* —*a.* vierge. **be a ~**, (*woman, man*) être vierge. **~ity** /və'dʒɪnətɪ/ *n.* virginité *f.*

Virgo /'vɜːgəʊ/ *n.* la Vierge.

viril|e /'vɪraɪl, *Amer.* 'vɪrəl/ *a.* viril. **~ity** /vɪ'rɪlətɪ/ *n.* virilité *f.*

virtual /'vɜːtʃʊəl/ *a.* vrai. **a ~ failure**/*etc.*, pratiquement un échec/*etc.* **~ly** *adv.* pratiquement.

virtue /'vɜːtʃuː/ *n.* (*goodness, chastity*) vertu *f.*; (*merit*) mérite *m.* **by** or **in ~ of**, en raison de.

virtuos|o /vɜːtʃʊ'əʊsəʊ/ *n.* (*pl.* **-si** /-siː/) virtuose *m./f.* **~ity** /-'ɒsətɪ/ *n.* virtuosité *f.*

virtuous /'vɜːtʃʊəs/ *a.* vertueux.

virulent /'vɪrʊlənt/ *a.* virulent.

virus /'vaɪərəs/ *n.* (*pl.* **-uses**) virus *m.*

visa /'viːzə/ *n.* visa *m.*

viscount /'vaɪkaʊnt/ *n.* vicomte *m.*

viscous /'vɪskəs/ *a.* visqueux.

vise /vaɪs/ *n.* (*Amer.*) étau *m.*

visib|le /'vɪzəbl/ *a.* (*discernible, obvious*) visible. **~ility** /-'bɪlətɪ/ *n.* visibilité *f.* **~ly** *adv.* visiblement.

vision /'vɪʒn/ *n.* vision *f.*

visionary /'vɪʒənərɪ/ *a.* & *n.* visionnaire (*m./f.*).

visit /'vɪzɪt/ *v.t.* (*p.t.* **visited**) (*person*) rendre visite à; (*place*) visiter. —*v.i.* être en visite. —*n.* (*tour, call*) visite *f.*; (*stay*) séjour *m.* **~or** *n.* visiteu|r, -se *m., f.*; (*guest*) invité(e) *m.* (*f.*); (*in hotel*) client(e) *m.* (*f.*).

visor /'vaɪzə(r)/ *n.* visière *f.*

vista /'vɪstə/ *n.* perspective *f.*

visual /'vɪʒʊəl/ *a.* visuel. **~ display unit**, visuel *m.*, console de visualisation *f.* **~ly** *adv.* visuellement.

visualize /'vɪʒʊəlaɪz/ *v.t.* se représenter; (*foresee*) envisager.

vital /'vaɪtl/ *a.* vital. **~ statistics**, (*fam.*) mensurations *f. pl.*

vitality /vaɪ'tælətɪ/ *n.* vitalité *f.*

vitally /'vaɪtəlɪ/ *adv.* extrêmement.

vitamin /'vɪtəmɪn/ *n.* vitamine *f.*

vivac|ious /vɪ'veɪʃəs/ *a.* plein d'entrain, animé. **~ity** /-æsətɪ/ *n.* vivacité *f.*, entrain *m.*

vivid /'vɪvɪd/ *a.* vif; (*graphic*) vivant. **~ly** *adv.* vivement; (*describe*) de façon vivante.

vivisection /vɪvɪ'sekʃn/ *n.* vivisection *f.*

vocabulary /və'kæbjʊlərɪ/ *n.* vocabulaire *m.*

vocal /'vəʊkl/ *a.* vocal; (*person: fig.*) qui s'exprime franchement. **~ cords**, cordes vocales *f. pl.* **~ist** *n.* chanteu|r, -se *m., f.*

vocation /və'keɪʃn/ *n.* vocation *f.* **~al** *a.* professionnel.

vociferous /və'sɪfərəs/ *a.* bruyant.

vodka /'vɒdkə/ *n.* vodka *f.*

vogue /vəʊg/ *n.* (*fashion, popularity*) vogue *f.* **in ~**, en vogue.

voice /vɔɪs/ *n.* voix *f.* —*v.t.* (*express*) formuler.

void /vɔɪd/ *a.* vide (**of**, de); (*not valid*) nul. —*n.* vide *m.*

volatile /'vɒlətaɪl, *Amer.* 'vɒlətl/ *a.* (*person*) versatile; (*situation*) variable.

volcan|o /vɒl'keɪnəʊ/ *n.* (*pl.* **-oes**) volcan *m.* **~ic** /-ænɪk/ *a.* volcanique.

volition /və'lɪʃn/ *n.* **of one's own ~**, de son propre gré.

volley /'vɒlɪ/ *n.* (*of blows etc.*, in tennis) volée *f.*; (*of gunfire*) salve *f.* **~-ball** *n.* volley(-ball) *m.*

volt /vəʊlt/ n. (electr.) volt m. **~age** n. voltage m.

voluble /'vɒljʊbl/ a. volubile.

volume /'vɒljuːm/ n. volume m.

voluntar|y /'vɒləntərɪ/ a. volontaire; (unpaid) bénévole. **~ily** /-trəlɪ, Amer. -'terəlɪ/ adv. volontairement.

volunteer /vɒlən'tɪə(r)/ n. volontaire m./f. —v.i. s'offrir (to do, pour faire); (mil.) s'engager comme volontaire. —v.t. offrir.

voluptuous /və'lʌptʃʊəs/ a. voluptueux.

vomit /'vɒmɪt/ v.t./i. (p.t. vomited) vomir. —n. vomi(ssement) m.

voracious /və'reɪʃəs/ a. vorace.

vot|e /vəʊt/ n. vote m.; (right) droit de vote m. —v.t./i. voter. **~ in**, (person) élire. **~er** n. élec|teur, -trice m., f. **~ing** n. vote m. (of, de); (poll) scrutin m.

vouch /vaʊtʃ/ v.i. **~ for**, se porter garant de, répondre de.

voucher /'vaʊtʃə(r)/ n. bon m.

vow /vaʊ/ n. vœu m. —v.t. (loyalty etc.) jurer (to, à). **~ to do**, jurer de faire.

vowel /'vaʊəl/ n. voyelle f.

voyage /'vɔɪɪdʒ/ n. voyage (par mer) m.

vulgar /'vʌlgə(r)/ a. vulgaire. **~ity** /-'gærətɪ/ n. vulgarité f.

vulnerab|le /'vʌlnərəbl/ a. vulnérable. **~ility** /-'bɪlətɪ/ n. vulnérabilité f.

vulture /'vʌltʃə(r)/ n. vautour m.

W

wad /wɒd/ n. (pad) tampon m.; (bundle) liasse f.

wadding /'wɒdɪŋ/ n. rembourrage m., ouate f.

waddle /'wɒdl/ v.i. se dandiner.

wade /weɪd/ v.i. **~ through**, (mud etc.) patauger dans; (book: fig.) avancer péniblement dans.

wafer /'weɪfə(r)/ n. (biscuit) gaufrette f.; (relig.) hostie f.

waffle¹ /'wɒfl/ n. (talk: fam.) verbiage m. —v.i. (fam.) divaguer.

waffle² /'wɒfl/ n. (cake) gaufre f.

waft /wɒft/ v.i. flotter. —v.t. porter.

wag /wæg/ v.t./i. (p.t. wagged) (tail) remuer.

wage¹ /weɪdʒ/ v.t. (campaign) mener. **~ war**, faire la guerre.

wage² /weɪdʒ/ n. (weekly, daily) salaire m. **~s**, salaire m. **~-earner** n. salarié(e) m. (f.).

wager /'weɪdʒə(r)/ n. (bet) pari m. —v.t. parier (that, que).

waggle /'wægl/ v.t./i. remuer.

wagon /'wægən/ n. (horse-drawn) chariot m.; (rail.) wagon (de marchandises) m.

waif /weɪf/ n. enfant abandonné(e) m.(f.).

wail /weɪl/ v.i. (utter cry or complaint) gémir. —n. gémissement m.

waist /weɪst/ n. taille f.

waistcoat /'weɪskəʊt/ n. gilet m.

wait /weɪt/ v.t./i. attendre. —n. attente f. **I can't ~**, je n'en peux plus d'impatience. **let's ~ and see**, attendons voir. **while you ~**, sur place. **~ for**, attendre. **~ on**, servir. **~ing-list** n. liste d'attente f. **~ing-room** n. salle d'attente f.

wait|er /'weɪtə(r)/ n. garçon m., serveur m. **~ress** n. serveuse f.

waive /weɪv/ v.t. renoncer à

wake¹ /weɪk/ v.t./i. (p.t. woke, p.p. woken). **~ (up)**, (se) réveiller.

wake² /weɪk/ n. (track) sillage m. **in the ~ of**, (after) à la suite de.

waken /'weɪkən/ v.t./i. (se) réveiller, (s')éveiller.

Wales /weɪlz/ n. pays de Galles m.

walk /wɔːk/ v.i. marcher; (not ride)

aller à pied; (*stroll*) se promener. —*v.t.* (*streets*) parcourir; (*distance*) faire à pied; (*dog*) promener. —*n.* promenade *f.*, tour *m.*; (*gait*) (dé)marche *f.*; (*pace*) marche *f.*, pas *m.*; (*path*) allée *f.* ~ **of life**, condition sociale *f.* ~ **out**, (*go away*) partir; (*worker*) faire grève. —**out** *n.* grève surprise *f.* **to** ~ **out on**, abandonner. ~**over** *n.* victoire facile *f.*

walker /'wɔːkə(r)/ *n.* (*person*) marcheu|r, -se *m.*, *f.*

walkie-talkie /wɔːkɪ'tɔːkɪ/ *n.* talkie-walkie *m.*

walking /'wɔːkɪŋ/ *n.* marche (à pied) *f.* —*a.* (*corpse, dictionary: fig.*) vivant. ~**stick** *n.* canne *f.*

Walkman /'wɔːkmən/ *n.* (P.) Walkman (P.) *m.*, baladeur *m.*

wall /wɔːl/ *n.* mur *m.*; (*of tunnel, stomach, etc.*) paroi *f.* ~ (*mural.* —*v.t.* (*city*) fortifier. **go to the** ~, (*firm*) faire faillite.

wallet /'wɒlɪt/ *n.* portefeuille *m.*

wallflower /'wɔːlflaʊə(r)/ *n.* (*bot.*) giroflée *f.*

wallop /'wɒləp/ *v.t.* (*p.t.* **walloped**) (*hit: sl.*) taper sur. —*n.* (*blow: sl.*) grand coup *m.*

wallow /'wɒləʊ/ *v.i.* se vautrer.

wallpaper /'wɔːlpeɪpə(r)/ *n.* papier peint *m.* —*v.t.* tapisser.

walnut /'wɔːlnʌt/ *n.* (*nut*) noix *f.*; (*tree*) noyer *m.*

walrus /'wɔːlrəs/ *n.* morse *m.*

waltz /wɔːls/ *n.* valse *f.* —*v.i.* valser.

wan /wɒn/ *a.* pâle, blême.

wand /wɒnd/ *n.* baguette (magique) *f.*

wander /'wɒndə(r)/ *v.i.* errer; (*stroll*) flâner; (*digress*) s'écarter du sujet; (*in mind*) divaguer. ~**er** *n.* vagabond|e *m.* (*f.*).

wane /weɪn/ *v.i.* décroître. —*n.* **on the** ~, (*strength, fame, etc.*) en déclin; (*person*) sur son déclin.

wangle /'wæŋgl/ *v.t.* (*obtain: sl.*) se débrouiller pour avoir.

want /wɒnt/ *v.t.* vouloir (**to do**, faire); (*need*) avoir besoin de (**doing**, d'être fait); (*ask for*) demander. ~ **for**, manquer de. —*n.* (*need, poverty*) besoin *m.*; (*desire*) désir *m.*; (*lack*) manque *m.* **I** ~ **you to do it**, je veux que vous le fassiez. **for** ~ **of**, faute de. ~**ed** *a.* (*criminal*) recherché par la police.

wanting /'wɒntɪŋ/ *a.* **be** ~, manquer (**in**, de).

wanton /'wɒntən/ *a.* (*cruelty*) gratuit; (*woman*) impudique.

war /wɔː(r)/ *n.* guerre *f.* **at** ~, en guerre. **on the** ~**-path**, sur le sentier de la guerre.

ward /wɔːd/ *n.* (*in hospital*) salle *f.*; (*minor: jurid.*) pupille *m./f.*; (*pol.*) division électorale *f.* —*v.t.* ~ **off**, (*danger*) prévenir; (*blow, anger*) détourner.

warden /'wɔːdn/ *n.* direc|teur, -trice *m.*, *f.*; (*of park*) gardien(ne) *m.* (*f.*). (**traffic**) ~, contractuel(le) *m.* (*f.*).

warder /'wɔːdə(r)/ *n.* gardien (de prison) *m.*

wardrobe /'wɔːdrəʊb/ *n.* (*place*) armoire *f.*; (*clothes*) garde-robe *f.*

warehouse /'weəhaʊs/ *n.* (*pl.* **-s** /-haʊzɪz/) entrepôt *m.*

wares /weəz/ *n. pl.* (*goods*) marchandises *f. pl.*

warfare /'wɔːfeə(r)/ *n.* guerre *f.*

warhead /'wɔːhed/ *n.* ogive *f.*

warily /'weərɪlɪ/ *adv.* avec prudence.

warm /wɔːm/ *a.* (**-er**, **-est**) chaud; (*hearty*) chaleureux. **be** *or* **feel** ~, avoir chaud. **it is** ~, il fait chaud. —*v.t./i.* ~ (**up**), (se) réchauffer; (*food*) chauffer; (*liven up*) s'animer; (*exercise*) s'échauffer. ~**-hearted** *a.* chaleureux. ~**ly** *adv.* (*wrap up etc.*)

chaudement; (*heartily*) chaleu-
reusement. **~th** n. chaleur f.

warn /wɔːn/ v.t. avertir, prévenir.
~ s.o. off sth., (*advise against*)
mettre qn. en garde contre qch.;
(*forbid*) interdire qch. à qn. **~ing**
n. avertissement m.; (*notice*) avis
m. **without ~ing**, sans prévenir.
~ing light, voyant m. **~ing
triangle**, triangle de sécurité m.

warp /wɔːp/ v.t./i. (se)
voiler; (*pervert*) pervertir.

warrant /'wɒrənt/ n. (*for arrest*)
mandat (d'arrêt) m.; (*comm.*)
autorisation f. **~** v.t. justifier.

warranty /'wɒrənti/ n. garantie f.

warring /'wɔːrɪŋ/ a. en guerre.

warrior /'wɒrɪə(r)/ n. guerr|ier,
-ière m., f.

warship /'wɔːʃɪp/ n. navire de
guerre m.

wart /wɔːt/ n. verrue f.

wartime /'wɔːtaɪm/ n. **in ~**, en
temps de guerre.

wary /'weərɪ/ a. (-ier, -iest)
prudent.

was /wɒz, unstressed wəz/ see **be**.

wash /wɒʃ/ v.t./i. (se) laver; (*flow
over*) baigner. **—** n. lavage m.;
(*clothes*) lessive f.; (*of ship*) sillage
m. **have a ~**, se laver. **~-basin**
n. lavabo m. **~-cloth** n. (*Amer.*)
gant de toilette m. **~ down**,
(*meal*) arroser. **~ one's hands
of**, se laver les mains de. **~ out**,
(*cup etc.*) laver; (*stain*) (faire)
partir. **~-out** n. (*sl.*) fiasco m. **~-
room** n. (*Amer.*) toilettes f. pl. **~-
up**, faire la vaisselle; (*Amer.*) se
laver. **~able** a. lavable. **~ing** n.
lessive f. **~ing-machine** n.
machine à laver f. **~ing-powder**
n. lessive f. **~ing-up** n. vaisselle
f.; **~ing-up liquid**, produit pour
la vaisselle m.

washed-out /wɒʃt'aʊt/ a. (*faded*)
délavé; (*tired*) lessivé; (*ruined*)
anéanti.

washer /'wɒʃə(r)/ n. rondelle f.

wasp /wɒsp/ n. guêpe f.

wastage /'weɪstɪdʒ/ n. gaspillage
m. **some ~**, (*in goods, among
candidates, etc.*) du déchet.

waste /weɪst/ v.t. gaspiller; (*time*)
perdre. **—** v.i. **~ away**, dépérir.
— a. superflu; (*product*) de rebut.
— n. gaspillage m.; (*of time*) perte
f.; (*rubbish*) déchets m. pl. **lay ~**,
dévaster. **~ disposal unit**,
broyeur d'ordures m. **~ (land)**,
(*desolate*) terre désolée f.;
(*unused*) terre inculte f.; (*in town*)
terrain vague m. **~-paper**, vieux
papiers m. pl. **~-paper basket**,
corbeille (à papier) f. **~-pipe** n.
vidange f.

wasteful /'weɪstfl/ a. peu économique; (*person*) gaspilleur.

watch /wɒtʃ/ v.t./i. (*television*)
regarder; (*observe*) observer;
(*guard, spy on*) surveiller; (*be
careful about*) faire attention à.
— n. (*for telling time*) montre f.;
(*naut.*) quart. **be on the ~**
(*for*), guetter. **keep ~ on**, surveiller.
~-dog n. chien de garde m. **~
out**, (*take care*) faire attention
(for, à). **~ out for**, guetter. **~-
tower** n. tour de guet f. **~ful** a.
vigilant.

watchmaker /'wɒtʃmeɪkə(r)/ n.
horloger, -ère m., f.

watchman /'wɒtʃmən/ n. (pl.
-men) (*of building*) gardien m.

water /'wɔːtə(r)/ n. eau f. **—** v.t.
arroser. **—** v.i. (*of eyes*) larmoyer.
my/his/etc. mouth ~s, l'eau
me/lui/etc. vient à la bouche. **by
~**, en bateau. **~-bottle** n.
bouillotte f. **~-closet** n. waters
m. pl. **~-colour** n. couleur pour
aquarelle f.; (*painting*) aquarelle
f. **~ down**, couper (d'eau); (*tone
down*) édulcorer. **~ heater**,
chauffe-eau m. **~-ice** n. sorbet m.
~-lily n. nénuphar m. **~-main**
n. canalisation d'eau f. **~-melon**
n. pastèque f. **~-pistol** n. pistolet

à eau *m*. ~ **polo**, water-polo *m*. ~ **power**, énergie hydraulique *f*. ~-**skiing** *n*. ski nautique *m*.

watercress /'wɔːtəkres/ *n*. cresson (de fontaine) *m*.

waterfall /'wɔːtəfɔːl/ *n*. chute d'eau *f*., cascade *f*.

watering-can /'wɔːtərɪŋkæn/ *n*. arrosoir *m*.

waterlogged /'wɔːtəlɒgd/ *a*. imprégné d'eau; (*land*) détrempé.

watermark /'wɔːtəmaːk/ *n*. (*in paper*) filigrane *m*.

waterproof /'wɔːtəpruːf/ *a*. (*material*) imperméable.

watershed /'wɔːtəʃed/ *n*. (*in affairs*) tournant décisif *m*.

watertight /'wɔːtətaɪt/ *a*. étanche.

waterway /'wɔːtəweɪ/ *n*. voie navigable *f*.

waterworks /'wɔːtəwɜːks/ *n*. (*place*) station hydraulique *f*.

watery /'wɔːtəri/ *a*. (*colour*) délavé; (*eyes*) humide; (*soup*) trop liquide; (*tea*) faible.

watt /wɒt/ *n*. watt *m*.

wav|e /weɪv/ *n*. vague *f*.; (*in hair*) ondulation *f*.; (*radio*) onde *f*.; (*sign*) signe *m*. —*v.t.* agiter. —*v.i.* faire signe (de la main); (*move in wind*) flotter. ~**y** *a*. (*line*) onduleux; (*hair*) ondulé.

wavelength /'weɪvleŋθ/ *n*. (*radio & fig.*) longueur d'ondes *f*.

waver /'weɪvə(r)/ *v.i.* vaciller.

wax¹ /wæks/ *n*. cire *f*.; (*for skis*) fart *m*. —*v.t.* cirer; farter; (*car*) astiquer. ~**en**, ~**y** *adjs.* cireux.

wax² /wæks/ *v.i.* (*of moon*) croître.

waxwork /'wækswɜːk/ *n*. (*dummy*) figure de cire *f*.

way /weɪ/ *n*. (*road, path*) chemin *m*. (**to**, de); (*distance*) distance *f*.; (*direction*) direction *f*.; (*manner*) façon *f*.; (*means*) moyen *m*.; (*particular*) égard *m*. ~**s**, (*habits*) habitudes *f.pl*. —*adv*. (*fam.*) loin. **be in the** ~, bloquer le passage; (*hindrance: fig.*) gêner (qn.). **be**

on one's *or* **the** ~, être sur son *or* le chemin. **by the** ~, à propos. **by the** ~**side**, au bord de la route. **by** ~ **of**, comme; (*via*) par. **go out of one's** ~, se donner du mal pour. **in** ~, dans un sens. **make one's** ~ **somewhere**, se rendre quelque part. **push one's** ~ **through**, se frayer un passage. **that** ~, par là. **this** ~, par ici. ~ **in**, entrée *f*. ~ **out**, sortie *f*. ~ **out** *a*. (*strange: fam.*) original.

waylay /weɪ'leɪ/ *v.t.* (*p.t.* -**laid**) (*assail*) assaillir; (*stop*) accrocher.

wayward /'weɪwəd/ *a*. capricieux.

WC /dʌb(ə)lju:'si:/ *n*. w.-c.-*m.pl*.

we /wi:/ *pron.* nous.

weak /wiːk/ *a*. (-**er**, -**est**) faible; (*delicate*) fragile. ~**ly** *adv.* faiblement; *a.* faible. ~**ness** *n.* faiblesse *f*.; (*fault*) point faible *m*. **a** ~**ness for**, (*liking*) un faible pour.

weaken /'wiːkən/ *v.t.* affaiblir —*v.i.* s'affaiblir, faiblir.

weakling /'wiːklɪŋ/ *n.* gringalet *m*.

wealth /welθ/ *n.* richesse *f*.; (*riches, resources*) richesses *f.pl.*; (*quantity*) profusion *f*.

wealthy /'welθɪ/ *a*. (-**ier**, -**iest**) riche. —*n.* **the** ~, les riches *m.pl*.

wean /wiːn/ *v.t.* (*baby*) sevrer.

weapon /'wepən/ *n*. arme *f*.

wear /weə(r)/ *v.t.* (*p.t.* **wore**, *p.p.* **worn**) porter; (*put on*) mettre; (*expression etc.*) avoir. —*v.i.* (*last*) durer. ~ (**out**), (s')user. —*n.* usage *m*.; (*damage*) usure *f*.; (*clothing*) vêtements *m. pl.* ~ **down**, user. ~ **off**, (*colour, pain*) passer. ~ **on**, (*time*) passer. ~ **out**, (*exhaust*) épuiser.

wear|y /'wɪərɪ/ *a*. (-**ier**, -**iest**) fatigué, las; (*tiring*) fatigant. —*v.i.* ~ **of**, se lasser de. ~**ily** *adv.* avec lassitude. ~**iness** *n*. lassitude *f*., fatigue *f*.

weasel /'wiːzl/ *n*. belette *f*.

weather /'weðə(r)/ *n*. temps *m*.

—a. météorologique. —v.t. (survive) réchapper de or à. under the ~, patraque. ~-beaten a. tanné. ~ forecast, météo f. ~-vane n. girouette f.

weathercock /'weðəkɒk/ n. girouette f.

weave /wiːv/ v.t./i. (p.t. wove, p.p. woven) tisser; (basket etc.) tresser; (move) se faufiler. —n. (style) tissage m. ~r /-ə(r)/ n. tisserand(e) m. (f.).

web /web/ n. (of spider) toile f.; (fabric) tissu m.; (on foot) palmure f. ~bed a. (foot) palmé. ~bing n. (in chair) sangles f. pl.

wed /wed/ v.t. (p.t. **wedded**) épouser. —v.i. se marier. ~ded to, (devoted to: fig.) attaché à.

wedding /'wediŋ/ n. mariage m. ~-ring n. alliance f.

wedge /wedʒ/ n. coin m.; (under wheel etc.) cale f. —v.t. caler; (push) enfoncer; (crowd) coincer.

Wednesday /'wenzdi/ n. mercredi m.

wee /wiː/ a. (fam.) tout petit.

weed /wiːd/ n. mauvaise herbe f. —v.t./i. désherber. ~-killer n. désherbant m. ~ out, extirper. ~y a. (person: fig.) faible, maigre.

week /wiːk/ n. semaine f. a ~ today/tomorrow, aujourd'hui/demain en huit. ~ly adv. toutes les semaines; a. & n. (periodical) hebdomadaire (m.).

weekday /'wiːkdei/ n. jour de semaine m.

weekend /wiːk'end/ n. week-end m., fin de semaine f.

weep /wiːp/ v.t./i. (p.t. wept) pleurer (for s.o., qn.). ~ing willow, saule pleureur m.

weigh /wei/ v.t./i. peser. ~ anchor, lever l'ancre. ~ down, lester (avec un poids); (bend) faire plier; (fig.) accabler. ~ up, (examine: fam.) calculer.

weight /weit/ n. poids m. lose/put on ~, perdre/prendre du poids. ~lessness n. apesanteur f. ~-lifting n. haltérophilie f. ~y a. lourd; (subject etc.) de poids.

weighting /'weitiŋ/ n. indemnité f.

weir /wiə(r)/ n. barrage m.

weird /wiəd/ a. (-er, -est) mystérieux; (strange) bizarre.

welcome /'welkəm/ a. agréable; (timely) opportun. be ~, être le or la bienvenu(e), être les bienvenu(e)s. you're ~, (after thank you) il n'y a pas de quoi! ~ to do, libre de faire. —int. soyez le or la bienvenu(e), soyez les bienvenu(e)s. —n. accueil m. —v.t. accueillir; (as greeting) souhaiter la bienvenue à; (fig.) se réjouir de.

weld /weld/ v.t. souder. ~er n. soudeur m. ~ing n. soudure f.

welfare /'welfeə(r)/ n. bien-être m.; (aid) aide sociale f. W~ State, État-providence m.

well[1] /wel/ n. (for water, oil) puits m.; (of stairs) cage f.

well[2] /wel/ adv. (better, best) bien. —a. invar. as ~, aussi. be ~, (healthy) aller bien. —int. eh bien; (surprise) tiens. do ~, (succeed) réussir. ~-behaved a. sage. ~-being n. bien-être m. ~-built a. bien bâti. ~-disposed a. bien disposé. ~-done! bravo! ~-dressed a. bien habillé. ~-heeled a. (fam.) nanti. ~-informed a. bien informé. ~-known a. (bien) connu. ~-meaning a. bien intentionné. ~ off, aisé, riche. ~-read a. instruit. ~-spoken a. qui parle bien. ~-to-do a. riche. ~-wisher n. admira|teur, -trice m., f.

wellington /'weliŋtən/ n. (boot) botte de caoutchouc f.

Welsh /welʃ/ a. gallois. —n. (lang.) gallois m. ~man n. Gallois m.

rabbit, croûte au fromage *f.*
~**woman** *n.* Galloise *f.*

welsh /welʃ/ *v.i.* ~ **on**, (*debt,
promise*) ne pas honorer.

welterweight /'weltəweit/ *n.* poids
mi-moyen *m.*

wench /wentʃ/ *n.* (*old use*) jeune
fille *f.*

wend /wend/ *v.t.* ~ **one's way**, se
diriger, aller son chemin.

went /went/ *see* **go.**

wept /wept/ *see* **weep.**

were /wɜː(r), *unstressed* wə(r)/ *see*
be.

west /west/ *n.* ouest *m.* **the W~**,
(*pol.*) l'Occident *m.* —*a.* d'ouest.
—*adv.* vers l'ouest. **the W~
Country**, le sud-ouest (de
l'Angleterre). **W~ Germany**,
Allemagne de l'Ouest *f.* **W~
Indian** *a. & n.* antillais(e) (*m.
(f.)*). **the W~ Indies**, les Antilles *f. pl.* ~**erly** *a.* d'ouest.
~**ern** *a.* de l'ouest; (*pol.*) occiden-
tal; *n.* (*film*) western *m.* ~**erner**
n. occidental(e) *m. (f.).* ~**ward** *a.*
à l'ouest. ~**wards** *adv.* vers
l'ouest.

westernize /'westənaiz/ *v.t.* oc-
cidentaliser.

wet /wet/ *a.* (**wetter, wettest**)
mouillé; (*damp, rainy*) humide;
(*paint*) frais.—*v.t.* (*p.t.* **wetted**)
mouiller. ~ **the** ~, l'humidité
f.; (*rain*) la pluie *f.* **get** ~, se
mouiller. ~**blanket**, rabat-joie
m. invar. ~**ness** *n.* humidité *f.*
~**suit**, combinaison de plongée *f.*

whack /wæk/ *n.* (*fam.*) grand coup
m. —*v.t.* (*fam.*) taper sur.

whacked /wækt/ *a.* (*fam.*) claqué.

whacking /'wækiŋ/ *a.* énorme.

whale /weil/ *n.* baleine *f.*

wham /wæm/ *int.* vlan.

wharf /wɔːf/ *n.* (*pl.* **wharfs**) (*for
ships*) quai *m.*

what /wɒt/ *a.* (*in questions*)
quel(le), quel(le)s. —*pron.* (*in
questions*) qu'est-ce qui; (*object*)

(qu'est-ce) que *or* qu'*; (*after
prep.*) quoi; (*that which*) ce qui;
(*object*) ce que, ce qu'*. —*int.* quoi,
comment. ~ **date?**, quelle date?
~ **time?**, à quelle heure? ~
happened?, qu'est-ce qui s'est
passé? ~ **did he say?**, qu'est-ce
qu'il a dit? ~ **he said**, ce qu'il a
dit. ~ **is important**, ce qui est
important. ~ **is it?**, qu'est-ce que
c'est? ~ **you need**, ce dont vous
avez besoin. ~ **a fool/etc.**, quel
idiot/etc. ~**about me/him/etc.?**,
et moi/lui/etc.? ~**about doing?**,
si on faisait? ~ **for?**, pourquoi?

whatever /wɒt'evə(r)/ *a.* ~
book/etc., quel que soit le
livre/etc. (*no matter what*)
quoi que, quoi qu'*; (*anything
that*) tout ce qui; (*object*) tout ce
que *or* qu'*. ~ **happens**, quoi
qu'il arrive. ~ **happened?**,
qu'est-ce qui est arrivé? ~ **the
problems**, quels que soient les
problèmes. ~ **you want**, tout ce
que vous voulez. **nothing** ~, rien
du tout.

whatsoever /wɒtsəʊ'evə(r)/ *a. &
pron.* = **whatever.**

wheat /wiːt/ *n.* blé *m.*, froment *m.*

wheedle /'wiːdl/ *v.t.* cajoler.

wheel /wiːl/ *n.* roue *f.* —*v.t.*
pousser. —*v.i.* tourner. **at the** ~,
(*of vehicle*) au volant; (*helm*) au
gouvernail. ~ **and deal**, faire des
combines.

wheelbarrow /'wiːlbærəʊ/ *n.*
brouette *f.*

wheelchair /'wiːltʃeə(r)/ *n.* fauteuil roulant *m.*

wheeze /wiːz/ *v.i.* siffler (en
respirant). —*n.* sifflement *m.*

when /wen/ *adv. & pron.* quand.
—*conj.* quand, lorsque. **the
day/moment** ~, le jour/mo-
ment où.

whenever /wen'evə(r)/ *conj. &
adv.* (*at whatever time*) quand;
(*every time that*) chaque fois que.

where /weə(r)/ *adv., conj., & pron.*
où; (*whereas*) alors que; (*the place
that*) là où; *n.* **s.o's ~abouts**,
l'endroit où se trouve qn. **~by**
adv. par quoi. **~upon** *adv.* sur
quoi.

whereas /weər'æz/ *conj.* alors que.

wherever /weər'evə(r)/ *conj. &
adv.* où que; (*everywhere*) partout
où; (*anywhere*) (là) où; (*emphatic
where*) où donc.

whet /wet/ *v.t.* (*p.t.* **whetted**)
(*appetite, desire*) aiguiser.

whether /'weðə(r)/ *conj.* si. **not
know ~**, ne pas savoir si. **~ I go
or not**, que j'aille ou non.

which /wɪtʃ/ *a.* (*in questions*)
quel(le), quel(le)s. —*pron.* (*in
questions*) lequel, laquelle, les-
quel(le)s; (*the one or ones that*)
celui (celle, ceux, celles) qui;
(*object*) celui (celle, ceux, celles)
que *or* qu'*; (*referring to whole
sentence*, = and that) ce qui;
(*object*) ce que, ce qu'*; (*after
prep.*) lequel/*etc.* —*rel. pron.* qui;
(*object*) que, qu'*. **~ house?**,
quelle maison? **~ (one) do you
want?**, lequel voulez-vous? **~
are ready?**, lesquels sont prêts?
the bird ~ flies, l'oiseau qui
vole. **the hat ~ he wears**, le
chapeau qu'il porte. **of ~, from
~**, duquel/*etc.* **to ~, at ~**,
auquel/*etc.* **the book of ~, the
livre dont *or* duquel. **after ~**,
après quoi. **she was there, ~
surprised me**, elle était là, ce qui
m'a surpris.

whichever /wɪtʃ'evə(r)/ *a.* **~
book**/*etc.*, quel que soit le
livre/*etc.* que *or* qui. **take ~ book
you wish**, prenez le livre que
vous voulez. —*pron.* celui (celle,
ceux, celles) qui *or* que.

whiff /wɪf/ *n.* (*puff*) bouffée *f.*

while /waɪl/ *n.* moment *m.* —*conj.*
(*when*) pendant que; (*although*)

bien que; (*as long as*) tant que.
—*v.t.* **~ away**, (*time*) passer.

whilst /waɪlst/ *conj.* = **while**.

whim /wɪm/ *n.* caprice *m.*

whimper /'wɪmpə(r)/ *v.i.* geindre,
pleurnicher. —*n.* pleurniche-
ment *m.*

whimsical /'wɪmzɪkl/ *a.* (*person*)
capricieux; (*odd*) bizarre.

whine /waɪn/ *v.i.* gémir, se
plaindre. —*n.* gémissement *m.*

whip /wɪp/ *n.* fouet *m.* —*v.t.* (*p.t.*
whipped) fouetter; (*culin.*) fouetter, battre; (*seize*) enlever
brusquement. —*v.i.* (*move*) aller
en vitesse. **~-round** *n.* (*fam.*)
collecte *f.* **~ out**, (*gun etc.*) sortir.
~ up, exciter; (*cause*) provoquer;
(*meal: fam.*) préparer.

whirl /wɜːl/ *v.t./i.* (faire) tourbillonner. —*n.* tourbillon *m.*

whirlpool /'wɜːlpuːl/ *n.* (*in sea
etc.*) tourbillon *m.*

whirlwind /'wɜːlwɪnd/ *n.* tourbillon (de vent) *m.*

whirr /wɜː(r)/ *v.i.* vrombir.

whisk /wɪsk/ *v.t.* (*snatch*) enlever
or emmener brusquement; (*cu-
lin.*) fouetter. —*n.* (*culin.*) fouet
m.; (*broom, brush*) petit balai *m.*
~ away, (*brush away*) chasser.

whisker /'wɪskə(r)/ *n.* poil *m.* **~s**,
(*man's*) barbe *f.*, moustache *f.*;
(*sideboards*) favoris *m. pl.*

whisky /'wɪskɪ/ *n.* whisky *m.*

whisper /'wɪspə(r)/ *v.t./i.* chucho-
ter. —*n.* chuchotement *m.*;
(*rumour: fig.*) rumeur *f.*, bruit *m.*

whistle /'wɪsl/ *n.* sifflement *m.*;
(*instrument*) sifflet *m.* —*v.t./i.*
siffler. **~ at or for**, siffler.

Whit /wɪt/ *a.* **~ Sunday**,
dimanche de Pentecôte *m.*

white /waɪt/ *a.* (-er, -est) blanc.
—*n.* blanc *m.*; (*person*) blanc(he)
m. (*f.*). **~ coffee**, café au lait *m.*
~-collar worker, employé/e de
bureau *m.* (*f.*). **~ elephant**,
objet, projet, *etc.* inutile *m.* **~ lie**,

pieux mensonge *m*. **W∼ Paper**, livre blanc *m*. **∼ness** *n*. blancheur *f*.

whiten /'waɪtn/ *v.t./i.* blanchir.

whitewash /'waɪtwɒʃ/ *n*. blanc de chaux *m*. —*v.t.* blanchir à la chaux; (*person: fig.*) blanchir.

whiting /'waɪtɪŋ/ *n. invar.* (*fish*) merlan *m*.

Whitsun /'wɪtsn/ *n*. la Pentecôte.

whittle /'wɪtl/ *v.t.* ∼ **down**, tailler (au couteau); (*fig.*) réduire.

whiz /wɪz/ *v.i.* (*p.t.* **whizzed**) (*through air*) fendre l'air; (*hiss*) siffler; (*rush*) aller à toute vitesse. **∼-kid** *n*. jeune prodige *m*.

who /huː/ *pron.* qui.

whodunit /huːˈdʌnɪt/ *n*. (*story: fam.*) roman policier *m*.

whoever /huːˈevə(r)/ *pron.* (*no matter who*) qui que ce soit qui *or* que; (*the one who*) quiconque. **tell ∼ you want**, dites-le à qui vous voulez.

whole /həʊl/ *a.* entier; (*intact*) intact. **the ∼ house**/*etc.*, toute la maison/*etc.* —*n.* totalité *f.*; (*unit*) tout *m.* **on the ∼**, dans l'ensemble. **∼-hearted** *a.*, **∼heartedly** *adv.* sans réserve.

wholefoods /'həʊlfuːdz/ *n. pl.* aliments naturels et diététiques *m. pl.*

wholemeal /'həʊlmiːl/ *a.* ∼ **bread**, pain complet *m*.

wholesale /'həʊlseɪl/ *n*. gros *m*. —*a.* (*firm*) de gros; (*fig.*) systématique. —*adv.* (*in large quantities*) en gros; (*buy or sell one item*) au prix de gros; (*fig.*) en masse. **∼r** /-ə(r)/ *n*. grossiste *m./f.*

wholesome /'həʊlsəm/ *a.* sain.

wholewheat /'həʊlhwiːt/ *a.* = **wholemeal**.

wholly /'həʊlɪ/ *adv.* entièrement.

whom /huːm/ *pron.* (*that*) que, qu'***; (*after prep. & in questions*) qui. **of ∼**, dont. **with ∼**, avec qui.

whooping cough /'huːpɪŋkɒf/ *n*. coqueluche *f*.

whopping /'wɒpɪŋ/ *a.* (*sl.*) énorme.

whore /hɔː(r)/ *n*. putain *f*.

whose /huːz/ *pron. & a.* à qui de qui. **∼ hat is this?**, **∼ is this hat?**, à qui est ce chapeau? **∼ son are you?**, de qui êtes-vous le fils? **the man ∼ hat I see**, l'homme dont *or* de qui je vois le chapeau.

why /waɪ/ *adv.* pourquoi. —*int.* eh bien, ma parole, tiens. **the reason ∼**, la raison pour laquelle.

wick /wɪk/ *n*. (*of lamp etc.*) mèche *f*.

wicked /'wɪkɪd/ *a.* méchant, mauvais, vilain. **∼ly** *adv.* méchamment. **∼ness** *n*. méchanceté *f*.

wicker /'wɪkə(r)/ *n*. osier *m*. **∼work** *n*. vannerie *f*.

wicket /'wɪkɪt/ *n*. guichet *m*.

wide /waɪd/ *a.* (**-er**, **-est**) large; (*ocean etc.*) vaste. —*adv.* (*fall etc.*) loin du but. **open ∼**, ouvrir tout grand. **∼ open**, grand ouvert. **∼-angle lens** grand-angle *m*. **∼-awake**, éveillé. **∼ly** *adv.* (*spread, space*) largement; (*travel*) beaucoup; (*generally*) généralement; (*extremely*) extrêmement.

widen /'waɪdn/ *v.t./i.* (s')élargir.

widespread /'waɪdspred/ *a.* très répandu.

widow /'wɪdəʊ/ *n*. veuve. *f*. **∼ed** *a.* (*man*) veuf; (*woman*) veuve. **be ∼ed**, (*become widower or widow*) devenir veuf or veuve. **∼er** *n*. veuf *m*.

width /wɪdθ/ *n*. largeur *f*.

wield /wiːld/ *v.t.* (*axe etc.*) manier; (*power: fig.*) exercer.

wife /waɪf/ *n*. (*pl.* **wives**) femme *f*., épouse *f*. **∼ly** *a.* d'épouse.

wig /wɪg/ *n*. perruque *f*.

wiggle /'wɪgl/ *v.t./i.* remuer; (*hips*) tortiller; (*of worm*) se tortiller.

wild /waɪld/ a. (-er, -est) sauvage; (sea, enthusiasm) déchaîné; (mad) fou; (angry) furieux. —adv. (grow) à l'état sauvage. ~s n. pl. régions sauvages f. pl. run ~, (free) courir en liberté. ~goose chase, fausse piste f. ~ly adv. violemment; (madly) follement.

wildcat /ˈwaɪldkæt/ a. ~ strike, grève sauvage f.

wilderness /ˈwɪldənɪs/ n. désert m.

wildlife /ˈwaɪldlaɪf/ n. faune f.

wile /waɪl/ n. ruse f., artifice m.

wilful /ˈwɪlfl/ a. (intentional, obstinate) volontaire.

will¹ /wɪl/ v. aux. he ~ do/you ~ sing/etc., (future tense) il fera/tu chanteras/etc. ~ you have a coffee?, voulez-vous prendre un café?

will² /wɪl/ n. volonté f.; (document) testament m. —v.t. (wish) vouloir. at ~, quand or comme on veut. ~-power n. volonté f. ~ o.s. to do, faire un effort de volonté pour faire.

willing /ˈwɪlɪŋ/ a. (help, offer) spontané; (helper) bien disposé. ~ to, disposé à. ~ly adv. (with pleasure) volontiers; (not forced) volontairement. ~ness n. empressement m. (to do, à faire); (goodwill) bonne volonté f.

willow /ˈwɪləʊ/ n. saule m.

willy-nilly /wɪlɪˈnɪlɪ/ adv. bon gré mal gré.

wilt /wɪlt/ v.i. (plant etc.) dépérir.

wily /ˈwaɪlɪ/ a. (-ier, -iest) rusé.

win /wɪn/ v.t./i. (p.t. won, pres. p. winning) gagner; (victory, prize) remporter; (fame, fortune) acquérir, trouver. —n. victoire f. ~ round, convaincre.

wince /wɪns/ v.i. se crisper, tressaillir. without ~ing, sans broncher.

winch /wɪntʃ/ n. treuil m. —v.t. hisser au treuil.

wind¹ /wɪnd/ n. vent m.; (breath) souffle m.; (gas from stomach) gaz, vent; (Amer.) get ~ of, avoir vent de. in the ~, dans l'air. ~cheater, (Amer.) ~breaker ns. blouson m. ~ instrument, instrument à vent m. ~-swept a. balayé par les vents.

wind² /waɪnd/ v.t./i. (p.t. wound) (s')enrouler; (of path, river) serpenter. ~ (up), (clock etc.) remonter. ~ up, (end) (se) terminer. ~ up in hospital, finir à l'hôpital. ~ing a. (path) sinueux.

windfall /ˈwɪndfɔːl/ n. fruit tombé m.; (money: fig.) aubaine f.

windmill /ˈwɪndmɪl/ n. moulin à vent m.

window /ˈwɪndəʊ/ n. fenêtre f.; (glass pane) vitre f.; (in vehicle, train) vitre f.; (in shop) vitrine f.; (counter) guichet m. ~-box n. jardinière f. ~-cleaner n. laveur de carreaux m. ~-dresser n. étalagiste m./f. ~-ledge n. rebord de (la) fenêtre m.; ~-shopping n. lèche-vitrines m. ~-sill n. (inside) appui de (la) fenêtre m.; (outside) rebord de (la) fenêtre m.

windpipe /ˈwɪndpaɪp/ n. trachée f.

windscreen /ˈwɪndskriːn/, (Amer.) **windshield** /ˈwɪndʃiːld/ ns. pare-brise m. invar. ~ washer, lave-glace m. ~ wiper, essuie-glace m.

windsurf|ing /ˈwɪndsɜːfɪŋ/ n. planche à voile f. ~er n. véliplanchiste m.

windy /ˈwɪndɪ/ a. (-ier, -iest) venteux. it is ~, il y a du vent.

wine /waɪn/ n. vin m. ~-cellar n. cave (à vin) f. ~-grower n. viticulteur m. ~-growing n. viticulture f.; a. viticole. ~ list, carte des vins f. ~-tasting n. dégustation de vins f. ~ waiter, sommelier m.

wineglass /'waɪnglɑːs/ *n.* verre à vin *m.*

wing /wɪŋ/ *n.* aile *f.* ~s, (*theatre*) coulisses *f. pl.* **under one's ~**, sous son aile. ~ **mirror**, rétroviseur extérieur *m.* ~**ed** *a.* ailé. ~**er** *n.* (*sport*) ailier *m.*

wink /wɪŋk/ *v.i.* faire un clin d'œil; (*light, star*) clignoter. —*n.* clin d'œil *m.*; clignotement *m.*

winner /'wɪnə(r)/ *n.* (*of game*) gagnant(e) *m.* (*f.*); (*of fight*) vainqueur *m.*

winning /'wɪnɪŋ/ *see* **win**. —*a.* (*number, horse*) gagnant; (*team*) victorieux; (*smile*) engageant. ~**s** *n. pl.* gains *m. pl.*

wint|er /'wɪntə(r)/ *n.* hiver *m.* —*v.i.* hiverner. ~**ry** *a.* hivernal.

wipe /waɪp/ *v.t.* essuyer. —*v.i.* ~ **up**, essuyer la vaisselle. —*n.* coup de torchon *or* d'éponge *m.* ~ **off** *or* **out**, essuyer. ~ **out**, (*destroy*) anéantir; (*remove*) effacer.

wir|e /'waɪə(r)/ *n.* fil *m.*; (*Amer.*) télégramme *m.* ~**e netting**, grillage *m.* ~**ing** *n.* (*electr.*) installation électrique *f.*

wireless /'waɪəlɪs/ *n.* radio *f.*

wiry /'waɪərɪ/ *a.* (**-ier**, **-iest**) (*person*) nerveux et maigre.

wisdom /'wɪzdəm/ *n.* sagesse *f.*

wise /waɪz/ *a.* (**-er**, **-est**) prudent, sage; (*look*) averti. ~ **guy**, (*fam.*) petit malin *m.* ~ **man**, sage *m.* ~**ly** *adv.* prudemment.

wisecrack /'waɪzkræk/ *n.* (*fam.*) mot d'esprit *m.*, astuce *f.*

wish /wɪʃ/ *n.* souhait *m.*; (*specific*) vœu *m.*; (*general*) désir *m.* —*v.t.* souhaiter, vouloir, désirer (**to do**, faire); (*bid*) souhaiter. —*v.i.* ~ **for**, souhaiter. **I ~ he'd leave**, je voudrais bien qu'il parte. **best** ~**es**, (*in letter*) amitiés *f. pl.*; (*on greeting card*) meilleurs vœux *m. pl.*

wishful /'wɪʃfl/ *a.* **it is ~ thinking**, on se fait des illusions.

wishy-washy /'wɪʃɪwɒʃɪ/ *a.* fade.

wisp /wɪsp/ *n.* (*of smoke*) volute *f.*

wistful /'wɪstfl/ *a.* mélancolique.

wit /wɪt/ *n.* intelligence *f.*; (*humour*) esprit *m.*; (*person*) homme d'esprit *m.*, femme d'esprit *f.* **be at one's ~'s** *or* ~**s' end**, ne plus savoir que faire.

witch /wɪtʃ/ *n.* sorcière *f.* ~**craft** *n.* sorcellerie *f.*

with /wɪð/ *prep.* avec; (*having*) à; (*because of*) de; (*at house of*) chez. **the man ~ the beard**, l'homme à la barbe. **fill**/*etc.* ~, remplir/*etc.* de. **pleased**/**shaking**/*etc.* ~, content/frémissant/ *etc.* de. ~ **it**, (*fam.*) dans le vent.

withdraw /wɪð'drɔː/ *v.t./i.* (*p.t.* **withdrew**, *p.p.* **withdrawn**) (se) retirer. ~**al** *n.* retrait *m.* ~**n** *a.* (*person*) renfermé.

wither /'wɪðə(r)/ *v.t./i.* (se) flétrir. ~**ed** *a.* (*person*) desséché.

withhold /wɪð'həʊld/ *v.t.* (*p.t.* **withheld**) refuser (de donner); (*retain*) retenir; (*conceal, not tell*) cacher (**from**, à).

within /wɪ'ðɪn/ *prep. & adv.* à l'intérieur (de); (*in distances*) à moins de. ~ **a month**, (*before*) avant un mois. ~ **sight**, en vue.

without /wɪ'ðaʊt/ *prep.* sans. ~ **my knowing**, sans que je sache.

withstand /wɪð'stænd/ *v.t.* (*p.t.* **withstood**) résister à.

witness /'wɪtnɪs/ *n.* témoin *m.*; (*evidence*) témoignage *m.* —*v.t.* être le témoin de, voir; (*document*) signer. **bear ~ to**, témoigner de. ~ **box** *or* **stand**, barre des témoins *f.*

witticism /'wɪtɪsɪzəm/ *n.* bon mot *m.*

witt|y /'wɪtɪ/ *a.* (**-ier**, **-iest**) spirituel. ~**iness** *n.* esprit *m.*

wives /waɪvz/ *see* **wife**.

wizard /'wɪzəd/ *n.* magicien *m.*; (*genius; fig.*) génie *m.*

wobbl|e /'wɒbl/ *v.i.* (*of jelly, voice,*

hand) trembler; (*stagger*) chanceler; (*of table, chair*) branler. ∼y *a.* tremblant; branlant.

woe /wəʊ/ *n.* malheur *m.*

woke, woken /wəʊk, 'wəʊkən/ *see* **wake**¹.

wolf /wʊlf/ *n.* (*pl.* **wolves**) loup *m.* —*v.t.* (*food*) engloutir. **cry ∼,** crier au loup. **∼-whistle** *n.* stiflement admiratif *m.*

woman /'wʊmən/ *n.* (*pl.* **women**) femme *f.* ∼ **doctor,** femme médecin *f.* ∼ **driver,** femme au volant *f.* ∼ **friend,** amie *f.* ∼**hood** *n.* féminité *f.* ∼**ly** *a.* féminin.

womb /wuːm/ *n.* utérus *m.*

women /'wɪmɪn/ *see* **woman**.

won /wʌn/ *see* **win**.

wonder /'wʌndə(r)/ *n.* émerveillement *m.;* (*thing*) merveille *f.* —*v.t.* se demander (*if, si*). —*v.i.* s'étonner (**at, de**); (*reflect*) songer (**about, à**). **it is no ∼,** ce or il n'est pas étonnant (**that, que**).

wonderful /'wʌndəfl/ *a.* merveilleux. ∼**ly** *adv.* merveilleusement; (*work, do, etc.*) à merveille.

won't /wəʊnt/ = **will not**.

woo /wuː/ *v.t.* (*woman*) faire la cour à; (*please*) chercher à plaire à.

wood /wʊd/ *n.* bois *m.* ∼**ed** *a.* boisé. ∼**en** *a.* en or de bois; (*stiff: fig.*) raide, comme du bois.

woodcut /'wʊdkʌt/ *n.* gravure sur bois *f.*

woodland /'wʊdlənd/ *n.* région boisée *f.,* bois *m. pl.*

woodpecker /'wʊdpekə(r)/ *n.* (*bird*) pic *m.,* pivert *m.*

woodwind /'wʊdwɪnd/ *n.* (*mus.*) bois *m. pl.*

woodwork /'wʊdwɜːk/ *n.* (*craft, objects*) menuiserie *f.*

woodworm /'wʊdwɜːm/ *n.* (*larvae*) vers (de bois) *m. pl.*

woody /'wʊdɪ/ *a.* (*wooded*) boisé; (*like wood*) ligneux.

wool /wʊl/ *n.* laine *f.* ∼**len** *a.* de laine. ∼**lens** *n. pl.* lainages *m. pl.* ∼**ly** *a.* laineux; (*vague*) nébuleux; *n.* (*garment: fam.*) lainage *m.*

word /wɜːd/ *n.* mot *m.;* (*spoken*) parole *f.,* mot *m.;* (*promise*) parole *f.;* (*news*) nouvelles *f. pl.* —*v.t.* rédiger. **by ∼ of mouth,** de vive voix. **give/keep one's ∼,** donner/tenir sa parole. **in other ∼s,** autrement dit. ∼ **processor,** machine de traitement de texte *f.* ∼**ing** *n.* termes *m. pl.*

wordy /'wɜːdɪ/ *a.* verbeux.

wore /wɔː(r)/ *see* **wear**.

work /wɜːk/ *n.* travail *m.;* (*product, book, etc.*) œuvre *f.,* ouvrage *m.;* (*building etc. work*) travaux *m. pl.* ∼**s,** (*techn.*) mécanisme *m.;* (*factory*) usine *f.* —*v.t./i.* (*of person*) travailler; (*shape, hammer, etc.*) travailler; (*techn.*) (faire) fonctionner; (faire) marcher; (*land, mine*) exploiter; (*of drug etc.*) agir. —*v.i.* **s.o.,** (*make work*) faire travailler qn. ∼**force** *n.* main-d'œuvre *f.* ∼ **in,** (s')introduire. ∼**-load** *n.* travail (à faire) *m.* ∼ **off,** (*get rid of*) se débarrasser de. ∼ **out** *v.t.* (*solve*) résoudre; (*calculate*) calculer; (*elaborate*) élaborer; *v.i.* (*succeed*) marcher; (*sport*) s'entraîner. ∼**station** *n.* poste de travail *m.* ∼**to-rule** *n.* grève du zèle *f.* ∼ **up** *v.t.* développer; *v.i.* (*to climax*) monter vers. ∼**ed up,** (*person*) énervé.

workable /'wɜːkəbl/ *a.* réalisable.

workaholic /wɜːkə'hɒlɪk/ *n.* (*fam.*) bourreau de travail *m.*

worker /'wɜːkə(r)/ *n.* travailleu∣r, -se *m., f.;* (*manual*) ouvr∣ier, -ière *m., f.*

working /'wɜːkɪŋ/ *a.* (*day, lunch, etc.*) de travail. ∼**s** *n. pl.* mécanisme *m.* ∼ **class,** classe ouvrière f. **~-class** a. ouvrier. **in ~ order**, en état de marche.

workman /ˈwɜːkmən/ n. (pl. **-men**) ouvrier m. **~ship** n. maîtrise f.

workshop /ˈwɜːkʃɒp/ n. atelier m.

world /wɜːld/ n. monde m. **—a.** (power etc.) mondial; (record etc.) du monde. **best in the ~**, meilleur au monde. **~-wide** a. universel.

worldly /ˈwɜːldlɪ/ a. de ce monde, terrestre. **~-wise** a. qui a l'expérience du monde.

worm /wɜːm/ n. ver m. **—v.t.** **~ one's way into**, s'insinuer dans. **~-eaten** a. (wood) vermoulu; (fruit) véreux.

worn /wɔːn/ see **wear**. **—a.** usé. **~-out** a. (thing) complètement usé; (person) épuisé.

worr|y /ˈwʌrɪ/ v.t./i. (s')inquiéter. **—n.** souci m. **~ied** a. inquiet. **~ier** n. inquiet, -iète m., f.

worse /wɜːs/ a. pire, plus mauvais. **—adv.** plus mal. **—n.** pire m. **be ~ off**, perdre.

worsen /ˈwɜːsn/ v.t./i. empirer.

worship /ˈwɜːʃɪp/ n. (adoration) culte m. **—v.t.** (p.t. **worshipped**) adorer. **—v.i.** faire ses dévotions. **~per** n. (in church) fidèle m./f.

worst /wɜːst/ a. pire, plus mauvais. **—adv.** plus mal. **—n.** the **~** (one), (person, object) le pire etc. le plus mal. **—n.** the **~** (thing), le pire (that, que). **get the ~ of it**, (be defeated) avoir le dessous.

worsted /ˈwʊstɪd/ n. worsted m.

worth /wɜːθ/ a. **be ~**, valoir. **it is ~ waiting**/etc., ça vaut la peine d'attendre/etc. **—n.** valeur f. **ten pence ~ of**, (pour) dix pence de. **it is ~ (one's) while**, ça (en) vaut la peine. **~less** a. qui ne vaut rien.

worthwhile /wɜːθˈwaɪl/ a. qui (en) vaut la peine.

worthy /ˈwɜːðɪ/ a. (-ier, -iest) digne (of, de); (laudable) louable. **—n.** (person) notable m.

would /wʊd/, unstressed /wəd/ v. aux. he **~ do**/you **~ sing**/etc., (conditional tense) il ferait/tu chanterais/etc. he **~ have done**, il aurait fait. I **~ come every day**, (used to) je venais chaque jour. I **~ like some tea**, je voudrais du thé. **~ you come here?**, voulez-vous venir ici? he **~n't come**, il a refusé de venir. **~-be** a. soi-disant.

wound[1] /wuːnd/ n. blessure f. **—v.t.** blesser. **the ~ed**, les blessés m. pl.

wound[2] /waʊnd/ see **wind**[2].

wove, woven /wəʊv, ˈwəʊvn/ see **weave**.

wow /waʊ/ int. mince (alors).

wrangle /ˈræŋgl/ v.i. se disputer. **—n.** dispute f.

wrap /ræp/ v.t. (p.t. **wrapped**). **~ (up)**, envelopper. **—v.i. ~ up**, (dress warmly) se couvrir. **—n.** châle m. **~ped up in**, (engrossed) absorbé dans. **~per** n. (of book) jaquette f.; (of sweet) papier m. **~ping** n. emballage m.; **~ping paper**, papier d'emballage m.

wrath /rɒθ/ n. courroux m.

wreak /riːk/ v.t. **~ havoc**, (of storm etc.) faire des ravages.

wreath /riːθ/ n. (pl. **-s** /-ðz/) (of flowers, leaves) couronne f.

wreck /rek/ n. (sinking) naufrage m.; (ship, remains, person) épave f.; (vehicle) voiture accidentée or délabrée f. **—v.t.** détruire; (ship) provoquer le naufrage de. **~age** n. (pieces) débris m. pl.; (wrecked building) décombres m. pl.

wren /ren/ n. roitelet m.

wrench /rentʃ/ v.t. (pull) tirer sur; (twist) tordre; (snatch) arracher (from, à). **—n.** (tool) clé f.

wrest /rest/ v.t. arracher (from, à).

wrestl|e /'resl/ v.i. lutter, se débattre (**with**, contre). **~er** n. lutteu|r, -se m., f.; catcheu|r, -se m., f. **~ing** n. lutte f. (**all-in**) **~ing**, catch m.

wretch /retʃ/ n. malheureu|x, -se m., f.; (rascal) misérable m./f.

wretched /'retʃid/ a. (pitiful, poor) misérable; (bad) affreux.

wriggle /'rɪgl/ v.t./i. (se) tortiller.

wring /rɪŋ/ v.t. (p.t. **wrung**) (twist) tordre; (clothes) essorer. **~ out of**, (obtain from) arracher à. **~ing wet**, trempé (jusqu'aux os).

wrinkle /'rɪŋkl/ n. (crease) pli m.; (on skin) ride f. —v.t./i. (se) rider.

wrist /rɪst/ n. poignet m. **~-watch** n. montre-bracelet f.

writ /rɪt/ n. acte judiciaire m.

write /raɪt/ v.t./i. (p.t. **wrote**, p.p. **written**) écrire. **~ back**, répondre. **~ down**, noter. **~ off**, (debt) passer aux profits et pertes; (vehicle) considérer bon pour la casse. **~-off** n. perte totale f. **~ up**, (from notes) rédiger. **~-up** n. compte rendu m.

writer /'raɪtə(r)/ n. auteur m., écrivain m. **~ of**, auteur de.

writhe /raɪð/ v.i. se tordre.

writing /'raɪtɪŋ/ n. écriture f. **~(s)**, (works) écrits m. pl. in **~**, par écrit. **~paper** n. papier à lettres m.

written /'rɪtn/ see **write**.

wrong /rɒŋ/ a. (incorrect, mistaken) faux, mauvais; (unfair) injuste; (amiss) qui ne va pas; (clock) pas à l'heure. be **~**, (person) avoir tort (to, de); (be mistaken) se tromper. —adv. mal. —n. injustice f.; (evil) mal m. —v.t. faire (du) tort à. be in the **~**, avoir tort. go **~**, (err) se tromper; (turn out badly) mal tourner; (vehicle) tomber en panne. it is **~** to, (morally) c'est mal de. what's **~**?, qu'est-ce qui

ne va pas? **what is ~ with you?**, qu'est-ce que vous avez? **~ly** adv. mal; (blame etc.) à tort.

wrongful /'rɒŋfl/ a. injustifié, injuste. **~ly** adv. à tort.

wrote /rəʊt/ see **write**.

wrought /rɔːt/ a. **~ iron**, fer forgé m.

wrung /rʌŋ/ see **wring**.

wry /raɪ/ a. (**wryer**, **wryest**) (smile) désabusé, forcé. **~ face**, grimace f.

X

xerox /'zɪərɒks/ v.t. photocopier.

Xmas /'krɪsməs/ n. Noël m.

X-ray /'eksreɪ/ n. rayon X m.; (photograph) radio(graphie) f. —v.t. radiographier.

xylophone /'zaɪləfəʊn/ n. xylophone m.

Y

yacht /jɒt/ n. yacht m. **~ing** n. yachting m.

yank /jæŋk/ v.t. tirer brusquement. —n. coup brusque m.

Yank /jæŋk/ n. (fam.) Améri-cain(e) m. (f.), Amerloque m./f.

yap /jæp/ v.i. (p.t. **yapped**) japper.

yard[1] /jɑːd/ n. (measure) yard m. (= 0.9144 metre).

yard[2] /jɑːd/ n. (of house etc.) cour f.; (garden: Amer.) jardin m.; (for storage) chantier m., dépôt m.

yardstick /'jɑːdstɪk/ n. mesure f.

yarn /jɑːn/ n. (thread) fil m.; (tale: fam.) (longue) histoire f.

yawn /jɔːn/ v.i. bâiller. —n. bâillement m. **~ing** a. (gaping) béant.

year /jɪə(r)/ n. an m., année f.;

school/tax/etc. ~, année scolaire/fiscale/etc. **be ten/**etc. **be** ten/etc. **~s old**, avoir dix/etc. ans. **~book** n. annuaire m. **~ly** a. annuel; adv. annuellement.

yearn /jɜːn/ v.i. avoir bien or très envie (**for, to, de**). **~ing** n. envie f.

yeast /jiːst/ n. levure f.

yell /jel/ v.t./i. hurler. —n. hurlement m.

yellow /'jeləʊ/ a. jaune; (cowardly: fam.) froussard. —n. jaune m.

yelp /jelp/ n. (of dog etc.) jappement m. —v.i. japper.

yen /jen/ n. (desire) grande envie f.

yes /jes/ adv. oui; (as answer to negative question) si. —n. oui m. invar.

yesterday /'jestədɪ/ n. & adv. hier (m.).

yet /jet/ adv. encore; (already) déjà. —conj. pourtant, néanmoins.

yew /juː/ n. (tree, wood) if m.

Yiddish /'jɪdɪʃ/ n. yiddish m.

yield /jiːld/ v.t. (produce) produire, rendre; (profit) rapporter; (surrender) céder. —v.i. (give way) céder. —n. rendement m.

yoga /'jəʊgə/ n. yoga m.

yoghurt /'jɒgət, Amer. 'jəʊgərt/ n. yaourt m.

yoke /jəʊk/ n. joug m.

yokel /'jəʊkl/ n. rustre m.

yolk /jəʊk/ n. jaune (d'œuf) m.

yonder /'jɒndə(r)/ adv. là-bas.

you /juː/ pron. (familiar form) tu, pl. vous; (polite form) vous; (object) te, t**, pl. vous; (polite) vous; (after prep.) toi, pl. vous; (polite) vous; (indefinite) on; (object) vous (to) ~, te, t**, pl. vous; (polite) vous. **I gave ~ a pen**, je vous ai donné un stylo. **I know ~**, je te connais; je vous connais.

young /jʌŋ/ a. (-er, -est) jeune. —n. (people) jeunes m. pl.; (of animals) petits m. pl. ~**er** a. (brother etc.) cadet. ~**est** a. my ~**est brother**, le cadet de mes frères.

youngster /'jʌŋstə(r)/ n. jeune m./f.

your /jɔː(r)/ a. (familiar form) ton, ta, pl. tes; (polite form, & familiar form pl.) votre, pl. vos.

yours /jɔːz/ poss. pron. (familiar form) le tien, la tienne, les tien(ne)s; (polite form, & familiar form pl.) le or la vôtre, les vôtres. ~**s faithfully/sincerely**, je vous prie d'agréer/de croire en l'expression de mes sentiments les meilleurs.

yourself /jɔː'self/ pron. (familiar form) toi-même; (polite form) vous-même; (reflexive & after prep.) t; vous. ~**ves** pron. pl. vous-mêmes; (reflexive) vous.

youth /juːθ/ n. (pl. **-s** /-ðz/) jeunesse f.; (young man) jeune m. ~ **club**, centre de jeunes m. ~ **hostel**, auberge de jeunesse f. ~**ful** a. juvénile, jeune.

yo-yo /'jəʊjəʊ/ n. (pl. **-os**) (P.) yo-yo m. invar. (P.).

Yugoslav /'juːgəslɑːv/ a. & n. Yougoslave (m./f.) ~**ia** /-'slɑːvɪə/ n. Yougoslavie f.

yuppie /'jʌpɪ/ n. yuppie m.

Z

zany /'zeɪnɪ/ a. (-ier, -iest) farfelu.

zap /zæp/ v.t. (fam.) (kill) descendre; (comput.) enlever; (TV) zapper.

zeal /ziːl/ n. zèle m.

zealous /'zeləs/ a. zélé. ~**ly** a. zèle.

zebra /'zebrə, 'ziːbrə/ n. zèbre m. ~ **crossing**, passage pour piétons m.

zenith /'zenɪθ/ n. zénith m.

zero /'zɪərəʊ/ n. (pl. -os) zéro m. ~ **hour**, l'heure H f.

zest /zest/ n. (gusto) entrain m.; (spice: fig.) piment m.; (of orange or lemon peel) zeste m.

zigzag /'zɪgzæg/ n. zigzag m. —a. & adv. en zigzag. —v.i. (p.t. **zigzagged**) zigzaguer.

zinc /zɪŋk/ n. zinc m.

Zionism /'zaɪənɪzəm/ n. sionisme m.

zip /zɪp/ n. (vigour) allant m. ~**(-fastener)**, fermeture éclair f. (P.). —v.t. (p.t. **zipped**) fermer avec une fermeture éclair (P.). —v.i. aller à toute vitesse. **Zip code**, (Amer.) code postal m.

zipper /'zɪpə(r)/ n. (Amer.) = **zip (-fastener)**.

zither /'zɪðə(r)/ n. cithare f.

zodiac /'zəʊdɪæk/ n. zodiaque m.

zombie /'zɒmbɪ/ n. mort(e) vivant(e) m. (f.); (fam.) automate m.

zone /zəʊn/ n. zone f.

zoo /zuː/ n. zoo m.

zoology /zəʊ'ɒlədʒɪ/ n. zoologie f. ~**ical** /-ə'lɒdʒɪkl/ a. zoologique. ~**ist** n. zoologiste m./f.

zoom /zuːm/ v.i. (rush) se précipiter. ~ **lens**, zoom m. ~ **off** or **past**, filer (comme une flèche).

zucchini /zuː'kiːnɪ/ n. invar. (Amer.) courgette f.

French Verb Tables

Notes The conditional may be formed by substituting the following endings for those of the future: *ais* for *ai* and *as*, *ait* for *a*, *ions* for *ons*, *iez* for *ez*, *aient* for *ont*. The present participle is formed (unless otherwise indicated) by substituting *ant* for *ons* in the first person plural of the present tense (e.g. *finissant* and *donnant* may be derived from *finissons* and *donnons*). The imperative forms are (unless otherwise indicated) the same as the second persons singular and plural and the first person plural of the present tense. The second person singular does not take *s* after *e* or *a* (e.g. *donne, va*), except when followed by *y* or *en* (e.g. *vas-y*).

Regular verbs:
1. in -*er* (e.g. **donn|er**)

> *Present.* ~e, ~es, ~e, ~ons, ~ez, ~ent.
> *Imperfect.* ~ais, ~ais, ~ait, ~ions, ~iez, ~aient.
> *Past historic.* ~ai, ~as, ~a, ~âmes, ~âtes, ~èrent.
> *Future.* ~erai, ~eras, ~era, ~erons, ~erez, ~eront.
> *Present subjunctive,* ~e, ~es, ~e, ~ions, ~iez, ~ent.
> *Past participle,* ~é.

2. in -*ir* (e.g. **fin|ir**)

> *Pres.* ~is, ~is, ~it, ~issons, ~issez, ~issent.
> *Impf.* ~issais, ~issais, ~issait, ~issions, ~issiez, ~issaient.
> *Past hist.* ~is, ~is, ~it, ~îmes, ~îtes, ~irent.
> *Fut.* ~irai, ~iras, ~ira, ~irons, ~irez, ~iront.
> *Pres. sub.* ~isse, ~isses, ~isse, ~issions, ~issiez, ~issent.
> *Past part.* ~i.

3. in -*re* (e.g. **vend|re**)

> *Pres.* ~s, ~s, ~, ~ons, ~ez, ~ent.
> *Impf.* ~ais, ~ais, ~ait, ~ions, ~iez, ~aient.
> *Past hist.* ~is, ~is, ~it, ~îmes, ~îtes, ~irent.
> *Fut.* ~rai, ~ras, ~ra, ~rons, ~rez, ~ront.
> *Pres. sub.* ~e, ~es, ~e, ~ions, ~iez, ~ent.
> *Past part.* ~u.

Peculiarities of -*er* verbs:

In verbs in -*cer* (e.g. **commencer**) and -*ger* (e.g. **manger**), *c* becomes *ç* and *g* becomes *ge* before *a* and *o* (e.g. *commença*, *commençons*; *mangea*, *mangeons*).

In verbs in *-yer* (e.g. **nettoyer**), *y* becomes *i* before mute *e* (e.g. nettoie, nettoierai). Verbs in *-ayer* (e.g. **payer**) may retain *y* before mute *e* (e.g. paye or paie, payerai or paierai).

In verbs in *eler* (e.g. **appeler**) and in *-eter* (e.g. **jeter**), *l* becomes *ll* and *t* becomes *tt* before a syllable containing mute *e* (e.g. appelle, appellerai; jette, jetterai). In the verbs **celer, ciseler, congeler, déceler, démanteler, écarteler, geler, marteler, modeler,** and **peler,** and in the verbs **acheter, crocheter, fureter, haleter** and **racheter,** *e* becomes *è* before a syllable containing mute *e* (e.g. cèle, cèlerai; achète, achèterai).

In verbs in which the penultimate syllable contains mute *e* (e.g. **semer**) or *é* (e.g. **révéler**), both *e* and *é* become *è* before a syllable containing mute *e* (e.g. sème, sèmerai; révèle). However, in the verbs in which the penultimate syllable contains *é*, *é* remains unchanged in the future and conditional (e.g. révélerai).

Irregular verbs:

At least the first persons singular and plural of the present tense are shown. Forms not listed may be derived from these. Though the base form of the imperfect, future, and present subjunctive may be irregular, the endings of these tenses are as shown in the regular verb section. Only the first person singular of these tenses is given in most cases. The base form of the past historic may also be irregular but the endings of this tense shown in the verbs below fall (with few exceptions) into the 'u' category, listed under **être** and **avoir,** and the 'i' category shown under **finir** and **vendre** in the regular verb section. Only the first person singular of the past historic is listed in most cases. Additional forms appear throughout when these cannot be derived from the forms given or when it is considered helpful to list them. Only those irregular verbs judged to be the most useful are shown in the tables.

abattre	*AS* BATTRE.
accueillir	*AS* CUEILLIR.
acquérir	● *Pres.* acquiers, acquérons, acquièrent. ● *Impf.* acquérais. ● *Past hist.* acquis. ● *Fut.* acquerrai. ● *Pres. sub.* acquière. ● *Past part.* acquis.
admettre	*AS* METTRE.

aller ● *Pres.* vais, vas, va, allons, allez, vont. ● *Fut.* irai. ● *Pres. sub.* aille, allions.

apercevoir *AS* RECEVOIR.

apparaître *AS* CONNAÎTRE.

appartenir *AS* TENIR

apprendre *AS* PRENDRE.

asseoir ● *Pres.* assieds, asseyons, asseyent. ● *Impf.* asseyais. ● *Past hist.* assis. ● *Fut.* assiérai. ● *Pres. sub.* asseye. ● *Past part.* assis.

atteindre ● *Pres.* atteins, atteignons, atteignent. ● *Impf.* atteignais. ● *Past hist.* atteignis. ● *Fut.* atteindrai. ● *Pres. sub.* atteigne. ● *Past part.* atteint.

avoir ● *Pres.* ai, as, a, avons, avez, ont. ● *Impf.* avais. ● *Past hist.* eus, eut, eûmes, eûtes, eurent. ● *Fut.* aurai. ● *Pres. sub.* aie, aies, ait, ayons, ayez, aient. ● *Pres. part.* ayant. ● *Past part.* eu. ● *Imp.* aie, ayons, ayez.

battre ● *Pres.* bats, bat, battons, battez, battent.

boire ● *Pres.* bois, buvons, boivent. ● *Impf.* buvais. ● *Past hist.* bus. ● *Pres. sub.* boive, buvions. ● *Past part.* bu.

bouillir ● *Pres.* bous, bouillons, bouillent. ● *Impf.* bouillais. ● *Pres. sub.* bouille.

combattre *AS* BATTRE.

commettre *AS* METTRE.

comprendre *AS* PRENDRE.

concevoir *AS* RECEVOIR.

conclure ● *Pres.* conclus, concluons, concluent. ● *Past hist.* conclus. ● *Past part.* conclu.

conduire ● *Pres.* conduis, conduisons, conduisent. ● *Impf.* conduisais. ● *Past hist.* conduisis. ● *Pres. sub.* conduise. ● *Past part.* conduit.

connaître ● *Pres.* connais, connaît, connaissons. ● *Impf.* connaissais. ● *Past hist.* connus. ● *Pres. sub.* connaisse. ● *Past part.* connu.

construire *AS* CONDUIRE.

contenir *AS* TENIR.

contraindre *AS* ATTEINDRE (except *ai* replaces *ei*).

contredire *AS* DIRE, except ● *Pres.* vous contredisez.

convaincre *AS* VAINCRE.

convenir *AS* TENIR.

corrompre *as* ROMPRE.

coudre
- *Pres.* couds, cousons, cousent. ● *Impf.* cousais.
- *Past hist.* cousis. ● *Pres. sub.* couse. ● *Past part.* cousu.

courir
- *Pres.* cours, courons, courent. ● *Impf.* courais.
- *Past hist.* courus. ● *Fut.* courrai. ● *Pres. sub.* coure. ● *Past part.* couru.

couvrir
- *Pres.* couvre, couvrons. ● *Impf.* couvrais.
- *Pres. sub.* couvre. ● *Past part.* couvert.

craindre *as* ATTEINDRE (except *ai* replaces *ei*).

croire
- *Pres.* crois, croit, croyons, croyez, croient.
- *Impf.* croyais. ● *Past hist.* crus. ● *Pres. sub.* croie, croyions. ● *Past part.* cru.

croître
- *Pres.* crois, croît, croissons. ● *Impf.* croissais.
- *Past hist.* crûs. ● *Pres. sub.* croisse. ● *Past part.* crû, crue.

cueillir
- *Pres.* cueille, cueillons. ● *Impf.* cueillais.
- *Fut.* cueillerai. ● *Pres. sub.* cueille.

débattre *as* BATTRE.

décevoir *as* RECEVOIR.

découvrir *as* COUVRIR.

décrire *as* ÉCRIRE.

déduire *as* CONDUIRE.

défaire *as* FAIRE.

détenir *as* TENIR.

détruire *as* CONDUIRE.

devenir *as* TENIR.

devoir
- *Pres.* dois, devons, doivent. ● *Impf.* devais.
- *Past hist.* dus. ● *Fut.* devrai. ● *Pres. sub.* doive. ● *Past part.* dû, due.

dire
- *Pres.* dis, dit, disons, dites, disent. ● *Impf.* disais. ● *Past hist.* dis. ● *Past part.* dit.

disparaître *as* CONNAÎTRE.

dissoudre
- *Pres.* dissous, dissolvons. ● *Impf.* dissolvais.
- *Pres. sub.* dissolve. ● *Past part.* dissous, dissoute.

distraire *as* EXTRAIRE.

dormir
- *Pres.* dors, dormons. ● *Impf.* dormais. ● *Pres. sub.* dorme.

écrire
- *Pres.* écris, écrivons. ● *Impf.* écrivais. ● *Past hist.* écrivis. ● *Pres. sub.* écrive. ● *Past part.* écrit.

élire   *AS* LIRE.

émettre   *AS* METTRE.

s'enfuir   *AS* FUIR.

entreprendre   *AS* PRENDRE.

entretenir   *AS* TENIR.

envoyer   ● *Fut.* enverrai.

éteindre   *AS* ATTEINDRE.

être   ● *Pres.* suis, es, est, sommes, êtes, sont. ● *Impf.* étais. ● *Past hist.* fus, fut, fûmes, fûtes, furent. ● *Fut.* serai. ● *Pres. sub.* sois, soit, soyons, soyez, soient. ● *Pres. part.* étant. ● *Past part.* été. ● *Imp.* sois, soyons, soyez.

exclure   *AS* CONCLURE.

extraire   ● *Pres.* extrais, extrayons. ● *Impf.* extrayais. ● *Pres. sub.* extraie. ● *Past part.* extrait.

faire   ● *Pres.* fais, fait, faisons, faites, font. ● *Impf.* faisais. ● *Past hist.* fis. ● *Fut.* ferai. ● *Pres. sub.* fasse. ● *Past part.* fait.

falloir   (impersonal) ● *Pres.* faut. ● *Impf.* fallait. ● *Past hist.* fallut. ● *Fut.* faudra. ● *pres. sub.* faille. ● *Past part.* fallu.

feindre   *AS* ATTEINDRE.

fuir   ● *Pres.* fuis, fuyons, fuient. ● *Impf.* fuyais. ● *Past hist.* fuis. ● *Pres sub.* fuie. ● *Past part.* fui.

inscrire   *AS* ÉCRIRE.

instruire   *AS* CONDUIRE.

interdire   *AS* DIRE, except ● *Pres.* vous interdisez.

interrompre   *AS* ROMPRE.

intervenir   *AS* TENIR.

introduire   *AS* CONDUIRE.

joindre   *AS* ATTEINDRE (except *oi* replaces *ei*).

lire   ● *Pres.* lis, lit, lisons, lisez, lisent. ● *Impf.* lisais. ● *Past hist.* lus. ● *Pres. sub.* lise. ● *Past part.* lu.

luire   ● *Pres.* luis, luisons. ● *Impf.* luisais. ● *Past hist.* luisis. ● *Pres. sub.* luise. ● *Past part.* lui.

maintenir   *AS* TENIR.

maudire   ● *Pres.* maudis, maudissons. ● *Impf.* maudissais. ● *Past hist.* maudis. ● *Pres. sub.* maudisse. ● *Past part.* maudit.

mentir   *AS* SORTIR (except *en* replaces *or*).

mettre   ● *Pres.* mets, met, mettons, mettez, mettent. ● *Past hist.* mis. ● *Past part.* mis.

mourir
- *Pres.* meurs, mourons, meurent. ● *Impf.* mourais. ● *Past hist.* mourus. ● *Fut.* mourrai. ● *Pres. sub.* meure, mourions. ● *Past part.* mort.

mouvoir
- *Pres.* meus, mouvons, meuvent. ● *Impf.* mouvais. ● *Fut.* mouvrai. ● *Pres. sub.* meuve, mouvions. ● *Past part.* mû, mue.

naître
- *Pres.* nais, naît, naissons. ● *Impf.* naissais. ● *Past hist.* naquis. ● *Pres. sub.* naisse. ● *Past part.* né.

nuire *as* LUIRE.

obtenir *as* TENIR.

offrir, ouvrir *as* COUVRIR.

omettre *as* METTRE.

paraître *as* CONNAÎTRE.

parcourir *as* COURIR.

partir *as* SORTIR (except *ar* replaces *or*).

parvenir *as* TENIR.

peindre *as* ATTEINDRE.

percevoir *as* RECEVOIR.

permettre *as* METTRE.

plaindre *as* ATTEINDRE (except *ai* replaces *ei*).

plaire
- *Pres.* plais, plaît, plaisons. ● *Impf.* plaisais. ● *Past hist.* plus. ● *Pres. sub.* plaise. ● *Past part.* plu.

pleuvoir
- (impersonal) ● *Pres.* pleut. ● *Impf.* pleuvait. ● *Past hist.* plut. ● *Fut.* pleuvra. ● *Pres. sub.* pleuve. ● *Past part.* plu.

poursuivre *as* SUIVRE.

pourvoir *as* VOIR, except ● *Fut.* pourvoirai

pouvoir
- *Pres.* peux, peut, pouvons, pouvez, peuvent. ● *Impf.* pouvais. ● *Past hist.* pus. ● *Fut.* pourrai. ● *Pres. sub.* puisse. ● *Past part.* pu.

prédire *as* DIRE, except ● *Pres.* vous prédisez.

prendre
- *Pres.* prends, prenons, prennent. ● *Impf.* prenais. ● *Past hist.* pris. ● *Pres. sub.* prenne, prenions. ● *Past part.* pris.

prescrire *as* ÉCRIRE.

prévenir *as* TENIR.

prévoir *as* VOIR, except ● *Fut.* prévoirai.

produire *as* CONDUIRE.

promettre *as* METTRE.

provenir	*as* TENIR.
recevoir	● *Pres.* reçois, recevons, reçoivent. ● *Impf.* recevais. ● *Past hist.* reçus. ● *Fut.* recevrai. ● *Pres. sub.* reçoive, recevions. ● *Past part.* reçu.
reconduire	*as* CONDUIRE.
reconnaître	*as* CONNAÎTRE.
reconstruire	*as* CONDUIRE.
recouvrir	*as* COUVRIR.
recueillir	*as* CUEILLIR.
redire	*as* DIRE.
réduire	*as* CONDUIRE.
refaire	*as* FAIRE.
rejoindre	*as* ATTEINDRE (except *oi* replaces *ei*).
remettre	*as* METTRE.
renvoyer	*as* ENVOYER.
repartir	*as* SORTIR (except *ar* replaces *or*).
reprendre	*as* PRENDRE.
reproduire	*as* CONDUIRE.
résoudre	● *Pres.* résous, résolvons. ● *Impf.* résolvais. ● *Past hist.* résolus. ● *Pres. sub.* résolve. ● *Past part.* résolu.
ressortir	*as* SORTIR.
restreindre	*as* ATTEINDRE.
retenir, revenir	*as* TENIR.
revivre	*as* VIVRE.
revoir	*as* VOIR.
rire	● *Pres.* ris, rit, rions, riez, rient. ● *Impf.* riais. ● *Past hist.* ris. ● *Pres. sub.* rie, riions. ● *Past part.* ri.
rompre	*as* VENDRE (regular), except ● *Pres.* il rompt.
satisfaire	*as* FAIRE.
savoir	● *Pres.* sais, sait, savons, savez, savent. ● *Impf.* savais, ● *Past hist.* sus. ● *Fut.* saurai. ● *Pres. sub.* sache, sachions. ● *Pres. part.* sachant. ● *Past part.* su. ● *Imp.* sache, sachons, sachez.
séduire	*as* CONDUIRE.
sentir	*as* SORTIR (except *en* replaces *or*).
servir	● *Pres.* sers, servons. ● *Impf.* servais. ● *Pres. sub.* serve.
sortir	● *Pres.* sors, sortons. ● *Impf.* sortais. ● *Pres. sub.* sorte.

souffrir   *as* COUVRIR.

soumettre   *as* METTRE.

soustraire   *as* EXTRAIRE.

soutenir   *as* TENIR.

suffire   ● *Pres.* suffis, suffisons. ● *Impf.* suffisais. ● *Past hist.* suffis. ● *Pres. sub.* suffise. ● *Past part.* suffi.

suivre   ● *Pres.* suis, suivons. ● *Impf.* suivais. ● *Past hist.* suivis. ● *Pres. sub.* suive. ● *Past part.* suivi.

surprendre   *as* PRENDRE.

survivre   *as* VIVRE.

taire   ● *Pres.* tais, taisons. ● *Impf.* taisais. ● *Past hist.* tus. ● *Pres. sub.* taise. ● *Past part.* tu.

teindre   *as* ATTEINDRE.

tenir   ● *Pres.* tiens, tenons, tiennent. ● *Impf.* tenais. ● *Past hist.* tins, tint, tînmes, tîntes, tinrent. ● *Fut.* tiendrai. ● *Pres. sub.* tienne. ● *Past part.* tenu.

traduire   *as* CONDUIRE.

traire   *as* EXTRAIRE.

transmettre   *as* METTRE.

vaincre   ● *Pres.* vaincs, vainc, vainquons. ● *Impf.* vainquais. ● *Past hist.* vainquis. ● *Pres. sub.* vainque. ● *Past part.* vaincu.

valoir   ● *Pres.* vaux, vaut, valons, valez, valent. ● *Impf.* valais. ● *Past hist.* valus. ● *Fut.* vaudrai. ● *Pres. sub.* vaille. ● *past part.* valu.

venir   *as* TENIR.

vivre   ● *Pres.* vis, vit, vivons, vivez, vivent. ● *Impf.* vivais. ● *Past hist.* vécus. ● *Pres. sub.* vive. ● *Past part.* vécu.

voir   ● *Pres.* vois, voyons, voient. ● *Impf.* voyais. ● *Past hist.* vis. ● *Fut.* verrai. ● *Pres. sub.* voie, voyions. ● *Past part.* vu.

vouloir   ● *Pres.* veux, veut, voulons, voulez, veulent. ● *Impf.* voulais. ● *Past hist.* voulus. ● *Fut.* voudrai. ● *Pres. sub.* veuille, voulions. ● *Past part.* voulu. ● *Imp.* veuille, veuillons, veuillez.